LIBERTY COMMENTARY

On The

NEW TESTAMENT

Jerry Falwell, D.D., D.Litt.
Executive Editor

Edward E. Hindson, Th.D., D.Min.
Woodrow Michael Kroll, Th.D.
General Editors

Liberty Press
LYNCHBURG, VIRGINIA

ISBN 0-8407-51451

FOREWORD
by Dr. Jerry Falwell

The Bible alone is the Word of God and has stood the test of the ages. It is still the best seller of all time because the Bible is "profitable for doctrine, for reproof, for correction, for instruction in righteousness: That the man of God may be perfect, thoroughly furnished unto all good works" (II Tim. 3:16, 17). I have preached the message of the Bible for a quarter of a century now and have never found it wanting in meeting man's greatest needs. Every opinion we hold and every conviction that motivates our ministry is based on the Bible. To the best of our understanding we preach and teach God's word in its clearest and plainest sense. The Scripture alone is our final authority in all matters of faith and practice.

For these reasons we of the *Old-Time Gospel Hour* began the "Laymen's Library" as a series of Bible study aids for pastors, Christian workers, and laymen. I recently asked Dr. Ed Hindson and Dr. Woodrow Kroll to coordinate a team of Bible scholars from our Liberty Baptist Schools to assist me in producing a one-volume commentary on the entire New Testament. It is our prayer that this commentary will serve you greatly as an aid to effective Bible study. As the Ethiopian eunuch responded to Philip's question about whether he understood the Scripture, he replied: "How can I except some man should guide me?" (Acts 8:31), so we desire this commentary to be a wise guide to point men to the truth of Christ. Our interpreters do not claim infallibility, but each one is a born-again, Bible believer who accepts the inerrant inspiration of the Scripture and believes the Bible to be the only message of eternal life.

Open your Bible to the passage you are studying and then open the commentary to the appropriate page and use them comparatively. May God bless your study of His Word so that your life is changed by its impact upon your soul. The Apostle Peter said: "We have also a more sure word of prophecy; whereunto ye do well that ye take heed. . . .

For the prophecy came not in old time by the will of man: but holy men of God spake as they were moved by the Holy Ghost" (II Pet 1:19, 21). Let God speak to you through His Word as you read it, memorize it and meditate upon its truths.

Preface

The *Liberty Commentary* represents the first full-scale attempt by a single school faculty to produce a work of this nature. It is designed to meet the needs of pastors, teachers, and laymen alike. Therefore, it is critical, comprehensive, and devotional in tone and spirit. This work is not intended to cover every possible interpretation of every passage. Rather, the purpose of *Liberty Commentary on the New Testament,* is to provide a verse by verse exposition and interpretation of the entire New Testament. A similar commentary on the Old Testament will soon be forthcoming.

The uniqueness of this project rests in the common doctrinal commitment of each of the contributors. Most commentaries of this nature are produced by scholars who, while they are specialists in a given area, do not necessarily share a common doctrinal viewpoint. In this work each contributor has been allowed the freedom of his personal views, but the final material has been reviewed by an editorial committee that reflects the general position of our schools. Thus, while the author's personal preferences are often reflected in the individual commentaries, the following distinctive features of the commentary are consistent throughout.

Distinctively Baptist: Each of the commentators holds to the basic Baptist distinctives of the soul liberty of the individual priesthood of each believer, believer's baptism by immersion, the autonomy of the local church, separation of church and state, congregational church government, recognition of the Bible alone as our final authority in all matters of faith and practice, the ordinances of the local church, and the view that the Great Commission is given to the local church. Hence, the view of the New Testament church taken herein emphasizes the church's manifestation in autonomous local congregations, whose nature, discipline, and regulations are clearly defined in Scripture.

Aggressively Fundamental: We make no apology for the fundamentalist theology which is evident throughout this commentary. Each writer is personally committed to the fundamental doctrines of the Christian faith: the inerrant inspiration of the Scripture, the virgin birth and deity of Jesus Christ, His vicarious atonement, bodily resurrection, and literal Second Coming.

Historically Evangelical: The historic orthodox and evangelical doctrines of salvation by grace through faith are also evident throughout this commentary. The emphasis upon the evangelistic mandate of the church and the importance of individual conversion are also essential to the hermeneutic of this commentary. While academic and critical in its tone, this volume is warm and fervent in spirit.

Eschatologically Premillennial: The nature of predictive prophecy is viewed literally regarding its fulfillment. Thus, the eschatology of the commentators is both pretribulational and premillennial. However, many of the excessive divisions of extreme dispensationalism have been avoided. The rapture of the church is viewed as the next major coming event in Bible prophecy.

A note of appreciation should be extended to the entire faculty of Liberty Baptist College, who aided the production of the commentary by their total support of the project. We are especially grateful to the editorial staff of Thomas Nelson Publishers and Dr. Elmer Towns and the publications division of the Old-Time Gospel Hour ministries who gave many valuable insights to the final production of this volume. In all, it has been a very fulfilling experience to see a commentary of this nature come to fruition. It is our prayer that our Lord Jesus Christ will use it as a means of instruction to His church for many generations to come.

Edward E. Hindson
Woodrow Michael Kroll
on "Liberty Mountain"
Lynchburg, Virginia
September 1, 1978

CONTENTS

MAP SUPPLEMENTS

CONTRIBUTORS

James A. Borland, Th.D. Gospel of Luke, Philemon
Professor of Religion, Liberty Baptist College
B.A., Los Angeles Baptist College; M.Div., Los Angeles Baptist
Theological Seminary; Th.M., Talbot Theological Seminary; Th.D.,
Grace Theological Seminary.

Benjamin C. Chapman, Ph.D. Biblical Language Editor, I-II Thessalonians, Epistles of Peter, John, Jude
Professor of Religion, Liberty Baptist College
B.R.E., Grand Rapids Baptist College; B.D., M.R.E., Grand Rapids
Baptist Seminary; Th.M., Calvin Theological Seminary; Ph.D., Bob
Jones University. Additional graduate study at the University of
Michigan and University of Manitoba (Canada).

Edward G. Dobson, M.A. Gospel of John
Assistant Professor of Religion, Liberty Baptist College
B.A., M.A., Bob Jones University; Doctoral student at University of
Virginia.

Jerry Falwell, D.D., D.Litt. Executive Editor
Chancellor of Liberty Baptist Schools
Th.G., Baptist Bible College; D.D., Tennessee Temple University;
D.Litt., California Graduate School of Theology.

Edward E. Hindson, Th.D., D.Min. General Editor, Gospel of Matthew
Professor of Religion at Liberty Baptist College
B.A., Detroit Bible College; M.A., Trinity Evangelical Divinity
School; Th.M., Grace Theological Seminary; Th.D., Trinity
Graduate School of Theology; D.Min., Westminster Theological
Seminary. Additional graduate study at Eastern Michigan University
and Acadia University (Canada).

Woodrow Michael Kroll, Th.D. General Editor, Romans, Revelation
Professor of Religion, Liberty Baptist College
B.A., Barrington College; M.Div., Gordon-Conwell Theological
Seminary; Th.M., Th.D., Geneva Theological Seminary. Additional
graduate study at Harvard Divinity School; Princeton Theological
Seminary; the University of Strasbourg (France);Trinity Evangelical
Divinity School.

Daniel R. Mitchell, Th.D. Cand. I-II Corinthians
Assistant Professor of Religion, Liberty Baptist College
B.A., Washington Bible College; Th.M., Capital Bible Seminary;
S.T.M., Dallas Theological Seminary; Th.D. candidate, Dallas Theological Seminary.

Edward R. Roustio, Th.D. Galatians, Ephesians, Philippians, Colossians
Associate Professor, Liberty Baptist Seminary
A.B., William Jewell College; Th.M., Southern Baptist Theological
Seminary; Th.M., Th.D., Central Baptist Theological Seminary.

James D. Stevens, S.T.M. Gospel of Mark, James
Associate Professor of Religion, Liberty Baptist College
B.A., Bob Jones University; M.Div., Grace Theological Seminary;
S.T.M., Dallas Theological Seminary. Additional graduate study at
Eastern Michigan University and the University of Virginia.

Philip R. Stover, M.A.   Hebrews
Assistant Professor of Psychology, Liberty Baptist College
B.A., John Brown University; M.A., Rosemead Graduate School of Psychology. Additional graduate study at Baylor University and Southwestern Baptist Theological Seminary. Doctoral studies in progress at University of Virginia.

C. Sumner Wemp, D.D.   I-II Timothy, Titus, Philemon
Vice President and Professor of Religion, Liberty Baptist College
B.A., Samford University; Th.M., Dallas Theological Seminary; D.D., California Graduate School of Theology. Doctoral studies in progress at Trinity Evangelical Divinity School.

Harold L. Wilmington, D.D.   Acts of the Apostles
Dean of Thomas Road Bible Institute
Dip., Moody Bible Institute; B.A., Culver-Stockton College, D.D., California Graduate School of Theology. Additional graduate study at Dallas Theological Seminary and Ashland Theological Seminary.

LIST OF ABBREVIATIONS

Gen	Genesis	Nah	Nahum
Ex	Exodus	Hab	Habakkuk
Lev	Leviticus	Zeph	Zephaniah
Num	Numbers	Hag	Haggai
Deut	Deuteronomy	Zech	Zechariah
Josh	Joshua	Mal	Malachi
Jud	Judges	Mt	Matthew
Ruth	Ruth	Mk	Mark
I Sam	I Samuel	Lk	Luke
II Sam	II Samuel	Jn	John
I Kgs	I Kings	Acts	Acts
II Kgs	II Kings	Rom	Romans
I Chr	I Chronicles	I Cor	I Corinthians
II Chr	II Chronicles	II Cor	II Corinthians
Ezr	Ezra	Gal	Galatians
Neh	Nehemiah	Eph	Ephesians
Est	Esther	Phil	Philippians
Job	Job	Col	Colossians
Ps	Psalms	I Thess	I Thessalonians
Prov	Proverbs	II Thess	II Thessalonians
Eccl	Ecclesiastes	I Tim	I Timothy
Song	Song of Solomon	II Tim	II Timothy
Isa	Isaiah	Tit	Titus
Jer	Jeremiah	Phm	Philemon
Lam	Lamentations	Heb	Hebrews
Ezk	Ezekiel	Jas	James
Dan	Daniel	I Pet	I Peter
Hos	Hosea	II Pet	II Peter
Joel	Joel	I Jn	I John
Amos	Amos	II Jn	II John
Ob	Obadiah	III Jn	III John
Jon	Jonah	Jude	Jude
Mic	Micah	Rev	Revelation

AV	Authorized Version	Lat	Latin
RV	Revised Version	Eng	English
RSV	Revised Standard Version	viz.	namely
ASV	American Standard Version	e.g.	for example
NEB	New English Bible	i.e.	that is
NASB	New American Standard Bible	cf	compare
		ch.	chapter
NIV	New International Version	chs.	chapters
LXX	Septuagint	p.	page
MS	Manuscript	pp.	pages
MSS	Manuscripts	vs.	verse
Gr	Greek	vss.	verses
Heb	Hebrew	lit.	literally
Aram	Aramaic	ca.	around

Antiq.	*Antiquities of the Jews* by Josephus
Eccl. Hist.	*Ecclesiastical History* by Eusebius
Adv. Her.	*Against Heresies* by Irenaeus
Wars	*Jewish Wars* by Josephus

ORIGINAL LANGUAGE TRANSLITERATIONS

Hebrew Consonants	Hebrew Vowels	Greek Consonants and Vowels
א = '	ַ = a	α = a
בּ = b	ָ = a	β = b
ג = g	ֵ = e	γ = g
ד = d	ֵ = ē	δ = d
ה = h	ֵ = ē	ε = e
ו = w	ִ = ī	ζ = z
ז = z	ִ = i	η = ē
ח = ch	ֹ = ō	θ = th
ט = t	וֹ = ō	ι = i
י = y	ֻ = u	κ = k
כּ = k	וּ = ū	λ = l
ל = l	ְ = e	μ = m
מ = m		ν = n
נ = n		ξ = x
ס = s		ο = o
ע = '		π = p
פּ = p		ρ = r
צ = ts		σ = s
ק = q		τ = t
ר = r		υ = y
שׂ = s		φ = ph
שׁ = sh		χ = ch
ת = t		ψ = ps
		ω = ō

Note: The Hebrew Dagesh Lene and Dagesh Forte are not indicated. Every vocal Shewa is indicated by short e; silent Shewa is not indicated. In Greek, ι subscript is not indicated, and in diphthongs υ is indicated as u.

LIBERTY COMMENTARY

On The

NEW TESTAMENT

The Gospel According To

MATTHEW

INTRODUCTION

The four Gospels present a fourfold view of the life of Christ. With the exception of scant references by Tacitus and Josephus, our entire knowledge of the life of Jesus comes from these gospel accounts. Most likely, the early accounts were passed on verbally in the Aramaic language and then recorded in Greek manuscripts between A.D. 60-90. All four Gospels build upon genuine historical tradition and preserve different aspects of it.

The basic purpose of the Gospels is to present the Gospel message, the good news of the Redeemer-Saviour. They present Jesus as the Messiah of Israel, the Son of God, and the Saviour of the world. The gospels were written so that their readers would come to believe in Christ and receive eternal life (cf. Jn 20:31). They view Jesus as the Lord of Glory who is presently alive and active in heaven.

The New Testament was not given and received as a single volume, but it grew together by recognition and use. "The order in which we now read the books of the New Testament is that which on the whole, they have tended to assume; and the general internal arrangement, by which the entire collection forms for us a consecutive course of teaching, has been sufficiently recognized by the instinct and fixed by the habit of the church" (T. D. Bernard, *The Progress of Doctrine in the New Testament,* p. 23).

The order of the Gospels has been generally recognized by the church throughout its history. "The Gospel of Matthew occupies first place in all extant witnesses to the text of the four Gospels and in all early lists of the canonical books of the New Testament." (R. V. G. Tasker, *The Gospel*

According to St. Matthew, Tyndale New Testament Commentary, p. 11). Matthew's emphasis upon the Old Testament preparation for the gospel makes it an ideal "bridge" from the Old to the New Testament.

The four Gospels present four portraits of Jesus, each in its own characteristic manner. "The greatness of this person could not have been captured in one picture. So we have four portraits, each bringing out its own distinctive facets of the character of Jesus" (I. H. Marshall, The Gospels and Jesus Christ. In *Eerdman's Handbook to the Bible,* p. 470). Matthew, the Hebrew tax collector, writes for the Hebrew mind. Mark, the travel companion of Paul and Peter, writes for the Roman mind. Luke, Paul's physician-missionary, writes with the Greek mentality in view. John's Gospel is different by nature from the other three. It is an interpretation of the facts of Jesus' life rather than a presentation of its facts in historical sequence.

Authorship. The book itself is anonymous, but the earliest of traditions credits it to Matthew, the disciple of Jesus. Papias, the second century Bishop of Hierapolis, Irenaeus, the Bishop of Lyons, Origen in the third century, and Eusebius, who wrote his *Historia Ecclesiastica* in the fourth century, all agree that Matthew was the author of this Gospel and that he originally wrote it in Hebrew (probably meaning Aramaic, the common spoken language of the early Christians). However, there is no trace of this Aramaic "original" and the earliest quotations (early second century) from Matthew are in Greek.

It is difficult to determine at this time whether Matthew, as we know it today, is a Greek translation of his Aramaic original or whether it was originally written in Greek. Scholars, both conservative and liberal, are divided in their opinion on this matter. However, an examination of the Greek gospel does not substantiate the idea that it is a translation, for it has none of the characteristics of a translated work. Walvoord *(Matthew: Thy Kingdom Come,* pp. 10-12) points out that the gospel of Matthew includes a number of untranslated Aramaic terms. He comments: "These would be intelligible to Jewish Christians, but if Matthew was translated from Aramaic into Greek for the benefit of Gentile Christians, these terms would require an explanation. The fact that the terms are not translated tends to prove that the Gospel of Matthew was originally written in Greek, even though intended for an audience that also understood Aramaic" (p. 10).

A unique statement within the book of Matthew provides internal evidence to its authorship. The account of the call of Matthew (ch. 9) is followed by that of a meal taken by Jesus in the company of "publicans and sinners." The best translation of this passage says the meal took place "at home." The parallel account in Mark 2:15 makes it clear that this feast took place in Levi's (i.e. Matthew's) house. "The phrase 'at home' means 'in my (that is, in the author's) house.' Here, therefore, is a phrase that betrays the identity of the author" (B.F.C. Atkinson, The Gospel According to Matthew. In *The New Bible Commentary.* p. 771).

It is possible that Matthew wrote both an Aramaic "Gospel" of the sayings of Jesus and the Greek Gospel which now bears his name, since he was bilingual. Catholic scholars (Lagrange, Chapman, Butler) have tended to uphold the idea of an Aramaic original while liberal Protestants (Allen, Albright) have favored the idea of a Greek original based on the priority of Mark as its major source. Conservative scholars (Kent, Lenski, Walvoord) have generally rejected the idea that Matthew was dependent upon Mark as a source document and hold to the view that Matthew himself wrote the Greek version of his Gospel as an original apostolic witness to Christ.

Priority of Matthew. Two major critical views have been advanced in the twentieth century denying the priority of Matthew's Gospel: (1) the priority of Mark as the basic source document of both Matthew and Luke; (2) the previous existence of a common source document (Q) to all the synoptics. The "Q Theory" has recently fallen on rough ground among form-critics (cf A. M. Farrar, "On Dispensing with Q" in D. Nineham, ed. *Studies in the Gospels*). Neither view has really substantially proven its case even though many evangelicals hold to the priority of Mark (cf. Tasker, p. 17). W. R. Farmer and L. Keck are among several contemporary scholars to return to Griesbach's theory on the priority of Matthew. For a thorough discussion of the introductory matters regarding Matthew, see D. Guthrie, *New Testament Introduction,* pp. 19-48.

OUTLINE

III. Triumph of the Messiah. 28:1-20.
   A. His Resurrection. 28:1-8.
   B. His Reappearance. 28:9-15.
   C. His Recommission. 28:16-20.

COMMENTARY

I. COMING OF THE MESSIAH. 1:1-4:11.

A. His Ancestry. 1:1-17.

1:1-2. The book of the generation. The genealogy of Christ opens with a statement similar to the various divisions of the book of Genesis (showing the unity of the Scriptures). **Jesus Christ** is the title most often used of the Saviour. Jesus (Gr *Iēsous;* Heb. *Yehoshua*) is His earthly name, meaning "saviour". *Christos* is the Greek translation for "messiah" or "anointed". Technically: Jesus the Christ.

Son of David. By tracing Jesus' ancestry back to King David, through the line of Davidic kings, Matthew connects Jesus with His royal heritage. Despite six centuries of vacancy on the royal throne, the Messiah must be of royal descent. The genealogy here is that of Joseph, Jesus' legal father, whereas, the genealogy of Luke 3:23-38 is that of Mary, His actual parent, showing His blood line back to David. The author's purpose is to show that the messianic promises made to David's line are fulfilled in Jesus. **Son of Abraham.** He is also the fulfillment of the covenant promises to Abraham, the forefather of the Jews (cf. Gen 12:3; 13:15; 22:18). Since Matthew is writing primarily to Jewish readers, he naturally begins by emphasizing Jesus' Jewish parentage.

1-8. Judas is the Greek form of Judah, the father of the tribe so named. The promise of Jacob was that the leadership of the twelve tribes would come through Judah (cf. Gen 49:8-12) which the Jews understood to mean that the Messiah would come from the tribe of Judah. **Thamar . . . Rachab . . . Ruth . . . wife of Uriah.** Four "questionable" women appear in this genealogy in addition to Mary, the mother of Jesus. It was not customary to list the names of women in a genealogy; therefore, the inclusion of these names must be deliberate on the part of the author. Tamar was the mother of two illegitimate sons (Pharez and Zerah) by Judah. Rahab was the converted prostitute of Jericho and the mother of Boaz. Ruth, the wife of Boaz, was a godly foreigner (Moabitess). The wife of Uriah is none other than Bathsheba whose adultery with David is infamous. However, she later became the legitimate wife of David and the mother of Solomon. The curious feature of mentioning these women in this genealogy indicates that the evangelist wished to disarm Jewish criticism about the unusual virgin birth of Jesus by showing that irregular unions were divinely blessed in the Messiah's legal ancestry. "The evangelist's argument is that Jesus, born of a virgin mother, was none the less the true lineage of David because Joseph was in fact legally married to his mother Mary." (Tasker, p. 32).

9-10. Ozias is referred to as Uzziah (Isa 6:1) and Azariah (II Kgs 14:21). Three generations are omitted at this point. Matthew omits the names of Ahaziah, Joash, and Amaziah and then omits Jehoiakim after the name of Josiah. "The omissions are doubtless due to his arbitrary shortening of the list to give three groups of fourteen" (Kent, p.3). Being familiar with rabbinical thinking, Matthew uses a symmetry of numbers. He has, accordingly, divided the generations from

Abraham to Jesus into three groups of fourteen each: from Abraham to David (vss. 2-6), from David to the Babolynian exile (vss. 6-11), from the exile to the birth of Jesus (vss. 12-16). The significance of the number fourteen seems to come from the numerical values of the Hebrew consonants in the name David which add up to that number. The system of rabbinic sacred arithmetic was often based on hidden calculations. To what degree Matthew is following such a system is uncertain.

11-15 Jechoniah is also called Jehoiachin (II Kgs 24:8) and Coniah (Jer 22:24) and was cursed from having any descendant upon the throne of David according to Jeremiah 22:30. It should be noted that Jesus is not a natural descendant of his. He was recognized by the Jews of the exile as their last legitimate king. **Carried away to Babylon** refers to the seventy years' captivity of the Jews in Babylon during the days of Daniel the prophet.

12. Salathiel is named as the son of Jechoniah. This does not contradict Jeremiah 22:28-30 for the predicted childlessness of Jechoniah refers to reigning children, that is, that he would have no son who would rule Israel as king. The reference to Salathiel as the son of Neri in Luke 3:27 is better understood as being a totally different person, rather than the result of levirate marriage. It is assumed that the rest of this family record comes from Joseph's family annals.

16. Joseph the husband of Mary. The wording carefully inspired by the Holy Spirit avoids giving the impression that Joseph was the natural father of Jesus. As the husband of Mary, he was Jesus' legal father and the one through whom He had a right to David's throne. It is not said that Joseph "begat" Jesus, which is a deliberate change from the preceding genealogical expressions. Every emphasis of the text at this point reinforces the idea of the virgin birth of Christ. The marriage of Joseph and

Mary took place after the conception but before the birth of Jesus.

17. Fourteen generations is the literary grouping used by Matthew to emphasize the three major periods of Israel's national history: theocracy, monarchy, hierarchy. The use of "so" implies this is an artificial arrangement. The translation would be "so this makes fourteen generations."

B. His Advent. 1:18-2:23.

18. Espoused means that Mary was already bound or betrothed to Joseph, although they were not yet actually married. Among the Jews, marriage vows were said at the betrothal and required a legal divorce to end them. The custom of the day usually required an interval of one year of betrothal before the bride could actually take residence in her husband's house and consummate their union. It was during this interval that Mary **was found with child.** Her pregnancy naturally would have been assumed to be the result of an illegitimate union of adultery, a circumstance usually punishable by death (Deut 22:23). At this point, Mary had not yet explained her situation to Joseph. Indeed, she could hardly have expected Joseph to accept her story of the miraculous birth of the child by the Holy Spirit. **With child of the Holy Ghost** is the biblical explanation for the miraculous conception of Christ.

19-20. Because Joseph was a **just man,** he decided to divorce Mary privately (privily) but while he considered what should be done **the angel of the Lord** spoke to him in a dream. The angel is better translated as "an angel." Prior to His birth, Jesus Christ, the second person of the Trinity, often appeared to men in the form of a man. These appearances in the Old Testament are called theophanies or Christophanies. Since the Scripture clearly states that "no man hath seen God at any time" (Jn 1:18), these appearances evidently refer to Christ rather than God the Father. It is in-

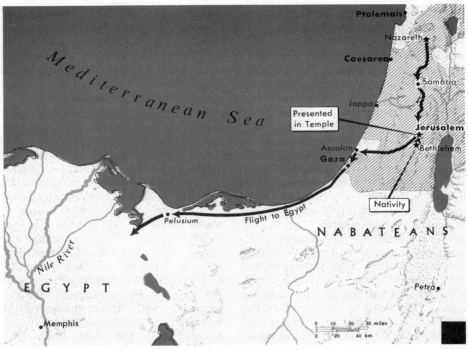

The Birth of Jesus and the Flight Into Egypt

teresting to note the references to God refer to Him as Lord (cf. Gen 18:2, 13, 17). After His birth as Jesus, there were no more temporary physical appearances of God to man. After His resurrection Jesus appeared to men as Himself in a glorified body.

Put her away means literally to divorce her. The Jewish betrothal had to be legally broken. Joseph's merciful attitude gives an insight into his true nature as a man. **Thou son of David** is the address by the angel to Joseph. In spite of his humble circumstances, he was a legitimate heir to the vacant throne of David. The angel orders him to take Mary as his wife because the baby she has conceived is **of the Holy Ghost**. This divinely born miracle-son is the fulfillment of God's miraculous promises to the Jewish nation, which promises began in the book of Genesis with God's covenant with Abraham.

21-22. Call his name Jesus. The naming of the child Jesus (Heb *Yehoshua*) means "Jehovah saves." This points to the very purpose of Christ's coming into the world to save sinners. Placed early in the New Testament, this statement becomes the foundational concept of the gospel. Jesus, by His very name and nature is the Saviour. **That it might be fulfilled.** This phrase (Gr *plēroō*) indicates the inevitability of the fulfillment of the words of the prophet, as well as the fact that Matthew saw Isaiah's statement as predictively fulfilled in the birth of Christ. "The verb pictures the promise or prophecy as an empty vessel which is at last filled when the event occurs" (R. Lenski, *Interpretation of St. Matthew's Gospel,* p. 52). Arndt and Gingrich list this use of the word as "the fulfillment of divine predictions or promises" (*A Greek-English Lexicon of the New Testament,* p. 677). There can be no doubt that Matthew firmly believed this reference was definitely a prediction of an event that was fulfilled in the birth of Jesus. One wishing to deny the predictive element of Isaiah or its acceptance by the early church cannot adequately do so on a philological-grammatical basis, nor on the basis of historical precedent.

23. A virgin relates Mary the mother of Jesus to the prediction found in Isaiah 7:14. Matthew uses the Greek word *parthenos* to translate the Hebrew word *'almah*. His contextual usage of "fulfill" is almost certainly indicative of his understanding the Isaiah passage to contain a definitely predictive element. He recognizes the prophecy as coming from God (the Greek preposition *hypo* introduces the direct agent with a passive verb, whereas *dia* introduces the mediate agent). The Lord is the source of the prophecy and the prophet is his mouthpiece. Thus, God is the cause and the prophet is the instrument which He uses. The quotation of Isaiah 7:14 follows the Septuagint (LXX) rendering where *parthenos* is also used to translate the Hebrew *'almah*. Perhaps no prophetic prediction has created a greater controversy than Isaiah's prediction of a virgin-born son which Matthew clearly claims to have been fulfilled in the birth of Christ (cf. *The Interpreter's Bible*, V, p. 218. It is interesting to note that the exegetical and homiletical sections of this work are done by different authors, and on the same page the exegete denies that Isaiah is predicting the birth of Christ and the Expositor claims that he is!). The liberal interpretation of this verse attempts to deny the validity of Matthew's use of Isaiah 7:14 as a prediction of the birth of Christ (cf. G. Cox, *The Gospel According to St. Matthew*, pp. 29-30; A. Argyle, *The Gospel According to Matthew*, p. 28; F. Filson, *A Commentary on the Gospel According to St. Matthew*, pp. 54-55).

There can be no doubt that the Greek term *parthenos* is always to be translated "virgin" (Arndt and Gingrich, p. 632). The real question is whether the LXX is correct in its translation of the Hebrew *'almah*. Since the weight of scholarship supports the translation of the Hebrew word *'almah*. as being the most accurate word possible for "virgin," one can only conclude that the LXX translaters were correct in their interpretation. The Dead Sea Scroll copy of Isaiah indicates the same usage (cf. G. Knight, *A Christian Theology of the Old Testament,* p. 310). For a thorough discussion of the Old Testament usage of *almah* see E. J. Young, *The Book of Isaiah, I,* pp. 284-291; *Studies in Isaiah,* pp. 143-198; C. Feinberg, "Virgin Birth in the Old Testament and Isaiah 7:14," *Bibliotheca Sacra* 119, pp. 251-58; E. Hindson, *Isaiah's Immanuel* and "Development of the Interpretation of Isaiah 7:14," *Grace Journal,* X, 1, 2 pp. 3-15, 19-25.

The virgin birth of Christ is undoubtedly the most essential doctrine underlying His deity. The prediction in Isaiah 7:14 of a virgin born son calls His name **Emmanuel** "which being interpreted is, God with us." This is a title describing the deity of the person of the Son of God rather than a name actually used by him. It implies God will come to dwell among His own people. For a discussion of the significance of the virgin birth of Christ see R. Gromacki, *The Virgin Birth: Doctrine of Deity;* H. Hanke, *The Validity of the Virgin Birth;* J. G. Machen, *The Virgin Birth of Christ.*

2:1-2. Bethlehem of Judaea was also called Ephrath. The town is five miles south of Jerusalem. Its name in Hebrew means "house of bread." This Judaean city was the birthplace of King David. It was the original city of Joseph's ancestors. According to Luke 2:1-7, Mary and he traveled there from Nazareth and Jesus was born in a stable after they arrived there. **Herod the king** was known as Herod the Great. and was the son of Antipater, an Edomite. He became king by Roman decree in 43 B.C. **Wise men** were originally the priestly caste among the Persians and Babylonians. These Magi from the east were experts in the study of the stars. Tradition claims there were three royal visitors who were also kings. However there is no real historical evidence to verify this. All we are told in the text is that there came wise men from the east to Jerusalem. **Born King of the Jews.** The wise men naturally came to Jerusalem, the royal capital of Israel, seeking one whom they thought was to be born a king, on the basis of their calculations of the stars. What exactly this meant to them we are not sure. Perhaps, through the science of astronomy they observed a new star and for some reason correlated that with the birth of a king. Why they would associate this star with Israel is uncertain. "It is entirely conceivable that these men had made contact with Jewish exiles, or with the prophecies and influence of Daniel, and thus were in possession of Old Testament prophecies regarding the Messiah" (Kent, p. 6). **His star.** It is unlikely that this star could only have been a natural phenomenon since it led the wise men to Jerusalem and later to Bethlehem. It almost certainly was a divine manifestation used by God to indicate the fact and place of the Messiah's birth and the place of His reign.

3-4. Naturally, such a question, seeking the birth of a new king, would upset Herod, the current ruler. He quickly gathered his scribes and demanded an explanation of them. The scribes belonged mainly to the party of the Pharisees and functioned as members of a highly honored profession. "They were professional students and defenders of the law . . . they were also referred to as lawyers because they were entrusted with the administration of law as judges in the Sanhedrin" (*Ryrie Study Bible*, p. 8). **Where Christ should be born.** This demand is highly

significant in that it implies the Jews of that day were anticipating the Messiah.

5-6. When they replied that he would be born in Bethlehem of Judaea, **for thus it is written by the prophet,** they clearly anticipated a literal fulfillment of the Old Testament prophecies regarding the coming of the Messiah. The quotation is from Micah 5:2 where the prophet predicts that Bethlehem of the tribe of Judah shall be the place where the governor or ruler of Israel shall originate. It is significant to note that Isaiah and Micah were contemporaries. Their prophecies of the coming of the Messiah interrelate to one another. The **Governor** who will come from Bethlehem is none other than the child-ruler predicted in Isaiah 9:6, "For unto us a child is born, unto us a son is given; and the government shall be upon His shoulder." The prophet goes on to proclaim that this ruler is the "mighty God" and that the increase of His government shall never end. He will sit upon the throne of David forever.

7-11. Herod's fear of a rival ruler caused him to question **what time the star appeared.** His subsequent slaughter of the children at Bethlehem from two years old and under was apparently calculated from the time given him by the wise men. The fact that the child was found in a **house** (vs. 11) and not the manger would indicate that Jesus was probably no longer a baby when the wise men found Him. They were guided to this place by the **star** which **went before them.** This again indicates the supernatural nature of this star. **The young child.** When the wise men arrived they found the child (not a baby) with His mother in a house. This would indicate that the family had now moved out of the stable into a rented home at Bethlehem. Whether the visit of the wise men occurred a few months after the birth of the child or one to two years afterwards is uncertain. Since the wise men brought three gifts, i.e. **gold, frankincense and myrrh,** it has been assumed that they were three in number (some traditions have even given them names but these are not necessarily established by fact). It has been suggested that the gifts were in recognition of Jesus as King, Son of God, and the Suffering Saviour. It is also significant that they **worshipped him**, indicating their recognition of the deity of the one whom they were worshipping. Again, Matthew has reasserted the importance of the deity of Christ. He is the virgin-born Son, "God with us," who deserves our worship.

12-15. Being warned of God. A special divine revelation in the form of a warning was given both to the wise men and to Joseph in the form of a dream. Thus instructed, the wise men did not return to Herod, and Joseph and Mary fled with the baby into Egypt. It should be remembered that there was a large Jewish population in Egypt at that time, especially in and around the city of Alexandria. The holy family would have been inconspicuous during their stay and would have been welcomed by members of their own race. **The death of Herod** occurred in 4 B.C. It should be remembered that our present calendar is off in its calculation by about six years (this would place the birth of Christ at ca 6-5 B.C.). Herod's death is recorded in detail by Josephus (*Antiq.* xvii. 6.5). The flight to Egypt by Jesus' family is related by Matthew to the statement in Hosea 11:1 which refers historically to the deliverance of the Hebrews from Egypt. Matthew records that this was done that it **might be fulfilled**. Since the Old Testament statement is not a direct reference to Christ, it is apparent that the writer saw this prophecy as a type of Christ. (On the significance and reliability of Matthew's quotations of Old Testament prophecies see R. H. Gundry, *The Use of the Old Testament in St. Matthew's Gospel*).

16-18. The bitter reaction of Herod when he **slew all the children** at Bethlehem was unrecorded in the history of that period. This should not surprise us because of the king's frequently outraged retaliation on people. He murdered his wife and three sons. Josephus calls him "a man of great barbarity towards all men." **Rachel weeping for her children** (vs. 18) is a quotation of Jeremiah 31:15. The calamity of Israel's mourning at the time of the exile is correlated here to this renewed calamity brought on by Herod, whose very act of ruling is a direct result of that captivity which had been caused by Israel's sin. **Rachel weeping** is a reference to Rachel, the mother of Benjamin, and thus the tribe of Benjamin. She stands as the symbol of the Benjamite mothers and their sorrow. Also, note that she died outside Bethlehem herself (Gen 35:19).

19-23. When Herod was dead refers again to the death of the king in 4 B.C. He was succeeded by his son **Archelaus**, the son of his Samaritan wife, Malthace. Archelaus was as brutal as his father. Thus, Joseph, again warned in a dream, returned to Nazareth, avoiding any further residence in Judaea. The phrase **He shall be called a Nazarene** is a reference to Christ's coming from the city of Nazareth. It should not be taken to mean that He was a Nazirite. A Nazirite was not to drink wine, touch anything unclean, or cut his hair. It was probably a misunderstanding that caused early Roman artists to depict Jesus with long hair. The proof that He was not a Nazirite is found in the fact that He did not keep the other two provisions of the vow. Many of the very people which He came to minister to were considered "unclean" by the people of His day. Since no particular Old Testament passage is referred to, it seems best to understand this verse as referring to a fulfillment of those prophecies which indicate that the Messiah would be of insignificant origin and despised by people (e.g. Isa 53:3).

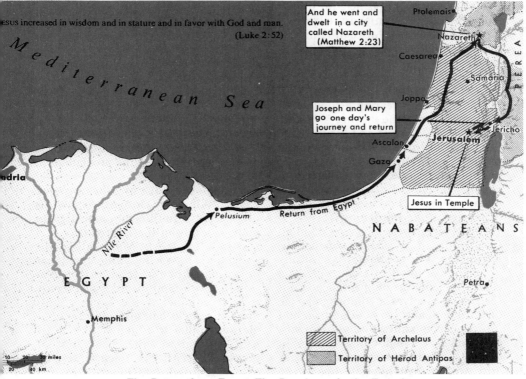

Jesus increased in wisdom and in stature and in favor with God and man.
(Luke 2:52)

And he went and
dwelt in a city
called Nazareth
(Matthew 2:23)

Joseph and Mary
go one day's
journey and return

Jesus in Temple

Mediterranean Sea

Nile River

Pelusium   Return from Egypt

NABATEANS

EGYPT

Memphis

Ptolemais

Nazareth

Caesarea

Samaria

PEREA

Joppa

Ascalon   Jerusalem   Jericho

Gaza

Petra

Alexandria

Territory of Archelaus

Territory of Herod Antipas

10   20   30 miles
20   40 km

The Return from Egypt; The Boy Jesus in the Temple

C. His Ambassador. 3:1-12.

3:1. The forerunner of Christ was **John the Baptist.** He was the son of Zacharias and Elisabeth, and a cousin of the Lord (cf. Lk 1:5-80). The significance of his preparatory ministry cannot be overestimated. Even Josephus (*Antiq.* xviii 5.2) refers to him by name. John was a child of promise whose birth had been announced by the angel Gabriel to his father who was a priest. His birth was accompanied by the promise: "He shall be great in the sight of the Lord . . . and shall be filled with the Holy Ghost" (Lk 1:15). Jesus said of him that there was none greater than John (Mt 11:11) during the Old Testament dispensation. This would imply that John the Baptist was the epitome of the message of the Old Testament itself.

Matthew's reference to John the

Baptist assumes that his readers were familiar with him. There is no connection anywhere in scripture to relate John to one of the Essene communities or to the Qumran sect (of the Dead Sea Scrolls). The real significance of John seems to be his appearance in the **wilderness of Judaea,** the eastern part of the province lying beyond the mountain ridge and west of the Dead Sea. This infertile area may rightly be called a "wilderness." John's appearance, preaching a message of repentance, is in fulfillment of Isaiah 40:3, "Prepare ye the way of the Lord." The words of the prophet originally formed the part of his message to the Babylonian exiles, who eventually returned to their own land. John, the last of the prophets of Israel, was now commissioned to prepare the way for the King. "The reign of God was immediately to be made manifest in Israel in all its fullness in the Person and the work of none other than the Messiah Himself'' (Tasker, p. 47). John is presented as the prophet sent in the spirit of Elijah "before the coming of the great and dreadful day of the Lord'' (Mal 4:5). His appearance (wearing a rough coat of camel's hair and having a leather belt around his waist and his dynamic and often scathing preaching) certainly depicts him in the life style of Israel's ancient prophet. Jesus would later proclaim, "I tell you that Elijah has already come!'' (For a recent study see M. Loane, *John the Baptist*.)

2. Repent means a change of mind that leads to a change of action. Repentance (Gr *metanoia*) is basically "a change of mind" which results in a change of conduct. Repentance is not sorrow. It involves a complete change of attitude regarding God and sin and is often accompanied by a sense of sorrow and a corresponding change in conduct. Such repentance does not arise within man himself, but is the result of God's mercy in leading man to it (cf. Acts 5:31; Rom 2:4; II Tim 2:25). Thus, repentance involves the very process of conversion whereby men are born again. (On the significance of repentance see H. A. Ironside, *Except Ye Repent*.)

John's message of repentance was necessary in order to prepare people for the **kingdom of heaven** which was **at hand**. The phrase "kingdom of heaven" is used only in the Gospel of Matthew and seems to be based on similar references in the book of Daniel. The phrase "the kingdom of God" is used more frequently by Mark and Luke. The change is perhaps due to Matthew's Jewish background and outlook. Since the Jews regarded it as blasphemous to refer to God by name, it is possible that Matthew substituted the word heaven for that reason. Usually the two phrases are used interchangeably in the Gospels. The kingdom of heaven is the rule of

heaven over earth. The Jews of Jesus' day were looking forward to the coming of a Messiah who would reign in a Davidic kingdom on earth. It is this kingdom which Christ proclaimed was a literal earthly kingdom, based upon spiritual principles, which would demand a right relationship with God for entrance into that kingdom. Therefore, John the Baptist's ministry is clearly seen as a time of preparation for the coming of Christ and the proclamation of His kingdom.

3-7. Spoken of by the prophet Esaias. All four Gospels relate this prophecy to a fulfillment in the life and ministry of John the Baptist (Mk 1:2; Lk 3:4; Jn 1:23). **Make his paths straight** refers to the straightening or preparing of one's life in a right relationship with God in order to prepare for the coming of the King. John's dress of **camel's hair and a leathern girdle** was similar to Elijah's clothing (II Kgs 1:8) and was the usual dress of prophets (Zech 13:4). **Locusts** were an allowable food (cf. Lev 11:22) and were eaten by the very poorest of people. The reference in verse 5 to **Jerusalem and all Judaea** relates to the people of those places. John's ministry was received with great enthusiasm in its early stages. So great was his success that even many of the **Pharisees and Sadducees** (vs. 7) came to this baptism.

8-10. Fruits meet for repentance. John rebuked the Pharisees, asking them to give evidence of **fruits meet for repentance** (vs. 8). There can be no doubt that the New Testament concept of repentance grows out of its biblical usage in the Old Testament where the term (Heb *shub*) means far more than an intellectual change of mind. Genuine repentance proves itself by the fruits of a changed life. John the Baptist further rebuked them for their belief in nationalistic salvation. **Abraham to our father** means they were trusting their physical descendence for salvation, rather than their spiritual relationship to the father of faith. **Of these stones** may be a reference to Isaiah 5:12, but is probably to be taken in the natural setting of the seashore. The **axe** about to chop the **root of the trees** is a reference to the impending judgment coming upon Israel (God's chosen tree, cf. Rom 11) if they reject the Messiah-King. Again, fruitlessness is depicted as a lack of conversion and spiritual life. No fruit means no life in the soul.

11-12. I baptize . . . with water. John's baptism in water was not Christian baptism. The death and resurrection of Christ had not yet occurred in order to be depicted by this baptism. John's baptism was similar to the Old Testament oblations (washings) that symbolized a cleansing of personal repentance on the part of a believer. Notice that Jesus submitted to this baptism to **fulfill all righteousness** (vs. 15). As God, He could not submit to baptism into the body of the church of which He is the Head. **He shall baptize . . . with the Holy Ghost** refers to the spiritual rebirth of the regenerate who shall receive the baptism of the Spirit (cf. I Cor 12:13, which clearly indicates that all believers have received the baptism of the Spirit). This experience began at Pentecost (Acts 1) and was repeated upon every new group of converts: Samaritans, Gentiles, John's disciples, etc. until it became normative for all Christian believers.

The term **and fire** is better translated "or fire". The immediate context certainly indicates that to be baptized with fire is the result of judgment (notice the reference to purging and burning in the next verse). Other than the visible tongues (billows) of fire which appeared over the disciples' heads at Pentecost, references to fire burning up unprofitable chaff refer to judgment rather than cleansing. The threshing **fan** (vs. 12) refers to a wooden shovel used for tossing grain into the wind in order to blow away the lighter chaff, leaving the good grain to settle in a pile. The chaff would then be swept up and burned, **the unquenchable fire** refers to the eternal punishment of hell or the lake of fire.

D. His Approval. 3:13-4:11.

1. Baptism of Christ. 3:13-17.

13-14. All four gospels relate this event (cf. Jn 1:31-33) with unquestioned historical verification. While this section of Matthew's gospel centers upon Galilee, Jesus now goes south to the Jordan River **to be baptized** (vs. 13). The word baptize (Gr *baptizo*) is an Anglicism. It means to dip or immerse in water, indicating the true form of baptism by immersion. John **forbad him** (vs. 14) for the obvious reason that Jesus needed no repentance of sin and John felt unworthy of this opportunity. The tense of the Greek verb emphasizes that John tried to hinder him. Thus, this was no casual hesitation on the part of the Baptist.

15. Suffer it to be so means allow it to be or let it happen. Jesus sought this outward identification with John's ministry **to fulfil all righteousness**. By identifying Himself with those whom He came to redeem, Jesus inaugurated His public ministry as the Messiah. In regard to the Jewish religious observances, Jesus always met the duties of a faithful Jew: synagogue worship, attendance at feasts, payment of the temple tax, etc.

16-17. In the process of His baptism, Jesus **went up . . . out of the water,** the prepositions indicating that He was completely in the water and came up out from it, again indicating the form of immersion. The descending of the **Spirit of God** fulfilled the predicted sign to John in order to indicate the true messiah (cf. Jn 1:33; Isa 11:2). "As the Spirit came upon Old Testament prophets for special guidance at the start of their ministries, so now He came upon Jesus without measure" (Kent, p.10). The **dove** was a symbol of innocence and purity (cf. Mt

10:16) and served as an ideal symbolic representation for the Holy Spirit since it is a totally defenseless animal. Jesus made it clear that the ministry of the Holy Spirit was to glorify Christ and not Himself (Jn 16:13-14). The **voice from heaven** is that of the Father (see also Mt 17:5; Jn 12:28 where He speaks at the transfiguration and just prior to the crucifixion) giving His verbal approval to the ministry of His **beloved Son**. There can be no doubt that all three persons of the Trinity are actively involved here as distinct persons of the Godhead. The Father speaks, the Spirit descends, the Son is baptized.

2. Temptation of Christ. 4:1-11.

4:1. Following His public baptism, Jesus was **led up of the Spirit into the wilderness** referring to the elevation of the Judaean wilderness. The historical setting of the temptation, which was directed against Jesus' human nature, indicates that this was a literal experience which He really conquered, not merely a mental victory over His own thoughts. The references to the work of the Holy Spirit make clear the interrelation of these two members of the Godhead. In His earthly work, Jesus depended upon the ministry of the Holy Spirit to empower Him.

That Jesus was **tempted of the devil** is clearly presented as a fact. The attack against Christ's humanity was a genuine temptation that would have overcome any normal man. However, Jesus was no ordinary man. As the virgin-born God-man, His divine nature could not sin (cf. I Sam 15:29) and thus held His human nature in check. Some have objected that the impeccability (i.e., He was not able to sin) of Christ denies the reality of Satan's temptation. Such an objection is meaningless when one remembers that Satan's rebellion against God has already been defeated in Christ's atonement, but his rebellion is nevertheless real, even though the outcome of God's victory is certain. The same is

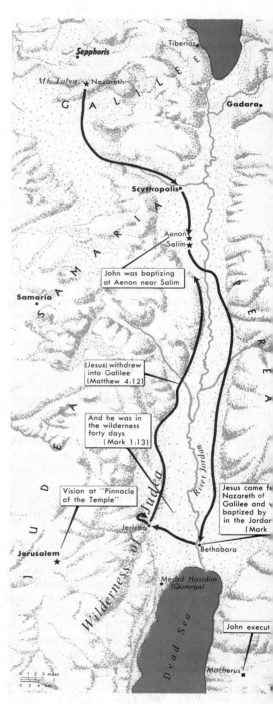

The Baptism of Jesus and the Sojourn in the Desert

true of the temptation of Christ. One may attack a battleship with a canoe. The outcome of the attack will be certain defeat for the canoe, but the attack is nonetheless legitimate.

2-3. Jesus had **fasted forty days and forty nights**, a remarkable feat of human endurance indicating the physical strength of the former carpenter. While the three major tests followed this period, other tests evidently had occurred throughout the forty days (Lk 4:2). His real physical hunger serves as the setting for the first temptation by the **tempter** (Satan). The incident is couched in the questioning aspersion **if thou be the Son of God**, indicating Matthew's purpose for including this record of Jesus' victory: it proves that He is, in fact, the Son of God! The urgency to turn the **stones** into **bread** appealed to Jesus' most basic human need in light of the extensive fast. The natural result of using His divine power in this regard would certainly have led to the desire to eat the bread. One mistake would have led to another. However, Jesus refused to use His divine prerogative to benefit Himself. In fact, He never did a miracle to benefit Himself. His heart was always reaching out to others.

4. The victory in each aspect of the temptation is related to Jesus' use of Scripture: **It is written**. First, He quotes Deuteronomy 8:3, "Man shall not live by bread alone, but by every word that proceedeth out of the mouth of God." The source of bread is more important than the bread itself. Later, Jesus would say, "I have meat to eat that ye know not of" (Jn 4:32). His source of strength was obedience to the Father's will and He would not even work a miracle to avoid personal suffering when such suffering was a part of God's purpose for Him. What a Saviour!

5-7. The second temptation took place in the **holy city** (Jerusalem) on the **pinnacle** of the temple, which towered above the Kidron Valley.

Evidently, Jesus was transported there by Satan's power and this time the devil quoted Scripture (out of context) in order to get Him to sin and to ultimately shake His faith in the Word. Satan used Psalm 91:11-12 urging Jesus to **cast thyself down**. Again, Jesus replied with Scripture (Deut 6:16) that He was not to **tempt . . . God** by such a presumptuous action. The very passage of Scripture quoted by Satan actually goes on to promise God's ultimate victory over him! Jesus' use of the Scripture again silences the tempter.

8. The third temptation takes place on an **exceeding high mountain**. That the mountain is real seems clear in the text, though its exact location is unidentified. Despite the grandeur and almost miraculousness of this temptation there is nothing in the passage itself to indicate that these temptations were only in the mind of Christ. Clearly they are depicted as being real experiences that actually occurred in the human life of the Messiah. Satan showed Him **all the kingdoms of the world**, which he promised to give Jesus if He would acknowledge and worship Satan as the prince of the world. The invalidity of the temptation is almost laughable. Satan, though the god of this world, is never depicted in Scripture as actually controlling or possessing any real power over the kingdoms of the world. While he may influence a king or a group of kingdoms, God is always depicted as being on the throne, over the earth which is His footstool. That Satan, the usurper, would attempt to give the kingdoms of the world to Jesus, the Messiah, the rightful King is the height of absurdity! Like many of Satan's temptations he offers something which in reality he cannot deliver.

9-11. For Christ to fall down and worship Satan would have been to acknowledge the devil's lordship over Him. In His direct rebuke **get thee hence, Satan**, Jesus clearly asserts His lordship over the old serpent whose head He will soon crush). Matthew's statement that Satan **leaveth him** shows that his order of the temptations is the chronological one (cf. Lk 4:1-13). In a demonstration of spirit and power, Jesus overcame the tempter showing that He is the One who enables us to overcome temptation as well. "Resist the devil and he will flee from you."

II. MINISTRY OF THE MESSIAH. 4:12-27:66.

A. In Galilee. 4:12-18:35.

12-16. Matthew designates four clear geographical areas in relation to the ministry of Christ: Galilee (4:12), Peraea (19:1), Judaea (20:17), and Jerusalem (21:1). The author then omits some of the early Judaean ministry and begins with Jesus at Capernaum in Galilee where he had first met Christ himself (cf. 9:9). **John was cast into prison** (vs. 12). The circumstances of the arrest and eventual beheading of John the Baptist are recorded in chapter 14. It appears that a widespread persecution of the followers of John and Jesus took place at this time. Luke 4:16-31 explains the reason for Jesus **leaving Nazareth** was an attempt on His life after a synagogue service at Nazareth. From this point on, Capernaum became the headquarters of Jesus' ministry to the house of Israel. This city was a Roman settlement near the Sea of Galilee and was the center of the Roman government of the northern provinces of Israel. **That it might be fulfilled** (vss. 14-16) refers to the coming of Christ into Galilee in fulfillment of the prophecy of Isaiah 9:1-2, ". . . beyond Jordan, in Galilee of the nations. The people that walk in darkness have seen a great light . . ." Jesus Himself was that great light that now would shine forth in His earthly ministry to the people of Galilee who had so long been despised by their Judaean cousins, in the south.

17. Repent for the kingdom of heaven is at hand. The message of John the Baptist is now clearly proclaimed by Jesus Christ. However, Jesus, as the Messiah, is not calling on His listeners to prepare for the coming of the kingdom but rather announces that the kingdom is here. In a very real sense the first coming of the King is an honest, straightforward presentation of the kingdom promised by the Old Testament prophets to the people of Israel. Thus, we find unusual miracles attending Jesus' presentation of this kingdom: incurable diseases and incomprehendable afflictions are cured by the power of His touch and His word. The kingdom blessings promised in Isaiah 35:5-6 to be fulfilled in a future kingdom, here become the credentials of the King in His first coming (cf. Walvoord, p. 39).

18-20. Simon called Peter, and Andrew became the first two disciples called publicly by Jesus. Andrew had earlier (cf. Jn 1:40) introduced his brother to Jesus on another occasion. The invitation, **Follow me,** called these earlier believers into a permanent ministry to be shared with Christ. **I will make you fishers of men** clearly indicates the nature of this ministry. They would receive special training in bringing men into the kingdom. These former fishermen would literally become fishers of men! There can be no doubt that aggressive personal evangelism was and still is a major priority in the believer's life. Our obedience to the lordship of Christ is evidenced by our carrying forth the mission to which He has committed us. Having **left their nets** these disciples entered into a new relationship and would never again be able to fully return to the occupation they once held so dear. There can be no greater calling than to serve Christ full time with every effort of our lives.

21-22. James and **John** were also brothers and fishing partners with Simon and Andrew. Matthew and

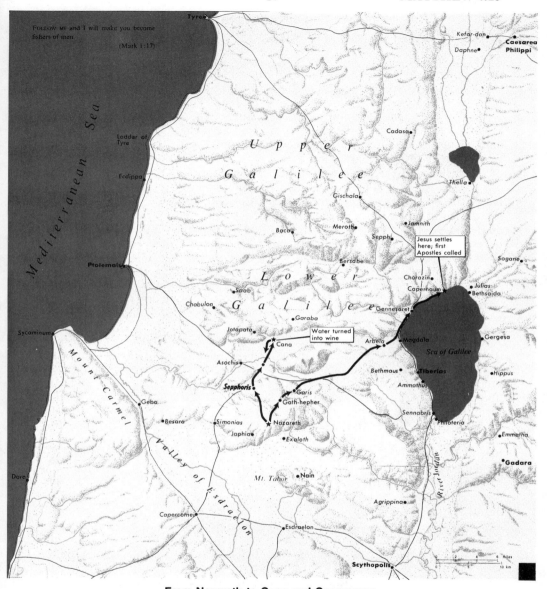

FOLLOW ME and I will make you become
fishers of men

(Mark 1:17)

From Nazareth to Cana and Capernaum

Mark agree that they were **mending their nets**, but Luke seems to differ. The two accounts can be simply harmonized. As two men were mending nets, the other two were fishing. Jesus then came upon them and called them all to follow Him. The statement in verse 22 that they **immediately** responded to His call gives us a perfect picture of true obedience to the lordship of Christ. To obey is to respond immediately in an attitude of faith.

23-25. The closing verses of the chapter summarize and survey the Galilean ministry of Jesus. This ministry concentrated on a presentation of the **gospel of the kingdom** to the Jews. Jesus as the Messiah (the annointed one) had arrived to set up the long-awaited kingdom. Accompanying this announcement were miracles of healing. Going from city to city throughout Galilee caused His fame to spread quickly, so that **great multitudes of people** (vs. 25) followed Him from Galilee, the Decapolis, Jerusalem, Judaea, and from beyond Jordan. Thus, followers were gleaned from virtually every geographical area of the nation of Israel, as it was in the days of Christ. This is no insignificant feat when one realizes that no prophet had arisen in Israel for over four hundred years. The silence of the Intertestamental period had been broken by the proclamation of the good news of the kingdom!

1. His Message: Sermon on the Mount. 5:1-7:29.

The nature of the kingdom which Jesus proclaimed has long been a controversial area of interpretation among Christian scholars. While these interpretations do not divide us between orthodoxy and heresy, they nevertheless formulate our fundamental understanding of the nature and message of the church today. Liberalism taught that the keeping of the Sermon on the Mount was to be regarded as the message of the Gospel. Thus it predicated a system of salvation by moral works. Some dispensationalists, at times, have tended to relegate everything related to the kingdom as being under the Old Testament dispensation, thus having no significant application to the church today. Still others recognize the truths within this kingdom message, but hold that its precepts are impossible to attain, thus, nullifying its significance for the Christian.

Nowhere in the presentation of the message of the kingdom does Jesus indicate that this message is significantly different from the proclamation of evangelism by the church. The difference, rather, seems to be in relation to those to whom the message is directed. During the early period of the gospels, the message of the kingdom of heaven was directed to the nation of Israel and contained the potential fulfillment of the promised kingdom to the Jews. To the Gentile nations of the Church Age the proclamation of the message is that God will gather a people for Himself from all nations into this great kingdom. The prerequisite for entrance into this kingdom included repentance (Mt 4:17), righteousness (Mt 5:20), faith (Mt 18:3) or, in summary, being born again (Jn 3). Because the people rejected these requirements, Christ taught that His earthly reign would not be centralized in the nation of Israel but in a gathering of a people from among the nations of the earth.

5:1-2. The opening verses of the Sermon on the Mount indicate that this message deals with the inner state of mind and heart which is the indispensable absolute of true Christian discipleship. It delineates the outward manifestations of character and conduct of the true believer and genuine disciple. A dispensationalist, Lawlor writes: "We do not find basic, fundamental Law here, for law cannot produce the state of blessedness set forth herein" (cf. G. Lawlor, *The Beatitudes Are for Today,* p. 11). Rather, the quality of life herein described is the necessary product of grace alone. As Jesus states the outward legal requirements of the law and then carries His listener beyond the letter of the law to the true spirit and intent of the law, He describes a life style which no human being could live in his own power. Thus, the life of the believer, described by Jesus in the Sermon on the Mount, is a life of grace and glory, which comes from God alone. To make this quality of life the product of man's human efforts (as does the liberal) is the height of overestimation of man's ability and underestimation of his depravity. To relegate this entire message, Jesus' longest recorded sermon, to a Jewish-only life style, as do hyper-dispensationalists, is to rob the church of her greatest statement of true Christian living!

The depth of spiritual truth proclaimed in this message of the kingdom, however, does not present the gospel of justification by faith in the death and resurrection of Christ. Pink states: "Its larger part was a most searching exposition of the spirituality of the law and the repudiation of the false teaching of the elders" (A. W. Pink, *An Exposition of the Sermon on the Mount,* p. 13). Jesus made it clear that the spirit of Christ goes beyond the outward demand of the law. The Christian, though not under the law, is to live above the law.

It has always been difficult to clearly draw the distinction between the relationship of law and grace. Dr. Martyn Lloyd-Jones has observed: "Some so emphasize the law as to turn the gospel of Jesus Christ with its glorious liberty into nothing but a collection of moral maxims. It is all law to them and there is no grace left. They so talk of the Christian, that it becomes pure legalism and there is no grace in it. Let us remember also that it is equally possible so to overemphasize grace at the expense of the law as again, to have something which is not the gospel of the New Testament" (D. Martyn Lloyd-Jones, *Studies in the Sermon on the Mount,* pp. 12-15). He goes on to note that the Sermon on the Mount and the message of the kingdom do have definite application to the Christian today. It was preached to people who were meant to practice it not only at that time but ever afterwards as well. Boice (p. 9) observes that that "World" of the Sermon on the Mount cannot be restricted to life in the future millennial kingdom, since it includes tax collectors, thieves, unjust officials, hypocrites, and false prophets.

Embodied in the Sermon on the Mount is a summarization of Jesus' basic ethical teaching of the life of a born-again man. While the Sermon on the Mount is not a way of salvation, neither is it only a message to those under the law, for it obviously goes beyond the law. It is a presentation of Christian discipleship which can be wrought in the soul of an individual only by the power of God. This message does not tell one how to be saved; it tells one what it is like to be saved. It explains the quality of the life changed by the saving grace of God. Its basic truths are reiterated everywhere throughout the New Testament epistles. There is no fundamental contrast between this message and the message of Paul. Both are in agreement that "the just shall live by faith!"

In the Sermon on the Mount Jesus states the spiritual character and quality of the kingdom which He wished to establish. The basic qualities of this kingdom are fulfilled in the church which He would establish. Virtually every section of this message is repeated in the substance elsewhere throughout the New Testament. There is nothing here to indicate that this message is to be limited in its application only to the people of Israel. Notice in the opening verse that **his disciples** had come to Him and **He . . . taught them** the following message.

a. The Beatitudes: Character Described. 5:3-20.

3. Blessed means "happy." This is a basic description of the believers' inner condition as a result of the work of God. Kent states that it is virtually equivalent to being "saved" (H. A. Kent Jr. Matthew, in *Wycliffe Bible Commentary,* p. 15). These Beatitudes, like Psalm 1, do not show a man how to be saved, but rather describe the characteristics of one who has been saved. The **poor in spirit** are the opposite of the proud or haughty in spirit. These are those who have been humbled by the grace of God and have acknowledged their sin and therefore their dependence upon God to save them. They are the ones who will inherit the **kingdom of heaven**. It is obvious in this usage that the kingdom of heaven is a general designation of the dwelling place of the saved.

4. Those that **mourn . . . shall be comforted**. The depth of the promise of these statements is almost inexhaustible. Those who mourn for sin shall be comforted in confession. Those who mourn for the human anguish of the lost shall be comforted by the compassion of God.

5. The meek . . . shall inherit the earth refers again to those who have been humbled before God and will inherit, not only the blessedness of heaven, but shall ultimately share in the kingdom of God upon the earth. Here, in the opening statements of the Sermon on the Mount, is the balance between the physical and spiritual promise of the kingdom. The kingdom of which Jesus preached is both "in you" and is yet "to come." The Christian is the spiritual citizen of the kingdom of heaven now.

6. These future possessors of the earth are its presently-installed rightful heirs and even now they **hunger and thirst after righteousness**. They experience a deep desire for personal righteousness which is, in itself, a proof of their spiritual rebirth. Those who are poor and empty in their own spiritual poverty recognize the depth of their need and hunger and thirst for that which only God can give them. To hunger means to be needy. It is joined with to thirst; the born-again man has a God-given hunger and thirst (inner passion) for righteousness. This hungering and thirsting continues throughout the life of the believer. He continues to hunger and to be filled and to hunger and to be filled. God supplies his every spiritual need daily. This act of hungering and thirsting after righteousness is the by-product of a regenerated life.

Lawlor (p. 60) rightly states that this is the description of a man who has already been saved. Nowhere does the Bible command unbelievers to hunger after righteousness in order to be saved. Rather, Paul clearly states "there is none that understandeth, there is none that seeketh after God" (Rom 3:11). The biblical writers make it clear that while man must come to Christ for salvation, it is not within man's normal ability and desire to want to come to God. Therefore, God is depicted throughout the New Testament as the seeking Saviour going after the lost. **They shall be filled** (Gr *chortazō*) refers to a complete filling and satisfaction. The psalmist proclaimed: "He satisfieth the longing soul, and filleth the hungry soul with goodness" (107:9). This filling comes from God, who is the total source of satisfaction of His people. It comes now and it will continue to come throughout eternity to those who hunger and thirst for it.

7. Those who are **merciful shall obtain mercy** has reference to those who have been born again by the mercy of God. Because divine love has been extended to them, they have the work of the Holy Spirit in them producing a mercy which defies explanation by unregenerate men. Jesus Himself became the ultimate example of this when He cried from the cross,"Father, forgive them for they know not what they do" (Lk 23:34). The form of proverbial teaching should not confuse the order of these statements; for example the believer does not show mercy in order to obtain mercy, he shows mercy because he has obtained mercy. In so continuing to show the evidence of the grace of God in his life he continues to receive that grace. In other words, he is not saved simply because he shows mercy and is kind to people. He shows mercy and is kind because he is saved.

8. Those who are truly saved shall **see God**. These are the **pure in heart**. Their lives have been transformed by the grace of God. They are not yet sinless but their position before God has been changed. They have the new birth, saving faith and holiness. The process of sanctification is ever conforming them to the image of Christ (Rom 8:29), which image consists in "righteousness and true holiness" (Eph 4:24). Purity of heart is both the end of our election and the goal of our redemption. We read in Ephesians 1:4, "He has chosen us that we should be holy" and Titus 2:14, "who gave himself for us that he might redeem us unto himself a peculiar people." To which we add Hebrews 12:14, "Follow peace with all men, and holiness, without which no man shall see the Lord."

9. The next description deals with the **peacemakers**. They are the ones who are themselves at peace with God and live in peace with all men (cf. Rom 5:1). They are called "the" peacemakers for these are not social reformers, but rather the ones reformed by the regenerating power of the gospel. They are peacemakers because they themselves are at peace with God. They have entered into the peace of Christ and thus are able ambassadors of God's message of peace to a troubled world. Hence, they shall be called **the children of God**. These only shall be called the sons of God! Throughout the Beatitudes Jesus clearly underscores that only those who have the life changing qualities herein described are citizens of His kingdom.

10. As Jesus develops His message He makes it clear that such a life causes His people to be in direct contrast to the world in whicht hey live. Therefore He reminds, "blessed are they which are **persecuted for righteousness' sake**." The plural use of ye in verse 11 indicates that He foresaw this persecution as touching all His followers. Notice II Timothy 3:12, "yea, and all that will live godly in Christ Jesus shall suffer persecution." The nature of this persecution (Gr *diōkō*) implies a driving or chasing away, a withstanding or keeping one

from his goal. This does not mean that every Christian will necessarily suffer physical abuse as evidence of true salvation. While many Christians have sealed their faith with their blood, many more have had to withstand the social temptations and pressures of the world in order to live effectively for Christ.

11. Again, Jesus warns that men shall **revile you and persecute you.** This became true during His own ministry, in the lives of the apostles and throughout the history of the church. But in Tertullian's words, "the blood of the martyrs became the seed of the church." The persecution spoken of here is twofold. First, it involves a physical pursuing of the persecuted and secondly a personal attack of slander against them.

12. Rejoice is the command that grows out of the blessedness of the believer. The phrase "rejoice and be exceedingly glad" means rejoice, but even more exalt! The believer who is the blessed one may not only rejoice in tribulation but he may rejoice exceedingly to the point of exaltation. Therefore, he glories in tribulation even as the Apostle Paul (cf. II Cor 1:3-7; 12:7-10). **Great is your reward in heaven** focuses attention upon the eternal, spiritual destiny of all things. If God is as real as He claims, if the Bible is true, if heaven is to be gained, then there is no temporary searthly trouble or persecution that can thwart the child of God from the eternal glory that lies ahead. In Romans 8:18, Paul proclaimed, "I reckon that the sufferings of this present time are not worthy to be compared with the glory which shall be revealed in us."

13. The Beatitudes are followed by a summary statement of the basic character of the Christian's life as salt and light. **Ye are the salt of the earth;** again the phrase "ye are" indicates that only the genuinely born-again person is salt and can help meet the needs of the world. The salt adds flavoring, acts as a preservative, melts coldness and heals wounds. Thus it is a very appropriate description of the believer in his relationship to the world in which he lives. The term "lose its savor" refers to its essential saltiness. Jesus was actually saying that if the salt loses its saltiness, it is worthless. The implication of this statement is that if a Christian loses his effectiveness, his testimony will be trampled under the feet of men.

14-16. Ye are the light of the world describes the essential mission of the Christian to the world. He is the condition (salt) to meet the world's needs and he has a mission (light) to the world. His light is to clearly shine forth into the darkness of human depravity. He is to set it up on a candlestick, not hide it **under a bushel,** e.g., basket. Inconsistent living and unconfessed sin in the life of the believer will become a basket-like covering which hides the light of God. God provides the light and it continues to shine, but as believers we must keep our lives clean before the Lord in order not to cover up the light which He has placed within us. Darkness is the absence of light and darkness alone cannot dispel the light, but the smallest light can dispel the greatest darkness. Therefore, let your light shine through a clean life before the Lord and before the world in which you live.

17. Having laid the foundation of the message in the summary statements of the Beatitudes, Jesus now proceeds to show the superiority of His message to that of the law of Moses. He makes it clear that **I am not come to destroy the law.** That is, the New Testament gospel is not contrary nor contradictory to the Old Testament law; rather it is the ultimate fulfillment of the spiritual intention of the law. Where the law had degenerated into legalism by the Pharisees, Jesus now takes the law beyond mere outward observance to the inner spiritual intention of God. For He had come **to fulfill** the law and

its fullest implications. In his earthly life Jesus accomplished this by meeting its strictest demands and going beyond its mere outward requirements. As our Saviour, Jesus not only bore our sins, but He has also established a perfect righteousness which is given to us as a gift of God. Our sin was thus imputed to Him and His righteousness was imputed to us (cf. J. Murray, *The Imputation of Adam's Sin*).

18. Verily I say is a unique form used by Jesus throughout His preaching to draw attention to the authority of His message. Verily means truly, certainly, or amen. It is used as a designation of authoritative teaching. **One jot or one tittle** refers to the minutest marks and letters of the Hebrew alphabet. He explained that even the smallest statement in the law must be fulfilled. A jot is the smallest letter of the Hebrew alphabet, called *yodh*. It functions as a "Y" in English and looks similar to an apostrophe. A tittle is a small projection on the edge of certain Hebrew letters to distinguish them from one another. For example, the Hebrew "D" differs from the "R" only by the use of the tittle.

19. Because of the seriousness of the law, Jesus emphasized the importance of keeping even its smallest details. However, in the ultimate plan of God, the law was not to become an extra burden on the souls of men. Rather than pointing the way to salvation, the law convinced men of the need of the Saviour. Therefore, whoever **shall teach men so** but shall not live what he teaches, he shall be made **least in the kingdom of heaven.** It is interesting to note that a person may be saved and a member of the kingdom of heaven, yet be hypocritical in his attitude toward the law. **But whosoever shall do and teach** the principles and precepts of the law shall be called **great in the kingdom of heaven.** This simply means that God will reward the faithfulness and effectiveness of our lives and there will be varying degrees of blessing and reward in the kingdom.

20. Because of the necessity of righteousness as a requirement to enter heaven, Jesus then declared that except their righteousness should **exceed the righteousness of the scribes and Pharisees** they could not enter heaven. The significance of this is seen in the fact that the Jews of Jesus' day considered these people to be the most religious in all Israel. However, their religion was merely an outward show of self-righteousness. What the Saviour demands is a kind of righteousness that is so godly that it cannot be the product of human effort but must be the gift of God. This righteousness Christ would establish in His life and death would be made available as God's free gift. This is the righteousness that would exceed that of the Scribes and Pharisees.

b. Six Illustrations: Character Applied. 5:21-48.

In communicating the depth of His message, Jesus used a series of contrasts between the outward demand of the law and the inner attitude of heart desired by God. In this series of contrasts we see the depth and dynamic of the teaching of Jesus Christ, the great Master Teacher. Here we discover the practical application of genuine Christian character to true spiritual living. Here we see the gospel in action. Here is piety on the pavement of life. The Christian may live above the demands of the law and the temptations of the world because he has an inner depth of character which is the product of the divine nature within him.

LAW	SPIRIT
Murder	No Anger
Adultery	No Lust
Divorce	Commitment
Oath Taking	Speak the Truth
Retaliation	Forgiveness
Hate your Enemy	Love your Enemy

(1) First Illustration: Murder. 5:21-26.

21-22. Christ begins this series of contrasts by quoting the statement of the law, **Thou shalt not kill** (Ex 20:13). The reference to killing is clearly understood in its context in both the Old Testament and New Testament as referring to an act of murder. It must be remembered that the God, who commanded the children of Israel not to murder one another, also commanded them at times to kill an enemy in order to defend their nation. Jesus goes beyond this outward demand of the law by stating that **whosoever is angry with his brother** is in just as great danger of judgment as a murderer. For anger is the emotion and inner intention that leads to murder.

The term *raca* (meaning "vain fellow" or "empty head") was a Hebrew or Aramaic expression of contempt (cf. II Sam 6:20). **The council** is a reference to the Jewish religious council called the Sanhedrin. **Thou fool,** (Gr *mōros*) means "stupid." We have developed the English word moron from this term. Those using such a malicious expression would be in danger of **hell fire.** This statement has often caused concern and confusion in the mind of many commentators. What does it really mean? The idea clearly seems to be that if one makes light of his fellow man he will be in danger of slander. But if one makes bitter, damning statements with reference to hell toward his fellow man, he shall actually be in danger of hell himself. The concept is that one making such statements is not likely to be a born-again person. The term hell (Gr *geenna*) is Gehenna, which was the hellenized form of the name of the Valley of Hinnom at Jerusalem in which fires were constantly burning to consume the refuse of the city. This valley provided a powerful and graphic picture of the ultimate destruction of hell and the lake of fire (cf. Jer 7:31; II Chr 28:3; II Kgs 23:10). Christ locates the root of murder in the heart of the angry man and states that God's judgment will be just as swift on anger as it will be upon murder.

23-24. Having made a comparison between the command not to murder and the inner motive and heart intention of hatred, Jesus then illustrated the seriousness of this matter by referring to one who would attempt to buy off his conscience by giving something to God without clearing his conscience with his offended brother. He reminded that **if thou bring thy gift to the altar** without reconciling with the offended party, God will not receive the intended gift. Bringing a gift to the altar refers to bringing it to the temple in order that it might be consecrated. Therefore if conflict exists between any two people, it is God's desire that they reconcile the conflict before attempting to give a gift or an act of service unto the Lord. Many people undoubtedly try to suppress the guilt of their sin by an outward act that they hope will please God in some way. Therefore, Jesus commands that we leave our gifts before the altar and **first be reconciled** to our brother before we offer them. To be reconciled means to be brought back into fellowship or favor with our fellow man. Having resolved the personal conflict, we have but then to return and perform the act of service unto the Lord. The performance of our duty to men does not free us from the obligation of direct service to God.

25-26. The Saviour then went on to remind that even if **thine adversary** (an opponent at law) disagrees with you, it is to your advantage to reconcile with him before he **deliver thee to the judge.** Many people make the foolish mistake of assuming that just because they think they are right in a given situation God will necessarily vindicate them. Jesus' exhortation here is to urge us to go out of our way to avoid legal conflicts before human judges (cf. vs. 40). The payment of debt and the **prison** referred to here simply mean the nor-

mal legal process that one would encounter in a civil suit. The term prison (Gr *phylakē*) does not refer to purgatory, as suggested by some Roman Catholic interpretors, but to the full measure of punitive justice.

(2) Second Illustration: Adultery Contrasted to Lust. 5:27-30.

27-28. Thou shall not commit adultery was the demand of the Old Testament law (Ex 20:14). Jesus went beyond this outward command to reveal that its act is the result of an inner attitude of lust. **Whosoever looketh** characterizes the man whose glance is not checked by holy restraint and results in an impure lusting after women. It has often been argued that there is a difference between an appreciation of beauty and a lustful, lurid look. The lustful look is the expression of a heart attitude that says in essence, "I would if I could." The act would follow if the opportunity were to occur. By taking his listener beyond the outward statement of the law to its real intention, Jesus was trying to get his attention off the physical and onto the spiritual.

29-30. Most men could claim that they had not committed the sin of adultery but very few could honestly say that they had not committed the sin of lusting, which could easily turn into adultery. Thus, the statement of cutting off one's hand or plucking out one's eye definitely is not to be taken literally. What Jesus implied is that if **thy right eye offend thee** then the logical thing to do would be to **pluck it out.** His point is not that one should literally pluck out his eye but that one should recognize that the source of lust comes from within the mind and heart of man, not from the physical organ itself. The right eye is not the source of sin, the heart of man is that source. Someone who had plucked out his right eye in an attempt to deal with lust would simply become a left-eyed luster! The real source of the sin of

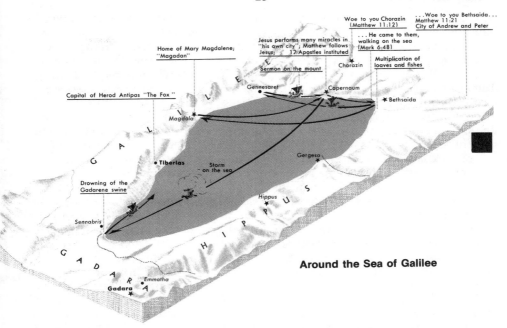

Woe to you Chorazin
(Matthew 11:12)

...Woe to you Bethsaida...
Matthew 11:21
City of Andrew and Peter

Jesus performs many miracles in
"his own city"; Matthew follows
Jesus;   12 Apostles instituted

...He came to them,
walking on the sea
(Mark 6:48)

Home of Mary Magdalene;
"Magadan"

Sermon on the mount

Multiplication of
loaves and fishes

Chorazin

Capital of Herod Antipas "The Fox"

Gennesaret

Capernaum

Bethsaida

Magdala

Tiberias

Storm
on the sea

Gergesa

Drowning of the
Gadarene swine

Hippus

Sennabris

Gadara   Emmatha

Around the Sea of Galilee

adultery comes from within man's **heart.**

The seriousness of the sin of lusting is thus illustrated by this graphic comparison. Ultimately, it would be better for a person to be physically maimed than to enter into hell forever. However, doing physical damage to one's self does not in any way guarantee entrance into heaven. What Jesus simply taught was that man must bring the passions of his heart under control of the Spirit of God.

(3) Third Illustration: Divorce as Contrasted to Marriage. 5:31-32.

31-32. It hath been said is again a reference to the Old Testament commandment of the Mosaic regulation (cf. Deut 24:1). The normal custom of the ancient Near East was for a man to verbally divorce his wife. The Arab custom was to say "I divorce you" three times and the divorce was consummated without any legal protection of any kind to the wife. In contrast, the ancient law of Israel insisted on a **certificate of divorce.** This written statement gave legal protection to both the

wife and the husband. Jesus explained elsewhere (cf Mt 19:8) that Moses' concession was not intended to be taken as license. In ancient Rabbinic Judaism Moses' statement had been variously interpreted from meaning adultery (Shammai) to the trivial matters of personal preference (Hillel). The only legitimate exception for divorce allowed by Christ is possibly for **the cause of fornication** (Gr *porneia*), meaning sexual unfaithfulness. Ryrie (p. 14) notes that fornication may mean adultery prior to or after marriage, as well as unfaithfulness during the period of betrothal.

These statements make it clear that adultery or fornication is a legitimate grounds for divorce. However, the legitimacy of the divorce does not necessarily establish the legitimacy of remarriage. That one *must* divorce an unfaithful wife or husband is nowhere commanded in Scripture. To the contrary, there are many examples of extending forgiveness to the adulterous offender (cf. Hos 3:1, Gen 38:26, Jn 8:1-11). Nor does the discovery of premarital fornication on the part of the wife necessarily demand a divorce as is indicated by Atkinson (p. 780). Sexual involvement alone does not necessarily constitute a marriage in the sight of God (cf. the example of Judah and Tamar, who were both widowed at the time of their illicit sexual involvement). Though this temporary union produced twin sons, it resulted in no permanent marriage. Great care needs to be exercised when interpreting the New Testament passages regarding divorce and marriage. It should be remembered that Jesus made His statements about divorce to people who were already married, so that they might take seriously the marriage relationship. These statements were not necessarily made to add an extra burden to the already divorced person.

The responsibility of divorce is clearly laid upon the one seeking the divorce. **Whosoever shall put away his wife** without biblical basis **causeth her to commit adultery.** Lenski (pp. 230-235) translates "brings about that she is stigmatized as adulterous" and regards the sin of the divorcer as bringing about an unjust suspicion upon the divorcee.

(4) Fourth Illustration: Oath Taking as Opposed to Speaking the Truth. 5:33-37.

33. The basis of Old Testament swearing, or oath-taking, is found in Leviticus 19:12; Deuteronomy 23:21; and Exodus 20:17. To **forswear** means to swear falsely or perjure one's self. Oaths taken in the name of the Lord were looked upon as binding and perjury of such oaths was strongly condemned by the law. Such phrases like "as the Lord liveth" or "by the name of the Lord" emphasize the sanctity of such oaths. Ryrie (p. 14) states: "Every oath contained an affirmation of promise of an appeal to God as the omniscient punisher of falsehoods, which made an oath binding." By the time of Christ, the Jews had developed an elaborate system of oath-taking, which

often formed the basis of actual lying. For example, one might swear that he had told the truth according to the dome of the temple, while another might swear by the gold on the dome of the temple! In other words, there were stages of truth and thus also of falsehood within the system of taking oaths. In our time this custom is found in phrases such as: "I swear by God," "cross my heart and hope to die," or "on my mother's grave."

34-36. All such oath-taking, Jesus would announce, was unnecessary if one were normally in the habit of telling the truth. Thus, His command was **swear not at all.** This does not have reference to cursing, as such, but to oath-taking. The Christian is not to take an oath by heaven, earth, nor the city of Jerusalem. He is not to swear on the basis of his own head or any other physical feature. He is to speak the truth in such a way that his "yes" means yes and his "no" means no.

37. Let your communication be yea, yea; Nay, nay. When you say yes make sure that that is what you mean. When you say no, make sure that also is what you mean. Mean what you say, say what you mean. Anything that is more than a simple affirmation of the truth **cometh of evil.** When we add an oath to our regular affirmation of the truth, we either admit that our normal conversation cannot be trusted, or that we are lowering ourselves to the level of a world which normally does not tell the truth. This does not necessarily mean that it is wrong to "swear to tell the truth" in a court of law. The point is that it should be unnecessary in a genuine Christian society to have to swear to tell the truth at all!

(5) Fifth Illustration: Retaliation as Opposed to Forgiveness. 5:38-42.

38. The principal of retaliation, *lex talionis,* is common in both Jewish and other ancient Near Eastern law codes (cf. the Code of Hammurabi). The judicial penalty of **An eye for an eye,**

and a tooth for a tooth is stated in Exodus 2:24 as a means of ending feuds. However, Jesus is clearly saying this method is not a license for vengeance. Many times an offended person will overreact to the offense and retaliate in such a way as to return injury for injury. The idea here is that to the Jews of Jesus' day it was common to attempt to retaliate upon the offender through the arm of the law, especially in a nation dominated by a foreign power.

39. The Saviour's point is that we should **resist not evil.** Evil is seen here, not as a state, but rather as the action of the evil ones or the malicious ones. It represents the evil and sinful element in man which provokes him to an act of evil. Jesus shows how the believer should respond to personal injury. He is not discussing the government's obligation to maintain law and order. The question of non-retaliation or non-violence is often discussed in relation to these verses. These passages alone do not mean that a man should not defend his family or his country, but rather that he should not attempt personal vengeance, even through the means of the law, to compensate for a personal injury.

Why would Jesus make such a statement? Certainly these words were spoken to remind those who would be His disciples not to expect divine justice from an unregenerate society. All justice ultimately is in the hand and heart of God. As long as human governments prevail, justice will be limited by man's finite abilities. The disciples of the kingdom are to look to the King Himself for ultimate vindication. The practical application of this truth is that the believer should not attempt to justify himself or inflict vengeance even through legal means. He is to place his total confidence in the ultimate sovereignty of God over the affairs of his life. (See Romans 12:19 where "give place unto wrath" means God's wrath.)

Jesus gives five examples of how the believer should react to unfair or unreasonable treatment. First, in retaliation to physical violence, he is to **turn the cheek.** Man's normal impulse is to strike back, but the disciple is not to be a normal man. He is to "overcome evil with good" (Rom 12:21). This is probably one of the most feared statements in all the Bible. People have gone to great lengths in an attempt to explain it away. Nevertheless, it remains the most pungent statement of Jesus' ethic. The life of the believer is to be lived with such a quality of spiritual verity and justice that he needs no physical retaliation in order to defend or justify his position. There is no greater example of this ethical truth than the life and death of Jesus Himself!

40. Secondly, whether robbed by personal assault or compulsory litigation, the believer is to respond with confidence in that which is eternal, rather than that which is temporal. If the believer is sued in order that the accuser may **take away thy coat,** he is to also let him have his **cloak.** The coat (Gr *chitōn*) is the undergarment or tunic. The cloak (Gr *himation*) is the more expensive outer garment worn over the tunic. Jesus taught us to have confidence in an almighty God who is completely aware of the injustices done to man and totally capable of evoking ultimate eternal justice. He must be trusted even when legal litigation goes against the believer. In our society, we would phrase Jesus' teaching, "If someone takes your suit coat, give him your overcoat as well."

41. Thirdly, in ancient times government agents were in a position to compel forced service upon a subjugated people. A Roman soldier, for example, could compel a Jewish native to carry his armor or materials for one mile, in order to relieve the soldier. Jesus now states that if someone compels you to walk a mile, **go with him twain.** The believer is to be willing to "go the extra mile." Doing double our duty not only proves the loyalty and faithfulness of our cooperation to human authority, but likewise proves the spiritual intention of our heart. It also provides an opportunity of conviction in order to witness effectively out of our life message. It would have been foolish for the believer of Jesus' day to reluctantly go only a mile with a Roman official and then attempt to share the gospel with him. By going the second mile he proved the innermost intention of his heart.

42. The fourth example is that of lending to **him that would borrow of thee.** Jesus made it clear that a loan should be looked upon as a potential gift. When we lend something to someone, we should not expect to receive in return. Is that not impractical, you ask. Yes it is! But that which is spiritual is not always that which is practical. There are many statements in Proverbs against borrowing, lending, and surety (cf. Prov 6:1; 11:15; 22:7; 27:13). While we are warned of the dangers of borrowing and lending, Jesus made it clear that the believer ought to be willing to lend to those in need.

Finally, even the beggar is to be ministered to through the provision of giving to **him that asketh thee.** This statement certainly forms the basis of all Christian charity and provides the proper social application of the message of the gospel to the physical needs of man as well as his spiritual needs.

(6) Sixth Illustration: Love Thy Neighbor Contrasted to Love Thy Enemy. 5:43-48.

43. The law of love, sometimes called the "law of Christ" summarizes the ethical principle of the Sermon on the Mount. "Love thy neighbor" summarizes the entire second table of the law (cf. Lev 19:18-34). But the unscriptural addition "hate thine enemy" was a popular concept in Jesus' day (cf.

The Qumran Manual of Discipline 1QS 1:4, "hate all that he has rejected"). The admonition **love your enemies** is one of the greatest statements Jesus ever made. The love enjoined in this passage is that which originates from God Himself! Man is not commanded to attempt to love his enemy on the basis of mere human affection but rather on the basis of a love which comes from God. This kind of love holds a unique place in the New Testament Scripture, for it is the gift of God and the fruit of the Spirit to the believer only. It is not something that man can muster within himself. Rather, it must come from God Himself into the life of the believer (cf. Gal 5:22; I Tim 1:5).

44. How does one love an enemy? Notice that the passage makes it clear that he does not have to attempt to work up an artificial feeling of love. The quality of love commanded here is expressed by giving. **Bless them** that curse you, **do good** to them that hate you, and **pray** for them that persecute you. Loving an enemy involves doing good toward that enemy in order to win him over to the cause that you represent. The message of the kingdom, therefore, is that we will win over those who oppose us more readily with love than with hatred. It is not in the divisiveness of contention that we win our greatest converts, but in the application of the heart of the gospel and the love of Christ.

45-47. In summarizing the importance of love, Jesus reminded that love was a necessary proof of salvation: "that ye may be the **children of your Father** which is in heaven." An initial reading of this text out of its context might seem to imply that loving one's neighbor automatically makes one a child of God. However, the New Testament is clear that love is an evidence of the one who is already saved by the grace of God (cf. 1 Jn 3:14). It is a natural tendency of human beings to love those who love them; therefore

Jesus reminds that we are to love our enemies as our **brethren, for even the publicans do the same.** Publicans were public officials of Jewish nationality who worked for the Roman government as tax collectors and were generally despised by the people. The idea here is that even the most hated people of the day loved their own friends. Therefore, the true child of the kingdom is to have a quality of love that goes beyond that of the world.

48. This section of the Sermon on the Mount is summarized with the statement **Be ye therefore perfect.** Since the New Testament makes it clear that even the believer is capable of sin, the term perfect here (Gr *teleios*) is not to be taken as absolute sinless perfection. Rather, it is used in relation to the matter of love in this context. "As God's love is complete, not omitting any group, so must the child of God strive for maturity in this regard" (Kent, p. 19).

c. True Spiritual Worship: Character Expressed. 6:1-7:12.

The nature of the true spiritual man previously described is not illustrated in acts of true spiritual worship as contrasted to traditional hypocritical worship. Again, Jesus goes beyond mere outward conformity to the law to the inward conviciton of the spirit. The following examples are given to illustrate this point: giving, praying, fasting, serving.

(1) First Example: Almsgiving. 6:1-4.

6:1. Jesus warns that we do not give **alms before men** just to gain human recognition to ourselves. That practical righteousness is in view is obvious. The one who does righteousness (or gives of his possessions) to the Lord merely to be **seen of men** has **no reward** from the Father in heaven. True worship is to result from the desire to serve God, not men, since pleasing God is far more important than pleasing men. Loss of reward is incurred by gaining the reward of human recognition as an end in itself. This does not mean that all human recognition is necessarily wrong. The implication of the text simply states that we are to serve the Lord because we love Him, not just because we desire something from Him.

2. Therefore in all of our giving we are not to **sound a trumpet** before us in a hypocritical manner of gaining attention to ourselves. This metaphorical phase means do not "publicize" your righteousness for such performers are **hypocrites** (from the Greek, "play actor"). Thus, Jesus warns against "acting like the hypocrites, whose aim is to win human praise . . . whose parade and pretense are spiritually futile" (Filson, p. 92). Those who parade their righteousness through the streets receive the honor of men and **They have their reward,** meaning that God will add nothing extra to that reward. But those who are willing to serve Him **in secret,** God will reward openly.

3. The phrase **let not thy left hand know what thy right hand doeth** means that one's giving of finances to the work of the Lord should be done so freely and spontaneously that his right hand cannot keep up with his left hand. He literally empties his pockets as fast as he can! Such giving is to be so spontaneous as to be unplanned at times. Notice that this passage does not state that it is wrong to give systematically, nor through church envelopes, nor receiving a tax deductible receipt. What it does teach is that one should not give by those means only. There are ample examples of systematic giving in Scripture in order to build the temple, to provide for the needs and welfare of the underpriviledged, etc. Planned giving is certainly biblical and encouraged; but all of our giving should not be limited to our foredetermined plan or system.

4. The real key to the success of this

kind of giving is found in the phrase: **thy Father which seeth in secret . . .** shall reward you. Giving by faith, out of a cheerful heart, depends upon our total confidence in the fact that God does indeed see us and knows our needs. The God who is there, sees in secret that which no man may observe, and that God rewards His own. The Christian is to give, not in order to receive reward, but that his love might be expressed to God who shall reward him. Our giving to the work of Christ spreads the message of the Gospel throughout the world. Notice again, that these verses certainly do not condemn public giving, but rather they speak against giving out of the wrong attitude and for the wrong motive.

(2) Second Example: Praying. 6:5-15.

5-6. Praying, like giving, is to be done unto the Lord, not unto man. Many professing Christians, if they were honest, would have to admit that they pray to be heard of men. Jesus said that the people of His day **love to pray standing in the synagogues.** Both a time and place for prayer were customary in the ancient Jewish synagogue (cf. Mk 11:25). Therefore, Jesus is not condemning the practice of public prayer, but rather the misuse of it! Because of the statement **enter into thy closet** some have suggested that all public prayer is wrong. This would be contrary to the rest of New Testament statements about prayer, commandments and restrictions regarding prayer, and examples of prayer meetings (cf. Acts 12:12).

The principle here is that the believer should not make a show of his prayer nor of the answers he receives to prayer in such a way as to call unnecessary attention to himself. Again, it is the God who sees in secret that rewards us openly. Here the intimate father-child relationship between God and man is clearly emphasized. It is the experience of private devotional prayer that ultimately prepares one to pray effec-

tively in public. Most people who say they cannot pray in public, do not pray effectively in private either!

7. Jesus warned that we **use not vain repetition** (Gr *battalogeō* denotes babbling or speaking without thinking). Such praying was characteristic of the heathen. A good example of this is found in the ecstatic babblings of the false prophets in the Old Testament and in the prophets of Baal who confronted Elijah on Mt. Carmel (cf. I Kgs 18:26-29). Jesus condemns the use of empty repetition as an attempt to overcome the will of God by wearing Him out. It is not the length of prayer, but the strength of prayer that prevails with God. Jesus Himself prayed all night prior to His crucifixion and on the other occasions prayed very briefly. He is not condemning lengthy prayers, although there is nothing particularly spiritual about them. He is merely emphasizing that prayer must be a sincere expression of the heart, not mere accumulation of verbiage. God is not impressed with words, but with the genuine outcry of a needy heart.

8. Many have questioned the meaning of the statement **your Father knoweth what things ye have need of before ye ask him.** "Then why should we pray?" they ask. Prayer is not man's attempt to change the will of God. God's method for changing our will is to bring it into conformity with His will. More than changing things, prayer changes people. Prayer is not conquering God's reluctance to answer, but laying hold of His willingness to help! Prayer, in the life of the true believer, is an act of total confidence and assurance in the plan and purpose of God. It is not an expression of panic and desperation.

The following sample prayer is given to the disciples as an example of a suitable prayer. It is neither lengthy nor irreverent. It contains a depth of piety and a pinnacle of power. This prayer, often called the "Lord's Prayer," is in reality a disciple's prayer, for Jesus gave it to His disciples as a sample of the true principle of spiritual prayer. In no way does the prayer itself embody all of his teaching about prayer and certainly, having just warned against vain repetition, He did not intend for this particular prayer to be merely recited with empty meaninglessness. This does not mean, however, that this prayer may not be recited as an act of public worship. There are those who feel such recitation is too liturgical, while there are others who feel that the omission of ever repeating this prayer is a failure to grasp its true significance. Certainly if we are to follow its example properly we may benefit from repeating it as it was given by the Lord Himself. To place this prayer under law and eliminate it from Christian usage is to deny the great essence of what the prayer is all about.

9. The very beginning phrase, **Our Father,** is completely uncommon to the prayers of the Old Testament. Martyn Lloyd-Jones (Vol. II, p. 54) has commented: "So when our Lord says, 'Our Father,' He is obviously thinking of Christian people, and that is why I say that this is a Christian prayer." By contrast see the ultra-dispensational approach of Gaebelein who refers to the Lord's Prayer as one of the rags of popery Luther brought with him from the Catholic church. He evaluates the Lord's Prayer as "decidedly unchristian!" (A. C. Gaebelein *The Gospel of Matthew,* p. 139). The two major elements of the prayer are adoration and petition. **Hallowed be thy name** addresses the attention of the prayer toward God and reverence for His name and his person. Hallowed (Gr *hagiazō*) means to be held in reverence and awe of holiness. God's name was so sacred to the Old Testament Jew that it was never pronounced by human lips. Thus His name is the expression of His very essence. The biblical usage of the concept of a name is a characteristic

description of the basic character of the person to whom the name is applied. Since the prayer is directed to our spiritual Father, only a child of God who has been born again can rightly pray this prayer.

10. The phrase **Thy kingdom come** refers to the eschatological nature of this prayer. Notice that the kingdom is to be prayed for, implying that it has not already arrived. The kingdom represents the full and effective reign of God through the mediatorial office of the Messiah. The disciples were not to think of their own convenience as their foremost expression in prayer, but the full and quick realization of the effective rule of God on earth in the hearts of men. That rule is realized through the regenerating process of the new birth in the lives of individuals. It will reach its pinnacle when the last enemy (sin and death, I Cor 15:24-28) has been destroyed at the Lord's return. The recognition of **Thy will be done** emphasizes the idea that prayer is to bring about the conformity of the will of the believer to the will of God. Prayer is an act of spiritual expression which brings us into conformity to the very nature and purpose of God.

11. The section of petitions begins with the request to give us this day **our daily bread.** Bread (Gr *artos*) may be applied to the provision of food in general. The term "daily" (Gr *epicusios*) denotes "indispensable" (Arndt and Gingrich, *Lexicon,* p. 296). The concept of daily provision of bread fits perfectly with the Old Testament example of the daily provision of manna to the Israelites while they were wandering in the wilderness (Ex 16:14-15). In a similar sense, while the Christian pilgrim takes his journey through a strange land that he does not yet literally possess, but which has been promised to him, it only stands to reason that God would make a similar provision to this New Testament, gospel-age wanderer.

12. The phrase **forgive us our debts**

refers to sins which are our moral and spiritual debts to God's righteousness. The request for forgiveness of sin is made here by the believer. In order to be saved one need not necessarily name all of his sins, but must confess that he is a sinner. For continued spiritual growth and cleansing the believer acknowledges his sins in particular. Notice that we seek forgiveness **as we forgive,** not because we forgive. Our expression of forgiveness does not gain salvation for us. We are to seek forgiveness in the same manner as we forgive others. Forgiveness is the evidence of a regenerate heart.

13. Lead us not into temptation is a plea for the providential help of God in our daily confrontation with the temptation of sin. James 1:13-14 makes it clear that God does not tempt us to do evil, but rather that we are tempted of our own lusts. However, God does test us in order to give us the opportunity to prove our faithfulness to Him. It is never His desire to lead us into evil itself. Therefore if we resist the devil, we are promised that he will flee from us.

The prayer closes with a doxology of praise **for thine is the kingdom, and the power, and the glory, for ever. Amen,** which is a liturgical interpolation from I Chronicles 29:11. Though omitted in some manuscripts, these words constitute a fitting climactic affirmation of faith.

In the first three petitions of this prayer of the Lord, our soul rises directly to God; in the three following we face the hindrances of these aspirations; and in the last petition we discover the solution to all these difficulties. Stier (*The Words of the Lord Jesus,* Vol. I, p. 198) draws a unique parallel between the two tables of the decalogue and the two sections of the Lord's Prayer. In the first petition the believer's soul is awed with the character of God, in the second petition with His grand purpose, and in the third petition with His moral condi-

tion. In the second part of the prayer the children of God humble themselves in dependence upon divine mercy in the fourth petition; they seek forgiveness in the fifth petition; gracious guidance in the sixth petition; and deliverance from the power of evil in the seventh petition. Thus, this arrangement may be readily suggested by dividing the prayer into two parts:

> Relationship to God—
> Hallowed be *Thy* Name;
> *Thy* Kingdom come;
> *Thy* will be done;

> Relationship to men—
> Give *us* this day our daily bread;
> Forgive *us* our debts;
> Lead *us* not into temptation;
> Deliver *us* from evil.

Finally the rich doxology expresses the certain hope that our prayers shall be heard and that God, in view of His great character, will bring to pass the highest good in our lives. Thus, prayer is the expression of the believer's confidence in the ultimate plan and purpose of God. In his *Commentary on the Holy Scriptures: Matthew* (p. 124), J. P. Lange has suggested the following comparison between the statements of the Beatitudes and the petitions of the Lord's Prayer:

BEATITUDES	LORD'S PRAYER
Blessed are the poor in spirit: for theirs is the kingdom of heaven	*Hallowed be thy name (the name of God which opens to us the kingdom of heaven)*
Blessed are they that mourn: for they shall be comforted	*Thy kingdom come (heavenly comfort into our hearts)*

Blessed are the meek: for they shall inherit the earth	*Thy will be done on earth as it is in heaven (this meekness, the characteristic of heaven, shall possess the new earth)*
Blessed are they that hunger and thirst after righteousness; for they shall be filled	*Give us this day our daily bread*
Blessed are the merciful for they shall obtain mercy	*Forgive us our debts as we forgive our debtors*
Blessed are the pure in heart: for they shall see God	*And lead us not into temptation*
Blessed are the peacemakers: etc.	*But deliver us from evil*

The comparison between these two pinnacles of piety is striking indeed. The inexhaustible expression of devotion and simplicity of language between the Beatitudes and the Sermon on the Mount give them a depth of expression which goes beyond the temporal and touches the eternal.

(3) Third Example: Fasting. 6:16-18.

16. When ye fast is a reference both to fasting prescribed under the Mosaic law in connection with the Day of Atonement (Lev 16:29) and the voluntary fast of that day. The Pharisees added two fast days, on Monday and Thursday of each week, as a case of public display and piety. The true purpose of fasting was intended, however, for deep contrition and spiritual communion. Fasting was especially emphasized as an effective means of dealing with temptation (cf. Isa 58:6). The Pharisees regarded the practice of fasting as meritorious (cf. *Taanith,* 8.3) and appeared in the synagogues negligently attired. Their sad disfigurement of face and the wearing of mourning garb gave them an opportunity to exhibit their superior ascetic sanctity before the people. The phrase **disfigure their faces** (Gr *aphanizō* literally denotes covering their faces and is a figurative expression for mournful gestures and neglected appearance of those wanting to call attention to the fact they are enduring. This was often done with dust and ashes (cf. Isa 61:3) and is similar to the modern Roman Catholic concept of Ash Wednesday. In the original, there is a play upon two cognate words meaning, "they make their faces unappearable," that they may "appear unto men."

17-18. This passage is not to be taken as a command against fasting but rather against the misuse of the spiritual exercise of fasting. Kent (p. 21) observes: "Fasting that requires spectators is mere acting." Though Jesus Himself instituted no fast for His disciples, voluntary fasting does appear in the early churches (cf. Acts 13:2). The injunction to **anoint thine head** relates to the ancient custom of anointing one's head when going to a feast. In other words, Jesus was saying that when we fast we are to do so secretly unto the Lord, while outwardly maintaining the appearance of joy and triumph which is the end result of true fasting.

Just as we have observed the interesting parallels within this sermon, so again we discover the contrast between outward acts of worship and inward attitudes of devotion. Outward worship stresses giving; inward worship stresses possessing. Outward worship manifests praying; inward worship manifests worrying. Outward worship is characterized by fasting; inward worship is characterized by judging.

The obvious contrasts are that a proper attitude toward giving will arise from the proper inward attitude toward one's possessions. Praying will resolve all worrying. Fasting, in judging one's self, is to be preferred over judging others.

(4) Fourth Example: Giving. 6:19-24.

The common error of Judaism was to regard material wealth as always indicating the blessing of God. While it is true that the book of Proverbs promises material blessings to those who honor God's financial principles, it does not imply that all wealth is a necessary sign of blessing. The Proverbs themselves indicate that many become temporarily wealthy because of ill-gotten gains. The contrast between these two sections of examples, both inward and outward, is directed specifically at the false spirituality of the Pharisees which arose from worldly-mindedness.

19. Because the false spirituality of men seeks to lay up treasures for themselves in a worldly sense, they "have their reward." Thus, their desire to be seen of men and to lay up treasure through the outward attention of men, as if some self-meritorious work could make them more acceptable to God and man, is provoked by their wrong attitude toward material possessions in the first place. Therefore, **treasures upon earth** are temporary and of short duration. These earthly possessions are at the mercy of **moth and rust . . . and . . . thieves.** Even if temporal possessions escape the clutches of the marauder, they are still likely to become moth-eaten and rusty. In other words, they do not last. Our materialistic, technological society in the late twentieth century all too often has overlooked the simplicity of this truth. Our attention to wealth, possession, social status, and retirement benefits too easily causes us to trust that which man can provide rather than that which God has already provided. Our simple appreciation of the natural provisions of God are frequently overlooked in favor of the plastic provisions of our contemporary technology.

20-21. The attention of the believer is directed toward **treasures in heaven.** The term "treasures" implies the addition or accumulation of things. The two kinds of treasures are conditioned by their place (either upon earth or in heaven). The concept of laying up treasure in heaven is not pictured as one of meritorious benefits but rather of rewards for faithful service, as is illustrated elsewhere in the teaching of Jesus. The ultimate destiny of our lives is either earthly or heavenly and the concentration of our efforts will reveal where our real treasure is. In contrast to the legalistic attempt of Judaism to establish a spiritual treasure upon earth, Jesus calls attention to His disciples to that true and eternal treasure which is heavenly. The only way man will ever overcome his natural inclination toward materialism and wealth is to place the priority of his possessions in heaven. If one were as concerned about spiritual benefits of his life as he were about the material possessions, his motivations would be pure indeed.

22-23. The **light of the body** is associated with the **eye.** The concept here is based on the ancient idea that the eyes were the windows through which light entered the body. If the eyes were in good condition the body could receive such light. Tasker (p. 75) notes that Jesus, using this language metaphorically, affirms that if a man's spiritual sight is healthy and his affections directed toward heavenly treasure, his whole personality will be without blemish. The phrase **if thine eye be single** indicates devotion to one purpose. The "single eye" refers to a single, fixed vision or goal. This reminds us of the statement of James, "A double-minded man is unstable in all his ways" (Jas 1:8). The phrase **if**

thine eye be evil refers to either disease or deception of vision. Though many commentators suggest the idea of disease, the context seems to imply deception. The "evil eye" is not necessarily something mysterious nor devilish, but rather a deceptive vision which causes the viewer to mistake the identity of an object. The mistake in this context is the darkening of the mind and thus **how great is that darkness!**

24. This kind of spiritual double vision causes one to believe that he can **serve two masters.** Total loyalty to God cannot be divided between Him and loyalty to one's material possessions. A master (Gr *kyrios*) is a lord or an owner. That God claims total lordship over His own is obvious in this passage. The concept of the lordship of Christ has often been greatly mistaken. Even in the face of the immediate denial of and on the part of His disciples, Jesus said to them: "Ye call me Master and Lord; and ye say well; for so I am" (Jn 13:13). There is no passage or command anywhere in the New Testament asking the believer to make Christ "Lord of his life" after salvation. The very experience of receiving Christ as Saviour is looked upon throughout the Scriptures as an acknowledgment of lordship and ownership. If perfect obedience were required in order to make Christ our Lord, He would be the Lord of no one! It is the fact that He is already Lord that makes our disobedience so serious. As Lord and Master He has the right to demand complete obedience. My disobedience as a believer is an act of sin against His lordship. The believer cannot sin away the lordship of Christ any more than he can His saviourhood.

Therefore, Jesus rightly proclaimed **Ye cannot serve God and mammon.** The term "mammon" is derived from the Aramaic term for possessions or wealth. Jesus is not condemning money or possessions in and of themselves, but the improper attitude of enslavement toward wealth. His point here cannot be overemphasized in light of the affluent society of our day. Outside the boundaries of North America the average Christian knows much more of the reality of poverty than do we. Within the depth of this message and its application we may certainly see afresh that it is the "gospel of the poor."

Double-mindedness is an attempt to sit on the fence in relation to spiritual matters. There is no halfhearted service for God. It is either all or nothing. Jesus gives the believer no option between loving God and loving the world. The regenerated heart is one which so longs for righteousness and desires the things of heaven that it lives above the temporal things of the earth.

(5) Fifth Example: Worry or Anxiety. 6:25-34.

25. Adding doubt to the danger of possessions, Jesus now deals with the equally dangerous tendency of those who have no possessions: worry! **Take no thought** (Gr *merimnaō*) means do not be anxious. Filson (pp. 100-101) notes that this word means to be so disturbed about material needs that we distrust God and are distracted from faithfully doing His will. The implication of the text is that all anxiety is provoked by worrying about material and temporal things. Such anxiety causes one to avoid the responsibility of work in order to cooperate with God's provison. Anxious care is an inordinate or solicitous concern or grief beyond our immediate needs. It is the direct opposite of carefulness, cautiousness, and faith. Therefore, even the poor are not to worry needlessly about what they should eat, drink, or wear. The question, **Is not the life more than meat, and the body than raiment?** indicates that inner mental stability must come from the spirit of a man and not from outward physical provisions. To set one's heart upon material possessions or to worry about the lack of them is to live in perpetual insecurity and to deprive one's self of the spiritual blessings of God.

26. Jesus illustrated His point by referring to objects in nature which were immediately at hand: the birds of the air and the flowers of the field. Though the birds which fly through the skies appeared not to labor, **your heavenly Father feedeth them.** How does God accomplish this? He does it through the normal process of nature. **Consider the lilies;** (vs 28) they appear to do nothing for themselves and yet God, through the process of nature which He controls, does **clothe the grass of the field** (vs 30). Even Solomon, the great and wealthy king of Israel, was not arrayed in any greater beauty than the flowers of the field which God has made.

27-30. The key point of this passage is found in the phrases "are ye not much better than they?" (vs 26) and "shall he not much more clothe you?" (vs 30). The Bible makes it clear that God is the Creator and Sustainer of nature. He is not divorced from the world which He has made. Indeed, "this is my Father's world!" Worry and anxiety are related to the length of one's life in the phrase **add one cubit unto his stature.** A cubit is a measurement of about eighteen inches. However, this reference is probably not to one's actual height but to the length of his life. The term "stature" (Gr *hēlikia*) may in this place mean "age." Thus the idea seems to be that a man cannot add the smallest measure to the span of his life by worrying. In fact, modern medicine would tell us that worry actually shortens one's life. This state of anxiety is related to having **little faith** (vs 30). Faith is total confidence in the provision of God. Faith in salvation is a total trusting of the complete work of Christ on the cross on our behalf. The Scripture reminds: "Whatsoever is not of faith is sin" (Rom 14:23). Therefore, a lack of

faith will lead to a life of psychological anxiety. Since this lack of faith is identified with sin, Adams is correct in asserting that man's emotional problems stem from his sin (J. Adams, *Christian Counselor's Manual,* p. 117 ff.). In the Sermon on the Mount we have then, not only a directive for spiritual well-being, but the model of a manual of mental health as well.

33-34. This portion of the Sermon on the Mount is summarized by the statement **seek ye first the kingdom of God.** The disciples who have pledged their allegiance to the King must continue seeking the kingdom and its righteousness. The present imperative form of the verb (Gr *zētō*) indicates a continual or constant seeking. The word first indicates one's first and ever dominant concern. The contrast between the spiritual and the material is again emphasized. The believer is to seek first the righteousness that is characteristic of God's kingdom and then **all these things** (i.e., material things) shall be added unto him. Seeking the kingdom of God involves a continued hunger and thirst after righteousness. We are not only to seek the kingdom of God in the sense that we set our affections on things above, we must also positively seek holiness in **righteousness.** The continual seeking here is similar to that of the seeking face of God. A true believer is never falsely content with what he has in Christ, but is continually seeking to know Him better. Thus, we could say: "keep seeking the kingdom of God" and as you do He will continually provide your needs. When our priority is spiritual, God will take care of the material, for where God guides, He provides. We need not even worry about tomorrow for **Sufficient unto the day is the evil thereof** (vs. 34). This means that each day has its own troubles and challenges to be responsibly handled, without worrying about the hypothetical problems which could arise tomorrow. God is ever pictured in Scripture as the God of the present. Today is the day of salvation.

(6) Sixth Example: Judging Others. 7:1-12.

7:1-4. Judge not refers to an unfavorable and condemnatory judgment. This does not mean that a Christian should never render judgment of any kind under any circumstances. The New Testament Scriptures are filled with exhortations to "mark those who cause divisions among you," "receive not" those who deny Christ, "exhort," "rebuke," etc. Certainly judging ourselves and those who have failed in their spiritual responsibility is a necessity of church discipline (cf. I Cor 5). The point being made here is that we are not to judge the inner motives of another. We are not to render a verdict based upon prejudiced information. Nor are we to use ourselves as the standard of judgment for **with what ye mete** you shall be judged. If we were judged in eternity merely on the basis of the verbal judgments we have rendered others, we would all condemn ourselves! **That ye be not judged** seems to refer to the ultimate judgment of God rather than our own judgment. The terms "mote" (Gr *karphos*) and *"beam" (Gr dokos)* are used metaphorically for a small fault and a great fault. The mote was literally a small speck of sawdust whereas the beam was literally a rafter used in building. Thus, the idea of the text is that one cannot remove the speck from his brother's eye until he has removed the rafter from his own eye!

5-6. Thou hypocrite is the only statement that can be made for this play actor who pretends to be a physician when he himself is sick. Filson (p. 104) comments: "His concern to criticize and reform others is marred by uncritical moral complacency as to his own life." The dogs and swine refer to those who have deliberately rejected the message of truth. These particular animals were especially repulsive to Jesus' audience. The connotation in verse 6 is not that we should not present our message to those who are the outcasts of society, for Jesus Himself went to the poor sinners among His people. Rather, the idea is that it is futile to continue to present truth to those who have refused what they have already heard. A man cannot appreciate new truth until he has responded to the truth which he has already received. Since the context deals with the matter of discernment and judgment, it may rightly be assumed that there is a proper place for such activity in the Christian's life. The main difference between judgment and discernment is that a judge merely pronounces a verdict, while discernment seeks a solution.

7-10. Earlier a paralleling contrast was drawn between the outward acts of worship (giving, praying, fasting) and the inward attitudes of devotion (possessing, praying, judging). Since the opposite of judging is fasting, it seems fitting that Jesus here makes a lengthy statement on the importance of prayer. This statement is not out of place as some have assumed; rather, it is the Christian alternative to judging. we would sincerely pray for those whom we are prone to criticize we would ultimately do them much more good. The three imperatives **Ask, seek, knock** are, in the original, in the present tense suggesting both perseverance and frequent prayer. In the English language the first letter of each word forms the acrostic A-S-K. Fervent and continual prayer is to be made on behalf of those for whom we are concerned.

God promises to answer all genuine prayer (vs. 8). Everything that we need for spiritual success has been promised to us. God leaves us no excuse for failure. **Ask and it shall be given you, seek and ye shall find, knock and it shall be opened unto you,** for everyone that does such will receive an answer.

You are not cut off in any way from the blessings and provisions of God for these are available to every one of His children.

11-12. Jesus illustrated His point by comparing the willingness of a human father to give his child a gift, contrasted to our heavenly Father who shall gladly give us what we need. The term **evil** (vs. 11) is used here of man's sinful nature. Even sinful men are kind unto their children; therefore, **how much more** shall your heavenly Father delight to answer your prayers. Hence, rather than judging others, we are to treat them as we would like to be treated. The statement in verse 12, **Therefore all things whatsoever ye would that men should do to you, do ye even so to them,** is the biblical injunction which has often been called "the Golden Rule." Similar statements are found in both Jewish and Gentile sources, but usually in the negative form. The phrase, **this is the law and the prophets,** indicates that the statement made here by Jesus is not intended to be unique, but rather a summarization of the second table of the law. Verse 12 is not intended to be a total summary of Jesus' teaching and in no way exhausts or explains the gospel itself. Any atheist could readily accept this statement alone. However, it is when we see this statement in the context of everything that Jesus taught that we understand its true signigicance. Rather than judge others we ought to pray for them. If we would rather have people pray for us than criticize us, then we ought to be willing to do the same to them.

d. The Two Alternative. 7:13-27.

The closing section of the Sermon on the Mount presents two choices to the listener. These are presented in a series of contrasts: two ways (vss. 13-14); two trees (vss. 15-20); two professions (vss. 21-23); and two foundations (vss. 24-29). This was a common method of teaching in both Jewish and Greco-Roman thought.

13-14. Enter ye in at the strait gate (narrow gate) means that one must come in the narrow way of the gate in order to reach the path which leads to eternal life. The order of the gate first and then the way suggests the gate is the entrance by faith in Christ into the way of the Christian life. It is interesting to recall that Christians were first called those of "the way" (cf. Acts 9:2; 19:9; 22:4; 24:14). Though the many are on the **broad way which leads to destruction** (eternal death), the gate which leads to life is so narrow that **few there be that find it.** Christ Himself is both the gate and the way (cf. Jn 14:6), and God enables men to find that gate (cf. Jn 6:44). In the immediate context of Jesus' day it could be assumed that His way was presented as that which is narrow and the way of the Pharisees as that which is broad. The contrast here is one between the way of grace and the way of works. There are many on the broad road of life who are seeking to arrive in heaven by means of their own works, but only a few have received the grace of God which guarantees them heaven. We are reminded of Jesus' statement, "Many are called, but few are chosen" (22:14).

15. The warning to **Beware of false prophets** fits appropriately with the concept of the two ways. Since many are being misled in the wrong way, it is obvious that they are being misled by wrong ones. False prophets were prevalent in the Old Testament, whereas God's true prophets were often in the minority (as in Elijah's confrontation with the prophets of Baal). These appear in **sheep's clothing** but are in reality **ravening wolves.** This is a perfect description of those preachers who have denied or distorted the truth of the Gospel. They look like a lamb but they act like a wolf. Their description is similar to that of the great false prophet in Revelation 13:11.

16-20. A true test of a prophet was

the conformity of his doctrine to that of the Scripture (cf. I Cor 14:37; Deut 13:1-5). **Their fruits** not only refer to actions of their lives, for these men are very, very sheepish, but to the doctrines which they proclaim. Having warned us against falsely judging others, Jesus now must remind us to beware and know such people. We are to be discerning enough not to be taken in by their cleverness.

The two trees are contrasted in relation to the fruit which they produce. The searching question, **Do men gather grapes of thorns?** reminds us of the origin of spiritual life which produces spiritual fruit. Man cannot produce such fruit out of his own unregenerate nature. Because he is a sinner by nature, he is a sinner by choice. Not only must his choice be changed, but so must his nature in order for him to make the right choice. **Every good tree produces good fruit** consistently, while a **corrupt tree produces evil fruit** continually. Therefore, the normal and consistent production of fruit, whether good or evil, in a person's life will bear evidence whether or not that life is of God. Verse 19 makes it clear that the unfruitful life is a picture of the unregenerate which is **cast into the fire.** The term "fire" is used as an apparent picture of eternal punishment in hell. The evil (Gr *sapros*) trees are literally rotten and useless. While the production of fruit in the life of a Christian may vary, some thirtyfold, some one hundredfold, no true Christian has the option of producing no fruit at all. No fruit means no life. The absence of life is the absence of the regenerating power of the Holy Spirit. Thus, the fruitless life is the proof of an unregenerate heart which can only be cast into hell. Always in the New Testament the changed life is the proof of one's profession of conversion (cf. II Cor 5:17).

21-23. Not everyone professing Christ is genuinely saved. Even the outward verbal acknowledgment of His Lordship is in itself not enough to save the unbeliever apart from true repentance and faith. A genuinely saved person is one **that doeth the will of My Father,** the Greek present tense meaning that he is continually living in obedience to the will of God as the normal course of his life. He may fail at times, but his general course of consistency is to obey the will of the Father. It is tragic to note that many will proclaim in that day, **Lord, Lord** and yet will be lost. On what do they base their profession? Their **many wonderful works** cause them to think that they have attained salvation and yet the response of Christ, pictured here as the Judge, will be **I never knew you: depart from me, ye that work iniquity.**Those who are continually living in sin, as the normal course of their lives, have no assurance of salvation whatever. This does not mean that one must experience basic and initial changes in one's life to validate his claim to conversion. The phase "work iniquity" is also progressive in Greek (i.e. they continue to work iniquity).

24-27. In drawing His concluding illustration of the two foundations, Jesus begins with the word **Therefore.** On the basis of all that He has taught and illustrated, He concluded that all who both hear and do His sayings shall be saved. He is not adding works to faith, but, as James reminds us, He is showing faith by its works. Faith is the root of salvation and works are its fruit. The works of man do not produce his own salvation. In fact, to the contrary, this entire message shows that man's human efforts alone are futile in gaining his salvation. Having made His point, Jesus also clearly stated that while salvation is by faith, it is by a faith which shows itself in a changed life. There is a repentant faith, a life-changing faith, a faith that works!

The contrast here is threefold: the wise man is the one who hears and practices upon a foundation of rock;

the foolish man does not practice these sayings and builds upon a foundation of sand. As a great master counselor, Jesus reminded His listener that hearing this message alone will not change his life. He must both hear and do what Jesus has said. The elements of the closing illustration are drawn from the simplicity of nature itself, the **rock,** the **rain,** the **winds.** The rain (Gr *brochē*) pictured here is that of a natural storm. However, it is implied as relating to the troubles and persecutions of life. The man whose house collapsed was at fault, not because he failed to labor, but because he did not lay the proper foundation. How lively must this imagery have been to an audience accustomed to the fierceness of an eastern temptest and the suddenness and completeness with which it sweeps everything unsteady before it! The sand represents human opinion and the doctrines of men as opposed to **these sayings.** (vs. 28).

28. The entire Sermon on the Mount is addressed to believers and presupposes faith in Jesus as Messiah. The works which are done by the believer are not based upon himself but upon the **rock** (vs. 24), who ultimately is Christ Himself (I Cor 10:4). He is the personal embodiment of all of His teachings. Thus, when He had finished the discourse, **the people were astonished.** Lenski (p. 314) notes that as Jesus spoke, crowds were in rapt attention, but when he ceased, attention relaxed and shocking amazement engulfed them.

29. The outstanding feature of His teaching was His **authority,** meaning the divine approval and authoritative constraint with which He delivered His message. Such straightforward preaching, based on the depth of one's own life, was in direct contrast to that of **the scribes.** The scribes were the copyists of the law and the theologians of their day. The scribes had to rely on tradition for their authority, whereas Christ was His own authority. This un-

doubtedly disturbed the Pharisees for He had no approval as an official teacher in their system. Rather than quoting the opinion of tradition, Jesus spoke as if He personally knew what He was talking about. He did!

The note of authority in the Sermon on the Mount warns the readers of Matthew's Gospel that they cannot ignore or reject Jesus' teaching without ruinous consequences. Why should we practice this sermon? Because of the beauty of its diction, its impressive pictures, its striking illustrations? No, we practice it because beyond its moral, ethical, and spiritual teaching is the person of the Preacher Himself! In the closing verses of this chapter we see that, without an ostentatious parade, our Lord calls attention to Himself as the focal point of the entire message. This is no mere restatement of the law but is the highest expression of the quality of Christian living which Christ alone can produce. The gospel is the message of the person and work of Jesus Christ. Its amazing "good news" is that He can do for us what we cannot do for ourselves. He can change a sinner into a saint!

2. His Miracles: Signs of Divine Authority. 8:1-9:38.

a. The Cleansing of a Leper. 8:1-4.

8:1-4. Make me clean. By the law of Moses, ceremonial uncleanness was attached to leprosy (see Leviticus 13, especially vss. 45-46). **Jesus . . . touched him,** a remarkable action, which normally would bring ceremonial uncleanness. In the case of Jesus, on the contrary, cleansing was brought to the leper. **See thou tell no man.** The purpose of Jesus in giving this command, as He did on several occasions, has been variously interpreted. It is probable that He did not wish crowds to be attracted by miracles alone, without spiritual hunger, or to appear in the role of a popular wonderworker. **Shew thyself to the priest,** i.e.

in obedience to the Mosaic Law (see Leviticus 13). **Offer the gift that Moses commanded.** The Mosaic directions for the cleansing of the leper, which are typical of Christ's atonement, are to be found in Leviticus 14:2-32. **For a testimony unto them,** i.e. as evidence to the priest that the leper had been cleansed.

b. The Healing of the Centurion's Servant. 8:5-13.

5-9. A rather fuller account of this miracle is given in Luke 7:2-10. **A centurion.** The rank of a centurion was between that of an officer and a non-commissioned officer. Perhaps the nearest modern equivalent is that of regimental sergeant-major. The position was one of considerable responsibility. **Servant** (vs. 6). The word (Gr *pais*) could mean "child" or "servant." **Sick of the palsy, grievously tormented,** i.e. paralyzed and greatly afflicted. The phrase does not necessarily mean that he was not personally present, as is plain from the parallel account in Luke 7:1-10. The answer was given through messengers. For a similar use of the word "said" see 11:3. **Servant** (vs. 9). Here the word means slave (Gr *doulos*).

11-13. In likening Jesus to himself as one **under authority,** (vs. 9) the centurion indicated that he believed Jesus had all the power of God behind Him and that His word would be instantly obeyed even in the realm of illness and death. **From the east and west.** The words are taken from Psalm 107 (see also Isa 49:12; 59:19; Mal 1:11). The Lord is referring to the gathering in of Gentiles through the Gospel, culminating in the final gathering together at His coming. **Sit down,** i.e. recline (Gr *anaklinō*) to eat. The ancients reclined at meals, resting on the left elbow. This eastern picture of the world to come as a great banquet is used by our Lord again in the parables of the wedding feast (22:1-14). **The children of the kingdom,** i.e. those to

whom the kingdom really belongs, the Jews. **Outer darkness,** i.e. destruction, the second death. **There shall be weeping and gnashing of teeth.** "There" is emphatic. The phrase looks back to Psalm 112:10. **As thou hast believed.** Faith is always the measure of blessing.

c. The Healing of Peter's Mother-in-Law. 8:14-17.

14-16. Laid (Gr *balō*) literally laid out, meaning sick in bed, the bed being a mattress placed on the floor. **Ministered unto them,** i.e. attended to their needs. This observation is included, perhaps, to stress the immediate and complete nature of the cure. **He cast out the spirits,** i.e. evil spirits, meaning the devils or demons. These beings belong to a higher and invisible world which our scientific knowledge has not yet pierced so that we know little of their nature and characteristics apart from Scripture.

17. With his word (vs. 16), better "with a word." **By Esaias**; RV margin, "through Isaiah." **Himself took our infirmities, and bare our sicknesses.** This is taken from the Hebrew of Isaiah 53:4. It is an important quotation that establishes the meaning of the first sentence of Isaiah 53:4, which refers to healing. Jesus deals with the cause of sickness, which is sin. It appears from Mark 5:30 and Luke 8:46 that there was a physical cost to the Saviour when He healed.

d. The Calming of the Storm. 8:18-27.

18. He gave commandment to depart. The Lord often wished to escape the crowds, partly to be alone with God, and partly for the disciples' sakes.

19-27. A certain scribe. The scribes are nearly always spoken of in the plural. **Master, I will follow thee.** These words have an underlying spiritual meaning in addition to the literal. (See Rev 14:4.) **Master** (Gr *didaskalos,* "Teacher.") Notice that our

Lord did not make it easy to follow Him, but insisted on the counting of the cost. **The Son of man.** This is the title by which our Lord most frequently referred to Himself. It was probably taken originally from Daniel 7:13, where it has a messianic significance. In the vision of Daniel, the kingdom of the Son of Man followed and superseded those of the four wild beasts. In the apocalyptic thought of our Lord's day the title was used for the Messiah. This is undoubtedly the aspect which the Lord emphasized by its use. By applying it to Himself He was testifying that He was the Messiah. **Another of his disciples.** We must infer from this that the man who found difficulty in following unconditionally was a professed disciple. **Bury my father.** This probably means to stay at home until the father's death. **Let the dead bury their dead,** a rather strong answer. It probably means that we are to leave the people of the world to live the ordinary life of the world and to devote ourselves to the highest that life can give, even over the claims of one's family. **Tempest.** A disturbance (Gr *seismos*) or violent tempest. **His disciples.** "They" is the better reading. **Fearful.** The adjective (Gr *deilos*) means cowards.

e. The Healings of the Gadarene Demonics. 8:28-34.

28. See notes on Mark 5:1-20; Luke 8:26-39. **Gergesenes.** A better reading is "Gadarenes." Gergesa was a town on the eastern shore of the Sea of Galilee. The town was included in the district of Gadara which took its name from that of a town of the same name; one of the cities of the Decapolis. The whole was included in the larger administrative district of Gerasa, whose center was the town of Gerasa in Gilead. **Two possessed with devils.** The mention of two demoniacs is peculiar to Matthew, the parallel passages in the other synoptists mentioning only one. A possible explanation is that the case

of the one was outstanding in view of his conversation with Christ and subsequent witness in the district, so that he would be the only one of the two of whom the evangelists Mark and Luke had heard. The evangelist Matthew, on the other hand, even if he was not himself present (his call is described in chapter 9), was intimate with those who had seen the double cure.

29-34. What have we to do with thee? The meaning seems to be, "What is there in common between us?" and a better translation would perhaps be, "What have you to do with us?". The question was an expression of resentment at intrusion. **To torment us before the time?** In the New Testament this word torment (Gr *basanizo*) does not seem to be used in its earlier, narrower sense of torture, but to express the wider meaning of "to cause suffering" or loss in any way. Note that the evil spirits appear to be aware that retribution awaits them in the future. **A herd of swine.** Swine were unclean animals by the ordinances of the mosaic law. To keep them was illegal for the Jews. **The whole herd . . . perished.** This is the only recorded miracle of our Lord which was destructive of animal life. The fact that He granted the demons' request is because of His concern for the man. The principle involved may be that those who are knowingly disobedient, as was the case of the pig-breeders, deprive themselves of divine protection and place themselves at the mercy of the forces of evil. **They besought him that he would depart.** The incident ends in tragedy. The people preferred their business to the Saviour whose power they feared.

f. The Healing of the Paralytic, and Lessons on Righteousness. 9:1-17.

9:1-8. See notes on Mark 2:1-12; Luke 5:17-26. **He entered into a ship, and passed over.** Jesus never stayed where He was not wanted. **His own city,** i.e. Capernaum (see Mt 4:13). **Thy sins be forgiven thee.** Jesus attended first to the man's spiritual need, which of course was the greater. Some versions render "are forgiven." **This man blasphemeth.** The supposed blasphemy lay in the claim to forgive sins. Jesus knew instinctively in His own heart the nature of their wicked reasoning and asked a pointed question. It is left unanswered perhaps because the scribes, who regarded Jesus as an impostor, thought it easier to say glibly, "Thy sins are forgiven," since no outward result could be observed. In the face of this the implication may be that it is, in fact, an easier task to deal with man's physical needs than with his spiritual needs. Another answer may be that both alike are equally easy with God. **Power,** i.e. authority or right. **They marvelled,** better texts read "they were afraid."

9-12. The receipt of custom, i.e. the toll booth in the street where the tax collectors sat to receive the taxes and dues. **In the house** means "at home." We know from the other synoptists that the house was Matthew's (Mk 2:15; Lk 5:29), where the expression used is "in his house." The only possible alternative meaning of the expression in Matthew's Gospel is that the owner of the house was the one who was writing. This then is a piece of internal evidence for the Matthean authorship of the Gospel. **Publicans.** The quotation is lit with a fresh glory as Jesus applies it to the salvation of sinners.

13-15. The righteous. The word is ironic. It means the self-righteous. Scripture tells us that "there is none righteous, no, not one" (Rom 3:10). **To repentance.** Some older manuscripts omit these words but the principle taught by our Lord here is that fasting is not an end in itself, but is to be practiced only under appropriate circumstances. The Pharisees' fasting was part of the righteousness which the Lord had just condemned (see vs. 13 above). **The children of the bride-chamber,** i.e. the wedding guests. **As long as the bridegroom is with them,** i.e. while the wedding festivities last, which might be for some days. **When the bridegroom shall be taken from them.** This is an allusion to His own death and ascension.

16-17. The principle expressed is that Jesus Christ has come to bring in a new dispensation altogether, which cannot be fitted into the forms of the old Jewish economy. The rule of the law must go, that grace may have free reign. **New cloth** means unbleached cloth. RSV reads "unshrunk." **Bottles,** i.e. skins, which were frequently used in the East as containers for liquids. The strength of fermentation of the new wine would be too much for partly worn, old, or inelastic skins and they would break.

g. The Healing of the Woman with the Issue and the Raising of the Ruler's Daughter. 9:18-26.

18-19. See notes on Mark 5:22-43; Luke 8:41-56. **A certain ruler,** i.e. a magistrate. We know from the other synoptists that his name was Jairus. **Worshipped.** This suggests that he recognized Jesus' deity. **Is even now dead.** In the other Gospels we are told that she was dying when the father first came and that she had died. Matthew combines these two phases into one.

20-22. I shall be whole, literally, "I shall be saved." The use of this word for the restoration of physical health makes it easier to understand that miracles picture spiritual healing. **Daughter.** The usual mode of address from a rabbi. **Be of good comfort** means, "cheer up". **Thy faith hath made thee whole.** The incident is an outstanding illustration of faith in action.

23-25. Verse 23 describes the usual scene in a Middle East house where someone lay dead. Mourners were hired to make a noise. The **minstrels** were fluteplayers. **The maid is not dead, but sleepeth.** The Lord meant that her death had been turned into a temporary sleep by the fact that He was shortly going to raise her. On the same principle, the dead in Christ are said to be asleep in view of the certainty of their resurrection. **Took her by the hand.** Perhaps He did this so that she should not be startled on such a tremendous awakening.

h. The Healing of the Blind and Dumb Men. 9:27-38.

27-32. See also Luke 11:14-26. **Crying,** better "crying out." **Thou son of David.** This appears to have been an expression in use at the time that implied messiahship. The blind men had apparently put their faith in Jesus as the Messiah. **Into the house.** This may have been His own home in Capernaum, or perhaps Matthew's house as in verse 10. **Believe ye . . . ?** Notice the emphasis laid in this, as in other miracles, upon faith. **See that no man know it** (see note on 8:4). This disobedience may have made the Lord's ministry more difficult and brought around Him large crowds with no spiritual hunger, thus contributing to the necessity of His use of parables (see ch. 8).

33-38. In verse 33 notice the connection between the spiritual evil and the physical disability. By the **prince of devils** is meant Satan. **Fainted** means were distressed. **As sheep having no shepherd** is quoted from Numbers 27:17. The words are taken substantially from LXX, but with an altered construction. Verses 37 and 38 constitute one of the great missionary passages of the New Testament. (cf. Lk 10:2; Jn 4:35-38).

3. His Missionaries: Sending of the Twelve. 10:1-12:50.

10:1. Power against unclean spirits, i.e. authority over demons. **Apostles** (Gr *apostolos*). This is the technical term that later came to be applied to the twelve men who are called in verse 1 by the more general term of "disciples." Note that their twelve names are ar-

ranged in six pairs, which perhaps correspond to the arrangement in which they were sent out on their mission.

2-4. The first, Simon. Peter heads all four lists of the Twelve (cf. Mk 3:16; Lk 6:14; Acts 1:13). In both the Gospels and Acts he is the most prominent and it may well be that he exercised a natural leadership among them. It does not follow from this, however, that his leadership was ever passed on to successors. **Bartholomew** is generally considered to be identical with the Nathanael of John 1:45-51. **Lebbaeus, whose surname was Thaddaeus.** Better texts read simply "Thaddaeus." Luke gives his name as Judas (6:16; Acts 1:13). **Simon the Canaanite.** This does not mean an inhabitant of Canaan. A more correct term is the "Cananaean." Simon had been a member of the nationalist party known as "Zealots" which party had resisted Herod the Great and was ready to resist all foreign rule by force of arms. They were a kind of *maquis.* **Judas Iscariot.** The name Iscariot may mean a member of the tribe of Issachar, or an inhabitant of Kerioth (Joshua 15:25; Amos 2:2), or the one who carried the purse (from Aram *secariota* "purse"), or the one who was strangled (from Heb *iscara* "strangling"). The second is the most probable. Thus, he was the only disciple who was not a Galilean.

5-10. The way of the Gentiles. There were Greek cities in Galilee which lived a separate life from that of the Jews. The apostles were to confine themselves to the Jewish towns. **The Samaritans** occupied the central portion of Palestine between Judaea and Galilee. They were descended from the peoples imported by the Assyrians and were intermarried to Jews after the destruction of the northern Israelite kingdom. Since the days of Nehemiah they had been the bitter enemies of the Jews (cf. Jn 4:9). **The house of Israel.** This term is not confined in either Old Testament or New Testament to the ten northern tribes. **The kingdom of**

heaven is at hand. This was the message of John the Baptist (see 3:2) and Jesus Himself (4:17). **Provide,** better "Get," as AV margin. **Purses** (Gr *zōnē*), literally belt. The fold of the robe or the girdle acted as do our pockets. **Scrip** means a wallet. It was a small bag. **Coats** was the outer robe or tunic, corresponding to the Roman toga. **Staves** (RV "staff"). The Greek is singular. With this Luke 9:3 agrees. The meaning of Mark 6:8 is perhaps that they were to have one walking stick between a pair. Perhaps our Lord did not wish them to look like ordinary travelers. **The workman is worthy of his meat.** They were to rely upon the gifts and hospitality of those to whom they preached. These words are quoted in I Timothy 5:18 in their Lucan form.

11-16. Inquire means search out. The accepted code of Eastern hospitality was such that many offers of accommodation would probably be received. But they were not to rely on hospitality from any who rejected their message. **Salute it,** i.e. with the customary greeting of "Peace," which explains the meaning of verse 13. **Shake off the dust of your feet.** This was a symbolic act of rejection and condemnation. Not even the dust of the wicked city was to cling to them. **Verily** (Gr *amēn*) is a transliteration from Hebrew meaning "truly" and gives emphasis to the statement that followed. **Sodom and Gomorrha.** For the story of the destruction of these cities see Genesis 19. For an application of this statement to Capernaum itself see Matthew 11:23-24. **Wise as serpents** (cf. Gen 3:1). The phrase emphasizes the amount of wisdom needed since the serpent was commonly regarded as the wisest of beasts. The quality of the wisdom to be shown is very different, as the next phrase shows. For an example of such wisdom in action see I Corinthians 9:19-23. Notice that it is because of fierce opposition that these qualities are to be exercised.

17-22. See also Mark 13:9-13; Luke 12:11-12; 21:12-19. **Take no thought.** Be not anxious. **It shall be given you.** As the next verse shows, this will be by the inner prompting of the Holy Spirit. **The brother.** In both cases the definite article is better omitted. **Children shall rise up against their parents.** This is a summary of Micah 7:6. **For my name's sake,** i.e. because you belong to me. **But he that endureth to the end shall be saved.** Not a teaching that salvation may be lost but rather that perseverance in a life of faith proves that one is saved.

23-24. It has been suggested that in the latter part of verse 23 the Lord was referring to a meeting with the apostles later during the course of His ministry. But such an interpretation seems out of harmony with the meaning attached in this Gospel and throughout the New Testament to the conception of the coming of the Son of Man. These rather difficult words seem to lift the commission here given to the apostles out of purely local circumstances and prove its application to the missionary work of the whole church in every generation.

25-31. Beelzebub. The name refers to an evil demon and is most probably a contemptuous name for Satan. **Fear . . . not.** The worst that our enemies can do is to destroy our physical life, but this does not prevent a blessed resurrection to life everlasting. To God, however, belongs the power of the second death, which is eternal destruction. By **soul** is meant the personality or personal identity. The contrast here made is between this world and the next. **Hell,** i.e. Gehenna, as a description of the second death. **A farthing,** the Roman *as*, equal in the time of our Lord to one-sixteenth of the denarius, and worth about a halfpenny or less. **Without your Father,** i.e. without His being concerned.

32-37. Confess me, i.e. acknowledge that he belongs to Me. In reality, secret discipleship is an impossibility. But, as verses 34-39 show, open confession of Christ leads to division and conflict. See the parallel passage in Luke 12:49-53. The message of "peace on earth" proclaimed by the angels at the Lord's birth is not to be fulfilled outwardly in this present world. It is fulfilled now in the hearts of those who believe, and perfectly so in the world to come. **A sword,** a vivid figure of division, and so rendered by Luke (12:51). Verses 35, 36 are taken from Micah 7:6. The words come apparently from the Hebrew, with reminiscences of the LXX. Verse 37 teaches that every man must choose between even his nearest and dearest personal relationship on the one hand and Christ on the other. **Worthy of me,** or fit to follow me, and so in verse 38.

38-40. Taketh not his cross. This is the first mention of the cross in the Gospel and, therefore, in the New Testament. On the theological significance of the cross, see L. Morris, *The Cross in the New Testament* and *The Apostolic Preaching of the Cross.* It was the custom for the condemned man to carry his cross on the way to execution. There is plenty of evidence that our Lord anticipated the mode of His own death. These words come as the climax of His warning to the apostles that their mission would involve arrest and persecution, culminating in condemnation to death, as in His own case. These important words also have a deep spiritual significance and constitute the basis of the Apostle Paul's teaching about the identification of the believer with the cross of Christ (see e.g. Gal 2:20). **Findeth his life,** i.e. gains, or gets something out of it for himself. Here the word means the self-life, or natural life, as opposed to the spiritual life. **Shall find it,** i.e. in the world to come. A life emptied and poured out in the service of Christ in this world will find full enjoyment and expression in life everlasting.

41-42. In the name of a prophet, i.e. as a prophet. **A prophet's reward . . . a**

righteous man's reward, i.e. the reward due for receiving a prophet or a righteous man respectively. **These little ones.** As used here this is perhaps a general term for the disciples or believers in general.

a. Excursus: John the Baptist and Christ. 11:2-30.

11:2-7. Verses 2-19 are parallel with Luke 7:18-35, where see notes. **In the prison.** This imprisonment has already been mentioned (see 4:12), but the circumstances leading up to it are not described until 14:3-12, where the manner of John's death is also recounted. **The works of Christ,** i.e. His miracles. **He that should come,** i.e. the Messiah of Old Testament prophecy whose coming John had proclaimed. **The blind receive their sight,** and allusion to Isaiah 35:5; 61:1 where, with some of the other miracles mentioned in this verse, this is stated to be one of the works to be performed by the Messiah. John would understand the allusion. **The poor have the gospel preached to them** is another allusion to a prophecy in Isaiah (61:1) concerning the Messiah. **A reed shaken with the wind,** i.e. a commonplace event which no one would go out of his way to see.

8-11. But what went ye out for to see? . . . A prophet? . . . More, i.e. much more (Gr *perissos*). The quotation in verse 10 is from Malachi 3:1. Only the first few words follow the LXX. John was the foreordained forerunner of the Saviour and, as verse 11 implies, the last of the Old Testament prophets (see also vs. 13). He belonged to the Old Testament dispensation. This latter verse may be interpreted in various ways. The weakest believer who has the knowledge of the glory of God in the face of the risen Lord Jesus Christ is in a more privileged position than was John. The expression **them that are born of women,** meaning mortal men, also gives to the saying an emphasis upon life in this world. John may be the greatest of all in this life; but no position in this life can be compared with the glory of the life to come.

12-15. The kingdom of heaven suffereth violence (Gr *biazomai*). The meaning of this saying and the connection of verses 12-14 with the preceding and following contexts are uncertain. The line of thought seems to be as follows: John threw open the kingdom of heaven (by baptizing sinners) to those who would never before have been supposed fit to enter. He was the culminating point of Old Testament witness. He was the fulfillment of the prophecy of the coming of Elijah. If "suffereth" is in the passive voice, the sentence immediately following seems to mean that beginning with John, the heralds and messengers of the kingdom are treated with violence and persecuted. There is no need to support this view by supposing that the words are not the words of our Lord at all, but those of an editor looking back to the days of John through a generation or two of early church history. The expression "from the days of John the Baptist until now" can mean "from the days when John was preaching." Compare also the parallel passage in Luke 16:16 where the same verb is used. Assuming this interpretation, the saying would mean that the kingdom of heaven is pressing its way on in the world and communicating its force and enthusiasm to those who receive and enter it. **This is Elias.** See Malachi 4:5-6. Our Lord here distinctly states that this prophecy of the coming of Elijah was fulfilled in John the Baptist. This is a valuable hint that we are not to over-literalize Old Testament prophecy. The meaning of Malachi 4:6 seems to be that John was to form a link between the Old Testament and the New Testament.

16-19. This generation refused to exercise its capacity to hear, but made excuses for disregarding both John and Jesus. Our Lord likens them to children playing out-of-doors. Some interpret verse 17 as describing first a

game of "weddings" and then a game of "funerals." The application of His hearers' contrary attitudes to John (vs. 18) and Himself (vs. 19) is obvious **But wisdom is justified of her children** (vs. 19). Some texts read "works" for "children." "Children" is the reading in the parallel lucan passage, and may have been introduced from there. On the other hand, "works" may be a gloss on "children." The meaning of either word is the same, i.e. results. The saying means that the wisdom of both John and Jesus, in adopting differing modes of life, was justified in either case by its results.

20-24. The denunciation of Galilean cities which follows is recorded by Luke, but in a different connection (see Lk 10:13-16). **Chorazin** was about an hour's journey on foot north of Capernaum. **Bethsaida** was on the west of the Sea of Galilee about three miles southeast of Chorazin. **Tyre and Sidon** were both on the Mediterranean coast of Syria, beyond the northern boundary of Palestine. The saying is an allusion to Isaiah 14:13, 15, where it is spoken of the king of Babylon and probably refers to Satan.

25-30. Answered. The words that follow are the response of Jesus' heart to the circumstances just described. **Thank** (Gr *exomologeō*) is literally "acknowledge." **Babes,** i.e. spiritual babes, who receive God's revelation in simple faith; with verse 27 compare John 3:35; 17:2. Verses 28-30 are a figure which would appeal immediately to an agricultural community. The **yoke** probably represents the teaching of Christ, and there is an implied contrast with the burdensome teaching of the Pharisees (see Mt 23:4). **Ye shall find rest unto your souls.** The words are taken from Jeremiah 6:16. The LXX has "Ye shall find purification unto your souls," and is corrected in the gospel to the meaning of the Hebrew. **Easy** means good or kind. The passage is peculiar to Matthew's Gospel.

b. *Excursus: A Dispute with the Pharisees. 12:1-45.*

12:1-9. See notes on Mark 2:23-3:6; Luke 6:1-11. **The sabbath day**, i.e., the seventh day of the week, corresponding to our Saturday. It began at sunset on Friday and lasted till the following sunset. The Pharisees had burdened the sabbath with a multitude of detailed observances which were not laid down in the Mosaic law. Apparently what they objected to in this case was the rubbing of the ears in the hands. **Have ye not read?** The passage referred to is I Samuel 21:1-6. The point is that in a case of necessity the ceremonial law might rightly be overruled. **The shewbread.** For this see Leviticus 24:5-9. The loaves were placed on the table in the holy place in the tabernacle each Sabbath, and when taken out were eaten by the priest and his family. For the allusion in verse 5, see Numbers 28:9. The priests prepared the sacrifices on the sabbath in spite of the general prohibition of work. If the necessities of temple worship permitted the priest to **profane the sabbath**, there was all the more reason why the service of Christ should allow a similar liberty. **I will have mercy, and not sacrifice** (see 9:13). The application of this principle, which is that ethics are more important than ritual, is easily seen in the present context. Verse 8 asserts that Jesus Christ has the right to interpret the Mosaic ordinances, so that they do not interfere with His service.

10-27. Withered, i.e. paralyzed. Notice in verse 13 how the power to obey was given with the command to act. **Held a council**, better, "took counsel." **My servant.** In the original Old Testament passage the reference is to Israel, i.e. the true Israel of God. This true Israel is gathered up in the person of the Messiah. **He shall shew judgment to the Gentiles**, a prophecy that the righteousness of God would be made known to the Gentiles by the gospel. Verses 19 and 20 refer to the gentleness of Jesus. He never brushed aside or trampled on the weakest faith or wounded conscience. **Till he send forth judgment unto victory**, i.e. till the final triumph of righteousness. **Is not this the son of David?**, a messianic title; see 9:27. **Beelzebub.** See 10:25. Here Beelzebub seems to be identified with Satan. **Jesus knew,** i.e. He realized, or understood, the true meaning of their thoughts. **Your children**, better "sons." A reference to the disciples of the Pharisees.

28-30. The kingdom of God. Matthew's usual expression is the kingdom of heaven; they mean the same thing. **Is come unto you,** i.e. has come upon you unawares. The Lord's power over the demons was evidence enough that He was the Messiah. In verse 29 Satan is "spoiled" by the capture of souls from him for Christ by the gospel. **He that is not with me is against me**. There is no middle course. Everyone either gathers souls with Christ or scatters them from God. In Mark 9:40 we have the converse truth stated. The present passage applies to any teaching which is positively unscriptural. That in Mark should be borne in mind when confronted, for example, with denominational differences among fellow believers.

31-38. The blasphemy against the Holy Ghost. This sin is deliberate rejection of Christ and His salvation, the only sin that by its very nature puts a man beyond the sin offering was for those who sinned "through ignorance," not for those who sinned "presumptuously." To act presumptuously was to reproach (RV "blaspheme") the Lord (see Mk 3:28-29; cf. Lk 12:10). At first sight the contrast in verse 32 may seem strange. The reason for it seems to be that it is the Holy Spirit who brings the offer of salvation to the heart of man. **The tree is known by his fruit.** The point of this verse seems to be that the good works done by Christ were evidence of His goodness and should have prevented any such blasphemous saying as that spoken by the Pharisees. But the illustration of the tree is double-edged and, as verse 34 indicates, it proves the wickedness of the Pharisees as well as the goodness of Christ. **By the words**. Words are not the cause of justification or condemnation, but the evidence of either. **Answered**. The thought carries on from the previous verses. In view of the Lord's claims the Pharisees ask for evidence, though they should have seen it in the miracles.

39-42. The word **adulterous** means unfaithful to God; it was a metaphor frequently used in the Old Testament. **The prophet Jonas**. For the prophet's story see the book of Jonah. The reference in verse 40 is to the LXX of Jonah 1:17. **Three days and three nights**. The actual period was either minimally from Friday evening to Sunday morning (covering parts of three days) or maximally from Wednesday evening to Sunday morning (covering seventy-two literal hours). **The whale's belly** (v. 40). This is the only occurrence of the English word "whale" in connection with the story of Jonah. The Greek word *ketos* means a great sea monster. **The men of Nineveh**. Notice that our Lord places them on the same level of historical reality as those whom He was actully addressing. **The queen of the south**, i.e. the queen of Sheba (see I Kgs 10). Our Lord is contrasting her eagerness to hear the wisdom of man with the refusal of His hearers to listen to one **greater than Solomon**. Notice also the claims made by our Lord in verses 6 and 41.

43-45. A reference to the fact that, though the Jews were cleansed by the Babylonian exile from idolatry, their unbelief and hardness of heart had produced in them a worse moral condition than when they were idolaters before the captivity. By asking **Who is my mother?**, (vs. 48) Jesus calls our attention away from earthly relationships to spiritual relationships. A believer is closer to Christ than even a physical relative. Kent (p. 44) notes: "This saying offered no disrespect to Mary, nor to His brothers, for at a later time we find them sharing this spiritual relation. Yet neither is there any suggestion that the mother of Jesus had any special access to His presence."

4. His Mystery: Secret Form of the Kingdom. 13:1-58.

13:1-2. On one of the busiest days of Jesus' earthly ministry He gave an extended series of parables (seven in Matthew and four in Mark, including one not given in Matthew). In the overwhelming press of the crowd at a **house,** Jesus could not be reached by people, so He went **into a ship** from which **He** taught the multitude. This is the turning point in Matthew's Gospel. Already sensing His impending rejection, Jesus now expresses the "mystery" form of the kingdom which will be the church. His early ministry involved a proclamation of the spiritual principles of the kingdom. The Jews, seeking a political and nationalistic kingdom, were now rejecting Jesus' concept of a kingdom of spiritual character. To bring in a political kingdom before men were born again would be a travesty. Therefore, an interval is now announced between the Messiah's original appearance and His final return. That interval is the Church Age, during which believers are citizens of the kingdom which is within them (Lk 17:21). The distinction between the church and the kingdom is not that one is more spiritual than the other. The church is the present (realized) form of the kingdom of God. The Millennial Kingdom, which is to come in the future (Rev 20:4) is another transitional form of the kingdom which will ultimately be presented to the Father to be the eternal kingdom of God (Rev 21).

3. Walvoord (p. 96) notes that this section introduces a new subject, a new approach and a new method of teaching by parables. **He spake . . . in parables,** a common method of teaching in the Near East, used to convey spiritual truth through a series of earthly comparisons. Jesus was an expert at this form of teaching. It should be noted, however, that parables did not always convert unbelievers who were often confused about their meaning. Tasker (p. 134) comments: "Jesus deliberately adopted the parabolic method of teaching at a particular stage in His ministry for the purpose of withholding further truth about Himself and the kingdom of heaven from the crowds, who had proved themselves to be deaf to His claims . . . from now onwards, when addressing the unbelieving multitude, He speaks only in parables (thirty-four in number) which He interprets to His disciples in private."

a. The Parable of the Sower. 13:4-23.

4-10. The first parable is set in an agricultural context. **A sower went forth** refers to the ancient seed sower, planting a crop. The Greek definite article here is generic. Jesus later interpreted this parable Himself. The seed depicts the Word of God (vs. 19) and thus the sower is the gospel evangelist. The **wayside** is the path trampled through the field. It was hard-packed and the seed found no root, thus the **birds** (demons? vs. 19, "wicked one(s)") snatched it away. Here there was no response at all to the gospel. The second category is called **stony places** or the rock ledge beneath a thin, shallow layer of soil. This thin crust would warm quickly causing the seed to sprout instantly but without adequate rootage or moisture. Thus, the **sun . . . scorched** the crop and it **withered away.** The third group of seeds fell **among thorns** which had not been plowed. The thorns (wild growth) choked out the crop. The **good ground** represents well-plowed and prepared soil capable of producing a large crop. The statement, **Who hath ears to hear,** goes beyond physical hearing and implies an inner spiritual reception of truth. This prompted the disciples' question as to why He had spoken to them in **parables.** Whereas before, He had used parables to illustrate His messages, now they formed the basis of the message.

11-13. The Saviour's reply was that only the disciples were to know the **mysteries of the kingdom of heaven.** The mystery implies a secret into which one must be initiated in order to understand it. The mystery revealed would be the new form of the kingdom during the interval between the first and second advents. Kent (p. 45) notes, "These parables describe the strange form of the kingdom while the King is absent, during which time the gospel is preached and a spiritual nucleus is developed for the establishment of the messianic reign." This special revelation is given only to the apostles who will become the foundation of that church. Those to whom this revealed secret is **not given** are those who have already rejected Christ. Thus, to the unbeliever, the parable form leaves him without understanding. Their rejection of Him leads to His rejection of them.

14-17. The quotation from the **prophecy of Esaias** (i.e. Isa 6:9-10) follows the LXX, emphasizing the obstinate unbelief of the people. As in Isaiah's day, the Jews had hardened themselves against God's truth and He had further hardened them in their unbelief. Their hearts had **waxed gross** (fat) and they would not, nor should not **be converted,** i.e. changed or saved. The faith of the disciples was evidence of their conversion and caused them to see and hear the truth which the **prophets** (vs. 17) had desired to know (cf. I Pet 1:10-12).

18-19. Jesus interpreted this parable Himself in verses 18-23. **The sower** is Christ working through the agency of His disciples to spread the gospel throughout the world. No longer is the message to be restricted to the house of Israel, but is to be declared to all men. The **word of the kingdom** is the gospel proclamation of Jesus the King and is not to be limited to an Old Testament Jewish-only message. Remember, these parables make it clear that the church is the present-day form of the kingdom. The key to interpreting the reception of the seed into the ground is the term **understandeth**, meaning to comprehend by believing faith (cf. vs. 23). The unsaved listener "understands" not and does not receive the seed, whereas the believer is one who both hears and "understands" the message and his life produces fruit to prove it. The reference to the **heart** in relation to the ground indicated that the quality of the soil represents man's heart response to the message.

20-23. The **stony places** are those shallow-hearted individuals who **anon,** "at once," receive (outwardly) the message with **joy,** i.e. enthusiasm or excitement. This emotional convert is not truly born again at all, for he **hath not root** and withers away. The one who is among the **thorns** (cares of this world) is the carnal, wordly convert, who never really breaks with his past. Worldliness and materialism **choke the word** in his life and he is finally **unfruitful** (unsaved). The one who received seed in the **good ground** is the one who both heard the word and understood it, **which also beareth fruit** (evidence of true conversion). While such evidence may vary in its amount, all true believers will produce some fruit. No fruit means no spiritual life.

The Parable of the Sower has been variously interpreted. Some hold that only the first one was lost, while others believe that examples two and three lost their salvation. To the contrary, only the last one was genuinely saved and produced fruit to prove it. The others fell away (not from salvation, but their profession) and were unfruitful. Jesus said that the believers' fruit would vary, but He gave no one the op-

tion of being His follower and producing no fruit at all!

b. *The Parable of the Tares. 13:24-30; 36-43.*

24-27. This parable serves as a warning to the laborers in the field (which is the world, vs. 38). Unlike the Jewish form of the kingdom in the Old Testament where citizens could be easily recognized, during the Church Age converts will be made from all over the world and received upon their profession of faith. Thus, it will be easier to slip in some counterfeits who profess what they do not possess. **The kingdom of heaven** must refer to the church, which is the subject of these parables. The **enemy** is Satan and the **tares** (Gr *zizanion,* denoting "darnel," *lolium temulentum*) are false converts. The darnel was a weed that resembled wheat but did not come to fruition. The **good seed . . . sprung up, and brought forth fruit** again, emphasizing that true converts produce fruitful lives. By contrast, false (professing) converts produce no lasting fruit. It should be noted that a "fruit" is something which God must produce in us by His power (cf. Gal 5:22 ff.), whereas, a "work" is something which man can do by his own effort. Singing preaching, ushering, teaching, witnessing are all works; by contrast, loving people, having a deep-seated inner joy, being at peace with people, etc., are fruits of the Holy Spirit, as is righteousness and holiness. False converts may produce outstanding works but no real fruits.

28-30. The servants questioned what could be done with these tares. To uproot them would be to damage the entire crop: **root up the wheat with them.** The implication seems to be that too much scathing of people's genuineness of faith may damage the saved before it exposes the lost. **Let both grow together** indicates that there will always be some false professors among true Christian believers until the **time**

of harvest or judgment. Note that the tares are gathered, bound, and burned first, whereas, the wheat is gathered into **my barn** (heaven). The same progression of judgment, then blessing, follows in Revelation 19-22.

The Parable of the Tares is interpreted later by Jesus in verses 36-43. It should be observed that only the main details are symbolic in a parable, the minor incidents (e.g. the servants) merely give substance to the story. **The field is the world,** not the church. The sower of the good seed is the **Son of man,** or Christ Himself who will also be the final Judge who evaluates the fruit. The Gospel is to be sown where lost people are and where converts need to be made in the world. As Lord of the harvest, Christ directs this sowing process, i.e., the missionary mandate of the church. The **children of the kingdom** are the saved believers of the church, who are Christ's true followers. The **harvest** is the end of the world and the **reapers** are angels who play a decisive role in the final judgment. The **fire** represents hell, or the lake of fire. The destination of all unbelievers and false professors who deny Christ. By contrast, the righteous shall enjoy the eternal **kingdom of their Father.**

c. The Parable of the Mustard Seed. 13:31-32.

31-32. See Mark 4:30-43; Luke 8:18-19. The **mustard seed** is usually small and yet grows to a great size, though not as great as described here. The idea seems to be that the tiny beginning of the church will eventually culminate in great growth. **Herbs** (Gr *lachanon*), plants or vegetables. However, such numerical growth will come to harbor the **birds,** i.e. evil ones. Atkinson (p. 790) holds that, "The parable accordingly foreshadows the growth of the church into a world power . . . we have here a perfect picture of the apostasy not condemned, as such, we are reminded that outward growth is not

always a true picture of spiritual depth. Again, as with the tares, false professors clutter the branches of the true tree (Rom 11) of God's fruitful people, seeking to benefit their own interest."

d. The Parable of the Leaven. 13:33-35.

33-35. Kingdom of heaven is the spiritual form of the kingdom in the church. **Leaven** is a lump of old dough in a state of fermentation which contaminates the bread. Leaven is virtually always used as a symbol of evil (cf. Mt 18:6-12; Mk 8:15; Gal 5:9). **Three measures of meal,** a common baking quantity (cf. Gen 18:6), equivalent to one and a half gallons (Gr *saton;* Heb *seah*). Kent (p. 47) sees the **woman** here as the false prophetess, Jezebel (Rev 2:20) and the great harlot (Rev 17). Thus, the leaven is not just false profession of unsaved church members but false doctrine which they will attempt to bring into the church.

e. The Parable of the Hidden Treasure. 13:44.

44. This tiny parable has been subject to widely diverse interpretation. Some see Christ as the **treasure hid in a field,** for which the sinner must forsake all in order to obtain (cf. H. Kee, Matthew, in the *Interpreter's Commentary on the Bible,* p. 626). However, this view smacks of self-effort in obtaining that which only grace can give. It also violates the imagery of the other parables where Christ is the man. The treasure, then, represents His treasure people whom He bought and hid with Himself in God (Col 3:3).

f. The Parable of the Pearl of Great Price. 13:45-46.

45-46. The **merchantman** is Christ who comes to purchase, through His atonement, sinners who shall become **goodly pearls.** The **one pearl of great price** is the church for whom Christ gave His life, i.e. **all that he had.** If the pearl is Christ or the kingdom for

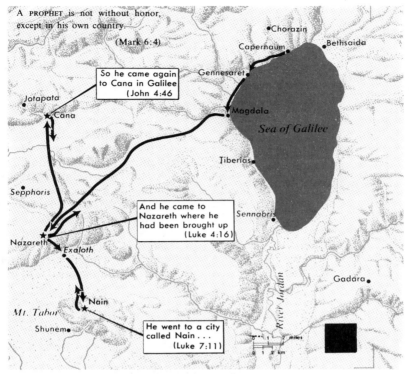

A PROPHET is not without honor,
except in his own country.
(Mark 6:4)

So he came again
to Cana in Galilee
(John 4:46

And he came to
Nazareth where he
had been brought up
(Luke 4:16)

He went to a city
called Nain . . .
(Luke 7:11)

Cana and Nazareth Revisited

whom a man must give all in order to obtain, then no man has ever yet given **all** that he has for Christ. While we receive Him as Saviour, we also progressively continue surrendering areas of ourselves to Him as we come to know better His will for our lives.

g. The Parable of the Dragnet. 13:47-50.

47-50. The **dragnet**. H. Stagg (Matthew, in the *Broadman Bible Commentary*, p. 159) states, "It was pulled between two boats or taken out into the water by a single boat and drawn to shore by ropes." In such a process all kinds of fish and other objects would be caught together. The **good** were put into **vessels**, while the **bad** were cast away to be burned **of fire** (in hell). The imagery is similar to the Parable of the Tares.

h. Excursus: The Use of Parables. 13:51-58.

51-52. The disciples have been given the parables and the principles of interpretation. Thus, they reply **Yea, Lord,** or "yes," we understand. Since they clearly understood these parables, then obviously we are to understand them as well. An informed disciple is a true **scribe** who comprehends new and old truths and can rightly discern between them.

53-58. Jesus then gave His disciples a first hand opportunity to witness the truth of these parables in action by teaching at the **synagogue** in His home town (Nazareth, not Capernaum). The people were **astonished**, i.e. greatly amazed or astounded. **Carpenter's son** refers to the family trade of Joseph, Jesus' legal guardian and earthly "father," being the husband of Mary.

The word "carpenter" (Gr *tektōn*) may refer to either a carpenter or a stone mason. The indication is that Jesus had learned His family's trade. There is no valid reason for understanding **brethren and sisters** in any sense but the normal one. They are Jesus' half brothers, the children naturally generated by Joseph and Mary after Jesus' virgin birth (cf. J. Broadus, *Commentary on the Gospel of Matthew,* pp. 310-312). Two of them, James and Judas (Jude), wrote New Testament epistles and played a prominent role in the early church. Some suggest that the family had moved to Capernaum, but that the sisters had married and remained at Nazareth ("with us"). Because they were **offended** at His message He did no **mighty works** (miracles) there due to their **unbelief**. His power was not limited by man's faith, but was exercised in response to it.

5. *His Malediction: Seriousness of Rejection. 14:1-16:28.*

a. *The Death of John the Baptist. 14:1-12.*

14:1-2. The occasion of John's death signaled a time for Jesus to retreat, lest He provoke an early death, before the appointed time. **Herod the Tetrarch** is Herod Antipas, the son of Herod the Great, the ruler of Galilee and Peraea. His ignorance of Jesus prior to this time is probably due to his self-indulgent, luxurious life style that had little contact with religious figures. His guilty conscience over John's death caused him to think Jesus was John the Baptist **risen from the dead**. His fear of the resurrection indicates its widespread belief in those days. Matthew, then, recounts the story of John's murder at Herod's hands.

3-8. John had been arrested because of challenging the illegitimacy of Herod's divorce and incestuous remarriage. **Herodias** was the daughter of Aristobolus, a half brother of Antipas. She had been married to her uncle, Herod **Philip**, and had borne him a daughter, Salome. However, she divorced her husband and married Antipas, who was already married himself. The king's own anger was already against John, but he **feared the multitude** and kept him alive because the people believed he was a **prophet** and indeed he was the last of the Old Testament prophets. Herodias was a guilty and vindictive ungodly woman who wanted John dead and devised a plan to get rid of him. At the king's birthday party, her daughter performed a provocative and sexually-enticing dance which so appealed to the drunken Herod that he **promised with an oath** that she could have whatever she wanted. Set up by her mother, she asked for **John Baptist's head in a charger**, i.e. a table platter.

9-12. The weak King complied and the forerunner of Jesus was slain. However, the vindication of the family was short-lived. Historical records confirm that the Herodian family never escaped bloodshed and violence (cf. H. Hoehner, *Herod Antipas* and S. Perowne, *The Life and Times of Herod the Great).* John's loyal **disciples** came bravely and obtained his body for burial and then informed Jesus, who departed into a **desert place apart**. We cannot fully comprehend the pressure Jesus was under at this time. Yet, in spite of His own heartache over John's death, He performs two major miracles for the multitude whom loving He cannot avoid healing and feeding.

b. *The Feeding of the Five Thousand. 14:13-21.*

13-19. The stage was now set for the miracle of the feeding of the five thousand, which is the only miracle recorded in each of the four Gospels (see Mk 6:30-44; Lk 9:10-17; Jn 6:1-13). It became **evening** may refer to either three o'clock or sundown. Both times were used in Jewish reckoning and both may appear in the harmonization of the various accounts. While towns were nearby where food could have been late in the evening (cf. Lk 9:12). Jesus' suggestion to the disciples **give ye them to eat**, placed the burden of responsibility on them. According to the Gospel of John, **Andrew**, who had brought Peter to Jesus, now brought a boy's lunch consisting merely of **five loaves and two fishes**, i.e. small baked rolls and dried fish (an adequate lunch for a boy, but hardly a crumb compared to the immense crowd).

The simplicity of the story and its inclusion by all four evangelists eliminates any doubt of its true historicity. Old liberal interpretations are totally inadequate. Albert Schweitzer suggested that in actuality each person received only a small crumb or fragment and yet felt satisfied. Barclay hints that the boy's offering of his lunch convicted the crowd, so that they all got out their previously concealed lunches and shared them. None of these approaches is suggested in the text. Even Schweitzer's crumbs would add up to gigantic, unbelievable loaves in order for five to feed five thousand! The obvious miracle was the result of Jesus' divine person and power. As the Creator-God, He multiplied the bread, so that, as each piece was broken off the original roll still remained intact. No wonder the crowd came back the next day seeking more. If the liberal interpretation of this passage were true, no one would have returned seeking more bread from Jesus (Jn 6:22-26)!

20-21. Not only is the miracle itself amazing but its result is equally stunning. **Twelve baskets full of fragments** remained over and above that which was eaten. The baskets (Gr *kophinos*) were small baskets carried on the arm and used as a satchel. These may have belonged to the disciples, who now receive a basketful of blessings as a result of their labor to feed others. Collection of the fragments emphasizes the adequacy and immensity of Christ's provision. Besides the **five thousand**

men a large uncounted group of women and children were fed.

c. The Walking on the Water. 14:22-36.

22-27. Following the miraculous feeding, which John relates to the discourse on the Bread of Life, the disciples departed across the **sea** (of Galilee) by rented ship. Jesus dismissed the crowd and went up **into a mountain apart to pray**. That night the disciples encountered great difficulty from a **contrary wind** about three miles out in the lake (Jn 6:19). During the **fourth watch**, three o'clock to six o'clock A.M. Jesus came to them **walking on the sea** (another obvious miracle not to be explained away by His supposedly walking on stones out in the middle of the lake)! The nearly exhausted disciples, who had been rowing all night, were afraid, thinking he was a **spirit** (Gr *phantasma*), i.e. a ghost or apparition. Jesus reassured them, **It is I.**

28-32. Peter answered him in his characteristic impulsive manner. This part of the story is recounted only by Matthew, on whom it must have made a deep impression. Remember that he was in the boat at the time; perhaps he got wet when Peter climbed back into the ship. The incident is not presented as a parable, but an actual event involving three miracles (cf. Filson, p. 174): Jesus walks on the water, Peter temporarily does so, and the wind ceases immediately. Peter urged Jesus, **bid me come unto thee upon the water**, not an unreasonable request for one who had just that day participated with the Saviour in the miracle of the feeding of the five thousand! However, Peter takes his eyes off the Saviour and fixes them on the surrounding conditions and begins to sink. With the concentration of his faith broken, Peter comes back under control of the natural forces. The incident served as a good lesson in spiritual truth for all the disciples, to urge them not to be

little faith and **doubt,** i.e. doubting feeble believers.

33-36. The disciples **worshipped him** and recognized Him as **the Son of God.** Their spoken Aramaic of this phrase was a clear recognition of the deity of Jesus. No mere man deserved their worship and no mere man could do what He had done. It is no surprise, then, that the people of **Gennesaret,** on the plain to the northwest of the Sea of Galilee, were healed by simply **touching the hem of his garment.** This procedure may have been motivated by reports of the cure of hemorrhage which had previously occurred in this same region (cf. 9:20).

d. The Conflict with the Pharisees over Ritual. 15:1-20

15:1-2a. See Mark 7:1-23. **Of Jerusalem.** It appears that the central religious leaders came to investigate the ministry and teaching of Jesus. **The tradition of the elders.** The Jews of our Lord's time believed that, in addition to the written law of Moses, there was an oral law given to Moses on Sinai and passed down from him by word of mouth till it reached the Great Synagogue or Council of Elders which succeeded Ezra after the return from the exile. This council lasted till 291 B.C. and seems to have been the source of the many accretions to the law of God which have been found in Judaism ancient and modern.

2b-9. Wash not their hands. The washing consisted of pouring a trickle of cold water over the outstretched hands. The Jews were not concerned with cleanliness but with ritual. **Why do ye also transgress?** The Lord here shows that additions to the Word of God ultimately contradict it. **Honor thy father and mother.** This is the fifth commandment of the Decalogue (see Ex 20:12; Deut 5:16). **He that curseth . . . let him die the death** (taken from the LXX of Ex 21:17). **It is a gift.** It was possible for a Jew by a legal quibble to dedicate his property to the tem-

ple, thus avoiding the necessity of supporting his parents, although he could continue to enjoy the proceeds himself. Notice that the Lord interprets the command to honor our parents in a practical sense. For children it means to obey them (Eph. 6:1-3) and for adults to support them. Our Lord condemns this common practice based on tradition since it completely defeats the purpose of the law. **Commandments** should rather be "Word of God." Verses 8 and 9 are from Isaiah 29:13 and follow the LXX where it differs from the Hebrew.

10-14. Defileth, i.e. makes him profane. The term is a technical one. The idea in Judaism was that to eat the wrong sort of food deprived a man of holiness and ultimately, therefore, of acceptance with God. The Jewish leaders showed offense at this deliberate contradiction of their own teaching. In two vivid pictures (vss. 13-14) our Lord tells His disciples that the Pharisees have no real mission from God and are themselves blind. They and all that their religion stood for would be destroyed.

15-20. Peter, acting on behalf of the others, asks for an explanation of the saying which had given such offense. Our Lord proceeds to elaborate the teaching for their benefit. **Draught** (Gr *aphedrōn*) means literally "latrine". **They defile.** The "they" is emphatic. **Evil thoughts,** i.e. evil schemes. **Blasphemies,** not only blasphemy in the modern, narrow sense of the word, but also criticism or libel of others.

e. The Healing of the Canaanitish Woman's Daughter. 15:21-28.

21-25. This second withdrawal of Jesus followed John's death and further rejection by the religious leadership of Israel. Thus, Jesus actually left the country and went into parts of **Tyre and Sidon** leaving Herod's jurisdiction to retire to Phoenicia for a time of seclusion, which was interrupted by the

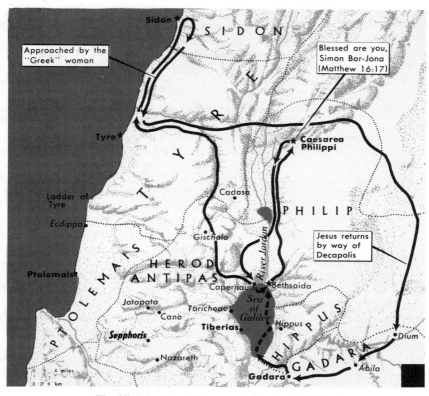

The Visit to Tyre, Sidon, and Caesarea Philippi

woman of Canaan, literally "Canaanitish woman." Mark 7:26 calls her a Syro-Phoenician woman. The word translated "coasts" (Gr *meros*) means districts. This is the only known occasion during His ministry that our Lord went outside the boundaries of Palestine. The woman was a Gentile and descended from the Canaanites who inhabited Syria and Palestine before the conquest of the latter by Joshua.

26-28. By **children** the Lord means Jews, and by **dogs**, Gentiles. Our Lord's attitude was intended to test the woman's faith, which was rewarded by a miraculous healing. Jesus is not angry with her, but is trying to teach the disciples a valuable lesson. Having been rejected by the Jews, He now turns to the Gentiles, a move that will later shock some of His followers. He

had healed Gentiles earlier, but here in Phoenicia He does not want to give the impression that he has totally abandoned Israel. The term used for "dogs" (Gr *kynarion*) means little dogs (pets), not wild, scavengering beasts. She replied that such **dogs eat the crumbs which fall from their master's table**. She knew what could be hers, even as a Gentile and, thus she became an illustration of millions of Gentiles who would later be blessed by **the Messiah of Israel. Great is thy faith.** Jesus again commends Gentile belief (cf. 8:10).

f. The Feeding of the Four Thousand. 15:29-39.

29-38. See also Mark 7:31-8:10. The supposition that this is a confused duplicate account of the feeding of the five thousand must be rejected. Both

Matthew and Mark include the account of the two events and do so in such a way as to indicate that they quite clearly thought of them as two separate miracles. The incident evidently took place on the southeast shore of Galilee, near the Gentile Decapolis. Therefore, many Gentiles seem to be among His listeners who **glorified the God of Israel.** This feeding took place after the crowd had been with Him for **three days** and were fed with **Seven** loaves and **a few small fishes** which were then distributed in a manner similar to the other feeding. This time **seven baskets full** remained. These baskets (Gr *spyris*) were much larger than those in 14:20.

39. The lesson to the disciples seems obvious: What you accomplish among the Jews will be duplicated among the Gentiles. **Magdala** (vs. 39) is Magadan, perhaps a suburb of Tiberias. In 16:9-10 Jesus refers to both feedings as separate events, even referring to the different numbers and using the different words for the baskets.

g. The Pharisees and Sadducees Rebuked. 16:1-12.

16:1-12. The unbelieving leaders came seeking a **sign from heaven,** i.e. an outward miraculous manifestation, of which Jesus had already given many. Notice that miracles alone never save anyone. They only serve to authenticate and call attention to the message, which must be believed in order for salvation to be experienced in the soul. Instead of another miracle, He points them to the **signs of the times,** eschatologically related to the sky and His second coming. He referred to their ability to discern the coming weather by the sky and implied that they should have been able to discern the time of His coming also. The **adulterous generation** is used here in a spiritual sense, unfaithful to God, though the two often interrelate. The **sign of the prophet Jonah** is one of Jesus' favorites for it relates to His

resurrection (see 12:38-40; Jn 2:18-22). This sign gives hope to the believer but is an indication of judgment for the unbeliever, who will be judged by the risen Christ at His second coming.

h. Peter's Confession. 16:13-28.

13-17. See Mark 8:27-33; Luke 9:18-21. **The coasts of Caesarea Philippi.** This was a town in the extreme northeast of Galilee, near the source of the Jordan. **Coasts** (Gr *meros*) means districts. Verse 14 shows that public opinion placed our Lord on the highest human pedestal by identifiying Him with one of the national heroes of the past, i.e. **John the Baptist.** Herod himself was a victim of this particular superstition (see 14:2). From 21:26 we know that He was held in high esteem as a prophet by the people. The coming of Elijah (Elias) was prophesied by Malachi (Mal 4:5) and the Jews often linked the name of Jeremiah with the prophet foretold in Deuteronomy 18:15. **Thou art the Christ.** Simon Peter recognized and acknowledged openly our Lord's deity. He may have been speaking for all the disciples. Verse 20 suggests that it was a conviction which they all now shared. Peter further used the Greek definite article "the" to designate that Jesus was **the Son of the living God.**

18. Thou art Peter, and upon this rock I will build my church. The Greek word used for "rock" (Gr *petra*) is played against the name Peter (Gr *petros*) in the original. The Roman Catholic interpretation of this passage is that Peter was the foundation stone of the church, that he had a primacy among the apostles, that he became Bishop of Rome, and that his primacy was passed on to his successors, the popes. The verse will scarcely bear the first of these propositions and certainly none of the others. Protestant interpreters, with some patristic support (Chrysostom, Justin Martyr, and Augustine), have tended to identify the rock with Peter's faith or confession, or with our Lord Himself. The most straightforward interpretation seems to be that Peter is meant by the rock, but that he is not the exclusive foundation (F. Broadus). For the twelvefold foundation of the church see Ephesians 2:20; Revelation 21:14. This view seems borne out by the fact that the same words are spoken to all the disciples in Matthew 18:18 as are spoken to Simon Peter in 16:19. Therefore, the rock or foundation of the church is the confession (ultimately, the doctrine) of the apostles, which became normative for the true church.

The word here translated **church** (Gr *ekklēsia*) means literally "a chosen or called-out assembly." Thus the use of the word as a technical term for an assembly or group of believers in Christ was quite natural. It is not viewed as an external organization, denomination, or hierarchical system. The New Testament church, therefore, is a local, autonomous congregation or assembly of believers which is a "church" in and of itself. This is the first occurrence of the word in the New Testament and probably is used in prophetic anticipation. Jesus' prediction, **I will build** could be translated, "I shall continue to build" (Greek progressive future) (see B. Chapman, *New Testament Greek Notebook,* p. 68). Since the commission in Matthew 10 sent the apostles only to the "house of Israel," and no further commission was given until chapter 28, there was no worldwide task for the disciples until the physical manifestation of the church at Pentecost. The same word was used in the LXX to translate "congregation" (Heb *kahal*) again emphasizing the local independent function both of a synagogue and a church.

Jesus promised that **the gates of hell shall not prevail** against the church (assembly). Some have viewed this as the inability of hell to overpower the church and see the church as being on the defensive against Satan. However, the phrase "shall not prevail" may be understood as meaning, "shall not stand against." The imagery would then picture the church as being on the attack against the gates of hell. Here hell (Gr *hadēs*) probably represents the kingdom of Satan, not just death and the grave. While Jesus' resurrection certainly will overcome the sting of death, it will also enable His church to aggressively and offensively attack the gates of hell (cf. usage as Satan's kingdom in Job 38:17; Isa 38:10; Ps 107:18) by snatching out victims from darkness into His glorious kingdom of light. One does not attack with gates, he defends. It is the church which is on the attack here and hell is on the defensive.

19-20. Our Lord then promised to Peter and the other apostles **the keys of the kingdom.** This means that Peter would have the right to enter the kingdom himself, would have general authority therein, symbolized by the possession of the **keys,** and preaching the gospel would be the means of opening the kingdom of heaven to all believers and shutting it against unbelievers. The book of Acts shows us this process at work. By his sermon on the day of Pentecost (Acts 2:14-40), Peter opened the door of the kingdom for the first time. The expressions **bind** and **loose** were common in Jewish legal phraseology meaning to declare forbidden or to declare allowed. Peter and the other disciples (see 18:18) were to continue on earth the work of Christ in preaching the gospel and declaring God's will to men, and were armed with the same authority as He Himself possessed. Christ in heaven ratifies what is done in His name and in obedience to His word on earth. There is also a definite reference here to the binding and loosing of church discipline which will be further explained in chapter 18. The apostles do not usurp Christ's lordship and authority over individual believers and their eternal destiny, but they do exercise the authority to discipline and, if necessary, excommunicate disobedient church members. **They should tell no man.** The revelation was to remain the property of the disciples until after the Lord's resurrection.

21. Jesus then announced His coming rejection and death at Jerusalem. All this would be necessary in order to initiate the church as the spiritual form of the kingdom on earth. **From that time forth.** He would openly reveal His coming rejection since the disciples' faith was now established enough to bear it. Thus, from this point onward, our Lord's ministry takes on a somewhat different complexion as He seeks to prepare His followers for the suffering which awaited Him and which would so disappoint their hopes. **Elders,** i.e. the religious leaders. The word probably denotes members of the Sanhedrin. The words **killed** and **rise again the third day** clearly indicate the divine Messiah's awareness of His earthly mission and destiny. To predict His death in view of His rejection was human, but to predict a supernatural resurrection could only be done by the God-man!

22-28. Be it far from thee. Notice the marginal readings of both AV and RV. The sentence seems to mean literally "Have mercy on yourself." Peter's instantaneous reaction to our Lord's new teaching shows how foreign to their way of thinking was this conception of His suffering. **Satan.** The Lord recognized in Peter's words a repetition of the temptations to avoid the cross which He had undergone in the wilderness. The word translated **offence** (Gr *skandalon*) means a trap or snare. **Savourest** (Gr *phroneō*) is very difficult to translate. It occurs in Romans 8:5 and Philippians 2:5, meaning to adopt and maintain an attitude of mind upon which the life and actions are based. **Deny himself,** i.e. refuse his own claims upon himself. **Take up.** The meaning is "lift up." It is a stronger word than that used in 10:38, and implies a lifting

of the cross on high, so that all may see it. This is the strongest statement in the New Testament about the disciple's need to crucify himself to the claims of Christ's lordship over him. **Lose his own soul** means to lose one's life and perish. **Shall reward every man according to his works.** The words are adopted from the LXX of Psalm 62:12 and Proverbs 24:12. This great fundamental moral principle of the Old Testament is made more explicit here by our Lord in explaining that it will find its fulfillment at His return. Verse 28 has caused much difficulty and needless misunderstanding. Its fulfillment may be looked for in the transfiguration which follows immediately, an occasion on which the Apostle Peter asserts that the three disciples saw Christ's coming (cf. II Pet. 1:16, ff) and also in the Lord's resurrection and subsequent glory.

6. His Manifestation: Special Transfiguration. 17:1-27.

17:1-9. See Mark 9:2-13; Luke 9:28-36. **Peter, James, and John** represent the "inner circle" of leadership among the disciples (cf. Lk 8:51; Mt 26:37) and serve here as ample witnesses according to mosaic law. They went into a **high mountain apart,** i.e. privately, by themselves. Tradition claims this took place at Mt. Tabor, but a more probable location would be Mt. Hermon, near Caesarea Philippi. Jesus was **transfigured** before them. The verb (Gr *metamorphoō*) indicates a transformation of essential form, proceeding from within. See Romans 12:2 and II Corinthians 3:18 where it is used of the spiritual transformation of the believer's new nature. The witness of Peter in II Peter 1:17-18 verifies the testimony that this was a real experince, not a vision. In His transfiguration, Jesus, as the personal manifestation of God's glory (cf. Jn 1:14, "we beheld his glory, even as the only begotten of the Father, full of grace and truth") reveals that glory tem-

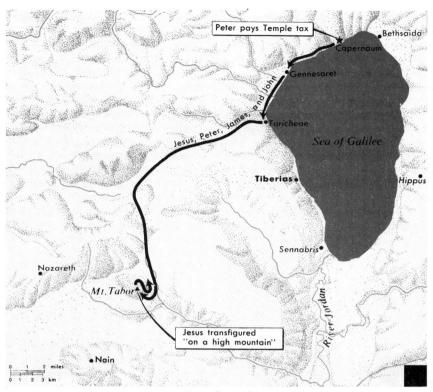

The Transfiguration

porarily to these key disciples. Later, in Revelation 1, His glorified resurrection form is permanently transfigured. **Moses and Elias** were the representatives respectively of the law and the prophets (see Jude 9, where Moses' resurrection is implied, and II Kings 2:11 for the account of Elijah's being taken up into heaven). **It is good for us to be here.** Peter wished to retain the situation and so suggests building **tabernacles** or tents. **A voice,** i.e. the Father's voice (for the words spoken compare 3:17). God the Father clearly indicated that Christ's authority completely superseded that of the Old Testament law and prophets. The warning, **tell . . . no man,** is to avoid a premature popular, but misdirected, awakening in His favor (cf. Jn 6:14-15).

10-14. The point of the disciples' question in verse 10 seems to be that,

supposing that Jesus' resurrection meant the end of the world and the inauguration of the kingdom, they thought it would be necessary for Elijah, of whom they had been reminded by seeing him on the mountain, to come and appear publicly first. Our Lord's answer is a quotation from Malachi 4:5-6, where the coming of Elijah was prophesied. (For the meaning of **restore all things** see Luke 1:17). He then repeats what He has told them already, i.e. that the prophecy foretelling the coming of Elijah was fulfilled in John the Baptist (see 11:14). He does not name him directly but recalls his suffering and compares with it the treatment which will be accorded to Himself (vs. 12). On the significance of the transfiguration, see E. Harrison, *A Short Life of Christ,* pp. 150-164.

15-23. The return down the mountain brought Jesus upon His powerless disciples who were attempting to cure a **lunatick.** The RV has "epileptic." **Sore vexed,** i.e. very ill. **How long shall I suffer you?** i.e. "can I endure you?" **Unbelief.** A better reading is "little faith," as in RV. **As a grain of mustard seed.** This seems to mean that faith, once implanted in the heart, grows naturally like a living organism. **This mountain,** i.e. any seemingly impossible obstacle or difficulty that stands in the Christian's way. Verse 21 is omitted by the more reliable texts. It seems to have been interpolated from Mark 9:29. The purpose of this incident is obvious. Since Christ alone is the glorified Saviour, the disciples' ability to work depends totally upon His empowerment. **Bring him . . . to me** clearly emphasizes this. It is never adequate to bring people to ourselves for our ideas; the true Christian evangelist must bring them to Jesus Himself. Christ emerges from this scene as totally dominant and the disciples as completely dependent upon Him, even to the point of being **exceeding sorry** or "greatly distressed" by His further announcement of His coming death, which so shocked them His prediction of His resurrection did not even register with their minds.

a. Excursus: Paying the Temple Tax. 17:24-27.

24-27. Jesus, as the glorified Son of God is greater than demons and also the temple itself. The two incidents following the transfiguration clearly reassert His supremacy. **Tribute money,** literally two drachmae, a technical term for the tax of half a shekel, which every Jew over twenty was expected to contribute to the upkeep of the temple. The amount was about fifteen or eighteen pence. **Prevented,** used here with its seventeenth century meaning of "anticipated." **Of strangers.** It was the subject races which were taxed first and most heavily. The **children,** i.e. the

king's own race, were **free.** The Lord Jesus Christ was the Lord and owner of the temple, and therefore it was not for Him to pay the tax. Action based on this fact might obviously be misunderstood, however, and under such circumstances our Lord would not give offense by seeming to be a lawbreaker. But note that in any matter where a fundamental principle was at stake, our Lord did not tone down His message in order not to offend (cf. 15:10-14). **A piece of money,** the silver tetradrachma, equivalent to the shekel and therefore the exact amount of the tax for two persons (cf. Atkinson, p. 794).

7. His Mercy: Sanctification of Forgiveness. 18:1-35.

a. Personal Forgiveness. 18:1-14.

See Mark 9:33-37; Luke 9:46-48. This chapter forms Jesus' longest recorded statement regarding the principle of forgiveness. The act of forgiving one who has wronged us is one of the most responsible and spiritual activities in our lives and must be repeated continually throughout one's life. This serves as the last great discourse before the journey to Jerusalem and is given in response to the disciples' jealousy of one another and to prepare them for the crucifixion, an act they will have to learn to forgive. Mark 9:33 indicates the message was given "in a house," probably Peter's.

18:1-4. The dispute over **Who is the greatest** was settled by Jesus' emphasis that it was the one who was willing to forgive the most! Thereby, He cut down the basic human motivation of pride in order to be the greatest by calling for the "greatest" to be the one most willing to forgive, which is contrary to proud human nature. Atkinson (p. 794) suggests that the **little child** may have been a member of Peter's family. **Be converted** means a "turning" (Gr *strepho*) of one's whole life and person toward God. This is the true biblical picture of conversion. It is far more than mental acknowledgment of the truth or intellectual assent to certain ideas. He now speaks generically of man's need to turn to Him and of the evidence of that turning in an attitude of humility. Thus, He challenges the disciples' selfishness by making them examine the reality of their own conversion. To **become as little children** means to be born again (converted) as a new-born spiritual child, characterized by faith and humility.

5-7. Thus, the **little child** represents a new convert or young believer. To **receive** such a fellow believer is to welcome Christ Himself. Therefore, the basis of true Christian fellowship is established in Christ Himself. There can be no real fellowship with those who deny Him and have not been converted, but with any true believer fellowship may exist. This, of course, does not overlook the discipline of an errant believer. **Offences** are viewed as a reality which must be accepted in the present world, but **woe** (the prophetic condemnation to death) to the one who is the source of the offense. Jesus very definitely took this matter seriously. A **millstone** is literally an "ass-stone," or a large grinding stone turned by an ass.

8-14. Verses 8-9 repeat the same idea as in the Sermon on the Mount (where see notes). The **hand, eye, foot** are not the real source of temptation nor are they the real cause of offending others. Just as temptation arises from within, so does offending others and being offended. It should be noted that this message is dealing with both aspects of the problem. We are most likely to offend others when we are selfish and proud. At the same time, however, we are also most likely to be offended when we are selfish and proud. The reference to **their angels** (vs. 10) supports the idea of individual guardian angels for believers (not all children, in general). See Hebrews 1:14 also. Verse 11, while legitimate in Luke 19:10,

seems to be inserted here, since the more reliable texts omit it. The truth of the statement, however, is reinforced throughout Scripture. Salvation is not just a privilege to be enjoyed by the elect, but is also to be shared with the lost that they too may be saved. Thus, it is not the Father's **will . . .** that any of these "little ones" **should perish.** The immediate context in Matthew relates "little ones" to believers but the cross reference in Luke 15:3-7 clearly refers to lost sheep. Thus, we may conclude that it is not the ultimate wish (or desire) of God that anyone perish. While God permits man to perish in his unbelief, He does not reprobate him to such condemnation against his will. Rather, all of heaven **rejoiceth** over every lost sheep which is saved. The contrast of the immanent danger to the lost sheep and the safety of those in the fold (of faith) clearly expresses where the majority of our attention and concentration should be in the ministry and activity of the church as we fulfill our commission to the world.

b. Church Discipline. 18:15-35.

The setting of these verses fits into the context of church discipline. If a church member offends someone or refuses to forgive someone, what must be done? Three basic views have been given here for the synagogue or the church (Gr *ekklēsia*). In either case the action is the same. The responsibility of action is threefold: (1) personal, "go tell him"; (2) "two or three witnesses"; (3) corporate, "tell it to the church."

15-18. Tell him his fault means to honestly express the point of offense. This should not be done in vindictive anger, but it must be done in straightforward honesty. To fail to speak up is to be dishonest and will lead to harboring continued bitterness. The last phrase of verse 16 is taken from Deuteronomy 19:15, substantially from the LXX. This just and sensible principle of the mosaic law is thus brought over by our Lord into the New Testament and established for the advantage of the Christian church. **Neglect**, better, "refuse," **as an heathen man and a publican,** i.e. as those who would not be admitted into the church. The obstinate sinner is to be cut off, at least temporarily, from Christian fellowship. Examples of this are to be found in I Corintians 5:4-5 and I Timothy 1:20. The promise is here addressed to all the disciples.

19-20. Verse 19 is one of the great Gospel promises with regard to prayer. But note the close connection of the verse with those that precede and that which follows. The promise is specifically given to a gathering of disciples with Christ **in the midst** (vs. 20), called to discipline an erring brother (vs. 17). Their authority to do this is restated (vs. 18) and the promise can be claimed because they are acting on behalf of the Father, in the name of the Son. **In my name,** i.e. claiming and using My authority. Notice, that the church in view here is operating in the future, in Christ's absence but by His authority.

21-22. All this teaching on forgiveness seemed overwhelming to the disciples, thus promoting Peter's question: **Lord, how oft shall my brother sin against me?** Peter wrongly assumed that **seven times** were ample to forgive anyone. Jesus responded that seven was not only insufficient but that one should forgive **seventy times seven,** in other words, unlimited forgiveness must characterize the true disciple, not retaliatory listing of other's offenses in an attitude of limited forgiveness.

23-27. The Parable of the Unforgiving Servant (vss. 23-35) was used by Jesus to reinforce the power and importance of the principle of forgiveness. **A certain king** represents God, the sovereign Father (cf. vs. 35), to whom the debt is owed. The **one** who **owed him** is a servant or satrap who had access to the king's money, and represents the individual sinner. **Ten thousand talents** was an insurmountable debt equivalent to millions of dollars in our society. It represents the debt of sin which the sinner cannot possibly pay by himself. The command that he be **sold . . . and payment to be made** indicates his being placed into a debtor's prison. However, an entire lifetime of service could never repay such a debt. The interpreter must stick to the main point of the parable and not be sidetracked by its minor details. The **compassion** of the king releases him and forgives (cancels) the **debt.** The picture illustrates God's total forgiveness when dealing with our sins at the point of salvation. The debt has been paid by Christ and we are set free from it forever!

28-35. The contrast in verse 28, where the **same servant** is unwilling to forgive his fellow servant a debt of **one hundred pence** (about ten dollars) is deliberately presented as a hideous hypothetical situation. As unbelievable as this action would be, that is how unbelievable it would be for a Christian disciple, who has been forgiven a lifetime of sin, to be unforgiving of others. In the story, such an unforgiving servant is called a **wicked servant** because no true believer would do such. The unforgiving servant is not one who was saved and then lost his salvation. The story is merely hypothetical; no one forgiven a debt of millions would behave this way, therefore, the intention of the parable is to challenge the genuineness of the disciples' conversion. A truly saved man would never behave like the man in the story, who was delivered to the **tormenters** (Gr *basanistēs* meaning "torturers" or "jailers"). This is certainly not a reference to purgatory. One behaving in this manner falls into the condemnation of the lost. The searching threat of verse 35 does not mean that a true believer will be lost, but if he claims to be born of God, he will act like a born-again person. True forgiveness "from the heart" of a

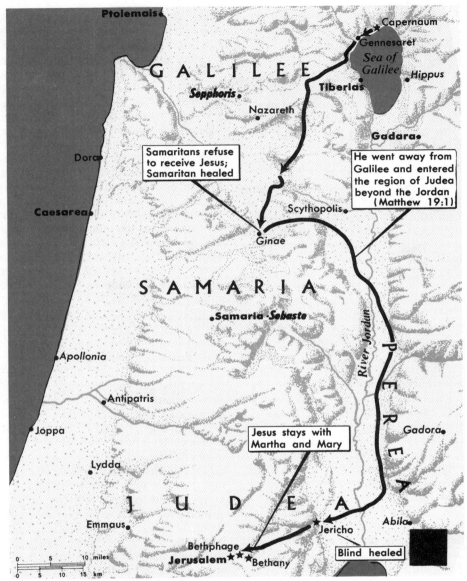

Jesus' Last Journey to Jerusalem

regenerate man is one of the true signs of genuine salvation and conversion (cf. Eph 4:32). Saved people are both forgiven and forgiving. Unforgiving people prove that they have never been born of God.

B. In Judaea. 19:1-27:66.

19:1. Verse 1 of chapter 19 indicates the close of another division of the gospel (see 7:28). With verse 2 it describes very briefly a journey from Galilee into the district of Judaea **beyond Jordan** (i.e. Peraea) which must have taken considerable time and into which the events of Luke 9:51-18:34 must largely be fitted. The teaching and incidents which follow in 9:3-20:34 also took place during the stay in Peraea.

1. His Presentation as King.
19:1-25:46.

a. His Journey to Jerusalem.
19:1-20:34.

19:1-2. During the various movements on the way to Jerusalem, Matthew presents a varied series of events: Jesus' teaching on divorce, the confrontation with the rich young ruler, a parable, and a miracle.

(1) Jesus' Teaching on Divorce. 19:1-12.

3-6. The Pharisees came **tempting** him with a difficult question. They wanted to test His wisdom with one of the most controversial questions of their day and Jesus proved far superior to their expectations. **Is it lawful** they asked to challenge. His interpretation of mosaic law in Deuteronomy 24:1-5, where a "bill of divorcement" was allowed. The more strict school of Shammai held that divorce was lawful only upon a wife's shameful conduct; whereas, the more liberal school of Hillel gave the widest possible allowances for divorce. Kent (p. 67) is correct when he explains: "Thus Jesus was being asked, "Do you agree with the most prevalent interpretation?' (Hillel's)." By asking **Have ye not read,** Jesus refers them back to God's original purpose in creation that they be **one flesh.** The passage in Genesis 2:24 indicates that being one flesh is one "person", and is not to be limited to sexual union. The Bible clearly indicates that sexual union does not itself constitute marriage, which is fundamentally a covenantal agreement between two partners for life (cf. Prov 2:17; Mal 2:14, "wife of thy covenant").

7-9. The question, **Why then did Moses command,** revealed the misuse of Deuteronomy 24 by the Jews of Jesus' day. Moses did not command, he permitted divorce. God had instituted marriage in the Garden of Eden. He is not the Author of divorce; man is its originator. However, to protect the Hebrew woman from being taken advantage of by a verbal divorce, Moses commanded that it be done with a **writing of divorcement,** i.e., official written contract, permitting remarriage. The Jews tended to take this as an excuse or license to get divorced whenever they pleased. The original provision was for the protection of the wife from an evil husband, not an authorization for him to divorce her at will. Therefore, Jesus gave one exception to the no divorce intention of God, **for fornication** (Gr *porneia*) "sexual sins," not to be limited to premarital sex only, but it includes all types of sexual sin: adultery, homosexuality, beastiality, etc.). Among the Jews only the male could divorce, so Mark 10:12 reverses the statement for his Gentile audience.

10-12. Since divorce, on any grounds, was common in those days (cf. rabbinical literature) the disciples felt **it is not good to marry.** The severity of Jesus' statement was in total contrast to the society of that day and represented the true intention of God. While divorce appears to be allowed in both testaments (cf. Deut 24:1-5; I Cor 7:15, 27-28) it is never encouraged because it always violates God's original intention in marriage. Jesus' reply, **All men cannot receive this saying,** indicates that some are called to be married and remain married; others (who cannot receive this) are called to be single (never to marry). If God calls you to be married, He will enable you to remain married. On the other hand, some are called to be single and never marry **for the kingdom of heaven's sake.** A **eunuch** was a person who never married and often served as a royal official. Some were **so born,** due to physical or mental deficiency; some were **made eunuchs of men,** either by choice or by force; some had deliberately chosen to be single for the purpose of serving God without being tied to regular family responsibilities (e.g. Origen). Unfortunately the early church began to take this statement to mean that it was more spiritual to be single than to be married, and eventually celibacy became legislation within the Roman Catholic Church. The single life is not to be forced on anyone. Those who are called to it are able to **receive it** (i.e. accept) gladly.

(2) The Rich Young Ruler. 19:13-30.

13-17. Much assimilation from the parallel accounts in Mark 10:17-31 and Luke 18:18-30 has been done in some texts; see ASV for a better rendition of Matthew's original. The **little children,** for whom Jesus cared so much, were evidently of sufficient age to respond to him (not infants) and He bade them **come unto me** revealing that, while all childhood professions may not be genuine, a child may follow Christ. By contrast to their simple obedience came the complex young rich man with all of his "hangups" calling Jesus **Good Master,** which the Saviour challenged, not as a denial of His deity, but to impress upon this seeker the seriousness of the implication. "Are you sure you really mean that?" would be a modern paraphrase. The young man's question, **What good thing shall I do?** implies that he wanted to perform some work that might gain him **eternal life** (salvation). Jesus' challenge was intended to elevate his concept of "good." The glib comment "good master" is followed by a request for something "good" that he may do to gain heaven. Jesus' concept of good was that which is divine. Therefore, only an act of God could grant eternal life. The Master's reply, **If thou wilt enter into life,** implies that the young man was still on the outside of such life.

The idea is this, if you want to gain eternal life, you must first of all enter it! The imperative, **keep the commandments** (vs. 17) was intended to hit his point of pride, i.e. self-righteousness. Jesus did not believe that mere outward keeping of the commandments of the law brought anyone

salvation. He had already told Nicodemus earlier that he must be born again (cf. Rom 3:20; Gal 2:16). Why, then, did He tell this young man to keep the commandments? The rest of the story reveals the answer. Jesus will go to great lengths now to show him that he has not kept the commandments and, therefore, is in need of God's grace.

18-22. This list of commands in verse 18 centers on outward duties, rather than inward nature, which was the young man's real problem. He protested that he had kept these outward demands. Jesus then revealed his real weakness. The law had been summarized earlier by our Lord: "Love the Lord thy God, with all thy heart" and "love thy neighbor as thyself." Herein was the young man's real failure. His self-centered wealth and luxurious self-righteousness had blinded him to his real weakness. To expose this Jesus ordered, **go and sell** all your possessions **and give to the poor . . . and come follow me** (vs. 21). This he would not do and went away **sorrowful** (grieved). What had Jesus done? Simply, He had shown him that he had not kept the commandments at all. He loved himself more than his neighbor (the poor) and he loved his possessions more than God (follow me). This passage teaches the seriousness of true discipleship, but it in no way teaches the average man that he must sell his possessions in order to be a Christian, or even a good one.

23-26. The further comment, **That a rich man shall hardly enter into the kingdom of heaven** shocked the disciples (note verse 25, "Who then can be saved?") who accepted the common notion of the day that the rich were blessed of God and therefore certainly saved. To correct that misunderstanding, Jesus explained the human difficulty for the rich to be converted. **Hardly** (Gr *dyskolos*) implies with extreme difficulty, though not hopeless. The illustration of a **camel** going through the **eye of a needle** has been interpreted as a camel hair rope going through a needle; or an actual camel squeezing through a small gate, "the eye of the needle," next to the main gate at Jerusalem; or the absolute impossibility of a literal camel (Palestine's largest animal) literally going through a tiny needle's eye. The latter usage is most likely, following a similar Talmudic proverb about an elephant. Note, that they were not in Jerusalem at this time and that the first two suggestions, while very difficult were within the realm of possibility, whereas, the salvation of the rich is called humanly **impossible** (vs. 26). In fact, all human nature is incapable of saving itself and must rely on God's efficacious grace for that which is humanly impossible to become **all things . . . possible** with God. The salvation of a rich sinner is just as miraculous as the salvation of a poor sinner. Both are only possible with God!

27-30. Peter's response, **we have forsaken all . . . what shall we have?** was most ill-timed and certainly reflected a selfish motivation which would have to go. Nevertheless, Jesus answered the question. **In the regeneration** (Gr *palinggenesia*) refers to the renewed world of the future, the kingdom of righteousness which is yet to come: "the new heavens and the new earth." While the term is used for individual rebirth in Titus 3:5, here it looks to the future Millennial Kingdom where the apostles will judge **Israel** (literally). Forsaking earthly benefits will bring a **hundredfold** blessing and **everlasting life.** Yet, while rewards will be abundant, attitudes are still crucial and **many** who would be **first** shall be **last** and the **last shall be first.** On the believer's rewards see W. Kroll, *It Will Be Worth It All.*

(3) The Parable of the Laborers. 20:1-16.

20:1-14. This parable reinforced Jesus' teaching regarding true Christian service and riches. The **householder** is Christ Himself, the Master of the **vineyard,** the field of labor (service to the world through His church). **Early in the morning,** the first workers were hired at dawn. **A penny** (Gr *denarion*) represents a denarius, or a common day's wage. **Others standing idle in the market place** were not lazy but were in the common place of seeking employment. From this unemployed group, the householder hired additional workers at 9 A.M., noon, 3 P.M., and 5 P.M. The pay scale will be **whatsoever is right,** indicating Christ's justice to His laborers. **When even** (evening) **was come,** i.e. at the end of the day, every man was paid the same wage. Therefore, the first hired laborers **murmured against the goodman.** However, he reminded them that he had been just in paying them that for which they bargained. The statement, **I will give unto this last even as unto thee,** is Jesus' interpretation of the "last shall be first and the first last" (vs. 16). There is here, perhaps, a sweeping view of church history, in which those working in the last hour are promised equal blessing to His original disciples. Thus, Jesus warns against jealousy and impurity of motive in serving Him.

15-16. Verse 15 shows that, everything being of grace, God has the right to give or withhold at will. We must take care that this goodness of God does not provoke us to complaint. The point of verse 16 is that all Christians receive the same, the reward being everlasting life given on the ground of Christ's death for them. By earthly standards of judgment, expressed clearly in verses 11 and 12, such action is regarded as putting the last first and the first last. **For many be called, but few chosen** refers to the general call of the gospel and the efficacious call of grace. He speaks of the difficulty that many experience in believing and obeying the gospel because their minds are fixed on what they can get for themselves, whether in this world or the next.

(4) The Coming Suffering of Christ and His Disciples. 20:17-28.

17-28. See Mark 10:32-34; Luke 18:31-34. The journey to Jerusalem is now resumed after the stay in Peraea. As the final events of His life draw nearer, our Lord again seeks to enlighten His disciples. Again they failed to understand, as is evidenced by the request of Zebedee's sons which immediately followed. But the fulfillment of these detailed predictions would strengthen their faith when the time came. **Zebedee's children.** From Matthew 4:21 we know that the two sons were the apostles James and John. **Grant,** better, "command." The request and the indignation of the others which followed show that the disciples were still thinking in terms of the setting up of an earthly kingdom, in spite of the clear prediction of suffering and death which our Lord had just made. Some texts omit the last part of our Lord's question in verse 22 and it may have been inserted from the parallel passage in Mark 10:38. The same is true of verse 23. The cup and the baptism both refer, of course, to our Lord's suffering and death. **To be ministered unto.** It is not wrong to accept ministry. Christ accepted it. But it was not the purpose of His life and should not be the purpose of ours. **His life** (Gr *psychē*) literally "his soul." **A ransom.** This important phrase provides one of the few occasions on which the doctrine of substitutionary atonement is mentioned in the Synoptic Gospels. It implies a price paid for the deliverance of captives. The price lay in the necessity for His life to be laid down. His life thus became the cost of our redemption. **Many** does not necessarily restrict the extent of His death (as contrasted to "all"), but it does indicate that not all would receive His offer of salvation.

(5) The Healing of the Two Blind Men. 20:29-34.

29-34. See parallel accounts in Mark 10:46-52; Luke 18:35-43. The problems of harmonization prohibit any suggestion of "collusion" (Kent, p. 71). Luke places this event on the approach to the city, whereas, Mark and Matthew state **as they departed from Jericho** (vs. 29). In actuality there were two Jerichos. The Roman city lay about a mile east of Herod's winter headquarters (also called Jericho) where the wealthy friends of the Herodian family lived near the palace and fortress. The healing of the blind man, evidently, took place while Jesus was going from one city to the other. Luke's attention would be on the Herodian city, for his next recorded event, the calling of Zacchaeus, took place there. **Two blind men** are mentioned by Matthew, while the other synoptists refer to only the more prominent Bartimaeus. Rebuked by the crowd, they cry the louder, **thou son of David,** a messianic title, earlier avoided by Jesus in public, but now accepted as He approaches Jerusalem. The miracle of restoring their sight was so total that afterwards even **they followed him.** What a contrast! The rich young ruler rejects Him for worldly possessions; His own disciples argue over who will be the greatest; the laborers in the parable murmur. Yet, now two transformed blind begging gladly follow Him! Of such is the kingdom of heaven!

b. His Joyful (Triumphal) Entry. 21:1-46.

1. The Messianic Arrival at Jerusalem. 21:1-11.

21:1-9. This event is traditionally known as the "Triumphal Entry," in which Jesus officially offers Himself to the nation of Israel as her long-awaited Messiah. However, in many ways it is far from a triumph, for the day ends in Jesus' public prediction of His rejection by His own people (see Mk

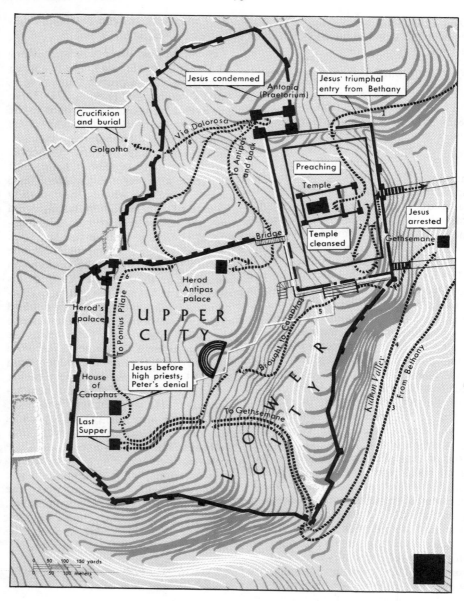

Jesus' Trial, Judgment, and Crucifixion

11:1-10; Lk 19:29-39; Jn 12:12-15). **Bethphage** was a village near Bethany, about a mile east of Jerusalem and apparently hidden from it by the summit of the Mount of Olives, which was the hill on the east of Jerusalem. **The Lord hath need of them.** The account of these closing events in our Lord's life shows that there were men and women in Jerusalem and its neighborhood who recognized Jesus as Lord. They may have become disciples during the earlier Jerusalem ministry described by John. The quotation in verse 5 is a combination of Isaiah 62:11 and Zechariah 9:9, taken substantially from the LXX. **Thereon,** that is, on the clothes. **Hosanna** is the transliteration of a Hebrew term meaning "please save," and occurs in II Samuel 14:4 and Psalm 118:25. From the following verse of this Psalm the acclamation **Blessed is he that cometh in the name of the Lord** is taken.

10-11. In verses 10 and 11 there is a contrast between the men of **the city,** who were ignorant of our Lord's identity, and the **multitude** who were able to answer their question. There were probably many Galileans in the latter who had come up for the feast and who already knew our Lord through His preaching and healing ministry in the north. In Jewish history and tradition the quoted Psalm was considered a messianic royal psalm and the riding of an ass's colt (not a horse) marked the official entry of the king (see A. Edersheim, *Life and Times of Jesus the Messiah,* II, p. 736).

(2) The Cleansing of the Temple. 21:12-17.

12-17. See Mark 11:15-19; Luke 19:45-47. A similar cleansing is recorded at the beginning of Jesus' ministry (cf. Jn 2:13-22), indicating His disdain for the corruption of organized religion which lacked purity of life and the power of God. Such a violent move was not to provoke a revolution, as such, but to bring about true spiritual conviction. In light of the seriousness of what He had come to do, Jesus could not tolerate such gross perversion of **the temple,** i.e. the whole temple area on Mount Moriah including all the precincts and courts. Note that some texts omit the words **of God. Money changers.** Temple dues could be paid only in sacred coinage, and it was necessary to change one's money. The selling of doves was, of course, for purposes of sacrifice. This exchangement became a source of extortion for the High Priest's family who personally controlled it. In reality, it amounted to a public bazaar. **It is written.** In his condemnation, our Lord quotes from the LXX of Isaiah 56:7 and Jeremiah 7:11. **They were sore displeased.** It was not just our Lord's popularity that angered them; the title "Son of David"which the children kept calling out implied messiahship. The cavils of the enemy were stilled, however, by the children's praise, as is suggested by the context of the psalm from which our Lord quotes (Ps 8:2). **Bethany** was a village on the eastern shoulder of the Mount of Olives, a little more than a mile east of Jerusalem. It was the home of Lazarus and his sisters.

(3) The Cursing of the Barren Fig Tree. 21:18-22.

18-22. See also Mark 11:12-14, 20-26. **The fig tree** fruit generally appears in February, followed by leaves, which are not formed until late spring. Thus, there should normally have been some fruit on the tree. The fig tree was often used as a symbol of the nation of Israel (cf. Hos 9:10; Joel 1:7) and while Jesus literally came upon a barren fig tree, He used the incident to fully illustrate Israel's desperate condition. The curse **Let no fruit grow . . . for ever** resulted in the almost immediate withering of the entire tree. While trees are non-moral, they, like all of nature, are subject to the word of Christ. The **disciples . . . marvelled** at how this could happen so fast. Notice, that none of them questioned the morality of this incident, as have misguided modern commentators (cf. Kee, p. 636). Jesus told them how to do such astounding things: **Have faith** or absolute confidence in the power of God. The removal of the **mountain** may indicate eliminating obstacles to giving the gospel to the Gentiles. Such appears to be the most likely meaning of the entire incident. Israel is the fruitless fig tree and the Gentiles are the mountain which shall be moved for God by the power of prayer.

*(4) The Question of Authority.
      21:23-46.*

23. On Jesus' third day of successive visits to the **temple** (i.e. Herod's temple) His authority was challenged by the ever-threatened **chief priests** (Stagg, p. 201), including the High Priest, who was also president of the Sanhedrin, and **elders,** who were laymen or Scribes and also served as members of the Jewish high court. In their own view, they were attempting to protect their laws and traditions against one who appeared to be a usurper who reinterpreted the law, rejected tradition and overthrew the money changers. Jesus had spoken with authority on matters which they considered their responsibility. Jesus did not challenge their right to question Him, but their hypocrisy and insincerity in such questioning.

They asked **By what authority** He had done these controversial things. Knowing that they would never recognize any authority but their own, He refused to answer them. Instead, He asked them about the authority of the **baptism of John,** which they had never officially sanctioned. To acknowledge that it was **from heaven** would be to condemn themselves for not receiving it and to claim it was **of men** (i.e. human origin) would upset the people. Their reply **We cannot tell** was begging the question and brought His clever response: **Neither tell I you by what authority I do these things.**

This incident forms the setting of the all-out attempt by the various religious authorities to expose and humiliate Jesus in chapter 22, which ends in their total frustration and embarrassment. The beauty and dynamic of these incidents reveal Jesus' mental prowess over the greatest minds of Israel. The divine Saviour is a genius, with no human peer. He can stump the Jews, mystify the Romans, and challenge the mind of any mortal man!

24-32. The Parable of the Two Sons (vss. 28-32) follows as an exposé of the hypocrisy of the religious leaders and as a vindication of John's ministry and the true work of God in general. The first son initially said **I will not** go (vs. 29), representing the immoral disobedience of the **publicans** and **harlots** who later **repented** under John and Jesus' preaching. Notice again, the connection between genuine repentance and changed action in verse 29 (repented, and went). No one who truly repents fails to show clear evidence of his inner heart change by his outward obedience. The **second** son promised to go but did not follow through with obedience. Jesus asked, "which **did the will of his father?**" By answering, **The first,** the religious leaders had condemned themselves. This very effective teaching method is commonly used in the Bible as the juridicial parable, whereby the answerer condemns himself by the obviously implied answer (e.g. Nathan's parable to David about the lamb; the Parable of the Good Samaritan, answering the prejudiced question, "Who is my neighbor?"). John had preached the **way of righteousness** (cf. II Pet 2:21) and the leaders had rejected him, even while claiming to be God's obedient servants. Thus, repentant sinners are more ready for the **kingdom of God** than disobedient religious leaders. The MSS support question on the variant reading in the Western Text must be decided in favor of the obvious intention of the parable (cf. discussion in Stagg, p. 202).

33-39. Jesus quickly gave another parable, the Parable of the Wicked Husbandmen. Again, Jesus makes clear His divine authority by presenting Himself as the Son sent by the Father. The **householder** represents God the Father and the **vineyard** is Israel, a symbol of the theocracy which was familiar to the Jewish leaders (cf. Ps 80:8-16; Isa 5:1-7). The **husbandmen** were the priests and religious leaders and the **far country** is heaven. The anticipated **fruit** represents spiritual evidence of true conversion, which was to be the end result of the work of the husbandmen. Instead, the religion of Israel had degenerated into a formal system for the benefit of the priests who were now more concerned about perpetuating their own interests. The **servants** sent by the owner represent the Old Testament prophets who came to correct religious abuses in the nation and were also rejected by their contemporaries (though venerated by subsequent generations). **Last of all** indicates that Jesus was God's final emissary to Israel. None has ever appeared since Him and none ever will until the Jews recognize Christ as their final Prophet and Messiah! The desire to kill the rightful heir of the Father had already been expressed by the Jewish leaders (cf. Jn 11:47-53). Jesus clearly foretold His coming rejection and death with the statement **they slew him.**

40-43. Verse 40 represents the condemning question of the judicial parable, **what will he do unto those husbandmen?** Their reply again unwittingly condemned their own attitude of rejection toward Jesus. The **other husbandmen** will become the Gentiles (vs. 43). Jesus quoted Psalm 118:22-23 exactly from the LXX, relating His present rejection to His ultimate triumph (cf. Acts 4:11; I Pet 2:6-7 where the **stone which the builders rejected** is also quoted in relation to Christ). The Sanhedrinists represent the builders of Israel's religion, who rejected the real cornerstone of God, i.e. Jesus the true cornerstone of the foundation of the church, which will be that **nation bringing forth . . . fruits** (cf. I Peter 2:7-9 where the church is called a "holy nation"). Equating the vineyard with the kingdom of God, McClain. (*The Greatness of the Kingdom*) notes that this clearly shows the kingdom as mediated to Israel through divinely appointed kings and now being transferred (mediated) to the church during the interval between Christ's advents.

44-46. The warning **the kingdom of God shall be taken from you** (vs. 43) was fulfilled at Pentecost when the "kingdom" was mediatorily transferred to the church (cf. Romans 9-11 which clearly promises Israel's restoration at the time of the Tribulation Period and the Millennial kingdom). Yet within this warning of judgment, Jesus offers mercy by falling **on this stone,** i.e. falling upon Him in repentance and faith. But, His falling upon man in judgment will **grind him to powder.** Finally, the Pharisees and chief priests **perceived** that He was speaking **of them** and wanted to kill Him but **feared the multitude** because they looked on Him as a **prophet.**

c. His Jealous Critics. 22:1-23:39.

(1) The Parable of the Marriage Supper. 22:1-14.

22:1-3. In preparation for the major confrontation which was coming, Jesus gave the Parable of the Marriage Supper. While similar to the parable in Luke 14, this one differs in its occasion and details. Again, the **kingdom of heaven** must refer to the mediatorial aspect of the kingdom in the Church Age. The **king** is the Father and Christ is the **son.** The **marriage** must be taken in the full aspect of salvation, including union with Christ, culminating in glorification at the marriage supper which inaugurates the Millennial Age. Rejection of the invitation to attend constitutes disloyalty to the King, as well as discourtesy to the Son, and accounts for the severe treatment of the rebels (vss. 6-7) which included their city being **burned up,** an obvious reference to the coming destruction of Jerusalem in A.D. 70.

4-14. The **bidden** guests are the people of Israel, whereas those in the **highways** are the Gentiles. **Both bad and good** refer to moral and immoral sinners who alike need God's gracious invitation. The "highways" implies crossroads, as opposed to backroads. History has revealed the success of urban evangelization, which may be implied here. The man without the **wedding garment** came to the feast but had disregarded the propriety of the king's provision, since such garments were normally supplied by the host. The reference seems to be to the "robe of righteousness" which we must receive from the Lord in order to enter the marriage feast. Casting the unclad guest into **outer darkness** symbolizes the eternal judgment of the lost. Again the phrase is repeated, **many are called, but few are chosen,** to emphasize to the Jewish audience, who considered themselves to be God's chosen people, that the outward call of God was not sufficient for salvation apart from the efficacious call of grace.

(2) The Herodians: Question of Tribute. 22:15-22.

16-21. See Mark 12:13-17; Luke 20:20-26. **The Herodians** were a party that favored the dynasty of Herod and stood for the Roman connection. They cared little or nothing for religion and normally were bitterly opposed by the Pharisees. The statements recorded in verse 16 were insincere and intended as hypocritical flattery. Their question was intended to place the Lord in a dilemma. If He said yes, He could be held up to the people as a traitor. If He said no, He could be denounced to the Roman authorities. **Caeasr,** i.e. the Roman emperor and head of the Roman state. Caesar was the family name of Julius Caesar, the first man who aspired to autocracy, and was taken over from him by his adopted son, afterwards the Emperor Augustus. It soon came to be regarded as a title. **Penny.** See 20:2. **Render therefore unto Caesar.** The Lord means that we are to give the civil magistrates all that is due to them, so long as it does not interfere with the honor due to God. Jesus had broken the Herodian's

dilemma by making light of the ultimate significance of Caesar's claim. The idea is: "if this penny is his, let him have it!" Jesus' response, render **unto God the things that are God's** exposed the spiritual failure of the Herodians. In essence, Jesus made light of Caesar's temporal claim in favor of God's greater claim over men's lives.

(3) The Sadducees: Question of the Resurrection. 22:23-33.

23-29. The Sadducees made the next attempt to discredit Jesus and were even more severely humiliated. As the liberal party within first century A.D. Judaism, they rejected belief in the supernatural, especially angels and the resurrection of the dead (See Paul's encounter in Acts 23:8ff.). **Moses said** is a reference to Deuteronomy 25:5, where the practice of levirate marriage called for an unmarried brother to take his widowed brother's wife to be his own (cf. Gen 38:8). This ancient practice was recognized by the Jews but rarely followed in those days. The absurd hypothetical case which follows represents another theological dilemma, this time attempting to discredit the legitimacy of the resurrection, which the Sadducees rejected. Thus, their question: **whose wife shall she be?** This extreme example must have been thought by them to be the ultimate proof of the foolishness of this doctrine. All seven brothers had been married to her, **Therefore in the resurrection whose wife shall she be of the seven?** They must have snickered as they asked such a ridiculous question, but the smile would soon be wiped off their faces by Jesus' reply. **Ye do err, not knowing the scriptures.** Jesus had extreme contempt for the Sadducees because they made light of the Bible and the **power of God** (i.e. His resurrection power, cf. Phil 3:10). This is His strongest recorded rebuke of this Jewish party.

30. Jesus then explained that **in the resurrection** men do not **marry** but are asexual **as the angels.** The infantile illustration of the Sadducees showed that they had no confidence in the power of a glorious resurrection to a new life. They thought that a resurrection would be to the same kind of life as on earth and probably "spiritualized" their rejection of such a concept. To be as the angels means that resurrected believers will have a glorified, non-mortal body (capable of neither reproduction nor destruction). The reference is not intended to imply that glorified men become angels nor that all earthly family relationships are lost in heaven. All resurrected (or raptured) believers will be in a state of perfect glorification and fellowship without any clannish prejudice.

31-34. Jesus further attacked the Sadducees' major belief in no resurrection at all, by quoting Exodus 3:6, a statement from the only part of the Old Testament which the Sadducees unquestioningly accepted. He related the eternal "I am" of God to the Patriarchs (Abraham, Isaac, and Jacob) to demonstrate that they were **of the living,** or immortal (a fact unlikely to be denied by the Sadducees in a public dispute. **God is not the God of the dead** does not mean that He has no relationship to those who have departed; it means that the departed are not really dead, and are thus still responsible to the living God (cf. Heb 10:31). Thus the crowd was **astonished** and the Sadducees were **silenced.**

(4) The Pharisees: Question of the Law. 22:34-46.

35-40. Each group came with their most difficult question, representing their expertise and their point of departure from Jesus' doctrine. In other words, each came representing his own "hangups." Remember that each of these groups normally hated each other, but were united in their rejection of Christ. **A lawyer,** i.e. an expert expounder of the Old Testament law, equivalent to a Doctor of Theology to-day, asked Him, **which is the great commandment in the law?** The phrase "tempting him" implies that he was trying to draw Jesus into an argument regarding the Pharisees' extensive interpretations of over six hundred laws. Instead, Christ summarized the two tables of the law (1. responsibility to God; 2. responsibility to man) by paraphrasing Deuteronomy 6:5 and Leviticus 19:18. **Love the Lord thy God** and **love thy neighbor as thyself.** The phrase **with all thy heart**, indicates the total being of a man in Hebrew thought and is part of the "shema," the Jewish confession of faith consisting of Deuteronomy 6:4-9; 11:13-21; Numbers 15:37-41. As the greatest commandment, it was of supreme importance and priority (cf. Filson, p. 237). No Pharisee could fault such an answer.

41-46. Jesus then counterquestioned the Pharisees: **What think ye of Christ? Whose son is he?** By asking them who is the Messiah, He gave them a clear opportunity to acknowledge Him. Tasker (p. 213) states that Jesus "asked the all important question 'What is your view of the Messiah?'" The question is similar to that earlier asked of the disciples in 16:15, where they gave the correct answer. The Pharisees' response, **The son of David,** was the common teaching of the Scribes who accepted the Davidic lineage of the Messiah (cf. Mk 12:35). Jesus then called their attention to Psalm 110 which they already recognized as messianic (Edersheim, App IX). The psalm, whose Davidic authorship Jesus affirms, was given **in the spirit,** i.e. by inspiration of the Holy Spirit (so Atkinson, Hendricksen, Kent, Lenski) and in it David refers to the Messiah as his Lord, thus He is more than just his "son." Thus, the verse says: "The **Lord** (God) said to my Lord (the Messiah), Sit on my right hand, until I (God) put your enemies (the enemies of the Messiah) beneath your feet (the final messianic victory over all who oppose Christ).'' Jesus totally stumped the Pharisees who wanted to believe in a human Messiah but not a divine Messiah. Thus, no one **was able to answer him,** i.e. defeat Him by question or debate and, therefore, no one dared ask Him **any more questions.** In one day Jesus had annihilated and humiliated the wisdom and craft of the leaders of each of Israel's religious organizations. ''Hallejulah, what a Saviour!''

23:1-2. Jesus' final condemnation of the Pharisees fills the entire twenty-third chapter. This now represents His final and official rejection of them at the temple, their very own stronghold of influence and security. Our Lord exposes the true hostility and hypocrisy of the religious leaders of Israel. See parallel passages in Mark 12:38-40; Luke 20:45-47. **Sit in Moses' seat** (Gr *kathedra* seat of authority) representing the synagogue chair which symbolized the origin and authority of their teaching.

3-6. Whatsoever they bid you observe, that . . . do. Bearing in mind the Scriptures that follow, it seems clear that this means all lawful things, i.e. it depends on the extent to which they do really sit in Moses' seat. It cannot include, for example, the traditions of the elders (see the condemnation of some of these in 15:1-20). But, as the verse goes on to show, the sin of the Pharisees lay more in their evil practices than in their teaching, for they themselves did not practice what they preached. **They make broad their phylacteries.** A phylactery was an amulet consisting of a strip of parchment on which was inscribed certain portions of the Pentateuch and which was rolled and placed in a small metal cylinder inside a square leather case. The cases were attached by the Jews with straps to their foreheads and to the back of their right hands, following a strictly literal interpretation of Deuteronomy 6:8-9. They were normally worn only during prayer, but the

Pharisees appear to have worn them always and to have made them especially conspicuous. **The borders of their garments** were the fringes worn in obedience to Numbers 15:38-39. **Uppermost rooms** better, ''chief place.''

7-12. Rabbi is from a Hebrew word meaning literally ''my teacher''. **Master,** i.e. teacher. **Call no man your father,** i.e. in a spiritual sense. This appears to condemn the use of the word ''Father'' used in addressing the clergy in the unreformed churches, and to render of doubtful propriety the use of the word ''padre'' (Italian for ''Father'') as a synonym for a chaplain. **Masters,** literally guides or leaders, i.e. teachers. **Servant** means minister or attendant. Verses 10-12 are very typical of our Lord's teaching (cf. Lk 14:11; 18:14).

13-15. Ye shut up the kingdom of heaven against men, i.e. you put stumblingblocks in the way of the sinner coming to repentance and conversion. **Devour widow's houses,** i.e. extort money from the helpless and bring them into debt and bondage, while making an outward show of religion. **The greater damnation,** i.e. a more severe sentence. **Proselyte.** The Jews recognized two sorts of proselytes: those who agreed to the so-called seven precepts of Noah, and those who submitted to circumcision and became full Jews by religion.

16-22. These verses give illustration of the Pharisees' casuistry with regard to oaths. **Temple** (Gr *naos* actually the ''sanctuary''). Our Lord teaches that all oaths are equally binding, and no man can expect to escape their consequences before God by making distinctions such as these.

23. Pay tithe of. A tithe or tenth of all produce was, by the Mosaic law, to be given for the use of the priests and Levites (see e.g. Lev 27:30). Several species of **mint** grow in Palestine. **Anise** (Gr *anethon*) is better rendered ''dill.'' It grew both wild and cultivated, its fruits being used for medicine. The seeds of **cummin,** which resemble caraways, were used as spice in seasoning. In such little matters the Pharisees were most careful to keep the law; yet they had completely overlooked its more important precepts.

24-26. Strain at a gnat, better "strain out a gnat." The Jews strained (Gr *diylizo*) wine before drinking it so as to avoid touching or swallowing anything unclean. **But within they are full of extortion and excess.** For "of" read "from." The Pharisees' living was obtained by extorting wrongfully from others.

27-33. Whited sepulchers. Since contact with a dead body rendered a person unclean according to the Mosaic law, it was the custom to paint graves white in order to make them conspicuous, and so to give the opportunity of avoiding contact with them. **The children of them which killed** literally "those who murdered." **Generation** or "offspring." **The damnation of hell,** i.e. being judged worthy of Gehenna.

34-39. That upon you may come. The generation to which these words were addressed represented the culminating point of the whole sinful history of the nation, beginning with the murder of **Abel** by his brother Cain (see Gen 4; Heb 11:4) and going on to the murder of **Zacharias son of Barachias.** In II Chronicles 24:20-21 we find the account of the murder of Zechariah son of Jehoiada "in the court of the house of the Lord." Since the books of Chronicles closed the Hebrew Old Testament canon, if this is the incident here referred to, the mention of Abel and Zacharias may be intended to cover the whole Old Testament revelation. The difficulty is that the Zechariah murdered in II Chronicles 24 was not the son of Berechiah. This Zechariah was the prophet (Zech 1:1). Though he lived after the exile and toward the close of Old Testament history there exists no tradition or record that he was mur-

dered. Another possibility is that the Zechariah referred to here is identical with "Zechariah the son of Jeberechiah" mentioned in Isaiah 8:2, but nothing further seems to be known of him. This passage is also recorded by Luke (Lk 11:49-51) and was evidently understood by His listeners. Jesus' statement that they would **not see me henceforth** foreshadows His death, resurrection, and ascension. Following His resurrection, Jesus only appeared to His followers and not to the world in general. From now on He must be received as personal Saviour by faith.

d. His Judgment: Olivet Discourse. 24:1-25:46.

24:1-4. This section forms Jesus' last major discourse and His most prophetic and apocalyptic message of the coming of the end of the world (or the present age). While the message includes a prediction of the imminent fall of Jerusalem, it also goes far beyond to point us to the distant future during which the "times of the Gentiles" will continue until the end of the Great Tribulation. **Temple** (Gr *hieron*) means the temple precincts. This prophecy of the very stones of the temple being cast down was fulfilled in the time of the Emperor Julian who, in a futile attempt to rebuild the temple, removed even the stones that had been left at the time of its destruction by Titus in A.D. 70. Jesus then left the city, crossed the Kidron Valley, and went east of Jerusalem to the **Mount of Olives** from which He could look down on the temple courtyard. Here His disciples asked Him three questions: **(1) when shall these things be?** (i.e. the destruction of the temple); **(2) what shall be the sign of thy coming?** (Gr *parousia*, technical term for the coming of the King); **(3) and of the end of the world?** (Gr *aion* "the age"). Therefore, the entire discourse must be looked upon as answering all three of these questions. On the significance of the signs of the end of the age see Walvoord (pp. 179-

195). He comments:"Premillenarians, accordingly, interpret the discourse as an accurate statement of end-time events, which will lead up to and climax in the second coming of Christ to set up His millennial kingdom on the earth" (p. 181).

Interpretation of the Olivet Discourse ranges widely from liberal (Allen, Moffat, McNeile, Kee, etc.) to conservative (among whom there is variation from amillennial, Hendricksen; to post-tribulational, Morgan; to pretribulational, Kent and Walvoord). Difference of interpretation may even be noted between Walvoord who views Matthew 24:4-14 as events of the Church Age leading up to the Tribulation Period and Kent (p. 85) who sees them as happening during the first part of the Tribulation Period. The key to interpreting this section rests in one's view of the "gospel of the kingdom" (vss. 13-14). Since Matthew has already shown in his selection of parables that the present form of the kingdom of heaven is the church, it seems more proper to view the events in these verses as relating to the entire Church Age and culminating especially at the end of it (thus John could say in general that he was a "companion in tribulation and in the kingdom," though he was still in the Church Age, of Revelation 1:9). Therefore, the "signs" of the end are general characteristics of the present age which shall be intensified as the age moves on to its conclusion. These are followed by more specific signs (vss. 15-26) of the Tribulation Period and the final return of Christ in judgment (vss. 27-31).

(1) Signs of the Present Age. 24:4-14.

5-14. Many shall come refers to the parade of false messiahs who have now spanned the centuries of church history and have led many astray into false religious cults. **Wars and rumors of wars** refer to peace being taken from the earth and the constant wars that have continually marked the "age of the Gentiles." **Famines and pestilences.** These events only mark the **beginning of sorrows** (Gr *odin*) "birth-pangs." This is followed by martyrdom and the rise of **false prophets** and the abounding of **iniquity.** While Kent makes an interesting parallel of these events to the seven seals in Revelation, it still remains that the "gospel of the kingdom" refers to the missionary expansion of the church **into all the world.** It is hardly reasonable to hold that the Jews will spread the Gospel throughout the entire world during the first half of the Tribulation Period of three and a half years when most conservative scholars view their coming national conversion at about the middle of the Tribulation (cf. Ez 37-39; Dan 9; Zech 12:10; 13:1-6). The gospel shall be preached in all the **world** (Gr *oikoumenē*), i.e. the inhabited world and unto **all nations** (Gr *ethnos*), "Gentile nations," as contrasted with the Jews. **Then shall the end come** would then refer to the end of the Church Age.

(2) Signs of the Great Tribulation. 24:15-28.

15. Ye must be taken generically, since the disciples have not lived to see this take place. The **abomination of desolation** refers to Daniel 9:27; 11:31; 12:11; where Antiochus Epiphanes' profanation of the Jewish temple worship would foreshadow a similar and more severe act by the eschatological Antichrist. Whereas, Antiochus offered a pig on the sacred altar of the Temple, the Antichrist will offer himself (II Thess 2:4)! The action of desecration by Antiochus, which David had predicted, will now be repeated in the future by the Antichrist as the signal of the beginning of the Great Tribulation and the breaking of the covenant "in the midst of the week" (Dan 9:27), i.e. the seventieth week of Daniel's prophecy, whose length is forty-two months (Rev 11:2), 1,260 days (Rev 12:6), or "time, and times, and half a time" (Dan 7:25; Rev 12:14). **The holy place,** i.e. temple, which will be rebuilt. Kent (p. 86) rightly observes that this cancels limitation of Daniel's prophecy to just the days of Antiochus (Allen, p. 256) since Jesus, in His day, was still awaiting further fulfillment, and it likewise goes beyond the catastrophe of A.D. 70 (Stagg, p. 200), since it is called the greatest tribulation of all time (Mt 24:21).

16-27. The warning to **flee into the mountains** eschatologically looks beyond the first century to the Jews' flight from the persecution of the Antichrist, (cf. Rev 12:6-14). Every Jew must flee and not look back. The reference to the **sabbath day** indicates these events will occur in a Jewish area, where such restrictions would be observed. **Then shall be great tribulation** makes our Lord's reference to Daniel 12:1 clearly evident as taking place just prior to the resurrection in Daniel 12:2. The terrible **days** of that time shall **be shortened** by the sudden return of Christ to destroy the Wicked One (II Thess 2:8). The **false Christs** may even refer to the False Prophet who aids the Antichrist with his miracle-working powers (Rev 13:11 ff.). The phrase, **if it were possible . . . shall deceive the very elect** clearly indicates that those who have been truly saved cannot be deceived and fall away. For even if it were humanly possible, the Lord will stop it by shortening (hastening) His coming. The exclamation, **Behold, I have told you before,** indicates Jesus' belief in the predictive nature of this prophecy. The **lightning** shining from **the east . . . even unto the west** refers to the final aspect of Christ's return (not the Rapture) in judgment upon the earth. In I Thessalonians 4, He comes in the clouds for the church; in II Thessalonians 1-2, He comes to the earth with the church to judge the world.

(3) Signs of the Coming Son of Man. 24:29-42.

29-31. The reference to the events **Immediately after the tribulation,** such as the sun being darkened and the stars falling, etc., refer to the cataclysmic events that will accompany Christ's return at the end of the Tribulation Period to establish His Millennial Kingdom on earth (see W. Price, *Jesus' Prophetic Sermon,* p. 118 ff.). His return will be marked by the **sign of the Son of man in heaven** which will identify His coming to the **tribes of the earth.** What this sign (Gr *semeion*) will be is not explained here. Ancient commentators (e.g. Chrysostom) thought it to be the appearance of a cross in the sky, whereas, Lange (p. 428) suggests it will be the shekinah glory of Christ Himself. It may, perhaps, even be the return of the star that marked His birth. In some way a visible manifestation will mark the graduai (cf. Acts 1:11, "in the same manner") return of Christ in judgment at the end of the Tribulation Period. As the earth revolves the various nations and tribes will be able to see this sign. Instead of repenting, though, they shall **mourn.** This indicates a severe, ritualistic mourning (cf. also Zech 12:10-12). The **clouds of heaven** indicate that Christ will come from heaven to the earth (cf. also Dan 7:13-14; II Thess 1:7-9). The **angels** are the same agents of judgment as in chapter 13. The **elect** are the saved who have come to faith in Christ by the grace of God and are gladly anticipating their Lord's return.

32-33. The illustration of the **fig tree** is referred to as a **parable.** The immediate context seems to refer to the fig tree in a natural (not symbolic) sense (so, Walvoord, p. 192). While it is clear in Scripture that Israel is symbolized, at times, by the fig tree (ch. 21), the usage here simply seems to be that as these events reach the apex of their fulfilment, the actual and ultimate return of Christ follows immediately. Just as God has built into nature certain time indicators (e.g. trees budding), so He has built into history certain time indicators of coming future events. Jesus' reference to **when ye shall see all these things** has caused some to speculate that these predicted events only relate to the coming destruction of Jerusalem in A.D. 70, within the disciples' lifetime (cf. Tasker, p. 227; G. C. Morgan, p. 286, does not even attempt an explanation). Kent (p. 86) views the fig tree as Israel "budding" in the last days as a reborn nation. Walvoord (p. 192) agrees with Lenski (p. 951) that "all these things" refers to the preceding context of the Olivet Discourse.

34. Thus, the **generation** that **shall not pass** is the generation in whose lifetime all these signs occur and it is that generation that will not pass away until **all these things be fulfilled.** While some have attempted to relate "generation" (Gr *genea*) to the race of the Jews, indicating the survival of their race until Christ's return, this seems somewhat stretched. Arndt and Gingrich (p. 153) prefer "age" or "period of time." In other words, the previously listed signs will continue to multiply throughout the Church Age and reach their ultimate climax at the end of the age in the generation of those who will live to see the entire matter fulfilled in their lifetime. However, no time indication of length is clearly given so that all may anticipate the imminent return of the Master. Those who object that the "last days" began at Pentecost should also see II Timothy 3:1, where "last days" are yet coming (shall come) in the future. On the one hand, the final age began with the manifestation of the church and continues today. On the other hand, though, the final aspect of this age will be a last day of perilous times which will occur at the end of the age. Even Filson (pp. 257-258) agrees that Matthew certainly understood Jesus to be saying that "all these

things" referred to the end of history in the distant future.

35-38. Verses 35-36 warn against attempts to set an exact date for Christ's return at the end of the Church Age (a warning unheeded by the Adventists in 1844, the Jehovah's Witnesses in 1916, and many others). To speculate that "day" and "hour" do not eliminate "year" is a gross oversimplification. The **Father only** knows the time of Christ's return since it has been set by His authority (cf. Acts 1:7). However, we are given a comparison to the **days of Noe,** i.e. Noah (and the flood) which illustrate and prefigure the condition of humanity at the time of Christ's return. The last generation, like the one of Noah's day, is pleasure-oriented and self-gratifying by **eating and drinking.** The reference to **marrying and giving in marriage** may refer to carrying on the normal course of life without heeding the impending judgment. However, the indication may even be stronger in that Noah's generation was judged as the result of the collapse of the godly line of Seth by spiritual intermarriage with the ungodly line of Cain's descendants (see Genesis 4-6 for the setting of the flood story). The drastic destruction of the godly families of Noah's day was due to a casual and indifferent attitude about whom one married or to whom he gave his children in marriage. Thus, Jesus' warning is that the last generation will also be so pleasure-oriented that its families will collapse (a shocking observation in view of the current failure of the American family with one million new divorces every year!).

39-42. The observation that the people of Noah's day **knew not** the severity and suddenness of the coming destruction indicates that this last generation will be totally unprepared for the **coming of the Son of man** (i.e. the return of Christ to judge the world, see II Thessalonians 1:7-8). The reference to **two** being in the field or at work at the time of Christ's return implies the suddenness of His coming to separate the lost and the saved. The **one taken** and the **other left** has been variously interpreted as one being taken in the Rapture and the other left to impending judgment, or as the taken one being taken to judgment and the one left being spared (so Walvoord, p. 193 and Kent, p. 88-89). Kent notes that this separation occurs after the tribulation (vs. 29) and correlates to "took them all away" (to judgment) in verse 39. The warning to **watch therefore** is repeated in 24:44; 25:13 and relates to the **hour** (a general period of time). **Watch** (Gr *grēgoreo*) is a Greek present imperative, meaning "be continuously on guard."

(4) The Parable of the Two Servants. 24:43-51.

43-51. The Parable of the Two Servants follows to illustrate the seriousness of Christ's second coming, a fact which Jesus never allegorized or spiritualized, but spoke of in the most serious terms: **cut him asunder . . . weeping and gnashing of teeth.** Kent (p. 89) notes that the **evil servant** (a usurper and impostor) "mistakes the uncertainty of the time of coming for a certainty that it will not be soon." At Christ's return, however, all hypocrites will be suddenly exposed and judged by the **Lord.**

(5) The Parable of the Ten Virgins. 25:1-13.

25:1-13. The Parable of the Ten Virgins explains the place of Israel's true converts of the Tribulation Period in relation to the church. These **virgins** (Gr *parthenos,* cf. 1:23) are the attendants at the wedding, not multiple brides. The one bride of Christ is the church, John the Baptist is the best man (Jn 3:29, i.e. friend of the bridegroom) and the prepared virgins are the saved of the Tribulation Period. While all share as the people of God, the church is accorded a unique relationship to the Master. The number

five in each group does not necessarily indicate that half of humanity will be saved but that there are two types of people. The **lamps** seem to refer to their lives which are either prepared or unprepared. The **oil** refers to that which prepares them to give forth light and may properly be illustrative of the regeneration of the Holy Spirit. The fact that they all **slept . . . While the bridegroom tarried** implies a period of Jewish inactivity during the Church Age, while the Bride is gathered. **Foolish** (Gr *miros*) means "stupid," and is the designation for those who are carelessly unprepared. They had no oil at all, not an insufficient amount. The refusal of the five prepared virgins to share with those unprepared must not be taken as cruelty. If the oil represents personal possession of the Holy Spirit, He cannot be shared but must regenerate each person individually. Thus, the Lord responds, **I know you not** (vs. 12), indicative of 7:23. False profession will save no one and only brings the final judgment of Christ upon the unsaved.

(6) The Parable of the Talents. 25:14-30.

14-23. The Parable of the Talents further emphasizes the need for personal preparation and faithful service to the Master. See also Luke 19:11-28. The **talents** represent monetary values and are distributed according to **ability** (vs. 15). **Far country** indicating the time between Jesus' first coming and His final return during which He is in heaven. The three **servants** are typical of three tyes who are entrusted various tasks in accordance with their own ability. Not all are expected to produce the same results, but all are to be faithful with what they have had entrusted to them. Thus, the first two double their money, while the last one hides the **one . . . in the earth.** The phrase **After a long time** gives a veiled indication of the length of Christ's departure to heaven during the present age. Each of those producing results is commended by the Master: **Well done . . . good and faithful servant** and is promised to be a **ruler over many things,** with a view to continued service in the Millennial Kingdom.

24-25. The great mistake of the unfaithful servant was in misjudging the character of his Master: **thou art a hard man.** He could not have known the Master well to assume him to be severe and merciless. Atkinson (p. 801) observes, "The slave seems to have thought that whatever he did his master would be unjust to him." He failed to understand the real generosity of his Master who wanted him to experience the joys of service. Whereas the Parable of the Ten Virgins emphasized personal preparation for the coming of Christ, the Parable of the Talents stresses the importance of faithful service during His present absence.

26-30. The fact that the latter man is called **wicked and slothful** and an **unprofitable servant** (vs. 30) who is cast out into **outer darkness,** certainly indicates that he was not a true disciple of the Master. The idea of this illustrative parable is that all true believers will produce no results (elsewhere, "fruits") in varying degrees. Those who produce no results are not truly converted. Those who deny soul winning, personal evangelism, and church growth will find no comfort in this story. Those who hide their treasure (probably, the life-changing message of the gospel), because of a harsh view of the Master's sovereignty over them, reveal that they do not really love people and, therefore, their own salvation is questionable!

(7) The Judgment of the Nations. 25:31-46.

31-46. The Judgement of the Nations concludes our Lord's prophetic discourse. Christ's return **in his glory** to be enthroned on the **throne of his glory** marks the great interruption of history as He brings the Tribulation Period to an end and ushers in the Millennial Kingdom. This judgment of **all nations** must be distinguished from the Great White Throne Judgment at the end of the Millennium. The **nations** (Gr *ethnos*) are those peoples living through the Tribulation on earth at the time of Christ's return. This is a judgment of separation: **sheep on his right . . . goats on his left.** At this judgment all nations (better, "all Gentiles") stand before Christ who then separates the sheep (the saved) from the goats (the lost) in a manner reminiscent of the wheat and tares parable. Some view this as the last general judgment (Atkinson, p. 801), whereas premillennial commentators see this as the judgment of the nations who have survived the Tribulation Period, with the saved going into the Millennial Kingdom. Note that these are living nations, whereas the Great White Throne Judgment is one of the wicked dead whose bodies are resurrected to face the final judgment of the lost. Thus, the saved are invited to come into and share the blessings of His Kingdom: **Come, ye blessed of my Father, inherit the kingdom.** The basis of their acceptance seems to be their treatment of the **least of these my brethren,** i.e. the saved of the Tribulation. The acts of kindness (vss. 35-38) were done by these sheep nations unto the persecuted Jewish believers and their converts during the reign of the Antichrist and now bring the blessing of God's salvation upon these nations. The acts of kindness do not themselves merit salvation apart from the atonement of Christ. Since the nations are the Gentiles and "my brethren" are neither, they must be the Jews. The goats are banished into **everlasting fire** or hell. Both the judgment and the blessed life are designated by the same adjective, "eternal" (Gr *aionios*), clearly indicating their equal duration. This eternal judgment is in keeping with Revelation 14:11; 19:15.

No unsaved adults are admitted into the Millennial Kingdom when it is begun on earth. A natural and legitimate conclusion, then, is that the Rapture must occur before this event. Thus, the Rapture precedes the Tribulation Period, which itself precedes the Millennial Kingdom.

2. His Rejection as King. 26:1-27:66.

These chapters describe the plot of the priests, the anointing of the Lord in Bethany, the betrayal, the institution of Lord's Supper, the agony in the garden, the Lord's arrest, His trial before the priests, Peter's denial, the trial before Pilate, and finally the crucifixion and resurrection.

a. His Denial by His Disciples. 26:1-56.

26:1 See also Mark 14:1-2, Luke 22:1-2. Jesus makes a final prediction of His death two days before Passover, which was eaten on the evening of Nisan 14. Thus the prediction was made on the twelfth of the month (April). The **feast of the passover** was the first feast on the Jewish yearly calendar and was kept in commemoration of the national deliverance from Egypt in the exodus under Moses. Passover takes its name from the Hebrew term related to the Death Angel passing over those who had applied the blood to their homes (cf. Ex 12). The Hebrew root *pesach* was transliterated into "pashcal" from which Christ's suffering is often referred to as His "passion." Passover time was a great high day among the Jews and thousands of pilgrims flocked to Jerusalem to observe it each year. Our Lord's death was the ultimate fulfillment of which the annual feast had been a shadow. It was followed by the seven day Feast of Unleavened Bread (Nisan 15-21). Sometimes the entire period was generally referred to as Passover.

2-5. Jesus also predicted His betrayal. **Son of man** is His favorite designation for Himself. **Betrayed** (Gr *paradidomi*) is better translated here as "delivered up" or "handed over." The assemblage of the Sanhedrin takes place at the **palace,** (Gr *aule* meaning the courtyard of his residence). **Caiaphas** was a Sadducee who had been appointed High Priest a few years earlier, about A.D. 18, just before Christ's earthly ministry began. **Not on the feast** means "not during the feast." Since many of Jesus' supporters from Galilee would be in Jerusalem during this time, the leaders did not want to upset the crowd whose emotions were at a high anyhow. Jesus ultimately foiled their plan and died at the very hour of the slaying of the Passover lambs.

6-16. The anointing at Bethany (cf. also Mk 14:3-9; Jn 12:1-8) is related by John as taking place six days before Passover, indicating the one version is topical and the other chronological, since neither Matthew nor Mark dates the event. The chronological problems with the crucifixion have long been wrestled with by scholars but the detailed accounts of factual material relating to such highly emotional material, make their veracity all the more certain. These are no mere legendary accounts, embellished by Church tradition. They are highly factual and readable accounts of the most sublime narratives in Scripture. **Simon the leper** is mentioned only here and in the parallel Mark 14:3. By a comparison with John 12:1-8, it becomes a reasonable deduction that he was the father of Lazarus, Martha, and Mary. **She did it for my burial.** The point seems to be that the action was appropriate in view of His burial which was soon to take place, and that it might be regarded as symbolic or prophetic of the burial. **This gospel,** i.e. the good news of the Lord's death and resurrection (see also Mk 14:10, 11; Lk 22:3-6). **Judas Iscariot** (see Mk 3:19) **and they covenanted with him for thirty pieces of silver.** Actually, they weighed the amount to him, representing about a month's wages or the price of a common slave (see Stagg, p. 231). These words are substantially from the LXX of Zechariah 11:12. **Betray him,** i.e. hand Him over. The same verb is translated "deliver" in verse 15. The last Supper is also related in Mark 14:12-16; Luke 22:7-13; and John 13:1-29. The synoptics agree in the basic details and seem to assert that this was the Passover meal, whereas John clearly indicates that it was eaten before the Passover, with Jesus dying at the very hour the Passover lambs were slain (Jn 18:28; cf. I Cor 5:7). Liberal interpreters see the accounts as contradictory (Kee, p. 640); others suggest that Jesus followed the Essene custom of the Qumran community in taking the Passover meal on Tuesday (J. Walther, "Chronology of Passion Week," *JBL,* 1958, pp. 116ff.) However, it seems most likely that John, writing later, is simply clarifying the ambiguous points in the chronology, as he does elsewhere in his gospel in regard to other matters. Kent's material (pp. 97-109) on the chronology of the passion week is excellent and should be thoroughly considered.

17-24. The first day . . . of unleavened bread, or the fourteenth of Nisan (cf. Mk 14:12; Lk 22:7). The day actually began at sundown on the thirteenth. While Jesus said, **I will keep the passover,** the cross reference in Luke 22:16 notes He added, "I will not eat it," implying an interruption. Perhaps, He did not want Judas to be aware of His certainty of the details. Only Jesus and the Twelve were present. At this crucial time Jesus announced **one of you shall betray me.** We cannot imagine the shock with which this statement must have jolted the disciples. For the first time, Jesus had clearly indicated that the betrayer would be one of the Twelve! They were **exceeding sorrowful,** indicating their grief over such an announcement. In the original language, the question **Lord is it I?** suggests that a negative answer was cautiously expected by each one, "It is not I, is it?" Coupled with Peter's later defensive protest and subsequent failure, it seems clear that the entire group feared the possibility of failure. What a transformation would have to take place to change these cowards into the mighty apostles of the book of Acts!

25-26. Judas repeated the same question and Jesus' reply, **Thou hast said,** means "yes." The statement, **He that dippeth,** reveals the personal and intimate nature of the betrayal. **Jesus, took bread.** The head of the Jewish household was accustomed to doing this during the Passover feast. Jesus gave a completely new significance to the action. **This is my body.** If the words of the Lord had intended to convey a transformation of the bread into His body they would have read "This has become my body." During the Passover feast the Jewish householder took bread in his hand and said, "This is the bread of affliction which our fathers ate in the land of Egypt," meaning, of course, that the one represented the other. By His words the Lord changed the whole significance and emphasis of the feast from looking back to the typical redemption from Egypt to faith in the redemption from sin accomplished by His death. For a clear example of the use of the word "is" as "represents" see Galatians 4:25. The bread and wine were only outward symbols of our Lord's death and a reminder to us of the cost of our redemption during our Lord's absence (cf. Lk 22:19). Nothing in the gospels indicates that these were to be viewed as a means of grace, sacraments, or that they were physically necessary for one's salvation.

27-30. The cup. Three cups were passed around by the Jewish householder during the Passover meal, the third, which is probably that referred to here, being known as "the cup of blessing." **My blood of the new testa-**

ment taken from the LXX of Exodus 24:8 with allusions to Jeremiah 31 and Zechariah 9:11. The covenant in Exodus 24:8 was sealed with blood. The word **testament** (Gr *diathēke*) did not mean a covenant, which is an agreement between equals, but a settlement by a great or rich man for the benefit of another. As the most common form of settlement was, and still is, by testament or will, the word came to have this meaning almost exclusively. **Shed for many for the remission of sins.** Here is a clear statement that the death of Jesus was necessary to enable God to forgive sins. It, in fact, made it right or morally justifiable for Him to do so. **That day,** i.e. when He comes again in glory.

31-35. The quotation in verse 31 is taken from the LXX of Zechariah 13:7. **Go before you,** literally, lead you forth, going at your head, as an eastern shepherd leads his sheep. This does not mean that the Lord would go first to Galilee in the sense that the disciples must go there to find Him, but that He would appear to them at Jerusalem and lead them to Galilee. **Though I should,** better, "Even if I must." Peter's boast later sets the stage for his bitter denials of his Master. He promised to be more faithful than the others, thus, later provoking Jesus' question, "Lovest thou me more than these?" (probably referring to the other disciples of John 21:15).

36-39. The scene in the Garden of Gethsemane is one of the most moving in all the New Testament. **Gethsemane** means "olive press" and was a lush garden east of the city near the slopes of the Mount of Olives. Jesus often resorted there for peace and quiet. He took the same inner circle as at the transfiguration (Peter, James, and John) further into the garden. **My soul is exceeding sorrowful** is found in the LXX of Psalm 43:5. The imperative **watch** means to keep awake in order to be prepared for whatever might come. The prayer for the **cup** to **pass** is not due to Jesus' fear of death. Many martyrs have faced terrible deaths without great fear. Jesus questions the **will** of the Father as to the necessity of drinking the cup. While this may refer to death ("he tasted death") it is more likely that the cup represents the wrath of God against sin, which divine wrath Christ would incur on the cross as man's sinbearer. In the awful anguish of that moment, the sin of the world was poured on Christ and He became "sin for us" (II Cor 5:21). His total submission to the will of the Father causes Him to be obedient, even unto a substitutionary death. The Innocent and Righteous One dies for the guilty. Herein is His ultimate exaltation as Lord (Phil 2).

40-46. In the meantime the **disciples** were **asleep** due to emotional fatigue and physical exhaustion. Again, He urged them to **watch and pray, that ye enter not into temptation.** Several commentators unnecessarily relate this temptation to Christ (see Atkinson, p. 803), whereas in the context, He relates it to the disciples. Because they are not prayerfully watching, they will not be prepared for the tragedy that is about to happen. He reminded them that the **spirit . . . is willing but the flesh is weak.** Man's regenerated spirit may have good intentions, but it must control his body (cf. Rom 12:1) in order to gain spiritual victory. The Greek present imperative indicates that they were to "continually keep watching." However, their fatigue causes the remark, **Sleep on now.** The immediate interruption of the soldiers causes Him to awaken them, **let us be going.**

47-50. The arrest took place in the garden during the middle of the night as a mixed mob arrived to take Jesus. There can be little doubt that Jesus saw them approaching as there is always a full moon at Passover, and they probably also carried lighted torches (see Filson, p. 280). The Roman soldiers carried **swords** and the Jewish temple police had **staves** (clubs). The **sign** was necessary to identify Jesus to the Romans to whom He was unknown. Judas **kissed him** as the sign of betrayal to the one he still glibly called **master** (cf. Mt 7:23 ff.). In response Jesus asked, **friend wherefore art thou come?** This convicting question was far more effective than an accusation, since Judas could not answer it.

51-56. One of them was Peter (Jn 18:10) who **drew his sword,** probably one of the short swords referred to in Luke 22:38. Attempting to defend Jesus, Peter **struck a servant of the high priest's, and smote off his ear.** In a typically impetuous move Peter had struck the one person who could have embarrassed them the most at the trial. Luke, a physician (22:51) tells us that Jesus healed him by replacing the ear (His last miracle) and John (18:10) tells us his name was Malchus. Jesus' rebuke: **Put up again thy sword** clearly revealed that His kingdom would not be brought in by force at that time. The statement **they that take the sword shall perish with the sword** is a statement of fact, but cannot be taken alone to teach nonviolence in all situations. Jesus has no lack of power by which to deal with these few enemies. **Twelve legions of angels** could be called to His aid. Each Roman legion has six thousand soldiers. Christ's restraint is due to His willingness to obey the will of the Father and so fulfill **the scriptures.** Even a well-intentioned defense by one of His disciples will not deter Jesus from the cross (on the meaning of these events see F. W. Krummacher, *The Suffering Saviour*).

b. *His Denunciation by the Sanhedrin. 26:57-75.*

57-65. See Mark 14:53-72; Luke 22:54-65; John 18:13-27. **Palace,** the open court around which the main buildings were built. **Servants** (Gr *hyperetēs,* "officers"). The evidence which was eventually brought forward (vs. 61) was based upon the Lord's words recorded in John 2:19, 21, nearly three years earlier! **I adjure thee by the living God.** This statement put a man on his oath and compelled an answer. The High Priest was seeking an admission which could be the foundation of a charge of blasphemy. **Thou hast said,** this means "yes." **Hereafter,** "Henceforth." The session at God's right hand began at the ascension (even, perhaps, at the resurrection). Note the allusion in our Lord's reply to Psalm 110:1 and Daniel 7:13. The second part of the phrase may refer as much to the ascension as to the second coming. The Jewish religious leaders would be witnesses of the victories of Christ after His resurrection. **Buffeted,** i.e. punched. Verse 68 is a sarcastic demand to be told the names and identities of those who were strangers to Him as a sign of supernatural knowledge. The incident ends with the charge of **blasphemy** and the indictment that He is **guilty of death.** There can be no doubt that the Sanhedrin took Him to be claiming to be the Messiah, which claim they violently rejected.

66-72. Peter's three denials occurred during the trial proceedings. **Peter sat without in the palace** or courtyard. We know from the synoptics that he was warming himself by a fire, prepared by servants of the priests. The first denial was prompted by a **damsel,** or young maid, and the porters who had admitted him and John. Somehow she recognized him from an earlier meeting. The form of the denial, **I know not what thou sayest,** was merely a pretense of ignorance on Peter's part (similar to, "I don't know what you mean"). Feeling the pressure of the interrogation, Peter went **into the porch,** a passageway leading to the street. Then he was confronted by **another maid,** probably the outer gatekeeper who alerted the men (thus Luke's reference to a man as the interrogator) that **This fellow was also with Jesus of Nazareth.** The terms "Galilean" and "Nazarene" were probably used in a derogatory manner by these Judaeans. This time his denial was stronger, **with an oath,** in spite of Jesus' earlier warning against oath-taking (5:34). No pretended ignorance this time either; **I do not know the man** he exclaimed.

73-75. The third denial came **after awhile** (less than an hour) when he was accused because **thy speech bewrayeth thee** or "makes you evident" (ASV) or "gives you away." Under the mounting emotional pressure and fear of being condemned along with Jesus, **he began to curse and to swear.** This emotional and sinful outburst was intended to make him appear unattached with Jesus. Later, this last great outburst of denial will be corrected by an emotion-packed reaffirmation of loyalty to the Saviour (cf. Jn 21:17). **And immediately the cock crew,** probably "cockcrowing" (i.e. the end of the Roman watch from midnight to 3:00 A.M.), verifying the illegitimacy of the trial which was being conducted during the middle of the night. **And Peter remembered** not because he heard the noise, but as Luke (22:61) records: The Lord turned and looked upon him with a convicting glance from the balcony of the High Priest's house. Then, he remembered the Saviour's warning and **went out and wept bitterly.** All these events related to the betrayal, arrest, and trial of Jesus show that He was completely in control of each situation even while being in the hands of His captors! See J. Stalker, *The Trial and Death of Jesus Christ* for a devotional discussion of these matters. On the theological significance of Christ's death see J. Denney, *The Death of Christ;* L. Morris, *The Cross in the New Testament;* J. Owen, *The Death of Death;* G. Smeaton, *The Atonement According to Christ and His Apostles.*

C. His Deliverance to Pilate. 27:1-31.

27:1-2. See also Mark 14:1-15; Luke 23:1-25, John 18:28-19:16. **Pontius Pilate the governor.** Pontius Pilate was the Roman procurator of Judaea from A.D. 26 to 37, holding his office under the Prefect of Syria. His usual place of residence was Caesarea, but he was in Jerusalem during the festival in order to deal with any insurrection or trouble.

3-8. When he saw that he was condemned, which would be evident from seeing Jesus being taken to Pilate (a move that Judas may not have anticipated), he **repented himself** (Gr *metameleomai,* "to regret"). This word is different from the term for repentance to salvation (Gr *metanoia*). Judas shows every indication of still being unsaved: he betrays innocent blood for money, becomes guilty, returns the money, and commits suicide. These are the actions of a guilty conscience, not a forgiven and regenerate one. His admission **I have sinned** is not necessarily a true confession to faith. The reply of the priests reveals the real cruelty of their hearts: **What is that to us? See thou to that.** A. W. Tozer calls this the "great double cross," wherein Judas betrays Christ in collusion with the priests, who in return, reject him! Judas then threw the money **in the temple** (Gr *naos* means "sanctuary") and **hanged himself.** It is generally supposed that "falling headlong" (Acts 1:18-19) happened while he was attempting to do this. Perhaps, hanging himself over the ledge, he then fell into the valley below. **Bought,** in such cases the purchase was made in the name of the man to whom the money had been paid and to whom the money by a legal fiction was supposed all the time to belong. By law, therefore, the man himself purchased the field (see Acts 1:18).

9-10. Much difficulty has been felt at the mention of Jeremiah in this passage on the ground that the quotation comes from Zechariah. Various ingenious theories have also been put forward to account for it. There is an allusion, it is true, to Zechariah 11:12-13, but the words do not agree closely either with the Hebrew or the

LXX. The most important addition is the word "field," upon which the fulfillment just described by the evangelist largely hangs. This word and the conception behind it come from Jeremiah 32:6-9, a passage in which occurs the purchase of a field for so many pieces of silver. The comparison between prophecy and fulfillment, therefore, which the evangelist is attempting to make, depends upon both Old Testament passages. It is natural, therefore, that he should mention Jeremiah, who was the greater of the two and the earlier of the two, from whom also was derived the word that gave the real point to the matter.

11-15. The Roman trial evidently began early in the morning with Jesus being condemned before noon. Pilate's question, **Art thou the king of the Jews?** was prompted by the formal Jewish charges. Jesus' reply, **Thou sayest** means "yes." Yet to the accusation of the priests He gave no answer at all and then no further answer to Pilate. Notice how totally Jesus dominates the scene of the trial. Even at this moment of impending tragedy, He rises above His accusers. Jesus' silence must have frightened Pilate who attempted to release a prisoner, hoping the people would call for Jesus' release.

16-31. Barabbas, the name means in Aramaic "father's son." There seems a designed contrast with Jesus the Father's Son. Pilate's question, **Why, what evil hath he done?** comes at the end of the trial and is an incidental acknowledgment of the innocence of Christ. No wonder that Pilate tried to shift the guilt of putting Him to death from his own shoulders to those of the Jews. The dramatic answer of verse 25, **His blood be upon us,** marked the final tragedy in the history of the Jews. The curse which they called down upon themselves has been upon them ever since. With this assurance from them, Pilate allowed his weakness and fear of a disturbance to override his sense of justice. Pilate then **scourged Jesus,** perhaps in hope that a bloody beating would appease the Jews (cf. Jn 19:1-6). This left Jesus extremely weak, causing His early death (some people survived on crosses for up to seven days). The scourging was a whipping with a leather whip with pieces of metal embedded in its thongs. Then Pilate **delivered him,** i.e. officially ordered the soldiers to execute Him. They took Him into the **common hall** (Gr *praitōrione;* Lat *praetorium,* the technical name for the governor's quarters, probably in the castle of Antonia). The soldiers mocked Jesus' claim to be King by clothing Him with a **scarlet robe** (Gr *chlamys*). This was a military robe, usually fastened at the right shoulder. The crown of **thorns** and the **reed** for a scepter added to their mockery.

d. His Death for Mankind. 27:32-66.

32-35. A man of Cyrene, Simon by name. Cyrene was a district in North Africa where many Jews lived. They had a synagogue in Jerusalem (Acts 6:9), so that numbers of them must have been constantly there. Simon's two sons, Alexander and Rufus, afterwards became well-known Christians (see Mk 15:21). **Compelled** (Gr *anggarevō*). This is a technical term for "requisition." **To bear his cross.** The cross was carried by the prisoner, a custom which was at first followed in the case of the Lord (Jn 19:17), but He evidently found the weight too great for Him. The transverse bar was at this stage usually attached by a piece of rope, and was fastened in its place on arrival at the scene of execution. **Golgotha . . . a place of a skull.** The reason for the name is not certain. The word is, a transliteration of the Aramaic word meaning "skull" and is equivalent to the Latin *calvaria* perhaps due to the appearance of the hill. Presently two sites have been claimed as Golgotha: the site of the Church of the Holy Sepulchre, which at that time, though not now, was outside the wall, and the hill on the north of Jerusalem usually known as "Gordon's Calvary." **They gave him vinegar to drink mingled with gall,** an allusion to Psalm 69:21. The act appears to have been usual in the case of all who were condemned, the drink being intended as an anodyne. **Vinegar** (Gr *oinon,* literally "wine"). **He would not drink.** The Lord refused any mitigation of His sufferings. The horror of the moment is very simply stated: **They crucified him.**

Crucifixion was a common means of execution by the Roman government. It was a torturous way to die with the victim eventually suffocating or gagging to death. It should be observed that death by crucifixion does not cause the victim to bleed to death. It was the fact that Jesus bore our sins and shed His blood for us that saves us, not the amount of blood He shed. His was a vicarious atonement as the substitute for our sins. We do not have to pay for our sins because He has paid the debt in full for us. The quote **They parted my garments** is from the messianic Psalm 22:18, and forms one of the many literal fulfillments of this Psalm in the death of Christ.

36-44. Pilate placed a placard over Jesus' head with the accusation: **THIS IS JESUS THE KING OF THE JEWS.** Little did he realize how true this intended mockery lof the Jews really was. Indeed, as Matthew shows, Jesus was the King of Jews, who they had rejected. The priests **wagging their heads,** an allusion to Psalm 22:7, said **Thou that destroyest the temple . . . save thyself.** However, that was the one thing Jesus could not and would not do. To save Himself would have meant the loss of the entire world. No wonder He had to have endured Satan's earlier temptation to satisfy Himself, for now He would conquer Satan's power forever by denying Himself! The further accusations, **He saved others . . . He trusted in God . . . He said I am the**

Son of God were actually true in the opposite sense in which the priests intended them. **The thieves** (Gr *lēstēs*) were robbers, perhaps cohorts of Barabbas. The statement, **cast the same in his teeth** means they repeated similar taunts to Him.

45-50. From the sixth hour . . . unto the ninth hour means from noon until 3:00 P.M. Mark (15:25) indicates Jesus had been placed on the cross at the third hour (9:00 A.M.). It is questioned whether this is Jewish or Roman time. The **darkness** was evidently supernaturally imposed since an eclipse of the sun at full noon is impossible. God's wrath was poured upon His Son during this time of darkness. At the ninth hour (3:00 P.M.) Jesus cried: **Eli, Eli, lama sabachthani** (Aramaic) for **My God, my God, why hast thou forsaken me?** Here we have the high cost of the atonement to Christ, who was accursed of God for us as our sin-bearer (cf. II Cor 5:21; Gal 3:13) and suffered the agony of spiritual death for us. The sense of being forsaken was not necessarily caused by God the Father looking away from Him, but from His looking at Him in wrath, as He would look in judgment at a condemned sinner. **He . . . cried . . . with a loud voice,** as a shout of triumph, and **yielded up** His Spirit. In other words having borne the wrath of God's judgment against sin, He knew that He had triumphed over Satan and the curse of sin. His heel was "bruised," but the serpent's head had been "crushed." The yielding of His life was the result of His voluntary surrender of His life for the sake of His own.

51-53. The events immediately following Jesus' death were remarkable indeed. **The veil of the temple** refers to either the curtain over the entrance to the Holy Place (which could be viewed from the porch) or to the curtain separating the Holy Place from the Holy of Holies (cf. Ex 26:31). The latter is most likely here and symbolizes the permanent opening of God's presence to man and man's direct access to God through the atoning death of Christ. Henceforth, all ceremonial services of priests and sacrifices would be done away for the Christian believer (cf. comments on the book of Hebrews). The **earthquake** was a visible manifestation of God's judgment on those who had wrongly crucified the Lord of Glory and it caused the **graves** to be **opened** and the **saints which slept** (departed Old Testament believers) **arose.** This incident is stated only by Matthew and indicates that the Old Testament believers were resurrected **after His resurrection** and **appeared unto many.** It is properly supposed that they were resurrected from "paradise," or "Abraham's bosom" and taken to heaven by the resurrected Christ (cf. Eph 4:8-9). For a discussion of a wide range of views on this see Lange (p. 528).

54-56. The **centurion and they that were with him** exclaimed: **Truly this was the Son of God** (vs. 54). Whether this was an affirmation of genuine faith (based on all they had witnessed) or merely a pagan appreciation of the awesomeness of the circumstances is not clear. However, we dare not minimize the spiritual effect these events could have had on them. Certainly the incident reveals how Jesus' life and character, even in the face of death, rose above the greatest qualities of pagan Rome. The witnesses also included several key women: **Mary Magdalene** (cf. Magdala, in Galilee. Some suggest she is the woman out of whom Jesus cast seven devils in that region. However, her identification as Mary is not clear); **Mary the mother of James and Joses** was the wife of Cleopas (Jn 19:25); the "other Mary" of verse 61; The **mother of Zebedee's children** was Salome (cf. Mk 15:40) and apparently a sister of the Virgin Mary.

57-61. The burial of Jesus' body was seen to by **a rich man of Arimathaea, named Joseph.** In fulfillment of Isaiah 53:9, Jesus made His death with the rich. Joseph was a Sanhedrinist, who had become a **disciple.** His wealth enabled him to own a tomb at Jerusalem even though he lived nearly twenty miles away. Wealthy people in those days often selected their tombs while they were still living. He **asked for the body** from Pilate and got it, undoubtedly not without personal risk on his part. With help from Nicodemus, a believing Pharisee (cf. Jn 3), he took the body from the cross and wrapped it in a **clean linen cloth** or shroud, in the typical burial custom of the day. The body was then placed in Joseph's **own new tomb . . . hewn out in the rock** and covered with a **great stone,** generally rolled in a groove and into place securely over the opening of the tomb. Such a stone would be humanly impossible for one man to roll back by himself from the inside, thus nullifying the ridiculous view that Jesus had only passed out and later "revived" and got out of the tomb. All such anti-supernatural compromises with the text cause more interpretive problems than they supposedly solve. According to the text only the two Marys watched the burial and no disciples were present.

62-66. The **next day . . . followed the day of preparation.** There is some question as to whether this was Saturday (the Sabbath), following a Friday crucifixion. However, John 19:14, 31 indicates that this "preparation day" was the day before the Passover feast day. This may account for Matthew's not using the term "Sabbath" here (cf. Kent, p. 709). He favors a Wednesday crucifixion, with the burial lasting a full seventy-two hours and taking literally the terms **After three days** and **on the third day;** by contrast see Atkinson (p. 805) who favors a Friday crucifixion based on Jewish "inclusive reckoning" of any part of a day equal to a full day. In favor of the Wednesday crucifixion it should be observed that the text does not specify

"Friday," and this view can harmonize all the Sabbath references and resolve the problems of the Jewish leaders meeting with Pilate on the Sabbath and the women preparing spices on the Sabbath (see chart on "Chronology of the Crucifixion" and the detailed discussion and diagrams in W. Scroggie, *A Guide to the Gospels,* pp. 568-577.

III. TRIUMPH OF THE MESSIAH 28:1-20.

A. His Resurrection. 28:1-8.

28:1-8. See also Mark 16:1-20; Luke 24:1-12; John 20:1-31. All four Gospels essentially agree in reporting the facts of the resurrection. The variety of details in each account supplement rather than contradict each other. The empty tomb was discovered **In the end** (Gr *opse*, used as improper preposition for "after") **of the sabbath** agreeing with the other evangelists. By Jewish reckoning the day ended at sunset and the new day began at the same time. Thus, Saturday night by our reckoning was actually Sunday by their calendar. Accordingly, the resurrection actually occurred sometime during the night, for by the time the women arrived **as it began to dawn** He had already risen from the dead. The **earthquake** and the **angel** (Mark's "man in white"), who rolled the stone away, did not come to let Jesus out of the tomb, but to reveal that it was empty and that He was gone already! Evidently Mary Magdalene left immediately to tell Peter and John. The angel told the other women, **Fear not . . . He is not here: for he is risen, as he said.** The pronoun "you" is emphatic: "you women, only, do not fear me" (as the guards did, who were paralyzed with terror). "They have come to see the grave drawn there by sorrow, love, and, perhaps, inarticulate hope. For their loyalty and persistent love they hear first the news of the resurrection" (Filson, p. 302). The angel then in-

instructed them to go unto Galilee to meet Him.

B. His Reappearance. 28:9-15.

9-15. Running ahead with **fear and great joy** they actually met Jesus and worshipped Him. We cannot imagine their emotional attitude at this moment when fear and joy gripped them simultaneously. Again, they were instructed to go before Him into Galilee. Here Matthew's account is considerably briefer and less detailed than the other Gospels (where we have specific accounts of Peter and John running to the tomb; Mary meeting Jesus; the appearance in the upper room; the appearance to more than five hundred believers at once; and the undeniably literal incident on the seashore in John 21). The one addition by Matthew is the falsified report of the guards in verses 11-15. Pilate had put the soldiers at the disposal of the Jewish Sanhedrin so they reported first to them. The assemblage **gave large money** or a large bribe to the soldiers to hide the truth of the resurrection with the lie, **saying . . . His disciples came by night, and stole him away while we slept,** a ridiculous statement in view of the disciples' earlier defection in the garden. How could this band of cowards overpower an armed Roman guard? Thus, Matthew observed that this explanation was still **commonly reported among the Jews** in his day. On the theological significance of the resurrection see E. Harrison, *A Short Life of Christ* (pp. 231-246); G. Ladd, "The Resurrection of Jesus Christ," in *Christian Faith and Modern Theology,* pp. 261-284; W. Sparrow-Simpson, *Our Lord's Resurrection;* M. Tenney, *The Reality of the Resurrection.*

C. His Recommission. 28:16-20.

16-17. Now instead of sending His disciples back to the house of Israel, they are sent into all the world. The kingdom rejected by Jews will now be offered to the Gentiles in accordance with Jesus' earlier parables. This appearance in **Galilee** is not to be confused with the appearances at Jerusalem and is probably the same as the appearance to "above five hundred brethren" (cf. I Cor 15:6), with the **eleven** being among them. This is further implied by the statement, **they worshipped him: but some doubted,** which would be unlikely of the eleven after the earlier appearances and the "doubting Thomas" incident (Jn 20:28). This also implies a difference in Jesus' appearance after His resurrection, as also described by John, His own beloved disciple, who barely recognizes the resurrected-glorified Christ in Revelation 1. Lange (p. 556) adds the further explanation that "doubted" (Gr *distazō*) may also be translated "hesitated," in the sense that while they obviously saw Him, they hesitated to offer Him such unbounded worship. Prior to Christ's death and resurrection, His disciples, while recognizing His divine messiahship, did not openly worship Him in the manner that would now become customary. Otherwise, why would Matthew, writing to convince the Jews of Jesus, say so close to the end of his Gospel that some "doubted"? The more obvious explanation is that as he wrote to the hesitant Jewish community, he was saying he understood their hesitation for he too was a Jew who had become a Christian.

18-20. The Great Commission brings this first Gospel to its grand finale. Christianity is not represented here as the mere reverential devotion of disappointed men who honor their martyred leader. Here is a far different scene. The triumphant living Lord sends forth His ambassadors to proclaim His gospel throughout all the world. The commission is not just an order but a pronouncement of victory (*munus regium Christi*) by the risen Saviour through His disciples. **All power** or authority (Gr *exousia*) was

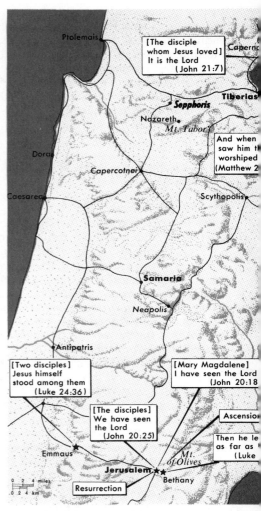

The Resurrection and Ascension

now in the hands of Christ, in heaven and on the earth. On the basis of that authority and power the Christian disciple is to carry out the great commission of the church. **Go ye** is actually a participle and conveys not a command to go, but the assumption that the listener will automatically be going. In other words, the idea expressed is that "as you are going" make disciples, and **Teach all nations** could be translated "convert all Gentiles," or "disciple all nations." Thus the converting influence of the gospel is indicated here. Reaching the nations is not merely a matter of education but the full process of discipleship, i.e. teaching and training, beginning with conversion. The "all nations" makes it clear that the commission to the church is a world-wide one, encompassing the entire missionary effort. The church is not to be merely "missionary-minded." The church is the vehicle of Christ's mission to the world and the two (church and mission) are inseparable. Every local church has a mission to its world. To attempt to eliminate this commission from the Church Age (as do the hyperdispensationalists) would be to leave the church without an assigned purpose from her Lord.

Baptizing the converted disciples is the first step of outward obedience to the Lord and brings entrance into the membership of the local congregation. "Baptize" (Gr *baptizō*) is an English transliteration, and means to "dip," or "dunk," or "immerse," thus indicating its proper mode. Nowhere does this term ever indicate "sprinkling." On baptism see A. Carson, *Baptism in the New Testament*; E. Hulse, *Baptism and Church Membership*; J. Warnes, *Baptism*; contra see J. Murray, *Christian Baptism*. These converts are to be baptized **in the name of the Father, and of the Son, and of the Holy Ghost.** The "name" is singular, followed by an elliptical clause indicating that the one name is the name of each person of the Trinity. While baptismal references in Acts refer to being baptized in Jesus' name (emphasizing His deity as Saviour) they in no way eliminate the significance of this formula given by Christ Himself. Nor do the three persons of the Godhead necessitate a trine immersion in each name. Furthermore, these baptized converts are to be taught **all things** that Jesus taught, thus the edifying and exhorting ministry of the church is seen as it develops in the book of Acts.

The closing promise, though given to the apostles, is transmitted by every generation of believers (cf. Jn 17:20). Christ's promise of His presence, **I am with you alway,** guarantees the success of the church's mission because it is really His mission carried out by His called-out disciples. The phrase **unto the end of the world** means until the end of the "age" (Gr *aiōn*). Therefore, the empowerment of Christ to the church to evangelize the world is available in every age, even unto the end of the church age. There is no excuse, then, for failing to exercise that power in our age. No time of apostasy will ever be so great as to nullify the true gospel ministry of the Bible-preaching church. In comparing the Great Commission with Jesus' promise to continually build His church (ch. 18), we must conclude that He intended His church always to be spiritually militant and evangelistically aggressive as we take His claims of lordship to the entire world of our generation. **Amen!**

BIBLIOGRAPHY

Allen, W. C. A Critical and Exegetical Commentary on the Gospel According to St. Matthew. In *International Critical Commentary*. New York: Scribners, 1925.

Alexander, J. A. *The Gospel According to Matthew.* New York: Scribner, Armstrong & Co., 1873.

Atkinson, B.F.C. The Gospel According to Matthew. In *New Bible Commentary*. Grand Rapids: Eerdmans, 1953.

Barclay, E. *The Gospel of Matthew*. Philadelphia: Westminster Press, 1958.

Boice, J. M. *The Sermon on the Mount*. Grand Rapids: Zondervan, 1972.

* Broadus, J. A. Commentary on the Gospel of Matthew. In *American Commentary Series*. Philadelphia: American Baptist Publication Society, 1886.

Brown, J. *Discourses and Sayings of our Lord Jesus Christ*. London: Banner of Truth, 1967.

Calvin, J. *Commentary on a Harmony of the Evangelists*. Trans. A. W. Morrison. Grand Rapids: Eerdmans, 1972.

Davies, W. D. *The Sermon on the Mount*. Cambridge: University Press, 1966.

Ellison, H. L. The Gospel According to Matthew. In *A New Testament Commentary*. Ed. G. Howley. Grand Rapids: Eerdmans, 1969.

Filson, F. *A Commentary on the Gospel According to St. Matthew*. New York: Harper & Brothers, 1960.

Gaebelein, A. *The Gospel of Matthew*. New York: Our Hope, 1910.

* Hendricksen, W. *Exposition of the Gospel According to Matthew*. Grand Rapids: Baker, 1973.

* Kent, H. A. Jr. Matthew. In *Wycliffe Bible Commentary*. Ed. C. Peiffer and E. Harrison. Chicago: Moody Press, 1962.

Lange, J. P. *Commentary on the Holy Scriptures: Matthew*. Grand Rapids: Zondervan, n.d.

Lawlor, G. L. *The Beatitudes Are For Today*. Grand Rapids: Baker, 1974.

Lenski, R. C. *The Interpretation of St. Matthew's Gospel*. Minneapolis: Augsburg, 1961.

* Lloyd-Jones, D. M. *Studies in the Sermon on the Mount*. Grand Rapids: Eerdmans, 1962.

Pink, A. W. *An Exposition of the Sermon on the Mount*. Grand Rapids: Guardian Press, 1975.

Plummer, A. *An Exegetical Commentary on the Gospel According to St. Matthew*. London: Robert Scott, 1909.

Ridderbos, H. *Matthew's Witness to Jesus Christ*. New York: Association Press, 1958.

Ryle, J. C. *Expository Thoughts on the Gospels: Matthew*. London: James Clarke, 1954.

Stonehouse, N. B. *The Witness of Matthew and Mark to Christ*. Grand Rapids: Eerdmans, 1958.

* Tasker, R. V. G. The Gospel According to St. Matthew. In *Tyndale New Testament Series*. Grand Rapids: Eerdmans, 1961.

* Walvoord, J. *Matthew—Thy Kingdom Come*. Chicago: Moody Press, 1974.

Watson, T. *The Beatitudes*. London: Banner of Truth, 1971.

The Gospel According to

MARK

INTRODUCTION

Authorship. Mark is commonly accepted as the author, the Church Fathers affirming this without controversy. In fact, they felt it necessary to explain how a seemingly improbable person like Mark came to compose this account. He became a close associate of Peter and for many years listened to his sermons and conversations about the Lord's life. Tradition says that those who observed his notes of Peter's sermons urged him to formulate them into a systematized life story of Jesus; if this were true, the source of the material would be Peter. Papias, bishop of Hierapolis, in the first half of the second century testified, "And John, the presbyter, also said this, Mark being the interpreter of Peter, whatsoever he recorded he wrote with great accuracy . . . and he was in company with Peter, who gave him such instructions as necessary, but not to give a history of our Lord's discourses" (Eusebius, *Ecclesiastical History* III, p. 39). It is probable that Papias as a young man had met the Apostle John. Ireneaus, bishop of Lyons, agrees, "Mark the disciple and interpreter of Peter, did also hand down to us in writing what has been preached by Peter." Likewise, Justin Martyr refers to Mark's work as the memoirs of Peter. Thus, we can picture the younger disciple, after hearing innumerable eyewitness accounts of the Saviour, feeling compelled to commit them to writing for the benefit of future generations.

The author's full name was John Mark (Acts 12:12). His mother, Mary, had servants, indicating the family was not ill-furnished. Besides by his mother, Mark was influenced by his cousin, Barnabas, who took him with Paul on the first missionary journey (Acts 13:5). Halfway through the journey Mark returned home (Acts 13:13). The reason for the departure must have been questionable for when Barnabas and Paul planned a second journey, Paul's insistence on discluding Mark was so intense that the two leaders parted company (Acts 15:39), Barnabas setting sail for Cyprus with Mark. Whatever Paul observed as a weakness in Mark at this point, in later years he commended Mark's efforts in the ministry (II Tim 4:11).

Little else is known of this disciple. However, his gospel does include an unusual event in connection with Christ's arrest. A young follower hurrying to escape lost his garment and sprinted away naked (Mk 14:51-52). Although it cannot be proven, most scholars understand Mark to be speaking of himself; there would be no other apparent reason for including this event.

His close association with Peter is not based on tradition alone; Peter himself mentions Mark in a manner which supports it (I Pet 5:13). It has been commonly held that Mark moved to Rome with Peter and remained there until both Peter and Paul had died. He then moved to Alexandria and founded a church which later became quite influential (Eusebius, *Ecclesiastical History* II, p. 16).

Recipients. Tradition depicts Mark's work as arising from the entreaties of Roman Christians. The style and contents corroborates this belief including several "latinisms" such as those found in 4:21 (bushel), 12:14 (tribute), 6:27 (executioner), and 15:39, 44-45 (centurion). That Aramaic expressions are translated or explained (7:3-4), indicates the readers were not Jewish. Additionally, in Mark 15:21 where a man named Simon bears Jesus' cross, his sons are named, one of whom was Rufus, a resident of Rome (Rom 16:13). If the book were destined for another locality, this inclusion would seem peculiar.

Date and Place of Writing. The final composition took place after Peter's death, no earlier than A.D. 65, and before the fall of Jerusalem, A.D. 70. Papias, Clement of Alexandria, Origen, Eusebius, and Jerome all affirm or infer that the place of writing was Rome.

Purpose. If one finds specific emphases in the other Gospels (Jesus as King in Matthew, as Son of Man in Luke, and as Son of God in John), he may observe the Lord as Servant in Mark. A passage that lays stress on Christ's service says that He came "to minister" (10:45). Another factor which supports this is the growth of Roman intolerance toward Christianity, which was developing into open persecution. One author concludes, "The chief purpose of the gospel is to portray the personality of Jesus in such a way that the church in the hour of its severe trial would receive power to endure and remain faithful" (Davies, *The Abingdon Commentary,* p. 996).

The design of the narrative also concurs with John who declared, "But these are written, that ye might believe . . ." Jn 20:31).

Characteristics. Three areas of emphasis may be observed:

1. *Activities, rather than teachings of Christ.* The narration swiftly moves from one event to the next. In fact, the action itself is described frequently by the word "immediately" (Gr *euthus*). This style may reflect the impulsive, action-oriented personality of Peter, who furnished Mark with his information. Relatively few of Christ's teachings are included, the Olivet Discourse being the only one of substantial length (Mk 13).

2. *Geography.* The longest and initial location of Christ's ministry occurred in and around Galilee. A later phase describes extended trips to areas beyond. Finally, tension builds as He approaches and enters Jerusalem, where His rejection and death ensue.

3. *Vividness of detail and realism.* Looks, gestures and actions stand out. The author announces without hesitation that the Lord's relatives had concluded that He lost His senses (3:21) and that "all men" were looking for Him. (1:35-38). During the Crucifixion the expressions of mockery and the details of His suffering draw a graphic picture of ineffable endurance.

OUTLINE

COMMENTARY

I. THE INTRODUCTION TO CHRIST'S MINISTRY. 1:1-13.

A. The Title. 1:1.

The theme of Mark's book is the "Good News" (Gr *euangelion*) about Jesus Christ. The name, **Christ,** (Gr *Christos*) refers to His office (the Anointed One). His early life was only the **Beginning** of this Gospel, for the resurrection denies the story an ending.

B. The Preparation for His Ministry. 1:2-13.

1. John the Baptist. 1:2-8.

2-3. The forerunner had arrived according to divine prediction: **As it is written in the Prophets** (Mal 3:1 and Isa 40:3).

4. John's preparatory ministry included two basic aspects: baptizing and preaching. **Baptize** (Gr *baptizō*) literally means "to dip into" or "to immerse" and its connection with **Repentance** indicates that the ordinance held no inherent virtue or merit but merely symbolized an inward change of attitude toward sin. The root problem of

John's listeners parallels that of contemporary society. They not only were sinful, but were insensitive to their condition.

5. Mark employs a hyperbole when he uses the word **all** to describe the response to his preaching. The translation "all the people of Judea were going out and were being baptized" more clearly brings out the significance of the imperfect tense used in Greek. **Confessing** stems from two Greek words which together mean "to say the same thing as." Genuine confession is not merely admitting guilt, but it places the same appraisement upon it that God does.

6. A simple, if not crude, life style marks John's priorities. His ambitions and goals pertain to the One mentioned next, not to personal convenience.

7-8. This announcement contains inferences regarding Christ's person and His function. His person: to untie someone else's shoes is the task of a menial servant. So eminent is He, that to untie His is a privilege! His function: John is but a man announcing the message and baptizing those who respond; he himself cannot affect the inner person. The One whom John introduces also will baptize, but not as a physical sign. His baptism will transform the soul by "the washing of regeneration and renewing of the Holy Ghost" (Tit 3:5).

2. Christ's baptism. 1:9-11.

9. Jesus' baptism is related in surprisingly simple language. Mark recounts that He left His home town and submitted to the rite.

10. The significance of this event lies in God's public approval of Jesus. The whole Trinity is involved. The Son submits to the ordinance; the Spirit rests upon Him; and the Father voices His pleasure. The form assumed by the Spirit, **like a dove,** may be related to Genesis 1:2, which pictures Him hovering (AV, **moved**) over the waters, as a hen resides on her nest. The Spirit longs to overshadow men with His infilling power. This was accomplished perfectly in the Son, because He submitted without any reservations.

11. The heavenly voice both qualified and identified Jesus. Others have been called **beloved** and pleasing, but He alone can be termed **my Son.** There are many children, but He is the unique Son of God.

3. Christ's temptation. 1:12-13.

In verse 10 Jesus' baptism resulted in the Spirit's control and here one may observe the extent of His submission. **Driveth** comes from the Greek *ekballō* which may be translated "leads." It does convey a forceful guidance, which illustrates one area of Christ's self-humiliation. Matthew and Luke include the details of the temptation (Mt 4 and Lk 4), but Mark limits his account to a general statement.

II. THE MINISTRY IN GALILEE. 1:14-7:23.

A. The Initial Stage. 1:14-3:5.

14. In spite of all the miracles evidenced in Christ's life, the predominant characteristic of His ministry is described by the words **Jesus came ... preaching.** In the oldest manuscripts **the gospel of the kingdom of God** is simply "the gospel of God" which may be rendered "the gospel from God," stressing its source.

15. What causes **the kingdom of God** to be **at hand?** The presence of the King! What does the King require of His servants? The answer is twofold: Negatively, **repent** (Gr *metanoeō*) change their attitudes about their sin; specifically recognize its evil and forsake it. Positively, **believe** God's Good News centered in Christ.

1. Four disciples called. 1:16-20.

16. John 1:40-42 describes the first encounter **Simon** and **Andrew** had with Jesus. The reference to them as **fishers** names their business or livelihood, not their sport.

17. Jesus frequently appealed to people on the basis of their occupation or background. Instead of catching fish, would you not rather be netting men? The prerequisite: **Come ye after me!**

18. Their response to this unusual "call" indicates they had previous contact with Him. **Forsook their nets.** Their action involved more than sacrificing a few possessions. They were giving up their trade.

19. It is interesting that James' name captures the scene. John's name joins the former as "his brother." In spite of this, John became "the beloved disciple," penned five New Testament books, and outlived the other twelve apostles.

20. For **Zebedee** to have had **hired servants,** employees, indicates that his business was relatively prosperous.

21. Capernaum. Matthew and Luke mention a visit to Jesus' home town, Nazareth, prior to this event, and Matthew 4:13 informs us that Jesus made His residence in this city. **Straightway.** The Greek Word, *euthus,* translated "straightway, immediately, anon," is characteristic of Mark's style. Already it has been used in verses 10, 12, 18, and 20, and it is used over forty times throughout the book. Here it signifies that Christ Jesus began teaching on the first Sabbath after He arrived.

22. The Greek imperfect tense of **they were astonished** depicts action in motion. As Jesus taught, the people were not only astonished at His sermon as a whole, but they kept reacting with amazement at every truth that crossed His lips. **Not as the scribes.** The distinction in His manner was that He ignored the normal procedure of the scribes, who consistently quoted or made reference to the Old Testament and the ancient rabbis. Jesus taught authoritatively since His word was final!

23. The term **unclean** (Gr *akathartos*) bore special connotations to the Jewish mind. the Old Testament fre-

quently distinguished between what was lawful and unlawful, accepted and rejected, and therefore, may mean "ungodly." "Demon" is a designation used interchangeably with **unclean spirit.**

24. When He recognized Jesus, **I know thee,** the unclean spirit questioned His presence: **let us alone; what have we to do with thee . . .** The expression is a Greek idiom which could be translated, "What do we have in common?" It assumes that two parties have converged without a unifying bond. Therefore, they concluded, He must be here **to destroy us.**

25. Hold thy peace. Here and in verse 34 Jesus silences the demons, because they knew Him. Apparently His objection is that "unclean" persons should identify Him. Revelation would come at the proper time through pure vessels.

26. Torn. The unclean spirit caused the man to have convulsions before it left.

27. What new doctrine is this? Their question shows a basic purpose in healing. Jesus certainly was moved by physical suffering, but His eternal objectives outweighed temporal matters. Verses 14-15 named "preaching" as Jesus' primary ministry, and in this context the occasion of healing happens immediately after Jesus' authoritative lesson. At first the people responded negatively, because His method seemed bizarre, but when they witnessed Him casting out demons, they accepted His teaching on the basis of His power.

28. The phrase **his fame** (Gr *akoē*) commonly signified a news report or announcement. It relates to the event of the preceding verse rather than His person.

30. Simon's wife's mother. Although the disciples' families are rarely mentioned in the New Testament, because of the inclusion of this incident, we learn that Peter was married, and it appears that his mother-in-law and brother lived with him.

32-34. In verse 28 it is said that the news of healing had spread "immediately," and here the multitudes thronged after Jesus because they had heard. The same types of people were brought to Him as the ones recently healed: demon-possessed and diseased.

35-37. A great while before day. Two things may be noted regarding the time. First, He prayed very early, before other activities could distract or interfere. Secondly, the account comes the day after His encounter with many demons (AV, devils is better translated demons from the Greek *daimonion*). Ephesians 6:12 pinpoints the Christian's enemy; his actual battlefield lies in the realm of the spiritual. An even more remarkable aspect of this prayer is the lengths Jesus took to assure privacy. He went **into a solitary place.** The others, when they awoke, sought Him and finally when He was found, they complained that the multitudes were awaiting Him. He offered no apology for what He was doing was well worth time and effort.

38. Jesus' stated objective in His extended ministry is to **preach** in the next towns. The miracles He performed proved the validity of His authority, and thus, His message.

40. Leper. In New Testament times, because of the unsanitary conditions, lepers were numerous. This one's petition pertained to Jesus' desire, not His ability; he declared **thou canst,** "you are able"!

41. The Lord's response is not routine. The healing resulted because He was **moved with compassion.** Since He is the second person of the Trinity, why would He need to **put forth his hand** and **touch him**? Yet the Lord typically touched when He healed. Since miracles were designed to verify Jesus as Lord, the touch would remove doubts as to the source of the healings.

43. Straightly charged . . . sent him away. Both verbs in this sentence are

very strong. The first (Gr *embrimaō*) sometimes portrays a horse snorting in anger; the second (Gr *ekballō*) often was used to describe an excommunication from the synagogue. Although they are less forceful here, their presence indicates intense feelings. Jesus perceived that the man was more excited about his condition and experience than the One who had healed him.

44-45. Verses 44 and 45 contrast the man's instructions with his actions. The first command prohibited him from telling what had happened, yet he not only disobeyed, but he became so involved in sharing his story that he apparently disregarded the other instructions also. To follow what **Moses commanded** would have affirmed that Jesus believed and fulfilled the Old Testament law.

No more openly. Jesus' fame even in this initial stage of His ministry was incredible. Crowds followed so heavily that it became impossible for Him to make His way through any city without creating a commotion.

2. The healing of a paralytic man. 2:1-12.

2:1. His entrance into **Capernaum** was unknown by the public, but **it was noised.** Someone discovered His presence and the news spread like wildfire.

2. When they heard where Jesus was, the multitudes swarmed about Him. The author lays stress on the situation by saying there was no room, **not so much as about the door,** which indicates the problem that the friends of the paralytic man faced. **Preached.** Although Jesus' fame was due to miracles, the narration more frequently has Him preaching the gospel.

3. They come unto him, bringing one sick of the palsy, which was borne of four. Why does it not simply say, "Four men came bringing their sick friend"? The wording shows that there were more than four in the group. **Sick**

of the palsy (Gr *paralytikos*) refers to paralysis.

4. The crowded condition, **for the press,** prohibited an approach to the Lord. **Uncovered the roof.** Luke 5:19 identifies it as a tile roof, the tiles being made of hardened clay.

5. Perhaps many in the crowd reacted negatively to such an odd performance. A ceiling opening up, men lowering a pallet on which an invalid lay: what sort of group could this be? Jesus, however, **saw their faith,** not their deeds. His response may at first seem inappropriate. **Thy sins be forgiven.** Although their desire was physical, Christ's answer was very proper. First, the previous statement reveals Jesus' ability to discern beyond physical appearance (also Jn 2:24-25). The sin of the soul is worse than paralysis of the body. Secondly, this story testifies to Jesus' true identity as the Son of God. God alone can forgive sins, but the forgiveness of sins cannot be observed. Thus His identity was certified by a supernatural act.

6-7. The scribes immediately misinterpreted what Jesus declared. Instead of properly reasoning: He claims to forgive; only God forgives; therefore, He must be God; they conjectured on the basis of a false premise: this man cannot be God, therefore, He is blaspheming.

9. A proof test of His identity results from this encounter. Jesus indirectly claimed to be God, but the scribes refused to accept it. How could deity be proved while discussing forgiveness? An area which could be subjected to investigation was used, the healing.

10. The demonstration of divine power proves to sinners that He indeed can forgive sins. **Forgiven** (Gr *aphiēmi*) which means "to send away," does not merely overlook sin, but actually removes it.

11. **I say.** Healing is not the result of involved methodology. A word from the Son of God, whose command

brought forth the universe, is sufficient.

12. **Before them all.** Jesus' miracles were not obscure stories developed by isolated reports; the evidence was open for examination. **We never saw it on this fashion.** Occasionally, one reads that Palestinians in the New Testament era readily accepted the supernatural in Jesus, because they "saw" it frequently elsewhere, but this statement denies that.

3. The call of Matthew. 2:13-17.

13. **Resorted . . . he taught.** These verbs are in the imperfect tense in Greek, emphasizing progressive or continuous action. The following translation clarifies the expression: they "were coming to Him, and He kept on teaching them."

14. **Levi.** Both Mark and Luke use the Aramaic name, while Matthew employs the more familiar one. **Son of Alphaeus.** Since last names are uncommon, the father's name usually was added to prevent confusion. **Sitting at the receipt of custom.** Although Mark does not use the word publican, the description refers to a tax-collector. **Follow me** may be rendered "be following me" or "continue following me." Jesus prescribed a new life style, not a temporary errand. Matthew **followed.** He turned over his money and books to his employer and took up an occupation arranged in heaven.

16. **Scribes.** Professional interpreters of the Old Testament. **Pharisees.** An extremely strict and ritualistic religious party, who concerned themselves more with the letter than the spirit of the law. **How is it that . . .?** The question was not wrong in itself, for the Old Testament forbade wrong associations (Ps 1:1), but their attitude lacked compassion.

17. Jesus' compendious answer reveals the heart of God's Good News. Although the New Testament never condones sinful alliances, it consistently urges us to "win" sinners, for they

are spiritually **sick.** The statement, **I came not to call the righteous,** was not given to morally segregate people; the New Testament affirms that all are depraved and under sin (Rom 3).

4. Fasting. 2:18-22.

18. Fasting means more than abstinence from food; that may be practiced for physical reasons. Scriptural fasting always involves a spiritual application; its basic purpose being to so seek God's person that temporal concerns pass unnoticed.

19-20. Christ's illustration, given as an explanation to the question in verse 18, relates to a specific purpose of fasting. It could be done because an individual hungers after a deeper knowledge of God, but more often it results from a desperate situation. Since the **bridegroom** was with His disciples, they had no need to fast. John the Baptist's disciples knew their leader remained in prison, but Jesus' disciples could rejoice with their Master. **Children of the bridechamber** refers to members of the wedding party.

21-22. The illustrations about the new cloth and the new wine present a principle to which fasting may be related. A patch of new cloth has not previously been shrunk, and therefore would pull the old garment apart. Conversely, new wine expands as it ages and an old wine sack would have already reached its limit. Under the context of the ancient system, the Old Testament law, limitations had been reached, but Christ brought principles that stretched these. For instance, murder in the Old Testament is physical, but Jesus said that a man can murder by hating.

5. The Lord of the Sabbath. 2:23-28.

23. The word **corn** (Gr *sporimos*) actually refers to wheat or grain.

24. The Pharisees accused Jesus' disciples of breaking the **Sabbath.** Exodus 20:10 prohibits Sabbath work and

Exodus 16:22 illustrates how that instruction relates to eating.

25-27. Two principles govern the uniqueness of the Sabbath. The first is illustrated in verses 25-26 and stated in 27. Jesus related David's unlawful act in I Samuel 21. David and his soldiers fleeing enemies had little time to acquire food, so they ate the showbread which was restricted for priests. Jesus' silence condoned the action, because **the sabbath was made for man,** that is, God instituted it for man's benefit.

28. The second principle is greater, because it encompasses God's nature. By definition He must be above any law which He establishes.

6. Healing on the Sabbath. 3:1-5.

3:1. Returning to the synagogue, He noticed a man with a **withered hand.** The condition was atrophy, the decreasing in size of a member of the body because of its lack of use.

2. The Pharisees, still accompanying Jesus, carefully observed Him, not hungering for spiritual food, like the crowds, but **that they might accuse him.** Earlier some of them might have had honest questions; at this point their motive became clear.

4. The rhetorical question destroys their argument by forcing a logical conclusion: would your interpretation of the law ever demand you to destroy life or do evil? No answer.

B. The Results of Popular Growth. 3:6-35.

Christ's swift fame hardly could occur without affecting everyone. As the multitudes crowded after Jesus, the author relates His influence upon others also. Religious and political leaders began a conspiracy; Jesus Himself organized a team of apostles, His relatives disbelieved, and scribes publicly denounced Him as an emissary of Satan.

6. When they **took counsel,** they did not merely share their adverse feelings in general terms. After agreeing to His death, they arranged meetings in which they could carefully plan the murder. **Herodians** refers to a political party which was loyal to Herod's family.

11. Two facts should be mentioned regarding the words **fell down.** First, the Greek *prospipto,* being in the imperfect tense, signifies continuous action: "they kept on falling down before Him and crying." Secondly, it may be that the reason for this action was not to worship, but to confuse the multitudes. If they heard unclean spirits announcing His title as the Son of God, they might think that good and evil in the spirit world are not totally opposite each other.

1. The Twelve chosen. 3:12-20.

12. See the discussion in 1:25.

13. A mountain. Its identity is uncertain, but it was the same one where the Sermon on the Mount was preached (Lk 6).

14. Although Mark and Luke use different Greek words for **ordained,** both mean "appointed" or "chosen." **with him.** Their relationship to their Lord preceded their service for Him.

15. Although the power of healing is not included in some manuscripts, Matthew 10:1 clearly affirms it.

16-19. For more about the background of the Twelve see Matthew 10:2-4 and Luke 6:12-16.

20. Not so much as eat bread. This statement infers what their purpose was. After a full day, they were hungry, but people would not leave them alone long enough for them to eat.

21. The word **friends** may be misleading. In Greek it literally means "those near" (Gr *hoi par autou*) and is an idiom which may refer to friends or relatives. Since the apostles would be His friends and were present with Him, it speaks of members of His family. John 7:5 says His brothers had not yet believed, so one may understand how they could declare **He is beside himself.**

They sought to physically restrain Him from His irrational activities.

2. The unpardonable sin. 3:22-30.

22. These **scribes** probably were more prominent than others, because of their location, **from Jerusalem.** They presented an official evaluation of this new prophet to the public. Since His supernatural powers could not be denied, they were said to have originated in **Beelzebub,** a name referring to Satan.

23-26. In answer to the question of verse 23, **How can Satan cast out Satan?,** Jesus' remarks imply, "to even think so is ridiculous!" Divided kingdoms fall (vs. 24); divided houses fall (vs. 25); therefore, Satan warring against himself would be self-destruction (vs. 26). Furthermore, complete victory must precede enjoyment of conquered territory (vs. 27). The only way to establish the kindgom of God on earth is to remove the kingdom of evil. This explains why it is only rational to view exorcism as an act of God.

28-29. The attempt to generalize this offense to the persistence of unbelief ignores the correct definition of **blasphemies,** which specifically means "speaking against in order to hurt" (Gr *blasphēmeō*) the Holy Spirit. **In danger of eternal damnation** would be better translated "guilty of eternal sin," sin standing in place of "damnation" in the oldest manuscripts.

3. Family ties. 3:31-35.

31. His brethren and his mother (cf. vs. 21). One need not suppose that Mary agreed with her sons' conclusion about Jesus. She probably joined her sons to prevent them from doing something rash.

33-35. Jesus set forth a question to advance a spiritual principle: eternal relationships surpass earthly ones. Neither religious activities nor memberships draw the Lord's favor, but doing **the will of God.**

C. Parables. 4:1-34.

4:2. By parables: the Greek word *parabolē* comes from two others (*para, beside and ballō,* to cast). Thus, a parable is a rhetorical device to explain truth. Especially in His lessons on the kingdom Jesus employed these story illustrations and with two effects: to believers they disclose truth; to unbelievers they hide it.

1. The parable of the sower. 4:3-8.

4. Wayside. Some fell, literally, "alongside the road" (Gr *hodos*), the hardened surface adjacent to the road or path.

5. Stony ground does not refer to a mixture of dirt and small stones, but speaks of huge slabs of rock with only a thin layer of soil upon them.

7. Thorns (Gr *akantha*) may be taken simply as weeds, not just thistles, any wild plants which grow among the planted crops.

8. Brought forth. No mention is made of the kind of produce. The purpose of the illustration centers around the type of ground.

9. This verse contains an often used quote in the New Testament, which aims at man's tendency to ignore or make light of truth. The statement is another way of calling the listener to pay close attention.

2. Christ's use of parables explained. 4:10-12.

10-11. Unto you. Jesus said the truth is made clear to those who believe and follow Him. **Them that are without.** "Without" (Gr *exō*) would be better translated "outside" because it refers to those who are outside the kingdom of God.

12. Lest . . . they should be converted. A superficial understanding of this quote from Isaiah 6:9-10 has confused some about the Lord's instructions regarding evangelism. Here He explains that details about God's kingdom are not to be used to "prove" God's message to anyone. Faith pre-

cedes proof, not vice versa. People are won "through the foolishness of preaching" not scientific facts. If that were the case, faith would be nothing more than the recognition of revealed evidence.

3. The parable of the sower explained. 4:13-20.

15. Because the **wayside** was hardened, the seed remains on top; similarly, the word does not penetrate a hardened heart, and Satan removes it easily.

16-17. Stony ground may have enough soil to cause initial growth, but no depth is established. As weather may ruin weak plants, adversity destroys those who base their faith on emotions. A person with a solid foundation would have counted the cost, which includes hardships and sacrifices as well as benefits.

18. No criticism is offered regarding the ground in the third category. The dedication was genuine initially, but later they allowed "things" to affect them. Their separation to the gospel softened as new appeals and attractions gained their attention. That which began as a minor tangent ends choking the Word of God right out of their lives.

20. The virtue of the **good ground** lies in its function. Yet the amount of its produce is not the issue, for some ground brings forth more than others. Even though the fruit may appear relatively meager, the fact remains, it **brings forth fruit.**

4. The parable of the candle. 4:21-23.

21-23. Verse 21 raises the question of a candle's (Gr *lychnos*) primary purpose, and 22 relates that purpose to God's kingdom. Jesus was reassuring them that although there is a time of mystery, the truth will be revealed.

5. The parable of new standards. 4:24-25.

24-25. The two verses at first may

seem unrelated, perhaps even contradictory. They relate in that they are opposite; the careful wording shows agreement. First, our world system operates on the basic premise, "regardless of the method, gain equals success." But Jesus said, the way you measure (AV, **mete**) determines how you will prosper, the verb dealing with physical materials. Secondly, when gifts are distributed among people, the poor usually receive first, but Jesus announces possessors will receive first. Obviously, these principles apply to the kingdom of God. The selfish hording of physical goods (vs. 24) and unwillingness to accept absolute truth (vs. 25) are indirectly rebuked.

6. The parable about growth. 4:26-29.

27. As a farmer **knoweth not how** his seed becomes mature plants which produce fruit, Christians may enjoy fruitful lives without thoroughly understanding the process.

28. The emphasis of this parable is found in the expression **of herself,** which in Greek means "automatically" (Gr *automatos*). God's procedure for growth does not need to be intellectually perceived to be experienced.

7. The parable of the mustard seed. 4:30-32.

31. Mustard seed at the time of its sowing is extremely small compared to herbs, yet at maturity extends upward beyond any. As an illustration of the kingdom, the lesson stresses phenomenal growth; it would expand from a few to millions. That **the fowls of the air may lodge** in it suggests some impurity, since they are neither part of the plant nor permanent.

D. The Journey to Gadara. 4:35-5:20.

1. The storm calmed. 4:35-41.

35. The same day sometimes is referred to as the "busy day," because it includes everything from 3:22.

37. The **great storm of wind** was a whirlwind or cyclone. The mountainous regions surrounding the Sea of Galilee often gave rise to unusually fast and vicious weather changes.

38. Hinder part (Gr *prumna*), the stern.

39. Rebuked may be translated "commanded." The simplicity of the narrative stands out in such a dramatic scene. He sleeps; He arises; He commands; all is well!

40-41. Man is so reluctant to accept supernatural truth. Although they had seen demons cast out and diseases cured, the apostles perceived Christ as a prophet only. Witnessing His sovereignty over nature, they respond among themselves in fear, **What manner of man is this!** What emotions must have flowed as they pondered if their master indeed was God Himself!

2. The healing of the Gerasene demoniac. 5:1-20.

5:1. An apparent discrepancy has been cited between Matthew's and Mark's accounts. The people are called **Gadarenes** in Mark (and Luke) but "Gergesenes" in Matthew. The discovery of the ruins of Khersa (Gerasa) on the lake shore disproved these claims because this location was in close enough proximity to the larger city of Gadara that a single event could be identified with either place.

2. Mark mentions **a man,** but Matthew reports that there were two. However, Mark does not specifically limit it to one. Probably one stood out as a leader. **With an unclean spirit** means demon possessed.

3. His residence being **among the tombs,** the case was all the more unique. Even if a few tombs were abandoned, no rational person would choose such an environment.

3-4. All hope to bring this man under control had been abandoned. A few times others had tried to **bind him . . . with chains** only to see them broken and the man escape. His strength was supernatural, which can be accounted for by demonic presence. The word **tame** (Gr *damazō*) is better translated "subdue."

5. The demon had so affected the man's mental faculties that he had been **cutting himself.** This plus his continuous outcries must have kept people away from the area.

6. Although the Greek word *proskuneō* may mean **worshipped,** here it speaks of the more literal translation, "bowed down before Him." (For more about this approach, see R. Lenski, *St. Mark's Gospel,* p. 207).

7. See the discussion on 1:24 regarding the demon's outcry.

9. The demon's name, **Legion,** stresses the numerous spirits involved. A Roman legion consisted of six thousand soldiers, but this is used metaphorically. The New Testament often relates the seriousness of a problem to the number of demons at work (Mk 16:9; Mt 12:43; etc.).

11-13. That Jesus allowed the unclean spirits to enter the **swine** may be explained by two factors: First, it is better to have them away from their human victims, even if they do attack animals. And more importantly, pigs were unclean in the Old Testament law (Lev 11:7).

15-17. The response of the Gadarenes was typically human; they were afraid of the unknown. Fear had existed before because of the demoniac, but as long as he remained in his own domain, they could live with it. When Jesus restored the man, however, his radical change caused confusion and **they began to pray him to depart.** They preferred the status quo, where everything could be explained by natural means. Admittedly Jesus' apostles were frightened by their Master's supernatural powers (4:41), but they also believed and followed.

18-19. Naturally the liberated man wished to be **with him,** to listen at his feet, to observe every action, to express his gratitude, but even commendable desires are not always His will. The Lord sent him back to his family and relatives to testify of God's grace in his life. What greater way could the gospel reach them, for they must have known all too well of their relative's condition.

20. The former demoniac went beyond the call of duty. He undoubtedly made an immediate visit to his friends and relatives, but he was so enthusiastic about what Christ had done he shared his story with everyone he met. **Decapolis** (Gr *deka,* ten and *polis,* city) refers to an area of ten cities southeast of the Sea of Galilee.

E. Two Unique Miracles. 5:21-43.

21. Much people gathered unto him. Jesus' popularity had grown to such an extent that wherever He traveled word quickly spread and the crowds clustered.

22. Mark singles out **one of the rulers of the synagogue, Jairus.** The above description (Gr *archisynagōgos*) refers to a synagogue official who maintains the physical needs.

23. The despair felt by Jairus is evident in the narration. He calls his child **little daughter** (Gr *thygatrion*), connoting special endearment.

24. The scene exhibits the Lord's patience. Jesus walked away with Jairus and the people **thronged him,** continuously pressing toward Him. This word (Gr *synthlibō*) was used of a heavy load weighing upon a beast of burden.

25-26. The woman with the hemorrhage (AV, **issue of blood)** not only had the condition twelve years, but time and again endured painful treatments by many physicians. The doctors were unsuccessful, in fact the hemorrhage grew worse.

29. The years of suffering and worry ended in a single act. **Straightway** she was healed and she knew it.

30. Jesus' power (Gr *dynamis;* AV, **virtue)** never was released without His knowledge and will. It was not a magical touch that caused healing. Many sick people had touched Him, but this particular woman was healed because Jesus permitted His power to deliver her. **Turned him about in the press** means that He turned around in the crowd.

31. The reason the Lord asked the question was to allow the woman to confess her act.

33-34. The importance of direct communication with God is accentuated, because experiencing God's power is not as vital as knowing Him. The woman could walk away not only with a restored body, but with His words of peace ringing in her heart.

35. Master (Gr *didaskalos*) means teacher.

36. To reassure Jairus after the tragic announcement Jesus said, **Be not afraid, only believe,** the Greek tense of the prohibition actually meaning, "Stop being afraid."

37. Often **Peter** and **James** and **John** are referred to as the "inner circle" because they were occasionally included in situations where no others were allowed. The phrase, **the brother of James,** suggests that John was the less prominent of the two.

38. The scene typifies an ancient Jewish wake, where outward expression was a sign of deep remorse.

39. When Jesus stated that the child only **sleepeth,** He did not mean that she was not actually dead (Lk 8:55), but that she soon would be aroused as if she had been sleeping.

40. They laughed him to scorn (Gr *katagelaō*): they intended to ridicule Him, but His only reaction was to dismiss them.

43. Why did Jesus prohibit them from sharing the news of this miracle? Since opposition to Him had already grown from the religious leaders, raising a dead person might have terminated His ministry too early. Furthermore, He limited some of His greatest miracles to the witness of only a chosen few (Mk 9:2).

F. Home Town Response. 6:1-6.

6:1. His own country was His home town, Nazareth.

2-3. Doubts about Jesus erupted from those who could never accept Him as more than a **carpenter.** Facts about His family seemed to confirm their judgment. Among the four half-brothers of Christ, two are well known. James presided over the Jerusalem church and wrote the book bearing His name, and Judas or Jude wrote the last New Testament epistle. The summary response, **they were offended,** is incredible. He had come to "seek and to save that which was lost" (Lk 19:10), to draw all men to Himself (Jn 12:32), and to provide abundant life (Jn 10:10), and yet those who lived near Him the longest "stumbled" (Gr *skanalizō*) before His presence.

4. The proverbial statement, **a prophet is not without honour, but in his own country,** explains why pastors often find the least acceptance as leaders among their own family and friends.

5. By definition God's omnipotence cannot be limited. When Mark said the God-man **could there do no mighty work,** the repression was self-imposed, based upon His own principles and volition. Furthermore, if God cannot work where there is no faith, then He will act when a person genuinely trusts Him.

6. He marvelled. The Greek verb being in the imperfect tense, indicates continuous action. As His former neighbors continued to respond with questions full of doubt, He kept on marvelling at their lack of faith.

G. Activities, Pressures and Rest. 6:7-56.

7. Jesus broadened His ministry by sending out teams to preach, to heal and to cast out demons. They were sent **by two and two,** a practice which was recommended in the Old Testament (Eccl 4:9).

11. Degrees of judgment parallel the measure of revelation. **It shall be more**

tolerable for Sodom and Gomorrha, because they did not have the opportunity to witness any miracle-working apostle.

12-13. And they went out and preached that men should repent. The same message had been preached by John the Baptist and by our Lord himself, and now it was preached by the Apostles. The message was confirmed by genuine miracles.

1. The death of John the Baptist. 6:14-30.

14. King Herod, actually a tetrarch, was Herod Antipas, second son of Herod the Great (Mt 2:1; Lk 1:5). (For more background of this family, see J. A. Alexander, *Commentary on the Gospel of Mark,* pp. 151-152.)

Since John the Baptist played such an important role in Jesus' ministry, Mark felt compelled to include the account of his death. Also, the political scene was often overlooked, but here the governing official's reaction allows the reader to view another side of the story.

20. The secular world during the New Testament era was filled with mysticism and superstition. Thus, even though Herod did not understand his message, he **feared John.** Recognizing his dedicated life style, he was reluctant to harm John lest God be vengeful.

23. Note the absurdity of this rash promise: **Whatsoever thou shalt ask of me, I will give it thee, unto the half of my kingdom.** "Herod was not a king and did not possess a kingdom; the tetrarchy he ruled he did not rule in his own right but under the Roman emperor. It was not in his power to give the half or any part of it to whom he pleased " (R. Lenski, *St Mark's Gospel,* p. 255).

24. Unto her mother. Children naturally look to their parents for guidance, but this unfortunate girl had a mother who not only was ungodly herself, but who did not hesitate to involve her daughter in her depraved plan.

25. For the sake of an unscriptural oath (Lev 5:4) and Herod's audience, one of the greatest men who ever lived was murdered.

2. Pressures. 6:31-36.

32-33. Slipping aside from the crowds, Jesus and the apostles acquired a boat and embarked for a private place. Once they were offshore some noticed the boat and **many knew Him.** The word **knew** (Gr *epiginōskō*) means "recognized," and since **him** is not found in the better Greek manuscripts, "them" could have been supplied just as easily.

Verse 33 should then begin, "A great many people saw them leaving and recognized them, so that they ran on foot . . . ."

34. Tired and hungry Jesus could easily have been disturbed by their persistence; His response is incredible! He **was moved with compassion.**

36. Perhaps the apostles had a selfish motive when they asked Jesus to dismiss the crowds, **for they have nothing to eat.** Verse 31 would indicate that they themselves had greater hunger.

3. Feeding the five thousand. 6:37-44.

37. Hungry and tired, Jesus appeared as other men, but suddenly the supernatural erupted. **Give ye them to eat** was a command to do the impossible.

38-44. The details remove all possibility of minimizing the event as something less than miraculous:

  a. The materials: five loaves, two fish.
  b. The audience: very organized (unusual stories could understandably result from a chaotic situation).
  c. The leftovers: twelve baskets (no one could claim that the people ate little because the food was scarce).

d. The number of people: **five thousand men** (Gr *anēr*) definitely refers to adult males. The generic term (Gr *anthrōpos*) is not used here.

46. Verse 31 indicated that He wanted to rest, but here He feels an urgency to **pray.**

49-52. Jesus demonstrated His power not simply in order to aid the disciples, for He could have uttered an effective command from shore. This miracle aimed at confirming His identity. The apostles reacted **beyond measure.** The fact that they **considered not the miracle of the loaves** points to their reluctance to accept Jesus as God. They viewed His miracles as divine interventions upon His life.

4. Reception at Gennesaret. 6:53-56.

53. Gennesaret is located on the western shore of Galilee south of Capernaum and north of Tiberius and was well known for its fertile soil.

54-56. The enthusiasm displayed by these people was probably due to their close proximity to Capernaum, which functioned as a headquarters for the Lord. The news of miraculous healings continuously spread through their neighborhoods, and one day, unannounced, the Healer arrived. People hurried to their sick relatives and friends to bear them before His presence. So frantically was this performed that **whithersoever** He turned He met people with infirmities.

H. Pharisees and tradition. 7:1-23.

7:1. The Pharisees, and certain of the Scribes were undoubtedly sent by the nation's religious leaders **from Jerusalem** to observe and record any unlawful activity or teaching.

2. Mark 6:31 states that Jesus and His assistants were so busy that they often skipped meals. When they had time to eat, these "religious authorities" observed a breach of the law, eating with **unwashen hands.** Their

fanaticism is apparent because their negative attitudes, seizing an insignificant detail of tradition, completely overlooked the laborious service that was rendered.

3. The apostles were characterized by their involvement in serving people; the Pharisees by their pertinacious adherence to Jewish law and custom. **Holding** is an intense expression which infers a strong, tight grasp as a hawk would seize its prey. **Tradition** (Gr *paradosis*) comes from two words which mean "to give alongside of." Thus, Jewish tradition is men's statutes set alongside of God's law. It is not the law, but has been accepted and taught with equal authority.

5-6. Although it may appear that Jesus ignored their question, He actually strikes at the heart of the issue with such directness that they are offended. Why not keep tradition? Because **you** who practice it are just role playing. **Hypocrites** (Gr *hypokrites*) originally referred to someone who acted in the theatre. They were merely imitating true spirituality. Their conception of religion was false because it was based upon outward conformity to a set of rules.

8-9. Usually when man affixes tradition alongside of inspired truth he centers his attention so much upon what is added that the original is neglected. **Full well** (Gr *kalōs*) is idiomatic as in "that's just great!" The Lord used sarcasm to reaffirm the folly of their conduct.

10-13. These verses present an example of how their tradition nullified the law. The precept, **Honor thy father and thy mother,** which included "honoring" by financial support, is among the Ten Commandments (Ex 20:12). It became customary for supposedly pious Jews to claim that their funds were already designated as a **gift** to God, when they were confronted with their parents' need. More than that, a Pharisee could impose a certain amount upon a layman, and if he replied, "But I am obligated to help my mother and father!" he could insist, "You are freed from this commandment, because that money is **corban** (Greek transliteration of Hebrew *qarban,* meaning a gift for God); it is a God-appointed gift for His service."

18-19. Whatsoever . . . entereth refers to food, physical matter which contains no moral significance.

20-23. That which cometh out He interprets as non-physical, anything stemming from the mind or heart. If actions, words, or thoughts originate in an evil, rebellious heart, they certainly must be contrary to God and righteousness.

III. THE MINISTRY BEYOND GALILEE. 7:24-9:50.

At this point in the narrative a new phase in Jesus' ministry begins. Previously He had remained in Galilee or in the vicinity of the Sea of Galilee, but henceforth His travels extend farther, although He limited them to the North.

A. Tyre and Sidon. 7:24-30.

24. Tyre and Sidon were two port cities along the Mediterranean Sea northwest of Galilee, and **borders** refers to the regions or neighboring communities surrounding them. Jesus' intent on this trip was not evangelism. He **would have no man know** that He was present. Perhaps He sought to find solitude after the trying encounter with the Jerusalem delegation.

26. Two words identify the woman. She was **Greek** and **Syrophenician.** The former categorized her as non-Jewish, while the latter indicates the unification of two countries, Syria and Phoenicia. The word **besought** explains the apparent reluctance of Jesus to heed a Gentile. It is a mild word (Gr *erōtaō*) which simply means "asked." He replies by testing the entent of her desire and faith.

27-28. Jesus' illustration of **dogs** is not an expression of contempt for

Greeks. He is merely putting a test before her.

29. For this saying. Her words proved her heart attitude, and her request was granted. **Devil** (Gr *daimonion*) should be "demon."

30. The verb in the clause, **her daughter laid upon the bed,** does not adequately express the force involved. The Greek perfect passive may indicate she had been thrown upon the bed, the demon committing his last violent act before his departure.

B. Decapolis. 7:31-8:9.

31. From Phoenicia Christ journeyed southeast of the Sea of Galilee to **Decapolis,** the region of "ten cities."

1. A deaf-mute healed. 7:32-37.

33. Why did Jesus resort to this healing procedure when a word could do all that was necessary? It seems that He responded to people's attitudes and requests accordingly. Here they asked Him to touch the deaf-mute, so He obliged.

35. The **string** (Gr *desmos*) of his tongue is that which binds the physical member, preventing clear speech. The noun is translated "fetter" or "bond" when describing the instrument which restrains a prisoner.

36. Tell no man. See comments on Mark 5:43 regarding these instructions.

2. Feeding the four thousand. 8:1-9.

8:1. Notice that **Jesus called his disciples,** but prior to the previous feeding of the five thousand they had worriedly approached him about the need for food (Mk 6:35-36). Their faith had grown.

2-3. The bulk of these followers were from Decapolis, where Jesus was ministering (7:31), although some **came from far.** The latter perhaps had followed Him from Tyre and Sidon (7:31). Their desire to be with Him surpassed their feelings of hunger, for they had fasted **three days.**

4. The contrast between the need

and the location is emphasized, **From whence . . . here . . . in the wilderness.**

5. Of course the Lord could have created food out of nothing, but He chose to use what was available, even though it appeared insignificantly small.

6-7. As with the previous miraculous feeding the distribution was highly organized (6:39-40).

8. They . . . were filled (Gr *chortazō*). There was enough food for each to eat until his appetite was thoroughly satisfied. In fact, leftovers filled **seven baskets** (Gr *spyris*) which at times were large enough to hold men (Acts 9:25).

9. The number four thousand does not specify men as with the five thousand, so the size of the gathering could have been significantly smaller. Since there are those who attempt to merge the two accounts into one event, the significant differences should be noted: the number of people fed, the place, the time, the numbers of fish, loaves and baskets.

C. Passing through Galilee. 8:10-26.

1. The trip to Dalmanutha. 8:10-13.

10. The location of **Dalmanutha** is unknown, although the context implies it is on the western side of the Sea of Galilee. The parallel passage in Matthew (Mt 15:39) calls it Magdala.

11. The Pharisees' approach to Jesus had an apparent motive, **seeking of him a sign,** but they actually came **tempting him.** Their appeal implied that Jesus' previous miracles were insufficient evidence that He was of God.

12. Matthew 13:58 sets forth a principle which relates the Lord's response to this religious party, "He did not many mighty works there because of their unbelief."

2. The leaven of the Pharisees. 8:14-21.

15. Take heed, beware literally means "Continue taking heed, keep watching," because both imperatives are in the Greek present tense. **Leaven,** or yeast, is a substance which ferments in order to produce its effect and spreads throughout every fiber of the dough. The diffusion of this souring substance illustrates an evil quality of false teachers. The **Pharisees** and **Herod** seem to be an odd combination. Matthew unites the Pharisees and the Sadducees (Mt 16:6) with a common leaven. If Herod belonged to the Sadducee sect, as many scholars believe, the common denominator would be their attachment to false religion.

22. In **Bethsaida,** a coastal city on the northeast point of Galilee, a certain party led a blind man to Jesus.

23-25. This miracle is unique because most of Jesus' supernatural acts occurred in a single word or touch. **He put his hands again upon his eyes,** in order to bestow perfect vision.

26. Jesus wanted as little publicity as possible. Besides the direct command here, verse 23 explains that He led the blind man outside the town before He healed him.

D. Caesarea Philippi. 8:27-9:1.

27. Caesarea Philippi lay north and slightly east of the Sea of Galilee, approximately the same distance from it as from Tyre. The first half of the name, obviously referring to Caesar, was common. The latter half distinguished it from the coastal city, Caesarea, by identifying it as a part of Philip's realm. Jesus' inquiry, **Whom do men say that I am,** introduced the more direct question which followed.

28. The response was that of the masses rather than the religious leaders, who claimed that He was a messenger of the devil (Mk 3:22).

29. In Greek **ye** is emphatic; it was their conclusion about His person that was the issue. Peter retorted without any hesitation, **Thou art the Christ.** The Greek *Christos* comes from the word which means "to annoint," the "annointed one" being the Messiah (Heb *Mashiac*). Matthew adds to this title "the Son of the living God" (Mt 16:16). Although the apostles seemed to recognize His true identity, confusion remained because like other Jews they were looking for a military leader.

31. This verse marks a turning point in the book. If there had existed hopes for an earthly kingdom established by Christ, they were now dismissed, because at this point **he began to teach them** of His suffering, rejection, death, and resurrection.

32-33. Jesus' announcement was made **openly** but Peter led Him aside to **rebuke** Him. The impulsive apostle cringed in unbelief at what he heard, and he quickly let it be known that he was unwilling to accept it. The harsh statement, **Get thee behind me, Satan,** arose because the attempt to sway Christ from God's plan of salvation made him a tempter of the worst sort. Peter did not **savour** or set his mind on the things of God, but rather on what his finite wisdom deemed best.

34. The disciples believed and yet they misunderstood Christ's plan. Therefore, He set forth some basic principles that explain the real meaning of life. **Deny himself.** Asceticism has its end in itself, but the type of self-denial proposed here aims to give the Lord Jesus Christ the preeminence. He Himself said, "Not my will, but thine be done" (Mt 26:39). Although self-denial means giving up one's rights, God does not usually require abandonment of personal property.

35-37. What a man attempts to save or gain, he ultimately will lose. On the other hand, if one loses all for the sake of Christ and the gospel he actually is preserving his life.

38. A man may speak boldly and candidly among friends. The test of character for a Christian comes when he must stand for Christ in the midst of **adulterous** and **sinful** men. The Lord's day will come, but do our lives demonstrate that we really believe it now?

9:1. This verse belongs at the end of chapter 8; it is the final statement in Christ's lecture about self-denial. Although He had just emphasized the spiritual over the physical, men seek and need physical evidence. Thus, it is promised: **some . . . here, . . . shall not taste of death, till they have seen the kingdom of God come with power.** Various interpretations have been offered regarding this statement. Since the transfiguration occurs next in the narration, that event probably symbolizes His coming with power because of the outward glory revealed.

E. Mount of Transfiguration. 9:2-29.

2. Peter and James and John, Jesus' closest companions, consisted of what is often called the "inner circle." The high mountain perhaps refers to Mt. Hermon, the highest in the vicinity of Caesarea Philippi. The word describing His transfiguration (Gr *metamorphoō*) signifies an outward manifestation of an inward change.

3. Although Matthew and Luke's accounts mention Jesus' change in countenance, Mark restricts his comments to the Lord's apparel. A **fuller** was one who professionally cleaned clothing.

4. Elias (Elijah) and **Moses** appeared with Jesus because of their close connection with Him in prophecy. Elijah stands out as the more prominent figure because his ministry more closely correlates with the Messianic advents.

5-6. Peter misjudged in his suggestion primarily because his impulsive nature responded too quickly (Jas 1:19). Although he had just exalted Christ as the Son of the living God, here he placed Him on an equal plain with the two prophets.

7. Jesus' uniqueness is confirmed from heaven: **This is my beloved Son: hear him.**

9. Jesus frequently restricted people from proclaiming His miracles in order to allow God's plan of salvation to be carried out. Had His supernatural identity been revealed, people would not have permitted His death.

11-13. The three apostles became puzzled about Elijah's connection with the Messiah in prophecy. The scribes claimed that **Elijah must first come** (Mal 4:5-6), yet his recent appearance obviously was not before Christ. Jesus agreed with the scribes, but interpreted Elijah's coming spiritually. Verse 13 hints at Elijah's connection with John the Baptist and Matthew 17:13 confirms it.

15. Evidently the crowds were unaware that Jesus was near for when they saw Him **they . . . were greatly amazed** or surprised. **Saluted** means that they "greeted" Him.

17. The petitioner's desperation may be seen by his boldness. Jesus directed a question to the scribes but **one of the multitude** interrupted. **Master** means teacher. **Dumb spirit** may be rendered "a spirit of silence" or "a mute spirit."

18. The youth's problem was more than his inability to speak. The indwelling demon persistently gave him convulsions. Among other things, Jesus had impowered his disciples to cast our demons, but a terse indictment erupted from a despairing father: **they could not,** they did not have the power.

19. Jesus' expression of displeasure against the **faithless generation** was not specifically directed toward one person nor just a small group. The word, **generation,** refers to a whole race. The scribes continued to voice doubts, the disciples could not heal, and the father of the mute son came out of despair, not in genuine faith.

20. Tare means he caused his victim to have convulsions.

21-22. A full description is given of the condition. The length and severity are clearly expressed to dismiss any superficial conclusions that the ailment may have been temporary. The healing could only be interpreted as a miracle.

22b-23. The brief dialogue between the petitioner and the Lord teaches a fundamental principle about obtaining supernatural aid from God. As with this individual, human nature usually approaches God with doubts about His ability: **if thou canst do anything . . . .** But Jesus clarified the issue. The prerequisite for healing never is doubtful on God's part, only on man's. **If thou canst believe, all things are possible.**

24-27. The man, recognizing the burden laid upon him, confessed his imperfect faith: **Lord, I believe; help thou mine unbelief.** He longed for stronger faith, and God granted his request, not because He saw mature faith, but because He honored his desire for growth.

28-29. Jesus' answer to the question, **Why could we not cast him out,** is written three ways: (1) verse 29 says **by prayer and fasting;** (2) a few manuscripts including those on which the AV is based add **fasting;** and (3) Matthew records that the reason for failure was "unbelief," which a brief illustration about mustard seed type faith following (Mt 17:20). The two accounts harmonize for if a person seeks God in a season of prayer, faith will result. Mark and Matthew simply chose different emphases.

F. The Secret Trip through Galilee. 9:30-50.

30-32. The Lord Jesus knew that soon He would depart for Jerusalem (10:1). The final phase of His earthly ministry was drawing near. Therefore, this trip through Galilee was reserved for the edification of His disciples. Again He taught them about His death and resurrection, but they **understood not.** In fact, Matthew notes, "they were exceeding sorry" (Mt 17:23).

33-34. After they entered their house in Capernaum, Jesus asked the Twelve what they had been discussing on the journey. Apparently they felt guilty, for **they held their peace.** Even though no one answered, He began a discourse on the very subject that they had been disputing.

35-37. Humility characterizes those who genuinely **desire** to serve Christ and His kingdom. A disciple should esteem himself as a **servant** (Gr *diakonos*), one who willingly attends to menial tasks and eagerly receives children without recognition or reward.

38-40. John's experience occasioned an injunction against judging. The expression **He that is not against us is on our part,** often is exaggerated to opposite extremes. II John 10-11 exhorts Christians to guard against fellowship which condones false teaching, and yet we must be careful not to distort this command so as to foster spiritual cliques.

42. To **offend** (cause to stumble) **one of these little ones** is so serious that immediate death would be better than further involvement, and thus, greater · judgment. A **millstone** refers to a large stone used in a mill for grinding, this particular type being large enough to require a donkey to move it.

43-48. Jesus used a hyperbole to impress His listeners with the gravity of sin. It would be better to sever a member of the body than to keep it and go to **hell.** It is obvious, however, that the real problem lies in the heart and mind. The word translated **hell** (Gr *geennan*) is a transliteration of Hebrew, and means the "valley of Hinnom." Lying to the south of Jerusalem, it was used as a rubbage heap and gradually adopted a spiritual application. Fires burned continuously and worms multiplied throughout the debris. Thus the statement, **their worm dieth not and the fire is not quenched,** illustrates the eternal destruction of those who have not received the Saviour.

49-50. These concluding statements stand as a warning to would-be offenders. Lest one follows an unrepenting road to hell, **everyone shall be salted with fire,** that is, a certain amount of affliction befalls everyone in order to stir them toward God. This kind of fire acts

as **salt.** It takes something insignificant and adds meaning. On the other hand, if salt has **lost his saltness,** it becomes ineffective and even tribulation may not turn the sinner from his way. The last clause must be related to both the ideas which preceded. **Have salt** could be paraphrased, "Receive God's providential lessons" and **have peace** refers to their dispute over who was greatest.

IV. THE CONCLUDING MINISTRY. 10:1-13:37.

A. Paeraea (beyond Jordan). 10:1-31.

10:1. Although the other Gospel writers tell us that Jesus made former trips to the South, this one toward Jerusalem marks a definite break in Mark's narrative. The only other time Jesus journeyed south in Mark's account was for baptism, but at this point Jesus' departure from the North was permanent.

1. The discourse on divorce. 10:2-12.

3-8. The reference to Moses demonstrates Christ's authority over the Old Testament. Although Moses permitted divorce (Deut 24:1), it was allowed because of the people's **hardness of heart.** Jesus, however, proclaimed God's perfect and ideal plan: **they twain shall be one flesh.**

10-12. After they had left the Pharisees and had found some privacy, the disciples sought a clearer statement about divorce. Anyone who divorces his or her mate, Jesus replied, and marries another is committing adultery. Elsewhere He added an exception: "save for fornication" (Mt 5:32 and 19:9).

2. Jesus' attitude toward children. 10:13-16.

13. People commonly brought their sick friends and relatives to Jesus for healing, but on this occasion some **brought young children.** The disciples failed to see the potential that their

Master did. He not only observed what men were, but what by the grace of God they could be.

14-15. Of such is the kingdom of God. A child does not become distracted by all the complexities of life. When he trusts, his faith is simple and unwavering. In fact, to possess salvation one must become **as a little child.**

3. The rich young ruler. 10:17-22.

18. Jesus' reply, **Why callest thou me good,** does not deny that He is God. Many passages clearly state that He is God (Jn 1:1; Phil 2:6; Tit 2:13; Heb 1:8), and He Himself claims so (Jn 8:58; 10:30; 11:25). The response here is aimed at the young ruler's attitude toward himself. Verse 20 indicates that he considered himself to be good. Jesus wanted him to know of whom that adjective should be exclusively used.

19-21. The burden of keeping the whole law (Jas 2:10) was overbearing, yet this man claims adherence to its demands. As if those laws were not enough, Jesus adds to them, **sell whatsoever thou hast and give . . . .**

22. This was too much; he **went away grieved.**

Does this story teach that salvation is merited by good works? One must remember that prior to the acceptance of the gospel a man needs to recognize his need. Jesus was aware of the man's self-righteous attitude, trusting in his observance of rules. Therefore, his need was for Christ to point out **one thing thou lackest.** Men must be cognizant of their sin and guilt before they can be ready for "good news."

4. The perils of riches. 10:23-27.

23-24. It is almost impossible to find an extremely wealthy person who is not trusting in his riches.

25-27. Verse 25 imagines an impossible act, and verse 27 reassures the bewildered apostles: **with God all things are possible.** There is an inference of salvation by grace. The Lord

will make possible through Christ's death what man cannot do in himself.

28-30. Peter's claim, **we have left all,** may have been true, but it also reveals pride. Graciously, Jesus responds with a promise; whoever forsakes his life for the gospel will receive incomparable rewards. Since the relationships refer to spiritual ones in God's family, the things mentioned may speak of new homes opened in Christian hospitality as well as personal physical blessings.

B. On the Way to Jerusalem. 10:32-52.

1. On the road. 10:32-34.

32. They were afraid. Because they were going toward **Jerusalem,** they sensed impending doom.

33-34. Knowing their feelings, Jesus predicted what would happen to Him in greater detail than ever before.

2. James' and John's request.
   10:35-46.

37. The petition exposes the instability of the apostles. They did not understand the salvation which was about to be accomplished, nor its implication on their life styles. Notice how contrary this desire is to Jesus' recent discourse on humility (Mk 9:33-35).

38-39. The display of ignorance continues, for instead of admitting their frailty, they claimed ability to partake of the Lord's **cup** and **baptism.** Kindly, Jesus refrains from rebuking them.

40. God will reward His servants according to faithfulness. A postion in heaven is granted, not upon request, but **for whom it is prepared,** based on faithful service.

42-44. The **Gentiles'** system of success (that of the secular world) is based on "getting ahead of the other guy." The philosophy of Christ refutes this. Christians are to serve and help others, to be other-centered and not self-centered.

45. The greatest example of this philosophy is our Lord Himself. He came **not to be ministered unto, but to minister.** The verb (Gr *diakoneō*) means to serve as an attendant, to wait on tables. The greatest service the Lord Jesus Christ could ever render for man was **to give his life a ransom for many.** He had foretold His death and resurrection several times, but this occasion bore special significance, because He interpreted His death. The impending doom would lead to ultimate victory. The **ransom** would be paid; slaves of sin set free. The last three words of this phrase merit individual treatment. **Ransom** (Gr *lytron*) signifies a loosing, debtors freed. **For** (Gr *anti*) specifically means "in behalf of" indicating a substitutionary death; He died in our place. **Many** simply emphasized a contrast in number: one person died, the ransom is paid for many.

3. In Jericho. 10:46-52.

46. Jericho was the "City of Palms," located just a few miles from the Jordan River.

47. Since **Jesus** was a rather common name, the phrase **of Nazareth** (literally, the Nazarene) clearly identified Him. Remarkably, Bartimaeus addressed Him as **Son of David,** aware of Jesus' ancestry and right to the Davidic throne.

48. The imperfect tense is employed in the Greek verb, stressing continuous action. They were attempting to silence this annoying cry, but he began calling even louder.

49-51. Jesus responded differently, **commanded him to be called,** because He preceived the man's need and his faith.

52. In reality it was the power of God that healed, but the man's faith was the channel by which that strength could flow.

C. Near Jerusalem. 11:1-13:37.

1. The triumphal entry. 11:1-11.

11:1. Bethphage and Bethany were very near Jerusalem, located on the opposite side of the Mount of Olives.

2. Jesus' knowledge of the animal's presence, **ye shall find a colt,** assumes that previous contact had been made with the owner (see the next verse). Its description, **whereon never man sat,** relates to a custom from the Old Testament (Deut 21:3; I Sam 6:7), which specifies that animals to be used for certain religious rites must not have previously been ridden, burdened, or harnessed for labor.

3. The statement, **the Lord hath need of him,** presupposes that the owners of the colt knew and wanted to obey Christ. It is possible, but very doubtful, that Jesus would have supernaturally imparted such a reaction.

7. Their garments refer to the long, thin outer robes. Zechariah 9:9 foresaw this event.

9-10. The jubilant exclamation exalted Jesus as "one who comes" or "the coming one," a Jewish title used for Messiah. The Hebrew equivalent of **hosanna** means "grant salvation," but here it signifies little more than an emotional expression. The people were expecting an earthly kingdom to be established, **the kingdom of our father David.** Their cry includes quotes from Psalm 118:25-26 and was chanted customarily at the Passover celebrations.

11. Mark is very brief, but Matthew informs us that Jesus healed many and had an encounter with the chief priests and scribes (Mt 21:14-15).

2. Bethany. 11:12-26.

12. The morrow would have been Monday of the passion week, the day after Palm Sunday. The expression, **he was hungry,** is one among many that proves Christ's humanity. The Second Person of the Trinity was a genuine man and felt the same physical needs as we do.

13. The normal order of growth in fig trees was that the fruit preceded the leaves. Therefore, the **leaves** presented a false picture, that fruit not only was present, but it was large and ripe.

14. Jesus' curse upon the fruitless tree was not the result of a quick temper; He used the occasion as an object lesson against hypocrisy and misrepresenting the truth.

15-16. The close proximity of the curse and the cleansing was not accidental. Jesus displayed His feelings toward false claims through the fig tree, and those businesses in the temple undoubtedly professed to be helping worshippers by making objects of sacrifice available. Jesus recognized that their real motive was greed.

17. The quote from Isaiah 56:7 significantly includes **of all nations.** God's house is revered even by Gentiles as a place of prayer. What would visitors think of the temple with such a worldly market within its gates? Even more important, how would they view the God of such a religion?

18. The religious leaders hated Jesus for His indictments against their hypocrisy, but here they began to conspire as a result of jealousy over His popularity as a teacher.

20. In the morning was Tuesday of the passion week.

21-22. The cursing of the fig tree is given a spiritual application. By faith this tree was destroyed; all things are possible if you **Have faith in God.**

23-24. The Lord's illustration is extreme so that it may dismiss all excuses which limit the faith principle. What could be more difficult than a mountain being **removed** and **cast into the sea?**

25-26. The request for forgiveness, besides needing faith as with other petitions, requires a willingness to forgive others. **Trespasses** (Gr *paraptōma*) are offenses, false steps, or blunders.

3. Jerusalem. 11:27-12:44.

27-28. The chief priests and the scribes and the elders came to Christ in an official capacity putting forth the question regarding His authority, which was the paramount issue between them.

30-33. These leaders were not men of principle, for they considered answering Jesus' question according to popular response and not by conviction. Since either of the possible answers would create a negative reaction, they remained silent, claiming ignorance. Jesus, however, was straightforward, **Neither do I tell you.**

12:1. Christ used parables constantly in His ministry. He **began** to do so here with the prominent Jewish leaders. **Hedge** (Gr *phragmos*) means fence, probably a stone wall. The **winevat** (Gr *hypolēnion*) was a receptacle below the winepress, into which the grape juice flowed through a wooden grate. The **tower** was erected to provide a safe storage area. **Let it out** (Gr *ekdidōmi*) may be translated "rented it" or "leased it." All these details are listed to suggest the thorough business manner of the owner.

2. At the season, the time of harvest, the owner sent for the rental price which was paid not in cash, but **of the fruit.**

3-5. Many servants were sent to these vine-growers to collect the owner's share. None accomplished his mission. In fact, they were beaten, mistreated, and some even murdered. It seems hardly possible that a landowner would continue to send small parties when he could have sent a large band to forcibly take the land, or that servants would obey such dangerous orders. These facts not only are included for the purposes of the story, but they illustrate God's long-suffering with His people in the Old Testament.

6. The **son** obviously represents Jesus Christ Himself. The attitude with which the Jews should have accepted Him is expressed in the statement: **They will reverence my son.** However, God's eternal purpose was to send His Son to die for our sins. (I Jn 2:2).

7-9. The ultimate act of violence, the slaying of the son, brought swift and final judgment upon those greedy men. Likewise, God endured the rebellious actions of His people for centuries. Their leaders had drifted so far from the truth that when the Son of God appeared, they rejected and murdered Him.

10-11. Psalm 118:22-23 is here fulfilled. The picture of a building parallels that of the church, of which Christ is **head.**

13. They (chief priests, scribes, and elders; Mk 11:27), having determined to destroy the Son, sent some **Pharisees** (2:16) and **Herodians** (3:6) to trap Him by something they might get Him to say.

14. The delegation introduced a "loaded" question, cleverly attempting to influence the way He answered. **Carest for no man** means not partial to any man (not even to the highest person in government). They wanted His answer to declare or imply disloyalty to Rome. **Teachest the way of God in truth** does not express their conviction, but hoped to appeal to Jesus' integrity. They judged that if He answered honestly, He would be "caught" by His own words.

15. Denarius (Gr *dēnarion*) was the actual name of the coin called **penny.**

16-17. The Lord's question draws their attention to Caesar by the **image** and **inscription.** However, the principle that He sets forth calls for obedience to both the government (Rom 13) and God in their respective areas. **Render** (Gr *apodidōmi*) does not limit the expectation to paying tribute as in verse 14. It means "to pay back in full" whatever is owed. The word **image** suggests a further idea. Although the coin bore Caesar's image which pointed to his authority, man himself was created in God's image (Gen 1:26). Therefore, the picture was an image of Caesar immediately, but of God ultimately, implying that the emperor's authority is under divine sovereignty.

18. The **Sadducees** were a religious party, like the Pharisees, but differed from them in their liberal interpretation of the Scriptures. A foremost example of their liberal teaching is mentioned here, **they say there is no resurrection.** They recognized the fact of the doctrine of the resurrection in the Old Testament, but they refused to accept it literally.

19. Deuteronomy 25:5 is the passage referred to. **Raise up seed** (offspring) expresses a practice of levirate marriage whereby a brother of a childless, deceased man would marry the widow and rear children, designating the firstborn as the legal descendant of his brother.

20-23. The story obviously was an invention aimed at exposing the absurdity of relationships after the resurrection. If there really were a resurrection, they conjectured, seven men would be married to one woman in heaven.

24. The Sadducees' question reveals their unbelief in two fundamental areas: the Scriptures and God's power. Surprisingly, these men held prominent positions among the chosen people, yet did not recognize how foundational the resurrection was in Old Testament doctrine and living. Their problem began with the denial of the supernatural, **the power of God.**

25. The change which transpires in man from earth to heaven is extreme: **they neither marry nor are given in marriage: but are as the angels which are in heaven.**

28. One of the scribes. A scribe was a professional interpreter of the Old Testament.

29-30. Jesus quotes what is termed the "shema" from Deuteronomy 6:4-5; **Hear,** the first word in the Old Testament passage being *shamac* in

Hebrew. The distinctive feature of ancient Judaism was that it held to monotheism among predominantly polytheistic cultures. In fact, "going after other gods" was one of the greatest sins. **Love the Lord thy God with all thy heart and with all thy soul and with all thy mind and with all thy strength.** The multiplicity of words emphasizes the thoroughness and fervency that our love for God should embrace.

31. The second commandment (Lev 19:18) fittingly joins the first, because genuine love for God naturally results in a love for others. "On these two commandments hangeth the whole law and the prophets" (Mt 22:40).

33-34. The scribe's response shows deep insight. **To love . . . is more than . . . .** The man recognized that loving God must be the foundation of any worthwhile service or sacrifice.

35-37. After numerous questions, Jesus reversed the situation by asking them one. It deals with David's relationship to the Messiah, **Christ.** He is both David's **Lord** and **son.** How could this be possible? The **scribes** remained silent, but the answer was not the issue anyhow. Jesus merely wanted to reveal that even the knowledgeable scribes with all their questions had their limits. The New Testament describes Christ as God-man; as incarnate God He was David's Lord; as man He was born in his line. **Son** means descendant.

38. Long clothing customarily was worn by distinguished persons for special occasions. **Salutations** or greetings were not simply acts of friendly courtesy; they loved recognition for their high positions.

40. Their love for praise paralleled their greed for money. **Widows** needing assistance to administer their estates often turned to "spiritual" leaders. Scribes gladly aided, managing a contrived plan for their own personal gain. **For a pretense** or "for appearance sake" declares the motive of **long prayers. Greater damnation**

(judgment) results from this hypocrisy; it also tells us that there will be degrees of punishment.

41. The treasury speaks of an area where thirteen receptacles were placed to receive offerings and taxes for the temple.

42. Two mites (Gr *lepton*) **which make a farthing** (Gr *kodrantēs*); approximately one fortieth of a penny (Gr *dēnarion*) (Mk 12:15). Thus, the gift was very small. Amazingly, she did not keep one coin.

43-44. The amount of an offering does not always signify the measure of love of the one who gives. Often a more important factor is what is held back. **She of her want** (poverty) **did cast in all,** everything she needed to live by.

4. Mount of Olives. 13:1-37.

13:1. The disciples' interest in the attractive stones and buildings did not arise from aesthetic appreciation only. Matthew's account of the afternoon's events includes a significant statement just prior to their exit from the temple: "Behold your house is left unto you desolate" (Mt 23:38 as quoted from Jer 12:7). Thus, they probably wondered why such beautiful buildings would be abandoned.

2. Jesus prophesied the thorough destruction of these edifices. **There shall not be left one stone upon another.** The Greek emphatic negative construction, has the idea "by no means" or "never."

3-4. Although the city of Jerusalem and its temple were destroyed by Titus in A.D. 70 the apostles' question initiates a discourse (called the Olivet Discourse because of its location) regarding the events of the Tribulation Period. It is common in prophetic literature to predict in a single message events with both contemporary and eschatological fulfillments (Ezk 28; Isa 7:14).

5-6. One characteristic that marks

the end of this age is the rise of many impostors. Even though the word **Christ** is supplied in the AV, the previous clause identifies their claim to Him, **in my name.**

7-8. Such things must needs be, that is, even these wars come from God's perfect plan. The word **troubles** is not found in some of the oldest manuscripts. **Beginnings** suggests that even worse judgments will follow (Rev 6-9; 16).

9-11. Verse 10 appears parenthetical; world evangelism shall precede these afflictions. Problems in bearing witness are everywhere, but they are a necessary part of God's plan. Under the pressure, disciples may take comfort in the Holy Spirit's special guidance: **for it is not ye that speak, but the Holy Ghost.**

12-13. The extreme cruelty is illustrated not in physical terms but by the destruction of family ties. **He that shall endure unto the end . . . shall be saved** is used to support a good-works gospel. However, the New Testament teaching on this subject dismisses such an interpretation. Romans and Galatians specifically discuss this issue and clearly declare that salvation is based on faith (Rom 1:16; 3:20, 28; 4:3, 16; 5:1; Gal 3:10-14, 23-26). In this passage "one who endures" speaks of a genuine believer who perseveres to the end of his life. **Be saved** should be taken in a spiritual sense; it does not merely mean one will be delivered from earthly trials.

14. The abomination of desolation, meaning the abomination that desolates or appalls (Dan 12:1), has been applied to ancient events. Many Jews thought that Daniel's prophecy was fulfilled in 186 B.C. when Antiochus Epiphanes, the king of Syria, erected an idolatrous altar in the temple of Jerusalem and sacrificed a pig thereon to the heathen god Jupiter Olympus. Others believe it referred to the entrance of Roman soldiers into the Holy Place before the destruction of Jerusalem in A.D. 70. Nonetheless, the entire discourse speaks of eschatological events, and the actions of the "man of sin" in II Thessalonians 2 corresponds to this description.

16-20. These verses vividly describe the terror involved; no other tribulation is equal to it, **neither shall be.** It, therefore, must be the Great Tribulation of the book of the Revelation.

21-23. The **false Christs and false prophets** are so persuasive that they would deceive even God's **elect, if it were possible.**

26. Son of man. He who is King of Kings and Lord of Lords returns to judge men as a man.

28-29. The **parable of the fig tree** encourages readiness and alertness. As a blossoming fig tree signifies the nearness of summer, the fulfillment of Jesus' prophecy announces the end of the age.

30. During the first century, **this generation** did undergo the prophecies uttered in a general sense, but their full force awaits the Great Tribulation and Christ's coming in glory. In the latter sense the generation would be speaking of race or nation.

31-32. Jesus' divine and human natures may be observed in these verses. As God, He claimed infinite authority for His words. As man, His "kenosis" (or self-emptying) is stated regarding His knowledge: **neither the Son.**

33. Ye know not when the time is reminds the disciples of their priorities. The imminence of Christ's return should stimulate a new realization of the temporal nature of this life.

34-37. The following illustration aims at the attitudes of **servants.** They receive their orders and are to faithfully perform them until their master returns. Since they **know not when the master of the house cometh,** they must watch (Gr *gregoreō*), a word which specifically implies watching with alertness, staying awake. Unfortunately, disciples often conform to the world's emphasis on the temporal.

V. CHRIST'S DEATH AND RESURRECTION. 14:1-16:20.

A. The Events Preluding His Arrest. 14:1-42.

14:1. The two designations, **the Passover** and **unleavened bread,** refer to the same event which is described in Exodus 12:1-20.

1. Mary anoints Jesus. 14:3-9.

3-5. Although Mark spends little time introducing the occasion, John implies that it was a special celebration in honor of Jesus with Mary, Martha, and Lazarus present. **Simon the leper** bears that title as a testimony to his healing, but that is all we know about him.

The story was included because of the manner by which Mary honored her Lord. The special significance of the anointing was its cost, around **three hundred pence**. A penny (Gr *dēnarion*) was a day's wages and thus the ointment would have sold for close to a year's wages. The statement, **she brake the box**, refers to a jar sealed in a manner which required breakage at the neck, and therefore its contents would be used at one time. **Some** of the disciples viewed this as an unnecessary extravagance.

6-8. Jesus defended her deed. It would have been commendable to give the money to the poor, but she had a better use. **She hath done what she could** to show her love for her Lord.

10-11. Judas' betrayal at least in part was a reaction to Mary's act of reverence. It was he who "held the bag" (acted as treasurer) and regularly pilfered it. His love for money provoked an indignant response when three hundred pence worth of ointment was "wasted" on Jesus. Thus, he sought to **betray**, to give Jesus over to His enemies for just thirty pieces of silver (Gr *argyrion*).

2. Preparation for the Passover. 14:12-16.

12. The question, **"Where . . ."** rather than "should we make preparations" indicates that Jesus and His apostles faithfully participated in this ritual.

13-16. Jesus' instructions are based partially upon His omnipotence. That they would encounter a **man bearing a pitcher** obviously could not have been perceived by human wisdom. On the other hand, He likely had already made arrangements with the **goodman of the house** (Gr *oikodespotēs*), the manager.

19. The translation of their question, **"Is it I?"** would be improved by "It is not I, is it?" for the Greek construction suggests that they expected a negative reply.

20. John's account (Jn 13:24-26) indicates that He actually did not expose Judas by this statement. It merely emphasized the close friendship that the betrayer appeared to have with Christ.

3. The Lord's Supper. 14:22-25.

22-24. This is my body was spoken symbolically, as when He called Himself the Door or the Vine. The **New Testament**, prophesied in Jeremiah 31:31-34, is associated with regeneration (Jer 31:33), for the Mosaic law never provided the way to heaven. "All have sinned and come short of the glory of God" (Rom 3:23). Therefore, a new testament or covenant (Gr *diathēke*) was needed. Jesus' blood was **shed for many**, the word **for** meaning "in behalf of" (Gr *hyper*) which specifies a substitutionary death.

25. Indirectly Jesus informs them that His earthly life is almost over.

4. On the Mount of Olives. 14:26-31.

26. The **hymn** must have been one or more of the Hallel Psalms which was customarily included in the

Passover celebrations (Alfred Edersheim, *The Temple*, p. 223).

27-28. Quoting Zechariah 13:7, the Lord predicted their disloyal flight of escape. Knowing that they would return to their home country, He speaks of His resurrection in specific terms. He would see them **in Galilee.**

29-31. Impulsively **Peter** responded to Christ's prediction in a forceful manner. Instead of defending himself, he might have obeyed the Lord's added command, "Watch ye and pray," in connection with I Corinthians 10:13. Overconfidence often precedes failure. The time, **before the cock crow twice,** refers to the third watch of the night.

5. In the Garden of Gethsemane. 14:32-41.

32. Although the Garden of **Gethsemane** was located on the same mountain, the Mount of Olives, it is mentioned separately as a special place of prayer and privacy for the Lord.

33-34. The inner circle, **Peter and James and John,** observed Jesus' agony. Significantly, it is Luke the physician who adds, "his sweat was as it were great drops of blood. . ." (Lk 22:44). Three expressions picture His inner feelings: (1) **began to be sore amazed,** (2) **to be very heavy,** and (3) **exceeding sorrowful unto death.** The first reveals His initial shock at what was to come; the second, His overwhelming sense of distress; the third describes the extent of His emotions. "Its (the agony) terrors exceeded his anticipations. His human soul received new experience—He learned upon the basis of things suffered (Heb 5:8)" (Kenneth Wuest, *Mark in the Greek New Testament*, p. 264).

35-36. Nowhere else in Scripture can one find a clearer picture of Jesus' humanity. His response to the **hour** lacks none of the emotions that other men would have felt. He, however, refused to allow inner feelings to direct Him, submitting to the Father's plan: **nevertheless not what I will, but what thou wilt.**

38. The command **Watch ye and pray** may be translated "Keep watching and praying . . . ." The spirit is described as **ready** (Gr *prothymos*), willing and eager to serve. Inwardly the disciples desired to keep praying, but fatigue won over their wills.

B. The Arrest and Trials. 14:42-15:14.

43-45. Mark identifies **Judas,** not by Iscariot, but after a fashion which emphasizes how incredible the feat was; he not only was among the followers, but **one of the twelve.** The company he brought included Roman soldiers and temple police, who were sent by the Jewish leaders named. The former carried **swords,** while the latter had **staves** (stout sticks). Judas' greeting was that customary of a disciple to his rabbi: **Master, master; and kissed him.**

46-47. John 18:10 informs us that it was Peter who drew the sword and cut off Malchus' ear.

48-49. The party came out at night with weapons as if Jesus were a violent criminal against whom cunning and force must be applied. He could have been taken easily during the day; He had been teaching in the temple publicly for the past three days. **But the scriptures must be fulfilled** refers to general prophecies of this violent hour.

50. The prediction found in verse 27 comes true.

51-52. This incident appears in Mark's account alone, and since no other purpose for its inclusion can be found, the **young man** was probably the author himself.

1. The trial before the Jewish leaders. 14:53-65.

53. The three groups mentioned along with the **High Priest** comprised the Sanhedrin or "counsel" (vs. 55), an official group of seventy men who held religious and civil authority in Israel. However, during the last forty years before the fall of Jerusalem (A.D. 70) executions were restricted to Roman authorities. That explains why the trial before Pilate followed this one.

55-59. The fundamental purpose of a court's existence is to execute justice, but this dishonorable court only **sought for witness against Jesus to put him to death.** Not succeeding, they resorted to **false witness,** but again they failed.

60-64. The High Priest turned directly to the defendant in hopes of clearer "evidence." While the response to **Answerest thou nothing** causes us to admire Christ's submission, the inquirer actually was seeking a statement of self-condemnation; **he held his peace.**

61-62. Art thou the Christ? Besides His affirmative reply, **I am,** Jesus quotes two Old Testament passages which clearly are Messianic (Ps 110:1 and Dan 7:13).

63-64. The verdict reveals their spiritual ignorance. Jesus' confession should have initiated at least some investigation, and with all the facts, its veracity. Instead, they cried **blasphemy!**

65. The unbelievably foul treatment against the holy Son of God seems worse in that it was commenced by national dignitaries. Isaiah 52:14 predicted hundreds of years before, "his visage was so marred more than any man."

2. Peter's denial. 14:66-72.

66-68. The scene was just outside the palace of the High Priest who was conducting the trial in the upper story. The girl, **one of the maids of the high priest,** noticed Peter and then paused to get a closer look (Gr *emblepō*). Her accusation caught Peter off guard. He who had claimed allegiance even in the face of death quickly disowned his Lord. He then retreated **out into the porch,** a vestibule between the courtyard and the street.

69-71. The pressure increased as accusations continued, and added denials only led to further accusations: **thou art a Galilean and thy speech agreeth thereto.** The Judaeans detected a Galilean accent in Peter's words perhaps as a Georgian could recognize a New Englander. **To curse and to swear** (Gr *anathematizō* and *omnyō*) means Peter took oaths in God's name and called down curses upon himself in the event he was lying.

72. The **cock crew** and its sound immediately reminded Peter of the Lord's prophetic words. Luke adds that "the Lord turned and looked upon Peter" (Lk 22:61) which must have occurred while Jesus was being transferred to a temporary cell. The apostle's reaction, **wept,** pictures an extended time of bitter weeping.

3. The trial before Pilate. 15:1-14.

15:1. The Sanhedrin regathered in the morning to make the trial official and Matthew 27:1 reiterates their singular purpose, "to put him to death." They discussed in detail the charges and how they would present them in order to gain the death sentence.

2. The insidious conspirators charged Christ with rebellion against the government (Lk 23:2), which explains Pilate's question, **Art thou the King of the Jews?** This simple affirmation does not include His detailed response (Jn 18:28-37), where He disassociates His kingdom from this physical and temporal world.

3-5. He answered nothing, "as a sheep before her shearers is dumb, so he openeth not his mouth" (Isa 53:7). Mark's account briefly reports that **Pilate marvelled,** but in John 19:8-12 he is pictured with "fear" attempting to free Jesus.

6-7. The narration of Barabbas' release is introduced by two facts: verse 6 explains the annual custom at the Passover of freeing one prisoner of the people's choice, and verse 7 characterizes Barabbas as an insurrectionist and a murderer.

8. The crowd reminded Pilate of this precedent; they **began to desire**, or more accurately, "to ask" (Gr *aiteō*).

9-10. Pilate hoped the people would choose Jesus because he was beginning to discern the true source of the charges: **the chief priests had delivered him for envy.**

11. Precisely how the **chief priests moved the people** is conjecture, but it probably included special appeals for the rebel as a political and social leader and as a local resident. Conversely, they agitated the crowd against Christ, because He claimed to be God. More than factual evidence, their awesome power and position must have been the determining factors.

12-14. The extent of that influence was incredible for less than a week before the people of this same city had honored Christ in His "triumphal entry."

C. The Crucifixion. 15:15-47.

15. Scourged him (Gr *phargelloō*). The Romans used short-handled whips with many leather lashes. On the ends of the lashes were tied small bits of metal or bone to cruelly rip the victim's flesh. They usually tied the prisoner to a low pillar so that his back was bent forward. This type of punishment would leave deep gashes, often exposing the bones.

16. The **hall** refers to the palace of 14:54 (Gr *aulē*), an open courtyard, which Mark identifies as **Praetorium. Band** (Gr *speira*), sometimes translated "cohort," technically included six hundred men though on occasion was used when the number was much less.

17-20. The "band" was gathered to make a spectacle of their prisoner. The royal color, **purple**, and a crown of needle-like thorns served to mock the king while adding further torture. The **reed**, a royal staff, not only was painful in itself, but also drove the thorns further into His skull. Their abuse continued (imperfect tense in Greek) for some time until they wearied of their sport, and He was led away for execution.

21. The only information about **Simon** is his national origin, **a Cyrenian**, and the names of his sons. Since **Rufus** appears in Romans 16:13, and Mark's Gospel was written in Rome, the readers must have known the two brothers. Some commentators suggest that Simon's experience here eventually led to his conversion. At this time he was not a disciple for they forced (AV, **compel**) him into service.

22. Mark identifies the place of the crucifixion in Aramaic, **Golgotha**, and interprets it as the place of the skull. Two views exist regarding the location: 1. The traditional view, going back to the 4th century, places it at the Church of the Holy Sepulchre and argues that the name arose from the presence of skulls, because it was a place of execution. 2. Gordon's Calvary bases its location on the skull-like appearance of an adjacent cliff and a garden of tombs nearby. The Gospels mark it outside the city, but the location of the ancient walls cannot be conclusively determined, since Jerusalem was destroyed in A.D. 70.

23. They gave, or better, they were going to give (Greek imperfect tense) **wine mingled with myrrh**. The beverage acted as a stupefying drug commonly given to lessen the torture.

24. Psalm 22:18 predicted the disrespectful distribution of His clothing. Usually in Scripture **casting lots** involves religious connotations, a means to discover God's will, but here it is merely gambling.

25. The **third hour** was nine o'clock in the morning according to Jewish time.

26. Pilate's superscription, **THE KING OF THE JEWS**, caused a harsh reaction among the Jewish leaders (Jn 19:21-22).

The physical suffering in those final three hours on the cross was bad enough, but the Lord also endured continuous insults and mockery by those who observed.

29-30. They that passed by railed on him would be better translated "kept on blaspheming" (Greek imperfect tense). When Christ prophesied about the temple He had referred to His body (Jn 2:19-21), but these accusers derided Him because they thought He spoke of the building and thus His word had failed. The claim would be fulfilled just three days later.

31-32. He saved others; himself he cannot save, though not true, indirectly emphasizes the fact that He would not save Himself because He was willing to save others. **Descend now from the cross, that we may see and believe.** Typical of fallen man, they confused the order of revelation. When a person believes in Christ, he begins to see. Spiritual understanding and discernment are results of spiritual illumination, which is accomplished by the new birth through the Holy Spirit.

33-34. The **darkness** which occurred at the sixth hour (noon until three o'clock) along with the outcry **My God, my God, why hast thou forsaken me** (Ps 22:1) bespeak of the harshest hour of human history. Although the exact meaning of the separation is debated, Bible students agree that it induced the greatest anguish.

35-36. The reaction to His outcry, **he calleth Elias,** implies His condition; He lacked the physical strength to speak clearly.

37-38. John 19:30 informs us of Jesus' final words before He **gave up the ghost:** "It is finished." And that declaration explains why the **veil of the temple** was torn from top to bottom. Jesus had paid the penalty of sin, and thus there was no longer a barrier between God and man. He Himself had said, "I am the way, the truth, and the life" (Jn 14:6). This **veil** was a heavy curtain that separated the Holy Place from the Most Holy Place, which the

book of Hebrews relates typologically to Christ (Heb 10:19-20).

39. Officially a **centurion** had one hundred men under him, but his assignment undoubtedly warranted but a small band. **Over against** means he was facing Jesus as He expired. The meaning of the confession, **Truly this man was the Son of God,** may not have come from understanding lips. The word **son** does not have a definite article before it, so it should be translated "a" son of God. As a Roman the title he employed could have merely recognized Jesus' righteousness (Lk 23:47).

40-41. Luke 8:2 describes the former life of **Mary Magdalene.** She had been demon-possessed. The other Mary was the mother of **James the less,** one of the Twelve. **Salome** was the wife of Zebedee and the mother of James and John (Mt 27:56).

42. The time factor is mentioned to explain the necessity of hasty action. The next day, the Sabbath, would begin at 6:00 P.M. according to Jewish time, and it was already past 3:00 P.M. Since burial was unlawful on the Sabbath, both permission and the act itself required swift achievement.

43. Joseph's home, **Arimathea,** is given to distinguish him from others bearing the same name. **Honorable counsellor** identifies him as a prominent member of the national religious council, the Sanhedrin. Luke 23:51 adds that he did not condone the illegal trial which condemned Jesus. **Craved** (Gr *aiteō*) means "asked for" the body.

44. Pilate **marvelled** at Joseph's request, because he was surprised that Jesus had already died. This implies how intense the Lord's suffering was. Prior to the Crucifixion, His body had been terribly and repeatedly beaten, so much so that He later was unable to bear His cross.

46. Matthew 27:60 says the **sepulchre** or tomb was Joseph's, and John 19:39 adds that Nicodemus helped him.

D. The Resurrection. 16:1-20.

16.1-3. The narration of the resurrection begins with an explanation of the presence of the women at the tomb. As they journeyed, they wondered how they would remove the stone which was wheel-shaped and large enough to block the entrance of the sepulchre. Besides its size, the area immediately in front of the entrance was lower, and thus its removal was accomplished only with extreme difficulty.

4-5. Two angels were present (Lk 24:4), but one must have been the more prominent, as in Mark's narrative.

6-8. Be not affrighted is a negative command in the present tense in Greek which is accurately translated "stop being afraid." **Neither said they anything to any man** appears to be a direct contradiction to the other Gospel accounts, which affirm that the women reported the news to the apostles. The purpose of these verses, however, centers around their immediate reaction, not the final outcome. They were afraid to tell anyone along the way, but when they found the apostles, they privately shared what had happened.

This concluding section (vss. 9-20) was not included in the two oldest manuscripts nor in other ancient reliable sources. Therefore, many Bible scholars conclude that Mark ended his Gospel with verse eight. However, the final twelve verses are discussed in this commentary. (For its inclusion in the original text see R. C. H. Lenski, *Commentary on St. Mark's Gospel*, pp. 750-755.)

9. Mary Magdalene was probably given the privilege of being first to witness the resurrected Christ because of her unreserved dedication. Having been delivered from her former condition, **out of whom he had cast seven devils,** she committed herself to Christ with ineffable gratefulness.

10-13. Three times in this passage the disciples' resistance to believe is mentioned. This negative emphasis parallels the need for signs mentioned in verses 17 and 18. The **two . . . as they walked** refers to Cleopas and his companion as they journeyed to Emmaus (Lk 24:13-35). The **residue** speaks of the rest of the disciples with the exception of Thomas who would see the Lord eight days later (Jn 20:24-29).

14-16. A striking peculiarity about this particular rendering of the Great Commission relates to baptism: **He that believeth and is baptized shall be saved.** The ordinance may appear to be a prerequisite to salvation. However, the negative statement mentions believing alone: **he that believeth shall not be damned** (Gr *katakrinō* to be condemned). In addition, baptism in the early church was the outward declaration of conversion, so even though the ordinance has no saving merit, the close connection is natural because it is the sign of genuine faith.

17-18. The distinctive emphasis of **these signs** causes some to conclude that the disputed ending of Mark was added to support the spiritual gifts that are listed. Since exorcism, speaking in tongues, handling snakes, and healing occurred in the book of Acts with **drink any deadly thing** being the single exception, one must admit that the passage could be harmonized with the New Testament on this subject.

19-20. Because of brevity, one might assume that the events occurred within a short time, as if He addressed them once and then immediately ascended. But actually He remained with them forty days (Acts 1:3). **Signs following.** This describes the pattern of apostolic preaching and ministry. Both leading figures in Acts, Peter and Paul, performed many miracles as a confirmation of the reality of their claims.

BIBLIOGRAPHY

Alexander, J. A. *The Gospel According to Mark.* London: Banner of Truth Trust, 1960.

Bruce, A. B. The Synoptic Gospels. In *The Expositor's Greek Testament,* Vol. 1. Grand Rapids: Eerdmans, n.d.

*Cole, Robert Alan. The Gospel According to St. Mark. In the *Tyndale New Testament Commentaries.* Grand Rapids: Eerdmans, 1961.

*Cranfield, C. E. B. *The Gospel According to St. Mark.* Cambridge: Cambridge University Press. 1963.

Earle, Ralph. The Gospel According to Mark. In the *Evangelical Commentary on the Bible.* Grand Rapids: Zondervan, 1957.

*English, E. Schuyler. *Studies in the Gospel According to Mark.* New York: Our Hope, 1943.

Erdman, Charles R. *The Gospel of Mark.* Philadelphia: Westminster. 1917.

Hendriksen, William. Exposition of the Gospel According to Mark. In the *New Testament Commentary.* Grand Rapids: Baker, 1975.

Hiebert, D. Edmond. *Mark: A Portrait of the Servant.* Chicago: Moody Press, 1974.

Kelly, William. *An Exposition of the Gospel of Mark.* Ed. by E. E. Whitfield. London: Alfred Holness, n.d.

*Lane, William L. The Gospel According to Mark. In the *New International Commentary on the New Testament.* Grand Rapids: Eerdmans, 1974.

Lindsay, Thomas M. The Gospel According to St. Mark. In *Handbooks for Bible Classes and Private Students.* Edinburgh: T. & T. Clark, 1883.

Martin, Ralph P. *Mark: Evangelist and Theologian.* Grand Rapids: Zondervan, 1973.

*Morgan, G. Campbell. *The Gospel According to Mark.* New York: Revell, 1927.

Morison, James. *A Practical Commentary on the Gospel According to St. Mark.* 4th revised ed. London: Hodder and Stoughton, 1882.

Plummer, A. The Gospel According to St. Mark. In the *Cambridge Greek Testament for Schools and Colleges.* Cambridge: Cambridge University Press, 1938.

Riddle, Matthew B. The Gospel According to Mark. In *The International Revision Commentary on the New Testament.* New York: Scribner, 1881.

Scroggie, W. Graham. *The Gospel of Mark.* London: Marshall, Morgan and Scott, n.d.

*Swete, H. B. *The Gospel According to St. Mark.* Grand Rapids: Eerdmans, 1956.

*Taylor, Vincent. *The Gospel According to St. Mark.* London: Macmillan, 1963.

Wuest, Kenneth. *Mark in the Greek New Testament for the English Reader.* Grand Rapids: Eerdmans, 1950.

The Gospel According To

LUKE

INTRODUCTION

Each of the four Gospels is written from its own perspective to present Christ to a particular group of readers. Matthew, who writes primarily for the Jews, presents Christ as Messiah and King in fulfillment of prophecy. Mark stresses the servant aspects of Christ's ministry in writing for those of Roman background. John proves Christ to be the Son of God, deity incarnate. Luke's emphasis is on the humanity of Christ. In fact, the characteristic title for Christ, found in the key verse, is the "Son of Man" (Lk 19:10).

As you read the book of Luke other features will also stand out. Luke includes more than the other Gospels about women, children, the home, the Holy Spirit, prayer, and praise. As the Son of Man, Jesus has experienced our griefs and sorrows, and He is able to meet these needs. Naturally, Luke, the "beloved physician," gives special touches regarding sickness and healing too. There are also more unique parables in Luke than in any other Gospel.

Authorship. From the earliest of times, believers have witnessed to the fact that Luke wrote this Gospel. Irenaeus, Tertullian, and Clement of Alexandria, who all lived circa A.D. 180, positively state that Luke was the author. From that time to this, there has been no other opinion except in the case of some more recent radical theologians.

The proof that Luke was the author must be gleaned from the book of Acts. The same author evidently wrote both books and addressed them both to a man named Theophilus (Lk 1:3 and Acts 1:1). Neither book actually states who its author is, but there are enough clues in Acts to confirm the universal testimony of history that Luke penned both volumes.

The argument may be expressed simply in several points. (1) In Acts, the writer differentiates himself from others in the account by using the pronoun "we" when he is part of the action (Acts 16:10-17; 20:5; 21:18; 27:1-28:16). Otherwise, he simply says "they." Since the author refers to Paul, Silas, and Timothy (and a few others, cf. Acts 20:4) as "they," none of them could be the author of Acts. (2) The writer's awareness of sicknesses and the use of distinct medical terminology in both Luke and Acts suggest that he may have been a doctor. (3) Luke was both a doctor and one of Paul's closest companions and fellow-labors as shown in Colossians 4:14. The latter reference, with Philemon 24, proves Luke's association with Paul in Rome after the voyage of Acts 27 and 28. In addition, in II Timothy 4:11 at the close of Paul's second Roman imprisonment, he notes that only Luke is with him. Only Luke fits all the criteria for the authorship of history found in Luke and continued in Acts.

As for Luke's personal life, he is thought by many to have been a Gentile. His name is Greek and in Colossians 4:14 Paul lists Luke with other Gentile names rather than with the Jewish believers. In any event, he was a tremendous historian, missionary, church planter, traveller, and writer, as well as being a physician.

Date. It is evident that the book of Acts is a continuation of "the former treatise" (Acts 1:1), namely, the Gospel of Luke. This means that Luke had to have been completed prior to the writing of Acts. From the abrupt ending of Acts with Paul still in custody in Rome awaiting the outcome of his case, several ideas are suggested: (1) Luke may have intended to have the book of Acts end in Rome to present the Gospel as having spread from Jerusalem to the very capital of the empire. (2) More likely, the book of Acts ends where it does because Luke had nothing more to report. Paul's trial was at a standstill. The date of Paul's first two-year Roman detainment is usually pinpointed around A.D. 60-62, on the basis of the date Porcius Festus replaced Felix (Acts 24:27). Since Luke was written prior to this time, it is most logical to place it between A.D. 58-60 when Paul was imprisoned in Caesarea. This would have given Luke ample time to consult needed eyewitnesses and examine other official Roman and Palestinian records during the two-year stay in Caesarea.

Place. The precise place where Luke penned his Gospel is not known. However, since it appears to have been written prior to the book of Acts, which was published around A.D. 61 or 62, several possibilities arise: (1) Some feel it may have been written in Greece, possibly on either the first or second missionary journey. But, there does not seem to have been enough time at that point for Luke to have consulted the many "eyewitnesses" (1:2) who would necessarily have lived in Palestine. (2) Caesarea, the Roman administrative capital of Palestine, is perhaps the most ideal location that could be suggested. Luke was with Paul during Paul's two-year detainment in Caesarea awaiting trial (Acts 24:27). From that city Luke no doubt would have been able to consult various early disciples, deacons, and other believers to attain information for the writing of his Gospel, under the superintending work of the Holy Spirit (II Pet 1:21). The two-year interval also affords Luke ample leisure time for pursuing such activities as writing. (3) A third possibility would be Rome during Paul's two-year imprisonment there from about A.D. 60-62. But, such might crowd the writing of Acts which was accomplished during the same period. Thus, Caesarea in Palestine is perhaps the most ideal and most likely place for the Gospel to have been written, both from the chronological as well as the fact-gathering perspectives.

OUTLINE

COMMENTARY

I. THE PROLOGUE TO THEOPHILUS. 1:1-4.

The first eighty-two words of the text compose just one sentence, Luke's preface. It was customary in the first century to write a formal literary prologue for most works. The purpose of such a preface was to announce the reasons for writing, the methods followed, and the dedication of the work, often to the one paying for its production. Josephus, for example, a first-century Jewish historian, follows this same pattern in his *Antiquities of the Jews.* Luke's style and vocabulary in these opening four verses comprise perhaps the best example of classical Greek in the New Testament. It is also an indication of Luke's extraordinary education and his fitness for the task God gave to him of writing such a complete biography of Christ.

1:1. Many have taken in hand to set forth in order a declaration. Apparently there were a number of early attempts to record parts of Christ's life and work, and also the beginnings of the New Testament Church after His death and resurrection. These early narratives were probably written by other believers, with whom Luke seems to classify himself (vs. 3 "me also").

They may have been truthful, authentic, and genuine accounts, but they were not God-breathed (II Tim 3:16), and thus passed off the scene as they were replaced by the inspired documents penned by Matthew, Mark, Luke, and John. Luke is not referring here to the accounts drawn up by the other gospel writers.

Those things which are most surely believed among us. This is more accurately rendered "the matters which have been fulfilled or accomplished among us." The terminology Luke uses includes the material in the book of Acts as well as the Gospel, showing that at the outset he intended to pen a complete history of the events surrounding the beginnings, growth, and development of Christianity. The prologue to this Gospel should also be seen as prefacing the book of Acts. In Acts 1:1-2 Luke refers to the gospel account as including "all that Jesus began to do and teach, until the day in which he was taken up." Acts simply continues the narrative of what Jesus continued to do and teach after He was taken up.

2. **Even as they delivered them unto us, which from the beginning were eyewitnesses.** Luke received information that was handed over to him from eyewitnesses who had seen the very beginnings of the gospel account he relates. Who were these early eyewitnesses? Luke may have talked with Mary, the mother of our Lord, and with James and Jude, two of Christ's brothers who were prominent enough to have written New Testament books. James was also the leading elder in the church at Jerusalem (Acts 15:13, 19; 21:18; Gal 2:9). Naturally, Luke must have met some of the twelve original disciples. Luke even tells us that he spent some time with Mnason who was a disciple of long-standing, perhaps one who knew Christ personally (Acts 21:16). Of course, there were probably hundreds if not thousands still alive who had personally heard Jesus teach and had seen Him

perform miracles just thirty years previously. In addition, Paul recorded in A.D. 52 or 53 that a great number of the five hundred who all on one occasion saw Christ after His resurrection were still alive (1 Cor. 15:6). They apparently joined the ranks shortly after Pentecost, and were some of the original deacons, such as Philip, who conveniently lived in Caesarea, and with whom Luke lodged for a while (Acts 21:8-10).

3. **Having had perfect understanding of all things from the very first** is more literally rendered "having traced or investigated accurately all things from the first." Luke expresses several ideas: (1) The length of his search took him back to the beginning of things. Only Luke recounts the birth announcements of Gabriel to Zacharias, or Zechariah, and to Mary. (2) The breadth of his research has included "all things." He would naturally have to evaluate each piece of evidence in order to retain that which would be most useful. (3) The accuracy of his investigation is declared by his use of the Greek word *akribōs* which speaks of precision and exactness.

To write to thee in order, most excellent Theophilus. Luke's mention of "in order" perhaps hints that some of the other accounts then in existence were not only fragmentary and partial, but also somewhat disarranged. Theophilus is referred to as one would address a Greek noble. He may have had a title, or Luke may simply be honoring him in a special way as the patron who is presumably financing the writing of this work.

4. The purpose of Luke's Gospel, as stated here, is to certify the truthfulness of those things wherein Theophilus has been taught or "catechized" (Gr. *katecheō*), regarding the Christian faith. One's faith is no more sure than the object upon which it rests. We can thank God that our faith rests firmly upon the unshakable his-

torical facts recorded in His matchless Word.

II. THE PREPARATIONS FOR THE ARRIVAL OF THE SON. 1:5-2:52

A. Gabriel's Announcement to Zechariah. 1:5-25.

5. In the days of Herod, the king. Luke is very exact in giving precise historical and chronological information. This is seen in these words, as well as other references to major historical persons, events and dates as in 2:1-3; 3:1-2, 19, and 23. This Herod, known as Herod the Great, was a descendant of Esau (cf. Gen 27:39-40). Born in 73 B.C., he was appointed King of the Jews by the Roman Senate in 40 B.C. He ruled until his death in March or April, 4 B.C. Archelaus (Mt 2:22), Philip (Lk 3:1), and Herod Antipas (Lk 23:7-12, 15), were his sons. Herod Agrippa I of Acts 12:1-6, 19-23 was his grandson, and Herod Agrippa II of Acts 25-26 was his great-grandson.

6-10. Zechariah . . . and Elisabeth were very old and childless (vs. 7), a theme repeated throughout the Old Testament, as with Sarah, Rebekah, Manoah's wife, and Hannah. Zechariah was a priest, and he was serving for about a two-week period in the temple. This temple was built by Zerubbabel and others in 516 B.C., but since 20 B.C. was in the process of being enlarged and redone by Herod the Great (see Jn 2:20). Zechariah had the unique opportunity of offering incense before the Holy of Holies. The people outside prayed and awaited his blessing.

11-17. At that moment the angel Gabriel (vs. 19) appeared to Zechariah, who was suddenly shaken with fear, and said his prayers had been answered. Zechariah's prayer could have been (1) his long-standing request for a son, or (2) his general petitions for the coming of the Messiah, or (3) both. Both were shortly accomplished. This Gabriel was the same angel who ap-

peared five hundred years before to Daniel (Dan 8:15-16; 9:21). No recorded revelation from God had been given to men for over four hundred years. Naturally, Zechariah was stunned. The content of Gabriel's message was twofold. (1) Elisabeth was to bear a son and name him John. (2) John would have the spirit and power of Elijah and was to prepare the way for the Messiah.

18-20. Zechariah expressed doubt, and so as both a punishment as well as a sign, he was stricken speechless for the ensuing nine months.

21-25. When Zechariah left the temple he had no priestly blessing to bestow upon the people. Luke contrasts this initial occasion with the final episode of this gospel as Christ, our High Priest, ascended up into heaven while giving the apostles His blessing (Lk 24:50-51).

B. Gabriel's Announcement to Mary. 1:26-38.

26. And in the sixth month refers to the sixth month of Elisabeth's pregnancy. Once again, Gabriel was sent to announce a special birth, this time to Mary in Nazareth.

27. To a virgin. There is no doubt according to Scripture that Christ's birth was a virgin birth, totally without parallel either before or since. This is required for several reasons: (1) to fulfill Old Testament prophecy (Gen 3:15; Isa 7:14; Jer 31:22); (2) to avoid the Old Testament curse on the seed of Jeconiah (Jer 22:24-30), yet still be able to claim the Throne of David in the kingly line; (3) to be in accord with the theological implications of the inspiration of the Scriptures and Christ's sinless humanity. Through the miraculous virgin conception, Christ avoided receiving a sinful nature; (4) to avoid receiving a human father. Christ already had a Father, and it would be unsuitable to have a second one; (5) to avoid creating a new person, as is done in all normal conceptions. Mary's con ception of Christ was to be the incarnation of an already existing person.

28. Blessed art thou among women. Mary was perhaps the best female descendant of David suitable for this matchless ministry of rearing the very Son of God. We must be careful not to downgrade Mary, nor to exalt her too highly.

29-33. Mary was naturally perplexed by all this, though she accepted it. Gabriel went on to explain that the Messiah Himself was to be born to her. The importance of verses 32-33 is that of the fulfillment of the Davidic Covenant of II Samuel 7:13-16, and of the messianic reign described in Isaiah 9:6-7.

34. How shall this be, seeing I know not a man? This was a legitimate question, given Mary's present marital status. Unlike Zechariah's question in verse 18, Mary expresses no doubt, but rather a humble submission to the will of God. Note verse 38 in this regard also.

35. The Holy Ghost shall come upon thee, and the power of the Highest shall overshadow thee. These words express the completely miraculous nature of Mary's conception. It was accomplished by God alone in a unique, never-to-be-repeated way. But one asks, could not Mary transmit her sinful nature to the one conceived in her womb? Ordinarily this would be the case, but the phrase **that holy thing which shall be born of thee** declares that God supernaturally prevented this from occurring.

36-37. Gabriel's announcement to Mary concluded with the statement that Mary's elderly cousin Elisabeth had also conceived, and was in her sixth month of pregnancy. The words, **For with God nothing shall be impossible,** are applicable to what God was doing with both Mary and Elisabeth.

C. Mary's Visit to Elisabeth. 1:39-56.

39-40. Almost immediately after receiving Gabriel's message, Mary prepared to visit Elisabeth some sixty or more miles south of Nazareth in Judaean territory. She remained there about three months (vs. 56).

41-45. Elisabeth was suddenly filled with the Holy Spirit when she saw Mary. Elisabeth's words in verses 42-45 indicate that God gave her a prophetic knowledge of Mary's condition, and filled her lips with the fruit of praise to Almighty God.

46-55. And Mary said, My soul doth magnify the Lord. This section, commonly called the Magnificat, in many ways resembles Hannah's prayer of thanksgiving and praise to God recorded in I Samuel 2:1-10. It illustrates Mary's rich acquaintance with the Old Testament Scriptures and the closeness of her fellowship with the Lord.

56. Naturally, when Mary returned home after being away for three months, and was soon obviously with child, her fiancé, Joseph, was dismayed. Only revelation from heaven could substantiate Mary's explanation regarding her condition. Matthew 1:18-25 records how God met this need.

D. John's Birth in Judaea. 1:57-80.

59a. Eight days after the birth of Elisabeth's baby boy, he was to be circumcised in accord with the elements enumerated in God's covenant with Abraham in Genesis 17:10-14, and made part of the law in Leviticus 12. The idea of circumcision seems to include three truths: (1) purification of the flesh, (2) separation unto God, and (3) identification as God's very own.

59b-63. And they called him Zechariah, after the name of his father. And his mother answered and said, Not so; but he shall be called John. Zechariah in his speechless condition, had at least made known to Elisabeth the full content of the angel Gabriel's message in which the new son was to be named John. The friends and relatives were not aware of this fact; they wanted to name him after his father.

They were greatly surprised to see the boy called **John,** which means in Hebrew, "Jehovah is gracious," or "Jehovah's gift." Certainly both were true regarding this gracious gift to Zechariah and Elisabeth. When the relatives questioned this new name, Zechariah confirmed the naming by writing "John" on a small wooden or wax tablet.

64-66. Immediately God miraculously ended Zechariah's long involuntary period of silence and he began praising God. These actions attracted great awe and amazement in that entire region. People began to take note of young John, and of the fact that **the hand of the Lord was with him** (cf. I Sam 2:21, 26).

67-79. The prophecy of Zechariah, found exclusively in these verses, was spoken under the power of the Holy Spirit. His words are filled with messianic importance with references to redemption or salvation in verses 68, 69, 71, 74, and 77. That God's unchanging covenant with Abraham was being fulfilled is mentioned in verses 72-73. In fact, there are no less than sixteen direct quotations or allusions to the Old Testament contained in these few verses. Zechariah utters a remarkable prophecy which heralds the coming of the Messiah and His forerunner. It is in some ways the New Testament reiteration of the last chapter of the Old Testament.

80. As with Christ, there is but scant mention of the childhood of John the Baptist. His work was to begin some thirty years later.

E. Jesus' Birth in Bethlehem. 2:1-21.

2:1. A decree from Caesar Augustus. Augustus was the grandnephew of Julius Caesar, and was adopted as his son. After the murder of Julius Caesar, young Octavius Augustus ruled with Mark Anthony and Lepidus in a triumvirate. Then for more than forty years, from 27 B.C. to A.D. 14, Augustus served by himself as the first emperor of the Roman Empire. It was during his reign that Christ was born.

All the world indicates only the twenty-seven provinces ruled by the Roman Senate and the emperor. **Taxed** (Gr *apographō*), better translated as enrolled, signifies a census, upon which basis perhaps a future taxation would be made.

2. When Cyrenius was governor of Syria. Syria was the most important of all the Roman provinces, and Quirinius (Cyrenius) served in several capacities there at different times. Roman censuses came every fourteen years. The first one of which we have recorded knowledge came in A.D. 6. This earlier census then may have been set in motion in Rome about 8 B.C., while Quirinius was the military governor of Syria. Several years would be required to complete such a census.

3-6. Joseph had to travel from Nazareth, where he was living, to Bethlehem for the census, because he was a descendant of King David of Bethlehem. Mary accompanied Joseph on the sixty-five-mile journey.

7. Wrapped him in swaddling clothes. With no midwife to help, Mary wrapped baby Jesus in long bands of cloth such as were used in wrapping the bodies of the dead. That He was born to die is perhaps intimated here and in the later gift of myrrh from the wise men (Mt 2:11). **Manger** is a cattle-feeding trough. **No room for them in the inn.** All these things suggest poverty, loneliness, and even rejection (see II Cor 8:9). The exact date and place are not recorded by Luke, perhaps to guard against the vain worship which men often attach to such information.

8-11. God sent an angel to make the first announcement of the Saviour's birth to lowly shepherds. He is called the Deliverer, the Anointed One (Messiah) promised in the Old Testament, even the Lord Himself.

12. The uniqueness of the sign was the rarity of finding a baby in a manger.

13-15. Upon completion of his announcement, this angel was immediately joined by hundreds of dazzling angels who lit up the dark sky (see verse 9, "the glory of the Lord shone"). Nothing like this had happened for hundreds of years. It must have made the intended impression on these shepherds.

16-18. They quickly found the Christ, and then spread the news of the miraculous events associated with His coming. All who heard it marvelled.

19-20. Mary was beginning to see God's attestation of her boy who was also the Son of the Highest. This was apparently the first confirmation she had had since her visit to Elisabeth, and the dream Joseph had received some months earlier.

21. The Saviour was officially named **Jesus** upon His circumcision at eight days old.

22-24. About five weeks later, Mary and Joseph traveled five miles north to the temple in Jerusalem to offer the sacrifice required by the law of Moses (Lev 12:6-8). This ended Mary's period

F. Mary's Purification in Jerusalem. 2:22-38.

of uncleanness which had lasted forty days from Christ's birth. The circumcision of a male child was apparently seen as removing some of the uncleanness, because a female child would cause uncleanness to remain for eighty days (Lev 12:5). The poverty of Mary and Joseph is seen in their offering a pair of doves rather than the more expensive lamb and a dove. The wise men of Matthew 2:1-12, who brought gold and other gifts, had not yet arrived. They came later after Mary and Joseph had moved from the stable into a house (Mt 2:11).

25-35. Before Christ was born, the Holy Sprit had ministered in a unique way to a man named Simeon, informing him that he would behold the long-promised Messiah before he died.

Guided by the Holy Spirit, he entered the Temple at the precise moment that Mary and Joseph were there with the six-week-old child. He lifted the baby into his arms and uttered a special prophecy. He spoke of Christ as a light for the Gentiles, and as the glory of Israel. This made even Mary and Joseph take note (vs. 33). Verse 34 speaks of both the tremendous earthly and eternal differences it makes whether one trusts Christ to be his personal sin substitute. Verse 35 looks forward thirty-three years to the agony Mary will suffer while seeing her son crucified.

36-38. Anna a prophetess. Anna follows in the train of Miriam, Deborah, and Huldah in the Old Testament. Note that the tribe of Asher had not completely lost its identity. The godly of all Israelite tribes had come south to Judah prior to the 722 B.C. deportation of most in the northern tribes to Assyria. Later, James addressed all twelve tribes of Israel (Jas 1:1). Anna may have been over one hundred years old. She witnessed to the faithful remnant in Jerusalem regarding the newborn Messiah.

G. Jesus' Growth in Nazareth. 2:39-40.

39. After these temple experiences, the wise men visited Christ in Bethlehem, which precipitated Mary and Joseph's departure and sojourn in Egypt (Mt 2:1-14). This verse telling of the return to Nazareth corresponds with Matthew 2:19-23.

40. The boyhood of Christ was natural as far as physical growth was concerned, but extraordinary in relation to His attainment of wisdom and understanding of spiritual things.

H. Jesus' First Passover in Jerusalem. 2:41-52.

41. The Old Testament law required all Israelite males to appear before the Lord three times each year (Deut 16:16). Mary and Joseph were in the habit of attending Passover. At age twelve, Jesus accompanied them.

43-46. After three days they found him in the temple. Mary and Joseph had lost track of Jesus on the way back to Nazareth. They traveled a day out and a day back, and searched the city a third day before they found Jesus in the temple. He was engaged in a profound discussion of theological topics with the greatest religious leaders of the day anywhere on earth. They knew the Old Testament and Jesus questioned them, as well as answered their questions.

47. Christ's understanding astonished everyone, even as His miracles would two decades later.

49-51. At this early age, the son of Mary knew He was also the Son of God. Perhaps in the routine of daily living, Mary and Joseph's initial awareness of the true identity of this Messiah-child had faded somewhat.

52. During the so-called silent years, Jesus matured in four ways: (1) Mentally, i.e. wisdom; (2) physically, i.e. stature; (3) spiritually, i.e. favor with God; and (4) socially, i.e. favor with men.

III. THE PUBLIC PRESENTATION OF THE SON. 3:1-4:13.

A. The Words and Work of John the Baptist. 3:1-20.

3:1. In the fifteenth year of the reign of Tiberius Caesar. As always, Luke gives precise historical information. Tiberius took over as Roman Emperor after Augustus (see on 2:1). Augustus reigned from 27 B.C. until his death in A.D. 14. However, it appears that Augustus made Tiberius co-emperor during his final two years. Thus, his fifteenth year is probably to be equated with A.D. 26 or 27. This would correspond with Jesus being about thirty years old at that time (Lk 3:23), and with John 2:20 which says the temple renovation began by Herod in 20 or 19 B.C. had been going on for forty-six years.

2. The word of God came to John. John followed in the train of many other Old Testament prophets, and the same formula is used to indicate God's revelation to him as with Elijah (I Kgs 18:1), Jeremiah (Jer 1:4), Ezekiel (Ezk 1:3), and others. John's ministry was in the wilderness, a barren area between the hill country and the Jordan.

3. Preaching the baptism of repentance for the remission of sins. This should not be confused with Christian baptism which began on Pentecost. Christian baptism, as explained by Paul in Romans 6:1-4, pictures death, burial, and resurrection in union with Christ. That meaning could only have been possible after the cross, since not even the disciples themselves understood anything about Christ having to die until after it was an accomplished fact (see Mt 16:21-23; Lk 19:11). John's baptism must have pictured a cleansing of heart and a preparedness to receive the Messiah, as evidenced by repentance. John's converts could be saved, but they were saved just as any other Old Testament saint was, such as Abraham, Job, Isaiah, or Daniel.

4-8. John's ministry was to prepare the way for the Messiah's appearance. His message was that of repentance for sin, and of a resulting change in one's life. His baptism was to picture the reality of that change, cleansing, and remission of sins. His message was stern (vss. 7, 9) and demanded a change in one's life (vs. 8).

9. The axe is laid to the root. The judgment of God was imminent upon these people and their nation. Only repentance could save.

10-14. Three groups responded to John's warnings: the people or multitude (vss.10-11), the publicans or tax collectors (vss.12-13), and the soldiers (vs.14). John specified appropriate actions for each class of hearer.

15. The people were wondering whether John could be the Christ (Gr *Christos*), or Messiah (Heb *Mashiach*), repeatedly promised throughout the Old Testament (see Isa 9:6-7; 11:1-9;

Amos 9:11; and Mic 4:1-3; 5:2). The Baptist clearly indicated here, and in John 1:19-29, that he was not their Messiah, but only His forerunner.

16-17. He shall baptize you with the Holy Ghost and with fire. This prediction of John, which is found as well in the other Gospels (Mt 3:11; Mk 1:8; Jn 1:33), is repeated by Christ in Acts 1:5 just before His ascension into heaven. Later this baptism in (or with) the Holy Spirit occurred on the Day of Pentecost, as the Holy Spirit took up permanent residence in the bodies of the believing disciples. The baptism with fire seems to refer to a future judgment as explained in verse 17, perhaps that which purifies believers, or ultimately judges those who refuse to believe.

19. Herod the tetrarch. This Herod was one of the sons of Herod the Great who sought to kill the baby Jesus in Matthew 2. John, who was not afraid to preach against divorce, had publicly reproached this Herod for marrying Herodias, the wife of his brother Philip.

20. He shut up John in prison. Very early during Christ's public ministry (Jn 3:24; Mt 4:12), John was cast into prison at Machaerus, a fortress on the east side of the Dead Sea. As a result, he was not privileged to see many of Christ's miracles and later had personal doubts regarding Christ (Lk 7:18-23), which were soon dispelled.

B. The Baptism of Christ. 3:21-22.

21. The baptism of Christ was totally unique. It did not signify what John's baptism of repentance did, because Jesus had no sin of which to repent. Jesus' explanation was that it might "fulfill all righteousness" (Mt 3:15). It no doubt marks the beginning of Christ's public ministry and probably pictures for Christ a pledge of His future death, burial, and resurrection for the sin of the world.

22. Here, as in other places (the Great Commission, Mt 28:19; certain benedictions; II Cor 13:14; and other passages I Cor 6:11; I Pet 1:2), all the persons of the Godhead are mentioned together, and distinguished from one another. On two other occasions, the transfiguration (Lk 9:35), and the triumphal entry into Jerusalem (Jn 12:28), God the Father similarly testified audibly regarding Christ.

C. The Genealogy of Christ. 3:23-38.

23. About thirty years of age. At the time Jesus began His public ministry He was thirty years old, as were the Levitical priests when they began their service (Num 4:47). **Being (as was supposed) the son of Joseph.** Luke is careful to explain Christ's unique parentage in light of His virgin birth. Jesus had no earthly father.

24-38. This genealogy differs from that in Matthew 1 in several ways. Matthew traces the line of descent beginning with Abraham and through the line of kings who directly followed David. This line alone could claim the Davidic throne. Luke, however, apparently gives Mary's blood line working backward from her father Heli, who would be Joseph's father by marriage. Mary is also seen to be a descendant of King David, but her line is followed all the way back to Adam. This firmly shows Christ to be completely human, yet a true descendant of David. Jesus' genealogy through Mary avoided the curse placed on David's kingly line following Jeconiah (Jer 22:30), yet allowed Him to claim the throne legitimately as a true human descendant of David, and as the adopted heir of the kingly line of Joseph.

D. The Temptation of Christ. 4:1-13.

The temptation of Christ was both a testing and a tempting. From the divine point of view, the Holy Spirit arranged a testing to show that Jesus qualified as free from sin. If He were not free from personal sin, He could not bear our sins. For Satan, it was a temptation to see if he could make Christ fall as had the first Adam. The temptation was real, yet it was impossible for God the Son to sin.

4:1. The wilderness. A barren region between the hill country and the Jordan Valley. The traditional site is northwest of Jericho.

2. Forty days. Jesus fasted during this entire period, in part as a spiritual preparation for the ministry in which He was about to engage.

3-8. If thou be the Son of God. Satan approached Christ assuming that He was God and could exercise divine power. However, for Christ to exercise His divine prerogatives at this point would be to step out of the pathway leading to the cross. Jesus met each temptation as a man. He quoted Scripture each time (Deut 8:3; 6:16; 10:20).

9. Pinnacle of the temple. The pinnacle is normally taken to mean the place where the southern and eastern walls of the city and temple area met. This place even today stands several hundred feet above the depths of the Kidron Valley below it.

13. For a season. These words, only recorded by Luke, indicate the fact that Satan was to similarly attack Christ again and again. Matthew and Mark record the ministry of angels to Christ at this point.

IV. THE PREACHING OF THE SON IN GALILEE. 4:14-9:50.

A. The Preaching that Claimed Messiahship. 4:14-44.

14. Jesus returned in the power of the Spirit. The Lord Jesus Christ was constantly and consciously yielded to the Holy Spirit; (cf. Jn 3:34).

15. Taught in their synagogues. Practically every Jewish village had a synagogue. They were used to instruct in the Old Testament. When Jesus taught, as in the following account, He pointed to the fulfillment of the messianic Scriptures in Himself.

16. Nazareth. Nazareth is situated at the southern edge of the hill country of Galilee overlooking the beautiful Jezreel Valley. Jesus had grown up here, and everyone knew Him as the carpenter's son. **As his custom was, he went into the synagogue on the sabbath day.** Jesus set an example of regular attendance at the public worship services. They met on the Sabbath (Saturday), because they were still bound under the dispensation of law. After the resurrection and ascension of Christ, Christians began meeting on the first day of the week (Sunday, cf. Acts 20:7; I Cor 16:2).

17-19. Jesus participated in the service that day by opening the scroll (Gr *biblion*) and reading one and a half verses (Isa 61:1-2a). He read a portion that dealt directly with the earthly ministry of the Messiah (such as preaching and healing) and stopped just before the passage went on to describe His coming judgment in the end times.

20-22. The application was short and to the point, **This day is this scripture fulfilled in your ears.** This was a direct and full claim to be the Messiah.

23-30. Unfortunately, the people could not accept the fantastic claim of this thirty-year-old carpenter's son. Instead of believing Christ, and receiving the long promised earthly kingdom He proclaimed, they were indignant and sought to cast Jesus over the side of the mountain into the valley far below. However, God supernaturally prevented them from carrying out their wicked intentions and Jesus went away unhindered.

31. Came down to Capernaum, a city of Galilee. Since the elevation of Capernaum is six hundred fifty feet below sea level, Jesus had to go down from the higher elevations of southern Galilee. Christ taught several Sabbaths in their synagogue on the shore of the Sea of Galilee.

32. And they were astonished at his doctrine: for his word was with power. This statement characterizes all of Christ's teaching ministry (cf. Mt 7:28-29). Such words, supported by miraculous works, should have produced faith on the part of all. Most religious leaders, however, rejected His claims, and most common people followed Him for the wrong reasons.

33-37. Demon possession was prevalent in Christ's time, and on numerous occasions Christ cast out these fallen angels. In the synagogue at Nazareth one such demon spoke to Christ from out of his human captive's body. Jesus rebuked him as an improper source for proclaiming who Christ was. Jesus' fame was spreading rapidly in every direction.

38-41. That same Sabbath day, Jesus instantly and completely healed Peter's mother-in-law (cf. I Cor 9:5) of a fever. Instead of being left weak, she immediately arose and waited on her visitors. After sundown, hundreds of sick and diseased assembled at Peter's door (cf. Mk 1:33), and Christ healed them all. None were sent away unhelped, and faith is not spoken of as a condition for being healed. These miracles performed by Christ, and later by the apostles too, were for the purpose of authenticating their ministry as from God. The Bible neither offers nor requires such a ministry for today.

42-44. Went into a desert place. Mark 1:35 records the fact that Jesus went early by Himself, and for the purpose of praying. Even as constantly busy as He was in ministry, He knew the necessity of a time alone with the Father at the beginning of each day. Let us not ignore His example.

B. The Miracles that Supported His Messiahship. 5:1-39.

5:1. Lake of Gennesaret. This is the Sea of Galilee. Jesus referred to it as a "sea" but Luke accurately calls it a lake. It is six hundred eighty-five feet below sea level, about seven miles wide, and twelve miles long. In Christ's day, it was abundant with fish.

2-3. From Peter's boat, Jesus taught the multitudes who stood on the shore. Jesus had met Peter previously (see Jn 1:41-42) and he had followed Christ in an intermittent fashion for some time. After this experience, how-

ever (cf. Mt 4:18-19), **they forsook all, and followed him** (vs. 11).

4-9. The miracle was that Christ commanded Peter to let down his nets in the deep to take a catch of fish. This was against the common practice of fishing at night, and near the shore. However, Peter obeyed and let down the nets. The result was a magnificent catch that pointed to Christ's deity and exposed Peter's sinfulness in contrast.

10-11. Leaving the vast catch was not a sinful waste of food, as some have supposed, because Zebedee and his servants would have been perfectly able to care for the haul. Jesus promised Peter and Andrew, and James and John that they would catch men from that time forward. The promise was certainly fulfilled.

12-13. A man full of leprosy. Leprosy is a dreadful disease that eats away the fingers, toes, ears, nose, etc. This man had an acute case, but knew Jesus could heal him if He only desired to. Jesus did, and instantly the leprosy was completely gone, not just arrested.

14. Tell no man. Jesus gave this command on several occasions, and it may seem strange to modern readers. The answer as to why Jesus said these words seems to have several aspects. (1) He was first to go to the temple to show himself to the priest as the law required (Lev 14). If the priest heard before his arrival that Jesus had healed him, the case might be prejudiced against him. (2) Jesus did not want to be known or sought merely as a miracle worker. His primary work was to be spiritual rather than physical.

15. Christ's fame, however, continued to spread, nonetheless.

16. He withdrew . . . and prayed. Here is but another example Luke gives of Jesus' reliance on prayer. If Christ needed to pray much, how much greater must be the necessity with us.

17-19. Jesus' healing of the palsied man (Mk 2:1) is the backdrop for the great controversy that began to develop between Christ and the Jewish religious leaders. Luke noted (vs.17) that some of these leaders had come from as far away as Jerusalem, some eighty miles distance.

The crowd was so great around the house where Jesus was that the palsied man had to be lowered through a makeshift hole torn in the roof by his four determined friends.

20. He saw their faith. The palsied man is probably to be included as having faith that Christ would heal him, as he was at least a consenting party to the action of his four friends. Jesus loved to see men act in faith, and thus responded: **Man, thy sins are forgiven thee.** Jesus' words were calculated to draw a particular reaction from the unbelieving Jews present.

21-24. Jesus was silently accused of blasphemy. The men rightly reasoned that only God could forgive sins. But they failed to consider the possibility that Jesus was indeed God! The omniscient Christ read their very thoughts. He pointed out that it would be easy for someone to say that another's sin was forgiven. No one could prove any differently. But the harder thing would be to heal a hopeless case of bedridden palsy. Jesus then proved He had the authority to speak the one thing by doing the other. He healed the man.

25-26. The reaction of the multitude was that the charge of blasphemy had been disproved. Jesus was vindicated; God was glorified.

27. A publican, named Levi. In Matthew and Mark, Levi is referred to as Matthew. Levi was a tax collector who worked for the Roman government, and was no doubt well off financially.

28. Upon Jesus' call of **Follow me,** Levi **left all.** He no doubt lost his job as a result. His commitment to Christ was complete and final. Levi was the writer of our first gospel, Matthew.

29-31. Later, Levi's efforts to win his fellow tax collectors to faith in Christ was an occasion for the Pharisees to criticize Jesus and his disciples

for dining with such sinners. Jesus replied that only those who are sick realize their need of a physician. The Pharisees were in need, but refused to acknowledge it.

32. Jesus indicated His own departure from the world in this verse, probably for the first time. His death and resurrection had been personally foretold earlier (Jn 2:19-22). Jesus also said that fasting would become a practice of His disciples after His departure. This was fulfilled in New Testament Church practice in Acts 10:30; 13:2; 14:23 and I Corinthians 7:5. The purpose for fasting is usually that one may give himself more fully to prayer and seeking the mind of the Lord in making special decisions. There may be some physical benefits to occasional fasting as well. New Testament fasting is always voluntary, never mandatory.

36-39. The two parables in this short paragraph relate the same message, only in different figures. New Testament truth cannot be bound up in the structure of the Old Testament law.

C The Choice of the Twelve. 6:1-49.

6:1. The second sabbath after the first. This unique expression, which does not occur in some manuscripts, is either a manuscript error or a reference to the second of the seven Sabbaths between Passover and Pentecost (Lev 23:15-16). If it is the latter, then it helps to fully establish Christ's ministry as being about three and a half years in duration. This is easily marked by the three different passovers mentioned in John's Gospel (2:13; 6:4; and 12:1). Luke 6:1 would then refer to an additional passover between John 2:13 and 6:4, thus accounting for three years of ministry between the four Passovers.

Plucked . . . ears of corn, and did eat. Jesus and his disciples picked some grain (probably wheat) for immediate eating as they walked along.

2. The Pharisees considered this to be harvesting and, therefore a violation of the Sabbath. Thus, the great Sabbath controversy was continued by Christ's enemies who sought to destroy Him.

3-5. The Son of man is Lord also of the sabbath. After countering with the Old Testament example of David who once ate the sacred shewbread, Christ announced that He was Lord or supreme over the Sabbath. For one to claim personal sovereignty over an institution of God was practically to claim deity.

6-8. On another Sabbath, the Pharisees watched Christ as He was teaching in a synagogue to see if He would heal a man's withered right hand. This was clearly a test case. The Scribes and Pharisees were hoping Christ would violate the law, as they saw it, in order to accuse Him. A man could be put to death for violating the Sabbath.

9-10. Jesus turned the tables by asking the rhetorical question of whether it was permitted to do good on the Sabbath. Since no one would deny this, Jesus quickly restored the man's hand.

11. The envy of the Pharisees, however, only increased as a result. The pressure mounted as they sought means to put Jesus out of the way (cf. Jn 11:53).

12. The selection of the Twelve was made after Jesus spend a night in prayer. Much prayer is often needed before such important decisions.

13. Disciples: and of them he chose twelve, whom also he named apostles. From the larger company of learners (disciples), Jesus selected just twelve, no doubt a number with special significance (see Lk 22:30), this number was suited for group instruction and "discipling." Mark 3:14 gives the purposes of this selection as that they might be with Him, and that He might send them out to preach. These Twelve were to be special witnesses. The fact that they are called "apostles" (Gr *apostellō*) indicates their new position as "sent ones."

14-16. Besides this passage there are several other lists of the twelve apostles (Mt 10:2-4; Mk 3:16-19; Acts 1:13). The names sometimes vary because Bartholomew and Nathaniel are the same person, Matthew is also named Levi, and Lebbaeus was sometimes called Judas (not Iscariot) and also had the last name of Thaddaeus.

17-19. Jesus' healing ministry was extensive, both in the number of people healed, the places from which they came, and the maladies of which they were relieved. Unlike modern-day healers, Jesus healed all who came to Him.

20. He lifted up his eyes on his disciples, and said. This passage, which follows the selection of the twelve apostles, records some of their formal training from the lips of the Lord. Much of this sermon on "the plain" (vs. 17) parallels the Sermon on the Mount (Mt 5-7), but there are differences as well as similarities. Jesus no doubt spoke similar messages on various occasions, even as preachers do today.

Blessed be ye poor: for your's is the kingdom of God. Certainly no one gets to heaven simply because he is financially destitute. Matthew 5:3 adds poor "in spirit." One must realize his spiritual poverty before he will ever trust God's provision for his need, but material poverty sometimes teaches one to depend on God entirely. The phrase **Kingdom of God** is here equivalent to Matthew's "Kingdom of Heaven."

21. Hunger . . . shall be filled. Certainly not a prediction of more ample food supplies, this speaks of God meeting the spiritual needs of those who are hungry for what He has to offer.

22-23. Blessed are ye, when men shall hate you . . . for the Son of man's sake. There is no blessing for being hated because one is foolish, lazy, untrustworthy, inept, or unfaithful. One might deserve such treatment in these cases. But when one is hated simply because he is a good Christian, living a life of testimony for Christ, then he receives the blessing promised (cf. Jn 15:18-19; I Pet 2:19-20; I Jn 3:13).

24. Woe unto you that are rich. Money is not evil, but the love of money is (I Tim 6:10). Fortune sometimes causes one to live independently of God, and to believe in his own self-sufficiency. Wealth should be acknowledged as from God, and used in a sacred stewardship.

25-30. Here Jesus is seeking to inculcate a godly spirit which is exactly the opposite of how we normally react to situations around us. The point is that a man must be a Christian before he can exhibit Christian behavior.

31. This verse contains what is commonly called "The Golden Rule." Some have claimed that Buddha, Confucius, and even some rabbinical writings, all prior to Christ. contain the same teachings. This is only partly true, because their statements occur only in the negative: "Don't do to someone else what you wouldn't want him to do to you." No positive action is contemplated. Jesus, however, requires His believers to initiate helpful actions toward others.

32-35. Jesus told His disciples that their actions must go far beyond even what is considered good morality by the world. The believer's standards far surpass those of the "sinner."

36. The progression of instruction has moved from an attitude of "love your enemies" (vs. 27), to the positive general action of "The Golden Rule" (vs. 31), and then to the very specific activity of leading (vs. 35). Now Jesus says to be **merciful as your Father also is merciful.** The fatherhood of God comes only by being born into His family by the new birth (Jn 3:3-7). Christ said that prior to that experience, men are naturally the children of the devil (Jn 8:44).

37. Judge not, and ye shall not be judged. This statement, and its parallel in Matthew 7:1, is often misconstrued. It means not to act as God in passing

some final judgment on an individual. Because we cannot fully see motives, we often judge falsely. But we are to be discerning. We must be able to identify wolves in sheep's clothing in order to warn others and to flee ourselves. As Jesus suggests in verses 43-44, the fruit one produces is an indication of what he is like.

38-40. Give, and it shall be given unto you. Our Lord had a lot to say about money. This is because money is so important, touches every life, and is so liable to misuse. In fact, both Solomon and Jesus gave many warnings regarding wine, women, and wealth. Here the principle is that we cannot outgive the Lord. Naturally, all our substance belongs to God. But as we give it back to Him, He is always more generous in returning it to us again. Every cheerful giver knows both the joy of giving and joy of God's blessed provision. God entrusts more wealth to those whom He knows will properly dispense it.

41-42. The mote that is in thy brother's eye. It is only human nature to see our brother's faults while overlooking our own. But human nature is sinful. Jesus notes that if one first takes care of his own faults, he may be able to help his brother. This correct order must be followed.

43-45. It is an unchangeable law that outward fruit resembles and reproduces the inward qualities of the tree. So with man, the mouth simply echoes the thoughts of the heart. One's speech is a good barometer of his spiritual condition. Each person must examine hisown speech to see if it exhibits anger, bitterness, irritation, and gossip, or if it reflects cheerfulness, sympathy, and love.

46. Why call ye me Lord? If one calls Christ Lord, then he had better not say what Peter said in Acts 10:14, "not so, Lord." For he who acknowledges Christ as Lord, the only correct response is as Paul humbly said, "Lord, what wilt thou have me to do?" (Acts 9:6). Jesus said, "If ye love me, keep my commandments" (Jn 14:15). Nothing less will do.

47-49. The meaning of this short parabolic saying about the house built on the rock and that built on the sand concerns the foundation of one's life. Only those who actually do Christ's will have the sure foundation of Christ beneath them. All other ways, routes, and efforts will end in destruction.

D. More Miracles and Parables in Galilee. 7:1-8:50.

7:1. He entered into Capernaum. It seems that Capernaum, on the northwest shore of Galilee, was Jesus' primary resting place during His great Galilean ministry. Matthew 9:1 calls it "his own city." Since Jesus had no home of his own (Lk 9:58), He must have stayed with one or more of the disciples who lived there (i.e., Peter's wife's family or Matthew).

2. Centurion's servant who was dear unto him, was sick, and ready to die. A centurion was a Roman soldier in command of at least one hundred men. There are approximately ten centurions mentioned in the New Testament, and each is presented in a good light. This centurion had numerous noble qualities.

3. He heard of Jesus. This no doubt refers to the tremendous healing miracles Jesus had done. **He sent unto him the elders of the Jews.** This centurion had great influence with the Jews, which was unusual.

4-5. These elders give two reasons as to why this Gentile was worthy of having Jesus come to heal his servant: (1) he loved the Jews, not many Romans did; and (2) he built the Jewish synagogue in Capernaum. The present synagogue ruins in Capernaum date from the fourth century A.D., and are clearly Roman in architecture, but with the Star of David, vine and branches, and other Jewish emblems quite evident. Perhaps this earlier synagogue was styled along the same lines.

6-10. Naturally, Jesus could effect healings even from a distance (Jn 4:46-53), but He went toward the centurion's house. When He had nearly arrived, the centurion sent word that he knew Jesus could simply give the command and the servant would be healed. This was said because he felt unworthy to have Jesus come under his roof. Jesus marveled at such a display of faith, and complied with the centurion's humble request.

11. The very next day Jesus journeyed about twenty-five miles into the Jezreel Valley to the city of Nain. It was a good-sized town in Christ's day. Many disciples and "much people" were present. Luke records this event out of concern for stories about women, as well as the fact that this is one of only three recorded times Jesus raised someone from the dead. It had been approximately eight hundred years since Israel had seen someone raised from the dead. The last case was wrought by Elisha the prophet (II Kgs 4:14-37).

12. There was no doubt as to this man's condition. He was plainly dead, the funeral was over, the funeral procession was en route to the place of burial. Luke alone records that the dead man was the only son of his widowed mother.

13-15. Showing human tenderness and compassion toward the weeping mother, Jesus touched the open casket and said, **"Young man, I say unto thee, Arise."** The object of recording that the young man spoke after arising was to give evidence that he was really alive.

16-17. The people responded correctly by noting that Jesus was a great prophet, and the report spread throughout the surrounding region and even south into Judaea.

18-23. John the Baptist, the Old Testament's predicted forerunner of the Messiah, was cast into prison shortly after he introduced Christ to Israel. Since the kingdom had not materialized in the interim, he began to entertain doubts regarding Christ's mission (vs. 20). That very hour, Jesus performed miracles predicted of the Messiah in Isaiah 61:1-2, and told John's disciples to convey that information back to John, which must have reassured the great prophet.

27. Jesus declared that John the Baptist was more than just an ordinary prophet. He stood last in the long line of prophets and actually heralded the personal presence of the Messiah as predicted in Malachi 3:1.

28. Though John the Baptist was the greatest of the prophets, positionally he was still in the Old Testament period, and was martyred several years before the new dispensation of grace began after Calvary. He announced the coming kingdom, but never lived to see it. Thus, even the least of those who live on into the kingdom age will be in a far more advanced period of revelation, and will enjoy more privileges than did John.

29-30. The fact that God can be "justified" proves that the term signifies "to be declared righteous," not to make righteous. The people simply acknowledged God's righteousness.

31-35. John was ascetic, while Jesus ate normally, yet their severe critics found fault with both because these critics disagreed with the message proclaimed.

36-40. Upon one occasion Jesus was invited to eat in the home of Simon, a Pharisee. When a notoriously sinful woman came in and anointed Jesus' feet with valuable perfume, Simon thought evil of Christ for not refusing her favor. Christ's omniscience told Him Simon's thoughts, and He answered with a short parable.

41-42. Jesus said that a creditor forgave two debtors, one of whom owed ten times as much as the other. Jesus then asked Simon which debtor would feel the most love toward the creditor.

43-50. The answer, of course, is the one who was forgiven the most. The application Jesus makes to Simon and the sinful woman is that both have been forgiven, but that the one who has a greater amount to have been forgiven will appreciate that forgiveness most. The more we sense the lost and hopeless condition we were in, the more we will appreciate what Christ has done for us.

8:1. He went throughout every city and village preaching and shewing the glad things of the Kingdom of God. Jesus' ministry was very extensive in Galilee, but His message was not that he would die for the sins of the world, but that He had come to establish the kingdom prophesied in the Old Testament. The twelve disciples were gaining matchless experience by being with the Son of God during these days of teaching and healing.

2-3. Also accompanying Christ and ministering to Him were a number of formerly demon-possessed women, whose lives must have evidenced complete transformation. Joanna is only mentioned here and in 24:10 in Luke's gospel.

4-15. Jesus was famous for His parables. Parables are stories that are true to life and nature in every way, thus differing from allegories and fables. They are used to teach spiritual truths. Jesus used parables often, the New Testament recording about thirty separate stories. Jesus used parables for at least five reasons. (1) To attract attention. They have tremendous interest value, and everyone likes a story. (2) To prevent hearers from being repelled too quickly by normal direct statements. (3) To stimulate inquiry and to teach. These stories could easily be remembered, and were thus good vehicles for preserving the truth. (4) To reveal the truth as some could understand a story taught in parabolic form more easily than regular teaching. (5) To conceal the truth. Often a story would protect the truth from the mockery of a scoffer who could not understand the meaning. One's spiritual condition frequently determined how much he would understand of what Jesus said. The parable of the four soils is found in every Gospel except John's. The four types of soils could easily be located within the same field. The represent the hearts (vs. 15) or minds of men. (1) The wayside or pathway soil (vs. 12) is hardened and uncultivated, and the seed which represents God's Word cannot penetrate it. Note the influence of Satan in keeping this type person from believing (cf. II Cor 4:4). (2) The rocky ground (vs. 13) had a thin layer of dirt over solid rock. This one is completely superficial and emotional, but has *no* root. (3) The thorny ground (vs. 14) is a double-minded man. He makes a profession, but it is unreal. (4) Only the good ground (vss. 8, 15) bears any fruit and represents a really saved individual. Jesus taught His disciples that they would sow much seed, but should not be distressed by seemingly poor results, and some cases of apparent salvation which were in reality nothing but an outward emotional experience.

16-18. These verses contain a great principle regarding the outward indication of one's salvation: there should be no secret believers. Really saved people will grow in grace but mere professors will lose even that which they seem to possess.

19-21. His mother and his brethren. By today's standards, Mary and Joseph had a good-sized family. Four brothers and additional sisters are mentioned in Mark 6:3. Jesus was not here denying His normal family relationships or even downplaying their importance, but He was stressing the new and more important spiritual relationships resulting from belief in Himself.

22-25. Jesus stilled or walked upon the waters on several different occasions, here and again after the feeding of the five thousand (Jn 6:17-21). By it,

He demonstrated His complete and absolute sovereignty over the natural elements. Also these miracles proved Christ's deity to the disciples and to us.

26-40. The story of the maniac of Gadara took place at ruins today called Khersa in the eastern edge of the steep slopes overlooking the Sea of Galilee. The story illustrates several things about demon possession. Some characteristics are: (1) insanity (prior to the action of verse 35). He was out of his mind, it being controlled by the demon; (2) indecency (vs. 27), this often accompanied demonic control; (3) injury (vs. 29, cf. Mk 5:4-5), he cut himself; and (4) infamy—his poor family must have lived in shame. That is what the devil drives man to. But this poor soul was delivered by Christ spiritually, physically, and mentally. The result was that he readily proclaimed far and wide what great things Jesus had done for him.

Many demons had controlled this man, and called themselves Legion (vs. 30). A Roman legion usually consisted of six thousand men, or ten cohorts of six hundred. They feared that Christ would send them into the deep (Gr *abyssos*). Apparently, while on earth Jesus did cast many demons into a place of confinement from which they will not be released until the Tribulation Period (cf. Rev 9:1-11). Jesus was certainly not responsible for the destruction of the herd of swine in the vicinity. The incident does reveal that demons may affect animals.

41-42. Jairus had only had one child, a twelve-year-old daughter who was at the point of death when Jesus entered Capernaum. He came to Jesus for help, asking the Master to come quickly.

43. However, they were thronged with people, each with his own special needs, and progress toward Jairus' house was slow. In the multitude was a woman with an incurable hemorrhage. She was unclean according to Leviticus 15:19, and was not permitted to come near people, but she cared not for that if she could only be healed. She was desperate.

44-48. When she touched Jesus in faith she was healed. Jesus' omnisicence caused Him to perceive her actions and He asked for the woman to identify herself, probably to reveal her publicly to the crowd and to further instruct her. Jesus said her faith had saved her.

49-50. After this incident and delay, messengers from Jairus' house came and reported the death of his daughter. Jesus knew this tried his faith, and told Jairus to continue believing and his daughter would be made well.

51. Jesus took only the parents and Peter, James, and John into the house. He preserved the sanctity of the home by not parading twelve men into this private place.

52-53. The little girl was really dead, but the death of a believer's body may outwardly be likened to sleep, which it resembles (cf. Jn 11:11-14; I Cor 11:30; I Thess 4:13-14). The Bible teaches no such doctrine as "soul sleep" as do some. At death, an individual's soul is either consciously (1) with the Lord (Phil 1:21-23; II Cor 5:8), or (2) in torment in hades awaiting the final resurrection to death (Lk 16:23).

54-56. Jesus raised the girl from the dead and her spirit reentered her body. Mark, who received much of his information from the eyewitness, Peter, records (5:42) that she arose and walked. No one could doubt this fantastic miracle.

E. Christ's Dealings with His Disciples. 9:1-50.

9:1. Christ granted His twelve disciples power and prerogatives over demons and sickness never exercised by man either before or after. The purpose of this was to place a divine seal of approval upon their message as well as to meet the needs of people.

2-6. The disciples preached the good news (vs. 6) of the kingdom of God.

Spiritual birth into God's family was a requirement for entrance (Jn 3:3, 5) but the kingdom itself was to be earthly, with Jesus ruling the world from Jerusalem in fulfillment of Old Testament prophecy (Isa 2:1-4; 11:1-9; Amos 9:11-15; Mic 4:6-8).

7-9. Herod, who had beheaded John the Baptist (see Mt 14:1-12 and Mk 6:14-29), wondered if he had risen from the dead when he began to hear about the miracles Jesus was performing. His desire to see Jesus was met in Jerusalem during the mock trials prior to Christ's death (Lk 23:7-12).

10. The Twelve are called disciples prior to being sent out. They are called apostles (Gr *apostolos*), meaning "sent out ones" in verse 10. The feeding of the five thousand occurred shortly after the death of John the Baptist as Jesus felt the need of rest (Mk 6:31).

11. The plans for rest were laid aside when multitudes followed Jesus to a quiet area on the northern edge of the Sea of Galilee in the spring of the year (Jn 6:4).

12-17. All four evangelists record this great miracle, and each makes it clear that five thousand men, not counting women and children, were fed from the miraculous multiplication of five small barley loaves and two fishes. The miracle must have occurred as the disciples broke pieces from their tiny allotments and distributed them to the sitting crowds. The twelve baskets collected were like little travel bags and probably provided sustenance for the disciples as they went to the Passover which was approaching.

18-22. Peter's great confession at Caesarea Philippi near Mt. Hermon, occurred approximately six months prior to the crucifixion. It marks the beginning of any mention by Christ that He is going to be killed (vs. 22), which explains the reaction of Peter to such a prediction (see Mt 16:23). This time also marks the very first mention by Christ of the fact that He would establish His church (Mt 16:18). Jesus' use of the future tense in this initial prediction points to Pentecost when the church was first physically manifested.

23-24. Jesus' challenge to His disciples was faithfulness, denial of self, and daily sacrifice. Its results are stated in paradoxical terms. If one lives merely for this life, the following life will be lost. But if one cares not about this life in order to serve Christ, only then will he secure life eternal.

25-26. For what is a man advantaged. This is still true. No amount of earthly gain can ever make up for the unutterable loss of one's soul.

27. There be some standing here, which shall not taste of death, till they see the kingdom of God. This verse has to be a prediction that some of the disciples would see Christ in all his glory during the soon-coming transfiguration.

28. Peter, James, and John made up the inner circle of disciples. At the outer perimeter was the group of five hundred who saw Christ after his resurrection (I Cor 15:6). A bit closer were the seventy disciples who were sent out two by two to preach and heal (Lk 10:1, 17). Still closer were the Twelve, of whom these three were specially selected to witness this event, the raising of Jairus' daughter, and Jesus' agony in Gethsemane. Of these three, John the beloved was closest to Christ (Jn 13:23; 21:20). The mountain of transfiguration has been thought by some to be Mt. Tabor in the Jezreel Valley, but many feel that Mt. Hermon's slopes above Caesarea Philippi more naturally meet the idea of "high mountain" (Mk 9:2). Hermon's highest elevation is over 10,000 feet, while Tabor only reaches to 1,843 feet, but is a majestic solitary bell-shaped hill.

29. Christ's clothing and complexion were surrounded and filled with a magnificent glory that had not been seen by mortal man since God's glory left the Temple in Ezekiel's day.

30-31. Moses and Elijah stood as representatives of the law and the prophets, and discussed Christ's coming death at Jerusalem. It must have been a wonderful yet an awesome experience for Christ as He was encouraged by these two fearless and faithful Old Testament saints to finish the task for which He had come.

32-33. The three disciples were fast asleep while all this was transpiring, and were surprised by what they saw when they awoke.

34-36. God the Father spoke, **This is my beloved Son: hear him.** All attention was to be directed to Christ.

37-43. Jesus and the three disciples returned from the mountain to find the other disciples unable to cast a difficult demon out of a young boy. The boy's father was distraught. Apparently the disciples had not relied on God in prayer for the power they needed to cast out the demon (Mk 9:26). Jesus then immediately restored the lad. The full account is given in Mark 9:14-29.

44-45. For the second time in a month, Jesus clearly predicted His coming death in Jerusalem, but the disciples **understood not this saying.** They could not fit a crucified King into the kingdom plans which they were all so busily announcing to the people in every town and city. In fact, it was not until after the resurrection that they even began to understand how Christ's death fit into God's plan. The kingdom was to be postponed due to Jewish rejection of Christ, and the church age was to occupy the interval in between.

46-48. Jesus said that true greatness is achieved by humility. This is true, but must also be balanced with the biblical doctrine of labor, striving, pressing forward, and occupying till He comes. In all of our labors, and especially in our successes, we must not think more highly of ourselves than we ought (Rom 12:3).

49-50. Jesus was not in favor of a narrow sectarianism which looks askance at anyone not in "our group" or not approved by "our agencies." We should all serve the Lord the best we can, expose error and deceitfulness as Paul did, yet not be ruled by a spirit of divisiveness that would condemn all who do not conform to "our" way of doing things. Thus, Jesus reminded: **he that is not against us, is for us.** For the converse truth see Mt 12:30; Mk 9:40.

V. THE PERAEAN MINISTRY OF THE SON. 9:51-19:27.

This large section of material from 9:51-19:27 is almost totally unique to Luke. Only a few isolated events are recorded in the other Gospels. This section contains an account of Christ's basic ministry in Peraea, east of the Jordan. The great majority of the parables in Luke are included here, almost all of which appear nowhere else.

A. Christ's Determination to Go to Jerusalem. 9:51-62.

51-53. Between the October Feast of the Tabernacles (Jn 7:14-10:21) and Christ's final Passover, a period of about six months, His life was in constant danger, especially in Judaea. During this time Jesus spent most of His time in Peraea. When He ventured into Jerusalem for the Feast of Dedication or Hanukkah in December (Jn 10:22), He was practically stoned (vs. 13). Thereafter He spent some time in Peraea (Jn 10:40), interrupted only by His mission to raise Lazarus. Luke tells us that Jesus was determined to go up to Jerusalem.

54-56. The beloved disciple John, with his brother James, was not always so loving and kind, as this passage notes. They were called Boanerges, sons of thunder (Mk 3:17), and needed to be transformed just like any other sinners.

57-62. Let the dead bury their dead (vs. 60) probably means let those who are spiritually dead bury the physically dead. Doing Christ's bidding is far

more important than even attendance at the funeral of one's own father.

B. Christ's Ministry with the Seventy. 10:1-24.

10:1-2. Christ was a trainer of men. He gave these seventy men a burden for the souls of men. He told them that **The harvest truly is great, but the laborers are few.** He sent them out two by two to help meet this need.

3-11. For the laborer is worthy of his hire (vs. 7) is quoted by Paul in I Timothy 5:18 as "Scripture." Even New Testament writings were counted as Scripture from the time they were written (cf. also II Peter 3:15-16 where Paul's epistles are called Scripture).

12-16. These verses definitely teach degrees of punishment, based on degrees of sin according to how much light people had. Some will be judged more severely than others, and as a result receive greater punishment in hell than others. This doctrine is also taught by Christ in each of the other gospels (see Mt 10:15-16; 11:21-24; Mk 6:11; and Jn 19:11).

17-20. The seventy are thrilled that even demons are subject to them. Jesus sees the disciples' success as a foretaste of the complete defeat of Satan. The cross would signal Satan's final downfall (Jn 12:31) and his being cast into the lake of fire only follows naturally (Rev 20:10), though separated by a larger time interval.

21-24. Christ's disciples had tremendous privileges for which countless others before them longed. Their greatest joy, however, was to be regarding their own salvation (vs. 20).

C. Christ's Parabolic Teaching Ministry. 10:25-13:21.

25-29. The parable of the Good Samaritan was told by Jesus in answer to the self-justifying question of a lawyer, **And who is my neighbor?**

30. A certain man went down from Jerusalem to Jericho. He was probably a Jew. The way down is from approximately 2600 feet above sea level to approximately 800 feet below sea level and is through a treacherous wilderness. Thieves and robbers waited for lonely travelers. This man was attacked, beaten, robbed, and stripped of clothes.

31-37. Two Jews, a priest and a Levite, passed by but did nothing to help the poor man. Then a Samaritan (see Jn 4:9) came along and aided the robber victim; even seeing to his full recovery by paying for his stay at an inn. This Samaritan was a true neighbor. He had a compassionate heart, a helping hand, and unlimited concern. He gave up personal comfort, physical energy, and valuable time. As one preacher expressed it, the robbers beat him up, the priest and Levite passed him up, but the Samaritan picked him up. The thief said, "What's yours is mine, I'll take it." The priest and Levite reasoned, "What's mine is mine, I'll keep it." But the Samaritan said, "What's mine is yours, we'll share it." Let us heed Jesus' final injunction to the lawyer, **Go, and do thou likewise** (vs. 37).

38-42. Mary . . . sat at Jesus' feet, and heard his word, but Martha was cumbered about much serving. This familiar story appears only in Luke, and outside of this story Mary and Martha are only mentioned in John 11 and 12. Yet these two ladies are among the most famous of all Bible characters, and were some of our Lord's dearest friends. The lesson to be learned from this true story is that we must choose to do the best things, and not be overly concerned about ourselves through self-pity. There is nothing wrong with serving, but we must first sit at Jesus' feet and spend time with Him.

11:1. As He was praying . . . one of his disciples said unto Him, Lord, teach us to pray. Jesus set the example of prayer before His disciples (see a study of *Jesus' Habits of Prayer* by S. D. Gordon).

2-4. These verses contain what is commonly called the "Lord's Prayer," also found in Matthew 6:9-13. It is a model prayer to show us how to pray, not a pattern to be repeated in vain repetition. We are to (1) recognize God for who He is and glorify His name, (2) pray for His program and (3) His will to be accomplished, then (4) ask for daily food, (5) forgiveness of sins, and (6) deliverance from sin and evil. These points are elementary and not exhaustive. Mature prayer will not be limited to these initial requests, but should at least contain these basic points. An example of how Christ prayed is given in John 17, the second longest prayer in the Bible. The longest is found in I Kings 8 when Solomon dedicated the temple.

5-10. The parable of the friend who came at midnight was told to reinforce an aspect about prayer. Although importunity is important in prayer, this parable is probably trying to show a contrast between God and the friend who eventually opened the door. God is more than a friend, and will certainly grant our needs much more readily than the man who had gone to bed.

11-13. In addition, God is our Father and desires to give us freely all things. One of the most precious gifts is naturally the Holy Spirit who abides with all believers today, but who was not resident in the lives of Old Testament saints.

14-23. After casting out a demon, Jesus was accused of casting out demons through the chief of demons, i.e. Satan (vs. 15). This wicked accusation on the part of some was equivalent to blasphemy against the Holy Spirit (Jn 12:10). Jesus performed His ministry through the power of the Holy Spirit, and this should have been evident to all unbiased seekers. Jesus used a piece of logic, however, to clear up the situation, noting that if Satan cast out his own demons, then he would be divided against himself, an unimaginable state of affairs.

24-28. After casting out a demon, Jesus wanted to stress the fact that a man's life must then be filled with good things, namely Christ and His salvation, or the man would be even more susceptible to the same calamity recurring than he was the first time. Mere self-reformation has no guaranteed results.

29-32. Jesus continually claimed to be God (Jn 5:17-18; 10:33), the Messiah (Jn 4:25-26), and the only way to heaven (Jn 14:6). Here He says that failure to heed His direct plain message, supported by signs and wonders, will result in condemnation. Even the Queen of Sheba, and those who repented at Jonah's preaching in Nineveh had enough light to know what to do. How much more blameworthy will these be if they fail to trust Christ. Note that Jesus fully endorsed the historicity of Jonah in these verses. Critics who deny the biblical account of Jonah degrade Christ as well.

33-36. Since the eye admits into the life that which influences it, Jesus is concerned that it be fed light, in the moral sense of the term, rather than darkness. Then one will become as a shining light himself.

37-40. The Pharisees were very careful to maintain outward cleanliness, but sometimes were unconcerned about the inside. Jesus probably ate without washing on purpose to point this out to his host.

41-54. Notice how boldly Jesus spoke in these verses. Six times he uttered woes, and once called them fools (spiritually imperceptive), and once hypocrites. Jesus was just over thirty, and this did not set well with the older generation. Jesus rightly accused them of deceit (vss. 41-42), pride (vs. 43), inconsistency (vss. 44-46), condoning murder and conspiracy (vss. 47-51), and hindering people from being saved (vs. 53). Luke notes how heated the discussion got in verse 53 where it says the Pharisees were rudely provoking Christ to speak about many such sub-

jects in hopes (vs. 54) of being able to accuse Jesus of something in order to put him to death. Christ was their thorn in the flesh.

12:1. Beware of the leaven of the Pharisees which is hypocrisy. One way of teaching is to set the proper example. Jesus did that. Another way is to learn from the misconduct of others. Jesus pointed that out too.

2-3. It is sobering to think that everything we have ever spoken will one day be revealed. We must guard our hearts, minds, lips, and hands.

4-5. Jesus had much to say about hell. These verses tell us it is a place, that God has the power to cast into hell, and that this occurs after this life. The grave does not end it all.

6-9. But the child of God is secure in Christ, both now and forever. Nothing can ever harm a believer in this life apart from the permission of God according to His perfect will.

10. The sin of blasphemy against the Holy Spirit could refer to the sin of seeing the Holy Spirit's working, and openly opposing it, such as attributing the miracles Christ performed to the power of Satan (cf. Lk 10:15). Or it could refer to an act which shows a state of sin in which there is a wilful determined opposition to the power of the Holy Spirit. It could thus be the result of gradual progress in sin. Jesus accuses no man of such sin, but sternly warns against anyone coming to such a state of affairs. How do you avoid such a predicament? Harden not your hearts! Believe God, and trust Christ as your Saviour and Lord.

11-12. Jesus warned that believers would be persecuted, but He also held out assurance that He would guide in that day of trouble.

13-15. A man's life consisteth not in the abundance of the things which he possesseth. What an important reminder this is in our materialistic age. Many seek after things, but all find that they do not satisy. Jesuis counselled, "Seek ye first the kingdom of God and his righteousness; and all these things shall be added unto you" (Mt 6:33).

16-21. Jesus spoke the parable of the rich fool to two young inheritance seekers (vs. 13). There are more parables dealing with money than with any other subject. This is probably because there are so many snares and temptations that beset those who possess and/or seek to acquire money. The warning contained in this story is that of providing amply for the physical aspects of life, while ignoring preparations for the life to come. Wealth cannot secure one's salvation, but it can be used for heavenly good.

22-30. In these verses the Master exhorted His disciples not to fret about securing food or clothing. He goes from the lesser to the greater by noting how God provides food for the fowl (vs. 24) and coverings for the flowers (vss. 27-28). If that is true, how much more shall God provide for His own children.

31-33. As a summary statement, Christ promised **seek ye the kingdom of God; and all these things shall be added unto you.**

34. For where your treasure is, there will your heart be also. One of the greatest things a pastor can ever do for his people is to get them to give tithes and offerings to the Lord. If they do, their hearts will be attuned to God. Pastors who preach on godly giving do their people a great spiritual service.

35. Let your loins be girded about, and your lights burning. Even though God will provide, the servant of Christ is to be about His Master's business until He comes. The parable that follows is drawn from the familiar near-eastern wedding custom.

36. Men that wait for their Lord, when he will return from the wedding. In the Orient, the groom returned with his bride after claiming her at her father's house. This parable could be spoken mainly for the Jews who will welcome Christ back with His bride after the Tribulation Period, but it certainly has an application for the church today.

37-40. Several things are taught. (1) Expectancy. Servants should be looking for the Master's return. (2) Preparedness. Servants should have things in order. (3) Rewards. Verse 37 indicates rewards for the faithful servants, as is taught elsewhere (vss. 43-44; Lk 19:17). The figure of the thief is also given by Paul (I Thess 5:4). The coming of Christ is never to overtake a believer as a thief. We are to be waiting and watching for His return.

41-46. This portion is vitally connected to what precedes it, and acts as a further amplification. The obedient servants will be blessed and rewarded (vss. 42-44), but those "servants" who disobeyed will suffer punishment (vss. 45-46).

47-49. The fact that there will be degrees of punishment is taught here. The torment of hell will not be uniformly felt. The light one possesses helps determine how responsible one is. Some will be found more guilty than others, but no lost man can claim innocency in that day.

50. But I have a baptism to be baptized with. That which Jesus referred to as necessary for Him to undergo (see also Mk 10:38-39) was His own coming death which is referred to under several figures in the New Testament.

51-53. Christ is the ultimate divider. What men decide regarding Christ determines their ultimate destiny, and also draws the barrier lines between men.

54-56. Jesus declared that signs were clearly discernible relative to His ministry, yet men refused to heed these. Such men must bear the responsibility for their own destruction under such circumstances.

57-59. These verses teach that one must settle with his adversary (in this case God) before it is too late. Verse 59 does not indicate that eventually one would get out of hell, because there no one has anything with which to "pay." It is too late.

13:1-5. Except ye repent, ye shall all likewise perish. Twice Jesus repeated identical words to reinforce the necessity of repentance (vss. 3, 5). Calamity and destruction await all who refuse to heed the warning. Jesus perhaps has reference to the events of A.D.70, and certainly beyond to eternal punishment.

6-9. He spake also this parable; A certain man had a fig tree planted in his vineyard. This parable is found only in Luke, but both here and in the miraculous cursing of the fig tree in Matthew 21:18-21, the tree seems to stand for Israel. The lesson is that when God gives spiritual privileges, He has a right to expect fruit. One might also learn the danger of not producing fruit. Even though the Lord was merciful with Israel, He yet had to judge that nation. The three or four years in the parable are probably not meant to represent so many years of Christ's ministry, but rather an adequate time for testing fruitfulness.

10. And he was teaching in one of the synagogues on the sabbath. This was Jesus' habitual Sabbath day practice. It so happened that these occasions became times when Christ healed some as well. The religious leaders constantly tried to convict Jesus of breaking the sabbath restrictions with such miraculous works.

11. Only Luke records this case of healing. As a physician, he has an interest in and sympathy for stories about women, of which he records more than the other gospel writers. This woman had been bent over for eighteen years by Satan (vs. 16). Though all sickness cannot be uniformly blamed on Satan, the Bible does enumerate several cases as in Job 2:6-7; Acts 10:38; I Corinthians 5:5 and II Corinthians 12:7.

12-13. Thou art loosed. Here the Greek tense is perfect and indicates that the cure was complete and certain.

14. The speech of the synagogue ruler was a hypocritical and underhanded way of criticizing Christ. It naturally drew a severe rebuke from the Lord.

15-16. Jesus' reply was that the sabbath was not intended to prevent works of necessity or mercy. The application of this truth is as follows: some jobs today require Sunday employment, such as hospitals, law enforcement, and fire-fighting. Most other jobs, however, can often be performed on other days, even though Sunday of itself is not to be kept as the Jewish sabbath. As a rule, Sunday is regarded as a day of worship, and we should not needlessly violate that principle, even though we realize there are exceptions.

17. Jesus' rebuke had its proper effect. His adversaries were ashamed, while His admirers were amazed and rejoiced. Nevertheless, a polarity was developing regarding Jesus.

18-19. Jesus parabolically indicated that a mustard seed sprouting into a better than ten foot tree represented the kingdom of God. This probably signified the large or surprising growth of Christianity from a tiny seed. The birds that sat in the branches may picture evil as in Matthew 13:4 and 19, or they may simply be an indication of the fact that this herb was large enough to hold birds on its branches.

20-21. The kingdom of God was also compared to a woman who mingled leaven into several loaves of meal until they had all risen. Perhaps a majority of older interpreters have seen this as the spreading of good throughout the world via the church. But this would seem to contradict the fact that the wheat did not take over the tares (Mt 13) and Jesus' forecast in Matthew 24:37 that the end times would be as in Noah's day. Besides, leaven is a picture of that which corrupts, and represents sin (Ex 12:15; Lk 12:1; I Cor 5:6-8). It is better to view this as a picture of the externalism, unbelief, evil doctrine, and worldliness which tend to inflate the church. Only fire ends the work of leaven!

D. Christ's Growing Public Confrontation with Religious Leaders. 13:22-16:31.

22. Journeying toward Jerusalem. Here Luke brings us back to the theme of 9:51, that Jesus was on His final preaching tour and was to keep a divine appointment in Jerusalem.

23. Lord, are there few that be saved? This question drew a lengthy answer from Christ that was to serve as a warning against religious presumption.

24-27. Man's time of probation ends both suddenly and surely. Naturally, death ends man's opportunity for salvation. There is no truth to some so-called second chance theories. But apparently at the judgment some may presume upon having once seen or known Christ. But one must know Christ in the personal way that characterized true faith and trust in His shed blood for one's salvation from sin.

28. The kingdom of God. This phrase has several prominent usages, for which see George N.H. Peters, *The Theocratic Kingdom*, and Alva J. McClain, *The Greatness of the Kingdom*. Here it has reference to the Millennial Kingdom when the Old Testament patriarchs will be resurrected to join Christ and the redeemed of all the ages during His one thousand year earthly reign. This fulfills numerous Old Testament prophecies (Isa 11:1-9; Mic 4:1-3) as well as Revelation 20:1-6.

29. Coming from the four winds could speak either of the regathering of Israel which will take place as the kingdom age begins, or of the cosmopolitan makeup of the kingdom. Both will be true.

30. The last being first and the first turning out to be last must have been a thought of momentous proportions for any Jewish hearers who considered it. Just think, those who judged Christ and condemned Him to death will one day stand before Him who is the Almighty God of the universe. Things will be different then.

31-33. The Pharisees told Jesus that Herod Antipas (see on Lk 1:5) planned to kill Him. Jesus replied that He would continue His work according to schedule (the three days are not intended to be taken literally) and then His work of redemption would be completed in Jerusalem (Jn 19:30).

34-35. O Jerusalem, Jerusalem, which killeth the prophets. Christ knew that Jerusalem, not Herod, was the real threat to His life. The lament for Jerusalem realizes its bloody past, but also recognizes its blessed future, which will not occur until the end of the Great Tribulation.

14:1-6. Luke the physician is the only gospel writer to record this healing. Dropsy was literally internalized or excessive water in the tissues, and this is the only mention of it in the New Testament. This Sabbath situation was apparently a trap set up by Jesus' opponents. No man with this terrible dropsy disease would be invited to supper at the house of a chief Pharisee, let alone sitting right in front of Jesus. Verse one also indicates that **they watched him.** The Pharisees refused to answer Jesus' question, **Is it lawful to heal on the sabbath day?** If they had answered "yes" they could not condemn Jesus for healing. But if they answered "no" they would have condemned themselves as indifferent to human suffering. Their silence was Christ's justification. If it was illegal, they should have said so. Thereafter, Christ healed the man. Christ's final question placed this sabbath healing in its proper perspective as doing good or rendering help whenever necessary.

7-11. And he put forth a parable to those which were bidden. The conduct of the guests at this sabbath meal was such that Jesus commented on it with a parable. The idea of lowest and highest seats refers to the almost universal custom of designating places for honored persons at meals and other functions. Jesus warned against placing oneself at the "head table" unless invited to do so. Removal could result in dishonor. Contrariwise, if the lowly seat has been selected at first, the host would thereafter assign one to the proper dignity. This thinking is against our inclination. We want the best for ourselves. But Jesus would have humility before exaltation. We must be little in our own eyes before we can be large in His eyes.

12-15. Similarly, Jesus cautioned His followers to invite guests who could provide little promise of returning the favor. This action helps one's attitude to be correct with regard to giving and receiving. When we give without hope of return, we trust God to bless and provide any reward as He may or may not see fit either here or at **the resurrection of the just** (cf. Jn 5:28-29; Rev 20:4-6).

16. A certain man made a great supper, and bade many. This parable paints a picture of God's abundant provision and invitation of salvation, refused by the Jews, then offered with all speed and diligence to others not previously invited.

18-20. And they all with one consent began to make excuse. Literally, they began "to beg off." Someone once defined an excuse as "the skin of a reason stuffed with a lie." There are three classes of excuses, all false on the very surface. (1) No one should buy land without previously having examined it. (2) No one would ever purchase ten oxen without knowing their condition. (3) The excuse about marrying a wife was evidently based on Deuteronomy 24:5, but this application was certainly novel. The **I cannot come** (vs. 20) actually means "I will not come." These invited guests rudely, ungratefully, and purposefully refused to come, even though they fully understood their deceitful practice.

21-22. After that, all classes of previously uninvited guests were asked to come, and they did come. This probably speaks in part of the command to take the gospel to the Gentiles given after the rejection, crucifixion, burial, and resurrection of Christ (Mt 28:18-20; Mk 16:15).

23. Compel them to come in. This must be regarded as a moral persuasion, not the use of physical force. Every effort is to be made by Christ's servants to bring the lost to Him. His Word must be used diligently to overcome the sinner's despair, as well as the arrogance of the self-righteous. Jesus came to seek and to save that which was lost (Lk 19:10) and we are sent on the same task. God desires that all legitimate means be used to procure the acceptance of His gracious invitation. Many a soul has been led to Christ by the earnest, tearful, sincere pleading of a dedicated Christian worker yielded to the control of the Holy Spirit.

26. In the context of all other Scripture (Ex 20:12; Mt 5:44; Rom 12:10) this command must be interpreted in a comparative manner. Christ meant that one must place Him above all other relationships. To be Christ's disciple, He must be Lord. If He is not lord of all, He may not be Lord at all!

27. Bear his cross. For one to bear a cross means to experience the shame and humiliation, as well as the toil and suffering, that this form of punishment suggests. Bearing one's cross is not an easy assignment; it is just being a true Christian with all that entails.

28-33. The short stories about considering the cost before building a tower or placing an army in the field is a picture of fully considering what it will cost before one becomes a Christian: for some, it may seemingly cost more than for others.

34-35. If the salt have lost his savour. A disciple must have certain essential qualities. If these are gone, he is useless to Christ, and as the saying goes "not worth his salt." The salt in use during Christ's time was impure, and the sodium chloride could be leached out of that common salt. This represents the type of disciple Christ does not want.

15:1-2. Publicans and sinners. Three stories with a common theme are recounted by Christ in this chapter to illustrate His love and concern for sinful men and women. **The Pharisees and scribes murmured** because Jesus showed such love and kindness to sinners.

3. And he spake this parable unto them. Both sinners and Pharisees alike were to hear and apply this parable. The word parable occurs only once in this chapter, perhaps pointing to one parable with three connected parts. In each story something is lost: (1) a sheep; (2) a shekel; and (3) a son. In each case, the lost object is found and produces rejoicing. The sheep is innocently lost, the coin carelessly lost, but the son willfully lost. The percentage of loss grows in each case from one out of a hundred, to one out of ten, to one out of two.

4. The sheep is an exceedingly dumb animal, seemingly not having much sense. As such, it is sometimes used to picture the lost spiritual condition of people (Isa 53:6; Jer 50:6; Mt 9:36; I Pet 2:25). This parable tells of a shepherd going out in search of one lost sheep while he leaves ninety-nine safely in the fold. It is almost a universal human characteristic to go after that which one loses. Jesus sees the plight of lost sinners and goes to seek and to save (Lk 19:10), while the Pharisees care little about lost sinners.

5. Layeth it on His shoulders, rejoicing. The poor sheep was probably exhausted from wandering, exposure, and hunger. The shepherd did not mind the extra burden or journey because he rejoiced.

6-7. The friends and neighbors were summoned because of the shepherd's

great joy and because they may have aided in the search. Jesus' remark that there is also joy in heaven over a sinner that repents perhaps sadly implies that not many rejoiced with Christ here on earth regarding these matters.

8-10. The story of the lost coin was perhaps told for women listeners. The coin was lost right at home. People may be members of good churches and still be lost and go to hell. The sheep may have had a vague idea it was lost, but this coin could picture those with no knowledge of being lost. We need to search for those who are lost to bring them to Christ. Joy in the presence of God's angels over repenting sinners (vs. 10) shows that they are interested in our salvation (cf. I Pet 1:10-12), though they do not aid it.

11. A certain man had two sons. In the two previous stories Jesus told how the Pharisees should act when lost sinners were found. In this longer story he pictured how they did act. They can see themselves in the person of the elder brother, who had his good and bad points. He was morally straight, a hard worker, and an obedient individual (vs. 29), but he was also proud and had no fellowship with the father. He was more willing to think of his brother's sin than of his repentance.

12-32. The younger son's conduct can be summarized in an alliterative fashion with just nine key words. His rebellion resulted in riotous living as he hit rock bottom before his realization to repent and return, where he experienced reception, reconciliation, and rejoicing. Ralph Earle sees his movements as from possessor to prodigal to pauper to penitent to pardoned. His wicked conduct was willful and inexcusable, but his repentance was complete and his forgiveness absolute. He is a picture of every man born on this earth and in need of a Saviour. It is almost ironical that everything the prodigal son sought in the far country was right at home. There was abundance, freedom, and rejoicing.

The father's part pictures God's love for lost sinners. He is kind, waits for the son, goes to meet him, perhaps to save him the deserved punishment he might have received from others for disgracing his family and village, and forgets his past life. He **was dead, and is alive again; and was lost, and is found** (vs. 32).

16:1-12. The contextual connection of the story of the unjust steward with the parable of the prodigal son is perhaps that both deal with wasting and abusing worldly goods. Verse 14 also takes notice of the covetous audience. The plot is that a rich man, upon discovering wastefulness in his steward, was going to dismiss him (vs. 12). To protect his future, the steward immediately began making friends on the outside by juggling the goods in favor of those who owed the master (vss. 3-7). The story continues to have the master commend the unuust steward for his prudence (vs. 8).

Many see a problem as to why Jesus used such a character as the unjust steward, and even told of his commendation. Christ could simply be stressing the use of one's money and influence to aid others for Christ's sake (vss. 9-12), but this does not seem to be it entirely. There are, of course, some valuable character qualities in the unjust steward that are worthy of imitation, including his quick decisiveness, his self-collectedness, his energy, and his tact. But the main lesson seems to lie in the larger idea of realizing he is about to be dismissed and doing something about it. Men should realize that death comes as a certainty, and that they must prepare properly for what comes afterward.

13. Ye cannot serve God and mammon. This does not mean a man cannot be wealthy and still serve God. But the love of money is the root of all evil (I Tim 6:10). If a person desires wealth, then he ceases to please God. A man's loyalties cannot be divided, and God demands that everything be subservient to Him.

16. The law and the prophets were until John. Until the coming of John the Baptist and Jesus Christ, the only message Old Testament saints had was the law of Moses and the prophets. **Since that time the kingdom of God is preached.** John and Christ heralded a new order, the long-awaited kingdom age. John announced it as "at hand" (Mt 3:2) or as having come near. But even after John the Baptist was in jail and out of the picture, Jesus was still saying that the kingdom had not arrived, but was yet "at hand" (Mk 1:14-15). **And every man presseth into it.** Since the Jews rejected Christ's offer of the physical kingdom age and His rule over them, that dispensation and ministry was never inaugurated, though it shall be after the Great Tribulation (Mt 24:29-31; 25:31; Rev 19:11-20:6). But from the time of Christ to this day men can meet the spiritual requirements for entrance into that kingdom. In fact, the publicans and sinners often sought entrance with great earnestness and determination, while the Pharisees usually made no conscious efforts to enter. See John 3:1-16 for the story of one who did.

17-18. Jesus' teaching on divorce corrected the lax interpretation of the Jews based on their loose understanding of Deuteronomy 24, where Moses "permitted" divorce because of the "hardness of your hearts." While our Lord corrected and interpreted the Old Testament law, He did not eliminate it. The law was part of God's inspired truth and therefore it will not **fail.** No exceptions are given to the matters of divorce in this passage (cf. Mk10:11; I Cor 7:10-11ff. for further details). Some take the "exception clause" (Mt 19:9) to allow a divorce on the basis of "adultery." while others limit "fornication" (Gr *porneia*) to pre-marital sex. This view sees pre-marital unchastity as the only cause of "divorce" in breaking a Jewish engagement. A clear case of this was where Joseph suspected Mary of premarital unfaithfulness and desired to "put her away privily," (Mt 1:18-19). This interpretation allows no provision for divorce whatever. The seriousness of remarriage on non-scriptural grounds means that **whosoever marrieth her that is put away** (Gr *apolelumenen* from *apoluo* "to loose" or "divorce") also **committeth adultery.**

19-21. There was a certain rich man . . . and there was a certain beggar. This is the true account of a real history of two men, even though it is used much like a parable, i.e. to teach a particular lesson or to emphasize some principle. Some, however, contend that this is a parable saying that (1) the name Lazarus means "God helps" and is figurative or perhaps was intentionally chosen later because another Lazarus did come back from the dead; (2) it begins exactly as the preceding "parable" in Luke 16:1 (which incidentally is also not called a parable in the text); (3) it is used in parabolic fashion to prove a main point; (4) facts are presented in symbolic form; (5) it is in the context of other parables in Luke 15-18; (6) Christ would not have divulged such truths to unbelieving Pharisees; (7) the ability to see, hear, and communicate between heaven and hell after death is not possible; (8) the rich man would not have known Abraham and Lazarus by sight; and (9) in real life the names of rich men are given, while beggars' names are unknown. Some of these points are well-taken, but none prove that this account was only a parable.

There are numerous arguments for this account being a real history. (1) Parables are hypothetical illustrations and never name specific individuals. Here not only Lazarus is named, but also Abraham (vss. 22-25, 29-30) and Moses (vs. 31). (2) Jesus said "there was a certain rich man." Harry Ironside noted, "Was there, or was there not? He definitely declared that there

was." (3) Moses, Abraham, and the prophets are real people, whereas parables never refer to specific Old Testament saints. (4) Luke does not call this a parable as he does in thirteen other clear cases of parable so designated. (5) It is narrated like a real history. (6) Parables deal with the commonplace of what is known to be true to illustrate moral lessons, and come from natural life. This does not. (7) Hades is a reality, not a figure of speech. (8) There is no reason why Jesus could not have had in mind a particular case. He is describing what took place after death in the cases of two men for the moral profit of his hearers. (9) The conversation between the rich man and Abraham does not seem to lend itself to parabolic format. (10) Even a case history, as this is, could be used in parabolic fashion to teach a precise moral truth.

22. Abraham's bosom. This is a designation for where Abraham was, taken variously as being heaven itself or some other intermediate place.

23-25. And in hell he lift up his eyes, being in torments. Between death and resurrection the immaterial part of man goes either to be with the Lord, if he is saved (2 Cor 5:8; Phil 1:23), or into conscious torment as here. Resurrection reunites the body to the soul, and the state of existence continues to be either with Christ, or in the punishment of eternal duration (Mt 25:41, 46).

26. A great gulf fixed. Once a person passes from this life his probation is ended, and his eternal destiny is fixed. It has been appointed by God that once a man dies, then comes the judgment (Heb 9:27).

28-30. I have five brethren. The rich man's name and town are probably omitted in Christ's recounting of this history because of the embarrassment it might bring to his family that was still living.

31. If they hear not Moses and the prophets, neither will they be persuad-

ed, though one rose from the dead.
Another Lazarus did return from the
dead and the religious leaders sought
only to kill him, though some believed
through his testimony (Jn 12:9-11).
Several additional teachings about hell
are contained in this brief history.
Memory and personality continue
there even in the midst of untold anguish, misery, and suffering. There is
no returning or sending back of
messages from hell; thus, no reincarna-
tion, nor spiritism as it is thought of by
those who are thereby deceived.

E. Christ's Instruction of His Disciples. 17:1-19:27.

17:1. At this point Jesus began to
instruct His disciples more fully as the
time drew near for going to the cross.

**2. Should offend one of these little
ones.** The little ones could be children
as in a parallel passage (Mt 18:2-6), or
older believers as well (Mk 10:24). Our
lives must be carefully examined to see
how they affect those around us,
especially our families.

3-4. The rebuking of a brother who
sins against someone is to be done
privately, and forgiveness toward a
repentant brother is to be offered
unceasingly.

5-6. Asking God for anything, even
for a sycamore tree to be uprooted and
cast into the sea, will be accomplished
providing it is God's will. We may
never ask with assurance for anything
that is outside of God's will (I Jn 5:14).
To pray in the will of God we must
have His Word abiding in us (Jn 15:7),
because only His Word informs us with
certainty regarding His will.

7-10. This short parable of service
reflects upon what our attitude should
be when we have done all that God has
commanded. Instead of being proud
we are to be humble enough to consider ourselves as useless, because we
have simply done our duty. Compare
what we are to say of ourselves with
what Christ says to His faithful servants at the last day (Mt 25:21).

11. On His way to Jerusalem for the
final passover and his appointment
with the cross, Jesus passed between
the borders of Samaria and Galilee
across the Jordan and into Peraea.

**12. Ten men that were lepers, which
stood afar off.** This group of ten men
was composed of Jews and Samaritans
alike, their common leprosy having
erased the usual religious animosities
(Jn 4:9). They stood afar off because
of the command in Leviticus 13:45-46.

13-16. In reponse to their cry for
mercy, Jesus commanded them to go
show themselves to the priests (the
plural perhaps referring to their respective nationalities or districts), as commanded in Leviticus 14:2-7. Only as
they ventured off by faith did their
healings occur. Only one of the ten, a
Samaritan, returned to express thanks.

17-20. Why did the others not
return to give thanks also? Perhaps it
was because of superstition, ignorance,
self-interest, or plain ingratitude.

**21. The kingdom of God is within
you.** The word "within" (Gr *entos*) is
used in the New Testament only twice,
here and in Matthew 23:26.
Theological as well as contextual considerations suggest that it here be
translated "among" meaning that the
kingdom was present among the
Pharisees in the person of the King,
Christ Jesus.

22-24. Having spoken to the Pharisees of His Messianic Kingdom, Christ
now turns to the disciples (vs. 22) to explain how men shall one day desire to
see the kingdom, but will not be able
to. Those will be the hectic days of the
Great Tribulation (vs. 23, cf. Mt
24:21-31). At the conclusion of the
Great Tribulation, Christ will come to
set up his glorious kingdom, and His
appearing will be as evident to all and
as sudden as a great blinding flash of
lightning (vs. 24).

25. However, before that day can
come, Christ must, according to Old
Testament prophecy be rejected, suffer, and die (cf. Lk 24:25-27).

26-30. Jesus compared the days of Noah and of Lot to the time when He would return in judgment with power and glory. In those earlier days men went about their ordinary pursuits without thought of God. It will be the same when Christ comes to set up the kingdom.

31-33. In those days, Christ's judgment will center on Jerusalem, as predicted in Daniel 11:45, because that is where the Antichrist will be located. Any Jews there in that day are here warned to flee quickly away (vs. 31), remembering the tragedy that befell Lot's wife who lingered and looked back (vs. 32).

34-36. Likewise, Christ's judgment shall overtake the entire earth at once. Some shall be in bed at night, while in other places the sun will be shining. The taking is probably for judgment in this context. The Rapture which occurs seven years prior to these events will be similar in nature, though with a good end in view.

37. The saying about the vultures being gathered together to the carcass is a proverbial way of expressing the judgment that is depicted above. It corresponds with other portions of Scripture that speak of this same feast at the conclusion of the Great Tribulation (Ezk 39:4; Rev 19:17-18).

18:1-8. And he spake a parable unto them. The verses that follow are often called the parable of the unjust judge. This judge was blatantly bad, unprincipled, lawless, and void of moral fortitude to do what was right. The poor widow, on the other hand, was helpless, friendless, destitute, and with no hope. Yet through her great persistence, the wicked judge was so bothered that he finally granted her request. Although Jesus taught perseverance in prayer in other places (Mt 7:7-8), He is here using a form of logic that reasons from the lesser to the greater. Jesus said, regarding God's children, that **he will avenge them speedily** (vs. 8). The idea is this. If this poor woman with no hope received help from a wicked unscrupulous judge, how much sooner and greater will be the help a loving heavenly Father gives to his own dear children.

When the Son of man cometh, shall he find faith on the earth? (vs. 8). The implied answer is "no." The faith spoken of is probably the body of truth, or revealed doctrine, since the word is preceded by the definite article in the original. Improvement in the worldwide spiritual climate is not here predicted.

9-14. The former parable spoke of God's part in answering prayer. This one deals with man's part, and is addressed to the self-righteous. Jesus must have stunned His audience because the outcome of the parable was the opposite of what they would expect. The Pharisee really uttered no true prayer at all. The humble publican (tax collector) was forgiven and justified solely on the basis of repentant faith.

15-17. Little children . . . of such is the kingdom of God. Jesus loved children, and declared that adults must receive His message in simple trusting childlike faith if they would be saved.

18. What shall I do to inherit eternal life? This story of the rich young ruler illustrates several truths. Something usually stands in the way of a person coming to Christ. It may be pride, position, family, friends, a particular sin, or even wealth. In this man's case, it was money. Jesus does not ask every wealthy individual to **sell all that thou hast, and distribute unto the poor** (vs. 22), but in this case, refusal to do so indicated unwillingness to become a disciple.

24-27. This led Jesus to remark on the difficulty of the rich coming to Christ. But with God, this practical impossibility is overcome.

31-34. These verses indicate a point in time less than two weeks before Christ's crucifixion (vss. 31, 35; 19:11, 28), when He clearly announced His coming death to the disciples. **And they understood none of these things** (vs. 34, see also on 19:11).

35-43. The healing of blind Bartimaeus is recorded in all three synoptic Gospels, although he is named only in Mark, and presents several elements difficult to explain. Luke says the miracle occurred as Jesus drew nigh to Jericho (vs. 35), but Matthew says it was "as they departed" (Mt 20:29). Matthew and Mark may be referring to the old city while Luke speaks of Herod's newer city mentioned by Josephus and Eusebius. The healing may, therefore, have been performed between the two sites. **Thou son of David** (vs. 39) is a clear recognition by Bartimaeus of Jesus as Messiah. This terminology was also prominent in the triumphal entry into Jerusalem (Mt 21:15).

19:2. A man named Zacchaeus, which was the chief among the publicans, and he was rich. Zacchaeus is a good example of a man whose riches did not prevent him from coming to Christ. But like so many today, what he needed was someone to explain the way of salvation to him. This Jesus did. This story is found only in Luke.

10. The Son of man. This title of Christ was His favorite, and was never used by the disciples as they addressed Him. It speaks of His identification with mankind, yet it points to His uniqueness. **Is come to seek and to save that which was lost.** This is the key verse of Luke's Gospel. If this was the chief task of our Lord and Saviour Jesus Christ, it should surely loom large in our own set of priorities.

11. As Jesus approached Jerusalem with His disciples and others traveling to the Passover, He told a parable to show that the kingdom they had been announcing would not be established immediately as they had thought. Instead, since Jesus had been rejected by the Jewish people, the kingdom would be delayed, and during the interval something new (the church) would be set up (Mt 16:18). In this parable of the pounds, the activity of professing believers during the church age is in view. Here each servant was given one pound, speaking of equal opportunity, whereas in the parable of the talents (Mt 25:14-30), each was given according to his ability.

13. Occupy till I come. We have a dual assignment: to work, and to wait. We must do both faithfully.

14-27. Christ's first coming was as Saviour; but when He returns, it will be as Judge. False professors and Christ-rejectors will alike be cast away (vss. 26-27).

VI. THE PROFFER OF THE SON'S KINGDOM AND ITS REJECTION. 19:28-21:4.

A. Christ's Entry into Jerusalem. 19:28-46.

28-40. Christ's entry into Jerusalem was in direct fulfillment of such clear messianic prophecies as Zechariah 9:9 and Psalm 118:25-26.

41-44. These verses are both a lament and a prophecy. Christ laments His rejection and, as well, predicts the city's coming destruction. What was true of this city will also be true of each individual who rejects Christ. Jesus cared for them and He cares for men today.

45-46. Christ's judgment of those who were making merchandise in the temple was His second such action. Three years before, Jesus cast out a similar group (Jn 2:13-22).

B. Christ's Public Teaching in Jerusalem. 19:47-21:4.

47-48. Christ's final days before death were spent in public and private (Jn 13-17) teaching. In contrast, the Jewish leaders spent the time in conspiracy to commit murder.

20:1-8. The Jewish authorities (vs.1) wanted to know what authority Jesus had to cast money changers out of the temple (vs. 2). Instead of answering directly, Christ countered with a question about whether John the Baptist's ministry was of God or not. Since they refused to acknowledge or disown Jesus' forerunner (due to political expediency), they deserved no further revelation from Christ (vs. 8).

9-18. This parable is the New Testament parallel of Isaiah 5:1-7. In general terms, the householder represents God (yet not his mistaken optimism, vs. 13); the husbandmen stand for the Jewish religious leaders; the servants speak of the prophets; and the son represents Christ. In verse 15 Christ again predicted His own death. Verses 16-18 tell of future judgment and the final display of Christ's sovereignty (see also I Pet 2:6-7 and Dan 2:34).

19. The religious leaders knew instinctively that they were meant to be the wicked murderers in the parable.

20. As a result, they sought occasion to arrest Jesus and turn Him over to the Roman authorities for execution, since they had not the power of capital punishment (Jn 18:31).

25. Render therefore unto Caesar the things which be Caesar's and unto God the things which be God's. In these few words are clearly found the basis for the doctrine of the separation of church and state. Both are to exist, and neither is to be lord over the other as supreme.

27. The Sadducees were the Jewish religious liberals of that day. They denied resurrection, angels, and spirits (Acts 23:8).

28-32. The law of levirate marriage (a man required to marry his brother's widow) is found in Deuteronomy 25:5-10. It applied in the case of Ruth (Ruth 3:13-4:10).

33-36. Angels cannot be participants of either funerals or weddings. In the resurrection we shall be like them in these two respects also.

37-38. When God referred to Himself as the God of Abraham, Isaac, and Jacob, they had already died. Jesus pointed out that these three will live again.

39-40. Jesus' use of Scripture and logic was so correct and devastating that His opponents stopped questioning Him.

41-47. Jesus, however, pointed out the deity of the Messiah as seen in Psalm 110:1, where God the Father called Him Lord in distinction from Himself, and promised Him rulership.

VII. THE PROPHECY OF TRIBULATION TO COME. 21:5-38.

A. Prophecy about this Age. 21:5-19.

5-6. When Jesus finished teaching in the temple area (20:1), He passed through the temple treasury (21:1), and some commented on the splendor of the magnificent temple reconstructed, enlarged and beautified by Herod. Jesus predicted it would be torn down (vs. 6).

8-19. Jesus' words here are descriptive of the time leading up to the destruction of Jerusalem by the Romans in A.D. 70, and also of the events preceding the Great Tribulation period when the Antichrist will enter a future temple in Jerusalem to set himself up as God (II Thess 2:3-4).

B. Prophecy about Jerusalem. 21:20-24.

20-24. These verses graphically portray Jerusalem's destruction by Titus in A.D. 70. Titus' Arch still stands today in Rome near the Coliseum at the entrance to the Roman Forum. It commemorates his capture of Jerusalem. **And Jerusalem shall be trodden down of the Gentiles.** This is taken by most to mean Jerusalem will be under the governmental control of non-Jews. This has been the case (with the exception of the Bar Kochba revolt, A.D. 123-35) until Wednesday, June 7, 1967. **Until the times of the Gentiles be fulfilled.** On June 7, 1967, the "times of the Gentiles" were completed. Jesus did not predict what would happen after that time, but it may be assumed that Israel would come back into God's spotlight, and the return of Christ would be nearer. That is indeed the case. Jerusalem is today entirely under the governmental control of Israel, though they allow access to religious shrines for all faiths. Israel has constantly been on page one of our newspapers from that day to this.

C. Prophecy about Christ's Return. 21:25-38.

25-28. These verses are written for the Jews who will be looking for Christ to return at the end of the Great Tribulation. Satan will persecute the Jews, but God will protect them (Rev 12:13-17).

29-31. The fig tree is thought by many to be a symbol of Israel. This is seen in Luke 13. This parable probably means that Israel may be seen as a sign of the nearness of Christ's return and the setting up of His kingdom (vs. 31).

32. This generation shall not pass away, till all be fulfilled. The generation spoken of is probably the one which sees the signs (especially those regarding the fig tree) come to pass. That generation will see God conclude this present age prior to the inauguration of His Millennial Kingdom.

33. God's Word, the Holy Bible, is more unshakable than the universe itself. In fact, the universe shall pass away.

34-38. These verses speak of the universal extent (vs. 35) of the Great Tribulation, and are a warning to those who will await Christ's return in that day (Rev 7:1-16 tells of the Jews and of the great multitude who will be saved during the tribulation).

VIII. THE PASSION OF THE SON. 22:1-23:56.

A. Christ's Final Night with His Disciples. 22:1-46.

22:1. Feast of unleavened bread . . . which is called the Passover. The Feast of Unleavened Bread began the fifteenth day of the first Jewish month (our March or April) and continued for seven days (Lev 23:4-8). The Passover and Feast of the Firstfruits were both connected with the Feast of Unleavened Bread, and sometimes, as here, the term "Passover" stands for the entire observance. All Jewish men were required to be in Jerusalem for the Passover (Deut 16:16).

2-6. The Jewish leaders wanted to kill Jesus for what they considered to be the good of their nation. They reasoned that if people followed Christ as the Messiah, the Roman government would rise up and rush the "rebellion." (See John 11:47-53 for an exact statement of this.) However, they were not going to take Jesus during the Passover season because of the crowds. But, Christ was to die as our Passover (I Cor 5:7). Judas' conspiracy and betrayal made this possible.

8-9. And he sent Peter and John. These men were ever together serving Christ. First they were fishermen, then among the inner circle of three disciples (Peter, James, and John). After this joint mission of seeking a room to observe the Passover, they were together mourning and at the garden tomb (Jn 20:1-10), in a boat on Galilee (Jn 21:7, 20-24), and in preaching after Pentecost (Acts 3:1).

10-18. Christ's omniscience is clearly seen here as in numerous other clear predictions He made that were subsequently fulfilled.

19-20. When Christ instituted the Lord's Supper, Judas had apparently already departed (cf. Jn 13:21-30; Mt 26:26-30 and Mk 14:18-26). The bread and wine represented Christ's broken body and shed blood in a futuristic sense. Today these same symbols commemorate Christ's body and blood given for us at Calvary. The command is **this do in remembrance of me** (vs. 19).

The frequency of the observance is stated in I Corinthians 11:25 as "this do ye, as oft as ye drink it." The early church may have observed it quite often (Acts 2:42, 46; 20:7), but each local church is free to determine the frequency with which it will observe this ordinance.

The new testament, or new covenant, refers back to Jeremiah 31:31-34; Ezekiel 34:25-27; 36:26-27; and Zechariah 9:11. God promised Israel and Judah (the Jews) a new covenant in which He would restore them to their land, forgive their sin, and rule over them. This will be accomplished literally with God's chosen people, Israel, not with the church. However, the basis for that new covenant was the shed blood of Christ. We, as believers today, participate in the salvation aspects of that new covenant, but not in the other unique benefits promised to Israel.

24-27. The Christian should strive for mastery and work hard but his attitude must ever be that of humility. Remember Luke 17:10.

30. Sit on thrones judging the twelve tribes of Israel. During the millennial (one thousand years) reign of Christ, the twelve apostles (Matthias probably replaces Judas Iscariot, Acts 1:15-26) will have governmental authority over the regathered twelve tribes of Israel (Jer 23:3-8). These will be literal Jews who live through the Great Tribulation, and perhaps resurrected Old Testament saints as well (Mt 8:11).

31-34. We can be encouraged to know that Christ also prays for us as He did for Peter. He knows what we experience (Heb 4:15), and He makes intercession for us (Heb 7:25).

37. This that is written must yet be accomplished in me (vs. 37). Christ was very much aware of the Old Testament prophecies concerning the Messiah. Yet in no way did He contrive to fulfill these. He had nothing to do with Judas' wicked act of betrayal (Ps 41:9), nor the offering of vinegar to drink (Ps 69:21; Jn 19:28-30), nor the manner in which the soldiers at the cross parted His garments (Ps 22:18; Jn 19:23-24). The matchless providence of God ruled and overruled in the affairs of men. We may also rest assured that nothing happens to us without God's permission to work out His own unique will in each of our lives.

39. And he came out, and went, as he was wont, to the mount of Olives. At the conclusion of Christ's meal and final instruction of the disciples (the Upper Room Discourse, only in John 13-17), Jesus passed over the narrow ravine of the brook Kidron (Cedron) to the Garden of Gethsemane (Jn 18:1; Mk 14:32). Peter, James, and John were selected to be near Christ during His agony of prayer (Mt 26:36-38), while the others remained some distance away.

44. Father, if thou be willing, remove this cup from me. The cup refers to Christ's coming death (Mt 20:22-23) with its accompanying physical and spiritual agonies (Mt 27:46). That event was variously referred to by Christ as His cup, baptism, and hour (Mt 20:22-23; Jn 7:30; 12:23, 27; 13:1; 17:1). Christ's human nature, though without sin, did fear death (Lk 12:50; Heb 5:7), yet more so than other men because He was to bear vicariously the sin of the entire world (Isa 53:6; Jn 1:29) and suffer the temporary loss of fellowship with God the Father (Mt 27:46). **Nevertheless not my will, but thine, be done.** Christ's human will always completely yielded to the divine will. It was natural for Him to be perfectly obedient to the Father.

43-44. The visit of an angel to strengthen Christ in answer to His prayer is only found in Luke. Though sometimes questioned by textual critics, these two verses are attested by the overwhelming majority of manuscripts, ancient versions, and church fathers. **His sweat was as it were great drops of blood.** This does not necessarily mean that Christ actually sweat blood, though He may have.

B. Christ's Betrayal and Trial. 22:47-23:25.

47-48. Judas came to arrest Jesus with a Roman cohort (Jn 18:3), although the full cohort may not have been present. They were taking no chances.

49-53. John 18:10 identifies Peter as the one who chopped off the ear of **the servant of the high priest,** whom John also identifies as Malchus. Peter was probably aiming for the head. Only God's providence saved Peter from becoming a murderer. Luke the physician is the only one to record the healing.

54. Brought him into the high priest's house. This was the first of several illegal trials (see James Stalker, *The Trial and Death of Jesus Christ* and Simon Greenleaf, *The Testimony of the Evangelists*). **And Peter followed afar off.** How easy it is to promise (Mk 14:29-31), and so hard to fulfill.

55-60. Peter's denial was wicked and sinful; he even cursed and swore in his denial (Mk 14:71), but he did no more than that of which any of us are capable.

61. And the Lord turned, and looked upon Peter. This was one of Peter's lowest points. He had publicly denied Christ three times. Later, Christ made Peter publicly confess three times that he loved his Lord (Jn 21:15-19).

63-71. Though Jesus was violently abused, mocked, and ridiculed, He did not return the same (I Pet 2:21-23). The only accusation they could make was Christ's positive reply to their question as to whether or not He was the Son of God (vss. 70-71).

23:1. Led him unto Pilate. Pilate, the Roman governor of Palestine from A.D. 26-36, was in Jerusalem for the Passover feast. A stone inscription bearing his name was uncovered in A.D.

1961 in Caesarea, the ancient governmental headquarters.

2-5. Some of the charges the council (Sanhedrin) brought against Christ were manifestly false. Several times Pilate pronounced his verdict, **I find no fault in this man** (vss. 4, 14-15, 22). However, the Jewish leaders grew angry (vs. 5) and actually intimidated Pilate (Jn 19:12).

6-12. Pilate sent Jesus the Galilean to Herod Antipas, the governor of Galilee who was visiting Jerusalem for the Passover. He had earlier beheaded John the Baptist, and was desirous of seeing Jesus, but Jesus was silent before Herod and his mockers.

24. And Pilate gave sentence that it should be as they desired. Pilate had no backbone to stand up for justice, but instead, succumbed to mob rule. Both share the immediate guilt for Christ's death, but it is also true that Christ laid down His life and that no man could take it from Him (Jn 10:17-18).

C. Christ's Crucifixion. 23:26-56.

26. Simon, a Cyrenian. This devout black Jew must have become a Christian. Mark records (15:21) that Simon was the father of Alexander and Rufus.

33. The place, which is called Calvary. No one actually knows the exact place where the crucifixion or burial occurred. The Church of the Holy Sepulchre is the traditional site but many appreciate Gordon's Calvary and the Garden Tomb because they give a better picture of what the site is presumed to be like in the early centuries.

34. Father, forgive them; for they know not what they do. As Christ and the martyr Stephen, we must be so controlled by the Spirit that in our darkest hour we will be able to speak these words and mean them.

38. Greek, and Latin, and Hebrew. These three languages were: (1) the universal tongues, (2) the official language of the Roman Empire, and (3) the official speech of the Jews.

Compare all four gospel records to recover the complete reading of "This is Jesus of Nazareth the King of the Jews." This was probably written as a mockery to the Jews.

43. Today shalt thou be with me in paradise. The thief who asked Christ for salvation received it. The word "paradise," found only in two other passages (II Cor 12:4; Rev 2:7 cf. 22:2), indicates the domain of the righteous dead.

44. This darkness was supernaturally imposed.

45. Only the veil separated the priests from the Holy of Holies in the temple. Its parting signified the opening to all men of the way to God. It represents Christ's flesh (Heb 10:20) the rending of which made our salvation possible.

50-53. Joseph . . . of Arimathaea (perhaps equivalent to Ramathaim, I Samuel 1:1, about twenty miles northwest of Jerusalem) was a member of the council (Sanhedrin), but a devout and brave believer in Christ as Messiah. He, with Nicodemus (Jn 19:39), carefully wrapped Jesus' body in long strips of cloth, pouring in at the same time a sticky resinous mixture of myrrh and aloes. Both spices are obtained from trees. Nicodemus contributed about seventy pounds (by our weights), which was a rich amount fit for royalty.

54-56. The preparation (Gr *paraskeuē*) was a common designation for Friday, though it could also refer to the day before a special feast. If we assume a Friday crucifixion (Jewish inclusive reckoning), Luke's reference to the commandment of Sabbath obvservance (cf. Ex 20:8-11) would identify the next day as Saturday. The women, then, rested on the Sabbath (Saturday) and returned to the tomb the following day (vs. 56; 24:1), which would be Sunday. If a Wednesday crucifixion is assumed (literal seventy-two hours in the grave), the reference to the Sabbath would refer to the Passover itself.

IX. THE POWER OF THE SON OVER DEATH. 24:1-48.

A. The Events Surrounding the Empty Tomb. 24:1-12.

24:1. Upon the first day of the week, very early in the morning, they came. It was probably no earlier than 5 A.M. Matthew says that it was beginning to dawn (28:1), and Mark says that they arrived at the tomb as the sun was rising (16:2). "They" refers to the women of 23:55-56, who are identified in 24:10.

2. The stone rolled away from the sepulcher. First century sepulchers with round stone doors may still be seen in Jerusalem at the tomb of the kings, and at Herod's tomb. The openings are from the ground to about waist high. This explains why various persons are said to stoop down to look in (vs. 12; Jn 20:5).

3. These women, as well as others later, actually entered into the tomb and saw two features which proved to them the miraculous nature of Christ's bodily resurrection from the dead. (1) The body was gone. (2) The grave clothes, or strips of cloth that had encircled the body with gummy resinous spices inlaid were still intact. It must have looked like an empty mummy shell. The resurrected body of Christ had passed through the cloth wrappings, leaving them undisturbed. That was what convinced Peter and others of the truth of the resurrection (Jn 20:6-8). If the mummylike wrapping had been disturbed in any way, no one could have been sure of what had happened.

4. Two men stood by them. Naturally, these two angels confirmed the story. They looked just like other men except for their bright appearance.

B. The Walk to Emmaus. 24:13-35.

13. Two of them went that same day to a village called Emmaus. This is one of the most delightfully fascinating stories in the New Testament. One of the two was named Cleopas (vs. 18), who is mentioned elsewhere only in John 19:25, as the husband of a woman named Mary. The one returning with Cleopas may have been his wife, since both were in Jerusalem for the Passover. Emmaus was about seven or eight miles northwest of Jerusalem. It would take two to three hours to walk the distance.

14-16. As they walked they were discussing the events of the past several days, including Christ's crucifixion and the reports of His resurrection. As they walked, Jesus joined them, but they were supernaturally prevented from recognizing Him.

17-18. Jesus inquired as to their evident sadness, and was asked as if He were only a stranger to the area, and did not know all the things that had happened in Jerusalem that weekend.

19-24. With a great sense of drama, Jesus, the very one about whom all these events had centered, replied, **What things?** Then they unfolded the account of how they had thought Jesus was the Messiah until His crucifixion had shattered their hopes. Yet, they added the seemingly incredulous reports of His resurrection and the angels at the empty tomb who clearly said that He was alive.

25-27. At that point, Christ, still unknown to these two travelers, took the part of one familiar with the Scriptures. He pointed out from Genesis to Malachi how it was predicted that the Messiah would suffer prior to His exaltation as King. He must have quoted from Psalm 22 and Isaiah 53, and drawn from such types as the smitten rock (Ex 17:6; I Cor 10:4). What a glorious Bible lesson it must have been for them, but how it must have grieved the Saviour's heart to witness such a lack of faith and understanding in the very ones who claimed to be His followers.

28-32. When they neared Emmaus Jesus did not want to impose on His walking companions, but they had

learned so much and had such sweet fellowship that they insisted He spend the evening with them. We, too, can learn from such spontaneous Christian hospitality as these manifested. Jesus consented, and as they sat to eat, they asked their new friend (still not knowing He was the risen Christ) to ask God's blessing on their meal. He did so. Then when Christ broke the bread their eyes focused on His nail-pierced hands and they immediately realized it was their Lord. Jesus disappeared from their presence, and they recalled the walk and talk they had had with Him along the way.

C. The Meeting in the Upper Room. 24:33-48.

33. Having had the privilege of being a part of one of the most unique of the post-resurrection experiences, these two hastened back the eight miles into Jerusalem. They made their way to the upper room where they knew other disciples were gathered behind locked doors for fear of the Jews (Jn 20:19). The group present consisted of only ten of the apostles, Thomas being absent (Jn 20:24), the two from Emmaus, and others who had gathered. We do not know how large the crowd was, but it could have been close to twenty or more. "The eleven" is a collective term that was used to identify the group of disciples after the death of Judas, whether all were present or not.

34. As the two gained entrance, they were immediately told, **The Lord is risen indeed, and hath appeared to Simon.** This appearance is only mentioned here and in I Corinthians 15:5. Christ was no doubt further preparing Peter for the leadership role he would assume in the early days of the church.

35. Then Cleopas and his companion related what had happened to them that afternoon.

36. While they were just finishing their story, Jesus miraculously appeared in their midst and said **Peace be unto you.**

37. Of the apostles, apparently only Peter had, up to that time, seen the resurrected Christ. The rest had only heard the stories of the appearances. Now, when confronted with the reality themselves, they were shocked by the sudden and obviously miraculous nature of this appearance. Their immediate reaction was terror, and in that first impression they must have felt they were viewing some spiritual form of their resurrected Lord.

39. Jesus quickly corrected their mistaken theology by drawing attention to his completely physical body. He said, **Behold my hands and my feet, that is I myself: handle me, and see; for a spirit hath not flesh and bones, as ye see me have.** Even with these clear words, given in the context of correcting a false view of the nature of Christ's resurrection body, there still persist some false cults and "isms" who maintain the heresy of a "spiritual resurrection" of Christ. The fact that Jesus said "flesh and bones" rather than "flesh and blood" does not necessarily indicate that His body had no blood. One cannot say, but flesh and bones usually do operate with blood. However, the life principle in a resurrected body may not be in its blood, but in the spirit of God.

40-43. In order to further prove the fact of His material bodily resurrection, Jesus gave a public demonstration by eating some broiled fish and part of a honeycomb.

44-45. All things must be fulfilled, which were written in the law of Moses, and in the prophets, and in the psalms, concerning me. This verse opens up the Old Testament as to its prophetic and typical import regarding Christ. We know that Old Testament is revealed in the New, while the New is concealed in the Old. Christ then opened **their understanding, that they might understand the scriptures.**

46. Our Lord continued to point out to these disciples that **it is written** that Christ should suffer and rise again the third day. This must refer to such Old Testament passages as Psalm 16:20, Isaiah 53:10, and the typology regarding Jonah. Even Genesis 3:15 may be considered as teaching the Messiah's resurrection, otherwise the "wound to the heel" would have been fatal!

47-48. These verses point to a coming change in dispensations, for whereas Christ had before strictly limited the apostles in their preaching to the Jews only (Mt 10:5-6), He now enlarges the commission as extending to all mankind.

X. THE PROMISE OF THE SON TO THE DISCIPLES. 24:49-53.

49. In order for Christ's disciples to accomplish this task of the Great Commission, Jesus promised them **power from on high.** They were to remain in Jerusalem until the promised power was received. This promise involved the coming indwelling presence of the Holy Spirit mentioned the night before Christ's crucifixion (Jn 16:7-15), and previously at the Feast of Tabernacles (Jn 7:39). John the Baptist had also intimated this special ministry of the Holy Spirit for disciples after Pentecost (Lk 3:16), and Jesus reiterated this just prior to His ascension when he said, "Ye shall be baptized with the Holy Ghost not many days hence" (Acts 1:5).

50. The ascension of Christ occurred near Bethany, on the eastern side of the Mount of Olives. His ascension was in His physical bodily form, and Acts 1:11 assures us that "this same Jesus which is taken up from you into heaven shall so come in like manner as ye have seen him go into heaven" Christ's return will not be of a secret spiritual nature as some cults suppose, but He will return bodily.

51-53. He . . . blessed them. Christ, in contrast to the speechless Zacharias in chapter 1, had a blessing to give these man. **And they worshipped him.**

Jesus is entitled to worship only because He is Almighty God, the eternal, omnipotent Creator of the Universe. Compare what happened to John when he mistakenly tried to worship a created being in Revelation 19:10 and 22:8-9. The text of the Authorized Version renders verses 52-53 correctly regarding Christ's deity.

The Gospel of Luke begins by announcing **good tidings of great joy, which shall be to all people** (Lk 2:10), and it ends with disciples who are filled **with great joy; And were continually in the temple, praising and blessing God.** Like those of old, we should be ready to carry this joy to others all around us. Let us imitate our Lord, who "came to seek and to save that which was lost" (Lk 19:10).

BIBLIOGRAPHY

Alford, Henry. "The Gospel According to Luke." In *The New Testament for English Readers.* London: Revingtons, 1863.

Arndt, William F. *Gospel According to St. Luke.* St. Louis: Concordia, 1956.

Burnside, W. F. *The Gospel According to St. Luke.* Cambridge: Cambridge University Press, 1913.

Earle, Ralph. "The Gospel According to St. Luke," In *The Wesleyan Bible Commentary,* Vol. 4 Grand Rapids: Eerdmans, 1964.

Ellis, E. E. "The Gospel of Luke" in *New Century Bible.* New York: Thomas Nelson, 1966.

*Erdman, C. R. *Gospel of Luke.* Philadelphia: Westminster, 1956.

Farrar, F. W. "The Gospel According to St. Luke," In *The Cambridge Bible for Schools and Colleges.* London: Clay and Sons, 1899.

Gaebelein, Arno C. *The Annotated Bible,* Vol. 3. Neptune, N. J.: Loizeaux Brothers, 1970.

*Geldenhuys, Norval. "Commentary on the Gospel of Luke," In *New International Commentary on the New Testament.* Grand Rapids: Eerdmans, 1951.

*Godet, Frederick L. *Commentary on the Gospel of Luke.* Grand Rapids: Zondervan; reprinted 1957.

Henry, Matthew. *Matthew Henry's Commentary on the Whole Bible,* Vol. 5. New York: Revell; reprinted, 1965.

Ironside, Harry A. *Addresses on the Gospel of Luke.* Neptune, N. J.: Loizeaux Brothers, 1947.

Jones, W. B. and F. C. Cook. "St. Luke's Gospel,' In *The Bible Commentary.* Vol. 6, ed. by F. C. Cook. New York: Charles Scribner's Sons, n.d.

Luce, H. K. "The Gospel According to St. Luke," In *The Cambridge Bible for Schools and Colleges.* Cambridge: University Press, 1936.

McGee, J. Vernon. *Luke.* Pasadena: Thru the Bible Books, 1975.

Marshall, F. *The Gospel of St. Luke.* London: George Gill & Sons, 1921.

*Morgan, G. Campbell. *The Gospel According to Luke.* New York: Revell, 1931.

*Morris, Leon. "The Gospel According to St. Luke," *The Tyndale New Testament Commentaries,* ed. by R. V. G. Tasker. Grand Rapids: Eerdmans, 1974.

Plummer, Alfred, "A Critical and Exegetical Commentary on The Gospel According to St. Luke," In *The International Critical Commentary.* New York: Charles Scribner's Sons, 1925.

Ramsay, W. M. *Luke the Physician,* Grand Rapids: Baker, 1956 reprint of 1908 ed.

Rice, John R. *The Son of Man.* Murfreesboro, Tenn.: Sword of the Lord, 1971.

Robertson, A. T. *Luke the Historian in the Light of Research.* Grand Rapids: Baker, reprinted, 1977.

Ryle, J. C. "Luke." In *Expository Thoughts on the Gospels,* Vol. 2. Grand Rapids: Zondervan; reprinted, 1956.

Stonehouse, N. B. *The Witness of Luke to Christ.* Grand Rapids: Eerdmans, 1961.

*Tenney, Merrill C. "The Gospel According to Luke." In *The Wycliffe Bible Commentary,* ed. by Charles F. Pfeiffer and Everett F. Harrison. Chicago: Moody Press, 1962.

The Gospel According To

JOHN

INTRODUCTION

The Gospel of John remains today as a favorite among Christians. Many ministers recommend this book to new converts as a training manual for Christian development. William Hendricksen prefaces his commentary on this gospel with the words of Scripture, "Put off thy shoes from off thy feet, for the place whereon thou standest is holy ground." (William Hendricksen, *The Gospel of St. John,* p. 3). This gospel is uniquely different from the synoptics in that ninety percent of its content is not discussed by the other gospels even though John had these gospels at his disposal when he wrote. John carefully chose, under the inspiration of the Holy Spirit, only those events, miracles, and sermons that would supplement his literary intent. The result of his effort is a gospel that "is the most amazing book that was ever written" (Hendriksen, p. 3).

Authorship. Although the author of this book is not mentioned by name, there is ample evidence externally and internally to conclude that John the Apostle was the author.

External evidence. The writings of early church fathers often quote from the Gospel of John and attribute this Gospel to the Apostle John. "The external evidence for the early date and Apostolic authorship of the Fourth Gospel is as great as that for any book in the New Testament" (Henry C. Thiessen, *Introduction to the New Testament,* p. 162). Irenaeus, who was a pupil of Polycarp, a friend of the Apostle John, writes, "Afterwards, John, the disciple of the Lord, who also leaned upon his breast, did himself publish a Gospel during his residence at Ephesus in Asia" (Thiessen, p. 164). The importance of this statement is that Irenaeus quotes from the Gospel (21:20, 24) and attributes the authorship to the Apostle John.

Internal evidence. There are certain facts about the author that can be deduced from the content. When these facts are considered collectively, they complement the external evidence and indicated Johannine authorship. First, it is clearly evident from the context that the author was a Jew. He understood and quoted from the Old Testament (12:40; 13:18; 19:37) and he had a thorough knowledge of Jewish feasts and customs: wedding feasts (2:1-12), ceremonial purification (3:25), various religious feasts (2:13, 23; 6:4; 13:1; 18:28), and burial customs (11:38, 44; 19:40). Second, he must have been a resident of Palestine. Throughout the Gospel he gives detailed geographical descriptions that could be given only by a Palestinian resident. He knows the exact distance between Bethany and Jerusalem (11:18), that Jacob's well is deep (4:11), that Ephraim was near the wilderness (11:54), and many other important geographical details.

Third, the author was an eyewitness to the events he describes. He saw the glory of Jesus Christ (1:14), was at the crucifixion (19:33-35), knew the number and size of the waterpots used in Cana (2:6), knew the distance from the shore to the apostles' boat (21:8), and knew the number of fish caught (21:11). Fourth, he identifies himself with the disciple "whom Jesus loved" on five occasions (13:23; 19:26; 20:2; 21:7, 20). Since John's name is absent from the Gospel it would be logical to assume that he is its anonymous author.

Fifth, the style and vocabulary of the Gospel of John are strikingly similar to the epistles which bear his name. These five observations from the content of the fourth Gospel lead clearly to the conclusion that John the Apostle was the author.

Date and place of writing. Liberal scholars have placed the date of the book as early as A.D. 40, while other liberals have dated it around A.D. 140-170. However, conservatives agreed on a date late in the first century and between the years A.D. 85-95. This date is supported by the discovery of a papyrus fragment called P⁵². This papyrus manuscript is the earliest textual evidence of the New Testament so far discovered, and contains five verses of John (18:31-33, 37-38). Since this fragment is dated about A.D. 125, the original Gospel had to be in circulation before the end of the first century (Robert G. Gromacki, *New Testament Survey,* p. 133). There is general agreement that John wrote this book from Ephesus where he spent the latter years of his life.

Purpose. John's purpose in writing this book is clearly identified in two verses (20:30-31): "And many other signs truly did Jesus in the presence of his diciples, which are not written in this book: But these are written, that ye might believe that Jesus is the Christ, the Son of God; and that believing ye might have life through His name." There are three key words in these verses: *signs, believe,* and *life.* The *signs* (Gr *sēmeion*) are the miracles which John chose to describe in proving the deity of Christ. John selected eight signs to substantiate his thesis:

eight signs to substantiate his thesis:
1. Turning water into wine. 2:2-11.
2. Healing the nobleman's son. 4:46-54.
3. Healing the impotent man. 5:1-15.
4. Feeding the five thousand. 6:1-14.
5. Walking on the water. 6:15-21.
6. Healing the blind man. 9:1-41.
7. Raising Lazarus. 11:1-44.
8. Providing the catch of fish. 21:6-11.

The second key word in John's statement of purpose is the word *believe* (Gr *pisteuō*) which means to trust or commit. John describes the miracles to prove the deity of Christ so that the readers "might believe that Jesus is the Christ, the Son of God." The third key word describes the results of believing the person and work of Christ—"and that believing ye might have life" (Gr *zōē*). John's Gospel is not merely an intellectual exercise, but rather a historical narrative about the Son of God with the express intent of producing life in the hearts of those who believe in the Son of God. The heartbeat of the Gospel of John is evangelism—pointing men to the "Lamb of God, which taketh away the sin of the world" (John 1:29).

John further supplements his thesis that Christ is the Son of God by emphasizing the claims that Christ made about Himself. Christ claimed for Himself the very name of God. "Before Abraham was, I am" (8:58). In a review of familiar statements, John amplifies on the claim of Christ to be the "I AM."
1. I am the bread of life. 6:35.
2. I am the light of the world. 8:12; 9:5.
3. I am the door. 10:7.
4. I am the good shepherd. 10:11, 14.
5. I am the resurrection and the life. 11:25.
6. I am the way, the truth, and the life. 14:6.
7. I am the true vine. 15:1.

John uses all the miracles and sermons of this Gospel to develop an impeccable argument for the deity of Jesus Christ.

To those who have experienced this eternal life, a review study of this Gospel will produce a deeper understanding and greater appreciation of the One who "came unto his own, and his own received him not. But as many as received him, to them gave he power to become the sons of God, even to them that believe on his name: Which were born, not of blood, nor of the will of the flesh, nor of the will of man, but of God'' (John 1:11-13).

OUTLINE

I. Prologue. 1:1-14.
   A. The Word in the Beginning. 1:1-2.
   B. The Word in Creation. 1:3.
   C. The Word after the Fall. 1:4-5.
   D. The Word at Incarnation. 1:6-14.
II. The Public Ministry of Christ. 1:15-12:50.
   A. Christ Proclaimed by Individuals. 1:15-51.
      1. Testimony of John. 1:15-34.
      2. Testimony of disciples. 1:35-51.
   B. Christ Performs His First Miracle. 2:1-25.
      1. Wedding at Cana. 2:1-12.
      2. Cleansing of Temple. 2:13-25.
   C. Christ as Saviour. 3:1-36.
      1. Teaching of the new birth. 3:1-21.
      2. Testimony of John the Baptist. 3:22-36.
   D. Christ as the Master Soulwinner. 4:1-54.
      1. Samaritan woman's sins forgiven. 4:1-45.
      2. Nobleman's son healed. 4:46-54.
   E. Christ as the Son of God. 5:1-47.
      1. Healing of lame man. 5:1-18.
      2. Defense of His person. 5:19-47.
   F. Christ as the Bread of Life. 6:1-71.
      1. Feeding of the five thousand. 6:1-14.
      2. Walking on the water. 6:15-21.
      3. Sermon on the bread of life. 6:22-59.
      4. Many turn away. 6:60-71.
   G. Christ as the Master Teacher. 7:1-53.
      1. Teaching concerning His person. 7:1-36.
      2. Teaching concerning the Holy Spirit. 7:37-39.
      3. Division of people. 7:40-53.
   H. Christ as the Light of the World. 8:1-9:41.
      1. Adulterous woman forgiven. 8:1-11.
      2. Sermon on the Light of the World. 8:12-59.
      3. Application of sermon by healing blind man. 9:1-41.
   I. Christ as the Good Shepherd. 10:1-42.
      1. Sermon on the Good Shepherd. 10:1-21.
      2. Rejection of Christ's message. 10:22-42.
   J. Christ as the Resurrection and the Life. 11:1-57.
      1. Power of Christ: raising Lazarus. 11:1-46.
      2. Plan of the Pharisees. 11:47-57.
   K. Christ as the Messiah. 12:1-50.
      1. Supper at Bethany. 12:1-11.
      2. Triumphal entry. 12:12-19.
      3. Teaching on the cross. 12:20-50.

COMMENTARY

I. PROLOGUE. 1:1-14.

John begins his Gospel with a series of declarative statements about the deity of Christ. In contrast to the other Gospels, John begins his Gospel in eternity past. Matthew, who portrays Christ as the King, begins with a genealogy to prove His Davidic lineage. Mark, who presents Christ as the Servant, begins his Gospel with the public activity of Christ as a servant. Luke, who emphasizes the humanity of Christ, begins his Gospel with a lengthy description of the events that led to the birth of Christ. John, who presents Christ as the Son of God, begins his Gospel in eternity.

A. The Word in the Beginning. 1:1-2.

1:1. In the beginning. This opening statement is a repetition of the opening statement of the Bible (Gen 1:1). When time began, the Word was already in existence. **Was the Word.** This unique name for Christ (Gr *logos*) occurs only four times in the New Testament as a name (1:1,14; I Jn 1:1; Rev 19:13) and is utilized only by John the Apostle. Since words reveal the thoughts of one person to another, Christ as the Eternal Word is a revelation of God to man.

And the Word was with God. The words translated with God (Gr *pros ton theon*) could be rendered "face to face with God." Two important thoughts emerge from this statement. First, the Word is a distinct person. Second, the Word was enjoying communion and fellowship with another distinct person, God the Father. **And the Word was God.** Lest the reader assume that the Word as a distinct person is less than God, John concludes the verse with an emphatic statement that the Word was completely God. To lend the greatest possible emphasis to the importance of this statement, it literally reads "and God was the Word." The subject and predicate are reversed to underline the deity of the Word.

2. The same was in the beginning with God. This verse simply summarized the deep theological truths revealed in the first verse.

B. The Word in Creation. 1:3.

Having established the eternality of the Word, John now describes His involvement in creation.

3. All things were made by him; and without him was not any thing made that was made. This verse established Christ as the subject of creation and not the object of creation. He was the Creator, not the created. One scholar translates the latter part of this verse as follows: "and apart from him not a single thing that exists came into being" (William Hendriksen, *The Gospel of St. John*, p. 71).

C. The Word after the Fall. 1:4-5.

4. In him was life. This verse opens with the preposition (Gr *en*), which means "in." Life is not from Him, or through Him, or by Him, but life is in Him. The life (Gr *zōē*) spoken of is not life in a physical sense but rather in a spiritual sense. John uses life fifty-four times in his gospel and first epistle to refer to the spiritual realm. **And the life was the light of men.** Christ is the Light shining in contrast to the darkness of this sinful world.

5. And the light shineth in darkness. In the previous verse both verbs are in the Greek imperfect tense denoting a past action. However, the tense of the verb "shineth" (Gr *phainō*) is the Greek present tense. Christ, who was the Light, continues to shine as the Light. **And the darkness comprehended it not.** The darkness referred to here is the unbelief and sin of mankind (3:

19). It is the antithesis of the light. The verb used here (Gr *katalambanō*) means to "grasp, comprehend, put out, seize with hostile intent" (W. Wilbur Gingrich, *Shorter Lexicon of the New Testament*, p. 111). This implies a hostility between the Light and the darkness with the darkness unable to put out the Light.

D. The Word at Incarnation. 1:6-14.

6-8. These verses contrast Christ and John the Baptist. A review of the descriptive statement is given concerning John. First, He was not the *logos*, but rather a human individual. Second, he was **sent from God.** John was commissioned by God, he was not God Himself. Third, John was a **witness, to bear witness of the Light, that all men through him might believe.** John's purpose was to give testimony concerning Christ that would lead persons to a saving faith in the Light. Fourth, John **was not that Light.** The ministry of John the Baptist is similar to the ministry of Christians today. We are to give personal witness and testimony concerning the Light so that others might believe.

In the following verses John elaborates on the theme of Christ the Light. He studies the Light in a series of relationships: to the world in general (1:9-10); to the Jewish people (1:11-13); and to the disciples (1:14).

9-10. That was the true Light. Christ is the true, or genuine, or real Light. **Which lighteth every man that cometh into the world.** Christ is the one who gives to every man the light of reason and conscience. The result of this revelation was that the **world knew him not.** The verb used here (Gr *gnōskō*) means to acknowledge or recognize. The world rejected Him.

11-12. There is a very strong play on the words "his own" (Gr *idios*). In their first occurrence, they refer to what was his own, namely his own world (see vs. 10, and compare the same expression in John 19:27 where it refers to a man's home). In their second occurrence, the Greek gender has changed and the reference is to his own people, who by their rejection show him to be truly despised (cf. Isa 53:3; Lk 19:14).

There are two actions delineated in verse 12: The action of man and the action of God. Man's action is to receive and to believe. To receive means to accept for one's self, and to believe means to place one's trust in. Both of these concepts are a part of salvation. God's action is **to them gave he power to become the sons of God.** The word power (Gr *exousia*) means the right or authority to become the sons of God.

13. The spiritual birth spoken of in the previous verse is **not of blood.** It is not on the basis of lineage or Jewish heritage. It is **not of the will of the flesh** or a carnal desire. It is not **of the will of man** or human in its origin. It is **of God.** This birth is supernatural.

14. The Word was made flesh and dwelt among us. The verb translated "dwelt" (Gr *skēnoō*) means to tabernacle or live in a tent. The author testifies that **we beheld his glory.**

II. THE PUBLIC MINISTRY OF CHRIST. 1:15-12:50.

A. Christ Proclaimed by Individuals. 1:15-51.

In the remaining verses of chapter one, Christ is proclaimed as Messiah by several individuals including John the Baptist, Andrew, Simon, Philip, and Nathanael.

1. Testimony of John. 1:15-34.

15. The writer again discusses the **witness** of John (1:7). Although Jesus comes **after** John, yet **he was before** him; He existed in eternity.

The verses are interjected into the testimony of John the Baptist and describe the personal testimony of the author.

16. Of his fulness. This **fulness** is expressed in verse 14 and the writer now claims that **of his fulness have we all received, and grace for grace** (literally, grace upon grace).

17. Continuing the thoughts of verse 14, a sharp contrast is made between the law of Moses and Jesus Christ. **The law was given by Moses.** The law had its place in revealing man's condition (Gal 3:24). However, the law did not provide **grace and truth. Grace** was to forgive and pardon the sinner and the **truth** (or the reality) was that which the sacrifices pointed to. These are found only in Jesus Christ.

18. God is a Spirit and cannot be seen by man (I Tim 6:16). The **only begotten Son. He hath declared him.** Christ has declared (literally, exegeted Gr *exēgeomai*) or revealed God to man. The expression, **the only begotten Son,** has excellent manuscript evidence to support translating it, "the unique God."

19. And this is the record of John. The author now returns from a note of personal testimony to the record of John. This culminates in verse 34 with the words of John the Baptist. The Sanhedrin is alarmed at the ministry of John the Baptist, and so they send a delegation of theologians to ask him the question, **Who art thou?**

20-21. John denies that he is the Christ. He also denies being Elijah, whom the Jews expected to precede Messiah (Mal 4:5). John did minister in the spirit of Elijah (Lk 1:17) and was even called Elijah by Christ (Mt 17:12), but he was not literally Elijah. John also denies being **that prophet** (Deut 18:15-18) or Christ Himself.

22-23. Unsatisfied with John's negation of their questions, they ask, **What sayest thou of thyself?** John answered with the words of Isaiah 40:3. He was simply a **voice** to **make straight** the paths or prepare **the way of the Lord.**

24-28. The investigating committee now becomes concerned with John's baptizing. **Why baptizest thou then?**

John replies by stating that there is a vast difference between what he is doing with **water,** which is only a sign, and what Messiah will do with the real thing, the cleansing power of the Holy Spirit (Mk 1:8). Concerning Him, John states that he is unworthy of even untying His sandal straps. These events took place in **Bethabara beyond Jordan.**

29. John seeth Jesus. The day after the committee investigates John, Jesus Himself appears on the scene. John makes the now familiar statement, **Behold the Lamb of God.** Christ is the fulfillment of the Old Testament lamb (Ex 12,13; Num 28:4; Isa 53). **Which taketh away.** This is a Greek present participle which means "is taking away." What the Old Testament lamb could not do, the Lamb of God is doing. **The sin of the world.** The Lamb of God was not limited to the Jewish people but rather He reaches the entire world.

30-32. The message of John seemingly centered around this theme (1:15,27). The apostle assumes that the reader is familiar with the synoptics since **the Spirit descending like a dove** occurred at the baptism (Mt 3:13-17; Mk 1:9-10; Lk 3:21-22).

33-34. And I knew him not. The value of John's testimony to Christ is that God revealed it to him at the baptism of Jesus. Until that time John **knew him not.** This section relating John's testimony to Christ concludes with the statement **that this is the Son of God.**

2. Testimony of disciples. 1:35-51.

35-37. In the latter portion of this chapter, Jesus is revealed to certain disciples. These verses are the transition between the ministry of John the Baptist and the ministry of Christ. John the Baptist is with two of his disciples (Andrew and John, the author), and after pointing to **the Lamb of God,** they **followed Jesus.**

38-39. Jesus then asks an important question. **What seek ye?** In response to this question, the disciples ask with another question, **where dwellest thou?** They were interested in close communion and fellowship with Christ. Christ invites them to **Come and see** and **They came and saw.**

41. The true response of one who has found Christ is to bring others. Andrew tells his brother Simon **We have found the Messias.** Messiah (Gr *Messias*) means the anointed one; it is the transliteration of the Hebrew *Mashiach,* which is often translated by the Greek *Christos* which is then transliterated into English as "Christ."

42. Simon comes to Christ and gets a new name, **Cephas, which is by interpretation, A stone.**

43. The day following. This is the last of four successive days discussed in chapter 1. Christ now does the finding and commands Philip to **Follow** Him.

44-46. Philip immediately **findeth Nathanael** and states, **We have found him.** Nathanael responds with doubt that Nazareth could produce Messiah. But Philip gives the invitation, **Come and see.**

47. Jesus sees Nathanael coming and addresses him as an **Israelite indeed in whom is no guile.** This is a compliment to the honesty and sincerity of Nathanael.

48-49. Nathanael responds, **Whence knowest thou me?** Then Jesus reveals the penetrating eye of deity by telling Nathanael that even before **Philip called thee, when thou wast under the fig tree, I saw thee.** In a previous moment of quiet devotion, Jesus had seen Nathanael. Nathanael then proclaims Christ **as the Son of God** and the promised Messiah.

50-51. This verse is more of a promise than a question. Because of Nathanael's faith, he would **see greater things than these.** Jesus now describes these **greater things** by referring to the Old Testament story concerning Jacob's ladder (Gen 28). Christ Himself was to be the Ladder between

God and man since He was the son of God (1:49) and the **Son of man** (1:51).

B. Christ Performs His First Miracle. 2:1-25.

In this chapter there are two events detailed which illustrate the emptiness and deficiency of Judaism. The empty water jars at the wedding feast describe the condition of Judaism in meeting the spiritual needs of the Jewish people. This emptiness is further described in the cleansing of the Temple and Judaism is described as corrupt.

1. Wedding at Cana. 2:1-12.

2:1. And the third day. The third day after Jesus had attained two more disciples, Philip and Nathanael, He journeyed about eight miles north of Nazareth to Cana. **The mother of Jesus was there.** John does not mention Mary by name, which is consistent with his style, since he tends to leave himself and his close relatives anonymous (19:26-27).

2. Since the disciples had joined Christ so recently, there is the problem in resolving how they were all invited to the wedding feast. There are two possible answers: Jesus could have stopped in Nazareth on His way to Cana and accepted the invitation for His disciples; or second, Nathanael could have made the arrangements since he was from Cana.

3-5. When the wine failed, Mary came to Christ for help because she knew who Christ really was (Lk 1:26-38). Christ addressed her as **Woman** or "Lady"; no disrespect is intended. **What have I to do with thee?** Christ emphasizes that Mary should no longer think of Him as her son. **Mine hour is not yet come.** Throughout the gospels, Christ is conscious that He is doing the will of the Father and each act has an appropriate time (7:6; 8:20; 12:23). Mary acknowledges submission to the Son of God and tells **the servants whatsoever he saith unto you, do it.**

6-8. Jesus Christ uses the **six waterpots of stone** which could contain from 17 to 25 gallons of liquid each. After filling them with water, Christ commands the servants to **Draw out.** This refers to dipping out the water. They **were told to bear it (Gr** *pherō*) to the **governor of the feast.** The verb used here is in the Greek present tense (progressive action), and perhaps hints that the process of serving must be continued no matter how ridiculous it seemed. The total volume of water changed to wine was about 100-150 gallons.

9-10. When the wine was tasted, it was proved to be of superior quality. The governor compliments the bridegroom, **Thou hast kept the good wine until now.** The symbolism is clear. The power of Christ filled the emptiness of the waterpots and that same power is able to fill the emptiness of Judaistic religion.

11-12. This beginning of miracles. The word used here for **miracles (Gr** *sēmeion*) means signs, and the apostle gives the reason for the sign: **and manifested forth his glory.** The sign drew attention to the power and glory of the one who performed it. In this story, Christ stands as the pre-eminent One. The faith of the disciples was strengthened because of this sign. After this incident, Christ returned to Capernaum. This was the home of James and John.

2. Cleansing of Temple. 2:13-25.

13. The law required every male Jew being twelve years old and above to attend the **passover. Jesus went up to Jerusalem,** the political and religious capital of Israel, and because of its geographical elevation, the Jews always talked about going **up** to Jerusalem regardless of the direction they were traveling from.

14-17. Christ found in the court of the Gentiles a terrible scene. The Sanhedrin was permitting the selling of sacrificial animals at exorbitant prices and permitting the changing of foreign currency into Jewish money, which was required for the temple tax. Christ makes a whip and drives out both the animals and the wicked merchants. He overturns the tables and scatters the coins across the floor. He commands the dove owners, **Take these things hence.** Christ then justifies this striking action, **make not my Father's house an house of merchandise** (Mal 3:1-3). Again, the failure of Judaism is emphasized. The disciples recall that this is the fulfillment of prophecy (Ps 69:9).

18. The Jews, who have been shocked by the action of Christ, demand a **sign** to substantiate His authority and conduct. However, this was a ridiculous request since the cleansing in itself was a sign (Mal 3:1-3).

19. Christ answers with a deep spiritual truth. **Destroy this temple, and in three days I will raise it up.** Christ was referring to the destruction of His body and to His resurrection from the dead. The physical temple was a type of Christ's body, and when the body of Christ was destroyed, the purpose and existence of the Jewish temple were also destroyed. consequently, the destruction of His body also meant the destruction of the temple.

20-22. The Jews take Christ literally, and ignore the spiritual and true meaning of His statement. The author adds these words lest his readers miss the truth of Christ's statement. Even the disciples did not fully understand until **he was risen from the dead.** They **believed the scripture,** or the Old Testament prophecies, and **the word which Jesus had said.**

23-25. Jesus remained in Jerusalem for the Passover, and **many believed in his name, when they saw the miracles.** The word used to express belief (Gr *pisteuō*) is used in the next verse. **But Jesus did not commit himself.** Christ did not entrust Himself to them because they were not true believers. He concluded this because **he knew all men.** These were nominal believers

whose only interest was the miracles. He did not need their testimony **for he knew what was in man.** These people had not accepted Him with saving faith, but rather they accepted Him as a powerful miracle worker.

C. Christ as Saviour. 3:1-36.

There are two separate incidents detailed in this particular chapter: the interview with Nicodemus, and the last testimony of John the Baptist. The interview with Nicodemus is of primary importance since it reveals the doctrine of the new birth.

1. Teaching of the new birth. 3:1-21.

3:1-2. In these opening verses, Nicodemus is introduced as a **man of the Pharisees** and **a ruler of the Jews.** The Pharisees were the religious separatists and the rulers (Gr *archōn*) who predominantly formed the Sanhedrin. Nicodemus **came to Jesus by night** so that he could personally talk with Christ. **We know** seems to indicate that other influential religious leaders were convinced that Christ was a **teacher come from God** because of the miracles.

3. After Nicodemus came to Christ, Christ made a statement about the new birth. Nicodemus then asked three questions about that statement. **Except a man be born again.** The word "again" (Gr *anōthen*) means "from above." Unless a person is born from above **he cannot see the kingdom of God.** The kingdom of God is His rule over His people and refers to everlasting life.

4. Nicodemus' questions reveal that he did not grasp the spiritual meaning of the Lord's statement. Nicodemus expects a negative answer to his rhetorical question. However, Christ answers by explaining this new birth.

5. To be a part of God's kingdom, one must **be born of water and of the Spirit.** There are three interpretations as to the meaning of **water:** it refers to the washing of the water of God's Word (I Pet 1:23); it refers to baptism; or it refers to physical birth. The latter of the three seems to be the most logical.

6. Christ continues to contrast physical birth and spiritual birth. The **flesh** produces **flesh** while the **Spirit** produces that which is spiritual.

7. Marvel not. Do not be amazed or shocked. **Ye must be born again.** To become a part of God's spiritual kingdome, one must experience a spiritual birth.

8. The wind. (Gr *pneuma* which is the same word used for **spirit**) cannot be seen or explained. The wind can only be heard or observed in relation to its effect. **So is everyone that is born of the Spirit.** The new birth is inexplicable. One can only observe the results.

9-10. Nicodemus asks his third question, **How can?** He asks the same question as before (3:4). Christ rebukes him, and in doing so, brings Nicodemus to the point of submission. Both **master** (teacher) and **Israel** have a definite article in Greek. Christ rebukes Nicodemus by asking, "Are you not *the* teacher of *the* Israel and you are ignorant of those things?" Nicodemus needed a new heart (Ez 11:19).

The conversation now becomes one-sided. Christ teaches and Nicodemus listens.

11. Verily (Gr *amēn*, truly) **I say unto thee.** In speaking for His followers, Christ reminds Nicodemus that they were saying what they knew and were testifying to what they had seen. The reality of the new birth was known to them by experience. However, the question and blindness of Nicodemus led the Lord to say, **Ye receive not our witness.**

12-13. If Nicodemus did not accept **earthly things,** matters of spiritual nature which take place on the earth, then he would not believe **heavenly things.** Firsthand knowledge must come from **the Son of man.** Knowledge of heavenly things is only possible

through Him **that came down from heaven.**

14-15. Christ now illustrates, from Numbers 21, the nature of God's plan of redemption. Sin had caused God to punish the Israelites with serpents. God commanded Moses to make a brass serpent, so that when the sick looked to that serpent, they would be healed. The son of Man must **be lifted up** (on the cross) so that man bitten by the serpent of sin might **have life eternal.**

16. The Gospel in a nutshell. The love of God shown in action. (1) The source of love—**God.** (2) The extent of love—**the world.** (3) The sacrifice of love—**He gave his only begotten Son.** (4) The results of love—**whosoever believeth in him should not perish.**

17. The Jews understood that Messiah would come to **condemn** the Gentiles (Amos 5:18-20). Against this false teaching, Christ told Nicodemus that God's plan was to save the **world.**

18. Condemnation is reserved for the one that **believeth not.** There are only two kinds of people in the world: (1) Those who have everlasting life as a result of faith in Christ; and those who have not believed and as a result stand **condemned already.** They are already sentenced (condemned) and await only the execution of that sentence.

19-21. Christ as the Light is rejected by a dark world **because their deeds were evil.** Those who reject the Light **also hate** (Gr *miseō*, detest, abhor) that Light, lest their deeds be exposed. In contrast to those who abhor the Light, **he that doeth truth** gravitates toward the Light to show that his deeds are **wrought in God.** Christ concludes their interview with an invitation for Nicodemus to leave his darkness and unbelief and come to the Light.

*2. Testimony of John the Baptist.
3:22-36.*

22-25. After these things. Following the interview with Nicodemus, Jesus traveled to Judaea and baptized. John, who **was not yet cast into prison,** was performing a similar ministry near Salim. A debate erupted over the baptism of Jesus and the baptism of John as to which had greater **purifying** ability.

26-29. They came unto John. They were probably disciples of John since their statement carried a hint of jealousy toward Christ (**all men came to him**) and they refused to mention Christ by name. John's disciples were concerned about the decreasing popularity of their leader. John quickly replied that each person is given a place of service **from heaven.** John had no right to claim any importance other than what God gave him. John's position was as the forerunner of Christ. Rather than regretting his loss of popularity to Christ, John rejoices in being **the friend of the bridegroom. This my joy therefore I fulfilled.** The reports that the crowds are attracted to Christ causes John to have joy.

30. He must increase, but I must decrease. Notice the **must.** In God's plan John must diminish and Christ must continue to grow. The comparison between Christ and John the Baptist is continued and brought to conclusion in verses 31-36.

31. Christ is **from above** and is **above all,** whereas John is **of the earth** and **speaketh of the earth.** Christ, because of His origin, is above all earthly things (3:13).

32. Christ is the one spoken of here. He testifies concerning **what he hath seen and heard** (3:11, 13, 31). Again, the rejection of that testimony is discussed.

33. The one who accepts Christ's testimony concerning Himself **hath set his seal** (literally, to certify, attest, acknowledge) **that God is true.** The antithesis of this affirmation is found in I John 1:10.

34. Christ is the faithful witness who **speaketh the words of God.** Christ has received the fullness of God's Spirit **(not the Spirit by measure).** It is implied that all believers receive the fullness of God's Spirit. Beyond the fullness of God's Spirit, Christ has received **all things** as a result of the love relationship between the **Father** and the **Son.**

36. The Baptist's last testimony to Christ is perhaps his most powerful one. It calls for a decision. Believe and one has **everlasting life** (3:16-18). **And he that believeth not.** This second **believe** is a difficult word in the original that is used in the first part of the verse (Gr *apeitheō*, to disobey, be disobedient). Literally, the one who disobeys **shall not see life; but the wrath of God abideth on him.** Wrath (Gr *orgē*, anger, settled indignation) is abiding on the one who disobeys, (the Greek present tense is used to note a progressive and continual action).

D. Christ as the Master Soulwinner.
4:1-54.

There are two events described in this chapter. They are the contact with the Samaritan woman, and the healing of the nobleman's son. In the story of the woman of Samaria, we observe Christ as the personal soulwinner.

1. Samaritan woman's sins forgiven.
4:1-45.

4:1-3. The popularity of Christ was increasing to the extent that the Pharisees became alarmed. To avoid a confrontation, Jesus traveled north returning to Galilee.

4-5. He must needs go through Samaria. Christ had a compelling compassion that drove Him to a woman in need. This was also the most direct route to Galilee. His journey took Him to Sychar, a city a few miles southeast of Samaria and near Mt. Gerizim. According to Genesis 33:19, Jacob bought this parcel of ground and later gave it to his son Joseph (Gen 48:22).

6. Jacob's well was there. This was a well about one hundred feet deep. The writer now emphasizes the humanity of

Christ in that He was travel-weary **with his journey** and consequently rested **on** (literally, upon) **the well.** The time of this incident was probably six o'clock in the evening.

7. A woman of Samaria. Note the contrast between chapter 3 and chapter 4. In the former, Christ deals with a man; in the latter, He deals with a woman. In the former, He deals with a Jew; in the latter, a Samaritan. In the former, he deals with a moral person; in the latter, an immoral person. Yet, He saves both. **Jesus saith unto her, Give me to drink.** In receiving this woman, Christ transcends the barriers of race (He was a Jew and she a Samaritan), religion, and rank (He was a teacher and she was a prostitute). Soulwinning crosses any barriers.

8-9. The request for water was a logical one since the disciples had gone into **the city to buy meat.** However, the woman is amazed at this request because of the natural animosity between the Jews and the Samaritans. This hatred was caused when, after the fall of Israel, the Jews who remained in Palestine intermarried with the heathen and were called Samaritans. They were not full-blooded Jews.

10-12. Christ answers the woman's hesitancy with a spiritual riddle. The **gift of God** refers to the **living water.** The emphasis now is taken off Christ's need for physical water and placed on the woman's need for spiritual water (7:37-39). The woman understands Christ to speak of the **living water** as that which is at the deepest part of the well. **Art thou greater?** The woman realizes that if Christ can do this, He is a **greater** person than Jacob.

13-15. Christ continues by stating that if one drinks of Jacob's well, he will need to drink again, but if one drinks of Christ's well, **he shall never thirst.** This water produces a well that keeps on bubbling **into everlasting life.** With this statement, Christ appeals to the woman's craving for satisfaction. The woman is still thinking on the physical level. She wanted this **living water** so that she would not have to come all the way out to Jacob's well every day.

16. Christ commands her to call her husband. It would seem the Lord changed the subject. That is not true. In order for the woman to understand the **living water** (4:10) concept, she must be aware of her need for that **living water.** (4:10) Christ now begins to arouse her conscience and sense of guilt. Before anyone can be saved, he must see his need of salvation and be convicted of his sin.

17-20. Christ reveals her sinful condition. She was morally bankrupt. She acknowledges Christ as a **prophet,** and in so doing admits her personal sin which Christ revealed. The woman now desires to be taught by the prophet. Should she worship in Mt. Gerizim or in Jerusalem?

21-23. The hour cometh. Christ reveals to the woman that where a person worships is unimportant. It is not limited to Mt. Gerizim or Jerusalem. The Samaritans worshipped what they did not know; they had created their own religion. The Jews had divine guidelines for worship. Nevertheless, **the hour cometh, and now is** when God is to be worshipped in **spirit and in truth.** Two separate concepts are implied. The worship of **the Father** is not confined to a place but is rather an action of the heart. Second, all worship must be in keeping with **the truth** of God's revealed Word.

24. God is a Spirit. Spirit, the predicate, is mentioned first to emphasize the spiritual character of God. Notice the emphasis on the "must" of that type of worship.

25. The knowledge of Christ causes the woman to talk about Messiah (Deut 18:15-16). She is still confused and resolves this confusion by admitting that Messiah **will tell us all things.**

26. I that speak unto thee am he. The woman claimed that the only person who could answer her questions and doubt was Messiah. What a surprise! This type of Messianic revelation would have been dangerous in Jerusalem, but in this setting at the well, He deemed it safe. The Samaritan woman first saw a Jew, then a prophet, and finally Messiah.

27-30. At that decisive moment, the disciples returned and were amazed that their Master broke tradition in speaking with the woman. The woman left her **waterpot,** showing her intention to return, and went to **the men** proclaiming the news about **a man, which told me all things that ever I did.** The question was not assertive but rather she herself wanted an answer. **Is**

Jesus' Visits to Jerusalem

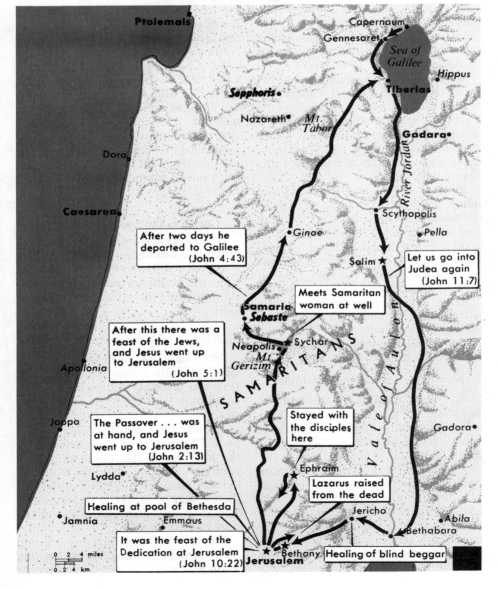

After two days he departed to Galilee (John 4:43)

Let us go into Judea again (John 11:7)

Meets Samaritan woman at well

After this there was a feast of the Jews, and Jesus went up to Jerusalem (John 5:1)

Stayed with the disciples here

The Passover . . . was at hand, and Jesus went up to Jerusalem (John 2:13)

Lazarus raised from the dead

Healing at pool of Bethesda

It was the feast of the Dedication at Jerusalem (John 10:22)

Healing of blind beggar

0 2 4 miles
0 2 4 km

not this the Christ? The men went out to see.

31-34. The disciples want their Master to eat. Christ replies that His **meat,** that which gives Him spiritual nourishment and satisfaction, was **to do the will** of the Father and **finish** (or bring to completion) **his work.**

35. He impresses the urgency of God's work on the disciples. Do not wait **four months** to harvest, **Lift up your eyes, . . . they are white already to harvest.** Christ was referring to the crowd of Samaritans now approaching them. The soul-harvest is a matter of immediate urgency.

36-38. In the spiritual harvest of souls, one **soweth** and one **reapeth,** but both are able to rejoice in the harvest. Christ had sowed the seed, and now the disciples were ready to reap. **Other** people have **laboured,** that is, planted seeds, and soulwinners reap the benefits of their labors.

39-42. The fruit was harvested and **many** believed. The response caused the Samaritans to invite Christ to stay and He remained **two days.** Afterwards, **many more believed.** It was concluded that Christ was the **Saviour** of the world—that is for Jews, Samaritans, and Gentiles.

43-45. Christ returned to Galilee where He was not honored and respected like He was in Judaea. Those who had **seen all the things** in Jerusalem **received** (welcomed) Him.

2. Nobleman's son healed. 4:46-54.

46. While in Cana, a **nobleman** (Gr *basilikos,* royal officer) visited Him with a problem: **whose son was sick.** It was a serious sickness **at the point of death** (4:47).

47-48. The royal officer was under two false impressions about the power of Christ. He thought Christ would have to travel to Capernaum to heal, and that Christ did not have power over death (**ere my child die**). Christ was concerned that the man's faith was based only on **signs and wonders.**

49-50. The nobleman compelled Christ to act, and Christ simply spoke the word. The man responded with a faith in **the word** of Christ and not the miracles of Christ. **And he went his way.** Faith is leaving our problem with Christ, accepting His word, and going on our way.

51-53. The man returned and was met by his servants who brought news of the child's recovery. He recovered the same hour in which Christ spoke the word. The result was that the entire house **believed** or placed their trust and confidence in Christ.

54. This was the second miracle in Cana. The first miracle of turning the water into wine showed His power over the physical universe and His disciples believed. The second miracle proved that Christ's power was not limited by a distance of sixteen miles and the entire house of the nobleman believed. Both miracles produced belief and life (20:30-31).

E. Christ as the Son of God. 5:1-47.

In this chapter Christ performs a miracle of healing on the Sabbath. He is questioned by the Pharisees and answers their criticism in a lengthy discussion proving Himself to be the Son of God.

1. Healing of lame man. 5:1-18.

5:1. There was a feast. Since the Greek definite article is missing, this feast was probably not the Passover. It could have been the Feast of Tabernacles.

2. Near the **sheep** gate there was a pool. There has been much debate over the location of this pool. In 1880 a painting depicting an angel **troubling** the water was discovered on the wall of the Church of St. Anne in Jerusalem. This discovery marked the site of the pool of Bethesda.

3-4. By this pool there lay a group of sick people **waiting for the moving of the water.** All the oldest manuscripts were copied without the latter part of verse 3 and all of verse 4.

5. Because the man had been sick for thirty-eight years does not mean that he had been at the pool for that length of time.

6. Note the three verbs: Jesus **saw**, Jesus **knew**, Jesus **saith**. Jesus sees each need, knows the depth of that need, and addresses Himself to meet that need. Christ's question seeks to probe man's will to be healed.

7-8. Note the three verbs, **Rise, take up, walk.** The first verb symbolizes spiritual healing (salvation). The second verb symbolizes a break with the past (picking up the bed), and the last verb symbolizes Christian growth (walking on).

9. Obedience brought complete and instantaneous healing. **The same day was the sabbath.** This phrase becomes the controversial issue that upsets the Jews.

10-14. They referred to the Old Testament law (Jer 17:19-27; Ex 20). The man replied that anyone who could heal him instantaneously and completely also had the authority to tell him to carry his bed. The Jews did not ask, "Who healed you" but rather, "Who told you to do this on the Sabbath?" The man did not know who healed him, and meanwhile, Christ had disappeared. The man goes to the temple (probably to give thanks for healing) and meets Christ, who tells him not to continue in sin **lest a worse thing come unto thee.** Christ does not insinuate that he was sick thirty-eight years because of sin, but rather since his sins were forgiven, he must walk in a new life.

15. The man told the Jews that Jesus healed him. He did not answer their questions concerning the Sabbath.

16. Persecute Jesus. This verb (Gr *diōkō*) refers to continued hostile activity even to the point of death (**sought to slay him**).

17-18. Christ answers by establishing His authority to work on the Sabbath. He was coequal with God the Father. The Jews were angered even more by this statement and **sought the more to kill him.**

2. Defense of His person. 5:19-47.

19-20. Christ continues His claim to be equal with God. He states that whatever **he seeth the Father do,** He does also. Because of the Father's love, the Father **sheweth him all things.** Consequently, all that the Father doeth, the Son doeth. Christ claims that the Father will show Him **greater works** than the healing of the impotent man.

20-24. Two of the **greater works** are listed: the raising of the dead and the pronouncing of judgment. The raising of the dead refers both to a physical and spiritual accomplishment. The former occurs through resurrection and the latter through regeneration. Second, the Father does not set apart from the Son in pronouncing judgment, but has **committed all judgment unto the Son.** The raising of the dead and the judgment are closely related eschatological matters. One day all the dead will be raised to stand before Christ in judgment (the saved through the rapture to the Bema Judgment, and unsaved through the final resurrection to the Great White Throne Judgment, Rom 14:10; Rev 20:11-15). The father **committed all judgment unto the Son** so that the Son would be equal in **honor** with the Father. Note also that the Son is equal in character (17-18), in works (19-22), and in honor (23). If a person accepts Christ's word and believes in the Father, even now he **is passed from death unto life** (spiritual resurrection) and **shall not come into condemnation** (judgment).

25-27. These verses discuss the power of Christ to quicken the dead **now.** Because the Son **hath life in himself** (like the Father), the Son gives this life to those **dead** who **hear** His voice.

28-30. These verses discuss the future aspect **(the hour is coming)** of Christ's quickening power. Here physical resurrection is discussed, and two results are listed: the good **unto the resurrection of life** and the **evil, unto the resurrection of damnation.** Again, the perfect harmony and unity of the Father and son relationship is discussed.

31-32. Christ had made the claim to be equal with God. He recognizes that the Jews would not formally accept the claim (witness) of one person. Jewish law required two witnesses. On the basis of one witness, Christ states that the Jews would accept that witness as **not true.** In the remaining verses, Christ calls several witnesses to establish validity for His claim: John the Baptist (33-35), His works (36), the Father (37-38), the Scriptures (39-47).

33-36. John's testimony is given in 1:19-28. Christ Himself did not need John's testimony, but He mentions it because it was true and if accepted one could be **saved.** John was a **burning and shining light.** However, although people were **willing . . . to rejoice in his light,** they were not willing to accept his testimony concerning Christ. Nevertheless, Christ had **greater witness than that of John.** His works (miracles) gave evidence to His deity. They were evidence that **the Father hath sent me** (Gr *apostellō*, to commission, send on a divine mission).

37-38. Christ continues with another testimony, that of His Father. This testimony refers both to what was said by the Father at Christ's baptism (Mk 1:11), and to what the Father had said through the Old Testament Scriptures. Christ reminds them that they had neither **heard his voice . . . nor seen his shape.** The **voice** of God and the **shape** (image, likeness) of God are Christ Himself (14:19, 24; II Cor 4:4). They did not have **His word abiding** in them (as a permanent possession).

39. Search the scriptures. This is not necessarily a command. It may be taken as the Greek present indicative and could be translated "ye are searching." The Jews were constantly searching the Scriptures because it was recognized that they contained the secret of **eternal life.** These same Scriptures bear testimony of Christ. Yet these pious Jews had missed the very key to understanding Scripture—Christ (Jn 5:46; I Pet 1:10-11).

40-43. Because of their hardness of heart, they had rejected Christ. Christ does not receive **honor** (glory or praise) **from men,** because God's love (literally, love for God) is not in them. Christ had come in the authority of His Father with mighty miracles to prove His deity. They rejected Him. If one comes in **his own name, him ye will receive.** This was proved in that the Jews accepted false messiahs such as Theudas and Judas of Galilee (Acts 5:36-37). They will also accept antichrist (II Thess 2:8-10).

44-47. The Jews could not believe because they derived praise from each other rather than praise from God. The name Jew means "praised."

45. The Jews had the utmost confidence in Moses and his writings. They claimed to be Moses' disciples (9:28), and yet they did not accept what Moses had said (Deut 18:15-18). If they had accepted Moses' writings, they would have accepted Christ, **for he wrote of me.** Moses' writing and Christ's words are both placed on the same level, divinely inspired and interrant.

F. Christ as the Bread of Life. 6:1-71.

In this chapter Christ reaches the height of His popularity. Because of His power to meet physical needs, the people wanted to make Him king. However, when they realized that His ministry was spiritual, they rejected Him. Such are the events of this chapter.

1. Feeding of the five thousand.
6:1-14.

6:1-9. Christ went across the Sea of Galilee to the vicinity of Bethsaida (Lk 9:10). The multitudes, impressed by His miracles, followed Him. Jesus went **up into a mountain.** From His high vantage point, Christ observed the crowd approaching and asked Philip if they had bread for the people to eat? Bread (Gr *artos*, flat, round bread like the shape of pancakes). Christ explained why He asked this question—**to prove him** (Gr *peirazō*, to put him to the test). The Lord **knew what he would do** and is now putting Philip's faith to the test (Jas 1:2). A **pennyworth** (Gr *dēnarios*) was equivalent to one day's wages (Matt 20:2, 9, 13). Phililp claims that two hundred days of wages would not be enough to give each **a little.** Andrew brings **a lad** (not necessarily a little boy) who has **five barley loaves, and two small fishes.** Andrew recognizes that this is so little to meet the need of so many. One commentator describes the problem this way: "Duty is not measured by ability, and ability is not measured by the sum-total of our resources" (J. D. Jones, *The Gospel According to St. Mark,* Scripture Truth).

10-11. Christ now takes command of the situation and has everyone sit down. The Lord gave **thanks.** Note the prayer of thanksgiving occurs before the miracle. The miracle provided **as much as they would,** whereas Philip's faith was so little.

12-14. The sufficiency of the miracle did not mean waste. All the leftovers were to be collected **that nothing be lost.** One should never waste God's blessings. The people saw the **miracle** (Gr *sēmeion*, sign) and were impressed. They proclaimed Him as **that prophet** (Deut 18:15-18) and probably thought Him to be the Messiah.

2. Walking on the water. 6:15-21.

15. Enthusiastic about this **prophet,**

they are ready to make Him **king,** even to the point of kidnapping Him. But Christ's kingdom was not of this world (18:36). Thus He went **into a mountain himself alone.**

16-18. The disciples put out to sea, but were hindered by the darkness and by a **great wind that blew.** The wind would blow strongly through the narrow gorges between the hills causing severe storms.

19-21. They rowed **twenty or thirty furlongs** (Gr *stadion*), about a total of three or four miles. They see Christ walking toward them on the water. The One who had fed five thousand was about to meet the needs of these twelve disciples. **It is I; be not afraid** (present imperative, "stop being afraid"). Matthew describes Peter's walking on the water (Matt 14:28-31). Although the disciples were far from the land when Jesus entered the boat, another miracle occurred: **immediately** (Gr *eutheōs*) **the ship was at the land.** Christ demonstrated His power over gravity (walking on the water), over the storm (stilling the winds), and over space (bringing the ship to land).

3. Sermon on the bread of life.
6:22-59.

22-25. The day following, those who had been fed by Jesus began looking for Him. Since they knew He did not cross the lake with His disciples, they were puzzled at His disappearing. They began a search that ended in Capernaum and they asked Christ **when camest thou hither?** These people still had the desire to make Christ king.

26. Christ rebuked their motives. He stated that although the people had seen the signs, they had not accepted them for what they were (proof of His true Messiahship), and they were only interested in the physical.

27. Labor not (Gr present imperative, "stop working for") the physical bread which **perisheth.** Rather, they should work **for that meat which en-**

dureth unto everlasting life, or work for the real food which produces everlasting life. That food is Christ Himself. His authority to give everlasting life rested in the **seal** (testimony) of the Father through His signs and miracles.

28-31. These people are confused. Christ offered to give them eternal life and they wanted to know what to **do.** Christ answered that acceptance with God or the **works of God** was to **believe on him.** The **work** is not something man does for God, but it is the act of receiving what God has done for man. The Jews ask for a sign to prove that they should **believe on him.** This shows what the Jews were thinking. They knew that Christ had made more bread out of already existing bread. Their claim was that Moses had done greater than Christ's miracles; he had brought bread from heaven. Now, if Christ wanted these Jews to **believe on him,** He had better perform a greater sign than Moses.

32-35. Christ explains that the manna which Moses gave is of different character than the **true bread.** The **true bread** is a person, **he which cometh,** and is capable of giving life. The Jews want this bread, but they still think it is merely physical bread much like Moses' manna. Christ identifies Himself as the **bread of life.** The life spoken of is spiritual and not physical. To partake of this life means that one's spiritual **hunger** and **thirst** will be fully satisfied. Note the verbs **cometh** and **believeth,** indicating salvation.

36-38. They had seen Him but had not believed. **All** who were given (Gr Everything which the Father gives to me will come to me) describes God's sovereignty in salvation. **Him that cometh to me I will in no wise cast out** emphasizes human responsibility. Here Christ emphasizes the unity of the Father's will and the Son's will. To reject the Son is to reject the Father.

39-40. The Father's will revealed is the preservation of those who believe.

A person cannot fall from grace. Everlasting life guarantees security because this is the Father's will. No one will be lost. Note the following references: Romans 8:29-30; Philippians 1:6; II Timothy 2:19; I Peter 1:4-5.

41-42. The Jews **murmured** (Gr *songuzō,* whispered) at these unusual claims of Christ. From a human perspective, Christ could not have descended from heaven because these people knew His human heritage. The Jews are almost cynical in their attitude. "Why, we have known you from your childhood, and now you make these ridiculous claims expecting us to believe in you."

43-44. Christ returns to His message of life. In order for a person to come to the bread of life, the Father must **draw him.** This verb (Gr *helkuō*) is also translated *draw* in the sense of "dragged" (Acts 16:19; 21:30). People cannot be saved at all unless God through the Holy Spirit draws them.

45-47. Christ describes this drawing process. It is accomplished through the Bible. When a man hears and learns, he comes to the Father. Salvation is impossible apart from hearing the Word of God. It is through this preaching that God draws people to Himself (Isa 54:13). The learning does not mean complete knowledge of the Father; this complete knowledge is only for the Son.

48. See verse 35.

49-50. Moses' manna was not eternal (see 32-35). In contrast to Moses' manna, this true bread will not let man die.

51. Christ further describes this bread. It is His flesh. He clearly refers to His vicarious death on the cross that will provide **life** for the **world.**

52. The Jews are still thinking of eating physical food rather than spiritual food.

53-54. Christ complicates the situation further by adding **except ye . . . drink his blood.** The Jews were forbidden to drink blood (Lev 7:26-27) and this additional statement must have added insult to injury. However, the Jews misunderstood. Leviticus 17:11 clearly states that life is in the blood. Accepting the sacrifice of the body and blood of Christ is the basis for eternal life.

55-58. As food and drink are offered to meet physical needs, so the **flesh** (meat) and **blood** of Christ are offered to meet spiritual needs. To assimilate this spiritual bread and drink is to be affected both spiritually (life) and physically (raised in the last day).

59. This message was preached at the **synagogue in Capernaum.**

4. Many turn away. 6:60-71.

60. The disciples were offended by the thought of eating Christ's flesh and drinking His blood (hard saying). These disciples are a general group larger than the Twelve.

61-62. Christ asks them if they would accept the fact that He came from heaven when they see Him return to heaven.

63. Christ now explains. He did not intend for them to physically eat of His flesh, that would profit **nothing;** rather, it is His **spirit** (person) which gives life. The **words** He spoke were **spirit** and **life.** They were not dead, but they carried the potential of producing life. Accept what He said (His words) and they would have life.

64-65. Unbelief stopped people from coming to Him. They did not accept His words, and consequently, they would not draw to Him (cf. 44).

66. Many of those who were impressed by the signs now left Christ because of their unbelief.

67. Christ turns to the Twelve and wants to know if they will **also go away?** This question is phrased in such a way as to expect a negative answer.

68. Peter had understood the teaching of his Master. The message of Christ was not dead words to Peter,

but they were full of spirit and life and were the **words of eternal life.**

69. We believe and are sure. Peter had partaken of the bread of life and had assurance of that belief. Assurance always follows true salvation (I Jn 5:13). Peter proclaims Jesus as the **Christ** (the anointed, holy, and chosen one).

70-71. Jesus knows that now all the Twelve have accepted Him. One was a devil (Gr *diabolos*, slanderer, false accuser).

The chapter ends differently than it begins. It begins with the crowds wanting to make Him king and closes with Christ questioning whether His Twelve will leave Him, as everyone else. The Twelve affirm their confidence through Peter, but even one of them is a devil and will eventually betray the Bread of Life.

G. Christ as the Master Teacher. 7:1-53.

1. Teaching concerning His person. 7:1-36.

7:1-5. After these things. After many people had forsaken Him (6:66), Christ remained in Galilee because of a Jewish plot **to kill him** (5:18). The Feast of Tabernacles was a harvest feast which commemorated the years of wilderness wandering. **His brethren.** His brothers (James, Joseph, Simeon, and Judas) perceived that Christ should go to the feast and exert His influence by performing mighty works. Their desire was that Jesus would impress all the people at the feast **openly.** They gave this bad advice because they themselves had not **believed** in the spiritual ministry of Messiah. They wanted someone who would unite the Jewish people and establish a kingdom.

6-7. Christ's **time** to go to the feast had **not yet come.** He knew that if He would go, the Jews would kill Him, and that time had not yet come. **The world** (people separated from God) could not hate Christ's brethren because they were part of that **world.** They hated Christ for his message that exposed sin.

8-9. My time is not yet fully come. Christ's time to go to Jerusalem and be crucified had not yet become full. He had no desire to gain popularity and influence people with His works.

10-13. The Lord eventually went to the feast in **secret** (that is, without public fanfare). Perhaps He traveled the back roads with only His twelve disciples. **The Jews** refers to the religious hierarchy. **Where is he?** They had hostile intentions (15:18). The people were divided in their opinion of Christ. Some thought Him a **good man** (moral, honest), while others thought He was a deceiver (interested only in leading people astray). Because the Jewish hierarchy had not stated their opinion, the people feared expulsion from the synagogue if their open opinion conflicted with the Sanhedrin.

14-16. Halfway through the feast, Christ went to the Temple and began to teach. The Jews were outraged at His boldness and objected to His teaching. They were amazed that he could be educated without ever having studied formally. Christ establishes a higher authority for His teaching than Jewish schools: God the Father.

17-18. To understand His teaching, one must have the desire to do the will of God. With this commitment a person could evaluate the authenticity of Christ's teaching. This person would also realize that Christ was not seeking **his own glory** but rather the glory of the One who sent Him.

19-20. To do God's will is to obey God's law. Christ is saying that these Jews had not kept the law, and consequently, they were not doing God's will. Therefore they were not in a position to properly evaluate His message. In fact, they wanted to break the sixth commandment by killing Christ. The people are unaware that the leaders have plotted to kill Christ, and they

assume that Christ is insane: **Thou hast a devil.**

21. One work. The healing of the impotent man on the Sabbath, recorded in chapter 5, caused them to plot His death (5:18).

22-23. Christ appeals to the Jewish law of circumcision which could be performed on the Sabbath. If that work of ceremonial cleansing could be performed on the Sabbath, then a work of complete healing should also be performed. The Jews had no logical answer for this convicting question.

24. Christ tells them to stop judging on the surface. **Judge righteous** (just) **judgment.**

25. The attitude of the Sanhedrin is found in verse 15, the attitude of the pilgrims in verse 20, and now the Jerusalemites who are aware of the leaders' plot react to Christ.

26. They are amazed that Christ spoke **boldly** (openly), and for a moment think that perhaps the rulers have been convinced that He is the Messiah.

27. This idea was quickly dismissed since they believed that Messiah would appear suddenly, but everyone knew that Jesus came from Nazareth. The true Messiah, according to the leaders, would come from Bethlehem.

28-29. Christ acknowledges their opinion about his earthly home. However, they were unaware of His divine origin. The Lord thoroughly knows the Father Who sent him. The Jerusalemites did not accept Him as the true Messiah.

30-31. Because of these divine claims with regard to origin, they were anxious to arrest Him. However, His **hour** of divine appointment had **not yet come,** and all the hatred and plots of the Jews could not harm Him. Many **believed on Him** (Gr. construction indicates saving faith) on the basis of His **miracles.**

32-24. The leaders have had enough. People are actually accepting this Jesus as Messiah, and the leaders decide to apprehend Him. Christ indicates that in a **little while** (about six months or the time between the Feast of Tabernacles and the Passover) He would return to the Father. The Jewish nation would then **seek** Him but their search would be in vain. They could not go to the Father, because in rejecting Him they had rejected the Father.

35-36. The Jews did not understand the spiritual meaning of Christ's statement. They thought that after Christ's failure in Judaea, He would go to the **dispersed** (Jews who lived around the world) and **teach the Gentiles** (Gr *hellēn*, Greeks). Unknowingly, these leaders had uttered a true prophecy. Christ, through His disciples, would spread His message around the world.

2. Teaching concerning the Holy Spirit. 7:37-39.

37. The last day. The seventh or eighth day of the feast. During the feast, a priest would fill a golden pitcher with water from the pool of Siloam and carry it to the altar at the Temple where he would pour it through a funnel leading to the base of the altar. Probably, after this ceremony, Christ invited those who thirsted to come to Him and drink. The emptiness of Judaism is emphasized in that it fails to satisfy.

38. The one who believes not only gets satisfied (37), but also that person becomes a channel of blessing to others, **out of his belly shall flow rivers of living water** (Isa 44:3, 4; 55:1-2).

39. This indwelling blessing would be available through the Holy Spirit after Christ was **glorified** (ascended into Heaven). The Spirit in the Old Testament came **upon** people, but Christ promised that the Spirit would come to live **in** people.

3. Division of people. 7:40-53.

40. Christ's invitation is responded to in different ways. Some thought He was a prophet.

41-42. Some thought He was the Messiah. Others said He could not be Messiah because Messiah was predicted to come from Bethlehem. They were correct about this, but they were incorrect in that they assumed Christ was born in Galilee. Consequently, their conclusion that Christ was not Messiah was also wrong.

43-44. There was division among the people.

45-46. The group whom the Pharisees sent to arrest Christ returned without Him. They were overwhelmed by the message and manner of Christ and were powerless to apprehend Him.

47-49. The Pharisees were mad and sought to instruct officers that an intellectual and spiritual leader would not believe in Christ. Only those who **knoweth not** God's law are deceived. They describe these people as **cursed,** the scum of society.

50-52. Nicodemus . . . being one of them, that is, being one of the rulers that were violating the law in judging a man without hearing him. They ignored Nicodemus's question and told him that if he would search the Scriptures, he would discover that no prophet had ever come out of Galilee. This again shows their ignorance of the Scripture, since Jonah, Nahum, and Hosea came from Galilee.

53. The Sanhedrin adjourns and the people go home.

H. Christ as the Light of the World. 8:1-9:41.

There has been debate over the authenticity of this story of the woman taken in adultery. Many older manuscripts do not include it. However, it is included in the AV and will be dealt with here.

1. Adulterous woman forgiven. 8:1-11.

8:1-6. This verse is colsely connected to 7:53. When everyone went home, **Jesus went unto the mount of Olives.** Afterward He returned to the Temple to teach. The scribes and Pharisees brought a woman to Christ who had been caught in adultery. The

Feast of Tabernacles had just been celebrated and acts of immorality during that festive week were not unusual. The scribes attempted to put Christ in a dilemma. If He answered that the woman should be stoned, He would be violating the Roman law which forbade such acts. If He answered that she should not be stoned, He would be violating Moses' law (Deut 22:24). They did this to **tempt** Him (Gr *peirazo*, "to entice to sin").

There are several theories about what Christ wrote on the ground. First, He wrote the sins of the scribes and Pharisees. Second, He wrote the Ten Commandments. Third, He wrote a message to the Pharisees.

7-8. After pressing the issue, Christ answered the accusers. In answering, He did not abolish Moses' law; rather, He applied that law to the lives of those who had accused the woman. Again, He wrote on the ground and silence convicted the crowd.

9-11. They left, probably not out of conviction, but rather they had been defeated in their attempt to trap the Son of God. The sinner is left alone with the only person who was perfect and able to condemn her. In mercy and love, He forgave her and told her to **go, and sin no more.**

2. *Sermon on the Light of the World. 8:12-59.*

12. Following the incident of the adulterous woman Christ made His second "I am" statement: **I am the light of the world.** Christ shines as the Light in the world of darkness and sin. **He that followeth.** If one accepts and trusts the leading of that Light, **he . . . shall have the light of life.**

13-14. The Pharisees objected to Christ's testimony because all testimonies must be substantiated by witness. Christ knew His origin and no man could testify to that. Consequently, the Pharisees could not disprove His testimony.

15-16. Christ accused the Pharisees of judging from an external perspective. **I judge no man.** Although Christ had perfect knowledge, He came, not to judge, but to save (3:17-18). **If I judge.** Those who reject the saving ministry of Christ must be judged, and they will be judged correctly. It is judgment from both the Father and Son.

17-18. The law required two witnesses (Deut 17:6). **Two men.** Two human witnesses. If the law required two human witnesses for accuracy, how much more dependable is the witness of two divine persons, the Father and the Son.

19-20. The Jews had rejected Christ and in doing so had rejected the Father. **His hour was not yet come** (see 7:30).

21-22. Again, Jesus pronounces the sentence on those who reject Him (7:33-34). **I go my way,** refers to His going back to the Father. Those who had rejected Him would **die** in their **sins** and would not be able to be with Christ and the Father. The Jews ignored His message to them and wondered what was going to happen to Christ.

23-24. The Jews who rejected Him were from a different **world** than Christ. Note the contrast: **from beneath** and **from above.** Failure to accept Christ is the basis for everlasting death (3:36).

25. Who art thou? (Literally, "You, who are you?") These Jews were blind and deaf. Christ had made it clear Who He was.

26-27. Christ had **many things** to tell them which would add to their judgment. Those **things** were **true** because He received them from the Father. The Jews were blinded by prejudice and unbelief. Christ had clearly explained on several occasions that the Father had sent Him (5:36-37), and yet they did not accept it.

28-29. When ye have lifted up. This refers to the cross and eventually to the glory that would follow. Then, they would **know** that Christ was Messiah and that He and the Father were in agreement (Phil 2:9-11).

30-31. Many believed. The test of their true faith is given in the conditional clause, **If ye continue in my word.** This is not the basis of true faith, but rather the result. This is true discipleship.

32-33. Abiding in His word gives greater knowledge of **the truth** and sets one free from sin (34-35, 37). They appeal to their religious heritage. They are not like the heathen who are in bondage to idolatry; they are **Abraham's seed.**

34-35. Christ eliminates the segregation of Jew and heathen, and declares that **Whosoever** is continually **committing sin** is the slave **of sin.** The slave is temporary and can be sold at any time. The son, who is related to the master, lives in the house **for ever.** Israel, as the slave, had the temporary blessing of God's house.

36-37. Everyone who wants freedom must be emancipated by the **Son** (compare the Son with **the truth** in verse 32). Even though these people had the advantages of being Abraham's seed, they desired to kill the One Abraham **rejoiced to see** (8:56). Their hearts were so filled with hatred that they had no place for Christ's **word.**

38. Note the contrast between **my Father** and **your father.** He would eventually tell them who their father was (8:44).

39. These people claimed Abraham as their **father.** Christ gives a logical sequence of statements. Given the assumption that they were Abraham's children, they would do the **works of Abraham** (he **believed in God,** Gen 15:6).

40. However, these people wanted to **kill** Christ. Such works were not characteristic of Abraham; consequently, these people were not Abraham's children.

41. They did have a **Father. We be not born of fornication.** The **We** is em-phasized. This is an insinuation that Jesus was illegitimate and that they were truly of God the Father.

42-43. Christ refutes this claim on the basis that they did not **love** Him. Their lack of spiritual understanding was attributed to the fact that they **cannot hear my word.** They could not because they had totally rejected Him.

44-45. Christ now identifies their **father the devil.** Physically, they were Abraham's children, but spiritually, they were the devil's children. They were acting like the devil. **He was a murderer** and they wanted to murder Christ. He **abode not in the truth** and they had rejected the truth. He is the father of lies. Since these people were the sons of a liar, they rejected the **truth.**

46-47. Christ substantiates His claim to be speaking the truth on the premise that no one could charge Him with sin. **Why do ye not believe me?** Christ answers His own question. They had rejected Christ because of their relationship to the devil. They were **not of God.**

48-51. Angered by the implications of Christ's accusations, they struck back by accusing Christ of being a demon-possessed Samaritan and not a true Jew. Such an accusation dishonored the **Father** and would result in judgment. To **keep** means to accept and rest upon. To those who did this was the promise of not seeing death.

52-53. The Jews state that now they **know** He has a demon. Every one of the great men of the Old Testament died disproving Christ's promise that whoever would keep His word would not die. The conclusion: the word of Christ was not true.

54-55. Christ answers their question by claiming that He does not seek glory for Himself, but for the Father. If He states that He does not **know** the Father, He will be a liar like the Jews.

56-58. The joy of Abraham refers to the birth of Isaac. Abraham saw in Isaac the hope of mankind and the promise of Messiah. He saw the promise afar off (Heb 11:13). Limited to physical understanding, the Jews could not comprehend how Christ saw Abraham. Christ now makes the strongest statement of this entire dialogue. Before Abraham existed, **I am.** Christ was from eternity and was the great I AM (Ex 3:14).

59. Angered by Christ's accusation that they belonged to the devil and that Christ was God, they attempted to kill Him. They were only doing the works of their father, the devil (8:44).

3. *Application of sermon by healing blind man. 9:1-41.*

This entire chapter illustrates the Light of the World in action as He reaches into the darkness of one man's life, opens his eyes, and sets him free.

9:1-2. Christ is confronted with a man **which was blind from his birth.** The disciples immediately raise a theological question. Was the blindness a result of the man's sin or his parents' sin? A common belief among the Jews was that physical sickness directly resulted from sin (Ex 20:5).

3-7. Christ is looking to the future not the past. The blindness gave opportunity for God's power to be manifested. I (Greek that was probably "We") **must work the works.** The disciples had asked the question, "Why?" but Jesus was interested in "What?" What could be done for the man's need? This statement is the premise for the action that is about to follow. No explanation is given as to why Christ chose this method in healing the blind man. He was probably testing the blind man's faith and obedience. Christ sent him to Siloam and told him to wash. This story is similar to that of Naaman. However, the blind man responded immediately and was healed.

8-9. There is confusion over the man's identity. The miracle had changed the man's complexion. Finally, the man said, **I am he.**

10-12. Having been accused that it really is the man who was blind, the next logical question was how he had received his sight. The man related the story and the neighbors responded by wanting to know the location of Jesus.

13-14. Because the man had been healed on the Sabbath, the neighbors took him to the Pharisees. To make clay on the Sabbath was illegal.

15. Again. The second time he was asked to tell his story of healing.

16-17. The Pharisees knew Christ had broken the Sabbath. Since Christ had broken the Sabbath, He could not be **of God.** Others argued that it was impossible for a sinner to perform miracles. Since Christ did perform a miracle, maybe He was not a sinner. **There was a division among them.** They asked the man his opinion of Christ. He responded that **He is a prophet.**

18-21. The Jews refused to admit the miracle until they talked to the man's parents, who confirmed that this was their son and that he **was born blind.** However, they did not explain the means of what happened.

22-23. Because they were afraid of the Jews, they wanted their son to speak for himself. The Jews had agreed that anyone who would recognize Christ as the Messiah would be excommunicated from the synagogue.

24. They recall the blind man. **Give God the praise.** They want the blind man to attribute the miracle to God alone and to admit that Christ **is a sinner.** Rather than being objective, the Jews had already made up their minds about Christ; He was a sinner.

25. Note the **I know not** and the **I know.** The Jews said **we know** He is a sinner, but the man says, **I know not** if He is a sinner, but **I know, whereas I was blind, now I see.** The receiving of sight is a fact, not an opinion.

26-27. Again, the Jews ask him what happened and how it happened. The man becomes impatient with their repeated questions. **Will ye also be his**

disciples? If I repeat it again, will you become Christ's disciples?

28-29. Angered by the fact that their authority has been questioned by a beggar, the Jews make a distinction between the followers of Christ who broke the Sabbath and the followers of Moses who obey the law.

30. The blind man now rubs salt in the wound. It is astonishing, he argues, that the religious leaders did not know where Christ came from when He had performed such an outstanding miracle. How could these leaders be knowledgeable and yet not know something so important?

31-33. The blind man continues his argument as follows: God only listens to those who do **his will** and not to sinners. This man performed a miracle that no one else had ever done, God helped him do it, therefore, Christ is not a sinner, for if he were, **he could do nothing.**

34. The Pharisees had been defeated by a poor beggar and so they **cast him out** of the synagogue.

35. Christ found the outcast and began to meet his spiritual needs. **Dost thou believe on the Son of God?**

36-37. The man is ready to believe but needs some direction. Christ reveals Himself.

38-39. The man responds in faith and worships Christ. Observing the man's humble response, Christ declares that He came to judge. Those who do not see but who want to see (the blind man), will see. Those who think they see (the Pharisees) will be **made blind.**

40-41. In disdain, the Pharisees ask, **Are we blind also? If ye were blind.** If you were ignorant of God's law, Jesus responded, and yet desired to be saved, then **ye should have no sin.** You would be saved. **Ye see.** You are proud in your religious enlightenment, and ye have rejected me. Therefore, **your sin remaineth.**

I. Christ as the Good Shepherd. 10:1-42.

This story is an allegory rather than a parable (vs. 6); this means that the details are relevant to the main idea. In this allegory Christ is referred to as the Good Shepherd and as the door into the sheepfold.

1. Sermon on the Good Shepherd. 10:1-21.

10:1. Thieves and robbers attempt to enter the **sheepfold** by climbing over the wall. The oriental sheepfold normally consisted of four walls of stone with one door and no roof. The fold refers to Israel (vs. 16), and the thieves and robbers refer to the Jewish leaders who are trying to lead Israel while avoiding the door (Christ).

2. The true leader enters **by the door** and is the only **shepherd of the sheep.**

3-4. The true shepherd has a unique relationship with his sheep. He **calleth** them by **name.** He **leadeth them, putteth** them forth, and **goeth before them.** The sheep respond by hearing **his voice,** knowing **his voice,** and following Him.

5-6. A stranger will they not follow (Greek emphatic negation; never follow). Their reaction to the **stranger** is totally opposite to that of the shepherd. They **flee.** They are not acquainted with **the voice of strangers.** They did not comprehend this story of the shepherd and the sheep.

7-8. Verily, verily. Christ begins His explanation with the same statement that He began His story. **I am the door.** Entrance into the fold is by Him and Him alone. The ones who **came before** were the scribes and Pharisees who attempted to enter the fold other than through the door.

9-10. Again, Christ emphasizes that He is **the door. If any man enter in, he shall be saved** (note vs. 10, **they might have life** refers to salvation). Also, that person will find pasture (in verse 10, referring to abundant life) or the constant nourishment necessary to maintain life. The scribes and Pharisees **steal, kill, and destroy.** Christ gives life (salvation) and gives it **abundantly.**

11. Besides being the only door into the sheepfold, Christ is also the **good shepherd.** He is good because He **giveth his life for** (Gr *hyper*), in behalf of, for the benefit of **the sheep** (Ps 23).

12-13. The scribes were merely **hirelings** (hired people) who had no true love and concern for the welfare of the sheep. In the moment of danger the hireling runs away.

14-16. The Pharisees are strangers, but Christ **knows** His sheep. The Pharisees have no love for the sheep, but Christ gives His life for them. Christ has a relationship to the sheep similar to His relationship with His Father. Christ now states that His fold will include both Jews and Gentiles (Acts 10:28).

17-18. The Lord further amplifies His statement saying that He will lay down His life in a voluntary act of sacrifice. **I lay it down of myself.** He had that **power** (right).

19-21. The Jews were divided in their opinion. Some thought He was mad and demon possessed, while others were impressed by His miracle on behalf of the blind man.

2. Rejection of Christ's message. 10:22-42.

22-24. About two months had elapsed between the previous account and these events. **Dost thou make us to doubt?** The Greek idiom means literally "lift up our soul." How long will you keep us in a state of suspense? **Tell us plainly.**

25-26. Christ had already told them (6:35; 7:37-39; 8:23-25). The problem was they had rejected what Christ had said about Himself. Christ had supplemented His claims by His works. The cause for their unbelief is rooted in the fact that they were not His sheep.

27-28. Note the verbs used to describe Christ's sheep. They **hear** and **follow** their shepherd. This obedient response is totally opposite that of the Jews. Note the verbs used to describe the shepherd. He knows and gives **eternal life.** He promises that they **shall never perish.** This is a Greek emphatic negation; "never perish." To further emphasize their security, He adds the phrase, "into the ages" (Greek idiom meaning "forever") or for all eternity they shall never **perish.** No one can take these sheep out of Christ's hand.

29. Besides being in the hand of Christ, these sheep are in the hand of **the Father** and **no man is able to pluck them out of my Father's hand.**

30. I and my Father are one. God the Father and God the Son are in agreement in the matter of the believer's eternal security. On the basis of this passage, no one should ever doubt the eternal security of his salvation. Once a person is genuinely saved, he is saved forever.

31. The Jews were angered that Christ would claim equality with the Father, and took **stones** to **stone him.**

32. Christ again makes the Jews face His works, and asks them to define which **good** work deserves such cruel treatment. These **good works** reflected His supernatural origin, and should be the basis for accepting Him as Christ and not the basis for stoning Him.

33-34. The Jews ignored what Christ did, and were judging Him on what He said. Christ had made Himself **God.** In defending His claims, Christ meets the Jews on their ground and makes His appeal to the **law. Ye are gods.** This refers to Psalms 82:6, and deals with Hebrew judges because they were interpreters of divine law and justice.

35-36. Christ states that if the Jews were willing to call these judges gods because **the word of God** had come to them, why did they accuse Him of blasphemy when the Father, who had sent the **word** to the judges, sent Him and set Him apart for a divine mission?

37-39. If His works do not substantiate His claim, then do not believe Him. Christ appeals to their unbelief. **I do.** If His works agree with His message, and if they still do not believe, Christ exhorts them to consider again His **works,** so that they **may know, and believe.** Now they try to arrest Him because of these blasphemous claims.

40-41. Christ retires from the public scene. However, they find Him, and the ministry of John the Baptist is remembered. Even though John **did no miracle,** yet all that he had said about Christ was true (1:19-36).

42. Many believed. (See Merrill C. Tenney, *John the Gospel of Belief*, pp. 163-167.)

J. Christ as the Resurrection and the Life. 11:1-57.

This chapter deals with the resurrection of Lazarus and the Jewish reaction to the miracle. It is apparent that the fame of Christ had reached national prominence, and that this was of great concern to the Jews who feared that the Romans would punish them if Christ influenced the people to follow him.

1. Power of Christ: raising Lazarus. 11:1-46.

11:1-2. The setting for this miracle is described. Lazarus had become ill; his sisters Mary and Martha send to Christ for help.

3. Note that they do not ask Christ to do anything. They simply make Him aware of their need, and know that because He loves and cares He will respond appropriately.

4. This sickness is not unto death. This means that the final result of Lazarus' sickness will not be death. The final result will be **for the glory of God.** Sin is not the source of all sickness. Sometimes God permits sickness in order to reveal His glory. Greater glory was manifested in raising Lazarus from the dead than if Christ had simply healed him.

5-6. Jesus **loved.** In the hour of crisis and need, remember that God loves us. Christ delays His going to Bethany. This might seem strange since Lazarus had a great need; however, note again the previous verse. His waiting is based upon His love.

7-8. The disciples are alarmed when Christ wants to return to **Judaea,** because the last time He was there they tried to stone Him (10:31).

9-10. Are there not twelve hours in a day? Christ alludes to the fact that His time on the earth is a final period of time and it cannot be changed. A person who walks in the **light** of God's will cannot be harmed, but the person who does not **stumbleth.**

11. Lazarus sleepeth. Death is often referred to as sleep (Gen 47:30; Matt 27:52; I Thess 4:13). However, in no way do these passages teach a state of soul-sleep or unconsciousness. Death for the saint is restful sleep from the problems of this world, but a full consciousness of another world (Phil 1:23).

12-13. The disciples thought that Lazarus was physically asleep and assumed that sleep would be good for his illness.

14. Finally, Christ clarifies His statements by telling them **plainly, Lazarus is dead.**

15. Christ is happy that He was not with Lazarus when he died. Had He been there, He would have healed him and prevented death. Now He must perform a greater miracle that will increase the faith of the disciples.

16. Thomas, **called Didymus** (Greek means "twin"), encourages the disciples to go with Christ, **that we may die with him.** The outlook for safety in Judaea is dim and Thomas feels that Christ will be killed, and as a result they will be killed as well.

17. Four days. Lazarus probably died around the same time that the messenger came to Christ (11:3).

18-19. Bethany was about two miles from Jerusalem. Many residents of Jerusalem had come to Bethany to comfort Mary and Martha.

20. Note the contrast in personalities. Martha is a woman of action, whereas Mary is a woman of quiet reflection (Lk 10:38-42).

21. This statement is not critical of Christ's action, but it is a statement of grief that if Christ could have been with Lazarus he would not have died.

22. This verse displays great hope in Christ's ability to ask from God; however, Martha did not have the resurrection of her brother in mind.

23-24. Christ assures Martha that her brother **shall rise again.** She interprets this to mean in the **last day.** Martha, like many Christians, does not appropriate the promises of God for now. God is able to meet our needs in the present as well as the future.

25-26. I am. This is the fifth of the seven **I am** statements (6:35; 8:12; 10:9; 10:11; 14:6; 15:5). Christ is the **resurrection** (He raises those who are dead in sin) and **the life** (He gives to them eternal life). Those who believe in Christ though they may die physically, they shall live. Beyond that, those who really have Christ's life **shall never die.**

27. Yea, Lord: I believe (Gr. perfect tense; emphasizes certainty, "I *do* believe"). Martha had accepted the **I am** (25) as the Christ (Messiah), **the Son of God.**

28. Martha returns and quietly tells Mary that Christ has arrived.

29-30. Mary now goes out to meet the Master.

31-32. The Jews observing her haste, and assuming that she is going to the grave, follow her to comfort her. Note that the words of Mary were the same as Martha's (11:21). How many times they had repeated these words to each other in the last four days.

33. He groaned in spirit. The verb used here means to become angry. Christ was probably angry at the root

cause of all this sorrow and grief, i.e. sin.

34-35. Jesus wept. Jesus broke out into tears. Here we are reminded of the humanity of Christ and His love and concern for His people.

36-37. The Jews saw the love of Christ, but some of them debated whether or not He could have prevented this tragedy by healing Lazarus.

38-39. Christ came to the tomb and ordered someone to roll away the stone. Martha objected to this strange request since Lazarus' body would stink.

40. Christ reminded her of His previous statements (11:25-26).

41-42. Christ offered a prayer before He performed the miracle. The prayer was one of thanksgiving rather than requesting. He is thankful that the **Father hast heard.** Because He is in close communion with the Father, this miracle is possible. He prays so that the **people** may **believe that thou hast sent me.**

43-44. Lazarus, come forth. The voice of omnipotence speaks and the dead responds. Here is a picture of many Christians who are alive in Christ but are still bound by the **graveclothes** of the world. They cannot work because their hands are bound, they cannot walk because their feet are bound, and they cannot witness because their mouths are bound. Christ Jesus orders: **Loose him.**

45. The miracle brought results. First, many **believed on him.**

46. Second, some went back to Jerusalem to report this incident to the leaders.

2. Plan of the Pharisees. 11:47-57.

47-48. Third, the Sanhedrin became angry and were afraid that if people continued to follow Christ, the Romans would think the Jews were planning a rebellion and would take their leaders into captivity.

49-50. Caiaphas presents a solution.

He reasons that if Jesus lives, the nation will die. Therefore, in the interest of patriotism, Jesus must die so that the nation will live.

51-52. Little did Caiaphas realize the real truth of what he was saying. Christ would die to save the nation spiritually, whereas Caiaphas intended Him to die to save the nation politically. Again, the cosmopolitan nature of Christ's death is emphasized (10:16).

53-54. The Sanhedrin had formally decided to kill Christ. Knowing about their plan, Christ removed Himself from the public view.

55-57. As the pilgrims came to Jerusalem for the Passover there was much excitement and enthusiasm over the ministry of Christ. Popular opinion among the common people was in His favor. However, the leaders made it clear that anyone who saw Christ should report it, **that they might take him.**

K. Christ as the Messiah. 12:1-50.

There are four separate sections in this chapter: the anointing of Jesus (12:1-11); the triumphal entry (12:12-19); the Greeks seek Christ (12:20-36); and the Jews reject Christ (12:37-50). In all these events, Christ emerges as the true Messiah.

1. Supper at Bethany. 12:1-11.

12:1-2. Six days before the passover. Although there is debate concerning which day Christ entered Bethany, most commentators conclude that it was Saturday evening. According to Matthew 26 and Mark 14, the supper took place at the house of Simon the Leper. Martha, true to her personality, was serving (Lk 10:40). Perhaps this was a meal designed to thank the Lord for what He had done for Lazarus and Simon.

3. A pound of ointment of spikenard. Mary took twelve ounces of this perfume and **anointed the feet of Jesus.** This perfume was extracted from the root of the nard plant which

is grown in India. It was a costly import. This was an act of love and devotion to the Lord. Nothing is wasted if it is given to the Lord.

4-5. Contrasted to the generosity of Mary is the selfishness of Judas. He had estimated the ointment to be worth **three hundred pence** or the amount of wages a person would receive for three hundred days' work.

6-7. Judas was not concerned for the poor. He had been stealing **(he was a thief)** from the treasury **(the bag).** If the perfume had been sold, he could have stolen some of the three hundred pennies. Christ rebuked Judas. Mary, anticipating the death of her Saviour, anointed the body of Christ. In doing this prior to his death, she was expressing her complete love and devotion.

8. What Mary did was more important than feeding the poor; however, Jesus implied that Christians must minister to the poor, since **the poor always ye have with you.**

9-11. Lazarus had become a phenomenon since Christ had raised him. However, the religious leaders wanted to kill Lazarus, because **many** had believed on Christ after observing what He had done for Lazarus.

2. Triumphal entry. 12:12-19.

12-13. On the next day. On Sunday, many of the people who had come to the feast took **branches of palm trees, and went forth to meet him.** It should be noted that those who sought to honor the Lord were pilgrims, not the residents of Jerusalem. **Hosannah.** The Greek is a transliteration of Hebrew meaning "Save, I beseech thee" (see Ps 118:25). They proclaim Christ as the **King of Israel,** and the one who comes in **the name of the Lord** (Ps 118:25-26). These people were expecting Christ to establish David's kingdom.

14-15. John now moves from the public scene to the private scene where Christ mounts a donkey. This action was in fulfillment of prophecy (Zech 9:9). The donkey was used in the Old

Testament by kings who were bringing peace, while the horse was used when the kings rode into battle. **Daughter of Zion.** This symbolically represents Jerusalem and its inhabitants. Jerusalem should stop being afraid because their own king was coming.

16. The disciples understood these things after the ascension of Christ and the coming of the Holy Spirit, who called these things to their remembrance (7:39; 14:26).

17-19. The raising of Lazarus had caused great excitement in Jerusalem. Many who proclaimed Him as the **King of Israel** did so because of the miracle He performed in raising Lazarus. The Pharisees responded to this excitement by concluding that the **world** (everyone) **is gone after him.**

3. Teaching on the cross. 12:20-50.

20-21. The attention is now turned from the Jews to the Greeks. Some Greek proselytes had come **to worship at the feast.** The Greeks approached Philip and asked for an interview with Christ.

22. Philip consulted with Andrew, and they both approached Jesus. Why did Philip consult Andrew? Probably because he was wondering whether Jesus would consent to a Gentile interview since His mission was to Israel.

23. Jesus did not talk directly to the Greeks. He conveyed His message through Andrew and Philip. **The hour.** This does not refer to a sixty minute period, but to the general time period when the **Son of man should be glorified.** This glorification is explained in the next verse.

24. Seeds which are not sown are alone. The seeds which are sown, die, and in so doing bring forth a harvest. Christ used this to illustrate His death, which will produce a rich spiritual harvest.

25-26. This principle of death producing life is applicable to the disciple as well as the Master (Mt 10:37-39; Mk

8:34-38). The reward for following Christ is honor with the **Father.**

27. The awful agony of approaching death grips Christ's emotions. **Save me.** This does not imply disobedience or weakness on the part of Christ. "A man may shrink from an experience which he, nevertheless, wants to undergo; e.g. an operation. So it is also with Christ" (Hendriksen, p. 200).

28. Christ's ultimate desire is to glorify His Father's **name.** The Father answers from heaven that His Name has been glorified (through the obedient ministry of His Son), and it will be glorified again (through the death, burial, and resurrection of the Son).

29. The people **heard** but did not understand. They assumed that an angel had spoken to Him.

30-31. The voice was also for the people so that they would recognize Christ as God. Christ is referring to His judgment of sin through His death, and His defeat of Satan (I Cor 15:54-57).

32-33. Christ would **draw all men** (including the Greeks) to Himself through the cross **(be lifted up).** Christ would die on a cross lifted up.

34. The Jews were expecting **Christ** to reign forever. They were puzzled that He was talking about death. Their Messiah would not die.

35-36. Christ answered their question with a solemn warning that if they did not receive the Light, darkness would **come upon** them. The Light would soon be removed.

37-38. In spite of all the miracles, they **believed not on him.** This rejection of Christ had been prophesied by Isaiah. They rejected what they heard **(our report)** and what they saw **(the arm of the Lord** in powerful miracles).

39-41. Could not believe. God does not prevent people from being converted. In his judgment, as a result of man's unbelief, God sometimes hardens the heart.

42-43. Many leaders **believed on**

him but were unwilling to confess Him for fear of the Pharisees.

44-45. The series of statements that conclude this chapter are Christ's final public messages to Israel. Knowing Christ means knowing the Father. Seeing Christ means seeing the Father.

46. See chapter 8:12.

47-48. Christ's purpose is not to judge, but to **save.** Those who rejected the words of Christ would be judged by those words in the **last day.**

49-50. The Father gave Christ to speak, and His words are **life everlasting.**

III. THE PRIVATE MINISTRY OF CHRIST. 13:1-17:26.

A. Christ as the Servant. 13:1-38.

The setting for chapters 13 through 17 is given in 12:36: **and did hide himself from them.** During this time prior to His death, Christ limits His ministry to His diciples.

1. Washing the disciples' feet. 13:1-20.

13:1. Christ's appointed time had come when he would leave this world. **He loved them unto the end** (or to the uttermost).

2-3. In the midst of this loving scene one can observe the work of Satan, for it was Satan who put the idea of betrayal into Judas' mind. To fully appreciate the Lord's humility, one must remember that **all things** had been given **into his hands.** The all-powerful One was about to wash His disciples' feet.

4-5. It was customary in oriental homes for the servant to wash the feet of guests to remove the dust. However, Christ had requested privacy for His supper and consequently, no servant was present. The disciples were too proud to perform this menial task; therefore, the Lord took the basin and washed the feet of His disciples.

6-7. Impulsive Peter strongly objected to this act of humility. Christ responded to Peter's question by implying that there is a deeper meaning in washing feet. One day Peter would understand that this was a graphic illustration of Christ's humility.

8-9. Peter responds. **Thou shalt never wash my feet.** In this statement, the double negative is used. "You shall never, ever wash my feet." Christ is thinking of His overall humiliation and death when He states that if Peter is not washed, he has **no part** with Christ. Peter is still thinking about physical washing.

10-11. A person who is **washed** (i.e. saved, Tit 3:5) does not need another bath. However, many times his feet may get dirty for the world, and he needs his feet washed (I Jn 1:7-9).

12. Christ now asks them if they have understood the meaning of what He has done.

13-14. If the **Master and Lord** is willing to humble Himself to the point of washing his disciples' feet, then the disciples should be willing to do the same thing.

15. Given you an example. Christ is not instituting and ordinance of footwashing, but is showing an example of humility. he does not command us to perform this act, but to acquire the attitude that this activity displays.

16-17. Blessing (**happy are ye**) is the result of practicing a life of humility and service.

18. I speak not of you all. Not all the disciples would have blessings on their lives because they were humble. One of the group who would eat with Christ would betray Him. Christ is speaking of Judas (Ps 41:9).

19-20. Christ forewarned the disciples that this would take place. The disciples did not later question Christ's choice of Judas since this was all a part of God's plan. To accept Christ means to accept the Father.

2. Predicting His betrayal. 13:21-35.

21-22. The time has come to clearly state that one of the disciples would betray Him. This brought sorrow and grief to the Lord. The disciples were shocked, and in amazement they **looked** (kept on looking) **one on another.**

23-24. John, the beloved disciple, was leaning on Jesus. This was the customary way to recline at the table. Simon probably assumed that John knew the identity of this betrayer.

25-26. John asked, **who is it?** Christ did not identify the betrayer by name, but stated that He would give the **sop** (a piece of bread dipped in sauce) to the betrayer. Sop was usually given as a token of friendship. Even in betrayal, the Lord loved Judas.

27. Now the progress of Satan; 13:2 states, "the devil having now put into the heart." Satan went a step further and took full possession of Judas.

28-29. The whole company of disciples did not understand this. Christ had addressed his statement about the sop to John and consequently, he was the only one who understood its implications.

30. It was night. Note the symbolism here. As Judas went out from the Saviour to betray Him, he was surrounded by darkness. This symbolizes the evil and sin surrounding the action of Judas.

31-32. With the exit of Judas the scene is now set for the death and ultimate glorification of Christ. God would glorify the Son through the Son's passion, and would show the close relationship between the two.

33. Little children. This is the only time this phrase is used in the gospels.

34. Christ commands them to love, **as I have loved you.** The love Christians should display for each other must be a sacrificial love similar to the Lord's love.

35. Grasp the meaning of this verse. In a day of church schisms and divisions, the words of Christ have deep significant meaning. The world should recognize us as followers of Christ because our relationship to each other is permeated with love.

3. Predicting Peter's denial. 13:36-38.

36-38. Peter is still a little confused. Christ tells him that he will follow **afterwards.** Peter's time of death had not yet come (Heb 9:27). Note Peter's impulsiveness. He wants to be with Christ now. Christ predicted the exact opposite of Peter's claims. Peter said he would die, but Christ died. Peter would deny his Master.

B. Christ as the Comforter. 14:1-31.

There is a close connection between the events of chapter 13 and the promises of chapter 14. In chapter 13 the disciples had been rebuked by their lack of humility. They were instructed that Christ would soon leave them. They were told that one of their number would betray his Master, and Peter had been rebuked. To offset the depression produced by this startling revelation, Christ brought a message of hope and encouragement.

14:1. Let not your heart be troubled. This is the foundational statement of the entire chapter. To settle the emotions of the disciples, Christ lists the reasons why their hearts should not be **troubled** (Gr *tarassō*, stir up, disturb, throw into confusion). **Believe.** Both times this Greek verb (*pisteuō*) can be interpreted as imperative. Christ stirs both their faith in God and their faith in Him. This settles a troubled heart.

2. The disciples should be comforted with the fact that Christ is going to **prepare** an abode for them in heaven (**my Father's house**).

3-4. I will come again. This is the promise that brings hope to troubled hearts. The emphasis of His coming is not the dwelling places but the prospect of being with the Saviour (Gr *pros,* literally, face to face). The **way** to heaven is through Christ Himself.

5. Overwhelmed with grief at the prospect of Christ's leaving, Thomas does not understand the meaning of Christ's statement. Thomas objects that since he does not know where Christ is going, how could he possibly know the **way** to get there?

6. Christ answers with another **I am** statement. **The way.** Christ is the only **way** to heaven (10:9). The **truth.** Christ is the embodiment of all truth (8:32). **Life** (1:4; 3:16). no man can approach the Father unless he does so through Christ.

7. From henceforth ye know him. To know Christ is to know the Father. The disciples knew Christ; therefore, they knew the Father.

8. Philip asks for a theophany (manifestation of God's glory) similar to Moses (Ex 33:18-23).

9. So long time with you. Christ had stated this truth about seeing the Father through the Son throughout His ministry (1:18; 10:30).

10. The **words** and **works** of Christ surely must indicate a unique relationship between the Father and the Son.

11. The disciples were weak in their faith. Christ exhorts them to **Believe** what He has said, or to simply believe on the basis of His **works.**

12. What a promise this is. **Greater works.** The works of Christ were limited to a small geographical area and to a specific people. The disciples' works would be worldwide in their reach and would affect all people. In this way, they were **greater.** Christ's going away would cause Him to send the Holy Spirit.

13-14. Note the relationship of works to prayer (Acts 1:14; 2:42; 3:1; 4:31). Effective prayer is **in my name.** This is prayer in agreement with the desires of Christ. The result of prayer is the glorification of the Father, not self-glorification.

15. Love is not sentimental emotionalism, it is obedience to the commandments of God.

16. Comforter (Gr *paraklētos*) one called alongside to help. Christ would **pray the Father,** and they would receive a Helper. **Another** (Gr *allos*, another of the same kind). This would

indicate that the Comforter would be of the same quality and character as Christ's. The Comforter would be God. **For ever.** Christ would go away (14:2), but the Helper would remain **for ever.**

17. Spirit of truth. The Helper is the Holy Spirit (16:13). The world cannot **receive** the Spirit. This Spirit would have a twofold ministry. He would dwell with them (be in their midst), and He would **be in** them (dwell within).

18. Comfortless (Gr *orphanos*), literally, I will not leave you as orphans. **I will come.** Christ would be with them through the ministry of the Holy Spirit.

19. Very soon the world that hated Him would no longer be able to **see** Him. The disciples would **see** Him. They would see Him because they were spiritually alive, and the Holy Spirit would glorify Christ to them (16:14).

20. At that day. In the day of the dispensation of the Holy Spirit they would recognize the relationship between the Father and the Son and themselves: Christ in the Father, the disciples in Christ, and Christ in the disciples.

21. True love is demonstrated by obedience to the Lord's **commandments.** This love and obedience to Christ will cause the Father to love them. Christ too will love those who obey, and will reveal Himself to them through the Spirit and the Word.

22. Judas is thinking of Christ's revealing Himself to the world as the Messiah, and cannot understand this limited revelation.

23-24. The answer of Christ is based on obedience. The Father and the Son will **come** only to those who love and prove their love by obedience. **Abode.** Through the Spirit, both the Father and the Son will make their home in the believer. Disobedience to the Word of Christ is also rejection of the Father's Word.

25-26. Christ had spoken **These things** while He was with the disciples, but the Holy Ghost would **teach** them **all things.** The Spirit would also cause them to remember the things that Christ had told them. The ultimate fulfillment of this promise is the completion of the canon of the New Testament.

27. Peace. In the hour of sorrow for the disciples, Christ promised a unique kind of **peace** that is different from the world's peace: **My peace.** This peace would calm troubled and fearful hearts.

28-29. True love would cause the disciples to **rejoice** because Christ was going away. This departure would bring glory to Christ and would enable the Holy Spirit to come. Christ foretold these events so that when they happened they would increase the faith of the disciples.

30. Christ would not continue to teach them. **The prince of this world cometh.** Satan, through the behavior of Judas, was coming. **Hath nothing in me.** Christ is the sinless Son of God, and Satan had no part in Him.

31. Christ will not resist those who come to kill Him. In obedience to the Father's commandment, He is ready and willing to die. **Arise, let us go hence.** The hour for which Jesus came had arrived. He must now go to the cross, and He is ready. He voluntarily goes forward to meet His death.

C. Christ as the True Vine. 15:1—16:33.

Although there is difference of opinion among commentators over the meaning of all that is discussed in this chapter, there is one basic truth upon which all agree. The basic truth of this chapter is that just as the branch cannot bear fruit unless it abides in the vine, Christians cannot bear fruit unless they have an abiding relationship with the True Vine, Jesus Christ.

1. Christ and the disciples. 15:1-17.

15:1. The true vine. In the Old Testament, Israel is referred to as a vine. However, in this verse, we find the True or Real Vine is Christ Himself. The **husbandman.** The Father is the **husbandman,** or the One who owns the vineyard and who takes care of it.

2. He taketh away. Just as the husbandman disposes of branches that bear no fruit, so the Father judges those who bear no spiritual fruit. **He purgeth it.** The **husbandman** prunes (Gr *kathaireō*) the branches which bear fruit in order for them to bear **more fruit.** In like manner, God the Father cleanses Christians who are bearing fruit to bring them to bear more fruit. Fruit is the natural product of a living organism. Spiritual fruit is a spiritual product of a spiritual union (Gal 5:22-23).

3. Cleansing is produced through the Word of God.

4. Abide in me. In order to be a fruitful Christian, one must learn to depend on Christ and let the power and Spirit of Christ flow through him.

5. Christ now clearly states the implications of this story. He is the **vine** and we are the **branches.** Note the total dependence upon the Vine. Without that abiding relationship **ye can do nothing.** In verse 2 it refers to **more fruit,** and in verses 5 and 8 it refers to **much fruit.**

6. This does not refer to everlasting punishment in hell. Note that there are results of not abiding in Christ as a branch. The man himself is not the branch; the branch represents the fruits of his relationship with Christ. When the Christian fails to abide in Christ, he withers, dries up, and his fruit or works will be judged by fire (I Cor 3:12-15).

7-8. Those who abide in Christ, and who permit His **words** to abide in them, have a blessed promise that Christ will perform whatever they ask. This is a blessed promise of the **Father.**

9-10. In the center of this unique abiding relationship is the love of God. Christ exhorts His disciples to continue in **my love.** It is interesting to note that this is the first fruit of the Spirit mentioned in Galatians 5:22. Christ remained in the Father's love because He obeyed Him. We remain in Christ's love because we obey His commandments (14:21, 23-24).

11. The second fruit of the Spirit of joy. The abiding relationship also gives us Christ's joy. Christ promises them fruit, answered prayer, love, and joy as the result of abiding in Him.

12. This is the second commandment found in chapter 15. The first is **abide in me** (7), and now Christ commands them to **love one another.** He defines the extent of that love in the phrase, **as I have loved you.**

13-14. Love is giving sacrificially for others. Love is not an emotional feeling, but it is the act of giving (John 3:16). To be a friend of Christ means to obey Him.

15. Because of their obedience, Christ could now call them **friends.** As His **friends,** they were told all the things that Christ had **heard** from the **Father.**

16. Although they were Christ's friends, this was by His choice, not their choice. **Ordained you** (Gr *tithēmi,* appointed you). **Bring forth fruit.** It is evident that the fruit refers to love and its results (15:8-14). Note the progression. To abide means to bear fruit; to bear fruit means to experience answered prayer (**he may give it you**).

17. Again Christ returns to the theme of love. Loving one another is a command, not an option.

2. Disciples and the world. 15:15-26.

18. Christ turns from the subject of love to the subject of **hate. Hate** (Gr *miseō*) occurs eight times in the rest of the discourse. **World** (Gr *kosmos*). This includes all who are not friends of Christ.

19. The **world** can **love** only those who are of the world. Since the friends of Christ have been **chosen out of the world,** the world, logically, hates them.

20-21. The disciples could expect the same treatment as their Lord received. Some would **persecute** them, while others would **keep** their message. The root of the world's rejection of the disciples was their rejection of the Father who had **sent** the Son.

22-23. If Christ had not come, the people would not have been guilty of rejecting Him. But He did come, and now they had no excuse for their sin. The Jews claimed to obey the Father, and yet they hated the Son. In reality, they hated both the Father and the Son.

24-25. Even though Christ had performed **works** that should have caused them to believe, they still rejected and hated Him. Yet even in their rebellion and hatred, the Jews were fulfilling God's plan (Ps 69:4).

26. Christ now concludes His discourse on hatred by reminding the disciples that they will not be alone. The **Spirit of truth** will **testify** (bear witness) of **me.** The witness of God's Spirit will cooperate with that of the disciples to give powerful testimony to the mission and purpose of Christ.

3. Disciples and the Spirit. 16:1-33.

16:1. These things. Christ had forewarned the disciples about the hatred they would encounter in the world.

2-3. The hatred would be so strong that eventually they would be excommunicated from the **synagogue.** This meant isolation from the social life of Israel. It meant loss of employment and rejection by their own families. **Doeth God service.** They would also be killed in the name of God (Acts 26:9-11). The root cause of this persecution is the world's rejection of both the **Father** and the Son.

4. Christ did not want the disciples to be unprepared for the trial of their faith. **At the beginning.** Since Christ was with them from the beginning, there was no reason to discuss this persecution. Now He was going away (Jn 14), and He wants to prepare them.

5-6. The disciples had not been interested in where Christ was going; they were concerned only about the **sorrow** that they were experiencing because He was going away.

7. I tell you the truth. He explains the necessity of His departure. If the disciples would understand this truth, they would have reason for triumph and not tragedy. It was necessary for Christ to go so that the Holy Spirit would come (14:16).

8-9. The work of the Spirit is now described. **Reprove** (Gr *elengchō*, convict or convince). The ministry of the Holy Spirit is a convicting and convincing ministry. He will convict of **sin,** of **righteousness,** and of **judgment.** The Holy Spirit through the Word of God and preaching convicts men of their sin.

10. Of righteousness. Although the world would reject the work of the Righteous One, the Father would accept it (**I go to my Father**). God's Spirit would convict men of true righteousness.

11. Of judgment. Satan, **the prince of this world,** had already been judged (Gen 3:15). The final judgment would come. The Spirit will convict men of this final judgment.

12. After describing the Spirit's work in the world, Christ now elaborates on the Spirit's work with regard to the disciples. The disciples were not ready spiritually to accept all that Christ wanted to tell them.

13. All truth. The Spirit would **guide** (lead) them into a complete knowledge of **all truth.** What the Spirit **hears,** He will **speak.** This indicates the close relationship of the Trinity. **Things to come.** The book of Revelation is an example of this.

14-15. The Spirit will **glorify** Christ. Again, the close unity of the Trinity is implied.

16. A little while. Very soon Christ would go away, but He promised them that **a little while** and they would see Him. This refers to both facts that the Holy Spirit would reveal Christ to them, and that Christ would return again (Jn 14:3). All this was possible because Christ was returning to the Father.

17-18. The disciples are confused by this statement, **a little while.**

19-20. Christ explains. The disciples would **weep** at the death of Christ, but the world would **rejoice,** thinking that they were finished with Christ. However, the sorrow of the disciples would be turned to joy through the resurrection, the coming of the Holy Spirit, and the return of Christ.

21. Using as an example the pain of childbirth and the joy that follows, Christ illustrates the future experience of the disciples at the death and resurrection of their Master.

22. I will see you again. This refers to both the resurrection and the advent of the Spirit. The permanent indwelling of the Spirit would produce a permanent **joy.**

23. The day would come when it would be impossible for the disciples to personally ask Christ for things. However, if they requested the Father in Christ's **name, he will give it you.** Since Christ has returned to the Father, the prayers of Christians must be made to the Father in the name of the Son.

24. Until then, prayer had been made directly to God. Now they were to pray in the merits of the finished work of Christ. Note the order: **ask, . . . receive, . . . joy may be full.**

25. Proverbs (Gr *paromoids*, veiled sayings). Christ had not spoken openly because the disciples would not understand. However, when the Spirit came, Christ would reveal the Father **plainly.** This occurred through the inspiration and writing of the epistles.

26-27. Prayer made in Christ's name was not so that Christ could somehow convince the Father to answer the prayers. The Father will answer prayer because of His love for the disciples.

28. Here is the entire purpose of

Christ. His eternity, His humiliation, and His exaltation are all implied in this verse.

29-30. The disciples now realize that Christ is speaking to them openly. They realize that Christ knows all things, and would reveal them without the disciples asking questions. Their conclusion is faith, that Christ came **forth from God.**

31-32. Thrilled with these revelations, the disciples are quickly reminded that soon they would scatter at the arrest of their Master. Christ would be **alone,** and yet in that hour the **Father is with me.**

33. Note the origin of **peace-in me.** They had peace in Christ, but in the **world** they would have **tribulation. Be of good cheer** (be courageous). Even though they would be opposed by the world, they should remember that Christ has overcome the world.

D. Christ as the Intercessor. 17:1-26.

This chapter contains the prayer of Christ for his disciples. In many aspects, it is a model prayer for all Christians.

17:1 Lifted up his eyes to heaven. This was a common practice when one prayed, since he was addressing himself to God. **Father.** Christ uses this term six times in His prayer. **The hour.** The moment of crisis had come when Christ would consummate His earthly ministry. **Glorify thy Son.** The hour that Christ referred to was not only the hour of death, but also His resurrection and exaltation.

2-3. Christ had been given **power** (authority) **over all flesh** (all mankind). This authority extended to the giving of **eternal life. As many as thou hast given.** This refers specifically to the disciples and generally to those of **all flesh** whom God has given to Christ. Eternal life results in a true knowledge of both God and Jesus Christ.

4. I have glorified thee. Christ has brought glory to the Father by fulfilling His will and completing His task

(4:34; 6:38). Note that Christ views His death as having been completed. He is so certain and sure of His atonement that He can speak as if it had already been completed.

5. Christ again asks the Father to glorify Him. He desires that glory which He had in eternity past, but which He voluntarily laid aside to redeem mankind (1:1-3,14).

6. Christ made known **(manifested)** the Father's name to those who followed Him. These disciples had been given to Christ by the Father. Note the results of Christ's revelation of the Father: **they have kept thy word.** An evidence of true conversion is obedience to the word of God.

7-8. The disciples had come to understand that **all things** (the message and the mission of Christ) which Christ had were ultimately from the Father. Christ was faithful in giving the Father's **words** to the disciples. The disciples accepted the message, and obtained a twofold knowledge: they understood that Christ had come from God, and that God had sent Him.

9. I pray for them. Christ's concern was for His own (Rom 8:34; Heb 7:25). **I pray not for the world.** This does not mean that Christ is unconcerned about the unsaved (Lk 23:34). However, His prayer for sanctification, glorification, and protection is only applicable to those who belong to Him.

10. Christ is praying to the Father in behalf of the disciples, and is confident that His prayers will be answered, since the disciples belong to the Father as well as the Son.

11. Note that Christ is again speaking as if His death had already occurred (17:4). **Keep** (Gr *tēreō*, keep watch over, guard, or preserve). Christ prays for the Father to stand guard over the disciples in the wicked world. **That they may be as one.** This does not mean that Christ wants all denominations to be as one; He is praying that the disciples would be united in their stand against the wickedness of the world.

12. Christ states that during His earthly ministry, He guarded the disciples. None of them perished (compromised with the wicked world). **The son of perdition.** The word **perdition** means the lost one. Note the synthesis of human responsibility and God's purpose. Judas was lost by his own volition, but his behavior was a fulfillment of divine prophecy (Ps 41:9).

13-14. Christ was about to leave the earth, and He was conscious of the void that He would leave with His disciples. He requests that His **joy** would fill them. It was the disciples' acceptance of Christ's **word** that caused the world to hate them.

15. Christ did not want the disciples taken out of the world because He would fulfill His purpose in their lives while they were in the world. He wanted them to be delivered from the evil one (Satan himself, Mt 6:13; I Pet 5:8).

16. The disciples did not belong to the world, they belonged to Christ (17:9-10).

17-18. Sanctify (Gr *hagiazō*, make holy, consecrate, dedicate, purify, set apart). This is the positive aspect of being delivered from the world. This process of becoming holy could only be accomplished through the Word of God. The disciples had been commissioned to go into the world.

19. I sanctify myself. Christ does not state that He is in the process of becoming holy; He is referring to His self-sacrifice and total commitment. It is His example that should stir His followers to that same type of surrender.

20. Beginning in this verse and continuing through the remainder of the prayer, Christ now prays for His entire church. The first part of the prayer was for the disciples; this part includes believers today. He prays for everyone who will **believe** on Him.

21. May be one (see 17:11).

22. The Father had manifested Himself through the Son, and now the Son manifests Himself through His followers. This is **glory.**

23. Made perfect. The idea here is that of completeness, not sinless perfection. The ultimate result of that unity will be that the world will see God's love revealed through the believers.

24. This is Christ's final request. He desires that all who believe on Him would see His **glory** (Rev 1:12-18).

25-26. Righteous Father. Because the Father is righteous, He will fulfill all that the Son has requested for His followers. To **declare** God's name is to declare God's love, for God is love.

In this prayer, Christ prays for Himself (vss. 1-5); for His disciples (vss. 6-19); and for His entire church (vss. 20-26).

IV. THE PASSION MINISTRY OF CHRIST. 18:1-21:25.

A. Christ and the Crucifixion. 18:1-19:42.

1. His arrest. 18:1-11.

18:1. After the prayer of chapter 17, Jesus takes His eleven disciples to a **garden** (Gethsemane). The **brook** mentioned refers to a stream that flows only during the winter season.

2-3. Ofttimes. Frequently Christ had taken His disciples to this place of seclusion. Judas came to the garden with a large crowd. **Band.** This (Gr *speira*) refers to a Roman cohort of six hundred soldiers. John, however, is using the term in its more general sense of "a detachment." Note the paradox: they came with **torches** to take the Light of the world, and they came with weapons to arrest the Prince of Peace.

4. Christ was completely aware of Judas' plan. **Went forth.** Probably Christ went from the garden to meet the crowd as they approached the gate. It was at this point that Judas kissed the Master (Mt 26:49).

5. Jesus of Nazareth. This was the name that appeared on the official arrest warrant issued by the Sanhedrin and the Roman government. **I am.** Again, Jesus states His deity (see 8:58).

6. The crowd was caught off guard by the unusual behavior of Christ. He calmly faced the crowd, identified Himself, and made no effort to escape.

7-8. Again He asked the crowd whom they sought. He requested that the disciples be left alone. In the moment of personal crisis, the Shepherd's concern was not for Himself, but for His sheep.

9. The Scripture mentioned deals with spiritual preservation rather than physical protection. Perhaps the disciples had already been arrested, and Christ knew that "it would have been too severe a test for their faith" (Hendriksen, p. 380).

10-11. Impulsive Peter proceeded to cut off a slave's ear with his **sword** (Gr *machaira*, denotes any long knife). Christ rebuked him by stating that He will drink of the **cup** which the **Father hath given me.** This **cup** refers to the suffering and agony of the cross.

2. His trials. 18:12-19:16.

12. The cohort and the temple guard take Jesus (arrest Him). They **bound** the One who had come to set them free (8:36).

13-14. They took Him to Annas. Although he was not at this time the High Priest, nevertheless Annas had a great influence over the Sanhedrin. Christ was taken there for a preliminary examination. Annas would then give his advice to Caiaphas. Caiaphas had already drawn a conclusion regarding Christ's destiny.

15-16. Another disciple. This probably refers to John. **Palace.** Here was the courtyard located in the center of the building. Peter could not enter the courtyard. John talked to the woman who controlled the entrance, and Peter was finally admitted.

17-18. John records only one of Peter's three denials. He was aware, however, that three were predicted by Christ (13:36-38). Here is a picture of a defeated man who had denied the Lord. He was warming himself by the fires of those who had arrested his Master.

19. The high priest. This refers to Annas (see 18:13). This was not a true trial since the Sanhedrin had not been assembled. The purpose of this inquisition was probably to gather evidence. Annas was interested in Christ's **disciples** and His **doctrine.** He was interested in the number of followers that Christ had gained.

20-21. Openly. Christ does not answer the question directly. He appeals to the fact that He taught His doctrine **openly. Why askest thou me?** Christ refused to be a witness for Himself. He asked Annas instead to produce witnesses who could testify about His teaching. Failure to produce reliable witnesses (those who **heard me)** would make the trial illegal.

22-24. One of the **officers** hit Christ in order to make Him answer the High Priest. Again Christ appealed to them to produce witnesses that could testify that He had done **evil.** If they could not, then the behavior of the officer and the arrest itself were wrong. Annas could not answer the Lord, and he sent Him to Caiaphas.

25-26. Prior to describing the trial before Caiaphas, John interjects Peter's last two denials of the Lord. The crowd around the fire asks Peter if he is one of Christ's disciples, and he denies it. Then one of the relatives of Malchus states that he saw Peter in the **garden.** Again, he denies the Lord. **Immediately the cock crew.** This refers to "the third of four watches into which the night was divided" *(Wycliff Bible Commentary, p. 363).*

28. The trial before Caiaphas is not mentioned in John's narrative (Mt 26:57-68). **Hall of judgment.** They took Him to the governor's place of residence. Note that the Jews did not enter their Gentile quarters. They were more interested in ceremonial purity than justice.

29-30. Pilate asks for the formal **accusation** that they were bringing **against** Christ. This was a logical question. The Jews had not prepared a formal indictment. They wanted Pilate to accept the fact that they would not bring a person to him if he were not a **malefactor** (evildoer).

31. Pilate, unaware that the Jews want to kill Christ, tells them to judge the case and pass sentence **according to your law.** The Jews could not legally execute anyone. They wanted Pilate to pass the death sentence on Christ.

32. The Jews used the method of stoning to execute criminals. If Pilate were to authorize death, it would mean crucifixion. This Roman method of execution had been predicted by Christ (Mt 20:17-19).

33. John does not describe all the details of the trial. It is assumed that the reader knows from the other gospels that a charge has been brought against Christ because He claimed to be the King of Israel. Pilate now questions Christ about this accusation. He may have asked this question with irony. It was ridiculous that this seemingly helpless prisoner would think Himself to be the King.

34-35. Christ desired to know whether Pilate was asking this question for the Jews or for himself. The Jews were looking for a political king and He was not at that moment their king. Pilate dismissed any prior conversation with the Jews. He simply wanted to know, **what hast thou done?**

36. Christ then explains the nature of His kingdom. He has no political motives in mind. His kingdom is a spiritual one which is not expanded or defended by military force.

37. Pilate wants to know if Christ is really a **king.** He was still confused about Christ's concept of a king and a kingdom. Pilate assumed Christ to be a political king. **To this end.** The pur-

pose for which Christ was born of royal inheritance (as King of Kings) was to bring **truth** to mankind. Those who are born again of that truth hear His **voice** (10:4).

38. Still confused about the spiritual purposes of Christ, Pilate asks the question, **What is truth?** The answer was standing before him (14:6). Satisfied that Christ is not a political threat to the Roman authorities, Pilate declares Christ to be innocent.

39-40. Pilate, although declaring the innocence of Christ, was fearful of the angry Jewish leaders. Since it was customary to release a prisoner at the Passover, Pilate attempted to place the responsibility of Christ's destiny in the hands of the Jews. It must be remembered, however, that each man is personally responsible for his relationship and actions to Christ. Pilate probably assumed that the majority would want Christ released since He was a popular person. Instead, the crowd asked for a **robber** (Mt 27:19-21).

19:1. Pilate orders Jesus to be **scourged,** hoping that the Jews would accept this rather than execution. The scourge was made of thongs to which were attached sharp pieces of metal and pieces of bone. The prisoners were beaten across the back, having the flesh and sometimes the organs torn. Many prisoners died from this cruel punishment.

2-3. The soldiers mock and torture Christ by their actions. They force a **crown of thorns** on His head, causing blood to flow down His face. They hit Him and dress Him like a king.

4-5. Pilate presents Christ dressed in a purple robe, with a crown and a reed. The robe is drenched with blood from the gaping wounds received from the scourging. **Behold the man.** Pilate clearly states that Christ is no king. He is simply a **man.** It is interesting to note that Pilate declares Christ innocent, yet subjects Him to a terrible beating.

6. Rather than being appeased, the

angry multitude chants, **Crucify, . . . Crucify . . .** Frustrated, Pilate tells them that if Christ is to be crucified, they will have to do it. **No fault.** This is the third time that Pilate declares the innocence of Christ.

7. According to Roman law, Christ was innocent. The Jews now appeal to their **law.** Christ had claimed to be God, and by Jewish law, He should die (Lev 24:16).

8-9. When Pilate hears that Christ claimed to be the Son of God, he is **more afraid.** Superstitious Pilate had already been warned by his wife about Christ (Mt 27:19) and now he realizes that he may be dealing with the Son of God. Pilate immediately attempts to discover the origin of this person standing before him. An answer would be useless, since Pilate was spiritually blind.

10-11. Fearful and confused, Pilate attempts to hide his weaknesses by the statement, **I have power.** Christ reminds him that the only authority he has is that which has been given to him by a higher source. **Greater sin.** Although Pilate was responsible for his actions to Christ, Caiaphas, who had planned the entire plot to kill Christ, had committed a greater sin and would be more accountable to God.

12. Fearful of Christ, and knowing that He was innocent, Pilate again attempted to release Him. The Jews made their final argument, **thou art not Caesar's friend.** If the Jews contacted Caesar, and explained that Pilate released a king who threatened Roman authority, Pilate would be guilty of treason against Rome.

13-14. Pilate was ready to make his decision. For a discussion of the chronology of the events of the crucifixion see notes on Matthew 26. **Behold your king.** It was apparent that Pilate hated the Jews and in scorn he gives them their king, poor, miserable, and beaten.

15-16. Driven by the crowd and not his conscience, Pilate succumbs to the wishes of the Jews.

3. His crucifixion. 19:17-37.

17. Christ was already weakened by the treatment of the soldiers, and now they make Him carry His cross. **Golgotha.** Called a **place of a skull** probably because its physical appearance resembles a skull, this place was also called Calvary (Lk 23:33).

18. They crucify Him between two criminals.

19-20. Since Christ had not been found guilty of a crime, Pilate placed a title above the cross. It was written in Aramaic, the language of the Jews; Greek, the language of culture; and Latin, the official language of Rome.

21-22. The **chief priest** was furious, and demanded that the title be changed from a statement to a claim. Pilate, vacillating in his character, now refused to change under pressure.

23-34. Four soldiers normally carried out the crucifixion sentence. Each soldier took one garment, and because of the value of the seamless inner coat, they **cast lots for it.** Unknowingly, the soldiers were actually fulfilling Old Testament Scripture (Ps 22:18). **These things therefore the soldiers did.** Bruised, beaten, mocked, tortured, compelled to carry His cross, Christ is now left hanging naked before the angry mob.

25. Contrasted to the soldiers and the crowd, John mentions three women who loved the Lord: Mary, His mother; Mary, **the wife of Cleophas;** and Mary Magdalene.

26-27. Woman. Although Mary was His earthly mother, Christ as her Redeemer and Saviour refers to her in that redemptive relationship. Here is love again. Christ tells John to take care of His mother. This teaches that everyone has a responsibility to provide for and take care of his parents.

28. The life and death of Christ was a constant fulfillment of prophecy (Ps

22:15). This statement was another evidence of His physical suffering.

29. Vinegar (Gr *unuo*). This was a very strong wine.

30. It is finished. (The Greek perfect tense denotes the certainty of the fact). **Gave up the ghost.** He died and gave His Spirit to God.

31. To permit a body to remain on the cross until the next day was a violation of Jewish law (Deut 21:22-23). **Legs might be broken.** Since the victim would press on his legs to lift his chest enough to breathe, if the legs were broken, this would hasten death. The victim would not be able to breathe.

32-33. When they came to Christ, they did not break his legs.

34. One of the soldiers took a **spear** and **pierced his side.**

35. John adds that he personally witnessed the events he has just described.

36-37. The importance of the piercing, and the fact that they did not break Jesus' legs, is given in that it was fulfilled prophecy (Ps 34:20; Zech 12:10). Even these wicked soldiers in their duties were completing the plan of God.

4. His burial. 19:38-42.

38-40. Joseph and Nicodemus, who were secret disciples, now came into the open, and prepared the body of Christ for burial. Both men were wealthy, and they were members of the Sanhedrin (Lk 23:51; Jn 3:1).

41-42. They quickly prepared the body for burial, and put it in a **new sepulchre** near the place of the crucifixion. They intended to finish their preparations after the Sabbath (Lk 24:1).

B. Christ and the Resurrection. 20:1-31.

1. Christ revealed to Mary. 20:1-18.

20:1. On Sunday, **Mary Magdalene** came to the tomb with spices to anoint the body of Christ (Mk 16:1; Lk 24:1).

Seeth the stone taken away. Mary would have had trouble removing the stone; now her problem is worse. The body is missing.

2. Mary runs to tell startling news to Peter and John (**the other disciple, whom Jesus loved**). These two were considered to be the leading disciples and were a part of Christ's inner circle (Lk 9:27-29).

3-4. Peter and John immediately made their way to the tomb, first walking together, and then running together. Perhaps John was younger than Peter, since he arrived there first.

5. John, **stooping down,** looks in, and observes the **linen clothes** lying there. However, the resurrection does not explain this phenomenon in the disciple's mind (20:9).

6-7. Impulsive Peter does not stop outside the tomb, but goes inside. What Peter saw was strange. Everything was neat and orderly in the tomb, except that the body of the Lord was no longer there. The headband was folded and lying in a separate place from the rest of the grave clothes. It was now obvious that the body had not been stolen.

8-9. John entered the tomb, and **saw** and **believed.** The teaching of Christ's resurrection now began to dawn on them, and their sight now turned to faith as they realized that Christ had risen **again from the dead.**

10. Overwhelmed with their observations and the faith it produced, they returned home.

11. It is logical to assume that Mary returned to the tomb after Peter and John have returned home. She has no knowledge of the Lord's resurrection. She too stoops down and looks into the tomb.

12. Two angels. No explanation is given for the appearance of the angels to Mary and not to the two disciples. It is interesting to note that heaven is interested in the resurrection.

13-15. Why weepest thou? This is a time of joy and triumph; therefore, the angels want to know why Mary is weeping. Mary wants to know where the Lord's body is lying so that she can complete the embalming process. Mary is so overcome with sorrow and grief that she does not even recognize Jesus. He asks the same question that the angels asked, and He receives the same answer.

16. Mary. She now recognizes the person to whom she is speaking and calls him, **Rabboni (Master).**

17. Touch me not (Gr *haptomai*, to cling to or to take hold of). Christ told Mary to stop (Greek prohibition with present tense) clinging to Him because, by doing so, she could not keep the Lord there with her. His destination was to go **to the Father.** Note the warm and close terminology used: **my brethren, your Father, your God.** This is the new relationship between the disciples, the Son, and the Father.

18. The command given to Mary is the command given to all Christians: go and tell that Jesus is risen.

2. Christ revealed to the ten. 20:19-23.

19. First day of the week. The Sabbath commemorates the creation of the world, but Sunday, the first day of the week, commemorates the redemption of the world. Fearful and confused, the disciples meet in secret. Christ appears to them apparently by coming through the wall. **Peace.** To the troubled disciples, Christ brings a message of peace.

20. Several important concepts emerge from this action: Jesus had a real body; His body had been resurrected (not just His spirit), and the nail prints proved that He was Jesus and not someone else.

21. The resurrection had certain implications for the disciples. It gave them **Peace,** and it implied a commission: **So send I you.**

22-23. He breathed. This gift of the Holy Spirit is connected with the action of forgiving or retaining sins. It was not the work of the disciples to forgive sins, but the work of the Holy Spirit through the disciples as they fulfilled the great commission (Mt 28:18-20). Christ gave the disciples authority to state that forgiveness of sins was possible.

3. Christ revealed to Thomas. 20:24-31.

24-25. No explanation is given for Thomas' not being with the other disciples. Perhaps he was alone mourning the death of his Master. When the other disciples tried to comfort him with the news of the resurrection, he refused to accept it until he had actually touched the hands, feet, and side of the Saviour.

26. One week later, Christ appears again to the disciples (including Thomas), and gives the same message of **Peace.**

27. Compare this verse with verse 25. Christ answers all of Thomas' requests. Christ commands him to do what he said was necessary for him to believe.

28-29. My Lord and my God. Thomas now recognizes both the resurrection and the deity of Christ. Thomas based his faith on sight. Christ promises a blessing for those who believe upon hearing instead of upon seeing.

30. Many other signs. The greatest sign found in the writings of John is the sign of the resurrection. (For a detailed description of the importance of this event see Josh McDowell's *Evidence that Demands a Verdict.*)

31. A detailed analysis of this verse is given in the introduction to the commentary.

C. Christ and the Commission. 21:1-25.

1. Miracle of the fish. 21:1-14.

21:1. Showed he himself. (Gr *phaneroō*, to reveal or make known; show or manifest). Jesus now reveals His glory to the disciples at the **sea of Tiberias** (Galilee).

2. Peter, Nathanael, James, John, and two other unnamed disciples were together.

3-4. Again Peter is the man of action. **I go a fishing.** Although the Greek present tense (I am going to fish) is used here and normally denotes continual action, this does not necessarily mean that Peter intended to return permanently to his former occupation. As they arrive at the shore after a frustrating night, they see Jesus, but for some providential reason, they do not recognize Him.

5-6. Children (literally, lads). This question and negative answer was a blow to these fishermen's egos. Fishermen would not usually respond immediately to this unusual request by a stranger on the shore. However, there was something compelling about this stranger that caused them to obey without an objection.

7-8. It is the Lord. John finally recognizes that this stranger is the Lord. Peter again is the first in action; he puts on his coat, for he **was naked** (literally, "stripped" of his overcoat). Peter's enthusiasm to be with the Lord would indicate that he was not fishing in disobedience to the Lord's command. The rest of the disciples now join the Lord and Peter.

9-11. Christ had already prepared a meal when they arrived. It consisted of **fish** and **bread. Bring of the fish.** They count the number of fish and discover that although there were one hundred fifty-three fish, **yet was not the net broken.**

12-13. Come and dine. Christ invites them to breakfast. The disciples are speechless in the presence of their risen Lord.

14. Shewed himself (see 21:1).

2. Message to Peter. 21:15-17.

15. After breakfast, the attention of the Lord is upon Peter. Peter had denied his Lord three times, and now the Lord asks Peter three times, **Lovest thou me?** Two Greek words for "love"

are played against each other in the original: *Agapaō*, when used in distinction from the other, connotes love as an emotion of deep appreciation based upon careful consideration. It means to recognize the worth of someone and esteem him highly. The synonym *phileō*, when used in distinction as here, connotes "love" as a pure, intense "feeling of love." It is a personal, warm, intimate relationship like that between family members. It is a love that is more spontaneous than philosophical. Jesus asks Peter, **lovest thou me more than these?** This refers to the other disciples. Peter had boasted of his loyalty, and yet had denied his Lord. The other disciples had not denied the Lord. Consequently, the Lord is really probing the sincerity of Peter's love. Peter answers, using a different word (Gr *phileō*). "I have a deep affection for You." **Feed** (Gr *boskō*, feed, graze, or tend to) **my lambs.** Christ is commissioning Peter to a pastoral office of caring for His sheep.

16. Jesus asks, **lovest thou me** (Gr *agapaō*)? Peter responds, **I love thee** (Gr *phileō*). **Feed** (Gr *poimainō*, shepherd) **my sheep.**

17. Jesus asks a third time, and the third question is the most convicting. The first two times, Jesus was asking Peter if he loved Him (using *agapaō*). Now the third time Jesus changes the verb to *phileō*. Peter is **grieved,** and he appeals to the omniscience of his Master. **Thou knowest all things; thou knowest that I love thee** (Gr *phileō*). It is interesting to note that in Christ's commissioning Peter to tend to the sheep, the first time He tells Peter to feed His lambs, the second and third times to feed His sheep (using two different Greek words).

3. Conclusion. 21:18-25.

18-19. Christ now prophesies that one day Peter's freedom would cease. **Old.** This indicates that Peter will have a long, useful life of service. **Thou**

shalt stretch forth thy hands. This language could refer to crucifixion, and church tradition concurs that this is how Peter died. **Glorify God.** What confidence the Lord gives to the one who had denied Him. Peter would be faithful to the end, and would bring glory to God through his death. **Follow me.** The Lord calls Peter to a life of total commitment to Him.

20-22. Jesus begins to leave, and as Peter follows Him, he turns around and sees John following. Having been told about his future, Peter wants to know about John's future. The emphasis of Christ's rebuke is that Peter should not be concerned about John, but about the job which he must do. The disciples misunderstand the rebuke. They had forgotten the **if.** The future of John was not their business.

24. The disciple. This refers to John. **Testifieth.** The entire book of John is a testimony to the deity of Jesus Christ. **We know.** The **we** probably refers to the elders in the church of Ephesus. They are not identified by name.

25. John concludes by reminding his readers that he has described only a small portion of all that **Jesus did.**

BIBLIOGRAPHY

Barclay, William. The Gospel of John. In *The Daily Study Bible.* 2 Vols. 2nd ed. Philadelphia: Westminster, 1956.

Barrett, C. K. *The Gospel According to St. John.* London: S.P.C.K., 1962.

Gaebelein, A. C. *The Gospel of John.* Wheaton: Van Kampen Press, 1936.

Godet, Frederic. *Commentary on the Gospel of John,* trans. Timothy Dwight. 2 Vols. Grand Rapids: Zondervan, reprint.

*Hendriksen, William. *A Commentary on the Gospel of John.* Grand Rapids: Baker, 1953.

Ironside, Harry. *Addresses on the Gospel of John.* New York: Loizeaux Brothers, 1942.

Kelly, William. *An Exposition of the Gospel of John.* Denver: Wilson Foundation, reprint, 1966.

*Kent, Homer A., Jr. *Light in the Darkness: Studies in the Gospel of John.* Grand Rapids: Baker, 1974.

Lange, John P. The Gospel According to John. In *Lange's Commentary on the Holy Scriptures,* trans. and ed. Philip Schaff. Grand Rapids: Zondervan, reprint, n.d.

Lenski, R. C. H. *The Interpretation of St. John's Gospel.* Columbus: Lutheran Book Concern, 1942.

Lightfoot, R. H. *St. John's Gospel: A Commentary,* ed. C. F. Evans. Oxford: Clarendon, 1956.

Luthardt, Christoph Ernst. *St. John's Gospel, Described and Explained According to Its Peculiar Character,* trans. C. R. Gregory. 3 Vols. Edinburgh: T. and T. Clark, 1876-78.

Morgan, G. Campbell. *The Gospel According to John.* Westwood, N. J.: Revell, 1933.

*Morris, Leon. The Gospel According to John. In the *The International Commentary on the New Testament*. Grand Rapids: Eerdmans, 1971.

*Pink, Arthur W. *Exposition of the Gospel of John*. 3 Vols. Grand Rapids: Zondervan, 1945.

Plummer, Alfred. The Gospel According to St. John. In *Cambridge Greek Testament for Schools and Colleges*. Cambridge: Cambridge University, 1905.

Scroggie, W. Graham. St. John, Introduction and Notes. In *Study Hours Series*. New York: Harper and Brothers, 1931.

*Tasker, R. V. G. The Gospel According to St. John. In *The Tyndale New Testament Commentaries*. Grand Rapids: Eerdmans, 1960.

*Tenney, Merrill C. *John: The Gospel of Belief*. Grand Rapids: Eerdmans, 1960.

Vine, W. E. *John: His Record of Christ*. Grand Rapids: Zondervan, 1957.

Westcott, B. F. *The Gospel According to St. John: The Authorized Version with Introduction and Notes*. Grand Rapids: Eerdmans, 1950.

THE ACTS

of the Apostles

INTRODUCTION

The Acts of the Apostles is unique among the books of the New Testament. One of the most influential books of all time, it forms the essential link between the Gospel accounts of Jesus and the only account of the beginning of His church. The book of Acts is our chief source of information about the first century. As Matthew, Mark, Luke, and John record the gospel as evidenced in the life of Jesus Christ, Acts records the gospel as evidenced in the lives of those who followed Him. Luke writes his first letter (the Gospel according to Luke) to tell what Christ did while on earth through His physical body (see Lk 1:1-4). His second letter (the Acts) was written to tell what Christ was doing while in heaven through His spiritual body, the church.

The story in Acts moves rapidly from one episode to another. It records the birth and the growing pains of the fledgling church. It reveals the vitality of the first century faith. It maps out the master plan for world evangelization. The first half of the book essentially records the ministry of Peter; the second half the ministry of Paul. Subthemes in the lives of Stephen, Philip, and others are also revealed. But essentially the book of Acts records the working of the Holy Spirit in the lives of the New Testament church.

Authorship. Although the book of Acts is anonymous, and not even its title indicates authorship, yet a nearly universal tradition ascribes this writing to Paul's physician-friend, Luke. In the prologue to both Luke and Acts the author refers to himself by the first person pronoun. Theophilus, the recip-

ient of both writings (Lk 1:4; Acts 1:1), obviously knew the identity of the author.

1. External evidence. The uniform tradition of the early church ascribes this work to Luke. The oldest extant list of New Testament writings, known as the Muratorian Fragment, which dates from the later half of the second century A.D., lists both the third Gospel and the Acts of the Apostles as the work of Luke. The so-called antimarcionite prologue to Luke (ca. A.D. 150-180), in discussing the third Gospel comments, "and afterwards this same Luke wrote the Acts of the Apostles." In his *Against Heresies* A.D. 185), Ireneaus takes for granted that Luke is the author of Acts. Clement of Alexandria (ca. A.D. 155-215) quotes from the Acts in *Stromata* and says, "As Luke in the Acts of the Apostles relates that Paul said, 'Men of Athens, I preceive that in all things ye are too supersticious.'" In his work *On Fasting,* Tertullian (ca. A.D. 150-220) frequently quotes from or alludes to Acts naming Luke as the author. And Eusebius, in his *Ecclesiastical History,* published in A.D. 324, explicitly mentions Luke as the author of two books, the Gospel and the Acts. Origen (ca. A.D. 185-254) and others add their voices to the testimony of scholars that spans a hundred years attesting that Luke is the author of the Acts of the Apostles.

2. Internal evidence. Likewise, there is an overwhelming abundance of internal evidence to the authorship of Acts by Luke. First, an analysis of the style and language of both the third Gospel and the Acts of the Apostles makes it clear that whoever wrote the

217

first also wrote the second. If Lucan authorship can be proved for the Gospel which bears his name, it can also be proved for the Acts. Secondly, the medical terminology which is characteristic of the vocabulary of the Acts necessitates that the author either be a physician or one well versed in that discipline. Since the traditional author is known to have been a physician (Col 4:14), it seems conclusive that Luke authored the Acts. Thirdly, there is a great deal of archaeological and epigraphal evidence which points to the fact that the author of Acts was well familiar with the first century world. As an educated man, Luke would have been well traveled and would have personally known the Mediterranean world of the first century. Finally, a reading of the book makes it clear that the writer was a companion of Paul in many of the adventures recorded in Acts. In the so-called "we" passages the author describes the situation in the first person (16:10-17; 20:5-15; 21:1-18; 27:1-28:16). A survey of Paul's close associates produces only one individual who could have authored the passages which record these experiences. Timothy was in the presence of those awaiting Paul's arrival at Troas. Neither Titus nor Silas was with Paul on the journey to Rome or in Rome. The only close associate who fits the facts is Luke.

Date and place of writing. There is strong evidence to date the Acts of the Apostles in the first century. The style and vocabulary of the writer is certainly that of this era. He has a command of facts that is best explained by his being an eyewitness to them. The tone of the writing seems to rule out the possibility that it was written after the organized attack on the church by the Roman emperor Domitian (A.D. 81-96).

Apparently Acts could not have been written beyond the turn of the second century, for there are possible references to the text of Acts in the *Epistle of Barnabas* (ca. A.D. 100) and in Justin

Martyr (ca. A.D. 150). Likewise, the earliest possible date for the completion of Acts is two years after Paul's arrival in Rome as a prisoner (Acts 28:30-31). Thus the book must have been composed sometime between A.D. 61-62 and approximately A.D. 95.

Although most conservative scholars place the date of writing between A.D. 62 and A.D. 68, a very good case can be made for the early 60's. First, there is an apparent excitement in the record of the "we passages" which most likely existed shortly after the events occurred. Secondly, the lack of any discussion of the fall of Jerusalem in A.D. 70 would seem to preclude a date of writing beyond that date. Thirdly, the abrupt ending of Acts is best explained by a drawing to a close of Paul's two-year imprisonment in Rome. Luke had to finish his writing in order to once again sail with Paul.

Although arguments can be advanced for other early dates, there seem to be no facts prohibiting a date of A.D. 62-63 for the writing of Acts. Even though the place of writing is not mentioned by name, it is reasonable to assume that if the A.D. 62-63 date is correct, then the place of writing is Rome. As attending physician to the Apostle, Luke would certainly have had time to write the historical account of Acts during that two-year house arrest of Paul at Rome.

Purpose. Although the book of Acts does not contain any indication of the author's purpose, it nevertheless cannot be divorced from the Gospel of Luke. Since these two works are an integral whole, with coherent purpose running throughout, it is safe to assume that the purpose stated clearly in the initial verses of Luke is still the purpose for the writing of the Acts. In the words of the author himself: "Forasmuch as many have taken in hand to set forth in order a declaration of those things which are most surely believed among us, Even as they delivered them unto us, which from the beginning were eyewitnesses, and ministers of the word; It seemed good to me also, having had perfect understanding of all things from the very first, to write unto thee in order, most excellent Theophilus, That thou mightest know the certainty of those things, wherein thou hast been instructed" (Lk 1:1-4)."

Since the church was growing so rapidly in the Roman world, those who joined its ranks needed an authoritative account of its birth and early history. Thus Luke sets himself to the task of giving a coherent account of the life of Jesus Christ as it was lived through those closest to Him. Thus the birth and development of the church, the preaching of Peter, and the missionary activity of Paul, became the motifs of the most accurate history of the first century, i.e. the Acts of the Apostles (see the discussion of Sir William Ramsey, *St. Paul the Traveller and the Roman Citizen,* p. 7 ff.).

OUTLINE

COMMENTARY

I. THE BIRTH OF THE CHURCH AT JERUSALEM. 1:1-3:26.

A. From Resurrection to Ascension. 1:1-14.

1:1-2. The former treatise have I made, oh Theophilus. The relationship between Luke and Acts has already been discussed. It is obvious that the gospel of Luke is the former treatise mentioned here. There is no reason to suppose that Theophilus was not a real person although some would translate literally as "dear to God." In that event, Luke would be addressing those Christian readers in general. However the title of respect, "most excellent" as found in Luke 1:3, makes it most improbable that the author is addressing a company of individuals. Whether Theophilus is a Jew or Greek cannot be absolutely determined. The absence of the honorific title here in Acts 1:1 may not mean a loss of affection but rather a deepening friendship between Luke and Theophilus.

3. Many infallible proofs. The resurrection ministry of the Lord was accompanied by unmistakable signs. Over a period of forty days between His passion and ascension Jesus appeared at frequent intervals to His apostles. No one could seriously doubt that He was alive. The adjective "infallible" (Gr *tekmērion*) is employed in the AV in order to extract the complete meaning. So infallible were the "proofs" of Christ's resurrection that

the author does not feel it necessary to list them for his first century readers.

4. Wait for the promise of the Father. Much ink has been used attempting to explain these five words, **the promise of the Father.** Various passages of Scripture make it clear that the promise of the Father (Joel 2:28; Acts 2:16) and also the promise of the Son (Jn 14:16, 26; 15:26; 16:7) were references to the arrival of the Holy Spirit of God.

6-7. Lord, wilt thou this time restore again the kingdom of Israel? Even after the resurrection ministry of our Lord, the disciples were yet confused about His true purpose in coming to live among them. Jesus did not answer the apostles' question concerning the precise time when God would restore the kingdom of Israel, but He did promise them something far more important in those seconds prior to the ascension.

8. But ye shall receive power, after that the Holy Ghost is come upon you. The power to which He referred was not political, but spiritual. When the Holy Ghost came upon the disciples they would be clothed with heavenly power. As Jesus had been anointed at His baptism with the Holy Spirit and and power, so now His disciples will share in that anointing. The Holy Ghost will come upon them in power. **Ye shall be witnesses unto me.** Jesus came to bear witness of the Father and His love for mankind. The apostles would bear witness of Jesus' death and resurrection, proving God's love for mankind. The references to **Jerusalem, Judea,** and **Samaria,** and **the uttermost part of the earth,** give the widening circles of the witness to God's love. Actually this verse provides a table of contents and divine outline for the entire book of Acts: (1) witnessing in Jerusalem (chs. 1-7); (2) witnessing in Judaea and Samaria (chs. 8-12); and (3) witnessing unto the uttermost part of the earth (chs. 13-28).

9-11. Having commissioned His disciples, the Lord was now prepared to disappear from their sight and make no further resurrection appearances. As the cloud received Him out of their sight, the Lord was once again restored to the glory which He had with the Father before the world began (Jn 17:4-5). As those gathered looked steadfastly toward heaven, two men in white appeared, whom Luke obviously intends his readers to understand as angelic messengers (cf. Mt 28:3; Jn 20:12). They gave to the followers of the Lord Jesus the tremendous promise, **this same Jesus . . . shall so come in like manner.** Not another and in a different way, but this same Jesus in the same way would descend for believers as they had seen Him ascend from them. Between ascension and His return for them, however, would be an interval of time in which the Holy Spirit would empower His church to carry on the ministry of worldwide evangelization.

12-14. To the disciples their duty was clear. They were to return to Jerusalem and wait there for the empowerment of the Spirit of God. Thus they came to the upper room where the Eleven **continued with one accord in prayer and supplication.**

B. Twelfth Apostle Chosen. 1:15-26.

15-17. Peter stood up in the midst of the disciples. It is clear that the Apostle Peter has now become the undisputed leader of the apostolic band. The bumbling, denying Peter has now become the rock and is the principal preacher of Christianity following the ascension of the Lord. Peter clearly understands that the defection of Judas and his subsequent replacement are both fulfillments of Old Testament prophecies. The Lord also applied Psalm 41:9 to the defection of Judas (Jn 13:18). Peter here adduces further "testimonies" from the Psalter indicating that they must continue following the plan of God, as they understand it to be.

18-20. Now this man purchased a field . . . insomuch as that field is called in their proper tongue, Aceldama, that is to say, The field of blood. "The account of Judas' faith (vss. 18-20) is not inconsistent with that set forth by Matthew (27:3-10). The field was probably bought by the legally-minded priests in Judas' name. Amid the crazed inconsistencies of despair he may have laid claim to it in consequence, and in bitter irony made it the scene of suicide. The two accounts preserve different but equally true details from the rest of the shocking story, and the field won its sombre name on more than one count" (E. M. Blaikock, *The Acts of Apostles,* p. 53).

Further evidence confirming the prophetic character of Judas' death is given by Luke in Peter's quote from the Psalms. The former, from Psalm 69:25 is a prayer that the final resting place of the foes of the psalmist will be a place of desolation. The latter, from Psalm 109:8 is a prayer to the enemy of the psalmist that a possible replacement will be found for the psalmist.

21-23. The essential criteria for the replacement for the apostolic band was twofold: this person must have been with the Lord from His baptism by John unto His ascension; and, more importantly, he must have been a witness of the resurrection, as the others were. **Joseph called Barsabas . . . and Matthias.** Of either man we know nothing. We even hear no more of

Matthias in the New Testament, although a legend of Ethiopian martyrdom is known.

24-26. A momentous dicision was about to be made. Immediately the disciples set themselves to praying, seeking the will of the Lord. Specifically, they asked that the Father would make known unto them which of the two candidates had already been chosen by God. **And they gave forth their lots.** The disciples did not now engage in a bit of gambling. We must remember that before lots were cast they selected two men whom they judged most worthy to fill Judas' vacancy. Having passed that difficult screening test, they were now prepared to receive the will of God. Casting lots to discern God's will was a very respectable Hebrew custom. The disciples believed in God's providence and perhaps even remembered, "The lot is cast into the lap; but the whole disposing thereof is of the Lord" (Prov 16:33). Divine will is now known; the lot fell to Matthias, and he was numbered with the eleven apostles.

C. Pentecost. 2:1-13.

Pentecost was the third great Israelite feast mentioned in Leviticus 23. It was a harvest festival fifty days after the Passover week. This particular Pentecost, however, was to have greater significance than those which had preceded it. Old Testament Pentecost occurred fifty days after Israel left Egypt and the Passover lamb was slain. New Testament Pentecost occurred fifty days after Christ rose from the dead, the Lord being our Passover Lamb. Old Testament Pentecost celebrated the birth of the nation Israel (Ex 19:5). New Testament Pentecost celebrated the birth of the church (2:41-47). Old Testament Pentecost witnessed the slaying of some three thousand souls (Ex 32:28). New Testament Pentecost witnessed the saving of some three thousand souls (2:41). The former pointed typologically to the latter.

2:1-3. They were all with one accord in one place. The words translated "with one accord" (Gr *homothymadon*), meaning likemindedness, occurs twelve times in the New Testament, eleven of which are found in the book of Acts. This shows the unity of purpose among these early disciples.

The coming of the Holy Spirit of God with power was accompanied by two manifestations. The first was the sound of a **rushing mighty wind,** and the second was **cloven tongues like as of fire.** The wind is symbolic of the Spirit of God. In Ezekiel 37, Ezekiel prophesies that the wind would blow upon the dead bones in the valley of his vision. He was actually prophesying the coming of the Spirit of God upon Israel. Here that same wind is used to symbolize the Spirit's presence. In addition to the audible wind, an appeal was made to their eyes as the cloven tongues of fire appeared. Again, Matthew and Luke both report that John the Baptist foretold of One who would baptize "with the Holy Ghost, and with fire" (Mt 3:11; Lk 3:16). Together the fire and wind make a graphic picture of the coming of the Spirit of God.

4. And they were all filled with the Holy Ghost, and began to speak with other tongues. Although glossolalia is not always a proof of the presence of the Spirit of God, for many pagans practiced speaking in other tongues, nevertheless here, as the Spirit gave them utterance, these men at Pentecost were given an unnatural ability to speak in tongues that were not their own. The word translated tongue (Gr *dialektos*) can mean language as well as dialect. The various languages being spoken corresponded to the nationalities of those present (cf. 2:8).

5-11. And there were dwelling at Jerusalem, devout men, out of every nation under heaven. From farflung lands and many languages, Jews had come from the diaspora to celebrate the Feast of Weeks in Jerusalem. This was because only at the Jerusalem

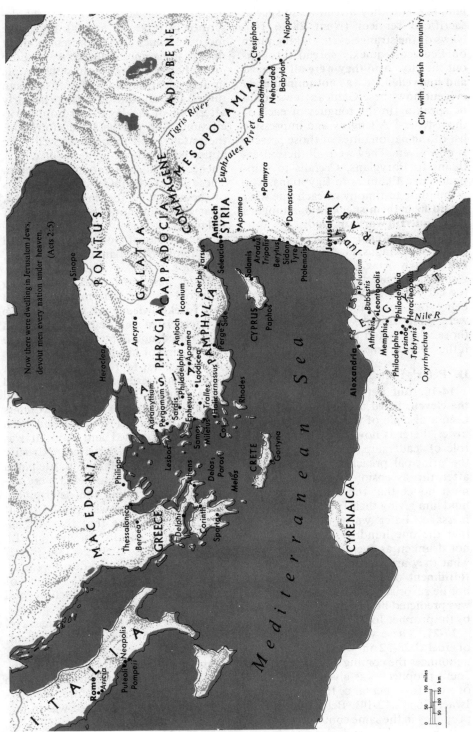

Now there were dwelling in Jerusalem Jews, devout men from every nation under heaven. (Acts 2:5)

• City with Jewish community

The Jewish Diaspora in the Time of Jesus

temple could they attend these special sacrificial services (Num 28:26 ff.). News of the strange events taking place on Pentecost quickly spread throughout the city. **And they were all amazed and marvelled.** It was not immediately evident how these Galilean Jews could be speaking in the tongues of each of the listeners. A lengthy and impressive list of the nationalities of those present is now given. They were all there: Parthians to Phrygians; Cretans to Cappadocians; Elamites to Egyptians. The astounding testimony of each one was, **we do hear them speak in our tongues the wonderful works of God.**

12-13. Although all were amazed, **others mocking said, These men are full of new wine.** The new wine (Gr *gleukos*) is "sweet wine." Pentecost is too early for new vintage wine, August being the next vintage. So different were these disciples at Pentecost that those who looked on mocked them as if they were drunk.

D. Peter's Preaching. 2:14-3:26.

14-16. But Peter, standing up with the eleven, lifted up his voice. Having been a disciple of the Lord, and a follower, Peter is now ready to assume a role of leadership. Even though he is the principal preacher of Christianity after the ascension, nevertheless, we must notice that the Eleven stand behind him giving their full support to his message. Peter warns the onlookers that the one hundred and twenty are not drunken as everyone thought, but what they are viewing is in actuality a fulfillment of prophecy. They should not be surprised at what they see for it was predicted hundreds of years before by the prophet Joel.

17-21. These verses are a quotation of Joel 2:28-32 in which the prophet announces the coming day of the Lord. Joel's prophecy was given in the midst of a call for repentance from the nation Israel (Joel 2:12-14). Peter quotes that prophecy in the same context.

"The wonders and signs to be re-vealed in the world of nature, as described in verses 19 and 20, may have more relevance in the present context than is sometimes realized: it was little more than seven weeks since the people in Jerusalem had indeed seen the sun turned into darkness, during the early afternoon of the day of our Lord's crucifixion. And on the same afternoon, the paschal full moon may well have appeared blood-red in the sky in consequence of that preternatural gloom. These were to be understood as tokens of the advent of the day of the Lord, 'that great and notable day,' a day of judgment, to be sure, but more immediately the day of God's salvation to all who invoked His name" (F. F. Bruce, *The Book of Acts*, p. 69).

22-24. Jesus of Nazareth . . . being delivered by the determinate counsel and foreknowledge of God, ye have . . . crucified and slain: Whom God hath raised up. Peter now gets to the main theme of his message. In the ears of his hearers, he rehearses the death, burial, and resurrection of the Lord Jesus Christ. One who accomplished mighty works and signs and wonders through the power of God had been taken and crucified and slain. It was the howling mob that cried, "Crucify Him!" However, all who participated in putting the Lord to death were unconsciously fulfilling the determinant council and foreknowledge of God. It was God's purpose that the Messiah should suffer death for us (cf. Lk 24:25, 46; Acts 17:3; 26:23). But if Messiah's suffering and death were ordained by the determinate council of God, so was His resurrection and glory.

25-28. As support for his message, Peter appeals to the Old Testament. His quote comes from Psalm 16:8-11. These prophetic words, so Peter argues, were fulfilled in Jesus of Nazareth and in no one else. Therefore, the Messiah which David promised was in fact Jesus of Nazareth.

29-32. Men and brethren, let me

freely speak unto you of the patriarch **David.** Peter now clarifies the prophecy which he has just quoted. It is evident that prophecy did not literally find its fulfillment in David, for the patriarch died and is buried and is in a sepulchre that very day. But Jesus Christ's triumph over death in the resurrection confirms the veracity of this Old Testament prophecy. Therefore the prophecy was not made of David himself, but of his descendant, Jesus of Nazareth. They are all witnesses of the resurrected Lord and could attest to the veracity of the prophecy.

33-36. Peter continues to illustrate that the patriarch David is not the Messiah, **For David is not ascended into the heavens.** The exaltation of Christ allows Him to sit at the right hand of the Father and thus send the Holy Spirit of God on His believers. This David could not do, for he had not ascended into the heavens. In proof of this, Peter appealed to Psalms 110:1 which he quotes as evidence that David addressed the Lord Jesus as One on high. Peter's conclusion: **that God hath made that same Jesus, whom ye have crucified, both Lord and Christ.**

37-40. Peter's preaching was tremendously effective, for those who heard **were pricked in their heart.** Those listening asked, **what shall we do?** Peter's answer to them, **Repent, and be baptized every one of you in the name of Jesus Christ.** This is one of the most controversial verses in the New Testament. In understanding it we must remember that it was originally stated as a message to Israel concerning their national crime of murdering their Messiah. It is unwise to link baptism with the remission of sins for nowhere do the Scriptures teach that salvation is dependent on baptism (see I Cor 1:17; cf. I Cor 15:1-4. Here Paul clearly states what the gospel is and baptism is not included). Those who insist upon baptismal regeneration literally "rob Paul to pay Peter" (see II Pet 3:15-16).

41-47. And they continued steadfastly in the apostles' doctrine and fellowship, and in breaking of bread, and in prayers. By the Holy Spirit of God, so effective was Peter's first sermon that three thousand souls were added unto the church that day. Not only is evangelism evident here but growth in the church is evident as well. Each one saved was then nurtured in the faith as he continued to learn the doctrine of the apostles, to fellowship with the believers, to sit in equality at the Lord's table, to pray and share his burdens with others of like precious faith.

And not only that, **all that believed were together, and had all things common.** The enjoying of all things in common among those of the early church should not be interpreted as communism. This was an early system of mutual ownership (2:45) which is distinct from communism. Communism says, "what is yours, is mine." "Common-ism" says, "what is mine is yours also." At the birth of the church, this system was absolutely necessary for many who came to know the Lord were repudiated by society and disinherited by family. This system was temporary, and had its problems (cf. Acts 5:1; 6:1). It is a system which gave rise to laziness (II Thess 3:7-10) and had to be clarified by the Apostle Paul.

Nevertheless, in the harmony of the early church, the people continued likeminded, **Praising God, and having favor with all the people.** This unity of purpose produced much fruit and daily the Lord added to His church.

3:1-6. So strong was the bond of love between these early believers, that people of diverse backgrounds found themselves strangely teamed together. A prime example is that of Peter and John. Peter was impetuous, forthright, and very bold. John was more quiet and retiring, one who was tender and compassionate. Yet at the established hour of prayer, Peter and John **went up together into the temple.** Their unity is rewarded by the Lord. As they entered the temple compound through the Gate Beautiful, probably given this name because it was a gate of Corinthian bronze, which had such exquisite workmanship that it "far exceeded in value those gates plated with silver and set in gold" (Josephus, *Jewish Wars*, vs. 5.3), they met a man that had been lame from his mother's womb. When the man asked alms of Peter and John, Peter intensely fixed his eyes upon the lame man and with a piercing gaze the apostle offered the lame man much more than silver and gold. Peter's classic response was, **Silver and gold have I none; but such as I have give I thee: In the name of Jesus Christ of Nazareth rise up and walk.** At that authoritative command, given in the authority of the name of Christ Jesus, the lame man did that which he could never do before.

7-11. The progression of verbs used by Luke to describe the activity of this lame man is very interesting. When Peter took the man's hand, immediately the feet and ankle bones of the lame man received strength which was not their own. The man leaped up, walked, putting one foot in front of the other, and accompanied the two disciples into the temple, **walking, and leaping, and praising God.** Those standing by looked on in amazement. Obviously they recognized the man as the lame beggar who had been a familiar sight at the Gate Beautiful. Having passed through this gate at the entrance to the temple, they made their way along the eastern wall of the outer court to the colonnade named after Solomon. Here a crowd of spectators thronged around the man and the disciples. They stood in amazement and were ready for some explanation.

12-18. The astute Peter immediately recognized an opportunity to preach his second great sermon. He begins with the question, **Ye men of Israel, why marvel ye at this?** Because he is appealing to a Jewish audience, he makes reference to the God of Abraham, Isaac, and Jacob, but quickly draws the focus of that reference to God's Son, Jesus. To accurately identify Him, and to cause them to feel remorse, Peter described Jesus as the One delivered up to Pilate, the One that they had denied, **the Holy One and the Just.** The Jewish mob of Jerusalem killed the Prince of Life, but God had raised Him from the dead. It was through His name, that name once humbled and cried out against, that this lame man had been healed. Peter pressed the point that he was not healed magically or naturally but supernaturally through the power invested in the name of Jesus of Nazareth. His purpose again was to bring them to the belief that Jesus was indeed the predicted Messiah and that which happened to Him, His suffering and death, had been foretold in the mouths of the prophets.

19-21. Repent ye therefore, and be converted, that your sins may be blotted out. Peter's second sermon follows the lines of his first. He makes reference to the Lord Jesus and His messiahship and then calls for repentance on the part of those who crucified the Lord of Glory. Interestingly, the gift of the Holy Spirit is not mentioned in this sermon, for he is speaking nationally to Israel and not individually to the Israelites. It is in the context of this national message that he mentions the **times of refreshing** and the **times of restitution of all things.** The word rendered "refreshing" (Gr *anapsyxis*) is and may be translated "respite" (cf. Ex 8:15). Prior to the time when God shall send Jesus Christ again, He who has now ascended into heaven, the believing remnant of Israel will repent and turn to God in preparation for the millennium which is to follow (cf. Deut 30:1-3; Zech 12:10-14). Peter implores national Israel to repent of their sins so that they may be part of that remnant when the "times of refreshing" come.

The word rendered "restitution"

(Gr *apokatastasis*) (vs. 21) should perhaps be rendered "fulfillment" or "establishment." It is a restoration to the former state in the program of God. Although at the time of writing things looked very bleak for national Israel, nevertheless Peter assures the Israelites that God will once again deal with Israel in a blessed and bountiful way (cf. Rom 11:26-27).

22-26. The apostle introduces the testimony of Moses to support his case in a call for national repentance. The words that follow are from Deuteronomy 18:15 ff. Moses is there warning the children of Israel not to follow after the practices of the Canaanites, but to trust God to raise up a prophet like Moses from among their brethren. Peter contends that that prophet was indeed the Lord Jesus Christ, whom the Jews had crucified.

The prophetic testimonies of Samuel and the subsequent prophets are added to that of Moses. The whole of Old Testament prophetic testimony is to show that Jesus was indeed the expected Messiah, but in the plan of God, was crucified, buried, and raised from the dead. In addressing the **children of the prophets,** Moses makes reference to the fact that the Israelites are the heirs to the covenants made to Abraham and others. Hence God is vitally interested in having the Israelites repent and receive Jesus Christ as Messiah and Saviour so that He may turn **away every one of you from his iniquities.**

II. PERSECUTION AND THE EXPANSION OF THE CHURCH. 4:1-9:31.

A. Persecution before the Sanhedrin. 4:1-22.

4:1-4. Such a crowd had gathered around Peter and John at Solomon's colonnade that the priest, the captain of the temple (an official referred to in literature as the chief *sagan*) and the Sadducees seized them. Traditionally the priests and High Priests came from the ranks of the aristocratic Sadducees. These three groups were angered at the fact that Peter and John **taught the people, and preached through Jesus the resurrection from the dead,** a doctrine to which the Sadducees were violently opposed. The end result was that Peter and John were bodily thrown into prison and incarcerated until the next day. However, from Peter's second sermon five thousand men believed, another great victory for the faith.

5-7. The next morning the Sanhedrin met to discuss this problem. Their meeting probably took place just west of the temple area, across the Tyropoeon Valley, in the open-air gathering place known as the Xystos (i.e. "polished floor"). Present were Annas, the senior ex-High Priest, his son-in-law Caiaphas, the present High Priest, John, Alexander, and other kinsmen of the High Priest who cannot be identified with certainty. They were not at all concerned that a man was healed or that a sermon was preached, but in **what power, or by what name, have ye done this?**

8-12. Always boldly ready to preach, and having been successful in his first two endeavors, Peter, **filled with the Holy Ghost,** now begins his third sermon. He boldly asserts that the man was healed in the power, by the authority of, and in the name of Jesus of Nazareth. Then, as has now become his practice, he preaches the death, burial, and resurrection of the Lord Jesus and links that to the well-known Old Testament Scripture, "The stone which the builders rejected is become the head of the corner" (Ps 118: 22). The once despised Jesus of Nazareth, now glorified and at the right hand of the Father, was the One by whose authority this man was healed. If the Sanhedrin insists on repudiating the name and power of Jesus, they must also insist in repudiating the possibility of salvation, **for there is**

none other name under heaven given, whereby we must be saved. Healing, tongues, the church, the Spirit of God, even God the Father Himself is not the point of contact with sinful man. Jesus Christ alone is the One by whom salvation comes to mankind.

13-22. These highly educated and sophisticated members of the Sanhedrin were completely astonished at the boldness of Peter and John. Obviously they had no formal training in the rabbinical schools, yet they ably defended their actions and sustained a theological disputation with the Supreme Court of the nation. There was but one answer: they had been with Jesus. Their only recourse was to release Peter and John.

After they had done so, the Sanhedrin then attempted to deal with their dilemma. A miracle had been performed in their midst and all of Jerusalem knew it. They could not deny the miracle. However, they could attempt to keep the news of that miracle from spreading to other communities. The decision: let us straitly threaten them, that they speak henceforth to no man in this name.

Peter and John were recalled to the chambers of the Sanhedrin and advised that they could never again speak or teach in the name of Jesus of Nazareth. Actually, the Sanhedrin had little hope that they would obey this command. There was only one course of action for Peter and John: we cannot but speak the things which we have seen and heard. This open defiance only provoked an additional threat by the Sanhedrin. Their arrest and release were only to increase the number of believers in Jesus of Nazareth. The New Testament church had been born, was expanding rapidly, and had two eloquent spokesmen in the persons of Peter and John. Nothing could stand in the way of its development. Persecution only hastened the inevitable growth of the church.

B. Character of the Persecuted Church. 4:23-5:16.

23-30. Having been finally released by the Sanhedrin, Peter and John returned to where the other disciples were gathered and recounted for them what had just taken place. It was an occasion for rejoicing and together, with one accord, they made their prayer unto God. It was a prayer of thanksgiving.

They addressed God as Sovereign Lord (Gr *despotēs*, cf. Lk 2:29; Rev 6:10). God is the Sovereign Creator of all, and as such was in complete control of the Sanhedrin situation. After addressing the Lord in typical Hebrew language, the disciples then quoted the opening words of Psalm 2 (vs. 25). Next came a rehearsing of Satan's attempts to thwart the purpose of God as represented by Herod Antipas, Tetrarch of Galilee and Peraea (cf. Lk 23:7 ff.), and Pontius Pilate. They are not concerned, however, with Satan's attempts for they are convinced that what happened to the Lord Jesus (and now to them) was foreordained by the council of God. The Sanhedrin and others may threaten them, but they can never defeat them. "If God be for us, who can be against us?" (Rom 8:31). In the midst of persecutions and threats, the disciples pray that with all boldness they may speak thy word, By stretching forth thine hand to heal. Here the medical language of Luke comes to the fore. The word translated "heal" (Gr *iasis*) is used elsewhere twice by Luke and by no one else in the New Testament. This offers good evidence for the authorship of Luke. The disciples' prayer closes with a petition that signs and wonders may be done by the name of thy holy child Jesus.

31. And when they had prayed, the place was shaken. This first century fledgling church was not only a persecuted church, and a Spirit-filled church, and a powerful church, it was also a praying church. They had found that prayer was the ground of power.

So evident was the Spirit of God that the place in which they were assembled shook as with an earthquake when their prayer was offered up. Again, **they were all filled with the Holy Ghost.** While this was a fresh filling of the Spirit, it cannot be considered a fresh baptism. The only baptism by the Spirit of God they would experience had already occurred at Pentecost. With increased filling came increased boldness to speak the Word of God.

32-37. Characteristic of a praying church is its lack of selfishness. Each member of this Jerusalem church was interested in the welfare of each other member. The expression, **of one heart and of one soul,** shows the remarkable unanimity of this Spirit-filled community. Richer members of the church made provision for those who were poor. No one was in want or hunger. Those who had houses or land sold them in order to see to the welfare of others. Money was brought and laid at the apostles' feet and distribution was made to everyone **according as he had need.** No one made windfall profits; no one was impoverished.

Joses . . . surnamed Barnabas . . . Having land, sold it. The exact etymology of Joses' name "Barnabas" is not clear, but he does show himself to be a true "son of consolation (encouragement)." As a Levite from the island of Cyprus, he was not unfamiliar with Jerusalem, for he had relatives there (see 12:12; Col 4:10). The land which Barnabas sold may have been great or little, but whichever, he brought the money and willingly laid it at the apostles' feet to be distributed to every man according as he had need. Here is a fine example of Christian commitment that goes beyond mere words.

5:1-6. The account of Ananias and Sapphira occurs within the context of, and right on the heels of, the account of the generosity of Barnabas in sharing with other believers. As Barnabas had sold a possession and brought the money and laid it at the apostles' feet, so too this husband and wife team, Ananias and Sapphira, **sold a possession.** The difference between Barnabas and them, however, is seen in the second verse, **And kept back part of the price.** Ananias and Sapphira had apparently not learned the lesson that there is no such thing as secret sin. The Psalmist David had to exclaim, "Oh God, thou knowest my foolishness, and my sins are not hid from thee" Ps 69:5; (see also Moses, Ex 2:11-14; and Achan, Josh 7:21-22).

When Peter confronted Ananias with whether or not Satan had filled his heart to lie to the Holy Ghost, the apostle made it abundantly clear that the practice of "common-ism" was definitely not communism. Peter asserted, **While it remained, was it not thine own?** What belonged to Ananias was indeed his and did not belong to the church, unless he gave it to them. Likewise, after he sold the land, Ananias could do with the money whatever he wished. If he shared it with the believers of Jerusalem that were less fortunate than he it would be out of concern and love for them, not out of requirement. Since he chose to give it to the church in the same manner that Barnabas had given, he should not have attempted to have lied to God and His servants by claiming that he had given his all. A lie to the servant of God was tantamount to lying to the Spirit of God Himself.

When Ananias learned that he had lied unto God, he fell down, **and gave up the ghost.** Ananias was struck dead for his sin against God, and the young men bound him in grave linen, carried him out, and buried him.

7-11. Unaware of what had happened to her husband, about three hours later Sapphira came before Peter and the other disciples. A similar question was asked her concerning the selling of her possession. Because she had conspired with her husband to lie to the Spirit of God, and attempted to increase her image in the eyes of the other believers, Peter predicted that the feet of those that carried out her husband would also carry out Sapphira. **Then fell she down straightway at his feet, and yielded up the ghost.** As predicted, the men quickly came and bore her body away to be buried alongside her husband. Satan first attacked the church from without, persecuting it as a roaring lion. Now he has attacked the church from within, persecuting it as a serpent. But the end result is still the same: **And great fear came upon all the church.** All who had assembled as believers in Jerusalem were brought into a right relationship with God because of persecution. This not altogether unhealthy effect of persecution must have caused havoc in the dominions of darkness.

12-16. The shock of the double death of Ananias and Sapphira apparently sparked the apostles to double their efforts in behalf of the Lord. **Many signs and wonders wrought among the people.** This paragraph is a summary of the great things that have been accomplished through the Spirit of God (cf. 2:43-47; 4:32-35). The sick were brought into the streets on beds and couches and so evident was the presence of the Spirit of God on these men that even the very shadow of Peter passing over someone may cause the healing of that person. For miles around the news spread and the sick and those possessed by unclean spirits were brought to the disciples. The end result was a record of performance that should cause distrust of modern day healing campaigns: **and they were healed every one.**

C. Persecution before the Sadducees. 5:17-42.

17-28. Not long before this Peter and John had been released from the court of the Sanhedrin with a stern warning. But the additional healings and the multitudes which crowded around the disciples caused the High

Priests and the Sadducees to become very indignant. They ordered that the disciples should be seized and thrown into the common prison. It was there that another miracle occurred. Their escape from the common prison was not accomplished by a *deus ex machina*, as in the Greek tragedies, but by a real angel or "messenger" from the Lord. They were released from prison and were told, **Go, stand and speak in the temple.** Having been warned and imprisoned, the disciples could not be deterred from this heavenly command.

Early the next morning they entered the temple and did as they had been commanded by the angel. When the Sanhedrin convened to discuss the matter of the disciples, whom they thought were in prison, they felt it necessary to bring the disciples before them once again. Thus an officer was sent to the prison to retrieve them, but returned with the news that the prison doors were securely shut and the keepers were on duty outside the doors, but no one was to be found in the prison. The immediate concern of the High Priest, the captains of the temple, and the chief priests was that the miraculous release of the disciples would be yet another story that would grow causing even greater popularity for the followers of the Lord Jesus. Thus the officers were commanded to bring Peter and the others from the temple, but without violence for fear of the people.

When they took their place before the Sanhedrin, the president of the court (the High Priest) reminded them that they had previously been warned about preaching in the name of Jesus. They thought the disciples were attempting to place responsibility for the death of Jesus on the leaders of the Sanhedrin. In questioning Peter, the High Priest attested to a fact that is truly miraculous in light of the great persecution the early church had received. In just a short time, due to the indwelling presence of the Holy Spirit of God, the High Priest exclaimed to the disciples, **ye have filled Jerusalem with your doctrine.** This remains as an example and a challenge to every church of every age to do likewise.

29-32. We ought to obey God rather than men.

Peter is not so much advocating open defiance against the state as he is absolute dependence upon God. Having yet another golden opportunity to preach Christ and Him crucified, Peter falls back upon his pattern of making reference to the slaying of Jesus and the cursed hanging upon a tree (Deut 21:23; Gal 3:13). Also his message contains a note of repentance and forgiveness of sin, as well as his repeated claims to be among the witnesses of these things.

33-40. So enraged at the defiance of the believers in Christ were the Sadducees that they were about to pass judgment on the disciples and sentence them to death. However, the pharisaic members of the court, although in the minority, still had a very powerful and persuasive voice in the judgments of that court. Perhaps the most respected man of the entire Sanhedrin was the renowned Pharisee named Gamaliel. This *rabban,* a doctor of the law, was the leader of the famous school of Hillel. He had many illustrious disciples, among them Saul of Tarsus (cf. 22:3). When this prestigious elder rose to speak, everyone listened.

With calmer heads now prevailing, Gamaliel cautioned the Sanhedrin concerning their intentions to put the disciples to death. First he reminded them of an insurgent named Theudas, **boasting himself to be somebody.** It is obvious that Gamaliel did not believe Theudas was anyone of importance, but his following grew to four hundred persons before he was slain and his patriots scattered. Nothing for certain is known of this man except that he was probably one of many insurgents that arose in Palestine about the time of Herod the Great in 4 B.C.

Again, Gamaliel reminded the San-

hedrin of a more successful insurgent, Judas of Galilee. This man had a larger following in his revolt of A.D. 6, when he incited a nationalist revolt against paying tribute to Caesar when God alone was Israel's true King (see Josephus, *Jewish War* ii. 8.1: *Antiq.* xviii. 1.1). The taxing for census referred to was that of Publius Sulpicius Quirinius when he was the imperial legate of Syria for the second time (A.D. 6-7).

Gamaliel's counsel and advice to the Sanhedrin is classic. It is this. If the movement which involves these disciples of Jesus of Nazareth is not of God, it will come to nothing. But, on the other hand, if it is of God, the Sanhedrin certainly would not want to fight against it. This put the Sanhedrin on the horns of dilemma. They hated the movement, but the reasoning of Gamaliel and his "wait and see" policy had to be adopted. The end result was that **when they had called the apostles, and beaten them, they commanded that they should not speak in the name of Jesus, and let them go.** A now common procedure, releasing the disciples and forbidding them to preach in the name of Jesus, took on one additional feature. This time the disciples were beaten before they were released.

41-42. Having received the harshest punishment to date, the disciples were in no way disheartened. On the contrary they were **rejoicing that they were counted worthy to suffer shame for His name.** Increased persecution simply evoked increased dedication. So much so that **daily in the temple, and in every house, they ceased not to teach and preach Jesus Christ.**

D. Persecution of Stephen. 6:1-8:4.

6:1-4. And in those days. This passage may be regarded as an epilogue to what has preceded. The time has now come for an important advance in organization in the New Testament church. This organizational advance arose out of a rift between the **Grecians**

and the **Hebrews.** Both of these groups were Jews, the Grecians were Greek-speaking Jews and the Hebrews were Aramaic-speaking Jews. As is so frequently the case, a conflict arose over a minute concern. Since the wealthy of the Christian community had sold their goods to provide for the poor, some of the Grecian Jews felt their poor and widows were being neglected in favor of the more traditional Hebrew-speaking Jews.

Thus the Twelve called the disciples together and asked them to seek out seven men of good reputation, men who would be responsible for administering the charitable allocations. Upon the appointment of such men, the Twelve could give themselves to the ministry to which they were called: **prayer, and to the ministry of the word.** The twentieth century church would do well to take this advice given by the Twelve. Many church leaders today are not free to devote themselves to the two prime aspects of their ministry, prayer and the preaching of the word. Members of the local assembly must assume positions of responsibility in order to free the pastor to do the job for which he has been called.

5-8. And they chose Stephen . . . and Philip and Prochorus, and Nicanor, and Timon, and Parmenas, and Nicolas. The suggestion of the Twelve was readily accepted by the church of Jerusalem. Seven men were chosen to fulfill the obligation of deacon. The first named is Stephen who is a **man full of faith and the Holy Ghost.** This description is not without substance as the next chapters of Acts portray. Philip is also mentioned and he too will figure heavily in the next chapters. Of the others, less is known. A later tradition suggests that Prochorus was an amanuensis of John the evangelist and became Bishop of Nicomedia and was subsequently martyred at Antioch. The last named man, Nicolas, is mentioned as not a Jew but a proselyte from Antioch. Some have speculated that he

was the founder of the Nicolaitans in Revelation 2:6, 15. This, however, cannot be said with great certainty.

And the word of God increased. At this point Luke interrupts the narrative of this organizational advance to give a progress report on the church's activities. Five other such reports punctuate this history of Acts (see also 9:31; 12:24; 16:5; 19:20; 28:31). Perhaps the interjection here is to indicate that the church need not choose between evangelistic zeal and the social and physical concerns of its constituency. Both advanced together.

9-15. Then there arose certain of the synagogue . . . disputing with Stephen. The ministry of Stephen is the link between the establishment of the church in Jerusalem and the conversion of the Apostle Paul. As Stephen entered the synagogue to preach in the name of Jesus Christ, he encountered opposition. Apparently this synagogue was one which catered to those who were either from the dispersion or descendants of those from areas outside of Palestine. Specifically, this synagogue of the Libertines was made up of those who were Cyrenians, Alexandrians, and Cilicians. The dispute with Stephen brought little success to the Jews. **They were not able to resist the wisdom and the spirit by which he spake.**

These stubborn men, however, did not give up when they were beaten philosophically. They simply resorted to baser tactics, slanderous charges of blasphemy against Moses and God. Apparently in the first century the charge of blasphemy included more than a profane use of the ineffable name of the God of Israel (*Mishnah, Sanhedrin* vii. 5). Since Stephen had said nothing against Moses or God, they had to introduce false witnesses, a common practice among the Jews (see also Mt 26:59-61; Mk 14:55-59). These false witnesses stirred up the people by saying that Stephen spoke **blasphemous words against this holy place, and the law.** The false witnesses then alluded to a portion of Stephen's message in which he quoted Jesus' statement about destroying the body, and it being raised again in three days (cf. Mk 14:58; Mt 26:61). As this statement was misinterpreted when Jesus uttered it, now it is misinterpreted when Stephen reported it. Thus the persecution of Stephen began and he was dragged before the council. There they looked upon him and saw **his face as it had been the face of an angel.** This is not to intimate that he had the gentle, effeminate face often portrayed in medieval paintings of angels. Rather his face was aglow with the love of the Lord Jesus for these his persecutors.

7:1. Then said the high priest, Are these things so? In response to the question of the High Priest concerning the false allegations leveled against Stephen, this Spirit-filled deacon replied with what amounts to be an early apology for the Christian faith. It is a general historical account of the moving of God in the lives of Abraham and his descendants. But when Stephen makes his application to this historical account (vss. 51-53) it is evident that he shows Christianity to be the natural fulfillment of the promises made to Abraham and the Patriarchs. He does not divorce his heritage from his newfound belief in the Messiah. Instead, he shows that Jesus of Nazareth is the fulfillment of his Jewish heritage and those who have not recognized Him as Messiah are indeed traitors to their forefathers.

2-5. Men, brethren, and fathers, hearken. As Stephen begins his apology, he addresses them in a polite manner, not what one would expect of false witnesses. In these verses he addresses himself to the call of Abraham (Gen 12) and to his removal by faith from Ur of the Chaldees to Haran. Also mentioned is the possession of the Promised Land and Abraham's faith that this land would be retained forever, **when as yet he had no child.**

6-10. His seed should sojourn in a strange land. This section records the rite of circumcision given to Abraham as a sign of God's covenant with him and the birth of Isaac, Jacob, and the twelve Patriarchs. Also the deliverance into Egyptian bondage is addressed here.

11-16. Joseph was made known to his brethren. In these verses the touching story of Joseph, sold into slavery, and risen to power, is recorded. When Jacob learns that his beloved on is still alive, he migrates to Egypt where there is corn and food for all his family. Here the Patriarch dies and his body is taken to Shechem for burial.

17-22. Till another king arose, which knew not Joseph. Stephen now relates the birth and early life of Moses. His learning and wisdom in the sciences of the Egyptians is noted, and that he was **mighty in word and in deed.**

23-29. It came into his heart to visit his brethren the children of Israel. Now Moses is forty years old and he spies an Egyptian beating one of his brethren. Moses' anger brings him to commit murder and he slew the Egyptian and hid him in the sand. When this atrocity was made known to him, Moses had to flee to the land of Midian **where he begat two sons.**

30-36. Next in order in Stephen's historical account of Israel is the call of Moses **in a flame of fire in a bush.** The speaker is obviously the God of Abraham, Isaac, and Jacob and the place where Moses stood was holy ground. Moses was commissioned to return to Egypt and to stand in the court of Pharaoh demanding that God's people be released from bondage. After showing the Egyptians great wonders, Moses would lead the children out of the land across the Red Sea and into the wilderness for forty years.

37-43. A prophet shall the Lord your God raise up unto you of your brethren. Although Stephen is yet a great distance from the conclusion of his apology, he begins to lay the groundwork for his contention that the New Testament church is a natural result from those who have received Jesus as Messiah. Even Moses proclaimed that God would raise a prophet up from among the Israelites, whom they should hear and obey. That prophet was Jesus Christ.

The church (Gr *ekklēsia*) **in the wilderness** is a reference to the assembly of the people of God at the foot of Mt. Sinai. Here Stephen makes reference to the idolatry of his forefathers and the worship of the golden calf. In addition the Israelites worship **the host of heaven,** represented specifically by the planetary deities **Moloch** and **Remphan.** His purpose is to show that the nation Israel has the history of needing prophets like unto Moses and Jesus Christ. They also have a history, however, of not receiving those prophets. Interestingly, Stephen had just been charged by the false witnesses with speaking blasphemous words against Moses. But now his purpose is to show that those guilty of disrespect to Moses are his heirs, the Israelites, and not his new companions, the Christians.

44-50. Our fathers had the tabernacle of witness in the wilderness. The attention of the deacon is focused on the building of both the tabernacle and the temple. He makes reference to the tabernacle in the wilderness and the fact that it was brought in **with Jesus into the possession of the Gentiles.** The Greek form of Joshua, which is here translated Jesus as in Hebrews 4:8, may be a purposeful illusion to the fact that the one who led Israel into the land of inheritance bears the same name of the one who can lead Israel into the land of eternal life.

Next, reference is made to the days of David and the fact that it was his desire to build the house of the God of Jacob. This his son Solomon was permitted to do. **Howbeit the most High dwelleth not in temples made with hands.** Stephen quickly draws his

apologetic to the person of Jesus Christ. At His trial, the Lord said, "I will destroy this temple that is made with hands, and in three days I will build another made without hands" (Mk 14:58). This reference is obviously to clarify the charge which the false witnesses brought against him (cf. 6:14). Stephen has shown that the temple, as well as the tabernacle which preceded it, was never intended to be the permanent dwelling place of God. Jesus of Nazareth gave a correct perspective to the temple of Jerusalem and its relationship to the God who dwells in the hearts of believers.

Stephen's argument has now been concluded. However, he must yet convince his hearers that what he says is legitimate. Therefore, he has to undertake concluding remarks which will make the application of this historical argument.

51-53. Ye stiffnecked and uncircumcised in heart and ears. In making his conclusion Stephen appeals to a descriptive term which had been used many times of the Jews. God Himself complained that His people were "stiffnecked" (Ex 33:5). That they were "uncircumcised in heart and ears" meant that while they were circumcised in the physical sense, nevertheless their disobedience in not receiving the message of the prophets caused them to be ungodly in their hearts and lives. The resistance of the present generation of Jews to the work of the Holy Spirit is something that their forefathers also exhibited.

The coming of the Just One. Stephen now addresses himself to the present hardness of this stiffnecked people. Characteristic of being a prophet of God in the nation Israel was undergoing extreme persecution and more often than not martyrdom. Stephen depicts the Lord Jesus as one in a long line of such prophets whom the Jews betrayed and murdered. Again the tie with Christianity is made in the history of Judaism. The fathers had killed the messengers who foretold of the coming of the Just One; but they themselves had gone even further in bringing the Just One Himself to a violent death.

54-56. When they heard these things, they were cut to the heart. The testimony of Stephen in his application to the council did more to carve their ire than anything imaginable. The verb used here, and in Acts 5:33 (Gr *diapriō*) expresses the cutting done by a saw. It is designed to show how deep their feelings were, and the similar expression, **they gnashed on him with their teeth,** although not literally done, was always an expression of rage.

Saw the glory of God, and Jesus. Stephen makes no retaliation to the irritated counsel. Instead he fastens his attention on the heavens, which during this transition period of Acts, are said to have opened so that Stephen could see the glory of God and (or "even") Jesus, standing on the right hand of God.

Although the "Glory of God" usually represents the Shekinah Glory of the Old Testament, Jesus is nevertheless the Glory of God. Now ascended into heaven, Jesus has again received the glory which He had with the Father before the world began (Jn 17:5). It is that glory that all men have come short of, and in essence, it is that glory that shows each of us to be sinners (Rom 3:23). Stephen was given the unique opportunity to view Jesus as the Glory of God in heaven.

57-60. Again incensed by the calm, quiet attitude of Stephen, the crowd rushed upon him, crying for his death. Dragging him out of the city, they **stoned him.** Since this is the Jewish form of death, it would indicate that the Sanhedrin and the members of the council provided the oversight for the murder of Stephen. Although this was not legal, and apparently Pilate either turned a deaf ear to the situation or was not apprised of it, nevertheless the action was carried out in the rage of the Jews.

As was customary, the witnesses cast the first stones. This duty was prescribed both in the Mishnah and also in the law itself (cf. Lev 24:24; Deut 17:7). In order to throw the first stone the witnesses would divest themselves of their outer garments. These garments were placed **at a young man's feet, whose name was Saul.** At this first introduction to the man Saul, one very important element is frequently overlooked. Nowhere is it stated or even intimated that Saul, later the Apostle Paul, actually participated in the death of Stephen. Saul consented to his death, guarded the garments of those who first stoned him, but is not said to have actually cast a stone himself.

Lord Jesus, receive my spirit. This utterance of Stephen and the one to follow, echoes the Lord's utterances from the cross. On his knees and being constantly bombarded with stones, Stephen's one concern was not for himself but for those who were his persecutors. As the Lord cried unto the Father, "Father, forgive them; for they know not what they do" (Lk 23:24), so too, Stephen cries unto the Lord in a loud voice, **Lord, lay not this sin to their charge.** When the men of Israel were at their worst, the man Stephen was at his best. He interceded to the Lord God of heaven for those who persecuted him. Even in death his concern was for their eternal life.

8:1-4. There was a great persecution against the church which was at Jerusalem. The murder of Stephen precipitated a persecution unlike any seen heretofore. This time the target was not just the individual, Stephen, but the church as a whole. The most severe persecution must have fallen upon the Hellenistic Jews, for from this time onward the church at Jerusalem appears to have consisted almost entirely of Hebrew or Aramaic-speaking Jews. Although the persecution was deadly, nevertheless it accomplished the direct will of God. This persecution caused the dispersion of the Jews of the

Jerusalem church throughout the regions of Judaea and Samaria, except for the apostles who remained in Jerusalem. Thus the Lord's command in chapter 1, verse 8 was fulfilled by the persecution of chapter 8, verse 1.

It was directly against the Jewish law to make lamentations at the funeral of an executed person (see *Mishnah, Sanhedrin* vi. 6). However, certain devout men gave Stephen the burial that was due this first Christian martyr. And what is the "young man" Saul doing while this is going on? He has become the prime mover in the campaign against the church. With papers of permission from the authority of the Sanhedrin and Chief Priest, Paul harassed the church, smashing down doors and arresting men and women in their homes, sending them off to prison. He did so as a zealous Pharisee fully believing that he was keeping the law pure from those of this new Christian sect whom he considered to have prostituted the law. Then what was the result of Saul's and the other's harassment? **They that were scattered abroad went everywhere preaching the word.** Not only was persecution the means by which the gospel spread to other regions in Palestine, but also it caused the gospel to go to much further fields as well (cf. 11:19 ff.).

E. The Ministry of Philip. 8:5-40.

5-7. Then Philip . . . preached Christ unto them. It is difficult to say whether "the city of Samaria" was actually the city that bore that name in the Old Testament. At this period of history it had been rebuilt by Herod the Great as a great city and given the name Sebaste in honor of the Roman Emperor (Gr *sebastos;* the Latin equivalent is *augustus*). It may be that he went to a city in Samaria the region and may even have been Gutta, which Justin Martyr (*Apology* i, 26) designates as the birthplace of Simon the Sorcerer. Whatever the case, Philip had great success in his preaching ef-forts there. These efforts were accomplished by healing, casting out of unclean spirits, and other signs of the presence of the Holy Spirit in him.

8-13. In the midst of the joy over those who had believed in Jesus of Nazareth as Saviour and those who had been healed, Luke introduces the infamous Simon the Sorcerer. Frequently known as Simon Magus, this man has been the subject of much of early Christian literature. Ireneaus (*Against Heresies* i.) names Simon as the founder of gnosticism. Justin Martyr (*Apology* i, 26) mistakenly ascribes an ancient inscription in the city of Rome to Simon. In the pseudo-Clementine *Recognitions* and *Homilies* the legend about Simon becoming the nemesis of Peter is greatly elaborated. Also the apocryphal *Acts of Peter* tell how the Christians of Rome were corrupted by this man's false teaching. Whether any of this is historical or not is presently beside the point. What is known is that this sorcerer had great sway over the people of Samaria. So bewitching was his sorcery that it was said of him, **This man is the great power of God.**

When those who had been bewitched by Simon came to know the Lord as Saviour, through the preaching of Philip, and were baptized, **Then Simon himself believed also.** There seems to be some little doubt about the legitimacy of Simon's conversion. There is no sign of repentance. There is no confession of sin. But there is the statement that he continued with Philip **and wondered, beholding the miracles and signs which were done.** Apparently Simon wanted the secret of Philip's power. His only concern was not for his own soul but for the ability to get close to Philip and learn the secret of his ability to heal the sick and perform miracles.

14-24. They sent unto them Peter and John. When the news of Philip's preaching, and the subsequent conversion of the Samaritans reached Jerusalem, it was necessary for the Jewish church there to send their two key representatives in order to investigate these "conversions." The church at Jerusalem had been all Jewish; this assembly was all Samaritan. Thus Peter and John descended the heights of Jerusalem into Samaria and prayed that these believers would receive the Holy Spirit. The Samaritan believers had been baptized in water in the name of the Lord Jesus, but as yet the Holy Spirit had fallen on none of them. Therefore, Peter and John placed their hands upon them and **they received the Holy Ghost.**

This special function of Peter and John was not to be repeated. The first instance of the Holy Spirit coming upon a group of individuals was in the upper room with the one hundred twenty. They were Jews; these Samaritans were not present. Thus Peter and John bring the power of Pentecost to another group of people. This will occur twice again in this transition period of Acts: at the household of Cornelius when Gentiles received the Holy Spirit (ch. 10) and when the disciples of John the Baptist received the Holy Spirit (ch. 19). The baptism of the Holy Spirit, as it occurred in each of these groups, was never to be repeated again. Every believer is baptized into the body of Christ the instant he believes (I Cor 12:12-13). Subsequent baptisms of the individual by the Holy Spirit are unknown in Scripture.

He offered them money, Saying, Give me also this power. In further proof of the spurious character of Simon's so-called conversion, one can see his materialistic view of God. He attempted to buy that which is God's prerogative alone to give.

Simon was quite taken back by the stern rebuke he received from Peter. Peter sized up the situation and immediately diagnosed the problem: **for thy heart is not right in the sight of God.** A call for repentance was accompanied by Peter's perception that Si-

mon was yet caught up in the bitter gall-root of superstition and his fascination with magic and sorcery was still for him a bond of iniquity. Terror stricken, Simon begged Peter to pray for him, **that none of these things which ye have spoken come upon me.**

25-29. With the conclusion of the matter concerning Simon Magus, Peter and John returned to Jerusalem, apparently accompanied by Philip. Their evangelistic efforts among the Samaritans continued along the road. However, an angel of the Lord spoke unto Philip advising him, **Arise, and go toward the south.** Philip was specifically instructed to go into the region of Gaza, a narrow desert strip which provided access along the sea to the great Sinai Peninsula. Philip obeyed and, in consequence of that, encountered a man of Ethiopia.

This man had apparently come to Jerusalem to worship which may mean that he was a God-fearing Gentile. As a eunuch he was the chamberlain to the Queen of Ethiopia. **Candace** was not the name of the queen but rather a title given to the mother of each Ethiopian king (see Bion of Soli, *Aethiopica* 1). This Ethiopian eunuch had come to a position of great trust under the authority of the queen. Upon his return from Jerusalem, while sitting in his chariot reading from the prophet Isaiah, the spirit of the Lord moved upon Philip telling him, **Go near, and join thyself to this chariot.** This expression shows the definite moving of the Spirit of God in evangelism. What the Spirit of God commanded, Philip could not fail to do.

30-35. Understandest thou what thou readest? Having been moved by the Spirit of God to speak to this man, and recognizing the exact portion of Isaiah that the eunuch was reading, Philip received his cue to initiate conversation. The question concerning his ability to understand what he read was natural enough seeing that this man was Ethiopian and not Jewish. The eunuch's response also indicates this, **How can I, except some man should guide me?** The Ethiopian's need and Philip's apparent ability to meet it precipitated the invitation for Philip to come and sit in the chariot with the man. The actual passage which the man was reading was Isaiah 53:7 ff. This event recorded in the New Testament sets the New Testament seal of approval on the interpretation of Isaiah 53 and the servant passages as pertaining to Jesus Christ. When the eunuch asked Philip whether or not the prophet was speaking of himself as the sheep before the slaughter and the lamb dumb before his shearer, Philip boldly opened his mouth **and began at the same scripture, and preached unto him Jesus.** There was no question in the mind of Philip that the Suffering Servant of Isaiah 53 was Jesus of Nazareth. Luke recorded this as fact. We must accept it in the spirit in which it was recorded, i.e. as a prophecy concerning the sacrificial death of Jesus Christ.

Here is water; what doth hinder me to be baptized? We don't know how far or to what spot Philip and the Ethiopian had traveled. Perhaps it was the Wadi el-Hesi northeast of Gaza, which is the traditional sight. Wherever the spot was, there was sufficient water to perform baptism. Although some manuscripts do not include verse 37, it does fit perfectly into the story and gives the sense of what Philip must have told the Ethiopian Eunuch. **If thou believest with all thine heart, thou mayest.** Apparently this whole discussion concerning baptism was precipitated by Philip's instruction to the eunuch subsequent to salvation. He must have told the eunuch that the next step in a believer's life is a physical sign of baptism which outwardly speaks of the believer's death to the world and resurrection to new life in Christ. The confession of faith and the lordship of Christ made by the eunuch was absolutely sincere, **I believe that Jesus Christ is the Son of God.** Such public confession of new faith was a common practice when a convert was formally admitted to the Christian fellowship by baptism. Because of the evidence in the eunuch's life, and his sincere confession in the deity of Christ, Philip and the eunuch descended into the water and the eunuch was baptized.

Immediately another miracle occurs. After coming up out of the water the Spirit of the Lord caught Philip away so that he was no more seen by the eunuch. Philip next appeared at Azotus, the old Philistine city of Ashdod, some twenty miles north of Gaza. From there he proceeded along the coastal highway to Caesarea preaching in all the cities along the way. The ministry of Philip is a refreshing interlude in the great persecutions endured by the early church. It is as if Luke, guided by the Spirit of God, knew just when to put a note of encouragement into his history, for the next chapter deals again with the persecutions engineered by Saul of Tarsus.

F. Conversion of Saul. 9:1-31.

9:1-2. And Saul, yet breathing out threatenings and slaughter. This phrase (Gr *empneonapeiles*) is a difficult one to translate. Literally, Saul "breathed in" threatening and slaughter. Perhaps this is just designed to mean that with every breath he took, he became more adamant against the Christian believers.

As the narrative now returns to Saul of Tarsus, we may note that he pushes his campaign against the Christians far beyond the reaches of Jerusalem. Thus this zealous Pharisee procures extradition papers from the High Priest in Jerusalem to bring back **any of this way** who have fled to Damascus. For Christianity to be described as "The Way" is a common occurrence (cf. 19:9-23; 22:4; 24:14, 22). It was Saul's desire to bind the disciples and drag them back to Jerusalem for trial by the council of the Sanhedrin, of which the High Priest was president.

3-9. Suddenly there shined round about him a light from heaven. Armed with official papers from the High Priest, Saul set out for Damascus to bring back the refugees from Jerusalem and Judaea that had fled by dint of persecution. He almost made it to the capital of the Syrian Empire when one of the most phenomenal events recorded anywhere on the pages of history occurred. Although it was midday (cf. 22:6; 26:13), a light shined out of heaven that completely engulfed the light of the sun. So awesome was this light that Saul fell to the ground recognizing his inferiority to the One generating the light. In addition, he heard a voice, a phenomenon the Rabbi's call "the daughter of the voice (of God)." The voice of one far superior to him said, **Saul, Saul, why persecutest thou me?**

Here a great truth is seen. Although Saul had set out to Damascus to continue his persecution of Christians, it is the Lord who speaks to him and says, "Saul, Saul, why persecutest thou me?"All sin, regardless of its character, is ultimately directed against the Lord God. There is no such thing as private or personal sin. Every sin that is committed affects others, but in its terminal point, every sin affects God. Saul thought he was persecuting meaningless Christians; instead he was persecuting the Lord God of heaven. This is the same reaction given by the young Joseph when Potiphar's wife attempted to seduce him. He responded to her, "How then can I do this great wickedness, and sin against God?" (Gen 39:9). Even the prodigal son recognized this, for when he came to himself, he determined to return to his father and say, "I have sinned against heaven, and before thee" (Lk 15:18). In anger, sin might be directed against an object. In lust, sin may be directed against a person. But in actuality, all sin is directed against God.

Who art thou, Lord? Immediately this Pharisee recognized that he was dealing with someone superior to himself. The reply which he received was undoubtedly the least expected, **I am Jesus whom thou persecutest.** Naturally, this caused Saul to tremble in amazement, but his response was the only one possible when one meets his superior and is vanquished: **Lord, what wilt thou have me to do?** Saul was commanded to arise and enter the city, while those who journeyed with him stood speechless, hearing a voice, but seeing no man.

On the surface this statement appears to conflict with Luke's own statement in chapter 22:9, "They what were with me beheld indeed the light, but they heard not the voice of him that spake to me." This does not contradict 22:9. The verb "to hear" (Gr *akouō*) in Greek governs an accusative (22:9 or a genitive; 9:7). The genitive is partitive and in itself conveys the idea that they did not apprehend the sound in its entirety. Hence, the genitive at 9:7. It was correct to use the accusative in the second context. The accusative signifies the complete domination of the object, and the company did not understand the purport of the words. Admittedly this distinction is often blurred, but Luke is a careful writer" (E. M. Blaiklock, *The Acts of the Apostles*, pp. 92-93).

When his eyes were opened, he saw no man. When Paul finally arose from the Damascus Road he was unable to see. Thus, his companions led him by the hand to Damascus and **he was three days without sight.** It is not beyond the realm of possibility that the events recorded in II Corinthians 12:1-4 occurred during this three-day period.

10-12. And there was a certain disciple at Damascus, named Ananias. Ananias was apparently a Damascene Jew who believed in Jesus as Messiah. The Lord appeared unto him in a vision, calling his name, and he answered, **I am here, Lord.** The request of the Lord to Ananias was probably the strangest request this man would ever receive. It was, **go into the street which is called Straight, and inquire . . . for one called Saul, of Tarsus.** The escapades of the zealous Saul were well-known in Damascus. For Ananias to receive a vision from the Lord asking him to seek out a man who made it his religious practice to throw Christian men and women into prison, must have been almost too much for Ananias to take. Nevertheless, it was explained to him in the vision that Saul himself had had a vision in which he saw a man named Ananias coming toward him, placing his hand upon him, and causing him to receive sight.

13-16. As expected, Ananias was quick to object to this request. In explaining that he had heard of the evil this man had done to the saints in Jerusalem, Ananias is simply being cautious in living his Christian testimony and is not guilty of cowardice. His objections are overruled, however, and his concerns alleviated by the Lord who said, **for he is a chosen vessel unto me, to bear my name before the Gentiles.** Paul later would make frequent references to the fact that he was called of God to be the apostle to the Gentiles (see Gal 1:15-16). As Saul had been the minister of suffering to many believers, he himself would now be the recipient of much suffering, both at the hands of believers, and especially at the hands of his own kinsmen, the Jews.

17-22. And Ananias . . . putting his hands on him said, Brother Saul. What a difference three days can make in a man's life. Seventy-two hours earlier the chances of a Jewish believer addressing the threatening Saul as "brother" would have been nil. But now Saul and Ananias are all part of the same family. Ananias understands that Saul has come to him so that he might receive his sight and be filled with the Holy Ghost. **Immediately there fell from his eyes as it had been scales.** Probably speaking metaphorically, Luke here records that finally

after three days of temporary blindness Saul has now regained his sight. After being baptized, presumably at the hands of Ananias, Saul received strength and remained a number of days with the disciples at Damascus.

During those days Saul was not idle. **He preached Christ in the synagogues, that he is the Son of God.** This is the only reference to Jesus Christ as "the Son of God" in the book of the Acts. It is significant that it occurs very early in the preaching of Paul indicating that he immediately recognized not only the messiahship of Christ Jesus, but also His deity as well.

One can imagine the astonishment of those Jews in the synagogue at Damascus when they heard the man, whom they all respected and to whom they looked for leadership in quenching the spreading flame of Christianity, stand up in their midst and proclaim Jesus of Nazareth as God. The Damascus Jews were completely taken back; they could not believe their eyes or ears. But Paul proved that his conversion was real, in that he **confounded the Jews which dwelt at Damascus.**

23-25. And after that many days were fulfilled. In these verses the account of Paul's escape from Damascus is recorded. II Corinthians 11:32-33 adds even greater detail to the account of this escape. We know that it occurred during the reign of Aretas IV (9 B.C. - A.D. 40), the leader of the Nabataean Kingdom who extended his influence as far north as Damascus. The expression "many days" may lead us to the impression that his escape from the city occurred only a few days after his conversion. Such is not the case, for Galatians 1:17-18 clearly indicates to us that upon salvation Paul did not go to Jerusalem or confer with other of the apostles but once receiving his sight went to Arabia (the Nabataean Arabia), returned again unto Damascus, and apparently there communed with the Lord and preached for the space of about three years. His preaching was so successful that the Jews and Nabataeans **watched the gates day and night to kill him.** Their plans were foiled, however, when one of those who came to know the Lord through the ministry of Paul, who had a house built upon the wall, enabled Paul to escape by night by letting him down over the wall in a basket. From here Paul journeyed south to Jerusalem.

26-31. Paul spent the bulk of his life as a loner. He was one solitary man on a dedicated mission to the Gentiles. But when a friend was needed, God always saw to it that a friend was there. In Damascus that friend was Ananias. Now it is Barnabas' turn. **And when Saul was come to Jerusalem . . . But Barnabas took him, and brought him to the apostles.** Like that of Ananias, the initial reaction of the disciples in Jerusalem to the presence of Saul was one of fear. Thus Barnabas presented Paul as one who had been genuinely saved by the grace of God and who had spoken boldly of the Lord Jesus in Damascus. Now that he is in the great Jewish city of Jerusalem, Paul did not change his tactics. Back in Jerusalem for the first time since he left there with extradition papers from the High Priest, Paul is not warmly received as he would have been had he not had the Damascus Road experience. However, Paul again speaks out boldly against the Grecian Jews. Quite a little stir followed and they sought to slay Saul. Thus some of the brethren whisked him away to Caesarea, the Mediterranean seaport city built by Herod the Great, and from there he took a ship to his native Tarsus.

With Saul of Tarsus now safely entrenched on their side, and his defection to the ranks of Christianity so sudden that a replacement was not readily available, **Then had the churches rest throughout all Judaea and Galilee and Samaria, and were edified.** One great period of persecution has ended; others will follow; but for now the church has weathered its first great storm, withstood its first great critics, and won its first great adversary, Saul of Tarsus. Thus the local assembly of God's people, walking in the fear of the Lord, and in the comfort of the Holy Ghost, was multiplied.

III. PETER AND THE BEGINNING OF GENTILE CHRISTIANITY. 9:32-12:25.

A. Peter's Healing Ministry. 9:32-43.

32-35. The last time Peter was mentioned in the narrative of Acts was in 8:25 when he returned with John from their visit to Samaria. During this period Peter appears to be carrying on an itinerate ministry among those Christian communities of Judaea. Thus he comes to a stronghold of Jewry, the city of Lydda (Lod in the Old Testament). This city, in the ancient Philistine territory, had a Christian assembly. One of the believers in the church at Lydda was **a certain man named Aeneas, which had kept his bed eight years.** When Peter encountered this man, immediately he said unto him, **Aeneas, Jesus Christ maketh thee whole: arise, and make thy bed.** This command probably meant to get up and begin carrying on a normal life. This miracle caused many of the city of Lydda and the surrounding plain of Sharon to turn to the Lord.

36-38. Now there was at Joppa a certain disciple named Tabitha. Today known as Jaffa, Joppa was a Mediterranean coastal city about ten miles northwest of Lydda. There also was a Christian community in which a certain disciple was named Tabitha or **Dorcas** (Gr *dorkas*, meaning gazelle), who had endeared herself to that Christian community because she **was full of good works and alms deeds.** However, Dorcas had fallen ill and died and was prepared for burial having been placed in the upper chamber.

Apparently having heard of the healing of Aeneas by Peter, some disciple from Joppa sent to Lydda to fetch Peter, hoping that he could come and perform an even greater miracle on the behalf of their beloved Tabitha.

39-43. Peter quickly removed himself from Lydda and arrived in Joppa. There he saw the lifeless body of Tabitha already washed in accordance with the Jewish custom of "purification of the dead," and prepared in the upper room. She was surrounded by weeping widows who had come to display the coats and garments which Tabitha had made for them. "But Peter sent them and the other mourners out of the room, as he had seen his Master do before he raised Jairus' daughter from her death-bed; and then he uttered a short sentence differing only in one letter from the word of Jesus to Jairus' daughter. Whereas Jesus had said *Talitha cumi* (Mk 5:41), Peter now said *Tabitha qumi* (Tabitha arise) (F. F. Bruce, *The Book of the Acts,* p. 212). The result of the mighty power of the Spirit of God in Peter was that Tabitha opened her eyes, sat up, gave her hand to Peter, and he presented her alive to all the saints and widows who waited outside. Again, due to this miracle, many throughout the region round about Joppa believed in the Lord. Peter had a fruitful ministry there, being accommodated by the hospitality of one Simon a tanner.

B. Cornelius Receives the Gospel.
   10:1-48.

10:1-8. The city of Caesarea, the major seaport city of New Testament Palestine, was located some distance up the coast from Joppa. Here a man named Cornelius lived. He was a **centurion of the band called the Italian band.** The word translated "band" (Gr *speira*) is equivalent to the Latin word *cohors* (cohort). A cohort, or tenth part of a legion, may have consisted of up to six hundred men, and was divided into centuries each commanded by a

centurion. But when spoken of auxiliary provincial troops, it meant a regiment of a full thousand men. Thus Cornelius would have been one of the leaders of a rather sizable group of Roman soldiers.

In addition to Luke's information that this man was a Roman soldier, we also learn that he was a devout man, and one that feared God. This would place Cornelius among the "God-fearers" who were so prevalent in the first century. These were Gentiles who were not prepared to enter into the Jewish community as proselytes but were attracted to the morality and ethical standards of the monotheistic Jewish religion. Therefore some of them attended the synagogue services and were greatly knowledgeable in the practices of the Jewish religion. Hence, Cornelius gave much alms and prayed to God.

One day Cornelius had a vision of an angel of God coming to him with a vital message. At first he was afraid; but then was assured that his alms-giving and prayers had been looked upon by God with favor. The language of verse 4 is couched in similar sacrificial terms as are found in the book of Leviticus.

The message which the angel had for Cornelius was that he should call for one named Simon, whose surname was Peter, and who lodged with one Simon the tanner in the city of Joppa. Cornelius was assured that Simon Peter would be able to tell Cornelius why the Lord had appeared unto him in such an unusual way. The centurion wasted no time in dispatching two of his household servants, and a devout soldier as himself, south to the city of Joppa.

9-18. Peter went up upon the housetop to pray. The forthcoming meeting between Cornelius and Peter was well prepared by the Lord. Both Cornelius and Simon Peter had a vision paving the way for their meeting. Peter's vision came the day after that of Cornelius. The representatives of the Roman centurion were almost to Caesarea when Peter went to the top of Simon's house to pray. The quietest and most retiring spot in an Eastern house is the housetop (cf. I Sam 9:25-26). At about noon, as was the Jewish custom, Peter entered into a period known as "the midday prayer." While praying, and waiting for lunch to be prepared, **he fell into a trance.** In this trance Peter saw the heavens open and a vessel descending unto him that appeared to be **a great sheet knit at the four corners.** This huge sheet was being lowered from heaven and inside were **all manner of four footed beasts . . . and wild beasts, and creeping things, and fowls of the air.** The distinction between clean and unclean was very sharply drawn in the levitical law (Lev 11:41-44; 20:25; see also Deut 14:3-20).

To the complete amazement and astonishment of Peter, a voice came to him, **Rise, Peter; kill, and eat.** Peter's ancestral sensitivities at this point must have been at the breaking point. His Jewish conscience would never permit him to eat that which was prohibited by levitical law and thus his answer was, **Not so, Lord,** claiming that he had never eaten anything that was unclean. But Peter was about to learn his first major lesson in the new covenant. The abolition of Jewish ceremonial laws was about to be graphically illustrated to the apostle. Since the Lord Jesus' original command and commission to the disciples was "go not into the way of the Gentiles, and into any city of the Samaritans enter ye not. But go rather to the lost sheep of the house of Israel" (Mt 10:5-6). Peter could not readily accept the commission he was receiving now. But on the cross of Calvary God had already broken down the middle wall of partition (Eph 2:14-18) between the Jews and Gentiles and thus the voice from heaven spoke to Peter again a second time saying, **What God hath cleansed, that call not thou common** (unclean). Three times this interchange of conversation took place.

And while Peter doubted what he had seen in the vision, nevertheless he had no time to dwell on that doubt. Immediately the representatives of Cornelius appeared at Simon's house, standing before the gate and inquiring whether or not Peter lodged there. The apostle was still on the roof in a trance, but what he had learned was soon to be practiced. God is not looking for a debate from Peter, just obedience.

22-29. Upon hearing that the men from Cornelius had arrived, Peter immediately made his way down to greet them. This could have been a very tense moment, Jew meeting Gentiles, but in fact appears to be one filled with great hospitality. The men informed Peter that Cornelius was a centurion, a God-fearer, a man who was well respected among the Jews. Immediately Peter invited them in, undoubtedly to share the meal for which he had been waiting, and to give them lodging. It was now close to evening and the journey of more than thirty miles back to Caesarea could not have been undertaken immediately. Thus, the next day, Peter, accompanied by six other Christians from Joppa, went with the men to Caesarea.

The day after that they entered the city and found Cornelius anxiously awaiting their arrival. When Peter approached, **Cornelius met him, and fell down at his feet, and worshipped him.** Probably this reaction was evoked from the unusual character of the vision which instructed Cornelius to seek Peter's counsel. The word "worshipped" (Gr *proskyneō*) is one that is commonly used for any act of reverence or respect. But being a strict Jew, Peter could not allow Cornelius to behave in such a manner, and commanded him, **Stand up; I myself also am a man.**

When Peter was invited into Cornelius' house he undoubtedly did not expect to find the great company of kinsmen and friends of the centurion. His immediate thought was to justify his presence among them and give adequate explanation for this apparent breech of Jewish law. Jews and Gentiles had no ordinary social intercourse between each other. Thus it would be highly unlikely for Peter to enter the home of a Roman centurion. Because of the levitical dietary restrictions, the least likely practice Peter, as a Jew, would find himself engaging in was eating at the table of a Gentile. Nevertheless this was about to take place. In explaining how uncommon it was for a Jew to keep company with a Gentile, **or come unto one of another nation,** Luke uses a word (Gr *allophylos* "one of another nation") which is found only here in the New Testament. However, it is a common expression like "Philistines"(see Jud 3:3). Thus Peter is saying that it is highly unlikely that he would dine in the household of an "uncircumcised Philistine."

What then was his reason for doing so? **God hath showed me that I should not call any man common or unclean.** Hence, Peter immediately began to inquire of Cornelius the reason for which he requested Peter's presence.

30-33. In answer to the apostle's question, Cornelius explains that four days ago he was fasting when he received a vision from the Lord. He saw a man standing before him in bright clothing. This angel of the Lord instructed him to send to the house of Simon the tanner in Joppa and request a man named Simon, whose surname is Peter, to come to Caesarea and speak with him. Cornelius did not hesitate but immediately dispatched his representatives to bring Peter to this house. Cornelius still does not understand exactly why this has happened, but he shows a complete readiness to receive whatever Peter has to say. He says, **Now therefore are we all here present before God, to hear all things that are commanded thee of God.** On that occasion Peter had a captive audience, those who received willingly what the Holy Spirit of God impressed upon him to say. God has led both Peter and

Cornelius to this hour. It is evident in this transitional book of Acts that He has also led both the Jews and Gentiles to this hour. It is evident that the Gentile writer Luke recognized the importance of this hour because of the space he dedicated to it in his narrative. The program of God stands sure, but in the eyes of Peter and Cornelius, and those who witnessed these events, this program appears to be undergoing fundamental changes. For the first time Jew and Gentile could sit down with some measure of commonality.

34-43. Then Peter opened his mouth. This expression is a unique one which is generally used to introduce something of extreme importance. The weighty material which follows is perfectly in keeping with the expression. What Peter has to say in the next verses will run counter to centuries of racial prejudice between Jews and Gentiles.

The great lesson which Peter has learned is that God does not play favorites. **God is no respecter of persons.** Anyone from any nation may be saved, all on the same basis of faith. Any man who does justly and loves mercy and walks humbly before God, may receive the salvation provided by God (Mic 6:8). The animosity toward Gentiles and the unbelievability that Gentiles could even be saved, doesn't appear at all to enter into Peter's speech. What was once impossible, is now possible. What was once unacceptable is now, by the grace of God, acceptable. What was once unheard of, is now being boldly spoken by Peter. Gentiles may actually be saved in the same way that Jews have been saved.

At this point, Peter summarizes the life and teaching of the Lord Jesus, and the disciples' relationship to Him. He makes reference to the fact that Jesus' ministry was in both Judaea and Galilee after His baptism by John (vs. 37) and that the ministry of the Lord Jesus was not only approved by God the Father and God the Spirit, but was accompanied by signs of their approval (vs. 38). The disciples were witnesses to the death of the Lord Jesus (vs. 39) but many were witnesses to the fact that He was raised from the dead on the third day (vs. 40). Those who witnessed the post-resurrection activity of the Lord Jesus were chosen by God to do so and were commanded to testify to the world that Jesus Christ was indeed alive (vss. 41-42). The end result of the life and death of the Lord Jesus was not only predicted by the prophets but has proved to be the only entrance into salvation. **Through his name whosoever believeth in him shall receive remission of sins.** It is now obvious to Peter that "whosoever" included both Jews and Gentiles.

44-48. The Holy Ghost fell on all them which heard the word. Here is the second incident of a special, non-repeated, transitional baptism of the Spirit of God. The first was the descending of the Spirit to the Samaritans who believed (8:17). Like that incident, this too was the baptism of a group of believers, not an individual. Like that event, this baptism occurred to open a new field of evangelistic ministry and give validity to that new field. So unusual was this event that even those Jews who accompanied Peter were astonished **because that on the Gentiles also was poured out the gift of the Holy Ghost.** The baptism of the Spirit of God, and the subsequent speaking with tongues magnifying God, is clearly not in the context of everyday salvation experience. As the restrictive preaching of the original Twelve was broadened to the Samaritans and now to the Gentiles, it was necessary for them to have a similar experience to the Jews at Pentecost. This event, however, has been incorrectly called "the Pentecost of the Gentile World." This is not a Pentecost for non-Jews. It is a unique, one-time-only occurrence which was designed to show the Jews the validity of Gentile salvation. There would have been good reason to doubt whether Cornelius and his household were ac-

tually saved or not, had not his salvation experience been accompanied by the baptism of the Spirit and speaking in tongues. During that age these were characteristic evidences of salvation. The fact that this occurs in historical context should be reason enough not to assume that this will become a normative or continuing practice.

Can any man forbid water, that these should not be baptized. Peter recognizes that as they have received the outward manifestation of the Spirit of God in their hearts, it also necessary for them to show the world that they have identified with the death, burial, and resurrection of the Lord Jesus; thus, **he commanded them to be baptized in the name of the Lord.** Peter does not appear to have baptized these converts himself, anymore than Paul did his converts (I Cor 1:13-17).

C. Peter Defends His Ministry. 11:1-18.

11:1-3. Long before Peter returned to Jerusalem, the news of the conversion of Cornelius preceded him. Although the text makes specific reference to **the apostles and brethren that were in Judaea,** undoubtedly the character of Peter's revolutionary activities in Judaism must have come to the attention of the High Priest and others of more traditional Judaism. Thus both the more zealous Jewish believers and the greatly zealous Jewish unbelievers were waiting for Peter's arrival and explanation as to why he entered the house and ate with the heathen.

It is unnatural for Luke, a Gentile himself, to make reference to these Jews as **the circumcision.** The distinction is again seen in the record of what the Jews inquired of Peter, **Thou wentest in to men uncircumcised.** It is clear that the harmony which existed in Caesarea did not exist yet in Jerusalem.

4-17. Peter apparently understood his best defense to be a straightforward offense. Thus, **Peter rehearsed the matter from the beginning and ex-**

pounded it. In no way did Peter shrink away from giving complete details of what had happened at both Joppa and Caesarea. Quickly and completely he related to them of the trance into which he fell in Joppa (vs. 5) and the great sheet which he saw coming down out of heaven fastening his eyes on this unbelievable object, and noticing the content, Peter was shaken by a voice from heaven saying, **Arise, Peter; slay and eat** (vs. 7). As one would expect in rehearsing these events for the circumcision, Peter makes direct reference to his initial opposition to this proposition (vs. 8) but also makes sure that they understand that it is God who is speaking to him (vs. 9).

Again when he was approached by the representatives of Cornelius, Peter alludes to the fact that **the Spirit bade me go with them, nothing doubting** (vs. 12). Then too there was the account that Cornelius had been prepared by his own vision from the Lord to receive Peter. Cornelius was told that Peter would tell him words **whereby thou and all thy house shall be saved** (vs. 14).

Now Peter reaches the climax of his account. He makes reference to the fact that the Holy Ghost fell on them at Caesarea, in the same manner **as on us at the beginning.** In concluding the defense of his actions, he makes reference to the teaching of the Lord Jesus concerning baptism and, in accordance with that teaching, these Gentile believers were baptized with water. Finally, and most forcefully, Peter informs the circumcision that these Gentiles have **believed on the Lord Jesus Christ,** even as the Jews had done. Peter's terminal statement is phrased in the form of a question, to which there is no obvious answer, and from which there is no retreat: **What was I, that I could withstand God?** If the Jewish believers of the church at Jerusalem are to question Peter's action, they must first question the direct leading of God the Father, provision of salvation by God

the Son, and verifying signs of God the Spirit. Absolutely no one was ready to do that.

18. They held their peace, and glorified God. No rebuttal was made to Peter's argument; none could be. It has now become evident to the Jewish believers of Jerusalem that Gentiles may indeed become believers as well. It was also within the plan of God to grant **repentance unto life** to those with whom the Jews would not associate. In the minds of Jewish Christians, the evangelization of Gentiles would mean a drastic reappraisal of their own position before God. With this initial foray into previously untapped Gentile territory, the door has been opened for a flood of salvational activity on behalf of non-Jews throughout the world. The door which was cracked by Peter, was crashed by Paul. Most who read these words must do so out of thankfulness and gratitude toward God for the event that occurred on that day centuries ago in Caesarea.

D. Continued Persecution.
   11:19-12:25.

19-21. After a brief interlude in which the ministry of Philip, the conversion of Saul of Tarsus, and the varied ministry of Peter are elaborated upon, Luke now returns in his narrative to the point of the story at which he departed in 8:1. Under the dint of fierce persecution which arose when Stephen was stoned, the believing Jews of Jerusalem were scattered as far away as Phoenicia, Cyprus, and Antioch. Phoenicia is a narrow strip of coastline in northern Palestine, one hundred twenty miles long and only about twelve miles wide. It extends from the river Eleutherus southward to approximately the region of Mt. Carmel. Cyprus is an island just off the coast of, and in sight of, Phoenicia. The historians Philo and Josephus both speak of a Jewish colony on this island. Antioch, some fifteen miles from the mouth of the Orontes River, was the capital of the Greek kingdom of Syria. It was founded by Seleucus Nicator in 300 B.C. in honor of his father Antiochus, one of Alexander the Great's generals. Antioch was made a free city in 64 B.C. when Syria was incorporated into the Roman Empire. The ministry of persecuted Jews who fled north and westward to these areas was characterized by **preaching the word to none but unto the Jews only.**

However, there were some bold men of Cyprus and Cyrene (a city in the province of Lybia in Africa) who dared to speak **unto the Grecians, preaching the Lord Jesus.** These Grecians are not to be thought of as those Greek-speaking Jews mentioned earlier. There is good manuscript evidence that the rendering here ought to be "Greeks," instead of "Hellenists" (Grecian Jews). If this rendering is followed, it would more greatly substantiate the reason for the statement **unto the Jews only** in the preceding verse. Men of Cyprus and Cyrene had actually begun to preach the gospel to Greeks at Antioch. Also the reference to **preaching the Lord Jesus** tends to make an understanding of the Grecians being actually non-Jews all the more probable. If they were actually Jews, the evangelist would refer to Jesus as Messiah, the fulfillment of the hope of Israel. Instead, however, he refers to him in Greek terms, "Lord" (Gr *kyrios*), and "Saviour" (Gr *sōtēr*). Since the hand of the Lord was on these efforts, **a great number believed, and turned unto the Lord.** Although an Ethiopian eunuch and a Roman centurion have already been saved, this preaching of the gospel of Jesus Christ to the Gentiles is on a far broader scale than the Jews had ever seen before.

22-26. These things came unto the ears of the church which was in Jerusalem. It was only a short time until the events which had taken place in Antioch were made known unto the church at Jerusalem. As had been the situation when Peter and John were dispatched to Samaria to investigate the missionary activity of Philip there, so too now the Jerusalem church must send someone to Antioch to do the same. Who better to investigate the activites of Jews from Cyprus than a Jew from Cyprus. Thus Barnabas was sent forth by the Jerusalem church. Whatever report Barnabas returned with could be trusted, for Barnabas **was a good man, and full of the Holy Ghost and faith.** Thus, upon arrival at Antioch, when Barnabas viewed the situation there and saw that at Antioch a great number of Gentiles had been saved by the grace of God, he **was glad, and exhorted them all.**

Apparently Barnabas was to do more than just observe the activities of the Antiochene Christians. He must have become the advisor to them from the mother church in Jerusalem. But Barnabas quickly realized that the job was too big for one man, for Antioch was a large city, with a population at this time of perhaps five hundred thousand or more. Therefore he began to consider those who might assist him in this task. He needed someone who was of stellar quality and character, and yet someone who could sympathize with both the Jews and the Gentiles who were being saved. There was no question in the mind of Barnabas; there was only one man. **Then departed Barnabas to Tarsus for to seek Saul.**

Some years earlier Saul of Tarsus had been escorted to Caesarea by the Christians of Jerusalem, and from there he took a ship to his native Tarsus of Cilicia. Now Barnabas travels to Tarsus in order to seek out Saul who probably had been disinherited for his commitment to Christ (Phil 3:8), and was undoubtedly buried in the mass of humanity at Tarsus, engaged in tentmaking. All this time Saul was being prepared by the Lord for a greater work and he was patiently waiting for the time of the initiation of that work to come. Apparently Barnabas did not immediately locate Saul, for the verb "to seek" (Gr *anazēteō*) implies a searching with great difficulty. But when he had found him, he brought him unto Antioch. The next year in Antioch proved to be one of great accomplishment. Under the ministry of Barnabas and Saul, the Christians of Antioch grew both in depth and number. **And the disciples were called Christians first in Antioch.** This refers to a practice with which the nimble wits of Antioch prided themselves. They are known to have coined words to describe persons and events. Perhaps as a derogatory term originally, Antiochenes called those who had claimed Jesus as Messiah the "Christ-ones." Thus, as an accurate historian, Luke did not hesitate to record that the followers of the Lord first came to be popularly known as Christians at Antioch.

27-30. And in these days came prophets from Jerusalem unto Antioch. In the first century church, a prophet belonged to a recognized order in the church (cf. 2:17-18; 13:1; 20:23; 21:9-10; I Cor 12:28-29; Eph 4:11). One of these prophets was a man named Agabus who indicated, prophesying under the influence of the Spirit of God, **that there should be great dearth throughout all the world.** Luke is interested in pinpointing the exact time of this famine. Thus he goes one step further in identifying it by saying that the famine occurred in the days of Claudius Caesar (41-54 A.D.). Manys extrabiblical sources make note of a succession of bad harvests and extreme famine throughout the entire Roman Empire, especially Palestine, during the reign of Claudius.

In response to this prophetic announcement, the believers at the church of Antioch **determined to send relief unto the brethren** who lived in Jerusalem and its environs. Thus, they set aside a certain percentage of their income to collect a contribution to be sent to the believers of Judaea. This relief fund was to be sent to the elders **by the hands of Barnabas and Saul.** This social and communal interest the church at Antioch had for the church at Jerusalem is not only a pleasing expression of the love of the Lord Jesus for the brethren (Jn 10:35), but it marks the beginning of the Pauline practice of accepting the responsibility for caring not only for the souls of those to whom he ministered but for the bodies as well. The church at the end of the twentieth century could well take a lesson from the church at the end of the first century.

12:1-2. Herod the king. The Herod mentioned in this chapter is Herod Agrippa I. Agrippa I was the grandson of Herod the Great and his first wife named Mariamne. This Mariamne was a Hasmonean princess and therefore provided the tie between Herod and the Jews. Born in 11 B.C., Agrippa I was sent to Rome to live upon the execution of his father, Aristobulus in 7 B.C. While a young lad in Rome he became intimate friends with members of the imperial family, especially with Gaius, who was the grandnephew of the emperor Tiberias. In A.D. 37, Gaius succeeded Tiberias as emperor and, in consequence of their long friendship, he awarded the tetrarchies of Philip and Lysanias in southern Syria to his friend Agrippa. It was at this point that Agrippa took the title "king." Some two years later, Galilee and Peraea were added to Agrippa's kingdom when his uncle Herod Antipas was deposed by emperor Gaius. However, Agrippa's kingdom was even further enhanced by the addition of Judaea in A.D. 41 when, upon the assassination of Gaius, Claudius became the Roman emperor. In the fact that he was a descendant of the Hasmonean royal family, Agrippa enjoyed unusual popularity among the Jews. He went out of his way to win their support. Thus it is not surprising to find a notation in Luke's historical account concerning Agrippa's persecution of the nemesis of the Jews, the early church.

And he killed James . . . with the sword. The first of the apostles to fall victim to martyrdom, and the only one recorded on the pages of the Sacred Text, was James, the son of Zebedee. His death fulfills the promise of Jesus that he would drink of His cup and be baptized with His baptism (Mk 10:39). Although this promise was made to both James and John, John outlived all the other apostles, but nevertheless suffered "for the Word of God and the testimony of Jesus" (Rev 1:9). In his *Ecclesiastical History* (ii. 9) Eusebius preserves a tradition, which was first found in Clement of Alexandria, that the officer who was attached to James and commissioned with guarding him, was so impressed with the apostle's witness, that before James was martyred, this officer confessed Christ as Saviour and was beheaded with the apostle.

3-7. He saw it pleased the Jews. Agrippa's policy to maintain a spirit of goodwill with the Jews got a real boost in the death of James. So elated were they that this apostle was martyred, Agrippa next attempted to take the life of Peter. Peter was apprehended and put into prison on the first day of the festival of unleavened bread. He was therefore incarcerated throughout the entire festival with the intent to bring him to public trial after this period had ended.

The apprehension of Peter did not discourage the Jerusalem church. Rather it set them to praying (Jas 5:16). On the night preceding the day Herod Agrippa I would have brought Peter forth for trial and execution, a very strange phenomenon occurred in that prison. Sleeping between two soldiers, and bound with two sturdy chains, with the keepers of the prison standing guard just outside the door, **the angel of the Lord came upon him, and a light shined in the prison.** The light apparently emanated from the angel and Peter was quickly roused, probably unaware of what was happening to him. When the angel struck Peter on the side to awaken him, his chains, the passports to his execution, fell from his hands.

8-11. Gird thyself . . . Cast thy garment about thee, and follow me. The instruction of the angel to Peter was to prepare himself for leaving the prison. Peter was still in a daze, not fully knowing what was happening to him. He wasn't quite aware whether this was indeed a vision or in fact someone leading him from the depths of the prison. After leaving his cell, Peter successfully, by the leading of the angel, made his way through the first and second wards, the two guarded checkpoints before the gate that led to the city. Apparently with his garment cast about him, and in the obvious power of the Spirit of God, the guards permitted Peter and the angel to pass through these two wards. There would be no hope, however, of passing through the iron gate for it was securely shut. However, this miraculous escape would not be prevented by a locked gate **which opened to them of his own accord.** With the gate opening unaided by anyone, the angel and Peter passed on through one street, and at that point the angel departed from him. Once Peter found himself alone he had opportunity for the first time to appraise his situation. **And when Peter was come to himself.** With the cool night air in his face, and the immediate danger of the prison behind him, Peter could now fully appreciate **that the Lord hath sent His angel** to deliver Peter out of the hand of Herod and spoil the anticipation of the Jews the next morning. Peter sized up the situation correctly: this indeed was a miracle of God effected by the prayers of righteous saints.

12-15. Once Peter had come to his senses, his first reaction was to apprise the other disciples of his release. Therefore he made his way to a well-known meeting place for believers; **he came to the house of Mary the mother of John.** This is the first introduction to a man who will play a vital role in the transmission and recording of the gospel over the next thirty years. John Mark is the son of Mary and it is to their house that Peter made his way. As Peter knocked on the gate, his knock was answered by a young girl perhaps standing guard to warn the praying disciples of approaching Roman soldiers. The door upon which Peter knocked was the street door. This would give entrance to a courtyard or a long hallway from the street to the sanctuary of the home. When the young girl heard Peter's voice, and recognized it, **she opened not the gate for gladness.** So excited was Rhoda to hear the voice of the imprisoned apostle that in her excitement she neglected to let him in. Rather she ran and told the others that Peter was at the street gate. Their immediate response was one of disbelief. **Thou art mad.** So insistent was Rhoda that she had actually heard the voice of Peter, that those who prayed inside amended their assessment of Rhoda by assuming that perhaps she had heard a voice, although certainly not Peter's voice. Perhaps this was the voice of his angel who had come in Peter's stead.

16-19. But Peter continued knocking. Just as persistent as Rhoda was in insisting that Peter was outside the door, so persistent was Peter in knocking upon the door. There was but one way to solve this puzzle; those inside must answer the door. When they did, and they saw Peter standing there; **they were astonished.** Peter made a gesture which told them not to say a word for he was yet unaware that his escape had not been discovered. His immediate thought was for the others and he said, **Go show these things unto James, and to the brethren.** James, the brother of the Lord Jesus and a pillar of the Jerusalem church, and the brethren or elders (11:30) would have to be warned because, with the escape of Peter, their lives would be in danger as well.

Now as soon as it was day, there was no small stir among the soldiers. One can imagine the consternation that would have occurred in the minds of the two soldiers on either side of Peter, chained now to no one, the soldiers who stood guard outside the cell, now with no one to guard, and those who guarded the first two wards leading to the outside of the prison. No one had an explanation as to what happened to their prisoner. When Herod looked for him and the report came that he was not to be found **he examined the keepers, and commanded that they should be put to death.** The penalty for losing a prisoner was severe in the Roman Empire, and these men took very seriously their responsibility in keeping prisoners secure. But now nothing could be done; the prisoner was gone. Because of this, Herod Agrippa I departed from Jerusalem and went to reside at Caesarea, his other capital.

Although these verses do not advance the narrative, they do provide great insight into the death of Herod Agrippa I. Luke is always interested in keeping a historical perspective in the book of Acts. Thus he includes these verses.

20-23. For an unknown reason, the people of Tyre and Sidon have fallen out of favor in the eyes of Agrippa. This was a very precarious situation for them since the seaboard Phoenician cities of Tyre and Sidon depended entirely on the green fields of Galilee for their food supply. This had been the case for centuries (cf. I Kgs 5:9 ff.). Realizing that they must again be restored to the good graces of the king, residents of this town befriended the king's chamberlain, Blastus.

At this point Luke's account is paralleled by an extrabiblical account which provided confirmation of the accuracy and validity of Acts. Josephus (*Antiquities* xix. 8.2) records that on the birthday of the emperor (**upon a set day**), Agrippa held a large festival in which he donned a robe made of silver throughout. Entering the theater of Caesarea at the break of day, the silver glittered in the morning sunlight and was so resplendent that all who looked upon it were immediately enamored with the king. Luke records that **the people gave a shout, saying, It is the voice of a God and not of a man.** Josephus says the cry invoked by the crowd was, "Be gracious unto us! Hitherto we have reverenced thee as a man, but henceforth we acknowledge thee to be of more than mortal nature." Agrippa relished and revelled in the plaudits that had been thrown his way. He was claimed to be as a god; and he did not deny the claim. Therefore, **the Lord smote him, because he gave not God the glory.** Herod's receiving the praise due only to Jehovah, and his subsequent death, are not without precedent. But his own particular species of blasphemy is recorded by Luke to be the single cause of his death.

24-25. But the word of God grew and multiplied represents another of Luke's progress reports periodically seen in this historical account (cf. 6:7; 9:31). At this point Barnabas and Saul set out from Jerusalem taking with them John Mark. They apparently had just come to the city with the relief offering collected from the Antiochene believers and are now returning to Antioch. The death of Herod Agrippa I. probably occurred prior to their departure from Antioch.

IV. PAUL'S FIRST MISSIONARY JOURNEY: ITS EFFECT. 13:1-15:35.
A. Commissioning of Barnabas and Saul. 13:1-13.

13:1-3. The first official Gentile mission was carried on by Paul and Barnabas, who were sent by the **church at Antioch to** Cyprus and the cities in the southern part of the Roman province of **Galatia.** This church was characterized by many outstanding Christians and **prophets and teachers. Simeon . . . called Niger,** the Latin word meaning "black," was apparently a nickname for his dark complexion and

suggests that he was perhaps of African origin. Some have suggested that he may have been Simon of Cyrene (cf. Mk 15:21) who carried Jesus' cross. The designation for **Manaen . . . brought up with Herod** means that he was a "foster brother." This term was generally used of children who were brought up in the royal court and later the phrase was retained as an actual title. **Herod** is Herod Antipas who ruled Galilee and Peraea between 4 B.C. and A.D. 39. The relationship between them is one of the remarkable apologetic notices of the book of Acts. Ladd (*Wycliffe Bible Commentary,* p. 427) suggests that the **prophets** gave or were given direct revelation from God by the Holy Spirit and the **teachers** were gifted in the interpretation of that revelation. Thus, the utterance of the **Holy Ghost** probably came through a prophet. During a time of fasting and prayer, which was always especially significant for the early church, the Holy Spirit designated the two most eminent and gifted leaders among the entire group to become the first actual missionaries. While it is true that every Christian was to carry on the mission of the church (cf. Mt 28:20, notes), these men became the first actual "sent-ones." It should be noted that **they . . . laid their hands on them** refers to the church at Antioch as the sending agency. Thus in its purest form, the New Testament local church sent forth missionary representatives from the midst of its own congregation. In the book of Acts we find no reference to mission boards or organizations as such. Nor do we find single individuals sending forth missionaries apart from the commission of the church. In other words, as the Great Commission was given to the apostles who were to become the foundation of the church, it was, therefore, given to the church, not to individuals. The laying on of hands did not impart any special power nor qualification to the missionaries, but "expressed its fellowship with Barnabas and Paul and recognized them as its delegates or 'apostles'" (F. F. Bruce, p. 261).

4-6. Seleucia (vs. 4) was the port of Antioch from which they sailed for **Cyprus,** the large island off the shore in the Mediterranean Sea. It was formally annexed by Rome in 57 B.C. and later became a province governed by an imperial legate. After 22 B.C. Augustus gave its control to the Roman Senate and it was thereafter administered by a proconsul. Thus, Luke accurately indicates the magistrate's title as "governor." **Salamis** (vs. 5) was the eastern port of Cyprus and was its largest city. There were several synagogues there because of the large Jewish population. **John** Mark accompanied the apostles. He was the cousin of Barnabas whom they had recently taken with them from Jerusalem to Antioch (cf. 12:25). He was to serve as their **minister,** or "attendant." Some have suggested that his responsibility was that of instructing new converts in the Gospel. He later would write the Gospel of Mark. **Paphos** was the official capital of the province in those days. **Elymas** (vs. 8) is referred to as a **sorcerer** (Gr *magos*) and a **false prophet.** In essence he was a magician or astrologer attached to the political entourage as an "advisor" to the governor **Sergius Paulus.** Some have suggested that he is to be identified with Lucius Sergius Paulus who is known to have been one of the curators of the Tiber during the reign of Claudius.

8-12. Elymas was an alternate name for Bar-Jesus whose original Aramaic name means "Son of Salvation" but was in fact a "magician" and "false prophet." As he sensed the governor was accepting the message of Barnabas and Saul, he realized his own position would be endangered. Therefore, he attempted to sway Sergius Paulus **from the faith.** While this passage uses interchangeable names, it very interestingly shifts at this point from **Saul** to **Paul.** Paul is the Greek form of the Semitic name, Saul. Because of the correlation to the governor's name, and the fact

that they are now in distinctly Greek-influenced territory, Paul changes the outward usage of his name as a matter of cultural identification with the people whom he is trying to reach with the gospel. Paul's rebuke of this false prophet is stern and straightforward. He calls him a **child of the devil** and **enemy of all righteousness.** He rebukes his perversion of the truth and strikes him with temporary blindness. Amazed and stunned by the power of these servants of the Lord over his resident magician, the proconsul **believed . . . the doctrine of the Lord** (vs. 12). W. Ramsey (*The Bearing of Recent Discovery on the Trustworthiness of the New Testament,* p. 165) argues that there is evidence that the next two generations of his family were known as Christians.

13. Leaving Barnabas' native land of Cyprus, they sailed to the country bordering Paul's homeland. **Pamphylia** was a district on the coast of Asia Minor which included the city of **Perga,** some twenty miles inland. For some unexplained reason John Mark forsook them and **returned to Jerusalem.** Speculation at this point needs to be contained since we are not told why he left. It could have been due to news of an emergency, fear of strange territory, or uncertainty as to the new change of direction in their mission. It seems obvious later that Paul looked upon his action as inexcusable desertion and refused to give him a second chance (cf. 15:37). On the other hand, Barnabas reconciled with Mark and recovered him for effective ministry in the future.

A number of important and practical observations can be made from this incident. Paul, standing for the truth and the severity of their mission, demanded total allegiance which later led him to a new partner. Barnabas, however, equally a servant of the Lord, was able to restore one who had fallen as his new partner. An objective look at this incident makes it difficult to judge which was right or wrong, if indeed either were. The unavoidable "split" is ultimately overruled by the Lord to accomplish a double ministry.

B. The First Foray into Asia Minor. 13:14-52.

14-16. The phrase **Antioch in Pisidia** is mistranslated in the AV. Actually Antioch was not in Pisidia but near the region of Pisidia and, thus, came to be known as Pisidian Antioch. The so-called "South Galatian" theory and the "North Galatian" theory arise from the designation of this province. Most conservative commentators hold to Ramsay's view that the Epistle to the Galatians was written to these cities of southern Galatia (cf. Ladd, Tenney, etc.). Others (Bruce) hold the opposite. Ramsay (*St. Paul the Traveller,* pp. 94 ff.) infers from Galatians 4:13 that Paul caught malaria in the low-lying territory around Perga and went to recuperate in the higher altitudes of southern Galatia. Following their normal custom, Paul and Barnabas went to the synagogue of the Jewish community on the Sabbath day. Paul seemed to give great importance to the evangelization of Roman colonies (such as this one) which were stationed at strategic points along the imperial roads within the empire. The **rulers of the synagogue** were not clergymen but lay leaders or officers who were given the authority to invite anyone from the audience to give a word of exhortation. Notice that **Paul stood up** and that he beckoned **with his hand.** Thus, we observe something of the authoritative presentation of his message as he both stands to speak and gestures to the audience. The **Men of Israel** were Jews and **ye that fear God** were Gentiles who worshipped the God of the Jews and accepted the demands of the law (cf. 10:2).

17-41. Paul's sermon in the synagogue in Pisidian Antioch recounted the history of God's deliverance of the Jewish nation from the time of Moses through the reign of David. Several important dates are given within this message. The **forty years . . . in the wilderness** (vs. 18) and the **four hundred and fifty years** (vs. 20) **in the land of Canaan** (vs. 19). The **seven nations** conquered **in the land of Canaan** are listed in Deuteronomy 7:1: "the Hittite, the Girgashite, the Amorite, the Canaanite, the Perizzite, the Hivite, and the Jebusite." The **four hundred and fifty years** may be intended to cover the period up to David's reign or the entire four hundred year period of sojourn in Egypt, along with the forty years of wandering in the wilderness and ten years of the initial period of conquest until the actual distribution of the land (cf. Josh 14). Paul especially identifies the line of God's promised Messiah through **David . . . their king** (vs. 22). God's **promise** has been kept to Israel in providing a **Saviour, Jesus** (vs. 23). The reference to John the Baptist (vs. 24), his preaching, and **the baptism of repentance** seems to provide very early authoritative reference to the historicity of John's ministry as it is quoted here by the Apostle Paul. One should also note the connection between John's "baptism of repentance" and the people of "Israel," indicating, as do the Gospels, that John's ministry was not that of initiating the church but bringing to a conclusion the ministry of the Old Testament prophets.

The resurrection of Christ is the central theme of victory in Paul's sermon as it was in the majority of New Testament evangelistic messages. Notice that the gospel centers in the death, burial, and resurrection of Christ in this sermon. It should be observed that true gospel preaching does not really occur until this central theme of the person and work of Christ in relation to salvation has been declared. The agents of His message are called **witnesses** (Gr *martys,* from which we derive "martyr"). These messengers of God were declaring the **glad tidings** (vs. 32) of the

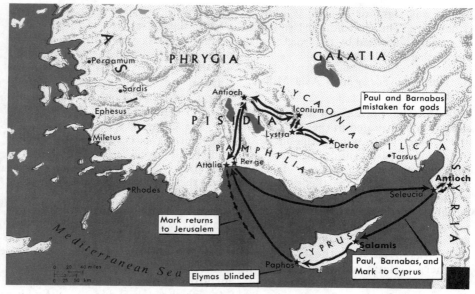

The First Missionary Journey of Paul

promise which God had made to their fathers and was now fulfilled in their lifetimes.

In verse 35 Paul quotes Psalm 16:10 as referring to Christ since it could not refer to David who had died and remained dead. Therefore it must refer to his promised descendant, the Messiah, whom Paul was now declaring to be Jesus Christ. The fact that Christ rose from the dead literally and physically is emphasized by the statement that he **saw no corruption** (vs. 37). On the basis of his triumphal death and resurrection, **forgiveness of sins** could now be offered to Paul's hearers. The key to receiving these benefits is faith. So that **all that believed are justified** (vs. 39). Justification (Gr *dikaioō*) involves the declaring of one righteous. This, then, is the good news ∙ or glad tidings of the gospel.

42-45. The excitement of this new message of forgiveness of sin and impartation of righteousness created a great deal of excitement. After the synagogue service, many indicated their readiness to accept the message. This reception seems to have been the greatest among the **religious proselytes** (vs. 43). During the week the report of the impact of this service was so great that by the next Sabbath the synagogue was filled with Gentiles desiring to hear Paul's message. Unfortunately, such a crowd of Gentiles provoked the Jews to envy and they began **contradicting and blaspheming** Paul's message.

46-52. In the face of this rejection by his Jewish listeners Paul reminded them that it was **necessary that the word of God should first have been spoken to** them and if they **judge** themselves **unworthy of everlasting life,** then he will **turn to the Gentiles** (vs. 46). This rejection on the part of the Jews at the synagogue, however, did not stop the influence upon the Gentiles, who **were glad, and glorified the word of the Lord.** Thus the response by the Gentile "God-fearers" seems to have been outstanding. Without a doubt this incident serves as the great turning point in Paul's missionary strategy. While he will continue to offer the gospel to the Jew first, he will concentrate his major attention on the most responsive element of society to whom he is preaching: the Gentiles. Thus, it is said that **as many as were ordained to eternal life believed** (vs. 48). At this point the primary significance of this reference to predestination is more historical than it is theological, though the one does not detract from the other. That God is sovereign in sending his messengers to carry his message wherever He will, is obvious from both Scripture and the history of the church. It is the living Lord of heaven, Jesus Himself, who directs the activities of His messengers and opens and closes the doors of opportunity which he sets before them! There can be no doubt that the apostles were to be personally responsible to carry the message of Christ to the hearts of men.

Again we notice that the "Acts of the Apostles" are really the Acts of Christ carried on through His apostles. Not only was the gospel rejected here by the majority of the Jews but they in turn **stirred up** the "devout and honorable women," or those of high and influential standing. The **persecution against Paul and Barnabas** is the first recorded such action against the missionary enterprise of the early church. The shaking of the **dust off their feet** implied their recognition of the rejection of their message and their rejection in turn of those who had refused Christ's salvation. Notice that the **disciples** were not discouraged by this incident but were **filled with joy and with the Holy Ghost** (vs. 52).

C. Iconium, Derbe, and Lystra.
14:1-28.

14:1-5. Following their previously established pattern, Paul and Barnabas went first to the **synagogue of the Jews** which was located ın **Iconium,** in the eastern district of **Phrygia.** The text indicates that **a great multitude** (vs. 1) believed of both Jews and Greeks. However the **unbelieving Jews** began to stir up opposition again to the message of the apostles. Since it took a while for

the opposition to become effective, Paul and his team were able to remain there preaching for a **long time.** In Luke's typically historical fashion, he does not indicate how long a period of time this actually was, making an exact chronology of Paul's travels almost impossible. Finally, the hostile Jews succeeded in inciting a riot which caused Paul and Barnabas to have to leave Iconium. Verse 3 indicates that the message of the gospel was the **word of His grace** and that their ministry was also accompanied by **signs and wonders,** or miracles.

6. The missionary team **fled into Lystra and Derbe** which are described as **cities of Lycaonia.** Luke's ancient contemporaries seemed to refer to these cities as being outside the district of Lycaonia, leading many scholars to challenge his accuracy. The investigation of this matter was the great turning point in archaeologist Sir William Ramsay's life as this reference caught his attention and careful examination of the matter proved Luke to be correct. Beginning as a critic of the veracity of the book of Acts, Ramsay became one of its strongest defenders (see *Bearing of Recent Discovery on the Trustworthiness of the New Testament,* ch. 3).

7-15. The missionary-apostles **preached the gospel** (Gr *euangelizomai*), or the "good news" of Christ's death and resurrection. The preaching was followed by the healing of a crippled man **who never had walked** (vs. 8). The miracle was based upon the man's **faith** and was total and instantaneous, for he immediately leaped and walked (vs. 10). The people became ecstatically overwhelmed and began to speak in their native dialect indicating that these men were **gods,** thinking that they were **Jupiter** and **Mercurius** (Mercury). Therefore, the **priest** of **Jupiter** brought a sacrifice unto them which resulted in their rebuking the people and reminding them that they were human beings who had come to turn them from **these vanities** unto the **living God.** Paul's usage of his term in pagan cities seems to be deliberate to distinguish God the Creator as the only God whom he represented. The names "Jupiter" and "Mercury" are the Latin equivalents for the Greek names of these gods, Zeus and Hermes, the father of the gods. Greek mythological literature is filled with references to these deities.

16-18. Paul's apologetic speech reminded them that **in times past** God had allowed the nations to go their own ways but had not left Himself **without witness.** The concept of this message was to show them that the great Creator-God was revealing Himself to them through nature, a message which Paul indicates in Romans 1-2 was sufficient to make men responsible to God, but not sufficient to bring them to salvation. The Lord had allowed the nations to go their own way, because they had previously rejected His way (cf. Gen 10-11, which forms the great turning point in God's dealing with man). The effect of the sermon was to restrain the people from honoring them as gods. There can be no doubt that the early Christian disciples did not consider themselves worthy of worship or sainthood. They rejected any special place of spiritual authority or recognition. They clearly saw themselves as men simply doing God's work by carrying out the commission which Christ had left to His church.

19-20. No reference is actually made to a Jewish synagogue in Lystra but probably such a synagogue existed for when the Jews from Antioch and Iconium came there they were able to raise up strong opposition against Paul. He was eventually **stoned** and left for **dead** (vs. 19). Paul evidently refers to this event in II Corinthians 11:24-25 where he mentions being caught up into the "third heaven." The abrupt nature of the narrative at this point seems to indicate a miraculous deliverance of some sort. Any man stoned in such a manner without receiving severe physical injuries, both

externally and internally, would be a miracle indeed! The reference in Galatians 6:17 to the "marks of Jesus" may well refer to the scars received from this stoning. There can be no underestimation of the shock which must have come upon the people of the city when Paul **rose up** (vs. 20) and came back into the city probably to continue his preaching. Note that the **disciples** were present at this "resurrection." The next day they left and went to **Derbe,** a frontier city of the province of Galatia. No opposition is recorded in this city where it is said they made many disciples.

21-25. Having completed this initial tour they returned to each city in reverse order. **Confirming the souls of the disciples** (vs. 22). This sets the pattern for the concept of "follow-up" work among new converts, whom they exhorted to **continue in the faith.** This does not mean that a born-again believer might stop believing and thus lose his salvation, but rather, emphasizes the importance of continued growth in the Christian life. This process of growth will bring us through **much tribulation** to enter **the kingdom of God,** which here must refer to heaven. The reference to "tribulation" is not to the Tribulation itself, but to the continued troubles and sufferings of the church throughout all ages. The fact that they **ordained them elders** in each church indicates that the leadership of each local congregation rested in the authority of its own men. While the leaders of the church at Jerusalem had spiritual influence over the local congregations, nowhere do we find any hierarchical structure in the early church. One predominant church did not overrule the affairs of another. Certainly the church at Jerusalem remained the spiritual standard during these early years because of its geographical proximity to the origin of the Christian faith. But even there great latitude was permitted toward the individual local congregations. The "elders" (Gr *presbuteros*) were spiritual leaders who shared the oversight of the church and from among whom a "bishop" or pastor was chosen as their leader. The elders were similar to the pastoral staff of most of our churches today. They engaged in the spiritual oversight of the church, whereas the deacons were designated as servants of the congregation.

24-28. The missionary team then **sailed to Antioch** from the seaport **Attalia.** Upon their return to their sending church they gathered them together and **rehearsed all that God had done.** Certainly this experience sets the pattern of sent missionaries returning to the sending church with a report of their evangelistic activities. Note that **God . . . opened the door of faith unto the Gentiles** (vs. 27). Again we observe that Christ, the Lord of the church, is sovereignly directing her affairs from heaven. The church in Antioch had now become independent of the "mother church" in Jerusalem. Thus they remained there a **long time.** This again is one of Luke's characteristically indefinite references to time. It is generally assumed that this first missionary journey took about one year and was followed by another year of recuperation. and preparation in Antioch.

D. The Council of Jerusalem. 15:1-35.

15:1-2. The Council of Jerusalem is one of the great turning points of the book of Acts, as are the conversions of Paul and Cornelius. The relation between the Jewish and Gentile believers in the terms of admission to membership in the church was the issue of this discussion. In the beginning, the church consisted almost entirely of converted Jews who had automatically been circumcised as Old Testament believers. Even Peter, earlier, had great difficulty making the transition to full fellowship with the Gentiles.

The establishment of a predominantly Gentile church in Antioch and now the success of the Gentile mission in Galatia, refocused attention upon fellowship with these growing churches. Church growth certainly underlies the basic themes represented by Luke in the book of Acts. The power of the message of the gospel is demonstrated by the fact that it gains reception and response almost everywhere. When the Jewish converts from Judaea arrived in Antioch, they insisted that **ye be circumcised** in order to **be saved** (vs. 1). The text later (vs. 5) indicates that these converts were from among the Pharisees, the strictest of the sects of the Jews. The disputations would also seem to indicate that some of the early believers still looked upon Christianity as a movement within Judaism at this point (cf. Ladd, p. 435).

It should be noted that a substantial difference of opinion exists among commentators as to whether or not this visit to Jerusalem is represented in Galatians 2 or not. Harrison, *Wycliffe Bible Commentary*, pp. 698-699, argues for this (cf. also Lightfoot, *Galatians*, pp. 125 ff. and Ladd, pp. 435 ff.) and others argue that the Epistle to the Galatians was written shortly before the council of Jerusalem which would adequately explain why that epistle makes no allusion to that council. Since the discussions and decisions of the council were distinctly relevant to the issue at hand in the Epistle to the Galatians it would seem highly unlikely that Paul would not have made reference to this decision. Thus, Paul's visit to Jerusalem in Galatians 2 seems to be equated with the famine-relief visit of Acts 11. No matter how important that interview was when Paul wrote to the Galatians, its importance was erased by that of the Jerusalem council which took place soon afterwards. According to the text of Acts the visit that Paul paid to Jerusalem at the time of the council was his third visit after his conversion (cf. 9:26; 11:30; 12:25). In the

Epistle to the Galatians Paul tells of two visits which he paid to Jerusalem after his conversion, the first being identified with that of Acts 9 and the second with that of Acts 11, rather than with this visit in Acts 15. Bruce argues that a "reasonable and satisfying sequence of events" can be reconstructed by accepting the view that the Epistle to the Galatians was written to the young churches founded by Paul and Barnabas during their first missionary tour and that it was written at Antioch shortly before the Jerusalem council. The rapid progress of Gentile evangelization in Antioch, Cyprus, and Asia Minor posed a serious threat to the Jewish Christians at Jerusalem. It was this issue which was settled by the epochal conference at Jerusalem.

3-6. The Jerusalem church welcomed the delegation from Antioch and listened eagerly to the story of their successful evangelization of the Gentiles in Galatia, which caused **great joy unto all the brethren.** Objections by the **Pharisees which believed** (or Christian converts from among the Pharisees) led to a formal conference of the **apostles and elders** with the delegation from Antioch. While the leaders were involved in the discussion, verses 12 and 22 show that the whole church participated in the ultimate decision. The wrong decision at this point would have thrown the church back under Jewish legal bondage to the law and would have stalled the expansion of the church as designed by her Lord.

7-11. Paul's earlier rebuke of Peter in Antioch (cf. Gal 2:11) had taken effect. Now, as the leader of the apostles, Peter reinforced his original position on the Gentile mission as he had with Cornelius. He reminded them that God had accepted the Gentiles by faith alone and not on Jewish terms. Peter emphasized that it was God's **choice** to give the gospel to the Gentiles and that He who directed this mission had given them **the Holy Ghost** even as He had done unto the Jewish believers. There-

fore, there exists **no difference** (vs. 9) between Jewish and Gentile believers, for both have their hearts purified **by faith.** The entire discussion of this matter and its final conclusion should have guarded the church over the centuries against any concept of salvation by works or faith plus works. Each speaker in this conference made it clear that salvation is by faith alone. Peter emphasized that salvation was **through the grace of the Lord.** Thus, the book of Acts is consistent throughout in emphasizing that salvation is of God and does not originate with man.

12-21. The impact upon the congregation was such that the **multitude kept silence,** giving Barnabas and Paul an opportunity to review the results of the Gentile missionary enterprise. Then the turning point came when **James, the brother of our Lord,** spoke decisively in regard to this matter. While all of the apostles appeared to be actively involved in this discussion it seems clear from this passage that James, the pastor of the church at Jerusalem, was the ultimate leader and his decision was accepted by the others. Rather than Peter or Paul being in the leadership role at this point, James alone assumes that responsibility. This incident gives great understanding of the authority of the pastor's leadership in the church. Even the leader of the apostles, Peter, and the church's outstanding missionary spokesman, Paul, could not overrule his decision. It should also be observed that all of these men essentially agreed in how to handle this matter. Spirit-directed ministry will always reflect harmony and fellowship in vital matters of this nature. The reference to the **tabernacle of David** which is **fallen down** (vs. 16) seems to be a reference to the spiritual leadership of the Jewish nation, not a literal reference to the Temple as such. Therefore, the rebuilding referred to here may not necessarily be to the reconstruction of the tribulation or millennial temple, but rather to the ultimate rebuilding of the nation of Israel itself at the time. James' decision was that they no longer **trouble** the Gentiles who had **turned to God** (vs. 19), referring to the drastic nature of their conversion. However, he suggested that they **write unto them** that they abstain from **idols,** from **fornication,** from things **strangled,** and from **blood** (vs. 20). Each of these prohibitions related to particular pagan offenses which were especially objectionable to orthodox Jews.

22-29. The final decision was reached with such unanimity that it **pleased . . . the apostles and elders, with the whole church.** Thus, we find the first major ecumenical council ending with total harmony. Messengers were then chosen to take a letter to Antioch explaining the decision. Judas and Silas (who appears later as Paul's companion) were to communicate the council's findings by word of mouth and also by carrying a letter from the apostles and elders at Jerusalem to the church at Antioch. Paul and Barnabas returned to Antioch where they remained and were accompanied by Judas and Silas as representatives from the Jerusalem church to which they returned. The letter is quoted in its entirety in verses 23-29. It is clear, direct, uncomplicated, and simple. It is neither artificially "spiritual," nor unnecessarily lengthy. The letter is referred to as **the epistle** (vs. 30).

30-35. The reception at Antioch was joyous and the issue was permanently settled in that church. Judas and Silas are referred to as **being prophets** (vs. 32). Paul and Barnabas were engaged in the activity of **teaching and preaching** (vs. 35). The reference seems to indicate that several men were involved in the teaching and preaching ministry of this congregation and that the entire membership was mobilized in the task of evangelism. The reference to "prophets" clearly seems to be that of the task of preaching or proclaiming the Word of God.

V. PAUL'S SECOND JOURNEY: CHRISTIANITY SPREADS WESTWARD. 15:36-18:22.

A. A New Team. 15:36-16:5.

36-41. After some time passed (again the amount of time is vaguely stated), Paul initiated to Barnabas the idea of returning to the cities where they had established churches. It should be noted that they did not merely establish believers who were unattached from each other in the cities to which they had gone, but rather they established churches, or local assemblies of believers, in each city.

The disagreement over **John, whose surname was Mark,** brought about the division of the first missionary team. Paul objected to taking Mark who had **departed from them from Pamphylia** earlier. The difference was so **sharp** that each took a new assistant and travelled in a different direction: Barnabas taking Mark and sailing to **Cyprus;** Paul choosing Silas and departing into Cilicia. Much speculation has been done over the nature of this division; however, it is presented by Luke in a matter-of-fact-tone. Evidently each man had a preference for his native land in his missionary work. Barnabas returned to Cyprus; Paul returned to his native Anatolia. As a missionary handbook, Acts indicates that immediate evangelization is most effective in a context where one is most familiar with the people and their needs. This does not mitigate against cross-cultural evangelism for Paul would be engaged in such throughout most of his career. However, as a training model, the immediate implication seems to be that one receives his best early training for evangelism within his own cultural context. The new teams evidently were both very effective. Barnabas was able to recover and rebuild the life of Mark whom Paul later referred to as one whom he appreciated (cf. Col 4:10; II Tim 4:11). In the meantime, Paul was able to develop the qualities which he had observed in Silas. In either case God's work was extended and again the Lord of the church must be seen as sovereignly operating over and above the affairs, and even the disputes, of men.

16:1-5. Paul returned to Derbe and Lystra where he selected **Timothy,** the son of a **Jewess** who was a believer. This outstanding young man would become his travel companion and later would be one of the leaders of the early church. He is the same Timothy to whom the epistles bearing his name were sent. The cultural barrier to evangelism of the Jews centered in the issue of circumcision. Therefore, since Timothy was a half-Jew, Paul **circumcised him** so that he would be acceptable to the Jews in their forthcoming Jewish ministry. This action can hardly be looked upon as a compromise of conviction in relation to chapter 15, since Paul had spoken so strongly in favor of the Gentile mission. It should be remembered, however, that Paul was not giving up on the Jews, though he must have experienced a growing awareness of the Gentile thrust of his mission. He would continue to go "to the Jew first" and then to the Gentiles. This incident teaches us that cultural accommodation in relation to missionary evangelism is often vital to the furtherance of the gospel. It should be observed, though, that such accommodation is made in matters of external preference and should not be made in matters considered morally sinful (see this principle expressed in I Corinthians 9:20). Ladd notes that it was probably at this time that Timothy was set aside by the elders in Lystra for missionary activity, referred to in I Timothy 4:14 (p. 441). The initial stage of the second missionary journey took them back to the churches which had been established on the first journey and were now **increased in number daily** (vs. 5), emphasizing again Luke's apologetic approach to church growth as proof of the power of the gospel. As in the earlier reference to the church at Jerusalem (2:42 ff.) these churches are said to have been growing in number daily. This would certainly mean that conversion was occurring as a result of every-member evangelism, not just evangelistic preaching on Sundays. While such preaching is never mitigated against in the New Testament, daily personal evangelism seems to have been the strength of the early church. Thus, the pattern of aggressively evangelistic, soul-winning church ministries is modelled for us in these early New Testament churches.

B. A New Direction. 16:6-40.

6-8. The geographical movement which ultimately led the missionary leader to Troas is viewed differently in relation to the "North Galatian theory" or the "South Galatian theory." The latter seems the most reasonable; that they came **to Phrygia and the region of Galatia,** not as separate regions but as a single area: Phrygian Galatia. Thus their journey would have taken them from Derbe and Lystra through this part of Galatia directly westward to the great cities of the province of Asia. It hardly needs to be mentioned that this is not a reference to the continent of Asia, but to the province of that name within a peninsula of Asia Minor. Nevertheless, a great deal of allegorical interpretation and preaching has often been done by those misunderstanding this reference. Travelling through this area they then turned northward toward **Mysia** and **Bithynia** and again were constrained by the Holy Spirit. Consequently they came to the seaport of Troas (ancient Troy). From this spot on the edge of the geographical continent of Asia, their attention would be turned across the straits to Greece and the continent of Europe.

9-12. The famous Macedonian vision takes place at this point. Paul had been postponed by the Holy Spirit from preaching in Asia Minor (a mission which would be engaged in later). At this point, certainly some sense of concern, perhaps even confusion, must have gone through the apostle's mind. Why had they traveled all the way to the seaport of Troas? It was here that **a vision appeared to Paul,** evidently sent by God and not merely the product of his own imagination. In the vision a **man of Macedonia** (northern Greece) called to them to **Come over . . . and help us.** We note the need to preach the gospel in each of these areas. It may be also said that they did not attempt to second-guess God. They had just come from the east, they had been forbidden to go south or north so they waited. God's ultimate will is not always the easiest thing to find, but once found, it becomes the most blessed! In the vision at Troas Paul saw the man of Macedonia and prepared a team of evangelists to enter Europe. Evidently, at this point, the author, Luke, joined the team. The reference to "we came" indicates that the story is now autobiographical. Luke was a physician, an intellectual, an author, and Greek by background. Thus, by adding an educated Greek doctor to the evangelistic team they would only enhance their effectiveness in the new mission. Whether Luke was a practicing physician in Troas at the time, or whether he was there for some other purpose, or whether he joined them along the way, is difficult to tell. Nevertheless from this point it is obvious that he continues in Paul's company to Philippi. Thus, the evangelistic team now consists of Paul the leader, Silas his assistant, Timothy the young man, and Luke the intellectual. While this four-man team is in no way designed to set a necessary precedent, it is interesting that the variety of their backgrounds added balance and flexibility to the team. On the "we" sections see also 20:5; 21:18; 27:1. The group took ship from Troas and sailed to the island of **Samothracia** and on to **Neapolis.**

13-15. They arrived at **Philippi,** a Roman **colony,** made up of transplanted Roman citizens. Colonies were usually located at strategic points throughout the empire and enjoyed such privileges as self-government. Evidently, there was no Jewish synagogue there, since Paul and his team went to the **riverside** seeking the Jewish "place of Prayer." There they met **Lydia** (perhaps a proper name, "the Lydian") designating the region in which **Thyatira** was located. She was a **seller of purple,** indicating that she had learned the dye and textile business of her hometown, and had brought it to Philippi. On the significance of this industry in Thyatira, see E. M. Blaiklock, *Cities of the New Testament,* pp. 107-111. She seems to have been a Gentile "God-fearer" (or Jewish proselyte). She was saved and baptized and **her household** followed her example. A woman of wealth and great position she undoubtedly had a number of servants and attendants. The reference to her "household" does not necessarily refer to small children. Conversions in the Book of Acts seem to be limited to adults or older young people.

16-18. The demoniac girl who followed Paul and disturbed his preaching services was miraculously healed. The **spirit of divination** (Gr *pythōn*). The priestess of Delphi was called "the python" after the serpent that had guarded the oracle, and the word was also used of soothsayers. Such a person was thought to be inspired by the god Apollo who was associated with the giving of oracles. This girl was demon-possessed and her uncontrolled utterances were considered to be the utterances of a god. Paul exorcised a demon from this slave girl and set her free. She had previously followed them around chanting **These men are the servants of the most high God** (vs. 17). Just as a demon had recognized Jesus as the "Holy One" (Mk 1:24), so this demon recognized the divine power upon Paul and his companions. The demon was cast out of her **in the name of Jesus**

Christ. Only by His personal power and authority resident in the one who uses His name can such be accomplished.

19-24. This miracle led to their being cast into jail, because of the complaint of **her masters.** Having delivered her from demon power, they had rendered the girl incapable of "soothsaying." Thus she was now a financial liability to those who owned her. Paul and his companions were taken to the **magistrates,** equivalent to the Latin *praetor*. They were especially criticized for **being Jews** (vs. 20). The objections against them were increased by the citizens of Philippi because of their being **Romans.** This later explains Paul's action in demanding a proper apology since he was also a Roman! The mob was incited to near riot and Paul and Silas were beaten, probably by "lictors," who attended the magistrates. Each lictor carried a bundle of rods

and an axe, symbolizing the power to inflict capital punishment. This symbol was later popularized by the Fascists in Italy in the twentieth century. Paul and Silas were then jailed as anarchists. The personal touches of the stories of Philippi have led Ramsay and Blaiklock (p. 124) to assume that Luke may have been a Philippian himself. On the other hand, Rackham, *Acts of the Apostles,* pp. 278-281, strongly rejects this. Most others are undecided. Bruce notes that the "double discomforts of the lictors' rods and the stocks was not calculated to fill Paul and Silas with joy" (p. 337).

25-34. However, **at midnight** Paul and Silas **prayed, and sang.** Such singing must have startled and surprised both the jailor and the prisoners. We thus have here the first "sacred concert" ever held in Europe and one that eventually "brought down the house"! The **great earthquake** shook the prison

The Second Missionary Journey of Paul

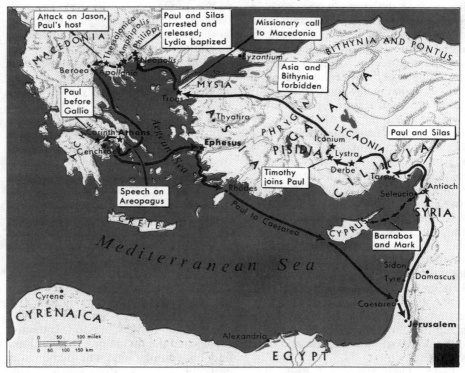

foundations to the point that the doors were opened and everyone's bands were loosed. While this may seem strange, modern day earthquake phenomena certainly verify the actual possibility of such an incident. The jailor, hearing that all the prisoners had escaped and that he had failed his responsibility, prepared to kill himself. Then Paul cried out, **Do thyself no harm.** The fact that he came in **trembling** and **fell down before** them implies that he was shaken not only by the incident but by the evident power of God which had been demonstrated in the earthquake. His question, **Sirs, what must I do to be saved?** appears to be genuine and Paul's answer is really the gospel in a nutshell: **Believe on the Lord Jesus Christ.** Using the tragedy of the moment as an opportunity to present the truth of the gospel, the two missionaries told him that faith in Jesus as Lord was the way of salvation for himself and his family. The jailor and his entire household believed their message and were baptized that very night. This evidence of "household conversion" does not imply that the family was saved simply because the father believed, but rather because each one in particular believed. Nor does it imply that infants were baptized along with the rest of the family. We are told nothing of the ages of the family members. The jailor's first Christian act of mercy was to wash the stripes of Paul and Silas, which before apparently had been left unattended.

35-40. After receiving apologies from the terrified city officials, who now learned that they had shamelessly beaten two Roman citizens, the team left Philippi and moved on to Thessalonica. Notice that Paul used his Roman citizenship as an opportunity to bring credibility upon the new believers in the community. Upon leaving the prison they returned to Lydia's house and **comforted . . . the brethren.** Apparently Luke stayed behind to oversee the new work and to add lead-

ership to its direction. The use of "we" is not mentioned again until 20:5, when Paul returns to Philippi on his third journey, when Luke evidently rejoins the missionary team.

C. Flight from Thessalonica to Athens. 17:1-34.

17:1-4. Paul, Silas, and Timothy journeyed westward along the great military road, *Via Egnatia.* They passed through **Amphipolis** and **Apollonia.** Why he passed by these cities we are not told. However, it should be observed that Paul followed definite missionary strategy in establishing churches in key centers which could form evangelistic outreach centers around their location. Thus, he moved on to **Thessalonica,** the chief city and capital of the province of Macedonia. In his epistle to this church (I Thess 1:8) Paul indicated that the gospel had gone forth from them into Macedonia and Achaia. The cities bypassed were not small towns for Amphipolis was itself a major community, though it declined in significance after this time. In Thessalonica Paul discovered a **synagogue of the Jews,** and went there three consecutive **sabbath days.** Paul spent at least these three weeks in the home of Jason oranizing a church from the Jewish converts, while working as a tentmaker that he might not be a burden to the believers (cf. I Thess 2:9; II Thess 3:7-12). However the three weeks only refers to the time Paul was allowed to present his case in the Jewish synagogue. Again Luke's chronological references are vague and it is possible that they spent a great deal of time in this community establishing an outstanding local church. Paul's method of evangelism was to "reason" with them **out of the scripture.** This does not mean that he merely used philosophic arguments, which he attempted to tie to the Old Testament, but rather that he presented prophecies that related to Christ, His death and resurrection, to prove to them that **this Jesus, whom I preach is . . . Christ.**

5-10. Some of the Jews believed and **a great multitude of the Greeks.** The gospel was once again opposed, however, by the unbelieving Jews who dragged Jason into court and unsuccessfully attempted to put him in jail. The **rulers of the city,** literally "politarchs," were responsible for reviewing the case. Since the term "politarch" was unknown in Greek literature until recent archaeological discoveries, some commentators wrongly accuse Luke of being inaccurate in his designation. The disciples were referred to as those who had **turned the world upside down** (vs. 6) referring to the impact of their ministry in the previous places. One needs to be careful not to allegorize this statement too strongly. They had obviously not yet won the world to Christ but they were in the process of bringing about a confrontation with the wills of men which left no doubt as to the clarity and definiteness of their message. They were literally shaking communities with the gospel! They were also accused of claiming to have **another king, . . . Jesus.** Ladd (p. 446) very vividly notes that this may explain why there is such little reference to Christ as king or to the "kingdom" in the epistles, since the term "king" was the common Greek designation for the Roman emperor and could be easily misunderstood. Rome was tolerant of many things but not rebellion against the emperor. This may explain Paul's preferred usage in the Gentile epistles of the term "Lord." The designation also helps us understand the concept of Christ's lordship, it is recognizing him to be king of one's life. Jason had to put up a **security** (or bond) which would be forfeited if there were any further disturbances. In the meantime, Paul and Silas slipped away at night unto Berea and went to the Jewish synagogue which was there.

11-14. In Berea Paul found the people here more open-minded than at Thessalonica for they received the word with all **readiness of mind.** This open reception to the gospel message caused them to spend a considerable amount of time establishing the church in this community where the people **searched the scriptures daily.** This would imply that the method of Jewish evangelism was again basically the same, concentrating on the fulfillment of Old Testament predictions of the Messiah as related to Jesus. We are told that **many of them believed.** It should be observed again that Luke continually emphasizes the numerical growth of the early church as proof of the power of its message. Eventually Paul had to escape because of the hostility of the Jews of Thessalonica who came to Berea and stirred up opposition to his message. Thus, Paul departed for **Athens.** In the meantime Silas and Timothy remain in Berea to minister to the believers, while awaiting the opportunity to rejoin Paul as soon as possible.

15-34. Athens was no longer a city of great political or commercial influence but had remained the world's most famous intellectual center of thinking. Even Roman students desired to go to Athens for their university training. It should be noted that Paul's original strategy did not include the evangelizing of this city. But as he waited there for Silas and Timothy he was greatly disturbed by the **idolatry** in which he saw the city engulfed. Again, he went to the synagogue daily to preach to the Jews and to the open market place to preach to the Gentiles. He was invited to explain his message at the open forum on Mars Hill by the **Epicureans** and **Stoics** who were the leading schools of thought among the Greek **philosophers.** The former group had been founded by Epicurus in about 300 B.C., believing in the existence of gods but never their interference in the affairs of men. Their philosophy of life was one of pleasure and freedom from fear of death. "Eat, drink, and be merry," was their motto. On the other hand, the Stoics founded by Zeno at approximately the same time believed in the brotherhood of all men and held to the high moral principles of a life of self-denial. To these men Paul certainly must have seemed to be a **babbler** (Gr *spermologus*), literally a "seed-picker."

Gaining the opportunity to share his personal philosophy with these **Athenians** Paul used the immediate surrounding as an opportunity in which to present his message. Observing the numerous temples, statues, and idols of their religious mythology, Paul began by announcing that he believed that they were too **superstitious** and, so much so, that he had even found an inscription **To the Unknown God** (vs. 23). This "unknown God" Paul then declared to them to be the creator, governor, saviour, and judge of the world. In essence, he was announcing to them that he knew the real God, who was unknown to them in spite of their extreme religiosity. Standing on the Areopagus and facing the crowd Paul had his back to the great temples of the city, which would be instantly observed by his audience to whom he announced that God **dwelleth not in temples.** Certainly his point would be vividly made to his listeners. It should be observed that in addressing these pagan philosophers Paul did not quote extensively from the Old Testament which would have related only to a Jewish audience. Nothing in the text itself indicates that Paul used the wrong approach with his audience. In fact, he actually quoted from two Greek poets: Epimenides of Crete and Aratus of Cilicia. By referring to men as the **offspring of God** Paul is not implying by any means that all men are saved, but rather, that they are all God's creatures and, therefore, responsible to Him. The ignorance of their past may have been overlooked (not "winked at," AV) but God was now calling **all men everywhere to repent.** This makes it clear that the message of repentance was not limited only to believers, nor to the Jews, but was issued to all men everywhere as the passage clearly says. On the nature and significance of the doctrine of repentance see H. Ironside *Except Ye Repent.* It is foolish to argue, as to some dispensationalists, that repentance is not necessary for salvation when the New Testament Scriptures clearly say that it is. On this matter see also E. Hindson, *Glory in the Church,* pp. 75-83. The central biblical theme of Paul's message was the resurrection of Christ from the dead. This was the crucial content of the gospel as proclaimed by the early evangelists and caused a mixed reaction in the audience: **some mocked ... Howbeit certain men . . . believed.** Among these converts was Dionysius the **Areopagite,** meaning that he was a member of the Areopagus itself. A woman named **Damaris, and others** also **believed.** Little is said in the New Testament of the converts at Athens. While a church does appear there later in history, there is no reference to a local church at Athens as such at this time. This does not mean that such a church was not organized there at this point, but that we have no record of it. Paul apparently stayed only a brief time in this city and moved on to Corinth where he would eventually spend a great deal of time and effort, and to whose church he would write two major epistles.

D. The Corinthian Ministry. 18:1-22.

18:1-17. Here Paul met a Christian Jew named **Aquila** and his **wife Priscilla,** who had recently been driven from Rome by the anti-Semitic activities of the empire at that time. There are inscriptions in the catacombs which hint that Priscilla was of a distinguished family of high standing in Rome. Later, in Ephesus a church met in their home (cf. I Cor 16:19). In later years they apparently moved back to Rome (cf. Rom 16:3-5). At this time Silas and Timothy caught up with Paul. They had been left behind at Berea with instructions to meet Paul in Athens, but this had evidently not worked out. Silas had left Berea for Philippi to help Luke with the new church there (cf. 18:5). Timothy, at Paul's request, had gone back to Thessalonica to oversee the work there (cf. I Thess 3:1). Both men now meet Paul in Corinth. Silas brought a financial gift for Paul from the Philippian church for his missionary support which is referred to in II Corinthians 11:8 and Philippians 4:15 and Timothy brought a good report concerning the work in Thessalonica. **Crispus** (vs. 8) was the chief ruler of the synagogue and was gloriously converted along with many other Corinthians, all of whom were baptized. So great was the response in this city that Paul remained there **a year and six months.** The conversion of **Crispus** and his family must have been tremendous defeat for the Jews and a great incentive to Paul's continued mission. However, the success of the ministry caused Paul to remain here for a full eighteen months, during which period he wrote I and II Thessalonians. In time, however, the unbelieving Jews dragged Paul into court before the governor Gallio accusing him of blasphemy. Because of the religious nature of the case, Gallio quickly dismissed it. **Gallio** (vs. 12) was the brother of the philosopher Seneca. Since procouncils ("deputy") served a two year term it is relatively certain that this incident must be dated in A.D. 51 or 52. The Jews evidently thought to put pressure on the new Roman governor by instigating a riot and bringing Paul before the **judgment seat,** accusing the evangelist of propogating a religion that was contrary to the Roman law, which recognized Judaism as a legitimate religion, but had not officially recognized Christianity as such. It was technically *illicita* as a religion in the eyes of the Ro-

man government. Therefore, Gallio's decision would have been epoch-making for the fate of Christians in the province of **Achaia.** Not to be denied, an unruly Greek mob (doubtless organized by the Jews to harm Paul) grabbed **Sosthenes** who had succeeded Crispus as **ruler of the synagogue** and severely **beat him** in the presence of **Gallio.** It has been suggested that this experience may have later led to his conversion to Christ (cf. I Cor 1:1)!

18-22. After remaining in Corinth **yet a good while** beyond the year and a half, he took Aquila and Priscilla and left for Ephesus. At this time we are told that he **had shorn his head . . . for he had** vowed **a vow** (vs. 18). Evidently, before leaving Corinth, he assumed a Nazirite vow and during the period of the vow allowed his hair to grow uncut and at the end of the period, cut his hair. While Paul strongly refused to allow the demand of the Old Testament law to be imposed upon Gentiles, he himself, as a Jew, continued to practice many of its demands in order to increase his effectiveness in Jewish evangelism. Arriving at **Ephesus** he left Aquila and Priscilla and there remaining only a short time himself and refusing their invitation to stay longer he **bade them farewell** (vs. 21), or bid their leave. He was determined to return to Jerusalem to **keep this feast.** While this phrase is lacking in the majority of texts, there is no other explanation for his hasty return to Palestine. He promised to return again to Ephesus **if God will** (vs. 21). Such an attitude should condition all of our plans in relation to the work of God (cf. Heb 6:3; Jas 4:15). Since Paul **landed at Caesarea** and went from there and **saluted the church** and from there went **down to Antioch** (vs. 22), the church referred to must be the one at Jerusalem to whom he reported and then returned to Antioch his sponsoring church. Again we notice a great deal about missionary strategy in the activities of the Apostle Paul.

VI. PAUL'S THIRD JOURNEY: RE-INFORCEMENT. 18:23-21:14.

A. The Prolonged Ephesian Ministry. 18:23-19:41.

23-28. Paul left again for Asia Minor (modern Turkey) visiting and encouraging the churches there. He covered the country of **Galatia** and **Phrygia** where he strengthened the **disciples.** About this time an eloquent Bible teacher named **Apollos** (born in Alexandria, Egypt) arrived in Ephesus on a preaching tour. Apollos had learned of the ministry and message of John the Baptist from Jewish pilgrims while still in Egypt but knew nothing beyond that point. He came to Jerusalem during the days of our Lord's earthly ministry. He had heard of the message of John the Baptist that the Messiah was soon to come and that this coming was fulfilled in the life of Jesus. Armed with these limited facts, he traveled afar faithfully proclaiming what he knew. Apollos is described as an **eloquent man** being **mighty in the scriptures,** meaning that he was an effective speaker and especially able to present the messiahship of Jesus to the Jews. He is described as being fervent in the spirit (vs. 25). This is an interesting statement in regard to the fact that his followers in chapter 19 are unaware of the Holy Spirit, giving us insight into the Old Testament believers who though they were regenerated and probably indwelt by the Holy Spirit, were unaware of a full understanding of the nature of His work in them. Aquila and Priscilla were impressed with his ability and took him in **and expounded the way of God more perfectly,** implying that they brought him to a full understanding of the Christian gospel. Eventually he felt called to Corinth and departed, carrying with him the written recommendations of fellow believers in Ephesus. In Corinth he was greatly used of God in the apologetic ministry of convincing the Jews **by the scriptures that Jesus was**

Christ (or Messiah). Notice that he used the Word of God as the focal point for his apologetic approach which resulted in a great number of conversions.

19:1-3. Paul's two-year stay at Ephesus was marked by three noteworthy events. The first was his confrontation with the disciples of John who had not **heard whether there be any Holy Ghost** (vs. 2). These followers of John's preaching had believed the truth that John had proclaimed but had not yet been informed of the full message of the gospel including the coming of the Holy Spirit at Pentecost. Several questions arise in relation to this incident. The Greek participle should be translated "when you believed" rather than "since ye believed" (AV). This passage does not imply that one receives the Holy Spirit *after* salvation since the rest of the New Testament makes it clear that the Holy Spirit is received at the time of salvation and that every true believer has received the Holy Spirit, or been a partaker of the Holy Spirit (cf. I Cor 12:3, 7, 11, 13). Paul then asks them unto what they had been baptized and they replied **Unto John's baptism** (vs. 3).

4-7. John's **baptism of repentance** in verse 4 clearly distinguishes the baptism of John from Christian baptism. It was a baptism of repentance in preparation for the coming of Jesus Christ. It was not a baptism of identification with the death, burial, and resurrection of Christ for at that point He had not yet died. Baptisms or "washings" were frequently employed in Jewish spiritual matters. Therefore, it is a mistake to regard John the Baptist as beginning a Christian ministry of baptism. Certainly, he was not the founder of the "Baptist" church! Upon hearing Paul's explanation, these disciples of John who were caught in a dispensational overlap from the Old Testament era were **baptized** (Gr *baptizō*) **in the name of the Lord Jesus.** Again, the use of **baptized**

indicates the form of baptism as immersion, or dipping or dunking into water (to symbolize death and resurrection). The identification with the name of Jesus was to emphasize the significance of this baptism as distinctly Christian as opposed to that of John in preparing the Jews for the first coming of the Messiah. The references to being baptized in the name of Jesus in the book of Acts do not necessarily imply that the baptismal formula given in Matthew 28 was not used, but that the emphasis was especially upon identification with the person of Christ. Paul then **laid hands** upon them and **the Holy Ghost came on them** and as a result they spoke with **tongues, and prophesied.** This experience is designated to illustrate the oneness and unity of the church. Since believers are baptized by one spirit into one body (cf. I Cor 12:13), there can be no offshoot groups of disciples outside the church. Ladd (p. 454) correctly observes, "It is beside the point to debate whether or not these disciples were Christians before Paul met them, even as it is futile to question whether the apostles were saved before Pentecost. They were disciples of the Lord Jesus but with an incomplete knowledge of the Gospel." Like the believers in Samaria (cf. 8:16-17) these followers of John who believed in the Lord to the point which they had truth revealed to them, now experienced an extension of Pentecost to include all believers. Like the other transitional groups in Acts, the original disciples, the Samaritan believers, the Gentile converts, and now these wandering followers of John the Baptist, each new group receives the baptism of the Holy Spirit in a dramatic outward manner, resulting in speaking in tongues. This is never intended to be normative for all believers and certainly not for all time. In writing to the Corinthian church which was completely over balanced in regard to the gift of tongues, Paul had to remind them that they all had received the baptism of the Spirit, but all of them were not intended in the first place to receive the gift of tongues (cf. I Cor 12:13; and 12:29-31).

8-12. For the next three months Paul continued his synagogue ministry and, upon being opposed there, rented a public hall and carried on the work. He probably taught from 11 A.M. to 4 P.M. and worked as a tentmaker both before and after this time period. God performed several unusual miracles through Paul at this time so that even **handkerchiefs or aprons** taken from his body caused healing of disease and the exorcism of evil spirits. The total ministry in Ephesus lasted for about **two years** and centered in the **school of one Tyrannus** (vs. 9). As a result of this concentrated ministry virtually all of the province of Asia (in Asia Minor) heard the Word of the Lord Jesus (vs. 10). The unique position of the ministry of the apostles, as the foundation of the early church, was attended by a series of unusual miracles. While the dynamic of their preaching and their gospel message was to be repeated in every age it has become obvious throughout church history that direct revelation from God ceased with the closing of the canon of New Testament Scripture as did other revelational gifts, such as tongues and predictive prophecy. While God still heals as a result of answered prayer, healing by means of a handkerchief is no longer legitimate for the church any more than raising the dead, which was also done by the early disciples.

13-20. A family of **vagabond Jews** composed of Skeva, a priest, and his seven sons had been watching Paul do his mighty miracles and decided to attempt an exorcism of their own. Traveling Jewish exorcists were common in the ancient world. Listening to the name of Jesus, which Paul used to command evil spirits to come out of people, they attempted to use the same name as a sort of magical charm. However the **evil spirit** replied: **Jesus I**

know, and Paul I know; but who are ye? Then the man who was demon possessed jumped upon them, beat them up, and stripped them **naked.** Exorcism is dangerous unless the exorcist is anointed by the Holy Spirit and is genuinely dealing with real demon powers. The story of the incident spread quickly and resulted in a great revival in which many people came to believe in the **name of the Lord Jesus** (vs. 17) and forsook their former practice of black magic. Over $10,000 worth of occult scrolls and magic charms were burned at a public bonfire. It was normally thought by magicians that if their magical secrets were made public they would lose their potency. Therefore, a public discrediting of their practice was seen as a genuine conversion of turning from evil to Christ. It is often noted, even today, by missionaries in such places as Haiti where voodoo is still practiced, that a private confession of faith is almost worthless until the individual is willing to go to his home, bring out his accult objects, and openly and publicly destroy them.

21-22. Paul's ultimate plan for his future ministry is revealed in his statement that he would **go to Jerusalem** and afterwards must **also see Rome.** He planned to revisit the churches in Macedonia and Achaia in order to collect money for the needy saints at Jerusalem and after taking this collection to the church he intended to visit Rome itself. Romans 15:24-28 seems to imply that he did not intend to stay in Rome for an extended period of time but merely stopped there on his way to Spain. It was his normal policy to preach the gospel where it had never been preached and to avoid building on another man's foundation. The personal motivational drive and dynamic of this man is almost incomprehensible to the modern reader. Having already extended himself throughout Asia Minor and the Peninsula of Greece, he now reveals his plan to move westward into Italy and ultimately to Spain,

which was the western extremity of the Roman Empire of that day. The extensive nature of his travels has rarely been repeated by missionaries even in the modern era. However, the next verse indicates that he **stayed in Asia** and sent Timothy and Erastus to Macedonia. Luke does not mention Timothy between the time he rejoined Paul at Corinth (cf. 18:5) and this point, but he obviously had continued with the Apostle Paul in Ephesus. Nor does Luke record the fact that Paul had previously sent Timothy to Corinth to deal with certain problems in the church (cf. I Cor 4:17; 16:10).

23-41. In the meantime a riot was instigated in Ephesus by a silversmith named **Demetrius** whose business of selling silver shrines of the Greek goddess Diana had been severely threatened by Paul's preaching. The statement that there arose a stir about **that way** (vs. 23) refers to the way of Christ or the Christian faith. Demetrius was able to rally several **workmen of like occupation** (vs. 25) with the objection that Paul's preaching was destroying their income. The statement: **This Paul hath persuaded and turned away much people** reveals the dynamic and extensive nature of the success of Paul's ministry in Ephesus. The New Testament later makes it clear that the church at Ephesus was one of the outstanding churches of the apostolic period. A church, who though she had left her first love in Revelation 2, nevertheless was an outstanding, warmhearted church whose first love was one of the greatest examples of the New Testament. It is amazing that the spiritual growth of the Ephesian church was contemporary to the spiritual confusion and carnality of the Corinthian church. Notice that Luke continually emphasizes the principle of church growth and numerical evaluation of evangelism throughout the book of Acts. Not only is Paul preaching the truth, but the truth is producing results! Obviously, Paul must have had more

The Third Missionary Journey of Paul

than just a handful of believers to cause the silversmiths to riot in the fashion in which they did. In many cities throughout the word today people are not opposed to the church because they are not even aware of the threat which she poses to their lifestyle!

Soon the huge city amphitheater, capable of seating twenty-five thousand, was packed with a howling mob that chanted hysterically for two uninterrupted hours: **Great is Diana of the Ephesians** (vs. 34)! The temple of Diana, whose Greek name was Artemis, was one of the seven wonders of the ancient world. The image within the temple was of a woman carved with many breasts to signify the fertility of

nature. The original stone from which the image had been carved was reported to have "fallen from heaven," leading many historians to believe that it may have been a meteorite. Paul determined to appear in the arena along with some of the believers who had been dragged there by the mob but was persuaded at the last minute by the Christians not to go there. It is very likely that had he appeared before the mob as the leader of the Christian movement he would have occasioned his death long before his arrival in Rome. The text indicates that the crowd was in such a state of hysteria that they were **confused** and many did not even understand why they were there. Apparently some of the Jews feared being condemned along with the Christians and put forth a man named **Alexander** to make a speech in defense of them, but he was shouted down by the crowd and chaos prevailed. Finally order was restored by the **townclerk** (vs. 35) who reminded them that the city was not in danger of being destroyed by these Christians since Ephesus was known throughout the world of her day as the **worshipper** (actually "temple keeper") of Diana. He also reminded them that the Christians in question were not sacrilegious men nor **robbers of churches** (literally "robbers of temples"). He then challenged the legitimacy of the procedure since the silversmiths had not gone to the **deputies** (proconsuls) to bring formal charges against these people through proper channels. Anything other than that he reminded them would be determined in **lawful assembly** (Gr *ekklēsia,* "congregation," and the same word used to designate the "church"). This reference shows us that not all assemblies referred to in scripture are church assemblies. The reference here is simply to the legal gathering of Roman citizens, which was a democratic local organization.

B. From Macedonia to Miletus. 20:1-16.

20:1-16. After the riot had ceased Paul was convinced of the stability of the church at Ephesus and was now free to depart **into Macedonia** to revisit and strengthen the churches there. The apostle's departure from Ephesus is recorded in II Corinthians in relation to his visit to Troas to await the arrival of Titus whom he had previously sent to Corinth to deal with the serious problems among the believers there. Titus' delayed arrival eventually brought news of improved conditions in the church and occasioned the writing of Paul's second letter to the Corinthians, which he sent to them by the hand of Titus and another brother. After

spending three months in **Greece** Paul was preparing to sail for Syria when he discovered a plot by the Jews against his life and decided to **return through Macedonia** instead. It is probably during this time that he wrote the Epistle to the Romans. Several people **accompanied him** including **Sopater, Aristarchus, Secundus, Gaius, Timothy, Tychicus, and Trophimus.** Again we note that Paul rarely worked alone and usually carried a team of evangelists and ministers with him. Many of these men are referred to elsewhere in the New Testament. Upon their arrival in Philippi, Luke also rejoined the team and the second "we" section of Acts begins at verse 5 and runs through verse 15 of chapter 20 and is resumed again in 21:1. The reference to the keeping of the **days of unleavened bread** (vs. 6) shows Paul's adherence to his Jewish past, and yet the reference to the gathering of believers at Troas **upon the first day of the week** to preach and celebrate the Lord's Supper clearly emphasizes the distinct non-Jewish nature of the New Testament church. Although Paul was in Troas for seven days (vs. 6), he apparently did not meet with the local church for the purpose of breaking bread until the first day of the week (vs. 7). The *New Scofield Bible* states: "the fact that Paul and others sometimes attended Sabbath services in Jewish synagogues (17:1-3) does not prove that the apostolic church kept the seventh day as a special day of worship. It only shows that the early missionaries took the gospel message wherever and whenever they found people gathered together (5:19-20; 13:5; 16:13, 25-33; 17:17, 19, 22; 18:7; 19:9; 25:6, 23). This witness was carried on daily (2:47; 17:17; 19:9) in every possible way (I Cor 9:19-22). The early churches were specifically warned against submitting themselves to the bondage of any legalistic observance of Sabbath days (cf. Col 2:16; Gal 4:9-11). On the other hand, in the exercise of their Christian liberty (Rom

14:5-6), these same churches voluntarily chose the first day of the week as an appropriate time for fellowship and worship (Acts 20:7; I Cor 16:2), the day on which the Lord arose and repeatedly appeared to His disciples (Jn 20:19-24, 25-29). It was a new day for a new people belonging to a new creation (II Cor 5:17), a day of commemoration and joy (Mt 28:9 Margin, "service" Mt 28:10), and spiritual rest (Heb 4:9-10). This observance of the first day of the week is corroborated by the early fathers in the writings of Barnabas (A.D. 100), Ignatius (A.D. 107), Justin Martyr (A.D. 145-150), and Irenaeus A.D. 155-202). The Edict of Laodicea (fourth century A.D.) did not change the day of worship from the seventh day to teh first day of the week, as sometimes alleged, but rather put the stamp of official approval upon an observance already long established in the early churches" (pp. 1194-1195).

7-16. The meeting at Troas **continued . . . until midnight.** The service was held in an upper room on the **third** floor, with illumination provided by many smoky lamps which would have made the air thick and stuffy. Tragically, a young man named **Eutychus** fell asleep and fell from the **third loft** and was **taken up dead** (vs. 9). It seems clear from early custom that the Christians often met on Saturday night as well as Sunday morning. Early Jewish reckoning observed the beginning of the new day at sunset, continuing through the night and the next day until sunset again. Rackham (p. 379) notes that the meeting was held in a private house in the uppermost room which was the most removed from any possibility of interruption. Either Eutychus fell out of the upper window and landed on the ground outside the house or he fell down through the house to the bottom floor of an open area. Paul came and embraced him after the manner of Elijah and Elisha and bade them **Trouble not yourselves** because **his life is in him.** This would seem to indicate that even though he had every outward appearance of being dead, his spirit had not yet departed from his body. This would also explain modern instances where people are pronounced legally dead for a few moments and yet are still brought back to life. Once the spirit leaves the body there is no possibility of life returning, except by direct miraculous resurrection from God Himself. Paul raised the young man **alive** to the thrill and amazement of the congregation. The next day Luke and the other members of the party sailed from Troas to **Assos,** while Paul travelled **afoot** (by land). Again we notice the reference to "we" in verse 14. The rest of the missionary party met the apostle at Assos and sailed to **Mitylene,** the chief town of the island of Lesbos, from which the myth of the homosexual girls (lesbians) originated. From there they sailed between the mainland and the islands of **Chios** and **Samos,** until they came to **Miletus,** on the mainland of Asia Minor. Paul wanted to take time to go inland from there to visit the church at **Ephesus,** but could not arrive in time for the **day of Pentecost,** so he arranged for the **elders of the church** to meet him at the seaport of Miletus a few hours away.

**C. Farewell to the Ephesians.
20:17-38.**

17-21. Paul's sermon to the Ephesian elders is important in revealing the simple structure of the early church, the nature of apostolic authority and the content of apostolic preaching. Paul sent for the Ephesian elders, who hurried to meet him at Miletus during a layover in his ship's schedule. On this occasion the apostle delivered his third main recorded discourse. He began his message by reviewing the past two years and the tears and toils he had while serving the Lord in Ephesus. The church leaders or elders (Gr *presbyteros*) were the **overseers** (vs. 28, Gr *episcopos*) or guardians of the church and "bishops." It becomes obvious from Paul's interchangeable usage of the two terms that a bishop was also an elder. It is also clear that there was a plurality of elders in the church. It seems that early church custom was for one of the elders to eventually become the bishop or pastor of the church. This would parallel the modern situation in most evangelical churches which are led by a pastoral staff (elders) who in turn are led by the pastor himself (the bishop). Paul's statement about his preaching clearly reveals the nature and content of early New Testament preaching of the gospel. The message which was **profitable** unto them which he had taught both **publicly** and **from house to house** (i.e. privately) was the same message for both . . . **Jews and Greeks** (vs. 21). That message had a twofold thrust: **Repentance toward God, and faith toward our Lord Jesus Christ.** This verse along with several others in the book of Acts makes it clear that repentance was an essential ingredient in the preaching of the gospel. Those who have argued that repentance is not to be preached to the unsaved, but only to the saved, or only to the Jews certainly do not develop such a view from this passage of scripture! Paul makes it clear that part of his essential message to both Jews and Greeks was that they repent and believe. Ironside (*Except Ye Repent,*) emphasizes that one must repent in his overall attitude toward God in order to have genuine saving faith in Christ. Therefore, both repentance and faith are essential to salvation and inseparable from salvation.

22-28. Paul exclaimed that he was going **bound in the spirit unto Jerusalem,** emphasizing the sense of divine compulsion which he felt. The **spirit** here must be identified with the Holy Spirit who is referred to in verse 23. Paul was determined to **finish my course with joy** and to **testify the gospel of the grace of God** to as many men as possible. This preaching he refers to as **preaching the kingdom of God** (vs. 25), which must refer to the gospel proclamation of the church which he was establishing. Again, we see that the present day form of the kingdom is the church. This in no way denies the literal nature of the coming Millennial Kingdom, but clearly indicates that the church is the mediatorial form of the kingdom at the present. Otherwise this reference would have to be looked upon as if Paul were still preaching a Jewish kingdom message (so, hyperdispensationalists). Paul could claim that he was **pure from the blood of all men,** meaning he had fully preached and testified to as many men as possible and had a clear conscience toward all men with whom he had contact regarding the nature of their soul. The book of Acts makes it very clear that Paul was an intense soul-winner and gospel evangelist. One should note, however, that being **pure from the blood of all men** does not mean that he had witnessed to every single person he had ever seen, or every single person in the world, which would obviously be a human impossibility. The point is that Paul had a clear conscience before God and man, knowing that he had used every occasion and opportunity to witness to those that he had come in contact with in his extensive travels. He was also pure of the blood of all men because he had fully declared unto them **all the counsel of God.**

He then reminded the elders to **Take heed . . . unto yourselves** and unto all the **flock** over which the Holy Spirit had made them **overseers.** The nature of pastoral care in the church is clearly placed in the hands of leadership. It should be observed that Paul did not call for the entire church to come to meet him in Miletus, which also would have been a human impossibility. Rather he called for the designated and ordained leaders of that church. The New Testament throughout clearly emphasizes the importance of pastoral leadership in the local church. While that church is an independent, local congregation, its authority has been invested, nevertheless, into certain designated leaders. These leaders are the representatives of the congregation, not its dictators. The church is the Lord's and not man's to begin with. Thus, Christ, the Lord of the church, invests His authority in men who are to lead and oversee the direction of His church. They are His undershepherds and thus carry His authority as revealed in the scriptures. However it should equally be observed that they are not dictators who rule after the whim of their own will, apart from the will of God. Their responsibility is to **feed the church of God** (vs. 28) which has been **purchased with his own blood.** This passage has varying manuscript support, and a problem has arisen centering around the idea of God purchasing the church with His blood, rather than the blood of Christ. Therefore some ancient texts read "the church of the Lord." However, the more favorable reading (followed by the AV) is **church of God.** Bruce (p. 16) suggests the translation, "which he hath purchased with the blood of his Own." The actual rendering is definitely to the blood of Christ which was shed for the church, which is ultimately the church of God. His blood was shed as an atoning death for all men. Christ's atonement is efficacious only for those who by faith receive Him as Saviour and become a part of His church.

29-38. Paul then previewed the future and warned them that after his departing **grievous wolves** would enter in among them not sparing the flock. He further reminded that some of these men would arise from among **your own selves.** Paul later wrote to Timothy who was in Ephesus concerning these "grievous wolves" (see I Tim 1:3-7). His warning was later fulfilled in the apostasy of such men as Hymenaeus, Alexander, and Philetus. In general, however, the church at Ephesus was an outstanding example of the early New Testament church and Paul finished his interview and last farewell to these Ephesian elders **with tears.** He knew that he could leave them because he was leaving them in the hand of God so he commended them to God and **to the word of his grace.** Here Paul seems definitely to express confidence in the inspired scriptures which were now becoming more and more available to the early church period. This sure word of prophecy is that which is able to **build you up.** Paul was "warning" the leaders of the church by admonishing them (Gr *noutheteō*) by "confronting" with their responsibilities in this matter. On the significance of "nouthetic confrontation" see J. Adams, *Competent to Counsel.* The touching farewell gives us a keen insight into the warm fellowship of the early church. **Paul kneeled down and prayed with** his converts and they all **wept . . . and kissed him** (following the common early Christian greeting of the "kiss of peace"). It is also interesting to note that they sorrowed most because they would not have the opportunity to hear him speak again, more so than sorrowing over missing his presence. The implication here is clearly that their loyalty to Paul was based on his message of truth rather than his personality.

D. Return to Palestine. 21:1-14.

21:1-7. Paul and his party resumed their trip by boat sailing between the islands of **Coos** and **Rhodes,** where they apparently anchored overnight. From there, they reached **Patara,** a city on the mainland, where they found shipping that would take them directly across the sea to **Syria** (or **Phoenicia**) on the near eastern mainland, just north of Israel. Landing at **Tyre,** Paul spent seven days with a group of disciples while the ship apparently unloaded its cargo (vs. 3). It was here that Paul was warned by a group of prophets in the church who disclosed **through the Spirit** that he should not go to

Jerusalem. It would seem that the apostle made a mistake here, though this is a highly debated issue. He had already been warned during the beginning of his ministry to: **Make haste and get thee quickly out of Jerusalem: for they will not receive thy testimony concerning me** (22:18). Paul's motive for going to Jerusalem at this time seems to have been his great love for his people and his hope that the gifts of the Gentile churches, sent by him to the poor saints at Jerusalem, would open the hearts of the law-bound Jewish believers to the gospel of God's grace. At any rate it is significant that his stop at Jerusalem was one of the very few where absolutely no fruit whatsoever was recorded. Whether he had a constraint of the Spirit which was stronger than that of the disciples at Tyre, or whether this must be seen as an act of disobedience to the will of God, since we are told that the men at Tyre spoke **through the Spirit,** is difficult to discern. Nevertheless Paul did go to Jerusalem and ultimately did go "bound unto Rome."

8-14. Paul next went to **Caesarea** where he visited the home of **Philip the evangelist,** previously one of the deacons of the Jerusalem church, who had engaged in evangelism in Samaria and on the coastal plain. He is the same fellow who led the Ethiopian eunuch to Christ. He last appeared in Caesarea (8:40) and apparently made his permanent home there. His **four daughters, virgins**, are referred to as "prophetesses." These girls are the last ones mentioned in the Bible who had this gift (others were Miriam, Ex 15:20; Deborah, Jud 4:4; Isaiah's wife, Is 8:3; Huldah, II Kgs 22:14; and Anna, Lk 2:36). While he was there, a **prophet named Agabus** came from Jerusalem and symbolically acted out the fate that he foresaw for the apostle in Jerusalem and predicted that he would be delivered **into the hands of the Gentiles.** He bound his hands and feet with the apostle's belt ("girdle")

and was joined by the other believers in pleading with Paul not to go on to Jerusalem. Luke indicates again by using "we," that he joined the appeal to Paul. Paul, fighting back the tears, told them not to weep for him because he was ready if necessary **to die at Jerusalem** for his Lord. No one could prevail over him. They committed him to **the will of the Lord** (vs. 14). Paul next stayed with **Mnason of Cyprus,** who is referred to as an **old disciple,** referring to the fact that he was a disciple from the earliest days (rather than being a reference to his age). With such a person Paul would feel most comfortable. On Paul's arrival in Jerusalem he was **gladly received** by the brethren and went unto **James,** the pastor of the church, who met him with **all the elders.** It would appear that there were no other "apostles" residing in Jerusalem at this time.

VII. PAUL'S JOURNEY TO ROME. 21:15-28:31.

A. The Apprehension of Paul. 21:15-22:29.

15-26. Paul met with the leaders of the church at Jerusalem and reported to them what **God had wrought among the Gentiles.** They were thrilled with the report and **glorified the Lord.** They reported to him that a rumor was making its rounds among the Christian Jews in Jerusalem (of whom verse 20 says there were "many thousands," indicating the gigantic size of the church there at that time) to the effect that he was telling all Jews who were among the Gentiles to **forsake Moses,** not to circumcise their children, neither to walk after the customs of their forefathers. In order to avoid misunderstanding and such a misrepresentation Paul submitted himself to a **vow** (vs. 23) to show them that the charges were **nothing** and that he himself walked **orderly** in his own personal life. The leaders then reminded him that as **touching the Gentiles which believed**

they would abide by their original decision. Therefore, it becomes obvious that while the church was large and the number of Christian disciples was great at this time in Jerusalem, there was still not yet a clear cut break with their Jewish heritage. It should be observed, however, that the law is not evil in and of itself, but that it is insufficient to bring a man to salvation. By retaining allegiance to the moral aspects of the law, these Christian Jews were retaining the good part of their cultural and spiritual heritage, while acknowledging Christ as Lord. After the destruction of the temple and the subsequent dispersion these Jewish Christians eventually discarded the Jewish distinctions. The believing Jews would later come to understand that it was unnecessary to retain outward observance of the ceremonies of Judaism, when the temple no longer existed. The future nature of the church in general was already being developed in the Gentile churches where Paul's missionary efforts were bringing about the most significant results. This should also be a reminder to us that many times the original mission station may eventually become a mission field. We in America need to remember that the gospel came to us from Europe, which today is desperately in need of the same gospel! We should also remember that the gospel has gone forth from us to Latin America, Africa, and Asia and that missionary statistics now claim that the greatest church growth of this century is actually going on outside of North America! The pattern of the expansion of the church throughout its history seems to indicate that God continues to move and bless where the gospel seed is being planted in fresh ground.

27-40. In spite of his submission to the vow Paul was set upon by a mob of unbelieving Jews who saw him in the temple and mistakenly concluded that he had brought a Gentile in with him. A riot was stirred up by **Jews which were of Asia,** where Paul had just completed his most extensive evangelism. These would appear to be related to the same people who had so violently opposed him during his missionary journeys. The **uproar** that resulted nearly brought Paul's death and he was spared only by the commander of the Roman garrison stationed there. Soldiers were normally housed in the Tower of Antonia, northwest of the temple area, having easy access to the temple courtyard by two flights of stairs. During the time of trouble these soldiers could run into the courtyard to restore order. The **chief captain** (Gr *chiliarchos*) brought a band of **soldiers** and **centurions,** numbering at least two hundred men, and intervened just in time to save Paul's life so that the Jews **left beating of Paul** (i.e. they stopped beating him). He was then arrested by the chiliarch, chained and carried by the soldiers to the top of the stairs and **into the castle** (i.e. "barracks"). The **violence of the people** (vs. 35) was so extreme that the soldiers literally had to fight off the crowd in order for the captain to speak personally to Paul. Upon arriving in the barracks Paul asked if he could speak to the captain who was surprised to find that he could **speak Greek** (note that there can be no doubt that Greek was freely spoken as the common language of that day as the form of communication between both Romans and Jews). The Roman chiliarch was surprised because he thought Paul was **that Egyptian** who had earlier rallied **four thousand men** in an attempt to overthrow the government. History records that this revolt was led by an Egyptian Jew who rallied supporters called in Latin, *sicarii*, dagger men, because each carried a dagger (Latin, *sica*), with which he might assassinate military and political leaders. The revolt had been crushed by the Roman procurator, Felix, but the Egyptian had escaped. Paul assured the tribune that he was a Jew and that he had the right to enter the temple precincts and that he was also a citizen of the important city of Tarsus, and it is also likely that he asserted his Roman citizenship in order to receive fair treatment from the Roman soldiers. It is interesting to note that Paul's citizenship was a protection to him which his Master Jesus did not have. Standing on the stairs he **beckoned with the hand** (an interesting reference to the use of gestures in speaking) and addressed the people **in the Hebrew tongue** (certainly a reference to the native Aramaic dialect which was the common Jewish language of both Palestine and western Asia at that time. Since many of the Jews of the Diaspora could speak only Greek, the apostle captured the attention of the native crowd by speaking in their own dialect. The New Testament makes it clear that the apostle was certainly trilingual, if not quadri lingual, speaking Hebrew, Greek, Aramaic, and probably to some degree Latin).

22:1-21. In the latter chapters of Acts we find the most extensive personal references to Paul's life and experiences. From these an extensive biography may be gleaned of this important early church leader. On his life see Conybeare and Howson, *The Life and Epistles of Paul* and Lenski, *St. Paul;* on the significance of his theology see Bruce, *Paul and Jesus;* Ridderbos, *Paul: An Outline of His Theology.* It is interesting to note that Paul made his defense on the same Roman stairway where Pilate had condemned Christ to death some twenty-six years earlier. The attitude of the Jewish mob also reflects a similar treatment of the Lord's servant who had returned, in one last desperate appeal for the Jews to come to Christ. Paul used the opportunity to relate his conversion on the Damascus Road. He also emphasized his Jewish heritage as one **brought up in this city** (i.e. Jerusalem) and educated by the outstanding Rabbi of that time, **Gamaliel,** and being a Pharisee in his zeal for the law. Then he reminded the Jews that he himself had originally **persecuted this way,** referring to the "way of Christ." Paul went on to explain the Damascus vision, the voice that cried to him, and his resulting question, **Who art thou, Lord?** and the response: **I am Jesus of Nazareth** (vs. 8). The statement in verse 9 that those that were with him saw the light but **heard not the voice** has been wrestled with by some commentators in comparing the statement in 9:7 where the soldiers also heard the voice of Christ. Kent, *From Jerusalem to Rome* (p. 166), observes, "it may be significant that the verb 'to hear' uses different grammatical cases for its object in these two instances. Perhaps in 9:7 the use of the genitive case implies that they heard a sound coming from some identified source, whereas the accusative case in 22:9 indicates that they did not hear it as intelligible speech." Paul further emphasized that he then was instructed to go into Damascus where he would meet a man that would tell him what to do. He then explained that man was **Ananias** who was a **devout man according to the law** (an obvious apologetic appeal), who then told him that the **God of our fathers had chosen** him to **know his will** and see that **Just One** (referring to Christ) and that he should be a **witness unto all men** of what he had seen and heard. Paul further referred to the incident of the **martyr Stephen** and his part in his death and how he had hoped originally to bring the message of Christ only to the Jews, but instead the Lord said **I will send thee far hence unto the Gentiles** (vs. 21).

22-30. Until this point the crowd had retained a hostile silence but with the mention of Paul's divine call to the Gentiles, they burst into rage, demanding that he be taken **away . . . from the earth** because he was **not fit to live.** The hostile Jewish mob tore their clothes, and threw dust in the air and made such a tumult that the chief captain brought him into the barracks. They then prepared to scourge him. At this point Paul reminded the man with the whip that it was unlawful to scourge a **Roman** who was uncondemned by lawful trial (vs. 25). The chief captain was amazed to discover that Paul was a Roman citizen and assumed that he had obtained **this freedom** with a **great sum** of money. To which Paul replied that he was **freeborn** (vs. 28), by virtue of having been born in the colony city of Tarsus. In fact, the chief captain was now even fearful of the fact that he had bound Paul in the first place, so he decided to allow him to appear before the **council of the Jews** (i.e. the Sanhedrin), to determine whether any adequate grounds existed for a legal proceeding against Paul.

B. Paul's Defense before the Sanhedrin and Pharisees. 22:30-23:22.

23:1-10. Paul began by protesting his innocence before the council, stating that he had **lived in all good conscience before God.** Throughout his epistles and recorded sermons there are numerous references by Paul to the importance of having a clear conscience with God and man. **Ananias** was the high priest of Israel from about A.D. 48-58. A crude and overbearing man, he was angered by Paul's claim and commanded someone who stood by him to **smite him on the mouth.** Jesus similarly had been struck during His trial (see Jn 18:22). In response to the action of the high priest, Paul replied: **God shall smite thee, thou whited wall** (vs. 3). The term "whited wall" suggests a white-washed coating over a precarious, tottering wall (cf. Bruce, p. 451). Paul's outburst might seem strong to some, until one realizes the tremendous pressure that he was under and the tension of the moment in which his life was literally at stake! Also note that the action of the high priest was **contrary to the law.** The crowd, however, was shocked by Paul's response in "reviling" the high priest. Paul then seemed to change the tactic of his defense. Realizing that the situation was "stacked" against him, Paul replied that he did not know that he was the high priest, probably the result of the action and character which he displayed, for certainly he would have been dressed in some manner to indicate who he was. Instead, Paul recognized that the Sanhedrin, of which many feel he was himself originally a member (cf. Blaiklock, p. 176), as the ruling body of the Jews was composed of both **Pharisees** and **Sadducees,** who held the majority, and who differed with each other on important matters of doctrine such as the resurrection, angels, and the nature of supernatural intervention. Paul used their difference to gain an opportunity to save his own life. He openly identified himself as a Pharisee and a believer in the resurrection of the dead, thus causing an immediate split between the assembled Pharisees and the resurrection-denying Sadducees. The clamor became so intent that Paul was removed by the Roman commander and the interview before the Sanhedrin came to a close. Paul's statement that he had been called into question because of the **hope and resurrection of the dead** (vs. 6) was true in light of the fact that he believed in the resurrection as the hope of the dead! The Pharisees naively arose to Paul's defense, but the **dissension** became so intense that Paul was returned to the barracks.

11-22. One of the heartwarming and encouraging statements of Paul's entire life occurred at this point when that night **the Lord stood by him,** referring to a literal appearance of Christ who came to tell Paul to **be of good cheer . . .** for he must bear witness also at Rome. Paul had often hoped to get to Rome, and at Ephesus he even made plans to go to Rome, but at this point he was not even sure he would get out of Jerusalem alive. But now, for the first time, God had confirmed his original plan. It is difficult to honestly state these many centuries later whether Paul made a mistake in going to Jerusalem, or whether the Lord knew all along that he would go to Jerusalem, and warned him so that he would be prepared for the ultimate consequences, and used his arrest as the opportunity to get him to the place where he ultimately wanted to go. Certainly Paul's life shows us time and again that God can overrule the most difficult of human circumstances in order to accomplish His will. He may even overrule our own will so that His ultimate will may be done. The next day **certain of the Jews banded together . . . under a curse** in a unified effort to kill Paul. The extent of their fanaticism can be understood when we realize that the execution of this plot certainly would have meant the death of many of them at the hands of the Roman guard who protected Paul. Such intense religious fanaticism was often common among the Jews of that day. **Paul's sister's son** (a nephew) learned of their **lying in wait** (ambush) and came to warn Paul. This is the only reference in the New Testament of Paul's family, and we have no clear indication as to who this person was. The Roman commander quickly removed Paul that night to **Caesarea** (vs. 23), protected by four hundred seventy armed soldiers. He sent a letter on ahead to Felix in Caesarea, explaining why Paul was being transferred to his authority.

C. Paul's Defense before Felix and Festus. 23:23-25:12.

23-35. Paul was transferred under heavily armed guard to **Felix the governor** (or procurator). The troop departed during the **third hour of the night** between nine and ten P.M. and brought him safely unto Caesarea. The transcript of the official letter sent by the tribune, **Claudius Lysias,** unto Felix is given in length, verses 26-30. The nature of the letter seems to in- dicate that the tribune was afraid that he might have accorded some improper treatment to this Roman citizen, and therefore, wanted to make sure that the situation was properly handled. In the morning they arrived at **Antipatris,** some forty miles from Jerusalem and well on the way to Caesarea. Being out of immediate danger of the Jews, the majority of the guard returned and seventy **horsemen** (cavalrymen) accompanied Paul the remaining distance. Learning that Paul was a citizen of **Cilicia,** the governor agreed to hear the case when his **accusers** arrived to bring formal charges against him.

24:1-9. Antonius Felix was the governor of Judaea from A.D. 52-59 and was a man of servile origin who owed his unprecedented advancement to the influence of his brother at the imperial court of Claudius. His governorship was marked by a period of unrest and several Jewish uprisings which resulted in ruthless response by Felix, which in turn alienated more Jews, and led to further revolts. Tacitus, the Roman historian, wrote of him: "Felix indulging in every kind of barbarity and lust, exercised the power of a king in the Spirit of a slave." (*Histories* V, 9). He had three successful marriages to princesses, which elevated his status among the Romans. The first of the three was the granddaughter of Antony and Cleopatra, the third was Drusilla, the daughter of Agrippa. After five days, **Ananias** arrived with the **elders** and a professional **orator** named **Tertullus** to present a formal case against Paul. As the official representative of his client he **began to accuse** (i.e. made his charges) to the governor against Paul. Years after this incident Ananias was assassinated and his son Jonathan became the high priest and was later assassinated by Felix! Paul was accused of treason, religious heresy, and desecration of the temple. Since Tertullus' name is a common Roman designation it may be that he was a Hellenistic Jew or that he was a hired attorney on behalf of the Jews. The reference to **our law** would seem to indicate the former to be true. The flattering speech was in fact the exact opposite of the truth; instead of **great quietness** (vs. 2) and **clemency** (vs. 4) Felix was noted for his ferocious temper and prevailing discontent throughout his realm. The charges brought against Paul claimed that he was a trouble-maker among **all the Jews throughout the world** and that he was the **ringleader of the sect of the Nazarenes** (vs. 5). The term "sect" was used by Josephus to designate the various parties and divisions within Judaism, indicating that even still the opposition considered the Christians as an unorthodox break within Judaism. This is the only place in the New Testament where the followers of Jesus are called **Nazarenes.** The term continued to be used as a derisive designation for Christians in Hebrew and Arabic. It is certainly not wrong to call the followers of Jesus, Nazarenes, but there is no precedent within the Scriptures for the church ever calling themselves by this term. "Nazarene" was at times a term of derision used by Judaeans against the Galileans within the Jewish nation, and therefore, did not necessarily carry any spiritual connotation.

10-21. Paul waited until the governor **beckoned unto him to speak.** Beginning with a modest compliment, he openly denied the charge of stirring up rebellion. To the first charge, he pointed out that he had only been in Jerusalem for twelve days and could not have possibly created all the alleged trouble in that brief time. In regards to the second charge, he showed that he was actually more orthodox than some members of the Sanhedrin who denied the doctrine of the resurrection. Concerning the third charge, he reminded the court that the Jews in Jerusalem itself could not make that indictment stick, which was the only legitimate charge that could have occasioned his

death according to the law. Felix wisely decided to defer any action until he received the official testimony of Lysias, the arresting Roman commander. The only charge which Paul accepted was to **confess . . . the way which they call heresy** (vs. 14). Notice again that Christianity is referred to as "the way" (of Christ). Paul emphasized the importance of having a **conscience void of offense** toward God and man (vs. 16). Having a clear conscience, was vital to the preparation for spiritual warfare. He proceeded to explain that the **Jews from Asia** (vs. 18) who had originally accused him were not even there to bring formal charges against him (since they had by now returned to their homeland). Paul ended his defense by pointing out that he was really called into question in regard to his view of the **resurrection of the dead** (vs. 21).

22-27. When Paul's defense was finished Felix had a **more perfect knowledge of that way** meaning that he had a more accurate understanding of the Christian faith. Eventually Paul had the opportunity to speak to both Felix and his wife Drusilla. This girl was the youngest daughter of Herod Agrippa I (the murderer of James, Acts 12) and the sister of Agrippa II and Bernice (Acts 25:13). She was not yet twenty years old and had already left an Assyrian king to marry Felix. She was a **Jewess** and died 21 years later in the eruption of Mount Vesuvius! When the passage says that he sent for Paul to explain to him **the faith in Christ** (vs. 24) and as Paul preached **righteousness, temperance, and judgment to come** the message was brought home with such conviction that **Felix trembled.** Obviously disturbed by what he heard he responded with his now infamous statement, **Go thy way for this time; when I have a convenient season, I will call for thee** (vs. 25). The closing verses of the chapter indicate that he had hoped for a bribe from Paul in order to release him; however, the bribe was never forth-coming and **after two years** Felix was recalled to Rome by the emperor Nero under an accusation of bad administration by the Jews of his dominion. **Porcius Festus** succeeded him as procurator of Judaea and Felix left Paul in prison for his successor to decide his fate. Thereby, he hoped to pacify the Jews who were now bringing the accusations against him.

25:1-2. In A.D. 58 Felix' soldiers put down a riot of Jews in Caesarea with such violence that he was replaced by Festus, a more fair and honorable ruler, but one who was unable to control the situation in Palestine which had now become a hotbed of revolution and within twelve years would come under the wrath of the emperor himself. Upon his arrival in the province, Festus went from **Caesarea to Jerusalem** (vs. 1). There, the **high priest** and the **Jews** again brought charges against Paul, requesting that he be sent to Jerusalem, in hope that they might ambush him on the way. Instead, Festus resisted their pressure and returned to Caesarea where the Jews were forced to come and make formal charges against the apostle before the **judgment seat** (Gr *bēma*). When Festus suggested that Paul return to Jerusalem to be tried, the Apostle then appealed to **Caesar's judgment seat** (vs. 10). It is clear that Paul was willing to accept the penalty of death if he had done anything **worthy of death** (vs. 11). Festus, seeing an immediate way out, honored the appeal to Caesar (who was Nero, having begun his reign in A.D. 54). The early years of his rule were gentle in nature and gave no hint of the awful cruelties which would soon follow.

D. Paul's Defense before Agrippa. 25:13-26:32.

13-22. Agrippa II was the son of Herod Agrippa (12:1) and Bernice, who was the sister of both Drusilla and Agrippa. She had previously been married to her uncle until his death, and was now living with her brother in a relationship widely rumored to be incestuous. She later left him for another pagan king, then deserted him and finally became the mistress of both the Roman emperor Vespasian and his son Titus, who later destroyed Jerusalem in A.D. 70. Upon hearing about him from Festus, **Agrippa** requested an audience with the famous prisoner. Paul was brought into the palace court and in chains preached Christ to his royal guests. It is interesting to note that **Agrippa,** who had come to power in A.D. 53, controlled most of Palestine at the time and supervised the appointment of the high priest in Jerusalem. His powerful influence in Jewish affairs certainly made Paul's interview with him one of extreme importance. Festus related how Paul had been left there from the time of Felix and how he **doubted of such manner of questions** (vs. 20) because of his lack of understanding of the nature of Jewish matters, since he was new to that territory. The term **Augustus** (vs. 21) is misleading since the word is a translation of the Latin *Augustus*, meaning the "revered" or "august one." This term was applied to all Roman emperors of whom Augustus Caesar had been the first. Again note that the emperor at this time was Nero. The modern equivalent for this term would be similar to "his majesty" (Gr *sebastos*). Because of Paul's appeal to Caesar no further action could be taken by these royal rulers.

22-27. A further hearing was set up before Festus, Agrippa, Bernice, and an advisory council consisting of the **chief captains** (or military tribunes) and **principle men of the city.** Luke's purpose in including these appearances before public officials in such lengthy detail seems to be of an apologetic nature in defense of Christianity. Such statements as he had committed **nothing worthy of death** (vs. 25), are used to verify the credibility of this great Christian leader. While the book of Acts first centered on the ministry of James and Peter, it has now shifted totally to that of Paul, undoubtedly due to Luke's close relationship to him. Festus went on to explain that the entire process **seemeth to me unreasonable**, since no proven charge had ever been established against Paul.

26:1-12. Paul's defense before Agrippa began again with a gesture of salutation as he **stretched forth the hand.** Paul expressed his gratitude that he was able to make his defense before Agrippa since he was an expert in Jewish customs and affairs. Paul's approach, notes Ladd (p. 478) was to convince him that faith in Christ was the ultimate fulfillment of Jewish belief. Therefore, the apostle outlined his upbringing as a Jew in the **straitest sect** of the Jewish religion as a **Pharisee** (vs. 5). Paul centered his appeal on the question of the resurrection and God's power to **raise the dead** (vs. 8). He went on to explain that he himself had thought and done many things **contrary to the name of Jesus of Nazareth.** Notice that the early Christian movement always identified itself closely with Jesus' name. He explained how he imprisoned believers ("saints," Gr *hagios*). He went on to explain that he even **compelled them to blaspheme.** A better translation would be "tried to make them blaspheme." The tense of the Greek word indicates that Paul failed in his attempt to bring them to blasphemy. An experience which certainly would have left a marked impression upon the young Jewish inquisitor!

13-23. This account gives more details into Paul's experiences as a persecutor than any other passage in the New Testament. Having laid this background, the apostle now began to explain the Damascus vision which occurred at **midday,** in which Christ appeared to him and called to him **in the Hebrew tongue** (vs. 14). The phrase **it is hard for thee to kick against the pricks** means that it was "painful" to

kick back against the "goads," used to prod beasts of burden. This was a proverbial saying in Latin and Greek, but is unknown to us in Hebrew or Aramaic. Paul's terminology is such that it would be most understandable to his Gentile listeners. Then, Paul clearly recounted the voice as identifying himself as **Jesus whom thou persecutest** (vs. 15). He went on to explain that Jesus was sending him to the **Gentiles . . . to open their eyes.** Paul was making it clear that his very defense before these earthly kings was a fulfillment of the mission upon which his Lord had sent him! Thus, he could offer **forgiveness of sins** (vs. 18) unto his Gentile listeners. He drew the story of his conversion to a close by announcing: **Whereupon O king Agrippa, I was not disobedient unto the heavenly vision** (vs. 19). He then quickly summarized his entire ministry preaching to them of **Damascus . . . Jerusalem . . . Judaea . . . and then to the Gentiles** (vs. 20). In each case, and to each group, he had preached that **they should repent and turn to God.** Again, there can be no doubt that repentance was an essential ingredient to salvation and was a vital part of Paul's apostolic preaching! He went on to explain that it was for **these causes** (that of his evangelistic mission) that the Jews had taken him and wanted to kill him. However, he explained that he had obtained the **help of God** (vs. 22) and that God had kept him alive until that day **witnessing both to small and great** of what Christ had suffered and that He had risen from the dead **to show light unto the people, and to the Gentiles** (vs. 23).

24-32. Festus, a Gentile who was unaware of Jewish thinking and Old Testament teaching, was shocked and uttered with a loud voice: **Paul, thou art beside thyself** (or insane). Reference to his **much learning** which had made him **mad** indicates that it was obvious that Paul was a man of unusual intelligence but must have gone crazy from all of these religious investigations. While the point is not made directly by the story, it seems obvious as Luke recounts this incident to show that Christianity could be no mere invention of the mind of man but only the revelation of the truth. Only the life-changing experience of conversion could drive a person like the Apostle Paul for so many years to remain faithful to what had happened in his life on one given day so many years before. Paul protested that he was **not mad** but was speaking the **truth** in **soberness** (Gr *sōphrosynē*, "temperate," "self-control," of "balanced mind"). He also appealed to Agrippa, that as an expert in Jewish affairs, he understood the things of which he were not spoken because these things were not **done in a corner.** He was reminding him that the events of the death and resurrection of Christ were hardly a secret and were openly known to anyone who had any knowledge of Jewish affairs at all. Paul's final appeal: **Believest thou the prophets? I know that thou believest** must be seen as an appeal to the king who evidently showed some outward indication of conviction and concern at that point. However, Agrippa, evidently embarrassed by the presence of Festus, was not about to make such an admission, and his response: **Almost thou persuadest me to be a Christian** is probably best understood as a parody on Paul's appeal: "In short, you are trying to make me play the Christian." Paul, however, went on to say that he wished they were **both almost, and altogether** true believers! After dismissing him, they conferred among themselves and decided that he had done **nothing worthy of death or of bonds** (vs. 31). Again, Paul's innocence was verified by Roman officials who agreed that he **might have been set at liberty** had he not **appealed unto Caesar.** Because of the formality of such an appeal, the legal process had to be carried through. It is most likely

that Festus and Agrippa sent some kind of letter of explanation to the emperor along with their unusual prisoner who was now finally on his way to Rome!

E. The Journey to Rome. 27:1-28:10.

27:1-14. Paul never seemed to be able to do anything half heartedly and the journey to Rome is itself an exciting and unusual story. A group of prisoners had collected at the headquarters of the Roman officials in Caesarea and Paul was sent with them to Rome under the charge of a centurion and the cohort of **Augustus' band** (an unidentified military formation). The final "we" section of the book picks up again with verse 1. Thus Paul was accompanied by Luke, who had originally arrived with him at Jerusalem, and is assumed to have remained nearby during the two year imprisonment in Caesarea. The obscure but faithful Aristarchus (as Blaiklock calls him, p. 189) also accompanied them. References to him appear in Collossians 4:10; Philemon 24. The ship of **Adramyttium** refers to a seaport on the Aegean opposite the island of Lesbos. They went north along the Palestinian coast to **Sidon,** where **Julius,** the centurion, allowed paul to go ashore briefly to visit his friends. Because the prevailing winds blow from teh west, the ship sailed between **Cyprus** and the mainland, rather than going directly into the winds which were **contrary.** Eventually they had to head out into the open sea below **Cilicia** and **Pamphylia** and finally came to **Myra,** a Lycian port, where larger ships could be found. There they transferred to an Alexandrian grain ship and headed for Rome. Sailing against the wind, they finally arrived with difficulty at **Cnidus,** on a promontory point at the southwest tip of Asia Minor. From this point they had to choose whether they would wait for a more favorable wind moving westerly, or whether they would sail

Paul's Voyage to Rome

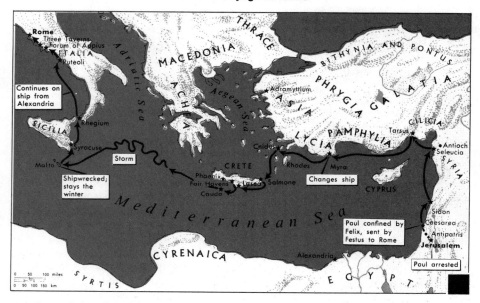

southward to Crete itself. The statement, **the wind not suffering us,** means the wind did not allow them to go on. Therefore, they chose the alternate route and sailed southward around **Salome** at the eastern end of Crete and coasted along westward on the leeward side of the island. Eventually they came to the port called **Fair Havens** which was, and still is, about halfway along the coast and beyond which the land slopes downward, exposing ships to the open wind. By the early fall the winter winds become fierce and by mid-November all sailing was an impossibility in the Mediterranean in those ancient times because the ships were not large enough to withstand the winter storms. **Paul admonished** his superiors not to attempt the journey under such dangerous circumstances. The **fast** (vs. 9) to which Luke refers is the Day of Atonement which generally falls at the end of September. Through the influence of the **master and owner** of the ship they attempted to sail to the more commodious port of **Phoenix** on Crete. Leaving the **Fair Havens** they were able to follow close along the shore of the island because the **south**

wind blew softly. Thinking they had made the right decision they got away from the safety of the port and were caught on the open seas by a **tempestuous wind** called **Euroclydon** (a hybrid word meaning "northeaster").

15-26. Luke then vividly recounts the story of the treacherous voyage which drove them twenty-three miles across the turbulent sea to the offshore island of **Clauda.** During this time the passengers had to aid the crew and struggled desperately to haul aboard the ship's boat, which was towing, water-logged behind. Fearing the **quicksands** *(Syrtis,* the graveyard of many ships off the north African coast), they **struck sail** (probably meaning they set storm sails) and were driven by the wind. When the storm did not abate the next day, they were forced to "lighten" the ship by throwing the cargo overboard and when it did not calm the following day, they threw over all the extra **tackling** and gear. The storm then continued for many days and the ancient sailors lost all hope of navigation because they could not see the stars. The reference to being **saved** (vs. 20) refers to the salvation of their lives from the storm. Paul's unusual leadership now arose to the forefront as he stood up in the midst of the storm and rebuked the sailors for not listening to his original advice and then reassured them that no man would die, in spite of the loss of the ship. He announced that the **angel of God** had appeared unto him in the storm to assure him that he would be **brought before Caesar** (vs. 24). There can be little doubt that Paul's unique experience on the road to Damascus was not limited by a one time event in his life. Time and again. God continued to put His miraculous mark of approval on His unusual servant. In the midst of our greatest personal dangers we can have the confidence that God is with us.

27-44. Blaiklock's (pp. 190 ff.) vivid description states: "they were, indeed, at the end of human resource. They had looped and tautened cables precariously round the hull, to bind the straining timbers against the stress of the violent seas, and the leverage of the mast; they cut loose all dispensable tackling and gear to lighten the vessel." As they drifted across the sea of **Adria** (a reference to the entire eastern Mediterranean, not the Adriatic Sea), they could tell they were approaching land, probably due to the sound of breakers crashing against the shore or the rock. As the depth soundings revealed that the water was becoming more shallow, they **cast four anchors** (vs. 29) in an attempt to secure the ship before drifting into the shore. The alert apostle frustrated an attempt by the **shipmen** (crew) to escape in the boat launch, leaving the rest on board. Therefore, the soldiers cut the ropes and let the smaller boat drift off. Toward daybreak, Paul then urged them all to have something to eat, a suggestion that paid off later. In unique Christian style he **gave thanks to God in presence of them all** (vs. 35). Certainly a true believer can never become reluctant or embarrassed to ask God's

blessing over his meal in a public situation in light of the example of the apostle Paul. The total number of people on the ship was 276. Finally, they cast even the remaining **wheat into the sea.** Therefore the ship owner's attempt to get his cargo to Rome in time to get the best price had now totally failed. At daybreak they attempted to run the ship aground in a creek which parted the shore. They cast off the anchors and using the **rudder bands** (two large steering oars on either side of the ship) they attempted to make the shore with a small "foresail." However, they did not make it and **ran the ship aground.** The bow of the ship was stuck on the shoal, while the force of the waves against the stern began breaking the ship in two. Had Paul not stepped to the forefront as he had and won the confidence of the centurion, all the prisoners would have been put to death by the **soldiers' counsel** (vs. 42). This action would have followed traditional Roman discipline to kill their charges rather than risk escape. The centurion, however, **willing to save Paul** and a lot of those who could swim did so and the rest floated in on **boards,** and some even on the **pieces of the ship.** Nevertheless, they all were able to reach land safely from the sandbar. The incident reveals the outstanding faith and character of the Apostle Paul who emerged as the hero of the story in spite of being a prisoner on the ship!

28:1-10. Again the reader is amazed that Paul's spiritual determination does not quit even under such difficult circumstances. In spite of his imprisonment, the series of trials, and now the traumatic shipwreck, Paul dominated the scene on the island of Melita (modern Malta) lying about a hundred miles south of Sicily. **Melita** is related to the Canaanite word "refuge" and was at one time part of the territory of Carthage, and the peasantry still spoke the Phoenician language. The term **barbarous** does not refer to primitive people, but rather those who spoke an unintelligible language. A better rendering would be "foreigner." A fire was kindled to warm them from the cold winter rain and Paul helped gather sticks for the fire, when a **viper** (snake, which had hibernated in the wood pile) **fastened on his hand** (i.e. bit him). The Melitians assumed that the snake bite had been inflicted in punishment of Paul's misdeeds. The common concept was that the goddess of justice, *Dike*, would use tragedy to catch up with her victims. When Paul shook off the snake unharmed, they **changed their minds** and decided that he was a **god** (vs. 6). Note that the verb **changed their minds** (Gr *metaballō*), meaning to change their "opinion," and is a completely different word from the theological term "to repent" (Gr *metanoeō*). As a result, the **chief man of the island** (the leading official), named **Publius,** lodged them for three days in his villa estate. His father **lay sick of a fever** and **bloody flux** (hemorrhage). Dysentery and fever were common on the island of Malta and often took many lives. Paul came to the man and **prayed, and laid his hands on him, and healed him.** These unusual miracles completely dominate the story of their three month winter sojourn on this island. Afterwards they continued "healing" the people of the island. Because of the change of the verbs for "healing" some have suggested that the subsequent "cures" may have been wrought by Luke the physician as well as by Paul. However, note the same use of the latter verb for the healing done by Peter in Acts 5:16. The ultimate concept seems to be that even in the presence of a medical doctor, miraculous healing was being done by the Apostle Paul!

F. Conclusion. 28:11-31.

11-16. Since the shipwreck had taken place during the early part of November, three **months** later would have put them near the end of Febru-

ary. Again they departed in a **ship of Alexandria** (vs. 11) which had wintered at Melita and which bore the sign of **Castor and Pollux.** Ancient sailing vessels often took their names from their figureheads, these being the *dioscuri*, meaning "the sons of Zeus," who were regarded as the patron deities of sailors. Sailing directly north they came to **Syracuse,** the most important city on Sicily at that time. The quaint archaism of the AV, **fetched a compass,** means they "made a circuit," or had to tack back and forth in order to reach **Rhegium** on the southern toe of Italy. They reached **Puteoli** on the bay of Naples, the regular port of arrival for grain ships coming from Alexandria. Here they spent seven days with **brethren.** By this time in the history of the early church Christian believers could be found almost anywhere throughout the entire empire. From **Puteoli** the land route was taken to Rome which normally included a barge passage through the Pontine Marshes and reached its terminus at the **Appii Forum,** some forty-three miles from Rome. **Three Taverns** was about ten miles closer and both were stopping places where travelers might lodge for the night. The reference in verse 16 is the last of the "we" statements in Acts. But since Luke is mentioned in Paul's letters which were written from Rome (cf. Phm 24; Col 4:14) it must be understood that he remained with Paul throughout this Roman imprisonment. It is not likely that Paul was actually put in jail or prison at this time, but was actually under personal attachment to a soldier whose responsibility was to bring him before the authorities at the proper time. Paul was able to dwell in a home.

17-31. The two-year imprisonment is briefly recorded by Luke in which Paul spent the greater amount of the time in a **hired house** (vs. 30), where he was allowed to receive visitors including many of the Jews and the Christians of the community. Very interestingly Paul put forth an aggressive attempt to evangelize the Jews at Rome who were totally ignorant of his disastrous encounters back in Palestine. To them he **expounded and testified the kingdom of God** (vs. 23) and **some believed . . . and some believed not.** Luke records the apostle's tireless effort to carry on his mission but then records the statement of **Esaias** (i.e. **Isaiah**), quoting 6:9-10, which describes the spiritual dullness of the Jews. Luke, himself a Gentile, seems convinced that only a minority of the people of Israel would be converted to the true gospel, therefore the statement is made again that **the salvation of God is sent unto the Gentiles** (vs. 28), reaffirming the ultimate Gentile mission of Paul. During the two-year wait for his court trial, Paul continued **Preaching the kingdom of God** and teaching the doctrine of **the Lord Jesus Christ.** Again the reference to the **kingdom of God** must refer to the church and not to continued Jewish preaching at so late a time in the apostle's ministry. His preaching was continued **with all confidence, no man forbidding.** The book obviously ends abruptly which has caused most commentators to believe that Luke wrote right up until the present time and closed the book at the point at which they had now arrived. No statement is made of Paul actually going to trial before Caesar, nor of his traditional release and a two or three-year interval, finally ending in his reimprisonment and death in A.D. 68. The two pastoral epistles (I Timothy and Titus) seem to reflect a continued traveling and preaching ministry of Paul which cannot be properly fitted into the narrative of the book of Acts, whereas II Timothy reflects the atmosphere of imprisonment awaiting final execution. In the early stages of these last events Paul seems confident of his release and looks forward to a continued ministry, whereas, in his last letter to Timothy he accepts the fact that he has "finished his course" and inevitable execution awaits him. Most writers agree that during the Roman imprisonment Paul penned the letters of Ephesians, Colossians, Philemon, and Philippians, and that he was eventually released and once more traveled throughout the empire preaching Christ, perhaps as far west as Spain, before his final arrest and martyrdom in Rome. It is not likely that Luke, who so carefully narrates the exciting experiences of Paul's encounter with worldly kings, would have omitted his appearance before Caesar had such already taken place at the time of the writing of this book. It would appear then that the narrative ends as it does because it had caught up with history. Luke has brought us up to the most contemporary point in the apostle's life at this time, so the narrative is closed and the message is sent off to the church who shall forever be grateful that a sovereign God was pleased to send into Paul's company one so capable and prepared under the hand of grace to recount in such accurate historic detail the events of the greatest servant of Christ in the history of the church. The unfinished ending of the Acts of the Apostles does not conclude beside the Tiber River, but in reality continues on in our own day and time as the Living Lord of the church continues to build His church, against which the gates of hell shall not prevail! Hallelujah!

BIBLIOGRAPHY

* Alexander, J. A. *A Commentary on the Acts of the Apostles.* London: Banner of Truth. reprint of 1857 ed.

Baumgarten, M. *The Acts of the Apostles or the History of the Church in the Apostolic Age.* Edinburgh: T. & T. Clark, 1854.

* Blaiklock, E. Acts of the Apostles. In *Tyndale New Testament Commentary.* Grand Rapids: Eerdmans, 1959.

* Bruce, F. F. *The Acts of the Apostles.* Grand Rapids: Eerdmans, 1951 (based on Greek text).

* ———Commentary on the Book of Acts in *New International Commentary.* Grand Rapids: Eerdmans, 1954.

Carter, C. and R. Earle. *The Acts of the Apostles.* Grand Rapids: Zondervan, 1959.

Erdman, C. *The Acts.* Philadelphia: Westminster Press, 1919.

Foakes-Jackson, F. J. and K. Lake, *The Beginnings of Christianity,* 5 vols. London: Macmillan, 1920-33.

Gloag, P. *A Critical and Exegetical Commentary on the Acts of the Apostles.* Edinburgh: T. & T. Clark, 1870.

Hackett, H. B. *A Commentary on the Acts of the Apostles.* Philadelphia: American Baptist Publication Society, 1851.

* Jensen, I. *Acts: An Inductive Study.* Chicago: Moody Press, 1968.

Ladd, G. E. "Acts" in *Wycliffe Bible Commentary.* Chicago: Moody Press, 1962.

Lindsay, T. *The Acts of the Apostles,* 2 vols. Edinburgh: T. & T. Clark, 1884.

Lumby, J. The Acts of the Apostles. In *Cambridge Greek Testament.* Cambridge: University Press, 1899.

* Morgan, G. C. *The Acts of the Apostles.* New York: Revell, 1924.

Rackham, R. *The Acts of the Apostles* (Westminster Commentaries). New York: Macmillan, 1901.

Ramsay, W. *Pictures of the Apostolic Church: Studies in the Book of Acts.* Grand Rapids: Baker, reprint of 1910 ed.

Ridderbos, H. *The Speeches of Peter in the Acts of the Apostles.* London: Tyndale Press, 1962.

* Scroggie, W. G. *The Acts of the Apostles.* London: Marshall, Morgan, Scott, 1931.

Thomas, W. H. G. *Outline Studies in the Acts of the Apostles.* Grand Rapids: Eerdmans, 1956.

The Epistle To The
ROMANS

INTRODUCTION

No other portion of Holy Scripture so completely sets forth the great doctrines of the Christian faith as does Paul's Epistle to the Romans. No other product of the pen has ever more powerfully confronted the mind of man with the great truths of God. All of man's alibis, all of his pretenses, all of his attempts at self-justification are mightily struck down by the truths of this book. In this, his *magnum opus,* every argument which man can muster against the claims of God are thoroughly demolished with unanswerable logic by the Apostle Paul.

Romans has rightly been called "the Constitution of Christianity," "the Christian Manifesto," "the Cathedral of the Christian Faith." There is nowhere to be found a more complete compendium of Christian doctrine. Herein are recorded the doctrines of justification, sanctification, divine election, condemnation, the perseverance of the saints, total depravity, the last judgment, the fall of man, the revelation of God in nature, the final restoration of the Jews, and many more. This epistle stands at the head of Paul's epistles as the brazen altar did before the Holy Place. You could not enter the tabernacle until you passed the brazen altar. Likewise, you cannot enter the great doctrinal portions of the New Testament without first passing Romans. It is the gateway to New Testament truth. It is basic training for the Christian. By the Holy Spirit of God, it is the masterpiece of Paul.

The Church at Rome. As the capital of the empire, Rome was the largest and most important city in the first-century world. Located about fifteen miles from the Mediterranean Sea, Rome was a teeming metropolis. In 1941 an inscription was discovered at Ostia which indicated that in A.D. 14 the city had a population of 4,100,000 (see Jack Finegan, *Light From the Ancient Past,* p. 288).

It is impossible to determine with great certainty who founded the church of this great metropolis. There are, however, several contenders for this honor who can be eliminated. First, it is evident that Paul did not establish the Roman church. Romans 1:10-11, 13, 15 all make reference to the fact that Paul had never been to Rome at the writing of this epistle. He obviously could not have founded the church there. Secondly, Peter must be ruled out as well. The view of the present Roman church, which adamantly holds to Petrine founding of the church in Rome, is based on an erroneous statement of Eusebius in his *Ecclesiastical History,* Book II, Chapter 14. This church historian inaccurately records that Peter went to Rome during the second year of the reign of the Roman Emperor Claudius to encounter the impostor Simon Magus, the sorcerer who tried to buy the power of the Holy Spirit (Acts 8:18-19). The second year of the reign of Claudius would have been A.D. 42. However, Peter was a pillar in the church of Jerusalem, not Rome (Gal 2:9). He is frequently mentioned as being active in Jerusalem (Acts 9). He was certainly in Jerusalem up until and through the Council of

Jerusalem (Acts 15). Since the Council of Jerusalem can be dated A.D. 49, it would have been highly unlikely for Peter to be in residence in Rome earlier than that.

Besides, in the salutation of the last chapter of Romans, Paul salutes twenty-seven individuals by name. If Peter was bishop of the church by that time, why did Paul not mention his name as well? Also, Luke has been demonstrated to be the most accurate historian of the first century A.D. (see Sir Wm. Ramsay, *St. Paul the Traveller and the Roman Citizen,* pp. 1-10). If Peter, as prominent as he was, had founded the church at Rome, how could Luke have overlooked such an important fact in recording the history of the early church in Acts? In addition, in Romans 15:20 Paul writes, "Yea, so have I strived to preach the gospel, not where Christ was named, lest I should build upon another man's foundation." If Peter had founded the church at Rome, why was Paul so anxious to preach there? (Rom 1:15). These considerations would make it appear impossible that Peter established the Roman church.

If neither Paul nor Peter established this church, then who did? Two possibilities exist. The first arises from those present at the Day of Pentecost. Acts 2:9-11 mentions that among those in Jerusalem on that eventful day were "strangers of Rome, Jews and proselytes." It is quite possible that believing Jews carried their new faith and the message of the gospel back to the imperial city and founded the church there. Another possibility is that families from Pauline churches in the East settled in Rome and, discovering the faith of each other, gathered together to worship independently of the Jewish synagogues. Either way the church at Rome apparently owed its origin to the migration of Christians from the eastern part of the empire who were converted through their contact with the gospel there.

It is generally accepted that when Paul wrote Romans there was a church of considerable size at Rome. The contents of this epistle make it evident that the Roman church was comprised of both Jews and Gentiles. There was a Jewish community in Rome as early as the second century B.C. It was greatly enlarged by Pompey's conquest of Judaea in 63 B.C. when Jewish prisoners-of-war marched in his grand procession. Cicero makes reference to the size and influence of the Jewish colony in Rome in 59 B.C. (*Pro Flacco* 66). In A.D. 19 the Jews of Rome were expelled from the city by a decree of Emperor Tiberius. Another mass expulsion took place in the reign of Emperor Claudius (A.D. 41-54). This expulsion caused Aquila and Priscilla to migrate to Corinth where they encountered Paul (Acts 18:2). But the effects of this expulsion order were temporary, for less than three years after the death of Claudius, Paul wrote of the Jewish Christians in Rome speaking of their faith as a matter of common knowledge. The original nucleus of the church must have been Jewish.

However, the Gentile element in the Roman church was predominant at the time of writing. Even though Paul addressed the Jews in 4:1 when he spoke of Abraham as "our father, as pertaining to the flesh," there are many direct references to the Gentiles. In his introduction Paul spoke of "obedience to the faith among all nations" (1:5). Paul desired fruit among the Romans, "even as among other Gentiles" (1:13). After he reviewed God's dealings with Israel in chapters 9-11, it is to the the Gentiles that Paul gives concluding admonitions (11:13). Later when he wrote to the Philippians from Rome, Paul intimated that it was among the Gentiles that the gospel had chiefly taken hold in Rome (Phil 1:13; 4:22). The church which had begun in Jewish hearts had taken on a decidedly Gentile tone.

Place of writing. The contents of the

Epistle to the Romans indicate that it was written from Corinth on Paul's third missionary journey. The events of this epistle fit perfectly into the chronology of Acts 20:1-5. Paul's eastern journeys were over; his face was set toward the West (Rom 15: 23-24; Acts 19:21). At this time Paul was heading to Jerusalem with the collection for the poor (Rom 15:24-27). This he did at the close of his three months' visit to Corinth (Acts 24:17). This collection was emphasized in his Epistles to the Corinthians (I Cor 16:1-4; II Cor 8:9). Romans must have been written about the same time as the Corinthian epistles, only a bit later. When he wrote the epistle, Paul mentioned that with him were Timothy, Sosipater, Gaius, and Erastus (Rom 16:21-23). Timothy, Sosipater (Sopater), and Gaius were all mentioned as being with Paul in Corinth during his three months' visit (Acts 20:4). By crossreferencing we note that those mentioned in Romans were the same men who were with Paul at Corinth and it was from there that he wrote the Epistle to the Romans.

Date of writing. It is possible to pinpoint the date of writing even further than simply Paul's three-month stay at Corinth. The absence of defensive tactics by Paul and the tranquil tone of the epistle suggest that it was written toward the end of his stay in Corinth, after the troubles at Corinth had been quieted. Since all navigation on the Mediterranean ceased between the middle of November and the middle of March, the plans of Phoebe to travel to Rome would hardly have been made before the spring. Thus it is likely that the date of the Roman epistle was the spring of A.D. 57, although estimations range from A.D. 56 to A.D. 58.

Purpose of writing. During the decade A.D. 47 to 57 Paul had spent most of his time intensively evangelizing the territories which border the Aegean Sea and planting churches throughout Asia Minor and Greece. His eastern campaign was now concluded, but his task was by no means complete. During the winter of A.D. 56-57, which he spent at the house of his Corinthian friend Gaius, he apprehensively looked forward to an immediate journey to Jerusalem where he hoped the gift he bore from the Gentile churches to the poor Jewish saints at Jerusalem would help salve the wounds of controversy and strengthen the bonds between the mother church and the churches of the Gentiles. Once this mission was complete, Paul could continue his dream to labor where no man had labored and build where no man had built. His choice was Spain, the oldest Roman colony in the West. But a journey to Spain would afford opportunity to realize another lifelong ambition, to visit Rome and spend some time with the believers there.

The purpose of his epistle to these Roman believers was as follows: (1) to enlist the co-operation and support of the church at Rome for the inauguration of his missionary campaign in the West. Paul realized the strategic and political importance of this city. He needed the assistance of the believers of Rome to launch him into missionary activity in the West as the church at Antioch had done in the East. (2) Paul also wanted to enlist the prayer support of the Roman Christians for his forthcoming venture at Jerusalem (15:30-33). He was concerned about the outcome of his journey there and rightly so. (3) Paul was emphatic in his claim to be the apostle to the Gentiles. Since Rome was the capital of the Gentile world it was entirely appropriate that he visit the church there. (4) Paul knew that the Roman church had come into existence without the authoritative leadership of an apostle of the Lord. Thus Paul wanted to add validity to their existence by instructing them in the faith through his epistle. (5) Paul desired to deposit a compendium of theological truth and the capital city of the empire was the natural place for him to do so. Besides, Paul was apprehensive about the immediate trip to Jerusalem and perhaps the Epistle to the Romans would be his final opportunity to draft a theology of the Christian faith in a written, changeless form. As Adam W. Miller says, "He bequeaths to them in the form of the Epistle the gospel that he would preach to them, should he be permitted to reach there, and if not, they have his letter to read and refer to again and again" (Adam W. Miller, *An Introduction to the New Testament*, p. 209). Paul certainly fulfilled these purposes. This epistle has proved to be one of the bulwarks of evangelical Christianity.

Authorship. That Paul was the author of the Epistle to the Romans is indisputable and universally acknowledged. On internal grounds, Paul claims to be the author (1:1). The writer makes personal references which can only apply to Paul (cf. 11:13; 15: 15-20). The style, argument, and theology are all Pauline. On external grounds quotations from this epistle are found in Clement of Rome. Ignatius, Justin Martyr, Polycarp, Hippolytus, Marcion, the Muratorian Canon, and the Old Latin and Syriac Versions. Romans was recognized as Pauline and a canonical writing since the time of Irenaeus, A.D. 130-202.

Although Pauline authorship is indisputable, some critics have questioned the authenticity of chapters 15 and 16. It seems certain that Marcion did not include the last two chapters in his canon. There is also evidence that the early Latin Version ended the epistle with chapter 14 and the doxology of 16:25-27. However, there is no extant Greek manuscript which omits these chapters.

These two chapters have been assaulted basically on three grounds. Critics charge: (1) the large number of personal greetings in chapter 16 is improbable if Paul had never visited Rome; (2) the commendation of Phoebe was not appropriate to a church Paul had never met; and (3) the suitability of 15:33 as an ending to the epistle makes the addition of chapter 16 unlikely. These criticisms, however, are weak and can be otherwise explained. The great Roman system of roads would have made it easy for Paul to have met the people mentioned in chapter 16 or to have known them before they moved to Rome. Since Paul was well enough known to the church at Rome to have written an epistle to them, he was well enough known to have commended Phoebe to them. And, although 15:33 does make an appropriate ending, nevertheless its style is unparalleled in all the Pauline Epistles. The word "grace" occurs in each of Paul's benedictions except 15:33 (cf. Rom 16:24; I Cor 16:23; II Cor 13:14; Gal 6:18; Eph 6:24; Phil 4:23; Col 4:18; I Thess 5:28; II Thess 3:18; I Tim 6:21; II Tim 4:22; Tit 3:15; Phm 25). Hence, there is no reason not to accept all sixteen chapters of the Epistle to the Romans as authentically Pauline.

The importance of Romans. It is likely that the importance of the Epistle to the Romans cannot be overstated. In the summer of A.D. 386 Aurelius Augustinus, a native of Tagaste in North Africa and Professor of Rhetoric at Milan, was on the brink of beginning a new life. Taking up his scroll he read, "Not in rioting and drunkenness, not in chambering and wantonness, not in strife and envying. But put ye on the Lord Jesus Christ, and make not provision for the flesh, to fulfil the lusts thereof" (Rom 13:13-14). "No further would I read," he said, "nor had I any need; instantly, at the end of this sentence, a clear light flooded my heart and all the darkness of doubt vanished away" (*Confessions* viii. 29). Such was the conversion experience of St. Augustine.

In November, 1515, an Augustinian monk and Professor of Sacred Theology at the University of Wittenberg,

Germany, began to expound this epistle to his students. As he prepared his lectures, he became more and more convinced that the just shall live by faith. "I greatly longed to understand Paul's Epistle to the Romans," he wrote, "and nothing stood in the way but that one expression, 'the righteousness of God.' . . . Night and day I pondered until . . . I grasped the truth that the righteousness of God is that righteousness whereby, through grace and sheer mercy, he justifies us by faith. Thereupon I felt myself to be reborn . . . " (*Luther's Works,* Weimar edition, Vol. 54, pp. 179 ff.). Through the reading of this epistle, Martin Luther was born into the family of God.

On the evening of May 24, 1738, John Wesley unwillingly attended a society meeting at Aldersgate Street where someone was reading Luther's Preface to the Epistle to the Romans. Wesley wrote in his journal, "About a quarter before nine, while he was describing the change which God works in the heart through faith in Christ, I felt my heart strangely warmed. I felt I did trust in Christ, Christ alone, for my salvation; and an assurance was given me that he had taken my sins away, even mine; and saved me from the law of sin and death" (*Works,* 1872, Vol. I, p. 103). This event, more than any other, launched the Evangelical Revival of the eighteenth century.

The great Swiss Reformer John Calvin said of this epistle, "When any one understands this Epistle, he has a passage opened to him to the understanding of the whole Scriptures." James I. Packer, twentieth century theologian, comments that, "there is one book in the New Testament which links up with almost everything that the Bible contians: that is the Epistle to the Romans. . . . From the vantage-point given by Romans, the whole landscape of the Bible is open to view, and the broad relation of the parts to the whole becomes plain. The study of Romans is the fittest starting-point for biblical interpretation and theology" (James I. Packer, *Fundamentalism and the Word of God,* pp. 106 ff.).

In his commentary on Romans the well-known Greek scholar Frederic Godet observed that "The Reformation was undoubtedly the work of the Epistle to the Romans, as well as of that to the Galatians; and the probability is that every great spiritual revival in the church will be connected as effect and cause with a deeper understanding of this book." One cannot say what might happen if Christians undertake an intensive study of this epistle. What happened to Augustine, Luther, Calvin, and Wesley, which left a mark on the world, could happen to us today. So, let the reader beware. Do not begin a serious study of this epistle unless you are willing to bear the consequences. Reading through Romans repeatedly results in revival.

OUTLINE

B. The need of the Moralist. 2:1-16.
   1. Condemned by his own judgment. 2:1.
   2. Condemned according to truth. 2-5.
   3. Condemned according to works. 6-10.
   4. Condemned without respect of persons. 11-16.

C. The Need of the Jew. 2:17-3:8.
   1. His law cannot make him righteous. 17-24.
   2. His circumcision cannot make him righteous. 25-27.
   3. His birth cannot make him righteous. 28-29.
   4. His arguments cannot make him righteous. 3:1-18.

D. The Need of the Whole World. 3:9-20.
   1. The charge against the whole world. 9.
   2. The indictment against the whole world. 10-18.
   3. The defense on behalf of the whole world. 19.
   4. The verdict against the whole world. 19-20.

III. The Righteousness of God Provided. 3:21-8:39.

A. The Provision for Justification. 3:21-5:21.
   1. Justification is by faith alone. 3:21-31.
   2. Justification is illustrated in the Old Testament. 4:1-25.
   3. Justification brings blessings to its recipients. 5:1-11.
   4. Justification is imputed to us as was sin. 12-21.

B. The Provision for Sanctification. 6:1-7:25.
   1. Sanctification and the principle of sin. 6:1-14.
   2. Sanctification and the practice of sin. 15-23.
   3. Sanctification and the law. 7:1-14.
   4. Sanctification and the conflict within. 15-25.

C. The Provision for Assurance. 8:1-39.
   1. The assurance of the righteousness of God. 1-4.
   2. The assurance of the indwelling Spirit of God. 5-13.
   3. The assurance of eternal heirship. 14-25.
   4. The assurance of present intercession. 26-27.
   5. The assurance of the eternal purpose of God. 28-34.
   6. The assurance of the eternal presence of God. 35-39.

IV. The Righteousness of God Exemplified. 9:1-11:36.

A. Righteousness Exemplified in Divine Sovereignty. 9:1-33.
   1. Sovereignty exhibited in Israel's identity. 1-8.
   2. Sovereignty exhibited in God's personal choices. 9-13.
   3. Sovereignty exhibited in God's powerful will. 14-24.
   4. Sovereignty exhibited in Israel's partial blindness. 25-33.

B. Righteousness Exemplified in Human Responsibility. 10:1-21.
   1. Nearness of the gospel: opportunity for responsibility. 1-10.
   2. Offer of the gospel: ground for responsibility. 11-15.
   3. Disobedience to the gospel: failure of responsibility. 16-21.

C. Righteousness Exemplified in Israel's Future. 11:1-36.
   1. Israel's rejection leaves a remnant. 1-10.
   2. Israel's rejection is not permanent. 11-24.
   3. Israel's restoration is prophesied. 25-32.
   4. Israel's restoration evokes praise. 33-36.

COMMENTARY

I. INTRODUCTION. 1:1-17.

A. Salutation to the Romans. 1:1-7.

The epistolary form which Paul uses is thoroughly consistent with other authors of the New Testament era. Paul begins each of his epistles with his own name, gives his salutation, adds a note of thanksgiving for his readers (Galatians is the only exception) and then, in epistles dealing with theological problems, he launches into a doctrinal section followed by a practical section. Finally, personal greetings and an autograph conclude his letters. This basic form does not essentially vary from epistle to epistle.

1:1. Paul, a servant of Jesus Christ, called to be an apostle. Paul calls himself a servant (Gr *doulos,* bondslave) of Jesus Christ. In his mind, since a Roman slave was answerable only to his master, Paul was not just servant to the Lord but slave as well and answerable only to Him (I Cor 4:1-4). In addition, he was a "called" apostle. Pual claimed apostleship on at least four grounds: (1) he was a chosen vessel of God (Acts 9:15); (2) he was personally commissioned by Christ (Acts 9:6); (3) he had actually seen the risen Lord (I Cor 9:1-2); and (4) he was the recipient of divine revelation (Gal 1:10-12; 16-17).

Separated unto the gospel of God. Paul was set apart for the ministry of the gospel long before the Damascus Road experience (Gal 1:15). With the pedigree of Paul (Phil 3:5-6), he would have made an excellent minister to his people, the Jews. But in the providence of God, Paul was separated unto the gospel of God as an apostle to the Gentiles (Acts 9:15). Thus a disastrous schism between the Jewish and Gentile factions of the early church was avoided through the unique ministry of Paul.

2. With the mention of the gospel (Gr *euangelion*) of God, the apostle begins an explanation of the person of that gospel, Jesus Christ. In the AV the first sentence of Romans includes one hundred twenty-six words and encompasses seven verses. We can proceed directly from verse 1 to verse 7 without losing Paul's train of thought. But the mere mention of the gospel of God prompts him to include the interlude of verses 2 through 6 in which he describes this gospel as that **Which he had promised afore by his prophets in the holy scriptures.** The gospel was not an innovation but had been preannounced by the Old Testament prophets from Genesis 3:15 to Malachi 4:2. By quoting sixty-one times from the Old Testament, Paul indicated to the Jews that their Scriptures were really speaking of Jesus Christ. **Concerning His Son Jesus Christ our Lord** expresses the subject of the gospel. The gospel is not about Jesus Christ, the gospel *is* Jesus Christ. **Which was made of the seed of David according to the flesh.** The Davidic descent of Jesus Christ was the fulfillment of the promise that one from the chosen line would sit on the throne of David forever (II Sam 7:13; Jer 33:17).

4. And declared to be the Son of God with power. Notice that although Jesus Christ was *made* of the seed of David according to the flesh, He was not *made* the Son of God. The word rendered "declared" (Gr *horizō*) has the meaning of "appointed" or "marked out by unmistakable signs." It is used in Acts 10:42; 17:31 of Christ's appointment as Judge. Christ was not *made* but eternally is the Son of God. This fact graphically and unmistakably was revealed to the world **according to the spirit of holiness, by the resurrection from the dead.** There is an obvious antithesis between **according to the flesh** and **according to the spirit.** Here is a distinction between the two states of Christ's humiliation and His exaltation. Christ's humiliation came when He voluntarily was made in the likeness of men (Phil 2:7) and His exaltation when He was resurrected by the Holy Spirit of God.

5-6. Grace and apostleship. Probably better translated "grace of apostleship," Paul regards his calling as a heavenly gift. The purpose of his apostleship is **for obedience to the faith among all nations, for his name.** Paul wants to bring the nations of the world, both Jew and Gentile, into obedience to the faith (i.e. the body of doctrine which he teaches). **Among whom are ye also the called of Jesus Christ.** The expression "the called" is a favorite one of the apostle to indicate those who have trusted the Lord Jesus as Saviour (cf. 8:28).

7. To all that be in Rome, beloved of God, called to be saints. Sainthood is not to be identified with the practice of canonization which later arose out in the Roman church. The saint is one called of God and "holy," that is (Heb *quadosh*) set apart to God. The saints of Rome were **beloved of God,** which marks them out as the undeserving yet grateful recipients of God's love, **Grace to you and peace.** One of the interesting features of the Pauline style is that in every one of the Pauline Epistles these two words appear together. Grace and peace are never separated by Paul (cf. Rom 1:7; I Cor 1:2; II Cor 1:2; Gal 1:3; Eph 1:2; Phil 1:2; Col 1:2; I Thess 1:1; II Thess 1:2; I Tim 1:2; II Tim 1:2; Tit 1:4; and Phm 3). The reason is that Paul, a Hebrew of the Hebrews but the apostle to the Gentiles, was the bridge between the Jews and Gentiles of the first century church.

Grace is the typical Greek greeting (*charis*) whereas peace is the usual Hebrew greeting (*shalom*). Paul always uses both to bind Jews and Gentiles together in the Lord.

B. Expression of Personal Feelings. 8-15.

8. Your faith is spoken of throughout the whole world. So strong was the faith of these Roman believers that, as the church of the Thessalonians (I Thess 1:8), Paul speaks of it in worldwide terms. The expression "throughout the whole world" is the common one for "everywhere."

9. Whom I serve with my spirit. Without ceasing I make mention of you always in my prayers. Paul's prayer life is intertwined with his life of service. The word the apostle uses for service (Gr *latruō*) is that of the function of a priest in the temple and is very frequently used by Paul to mean worship (cf. Phil 3:3; II Tim 1:3). A great deal of Paul's priestly service to the Lord was his regular program of intercessory prayer on the behalf of other believers (cf. Eph 1:16; Phil 1:3; Col 1:3; I Thess 1:2; II Tim 1:3; Phm 4).

10-13. Paul now states his purpose in wanting to come to Rome. He says, **For I long to see you** (in current idiom, "I am homesick for you"). This deep longing of Paul to be with the Roman believers arises out of three reasons. First, **that I may impart unto you some spiritual gift.** Paul wants to be more than a blessing to them, he wants to build them up in the most holy faith and explain to them more fully what it means to be "in Christ Jesus." Knowing that this local church had not had the apostolic stamp of approval placed on it, Paul wishes to visit them to do so. Secondly, Paul desires the Romans to reciprocate, **that I may be comforted together with you.** It has been the lifelong desire of the apostle to preach the gospel in Spain where no man had laid a foundation. Rome was to be a stopover for that journey. Paul would need

lodging, food, and Christian fellowship. He desires the Roman believers to provide these for him. Finally, verse 13 indicates that Paul's desire is not only to evangelize Spain but also the capital of the Gentile world. He says, **that I might have some fruit among you also.** An evangelist at heart, Paul does not look to Rome simply as a launching pad for further evangelistic effort but as a needy field itself.

Even as among other Gentiles would seem to indicate that although the nucleus of the Roman church was originally Jewish, it is now predominantly a Gentile church.

14. I am debtor. Paul views himself as a debtor to the whole world. He has been placed in debt by the love of Jesus Christ (II Cor 5:14). The Pauline concept of Christian service is that each believer is deeply in debt. It is probably this same concept that inspired Isaac Watts to pen the words of the hymn *At the Cross* when he said, "But drops of grief can ne'er repay the debt of love I owe. Here, Lord, I give myself away 'tis all that I can do." Paul felt he had a responsibility to give nothing less than himself to the propagation of the gospel by which he was saved.

To the Greeks and to the Barbarians. In the Jewish mind, there were but Jews and heathen; in the Greek mind there were Greeks and barbarians; but in God's mind there are but the saved and the lost (I Jn 5:12). From the golden age of Athens under Pericles in the fifth century B.C. until the decline of the empire, Greece was more highly civilized and educated than any other society of its time. However, when Paul contrasted the Greek with the barbarian, it is evident that he included the Romans with the Greeks. Rome was heir to Greek culture and learning. Most people looked upon Rome as a militarized extension of the Grecian Empire. This is not to say that the Romans had no culture of their own, but that it was successfully synthesized with the Grecian so as to form a new culture, the Graeco-Roman. The Roman orator-author Cicero (106-43 B.C.) places Greece and Rome in the same category in his treatise *De Finis, On Ends.* He says, "not only Greece and Italy, but also every foreign country." Therefore, Paul can readily say to the Romans that he is debtor both to the Greeks (Gr *Hellenes*), including the Romans, and the less civilized barbarians (Gr *barbaroi*).

15. I am ready to preach. This expression appears to be the middle statement of a trilogy of three first person statements concerning Paul's preaching of the gospel of Christ. The first segment is **I am debtor.** The third statement is **I am not ashamed.**

All of us are debtors to Christ. All of us should be unashamed of the gospel of Christ. But not all are ready to preach that gospel. Paul was not only able and willing, but he was ready to preach as well. He was a clean vessel, not just a chosen vessel. He was ready to be used of God. Paul was like the old country preacher who, when asked how he prepared his Sunday sermon, said, "I read myself full, think myself clear, pray myself hot, and let myself go." Many believers are not ready to be let go because they are not read full, clear-minded about Christian doctrine, or prayed up. Paul was ready to be "let go" and sent to Rome by any means.

C. Statement of the Theme. 16-17.

16. For I am not ashamed of the gospel. In stating the theme of the gospel as the good news that Christ died for our sins, Paul makes a bold claim that he is not ashamed of that news. He may have had our Lord's warning in the back of his mind (Lk 9:26). Someone might well ask why Paul could have been ashamed of the gospel. Perhaps he would be ashamed to spread the gospel because of the fierce persecution for those who had come to believe in this message. As a Jew, Paul could have been ashamed of the gospel because the Jews abhorred it as sub-

verting the law. As an educated man he might have been ashamed because to the wise Greek the gospel was sheer fooolishness. He may have been ashamed of the gospel of Christ because, by the pagans, Christians were branded as atheists, a brand no Pharisee could tolerate. This atheism was not a theoretical denial of the existence of the gods (Gr *asebeia*), but was a practical refusal to recognize pagan dieties as truly God (Gr *atheos*). For those whom the Romans considered to be "Christian atheists," the consequences were severe, perhaps forced labor in mines or even capital punishment.

Although for these and other reasons Paul could have been ashamed of the gospel of Christ, there is never a hint in the Pauline corpus that he ever was ashamed. Quite the contrary (see Rom 9:33; 10:11; II Tim 1:8, 11-12, 16). **It is the power of God unto salvation.** Paul now gives the reason why he is not ashamed of the gospel of Christ. It is the power of God, the great and admirable mystery which has been hidden with God from before the foundation of the world. The gospel, through the agency of the Holy Spirit of God, does what no amount of mere human reasoning or argumentation can do. The gospel compels men to face the reality of their own sin and guilt, the inevitability of divine judgment, and the need for a perfect substitute to make atonement for sin, if man is to survive at all. The gospel is the dynamite (Gr *dynamis*) which blasts away self-complacency, self-delusion, and sinful self-reliance. This nothing else can do, for nothing else is in itself the **power of God unto salvation to everyone that believeth.**

To the Jew first. Paul has deliberately proclaimed that the gospel is for everyone. He did so because there were many Jewish believers who thought the gospel was not for the heathen, the Gentile. Paul says no. The gospel is for all, it is the power of God unto salvation to everyone, without distinction of age, sex, race, or condition. But faith is the key to receiving the gospel and the gospel is to be proclaimed first to the Jew.

From the days of Abraham the Jews have always been highly distinguished from all the rest of the world in many and great divine privileges. They are the royal family of the human race. They are the rightful heirs to the Promised Land. They are the chosen nation of God. They were given the oracles of God. They had a covenant with Jehovah God. It was through the Jews that Christ Jesus came. Originally the preaching of the gospel was addressed to them exclusively (Mt 10:5-6). During His ministry on earth Jesus Christ was a minister to the circumcision only (Rom 15:8). The spread of the gospel was to begin in Jerusalem, the center of Judaism (Acts 1:8). Paul did not forget that the gospel was to be first directed toward God's chosen nation, Israel, but the words **and also to the Greek** indicate that Paul was well aware that the message of the gospel is a universal message, for everyone needs it. It is not for just the Jew or the Roman citizen, it is not just for the wise, but it is for the heathen and the Roman slave as well. The gospel is open to all, it is for everyone, but there is a condition or restriction put on that everyone. That restriction is faith. The gospel is for all who believe. It is efficacious to everyone **that believeth.**

17. For therein links verse 17 with verse 16; "for in it," that is in the gospel, is the rightness of God revealed. This explains why the gospel is the power of God.

The gospel is "dynamite" because through it the righteousness of God is revealed. Righteousness is that aspect of God's holiness which is seen in His treatment of His creatures. Simply, righteousness is how God treats us. Jesus Christ is our righteousness. He is how God treats us. We are unright-

eous, unholy, and unlovely. Yet Christ died for our sins (I Cor 1:30).

How is righteousness obtained? **From faith to faith.** Righteousness is received by faith in Christ Jesus and is in turn revealed in faithful living. Thus, in answer to the question, "How are the righteous to live?" Paul quotes Habakkuk 2:4, **"The just shall live by faith."** This faith implies more than mere acceptance of Christ's righteousness for salvation. It implies a life style that is characterized by faith and righteous living. It was this truth that excited Martin Luther and initiated the Protestant Reformation (1:18).

II. THE RIGHTEOUSNESS OF GOD NEEDED. 1:18-3:20.

A. The Need of the Heathen. 1:18-32.

With the introduction complete, thanksgiving made, and the theme of his epistle stated, Paul now turns to the heart of the doctrinal teaching in Romans. Paul has both good news and bad news for the world. The good news, which will shortly follow, is that God has provided an atonement for our sins. The bad news, which he explores first, is that all men need atonement for their sins. Before you can appreciate the good news, you must know that there is bad news. Before Paul tells us that the gift of God is eternal life, he tells ut that the wages of sin is death. Verse 18 begins the groundwork which Paul lays for his case against man's self-righteousness. His aim is to show that the whole world is morally bankrupt, unable to receive a favorable verdict at the judgment bar of God, and desperately in need of divine mercy and pardon.

1. The heathen have clearly seen God. 18-20.

For the wrath of God is revealed. God's attitude toward the sin of mankind is not one of tolerance. He does not simply hold man accountable for what may be reasonably expected of him in view of man's nature as a sinner. If God did, His holiness and purity would be soiled by complicity with our guilt. God hates man's sin. His wrath is a holy aversion to all that is evil. Wrath is as essential to divine righteousness as love and mercy are. God could not be free from wrath unless He were also free from all concern about His moral universe.

Against all ungodliness and unrighteousness of men. Ungodliness has to do with religion, our relation to a sovereign God. Unrighteousness has to do with morality, our relation to our fellowman. Ungodliness is sin against the being of God. Unrighteousness is sin against the will of God. Man is both a religious sinner (he is ungodly) and a moral sinner (he is unrighteous). The unrighteous man lives as if there were no will of God revealed. The ungodly man lives as if there were no God at all. God's wrath is against both.

Who hold the truth in unrighteousness. The word hold (Gr *katechō*), carries the meaning of "hold down," "keep back," or "suppress." Those who are unrighteous and ungodly restrain the truth of God's righteousness. The meaning of this word is clearly seen in the way it is used in Luke 4:42, "And when it was day, he (Christ departed and went into a desert place: and the people sought him, and came unto him, and stayed him, that he should not depart from them." Paul contends that the heathen have had the righteousness of God revealed to them, yet they suppress the truth of His righteousness for they are ungodly and unrighteous.

19-20. The apostle now anticipates the question: "If these ungodly men do not have full knowledge of God, are they then really lost?" The key word in Paul's answer is the first word of verse 19, **Because.** Paul will now present two lines of argument which will prove that the condemnation of the sinner does not rest upon the depth of his knowledge of God but upon what use he makes of that knowledge. **That which may be known of God is manifest in them.** Paul's first reason that the heathen are lost (or any man who willingly suppresses the knowledge of God) is because of the revelation of God in nature. Man has a sufficient knowledge of God to make him responsible to God. That knowledge arises from the fact that **the invisible things of him from the creation of the world are clearly seen** (cf. Ps 19:1). Man's mind is capable of drawing obvious conclusions from effect to cause. To the animals below us the phenomena of nature may just be a spectacle before their eyes, but make no impression on their minds. But to man, they have a language, a communication. They awake wonder, awe, a basic idea of God and His righteousness. **Even his eternal power and Godhead.** Nature does not simply give the impression that God is an abstract principle but a real person, the Supreme Person, transcendent above His creation and not part of it. The testimony of nature alone is sufficient to lead man to an understanding of the personal, righteous nature of God, **so that they are without excuse.**

2. The heathen have clearly rejected God. 21-23.

21-23. Paul's second line of argument is that the heathen are lost because of the revelation of God to the conscience. **They glorified him not as God.** As if the natural world around us isn't enough, God has planted in the heart of every man the knowledge that there is a righteous God. Though the heathen knew that He was God and deserved to be glorified, they willfully chose not to glorify Him as God. They did not ascribe to His person the holiness, perfection, and sovereignty which are His alone. **Neither were thankful.** To add injury to insult, the heathen accepted the good things of nature from the hand of God, but were not thankful for them. **But became vain in their imaginations.** In order to suppress the witness of the ordered structure of the universe, and the innate testimony of the conscience, fallen man had to develop a reasoning process of imagination. This reasoning is described by God as vain because the whole structure of man-made philosophy is devoid of divine truth and therefore invalid. Thus, by suppressing the truth of God and believing their man-made falsehood, they plunged their foolish heart deeper into darkness. When they exalted their human reasoning and paraded their wisdom before their peers, they acted as fools. The foolish heart is not one deficient in intelligence but one deficient in the moral understanding of who God is.

Laboring under the handicap of this extreme deficiency, the heathen **changed the glory of the uncorruptible God into an image.** By creating a god suitable to their own fallen conception of deity the heathen have violated the first commandment. They have devised their own concept of divinity and placed it above the one true God. **Made like corruptible man, and to birds, and four-footed beasts, and creeping things.** More than just conceptualizing what they thought God ought to be, the heathen actually created animal-like images of their concept of God. In so doing they violated the second commandment.

The apostle has thus given two reasons why the man without God is lost and deserving of condemnation: (1) because of the revelation of God in nature (vss. 19-20; and (2) because of the revelation of God in their conscience (vss. 21-23). The wrath of God is revealed from heaven against all who suppress the truth of these two witnesses. To the heathen who does not suppress this fundamental light, the Lord Jehovah grants additional enlightenment of His person. But whoever is guilty of suppressing the available truth about God does not receive light unto salvation.

3. The heathen have clearly become reprobate. 24-32.

24. Wherefore God also gave them up to uncleanness. Ungodliness and unrighteousness have a definite terminal point and that is idolatry. The word "wherefore" indicates that the retribution to follow finds its ground in the antecedent sins and is therefore justifiable. Because the heathen participated in idolatry, God gave them up to uncleanness. As seen by Paul's usage of this term elsewhere (cf. II Cor 12:21; Gal 5:19; Eph 5:3; Col 3:5; I Thess 4:7), "uncleanness" means sexual aberration by which they would **dishonor their own bodies between themselves.**

25. Who changed the truth of God into a lie. Suppression of the truth which God gave to the heathen became the basis for their idolatry and thus they **worshiped and served the creature more than the Creator.** They degraded themselves in that which they worshiped and exalted those things created to a higher position than the One who created them.

26-27. For this cause God gave them up unto vile affections. These "vile affections" (Gr *pathē atimias*) were passions of infamy. The apostle goes on to explain that **their women did change the natural use into that which is against nature.** Sexual perversion always accompanies idolatry. **And likewise also the men . . . burned in their lust one towards another; men with men.** Homosexuality is likewise the result of idolatry. Although today the world seeks to popularize and legitimize homosexuality, nevertheless it is despicable to God and condemned by Him. Increased homosexuality is a sign of the soon return of the Lord (II Tim 3:2). God never overlooks this blatant misuse of the body and consequently those who have engaged in this perversion receive **in themselves that**

recompense of their error which was meet.

28. God gave them over to a reprobate mind. The word "reprobate" means "unapproving" or "undiscerning." Since they had suppressed the truth of God revealed to them, the heathen did not retain God in their knowledge and consequently, for the third time in almost as many verses, the apostle records that God gave them up (or over) to what they wanted all along. When He did so, the results were disastrous. The effects of their abandonment result solely from the corruption of the human heart; this cannot be blamed on God.

29-31. Being filled expresses (by the Greek perfect tense) that the heathen were not simply tainted by the catalogue of sins that follow but were in fact saturated with them. Thus the ugly character traits listed as the result of abandonment by God include: **unrighteousness,** or injustice (Gr *adika*); **fornication, wickedness** (Gr *poneria*), **covetousness** (Gr *pleonexia,* grasping for more than is needed), **maliciousness** (Gr *kakia*, intending evil toward others), . . . **whisperers, Backbiters, haters of God, despiteful, proud, boasters, inventors of evil things, disobedient to parents, Without understanding, covenant breakers, without natural affection . . . unmerciful.** This gallery of iniquity was not only true of the first century heathen world but reads much like our newspapers today.

32. Who knowing the judgment of God . . . do the same, . . . have pleasure in them that do them. The heathen world is not unaware of God's displeasure with these activities. Therefore, fully cognizant of the consequences of their sin, they continue to defy the Lord God of heaven and take great pleasure in keeping company with those who do the same.

Paul's conclusion is that the heathen are never without a witness to the presence and personality of God. They have the witness of nature and the witness of their own conscience. However, the heathen have deliberately suppressed these witnesses to the truth and have consistently opted for a lie in place of the truth. They have chosen the course of idolatry, which is always accompanied by debauchery. Thus, God has revealed His wrath from heaven against all ungodliness and unrighteousness of men who suppress the truth of God. In addition, God has given them up to idolatry, to passions of infamy, and to an undiscerning and unapproving mind. Are the heathen lost? Yes, the entire heathen world is lost, deserving condemnation, desiring evil, and desperately wicked.

B. The Need of the Moralist. 2:1-16.

1. Condemned by his own judgment. 2:1.

2:1. Therefore thou art inexcusable, O man, whosoever thou art that judgest. In the last chapter Paul painted a picture of the deplorable condition of the heathen. The apostle knew, however, that there would be a whole class of men who would say "amen" to what he had said about the heathen. These were the self-righteous moralists. So Paul expands his argument to show that "all ungodliness and unrighteousness of men" includes the moralist as well as the debauched heathen. The moralist is inexcusable when he judges the heathen for sin but is blind to his own sin. He only condemns himself when he condemns another. **For thou that judgest does the same things.** It is obvious that the moral man was not involved in the sexual deviations of the heathen, else Paul could not call him a moral man. But he was inwardly living in an identical manner as the heathen was living outwardly. Perhaps the moral man did not commit adultery, but did he lust? Our Lord put them in the same category (Mt 5:27-28). Maybe the moral man did not steal, but did he covet? Stealing and covetousness are listed together in Mark 7:22. Perchance the moral man did not commit murder, but did he hate? The Bible says if you hate your brother you are guilty of murder (I Jn 3:15). No one dares judge another while he is doing the same thing because he is then condemned by his own judgment.

2. Condemned according to the truth. 2-5.

2. The judgment of God is according to truth. When God judges it is always according to truth or in accordance with the facts. The moralist may attempt to hide the facts, but God always exposes them. The searching eye of God always ferrets out the truth.

3-4. And thinkest thou this, O man, . . . that thou shalt escape the judgment of God? Or despisest thou the riches of his goodness and forbearance and longsuffering. Since the judgment of God is according to truth, it is foolhardy for the moralist to believe that God will judge the heathen and not him. Since he does in his heart what the heathen does in his life, the moralist must withstand the same judgment as the man he condemned. To put ourselves in the position of the moralist would mean to despise God's **goodness** (Gr *khrēstotēs,* literally kindness), **forbearance** (Gr *anochē,* the willingness to tolerate the intolerance of others), and **longsuffering** (Gr *makrothymia,* patience which forgives until there is no more hope of repentance). **The goodness of God leadeth thee to repentance.** In judging others, the moralist has completely missed the truth that the purpose of God's goodness is to lead to repentance. It never occurs to the moralist that he personally needs the goodness of God just as the heathen does. He is unaware of his need for repentance.

5. But after thy hardness and impenitent heart. After years of glossing over his personal sin and guilt, the pride of the moralist will not allow him to have a change of mind (Gr *metanoia*) which is repentance. Thus his pride and sinful heart stockpile the wrath of God so that in the day of wrath, the day of God's righteous judgment, the Lord God will deal as justly with the moral man as he does with the heathen.

3. Condemned according to works. 6-10.

6. Who will render to every man according to his deeds. When unsaved men appear before the final judgment bar of God, the Great White Throne Judgment, salvation will not be the issue there. This is a judgment to determine the degree of punishment. Thus God will mete out punishment in relation to the evil deeds of the individual. By the same token, at the Judgment Seat of Christ, where only believers appear, God will reward us according to our deeds.

7. To them who by patient continuance in well doing. Patient continuance in well doing does not mean that we are saved by doing good. Paul is expressing an eternal truth. Obedience to God does well in every dispensation. When Cain brought his fruit as an offering and God rejected it, God said, "If thou doest well, shalt thou not be accepted?" (Gen 4:7). Obedience to God in bringing the proper sacrifice would have been doing well. Today, in the age of grace, we do well by placing our faith in Christ Jesus as Saviour. Thus faith in Christ is patient continuance in well doing in this age. This is what will bring **glory and honor and immortality, eternal life.**

8-9. But unto them that are contentious, and do not obey the truth. The moralist is likened to "those who are of contention." This formula is similar to other such expressions as "those who are of the circumcision" (4:12; Tit 1:10); "they which are of faith" (Gal 3:7); "they which are of the law" (4:14). Those who create a spirit of rivalry or factionalism have promised to them, **indignation** (Gr *orgē*), **wrath** (Gr *thymos,* a sudden outburst of anger), **tribulation** (Gr *thlipsis*, affliction), and **anguish** (Gr *stenochōria,* distress). As the gospel was promised to the Jew first and also to the Greek, so likewise these fruits of unrighteousness are **of the Jew first, and also of the Gentile.**

10. But glory, honor, and peace to every man that worketh good. Opposed to the reward of the unrighteous, Paul now indicates that the reward of the righteous is glory, honor, and instead of immortality as in verse 7, peace. The formula of impartiality is then the same, **to the Jew first, and also to the Gentile.**

4. Condemned without respect of persons. 11-16.

11. For there is no respect of persons with God. An eternal truth is that as God deals in condemnation without favoritism, likewise He deals in salvation without favoritism. Respect of persons (Gr *prosōpolēmpsia*, literally "lifting the face") simply means partiality (cf. Deut 10:17; II Chr 19:7; Acts 10:34; Gal 2:6; Eph 6:9; Col 3:25; I Pet 1:17). God is impartial because He does not change His pattern "to the Jew first," whether righteousness or unrighteousness is involved.

12-13. Unchecked and unatoned sin leads to perdition whether we are in the law or without the law. If the moralist is to live by the law then **not the hearers of the law are just before God but the doers of the law shall be justified.** The antithesis between merely hearing the law and doing it is elaborated in James 1:22-25. "The doers of the law" is an expression also found in the literature of the Dead Sea Scrolls. The moralist (now identified with the Jews, verse 9) is no better off than the heathen if the moralist has the law but does not keep it. The reason follows in the next verses.

14-16. For when the Gentiles, which have not the law, do by nature the things contained in the law, these . . . are a law unto themselves. Although the Gentiles do not possess the Old Testament law, nevertheless they do those things which are contained in the law. This is because of **the law written in their hearts, their conscience also bearing witness.** The Gentiles manifested a moral principle at work in their hearts, because when they broke their own ethical code, their conscience (Gr *syneidēsis*) would prick them and cause them to feel guilt. The result of their guilt, however, was they would excuse themselves by making a defense for their actions. But Jew and Gentile alike must face a day of judgment with God when the **secrets of men** (Gr *ta krypta*) are judged by the Lord Jesus Christ according to the truth of the gospel preached by Paul.

C. The Need of the Jew. 2:17-3:8.

1. His law cannot make him righteous. 17-24.

17. Behold, thou are called a Jew, and restest in the law. Israelites who remained in Palestine, or who returned to it after the Babylonian captivity, were designated as "Jews," even though tribes other than Judah were included. Paul calls himself a "Jew" in Acts 21:39 but "an Israelite" in Romans 11:1 and "a Hebrew" in Philippians 3:5. All three names refer to the same people; but in a technical sense "Hebrew" is the racial name, "Israel" is the national name, and "Jew" is the religious name of the sons of Jacob. The Jews rested in the law because it was described as "wisdom and . . . understanding in the sight of the nations" (Deut 4:6). The Jew did not have to travel around the world to study in a distant university. He did not have to rely on the philosophy of the Gentiles. The Jew trusted his law to be all that he needed and the best education he could get. Thus he boasted in the God who gave that law.

18. And knowest his will, and approvest the things that are more excellent, being instructed out of the law. Because he had received catechical training in the law as a youth, and rabbinical teaching as a man, the Jew felt confident that he could prove (Gr *dokimazō*) or discern those things that are more excellent.

19-20. Confident that he would be saved by his law, the Jew was convinced that he had been made righteous and therefore was able to assume four roles: **a guide of the blind** (the blind being the Gentile in his unjewish darkness); **a light of them which are in darkness** (the Gentile need to be enlightened by the Jew who was enlightened by the law); **an instructor of the foolish** (because he did not know the law, the Gentile was a fool); **a teacher of babes** (the Gentile was immature, an object of Jewish disgust).

21-23. There is a touch of sarcasm in Paul's question, **Thou therefore which teachest another, teachest thou not thyself?** The Jews were prepared to teach the heathen Gentiles the commandments of the law, but were themselves breaking those commandments. **Dost thou steal?** (the eighth commandment), **dost thou commit adultery?** (the seventh commandment), **dost thou commit sacrilege?** (literally, "Do you rob temples"), (the second commandment). The Jews were ready to preach morality but their lives did not back up their message. They were stealing from one another, perhaps by collecting an extreme interest; they were committing adultery; they were profaning the house of God by commercialism, and thus Paul asked the biting question, **Thou that makest thy boast of the law, through breaking the law dishonorest thou God?** Transgression of the law brings dishonor to God. The Jews claim to have known the law but were silent in claims to have kept it.

24. For the name of God is blasphemed among the Gentiles through you. This quotation from Isaiah 52:5 confirms that the inadequacies in the life styles of the Jews caused the Gentiles to speak lightly of the God of Israel. The Word of God was actually being blasphemed among the Gentiles because of the inconsistency of the Jews. Much the same thing could be said today about hearers of the Word but not doers. The Jew rested in his law, but since he did not keep it, his law could not make him righteous.

2. His circumcision cannot make him righteous. 25-27.

25. For circumcision verily profiteth, if thou keep the law. Notice that the apostle did not say "Circumcision verily justifieth." That has never been true. But circumcision is not a meaningless rite if it aids in keeping the law. However, when the Jew does not keep the law, **thy circumcision is made uncircumcision.** If the Jew trusts in his circumcision for salvation, and does not keep the law, his circumcision is made void.

26-27. If the uncircumcision keep the righteousness of the law. Now the tables are turned completely. If an uncircumcised Gentile gives his heart to God, and lives in a righteous relationship to the law, he is more pleasing to God than the circumcised Jew who does not. **And shall not uncircumcision . . . if it fulfill the law, judge thee.** The sin of the circumcised but unworthy Jew will be graphically demonstrated by the example of the Gentile who, though uncircumcised, nevertheless pleases God. Lack of circumcision would not condemn a Gentile just as the possession of circumcision would not save the Jew. The key is the law. If the law was broken then the Jew became as helpless as the Gentile. Therefore, the circumcised Jew is in the same pitiful state as the uncircumcised heathen if the Jew has broken the law. Since all the Jews have, Paul's conclusion is that his circumcision cannot save the Jew, for he has broken the law.

3. His birth cannot make him righteous. 28-29.

28-29. For he is not a Jew, which is one outwardly . . . But he is a Jew,

which is one inwardly. Here we see the double sense in which the term "Jew" is used. Frequently people speak of "Christians" as a term in opposition to heathen. In another sense, true believers in the Lord are called Christians. Paul is making the case that not all who are called Jews are truly Jewish. Possession of the law does not make one Jewish. Circumcision does not make one Jewish. Even birth in a Jewish family does not make one Jewish. Paul says that two things are necessary to be truly Jewish: (1) to be born of Abraham through Isaac **(that circumcision, which is outward in the flesh);** and (2) to be spiritually in tune with Abraham's God **(circumcision is that of the heart, in the spirit).** No one can claim to be Jewish who is not born of Abraham through his son Isaac. But to the requirement of outward circumcision (ancestry from Abraham), Paul adds the requirement of the circumcision of the heart. This spiritual or ethical circumcision is seen throughout the Scriptures (e.g. "uncircumcised lips" (Ex 6:12); "uncircumcised ear" (Jer 6:10); "uncircumcised heart" (Lev 26:41). The Jew who is born after the seed of Abraham through Isaac but yet does not have his heart circumcised in the way that Abraham did, that is, "to love the Lord thy God with all thine heart" (Deut 30:6; see also Jer 4:4), is not truly a Jew. He is a Jew outwardly, but not inwardly. He is born of Abraham, but not born again by the Spirit of God. The only true Jew is one who is a Jew by race, and a believer by God's grace. Thus, birth alone cannot make a Jew righteous.

4. His arguments cannot make him righteous. 3:1-8.

At the beginning of chapter 3 Paul anticipates arguments in rebuttal to his conclusion that neither Israel's law, her circumcision, nor her birth could save her. These theoretical objections are stated in the even numbered verses and Paul's answer to each objection is stated in the odd numbered verses.

3:1. What advantage then, hath the Jew? If the Jews are condemned along with the heathen, what advantage is there in being the chosen nation of God? **Or what profit is there of circumcision?** Since circumcision is the sign of Israel's covenant relationship with God, what advantage is that relationship if being Jewish will not save?

2. Much every way. Paul contends that there are many privileges which God has granted to Israel. A list of them is given in chapter 11; it is not necessary for Paul to enumerate them here. Rather, he simply points out one as example of the others. **Unto them were committed the oracles of God.** One of the chief ancestral privileges of Israel is that they were the custodians of the oracles of God. Acts 7:38 and Hebrews 5:12 mention these oracles, the Old Testament Scriptures. It was a great advantage to the Jew to be singled out by God and entrusted with the reception, inscription, and transmission of the Old Testament Scriptures.

3. Now a second argument is anticipated. **Shall their unbelief make the faith of God without effect?** As keepers of the Old Testament, the Jews had in fact failed to comprehend the message of the Old Testament, especially the prophetic and messianic passages. The unbelief of the Jews is seen in their rejection of Jesus as Messiah, and consequently they did not believe the oracles of God which they so carefully guarded. The question is, "Shall the unfaithfulness of Israel in this respect alter God's faithfulness?" Paul's answer is a classic.

4. God forbid. This expression (Gr *mē genoito*) corresponds to the Hebrew *chalilah* which is translated the same in the KJV of Genesis 44:17; Joshua 22:29; 24:16; I Kings 21:3; et al. It is an expression which indicates a recoiling abhorrence, utter shock, and disgust. It has been variously translated as "good heavens, no," "may it not prove to be so," "perish the thought," etc.

Let God be true, but every man a liar establishes a principle which is found throughout this epistle. God does not purpose or will according to extraneous influences but according to what He Himself is. If men prove unfaithful to God's oracles, He is nevertheless faithful in His promises to them. The quotation which follows is from Psalm 51:4 where King David had broken the covenant of God and had found in himself no righteousness or integrity of any kind. Paul quotes this verse in order that his readers may clearly see the difference between the faithfulness and integrity of God and the lack of the same in man.

5. A third objection is now theoretically advanced. **But if our unrighteousness commend the righteousness of God, what shall we say?** This is a clever but illogical argument. It is twisting Scripture to make what is inherently evil appear to be ultimately good. Paul anticipates someone saying, "If my unfaithfulness causes God's faithfulness to be set in boldface type, is not my sin by contrast enhancing the world's concept of the absolute holiness and faithfulness of God?" And a second question is: **Is God unrighteous who taketh vengeance?** Would it not be unjust of God to punish me for contributing to a more pristine picture of His true character?

The expression **I speak as a man** should not be understood as an absence of divine inspiration in recording these questions, but rather that Paul is using the form of human reasoning to express this inspired truth about God. Since God's justice is not something that may be called into question, Paul indicates that only foolish human reasoning would attempt to do so.

The answer to these questions is an emphatic **God forbid.** The consequence of this line of reasoning would be to deny God the divine right to judge any man. If God cannot judge men, then who can?

7. For if the truth of God hath more abounded through my lie; . . . why yet am I also judged as a sinner? Paul had been slandered by the Jews for teaching salvation by grace apart from works. Therefore he uses that situation to theorize a final argument from the Jews. If the doctrine of salvation which Paul preaches is a lie, and the truth is seen in contrast to Paul's teaching, then why is Paul also judged as a sinner? Should not he be considered a saint if his alleged false doctrine more clearly indicated what was true? Paul has turned the tables on the Jews by using their own logic and putting them in an untenable situation. They could not admit that Paul's teachings were true. But if they claimed them to be false, by their own logic, they would have to say that divine good arose out of Paul's doctrine.

8. We be slanderously reported. It was the Jewish argument that Paul was teaching the lie, **Let us do evil, that good may come.** For those who regarded the practice of religion as merely a matter of keeping the law, Paul's emphasis on justification by faith indeed seemed to make the law and its keeping superfluous. But justification by faith never meant believers could blatantly disregard the precepts of the law. If they did, it is theirs **whose damnation is just.** Damnation, or better condemnation, is executed on all those who, in light of their unfaithfulness, turn God's faithfulness into lasciviousness and license. This Antinomian philosophy is further condemned in chapter 6:2 ff.

God is just in condemning the Jews for they have sinned against Him and that their sin enhances His own righteousness is but a diversion from their own culpability as sinners. The justified man, whether heathen, moralist, or Jew, must never do evil. Arguments to the contrary can never save anyone.

D. The Need of the Whole World. 3:9-20.

Paul has shown that the heathen are lost because, even though they had the witness of both nature and conscience, they suppressed God's truth to them. He has shown also that the moral man is lost because even though he outwardly put on a facade to judge the heathen, inwardly he was guilty of the same sins. Likewise the Jew is lost because he has not kept the law, and his circumcision, ancestry, nor arguments, can save him from the condemnation of disobedience. Now Paul wraps up his argument and the summation assumes the terminology of the courtroom.

1. The charge against the whole world. 9.

9. The Jews enjoyed certain privileges as the elect nation of God, but these privileges did not include special treatment at the judgment bar of God. So to the question, **are we better than they?**, Paul's answer is **No, in no wise.** His reason is simple. **For we have before proved both Jews and Gentiles, that they are all under sin.**

The first step in the judicial procedure is to make an accusation or charge against the offender. This Paul does when he says **they are all under sin.** The word **prove** (Gr *proaitiaomai*) is a combination of two Greek words, *pro* meaning "before" and *altiaomai* meaning "to bring an accusation against" or "press formal charges." Paul has charged the entire world with being innately sinful. If the evidence is sufficient and the charge can be proved, the whole world will be judged guilty before God. Notice he does not say "all have sinned" but that all are **under sin.** This means they are all under the penalty as well as the power of sin. The apostle has in mind here a very definite contrast between being "under sin" and being "under grace." Romans 6:14-15 speaks of being "under grace" with our sins pardoned and ourselves justified.

2. The indictment against the whole world. 10-18.

Next in the judicial procedure is an indictment. Webster defines indictment as "a charge; accusation; specifically, a formal written accusation charging one or more persons with the commission of a crime" (*Webster's New World Dictionary*). An indictment is then a formal, written charge and every indictment must have at least one count, one specific charge to it. The more serious the crime, the more counts to the indictment. Paul immediately follows this pattern by quoting from a series of Old Testament passages which demonstrate, in no less than fourteen counts, the perversity and depravity of the entire world (3:10). **As it is written, There is none righteous, no, not one.** This same theme is seen throughout the Old Testament and is summarized in Psalm 14:1-3. Righteousness is not only the key word in this epistle, it is also the criterion by which sin is judged.

11. There is none that understandeth. Not a verbatim quote, this charge is derived from Psalm 14:2; 53:3. Here understanding is not mental but spiritual. The world is totally lacking in spiritual discernment (Eph 4:18). The natural man may not be mentally deranged, but he is certainly spiritually deranged and incapable of spiritual understanding (I Cor 2:14).

There is none that seeketh after God. In Psalm 53:2-3 David remarked that there is no man who innately seeks after God because man is sinful. When the sinner is drawn by God, he then seeks the Lord Jesus Christ in repentance and confession (Jn 6:44). Because he naturally does not seek the Lord, man gives evidence of being guilty of unrighteousness.

12. They are all gone out of the way. Man has not only "missed the mark," he has also "perverted his path." In this quote from the LXX of Psalms 14:3; 53:4, the picture is of a camel caravan crossing the desert which has strayed from the route and cannot return to the proper path. Likewise man has lost his way by deviating from God's prescribed route of righteousness. **They are together become unprofitable** is the fifth count of the indictment. Man is unuseful, of no benefit. Like salt that has lost its savor or fruit that hast become rotten, so all men are viewed as useless, rotten, corrupted when compared to the righteousness of Christ.

There is none that doeth good, no, not one. Again the written indictment comes from Psalm 14. This means that he can do nothing of spiritual or eternal value. No matter what he does, as far as righteousness is concerned, it is nothing but filthy rags (Isa 64:6).

13. Their throat is an open sepulchre. This seventh count of the indictment is the first one that is specific. Paul addresses himself to the chief outlets through which the sinner can display his sin. He will speak to the sinners' throats, tongues, lips, and mouths. Paul shows his familiarity with the Old Testament by drawing on King David's prayer for protection in Psalm 5.

Nothing is more abominable than the stench rising from an open sepulcher. The apostle graphically portrays the conversation of the wicked by likening the filth that arises from their mouths with the stench of the open sepulcher.

With their tongues they have used deceit. The sugared tongue, which is used to butter up the boss, is next listed by Paul as characteristic of sinful men. He indicts the world for the Madison Avenue approach to life which makes something out of nothing and promises what cannot be performed.

The poison of asps is under their lips. This ninth indictment is reminiscent of the final speech of Zophar, one of Job's critical friends (Job 20:14-16). The poison of the asp was stored in a bag under the lips of the serpent. When he spoke of this deadly poison Paul probably had in mind the Egyptian cobra, *naja haje,* the reptile used by Pharaoh Tutankhamen as his imperial symbol. Of the evil and violent man David says, "They have sharpened their tongues like a serpent; adders' poison is under their lips" (Ps 140:3). The natural man's human speech is likened to this poison.

14. Whose mouth is full of cursing and bitterness. Psalm 10:7 indicates that man's mouth, which was created to speak the truth of God and praise Him continually, has been perverted to speaking of Satan and praising him through cursing and bitterness. You do not have to teach a man to curse; it is the common expression of the bitterness within him that is rooted in personal sin.

15. Their feet are swift to shed blood. Paul now turns his attention, not to man's words, but to his deeds. Quoting from Isaiah 59:7 ff., the feet which were created to carry the gospel to the ends of the earth have in every era of history readily carried men violently to commit injustice and war with their fellowman (see Prov 1:7-19).

16. Destruction and misery are in their ways. This twelfth charge in the apostle's indictment lists not only what man is seeking but what he shall certainly receive if he continues in his unrighteous path. Calamity and misery always follow the sinner's futile search for happiness apart from Jesus Christ (cf. Jas 4:2).

17. And the way of peace have they not known. Unregenerated man can never find peace with his fellowman until peace has been made with his Creator. The United Nations and other peace-oriented agencies are doomed to failure because man is a ferocious animal. The most savage of animals does not destroy his own species to appease his hunger, but man destroys his fellowman for much less. The world is filled with animosity, hatred, terrorists, and murderers. Man will never be at peace with himself until he is at peace with God (Isa 59:8).

18. There is no fear of God before their eyes. Quoted from Psalm 36:1, this final charge is the fountain from which all the others spring. All the characteristics of man, his lack of understanding, his unprofitableness, his lack of peace, etc. stem from the fact that man does not fear God (Ps 36:2). Since man has no spiritual understanding, and the fear of the Lord is the beginning of wisdom, man is caught in a vicious circle. Only the external force of the Holy Spirit of God can break the circle of man's ignorance, arrogance, and guilt. Paul presents these fourteen specific, written counts in his indictment against the whole world.

3. The defense on behalf of the whole world. 19.

Having charged the whole world with being under sin, and having listed fourteen counts to his indictment, Paul now moves in the judicial procedure to the defense on behalf of the world. He quickly anticipates the line of argument the Jew will use in his defense. The Jew will say that Paul's description of mankind in the preceding verses does not describe him but the heathen. So Paul makes it clear, **what things soever the law saith, it saith to them who are under the law.** Using "law" as the entire Old Testament Scriptures, the apostle presses that he was in fact speaking of Jews as well as the heathen for they had received the oracles of God and were bound by them.

Ordinarily, in a civil court, the time of the defense is usually given to flowery speeches, insinuation, discrediting of witnesses, muddling of the issues, etc. But this will not be the case at the judgment bar of God. When the evidence against the universal sinfulness and guilt of man is presented and the opportunity for defense comes, there will be no defense. **That every mouth may be stopped.** The mouth of the heathen will be stopped. The mouth of the moral man and religious man will be stopped. Even the mouth of the cursing and bitter man will be stopped. A silent world will stand in judgment before the bar of God and neither clever lawyers, plea bargaining, bribing the judge, nor an impassioned appeal will get the sinner off. The famous French infidel, Jean Jacques Rousseau, who refused to marry and sent his illegitimate children to an orphanage, exclaimed: "I will stand before God and defend my conduct!" Bad news for Rousseau. No one will utter a word in his defense, for no one will have a defense before the righteous God.

4. The verdict against the whole world. 19-20.

All that remains in the judicial procedure is the verdict. The charge has been made. The indictment has been read. No defense can be made for there is no supporting case for mankind. The verdict is now ready to he heard. **All the world may become guilty before God.** The verdict is guilty, the only thing it can be. The word guilty (Gr *hypodikos*) means to come under judgment. It does not presuppose guilt, but denotes the state of a man who has been justly charged with a crime and is both legally responsible for it and worthy of blame.

20. Therefore. Anytime we see the word "therefore" we ought to ask ourselves what is "therefore" there for. Better translated "because," Paul is now coming to the summation of his argument and is about to make an application and draw a conclusion. He began back in chapter 1, verse 18, by proposing that the wrath of God is revealed from heaven against all ungodliness and unrighteousness of men. He has shown that the righteousness of God is sadly needed in the world. It is needed by the heathen, the moralist, the Jew. The righteousness of God is needed by the whole world. Having given his proposition, and the facts assembled from the Old Testament and present experience, Paul is now ready to draw a conclusion. He begins with **therefore** or "because."

By the deeds of the law there shall no flesh be justified in his sight. This free rendering of Psalm 143:2 (cf. Gal 2:16; 3:11) does not have the definite article "the" before law in the original language and thus Paul concludes that there is no law anywhere that can justify any man. The law of the heathen, the law of nature, the law of morality, the law of conscience, the law of Moses, none can justify a man and make him righteous in the sight of God. Even the law of Christ, laid down in the Sermon on the Mount, cannot justify a man. It is by the law that the knowledge of sin comes, a point expanded in 5:20; 7:7 ff., but no law can save a man. The law can convict men of sin, it can define sin, but it cannot emancipate man from sin. Only the grace of God can do that. The whole world is sinful and desperately in need of the righteousness of God. But if that righteousness is to come to the individual, it must come through the agency of grace, sovereign grace, not human works.

III. THE RIGHTEOUSNESS OF GOD PROVIDED. 3:21-8:39.

Having clearly established that the righteousness of God is needed by man, Paul now proceeds to indicate that the righteousness of God is provided by God. Thus, the second major division of the Epistle to the Romans begins at 3:21 with reference to divine provision for human need.

A. The Provision for Justification. 3:21-5:21.

The apostle begins this section with the Greek phrase *nyni de* which is usually translated "but now." This phrase is used in the Pauline Epistles eighteen times and twice in Hebrews. It does not occur anywhere else in the New Testament. *Nyni de* is an adverb of time. It is a favorite expression of Paul when he makes a transition from

a dark, gloomy picture to something wonderful that God does for us. Man has gotten himself in so deep that only God can get him out. God must enter man's world or else man will never enter God's world. In establishing guidelines for writers of tragedies in his day, the Roman poet Horace said, "Do not bring a god onto the stage, unless the problem is one that deserves a god to solve it" (Horace, *Ars Poetica,* 191 f.). The predicament of man is not one that Horace's gods can solve, but one that only Abraham's God can solve.

There are two very important words which pervade this passage. They are "righteousness' and "justify." Although quite different in English, these two words are practically identical in Greek (*dikaios,* to be righteous; *dikaioō,* to justify). Justification is a legal declaration issued by God in which He pronounces the person free from any fault or guilt and acceptable in His sight. "To justify means 'to pronounce and treat as righteous.' It is vastly more than being pardoned; it is a thousand times more than forgiveness. You may wrong me and then come to me; and I may say, I forgive you. But I have not justified you. I cannot justify you. But when God justifies a man, He says, 'I pronounce you a righteous man. Henceforth I am going to treat you as if you never committed any sin'" (Alva J. McClain, *Romans the Gospel of God's Grace,* p. 107).

1. Justification is by faith alone. 3:21-31.

21. The righteousness of God. The righteousness of God is neither an attribute of God nor the changed character of the believer. As defined in Romans 1:17, the righteousness of God is Christ Himself, who met every demand of the law for us in our stead, and is "made unto us . . . righteousness" (I Cor 1:30). God's righteousness is demonstrated and communicated to us through the cross.

This righteousness is **without the law.** This expression, which is literally "apart from the law" (Gr *chōris nomou*) is a strong expression categorically stating that righteousness is given totally apart from any law. See the same use of this word in Hebrews 4:15 where the Lord Jesus was tempted in all points as we are "yet totally apart from sin." Just as sin and Jesus Christ have nothing in common, so too the righteousness was not manifested in keeping the law but it was manifested at the cross when "He (God the Father) hath made Him (God the Son) to be sin for us, who knew no sin; that we might be made the righteousness of God in Him" (II Cor 5:21).

Being witnessed by the law and the prophets. Every time a man took his sacrifice to the temple for a sin offering, confessed his sin, and killed the animal, he was testifying that he had faith in a righteousness that was not his own. Thus, the law bears witness to an external righteousness that God provides, but the law itself cannot provide. Likewise the prophets witness to this righteousness. (see Isaiah 53:6; the same thought that is expressed in II Corinthians 5:21 and in I Peter 2: 21-25).

22. The righteousness of God which is by faith of Jesus Christ. Since the genitive case is objective here, a more understandable rendering is that we are justified when the righteousness of God is applied to us "through faith in Jesus Christ." The righteousness of God then does not come to one who simply has faith in God but to those who by faith claim the name of Jesus Christ. Saving faith in Christ is a necessary part of the righteousness God provides (Acts 4:12). **Unto all and upon all them that believe.** Although the words "upon all" are not included in some manuscripts (S, A, B, D, and some other versions), nevertheless the meaning is still the same. God's righteousness is provided unto all men. We therefore go into all the world and preach the gospel to every creature (Mk 16:15). However, even though this righteousness is provided unto all, it is nevertheless applied upon only those who believe in Jesus Christ as Saviour. This is the only conditional element of the gospel. This righteousness is placed upon us as a cloak when by faith we receive Jesus Christ as Saviour. Righteousness is from God, through Jesus Christ, to all who receive Him by faith.

For there is no difference. This phrase "no difference" occurs in only one other place in the Epistle to the Romans. In this verse there is no difference between the need of the Jew and the Gentile. That need is explained in the expression **For all have sinned.** But just as there is no difference in human need likewise there is no difference in divine provision (Rom 10:12-13), the other place the expression occurs.

23. And come short of the glory of God. The brief but all-encompassing statement that "all have sinned" is further enhanced by the fact that both Jew and Gentile have come short of God's glory. What is the glory of God? The Bible frequently speaks of the glory of God appearing in the pillar of the cloud leading Israel (Ex 16:7-10); the tabernacle of the congregation at Kadesh (Num 14:10); the temple of Solomon (I Kgs 8:11); the Mount of Olives at Jerusalem (Ezk 11:23); etc. The glory of God now, however, rests in the person of Jesus Christ (Jn 1:14). The glory of God is the person of Jesus Christ.

When Stephen was stoned he looked steadfastly to heaven and saw the glory of God and (or even) Jesus standing at the right hand of God (Acts 7:55). The knowledge of the glory of God is said to be in the face of Jesus Christ (II Cor 4:6). When Paul says that we have come short of the glory of God he means that we do not measure up to the sinlessness of Jesus Christ. The Mosaic law served as God's standard of righteousness until the coming of

Christ. But when the Lord Jesus was made a curse for us, He redeemed us from the curse of the law (Gal 3:19; Rom 10:4). Thus, the standard of God's holiness today is not the Old Testament law but the person of Jesus Christ (3:24).

Paul makes three observations about the righteousness of God which brings justification. He says that the righteous man is **justified freely** and that this justification is **by his grace and** provided **through the redemption that is in Christ Jesus.** Being justified freely means being justified without any prior conditions being met. Being justified by God's grace (in the Greek this expression is in the dative of means or instrumental case) indicates that not only is our justification without prior conditions being met but, on the other hand, it is graciously given. We do not merit justification, but we enjoy it. You cannot have both merit and grace. Our justification was by the grace of God. Beyond this, it was through the redemption that is in Christ Jesus. Since the word redemption signifies a buying back, it must have been accomplished by the payment of a price. The price of our redemption was the blood of Jesus Christ (Mt 20:28; I Cor 6:20; I Pet 1:18-19). Therefore, we are justified in the sight of God when the righteousness of Christ is placed upon us by the grace of God, freely and without cause. Only then God views us as ransomed by the blood of Christ.

25-26. The main points of these two verses are: (1) God presented Jesus Christ as an atoning sacrifice, a propitiation. (2) This sacrifice was one of Christ's blood. (3) It is appropriated to the sinner by faith. (4) The sacrifice was necessary because in the past God had not fully punished sin. (5) It was also necessary to validate the justice of God. (6) This sacrifice demonstrated that it is God who justifies those who have faith in Jesus Christ.

God hath set forth to be a propitiation. The Bible is filled with types, which foreshadow future persons or events, and antitypes, which are the real person or events foreshadowed. The type is the arrow; the antitype is the target.

One of the most unique types in the Old Testament is the mercy seat. This was the lid on the ark of the covenant and was covered with gold. At each end was a golden cherub, whose wings stretched toward the center of the lid. The ark was the meeting place between God and man. It contained the tablets of the Mosaic law (Ex 25:16-22). Therefore, the mercy seat was that which covered the law of God.

When the translation of the Hebrew Old Testament was made into Greek, which is called the Septuagint, the Greek word chosen to translate "mercy seat" (Heb *kaphorah*) was *hilastērion* which means "the place of propitiation." To propitiate means to appease an offended party and the *hilastērion* (mercy seat) was the place where, by blood, the sins of Israel were atoned, the penalty paid, and wrath of God (the offended party) was appeased. It is certainly no coincidence that the word Paul uses here to describe Jesus Christ is the same word used for "mercy seat," the *hilastērion*. Jesus Christ is our mercy seat. He is the person by whom our sins were atoned, our penalty paid, and the offended party appeased. Jesus Christ is where God meets man.

Why did Jesus Christ become our propitiation? The answer is **to declare his righteousness.** This is done by atoning for sins, which prior to Calvary were not permanently dealt with (Ps 50:16-23; Acts 17:30). God made His statement about sin at the cross. He not only said something about it, He did something about it. The righteousness of God is declared by atoning for present and future sins as well as past sins. Therefore God is the justifier of any man, past, present, or future, who places his faith in the blood of Jesus Christ.

27-31. These verses represent some final questions concerning justification and the conclusion Paul draws. **Where is boasting then?** In view of the fact that it is God who justifies us by providing Christ Jesus as our propitiation, what does this do to boasting? Paul's answer is **It is excluded.** Boasting is shut out, there is no room for man's boasting in the plan of God. **By what law? Of works?** What is it that caused boasting to be inappropriate? Is it the law of works? Paul's answer, **Nay: but by the law of faith.** If man could work to be justified, then he would have reason to boast. But we are saved by God's grace through faith, not of works. And why? "Lest any man should boast" (Eph 2:8-9).

28. Paul now comes to a conclusion which is central to Pauline theology. He concludes **that a man is justified by faith without the deeds of the law.** This is the same conclusion which came to the heart of Martin Luther and spawned the Protestant Reformation. When this concept grasps our hearts we too come to the conclusion that salvation is *sola gratia, sola fide, soli Deo gloria* (by grace alone, through faith alone; to God alone be the glory).

29-30. Is he the God of the Jews only? This question naturally arises in the Jewish mind, which still cannot conceive of the heathen being loved and justified by faith alone. Paul's answer to the question is **Yes, of the Gentiles also.** The reason is, **it is one God.** There is not a god of the Jews and another god of the Gentiles. There is but one God of Jews and Gentiles. Paul is not here simply teaching monotheism as opposed to heathen polytheism. As a Jew, a Hebrew of the Hebrews, but the called apostle to the Gentiles, Paul is the bridge between the Jew and the Gentile. But his message has made both one in Christ (Gal 3:28). The law of faith is the universal law of salvation by God.

31. Do we then make void the law through faith? Because God saves through faith and not the deeds of the law, does this make the law useless? Paul gives his characteristic answer, **God forbid. Yea, we establish the law.** Faith in Christ is the proper response to the law, for what the law could not do, Christ alone can do. The teaching that justification is by faith alone does not destroy the law. It completes the law, fulfills it, makes it meaningful. Justification by faith alone honors the law, because prior to Jesus Christ no one ever honored the law by perfectly keeping it. Since the Lord Jesus did, faith in the finished work of Christ on Calvary brings the ultimate respect to the law.

2. Justification is illustrated in the Old Testament. 4:1-25.

Paul has just firmly established that the righteousness of God is apart from the law (3:21) and that man is justified by faith apart from the deeds of the law (3:28). He is aware, however, that the Jew will offer the case of Abraham as rebuttal to this teaching. Paul's own people were still engrossed with the idea that being Jewish ought to afford them certain judicial privileges in the eyes of God. Thus, in this chapter, Paul analyzes the principle by which God saved Abraham. The father of Israel is an illustration of God's message of salvation in the Old Testament.

4:1-2. Abraham our father, as pertaining to the flesh. Paul's use of the possessive pronoun "our" and the qualifying phrase "as pertaining to the flesh" indicates that he is identifying himself with his people, the Jews. The question is, was Abraham saved by his acts of good work and obedience or was he saved by the faith of which Paul spoke in the preceding chapter?

3. As a Hebrew, a Rabbi, a Sanhedrinist and a Pharisee, Paul knew exactly how to settle a Jewish argument. He could have debated the point, but instead he says, **For what saith the scripture?** This is a lesson we all should learn well. Whenever we are asked for a moral, ethical, or eternal answer, we should always ask ourselves, "What do the Scriptures say?" The apostle answers his own question by quoting what Moses records in Genesis 15:6. **Abraham believed God, and it was counted unto him for righteousness.** What do we mean when we say that faith was counted unto Abraham for righteousness? The word translated "counted" (Gr *logizomai*) is a commercial term which is used with regard to credits and debits. It means to set to one's credit or lay to one's charge. If you authorize your lawyer to write checks on your bank account, and he does so, although the check is written by him and money received by him, nevertheless the amount of the check is charged to you. This one word *logizomai*, occurs eleven times in this chapter and is translated by various words such as "count," "reckon," and "impute." Abraham was not righteous. Justification never means to make a man righteous. It only means that God reckons and treats a man as if he were righteous.

4-5. This principle is now further explained. Paul reasons that justification by works rests on the principle that men may earn their salvation by doing good. If this principle were true, good men would be saved by their good works and salvation would not be a gift at all. But justification by faith rests on the principle that God imputes righteousness to the ungodly as a free gift. Salvation is not, therefore, earned by the sinner but is freely given to him when he puts his faith in the blood of Jesus Christ.

6-8. Paul has made a case for Abraham's justification apart from works; now he strengthens that case with another Old Testament illustration. The purpose of introducing David's testimony is twofold. (1) the Jews' law regarding two witnesses (Deut 19:15; referred to by Jesus in Mt 18:16 and by Paul in II Cor 13:1 and I Tim 5:19). David corroborated what is said about Abraham and further illustrates salvation apart from works; (2) David gives witness that the same principle of justification was operative even for those living under the Mosaic law.

David also describeth the blessedness of the man, unto whom God imputeth righteousness without works. Even King David, the type of the Messianic King, knew the truth of the words he penned in Psalm 32:1-2, which Paul quotes in verses 7 and 8. As believers, our iniquities are forgiven and our sins are covered. The reason the believer's sins are not reckoned to him is that they have been imputed to Christ Jesus (see Isa 53, cf. I Pet 2:24-25).

9-12. Paul has well argued that justification is by faith alone. He has illustrated, by the lives of Abraham and David, that God has never worked on a principle of justification by works. Yet it is difficult for the Jews, the sons of Abraham, to accept that they may be justified in exactly the same way as the heathen Gentiles. Thus, these verses introduce another potential argument against justification by faith.

It is true that both pre-law Abraham and under-law David received righteousness. But, so the Jew would argue, both of them were also circumcised. Since circumcision is the sign of the covenant between God and His chosen people (Gen 17:9-14), is it not possible that this was the ground of their justification? **Cometh this blessedness then upon the circumcision only, or upon the uncircumcision also?** Paul answers, **faith was reckoned to Abraham for righteousness.** This immediately prompts the question as to the timing of the reckoning of righteousness. **How was it then reckoned? When he was in circumcision, or in uncircumcision?** The answer is clear. Faith was reckoned to Abraham while he was yet uncircumcised.

The facts are these. (1) Genesis 15:6

records the event of Abraham receiving righteousness from God. (2) Sometime after that, Abraham had a son by Hagar when he was eighty-six years old (Gen 16:16). (3) At least one year had to elapse between the two events so that at the outside Abraham was eighty-five years old when righteousness was imputed to him. (4) Ishmael was thirteen years old when both he and Abraham were circumcised (Gen 17:25-26). (5) Abraham had righteousness imputed to him at least fourteen years before he was circumcised. Paul concludes that circumcision had nothing whatever to do with the imputation of righteousness to Abraham.

This does not mean circumcision was unimportant. Abraham received **the sign of circumcision, a seal of the righteousness of the faith.** Circumcision did not bring righteousness, but was the visible sign to Abraham's descendants of the righteousness that was imputed to him by faith. Also, circumcision was God's seal of righteousness. Once righteousness has been imputed to the individual, it is sealed there forever. This is true also of Christian baptism. It does not bring about salvation but is an outward sign declaring salvation and is God's seal of approval on the finished work of Christ in behalf of the believer. Abraham received righteousness before he was circumcised that he might be the father of all them that believe, whether circumcised or not, who also **walk in the steps of that faith of our father Abraham.** Abraham, therefore, not only bears a physical relationship with the nation Israel but also bears a spiritual relationship with all who believe by faith, whether Jew or Gentile.

13-16. Each of Abraham's descendants expected to receive the inheritance of Abraham. That inheritance was no less than the world. **For the promise, that he should be the heir of the world.** Although not directly stated, this promise is drawn from Genesis 12:3 and the correlative promises given in Genesis 18:18, 22:18, etc. Abraham's heritage was limited in geographical terms to the land between Egypt and the Euphrates (Gen 15:18; cf. 13:14 f.). But the promise was made to Abraham and **to his seed.** In Galatians 3:16 the "seed" is obviously Jesus Christ. The promise of inheriting the world must be understood then in relationship to the Messiah's future domination of this earth as "KING OF KINGS, AND LORD OF LORDS" (Rev 19:16). This promise will come to reality when the seed of Abraham, Jesus Christ, sits on the throne of David during the Millennium and rules the entire world with a rod of iron. Because of this, it is impossible that Abrahaham's inheritance can be obtained by law. No heir of Abraham, save Jesus Christ, has ever been able to entirely keep the law. If fulfillment of this promise depended on law-keeping, man's inability to keep the law would insure that the promise would never be fulfilled and thus would be **the promise made of none effect.**

The law worketh wrath. Eventually failure to keep the law imposes penalties which bring to the law-breaker the wrath of God. **For where no law is, there is no transgression.** Paul appears to be drawing on a current legal maxim in the Roman Empire ("no penalty without law"), when here, as in 5:13, he claims that sin is not imputed where there is no law. The law simply declares what is right, and requires conformity to it. But the law does not give either power to obey it or atonement when it is not obeyed.

Therefore it is of faith, that it might be by grace. Since the promise of salvation is dependent upon faith, the blessings of salvation are afforded by the means of God's grace. Therefore they come **not to that only which is of the law, but to that also which is of the faith of Abraham.** Paul is insistent that only those who possess the faith of Abraham are the seed of Abraham and whether we be Jew or Gentile, if we have placed our faith in the salvation provided by Abraham's God, then Abraham is the **father of all of us.**

17. As it is written, I have made thee a father of many nations. Again Paul quotes from the Old Testament, this time from Genesis 17:5. Throughout this next series of verses it is noticed that in giving and confirming the covenant to Abraham, God interchangeably uses the words "I will" and "I have." The reason is that God is above time; He has no future nor past, only an eternal present. When in Genesis 17:5 God said, "A father of many nations have I made thee," Abraham was yet childless. But it didn't matter, the promises of God are better than money in the bank. They always come true. We can count God's "wills" as God's "haves." The same thing was true before the battle of Jericho when the Lord appeared unto Joshua and said, "See, I have given into thy hand Jericho, and its king thereof, and the mighty men of valor" (Josh 6:2). What was for Joshua yet to happen, was for God an accomplished fact.

God, who quickeneth the dead. Although this is a general designation for God in Judaism, it is used here with reference to Abraham's own body, now as good as dead, and to the deadness of Sarah's womb (vs. 19).

18. Who against hope believed in hope. Grammatically this is known as an oxymoron, a figure of speech in which contradictory ideas are combined (e.g. thunderous silence, sweet sorrow, etc.). Abraham against hope, or beyond hope, nevertheless believed in hope. When the promise was given that Abraham would become the father of many nations, there was no human ground for hope with regard to Abraham's wife Sarah bearing a child. Although beyond hope, Abraham believed God anyway and his faith generated hope.

19. And being not weak in faith. Abraham believed God in spite of the circumstances. He did not consider his lack of virility at one hundred years old. Neither did he consider the inability of his ninety-year-old wife to conceive and withstand the pain of childbirth. Adverse circumstances did not stand in the way of Abraham's faith.

20. He staggered not at the promise of God. The word translated staggered (Gr *diakrinomai*), means to separate, distinguish, and as a deponent means "dispute." In regard to faith in God, Abraham was not of a divided mind. How can we reconcile this with Abraham's laughter in Genesis 17:17? We need not understand Abraham's laughter as mocking. Jerome translated laughter as "marveled." Calvin and Augustine both translated it as "laughed for joy." Abraham's questioning how a child could be born of him at one hundred years of age was more an exclamation of holy wonder which was immediately overcome by holy faith. Therefore, he was **strong in faith,** as opposed to being weak in faith (vs. 19). Above all, Abraham gave God the glory, for great things He had done.

21. Abraham was not just wistfully hoping that God would make him the father of many nations, but was **fully persuaded that, what he had promised, he was able also to perform.** History teaches us that what God promises, He also performs.

22. This verse begins **And therefore** which means what is to be said is linked closely with what has just been said. Because Abraham had faith, because he believed God in the face of adverse circumstances, therefore, that faith **was imputed to him for righteousness.** All that Abraham had, his righteousness, his inheritance, and his posterity, he gained not by works, but by faith.

23-25. This illustration of the way in which Abraham received righteousness is not recorded for his sake alone, or applicable to him only. The expression, **But for us also,** indicates that all believers are justified by faith in the promises of God. **If we believe on him that raised up Jesus our Lord from the**

dead. The reviving of Abraham's generative power, and his faith that God could do so, foreshadows the faith that we must have in the resurrection of Jesus Christ.

Who was delivered for our offenses. God the Father delivered Jesus Christ to the cross of Calvary, not as an example, but to make atonement for our sins (II Cor 5:21). God the Father also raised Jesus Christ again **for our justification.** The meaning of the resurrection for us today is that Christ Jesus died on account of our sins, and was raised from the dead in order to render us righteous in the eyes of God. The righteousness that Abraham had, and David had, and which we enjoy, is the righteousness of the risen Lord.

What can we learn from this chapter? The noun "faith" occurs ten times in this chapter and the corresponding verb "believe" occurs six times. Together the idea of believing faith is found no less than sixteen times in Romans 4. The words "count," Reckon," or "impute," all of which mean to charge to one's account, occur eleven times in Romans 4. The word "righteousness" occurs in one of its forms eight times in this chapter and the corresponding verb "justified" occurs in one of its forms three times. Together the idea of righteousness is found no less than eleven times in Romans 4. It is significant that, apart from the common words of our language, these three words occur so frequently. The application of Romans 4 is simple: *faith imputes righteousness.* There isn't a thing anyone can do to become clothed with God's righteousness except have faith in Jesus Christ as his Saviour from sin.

3. Justification brings blessings to its recipients. 5:1-11.

Having established God's method of justifying sinners, and having provided an Old Testament example of that method, Paul now demonstrates that not only are there benefits derived from justification at the moment of salvation, but there are blessings that accompany justification throughout the believer's life.

Therefore indicates that there is a close link between chapter 4 and chapter 5. It is unfortunate that there is a chapter break here for there is no break in Paul's logical pattern of thought. "Therefore" is a bridge between the two chapters and the ideas of past justification and present blessings.

5:1. Therefore being justified by faith. The word translated "being justified" (Gr *dikaioō*) is an aorist passive participle in Greek. The time of action is in the past. The voice is obviously passive which means that the subject received and did not initiate the action. So Paul says that at some point in the past, without our help, God justified us, that is, He declared us and began to treat us as if we were righteous. Thus, we should understand this verse today "having been justified by faith" we have . . . .

Paul will now list the benefits of having been justified by God. The first is **we have peace with God.** This is not the peace of God, but peace with (Gr *pros*) God. This is not a feeling of peace but a state of peace. Between the sinner and God exists a state of enmity, hostility, and antagonism. Sinners are the enemies of God (Isa 48:22; Jas 4:4; Col 1:21). The state of war that exists between the unbeliever and God continues until a state of peace is declared. Therefore, having been justified by faith, we have a peace treaty with God **through our Lord Jesus Christ.** He is the mediator between the two parties at war (I Tim 2:5-6). As our mediator, Jesus Christ has worked out our peace treaty with God. But since He made peace through His blood, He is our peace with God (Eph 2:13-18).

2. By whom also we have access. If you have ever attempted to call the President of the United States, you know how relatively inaccessible he is. To the unbeliever, God the Father is even more inaccessible than the President. He cannot be reached for there is no common ground, no mediator between the unbeliever and God. To the believer, there is access to God because He has justified us. Jesus Christ provides immediate and consistent access to God for all those whom God has declared and treats as righteousness.

Wherein we stand. An age-old problem is this, "How can a sinner stand in the presence of a holy God?" The psalmist wrestled with this question (Ps 130:3). Men and women shall wrestle with this problem at the opening of the sixth seal in Revelation 6:16-17 (see also Ps 1:5). We do not have a leg to stand on when it comes to a defense of our sinful actions. How is it possible for a sinner to stand before God? The Swiss reformer Robert Haldane said, "And it is by Him (Jesus Christ) they enter into the state of grace, so by Him they stand in it, accepted before God; secured, according to His everlasting covenant, that they shall not be cast down" (Robert Haldane, *Romans,* p. 186). The only possible way we can stand before God is by His grace.

And rejoice in hope of the glory of God. The word "hope" confuses many new Christians. Of the one hundred forty-one times this word occurs in the authorized version, in all of its forms, only twenty-one times does it occur as a verb (excluding the Psalms). Hope is not nebulous, it is concrete. We have joy in hope. The glory of God, of which we have fallen short, is the perfect standard of Christ's righteousness (Jn 1:14; 17:22-23; Heb 1:3). We can rejoice in the fact that whatever we are like today, one of the benefits of having been justified is the hope that one day we shall be like Him (Rom 8:29; I Jn 3:2-3).

3-4. We glory in tribulations also. He who has been justified rejoices, not in spite of his tribulations, but in or because of his tribulations. In delineating the progression from tribulation to hope, Paul shows that there is a natural, logical connection between the four: tribulations—patience—experience—hope. The tribulations of which Paul speaks (I Cor 5:9-13; II Cor 1:4-10; 11:23-30; Phil 4:12; II Tim 3:11-12; etc.), result in patience (Gr *hypomonē*). This is not a passive quality but the ability to remain strong while bearing the burden of tribulation. The test of endurance in turn results in experience (Gr *dokimē*) or proof of the presence of the Spirit of God which makes patience possible. The end result of this proof proceeds to hope, the certain knowledge that we will one day be glorified as the Son of God and be "heirs of God, and joint-heirs with Christ" (8:17). Here is a perfect circle: we began with hope of the glory of God, passed through tribulation which caused us to be steadfast; this endurance proved that we are indeed a child of God and this proof encourages us in the hope of the glory of God.

5. And hope maketh not ashamed. Having already been justified we have a hope that cannot be humiliated. The hope we have is in the glory of God and even though it is tested in the caldron of fiery tribulation, it will be proved genuine **because the love of God is shed abroad in our hearts.** This passage began by speaking of faith, moved to hope, and now has come to the end of the trilogy with charity or love. Our hearts are flooded with God's love for us because we have been justified. But more than that, there is another benefit which accompanies justification and that is **the Holy Ghost which is given unto us.** It is the Holy Spirit who pours into the heart of the believer a sense of God's love for him. Not only did the Holy Spirit come to us at salvation communicating God's love for us, but the Scripture says He "is given" unto us. The verb "is given" (Gr *didōmi*) means to grant, impart, or put into the heart. The clear implication is that at the moment of salvation we received the gift of the Holy Spirit Himself. A justified man need not anxiously look to a future time when he will be baptized with the Holy Spirit. The Holy Spirit is God's gift to us at the moment of justification. Then Christ's righteousness is ours, God's love is ours, and the Holy Spirit's presence is ours. They are inextricably bound together in a package we call salvation.

6-8. The distinctive quality of God's love is that it operates irrespective of merit. Human love is given to those who are lovable; but God's love embraces even the unlovely. **When we were yet without strength.** This expression is parallel to the expression in verse 8, **while we were yet sinners.** Paul uses it to show man's utter helplessness in the face of his all-encompassing sin. In due time Christ died for the ungodly. This means that circumstances did not bring Christ to the cross, the divine plan of God did (Gal 4:1-5). At the time of man's greatest need, nothing but the blood of Jesus would satisfy that need.

Verses 7 and 8 expand what is implicit in verse 6. When Paul said that Christ died for the ungodly, he was indicating that the Lord did not die for those who were simply void of morality but for those who were actively opposed to God. **For scarcely for a righteous man will one die.** Here the just or righteous man is distinguished from the good or benevolent man. The just man is approved by God, and hardly anyone would think of dying for him. The good man is loved by men, and most would not think of dying for him, although some may be tempted. Paul's argument is that while you will rarely find anyone who will lay down his life for a righteous or good man, God demonstrated His love by sending Christ Jesus to die for us while we were yet sinners, something no one else would even consider doing. The sacrifice of Christ on the cross of Calvary arose out of the heart of God filled with the love of God. All these blessings are ours because at some point in the past, without our help, we

have been justified by God and are now being treated as if we were righteous.

9. In addition to the blessings we presently enjoy because we are justified, there is yet the promise that **we shall be saved from wrath through him.** All men are by nature the children of wrath (Jn 3:36). The prophet Nahum warns that the Lord has reserved wrath for His enemies (Nah 1:2). It is comforting for the believer to note, however, that "God hath not appointed us to wrath, but to obtain salvation by our Lord Jesus Christ" (I Thess 5:9). One of the future benefits of the fact that we have been justified is that we shall be preserved from the day of God's fierce wrath.

10. We shall be saved by his life. Paul makes reference to us who were once enemies of God, but now are reconciled to Him by the death of His Son. It is the death of Christ and His shed blood which provide our atonement and redemption (Eph 1:7; 2:13; Col 1:14; Heb 9:12-15). It is the death of Christ which effects our salvation; but it is the life of Christ which sustains it. Christ died for our sins and was raised for our justification to make continual intercession for us (Heb 7:25). The life of Jesus Christ did not take away the penalty of our sins, His death did. But Christ ever lives to take away the dominion of sin over us. This is how we are continually kept saved by His intercessory life.

11. Not only shall the justified man escape the wrath of God by the death of Christ, but also he shall obtain joy in God because of Christ's life. The word translated "joy" is the same as is translated "rejoice" in verse 2 and "glory" in verse 3. The blessings which justification brings to its recipients terminate in joy **through our Lord Jesus Christ.** This last expression is identical to that found in verse 1 of this chapter. All that we have we owe to Him, the Lord Jesus Christ.

4. Justification is imputed to us as was sin. 12-21.

Thus far in the Epistle to the Romans, Paul has dealt with two great doctrinal subjects: condemnation and justification. Before the apostle leaves the subject he enhances our understanding of them by contrasting the two. The contrasts which he draws are: a contrast between Adam and Christ (vss. 14-15). between condemnation and justification (vs. 16); between disobedience and obedience (vs. 19); between law and grace (vs. 20); between sin and righteousness (vs. 21); and between death and life (vs. 21). Since these verses are so doctrinal in nature, it will be helpful to keep in mind three very important truths established in Romans 5:12-21. They are: (1) one offense, by one man, made all the world guilty of sin; (2) the resultant guilt of Adam's original sin is imputed to each of us; and (3) Adam acted as our official representative when he cast his vote against God.

12. By one man sin entered into the world. Genesis 3 makes it abundantly clear that this one man, Adam, brought sin to the human race by disobedience. It was not the sins of Adam's lifetime, but the one original sin which allowed death, sin's close ally, to enter the world with it. On no less than five occasions in verses 15-19 the principle of one sin by one man is asserted (vss. 15, 16, 17, 18, and 19). One act of disobedience to God was sufficient to allow sin to enter and permeate the entire realm of humanity, **for that all have sinned.**

13-14. Sin immediately inundated the whole world and had a mortal effect on its inhabitants. **Sin is not imputed when there is no law,** but even before the law of Moses was given, physical death attested to the presence of sin in Adam and his posterity. So universal was this sin that its deadly effects were seen over them that had not sinned after the similitude of Adam's transgression. Adam is here contrasted with Christ and said to be a "figure"

(Gr *typos*) or "type" of Him that was to come. The only Old Testament character to be called explicitly a type of Christ is Adam. Here the contrast between the first Adam and the Last Adam begins.

15. But not as the offense, so also is the free gift. The continued contrast between Adam and Christ shows a correspondence both in similarity and dissimilarity. Through the offense of Adam the many (i.e., all of Adam's descendants) incurred the penalty of death. Similarly, the many (i.e., all the redeemed) have incurred the free gift of eternal life through the Last Adam, Jesus Christ. The dissimilarity is seen in the phrase, **much more the grace of God.** The grace of God, which is the ground of our justification, is contrasted with the sin of Adam, because it is greater in quality and greater in degree than Adam's sin. In Adam we got what we deserved, condemnation and guilt. In Christ we have received much more of what we do not deserve, mercy and grace.

16. Now the contrast turns to condemnation in Adam and justification in Christ. **For the judgment was by one to condemnation.** Not only is our guilt derived from one man's sin, but it is derived from only one sin of that man. Notice that Paul never refers to the "offenses" of one man, but to the "offense" (singular) of one man (vss. 14, 15, 17, 18, 19, and 20). It is not the sins of Adam's lifetime that have been imputed to us, but only his original sin. That one sin brought condemnation. However, the righteousness which is imputed to us by Christ, through the free gift of God's grace, covers not just that one offense but **many offenses.**

17-18. As the representative head of the human race, Adam's offense dethroned him as the ruler of God's creation. Consequently, death became the ruler of nature. Adam became the representative of a death-destined society. As long as we are born into that society, death is our destiny as well. The

Last Adam, Jesus Christ, is also the representative of a society. Through the gift of righteousness, He **shall reign in life.** Since all are born into the society of death, the only way to enter Christ's society, in which men are born unto justification of life, is to be born again. By the new birth experience we pass from our old relationship to Adam into a new and living relationship with Christ.

19. One man's disobedience . . . the obedience of one. Here the contrast drawn is between blatant disobedience and willful obedience. God's command to our representative Adam concerning the Tree of Knowledge of Good and Evil was, "thou shall not eat of it" (Gen 2:17). Almost immediately the head of the human race disobeyed that divine command. However, Christ Jesus, the Last Adam and Head of the heavenly race, totally obeyed the will of God and testified to that when He said, "I have glorified thee on the earth: I have finished the work which thou gavest me to do" (Jn 17:4). The difference between obedience and disobedience is the difference between life and death.

20. Moreover the law entered, that the offense might abound. At this point the Jew might ask, "Well, what is the law for?" The law is "the necessary yardstick of God's holiness which served to bring out into sharp relief the guilt of man in revolt against God, showing him the hopelessness of attempting to earn salvation by good works" (Gleason L. Archer, Jr., *The Epistle to the Romans,* p. 32). The law came not to make a man a sinner, but to show him how great a sinner he is. **But where sin abounded, grace did much more abound.** Grace did not set aside the law, but rather completely satisfied it. As deep as sin goes, God's grace goes deeper. As wide as sin is, God's grace is wider. When sin abounded, grace super-abounded. God's grace is greater than all our sin.

21. This verse contains the double contrast between sin and righteousness and between death and life. From the very moment sin entered the universe it has reigned bringing about physical and spiritual death. Its principle of rulership has been to separate mankind from his Creator and to cause his end to be a mortal one. But through the blood of Jesus Christ, sin has been dethroned and righteousness now rules in its stead. Whereas death was the order of the day in Adam's society, now life eternal is the order of the day for those who have believed in Jesus Christ. The contrast is a great one. It is a contrast between man's sin and Christ's obedience, between the wages of sin and the gift of God.

Some have thought that universal salvation is taught in this passage, thinking that just because all were condemned, now all will be saved. Such is not the case. New birth is mandatory for eternal life and the qualifying expression, **they which receive** in verse 17, teaches that faith in Jesus Christ is absolutely essential for salvation.

B. The Provision for Sanctification. 6:1-7:25.

Having established in 3:21-5:21 that justification is provided by faith alone, Paul now turns his attention to the provision for sanctification. In the preceding chapter he has drawn some conclusions concerning the contrasts between Adam and Christ. In chapters 6 and 7, however, the contrast is between justification and sanctification. There is noticeable smoothness in the transition between the discussion of justification in chapter 5 and that of sanctification in chapter 6. Although there is a sharp contrast between the two, nevertheless the intimacy of the relationship between justification and sanctification is clearly seen in the way they are connected in these chapters.

Basically the contrast between the two is this: justification deals with the penalty for sin; sanctification deals with the power of sin. As was seen in

5:1, justification is a declarative act of
God. As will be seen in chapter 6, sanctification is a progressive act of God.
Both works of God deal with the sinner: justification with the unsaved sinner; sanctification with the saved sinner. The end result of justification is
salvation; the end result of sanctification is obedience. Although distinctly
different, justification and sanctification are two aspects of the one work of
God in saving men.

*1. Sanctification and the principle of
sin. 6:1-14.*

**6:1-2. Shall we continue in sin, that
grace may abound? God forbid.** In
every age there have been those who
have denounced the doctrine of
justification by faith on the incorrect
supposition that this doctrine logically
leads to sin. "If the believer is treated
as righteous by God, and if good works
will not save him, then evil works will
not condemn him either. Why then
should he be concerned about his sin or
attempt to live a godly life?" Paul anticipated this very attitude in 6:1-2.
Theologically, this belief is known as
Antinomianism. Paul's answer is crystal clear. Just because where sin
abounded grace super-abounded, the
believer is not automatically drawn to
license in his life style. On the contrary,
a mature understanding of justification
by faith leads the believer to appreciate
God's grace, so that the end result is
obedience to God out of a heart filled
with gratitude. Paul's characteristic expression "God forbid," shows how ap-
palled he is at the mere suggestion of
continuing in sin once we have experienced the grace of God. We cannot
continue in sin because through our
identification with Jesus Christ we are
dead to sin. To die unto sin means that
we are dead to the guilt of sin. Sin can
no longer make any legal claim on the
believer because we are viewed by God
as if we ourselves had died that fateful
day at Calvary.
3-5. At this point Paul begins to
relate the secret of living a holy and
sanctified life, a life which is characterized by being dead to sin. The secret
of sanctification is not found in some
sanctimonious formula or some deeper
or mystical experience with the Lord.
The secret is found in three words: (1)
know (vs. 3); (2) **reckon** (vs. 11); and
(3) **yield** (vs. 13). We must be vitally
aware of these words as we seek to understand the relationship between justification and sanctification.

To show the immaturity of those
who would continue in sin after justification so that grace may abound,
Paul introduces the subject of baptism
as evidence that life in sin cannot co-
exist with death to sin. **So many of us
as were baptized into Jesus Christ.**
Baptism into Christ means to be incorporated into Him, to become a member of His body (I Cor 12:13), and to
share with Him those experiences
which, although were historically His,
are vicariously ours (i.e. His crucifixion, death, burial, and resurrection).
**Therefore we are buried with him by
baptism into death.** Burial with Christ
Jesus signifies that sin no longer judicially has a hold upon us. The ordinance of Christian baptism beautifully
portrays this burial into Christ in
which the old order of a death-con-
trolled life comes to an end and the
new order of a Christ-controlled life
begins. Therefore, having already been
justified, a believer tells that fact to the
world by submitting to the ordinance
of water baptism. When he has been
symbolically **raised up from the dead,**
even as Christ was physically, the purpose of his resurrection is that he
should walk in newness of life. This
should entirely preclude the foolish
idea of continued sin so that a display
may be made of the grace of God. Just
as we were buried into Him **in the likeness of his death, we shall be also in the
likeness of his resurrection.** Hence we
enter into His life and become a part of
Him spiritually, yielding to Him our
desires, our wishes, ourselves.

6-8. Paul is still expounding the first principle of true sanctification. Hence, as in verse 3, he repeats the word that is characteristic of this first principle. **Knowing this, that our old man is crucified with him.** The old man referred to here is our old self, the man we once were before we were crucified with Christ. This crucifixion is not a present, daily experience but is rather a past event, expressed by the aorist tense in Greek. I Corinthians 15:31 was spoken by Paul in the context of physical not spiritual death. Our old man is not constantly being crucified, day by day, but has been crucified at the cross of Calvary. The reason is **that the body of sin might be destroyed.** A better rendering of "might be destroyed" (Gr *katargeō*), is "might be rendered inoperative." At the cross of Calvary a victory was won which provided the believer with the power not to live as he once did, serving his old master, i.e. sin, but to live eternally serving his new master, i.e. Christ.

For he that is dead is freed from sin. All who have died to sin are no longer debtor to it. Death wipes the slate clean. The death of our Lord has completely removed the guilt and penalty of our sin. Consequently, because we have died with Christ, we shall also live with Him. Living with Christ precludes the possibility of carnally continuing in sin so that grace may abound.

9-10. Knowing that Christ being raised from the dead dieth no more. This is the third time Paul has used the word "know" or "knowing." These three instances teach that we have been baptized into Jesus Christ, that our old man is crucified with Christ, and that because Jesus died unto sin once, He never shall die again. Death is a completed transaction by which we have once and for all passed into the resurrection life of our Lord. Jesus Christ can never die again. When we died with Him to sin, we never die to sin again. **Death hath no more dominion over**

him. When He went to the cross and paid the debt in full for our sin, death could no longer claim Him or those who died with Him. Therefore, sanctification is knowing what Christ has already accomplished for us through His death. It is not primarily a matter of striving to live holy, but of knowing that we are holy in Him.

11-12. Knowing what has been accomplished on our behalf at Calvary is not in itself sanctification. It is but the first principle in the process of sanctification. Paul couples to that principle a second one. **Likewise reckon ye also yourselves to be dead indeed unto sin, but alive unto God.** The word "reckon" (Gr *logizomai*) means that we know something is true and then, moment by moment, day by day, consider it to be true. We take as a solid reality that which God has promised. Therefore, not only do we know what has been accomplished in our justification, but we continue to live as though we had already entered into the resurrection presence of our Lord. We do not die daily, we live daily unto the glory of God.

"This 'reckoning' is no vain experience but one which is morally fruitful, because the Holy Spirit has come to make effective in believers what Christ has done for them, and to enable them to become in daily experience, as far as may be in the present conditions of mortality, what they already are 'in Christ' and what they will fully be in the resurrection life" F. F. Bruce, *The Epistle of Paul to the Romans*, p. 139). When we daily count ourselves to be dead to the penalty of sin and alive unto God, there will be no temptation to continue in sin for we will refuse that temptation out of thankfulness to God for counting us and treating us as if we were righteous.

13. The third and final principle in living a sanctified life is the negative principle, **Neither yield ye your members as instruments of unrighteousness**

unto sin, and a corresponding positive principle, **but yield yourselves unto God.** As those who have been justified, we are not to allow our members (i.e., our hands, our feet, our tongues, etc.) to become the instruments or weapons of unrighteousness. In the original language, the words "neither yield" carry the idea of a continuous yielding. Knowing of our justification and reckoning ourselves dead to the penalty of sin, we are to continually keep ourselves from yielding to sin. But, on the other hand, we are to once for all, as the Greek implies, yield to God. Although we will yet sin, by yielding ourselves to God we will never again be caught in the trap of continuing in sin. Our life and all that we have will be given over to the One who has spiritually raised us from the dead.

14. Paul's concept of sanctification, then, is not a daily dying to one's self. It is rather being mature enough to rest wholly on the finished work of Calvary, knowing that we have been justified there, daily reckoning that work to be finished, and constantly yielding ourselves to be used of God. When one is obedient to these commands, the believer finds himself on a road climbing progressively toward the resurrection life of the Lord. For those who seek santification in this manner, the Lord has a definite promise: **For sin shall not have dominion over you.**

2. Sanctification and the practice of sin. 15-23.

15. What then? Shall we sin? The Antinomian argument of verse 1 is now repeated but with a significant difference. In verse 1 the question was, "Shall we continue in sin?" This dealt with the principle of continuation in sin after the believer recognizes he is dead to it. But now the question is, "Shall we sin?" Here he does not speak of a life style of sin, but rather an occasional excursion into iniquity. "Because we are not under law but under grace, is it not permissible to fall into sin once in a while?" Paul's abhorrence is seen in his typical answer, **God forbid.**

16. To whom ye yield yourselves servants to obey, his servants ye are. Paul uses the analogy of the slave market to illustrate that the sanctified believer dare not even occasionally fall into sin. His point is that if you start to obey sin, you are thereby admitting the mastery of sin in your life. Paul develops our Lord's words, "No man can serve two masters" (Mt 6:24). Yielding to the mastery of sin brings death; yielding to obedience to Christ brings righteousness.

17-18. But God be thanked, that ye were the servants of sin . . . ye became the servants of righteousness. Paul was ever mindful that God is to be thanked that these Roman believers obeyed from their hearts the traditions or "patterns of teaching" which were embodied in Christ Jesus. Because of Him they have been made free from service to sin and, in turn, have become the servants of righteousness. Freedom from service to Satan is, by definition, bondage to the Lord, who loved us and gave Himself for us.

19-20. I speak after the manner of man because of the infirmity of your flesh. Paul uses the human analogy of a slave in order that the weakest flesh may understand. He now counsels them to yield themselves to holiness with the same gusto they once yielded themselves to uncleanness. When they were servants of sin, it was their master. Now that they are servants of Christ, righteousness must be their master. They cannot serve the master of righteousness and dabble in sin at the same time.

21-22. What fruit have ye then in those things whereof ye are now ashamed? Paul now addresses a biting question to those who would dare to practice sin. He asks what fruit has been yielded from that sin. Paul knows well that sin always promises more than it can deliver. None of sin's fruit is worth having, and the final result of being a slave to sin is the ghastly horror of death. But for those who are freed from the bondage of habitual sin and who are servants of God, **ye have your fruit unto holiness, and the end everlasting life.** There is a drastic contrast between the outcome of the two bondages. Bondage to sin has shame as its by-product. Bondage to Christ has as its by-product the status of being positionally holy and in the process of becoming conformed to the image of Christ. This is biblical sanctification. Bondage to sin has as its end death. Bondage to Christ has as its end everlasting life.

23. For the wages of sin is death; but the gift of God is eternal life through Jesus Christ our Lord. The outcome of enslavement to sin is quite different from that of obedience to Christ. Remuneration is the principle by which we become heirs of death. Sin always pays a wage, and that wage is a drastic one. But just as remuneration is the principle by which we become heirs to death, unmerited favor is the principle by which we become heirs to eternal life. Death is earned, eternal life is purely gratuitous.

3. Sanctification and the law. 7:1-14.

Paul now continues his teaching on the sanctified life, but thoroughly changes his analogy. Although the slave market is an appropriate analogy for our former relationship to the Mosaic law, an even better analogy to depict the justified man's relationship to Christ is that of the bonds of marriage. This is because the marriage relationship involves a response of the heart and emotion. Paul draws upon it to show the proper correspondence between our sanctified lives as believers and that of a wife to her husband. The believer's life in Christ is likened to widowhood and a second marriage.

7:1. The law hath dominion over a man as long as he liveth. Paul speaks of the law of God (the Mosaic law) and the law of the state (Roman law). Both divine and civil law maintain a hold on mankind as long as he lives.

2-3. For the woman which hath an husband is bound by the law to her husband so long as he liveth. Both the Jewish and Roman law required that a woman remain with her husband until his death. Should a woman join herself to another man prior to the death of her husband, she was considered an adulteress (Mk 10:12). The Greek verb used here is *chrēmatizō* which means "to be publicly known as" (cf. Acts 11:26 where this verb was used in giving the name "Christians" to the followers of Jesus Christ). Only should her husband die was a woman free to marry another without publicly being branded an adulteress.

4-6. Ye also are become dead to the law by the body of Christ. Having given the analogy of marriage, Paul now draws this conclusion. The law confirms and seals our bondage to sin. As long as we are governed by the law, there is no possibility of being released from that bondage. The only alternative is death. But when Christ died at Calvary, we died to the law. Sin has no more dominion over us, neither does the law. **That we should bring forth fruit unto God.** The purpose of our being free from the law and married to another, the risen Lord, is that we may produce fruit unto God. Although this may be an extension of the marriage analogy, and the fruit mentioned is the progeny which is the result of marriage (i.e., the winning of others to the Lord), it is most likely that the fruit unto God is a righteous life which is characterized by those "good works, which God hath before ordained that we should walk in them" (Eph 2:10).

Having been justified by faith, we are now set free from that which held us in bondage. Since we are now free, we are also expected to produce the fruit of freedom, i.e. the sanctified life. Hence, we serve in newness of spirit, and not in the oldness of the letter. The holy law of God is not an external code of "do's" and "don'ts." Rather it is a law of love written on our hearts. We do not obey that law because we fear the Lord, but because we love Him. In our former marriage to sin and the law we attempted to do only that which would meet the minimum standard of God. Now in our marriage to Christ, we seek to be all that we can be and to do for Him all that we can do to please Him and demonstrate our love for Him.

7. What shall we say then? Is the law sin? God forbid. Still another series of Pauline questions concerns the relationship of the law to sin. Characteristic abhorrence is shown to the question, "Is the law sin?" **Nay, I had not known sin, but by the law.** Paul claims that the function of the law is to reveal what sin truly is. Man would not have known what covetousness was if the law had not commanded, **Thou shalt not covet.** A fifty-five mile per hour speed sign is not sin, but teaches us the parameters of sin. This too is the function of the law.

8. But sin, taking occasion by the commandment, wrought in me all manner of concupiscence. Not only does the law reveal sin, but it provokes it as well. Law does not cause sin, but sin takes "occasion" by the commandment. The word rendered "occasion" (Gr *aphormē*) has the meaning of "a base for military operation." The moment Paul attempted to keep the law, (abstaining from covetousness, for example) the very commandments which he attempted to keep (and could not) provoked him to acts of sin. Thus he says, **For without the law sin was dead.** Sin has no existence apart from God's law, since by definition sin is the violation of God's law.

9. For I was alive without the law once: but when the commandment came, sin revived, and I died. This verse records the dawn of conscience in the life of Apostle Paul. He had lived a self-complacent, self-righteous life in which he was free from conviction of

sin. It is difficult to say exactly when this period existed in Paul's life. Some have suggested that it was the first thirteen years of Paul's life, before his barmitzvah ceremony (the ceremony in which a Jewish boy becomes a "son of the commandment" and assumes personal responsibility to keep the commandments of the law). But it may not be necessary to restrict Paul's complacency to those early, unreflecting years of childhood. When the commandment came to him, an apparent reference to "thou shalt not covet" in verse 7, for the first time, Paul became conscious of his lack of ability to keep the law. At that point sin sprang back to life and, says Paul, "I died." This must be put in contrast with "I was alive without the law" and therefore should be understood as death to his complacent attitude toward sin.

10-11. And the commandment, which was ordained to life, I found to be unto death. This is a reference to the original purpose of the law. God had declared, "This do, and thou shalt live!" The law was intended to guard and promote life but man could not keep the law. Paul found that unheeded law produced death. The more law of which Paul became aware the more sin he found himself committing. The more sin Paul committed the more convinced he was that one day he would have to pay for that sin. Since "the wages of sin is death," we learn that the law not only reveals sin but also produces death.

For sin, taking occasion by the commandment, deceived me. The deception to which Paul referred was this. Since the commandment was intended unto life, Paul expected the commandment to yield life as a result. But instead it became the occasion for sin and consequent death. Since the commandment yielded the opposite of what Paul expected, he felt deceived. But the perpetrator of this deception was not the commandment itself, but sin. The commandment was merely the instrument by which sin deceived him.

12-14. Wherefore the law is holy.
From what Paul has just said in verses
7 through 11, we might expect a totally
different conclusion. But since the law
intrinsically and originally was intended to guide men to life, it is therefore a
holy law, just and good. Paul then expands on the principle that it is sin
which is the deceiver and not the law.
**Was then that which was good made
death unto me?** His vigorous denial is
again, **God forbid.** It is sin that works
death using the instrument of the law
and the purpose is that sin might be
shown to be sin. Death is brought by
sin, even though the instrumentality of
the law is good.

Paul's conclusion concerning the law
then is this: **For we know that the law is
spiritual.** The apostle is convinced that
the Mosaic law is holy and just and
good because it is derived from the Holy Spirit. The word "spiritual" (Gr
pneumatikos) is not used in contradistinction to corporeal, but is used to
intimate that the law finds its roots in
the Holy Spirit. (See this same use of
spiritual words, I Cor 2:13; the spiritual man, I Cor 2:15; spiritual songs,
Col 3:16; etc.).

*4. Sanctification and the conflict
within. 15-25.*

Paul has exclaimed that the Mosaic
law is spiritual. If it is holy and good,
why cannot the law bring holiness?
Paul immediately gives the answer, **I
am carnal, sold under sin.** In this section the apostle continues to speak in
the first person singular. He uses the
present tense. Here, there is inward
tension evident that was not evident in
his discussion of the law (7:1-13).
Autobiographically Paul points out
that even the believer is constantly
beset by the tugs and pulls of a self-
seeking and self-centered ego. Paul
designates this ego "the flesh." This is
no straw man which he sets up, but in
fact pictures the anguish of Paul's own
soul. He knows to do right and to obey

the law, but in himself he cannot do
either.

This passage presents the tension
between Paul's knowledge and his
ability in three phases: (1) **We know
that the law is spiritual** (vs. 14); (2) **I
know that in me (that is in my flesh,)
dwelleth no good thing** (vs. 18); (3) **I
find then a law, that, when I would do
good, evil is present.** (vs. 21). Each of
these phases presents significant
knowledge by Paul. Each of them is
immediately followed by proof that,
even though he knows what is right, he
cannot do what is right. The conclusion of the whole matter, which he
draws in verse 25, should be an encouragement to all believers.

**15-17. For that which I do I allow
not: for what I would, that I do not.**
While recognizing that the law is
spiritual because it is God's law, Paul
also must admit that he is carnal (Gr
sarkinos). As a slave to the power of
sin, Paul recognizes that those things
he wishes he could do, he cannot do;
and conversely, those things he knows
he must not do, he finds himself doing.
A historical parallel to this is Horace's
statement, "I pursue the things that
have done me harm; I shun the things I
believe will do me good" (*Epistle*
1.8.11). Paul differs from Horace,
however, in his conclusion. **Now then
it is no more I that do it, but sin that
dwelleth in me.** Paul is not attempting
to rid himself of responsibility for his
sin. He is aware that in the Christian
there are two wills, that of the fleshly,
sinful nature which causes him to sin,
and that which is born of God which
does not commit sin (I Jn 3:9).

**18-20. For I know that in me (that is
my flesh,) dwelleth no good thing.** In
the second phase of Paul's knowledge
he recognizes that in himself there is
not the ability to do good. He wills to
do good, but how to accomplish his
will is not known. He cannot do the
will of God for sin holds dominion
over him. Sin is his master, his lord, his
king. By himself he cannot break it. He

is a defeated Christian when he is controlled by sin. "It is not the new man in Christ who carries on this life of defeat, but it is the sin-principle in him, engendered by the unyielded flesh and occupying the Lord's temple as a trespassing squatter like the Tobiah whom Nehemiah expelled" (cf. Neh 13:7-9) (Gleason L. Archer, Jr., *The Epistle to the Romans*, p. 43).

21-23. I find then a law. The law which is referred to here has been variously interpreted as the law of God (vs. 22) and the law of sin (vs. 23). Either interpretation is plausible. It seems likely, however, that the law to which he refers prohibits him from doing good and therefore is the law of sin. **For I delight in the law of God after the inward man.** It is the desire of Paul, as it should be with every believer, to love and obey the law of God. However, opposed to the law of God is the law of sin, which brings his members (i.e., his body, his hands, his tongue, etc.) into captivity.

The law which he finds is the third phase of his knowledge. Paul has come to the conclusion that as long as the believer is alive there will be a constant warfare between the old sinful nature and his delight in the law of God. Unfortunately, when the believer attempts to win that battle in himself, he is always defeated. Self-attempts to rid our members of the tyranny of indwelling sin cause the frustration which underlies this passage.

24. O wretched man that I am! Who shall deliver me from the body of this death? Helplessly, Paul throws up his hands and exclaims what a wretched individual a believer is when he has not gained mastery over sin. "O wretched man" (Gr *talaiporos*) is an expression used in pagan Greek drama to express tragic misfortune and woe. Paul recognizes that he is in a helpless state of despair because he cannot rid himself of his bent toward sinning. **The body of this death** (literally, this body of death) probably does not refer to a physical body. Sin is much more deeply rooted than the body. Paul is speaking of human nature which has inherited guilt and sin from Adam. Paul knows there hangs over his life a cloud of guilt and death which is imputed with sin.

The main purpose of this statement, however, is in the question "Who shall deliver me?" Paul indicates that if he is to be delivered from the mastery of sin, that deliverance must come from without. He is unable to live the Christian life in himself. He is incapable of gaining mastery over sin. If Paul is to live a mature and godly life, and to delight in the law of God after the inward man, the strength to do so must come from outside himself.

25. I thank God through Jesus Christ our Lord. Paul inescapably comes to the conclusion that only Jesus Christ can enable us to live a sanctified life. He would like to serve the law of God, but his flesh causes him to serve the law of sin. The Lord Jesus turns that around.

Romans 7 is not a hypothetical case. It is an actual picture of the internal strife caused by the law of sin against the law of the Spirit in the Apostle Paul. This need not be the normal Christian experience, for Paul has already instructed us how to avert this internal strife. The preceding chapter presents the proper way to sanctification; this chapter presents the improper way (cf. D. M. Lloyd-Jones, *Romans*, pp. 1-13). To live a sanctified life we must know well what Christ has accomplished for us in our justification, daily reckon that we have died with Him and are alive unto righteousness, and yield ourselves completely to Him.

C. The Provison for Assurance. 8:1-39.

1. The assurance of the righteousness of God. 8:1-4.

8:1. There is therefore now no condemnation to them which are in Christ Jesus. The word "condemnation" (Gr *katakrima*) means more than just the opposite of justification; it indicates that we are not servants to the penalty for our sin, but that guilt and penalty have been removed at the cross. Therefore, for those who are "in Christ Jesus," we do not live under the constant threat of judicial punishment by God. In many ways this chapter is the consummation of Paul's argument concerning the depravity of man and the righteousness God provided to meet man's need. The expression, "who walk not after the flesh, but after the Spirit" is not in the original. There should be an exclamation point after the expression "therefore now no condemnation to them who are in Christ Jesus!"

2-4. The law of the Spirit of life in Christ Jesus has made me free from the law of sin and death. This expression is reminiscent of II Corinthians 3:17, "Where the Spirit of the Lord is, there is liberty." We should understand the law of the Spirit of Life here to be the principle upon which the Holy Spirit works. The reference to the Spirit of Life is the first time (with the exception of Romans 1:4 and 5:5), that the Spirit of God is mentioned in this epistle. However, during this chapter, the Spirit and His operation will be mentioned nineteen times. Even a casual reading of Romans 8 will leave us with the impression that the Spirit of God and the absence of an attitude of defeat go hand in hand. Life in the Spirit enables us to live free from the law or principle of sin and death. This does not mean that the believer is free from sin or free from the prospect of death, but that the principle of sin and death does not have dominion over him. It is possible for those for whom there is no condemnation to live a life that is not inundated with sin, a life which will not end in death.

For what the law could not do. The law of Moses could not justify us; it could not sanctify us because it was **weak through the flesh.** The Mosaic law is good and holy, but our flesh is weak and we are unable to keep the law; therefore, the law does not have the power to justify. However, **God sending his own Son in the likeness of sinful flesh and for sin condemned sin in the flesh.** What the law could not do, the Lord could. Paul chose his words carefully when he said that God sent His Son **in the likeness of sinful flesh.** Had he said that Jesus came "in sinful flesh" he would be guilty of the Docetic heresy. However, he says that Jesus Christ came in the flesh, in the likeness of a man, but was not Himself in sinful flesh for He "knew no sin" (II Cor 5:21). **And for sin.** The word "sin" (Gr *hamartia*) is the equivalent of the Old Testament "sin offering" (Heb *chattath*). This indicates that Jesus Christ came to be the sin offering for us and, since the law could not be that offering, God provided our atonement by offering the person of Jesus Christ. The reason, **That the righteousness of the law might be fulfilled in us.** We do not fulfill the law by walking in the Spirit instead of the flesh, but God fulfills the law in us when we walk after the Spirit of God. Thus we are assured of the righteousness of God which the law could not provide but the atonement of Christ does provide.

2. The assurance of the indwelling Spirit of God. 5-13.

5-6. For they that are after the flesh do mind the things of the flesh. The verb "mind" (Gr *phroneō*) means to have something as the habit of your thought; something in which you place a total interest. Those who place their total interest in the things of the flesh cannot have their interest in the things of God. **For to be carnally minded is death.** If the mind is not Christ-centered and our interest is constantly on carnal things, the results are the symptoms of spiritual death. However, if the interests of the mind are placed on the things of the Spirit of God, there is a peace in life that passes all understanding.

7-8. The carnal mind is enmity against God. The basis of carnality is that which is placed in the mind. If our minds have an interest in carnal things, they cause us to be the enemy of God. This is why James counsels, "Ye adulterers and adulteresses, know ye not that friendship with the world is enmity with God? Whosoever therefore will be a friend of the world is the enemy of God" (Jas 4:4). The carnal mind **is not subject to the law of God, neither indeed can be,** because it is natural. Paul is not speaking here of two types of Christians, one spiritual and one unspiritual. He is speaking of believers and unbelievers, as verse 9 plainly indicates. Therefore, **they that are in the flesh cannot please God.** Until faith is placed in Jesus Christ, a man in no spiritual way can be pleasing to God the Father (Heb 11:6).

9-10. But ye are not in the flesh but in the Spirit, if so be that the Spirit of God dwell in you. The Holy Spirit of God is the decisive factor in salvation. If a man does not have the Spirit, he does not have Christ, and he is "none of His." Paul clearly teaches that no one can receive Christ's atonement for salvation unless the Spirit of God dwells within him. It is therefore irrational to say that there are Christians who have not fully received the blessing of the Spirit of God. There is no scriptural basis for a second work of grace or a baptism of the Holy Spirit subsequent to salvation. At salvation either we have all of the Spirit of God or we have none of Him. There may be a time subsequent to salvation in which the Spirit of God gets more of us, but there is never a time when we get more of Him. **And if Christ be in you, the body is dead because of sin.** This does not mean that we have already died physically, but that the energizing Spirit of God within us has given us new life, a life of righteousness. The body is yet mortal (i.e. subject to physical death).

11-13. He that raised up Christ from the dead shall also quicken your mortal bodies by his Spirit that dwelleth in you. The resurrection of believers is always made dependent upon the resurrection of Christ (see II Cor 6:14; II Cor 4:14; I Thess 4:14; etc.). The same Spirit that raised Jesus Christ from the dead will energize our mortal bodies as well when we are "in Christ Jesus." Consequently, we are not debtors to the flesh for we have not received new life by the flesh. When the Spirit of God comes to us at salvation we are under new management and therefore we are debtors to that management. All things are new in Christ for "there is therefore now no condemnation to them that are in Christ Jesus." We must not give ourselves to life styles that are characterized by the flesh, for we no longer owe allegiance to it. If we continually serve the flesh our life is characterized by a state of death. However, **if ye through the Spirit do mortify the deeds of the body, ye shall live.** The deeds of the body are those fleshly activities which characterize one who is not alive in Christ Jesus. Paul exhorts us to mortify or reckon as dead (cf. 6:11) these deeds and no longer engage in them. When that is the case, and our thoughts and deeds are energized by the presence of the Spirit of God, we will truly have a born again behavioral pattern. Because of the fruit borne by our life, men shall know that the Spirit of God resides in us.

3. The assurance of eternal heirship. 14-25.

14. For as many as are led by the Spirit of God, they are the sons of God. There is one characteristic quality of all who are truly born again. That quality is that in their thoughts, behavioral patterns, and life styles they are constantly and habitually led by the Spirit of God (Mt 7:20; Jn 13:35).

15. For ye have not received the spirit of bondage again to fear. There is a contrast to be drawn here between the life of a servant and the life of a son. When Paul says that we have not received the spirit of bondage he is saying that when the Spirit of God dwells in us we are not treated by God as servants but as sons (cf. I Cor 2:12; II Tim 1:7). We do not fear God as the slave fears his master. Rather we love Him as a son loves his father. The slave does his master's bidding because he knows he will be punished if he does not. But to him in whom the Spirit of God dwells, to him there is no element of fear that can intrude into his service for the Lord. He serves the Lord as a son lovingly serves his loving father. **Ye have received the Spirit of adoption, whereby we cry, Abba, Father.** The son is on entirely different footing than the servant. The spirit of adoption, (Gr *huiothesia*) or sonship, enables us to enter into a relationship with God the Father that the unbeliever can never experience. In the first century A.D. the adopted son was one who was deliberately chosen to perpetuate the name of his father and inherit his estate. He was not at all inferior to a son born after the course of nature. Thus we are enabled to cry "Abba, Father." The word *abba* is an Aramaic word which was never used by the Jews in addressing God. But when the Holy Spirit dwells within us, our relationship to God the Father is such that we may address Him as freely as we would our own father.

16. The Spirit itself beareth witness with our spirit, that we are the children of God. How can we be sure that we are the children of God? Because we take God at His Word and we have the ever-present Spirit of God dwelling within us to give assurance that we are indeed the sons of God. As His children we look at the world a bit differently when our lives are responsive to His commands.

17. And if children, then heirs: heirs of God, and joint-heirs with Christ. Because we are no longer servants but sons (Gal 4:7), we then are rightfully

the heirs of God. But more than that, we share in the inheritance of Christ Jesus because we will inherit by grace the glory which is His by right (Jn 17:22-24). The status of sonship, however, involves not only the privileges of inheritance, but the responsibilities of suffering.

18-19. For I reckon that the sufferings of this present time are not worthy to be compared with the glory which shall be revealed in us. If the suffering we presently endure brings great hardship, cruel and unusual punishment, severe persecution or even death itself, none of these evils can compare with the heavenly bliss that is awaiting those who are in Christ Jesus.

20-23. For the creature was made subject to vanity. As the preacher of Ecclesiastes observed, there is nothing in this life (apart from Jesus Christ) which provides lasting significance to life. If the hand of God were today removed from His creation, all that existed would be found pursuing a course of ultimate frustration. Creation is not subject to vanity by its own desire, but **by reason of him who hath subjected the same in hope.** This can only mean God, for only God can subject His creation in hope. **Because the creature also shall be delivered from the bondage of corruption.** The word "because" could be instead translated "that." It tells of the connection between bondage and vanity. Apart from God, creation is meaningless; it is plunging headlong into decay and death. However, God promises that even creation will one day be delivered from bondage to liberty. **The whole creation groaneth and travaileth in pain together until now.** The pain with which the whole creation groans is not death pains but birth pains. Paul has in mind the Jewish expectation of a coming Messiah, but he knows that a time of distress will precede that Messianic Age. Both mankind and the rest of God's creation will share in these birth pains as they together anticipate the joy that follows the pain of birth. **And not only they, but ourselves also, which have the first fruits of the Spirit.** As the creation groans for the coming of the Messiah, so too the believer groans. We are said to have the first fruits of the Spirit. That is, the indwelling Spirit is the first installment or downpayment on the eternal glory that awaits both the believer and God's creation. This provides the assurance of our eternal heirship. As believers we await the adoption, that is, **the redemption of our body.** Though we may today be attacked by physical pain, surrounded by financial distress, discouraged by the failing health, nevertheless we know that because we possess the Holy Spirit as our downpayment, God will certainly redeem our bodies as He has already redeemed our souls. As the sons of God we will one day be clothed with immortal and incorruptible bodies (I Cor 15:5-55; II Cor 5:2-3; Phil 3:21).

24-25. For we are saved by hope. This expression does not imply that salvation comes through the instrumentality of hope. The uniform teaching of Paul, as well as Scripture in general, is that we are saved by faith (cf. 1:16-17; Eph 2:8). The words "in hope" refer to that ingredient which is inseparable from salvation and a natural accompaniment to it. Hope can never be divorced from salvation because salvation is the ground of our hope. **But hope that is seen is not hope.** Once we have realized the heirship that has been promised to us and the redemption of our bodies, we will no longer hope in them. Therefore, **if we hope for that we see not, then we with patience wait for it.** This expression of patience is a fitting conclusion to the chapter which deals with the provision of assurance. Looking to a future adoption of the body provides opportunity for our faith to grow and mature. Consequently the virtue of patience is developed in addition to hope and faith. Therefore, although

we are assured of eternal heirship, nevertheless we develop patience in waiting for the coming of the Lord.

4. The assurance of present intercession. 26-27.

26-27. Likewise the Spirit also helpeth our infirmities. The great consolation we have during this period of waiting for the Lord's return is the presence of the Holy Spirit. He is the One who helps our "infirmities," (Gr *astheneia*) which is better translated in the singular. We have one great infirmity while waiting for the Lord to return to us, and that is **we know not what we should pray for as we ought.** The only thing our Lord's disciples asked Him to teach them was how to pray. Each believer encounters that same difficulty in knowing how to pray and for what to pray. Consequently, God has given His Holy Spirit to make intercession for us **with groanings which cannot be uttered.** Even when we do not know what to say to God, the Holy Spirit interprets our innermost feelings and intercedes in our behalf. These inarticulate sounds are heard by God when intercession is made for us by the Holy Spirit. **And he that searcheth the heart knoweth what is the mind of the Spirit.** The Scriptures frequently speak of God as One who searches the heart (cf. I Chr 28:9; Ps 139:1, 23; Jer 17:10; I Cor 4:5; Heb 4:12-13). As the omniscient eye of God searches even the inarticulate groanings of our hearts, the Spirit of God makes intercession for the saint of God. Thus, intercession is made for us not only by God the Son, who sits at the right hand of God the Father, but also by God the Spirit who dwells within the believer.

5. The assurance of the eternal purpose of God. 28-34.

28. And we know that all things work together for good to them that love God, to them who are the called according to his purpose. In the midst of the distress of this world, Paul has presented the future adoption of our bodies at the coming of the Lord as a source of strength and hope. The Spirit of God within us is also given as a source of strength. Now the apostle lists a third source of encouragement for the believer. In the midst of the sufferings of this life, God has given us knowledge that He is working every detail of life to the end established in His eternal purpose. Grammatically, "all things" may be either subject or object of the verb. Therefore, it is God who works things out according to His will. **To them who are the called according to his purpose.** "The called" is not in the general sense of "many are called but few are chosen" but in the specific sense of those who comprise the family of God. Therefore, the promise of all things working together for good is given to a specific group, "the called" (i.e. those who are in Christ Jesus and justified by His blood). The world in general does not have this promise.

29-30. For whom he did foreknow, he also did predestinate to be conformed to the image of his son. The last word of the preceding verse is the "purpose" of God. Paul now expands on that purpose in verses 29 and 30 by means of a "sorites," a construction in which the predicate of one clause becomes the subject of the next clause. In the salvation provided by God, there is a link from eternity past, through the present, to eternity future. That link includes foreknowledge, predestination, calling, justification, and glorification. However, we must understand that the key word in this passage is the word "purpose." All the others arise out of the purpose of God and our understanding of them must be in consort with God's eternal purpose.

Probably no doctrine has evoked a greater variety of interpretations than that of God's foreknowledge. Although it is true that foreknowledge means "to know beforehand," in the context of God's purpose, to interpret

the expression in this way would be an oversimplification. For God to preview history in order to discern our response to the Gospel, and then act accordingly, would make the creature sovereign over the Creator. The word "foreknow" occurs infrequently in the New Testament, and therefore a clear understanding of its import must be seen from the way it is used in both Old and New Testament Scriptures. When God takes knowledge of His people it is more than just a basic understanding of them (cf. Amos 3:2; Hos 13:5; I Cor 8:3; Gal 4:3; etc.). It is the knowledge a father has of his child. God knows and loves the world, but His foreknowledge of His own is an intimate knowledge which results in an abiding love (5:8) for us that draws us to Him in salvation.

He also did predestinate to be conformed to the image of his Son. God's foreordination or predestination must not be equated with fatalism. Fatalism says that the world is plunging headlong toward an indeterminate end. Paul teaches that there is a very determinate end for those who are "the called." Their end or goal is to be conformed to the image of God's Son, Jesus Christ. We are not plunging downward but are progressing upward in being sanctified toward the Son of Righteousness. As believers, we should become more and more like the Master every day. But God has planned for us a final and complete conformity to the resurrection glory of the Lord for He is the **firstborn among many brethren** (I Cor 15:49; II Cor 3:18; Phil 3:21; I Jn 3:2). Since the term "firstborn" always implies a position of supremecy, it is the eternal purpose of God that we become increasingly more conformed to the image of Him who is the Supreme Being in the universe. **Them he also called.** As believers, we were foreknown and foreordained prior to our birth. Yet God does not manipulate us like puppets. Rather He calls us, He beseeches us to receive His offer of salvation. When we are quickened by the Spirit of God (Eph 2:2), and respond to His call in faith, we are then justified in His sight by faith.

Them he also justified. Justification is a vital doctrine in Pauline thinking. When God justifies us, He reckons us as if we are righteous because of the atoning death of Jesus Christ. He imputes the righteousness of Christ to our account. Therefore, **whom he justified, them he also glorified.** The final step in the purpose of God is the glorification of His people. We will ultimately be completely conformed to "the image of His Son." "When Christ, who is our life, shall appear, then shall ye also appear with him in glory" (Col 3:4; cf. I Jn 3:2). This is God's view of salvation. Foreknowledge and foreordination belong to the eternal past, in the eternal counsel of the Godhead; calling and justification take place in the believer's present experience; the glory which begins now will not ultimately and completely be known until the future. Although salvation from our viewpoint is an instantaneous act, it has in fact stretched from eternity past to eternity future and finds its basis, not in our merit or in the works of the law, but in the purpose of God. In the depression and turmoil of these days, nothing can be of greater encouragement to believers than to know that God is working all things together for our good and His glory.

31. Paul now asks a series of four rhetorical questions in relation to the eternal purpose of God. **What shall we then say to these things?** In essence, this verse is the conclusion Paul draws to the first eight chapters of Romans. What will our response be to what has been said? **If God be for us, who can be against us?** This is not one of the four rhetorical questions but rather the answer to the first question. Paul's only response is he has complete assurance that the eternal purpose of God will come to fruition because God is God. **Who can be against us?** does not

mean that we have no adversaries. Verses 35 and 36 list a great number of adversaries. By this Paul means that there is no adversary too great to thwart the eternal purpose of God.

32. As evidence of the fact that God will bring His eternal purpose to its proper conclusion, Paul argues that God **spared not his own Son, but delivered him up for us all.** These words are reminiscent of the classic example of the redemptive efficacy of martyrdom which is given in Genesis 22:12. There God says to Abraham, "Thou hast not withheld (Gr *pheidomai*, as here) thy son, thine only son from me." So much did God love us that He did not spare His own Son in providing atonement for us. Paul then argues from the greater to the lesser in the rhetorical question, **how shall he not with him also freely give us all things?** If God did not spare His own Son, but delivered Him up to the cross of Calvary, it isn't logical that He would fail to bring to its completed end the purpose for which Christ was sacrificed. Hence, all the gifts and blessings which accompany salvation are promised to us even as salvation is ours.

33. Paul's third rhetorical question is, **Who shall lay anything to the charge of God's elect?** This question is along the same line as that in verse 31, "Who can be against us?" Paul is issuing a challenge to the universe that if there is any man, any angel, any demon, anyone who can bring forth a charge and lay it at the doorstep of God's elect, let him do so now. In answer to this question Paul says, **It is God that justifieth.** Since "the called" are justified by God, therefore no one will be able to appeal God's verdict of justification. Every tongue that attempts to do so will be silenced (cf. Isa 50:8-9; 54:17).

34. Who is he that condemneth? This fourth rhetorical question belongs with the preceding statement, "It is God that justifieth." Paul is saying that anyone can issue a charge, but only One has the authority to condemn and that authority is committed into the hands of God the Son (Jn 5:22). In answer to this question he says, **It is Christ that died.** Only the Lord God could devise a plan in which the only person in the universe who can condemn us, is the very person who died for us. But more than His death is that He **is risen again, who is even at the right hand of God, who also maketh intercession for us.** The death of the Lord Jesus on our behalf would avail little apart from His resurrection. It is the living Lord that insures the security of God's eternal purpose. Consequently, He is now sitting at the right hand of God where He is highly exalted in glory and sovereignty. By the authority which is innate to His deity, the Lord Jesus makes intercession for us to God the Father. By His victorious death, His victorious resurrection, His victorious ascension into heaven, and His victorious intercession for us, the Lord Jesus has sealed the eternal purpose of God. In the whole universe there is nothing which can provide greater assurance than the finished work of Christ.

6. The assurance of the eternal presence of God. 35-39.

35. Who shall separate us from the love of Christ? Our assurance in the eternal presence of God is based upon the unfailing love of God. Again Paul asks a rhetorical question. The love of God keeps us in the palm of His hand and has been demonstrated to us through the atoning sacrifice of His son, Jesus Christ (5:8). Paul then amplifies the question by asking if it is possible that tribulation, distress, persecution, famine, nakedness, peril, or the sword can enter our lives and undo what Christ has accomplished on our behalf at the cross.

36. As it is written. Before Paul answers his question, there is a verbatim quote from Psalm 44:22. This quote is introduced to indicate that God's people shall endure affliction even as the faithful did in the Old Testament. However, the persecution and tribulation that enters our lives, which has featured so prominently in this chapter, is not sufficient to separate us from God's love, demonstrated at the cross of Christ.

37. Now for Paul's answer. **Nay, in all these things we are more than conquerors through him that loved us.** In the midst of illness, suffering, and myriad of life's afflictions, we have God's assurance of His eternal presence and therefore are said to be "more than conquerors." The word used here in the original language is *hypernikaō* which literally means that we are "superconquerors." We do not merely hold our own in the face of testing, but through suffering we are drawn closer to Christ and become more conformed to His image. Notice, however, the means by which we are superconquerors, **through him that loved us.** Personal heroism and inner strength are not contributors to success in the Christian life. As we owe our justification to Him and our sanctification to Him, we also owe our assurance to Him. All we have we owe to Him.

38-39. For I am persuaded . . . shall be able to separate us from the love of God, which is in Christ Jesus our Lord. Paul searches the entire universe to see if there is anything that can possibly separate us from the eternal presence of God. He goes first to the realm of death and finds nothing there. Then he turns to the realm of life and again finds nothing. He looks to the angels and they have no power to separate us. He turns to principalities which, in this case, may refer to the angelic hosts representing Satan. There is nothing there. He proceeds to examine "things present" and finds nothing. He explores the future and in the "things to come" there is nothing which can separate us. Nothing can happen now nor in the future which can remove the love of God from us or us from His eternal security.

Paul does not stop here for next he searches the entire universe and nothing in the expanses of space, "height nor depth" can be found to prohibit the presence of God from us. But just in case he has missed something, Paul then says that there is no other creature or creation of God that is able to separate us from the love of God in Christ Jesus. Nowhere can the apostle find anything in the whole universe of God which can sever the relationship that the children of God have with their father's love. This great assurance comes to those who are "the called" in Christ Jesus our Lord.

"Blessed assurance, Jesus is mine! Oh what a foretaste of glory divine! Heir of salvation, purchase of God, born of His Spirit, washed in His blood." Paul has completed this great chapter in the same way he began it. "There is therefore now no condemnation to them which are **in Christ Jesus**"(8:1). Paul is persuaded that nothing **shall be able to separate us from the love of God, which is in Christ Jesus our Lord.** All these wonderful promises belong to us because we belong to Him.

IV. THE RIGHTEOUSNESS OF GOD EXEMPLIFIED. 9:1-11:36.

Although in many ways Romans 9-11 is parenthetical, nevertheless it is an integral part of Paul's argument for justification by faith alone. Paul may have been accused of being so dedicated as the apostle to the Gentiles that he had completely forgotten about his Jewish kith and kin. Therefore he addresses the problem of Israel before proceeding to the practical section of this epistle. Also, the original believers in Rome appear to have been Jews; but in Paul's day the church was predominantly Gentiles. Those Jewish believers at Rome needed Paul's reassurance of their place in the kingdom of God. But above all, the many messianic promises to the Jews of old necessitated an understanding that God

would yet honor those promises. If Paul's message of salvation by faith is true, then why did not Paul's own people receive that message? Paul must deal with the problem of Jewish unbelief before he can proceed to a conclusion concerning the life we live in Christ Jesus.

Paul's treatment of the problem is daring. He readily admits that the Jewish nation has rejected the gospel, and yet he takes a firm stand in declaring that God is not finished with the Jew. Paul views everything that happens as part of the eternal purpose of God and therefore moving toward God's desired end.

A. Righteousness Exemplified in Divine Sovereignty. 9:1-33.

9:1-3. I say the truth in Christ, I lie not. Paul arrests the attention of his readers by certifying the truthfulness of what he is about to say. He adds the negative "I lie not" to emphasize the veracity of his statement (cf. II Cor 11:31; Gal 1:20; I Tim 2:7). To this he adds **my conscience also bearing me witness in the Holy Ghost.** This indicates that to what his tongue will speak, his conscience will attest.

In the midst of Paul's expression of joy and great assurance, he also bears witness **That I have great heaviness and continual sorrow in my heart.** This unceasing pain and sorrow which Paul bears is for his kinsmen, the Jews. **For I could wish that myself were accursed from Christ for my brethren.** This statement about being anathema from Christ is reminiscent of Moses' statement made upon returning from Mt. Sinai. As the great leader viewed the children of Israel involved in the wicked worship of the golden calf, he desired to have his name blotted out of God's book in return for the salvation of Israel (Ex 32:30-33). The understanding of Paul, however, in relation to justification by faith, does not allow him to actually wish himself accursed from Christ (i.e. separate from Christ for everlasting destruction). Paul knows that his life is not his own. Therefore he is not the master of his own life and does not have the power to cast away the eternal life that was purchased for him by the blood of Christ. The verb is in the imperfect tense ("I could wish"), meaning that Paul would accept everlasting destruction in return for the salvation of Israel, but God will not allow him to do so.

Who are Israelites: to whom pertaineth . . . Paul does not address his kinsmen according to the flesh by their racial name, but as "Israelites," their theocratic name. Unto them pertain **the adoption** (i.e. sonship; cf. Ex 4:22-23; Deut 14:1-2; Hos 11:1; Mal 1:6); **the glory** (which appeared on Mt. Sinai, Ex 24:16-17 and filled the tabernacle, Ex 40:34-38); **the covenants** (made to Abraham, Moses, and David); **the giving of the law** (the Mosaic constitution); **the service of God** (the ordinance of worship and sacrifice in the sanctuary, Heb 9:1-6); **and the promises** (that of forgiveness of sins, the inheritance of the Promised Land, but most especially the promise of the Messiah, Gal 3:16).

Whose are the fathers, and of whom as concerning the flesh Christ came. All of these privileges pertain to the Patriarchs and their seed. Notice that Paul does not say that Christ belongs to them but that He came from their flesh. This is to indicate that the culmination of all the promises given to the Patriarchs is seen in the person of Jesus Christ. Each of these privileges finds its focus in Him, **who is over all, God blessed for ever.**

6-8. For they are not all Israel, which are of Israel. Paul now repeats the distinction he made in 2:28-29 between Israel of natural destiny and the true Jew. Often distinctions have been made between Israel and those who are truly of Israel (cf. Jn 8:30-32). The Lord Jesus spoke of Nathanael as "an Israelite indeed, in whom is no guile"

(Jn 1:47). Paul speaks of the Israelites as being true Israel when they are "born after the Spirit" (Gal 4:29). Being of the seed of Abraham does not make one an Israelite, for Abraham had two sons, Ishmael and Isaac. "In Israel shall thy seed be called" (Gen 21:12). **But the children of the promise are counted for the seed.** In Paul's understanding, the children of promise are those who believe in the God of Abraham and their faith is imputed to them for righteousness, as was his. Since not all of Abraham's descendants through Isaac have experienced this type of faith, not all of Israel are truly of Israel.

2. Sovereignty exhibited in God's personal choices. 9-13.

9. For this is the word of promise, At this time will I come and Sarah shall have a son. This quotation from Genesis 18:10 is in accordance with the promise that Isaac would be born, a promise which seemed so unlikely that it provoked Sarah to laughter (Gen 18:12). Nevertheless, Isaac was born and, although not the firstborn of Abraham, he was God's choice as the son through whom the promises of God would be manifested. God chose Isaac. It was His purpose that in **Isaac shall thy seed be called.** Paul advances Isaac as an illustration that God deals on the principle of His sovereignty.

10-13. And not only this. Paul concedes that someone might say that the example of Isaac is inappropriate because Ishmael was the son of the bondwoman and therefore not truly legitimate. Consequently, Paul introduces a second example of God's election of grace. This time the example is Jacob. Had the principle of sovereign election been seen only in the life of Isaac, it would not have produced a biblical pattern. But this principle is seen as well in God's choice of Isaac's sons.

Rebecca also had conceived by one, even by our father Isaac. There is no question that the sons Jacob and Esau are both legitimately in the line of Isaac, the promised child. Yet Paul advances that God, in His sovereignty, supersedes the process of natural primogenitureship and chooses Jacob the younger to be served by Esau the elder. The reason for this choice is that **the purpose of God according to election might stand.** Every action of God arises out of His eternal purpose (8:28). The selection of Jacob to be the heir of the promise instead of his older brother Esau is a perfect example of the sovereignty of God exhibited in God's personal choices. Jacob was chosen **being not yet born, neither having done any good or evil.** Salvation is never upon the basis of human merit, **not of works, but of him that calleth.** Salvation is always upon the basis of divine grace which arises out of the eternal purpose of the Sovereign God.

As it is written, Jacob have I loved, but Esau have I hated. The expression "Esau have I hated" cannot simply mean to love less but must mean, in the context of Malachi 1:1-5, that God has actually directed his wrath toward Esau and his descendants. The judgments upon Edom are positive judgments and not merely the absence of blessing. God displays His wrath upon the sins of Edom not in unholy rancor but in righteous judgment. He does the same with individuals.

3. Sovereignty exhibited in God's powerful will. 14-24.

14. What shall we say then? When Paul asserted this teaching on the election of God's grace, he was well aware that many would object. Their objection was embodied in the question, **Is there unrighteousness with God?** Would not God be unrighteous if He chose one man and not another? To the human observer the choice of Jacob in preference to Esau, prior to their birth, must appear to be arbitrary and unjust. This is because the human observer is acting on the basis on his limited knowledge. Paul's response to the thought that God is unrighteous in choosing one over another is the strongest negative he can express, his characteristic, **God forbid.**

15-16. I will have mercy on whom I will have mercy. This statement is a quote from Exodus 33:19 and is God's response to Moses' request, "I beseech thee, show me thy glory" (Ex 33:18). Paul quotes this verse without commentary. He intends to show that even Moses had no particular claim to any favor before God. God operates on the just principle of His eternal purpose. **So then it is not of him that willeth, nor of him that runneth, but of God that showeth mercy.** Again it is emphasized that God's mercy finds its cause in Himself and not in any activity of man. As in Galatians 2:2 and Philippians 2:16, "running" is symbolic of human activity and has no effect whatsoever on the mercy or purpose of God.

17. For the scripture saith unto Pharaoh. The case of the Pharaoh of the Exodus strikingly illustrates this principle of divine mercy. Pharaoh is said to have been raised up by God. **That I might show my power in thee and that my name might be declared throughout all the earth.** Not even the power of the great Egyptian Pharaoh was sufficient to thwart the eternal purpose of God or to prohibit Him from blessing and delivering His people. The Scripture which Paul quotes is Exodus 9:16 where the Hebrew verb *amadth* meaning "stand" is used for the expression "have I raised thee up." God put Pharaoh in a position of being the Egyptian king. He also preserved him there in spite of his disobedience, so that the purpose of God may be fulfilled. The purpose was that His name might be declared throughout the earth (cf. Ex 15:14; Josh 2:10; 9:9; I Sam 4:7-9).

18. Therefore hath he mercy on whom he will have mercy, and whom he will he hardeneth. The initial phrase of this verse echoes Exodus 33:19 but the later phrase refers to the occasions on which the heart of Pharaoh was hardened. It must be recognized that Pharaoh hardened his own heart (cf. Ex 5:2; 7:3; 13) by his deliberate opposition to the will of the God of Israel. However, a time came when he was judicially bound over in hardness by God, and the initial indifference of Pharaoh's heart was cemented by God into a permanent hardness (cf. Ex 5:21; 7:23; 9:12; 10:1, 20, 27; 11:10; 14:4, 8). **19-20. Why doth he yet find fault? For who hath resisted his will?** Paul knows that the unbeliever will object to his teaching, saying that God cannot find fault with him because that is the way God made him. If God is sovereign, it is impossible to resist His will and therefore man is not accountable for his lost condition. Although there is a fallacy in this type of reasoning (God did not make man the way he is; He created him in His own image and man is what he is today because of his own sin), Paul does not argue that point. Rather his reply is, **Nay but, O man, who art thou that replieth against God?** Paul maintains that the creature is not competent to sit in judgment on his Creator. To judge the validity of God's actions is to imply that man is more righteous than God; to judge the wisdom of God's movements is to imply that man is wiser than God. Thus Paul sternly rebukes any type of reasoning which inverts the divine order of creature to Creator. **Shall the thing formed say to him that formed it, Why hast thou made me thus?** God is not answerable to man for what He does, but He must act consistent with His character. Divine sovereignty does not permit God to do what divine character will not allow. If we can trust the character of God, we can trust the wisdom of His sovereignty as well. **21-24.** The apostle now engages in a bit of philosophical argumentation. **Hath not the potter power over the clay? . . . What if God, willing to show his wrath, and to make his power**

known, endured with much long-suffering the vessels of wrath fitted to destruction. Here Paul argues that man displays the justice and grace of God, both through the persistent unbeliever (whom he calls a vessel fitted for wrath), and through the believer, (a vessel of mercy). We must remember Paul does not say that God created one vessel to wrath and another to mercy. He endured the vessels of wrath which were fitted to destruction and made known the riches to His glory on the vessels of mercy **which he had afore prepared unto glory.** As the potter does not take one lump of clay and make it a good lump, and another lump and make it bad, so too God does not make one person evil and another one good. We must notice that the expression "fitted for destruction" is in the Greek middle voice, and should be interpreted that man fits himself for destruction. God never does that. On the other hand, are those who were prepared by the grace of God through faith in His Son and are fitted by God for eternal life. With a thankful heart Paul notes that God has sovereignly called to glory both those of the Jews and also those of the Gentiles. As believers, whether Jew or Gentile, we have been the recipients of God's mercy and have been prepared for the glory of His presence. For this we should be intensely thankful.

4. Sovereignty exhibited in Israel's partial blindness. 25-33.

25-26. As he saith also in Osee. Paul now appeals to a number of Old Testament prophecies concerning God's people and the principle of election. He paraphrases Hosea 2:23, **I will call them my people, which were not my people: and her beloved, which was not beloved.** In the tragedy of his domestic life, this Old Testament man of God saw a parable of the relationship between God and Israel. Hosea took Gomer to be his wife and a child was born which he named Jezreel. But when Gomer's second and third children were born, of whom Hosea was not convinced he was the father, names were given which expressed his dismay. They were named in Hebrew, Lo-ammi ("no kin of mine") and Lo-ruhamah ("one for whom no natural affection is felt"). These names strikingly indicate God's attitude toward His people Israel when they broke their covenant with Him and forsook His commands. **And it shall come to pass, that in the place where it was said unto them, Ye are not my people; there shall they be called of the living God.** Paul does not make an application here to the prophecy of Hosea but it is evident that he is extracting from this prophecy the principle of divine election. He shows that great numbers of Gentiles, who had never been "the people of God," could now lay claim to the same relationship with God which Israel had.

27-28. Next Paul appeals to the prophecy of Isaiah 10:22-23. The meaning of Isaiah's prophecy is that although Israel is numerous as a people, nevertheless only a small minority will survive the judgment of God by the Assyrian Empire. **A remnant shall be saved.** If only a remnant of Israel will survive, there will be at least a remnant. God has always had a people. Paul applies Isaiah's teaching of the remnant to his own day. Although Israel has rejected God, nevertheless there are some who, through the grace of God, have received the salvation of God. The teaching of verse 28 is that the punitive judgment of God will exhibit both thoroughness and great dispatch. God will cut short His working upon the earth to prevent Israel from spiritually destroying herself. In His eternal purpose a remnant, at least, will be saved.

29. Except the Lord of Sabaoth had left us a seed, we had been as Sodom and been made like unto Gomorrha. This quote from Isaiah 1:9 reveals that Isaiah placed squarely on the grace of

God the fact that a seed (i.e. a remnant, the very germ of the nation) had been saved and they had not been obliterated like Sodom and Gomorrah. To the Lord of Hosts alone belongs the praise for the salvation of any of the wicked Israelites.

30-31. What shall we say then? Paul's summary question in this chapter follows the same form as we have seen elsewhere in this epistle (cf. 3:5; 4:1; 6:1; 7:7; 8:31; 9:14). **The Gentiles . . . have attained to righteousness . . . but Israel . . . hath not attained to the law of righteousness.** God has always saved on the basis of faith and never on the basis of good works. Therefore Gentiles can come to the Saviour and follow after the righteousness which is of faith, even without the privileges of the Jew, and with no prior knowledge of the Scriptures. The Jews, on the other hand, who had great privileges and knew well the Old Testament Scriptures, tragically attempted to establish their own righteousness by adherence to the works of the Mosaic law. Consequently Paul concludes that the partial blindness of Israel exhibits God's sovereignty in allowing those who were most distant from Himself (the Gentiles) to come unto Him by faith.

32-33. How can such as has just been described possibly happen to Paul's kinsmen according to the flesh? **Because they sought it not by faith, but as it were by the works of the law. For they stumbled at that stumbling stone; As it is written, behold I lay in Zion a stumbling stone and rock of offense.** The great tragedy of the Jewish nation was that the Messiah they so long awaited became to them a stumbling stone rather than a shelter in which to hide. The quotation here is from Isaiah 28:16, which is set in the context of Israel trusting Egypt for deliverance from the Assyrians instead of trusting in the power of God. Those who trust in God need never fear that their trust has been ill-placed or is ill-founded.

Whosoever believeth on him shall not be ashamed. Had Israel trusted in her God rather than her law and her neighbors, she would not have been confounded and dispersed throughout the world. But the partial blindness of Israel, in the eternal purpose of God, has wrought good to the Gentiles and to the world in general. God is now calling out a people unto His name from both Jews and the Gentiles.

B. Righteousness Exemplified in Human Responsibility. 10:1-21.

The groundwork for chapter 10 has already been laid in 9:30-33. The emphasis here is on righteousness and why Israel lacks it. Paul will lay the responsibility for the lack of righteousness squarely on the shoulders of the individual. He knows that when sinners are brought into the presence of divine sovereignty their frequent response is to justify themselves by placing the responsibility for their sin on God. Paul does not apologize in any way for what he has said about God's sovereignty in chapter 9. He does not retreat at all from his strong belief that God has always worked by the principle of election. However he does demonstrate that God is not responsible for the unbeliever's lost condition. Man alone is responsible and it is futile to try to hide behind divine sovereignty and the doctrine of election as an excuse for personal sin.

1. Nearness of the gospel: opportunity for responsibility. 10:1-10.

10:1-3. Brethren, my heart's desire and prayer to God for Israel is, that they might be saved. In the first three verses of chapter 10, Paul reiterates his feeling for his kinsmen the Jews. He has already expressed this in the first three verses of chapter 9. Even though he is the apostle to the Gentiles, Paul takes no satisfaction in Israel's rejection of God. He bears witness to the fact that the Jews have a definite zeal for God, **but not according to knowledge.** The problem with Israel is that her improper motives have caused her to have a zeal for keeping the law, but not for being the nation God would have her be. They have read the law and memorized the law, but have never internalized the truth of the law about God's righteousness and consequently they are **going about to establish their own righteousness,** and in so doing they **have not submitted themselves unto the righteousness of God.** To earn righteousness is to gain spurious righteousness. Any attempt to establish one's own righteousness is open rebellion against God and His method of establishing righteousness in us.

4. For Christ is the end of the law for righteousness to everyone that believeth. In what respect is Christ the end (Gr *telos*) of the law? The word may mean, on the one hand, that Christ is the goal or purpose for which the law was given. In this respect it would mean that the law was aimed at bringing us to Christ and that He came to fulfill the law and thus give it validity (cf. Isa 42:21; Mt 5:17). But on the other hand, this word may properly mean that Christ is the terminal point of the law. With the advent of the Lord Jesus, the old order, of which the law was a significant part, has been done away and the new order of the Holy Spirit of God has been instituted.

There is one qualification to Christ being the end of the law for righteousness. He is only the end, **to everyone that believeth.** Those who yet attempt to establish their own righteousness do not find Christ as the end of the law and consequently do not discover true righteousness.

The antithesis seen in verses 3 and 4 between self-established righteousness and God-established righteousness is now alluded to as recorded by Moses. Moses speaks both of the righteousness which is of the law and of the righteousness which is of faith. For the righteousness of the law he quotes Leviticus 18:5.

5-8. That the man which doeth those things shall live by them. In reference to Moses' teaching concerning the righteousness which is of faith, the apostle quotes Deuteronomy 30:12, 14, **Say not in thine heart, who shall ascend into heaven?** The righteousness which is of the law taught men to do and live. But the righteousness which is by faith teaches men to believe and live (10:6). The Pentateuch clearly shows that the law is to be written upon the hearts of men. It was not to be an external means of external justification. Unfortunately, the Jews mistakenly perverted the law and were attempting to keep the law outwardly without the right inward heart attitude.

Throughout this passage Paul is interested in establishing the accessibility of the message of God's righteousness. To that end he counseled the Jew, **Say not in thine heart, who shall ascend into heaven? (That is, to bring Christ down from above).** This appears to be a taunt. The Jew feels the righteousness of God is inaccessible because no one can ascend into heaven to inquire about it. Paul teaches, however, that we do not have to ascend into heaven for God came and tabernacled among us in the person of Jesus Christ, to show us the righteousness of God. Similarly he asks, **Who shall descend into the deep? (That is, to bring up Christ again from the dead).** Again, a taunt of unbelief. This smacks of a denial of the resurrection of Christ. We do not need to descend into the abyss to learn of God's righteousness for Christ is alive and is living proof of that righteousness.

In putting an end to these foolish questions the apostle quotes Deuteronomy 30:12-14, "The word is nigh unto thee, even in thy mouth, and thy heart; that is, the word of faith which we preach." Paul maintains that the true word concerning the righteousness of God is near the Jews. He even goes so far as to say that it is in their mouths and in their hearts. How can this be?

The answer is that when entering a town to preach, Paul immediately proceeded to the synagogue. Whether the Jews believed his message or not, when he left, they remained behind to discuss what Paul had taught. The very message of the gospel of Christ had been in their mouths and in their hearts, but they did not believe. The truth of righteousness was as close to them as it could possibly be, but they failed in their responsibility to receive that truth.

9-10. That if thou shalt confess with thy mouth the Lord Jesus. Paul has just made reference that the gospel has been in the mouths of the Jews. Now he builds on that thought. He explains that the confession "Jesus is Lord" refers to the lordship which Jesus exercises as the exalted Christ. Salvation must entail faith in One who is Lord. Confession of the lordship of Christ presupposes the incarnation, death, and resurrection of the Lord. The apostle goes on to say that in order to be saved one must **believe in thine heart that God has raised him from the dead.** Necessary belief in the resurrection is mentioned because new life to the believer is contingent upon a living Lord.

Token assent that Jesus is Lord and the fact of His resurrection is not sufficient for salvation. **For with the heart man believeth unto righteousness.** Belief in the saving power of the risen Christ must come from the innermost part of man's being. This is described as man's heart. But more than that, **with the mouth confession is made unto salvation.** Confession with the mouth is evidence of genuine faith in the heart. Frequently both our Lord and the Apostle Paul indicate the coordination of faith and a confession (cf. Mt 10:22; Lk 12:8; I Tim 6:12). The natural response of the lordship and resurrection of Jesus Christ believed is the lordship and resurrection of Jesus Christ confessed. Confession with the mouth does not bring about genuineness of belief in the heart, but it gives evidence to it.

2. Offer of the gospel: ground for responsibility. 11-15.

11-13. For the scripture saith. As is Paul's customary habit, he always appeals to Scripture to validate his teaching. **Whosoever believeth on him shall not be ashamed.** The key element in salvation is again seen to be faith. Salvation is not appropriated to the sinner's life until there is a heart-felt belief in the Lord Jesus. But just as the gospel is near all, likewise it is offered to all. The word "whosoever" is used to indicate the universality of God's offer of salvation. **For there is no difference between the Jew and the Greek.** The immediate purpose of the universal offer of salvation is to show the Jew that it is possible for the heathen Gentile to be saved. God's prerequisite to salvation is faith, not racial distinction. Therefore the call to salvation is to whoever will believe, whether Jew or Gentile. The reason is that **the same Lord over all is rich unto all that call upon him.** The Lord God is rich in His attitude toward all sinners and ready to receive anyone who calls on Him for salvation.

For whosoever shall call upon the name of the Lord shall be saved. Paul restates his belief that the gospel is offered to all by quoting the prophet Joel (Joel 2:32). The expression "call upon the name of the Lord" is a common Old Testament expression of worship to God (cf. Gen 4:26; 12:8; I Kgs 18:24; Ps 79:6; Isa 6:47). Paul's application of this formula to Christ is another example of his practice of taking Old Testament passages which refer to God the Father and, without any qualification whatsoever, applying them to Christ. Thus, in the New Testament, sinners are advised to call upon the name of the Lord Jesus Christ (cf. Acts 9:14, 21; 22:16; I Cor 1:2; II Tim 2:22). The ground for human respon-

sibility in salvation arises out of the fact that the gospel is offered to all, irrespective of national heritage. Both Jew and Gentile may be saved by the grace of God.

14-15. Paul now gives a rationale for his responsibility to present the gospel worldwide. Men are told that they must call upon the name of the Lord to be saved. However, they will not call unless thay have been moved to believe in Him, and they cannot believe in Him unless they hear about Him. Furthermore, they cannot hear about Him unless the good news of the gospel is brought to them. The gospel message will not be taken to the unbeliever until someone is sent to him. Consequently salvation begins with God's sending process. Isaiah was asked the double question, "Whom shall I send?" and "Who will go for us?" Isaiah's answer was, "Here am I; send me" (Isa 6:8). Isaiah was willing to go with the message, but he could not go until he was sent by God. Consequently, Paul indicates that each of us has been sent by the Lord Jesus (Jn 20:21) and the success of getting the gospel message to those who need it is now dependent upon our obedience as servants of the Lord. We must proclaim the gospel message in every nook and cranny of the globe, because we are commissioned to do so; for unless they hear they cannot be saved.

How beautiful are the feet of them that preach the gospel of peace. Probably these words were originally intended to describe those who carried the good news home to Jerusalem that the days of Babylonian exile were passed. But in the context of the New Testament, these words indicate that the feet of a gospel messenger are beautiful things to those who believe the message and place their faith in the Lord Jesus. They become new creations in Christ Jesus. This may happen to any man who hears the gospel and believes.

3. Disobedience to the gospel: failure of responsibility. 16-21.

16-17. Paul now comes to the crux of his argument concerning human responsibility and the righteousness of God. He claims that God takes the responsibility for Jewish unbelief and places it squarely upon the shoulders of the Jews. The gospel has been near unto them, it's been offered unto them, but it has not been believed by them. As proof of this he again quotes from the Jews' own Scripture as recorded in Isaiah 53:1, **Lord, who hath believed our report?** The report was Isaiah's message of the gospel concerning the Messiah. It was brought to the mouths of the Jews and offered to them, but that message was not obeyed. **So then faith cometh by hearing, and hearing by the word of God.** The word translated "report" (Gr *akoē*) in verse 16 is the same word in the original language as that translated "hearing" in verse 17. We must understand that hearing alone does not bring salvation, but faith in the message heard does. The heathen is not saved by looking at a tree and conceptualizing a god-form represented in that tree. The moralist is not saved by leading a moral life style. Salvation comes when the message of the gospel is preached, believed, and then confessed by men. That message must come from the Word of God.

18. But I say, Have they not heard? In typical Pauline style the apostle anticipates an objection from his Jewish readers. Is it not possible that some of his Jewish brethren have not heard the message of the gospel? Paul uses the language of Psalm 19 to remind them of the testimony of the stars and the heavens. The gospel had gone out through the entire Jewish world and therefore there was no excuse for ignorance of its claims.

20. But Isaiah is very bold, and saith, I was found of them that sought me not. Now Paul very convincingly turns to the greatest of the Jewish prophets and quotes Isaiah 65:1. The prophet's statement is very bold because he utterly ruled out any merit or privilege on the part of the Jews, and said that the Gentiles, who had been indifferent to God, would someday have the gospel preached to them and would come to a knowledge of God. Paul proclaims that this is that day and that the gospel is open to anyone who believes on Jesus Christ.

21. Paul now brings to a conclusion the exemplification of righteousness and human responsibility. He places the blame on men and not on God. **All day long have I stretched forth my hands unto a disobedient and gainsaying people.** The Lord God has patiently dealt with Israel throughout history ("all day long") but she has been disobedient to His love. She is therefore guilty of spurning the love of God, and the responsibility for her future is clearly her own.

C. Righteousness Exemplified in Israel's Future. 11:1-36.

1. Israel's rejection leaves a remnant. 11:1-10.

11:1. I say then, hath God cast away his people? God forbid. The problem of the unbelief of Israel as a "disobedient and gainsaying people" was prevalent in chapters 9 and 10. Paul now anticipates this theme will cause the Jews to wonder if God is finished with Israel as a nation. Thus he frames his question in Greek in such a way as to require the answer "no." The answer to the question is **God forbid.** He will give several lines of proof.

As exhibit A, Paul offers himself. **For I also am an Israelite, of the seed of Abraham, of the tribe of Benjamin.** There are two views why he offers this biographical material but the most probable one (which may boast exponents in Luther, Calvin, Hodge, Godet, etc.) is that Paul is appealing to his own salvation as proof that God has not completely abandoned Israel.

Paul was enjoying the promises of God and as long as he did, he offered a living example of God's continuing relationship to Israel.

2. God hath not cast away his people which he foreknew. As exhibit B, Paul now offers the faithfulness of God. God's foreknowledge is the guarantee that He has not cast off His people. Had He done so, it would mean a revocation of God's promises to Abraham, Moses, David, and others which guaranteed to them an ultimate restoration of the seed of Abraham.

As exhibit C, Paul offers an Old Testament quotation. The reference is to I Kings 19:10, 14 where Elijah is the speaker. **Wot ye not what the scripture saith of Elijah? How he maketh intercession to God against Israel, saying.**

3-4. Although apostasy has been present many times in the life of Israel, yet God has always preserved a remnant of true believers out of that apostasy. The Northern Kingdom in Elijah's day had grossly violated her covenant relationship with God and had slain His prophets. So bleak was the situation that Elijah felt he was the only believer left. **But what saith the answer of God unto him?** The Greek expression for "the answer" is *chrēmatismos* which is used of a divine response. To his question, Elijah received a divine and therefore certain reply, **I have reserved to myself seven thousand men, who have not bowed the knee to the image of Baal.** The presence of a remnant of believers in the Northern Kingdom meant that God would preserve that kingdom. He did so for another one hundred thirty years. Even after the Assyrian captivity, there were a few of believing Israel from the ten tribes who returned to form the nucleus of the Hebrew population in Galilee during the days of Paul.

5-6. Having presented three lines of evidence to support his answer to the question "Hath God cast away His people?", Paul now draws a conclusion. It is utterly ridiculous to think that the nation Israel has been entirely rejected of God, for even at the present time, **there is a remnant according to the election of grace.** This remnant of Israel is not saved by her line of descent, nor by personal righteousness, but upon the same ground that Gentiles are saved is the grace of God. No claim to special merit can be made even by this remnant. **And if by grace, then it is no more of works: otherwise grace is no more grace.** *A priori* grace cannot include works. They are mutually exclusive. If works are to be added to grace, as the Jews thought, then grace is completely cancelled out. Salvation is a free gift and no payment at all can be made, else it would cease to be free.

7. What then? Israel hath not obtained that which he seeketh for. What was Israel seeking for? Righteousness. Chapter 10 indicates that while seeking to establish their own righteousness, the Jews did not recognize the divine method of imputed righteousness. It was their own fault that they did not receive what they sought, for they sought it by works and not by faith. However the remnant did obtain the righteousness of God through the grace of God. The rest of national Israel has been blinded. The Greek verb *pōroō* which is used for "blinded," means to "render insensitive." Because they sought not the righteousness of God, the rest of Israel became insensitive to God. Such moral insensitivity was the judicial penalty inflicted on them for their refusal to heed the Word of God.

8. God hath given them the spirit of slumber. This quote from Deuteronomy 29:4 and Isaiah 29:10 gives reference to the unseeing eyes and unhearing ears of those who refuse to recognize the truth of God. Each of the gospel writers used this expression to indicate the Jews' failure to recognize Jesus as the Messiah (cf. Mt 13:14; Mk 4:12; Lk 8:10; Jn 12:40). The spirit of "slumber" (stupor or torpor) literally means "the spirit of stinging." The word (Gr *katanyxis*) is used of the numbness which is the result of a bite or poisonous sting. Israel had refused to seek righteousness after the manner of God and had attempted to establish her own righteousness. Thus God gave them to a blinding stupor and poisoning insensitivity toward the truth of God.

9-10. And David saith, Let their table be made a snare. The words "snare," "trap," and "stumbling-block" are closely related. Their combination serves to enforce the turning of the table to its opposite intent. The table is indicative of the bountiful mercy and blessing of God to Israel. Israel has not partaken of the good things of God's table. The recurring motif of the unseeing eyes indicates the principle that the temporary "blindness" has overtaken all of Israel, with the exception of the believing remnant. Thus the application is clear. Those who seek their own righteousness must **bow down their back always** to the bondage of sin. But those who seek the righteousness of Christ receive it by grace and are the believing remnant of God.

2. Israel's rejection is not permanent. 11-24.

11-12. I say then, Have they stumbled that they should fall? God forbid. Again Paul introduces his thought with a question and his reply of abhorrence. **But rather through their fall salvation is come to the Gentiles, for to provoke them to jealousy . . .** One of the purposes of the fall of the Jewish nations, in the eyes of God, is that the Gentile nations may come to Him in salvation. In return this will provoke the Jews to jealousy, as was suggested in Romans 10:19 where Deuteronomy 32:21 was quoted. When the Jews see the Gentiles feasting on bread from the banquet table of God and enjoying the salvation which could have been theirs, they will be convinced of their apostasy and foolish rejection of Jesus as their Messiah. However, if the fall of the Jews brings the riches of salvation to the world, **how much more their fullness,** or large-scale conversion, will bring riches to the Gentile nations and glory to God. Thus Paul begins to lay the groundwork for the proof that Israel's rejection is not permanent. She will be restored to God.

13-14. For I speak to you Gentiles . . . I magnify mine office. The apostle now addresses the Gentiles directly in response to their anticipated question, "Paul, as the apostle to the Gentiles why are you concerned about the salvation of Jews?" Paul's answer reflects both his conviction concerning his divine calling and the compassion he has for his own people. He magnifies his office in that the salvation of the Gentiles will provoke to jealousy the Jews and bring them to salvation as well. The swelling of the ranks of true believers among Paul's own countrymen will also cause the swelling of the ranks among the Gentiles and the ministry of the apostle will then be a greater ministry.

15. For if the casting away of them be the reconciling of the world, what shall the receiving of them be, but life from the dead? Here we have an *a fortiori* argument. The "receiving" is being contrasted with the "casting away." The rejected Messiah of Israel was taken by her to the cross and there He reconciled the world to Himself. But if Israel's blindness brought salvation to the Gentile world, what will her reception by God bring? The ultimate reception of a repentant Israel will bring revival on an unprecedented scale. We may expect to see a mighty evangelistic movement in the last days which will be characterized by large numbers of Jews coming to receive Jesus Christ as their Messiah and Saviour.

16-17. If some of the branches be broken off, and thou, being a wild olive tree, were grafted in among them. In preparing to warn the Gentiles, Paul introduces the principle of dedication of firstfruits to God (cf. Num 15: 20-21) and the organic relationship between the root of a tree and its branches. These two metaphors illustrate one central truth: Israel is not only the firstfruits in God's program of salvation, but also the nation in which that salvation is rooted. However, some of the branches of Israel have been broken off through unbelief. The Gentiles, being wild olive trees, have been grafted into the life of the Abrahamic root in place of those dead Jewish branches which have been discarded. Gentiles must remember, however, that not all branches of Israel have been discarded. Just unrepentant Israel is broken off. The life of the tree of Abraham has not been removed. The wild branches gain sustenance from the root which still bears a remnant of Jewish believers.

18-24. The apostle issues a strong warning to the Gentiles about their understanding of what has happened to unbelieving Jews. **Boast not against the branches . . . because of unbelief they were broken off, and thou standest by faith . . . for if God spared not the natural branches, take heed lest he also spare not thee . . . And they also, if they abide not still in unbelief, shall be grafted in: for God is able to graft them in again.** The great lesson of this passage is certainly that just as the Jews of the Old Testament became proud, assuming that they alone knew God, the same thing may happen to Gentiles in the New Testament era. Gentile believers must not yield to the temptation to disrespect the Jews. If it had not been for the grace of God, Gentiles would never have been grafted into the life of God which the Jews enjoyed. The new life which enables them to produce fruit grows from the same root that the old stock of Israel grows. New Testament believers must not assume that they are better than the Jews because they were cut off for their unbelief. The Gentile church must never

forget its reliance upon the divine grace of God, else her end will be the same as that of the old branches. The process of being grafted into the life of God finds its basis in the grace of God. We must never lord the grace of God over those who have been cut from the tree, for it is much easier to put the natural branches back, than to graft different branches in their place. We therefore must rest totally on the grace of God for our salvation, as the remnant does.

3. Israel's restoration is prophesied. 25-32.

25. The expression **For I would not, brethren, that ye should be ignorant** (cf. 1:13; I Cor 10:1; 12:1; II Cor 1:8; I Thess 4:13) indicates that what Paul is about to say is of extreme importance. He is in the process of revealing a mystery **lest ye should be wise in your own conceits.** The Gentiles dare not fall into the trap, as those in Rome apparently had done, of disparaging the Jews as a nation lest they become self-complacent in their new-found position. Paul reveals to them a mystery, not in the sense of a secret, but in the sense of a divine truth previously unknown. The mystery is **that blindness in part is happened to Israel. Until the fulness of the Gentiles be come in.** The spiritual blindness of Israel is not only to be understood as partial and not total, but also as temporal and not eternal. This blindness holds sway over the nation Israel until the "fulness of the Gentiles" is come. According to Acts 15:14, God is visiting the Gentiles today to call out a people for His name. Luke 21:24 says, "Jerusalem shall be trodden down of the Gentiles, until the times of the Gentiles be fulfilled." This means that when the complete number of Gentiles has entered the kingdom of God, the spiritual blindness on the nation Israel shall be removed.

26. And so all Israel shall be saved. The Greek *houtōs* (translated "and so") is important and must not be missed. It shows the relationship of what has preceded to what follows and can be translated "and accordingly." Throughout this passage Israel has been taken to mean a nation in contradistinction to the Gentiles. It must mean the same here. However, this may not be interpreted as implying that, in the time of fulfillment, every Israelite will be converted simply on the basis of his inheritance. The German theologian Adolph Harnach (*The Date of the Acts and of the Synoptic Gospels,* pp. 40-66) attacked Paul for this statement saying that he allowed his patriotism to override his logic. But when Paul says "all Israel shall be saved" he is not repudiating the doctrines he expounded in chapter 2 (that the Jews' law, circumcision, birth, or arguments could not make him righteous). We must understand the "all" (Gr *pas*) to be taken in the proper meaning of the word, i.e., Israel as a whole or Israel as a nation and not necessarily including every individual Israelite. This clearly is the way the Jews used the phrase "all Israel." The Mishnah tractate *Sanhedrin* X.I. says, "All Israel has a portion in the age to come" and then proceeds immediately to name the Israelites who have no portion in that age. Thus we must understand this expression to mean Israel as a company, rather than every Jew without single exception. No one is ever saved without a personal relationship with the Saviour.

Paul seals the restoration of Israel with a prophecy from Isaiah 59:20, **There shall come out of Zion the Deliverer, and shall turn away ungodliness from Jacob.** This reference is to a manifestation to Israel of her Redeemer and Messiah. When He comes, Israel shall be restored to the root of God.

27. For this is my covenant unto them, when I shall take away their sins. Paul continues the quotation of Isaiah 59:21, but then passes into the promise of Jeremiah 31:33 to indicate that God will not fail to keep His covenant with Israel.

28-29. They are enemies for your sakes . . . they are beloved for the fathers' sakes. The Jews have been alienated from God's favor and blessing, and thus are said to be enemies concerning the gospel. At the same time they are beloved as the election of God. Israel is still God's chosen people, regardless of her present condition. This proves that **the gifts and calling of God are without repentance.** Those privileges and prerogatives in 9:4-5 have never been abrogated. What God promises, He also performs. Israel will one day be restored to the favor and blessing of God. Her restoration is prophesied; it will happen.

30-32. For God hath concluded them all in unbelief, that he might have mercy upon all. The apostle is still addressing the Gentiles. Verse 30 is a repetition of what he has stated in verses 11, 12, 15, 28, that the Gentiles have received God's mercy by way of the unbelief of Israel. Verse 31 indicates the relationship which the salvation of the Gentiles has to the restoration of Israel. Verse 32 shows the relationship of God's mercy to all. Jew and Gentile alike must realize that both are undeserving sinners and the expression of the love of God on their behalf is an act both of mercy and grace.

4. Israel's restoration evokes praise. 33-36.

33. In the first eleven chapters of this epistle Paul shows that the human race is split into two segments: Jew and Gentile. The promises of God came to the Jews but they failed to receive those promises and crucified the Lord of Glory. This resulted in the expansion of those promises to the Gentiles. The day is prophesied, however, when Israel will once again be restored to the Father and God will have mercy upon all, both Jew and Gentile. This plan of God calls forth transcendent praise. **O the depth of the riches both of the**

wisdom and knowledge of God! Paul exclaims in this final doxology that the wisdom and knowledge of God are much greater than that of humanity, for the human mind could never conceive of a solution to the problem of how God could punish sin and still justly save the sinner. God's wisdom provided that solution. The depths of that wisdom are far beyond man's power to comprehend them.

How unsearchable are his judgments, and his ways past finding out! Paul employs two emphatic words in describing God's wisdom. They are "unsearchable" and "untrackable" (cf. Eph 3:8). So unfathomable are the wisdom and knowledge of God that man can never descend to the bottom of that wisdom to search it out nor can he trace it through history, because it is beyond possibility to follow it completely.

34. For who hath known the mind of the Lord? Or who hath been his counselor? The expression **Who hath known the mind of the Lord?** tells of the unsearchable depth of God's knowledge. No one can completely know it. The expression **Who hath been his counselor?** implies that God, without dependence on any creature for counsel, devised the plan of our salvation (Eph 1:9-11).

35-36. Or who hath first given to him, and it shall be recompensed unto him again? In echoing Job 41:11, Paul cannot resist going back to the principle of grace. The salvation that both Jew and the Gentile enjoy is based, not on what God must give back to them for what they have first given to Him, but on the basis of the grace of God alone. **For of him, and through him, are all things.** God is the very reason for our existence. Out of God all things have come: He is their origin. Through God all things exist: He is their sustainer. Unto God all things repair: He is their goal. In the circle of eternity, past, present, and future, God is all and

to Him all the praise for salvation must go. **To whom be glory for ever. A-men.**

V. THE RIGHTEOUSNESS OF GOD ENACTED. 12:1-15:13.

A. Righteousness Produces a Life of Transformation. 12:1-21.

1. Transformation exhibited in humility. 12:1-8.

In the last eleven chapters Paul has taken his readers through quite heavy doctrine. But doctrine is never taught in the Bible as an end in itself. It is always taught in order that doctrine may be translated into practice. John 13:17 declares, "If ye know these things, happy are ye if ye do them." Consequently, it is the Pauline practice to follow a doctrinal section of Scripture with a practical section, and usually these two are linked together with the word "therefore" (cf. Eph 4:1; Col 3:5).

This section begins with the third and final "therefore" in the Epistle to the Romans. Each of these "therefore's" marks a great division in the book. "Therefore being justified by faith, we have peace with God through our Lord Jesus Christ" (5:1). "There is therefore now no condemnation to them that are in Christ Jesus" (8:1). "I beseech you therefore . . ." (12:1). It is now Paul's purpose to tie together all the doctrinal material he has presented. Hence, the rest of this epistle will be as intensely practical as what has preceded was intensely doctrinal.

12:1-2. I beseech you, therefore, brethren, by the mercies of God. The word **brethren** identifies the group to whom these words are addressed. Paul is speaking to Christians, whether Jews or Gentiles. The **mercies of God** are all those good things we have because we are in Christ Jesus. Most especially he is referring to those mercies enumerated in 8:35-39. The progression of Pauline thought moves very easily from the end of chapter 8 to the beginning of chapter 12. He is now dealing again with what our responsibility is to those who have received the righteousness of God.

That ye present your bodies a living sacrifice, holy, acceptable unto God, which is your reasonable service. This request is eminently linked to his discussion of sanctification in chapters 6 and 7. In fact, the word rendered **present** here (Gr *partisēmi*) is the same as translated "yield" in 6:13, 19. Paul now deals in greater detail what it means to present ourselves to God.

The Lord God wants the sacrifice of our life, not our death. Consequently the sacrifice we are to make of our bodies (representing our whole person) is a **living** sacrifice. This is in contrast with the Old Testament sacrifices which were put to death on the altar. Since we know that we have died with Christ Jesus, we are in a position to present Him with our lives that are hidden with Him. Not only is the presentation of our bodies a **living** sacrifice but it is also a **holy** and **acceptable** sacrifice. Holiness is contrasted with the defilement which is the usual characteristic of the sinful man. When the sacrifice of ourselves to God is holy it is inherently acceptable to God and well-pleasing to Him. More than this, says the apostle, the sacrifice of ourselves to God is our **reasonable** service. The word **service** (Gr *latreia*) is a term used for the function of priests in the tabernacle. The adjective (Gr *logikos*) which precedes it may translated either reasonable (i.e. rational) or spiritual. But our worshipful service can only be spiritual in the biblical sense when it is characterized by our conscious, intelligent, rational service to the Lord God. In Paul's theology, spirituality is not some mindless flittering of the heart but is the presentation of an entire life to the Lord.

Not only is the presentation of our bodies the subject of Paul's request, it is the pattern of our behaviour as well. **And be not conformed to this world.**

Paul cautions the believer not to be fashioned after this world or age (Gr *aiōn*). The world system of this age is an evil one (Gal 1:4), and is dominated by "the god of this world" (II Cor 4:4). The new creation in Christ is to live with the understanding that "old things are passed away; behold, all things are become new" (II Cor 5:17). We are therefore not to have our lives governed by the thought patterns and dictates of this evil world system.

But how can we prevent that? **Be ye transformed by the renewing of your mind.** The only possible way for the believer not to be fashioned (Gr *syschēmatizō*) after this world is to be transformed in mind. The word "transformed" (Gr *metamorphoō*) reaches far deeper than conformity to the world. This implies a fundamental change in the Christian's inward nature and a following pattern of character which corresponds to that new nature. Thus the mind (Gr *nous*, the center of logical reasoning, ethical judgment, and moral awareness) must be completely changed if we are to live a life that is holy and acceptable unto God. The reason this change must be undertaken is **that ye may prove what is that good, and acceptable, and perfect, will of God.** To prove (Gr *dokimazein*) something is to test, scrutinize, or examine it. When we put the will of God to the test of actual experience we will find that it is **good, acceptable** (Gr *euarestos*) and **perfect** (Gr *teleios*). God's will is good in that, even when we cannot conceive it to be so, it is never mistaken. It is acceptable in that when you recognize it as good, it will be heartily endorsed by the believer. It is perfect in that it achieves the desired end that God has in mind. When the righteousness of Christ is placed upon us like a cloak, a life of transformation is produced that conceives of God's will in these ways.

3. For I say, through the grace given unto me. Paul now expands the biblical idea of the transformed life. His authority to speak in the way he does comes from the **grace** which is given unto him. That grace is the spiritual gift of apostleship (cf. 1:5; 15:15). From his position as an apostle Paul counsels, **every man that is among you, not to think of himself more highly than he ought to think; but to think soberly.** The transformation which comes through imputed righteousness is first exhibited in humility. The believer must be careful of being "above-minded" (Gr *hyperphroneo*), having an attitude of superiority. Rather we are to have a sober assessment of ourselves. This assessment is properly based in Galatians 2:20 where we recognize that we have been crucified with Christ and He lives through us.

4-5. Paul uses the metaphor of the body to indicate that the life of humility must be lived in relationship to other believers. Each of us must recognize that we possess a special "gift" (Gr *charisma*) as an outgrowth of our salvation and the indwelling gift of the Holy Spirit. There are many members in the body of Christ, and each of us, regardless of how humble our station in life or how deficient in education or expert we may be, has a gift from God to contribute to the whole body. In His sovereignty, God has just the proper place for each of us.

6-8. What is the believer to do with his gift? Since the members of the body of Christ have gifts which differ, each of us is to use his gift in the way that God intends. **Whether prophecy, let us prophesy.** Prophecy is the gift of inspired utterance (I Cor 14:1). This activity is to be done **according to the proportion of faith** or in harmony with that which has already been spoken by God. **Or ministry, let us wait on our ministering.** Ministry (Gr *diakonia*) is the general work of deaconing. This denotes a very broad office that may cover almost any kind of service in the local church. **Or he that teacheth, on teaching.** Teaching is the art of making the unchanging message of God understandable to the unlearned. Teaching is a gift of God; those who have that gift must not neglect to give attention to teaching. **Or he that exhorteth, on exhortation.** Unlike the teacher who appeals to the mind, the exhorter takes his brother aside and appeals to his heart in order to console or encourage him. Exhortation (Gr *paraklēsis*) is a specific and highly necessary ministry in the local church, especially in times like these. **He that giveth, let him do it with simplicity.** Each member of the church has the opportunity to give. The term **simplicity** (Gr *haplotēs*) sometimes means liberally (cf. II Cor 8:2; 9:11-13), and sometimes it means in singleness of heart or motive (cf. II Cor 11:3; Eph 6:5; Col 3:22). Essentially when we give, whatever we give, we are to do it with all our heart. **He that ruleth, with diligence.** The exercize of leadership in the church is as much a spiritual gift as any of the others. He who presides (Gr *proistēmi*) is not to do so sluggishly but responsibly and diligently. **He that showeth mercy, with cheerfulness.** This is the Christian gift of engaging in practical deeds of kindness. There is a place in the local church for those who cannot teach or cannot minister. Many there are within the church who go about their business in an unspectacular way doing a much needed work in showing kindness and helpfulness to their fellow believers. Each of these gifts is necessary for the proper functioning of the body of Christ. Since that is the case, one gift cannot be exalted over another and therefore the transformed life exhibits humility in its relationship to others in the local church.

2. Transformation exhibited in love of the brethren. 9-16.

9. The injunctions in this section are a practical outworking of the Sermon on the Mount. The brotherhood of believers is expected to have a mutual love toward one another. Thus the apostle says, **Let love be without dis-**

simulation. Dissimulation (Gr *anypo-kritos*) literally means without hypocrisy or insincerity. We must genuinely love one another. **Abhor that which is evil: cleave to that which is good.** We should not expect God to remove sin from us until we actually hate it and have rooted out of our transformed lives any secret love that we still hold for that which is evil.

10. Be kindly affectioned one to another with brotherly love. We must have a tender regard for those who are our brothers in the Lord. Brother-love (Gr *philadelphia*) is a love for all members of the local assembly, regardless of their heritage or financial status. **In honour preferring one another.** Since the root of all "above-mindedness" is taken away by the basis of our salvation, which is grace, therefore we must not count ourselves better than our brother (Phil 2:3). We need a devalued opinion of our own worth before the Lord, but a greatly inflated opinion of what He can do through a devalued person who is yielded to Him.

11. Not slothful in business. The local church must be run in just as businesslike fashion as any secular corporation. We dare not be sluggish or unenthusiastic about the business of the church. **Fervent in spirit; serving the Lord.** This expression, which was used of Apollos in Acts 18:25, means to be boiling or bubbling up (Gr *zeō*) or aflame with the Spirit of God. Not only must we serve the Lord as a slave would serve his master, but we must do so in an energetic and enthusiastic manner (cf. Eccl 9:10; Col 3:23).

12. Rejoicing in hope; patient in tribulation; continuing instant in prayer. The life of love among the brethren never allows adverse circumstances to restrain the joy of the local congregation. The believer must bear up steadfastly under the great weight of tribulation which the church will sustain and the only possible way to do that is to be steadfastly given to prayer, seeking the comfort and aid of the Lord.

13. Distributing to the necessity of the saints; given to hospitality. The transformed life exhibits love among other believers in such a way as to be tangibly moved by those of the brethren who have a financial lack. We need a genuine concern for those who are poor and needy and our hospitality must extend to them as automatically as did Abraham's extend to the three strangers (Gen 18:2-3).

14-15. Bless them which persecute you. Paul is a good example of one who lived up to this admonition (cf. I Cor 4:12-13; Acts 28:19). **Rejoice with them that do rejoice, and weep with them that weep.** That this practice can be found in the life of Christ proves that this is not just a Stoic philosophy. Jesus Christ rejoiced at the marriage feast with those who rejoiced (Jn 2:1-12) and wept at the graveside of Lazarus with those who wept (Jn 11:1-44). We need to be so intimately involved with the lives of other believers that we know of their joys and their sorrows, and can identify with each.

16. Be of the same mind one toward another. Although we may not always see eye to eye with other believers, nevertheless we must preserve the unity of belief and practice which characterized the early church. When we are told to **Mind not high things, but condescend to men of low estate,** the apostle brings us right back to the base of humility. The believer who is concerned about exhibiting his transformation in an attitude of love for the brethren will not attempt to cultivate friendships only among the attractive or wealthy of the church, but will especially befriend those who are not befriended by others. **Be not wise in your own conceits** is a quotation from Proverbs 3:7 and summarizes the teaching of this section.

3. Transformation exhibited in honor before the world. 17-21.

17. Not only is the life transformed by the righteousness of Christ to be lived in love toward the brethren, but it is to be lived in honor toward those who are outside the church as well. **Recompense to no man evil for evil.** When we are wronged our natural instinct is to fight to assert ourselves and right the wrong. But in the believer's life there is no place for retaliation. **Provide things honest in the sight of all men.** Because retaliation can mean a complete loss of our Christian testimony, we are advised to let our aims be such as men consider honorable. The quotation from Proverbs 3:4 (LXX) means that we have to live honorably and righteously before the world just as we must live godly before the Lord.

18. If it be possible, as much as lieth in you, live peaceably with all men. In so far as it is consistent with our obedience to God, the Christian is to labor in the utmost harmony with men of the world. We must live in good will toward men and attempt not to be offensive or obnoxious toward them, unless our offense comes through loyalty to God and our refusal to participate in those activities which are prohibited by God.

19-21. Dearly beloved, avenge not yourselves, but rather give place unto wrath. Self-vengeance has no place in the Christian life. We are told to make room for divine retribution to operate and therefore to **give place to wrath** means to allow God to bring His vengeance to bear on those of the world, rather than us avenging them. We are not to give a place for wrath in our dealings with men, but rather to give that place to God's wrath. Thus the apostle introduces the quotation from Deuteronomy 32:35 that **Vengeance is mine; I will repay, saith the Lord.** In light of this, and quoting from Proverbs 25:21, we are to treat our enemy kindly and not vengefully. If he is hungry, we are to give him food; if he is thirsty, we are to give him drink. **For in so doing thou shalt heap coals of fire on his head.** There are two main lines of interpretation to this phrase. One is that this quotation from

Proverbs 25:22 reflects an Egyptian ritual in which a man showed his repentance by carrying a pan of burning charcoal on his head. This was a dynamic symbol of the change of mind which had taken place in his life. The meaning would then be that our act of love in giving him food or drink would bring about a change of attitude toward us. The prevailing view, however, is that heaping coals of fire on the head refers to the sense of shame, punishment, or remorse which is engendered in the mind of our enemy when we show kindness to him. Whichever meaning is to be held, it is obvious that verse 21 is closely linked with it. **Be not overcome of evil, but overcome evil with good.** As believers we must resist the impulse to retaliate but rather we promote our sanctification by doing good to those who do evil to us. Therefore we exhibit our life of transformation before a watching world.

B. Righteousness Produces a Life of Subjection. 13:1-14.

1. Subjection to the state. 13:1-7.

When one receives the righteousness of Christ and begins to live out that righteousness, it not only produces a life of transformation but also a life of subjection. It was inevitable that Paul would have to say something with regard to the believer's relationship to the state. The men and women of the first century were vitally interested in their position before the Roman Empire. Jesus was questioned in Mark 12 by the Jewish leaders concerning His attitude toward the Roman government. The Corinthian Jews dragged Paul before Gallio, the proconsul of Achaia, and charged him with propagating a religion that was illegal in the empire (Acts 18:12-13). Paul's opponents at Thessalonica went to the civil magistrates and accused the Christians of subversion to the state (Acts 17:6-7). The question of religion versus state was very much on the minds of those of the first century.

13:1. Let every soul be subject unto the higher powers. Even though governments are generally carried on by nonbelievers, the teaching of the Lord Jesus (Mk 12:17), the teaching here of the Apostle Paul, and historic position of the church (cf. the *Westminster Confession of Faith,* Chapter XXIII, Section IV) has always been that the believer must live under the law, governed by a magistrate. The reason, **For there is no power but of God: the powers that be are ordained of God.** There is no governmental authority except that which is ordained of God. It is God who establishes kings and dethrones kings (cf. Dan 4; see also Prov 21:1). This truth was strikingly illustrated of Pilate by the Lord Jesus. In his anger Pilate said, "Speakest thou not unto me? knowest thou not that I have power to crucify thee, and have power to release thee?" Jesus put this magistrate in his place when He answered, "Thou couldst have no power at all against me, except it were given thee from above" (Jn 19:10-11). Since all power comes from God, the believer is to be subject to that power.

2. Whosoever therefore resisteth the power, resisteth the ordinance of God. As a general rule, God condemns civil disobedience toward the lawfully-existent government. Those who would riot and rebel must know that opposition to government is opposition to God. However, the obedience which the Christian owes to the government is never absolute and must be carefully weighed in light of his subjection to God. To unlawfully and unethically resist government brings the judgment (not "damnation") of God upon the believer.

3. For rulers are not a terror to good works, but to the evil. Since God's purpose in ordaining government in the days of Noah was to restrain wickedness and promote virtue, we are to be in subjection to any government which fulfills this purpose. However, the Declaration of Independence was composed to rebuke George III's government for punishing virtue while at the same time rewarding wickedness. Christians are never under subjection to injustice or a government of wickedness. Rulers are to be established to be a terror to evil and to promote the good. That is the basic principle of good government. Consequently, we are to respect any government which does so and reject any government which does not.

4. For he is the minister of God to them for good. The officer of the state is ordained of God to minister that which is good. Therefore the town mayor is as much a minister of God as the local pastor, but in a very different way. We ought to have as much respect for a good mayor as we do for a good minister. **For he beareth not the sword in vain: for he is the minister of God.** God has granted human government the power of enforcing itself and therefore this verse unquestionably provides New Teatament justification for capital punishment. The divine directive was established in Genesis 9:6, "Whoso sheddeth man's blood, by man shall his blood be shed." The hands of good government should never be so tied that they cannot execute good judgment and the wrath of God upon those who do evil.

5. Wherefore ye must be subject ... but also for conscience sake. At this point Paul reiterates God's general rule that we need to be subject to the higher powers, but he introduces the question of the conscience as well. The Christian always lives in a tension between the two competing claims of obedience to the state and obedience to God. The state has a right to demand our respect and conformity. Thus, we are to be in subjection to those in authority over us, not only out of fear and respect, but also out of a good conscience before God. However, the believer dare not blindly bow to the state if his conscience is offended by the wickedness of the state. There may be times when "we ought to obey God rather than men" (Acts 5:29; cf. 4:19). Since the state and its magistrate are not infallible, the believer may at times have to conscientiously object to what the state requires that is in direct contradiction to the law of God.

6-7. For this cause pay ye tribute also . . . render therefore to all their dues: tribute to whom tribute is due; custom to whom custom; fear to whom fear; honor to whom honor. To be a good citizen of the state we must **render . . . to all their dues,** that is, to discharge our obligation to all men. Tribute is today called tax, that which is levied on persons and property (cf. Lk 20:22; 23:2). Custom refers to the tax levied on goods and corresponds to the tax paid on those things we import or export. Fear (Gr *phobos*) is the same word that is rendered **terror** in verse 3. This word means both concern and rev erence. If we disobey the state, we are to fear those who have been charged with the responsibility of punishing disobedience. At the same time we are to respect the laws of the state and those who make the laws. Honor means that it is not right for a Christian to speak in a disrespectful way of the state or officers of the state. For the sake of the Lord Jesus we are to give honor to those who are His ministers as evidence that we give honor to Him.

Frequently twentieth century Christians try to rationalize their infidelity to the state by saying that Paul simply could not understand what it meant to live in such a corrupt society as we do. We must remember, however, that as Paul wrote these words he was living under the reign of the wicked Emperor Nero. Nero's mother, Agrippina (sister of Emperor Caligula, who killed and tortured thousands for pleasure), had Nero's stepfather assassinated with a dish of poisoned mushrooms. Nero himself killed his stepbrother, Britannicus, when the boy was just fourteen years old. Later when he feared that his mother would attempt to exercise the power of the throne, Nero killed her as well. He banished his first wife, Octavia, to an island and had her killed. Still later he slew his second wife, Poppaea. In light of these facts, if Paul can so tenaciously hold that the believer should be subject to the higher powers, the twentiety-century believer must be very careful not to jump to the conclusion that he should not be subject to the present day powers.

2. Subjection to the citizens of the state. 8-10.

8-10. Owe no man anything, but to love one another. The key word in determining that the believer's relationship should be to other citizens of the state is **love.** Love enables us to perfectly fulfill all our obligations, whether to the state, to the citizens, or to God. More than anyone, Christians ought to pay their debts and honor their obligations. To be ever-increasingly in debt is to show a lack of regard and love for the one to whom you are indebted. We should not buy what we cannot reasonably afford.

Good citizenship in financial matters brings Paul to quote the seventh, sixth, eighth, ninth, and tenth commandments of the Mosaic law (cf. Ex 20:13-17; Deut 5:17-21). To these he adds the chief commandment in which the law is fulfilled in one word, **Thou shalt love thy neighbor as thyself** (Gal 5:14). Love adds to the complete performance of the law, because it shows that we do not conform to the law out of duty but out of a right heart attitude. No man will commit adultery, murder, or steal if the love of Christ motivates his heart. No man will cause ill to this neighbor if the seat of his action is love. **Therefore love is the fulfilling of the law** (literally "the fulfillment of the law"). If the law is filled to the brim with love, it is a law which can easily be obeyed. The believer will have no difficulty in subjection to the citizens of the state if his heart is filled with love toward them.

3. Subjection to the timetable of God. 11-14.

11. It is high time to awake out of sleep. The duty of spiritual vigilance with relation to the timetable of God was constantly enjoined by the Apostle Paul (cf. I Thess 5:4). The urgent nature of these days in the endtime necessitates that the Christian awake out of his lethargy and fervently pursue his calling as an evangelist. It is time for believers to stand up and be counted and to make a mark for God. **For now is our salvation nearer than when we believed.** The salvation of which the apostle speaks is "the adoption, to wit, the redemption of our body" for which believers wait (8:23). We are now much closer to that day than the day we first believed. This behooves us to be the transformed believer we ought to be and more actively engaged in the transforming process of others.

12. Let us therefore cast off the works of darkness, and let us put on the armor of light. The Christian must recognize that he is engaged in a warfare with the powers of darkness. It is therefore absolutely necessary that we discard the works and values of that darkness and replace them with the armor of light. A detailed description of this armor is given in Ephesians 6: 14-17. We constantly live in subjection to the timetable of God and time is running out.

13. Let us walk honestly as in the day. Those who have received the light, must walk in the light. The manner of life which spawns riotous living, drunken bouts, sexual orgies, and all forms of wanton revelry cannot be that of those who walk honestly or honorably. When a person claims to be a Christian, if he cannot change his life style, he had better change his name.

14. But put ye on the Lord Jesus Christ. Paul urges his Christian converts to **put on** Christian virtues in the same manner that they would put on their clothes (Col 3:12). When they had "put on the new man" (Eph 4:24) they had in fact been baptized into Christ and had "put on Christ" (Gal 3:27). Putting on Christ means to allow Him to envelop us so that when others view us they see His righteousness. He therefore not only lives in us and through us, but on us as well. When that is the case, we need not take thought of satisfying our bodily lusts or carnal desires, but our prime concern will be to live in honor to the Lord. When Christ is on us and in us, we will not feed our fleshly desires but will feed a soul striving to be more like Him, and much more so realizing our subjection to the timetable of God.

C. Righteousness Produces a Life of Consideration. 14:1-15:13.

1. Consideration for a brother weak in the faith. 14:1-13.

14:1. Him that is weak in the faith receive ye. This verse more accurately reads, "Him that is weak in *the* faith" not merely weak in faith. What was the nature of the weakness? Scholars differ dramatically on the root of the weakness in the lives of the Roman believers. But whatever were the particular religious scruples which caused differences between them, the basic problem was that some of the believers had not grasped the great truths Paul has just expounded in his epistle. Those who are weak in the faith were Christians who did not have full understanding that salvation is the free gift of God and that the believer faces no condemnation whatever because of the atonement of Christ. Paul enjoyed his Christian liberty to the fullest and was totally emancipated from foolish superstitions and unbiblical taboos. Some of the Romans, however, were yet clinging to these taboos for they did not fully accept the doctrine of justification by faith alone. In relation to this, Paul addresses both those living freely in

Christ and those in Christ who are still bound by fleshly legalism. The strong who had internalized Bible doctrine, were to receive the weak, those who did not fully rest in the grace of God. But they were not to argue with them over secondary points of difference.

2-3. For one believeth that he may eat all things: another, who is weak eateth herbs. Let not him that eateth despise him . . . and let not him which eateth not judge him. So that he may be easily understood, Paul immediately advances two concrete examples of the weak in the faith versus the strong in the faith. What is the proper diet for the separated Christian? Some believers (whom Paul characterizes as the weak in faith), in order to avoid eating the flesh of animals that had been consecrated to pagan gods (cf. Dan 1:8), refused to eat anything but vegetables. Converts from heathenism would be especially sensitive to the eating of such meat. Paul's contention is that the meat itself is not destroyed of nutritional value because it was offered to idols. Since these idols have no validity before God, there is no reason not to partake of this meat. However, he counsels those who do eat not to despise those who do not. Those who feel no compelling reason not to eat are to refrain from ridiculing those who have definite scruples against meat. The reason is God has received this brother who is weak in the faith and we must as well.

4. Who art thou that judgest another man's servant? Essentially addressing the weak in faith, Paul draws a principle which is found many times in Scripture (cf. Mt 7:1; Lk 6:37; I Cor 4:3 ff). Each Christian is the property of God and we are not in a position to see the inner motives of others. God's jurisdiction over all believers is not to be infringed upon by either those who are weak or those who are strong. God is judge and not we ourselves.

5-6. A second concrete example is now given of the differences between those who have laid hold on the truths of God's Word and those who tenaciously cling to some legalistic practice. It is the keeping or honoring of certain days. **One man esteemeth one day above another: another esteemeth every day.** Some of the brethren, those who are weak, pick out a certain day and proclaim it holy, more holy than other days. Those who, like Paul, understand the liberty we have in Christ Jesus, do not observe days but rather serve and worship Him consistently seven days a week. Paul clearly aligns himself with those who are seven-day-a-week Christians, those who view one hundred percent of their income as holy to the Lord, not just one-tenth. But he says that even though believers disagree with regard to this issue, they must respect the opinion of others for the motive of both the weak and the strong is to honor God with thanksgiving.

7-9. For none of us liveth to himself . . . whether we live therefore, or die, we are the Lord's . . . For to this end Christ both died, and rose. The adage "no man is an island unto himself" is the modern outgrowth of these verses, but that is not the central truth taught here. The basic teaching is that each Christian must live his life in the full view of the Lord Jesus Christ. We do so as servant to master and therefore our relationship to Him will affect our relationship to the brethren. We must interact with others in a method pleasing to the Lord and not in judging the strong or demeaning the weak. The ground of our actions toward one another is the absolute lordship of Christ Jesus as established in His death, burial, and resurrection. From His authority as resurrected Lord He bids us live in harmony with one another.

10-13. But why dost thou judge thy brother? Paul addresses this question to the weak in faith. **Or why dost thou set at nought thy brother?** This question is addressed to the strong. **For we shall all stand before the judgment seat**

of Christ. As Paul, each believer must live with the Judgment Seat of Christ in view. All that we do will be judged at that heavenly *bēma* or judgment seat (cf. II Cor 5:10). On that day all meaningless differences between Christians will fade away and we will not be concerned about the validity of what others have done for **every one of us shall give account of himself to God** (see Woodrow Michael Kroll, *It Will be Worth it All*). The weaker brother does not have to defend the actions of the strong. The stronger brother will not have to answer for the actions of those weak in the faith. We must give an account of our life and activities for the Lord, individually, one-on-one, with the Lord of Glory. To indicate the certainty of this event, Paul quotes from Isaiah 49:18 and Isaiah 45:23, a passage he also applies to Christ in Philippians 2:10 ff. Under the lordship of Christ we must live with the convictions we have and not those of others. This responsibility naturally drives us to constantly take inventory of our religious scruples and convictions to make sure that they are based in the infallible Word and not in the traditions or whims of men.

2. Consideration for our neighbor. 14-23.

14-15. Martin Luther, in his treatise *On the Freedom of a Christian Man*, wrote, "A Christian man is a most free lord of all, subject to none. A Christian man is a most dutiful servant of all, subject to all." By this he meant that even though our liberty in Christ may permit us to engage in a certain activity, we nevertheless may not be wise in doing so. **I know, and am persuaded by the Lord Jesus, that there is nothing unclean of itself.** Paul casts his lot with the strong in faith who are not given to the legalism of the weak. However he is well aware that he may become a "stumblingblock" (Gr *proskomma*) to the weaker brother for the conscience of the weak will not allow him to en-

gage in the activities of Paul. There is no virtue in flaunting Christian liberty. **But if thy brother be grieved with thy meat, now walkest thou not charitably.** Believers must not insist on their liberty in the presence of those whose consciences would be offended. To do so is not to walk in love under the lordship of Christ. To the strong in faith Paul admonishes, **Destroy not him with thy meat, for whom Christ died.** If we are to live a life of consideration for our neighbor then we must learn that even though there are things we feel we biblically may do, many of those same things, for the sake of others, we should not do.

16-19. Let not then your good be evil spoken of. Paul reaffirms that the position of the strong is right and good, but advises them not to let what is good become the object of misunderstanding. **For the kingdom of God is not meat and drink; but righteousness, and peace, and joy.** The kingdom of God does not consist in observing or not observing days, eating or not eating meats, or any other secondary issues of religious scruples, but in **righteousness** (perfect uprightness in our daily walk), **peace** (perfect peace with God and a consistent attempt to be a peacemaker of the brethren), and **joy** (perfect union and intimate love through the Holy Spirit, cf. Mt. 6:31; 5:6, 9, 10, 12). **Let us therefore follow after the things which make for peace, and things wherewith one may edify another.** Paul cautions the Romans not to ride moral or theological hobby horses but to pursue those issues which will tend toward building the common bond of faith between the weak and the strong. The basis of fellowship is not peripheral matters of eating or drinking but the salvation which both enjoy in Christ.

20-21. For meat destroy not the work of God. Convictions are fine, says the apostle, but not at the expense of the work of God. The reason is simple. All foods are clean in themselves but they become unclean to the one who eats them when his conscience tells him otherwise. For conscience' sake that man should avoid them. To the strong Paul advises, **It is good neither to eat flesh, nor to drink wine, nor any thing whereby thy brother stumbleth, or is offended, or is made weak.** What a beautiful picture: a Christian that knows he is at liberty to do something but does not for the sake of another. That is living under the lordship of Christ. The best thing one who is strong in the faith can do is to assist one who is weak in the faith become strong. This will never be accomplished if we parade our liberty in the face of the weak and offend him.

22-23. Hast thou faith? Have it to thyself before God. "Faith" here means a firm conviction before God that what you believe is right. Paul remarks that it is proper to have and cherish a conviction, but we must not force our convictions upon others. We do not have the prerogative to do so. We must hold that conviction before God. **And he that doubteth is damned if he eat.** For the translators of the AV the word **damned** did not have the force it does today. It did not mean that if someone violates his conscience by eating that which he feels is wrong he will be damned to irrevocable perdition. Rather the meaning is that he is condemned in his conscience for doing that which it will not allow. If he does not eat in faith believing that it is acceptable to God, he eats in sin **for whatsoever is not of faith is sin.** If our actions do not arise from our convictions then they are sinful actions and unacceptable to God.

3. Consideration as we have Christ as example. 15:1-13.

15:1-3. We then that are strong ought to bear the infirmities of the weak. Again, Paul casts himself as one of the strong, one who has grasped the principle of Christian liberty and freedom from manmade taboos. But

note that he does not relish in his strength of understanding doctrine but rather he uses his strength to assist the weak in doctrine. His desire is that the strong bear with those whose scruples he regards as weaknesses or sicknesses (Gr *asthenēma*). **For even Christ pleased not himself.** As the prime example of one strong in the faith, living in light of those weak in the faith, the apostle proposes the Lord Himself. The Lord Jesus had every right to please Himself for what He would do of necessity would be right. Yet He was willing to set aside His own desires and follow the Father's directives. The quote from Psalm 69:9, **The reproaches of them that reproached thee fell on me,** is applied to the life of the Lord in that He obeyed the will of the Father even when He Himself might have chosen an easier path. He did not exercise His perfect freedom so that the ultimate task of salvation could be accomplished.

4. For whatsoever things were written aforetime were written for our learning. This is akin to the apostle's statement in II Timothy 3:16 about the profitableness of Scripture. An earnest study of the Word of God will not only make the weak strong but will enable us to bear the burdens and weaknesses of others. The instruction which the Scriptures impart is directed to patience and comfort. Patience is steadfastness or endurance and comfort (Gr *paraklēsis*) is more properly understood as encouragement or consolation. These culminate in hope, not some wistful desire that everything will turn out all right, but in the confidence that "all things work together for good" (8:28).

5-7. Now the God of patience and consolation grant you to be likeminded one toward another. The reference to the God of patience and consolation indicates that behind the patience and comfort that the Scriptures bring is a God who energizes them through the Scriptures. Paul appeals to this God to bring the strong and weak together and advises, **Receive ye one another, as Christ also received us to the glory of God.** In the same manner in which we were received of Christ the Lord, we are encouraged to receive each other as believers. Paul's point is that if the Lord can receive us with the great chasm that existed between Him and us, should we not also be able to accept one another even if there are minor difference between us? The result of such acceptance of one another will be the harmonious praise **That ye may with one mind and one mouth glorify God.** Since the Lord Jesus found it possible to embrace us and reconcile sinners to Himself, it should be an easy task to **receive ye another, as Christ also received us to the glory of God.**

8-13. Paul turns his apostolic guns squarely on Jew/Gentile acceptance of each other. As we have Christ our example, the Jew must receive the Gentile and the Gentile the Jew. Jesus Christ came to be a **minister of the circumcision.** This word **minister** is the word *diakonos* in Greek. Paul's assessment of the Lord's ministry squares with the Lord's own assessment. "The Son of man came not to be ministered unto, but to minister (Gr *diakoneō*, Mk 10:45). The truthfulness of God's Word is seen in the fulfillment of His promises to the Patriarchs. **And that the Gentiles might glorify God for his mercy.** The fulfillment of promises to the Jews evokes praise to God from the Gentiles. Paul also appeals to Psalm 18:49 where David included Gentile nations in the heritage of God to Israel, **as it is written, For this cause I will confess to thee among the Gentiles, and sing unto thy name.**

Not content with that, the apostle begins a series of quotations from the Old Testament. From the Song of Moses, **Rejoice, ye Gentiles, with his people** (Deut 32:43). Then, from Psalm 117:1, **Praise the Lord, all ye Gentiles, and laud him all ye people.** Next a quote from Isaiah 11:10, **There shall be a root of Jesse, and he that shall rise to reign over the Gentiles; in him shall the Gentiles trust.** Paul's purpose is to indicate that Gentiles as well as Jews will be included in the family of God. The *goyim* (Hebrew for Gentiles) will put their trust in the Root of Jesse (the Lord Jesus) the same as believing Jews will. Although there are many differences between these two groups of believers, nevertheless their common bond is faith in Christ. As a result, Paul's prayer is, **Now the God of hope fill you with all joy and peace in believing, that ye may abound in hope, through the power of the Holy Ghost.**

VI. CONCLUSION. 15:14-16:27.

The Apostle Paul begins to conclude this letter long before he actually does so. The change from doctrine to practice has made it difficult for him to say goodby to these Roman saints for they were apparently weak in both. He has intense personal feelings for them even though he has never been to Rome. Since he has met many of them in other areas of the Mediterranean world, he must express personal greetings. A lengthy list of final greetings is capped by a final note of praise to the Lord.

A. The Presentation of Personal Feelings. 15:14-33.

1. Explanation for writing. 15:14-16.

14-16. And I myself also am persuaded of you . . . nevertheless, brethren, I have written the more boldly unto you . . . That I should be the minister of Jesus Christ to the Gentiles. Paul did not want the Roman believers to think that he considered them spiritually immature. Thus the admonitions which he gives in this epistle are not to be received by them alone but by every reader of the Epistle to the Romans, in every country, in every age. Paul knew that the Roman believers were full of goodness and kindness and that they were adept enough in doctrine to be able to admonish one another. Nevertheless the apostle has spoken boldly **in some sort** (Gr idiom, "in part," or "on some points," e.g. 6:12; 8:9; 11:17; 12:3; 13:3; 14:3, 10, 15). Clothed in the vocabulary of worship, Paul asserts that the reason for his writing the way he has is the grace of God has made him an officiating-priest (Gr *leitourgos*) to preach the gospel as a priestly service (Gr *hierourgeo*). This is done to present the Gentiles as an acceptable thank-offering (Gr *prosphora*) to the Lord God. They are sanctified, not by circumcision, but by something much better, the Holy Spirit. He wants to include the Gentiles of the church at Rome in that offering.

2. Vindication for writing. 17-21.

17-19. I have therefore whereof I may glory through Jesus Christ . . . so that from Jerusalem and round about unto Illyricum, I have fully preached the gospel of Christ. Though there were many triumphs already in the life of the apostle about which he may boast, Paul is careful to give the praise to the Lord Jesus. His only glory is **through Jesus Christ.** Through the grace of God Paul has preached the gospel of God with mighty signs and wonders in a wide radius from Jerusalem through Macedonia to the area round about Illyricum, the Roman province bordering the eastern shore of the Adriatic Sea. What God has chosen to do through Paul gives him vindication for writing to a church he has never visited.

20-21. Yea, so have I strived to preach the gospel, not where Christ was named, lest I should build upon another man's foundation. Paul made it his ministerial ambition to break up fallow ground with the gospel. He wanted to be missionary as well as theologian, scholar, and soul-winner. His intent was to lay a foundation where other men had not labored and in so doing the Lord drew him to various metropolitan centers such as Ephesus, Philippi, and Corinth. Each time Paul encountered first-time hearers of the message he bore.

3. Paul's plans following the writing. 22-29.

22-24. For which cause also I have been much hindered from coming to you. The pioneering spirit of Paul to spread the gospel where no man had done so has thus far prohibited the apostle from coming to Rome. However, years of desire are about to give way to an actual journey to Spain which will necessitate a stopover in the capital city of the empire. The activity in Spain will likewise be cultivating virgin soil but before he arrives there he wants his visit to Rome to be one of mutual benefit for both the Romans and himself. He has spiritual benefit to impart to them as a teacher of the Word and they have comfort, fellowship, and lodging to give to him. He desires to be filled with their company.

25-29. But now I go unto Jerusalem . . . to make a certain contribution for the poor saints which are at Jerusalem. Paul cannot immediately embark on his way to Rome for he must travel first to Jerusalem. He must deliver to the poor saints there an offering which the apostle had collected from the Christians of Macedonia and Achaia. This was not only an act of Christian love but a way of cementing the relationship between the Jewish and Gentile factions of the early church, since the Christians of Macedonia and Achaia were predominantly Gentile. The contribution (Gr *koinōnia*) or sharing of their wealth was a voluntary gesture on the part of the Gentile churches, yet it also recognized the moral debt they owed to the mother church which had first disseminated the gospel.

When therefore I have performed this . . . I will come by you into Spain . . . in the fullness of the blessing of the gospel of Christ. Paul again returns to the thought of his arrival in Rome en route to Spain. He is convinced that his coming to them will be more than a blessing. It will be "the fullness of the blessing of the gospel of Christ" (cf. Eph 3:8, 19). At the time he was unaware that when he finally arrived in Rome, he would be in chains. Even so it was in the fullness of the blessing of the gospel. This is exhibited in the fact that Colossians, Philemon, Ephesians, and Philippians were all written from Rome during his first imprisonment there.

4. Paul's plea for prayers on his behalf. 30-33.

30-33. Paul appeals for the support of Roman prayers in the face of the imminent dangers he must face before he comes to them. His requests are: **that ye strive together with me in your prayers . . . That I may be delivered . . . that my service which I have for Jerusalem may be accepted . . . That I may come unto you with joy . . . and may . . . be refreshed.** Paul knows that dangers threaten him in Judaea, for there are many that mark him as a traitor to the Jewish cause. Coupled with the hatred of unbelieving Jews is the danger that the church at Jerusalem might misread his intentions in bringing a monetary gift. Perhaps they might not receive it because it was given by the Gentiles. Also, he desires to come to Rome **with joy by the will of God,** that is, only if it be the will of God. He desires to be refreshed both physically and spiritually there. Since these requests are couched in the language of prayer, it is appropriate for him to close with a doxology. The beautiful benediction, addressed to the weak as well as the strong, to the Jew as well as to the Gentile, is, **Now the God of peace be with you all. Amen.**

B. The Presentation of Personal Greeting. 16:1-23.

1. Commendation of Phoebe. 16:1-2.

16:1-2. I commend unto you Phoebe our sister, which is a servant of the church which is at Cenchrea. Phoe-

be, whose name means "radiant," was apparently a businesswoman from the city of Cenchrea, the seaport city of Corinth on the Saronic Gulf (cf. Acts 18:18). She was a servant (Gr *diakonos*) of the church in that location. Paul designates her "our sister," as a term of Christian endearment. Likewise she is said to be a **succourer** (Gr *prostatis*) or befriender of many including Paul. Apparently Phoebe was a widow else she would not have been able to travel so freely in the Roman Empire. This woman was preparing for a business trip to Rome and Paul seizes that opportunity, since as a private citizen he was not permitted to use the official Roman postal system, to send his epistle to Rome. Thus he advises the Romans **That ye receive her in the Lord . . . and that ye assist her in whatsoever business she hath need of you.**

2. Greetings for friends in Rome. 3-16.

3-4. Greet Priscilla and Aquila my helpers in Christ Jesus. This Jewish couple moved, under the dint of persecution and in their quest for souls, from Rome to Corinth, to Ephesus and back to Rome again. They supplied lay leadership in various evangelistic endeavors. **Who have for my life laid down their own necks.** Just when these two risked their lives for Paul is not known, but their friendship with the apostle was so intense that he mentions them in the salutations of two other epistles (cf. I Cor. 16:19; II Tim 4:19).

5. Salute my well-beloved Epaenetus, who is the firstfruits of Achaia unto Christ. The translation here should undoubtedly be "Asia" not "Achaia" and such rendering is supported by manuscripts P[46], A, B, D★, G and others. According to I Corinthians 16:15, "the household of Stephanas" was the firstfruits of Achaia. As a convert, and especially among the first in Asia Minor, Paul had a special love for Epaenetus.

6. Greet Mary, who bestowed much labor on us. The labor which this woman bestowed probably refers to her association with Priscilla and Aquila from the inception of the Roman church. We know nothing of her but that she bore the name Mary, one of the six persons so named in the New Testament.

7. Salute Andronicus and Junia, my kinsmen, and my fellow prisoners. It is impossible to know for sure if the second of the names is the feminine, Junia, or masculine, Junias. When Paul says they are his "kinsmen," he need not be referring to a close family relationship for all Jews were his kinsmen (cf. 9:3). Since the apostle's imprisonments were many (cf. II Cor 6:5; 11:23), it is difficult to say in which of these they shared. They were of note among the apostles (using this term in the general sense of "messenger," cf. II Cor 8:23; Phil 2:25) and came to know the Lord as Saviour even before the Apostle Paul.

8. Greet Amplias my beloved in the Lord. Amplias is an abbreviated form of Ampliatus, a common name in the empire. "A branch of the *gens Aurelia* bore this cognomen. Christian members of this branch of the family are buried in one of the oldest Christian burying-places in Rome, the Cemetery of Domitilla, the beginnings of which go back to the end of the first century. One tomb in that cemetery, decorated with paintings in a very early style, bears the inscription AMPLIAT in uncials of the first or early second century" (F.F. Bruce, *The Epistle of Paul to the Romans*, p. 272).

9. Salute Urbane, our helper in Christ, and Stachys my beloved. Urbane, or Urbanus, by his very name, must have been a native of Rome. He is said to be a helper in Christ but not a fellow worker as Priscilla and Aquila. Stachys, a name meaning "ear" (of grain), is not a common name and occurs with no further amplification other than "my beloved."

10. Salute Apelles approved in Christ. Apelles is distinguished as **approved in Christ** but we are not left with a clue as to why. His is a common name, found in Roman inscriptions, sometimes related to the imperial household. **Salute them which are of Aristobulus' household.** Although it cannot be said with certainty, J. B. Lightfoot suggests that this Aristobulus was the grandson of Herod the Great and the brother of Herod Agrippa I. If so, he lived in Rome as a private citizen and enjoyed a close friendship with the Emperor Claudius. He is not saluted himself, but the slaves of his household are being greeted as Christians.

11. Salute Herodion my kinsman. This name, and the context of the preceding verse, would suggest that this man was one of Herod's household. He was a kinsman of Paul and therefore Jewish. **Greet them that be of the household of Narcissus, which are in the Lord.** It may be possible to identify this man with Tiberius Claudius Narcissus, a wealthy freedman of the Emperor Tiberius. Narcissus was executed by order of Agrippina, Nero's mother, shortly after her son's accession to the throne in A.D. 54. If his possessions were at this time confiscated, his slaves would become imperial property and would be known as the *Narcissiani* or **household of Narcissus.**

12. Salute Tryphena and Tryphosa, who labour in the Lord. Tryphena and Tryphosa were probably sisters and possibly even twins. It was a common practice to name twins of the same root word. The name means "those who live voluptuously." Although these names stem from a pagan, Anatolian root, Paul nevertheless associates them with labor in the Lord. **Salute the beloved Persis, which labored much in the Lord.** Persis (the name means "Persian woman") is said to be **beloved** but with a woman Paul delicately avoids using the phrase "my beloved." Her name appears on Greek and Latin inscriptions as that of a slave or freedwoman.

13. Salute Rufus chosen in the Lord, and his mother and mine. It may be possible to make an identification between this Rufus and the man of the same name who Mark records was the son of Simon of Cyrene (cf. Mk 15:21). Mark says, "And they compel one Simon a Cyrenian, who passed by, coming out of the country, the father of Alexander and Rufus, to bear his cross." That Simon would be identifiable by the name of his son Rufus must mean that the son was a man of some reknown. F. F. Bruce, in addressing how Rufus' mother could act as mother to Paul, hazards the guess that when Barnabas brought Paul from Tarsus to become his missionary colleague, one of the teachers of the church at Antioch permitted Paul to lodge with him, a certain Simon surnamed Niger, "the dark-skinned," cf. Acts 13:1 (whom Bruce identifies with Simon of Cyrene). In the course of Paul's lodging there, Simon's mother cared for or "mothered" the apostle. Although interesting, this must be considered speculation.

14. Salute Asyncritus, Philegon, Hermas, Patrobas, Hermes. Little is known of these believers other than that they were apparently of one community and were all men. Hermas is an abbreviation of some names such as Hermogenes or Hermodorus and very common (cf. *The Shepherd of Hermas* in apocryphal literature). Patrobas was abbreviated from Patrobius. Hermes was the name of the god of good luck and became a common slave name.

15. Salute Philologus, and Julia, Nereus, and his sister, and Olympas. Philologus and Julia were perhaps husband and wife. Both names occur several times in connection with the imperial household of Rome. Nereus, according to a tradition which goes back to the fourth century, is associated with Flavia Domitilla, a Christian woman who was banished to the Island of Pandateria by her uncle Emperor Domitian in A.D. 95. She was released after his death the following year. Olympas is an abbreviated form of Olympiodorus. These all appear to have been a community of faith.

16. Salute one another with an holy kiss. The "holy" kiss was a common feature of Christian greeting (cf. I Cor 16:20; II Cor 13:12; I Thess 5:26; I Pet 5:14). Justin Martyr mentions that it was a common feature in early Christian worship (*First Apology*, 66). It was "holy" as opposed to that in the question, "betrayest thou the Son of man with a kiss?" (Lk 22:48). Although a feature in the liturgy of the Eastern Church to this day, the holy kiss is noticeably absent in the Western Church.

3. Warnings to friends in Rome. 17-20.

17. Now I beseech you, brethren, mark them which cause divisions . . . and avoid them. Paul's admonition and warning to his friends at Rome concerns those who would cause divisions among the brethren. He commands two things; mark (Gr *skopeō*) them as to who they are, and then avoid them (Gr *ekklinō*). Those who cause divisions may have been Antinomians who pushed their liberty in Christ to the "nth" degree. They may have been the ubiquitous Judaizers who seemed to incessantly plague Paul. But Paul characterizes them as those **which cause divisions and offenses contrary to the doctrine which ye have learned.** This may mean any group which denied the teachings of the apostle.

18. They . . . serve not our Lord Jesus Christ, but their own belly. In further description of these divisive teachers, Paul describes them, not as servants of the Lord, but in service to their own carnal desires and self-interests. This is characterized by the symbol of their belly. In Philippians 3:19 the apostle warns the Philippian

Christians against people "whose God is their belly." **And by good words and fair speeches deceive the hearts of the simple.** These smooth-talking teachers have ensnared innocent (**simple**) believers in their doctrinal trap.

19. I would have you wise unto that which is good, and simple concerning evil. In Matthew 10:16 we are counselled to "be ye therefore wise as serpents, and harmless as doves." The Greek adjectives, *sophos* and *akeraios*, are used both in Matthew and here. Paul cautions the Roman Christians to be alert and discerning in relation to false doctrine (cf. I Cor 14:20).

20. And the God of peace shall bruise Satan under your feet shortly. In echoing Genesis 3:15, Paul reminds the believers at Rome that God has promised ultimate victory to His church and shortly, despite Satan's crafty attacks, the enemy will be defeated as promised. God will crush Satan, under the feet of the faithful, and that right speedily.

4. Greetings from friends with Paul. 21-23.

21. Timothy my workfellow, and Lucius, and Jason, and Sosipater, my kinsmen, salute you. Timothy, Paul's convert from Lystra and subsequent colleague, was of particular affection to Paul. Of him Paul said to the church at Philippi, "For I have no man likeminded, who will naturally care for your state . . . But ye know the proof of him, that, as a son with the father, he hath served with me in the gospel." (Phil 2:20, 22). Lucius, Jason, and Sosipater are mentioned as Paul's kinsmen and therefore as Jewish Christians. Jason may have been Paul's host on his first visit to Thessalonica (Acts 17:6, 7, 9). Sosipater is probably Sopater of Beroea, the son of Pyrrhus, according to Acts 20:4.

22. I Tertius, who wrote this epistle, salute you in the Lord. Tertius, probably a native Italian, was the stenographer or amanuensis of the apostle.

Paul's practice of using an amanuensis is attested in other epistles (I Cor 16:21; Gal 6:11; Col. 4:18; II Thess 3:17). Apparently Tertius interjects his own greeting into Paul's narration because he too knows and loves the believers at Rome.

23. Gaius mine host . . . Erastus the chamberlain of the city saluteth you, and Quartus a brother. Gaius is to be identified with the man whom Paul baptized at Corinth (I Cor 1:14) and may be identified as well with Titus Justus of Acts 18:7 who extended the hospitality of his house to Paul when the fledgling church of Corinth was expelled from the synagogue next door. The Roman system of naming a citizen was by the use of three names (*praenomen, nomen,* and *cognomen*) and Gaius was a common *praenomen*. His full name would then have been Gaius Titus Justus. Erastus the chamberlain of the city was in fact the city treasurer of Corinth. Quartus, of whom we know nothing, is simply mentioned as "a brother."

C. The Concluding Doxology. 16:24-27.

1. The worthy recipient of praise. 16:24.

24. The grace of our Lord Jesus Christ be with you all. Amen. Some older manuscripts do not include this phrase in the doxology. Its truth is evident from similar language in II Thessalonians 3:18.

2. The ascription of praise. 16:25-26.

25-26. To him that is of power to stablish you according to my gospel. Paul's readers are commended to the only God who has the power to establish them and keep them from falling. When Paul says **my gospel** (cf. 2:16) he is referring to the gospel of Christ which he preaches. Equivalent to that is **the preaching of Jesus Christ** for that was the apostle's calling. **According to the revelation of the mystery.** The preaching of Christ was not a new innovation in the plan of God, but the fulfillment of the Old Testament prophecies. This, Paul explains, is a mystery for the Old Testament prophets did not fully appreciate the new life which we have in Christ.

26. But now is made manifest. That which was not clearly known in the Old Testament is now clearly known **by the scriptures of the prophets,** i.e., the fulfillment of the Old Testament prophecies concerning the Messiahship of Christ (cf. Isa 9:6; 53:1-2; Jer 23; Mic 5; Zech 9; etc.). The purpose of manifesting God's plan in Christ Jesus is that He may be **made known to all nations for the obedience of faith.** The preaching of the gospel is not just for intellectual acceptance but that nations may come to place their faith in the Christ of the gospel.

3. The benediction. 16:27.

27. To God only wise, be glory through Jesus Christ for ever. Amen. This great hymn of praise ends with the glory for man's salvation being directed toward God, exactly where it belongs. But inherent to Paul's theme throughout the epistle is that it is **through Jesus Christ** that praise and glory are channelled toward God. Thus, **To God only wise, be glory through Jesus Christ for ever. A-men.**

BIBLIOGRAPHY

Barnhouse, Donald Grey. *Exposition of Bible Doctrine Taking the Epistle to the Romans as the Point of Departure.* 10 Vols. Grand Rapids: Eerdmans, 1952-63.

Barth, Karl. *The Epistle to the Romans.* Trans. by E. C. Hoskyns. London: Oxford University Press, 1933.

* Bruce, F. F. The Epistle of Paul to the Romans. In the *Tyndale New Testament Commentaries.* Grand Rapids: Eerdmans, 1963.

Calvin, John. *Commentaries on the Epistle of Paul the Apostle to the Romans.* (Published 1539). Trans. and ed. by John Owen. Grand Rapids: Eerdmans, 1947.

Denny, James. St. Paul's Epistle to the Romans. In the *Expositor's Greek New Testament.* Grand Rapids: Eerdmans, reprint, n.d.

Erdman, Charles. *The Epistle to the Romans.* Philadelphia: Westminster Press 1925.

Godet, Frederic. *Commentary on St. Paul's Epistle to the Romans.* Grand Rapids: Zondervan, n.d.

* Haldane, Robert. *Exposition of the Epistle of the Romans.* London: Banner of Truth Trust, reprint.

* Hodge, Charles. *Commentary on the Epistle to the Romans.* Grand Rapids: Eerdmans, reprint, 1950.

Ironside, Harry. *Lectures on the Epistle to the Romans.* New York: Loizeaux Brothers, 1951.

* Lloyd-Jones, D. Martyn. *Romans.* 6 Vols. Grand Rapids: Zondervan, 1970-.

Luther, Martin. *Lectures on Romans.* Trans. by Wilhelm Pauck. Philadelphia: Westminster, 1961.

McGee, J. Vernon. *Reasoning Through Romans.* 2 Vols. Los Angeles: Church of the Open Door, n.d.

Moule, H. G. G. Romans. In *The Expositor's Bible*. Grand Rapids: Zondervan, n.d.

* Murray, John. The Epistle to the Romans. 2 Vols. In the *New International Commentary on the New Testament*. Grand Rapids: Eerdmans, 1959-65.

Newell, William R. *Rfomans Verse by Verse*. Chicago: Moody Press, 1938.

Shedd, W. G. T. *A Critical and Doctrinal Commentary on the Epistle of St. Paul to the Romans*. Grand Rapids: Zondervan, 1967.

Steele, David N. and Curtis C. Thomas. *Romans: An Interpretive Outline*. Philadelphia: Presbyterian and Reformed, 1963.

Stifler, James M. *The Epistle to the Romans*. Chicago: Moody Press, 1960.

Thomas, W. H. Griffith. *St. Paul's Epistle to the Romans*. Grand Rapids: Eerdmans, 1946.

Vine, W. E. *The Epistle to the Romans: Doctrine, Precept, Practice*. London: Oliphants Ltd., 1948.

Wuest, Kenneth. Romans, In *The Greek New Testament*. Grand Rapids: Eerdmans, 1956.

The First Epistle To The

CORINTHIANS

INTRODUCTION

Falling second in the corpus of Pauline literature, I Corinthians both complements and contrasts the great doctrinal epistle which precedes it. Where Romans emphasizes matters of biblical theology, I Corinthians is concerned with practical theology and its application to a particular local assembly.

Yet, this is not to say that Romans is not a practical epistle (as chapters 12-15 demonstrate). Nor is this to suggest that Paul does not give attention to doctrine in I Corinthians (note especially chapters 7-15). But, the predominant thrust here is that of a pastor concerned with the spiritual welfare of a wayward assembly. And that concern does not appear to be misplaced, as a closer look at the city of Corinth will show.

The city of Corinth. Corinth was a wealthy commercial center located on a narrow neck of land (four miles wide) that connected the Peloponnesus and Northern Greece. Situated as it was, it became a crossroads for travel and commerce both north and south, east and west. It had two harbors, one (Lechaeum) facing toward Italy, and the other (Cenchrea) facing toward Asia. The wealth of Corinth was acquired by hauling freight and smaller vessels across the isthmus, and by politicians who would levy tolls on the commerce.

The history of the city may be divided into two periods—the old and the new. The old city (which gave to the world the classic Corinthian pillar) was founded ca. 1500 B.C., and was destroyed in 146 B.C. by the Roman general, Lucius Mummius. A century later, the new city was built on the same location. The old city of Corinth rose to wealth and fame during the period of the Greek city-states. It was known for its cosmopolitan culture and luxurious temples. On the gray, rocky hill to the south of the city (called Acrocorinth), the shining sanctuary to Aphrodite was located. Visible far out to sea, this temple was serviced by a thousand slave girls who doubled both as temple prostitutes and as entertainers for the city's night life (E. F. Harrison, *Introduction to the New Testament,* p. 267). The destruction of the old city (together with the sacking of Carthage) largely became the means by which Rome rose to wealth and power.

The new city was built by Julius Caesar in 46 B.C. and elevated to the status of a Roman colony with the title *Colonia Laus Julia Corinthiensis.* When Paul came to Corinth in A.D. 51, it was again a thriving metropolis, the capital of Achaia, and ruled by a Roman proconsul. Its population, vastly different from the old city (a mixture of Roman, Greek, and Oriental), was nearly half slaves. This rich cosmopolitan city boasted that it was heir to the glories of ancient Greece.

The city knew every type of religion its pluralistic society could bring to it. There was also a synagogue and a sizable contingency of Jews.

Corinth was known for the Isthmian Games held in the stadium on alternate years. These were second in popularity only to the Olympics. An outdoor theater, accommodating twenty thousand people, was the arena for the gladiatorial games and contests with wild beasts. There was also a smaller indoor theater (capacity of three thousand) for those interested in plays and music.

From such a cultural hub, a strong gospel witness might well be heard all over the world. It was no wonder that Paul felt constrained to bear a testimony to such a city.

But the moral depravity most vividly reflects the spiritual need of Corinth. The vile character of the old city carried over into the city of New Testament times. The Greek work *Korinthiazomai* (literally "to act the Corinthian"), came to mean, "to commit fornication." Corinth was a seaman's paradise and a moral cesspool. Divorce was rampant. Prostitution plagued the streets, and the moral air was polluted with the luring aroma of sin. It was famous for all that is debauched. It was, no doubt, the inspiration for the catalogue of man's sins in Romans 1:18-32 (written by Paul while a guest of Gaius in this wicked city)!

Inebriated by the swaggering pride of supposed Greek wisdom, they had even reduced their religion to a quagmire of gross sensualism. And it was from this filthy slough of sin that Paul's converts were extracted (cf. 6:9-11).

The founding of the church. Luke records the origin of the Corinthian church in Acts 18:1-17. Paul came to Corinth in A.D. 51 after a very unfruitful evangelistic effort at Athens (Acts 17:16-34). His experience at Athens, no doubt, influenced Paul's methodology when he moved on to Corinth. When he came to Corinth, Paul determined (the Greek suggests the idea of "predetermined") to preach nothing but "Jesus Christ, and him crucified" (I Cor 2:2). It was not with human wisdom but the gospel with which God built a thriving assembly in this heathen city.

Upon arrival in the city Paul accepted the hospitality of Aquila and his wife Priscilla, exiled Jews from Rome. During the week, he worked with them making tents (Acts 18:1-4). On the Sabbath he would go to the synagogue where he reasoned with the Jews concerning Christ.

After the arrival of Silas and Timothy, Paul no longer required secular employment, and thus devoted himself entirely to an aggressive evangelistic effort. One of his earliest converts was Crispus, the leader of the synagogue. Subsequently, the man's entire household believed, along with many Corinthians (Acts 18:8). Incurring opposition from the Jews, he was forced to find another meeting place. Providentially, he was led to the home of Titus Justus (probably the "Gaius" of I Corinthians 1:14) next door to the synagogue!

Later, the Jews had Paul arraigned before Gallio where the proconsul dismissed their charges and demonstrated his contempt for the Jews by looking the other way as their new leader, Sosthenes, was flogged in the street.

Paul ministered in Corinth eighteen months (Acts 18:11) during which time he also wrote I and II Thessalonians. It is noteworthy that another church was started in the eastern port of Corinth in Cenchrea (cf. Rom 16:1). Whether Paul initiated this during his first visit or at a later time is not known for certain. The leadership of the assembly was assumed by Apollos, an eloquent preacher from Alexandria, at the conclusion of Paul's first visit (Acts 18:24-19:1). Paul then moved on to Ephesus where he enjoyed the longest ministry that he was ever to have in any one place.

Paul's relations with the church. In order to understand the occasion for the writing of I Corinthians, it is necessary to outline Paul's involvements with the church subsequent to going to Ephesus. While it is true that much of this is open to debate, the best that can be done here is to outline the most conspicuous details.

1. Those of Chloe's household reported a lack of harmony (I Cor 1:11).

2. Although Paul promised a second

visit (I Cor 4:19), he did not have occasion to see them again before writing I Corinthians.

3. After his initial visit described above, Paul wrote the church a letter, known as the "previous letter" in which he warned the Corinthians not to associate with immoral persons (I Cor 5:9). This letter was misconstrued by the people and required further explanation in I Corinthians 5:10-11. It is doubtful that this "previous letter" is incorporated in any way into the text of the canonical book of I Corinthians, as suggested by some (Moffatt, *Introduction to the Literature of the New Testament,* p. 109).

4. A letter was sent to Paul containing several questions (note the recurring phrase "now concerning" or the similar "as concerning" or "as touching." I Cor 7:1, 25; 8:1; 12:1; 16:1, 12). This letter may well have been delivered to Paul by the three men mentioned in I Corinthians 16:17.

5. After writing I Corinthians, Paul sent Timothy to check into conditions in the church with the promise that he would come in person to deal with their carnality (I Cor 4:17-19; 16:10, 11; Acts 19:22). It is not known whether Timothy ever made it. He may have also requested Apollos to take time out to help with the situation (I Cor 1:12).

6. With the problems apparently unresolved, Paul was forced to pay a brief but "painful" visit (II Cor 2:1-4; 12:14; 13:1-2).

7. Upon his return, Paul sent a third letter to Corinth which was of such a severe nature that he later regretted having sent it (II Cor 2:4). This letter was carried by Titus, who was to meet Paul at Troas to give him a status report. This letter (along with the "previous letter") has been lost, and may well have been destroyed after Paul's final visit with them.

8. When Paul failed to meet Titus at Troas, his anxiety was so great that he was unable to even preach, though he had the opportunity (II Cor 2:12-13).

He hurried on to Macedonia where he met Titus en route. Titus' report was very encouraging. Paul immediately sat down and penned II Corinthians to express his great relief at improved conditions (II Cor 2:13-14; 7:5-16), and to deal with some of the remaining problems in anticipation of another visit.

9. He followed this letter with his last recorded visit when he spent the winter in Corinth on his way to Jerusalem with the collection for the poor (Acts 20:1-4).

Purpose. From the foregoing data, it is discerned that Paul's letter was occasioned by at least two factors. First, he had received word from two sources of divisions in the church (I Cor 1:11; 16:17). This sectarianism probably rose more out of the sophist spirit in Corinth than from Judaistic tendencies (as at Galatia). The tendency to faction had long characterized the Greek race (D. Stanley, *Epistles of St. Paul to the Corinthians,* p. 8). They split on politics, sports, and philosophy. Thus it is not surprising to see them carry this habit over into the church. Paul was to show them that this was totally incompatible with the gospel of Christ (I Cor 1:18-25).

Secondly, Paul had received a letter from the assembly requesting answers to a series of questions. Paul felt obliged to respond.

In addition to these factors, there were apparently other reports not recorded (such as that mentioned in 5:1) that concerned the apostle. Thus, with pen in hand, Paul purposes to: (1) rebuke the party spirit in the assembly; (2) encourage them to moral purity; (3) instruct them regarding specific doctrinal problems; (4) urge their participation in the collection for Jerusalem; and (5) inform them of his immediate plans.

Authorship. The authorship of I Corinthians is so well attested that only a brief sketch is necessary here. External evidence derives from references to the epistle from the first century onward. Clement of Rome, the *Epistle of Barnabas* (3:1, 16), the *Didache* (ch. 10), Polycarp, Hermas, Justin Martyr, Athanagoras, Irenaeus, Clement of Alexandria, Tertullian, the Muratorian Canon, Marcion, the Old Syriac and Old Latin texts all attest to the authority and Pauline authorship of I Corinthians.

Internal evidence is equally strong. The writer calls himself Paul (1:1; 3:4, 6, 22; 16:21). The epistle harmonizes well with Acts and other Pauline letters. Frequent mention is made of contemporaries of the mid-first century (thus eliminating a second-century forgery). This, without doubt, is a genuine product of the apostle.

Date and place of writing. Paul himself tells us that I Corinthians was written from Ephesus (I Cor 16:8-9, 19). The subscription in the TR and the AV is probably due to a misunderstanding of I Corinthians 16:5. If it were written toward the end of Paul's stay at Ephesus, the time would be spring of A.D. 55. This is suggested since he says he planned to stay in Ephesus till Pentecost (I Cor 16:8) and he was in Jerusalem on or about Pentecost in A.D. 56 (Acts 20:16). In the interim, he visited Corinth briefly (II Cor 2:1-4), spent some time in Macedonia (Acts 20:1-6), wrote II Corinthians (fall, A.D. 55), came to Corinth a few weeks later and stayed about three months. He spent the Passover season of A.D. 56 in Philippi on his way to Jerusalem (Acts 20:6).

Argument. Particular problems as they are brought under the gaze of the apostle actually form the outline of the book. However, his discussion falls basically into two categories; unsolicited advice (chs. 1-6, 15), and solicited advice (chs. 7-14). They have requested his counsel on some problems they knew about. Paul responds to these, but not until he directs their attention to a few problems they didn't know about. Hence, he opens the epistle with a rebuke: (1) The disorders in the assembly (namely, misconceptions regarding the nature of the body of Christ, the message of the gospel, and the nature of the ministry (chs. 1-4). (2) Then he deals with the matter of discipline as it was necessary in the cases of lust, lawsuits, and license (chs. 5-6). Having taken care of these matters, Paul (3) answers the specific questions addressed to him on matters of doctrine and church polity. Here he focuses his attention on Christian marriage, Christian liberty, worship, and spiritual gifts (chs. 7-14). (4) His chapter on the resurrection is directed to an additional problem of certain Greeks in the assembly who had problems with the concept of the bodily resurrection (ch. 15). This is the only doctrinal "error," as such, that Paul has to deal with in the epistle, and it does not appear to have been one of the questions asked of him.

OUTLINE

      2. Concerning the permanence of marriage. 7:8-16.
        a. For the unmarried and widows. 7:8-9.
        b. For the married believers. 7:10-11.
        c. For the mixed marriages. 7:12-16.
      3. Concerning the place of marriage. 7:17-24.
        a. The selection of God. 7:17-20.
        b. The service for God. 7:21-24.
      4. Concerning the priorities of marriage. 7:25-40.
        a. The personal judgment of Paul. 7:25-26.
        b. The prospect of tribulation. 7:27-28.
        c. The passing away of worldly fashions. 7:29-31.
        d. The problem of divided allegiance. 7:32-35.
        e. The pattern for advising virgin daughters. 7:36-38.
        f. The preference of Paul. 7:39-40.
  B. Doctrine of Christian Liberty. 8:1-11:1
      1. The principle of liberty. 8:1-13.
      2. The picture of liberty. 9:1-27.
      3. The practice of liberty. 10:1-11:1.
  C. Doctrine of Worship. 11:2-34.
      1. The order of authority. 11:2-16.
      2. The ordinance of communion. 11:17-34.
  D. Doctrine of Spiritual Gifts. 12:1-14:40.
      1. The Partitioning of gifts. 12:1-11.
        a. The assignment of the gifts. 12:1-6.
        b. The allotment of the gifts. 12:7-10.
        c. The administration of the gifts. 12:11.
      2. The proportion in the body. 12:12-31.
        a. The indivisibility of the members in the body. 12:12-19.
        b. The interdependence of the members in the body. 12:20-26.
        c. The induction of the members into the body. 12:27-31.
      3. The primacy of love. 13:1-13.
        a. Contrast of love. 13:1-3.
        b. Character of love. 13:4-7.
        c. Constancy of love. 13:8-13.
      4. The prominence of prophecy. 14:1-40.
        a. In the edification of the assembly. 14:1-17.
        b. In the example of Paul. 14:18-19.
        c. In the essential purpose. 14:20-25.
        d. In the exercise in the assembly. 14:26-40.
  E. Doctrine of the Resurrection. 15:1-58.
      1. A defense of the doctrine of the resurrection (based on known truth). 15:1-34.
        a. Resurrection is vital to the historical preaching of the gospel. 15:1-19.
        b. Resurrection is vital to the prophetic preaching of the gospel. 15:20-28.
        c. Resurrection is vital in suffering persecution for the gospel. 15:29-34.

COMMENTARY

I. Introduction. 1:1-9.

Paul's introduction to I Corinthians consists of (a) the salutation, where he introduces himself and the recipients of his letter; and (b) the setting of the epistle, where he introduces the direction he intends to take in his writing.

A. The Saluation of the Apostle. 1:1-3.

1. Addresser: Paul and Sosthenes. 1:1.

1. Paul. Tne addresser of this letter is Paul, the great apostle, the one whom God used to establish this young assembly. **Called to be an apostle.** There is particular stress on Paul's authority as an apostle through divine call. This, together with the expression **through the will of God,** answers at the outset those who had questioned Paul's right to speak (cf. 9:1-2; II Cor 10:10). **Sosthenes our brother.** Rather than exalt himself unduly, Paul joins with him in writing the well-known brother Sosthenes. This man was not a fellow apostle, but certainly a fellow minister of the gospel. He was probably the ruler of the Jewish synagogue mentioned in Acts 18:17, although this cannot be established beyond question. However, if this is the case, it is noteworthy that the Jewish synagogue in Corinth had no little trouble retaining their leaders! Acts 18 also mentions Crispus, the synagogue ruler when Paul first arrived, as one of the first converts (Acts 18:8). Sosthenes is the man who had been elected to take his place, and subsequently, in a display of anti-Semitism in Corinth, had been beaten. Now he appears as a fellow Christian and minister of the gospel. In light of the opposition facing Paul at the Corinthian church, it is no doubt possible that he uses Sosthenes, probably a native Corinthian, to help ingratiate himself with his readers.

2. Addressees: Church in Corinth. 1:2.

2. Unto the church of God which is at Corinth. Humanly speaking, Paul could have taken some credit here. But, for purposes of the epistle, he identifies the church as "of God." And to add additional force to this, he adds the phrase **to them that are sanctified** (literally, "having been sanctified") **in Christ Jesus.** Here Paul has special reference to the Corinthians' correct standing before God. That is, they were set apart for God's special use. His aim in the epistle is to bring the Corinthians' "state" into closer alignment with their positional "standing." **Called to be saints, with all that in every place call upon the name of Jesus Christ our Lord, both theirs and ours.** Since the Corinthians are claiming the family name, Paul expects that they will live in conformity to the family way. The emphasis, of course, is upon the unity of all who call upon the name of the Lord.

3. Address. 1:3.

3. Grace . . . and peace. In the former, Paul contemplates all that is understood in God's love as it is exercised toward sinners. The latter has in mind those benefits which fall from the exercise of God's love. Note that this grace and peace come from God, who is identified as **our Father and . . . the Lord Jesus Christ.** Here the Father and the Son are shown to be of equal status, yet clearly distinguished (cf. Phil 2:6).

B. The Setting of the Epistle. 1:4-9.

This takes the form of genuine thanksgiving to God for specific benefits enjoyed by the Corinthian assembly.

1. The regularity of Paul's thanks— always. 1:4.

4. I thank my God. The direction of Paul's thanks is to God. The very fact that a church should have been brought into existence at all in so wicked a place as Corinth was evidence of God's grace and power. The regularity of Paul's prayer is expressed in the term **always.** The concern of Paul's prayer was **on your behalf.** This is a good illustration of what the theologians like to call the "communion of the saints;" that is, to give thanks to God for the mutual benefits that he extends to all believers. In this case, it is for **the grace of God which is given you.** Here Paul hints on that important subject which he mentions in the next verse and will enlarge upon later in chapters 12-14.

2. The cause of Paul's thanks— enrichment. 1:5-8.

5. That in every thing ye are enriched by him, in all utterance, and in all knowledge. The cause of Paul's thanks was that the Corinthians had been enriched, and that this enrichment was "in all utterance and knowledge." The extent of this enrichment is expressed in verse 7 that they **come**

behind in no gift. While the term "gift" (Gr *charisma*) has a wide variety of meanings, here it probably has reference to spiritual gifts later developed in the epistle.

6. Testimony of Christ was confirmed in you. Here is the most significant result of their enrichment. This is that message of the gospel concerning Jesus Christ that Paul faithfully preached at Corinth (cf. I Cor 2:2).

7-8. Waiting for the coming of our Lord Jesus Christ. Since the gospel had been faithfully preached and responded to by the Corinthian believers, they are now privileged to wait upon the Second Coming of Jesus Christ, who in turn **shall also confirm you.** Historically, the gospel had been confirmed in them. Now they anticipate the prospect of that blessed event when Jesus Christ shall also confirm them blameless before the throne of God.

4. The ground of Paul's thanks— God. 1:9.

9. God is faithful. Just as Paul directed his thanksgiving toward God, so the ground of his thanksgiving is that same God. For it is God who "is faithful." And it is also that same God by whom **ye were called unto the fellowship of his Son.** The term "fellowship" (Gr *koinonia*) includes both union and communion. The Corinthian believers had been brought into union with the Lord Jesus Christ. Accordingly, this great truth implies that they had been brought into communion with one another. It will be upon this basis that Paul attacks their sectarianism.

II. DISORDER IN THE FELLOWSHIP. 1:10-4:21.

A. Denunciation of Division. 1:10-31.

The first major concern of the Apostle Paul has to do with the divisive spirit in Corinth. He approaches the problem by first denouncing their factional spirit (1:10-31), then by demonstrating the quality of divine wisdom as contrasted with human wisdom (ch. 2). In chapter 3, he develops those qualities that make for mature Christian service. And finally, in chapter 4, he defends his own ministry, and that of Apollos and the apostles, contrasting personal discomfort whilch he himself endured, with the arrogance of the Corinthians who are now criticizing him.

1. Paul's exhortation. 1:10-17.

10. Now is adversative. With this, Paul introduces his appeal for unity. **I beseech you, brethren, by the name of our Lord Jesus Christ.** Paul does two things here. First of all, notice the significant way in which he addresses them as brethren. He is about to exhort them to unity, which is characteristic of brethren in Christ. Paul establishes his authority when he says, **I beseech you . . . by the name of our Lord** (cf. Rom 12:1; II Thess 3:12). Their reverence and love for Christ should induce them to yield obedience to the apostle. Since Paul's own integrity has been called into question, he appeals to the authority of Christ. **That ye speak the same thing, and that there be no divisions among you.** Quarrels had split the congregation into factions. The appeal is to unity in speech, and fellowship. **But that ye be perfectly joined together** (this is translated "mending" in Mark 1:19). The force of this term (Gr *katartizō*) is that they be adjusted to one another in **mind and . . . judgment** (literally "thought" or "opinion").

11. Word had come to the apostle concerning the condition of the assembly at Corinth by **them . . . of Chloe** (probably slaves of Chloe's household who were in Ephesus on business). The report was that there were **contentions among you.**

12. There appear to have been four rival parties. Those who professed to follow **Paul;** perhaps as the most sublime teacher. Then there were those who professed to follow **Apollos,** the gifted orator from Alexandria. Others claimed to follow Peter, or **Cephas** as it is given in the text. These may have been Judaists or, more likely, they were those who preferred Peter as representing more authority, as he was with Christ in His earthly ministry. Then there were those who renounced all the others, and claimed only **Christ.** What special advantage this last party claimed is not certain. But they were as much sectarian as the others since they degraded the Lord to the level of a party leader (also notice II Cor 5:15; 10:7; and 11:23).

13. Is Christ divided? The implied answer is "no." There is but one Christ. **Was Paul crucified for you?** Paul asks, "was I ever your saviour, or did I ever pretend to be?" **Were ye baptized in the name of Paul?** "You never swore loyalty to me."

14-16. In view of the divisions in the assembly, Paul is thankful that very few in Corinth were even baptized by him. No one could ever accuse him of trying to gather a following in this way. The implication of this is rather significant. Baptism is not necessary to salvation, else the apostle would have been giving thanks to God that he saved so few.

17. The point is that baptism was not part of the apostle's commission, rather, he asserts **Christ sent me . . . to preach the gospel.** Paul concludes his exhortation regarding the divisions in the assembly with a call to evangelize. **Not with wisdom of words.** This looks ahead to the next segment of the apostle's argument when he deals with the problems of human wisdom as opposed to divine. **Lest the cross of Christ should be made of none effect** (Gr *kenoō* means "to empty or deprive of substance"). The success of the gospel lies in the plain doctrine of a crucified Lord. Paul was not about to ascribe its power to the flourish of oratory, or the intricacies of Greek philosophy. In spite of his learning at the feet of Gamaliel, the Apostle Paul lays his learning aside when he preaches the simple gospel of Christ. This truth needs no artificial dress. It alone carries with it the "power of God unto salvation" (Rom 1:16). Having exhorted the people to unity, the apostle now goes on to correct a misconception that they have regarding the nature of the gospel.

2. Paul's proclamation. 1:18-25.

18. Paul directs his attention first to the word of the cross (vss.18-20). **For** introduces the reason he did not come in wisdom of words. **The preaching** (Gr *logos*) **of the cross.** The content of Paul's message was the cross, not wisdom. **To them that perish foolishness.** In its effect on man, Paul singles out two groups. Those that perish deem the word of the cross foolishness. For men of wit and learning, and of the cultivated arts and sciences, the word of the cross was met with scorn and contempt. As those who cried out on Golgotha's hill, "he saved others, himself he cannot save." Another group Paul identifies with the words **unto us which are saved.** The language here is strongly reminiscent of our Lord's instructions regarding the broad way that leads to destruction, and the many that enter by it, and the narrow way that leads to life, while there are few who find it (Mt 7:13-14). To the saved, the pure, simple message of the cross is the power of God.

19-20. Paul further buttresses his argument by the appeal from inspired Scripture (Isa 29:14; 19:12; 33:18). The "wise" of Corinth are no more effectual to the saving of souls than the "wise" of Judah in staving the threat against Sennacherib. The great stress in these verses is upon the activity of God. God will **destroy** human wisdom, and make the wisdom of the world **foolish.** But where is the wisdom of God, and how is it demonstrated? Paul's answer to this question is given in verses 21-25. It is the wisdom of the cross.

21. The world by wisdom knew not God. By leaving man to his own wisdom, God demonstrates his folly. For he is not only incapable of knowing God, but in fact, has degraded Him to the level of the creature (cf. Rom 1). Why are these Corinthian believers taken up with sophistry when history affirms that through wisdom, the knowledge of God is impossible. By way of contrast, Paul says that the knowledge of God is possible to **them that believe.** Here is the wisdom of God. Salvation comes through the foolishness of **preaching** (Gr *kēryoma*). The emphasis of the apostle here is not upon the act of preaching, but upon the content of preaching (viz. the message of the cross, cf. vs. 18 above).

22-25. Verse 22 deals with the matter of man's curiosity. **Jews require a sign, and the Greeks seek after wisdom.** For the Jew, it was necessary that the message be accredited by physical wonders. For the Greeks, they required intellectual splendor. Both found it equally difficult to accept a dead man on a cross as an eternal Saviour. **But unto . . .** (the) **called . . . Christ** (is) **the power . . . and the wisdom of God.** The superiority of the cross is seen in that it is both a sign and wisdom. But only to the "called" (these are to be identified with those above who "believed," verse 21).

3. Paul's evaluation. 1:26-31.

The factional spirit at Corinth was wrong because it represented an attitude that was incompatible with the gospel of Christ. It was also wrong because it represented a misunderstanding of the nature of the gospel. Paul goes on, now, to show it is wrong because their own experience belies such a haughty spirit.

26. For introduces the negative side of Paul's argument. **Ye see . . . not many wise . . . mighty . . . noble.** Look around you, the apostle says, and tell me the kind of men God is calling. Are they the wise, mighty, or noble? Obviously not. The nature of Paul's argument here tells us that most of the Corinthian congregation was poor and of the lower element of society. They certainly had very little to offer in themselves.

27-29. God hath chosen . . . the foolish, . . . the weak, . . . and things which are not. The selection of God is designed to bring to silence the wisdom of man. He selects the foolish to shame the wise; the weak to shame the strong; and the "nobodys" to shame the "somebodys."

30. But introduces the positive side of Paul's argument. Paul concludes that all the riches of salvation are lodged in Jesus Christ. All that the Corinthian believers are, they owe to Him. Thus, it is not in oneself, or in party alignment, or in supposed human ability, that any believer ought to glory, but **of him are ye in Christ Jesus.** To answer the implied question, "what am I in Christ?", Paul tabulates those qualities which belong to the believer. **Wisdom.** This is positional. It does not contemplate the acquisition of cognitive skills, but the wisdom of God as demonstrated in the Cross. **Righteousness** is a legal concept, and has in mind that righteousness that is registered to the believer's account the moment he believes (Rom 5). **Sanctification** has in mind that which Paul has already introduced in 1:2 in the words: "sanctified in Christ Jesus." This contemplates the work of Christ "in" the believer. It has in mind both a positional and a progressive truth. In justification, there is the idea of righteousness applied to one's account. In sanctification, the idea is that of righteousness activated in the believer's life, equipping him for service to the Lord. **Redemption.** If the order of these terms is logical, this would have in mind more the eschatological prospect of the resurrected body. However, the apostle is more emotional than logical in this passage, and it is more likely that he has injected this as a factor which underlines all the above. As the twenty-four elders put it, "Thou art worthy . . . for thou wast slain, and hast redeemed us to God by thy blood out of every kindred, and tongue, and people, and nation" (Rev 5:9). It was the atonement which opened the way for God to extend His grace to sinful man, and pour out upon him such benefits as wisdom, righteousness, sanctification, etc.

31. That indicates purpose. If there is to be boasting, it is to be properly directed. That is, to **the Lord.** If the gospel were shackled with human contingencies, this would not be possible. But because salvation is of Jehovah, to Him alone must be the praise.

B. Demonstration of Divine Wisdom. 2:1-16.

Having denounced the divisive spirit which characterized the Corinthian assembly, the Apostle Paul in chapter 1 has shown that the real genius of the Christian assembly is unity, not controversy. Chapter 2 is related to the preceding in that while the former deals with a worldly attitude, the latter deals with a worldly mentality. Paul's message was in demonstration of divine wisdom. He is about to show the Corinthians that divine wisdom is unlike any they had ever seen before. Paul characterizes it as: (1) wisdom of divine power (2:1-5); (2) wisdom of divine origin (2:6-9); and (3) wisdom of divine perception (2:10-16).

1. Wisdom of divine power. 2:1-5.

2:1-2. In pursuing his argument, Paul reflects upon his initial ministry with the Corinthians. His message was not characterized by eloquence (although he certainly was capable of it). Rather, it was a declaration of the **testimony of God.** This was not Paul's testimony of God, but God's testimony of Himself (viz. "the cross").

I determined (literally, "I decided not"). The implication is that Paul gave careful thought to his approach, and resolved to lay aside the ornaments of speech and philosophical skill to announce **Jesus Christ, and him crucified.** Not only was Paul's message of divine wisdom, but his method also reflected the same.

3. Weakness . . . fear . . . trembling. To some of Paul's enemies, this approach was a stumbling block (cf. II Cor 10:10).

4. But Paul resolved to come **not with enticing words . . . but in demonstration of the Spirit and of power.** With a deep sense of his own insufficiency, Paul carried on a ministry characterized by modesty and humility. Paul was determined, as John the Baptist, that "he must increase, but I must decrease." Instead, his ministry demonstrated the Spirit and power. Obviously, the power was not in respect to any human agency, but the power of divine wisdom. Paul's mention of the Spirit here is significant. The Corinthians thought they knew much about the Holy Spirit, for as no other church in apostolic times, they had experienced the gifts of the Spirit. But, they still had a lot to learn, and Paul will have many things to say about this important subject.

5. That your faith should . . . stand . . . in the power of God. Paul has a motive. Paul knows that his clever speech and polished oratory can save no one. Furthermore, he knows that if they are merely drawn by the logic of his arguments, their faith will be at the mercy of the next man that comes with a more clever presentation. Paul's motive is that their faith should "stand," and that it should stand in the "power of God."

2. Wisdom of divine origin. 2:6-9.

6. Paul does not depreciate wisdom as some anti-intellectuals do today. On the contrary, what Paul proclaims is the only true wisdom. **We speak** (literally, "go on speaking"). Contrast the historical aorists in Greek in verses

1-3. Paul wants them to know that his message has not changed.

But this wisdom could only be fully appreciated by **them that are perfect** ("mature," Gr *teleios,* cf. I Cor 14:20; Phil 3:15; and Heb 6:1). Paul cannot resist the use of irony here. **That come to nought** (Greek present passive participle, "who are being made ineffective").

7-9. This wisdom is also a hidden wisdom. This is the **wisdom of God.** In contrast to the groping speculation of fallen men, Paul's message is the unchanging truth of God. **In a mystery.** "In" has an instrumental force. Mystery (Gr *mystērion*) refers to some work or purpose of God hitherto unrevealed (Rom 16:25-26). In this case, the reference is to the **hidden wisdom, which God ordained . . . unto our glory.** The counsels of God concerning our salvation are from eternity, and directed toward the same everlasting glory (cf. Rom 8:28-32; Phil 1:10). That this wisdom was hidden from men has the horrible consequence that the **Lord of glory** was crucified (on the expression "Lord of glory," meaning perhaps "the Lord whose attribute was glory," see Ps 29:1; Acts 7:2; Eph 1:17; Jas 2:1). **Eye hath not seen . . .** Paul employs the language of Isaiah 64:4 in order to demonstrate that the wisdom of God is not of human origin, and also to contrast the thought of verse 10.

This wisdom which is of divine power, and of divine origin, is also shown by the apostle to be of divine perception (vss. 10-16).

3. Wisdom of divine perception. 2:10-16.

Paul develops his thought here by showing, first of all, that this perception is through the spirit, then by contrasting the perception of the soulish man in verse 14 with the perception of the spiritual man in verse 15.

10. The truth of which the apostle is

speaking is not truth that remains hidden to every human heart; on the contrary, it is **revealed . . . unto us** ("unto us" is in the emphatic position in the original). For the mature believer, all that God has revealed is open unto him. In verses 10-13 the apostle deals with three vital doctrines. In verse 10 he deals with the doctrine of revelation. For the believer today, the truth which Paul is talking about is contained in that record which God has given to us, the Bible. This is eternally and unchangingly the truth of God. Verse 11 deals with the doctrine of illumination, which has to do with human perception of divine truth. **The Spirit** (see Rom 8:4). The things of God can only be recognized by the highest element of human personality. They have not entered into the heart (vs. 9) but into the spirit, which is the principle point of contact with God. Since the truth of God is of divine origin, it requires divine enablement to properly understand it.

The subject of verses 12 and 13 is the doctrine of inspiration. In verse 12 Paul talks about the content of inspiration. **That we might know the things that are freely given to us of God.** In verse 13 his concern is with the communication of inspiration **which things** (the things freely given) **also we speak.** Paul's message was not of human contrivance. He was a channel, simply communicating God's truth. The faithful minister of the gospel today does the same thing. He takes of that truth, God's Word, and communicates it to man. **Comparing spiritual things with spiritual.** The term "comparing" (Gr *synekrinō*) occurs only here and in II Corinthians 10:12 where the meaning is clearly "compare." However, in classical Greek, the term was always used in a sense of "to compound" or "to interpret" (cf. LXX Gen 40:8). Probably the most satisfactory interpretation is "combining spiritual things with spiritual words," or "doing spiritual things by spiritual means." After speaking of spiritual things (11-13),

Paul now speaks of the forms in which they are conveyed. In other words, spiritual truth is conveyed in language that is given by God's Spirit. This would not be the case if he uttered the revelations of the Spirit in the speech of human wisdom (cf. Vincent, *Word Studies in the New Testament,* Vol. II, p. 197). Having established the principle by which God's truth is made known, the apostle contrasts two kinds of men to whom the truth comes, i.e. the natural and the spiritual man.

14. Natural man (literally, "soulish man"). Paul contrasts the soulish man (the soul as the organ of human cognition) with the "spiritual" (the spirit as the organ of spiritual cognition). The former, when confronted with spiritual truth, **receiveth not.** He is unreceptive. He does not admit the truth into his heart (cf. Lk 8:13; Acts 8:14; 11:1; I Thess 1:6; Jas 1:21). **They are foolishness.** He passes it off with scorn. **Neither can he know** (literally, "he cannot know"). As spiritual discernment is generated only by the Holy Spirit, the capacity to know spiritual truth is beyond the innate powers of the natural man.

Because they are spiritually discerned shows that the natural man is incompetent. The fundamental idea of "discerned" (Gr *anakrinomai*) is that of examination or scrutiny. It is used only by Paul and Luke, and mostly of judicial examination (cf. Luke 23:14; Actrs 4:9; I Cor 9:3; 10:25, 27). It speaks of the impatient human spirit which prejudges the truth and wants to anticipate the full judgment. On the spiritual plain, the natural man does not even have the ability to sift the facts.

15. But introduces the contrast with **he that is spiritual** (he who is dominated by the spirit). Such a man **judgeth** (Gr *anakrino* "discerns") **all things.** The difference between the natural man and the spiritual man is primarily that the spiritual man has been exposed to God's revelation, has received it, and founded his faith upon it. He can judge now both earthly and heavenly things. He can discern what is and what is not of the gospel and salvation, and whether a man truly preaches the truth of God. It is important to observe that the spiritual man does not lose his power of reasoning. Nor does Paul renounce the concepts of reason and logic. Rather, he elevates revelation above reason, and subjects the imaginations of human reason to the objective truth of God. The natural man operates in reverse. Discerning all things, the spiritual man is **judged of no man** who is not spiritual.

16. But we have the mind of Christ. This answers the question that Paul puts in the same verse, "who has known the mind of the Lord?" The answer is, "we do!" The term "we" no doubt includes the Apostle Paul and all true believers.

C. Development of Mature Service. 3:1-23.

In chapter 1 Paul has denounced their divisive spirit. In chapter 2 he has shown that they have totally misunderstood the message of the gospel. The burden of chapter 3 is the development of mature service. Paul develops his thought by, first, citing the fleshliness in Corinth (vss. 1-3), then by showing that he, Apollos, and others who assisted with the ministry in Corinth were not party leaders, but rather, fellow workers in the gospel (vss. 4-17). Then, in verses 18-23, he shows the utter folly in human wisdom.

1. Fleshliness in Corinth. 3:1-3.

1-3. In the opening verses, Paul notes that the fleshliness in Corinth had hindered his ministry. **And I, brethren could not speak.** The pronoun "I" is emphatic. Paul calls them brethren not simply to ingratiate himself with them. But, it is important to observe that they cannot be robbed of their relationship to Jesus Christ in spite of their immaturity and sin. The apostle observes that even on his first encounter with them, he was unable to speak as to spiritual men. Paul recalls this to mind briefly in order to compare the present state of the Corinthians with their beginnings in the faith, a comparison that must have filled them with shame. They still are acting like spiritual babes (cf. Lenski, *The Interpretation of I and II Corinthians,* p. 120). **I have fed you with milk, and not with meat.** As newborn babes, this would be natural and to be expected I Pet 2:2). But, at this stage in their development, it is embarrassing. Their problem was that they were still **carnal** (literally, "fleshly"). The warfare between the flesh and the Spirit receives continual emphasis in Paul's writings (cf. Gal 5:17; Rom 7:14-8:13). The factions which have destroyed the unity in Corinth indicate that these believers were not walking by the Spirit, but were allowing the flesh to direct their behavior. They were acting just like fleshly men, with no uplifting power of the Holy Spirit. They were soldiers of the Lord's army trying to march to the beat of Lucifer's drums.

Such an attitude also hindered the spiritual maturity and development of these people. They are still **babes** ("non-speakers" or "infants"). This strongly contrasts with the "perfect" in 2:6. **Milk,** the drink suitable for babies, suggests their undeveloped spiritual state. **Envying, and strife, and divisions,** all works of the flesh, are symptomatic of their carnality. **Walk as men.** Paul does not say that they "are" men, but they are "as" men (the inference is "natural" men, cf. 2:14). Having finally labeled the wranglings at Corinth for what they were (carnality), Paul goes on to show the absurdity of such party alliances, since he and Apollos and the other apostles were actually fellow workers in the gospel (3:4-17).

2. Fellow workers in the gospel. 3:4-17.

4-5. In verses 4 and 5, the Apostle Paul shows that he and Apollos were united in service. **Another** (Gr *heteros,* "another of a different kind"). **Carnal.** The better texts read "men." In other words, Paul is saying, "Are you not mere men?" Who (Gr *ti* "what"). Function is emphasized in this expression. What then are Paul and Apollos? **Ministers by whom ye believed, even as the Lord gave.** Paul comes now to the crucial question, "What are these men around whom the Corinthians had built their little coteries?" They are simply ministers (Gr *diakonos*) serving the Lord. The apostle was not there to extend his own influence and popularity; rather, he was in Corinth in obedience to God (note especially Acts 18:9-10).

6. These ministers were also united in sowing (vss. 6-8). **I have planted, Apollos watered; but God gave** (Greek imperfect tense, "was giving") **the increase.** Men are used to accomplish specific tasks in the economy of God, but in the process, God is giving the increase. While men can be used to plant and cultivate things, only God can make things grow.

7. Neither is he that planteth any thing. The point is that men are unimportant when compared to God who makes our efforts effectual.

8. Are one ("of one purpose"). **Every man shall receive his own reward.** Just as there are differences in quality of workmanship among craftsmen, even so among God's ministers. The quality of one's work and service will be directly related to the rewards he receives. We each have a responsibility to serve God faithfully, knowing that our best results are but the work of His grace.

Paul's servants are also united in structure. This is the essence of Paul's argument in verses 9-17.

9. Here is the key to this chapter.

The principle is expressed in the words, **we are laborers together with God** (literally, "fellow workers of God"). This, in effect, restates the phrase in verse 8, **he that planteth and he that watereth are one.** Then Paul employs two illustrations to explicate this principle. The first looks back to verses 6-8, **ye are God's husbandry.** The second he introduces by saying **ye are God's building.** This is the imagery which dominates the remainder of the chapter. The use of the architectural metaphor is best understood if one remembers the magnificent temples and buildings common in Corinth. The important thrust of this metaphor applies to the believer's works.

10. First a reminder. **I have laid the foundation.** The foundation is always the least noticed and the most important part of any building. Paul had laid the foundation of the church among them in that he had "begotten (them) through the gospel" (cf. 4:15). **Another buildeth thereon** corresponds to the phrase, "Apollos watered" above. **Let every man take heed how he buildeth thereupon.** We are urged to examine *how* we build, not *what* we build. The warning is necessitated by the nature of the foundation which is **Jesus Christ** (cf. Acts 4:12, cf. Lk 6:46-49).

12-14. The second factor which is important to the apostle is that there is to be a time of reckoning. Verse 12 deals with the materials employed in the building. Verses 13-15 deal with manifestations of every man's work.

12. Gold, silver, precious stones. There are two kinds of material that can be employed in the superstructure of the building. The first are eternal. These are consistent with the quality of the foundation. A second kind of material is temporal. **Wood, hay, stubble.** In contrast to the above, these will not withstand the trial by fire.

13. Every man's work shall be made manifest. While it is possible to hide the true quality of one's service for

Christ in this life, there is coming a time when it will be openly displayed for what it is. The time is given in the words **the day.** This is the day of the Judgment Seat of Christ (cf. 4:5; II Cor 5:10). **Fire.** This is figurative for judgment. More specifically, it speaks of the absolutely righteous judgment of God. Fire is used here, not for its enlightening power, but its consuming power. Of the six types of material mentioned, three are combustible and three are incombustible. (see also Deut 4:24; Mal 3:2; II Thess 1:8; Heb 12:29).

14-15. Abide . . . reward . . . burned . . . loss. The results of the judgment are broken into two categories. If a man's work remains undamaged by the fire, accordingly, he receives rewards (Gr *misthos,* "wages," cf. 3:8). Of course, it goes without saying that even the "wages" mentioned here are entirely a gift of grace (cf. Dan 12:3; I Cor 9:17; II Jn 8; Rev 4:4; 11:18). If a man's work does not endure, and is consumed in the fire, then he shall "suffer loss." Everything he has devoted himself to in this life shall be suddenly swept away. **But he himself shall be saved; yet so as by fire.** It is important to notice that such a man does not suffer the loss of his salvation, but the loss of reward. The stress in this entire passage is not upon a man's relationship to Christ, but upon service to Christ. (On the believer's rewards see, W. Kroll, *It Will Be Worth It All.*)

Then Paul directs his attention to the fact that the building being erected is a residence of Almighty God (vss. 16-17).

16. Ye are the temple of God. Here the temple is the local church, not the individual believer (cf. Eph. 2:21; II Cor 6:16). **The Spirit of God dwelleth in you.** This expression does not vitiate the doctrine of the omnipresence of the Holy Spirit. Indeed, the Holy Spirit is everywhere, but He does not "dwell" everywhere. He dwells in the local church because He has taken up residence in every believer (cf. Jn 14:16).

17. Defile . . . destroy (Gr *phtheirō*, has the idea of dishonoring or destroying). **Him shall God destroy.** This is a much stronger expression than "suffer loss" above. Paul seems to have in mind unsaved people who may or may not be in the assembly, but who, in fact, are false believers. The prospect for such a one is a fearful one. **The temple of God is holy, which temple ye are.** Paul has built a syllogism here. In verse 16 he has said, "you are a shrine of God." Now he says, "the shrine of God is holy." Therefore, the conclusion is, "you are holy."

3. Folly in worldly wisdom. 3:18-23.

18. Here the apostle gives the formula for Godly wisdom. **Let no man deceive himself.** Do not be led away from the truth and simplicity of the gospel by having too high an opinion of human wisdom. **If any . . . seemeth to be wise in this world, let him become a fool.** Do not have too high an opinion of yourself. Learn to resign your own understanding to follow the instruction of God. This is the way to truth and everlasting wisdom. In order that **he may be wise.** One must learn to prefer the infallible revelation of God to his own shallow reasonings.

19-20. There can be no comparison between God's wisdom and man's. **He taketh the wise in their own craftiness** (cf. Job 5:13, cf. Ps 94:11).

The conclusion to chapter three is very much like the conclusion to chapter 2. If you must boast, then by all means, do not boast within yourself or man, but in Christ.

21. For all things are yours. The man who belongs to Christ is a child of God, and his Father will do anything for him. Nothing of the Father's resources shall be begrudged to the believer (cf. Rom 8:32).

22. Whether Paul, or Apollos, or Cephas. The absurdity of their dividing over allegiances to any of these men is that God gave them "all" to the Corinthians. **Or the world,** a rebuke to the legalists of Paul's day. **Or life, or death,** the former denoting **things present,** the latter, **things to come.** The believer in Christ "shall want no good thing" (Ps 84:11).

23. But it must be remembered that **Ye are Christ's.** It is only because of our relationship to Christ who is Lord of all, that all of these benefits accrue. **Christ is God's.** Christ is not subordinate to God, as the believer is to Christ; rather, He is the anointed one of God. He is God in the flesh, "reconciling the world unto himself" (II Cor 5:19).

D. Defense of a Faithful Steward. 4:1-21.

Since all who ministered at Corinth were servants of God (cf. 3:5), and since the church belongs to God and was His temple (cf. 3:16-17), then the Corinthians were not justified in qualifying these ministers by some arbitrary standard. It is God whom these men serve, and He must be their Judge. Paul, Apollos, and Peter were simply faithful ministers of Christ, and along with the other apostles, were simply obeying God in extending the gospel around the world. In this chapter, Paul shows that the wranglings in Corinth were inappropriate, unfair, and intolerable.

1. Execution of faithfulness. 4:1-5.

4:1-3. The character of a faithful steward of God is that his ministry is centered in Christ and he is committed to Him. **Ministers** (Gr *hypēretēs,* "under rower," "a subordinate," or "servant," J. H. Thayer, *Greek-English Lexicon of the New Testament,* p. 641). This term is used only here in Paul's epistles. It differs from the word translated "ministers" in 3:5 in that it has the idea of an attendant or helper that assists a master. The apostle and minister of Christ is simply an underling, or an attendant of Christ. He takes orders and executes them. **Stewards,** (Gr *oikonomos*). Generally, a slave in the master's household who is entrusted with property. Both of these terms emphasize subordination to the master. However, in the latter, there is particular stress on accountability. He must render account for the manner in which he carries out his master's orders. **That a man be found faithful.** In verse 2, Paul moves from the plural to the singular ("stewards"—"a man"). This is characteristic of Paul. He moves from principle to particular: i.e. it is sought for in all stewards, that each one be found reliable and trustworthy. The subject of verse three is the criticism of a faithful steward. **A very small thing.** It amounts to very little that the apostle finds himself subject to the judicial examination of the Corinthians. **Man's judgment** (literally, "man's day"). This is an implied contrast with the day of the Lord (cf. vs. 5). **I judge not mine own self.** If Paul were to resort to introspective critical examination of himself, then he too would be guilty of usurping a responsibility which belongs only to God.

4. Verses 4 and 5 deal with the manner by which this faithful steward is certified. **I know nothing by myself** ("I know nothing against myself"). It was this sort of total commitment that gave Paul the authority to make such a statement as "be ye followers of me" (cf. I Cor 4:16; 11:1). **Yet am I not hereby justified.** Paul recognized that even he himself was not competent to adequately examine himself. Arthur Custance observes, "man is totally irrational in his attitude and assessment of his own nature. He is a fallen creature with a heart that is desperately wicked above all else (Jer 17:9), and a mind that has to be renewed (Rom 12:2)" (A. C. Custance, *Man in Adam and in Christ,* p. 17).

5. The Lord alone is the Judge. Therefore the examination must await His time, that is, "when He comes" (cf. 1:7). Then He will shed light on the **hidden things,** which Paul defines as **the counsels of the hearts: and then shall every man receive praise of God** (literally, "praise from God"). God who knows the mind and the hearts will apportion to each his due praise.

2. Example of faithfulness. 4:6-13.

Paul goes on in verses 6-13 to use himself, Apollos, and the other apostles as examples of faithfulness. In an effort to shame the Corinthians into recognizing the nature of their behavior, Paul first contrasts the efforts of Apollos and himself to accommodate the Corinthians (vs. 6) with their continued arrogance (vss. 7-8). Then in verses 9-13, he attacks their haughty spirit by citing the continued abuse of all the apostles.

6. I have in a figure transferred (Gr *metaschēmatizō* , "exchanged the outward fashion"). Paul adapted himself for the purpose **that no one of you be puffed up one against another.** The expression, **not to think . . . above that which is written,** is a proverbial expression. The Apostle Paul is enjoining the Corinthians not to go beyond scripture. In other words, learn to live by the Book, and stop following men.

7-8. Three pointed questions puncture the bubble of the Corinthian pride. **For who maketh thee to differ.** There is no room for pride and self-conceit, when all the distinction made among them is owing to God. **What hast thou . . . received?** Everything they had, including their gifts in the ministry were given them by God. To take personal pride in them was tantamount to insulting God. Irony exudes from the apostle in verses 7 and 8 in the words, **Now ye are full, now ye are rich, ye have reigned as kings without us.** These are three blessings promised in the coming Messianic Kingdom. The Corinthians were boasting each with

his own party as if he had already arrived in that kingdom. And so Paul says, **I would to God ye did reign, that we also might reign with you.** The Corinthians had already arrived while the apostle was still waiting (vs. 5)!

9. For I think. The apostle is about to level the arrogance of the Corinthians. With the consideration of my own suffering and the abuse of the apostles, since you are already reigning, God must have placed **the apostles last.** We have not come into the kingdom yet! To the world, we are a **spectacle** (Gr *theatron,* "a theatre"). The apostles were like exhibits in a side show. Notice the verb form of this term in Hebrews 10:33.

10-13. The series of growing distinctions between Paul and the Corinthians must have been nothing short of embarrassing to his readers. **We are fools for Christ's sake, but ye are wise.** The apostles were considered fools because they knew and preached nothing but Christ. On the other hand, the Corinthians used their Christianity as another philosophy to extend their reputation as wise and enlightened people. **We are made . . . the offscouring of all things unto this day.** Some find an illusion to an ancient Athenian custom of throwing certain worthless persons into the sea in case of plague or famine, saying "be our offscouring" in the belief that they would wash away the nation's guilt (Vincent, *Word Studies in the New Testament,* vol. II, p. 208).

3. Exhortation to faithfulness. 4:14-21.

Here Paul's tone changes. He lays aside the irony which characterizes so much of this chapter, and he entreats them as a loving father his wayward children.

14. I write not . . . to shame you. Paul realized that if all he does is expose his readers to open shame, he will only provoke them to obstinacy. And so, while wishing to expose their sin, he does not wish to exasperate them. **As**

my beloved sons I warn. With great love and affection, the apostle admonishes his children in the faith. He was not interested in making them cringe before him, but in correcting them, and offering them a chance to respond and be restored.

15. Though ye have ten thousand instructors (Gr *paidagōgos*, "slave guardians"). The guardians to which Paul refers are not strictly instructors, or even tutors, but they were guardians that were common in wealthy families to oversee the children. **Yet not many fathers.** No matter how many guardians a man may have had to assist him through his early life, there is only one person who brought him into this life, and that is his father. If Paul was just a stranger, he could not have spoken so freely. But he was their father. Hence, he was probably the only one who could speak to them in this way. Not only that, he was under obligation to do so. **I have begotten you** ("I" is emphatic). Paul alone was responsible for the beginning of the Corinthian assembly. The term "begot" does not have in mind so much the conversion of these people, but the fact that it was Paul who laid the foundation (3:10). **Through the gospel.** Not through the power of Paul's personality, or through the sagacity of his wisdom, but the gospel of Christ and Him crucified (cf. 2:1-5).

16-17. Be ye followers of me (cf. 11:1, literally, "continue to imitate me"). No doubt Paul has in mind those characteristics which are common to him and the other apostles, listed in verses 11-13. But his thinking goes further to include his doctrine and his teaching, as shown in the expression: **my ways.** If they have any questions as to how to follow the apostle, Timothy was on his way, and would clarify any problems they had.

18-20. The Apostle Paul assures them that he is coming to see them. He warns that when he comes he will know **not the speech of them which are puffed up, but the power.** Paul was well known for confronting trouble head on (cf. Gal 2:11). **The kingdom of God is not in word, but in power.** We will see if the millennium has come to Corinth!

21. Finally an alternative is extended to them. **Shall I come unto you with a rod or in love?** It is all up to them. "The rod" introduces the note of discipline which is Paul's primary concern in the next section.

III. DISCIPLINE FOR THE FELLOWSHIP. 5:1-6:20.

In coming to this, Paul's second major division of the epistle, it is well to remember the vile surroundings out of which the Corinthian converts had come. They had been truly won to Christ. They had broken from their idolatries, and formed a local church. They had indeed come out of the corruption of Corinth to form a community of saints. But the question was now, could they get Corinth out of the assembly? It is imperative that they learn that the gospel does not tolerate compromise. There must be a clean break. This is the thrust of I Corinthians 5-6. "The Holy Spirit is grieved and thwarted in the assembly where sin is allowed a footing" (J. S. Baxter, *Explore the Book,* Vol. 5, p. 109). Here Paul confronts successively: the problem of lust (5:1-33), the problem of law suits (6:1-11), and the problem of license (6:12-20).

A. Relating to Lust. 5:1-13.

1. A common report. 5:1.

5:1. It is reported commonly. "It is a fact" that the report had come to Paul's hearing of fornication existing in the Corinthian assembly. The word **fornication** (Gr *pornēia*) is used in a comprehensive way ("sexual sins"). Perhaps implying that the offense in different forms more or less prevailed in the Corinthian assembly. But one case in particular is so gross that it is not so much as named among the Gentiles. Cicero (*Oratio Pro Cluent.* 5, 6) refers to this sin as *"scelus incredibile, et praeter unum in omni vita inauditum"* ("incredible wickedness, such I never heard of in all my life besides"). The crime was that one should have his father's wife. One of the members of the church had taken his stepmother (cf. Lev 18:8) and had married her (the expression "to have a woman" always means "to marry," cf. Mt 14:4; 22:28; I Cor 7:2, 29). Hence, this man's crime is worse than adultery. It is incest. Otherwise, the apostle would not have spoken of it in such terms.

2. A critical rebuke. 5:2.

2. And ye are puffed up, and have not rather mourned. The problem with the assembly was that they were laden with pride and lacking in discipline. Such an outrageous and detestable sin should have provoked the strongest response from the congregation. But because of their pride and carnality, they were immobilized when it came to dealing with a real problem in their midst.

3. A corrective remedy. 5:3-8.

3-5. "In verses 3-5 we have an interesting indication of the manner in which discipline was administered in the early church. The congregation would be called together, with an apostle presiding if available, and the person accused would be arraigned before them. After the evidence had been heard, and the accused had said what he had to say in defense of himself, the judgment of the congregation would be pronounced by the president. Paul, though absent in person, yet pictures himself present and presiding in spirit, and he leaves them in no doubt concerning the verdict which ought to be pronounced: the offense should be condemned and the offender excommunicated" (P.E. Hughes, "I Corinthians," *The Biblical Expositor,* Vol. 3, p. 267).

To deliver . . . unto Satan. Concerning this difficult and obscure passage, several observations must be made. (1) It involved excommunication from the church (vs. 2). (2) It involved the chastisement of the man (it was the body which was to be handed over). Paul elsewhere conceives affliction, disease, or loss as Satan's work (I Thess 2:18; II Cor 12:7, cf. I Tim 1:20). Destruction nowhere means annihilation. The reference seems to be to the destruction of the physical appetites which prompted this gross immorality. (3) Paul has the restoration of this man ultimately in view. That the spirit may be saved. This last purpose shows that the phrase "destruction of the flesh" cannot mean that the person could be brought to death. This is asserted for several reasons: (a) because nowhere in Scripture is Satan asserted as God's executioner, (b) because restoration would be impossible if the man were put to death. God does not want him killed, He wants him restored (cf. Mt 18:15; Gal 6:1; II Cor 2:1-11). The implications of Paul's instruction are given in verses 6-8.

6. A little leaven leaveneth the whole. No sin can be considered an isolated event. Just as with the sin of Achan (Josh 7:11), the sin had to be purged out or else it would contaminate the whole "lump" (on this see Rom 12:21). The stress is on the church as a singular unity.

7. Cleansing is essential. Purge out therefore the old leaven. Here the leaven does not signify the sinful man, *per se,* but evil of any kind in accordance with the more general statement of the leavening power of evil in verse 6. The background for this metaphor is Exodus 12:19 and 13:7. The larger scope of the apostle's imagery here is that he sees Christ as the fulfillment of the Old Testament passover feast of unleavened bread. The Passover depicted, typically, Christ's vicarious death on behalf of His own. That is, "the Lamb of God, which taketh away the sin of the world" (Jn 1:29). The Feast of Un-

leavened Bread accompanied the Passover. It involved a period of seven days during which no leaven was to be found in the homes of the Israelites. This was typical of the holy life that was to accompany partaking of the paschal lamb. The expression, **ye are unleavened** denotes a positional truth. Paul is interested that their practice match up to their position. **Christ our passover is sacrificed for us.** Since sin required the sacrifice of the Lamb of God, it is inconceivable that it would ever be tolerated in the assembly of believers.

8. Therefore let us keep the feast (Greek present subjunctive, "go on keeping"). By purging out **malice** (chs. 1-4) **and wickedness** (ch. 5) **let us go on to celebrate holiness of living. Sincerity and truth** are those qualities on which the believer is to feed.

It is not surprising that the apostle uses the Passover as an illustration here. I Corinthians was written just before the passover (cf. I Cor 16:8) and the celebration of the feast is on Paul's mind. This is a good example of how God used the experiences of the biblical authors in the writing of Scripture.

4. A commanding regulation. 5:9-13.

9. I wrote unto you in an epistle. This is the "previous epistle" discussed in the introduction. This letter is now lost but we know that at least one subject discussed in this letter was that they were **not to company with fornicators.** The intent of the apostle in this epistle was misunderstood, and so he finds it necessary to clarify himself in verses 10 and 11.

10. Yet not altogether. Of course Paul does not intend to say that they are not to have any association with vile and sinful men. In order to do this, one would have to **go out of the world.** As long as the believer is "in" the world, it will be necessary to rub shoulders with sinners. A parallel idea is contained in the words of our Lord in John 17:15-18.

11. Not to keep company. The key to Paul's thought is here. The term translated "to keep company" (Gr *synanameignymi*) is found only here and in II Thessalonians 3:14. It is a compound of three Greek terms, and means "to mingle together with." It has the idea of close, habitual intercourse. **If any man that is called a brother.** Paul's instruction relates to those who are in the assembly calling themselves brethren in Christ. If such a person is a **fornicator** or covetous, etc., then this person is not to be included in fellowship. **With such a one, no, not to eat.**

12. Them . . . that are without. Those outside of the church (cf. Col 4:5; I Thess 4:12). The command of the apostle had reference only to those who were in the church, but it was not his prerogative to judge those outside of the church. The Corinthians should have understood this.

13. Them that are without God judgeth. The Greek present tense of this verb fits well with Paul's thought in Romans 1:18, "For the wrath of God is being revealed (presently) from heaven against all ungodliness." There is a vitally important truth to be observed here. It is true, as the Apostle John said, that "the whole world lieth in wickedness" (I Jn 5:19). But, it will not do to simply curse the darkness. It is the task of the believer to proclaim the positive truth of the gospel. The saints are obligated to be faithful stewards; as for the world, God will take care of it.

Paul summarizes: **Therefore put away . . . that wicked person.** As for this person who is committing open sin, remove him from the assembly, and have no further fellowship with him.

B. Relating to Lawsuits. 6:1-11.

Paul has already introduced the subject of judging in the previous chapter. Accordingly, he has shown that the responsibility for judging sin lies with the assembly. Now he goes on to show that even in matters of civil dispute, the responsibility for settling such matters lies with the leadership of the local church. Paul develops this matter by first introducing the problem (vs. 1). Then in verses 2 and 3 he shows the absurdity of stooping to a pagan judge to adjudicate some matter between two brethren in Christ. Finally, in verses 4-11, he traces the biblical principles underlying his instructions.

1. An inquiry. 6:1.

6:1. Dare any of you (this is very emphatic). "Is anyone so bold as to shock the Christian sense of propriety?" (Hodge, *Commentary on the First Epistle to the Corinthians,* p. 93). **Go to law before the unjust, and not before the saints?** The terms "unjust" and "saints" are generic, referring to all unbelievers as opposed to all believers. How incredible that the just should go before the unjust for justice!

2. An inference. 6:2-3.

2-3. Here the apostle argues *a majori ad minus.* That is, he cites a major premise in order to contrast and establish a minor premise. The first is that **the saints shall judge the world.** Certainly the Corinthians must have known this elementary truth (cf. Dan 7:22; Mt 19:28; Rev 2:26; 3:21; 20:4). Now, if this be the case, Paul goes on, **are ye unworthy to judge the smallest matters?** (literally, "on the lowest tribunals"). You who shall comprise the Supreme Court of the world, do you not feel qualified to sit on some tiny local court? But Paul goes on with another major premise. **We shall judge angels** (Isa 24:21; II Pet 2:4; Jude 6). The contrast now borders on the ridiculous. **How much more things that pertain to this life** (literally, "to say nothing of common life affairs"). Here is the minor premise.

3. An inconsistency. 6:4-11.

4. Things pertaining to this life (Gr *biōtikos,* "common life affairs"). Paul connects what is to follow with the above. **Then** is inferential. **Judgments** may mean "legal causes," or it may simply mean "trials." The former is more consistent with the normal usage of the term. **Set them to judge who are least esteemed.** In the original, this may either be taken as indicative or interrogative. If the latter, then Paul is being sarcastic. That is, if you are going to go to a civil court, you might just as well put your least qualified members as jurors. If it is a question, then it is emphatic, "are you setting them to judge who are least esteemed in the church?" (that is, "the heathen"). This would render a statement of shock and surprise that they were doing such a thing. The latter seems more in keeping with the context.

5-6. I speak to your shame (i.e., "to move you to shame"). This suggests Paul's purpose in speaking as he does. **Is it so, that there is not a wise man among you?** This is a rather ironic question to be asking the Corinthians who boasted in their wisdom. Apparently this is the case, since in verse 6 Paul says **brother goeth to law against brother, and that before the unbelievers.** The apostle is incensed for at least two reasons: (1) that they went to law; and (2) that they went to law before heathen judges. In verses 7-11, the apostle probes some of the underlying causes for this situation existing in Corinth.

7. They have a defect. **There is utterly a fault among you.** They were defective in that they would even consider taking a problem between each other before a heathen judge. Before doing this, the apostle says it would be better to **take wrong** (and) **. . . be defrauded.**

8. Instead of following the correct course when they were wronged, they were defrauding one another. The very opposite of what they should have done. It would be better to accept the wrong committed than to pursue it and inflict further injury on anyone else.

9-10. They are also deceived. Those who would accuse the Apostle Paul of bifurcating works and faith should take a closer look at these verses. **The unrighteous shall not inherit the kingdom of God.** It would seem that there were some in the Corinthian assembly who have professed Christianity as a system of doctrine, but not as a rule of life. The apostle warns that this is a fatal mistake. **Be not deceived.** No one who can allow himself the indulgence of known sin in his life can be saved. This passage proves that "Paul and James are in basic agreement. Both affirm that genuine faith produces good works (cf. Eph 2:8-10), and that the absence of good works indicates the lack of faith (cf. James 2:14-26)." (S. L. Johnson, "I Corinthians," *The Wycliffe Bible Commentary,* p. 1238).

11. Then Paul concludes this section with a positive appeal. He assures them that they have been delivered. **Such were some of you.** Here Paul cites the fact that there were some in the assembly who were formerly characterized in the catalogue of sins listed in verse 10. **But ye are washed . . . sanctified . . . justified.** Logically, one would expect to find these words in inverse order. That is, they are first justified, then they are sanctified, then they experience daily cleansing. Paul placed them in this order for emphasis. Now you are washed, indeed you have been sanctified or set apart to do God's special service. Indeed, you stand before God declared righteous. In such an exalted position, it seems incredible that such people would find it necessary to go before an inferior human court to arbitrate their dispute.

C. Relating to License. 6:12-20.

Paul now goes on to distinguish between proper Christian liberty and the problem of unbridled license. Some were presuming that all physical passions and appetites were as lawful as eating and drinking, and were to be freely gratified. In the pagan society of Corinth, prostitution was accepted as a normal thing. It was not difficult for some of the Christians to justify themselves with the argument that such behavior only involved the body and not the soul (cf. Acts 15:20 where the prohibition of certain foods was also joined with the prohibition against fornication). The teaching regarding this important subject is given in verses 12-14, and the thrust of it is applied in verses 15-20.

1. The teaching. 6:12-14.

12. Paul's principles may be summarized in three words. **Lawful . . . expedient . . . power.** The first is the principle of liberty. When Paul says "all things," we cannot understand this in an absolute sense. Obviously, what God forbids can never be allowed. Rather, it seems to have in mind those things about which the Scriptures are non-explicit. These matters are left to the Christian's own judgment. The apostle is careful not to vitiate the important doctrine of Christian liberty by leading these people back under Judaistic legalism. Rather, his intent is to circumscribe its application through proper restrictions. These are expressed, first of all, in the principle of "expediency." Not everything is of benefit. Whether a law of prohibition exists or not, it is simply wrong to do something to ourselves or others simply because it is beneficial (cf. Rom 14:15-23; I Cor 8:7-13; 10:23-33). A second restriction is expressed in the words, **I will not be brought under the power of any.** This is the principle of control. Certain forms of indulgence become wrong when they bring the person into bondage. One of the character qualities of the believer is self-control (cf. Gal 5:22-23). The spiritual man of I Corinthians 2:15 is not in subjection to any appetite or habit.

13-14. Meats for the belly. Nature

demonstrates the law of mutual adaptation. This is illustrated by meat and the digestive system. **God shall destroy both.** The present bodily constitution is only temporary. **Now,** a mild adversative, better "but," **the body is not for fornication.** Contrary to the natural law of adaptation, the body is not designed for fornication, **but for the Lord.** The body is intended to be a member of Christ (vs. 15), and the dwelling place of His Holy Spirit (vs. 19).

Whereas God is to destroy the belly and meats, the ultimate purpose of the body is fulfilled in the resurrection. **And God hath both raised up the Lord, and will also raise up us by his own power.** With this argument, Paul dismisses the notion that the sexual drives are the same as all of the other physical appetites. Where the latter are considered temporary, the former are permanent. The one touches matters of indifference, the other tampers with the very nature of the design for which we were created.

Paul's usage of the pronoun **us,** shows that his use of the term **body** goes beyond its normal usage to signify the whole man. Note also its connection with the second person pronoun in verse 19, below. (On the destiny of the body, see also I Cor 15:15, 20 and 35-56; Phil 3:21; Rom 8:11; II Cor 4:14; and I Thess 4:14). Paul's argument runs something like this. It was an uncommon honor that God should raise up the body of Jesus Christ. It will be an undue honor that our bodies will also be raised by His own power. Therefore, let us not abuse those bodies through fleshly lusts.

2. *The thrust. 6:15-20.*

15-16. The real thrust of Paul's concern is now taken into account. In the first place, **your bodies are the members of Christ.** The body is not only for the Lord (vs. 13), but they belong to Him by virtue of His redemptive work, and because they are united with Him.

This union pertains not only to the soul, but also to the body (cf. I Cor 12:12-27; Rom 8:6-11; Eph 2:6-7; 5:30). It is this fact, above all else, that makes fornication such a wicked and malicious sin. It takes what belongs to Christ and makes them **the members of a harlot.** To this Paul recoils with **God forbid.** He then goes on to enlarge on this point to say that **he which is joined to a harlot is one body.** The verb "joined" (Gr *kollaō*) is used in Genesis 2:24 (Gr *proskallaō*) of the relationship of husband and wife. It is also used of man's relationship to God (Deut 10:20; 11:22; Jer 13:11). When fornication is committed, the parties involved share a common life. In the same sense, one cannot serve God and mammon, or share in the life of Christ and in the life of Belial. It is inconceivable that one can be simultaneously joined to Christ and to the body of a harlot. On the phrase **shall be one flesh,** compare Ephesians 2:15.

17. But he that is joined unto the Lord is one spirit. As if Paul's mundane analogies were not enough, he lays them aside to express, in eleven short words, a concept that "suggests to us the highest possible unity between the believer and the Lord. Many other forms are used to express this identification, but none approach this in the conception of inseparable oneness. The sheep may wander from the shepherd, the branch may be cut off from the vine, the member may be severed from the body, the child alienated from the father, and even the wife from the husband, but when two spirits blend in one, what shall part them? No outward connection of unity, even of wedlock, is so emphatically expressive of the perfect merging of two lives in one" (A. T. Pierson, *Knowing the Scriptures,* p. 108). This imposes the highest conceivable obligation to refrain from fornication.

18. Flee ("make it your habit to flee"). Compare Joseph's response (Gen 39:1-12). **Without the body.** The body is not the instrument, but the subject. But when man commits fornication, then he **sinneth against his own body.** Here the body becomes the instrument of the sin.

19. Your body is a temple of the Holy Ghost. Not only is the local church a temple of the Holy Spirit (cf. I Cor 3:16), but the individual believer's body itself also is a temple of the Holy Spirit, **which ye have of God.** Notice, the thought here is indicative, not imperative. Paul is not telling them that they can become more spiritual by receiving the Holy Spirit. The fact is, they already received the Holy Spirit. He dwells within them. This fact, instead, introduces the imperative of verse 20.

20. The blessed fact that our body is the temple of the Holy Spirit has two sides. One, that He is ours, the other, that we are His. **For ye are bought with a price** (literally, "were bought"). The believer was purchased on Golgotha's hill. The price paid was the blood of God's only Son (Acts 20:28). While it is true that this is applicable to all men, even those who deny the Lord (II Pet 2:1), it has a very unique and special significance for the believer (cf. I Pet 2:9; I Tim 4:10). Paul concludes with the imperative **therefore, glorify God in your body.** In other words, use your bodies in order that other men may see that you belong to God.

IV. DOCTRINE FOR THE FELLOWSHIP. 7:1-15:58.

A. Doctrine of Christian Marriage. 7:1-40.

Up until now, the main thrust of the epistle has been on reproof and correction. Paul now turns his attention to matters of instruction. The Corinthians had written to Paul concerning several matters that perplexed them. Paul deals with each of these in order. The first concerns Christian marriage. It is not surprising, in light of the preceding, that there were evident problems in this area. Paul's advice may be broken into four broad categories: (1) concerning the precept of marriage (vss. 1-7); (2) concerning the permanence of marriage (vss. 8-16); (3) concerning the place of marriage (vss. 17-24); (4) concerning the priorities of marriage (vss. 25-40).

1. Concerning the precept of marriage. 7:1-7.

a. A prevention of sin through the marriage relationship. 7:1-2.

7:1:2. Now concerning. (Gr *peri de,* see also 7:25; 8:1; 12:1; 16:1, 12). This recurring formula indicates that Paul is dealing in turn with the points the Corinthians had raised in their letter. **It is good for a man not to touch a woman.** The manner in which the apostle introduces this subject suggests that there was a reactionary element in the church to the libertines dealt with in chapter 6. It is likely that they were recommending celibacy as desirable if not obligatory on all believers. Paul says, such a practice is **good** ("expedient" or "profitable," cf. Mt 17:4; I Cor 9:15). That the apostle does not intend to teach that marriage is morally wrong as compared with celibacy is clear from verses 2, 7, 9, and 26 (see also Gen 2:18; II Cor 11:2; Rom 7:4; Eph 5:28-33; I Tim 4:3; Heb 13:4). **Nevertheless.** Here and throughout this passage, Paul demonstrates balance. On the one hand, there is a principle established to be applied in extenuating circumstances (such as those in which the apostle finds himself). But, on the other hand, there is the more general rule to be applied to the majority of cases. **To avoid fornication.** Paul overrides his principle of expedience (vs. 1) with the principle of necessity. Because of the prevalence of immorality in Corinth, Paul's advice to these believers is that every man is to have his own wife, and every wife her own husband.

b. A pledge of persons through the marriage relationship. 7:3-4.

3-4. Persons are to, first, **render . . . due benevolence** (literally, "fulfill (their) duty"). Paul clarifies what he means by this in the next verse when he says, **The wife hath not power of her own body, but the husband; and likewise also the husband hath not power of his own body, but the wife.** Partners in a marriage no longer have the right to autonomous existence (cf. vss. 32-33). Thus, it is sin to sexually reject one's partner!

c. A parenthesis in the marriage relationship. 7:5-7.

5. Defraud ye not one the other ("stop depriving one another"). The biblical precept of marriage implies that conjugal rights will be regularly exercised. The only exception to this rule will be **for a time.** And then only for **fasting and prayer.** Again the apostle's advice is practical in nature. It is given in order that **Satan tempt you not.**

6-7. I speak this by permission . . . not of commandment. The apostle does not take sides with the extreme Jewish view that held that it was a sin if a man reached twenty years of age without being married. Instead, he regards the matter as optional. **Even as I myself.** Content, not necessarily single. As to Paul's marital status, he was probably a widower (cf. Vincent, *World Studies in the New Testament,* Vol. 2, p. 217). But that is not the point here. The point is that **every man hath his proper gift of God** (cf. vss. 17, 20, 24, and 27). Both marriage and celibacy are considered as gifts of the Holy Spirit.

2. Concerning the permanence of marriage. 7:8-16.

Here the apostle develops guidelines for three categories of individuals: the unmarried and widows (vss. 8-9), the married believers (vss. 10-11), and mixed marriages (vss. 12-16).

a. For the unmarried and widows. 7:8-9.

8-9. I say therefore to the unmarried and widows. The apostle is not being redundant when he singles out widows for special mention along with the unmarried. No doubt they would have special cause to consider their situation a sad one, and therefore desire to have it changed. **Abide even as I.** The personal reference here is not identical with that given in verse 7. The point of verse 7 has to do with being content with the gift God gives you. This verse merely points to the matter of remaining unmarried. **It is better to marry than to burn.** This expression is not to be taken to indicate that the apostle conceives of marriage in mere physical, brute terms. Rather, it is to be taken in light of the preceding. That is, if a person's gift is to be married, then let him not try to exercise a gift he does not possess by remaining unmarried.

b. For the married believers. 7:10-11.

10-11. And unto the married I command. Notice Paul's advice to the unmarried is given as optional; his advice to the married is given as a command. In case his readers miss this point, he reinforces it with the words, **not I, but the Lord.** No doubt, the apostle has in mind explicit instruction of our Lord recorded in Matthew 5:32; 19:3-9; Mark 10:2-12; Luke 16:18. **Let not the wife depart.** Paul's command here is in opposition to Greek and Roman law which permitted a woman to divorce her husband. The command is unequivocal; let her not depart. **And if she depart, let her remain unmarried, or be reconciled.** While Paul disapproves of separation on any grounds, he recognizes that there will be cases of unapproved separation. In these cases, they are to "remain unmarried." The Greek present tense emphasizes a permanent state. The only other option is reconciliation. **And let not the husband put away his wife.** This is tantamount to saying, "and the same thing goes for husbands."

c. For the mixed marriages. 7:12-16.

12-13. Now the apostle turns his attention to the special case of mixed marriages. **But to the rest speak I, not the Lord.** This is not to be taken as marking a contrast between inspired scripture and what Paul is about to say. On the contrary, while on the earth, the Lord explicitly gave instructions about marriage and divorce. However, He did not make any special reference to the case of a mixed marriage. Thus, it is incumbent on the Apostle Paul, under inspiration of the Holy Spirit, to give additional instructions regarding this kind of situation. The instruction is essentially the same. If a Christian person is married to an unbelieving spouse, and the unbeliever is **pleased to dwell** with the believer, then divorce or separation is prohibited. Paul's advice here is intended to answer any of his Jewish converts who might be inclined to make an unwarranted application of the situation recorded in Ezra 10:3.

14. In the event that his readers should have any misgivings, the apostle shows why his advice is sound. **The unbelieving . . . is sanctified.** And the children are **holy.** This is not to indicate that the children or the spouse of a believer are automatically born into the family of God. The words "holy" and "unclean" in this text are equivalent to "sacred" and "profane." Again, the apostle's thought has Old Testament antecedents (cf. Hag 2:11-13). The unbeliever and the children are considered holy in a positional sense. Hence, the principle of the communication of uncleanness given in the Old Testament does not apply here (cf. also Rom 11:16). Together with the believer, they share in God's blessing, and are more likely to become converted by the presence and influence of the saved partner.

15. But if the unbelieving depart (Gr chōrizō, in the middle voice, almost a technical term for divorce, Moulton & Milligan, *The Vocabulary of the Greek New Testament,* pp. 695-696). In the foregoing instruction, the apostle presumes that the unbeliever is content to remain with the believer. But what of the situation where the unbeliever takes the initiative in dissolving the marriage? In such a case, Paul's advice is that the believer is **not under bondage.** There is no conflict here between Paul's advice and that of our Lord in Matthew 5:32. The point is that the divine standard cannot be imposed upon the unregenerate. There is nothing the believer can do but submit to the divorce. The overriding principle is that **God hath called us to peace.** The mild adversative clues us as to Paul's meaning in the use of this principle. He does not herein justify the divorce, even though the believing partner is free. Rather, there should be every effort on the part of the believer to avoid the separation if possible. This understanding fits well with the previous context, and also helps us understand the intent of the next verse.

16. For what knowest thou, O wife, whether thou shalt save thy husband? The reason why every means should be taken to induce the unbeliever to fulfill his marriage covenant is that the unbeliever might be saved. To give up too soon on an unsaved partner, may mean that they will never come to Christ.

3. Concerning the place of marriage. 7:17-24.

Marriage, like everything else, is determined by the selection of God (vss. 17-20), and directed to the service of God (vss. 21-24).

a. The selection of God. 7:17-20.

17-20. But as God has distributed to every man . . . so let him walk. The apostle now builds on the principle stated in verse 6, that is, "every man hath his proper gift of God, one after this manner, and another after that.'' There is no special reason why a believer should change his occupation or position in life subsequent to being saved. When applied to marriage, this simply means that there is no reason why a believer should put away his unbelieving spouse. Paul illustrates his point with the rite of circumcision. There is no need for a Gentile convert to be circumcised. On the other hand, there is no obligation incumbent upon a Jewish convert to be uncircumcised. In the New Testament, this rite had no direct reference on the life of faith (cf. Rom 2:25, 29; Gal 5:6). Therefore, even though it means living with an unbeliever, Paul is able to say, **Let every man abide in the same calling wherein he was called.**

b. The service for God. 7:21-24.

21-24. Here, the apostle employs another illustration to show that, properly understood, marriage should be viewed as directed to the service of God. **For he that is called in the Lord, being a servant, is the Lord's freeman; likewise also he that is called, being freed, is Christ's servant.** As to one's social status at salvation, it matters little whether he was a slave or free. In reality, he has been set free from the bond of sin to serve the living and true God. Thus, the horizontal relationships have little significance when compared to the vertical. Again, when applied to the question of marriage, there is no reason why the believer cannot remain faithful to his obligation to God, whether he be single, widowed, married in the Lord, or married to an unbeliever. The overriding principle is again repeated **Let every man, wherein he is called, therein abide with God.** The prescription for peace and holiness is to remain in communion with God.

4. Concerning the priorities of marriage. 7:25-40.

Here the problem centers around how to advise young people contemplating marriage, and how to instruct the parents of young people who are of marriageable age. Without being dogmatic, the apostle begins the subject by giving his personal judgment (vss. 25, 26). Then he reminds them of the prospect of tribulation (vss. 27, 28), the passing away of worldly fashions (vss. 29-31), and the problem of divided allegiance (vss. 32-35). Then he suggests to parents a pattern for advising virgin daughters (vss. 36-38). And finally (vss. 39, 40), Paul gives his personal preference.

a. The personal judgment of Paul. 7:25-26.

25-26. Now concerning (Gr *peri de*). Paul is now about to deal with another subject about which the Corinthians had written him (cf. 7:1). **I have no commandment of the Lord.** In our Lord's instruction regarding marriage and divorce recorded in the Gospels, there is no record of Him speaking directly to this issue. And so, the apostle says, **yet I give my judgment.** This again is not to say his advice is less inspired than something he may or may not quote from our Lord. Rather, Paul gives advice under the inspiration of the Holy Spirit in order to fulfill this obligation to the Lord **to be faithful.**

It is good for a man so to be. That is, it is good for a man to remain single. In Paul's judgment, celibacy is to be preferred. Why? His answer is **for the present distress.** This expression is probably best understood in light of I Corinthians 15:30-31; and II Corinthians 11:21-33. The Apostle Paul had already experienced intense persecution, and no doubt anticipated it would get worse. History records all too well that he was right.

b. The prospect of tribulation. 7:27-28.

27-28. Because of this prospect of tribulation, Paul's advice is **Art thou bound unto a wife? Seek not to be loosed. Art thou loosed from a wife?**

Seek not a wife. Although what Paul has said can never justify the dissolution of a marriage, hopefully it will discourage some from getting married. Notice that "bound" refers to marriage and "loosed" to divorce. This verse warns the divorced not to remarry, but also states that it is not a sin to do so. If married, Paul says, **thou hast not sinned.** There is nothing morally wrong with getting married. **Nevertheless, such shall have trouble in the flesh: but I spare you.** The term "trouble" (Gr *thlipsis*) indicates that Paul understands this trouble will not come from within, as though marriage would necessarily be accompanied by turmoil and distress; rather, this trouble would come from without. This fits well with his emphasis on the persecution and trouble confronting the church at that time.

c. The passing away of worldly fashions. 7:29-31.

29-31. The essence of all worldly relationships constitutes an additional reason why one should not marry. **Brethren, the time is short: it remaineth** (or, "brethren, the time henceforth is short"). Life, at best, is exceedingly brief. Furthermore, the relationships contracted during this life are only transient. Indeed, it will be all too soon for all of us that marrying and weeping and rejoicing and buying (and every other earthly activity) will be all over and it will be as though they never occurred. Paul is not asking his readers to give up anything of eternal value, only temporal things: **the fashion of this world** (which) **passeth away.**

d. The problem of divided allegiance. 7:32-35.

32-35. In the light of the above, Paul notes that a person who is married has a problem with divided allegiance. As for the men, the unmarried **careth for the things that belong to the Lord,** but the married man **careth for the things that are of the world.** It is

only natural for the married man to be concerned about the welfare of his wife and family. But as noted above, these are only of passing value. The same problem also exists for the woman. If the woman is a virgin, she is unencumbered by worldly necessities, and her only concern is **for the things of the Lord.** On the other hand, **she that is married careth for the things of the world, how she may please her husband.** One must take care not to misconstrue the force of Paul's argument here. It is not that he views the married life as less spiritual than the celibate life, but that the celibate life is less distracted by worldly cares. Hence, the single man or woman enjoying greater freedom, also enjoys greater potential in terms of service. And so Paul is able to say, **and this I speak for your own profit.** It is not that the apostle is trying to ensnare them, nor much less that he is trying to mislead them. Nor is he impugning a divine ordinance. Rather, he is concerned about the distress which will surely accompany them should they be married, and **that ye may attend upon the Lord without distraction.** The focal point of Paul's advice is the promotion of faithful, undistracted devotion to the Lord.

e. The pattern for advising virgin daughters. 7:36-38.

36-38. If what Paul says is correct, then how does a parent advise his single daughter? It will help in understanding this passage, to remember the control which the father had over the marriage of his daughter in ancient times. The apostle's advice is first to the man who thinks **he behaveth himself uncomely toward his virgin.** In other words, the father who thinks that he is being unreasonable. In this case, his daughter is past **the flower of her age.** This is a euphemism for "full sexual maturity." And **need so require.** There seems to be some reason why marriage is necessary. Perhaps the daughter's happiness is involved. Paul does not elaborate. His advice is **let him do what he will, he sinneth not; let them marry.** In other words, in spite of Paul's foregoing advice, he does not intend to discourage marriage, especially in situations where it becomes necessary for the happiness of the individuals involved. Then he deals with the situation where there is no **necessity,** and the father **hath so decreed in his heart that he will keep his virgin.** Again, there is no hard, fast rule. And so Paul is able to say to this man, he **doeth well.** But all things being equal, the one who **giveth her not in marriage doeth better.** While there is no sin in marriage and no superior virtue in celibacy, in light of the "present distress," Paul still maintains that the single life is better.

f. The preference of Paul. 7:39-40.

39-40. To summarize, marriage is for life, broken only by death. In that event, a woman **is at liberty to be married to whom she will; only in the Lord.** But in Paul's personal judgment, **she is happier if she so abide.** The expression **I think also that I have the Spirit of God,** has been taken to suggest that Paul did not know for sure if he were writing under inspiration. This is not the case at all. The verb "think" (Gr *dokeō*) does not suggest doubt in any way (cf. Gal 2:6; I Cor 12:22). The phrase is better translated, "and I consider also that I have the Spirit of God."

B. Doctrine of Christian Liberty. 8:1-11:1.

The next matter concerning which the Corinthian believers had solicited Paul's advice had to do with the question of meats sacrificed to idols. The question was a serious one for these believers. There were many pagan temple rituals, state occasions, and festivals of various kinds which obligated them to participate. Generally, a part of an animal was burned at the sacrifice, and the rest was prepared for the feast that followed. Sometimes portions were taken home and eaten there. Meat unused at such feasts also found its way into the market place and the butcher shops. It had been determined earlier at the council at Jerusalem that the Gentile converts should "abstain from meat offered to idols" (cf. Acts 15:29). Although the apostle does not allude to this decision in this text, it is very likely that this constituted a legal precedence for the Jewish converts in the assembly. Paul's approach is to state the principle of liberty (8:1-13), then to cite himself as a picture of Christian liberty (9:1-27), and finally, to demonstrate to the Corinthians how they should put into practice their Christian liberty (10:1-11:1).

1. The principle of liberty. 8:1-13.

8:1. We know that we all have knowledge. To paraphrase this: "we both know that you consider yourself to be thoroughly informed about this matter." Apparently in their question to Paul, they inferred that they felt adequate to deal with the problem. Perhaps some in the assembly were disputing their approach. One should recall that it was this arrogance in regard to their knowledge that constituted one of their major problems. But knowledge alone will not suffice when dealing with Christian liberty. Paul is about to introduce a much higher principle. **Knowledge puffeth up, but charity edifieth.** Mere theoretical or speculative knowledge acquired in a vacuum has the effect of inflating a person and rendering him vain and conceited. On the other hand, love (Gr *agapē*) edifies. That is, it does not terminate upon itself as knowledge does, but goes beyond to seek the well-being and benevolence of others. And it is this incomparably higher principle which the apostle applies to this case.

2. If any man think that he knoweth any thing. If knowledge is simply a cognitive process, then Paul says, **he knoweth nothing yet as he ought to**

know. If, in a person's life, he simply acquires knowledge components, he is a seriously defective person.

3. In true knowledge, the intellect and the emotions go hand in hand. **If any man love God, the same is known of him.** The true knowledge of God does not come about through the acquisition of cognitive data concerning Him. It comes through loving Him.

4-8. As concerning therefore. Paul returns now to the main subject, which is **eating of those things which are offered in sacrifice unto idols.** The first thing Paul establishes is that **an idol is nothing.** Any thinking person knows that since there is **none other God but one,** if a person offers a sacrifice to an idol, he is, in fact, sacrificing to a nonentity. For, while we know that in the pagan world there are those **that are called gods,** we who are Christians know **there is but one God, the Father . . . and one Lord Jesus Christ.** And, of course, all things owe their existence to Him. **Howbeit there is not in every man that knowledge.** As irrational as it may seem, there are some who are still under the apprehension that heathen gods are real beings. For such a person to eat meat sacrificed to idols, **their conscience being weak is defiled.**

9-10. Since we know that our relationship with God is not necessarily affected by whether or not we eat meat, then, it ought not to be offensive to the stronger Christian to limit himself for the sake of the weaker. Here is where the principle of love is most conspicuously applied. **Take heed lest by any means this liberty of yours becomes a stumbling block to them that are weak.** The term "liberty" (Gr *exousia*) may be translated, "authority"or "lawful right." The availability of an option does not necessitate its exercise, especially when love and concern for someone else becomes a factor. The most serious danger to an unbridled latitudinarian approach to Christian liberty is the possibility of causing sin in the weaker brother. **For if any man**

see thee which hast knowledge sit at meat in the idol's temple. If the stronger brother publicly exercises his right to eat meat sacrificed to idols, he, in effect, encourages **him which is weak . . . to eat those things which are offered.** But the problem in the latter case is that he has violated his conscience, and has sinned. The expression **be emboldened** is literally, "be edified."The sense is ironic; edification should build up to righteousness. Here, one is edified or built up to sin.

11-12. And through thy knowledge shall the weak brother perish (literally, "for because of your knowledge, the weak one is destroyed"). Is Paul implying that this weak brother could lose his salvation? No. This is tantamount to what he says in Romans 14:23, "he that doubteth is damned if he eat." In other words, he is to be brought under the sure judgment of God for his sin. In the most extreme application of this principle, it would involve sinning unto death (cf. I Cor 5:5; 11:30; I Jn 5:16-17). **For whom Christ died?** The force of this expression here is practical, not soteriological. It is true that Christ died to secure this man's salvation, but speaking more to the point, He did so to put away his sin. Hence, if you, being a "stronger brother" should entice another brother to sin, then in effect, **Ye sin against Christ.** This truth is derived from two facts. First, and most immediate, the stronger brother has enticed a weaker brother to sin against the Saviour who died for him. Secondly, Jesus said in Matthew 25:40, "inasmuch as ye have done it unto one of the least of these my brethren, ye have done it unto me."

13. Wherefore directs us to the conclusion of the matter. It is not knowledge which forms the basis of the conclusion, but love. Hence, Paul says, **I will eat no flesh while the world standeth.** The latter half of this phrase is intended for emphasis. The apostle does not qualify this. He does not say he will refrain in public and exercise his liberty in private. In order to avoid offending a brother, he would permanently exclude the eating of meat from his diet. An additional comment that needs to be made on this subject has been very succinctly stated by S. L. Johnson. "In the first place the passage does not refer to legalists desirous of imposing their narrow-minded scruples on others. Such are not weak brethren, but willful brethren desirous of glorying in the subjection of others to their tenets (cf. Gal 6:11-13). This is tyranny, and Christianity must always be on guard against this. In the second place, it should be noted in this verse that the decision to follow the path of love rests with Paul, not with the weak. The strong are to yield to love's appeal voluntarily, not because the weak demand it, legalists always demand subjection to their laws." (*Wycliffe Bible Commentary*, p. 1242).

2. The picture of liberty. 9:1-27.

Having established the principle of Christian liberty, Paul is concerned that his readers understand that this principle does not just apply to meat sacrificed to idols. Rather, it cuts across every aspect of the Christian's life. The apostle appeals to his own experience to show how multi-faceted the problem is. He does this by defending his right to exercise Christian liberty (vss. 1-14), then by citing his own deportment in the exercise of his ministry (vss. 15-22), and finally by expressing his desire to run the race well, to keep his eyes on target, and to win the prize (vss. 23-27).

9:1-2. The seal of Paul's authority is the very existence of the Corinthian church. Whenever he speaks, he can do so with authority because of his relationship to the Corinthian assembly. **Am I not an apostle? Am I not free?** (In the original, these questions appear in reverse order.) The first question has to do with his freedom and liberty in Christ. He says, in effect, "am I not just as free as any other believer to re-gulate my conduct according to my own convictions? Yet more, I am an apostle as well." **Have I not seen Jesus Christ our Lord?** This follows to substantiate his claim to apostleship (cf. Acts 1:21-22; 9:3-9, 17). **Are not ye my work in the Lord?** Again if Paul is an apostle, then one would expect to see evidence of his ministry. The Corinthian assembly itself was that evidence. Hence, whether anyone else considered Paul an apostle, there was certainly no ground for doubt among the Corinthians. Conversion of men is a divine work performed through the agency of God's ministers. The fact that people were saved at Corinth and formed an assembly of believers, validates Paul's commission.

3-5. Mine answer to them that do examine me is this. As for those who are questioning Paul's authority, he answers, **Have we not the power to eat and drink?** "Power" here has the force of "right," or "authority" (and so throughout this context). **To lead about a sister,** that is, a sister in Christ; **a wife,** in other words. Paul had the authority to take a wife, and bring her on his journeys with him as **other apostles.** The inclusion of **the brethren of the Lord, and Cephas** shows the fallacy of those who promote celibacy among the clergy by citing the example of the apostles (cf. Mt 8:14).

6. Or I only and Barnabas, have we not power to forbear working? To paraphrase, "are Barnabas and I the only exceptions to the rule that ministers should be supported by their respective churches?" At the beginning of his ministry in Corinth, the apostle supported himself. Then, when financial aid did come, it did not come from the Corinthian assembly. This issue was no doubt an embarrassment to the Corinthians, and appears to have been an annoyance to the apostle.

7. That Paul has the right to expect remuneration for his labors is supported by natural law. Whoever heard of a soldier who went to war at **any time at**

his own charges? The same is true of the owner of a vineyard, or a flock of sheep. They have the right to expect to be supported by the vocation to which they devote themselves.

8-9. What Paul says is further supported by the Mosaic law. **Say I these things as a man? Or saith not the law the same also?** Is simply a secular principle, or can we expect to find biblical precedence? **For** introduces Paul's quotation of Deuteronomy 25:4. **Thou shalt not muzzle the mouth of the ox that treadeth out the corn.** Even the ox has the right to expect to be fed for his labors. **Doth God take care for oxen?** This question is not to be understood as irony, nor as a contemptuous question. Rather, the implied answer to the question is "yes." God cares for His entire creation (cf. Job 38:41; Ps 147:9; Mt 6:26; Lk 12:24).

10. For our sakes, no doubt, this is written. Certainly if this principle should apply to the brute beast, much more should it apply to mankind in general. **That he that ploweth should plow in hope; and that he that thresheth in hope should be partaker of his hope.** That is, of being rewarded. It is only natural and right, but more than that, it is scriptural that one should expect profit from his labors.

11-12. Spiritual things . . . we shall reap your carnal things. The contrast here is not of a moral sense, but a qualitative sense. Paul, as their minister and teacher, imparted to them spiritual things. Was it any great thing if he should expect remuneration to sustain the body? The former connoted things of infinite value, the latter, only of temporal value. Paul is not through with this argument yet, but he pauses here to interject a reminder, **Nevertheless we have not used this power.** In order not to **hinder the gospel of Christ,** the Apostle Paul continues to **suffer all things.** Paul is not justifying something he did, but only something that he has the right to do. A right

which he did not exercise. He continues.

13. Not only is Paul's position supported by natural law, and by scripture, but it is also supported by the temple law. **They which wait at the altar are partakers with the altar.** The point here is that with every sacrifice made at the altar, the priest would receive a protion. This was an institution ordained by God Himself in the Old Testament.

14. Even so, Paul concludes, **hath the Lord ordained that they which preach the gospel should live of the gospel.** The ministers of the gospel in the New Testament have no less holy a vocation than the priests of the Old Testament. So Paul establishes beyond question that he has the authority to receive financial support from the Corinthian assembly. But the bottom line of this entire discussion is not given until the next verse.

15. But I have used none of these things. "I never exercised that right." And the apostle is quick to add that he is not mentioning these things now in order to receive a remuneration belatedly. He would rather die **than that any man should make my glorying void,** or "that any man should pay me now for my labors in Corinth." The reason for this is simply because this policy of self-denial enabled the apostle to face his enemies squarely. He could never be accused of self-interest, nor could his integrity ever be questioned.

16. For though I preach the gospel, I have nothing to glory of. Paul is ironically answering now the questions he asked to begin with. "Am I not free, am I not an apostle?" The implied answer to the first is "no"; as for the second, "yes, but that is no cause for glorying." **For necessity is laid upon me; yea, woe is unto me, if I preach not the gospel!**

17. As proof of the fact that Paul had no grounds for boasting, he adds, **For if I do this thing willingly, I have a reward.** If it was optional for him to preach the gospel, then he would deserve remuneration. **But if against my will, a dispensation of the gospel is committed unto me.** By this, the apostle is not implying that he was an unwilling servant of the Lord (cf. Rom 1:5; 11:13; 15:15-16; I Cor 15:9; Gal 1:15-16; Eph 3:8). He is simply drawing a distinction between what was optional for him, and what was obligatory upon him. Paul was given a stewardship to preach. That was enough (cf. 4:1-2; Lk 17:10). A steward received no pay. He was merely a slave doing his assigned task faithfully.

18. What is my reward then? The answer to this question is twofold. **That . . . I may make the gospel of Christ without charge.** And secondly, **that I abuse not my power in the gospel.** The former discharges his obligation to God. The latter, discharges his obligation to man. In the context, it is important to note that Paul is not laying this down as a general principle for all ministers of the gospel to follow. The point is that it was a voluntary necessity. He had the authority to do many things, yet, he did not **abuse** (Gr *katachraomai*, "use to the full") that authority. The historical, social, and cultural context were the criteria by which Paul made this determination, as it is shown by what follows.

19. I be free from all men. When understood in the context of his Christian liberty, Paul was indeed free. But when understood in the light of his Christian responsibility, **yet have I made myself servant unto all.** With all the freedom in the world open to him, why did the apostle restrict himself so severely? The answer is **that I might gain the more.** His foremost interest was to preach the gospel and win men to Jesus Christ. Whatever it took in terms of personal freedom, he was prepared to pay the price. It is only fair to point out here that the apostle is not teaching that the end justifies the means. Or that compromise is in order. Certainly if there was anyone who was

prepared to stand rigidly upon matters of principle, it was the Apostle Paul (cf. Gal 2:5). But as for matters of indifference, they are luxuries, and therefore, dispensable.

20-22. Unto the Jews I became as a Jew. How far Paul was willing to go in this regard is recorded in Acts 21:18-27. Again, he did not accommodate himself to sin, or to error, but to social custom. Likewise, **To them that are without law, as without law.** He goes on to explain that he does not intend to say that he was antinomian. He was certainly **under the law of Christ.** What he has in mind are the Gentiles. And the extent to which he is willing to go to win the Gentiles is clearly reflected in this entire chapter. He summarizes his guiding principle in the words, **I am made all things to all men, that I might by all means save some.** "I am willing to concede Christian liberties at all points if in the process, the gospel is preached, and the lost are won to Christ." This implies a willingness to do more, not less than the law required. It certainly does not condone sinful activity and compromise in order to "win" some.

Paul's paramount interest is expressed in the closing verses of this chapter.

23. And this I do (better manuscripts have "I do all things"), viz. all the things mentioned above, I do **for the gospel's sake.** His ulimate criteria is not the prejudices of men, but the gospel. Notice, this is so much more than simply preaching the gospel. It is living the gospel.

24. Paul draws upon a very familiar scene to his Corinthian readers in order to drive home his point. The Isthmian games were an athletic event known to all of his readers and held on alternate summers within the vicinity of Corinth. It was an event not to be missed by anyone of importance in all parts of Greece. As a national institution, it was as familiar to his readers as football is in Texas. And so he says, **Know ye not.** He takes for granted that his readers understand the rules of the game. The most important rule is that while all participants run, only **one receiveth the prize.** And this is Paul's desire for his readers. **So run, that ye may obtain.** There was no legal compulsion which demanded that the runners strive to attain the crown. Why then, do they run? They run because they're athletes. And that is what they are there for. To achieve their final objective, it took great sacrifice on the part of all.

25. And every man that striveth for the mastery is temperate in all things. During the long days of preparation, the athlete is free to do as he pleases. He still has personal liberty. But if his intent is to win the crown, he restricts himself in all things: his diet, his activities, his associations, and probably even his friendships. He "laid aside every weight." And all for temporal glory. **But,** counters the apostle, the crown for which we strive is **incorruptible.** If temperance and self-discipline are so important in the temporal realm, much more in the spiritual.

26. I therefore so run. That is, like the athletes in verse 25. **Not as uncertainly** (this term, Gr *adēlōs*, appears only here in the New Testament). Paul does not run as one who has no specific objective. **So fight I.** Paul changes his metaphor to that of the boxer. **Not as one that beateth the air.** Paul does not swing wildly without hitting his target, but to reach his level of proficiency in the gospel ministry.

27. I keep under my body, and bring it into subjection. The expression, "I keep under" (Gr. *hypōpiazō*), loses much of the original sense. It has the idea of "to give one a black eye," "buffet," or "bruise." Paul's Corinthian readers knew that in the Isthmian games, the boxers wore gloves consisting of ox-hide bands covered with knots and nails and loaded with lead and iron. To prepare for such an event, a man would have to steel himself against all forms of physical abuse. **Lest . . . when I have preached to others, I myself should be a castaway.** It is unlikely in these words that the apostle intends to associate himself with the herald at the Grecian games whose task was to proclaim the rules, and to summon the competitors to their places. It is more likely that he drops the metaphor now, and applies it to the main subject at hand. The reason he, in effect, restrains himself so, sacrificing even his essential Christian liberties, is that he might never reach the point where he is no longer qualified to run the race. Again, this expression must not be construed to suggest that Paul was afraid of losing his salvation. His subject is still Christian liberty, and his point is that sometimes the mature Christian will have to restrict himself in order to accomplish the ultimate task.

3. The practice of liberty. 10:1-11:1.

Paul concludes his discussion of Christian liberty with an admonition to beware of temptation and unbelief (vss. 1-13), to be conscious of the association of tables with demons and idolatry (vss. 14-22), and to be guided by the principles of thankfulness and expediency (vss. 23-11:1).

In his opening section, Paul begins by illustrating his point (vss. 1-5), and then by applying it (vss. 6-13).

10:1. Moreover (Gr *gar,* "for"). He concludes chapter 9 with a discussion of the need for self-discipline. A classic case of what happens when self-control is absent is seen in the experience of Israel in the wilderness. The immediate connection is with the word, "castaway." Israel refused to deny self, and demanded the fleshpots of Egypt, and so became a castaway in the desert. **I would not that ye should be ignorant.** Here is one of Paul's favorite expressions introducing a matter of great importance (cf. Rom 1:13; 11:25). **How that all.** The five "alls" in verses 1-4 emphasize the five downward moral steps of verses 5-10. The very same people who enjoyed great privilege from God, also fell into serious apostasy from God. This also ties with 9:24, "all the runners run." Historically, in the case of Israel, all ran, but only Caleb and Joshua received the prize. The five privileges are enumerated as follows. **Under the cloud.** This speaks of divine guidance and protection (cf. Num 9:15, 23; 14:15; Deut 1:33; Ps 78:14; Mt 28:20). **Passed through the sea.** This has reference to divine deliverence (cf. Ex 14:15-22; I Pet 1:18-20).

2. All baptized unto Moses. This has neither a sacerdotal nor a soteriological import. Rather, it is a non-technical use of the term "baptism." The people were immersed in Moses' authority. Thus, the expression speaks of divine leadership (cf. Ex 14:31). Therefore, they came under the influence of his authority. The reference is not to water baptism.

3-4. Their fourth privilege was that they all ate of **the same spiritual meat.** The reference here is obviously to manna, spoken of in Psalm 78:25 as "angels' food." This speaks of divine provision. By employing the term "spiritual," Paul does not intend to imply that the manna was not literal food. It was clearly designed for ordinary nourishment (cf. Neh 9:15; Jn 6:49). It was spiritual in the sense that it was supernaturally provided by the Spirit of God. Likewise, **And did all drink the same spiritual drink.** The water that was received from the rock was real water. It was spiritual in the sense that it was given through the divine intervention of God. They drank of the spiritual rock that followed them, and **that Rock was Christ.** Here, Paul does not intend to advance an old Jewish fable that the rock that Moses smote actually was not part of the mountain, but rolled after them during their journeys. The rock was not a theophany. Rather, it was a "type" of Christ. It prefigured the character and provision that Christ would ultimately make for His people. But also, it is intended to mean that the ultimate supply was

Christ and not the rock. This spiritual Rock, even Christ, remained with them and followed them.

This passage is an impressive affirmation of the pre-existence of Jesus Christ (cf. also vs. 9; Jn 8:58; 12:41; Heb 11:25; and Jude 5). In the light of what follows, it is most probable that the expression, "spiritual meat" and "spiritual drink" are intended to be parallel with the elements employed in the Lord's Supper.

5. But. In spite of their great privilege, **God was not well pleased.** Divine privilege does not guarantee divine success. The evidence of this is that **they were overthrown in the wilderness** (literally, "their bodies were strewn about the wilderness"). Paul draws a pathetic picture of people, sated with providential privilege, paving the wilderness trail with their dead bodies (cf. Num 14:29).

The five successive backward steps are now enumerated.

6. Now introduces Paul's application of the preceding to the experience of his readers. **Examples** (Gr *typos,* "type or example"). The AV rendering here is no doubt correct. Unless we are careful, the history of Israel will be duplicated in our own experience. The first step was that they lusted **after evil things.** Not satisfied with the manna supplied by the Lord, the people lusted after the fleshpots of Egypt. Because of their inordinate desire, while the meat was yet in their mouths, God struck them with a plague (cf. Num 11:4-34). The specific application to the Corinthians' situation is hard to miss. The pot roasts of Egypt were no more unclean than the prime ribs of Corinth. But what a terrible consequence that they should become an obstacle between God and His people.

7. Neither be ye idolators, as were some of them. The second step down is to substitute a graven image for the Holy God. The allusion is to Exodus 32. What is significant here is that the Israelites considered that their golden calf was made in honor of Jehovah. Likewise, for Paul's readers, the inordinate exercise of Christian liberty was considered a celebration of their freedom in Christ. The evidence of idolatry was seen in that **The people sat down to eat and drink, and rose up to play.** Sensual amusement was always associated in the pagan world with their feasts and idolatrous practices.

8. The third step is **commit fornication.** Spiritual defection always leads to moral defection. If this was symptomatic of the spiritual decay in Israel, how much more in Corinth (cf. 5:1-5). Allowing immorality to persist in their assembly, they were no different from their neighbors who worshipped at the temple of Venus. Again, the same truth holds today. When men, even Christians, substitute anything for the God of the Bible, the results are the same. **In one day three and twenty thousand** is not a mistake. In Numbers 25:9, the total people who died is given as twenty-four thousand. The discrepancy may be accounted for in at least two ways. The actual figure may be midway between twenty-three and twenty-four thousand, and hence, in each case the figure is rounded off. Furthermore, it will be noted that Paul refers to the number slain in one day. Numbers refers to the total number that died. In any case, the precise number is only given in approximate terms.

9. The fourth step is to **tempt Christ** (cf. Num 21:4-9; Ps 78:19). This, in effect, reflects skepticism over whether or not God will discipline them for their sins. The exhortation is that one should not provoke the forbearance of God. If it comes as especially obnoxious that some of the Corinthians had to give up some of their better cuts of meat for the cause of the gospel of Christ, let them remember from whence they were delivered. To become overly concerned about temporal desires is to forget the great spiritual privilege they enjoy. Anyone who doubts that God can and will exercise

His option to punish sin should remember Israel and the fiery serpents.

10. The fifth step down is **murmur.** This implies a total rejection of divine leadership. The reference is to Numbers 16:41-50. But the spirit which prompted that situation is expressed in Numbers 14:4. The results are that they **were destroyed.** The parallel situation and obvious admonition is seen in the Corinthians' attitude toward their leadership (viz. Paul). Nothing provokes the anger of God more than to chafe under the yoke that we share with Christ (cf. Mt 11:29-30; I Cor 3:9).

11. Paul summarizes with both an admonition and an encouragement. **Now all these things happened . . . for examples** (literally, "now these things happened to them typically"). The expression emphasizes God's providential control over all the affairs of men (cf. Gen 50:20; Prov 21:1). Even though the Israelites rebelled against God and received subsequent judgment because of it, God intended to use their experience for His own good. **And they are written for our admonition.** The reason God had Moses to record the experiences of the children of Israel was because he had Paul and his Corinthian believers in mind. He knew that the Corinthians were going to face a similar crisis situation. When that time came, the example of the children of Israel would provide the deterrent to guide them from sin, and to lead them to spiritual victory. **Ends of the world.** That is, "for us who are living in the end times." Paul considered the second coming of Christ to be imminent. Thus, as far as he knew, he and his generation constituted the end times.

12. **Him that thinketh he standeth.** The one who thinks himself to be the strong Christian, who can exercise his Christian liberty at the expense of the weaker brethren, **take heed lest he fall.** Not from salvation, nor yet from his position of strength to that of weakness, but that he should suffer the

judgment of God, as the Israelites, and "fall in the wilderness."

13. Temptation. Paul is about to show that trials and temptations will be proportional to our strength. **Common to man** (Gr *anthrōpinos*). This term occurs mostly in this epistle. The trials you face are only normal problems (cf. also Rom 4:19; Jas 3:7; I Pet 2:13; I Cor 2:4, 13; and I Cor 4:3). **But.** A mild adversative. In the context of those temptations **God is faithful.** What great comfort Paul provides for his readers. Though men and the world about be false, God is true, God is faithful, and our strength and security are in Him. **Above that ye are able.** God knows our frame, and He knows exactly what we can take. Sometimes when the exigencies of life seem to overwhelm us, we think we can take no more. But take heart. If God did not know that you could take it, He would not have allowed you to suffer it. **Make a way to escape.** In early Greek usage, this term (Gr *ekbasis*) had the sense of a landing place. It was a nautical term. The idea is not that He will enable us to escape temptation, but that He will enable us to land safely on the other side victoriously. **To bear.** Often the only escape is to endure (cf. Jas 1:12).

Having shown the seriousness of abusing one's Christian liberty, the apostle now goes on to inform his readers that there is a direct relationship between heathen feasts and demonic activity.

14. Wherefore (Gr *dioper*, a strengthened form of *dio*, literally "for which very reason"). This term appears only here and I Corinthians 8:13 (14:13 in some MSS). In light of God's judgment upon Israel, **flee idolatry.** These words have a triple significance. They contain a concern because they are addressed to people whom Paul loved. They express a command, they are given in the imperative mode. And they express a consequence. Because of the expression of their Christian liberty, the Corinthians

are edging dangerously close to idolatry.

15. Wise men. This is not irony. Not wishing to be authoritarian or dogmatic on this issue, he appeals to their sense of wisdom. **Judge ye what I say.** "Consider for a moment the logic of my argument."

16-17. The cup . . . communion of the blood of Christ? The bread . . . communion of the body of Christ? Consider the Lord's table. When a believer participates, he partakes of Christ's blood and His body. This means to share and to participate in the benefits of Christ's saving work on Calvary. This being the case, all those who come to the Lord's Supper enter into communion with one another. They form one body in virtue of their joint participation of Christ. **For we being many are one bread, and one body: for we are all partakers of that one bread.**

18. This argument is further substantiated by the example of the altar of Israel. **Are not they which eat of the sacrifices partakers of the altar?** When a sacrifice was brought to the altar, it was not entirely consumed. Rather, the residue was divided between the priest and the offerer (cf. Lev 7:15; 8:31; Deut 12:18). Thus, it became an act of mutual sharing and worshipping of God. It is for this reason that non-Jews were forbidden to attend the sacrificial feasts of the Jews since it involved mutual sharing and joint worship of Jehovah. This passage must not be construed to indicate that the Lord's Supper is a sacrifice. The point of correspondence was not sacrifice, but communion.

19. What say I then? That the idol is any thing? The writer anticipates the obvious question. "But, Paul, you just said an idol was, in reality, nothing. Therefore, to worship an idol is to worship nothing. If one participate in fellowship with an idol, he would, in fact, participate in nothing."

20. It is very true, the idol is nothing. But the ones behind the idol are very real. **The things which the Gentiles sacrifice, they sacrifice to devils** (literally, "demons") **and not to God.** What is of grave concern to the apostle is that behind the idols are fallen angels; evil spirits. This is in keeping with Deuteronomy 32:17 and Psalm 106:37. Since Paul has already established that these religious feasts involved fellowship with the altar, should they attend a heathen feast, they will be having **fellowship with devils** ("demons"). And this was the last thing Paul hoped for his young converts at Corinth.

21. Ye cannot drink the cup of the Lord, and the cup of devils. It is not possible to be simultaneously related to the Lord and to demons. Paul does not merely indicate that this is an inconsistency, but an impossibility. We cannot expect that the Lord will allow this to continue. The consequences of such behavior have already been amply illustrated in the case of Israel. Thus, it is not necessary at this point for the apostle to do more than ask the simple question.

22. Do we provoke the Lord to jealousy? Unless they intend to provoke the greatest displeasure from the Lord, the Corinthians must be careful not to attend the heathen feasts.

So Paul has answered two questions. Question one, what about exercising my right to eat meat sacrificed to idols? Question two, what about my attendance at heathen feasts? The remaining question is, what about meat purchased in the market place? In answer, he returns to the original issue of Christian liberty, and the principles which govern it.

23. First, there is the principle of expedience. **All things are lawful for me, but all things are not expedient.** Two observations must be made on this point. When Paul says, "all things," he is speaking in an obviously restricted sense (cf. 6:12). He intends to mean all matters of indifference. The second observation has to do with

the significance of his advice. While on such matters all options are open to the believer, there is only one choice that is best. And there are some choices that will be of no help at all. Then, there is the principle of edification. **All things are lawful . . . but all things edify not.** Here he enlarges on his original statement of this principle in 6:12. If what I do subjects me rather than serves me, I must avoid it.

24. Wealth (better translated "welfare"). The principle of edification will place the concerns and needs of others first.

25-28. Then there is the principle of conscience. **The shambles** (Gr *makellō,* a Latin term used only here in the New Testament, refers to the "market"). In the sacrifices, usually only a part of the victim was consumed. The rest was given to the priest or sold again in the market. Anyone might therefore unknowingly purchase meat offered to idols. Concerning such purchases, Paul's advice is **Whatsoever is sold . . . that eat, asking no question for conscience sake.** Your conscience need not be activated on this issue. Going back to the original discussion, the idol is nothing; therefore, it can have no intrinsic effect upon the meat. While it is wrong to go to the heathen feast and to participate with demons in idolatrous worship, once the meat has been disassociated from that gathering, there is no reason why it cannot be eaten without scruple. Likewise, if you have been invited to a feast at the home of an unbeliever, and it is your desire to go, **whatsoever is set before you, eat, asking no questions for conscience sake.** On the other hand, if another brother in Christ (apparently a weaker brother) should turn to you and say **this is offered in sacrifice unto idols,** then the stronger brother is to **eat not for his sake that showed it.** The principle here is to bow to the weaker conscience.

29-30. Then there is the principle of thanksgiving. The question naturally arises, **why is my liberty judged of another man's conscience?** This is a legitimate question. The answer is: **I by grace be a partaker.** The word "grace" here (Gr *charis*) is used in the sense of thanksgiving. We use it today when we speak of "saying grace" before a meal. It is illogical to give thanks to God for something that will cause me to be **evil spoken of.** Whence the admonition in verse 31. **Whatsoever ye do, do all to the glory of God.** I fail in the proper exercise of my Christian liberty, if in the process I do not bring glory to God (see also I Pet 4:11; and Col 3:17).

32-33. Then there is the principle of evangelism. Care must be taken to **give none offense,** whether to **Jews . . . Gentiles** (or) **the church of God.** Thus, whatever we do in our public ministries or our personal lives should not deliberately bring offense to the church. **That they may be saved.** "Why should I go about offending people in the name of Christian liberty, and unnecessarily causing them to repudiate the gospel?" (cf. also 9:22).

11:1. The bottom line on the discussion of Christian liberty is the example of Christ as He is reflected in the Apostle Paul. The ultimate standard is Christ, and insofar as Paul is following Him, he is able to say to the Corinthian believers, **Be ye followers of me.**

To summarize then, in this section on Christian liberty, Paul is anxious to lead his assembly to maturity under grace. The Christian life is not governed by legalism. Yet on the other hand, this does not justify license. The best example of how it works is Jesus Christ. In Him we see ultimate sacrifice and supernatural love. And by these standards, every act is to be judged.

C. Doctrine of Worship. 11:2-34.

In this chapter, Paul is concerned with two vital matters. First, the order of authority (vss. 2-16), then the ordinance of communion (vss. 17-34). Since Paul does not begin with his characteristic expression, "now concerning" (Gr *peri de*), it is possible that this chapter falls into the category of unsolicited advice. Perhaps in their letter to Paul there was allusion to some of their public worship practices. Or perhaps his discussion of worship practices in the previous chapter prompted him to speak directly to this issue.

1. The order of authority. 11:2-16.

Paul develops this subject in two ways. First, he states the principle of headship (vss. 2-6). Then he defends this principle from scripture and nature (vss. 7-16).

2. Now indicates the transition to a new subject. **I praise you, brethren.** It is always a good practice to compliment someone before you rebuke him. **That ye . . . keep the ordinances, as I delivered them to you.** There is a play on the two words "ordinances" and "delivered." Both are derived from the Greek term *paradidōmi,* meaning "to give over." It is best rendered "oral teaching," or "tradition." Paul will have more to say about this in verses 17-34.

3. But is adversative. **I would have you know** is probably not intended as ironic, but it is difficult not to miss the irony of the situation. The Corinthians prided themselves in their knowledge, yet it is their knowledge that the apostle repeatedly finds deficient. **That** indicates purport. **The head of every man is Christ.** This is established by the fact that Christ is the head of the body, which is the church (Col 1:18; Eph 1:22-23). Whether "man" is taken generically (mankind), or "man" as opposed to "woman," the truth still stands. However, the latter sense seems to be dictated by the context. **The head of the woman is the man.** This constitutes the fundamental order in the race in the same sense that **the head of Christ is God.** It is important here to note that the concept of headship does not connote qualitative or essential difference. It connotes a functional subordination. The prototype is seen in the persons of the Trinity. The Father and Christ are co-equal, yet the Son is answerable to the Father (cf. Jn 6:38-40; 10:29-30; 14:9; I Cor 15:28; and Phil 2:6). It is unfortunate that Paul has been so misunderstood on this point. He is not a male chauvinist. On the contrary, he argues here for the equality of the sexes. Any other sense leads to Seballianism, which is heresy.

4. Since this constitutes the order of authority, it is inappropriate for a man to participate in public worship of God with something on his head. The covering would seem to indicate another authority coming between the man and Christ.

5. On the other hand, when a woman **prayeth or prophesieth with her head uncovered,** this is equally wrong. It is wrong for the same reason the opposite is wrong for the man. The covering is symbolic, indicating the authority that exists above the woman, yet still under Christ. A further teaching of this verse is that women did prophesy and pray in public worship. This, no doubt, involved edifying, exhorting, and comforting. And apparently this did not constitute a point of contention, since the apostle does not feel obligated to speak directly to it. Yet this is not a contradiction with I Corinthians 14:34-37. Here the context has reference to orderly participation. Chapter 14 refers to disorderly participation.

6. For if the woman be not covered, let her also be shorn: but if it be a shame for a woman to be shorn . . . let her be covered. In Corinth, it was not uncommon for prostitutes to shave their heads and don blonde wigs, thus signifying their availability to the men in the streets. This is not a point of indifference to the apostle. It is a serious matter. An unsubmissive woman standing before the congregation is tantamount to going out in public improperly attired (e.g. with her head shaven). But the force of Paul's words

here is poignant. Just as no respectable Christian woman would go out in public dressed as a prostitute, it is equally important that she not participate in public worship without proper dress.

Having established the principle of headship, Paul goes on to validate his position from Scripture (vss. 7-12) and from nature (vss. 13-16).

7. The image and glory of God. It must not be inferred from this that only the man is in the image of God. In Genesis 1:26-27 it is said that God created man in His own image, "male and female created he them." But, Paul uses the term "image" in a restrictive sense. The only sense in which the man is uniquely in the image of God is that to him was given dominion over the earth. This was done before the creation of the woman. Thus, in the same sense, **the woman is the glory of the man.** That is, whatever dominion and authority she has is delegated.

8-9. The order of creation also supports Paul's position. **Neither was the man created for the woman; but the woman for the man.** Chronologically, she came *after.* Constitutionally, she was made *for* the man (cf. Gen 2:21-25).

10. Power signifies here the symbol of authority **on her head.** A further reason is **because of the angels.** The reference is to the holy angels who elsewhere are spoken of as "worshipping spirits" (cf. Heb 1:4). The keynote of Paul's thought is submission to the divine order of things. Women should demonstrate the same sense of submission to God in recognizing their true position, and fulfilling its claims, as do the angels who know nothing of insubordination among their ranks. Since the angels have their very existence in the presence of God, they are also present whenever the congregation meets together to worship the Lord (cf. I Cor 4:9; Eph 3:10; I Tim 5:21).

11. Lest his readers understand this distinction in a qualitative sense, Paul hastens to add, **neither is the man with-**

out the woman, neither the woman without the man, in the Lord. Both are mutually dependent upon each other. The expression "in the Lord" has the sense of "according to the will and purpose of the Lord." Neither can exist without the other.

12. Even so is the man also by the woman. Just as the principle of submission is supported by the order of creation, the principle of mutual dependency is supported by the order of procreation. In Genesis 2, the woman came out of the man. In Genesis 4:1, the man came out of the woman. So have all men since. In the final analysis, **all things** (are) **of God.**

13-15. Nature itself ("the recognized constitution of things"). **If a man have long hair, it is a shame.** This is a difficult passage, especially in a culture where nature does not seem to be dictating it. It cannot mean that nature naturally grows short hair on men and long hair on women, since biologically we know this is not the case. Several factors must be considered. First, the context: Paul is talking about differentiating between the sexes. **Have long hair** (Gr *komaō*) means to wear long hair like that of a woman. It cannot be said that he has in mind a specific kind of haircut. He is simply saying that it is shameful for a man to wear his hair in an effeminate way. Another factor has to do with culture. In Paul's experience, he knew of no culture, whether Hebrew, Greek, or Roman, that did not consider long hair a disgrace to a man. The only exception to this rule was the Nazarite (Num 6:5; and Ezek 44:20). Thus, to Paul it was significant that just naturally, worldwide cultures emerged with the same sense of propriety regarding long hair on men. The same principle holds true today. The vast majority of cultures regard effeminacy of hair and dress as distasteful and shameful to a man. **But if a woman have long hair, it is a glory to her.** The logic is obvious. In the natural order of things, it only seems

appropriate to cover a woman's head and here her ultimate covering is her hair. The scripture does not dictate "spirituality" by the length of one's hair. The real issue here is submission to divine authority. Therefore, every aspect of the believer's life should reflect his obedience and submission to the Lord Jesus Christ and divinely established authority. Some suggest the long hair constitutes the "covering" of verses 5-6. However, it may be argued that the shorn head in verse 5 is equated only hypothetically with the absence of the covering.

16. If any man seem to be contentious. If someone desires to dispute me, then, **we have no such custom.** In other words, there is no other precedent. To violate this principle is to go against a standard that is maintained in every church of which Paul is knowledgeable. Having appealed to their sense of wisdom, and their sense of propriety, here Paul ultimately appeals to his own authority as an apostle. But he does so only last, and inserts it almost as a footnote. In keeping with his approach to Christian liberty, he hopes there will be a voluntary submission to the principles he has laid out in this chapter.

2. The ordinance of communion. 11:17-34.

The Corinthians were to be commended for keeping the ordinances (vs. 2). But they deserved sharp criticism for the manner in which they did so. In the observance of the Lord's supper, they have been guilty of carnality (vss. 17-22). They are desperately in need of correction (vss. 23-26), and they are in danger of chastisement from the Lord (vss. 27-34).

17. Now in this. The reference is to what follows. **Declare,** better rendered, "command." **I prasie you not.** An obvious contrast with verse 2. **Ye come together not for the better, but for the worse.** Your congregational gatherings are more debilitating than edifying.

Sometimes one may be worse for attending services if he goes out of the wrong motivation.

18. First . . . I hear that there be divisions among you (cf. 1:10). The expression is intended as irony to contrast with **when ye come together.** What is described is a party spirit in the assembly. It is evident in what follows that the factions were largely divided between the rich and the poor. **I partly believe it.** What Paul knew of the Corinthian assembly, compelled him to accept part of what he had heard. What Paul aspired of the Corinthian assembly compelled him to reject the rest.

19. For there must be also heresies (Gr *hairesis*, factions, the term is used in a non-ecclesiastical sense. Note Acts 5:17 and 15:5, translated, "the sect"). Paul was certain that some divisions would occur in the assembly, if only to bring to light those who defend the truth. It is significant that God in His sovereign purpose might even use dissension and disorders in the assembly to put His people to the test.

20. When ye come together . . . this is not to eat the Lord's supper. It is a supper, but not the Lord's. It is a disorderly gathering of people going through the motions.

21. For in eating . . . one is hungry, and another is drunken. In the early church, the Lord's Supper was commonly preceded by a fellowship meal, later known as the Agape Feast. Eventually, so many problems accompanied these feasts that at the Council of Carthage (A.D. 397), they were strictly forbidden. And such was the case at Corinth. In their coming together, they were not eating together; hence it could not be called communion, and their behavior was so dishonoring to the Lord, it could hardly be called the Lord's Supper. Some were actually getting drunk.

22. Despise ye the church of God, and shame them that have not? Paul's indictment is twofold. They disgraced the Lord's house, and they embarrassed the poor in their midst who were not invited to participate in the fellowship dinner. This being the case, they could just as well do this at home. The apostle is writing to correct these abuses in the church. His statement should not be taken as a prohibition against eating any food at all in the church.

23. Having given ample expression of his sentiments about how not to come to the Lord's Supper, Paul now goes on to give instruction as to how it ought to be done. **I have received of the Lord.** Paul traces his authority to the Lord Himself. He does not indicate how the Lord gave him the instruction. It is likely that he received it through the apostles. **That which also I delivered unto you.** Evidently, this was not the first time Paul had been through this with the Corinthians. Paul's method here is to take his readers back to the upper room to trace the events of the last supper. This says several things. In the first place, it bases what he has to say in history, not dogmatism. In the second place, it forces his readers to think back with him to Calvary, which, of course, is what the Lord's Supper is all about. Thirdly, he delineates precisely what the Lord said and did so that his readers cannot escape the significance of it.

24. Take, eat: . . . broken, are all omitted in the best manuscripts. **This is my body.** Certainly not literally, but figuratively. He was there in the midst participating with the disciples in the element of the bread which signifies His incarnation. **Which is . . . for you.** This signifies the sacrificial and vicarious character of the death of Christ. Christ is memorialized at this table, not as a great example, or teacher, or even prophet, but as the Lamb of God that takes away the sin of the world. **This do in remembrance of me.** In contrast to the often thoughtless and reckless gathering of Corinthian believers at their so-called love feast, Jesus asked of His disciples, "remember me."

25. This cup is the New Testament in my blood. Christ is the mediator of the new covenant who "by His own blood . . . entered in once into the holy place, having obtained eternal redemption for us" (Heb 9:12-15). Notice the emphasis on the blood. This signifies our Lord's death which in turn signifies the grounds on which an eternal salvation is applied to the heart of the believing sinner. **This do ye, as oft as ye drink it.** The observance is commanded. The frequency is not. In the apostolic church, it was generally a weekly occurrence.

26. Ye do show the Lord's death till he comes. The service at the Lord's table looks both back and ahead. It recalls the accomplishments of Calvary, and anticipates our Lord's glorious return. Incidentally, the fact that this is observed "till he come" indicates that our Lord intended this ordinance to be observed throughout the present age. Certain hyper-dispensationalists are inclined to see this as no longer applicable to the present age. Such a view does serious injustice to our Lord's stated purpose in the ordinance. Nor should this memorial ordinance be viewed as a sacrament ("means of grace").

27-28. Paul concludes his discussion of the Lord's Supper with a warning to his readers that they may be facing the sure chastisement of the Lord unless they correct their abuse of the Lord's Supper. **Wherefore whosoever shall eat . . . unworthily.** This is defined in verse 29 as "not discerning the Lord's body." In other words, there is an irreverent and careless attitude displayed at the table of the Lord. Such a one **shall be guilty of the body and blood of the Lord.** This expression is not to be taken to prove the doctrine of consubstantiation (cf. Lenski, pp. 477-479). Rather, the intent is to show that when one violates this sacred institution, he is, in effect, despising the body and

blood of our Lord. In the same sense as it is expressed in Hebrews 9:26, they profane the institution and crucify the Saviour all over again. Instead of being cleansed by His blood, they are guilty of His blood. For this reason, it is imperative that **a man examine himself.** Before one partakes of the Lord's Supper, it is essential that he take stock of himself as he takes stock of our Lord. There is no room here for callousness of heart or carelessness of mind.

29. Coming to the table with the wrong attitude and the wrong approach may cause a man to eat and drink **damnation to himself, not discerning the Lord's body.** "Damnation" (Gr *krima*) is best rendered "judgment." The kinds of judgment the apostle has in mind are enumerated in the following verse.

30-31. For this cause, many are weak and sickly among you, and many sleep. Paul knows that the judgments of God many times take the form of physical illness and even death (cf. Acts 5:1-10). It is his conviction that such judgment has already occurred in their midst. The verb (Gr *koimao*) "sleep" when referring to death, always refers to the death of believers (cf. Jn 11:11-12; Acts 7:60; I Cor 15:6, 18, 20, 51; I Thess 4:13-15; II Pet 3:4). Judgment here is physical and temporal, not eternal. The exhortation of verse 31 goes back to verse 28. **If we would judge ourselves** corresponds to self-examination. The benefit of such examination is that **we should not be judged.** Paul gives his readers a choice. They may either exercise their own judgment upon themselves, or they may await God's judgment.

32. Lest his readers misunderstand what he means by judgment, Paul adds, **But when we are judged, we are chastened of the Lord.** Chastening itself is evidence of sonship (cf. Heb 12:6). The purpose is **that we should not be condemned with the world.** The sin of which the Corinthians were guilty was worthy of the certain judgment of God. But it was certainly not unpardonable. And true to his previous exhortation to the church. Paul's primary interest is not reprobation, but restoration.

33-34. Tarry one for another. Paul concludes his discussion of the Lord's Supper with a practical exhortation that the Corinthian believers show proper concern for one another. He implies his disapprobation of the common love feast in the words **eat at home.** And he demonstrates again pastoral concern when he expresses the thought **that ye come not together to condemnation.** Paul takes no delight in the chastening hand of the Lord. **Will I set in order** (Gr *diatassō*) refers to outward practical arrangement, cf. Mt 11:1; I Cor 9:14; 16:1; and Gal 3:19). Any other details pertaining to the Lord's Supper, Paul will clarify upon his visit to the city.

D. Doctrine of Spiritual Gifts. 12:1-14:40.

In the eleventh chapter, Paul introduced the general subject of Christian worship. There he dealt a much needed corrective regarding authority as it is now demonstrated in public worship and the practice of the ordinances. He now turns his attention to a related subject concerning which the Corinthians had solicited his advice. This is without a doubt the most difficult section of I Corinthians to interpret. The comment made by Robertson and Plummer more than fifty years ago is as pertinent today, "The difficulty of this passage lies in our ignorance of the condition of things to which it refers" (*International Critical Commentary,* p. 257). This will be noted as we progress through the text. In this section Paul strives to achieve four objectives: (1) to show that the partitioning of the gifts is under the control of the Holy Spirit (12:1-11); (2) to show that the proportion of the gifts in the church is as diverse as the members of the human body (12:12-31); (3) to es-

tablish the primacy of love (13:1-13); (4) to show the prominence of the gift of prophecy over all other manifestations of the Holy Spirit (14:1-40).

1. The partitioning of gifts.

Paul begins by dealing with the assignment of the gifts (vss. 1-6). He then treats the allotment of the gifts (vss. 7-10), and finally, the administration of the gifts (vs. 11).

a. The assignment of the gifts. 12:1-6.

12:1. Spiritual gifts (Gr *pneumatikos,* "spiritual"). This term may be either masculine or neuter, referring to either "men" or "gifts." The context is determinative. Here it is best understood as neuter, denoting "spiritual gifts" (cf. vss. 4, 5, 31; 14:1 where the neuter is used). **I would not have you to be ignorant.** This is a common Pauline expression to denote a subject of importance (cf. 10:1; 14:38; II Cor 1:8; 2:11; Rom 1:13; 10:3; 11:25; I Thess 4:13).

2. Ye were Gentiles, carried away. Herein lie both a statement of fact and an insinuation. They need to face the fact that before they were saved they were led about into all forms of superstition and blind impulse. The pagan worship at Corinth not only involved the worship of **dumb idols** and temple prostitution, but it also involved a pagan exercise of "tongues." The practice of "ecstatic utterances" was very common in the cults and in the worship of various Greek gods and goddesses (Kittel, *Theological Dictionary of the New Testament,* I, p. 722). The insinuation is that they are still being **carried away.** This expression has the force of being controlled by an influence they could not resist (cf. Gal 2:13; II Pet 3:17).

3. While Paul is about to deal with the entire subject of spiritual gifts, it is clear from the start that emphasis will be on only one of them, tongues. **Wherefore** ties with verse 2 and indicates they are in need of instruction. In evaluating spiritual gifts there are two criteria to be employed. The first is negative. **No man speaking by the Spirit of God calleth Jesus accursed.** The second is positive. **No man can say that Jesus is the Lord, but by the Holy Ghost.** How a person speaks determines the nature of the spirit that is within him. His very recognition and reception of Christ is by the Holy Spirit.

4-6. In the first three verses Paul's burden is to show that the Spirit is in control. This says something of the quality of what is done in the exercise of them. In verses 4-6 he shows that the Spirit is central and, this says something about the consistency of what is done in the exercise of them. **Diversities of gifts . . . differences of administration . . . diversities of operations.** Paul is not necessarily classifying the gifts into three categories, but their relationship to **Spirit . . . Lord . . . God.** They are the gifts given by the Spirit, used in ministry by the Son, and energized by the Father.

b. The allotment of the gifts.
12:7-10.

7. Manifestation of the Spirit. It is improper to equate this expression with "diversities of gifts" in verse 4. Neither is Paul about to tabulate the gifts *per se,* but the manner in which they are demonstrated. **Given to every man,** may refer to every man in the body of Christ or every man with a spiritual gift. If the stress is on **given,** the former is preferred. If the stress is on **profit,** the latter is preferred.

8-10. Given by the Spirit. This is the Holy Spirit not just the spirit of unity (cf. vss. 3, 11, 13). **The word of wisdom.** This has to do with the exposition of wisdom. It is speech that has wisdom as its content (Grosheide, *Commentary on I Corinthians,* p. 285). **The word of knowledge.** This relates to the previous gift in that both are gifts of the Spirit. They are distinguished in

that the former has in mind the exposition of truths dealing with the being and nature of God. The latter, the experiential and personal knowledge of God. Where the one promotes sound theology, the other promotes sound living. **Faith.** This is not saving faith but the wonder working faith to "move mountains." **Gifts of healing.** This has in mind gifts whereby the healing of the sick was effected (cf. Acts 4:30). Two important facts should be noted here. First, the use of the plural ("gifts," "healings"). This indicates that a special gift is necessary every time a healing occurs. Second, the stress is on the results, not on the process. The gift does not produce divine "healers" but divine "healing" (cf. Jas 5:14-15). **The working of miracles.** This gift is more comprehensive than the gift of healings. It has in mind such manifestations as are recorded in Acts 5:1-12; 9:32-43; and 13:8-12. **Prophecy.** This is the communication of special revelation from God. It could have been in the sense of "foretelling" (Acts 11:28) or simply "forth telling." Most of the New Testament epistles fall into this category. The gift was temporary, no longer needed after the canon of the New Testament was completed. **Discerning of spirits.** During the period of time when Scripture was still being formulated a class of individuals gifted with discerning true prophets from false prophets was necessary. This seems to be what John has in mind in I John 4:1 (cf. 14:29; I Thess 5:20-21). **Tongues . . . interpretation.** The gift of speaking in tongues in the book of Acts appears to have been limited to speaking in "known languages" (cf. Acts 2:4; 10:46; and 19:6). In the Acts 2 passage it does not appear that the gift of interpretation was necessary, since "every man heard in his own dialect" (Acts 10 and 19 are not as clear). However at Corinth it seems that the exercise of tongues involved more than just speaking with "known" languages. This being the case, the gift of interpretation was vital in every instance. For a fuller discussion of the nature and exercise of these gifts see the exposition of 13:1 and 14:1-40.

c. The administration of the gifts. 12:11.

11. But all these. All the above mentioned gifts. **Worketh . . . one . . . Spirit.** While the gifts are diverse, the source is a common one. **Dividing to every man severally as he will.** The Holy Spirit not only produces these gifts but distributes them, and that according to His own will, not according to the wishes or merits of men. Notice here that the Apostle Paul attributes to the third Person of the Trinity one of the qualities of personality (viz. "will"). The Holy Spirit is not a force but a Person.

2. The proportion in the body. 12:12-31.

Paul uses the illustration of the human body in order to explain and illustrate the unity of Christ's body (vss. 12-19); the interdependence of each of its members (vss. 20-26); and the importance of each integral part (vss. 27-31).

a. The indivisibility of the members in the body. 12:12-19.

12. The body is one, and hath many members. The church is viewed as an organism. Like the human body it reflects both unity and diversity. **One body.** While there are many members there is only one body. This truth is further emphasized in Romans 12:4-5; Ephesians 1:23; and 4:4, 16. **So also is Christ.** That is, the body of Christ, which is the church. This expression is appropriate since Christ is the Head of that body.

13. One Spirit are we all baptized into one body. This is not the baptism of water but the baptism of the Spirit. This has the same force as the expression **and have been all made to drink into one Spirit.** This fulfills Matthew 3:11; John 1:33; and Acts 1:5. That this baptism is common to all believers at Corinth is implied by the fact that Paul does not further exhort them to be baptized by the Spirit. Rather he assumes that they have all been baptized. The believer does not tarry or pray for this baptism. It occurs at the moment of regeneration. While speaking in tongues occurred in conjunction with the baptism of the Spirit at Pentecost, this outward manifestation was not always repeated as the only proof of such baptism.

14-19. Here the illustration of the body is further developed with the emphasis on the diversity and placement of each member. One cannot escape the force of Paul's argument: for a body to be a body it must have diverse members. It is absurd to expect everyone to have the same gift. **God set the members every one of them in the body, as it hath pleased him.** Paul stresses the sovereignty of God in this process. It is not only foolish but disobedient to covet another man's gift. The place and gifts of each member are determined by the Lord.

b. The interdependence of the members in the body. 12:20-26.

20. And now are they many members, yet but one body. Based upon the theological fact of organic unity, Paul is now going to show that each member is interdependent upon the others.

21. I have no need of thee. There is no such thing as a free lance Christian. No part of the body can take leave of the other members as though they were not necessary.

22-23. Those members of the body, which seem to be more feeble, are necessary. Like the human body some members are weaker than others. Likewise, there are some **we think to be less honourable.** Some parts of the body seemingly receive more attention and exposure than others, while there are other parts of the body that are never noticed at all.

24. But God hath tempered the body together. As God views the body he does not see it in part but in the whole. "Tempered" was used to speak of mingling two elements to form a compound.

25-26. That there should be no schism in the body. Divisions and alienation of feelings should find no place in the body of Christ. Rather, **the members should have the same care one for another.** The body is one and it has a common life and consciousness, therefore, **whether one member suffer, all the members suffer.** Likewise, if **one be honored, all the members rejoice with it.**

c. The induction of the members into the body. 12:27-31.

27. Now ye are the body of Christ, and members in particular. In one succinct statement the apostle expresses both the unity and the diversity of the body of Christ. In the original the definite article does not appear before "body." The thought is not that this particular local assembly constituted the body of Christ. The stress is on quality. Since they are of the body of Christ their actions and their attitudes toward one another should reflect His character.

28. Paul gives a further listing of the gifts with some additions to those included in verses 4-11. Here the stress is twofold. First on the source, **God hath set.** And secondly on priority. The list is so arranged as to put the most important first and the least important last. In this arrangement **apostles** are first, **tongues** are last. It is doubtful that the apostle ever intended that this list be exhaustive.

29-30. Are all apostles? Just as a body possesses many different members, even so the members of the church possess a variety of gifts. It is both absurd and sinful to expect otherwise. Compare the assumption that all believers have the baptism of the Spirit (vs. 13) with the rhetorical question:

Do all speak with tongues? The implied answer is no! If all these had the baptism of the Spirit and not all had spoken in tongues, then tongues cannot be the confirming factor of Spirit baptism!

But covet earnestly the best gifts. This expression explains why the apostle has arranged the list in verse 28 in order of priority. He wants his readers to be clear in their own minds as to which gifts are the best. Obviously, his intent is to steer them away from the more spectacular gifts such as tongues. "Covet" here is not to be construed negatively but has the idea of "earnestly desire." **Yet I show unto you a more excellent way.** The import of this statement is to be seen in chapter 13. Paul will show that a better way is not through striving but through loving.

3. The primacy of love. 13:1-13.

Johnson is correct when he notes, "the last clause of chapter 12 has been misunderstood. Many feel that Paul is here showing how the gifts are to be administered, i.e. in love. However, the use of 'way' (Gr *hodos*) in the sense of 'a road' instead of the 'way' (Gr. *tropos*) in the sense of 'manner,' and the statement of 14:1 indicate that Paul was, rather, pointing out a path of life superior to a life spent seeking and displaying of spiritual gifts." (S. L. Johnson, *Wycliffe Bible Commentary,* p. 1251). Paul's interest here is not to instruct his readers how they may best use their gifts, but how to have their priorities straight. It is love for which they should strive, not spiritual gifts. The chapter breaks quite naturally into three sections: the contrast of love, verses 1-3; the character of love, verses 4-7; and the constancy of love, verses 8-13.

a. Contrast of love. 13:1-3.

13:1. Tongues of men and of angels. This expression is important in two ways. First, it shows that the content of chapter thirteen is directed foremost against the abuse of the gift of tongues (contrast 12:28 where tongues is listed last). Secondly, it shows that in the apostle's mind the gift of tongues involved both known and unknown languages. The Corinthians considered these tongues to be languages of the angels. Such was the association of tongues—speaking in pagan worship at Corinth. When a priest or devotee spoke in tongues it was considered that he spoke in the language of the gods (see J. Dillow, *Speaking in Tongues,* pp. 12, 13). The apostle is not so lacking in tact as to accuse his readers of actually incorporating a pagan activity into their worship. His approach in the next two chapters is to so circumscribe the exercise of the gift that the inordinate exercise of it will be eliminated.

2. And have not charity. (Gr *agapē,* "love"). The AV translation derives from the Latin and unfortunately does a serious injustice to the force of the Greek term. This is ultimately that which acts in conformity to the character and nature of God. It is not benevolence yet produces it. It is not motivated or moved by external circumstances yet always acts appropriately in response to them. It is no wonder that the apostle considered that though a man possessed any or all of the gifts but be destitute of love he was nothing.

3. Love has been shown to be superior to the very best of the spiritual gifts. It is also superior to philanthropy, **though I bestow all my goods to feed the poor,** and personal dedication, **though I give my body to be burned,** without love this **profiteth me nothing.**

b. Character of love. 13:4-7.

4-7. What is the character of love? Paul now proceeds to show the reader the character qualities of love. **Suffereth long.** It is not easily roused to resentment (cf. Jas 5:7). **Is kind** (Gr *chrēsteuomai*). This term appears only here in the New Testament in the finite verb form. It has the idea of "useful," i.e. inclined to be of good service

to others. **Vaunteth not itself.** It does not sound its own praises. **Not puffed up.** It is not swelled with pride (cf. 4:6; 8:1). **Easily provoked** (literally, "is not provoked or exasperated" Acts 17:16). **Thinketh no evil** ("does not reckon evil"). This expression of love does not keep track of the offenses committed against it. **Rejoiceth not in iniquity.** It does not take delight in that which is offensive to God. **But rejoiceth in the truth.** This may be taken in an instrumental sense "rejoiceth together with truth" (cf. Vincent, *Word Studies,* II, p. 265), or it may be taken in the locative sense as is reflected in the AV. The latter is probably more consistent with Paul's thought in the context (cf. also Rom 1:8; Jn 3:21; I Jn 1:6). **Beareth all things** (literally, "covers all things," cf. I Pet 4:8). **Believeth all things.** This does not suggest that it is gullible, but that it will believe well of others unless convinced otherwise. In any case, it always **hopeth all things.** Rather than having a negative and critical spirit, it is always positive and hopeful. **Endureth all things.** This is a military term; it means to sustain the assaults of an enemy (cf. also II Tim 2:10; Heb 10:32; 12:2).

c. Constancy of love. 13:8-13.

Unlike many of the spiritual gifts, love will never be outmoded, unnecessary, or eliminated.

8. Charity never faileth (Gr *ekpiptō,* "falls off," cf. Lk 16:17). Unlike the leaf or the flower, love never fades and falls off (cf. Jas 1:11; I Pet 1:24). **Prophecies, they shall fail** (literally "be abolished"). **Tongues, they shall cease.** The significance of the Greek word (*pauō*) indicates that tongues would soon be "cut off" as their necessity in the process of New Testament revelation ceased. It is important to note that tongues are never mentioned again in the New Testament after this warning. **Knowledge, it shall vanish away** ("be abolished"). This is the same word used in reference to prophecy above.

This is not knowledge in general but the "gift" of knowledge by direct revelation (cf. 12:8; 13:2).

9-10. For suggests reason. **We know in part, and we prophesy in part.** Knowledge and prophecy as we now know it are suited only to an imperfect state of existence. **That which is perfect.** This is best understood in light of I Corinthians 2:6, in the sense of "mature" or "complete" (cf. also Col 3:14; Heb 6:1). Conservative biblical scholars have proposed two main interpretations of **perfect.** It may be a reference to the completion of the canon of Scripture, with which partial revelation (by knowledge, prophecy, or tongues) came to an end, culminating in a complete revelation of God's Scripture or it may refer to the maturation of the Body of Christ (in the sense of Ephesians 4:11-16). Paul employs the neuter because he does not contemplate an individual. Thus, "that which is perfect" cannot refer to the coming of Christ Himself. **Then that which is in part will be done away.** Once the **perfect** has been achieved, there will be no need for that which is immature. It will not be needed or accepted and should not be desired.

11. The apostle illustrates his point by likening it to the maturation of a person from infancy to manhood. A child speaks, reasons, and assimilates knowledge at the level of his maturity. Paul's use of **spake . . . understood . . . thought** seem to correspond respectively to "tongues," "prophecy," and "knowledge" above. If this is the case, it is reasonable to expect changes to occur. The apostle goes on to say **when I became a man, I put away childish things.** A child's speech is undeveloped, his understanding crude, and knowledge incomplete. At that time his attention is focused upon developing the skill of speech, coming to terms with truth and assimilating knowledge. But when the child becomes a man his speech becomes subject to his mind, his understanding is tempered, and his

knowledge complete. Paul is not implying that they had reached or attained that level of maturity but, akin to Philippians 3:7-15, that is the end toward which they should be striving.

12. Now we see through a glass, darkly (literally, "for yet we see through a mirror in a riddle"). Paul seems to be alluding to the incident in Num 12:8. On another occasion Paul says the writings were an enigma compared to the revelations contained in the gospel (cf. II Cor 3:12-13). **But then face to face.** The apostle understands that complete maturity will not be achieved until we see the Lord face to face. At that time we will not only achieve complete maturity but perfect knowledge. As Paul puts it, **but then shall I know even as also I am known.** The gifts are fragmentary and only a means to an end. Paul's advice is keep your eyes on the goal and not on the means towards achieving that goal.

13. And now abideth faith, hope, charity. "Now" is best understood in a temporal sense (cf. Rom 8:24; II Cor 5:7; Heb 11:1). If the present Christian experience were to be reduced to three essential qualities they would be faith, hope, and love. **The greatest of these is charity.** Faith and hope will one day vanish from sight. Love alone abides. Its clearest expression is to be seen on Golgotha's hill. Thus Paul's approach is not to decry the possible abuses at Corinth but to challenge them to something much better.

4. The prominence of prophecy 14: 1-40.

While the acquisition and exercise of spiritual gifts in general constituted a problem at Corinth, it appears that the most serious difficulty was centered on the gift of tongues. Earlier (12:10) in Paul's tabulation, he listed tongues among the least of the spiritual gifts. In this chapter he is going to compare it with the greatest of the gifts, i.e. prophecy.

a. *In the edification of the assembly. 14:1-17.*

Comparing the gift of tongues with prophecy as they are used in the edification of the assembly, Paul, first of all, cites a contrast in usefulness (vss.1-6); then he notes a contrast in understanding (vss 7-17).

14:1. Follow after charity (literally, "pursue love"). This ties the preceding thought to what follows (cf. 12:31; 13:13). **And desire spiritual gifts.** Paul is anxious that his readers do not misunderstand him. He does not intend to mean by what he says in chapter 13 that spiritual gifts have no value at all; his concern there is only that they keep the gifts in the proper perspective. **But rather that ye may prophesy.** Now, as for desiring spiritual gifts, it is only proper to seek after those gifts which will best fulfill the mandate of love. Since prophecy issues in the greatest benefit to the greatest number of people then it is only appropriate that one seeks that gift above all others.

2. Unknown tongues (literally, "tongue"). Omit "unknown" throughout this chapter whenever it occurs with tongues as it has no support in the Greek text. **For no man understandeth him.** That is, apart from an interpreter. **Howbeit in the spirit he speaketh mysteries.** Even though he may be speaking spiritual mysteries the benefit to the hearers is nil because they cannot understand. This, of course, is in contrast to the gift of prophecy.

3. But he that prophesieth. Continuing his contrast, Paul returns to prophecy. **Speaketh unto men.** Communication is taking place. The results are **edification, and exhortation, and comfort.**

4. On the other hand, **He that speaketh in an unknown tongue edifieth himself.** When a person speaks in tongues only one person is benefited. By way of continuing contrast, **he that prophesieth edifieth the church.**

5. I would that ye all spake with tongues. It must not be misconstrued with Paul's argument that he undervalued the gift of tongues. He did admit its importance. **But rather that ye prophesied.** Admitting the value of tongues, it would still be better if you prophesied. The reason, of course, is **that the church may receive edifying.**

6. If I come to you speaking with tongues, what shall I profit you? The question is, what benefit is it to you if I come speaking in tongues. Paul really doesn't answer the question except by way of contrast. **Except I shall speak to you.** If you are benefited I must speak **either by revelation** (apostolic gift), **or by knowledge** (the gift of knowledge) **or by prophesying** (the gift of prophecy), **or by doctrine** (the gift of teaching). Any of the above gifts are far superior to the gift of tongues because they communicate and they edify and they profit.

7-8. Even things without life. Paul goes on to add additional examples to prove his point. An instrument **giving sound** must also be distinctive to be understood **whether pipe or harp.** This is clearly understood by the soldier who follows the sound of a trumpet. How could he **prepare himself to the battle** if the signal is **uncertain?**

9-10. So many kinds of voices in the world. That is, so many kinds of languages. **And none of them is without signification.** They are all intelligible to those who understand them.

11. On the other hand if I do not know a specific language **I shall be unto him that speaketh a barbarian.** Paul's use of "barbarian" here simply has the general sense of "foreigner" (cf. Rom 1:14; Acts 28:24; Col 3:11).

12. Seek that ye may excel to the edifying of the church. If you must be zealous of spiritual gifts then seek after one that will benefit the church.

13. Pray that he may interpret (pray in order that he may interpret). Paul is not saying that speaking in a tongue and praying are coterminous, but that if one is seeking to speak in a tongue it would be well to ask God for the gift of interpretation also. Notice that the tongue-speaker was to provide his own interpretation.

14. For indicates the reason for Paul's advice in verse 13. **My spirit prayeth.** This is a difficult expression but probably means "the Holy Spirit in me" in the sense that my spiritual gift is being exercised. **But my understanding is unfruitful.** I do not understand what I am saying. This further evidences that "unknown languages" are in view here, else the apostle would have knowledge of what he was saying (cf. Acts 2).

15. What is it then? What is the conclusion to all this discussion? **Pray with the spirit . . . sing with the spirit.** These expressions must be defined by verse 14. Paul, no doubt, has in mind praying and singing in tongues. **Pray with the understanding also . . . and . . . sing with the understanding.** If I should pray or sing in tongues then it will also be accompanied with intelligible praying and singing (viz. the tongues interpreted).

16-17. How shall he . . . say Amen at the giving of thanks. Even if a person should bless the Lord in tongues it would be impossible for anyone else to join in because no one would know it. **For thou verily givest thanks well, but the other is not edified.** What has been said may be well and good but no one has been edified.

b. In the example of Paul. 18-19.

18-19. I speak with tongues more than ye all. Paul possessed the gift of tongues. It is interesting that this is the only place that he makes mention of it. **Yet in the church** (emphatic) **I had rather speak five words with my understanding . . . than ten thousand words in an unknown tongue.** Words have meaning only as they are understood and it is Paul's intent that he might **teach others.**

c. In the essential purpose. 14:20-25.

20. Continuing his contrast with prophecy Paul goes on to show that in the essential purpose of spiritual gifts, prophecy was to be preferred. **Be not children.** This is the second time the apostle has measured their spiritual maturity by this term (cf. 13:11). **In understanding be men.** Paul associates the gift of tongues with spiritual immaturity. He anticipates that as the church matures her concerns will be less in the arena of the spectacular and more in the stimulation of understanding.

21. In the law it is written. "Law" has in mind the entire Old Testament Scriptures. In this case he has in mind Isaiah 28:11-12 (cf. Jn 10:34; Rom 3:20).

22-23. Wherefore tongues are for a sign. This is best understood as a general reference to divine power evidenced in the exercise of the gift. It does not profit the believer but **them that believe not.** Its purpose was to demonstrate divine power to the unbeliever. **But prophesying serveth not for them that believe not, but for them which believe.** Insofar as the assembly is the gathering of saints and not of unbelievers, prophecy is, by far, the more appropriate gift. Yet Paul's concern goes even beyond this. He asserts that the main purpose of the gift was as a sign. However, if an unbeliever should visit the congregation where gifts are being exercised without regard for order or understanding the results will be just the opposite. Paul asks, **will they not say that ye are mad?** In other words, the very purpose of the gift is mitigated by the unbridled exercise of it.

24-25. On the other hand, it is almost impossible to misuse the gift of prophecy. Should an unbeliever wander into the assembly and be exposed to the truth of God being taught through prophecy **he is convinced of all, he is judged of all.** Thus, instead of being repelled by the service, **falling down on his face he will worship God.** He will be convinced of his sin, of God's righteousness, and repentance and faith in God. And, so far as Paul is concerned, it is far more important that the unbeliever hear each message and testimony clearly in his own language.

d. In the exercise in the assembly. 14: 26-40.

In the concluding verses Paul circumscribes how these gifts are to be utilized in the assembly. He deals, first of all, with rules regulating the gift of tongues (vss. 26-29) and then rules regulating the gift of prophecy (vss. 30-35). He concludes the chapter with a challenge (vss. 36-40).

26. The key in the exercise of any gift is **Let all things be done unto edifying.** Throughout this chapter this has been the overriding principle and continues to dominate the apostle's thinking as he regulates the proper exercise of these gifts. Incidentally, this paragraph is also significant because it gives "us the most intimate glimpse we have of the early church at worship. Here we are able to see something of what the early Christians actually did when they assembled to worship God" (L. Morris, *The First Epistle of Paul to the Corinthians*, pp. 198-199).

27. If any man speak. The worship services of the early church do not seem to have been dominated by one individual, rather there seems to be the open and free participation in the worship service by all who would choose to participate. Thus, in this situation if a man should speak in a tongue, Paul says, **let it be by two, or at the most by three.** It is permissible for as many as three to speak in tongues and **that by course.** That is, one at a time, not all together. And **let one interpret.**

28. But if there be no interpreter, let him keep silence. To speak in tongues without an interpreter is forbidden in the church.

29-30. Let the prophets speak two or three, and let the other judge. Likewise, those who would share a special truth revealed to them by God

were to do so in order and no more than two or three. The only exception to this would be in the event that a person felt unusually constrained, while someone was speaking, to inject a thought and in this situation **let the first hold his peace.** In other words, the new communication was entitled to be heard at once.

31. Ye may all prophesy one by one. Again this is to be understood in the light of verse 29. Paul is not now saying that any number of people may prophesy but that the two or three will prophesy one at a time. And in the case of possible interruption the two are not to prophesy simultaneously, but one at a time.

32-35. And the spirits of the prophets are subject to the prophets. In contrast to tongues where it appears that the spirit of an individual is out of control, in the exercise of the prophetic gift, all is done decently and in order. **God is not the author of confusion.** The service that is disorderly, confusing, and disruptive is not of God, for God is the author of **peace. Let your women keep silence in the churches.** Obviously, this must be interpreted in light of 11:5 where it is clear that Paul understood that women were permitted to prophesy and to pray in public worship so long as they were properly dressed. The expression may have reference to speaking in tongues. That is, they were denied the privilege of exercising the gift of tongues in the assembly. Alternatively, it may have reference to what follows. **And if they will learn any thing, let them ask their husbands at home.** They were not allowed to disrupt the service by asking questions and talking while the service was going on. Certainly, they were not to speak out in tongues either.

36-38. Paul asks a sarcastic question. **What? Came the word of God out from you? or came it unto you only?** Are you the only repository of God's truth? If there is anyone in the assembly that considers himself a prophet or spiritual he must acknowledge that **the things I write unto you are the commandments of the Lord.** Here Paul unequivocally asserts his apostolic authority. **If any man be ignorant, let him be ignorant.** If there was anyone who would refuse to acknowledge divine authority he was not going to waste his time trying to convince him.

39. Covet to prophesy, . . . not to speak with tongues. Again, Paul compares the two gifts and in so doing asserts the legitimacy of the gift of tongues and the primacy of the gift of prophecy.

40. Let all things be done decently and in order. Public worship was to be reflective of the one to whom it was directed, thus it was to be beautiful and harmonious. While the revelational gift of tongues was still being given, they were to **forbid not to speak with tongues.** Today, however, this original apostolic gift has ceased and forbidding its misuse by modern day "Corinthian" churches is valid.

E. Doctrine of the Resurrection. 15:1-58.

The only doctrinal "error" to which the apostle addresses himself in this epistle is contained in this chapter. What were the historical factors behind this problem? One possibility is that the individuals to whom Paul addresses himself constituted one of the parties mentioned in 1:12. By process of elimination the party of Apollos is usually suggested. However, this does not agree with what we know of Apollos and of his ministry (cf. also Acts 18:27-28; I Cor 16:12). Another possibility is that they were the moral libertines mentioned in chapter 6 and against whom the apostle urges the resurrection in 6:14. The problem with this is if they doubted the resurrection Paul could hardly have used this as an argument for moral purity. Another view is that the problem came from converted Sadduccees (cf. also Acts

24:6-9; 26:6-8). However, there is no evidence of any such maverick breed at Corinth. Others suggest that the opponents of the doctrine were Epicureans (note the reference to material indulgence in 15:32). However, again there is no indication that such a party existed in the Corinthian assembly. Furthermore, the reference in 15:32 argues that the careless lifestyle is a consequence and not a cause of the denial of the resurrection. Probably the best view understands this problem in light of Acts 17:32. The tenets of Greek platonic philosophy had generally pervaded the Hellenistic world. Generally it was considered that the material universe was unsuited to a spiritual existence. The Gnostics, for example, even went so far as to suggest that the body was intrinsically evil. It is this kind of skepticism that formed the background for both I Corinthians 15 and Colossians 2:8-23. See also II Timothy 2:17-18.

Paul develops his thought first, by defending the doctrine of the resurrection (15:1-34) and second, by developing the doctrine of the resurrection (15:35-58). In the opening section he shows that: (a) Resurrection is vital to the historical preaching of the gospel (vss. 1-19); (b) Resurrection is vital to the prophetic preaching of the gospel (vss. 20-28); and (c) Resurrection is vital in suffering persecution for the gospel (vss. 29-34).

1. A defense of the doctrine of the resurrection (based on known truth). 15:1-34.

a. Resurrection is vital to the historical preaching of the gospel. 15:1-19.

1-2. Moreover, tells us that Paul has finished his answers to the Corinthians' questions and he now goes on to a new subject. **I declare unto you,** primarily looks ahead to verses 3 and 4. **The gospel which I preached unto you.** The good news which the Corinthians **have received . . . stand . . . are saved.** Paul is now at the very heart of the gospel message. **Unless ye have believed in vain.** "In vain" may mean "without cause" i.e. blind faith (cf. Gal 2:21). Or it may mean "without effect," i.e. to no purpose (cf. Gal 3:4; 4:11). The latter idea seems to be best. If, as some are saying in Corinth, there is no resurrection, then faith is vain and worthless (cf. vs. 14).

3-4. First of all, that is, in order of priority. **I also received.** Paul is not speaking of his personal salvation experience but the fact that the gospel which he preached was from direct revelation of God (cf. 11:23; Gal 1:12). Four vital truths are asserted here, identified by **that. Christ died for our sins.** This is a substitutionary and propitiatory sacrifice (cf. Rom 3:23-26). **That he was buried.** This evidences the reality and totality of his death. **That he rose again.** The Greek perfect tense stresses the certainty of the fact. **According to the scriptures.** The facts of the gospel are not only important historically, but prophetically as well. They occurred as had been predicted (cf. Jn 20:9; Acts 26:23; Ps 16:10).

5-7. That he was seen of Cephas. The fourth vital truth of the gospel is that Christ appeared after the resurrection, not to a few but to **Cephas, then of the twelve: After that . . . of above five hundred brethren at once.** It is not certain when this last event occurred. The most likely possibility is Matthew 28:16-20. Since Jesus had previously announced this meeting (cf. Mt 26:32; 28:10, 16) it is unlikely that anyone would have intentionally missed it. **Seen of James.** Probably the Lord's brother (Mt 13:55). He was earlier mentioned as an unbeliever (cf. Jn 7:5) and later with the assembly of believers (cf. Acts 1:14; 12:17; 15:13; 21:18). One wonders if this was not the turning point of his life.

8-9. Last of all he was seen of me also. In Paul's characteristically self-effacing way, he cites the fact that he too had the honor of seeing the risen Lord (cf. Acts 9:1-6). **For I am least of**

the apostles. Not because he was simply the last to see the risen Lord but because he was **not meet** (unworthy). Paul has not yet recovered from the "wonder of it all" that he should be elevated to the honor and office of apostleship, **because I persecuted the church of God.**

10-11. But by the grace of God I am what I am. Paul does not magnify his personal credentials but only the sovereign grace of God. Yet this least of the apostles **laboured more abundantly than they all.** Whether this is taken to mean any of the apostles individually or all of them collectively the intent of the apostle is not to boast but to magnify **the grace of God which was with me. . . . so we preach.** Paul's message and that of the other apostles is the same. Furthermore, both included the message of the resurrection. **And so ye believed.** If some of the Corinthians are now questioning the resurrection they are departing from their initial starting point. If they believed the message of the gospel they believed in the resurrection.

12. This verse stands as a focal point around which the first nineteen verses revolve. **Now if Christ be preached that he rose from the dead** directs our attention to the first eleven verses. **How say some among you that there is no resurrection?** This question looks ahead to verses thirteen through nineteen. Paul has established first of all that resurrection is an essential fact of the gospel. He now tabulates the logical consequences of denying the resurrection.

13. Then is Christ not risen. The first consequence of denying the resurrection is that Christ is still in the grave. The nature of Paul's argument here does not suggest that his objectors admitted the resurrection of Christ, only that it led to an unthinkable conclusion for any genuine believer.

14-19. The logic is inescapable. **If Christ be not risen, then is our preaching vain.** The proclamation of the gospel as outlined in verses 1-11 is hollow. Not only that, but **your faith is also vain,** that is, "groundless." Faith in a dead Saviour is both preposterous and pathetic. And not only so, but **we are found false witnesses of God** (literally, false witnesses against God). If Paul's preaching affirms something that God did not really accomplish, his message and ministry are opposed to God. They perpetrate a lie about Him. Paul summarizes his logic here and goes on to suggest yet another consequence. **Ye are yet in your sins.** Since the resurrection of Christ is essential to our justification (Rom 4:25), then the denial of it vitiates the forgiveness of sins. Not only that, but **they also which are fallen asleep in Christ are perished.** "Fall asleep in Christ" is used to speak of those who die in Christ (cf. I Thess 4:14 and Rev 14:13). "Perish" is tantamount to "perdition." **Only** is to be taken with the entire opening clause. If our hope in Christ does not take us beyond this present life, then **we are of all men most miserable.** Indeed, we are both deceived and unwitting deceivers. What a sad lot among men the Christian becomes.

Having shown the relationship of the doctrine of resurrection to biblical soteriology Paul now goes on to show its vital link to biblical eschatology.

b. Resurrection is vital to the prophetic preaching of the gospel. 15:20-28.

20. The first important truth is that Christ has **become the first fruits of them that sleep** (cf. Lev 23:9-14). The "first fruits" in Israel always anticipated a harvest.

21. For since by man came death is to be understood in the light of the parallel idea in verse 22. **By man came also the resurrection of the dead.** If the death which Adam brought is physical death then the life which Christ brings also includes physical life.

22. As in Adam all die. The plight of all the descendants of Adam is that they must pay the consequences of his sin. **Even so in Christ shall all be made alive.** The two occurrences of "all" are to be

understood in a restricted sense. In the first instance it is qualified "in Adam." In the second instance it is qualified "in Christ." Paul does not subscribe to universalism, i.e. that all are saved, as some liberal theologians aver: It is only in Christ that the sinner receives life.

23-26. Order (literally, "rank"). **Christ the first fruits.** He was the first to experience the resurrection of the body from the dead. **Afterward they that are Christ's at his coming.** When Christ comes for the Church at the Rapture then the believers will also experience the resurrection (cf. I Thess 3:13; 4:14-19). **Then** suggests an interval in the same way "afterward" (cf. vs. 23) suggests an interval of an indeterminate length of time. **The end** refers to the end of the **kingdom of God.** At that time he will have **put down all rule.**

27-28. Then shall the Son also himself be subject unto him. This is a difficult expression and has often been misunderstood to suggest that the apostle subordinated the Son to the Father. However, two facts must be accounted for here. First, when Paul says that the Son is subject to the Father he is not speaking of the Son in terms of his essence, but in terms of his function, or ministry, as the incarnate Son. Second, the force of Paul's statement is best understood dispensationally. At this present time the administration of the Messianic Kingdom is given to the Son (cf. Mt 28:18). However, at the conclusion of the Messianic Kingdom this function will be returned to the triune God **that God may be all in all.**

c. Resurrection is vital in suffering persecution for the gospel. 15:29-34.

Not only is the resurrection vital to both the content and the implications of the gospel but such a hope is also vital to the enduring of suffering for the gospel.

29. The expression **they . . . which are baptized for the dead** is obscure. The practice of vicarious baptism such as that which is practiced by Mormons today, appeared as early as the second century (Leon Morris, *The First Epistle of Paul to the Corinthians*, p. 219). Some suppose that this custom had already been introduced into Corinth (Hodge, *Commentary on the First Epistle to the Corinthians*, p. 337). It is extremely doubtful that the apostle would have made reference to this heretical practice without, in the same breath, condemning it. The context clearly indicates a different concept. Two more satisfactory views are as follows. First, the expression may refer to young converts who took the place of the older brethren in the church who had died so that it would be properly rendered "baptized in the place of" (Gr *hyper)* which has this sense (cf. II Cor 5:15; Phm 13).

Since the context centers on the reality of the resurrection, it seems that Paul would be questioning why they are continuing to baptize new converts "over" or "in place of" the dead ones, if there is no resurrection, since baptism symbolizes our death and resurrection. To continue to baptize new converts, then, in place of the dead ones, would be meaningless if there were to be no real resurrection of the dead.

A second alternative is that the expression is to be taken synonymously with verse 30, thus being rendered "baptized with reference to the dead." This would be a nonsacerdotal use of the term "baptism." That is, the people of whom Paul was speaking were being literally immersed in such severe persecution that they were dying for their faith.

30. Why stand we in jeopardy every hour? Certainly if there is no resurrection there is no sense in suffering persecution for Christ. On the contrary, it is only logical that one would do whatever is necessary to prolong life on earth.

31. I die daily. This does not teach that Paul mortified the flesh every day. The context tells us that he, in effect, faced the wild beasts every day. Paul's life was in such constant jeopardy that he never knew when he might be called upon to give his life for the gospel.

32-33. What advantageth it me? If one's existence is terminated in the arena for the sake of a gospel which can only provide empty hopes we may as well **eat and drink; for tomorrow we die.** Borrowing a proverb from the Greek poet Menander, Paul warns **evil communications corrupt good manners.** Evil is contagious. By this the apostle implies that those who are denying the resurrection are in fact false teachers.

34. Awake to righteousness and sin not. Wake up to righteousness, open your eyes to the delusion of your spiritual superiority. **For some have not the knowledge of God.** The denial of the resurrection suggests that those who hold to such a view are literally "ignorant of God" (cf. Mt 28:22). **I speak this to your shame.** It is both incredible and shameful that such a church so gifted of God could have allowed persons in their assembly to have called such a cardinal truth into question.

2. A development of the doctrine of the resurrection (based on revelation). 15:35-58.

In the first half of this chapter Paul argues on the basis of known truth and thereby commends the preaching of the resurrection. In the remaining part of the chapter he develops the doctrine, based on new revelation, to provide his readers with insights into the blessed hope of the believer.

a. The nature of the resurrection of the dead. 15:35-49.

35-36. The first question Paul answers is **How are the dead raised up? and with what body do they come?** While both questions are distinct they must be taken together. The first deals with how life can come from death and the second deals with the nature of the resurrection body. The first question is answered with an analogy from common life. **That which thou sowest is not quickened, except it die.** Whenever a seed is sown in the ground it must first die before it can germinate (cf. Jn 12:24). As to the second question the apostle requires more explanation.

37-38. Thou sowest not that body that shall be, but bare grain. That which is produced is very different from that which is planted. A grain is sown, a plant is the result. **God giveth it a body.** All of nature illustrates the providential control of God. The precise nature of the body of every living thing is determined by the good pleasure of God.

39-41. All flesh is not the same flesh. Furthermore, it is clear in nature that diversity exists among all living beings. Such diversity is not only reflected in the earthly sphere but also in the heavenly.

42. So also is the resurrection of the dead. It is to be understood in the context of reaping and sowing. It thus reflects the same principle of unity and diversity. The resurrection body is related to the earthly body in the same sense that the plant is related to the seed. Yet, it will be different. **It is sown in corruption; it is raised in incorruption.**

43-44. Paul enlarges upon the contrast between the two. The one is **sown in dishonor . . . weakness . . . a natural body.** It is **raised in glory . . . power . . . spiritual.**

45. So it is written. Tantamount to saying, "and this agrees with scripture." **Adam was made a living soul** seems to have in mind the earthly animal nature given to Adam in the original creation. This seems to suit the parallel ideas in verses 46 through 49. **The last Adam was made a quickening spirit** (literally, "the last Adam became a quickening spirit"). The expression "last Adam" was coined by the Apostle Paul as a reference to Christ (cf. also Rom 5:14). The contrast here is not so much between the soul and the spirit as it is between "living" (Gr *zao*) and "life giving" (Gr *zōopoieō*). The principle of life is common with all men. The last Adam is infinitely more than that (Jn 5:26). The one partakes of temporality, the other of eternality.

46-48. However, it was the **natural** which came first; it was the **spiritual** which came afterward. Adam is **of the earth,** Christ is **the Lord from heaven.** The former is thus earthly, the latter is heavenly.

49. The certainty of the resurrection is verified by the reality of human, earthly existence. **As we have borne the image of the earthly, we shall also bear the image of the heavenly.** Thus the human body, instead of becoming an argument against the resurrection becomes an argument in its favor.

b. The nature of the resurrection for the living. 15:50-58.

But what of those who are alive at the coming of Christ? How shall they be distinguished from those who have died? Paul's final statement in the chapter is to turn his attention upon the nature of the resurrection for those who are still living at the time of the Second Coming of Christ.

50. First the statement of a principle, **flesh and blood cannot inherit the kingdom of God.** A change is mandatory if the believer is ever to realize his promised blessings.

51. I show you a mystery (cf. 2:7). Not all believers will **sleep** ("die") but we can all be assured of one thing. **We shall all be changed.** How will that occur?

52. In a moment, in the twinkling of an eye, expresses the suddenness with which it will occur. The time is indicated **at the last trump.** This is not the last trump of Revelation 11:15 but the last trump of I Thessalonians 4:16. It is so designated because it signals the end of the present age. Two groups are distinguished. **The dead shall be raised incorruptible, and we shall be changed.** The term "dead" refers to those who have died in Christ. The term "we" refers to those who are still living at the time of the Rapture.

53-54. Both groups are alike in that they are **corruptible** and **mortal.** That to which both groups are changed is likewise the same, designated as **incorruption** and **immortality. Death is swal-**

lowed up in victory is taken from Isaiah 25:8.

55. Such hope and assurance issues in a great song of triumph. **O death, where is thy sting? O grave, where is thy victory?**

56. The sting of death is sin and Paul would answer "and yet am I forgiven." **The strength of sin is the law,** and Paul would exclaim "and yet I am pardoned."

57-58. No man can take credit for this victory. It comes **through our Lord Jesus Christ.** And this blessed hope, this blessed assurance, issues forth in a challenge in verse 58. **Be ye steadfast, unmovable, always abounding.** How does this relate to the doctrine of resurrection? Paul answers **ye know that your labor is not in vain.** For Paul it was more than faith. It was knowledge. It was the sure conviction that one day he would share in the glory of the resurrection.

V. CONCLUSION. 16:1-24.

The concluding chapter is taken up with practical and personal matters concerning: (a) The contribution for the support of the Jerusalem church (vss. 1-9); (b) Paul's personal efforts on behalf of the Corinthian assembly (vss. 10-12). And then a concluding challenge (vss. 13-24). It is here that the apostle reiterates the theme of the epistle, i.e. "called unto the fellowship of Jesus Christ our Lord" (1:9) in the most practical of terms.

A. The Contribution. 16:1-9.

1. Its instruction. 16:1-4.

16:1. Now concerning. The common formula used in this epistle to introduce matters about which the Corinthians had queried the apostle. In this case it had to do with **the collection for the saints.** The believers at Corinth were aware that the apostle was gathering funds for the Jerusalem church, and apparently they had written to inquire to what extent they could participate in this collection. **I have given orders** suggests that this was not an optional matter for the Corinthian believers any more than it was for the **churches of Galatia.**

2. The procedure by which they were to gather these funds was **Upon the first day of the week.** Their giving was to be systematic and planned. **Let every one of you lay by him in store.** This obligation extended to everyone. **As God hath prospered him.** The amount of each gift was proportionate to the giver's income. **That there be no gatherings when I come.** The apostle was desirous that the collection be taken before he came. This was for two reasons. First, through systematic and planned giving he knew that the amount would be more. Second, he did not want to apply pressure when he came.

3-4. And when I come. While his arrival in Corinth was yet indefinite, Paul is stressing here that they be prepared with the collection at any time. **Whomsoever you shall approve by your letters.** Placing himself above suspicion the apostle shows that he is not so much interested in handling their money as in assuring that it got to Jerusalem. He suggests that they appoint stewards to carry their money. **And if it be meet.** If it be substantial enough **that I go also,** then they would all go together. Paul was willing, if their contribution was especially large, to rearrange his schedule and go with the group to Jerusalem.

2. Its collection. 16:5-9.

5. Now I will come unto you, when I shall pass through Macedonia. Paul here changes his original itinerary and subsequently came under the charge of being fickle (cf. II Cor 1:15-17).

6-7. Paul's plans at this time are to spend the winter at Corinth. **If the Lord permit.** The apostle was always subject to the will of God above his own.

8. I will tarry at Ephesus till Pentecost. The time is near the close of Paul's three-year stay at Ephesus and the season is early spring.

9. A great door. "Door" is used here metaphorically for "opportunity."

Many adversaries. This is best taken with the previous expression. The apostle seems to have in mind his pending trip through Macedonia and is accounting for why he is staying a little longer in Ephesus (cf. 15:32; Acts 19:1-4).

B. The Collector. 16:10-12.

10. Now if Timothy come (cf. Acts 19:22). At this time Timothy was traveling throught Macedonia and the apostle anticipated that he would be reaching Corinth eventually (cf. 4:17). **See that he may be with you without fear.** The apostle hoped that the Corinthians would not intimidate Timothy, being a somewhat young and timid individual (cf. I Tim 4:12; 5:21-23; II Tim 1:6-8; 2:1, 3, 15; 4:1-2). Paul commends his ministry to them for **he worketh the work of the Lord, as I also do.**

11. Let no man therefore despise him. This advice is reminiscent of the advice given to Timothy in I Timothy 4:12.

12. As touching our brother Apollos. Paul had asked Apollos if he would be willing to go to Corinth in order to adjudicate some of their problems. Apparently, at that time he was not able but **he will come when he shall have convenient time.** Now, Paul begins a series of closing remarks, exhortations, challenges, and greetings.

C. The Close. 16:13-23.

13. As a military leader he exhorts the brethren to **Watch ye,** i.e. be wakeful and alert to your spiritual enemies. **Stand fast in the faith.** Don't be unsettled in your mind. Don't be afraid to be firm in your convictions. Don't be as the Sophists who called everything into question. **Quit you like men.** Be courageous. Be strong. Characteristic of Paul, he sees the Christian life as though he were in the arena. Faith, conviction, and courage are the essential ingredients for success and victory.

14. So that his readers do not understand his words to legitimize a careless and uncaring attitude, Paul moderates his advice with **Let all your things be done with charity.** This, of course, calls to mind all that he said in chapter thirteen.

15-16. The house of Stephanas (cf. 1:16). **Addicted themselves,** i.e. they devoted themselves in a self-imposed duty to the believers. This was the very first family to receive Christ in Paul's ministry in Achaia. This does not conflict with Romans 16:5, which in the better texts do not read "Achaia" but "Asia."

17. Stephanas and Fortunatus and Achaicus were three members of the Corinthian assembly who ministered to Paul's needs in Ephesus. Note the Latin names. This is not surprising since the new city of Corinth was largely composed of Romans.

18. They . . . refereshed my spirit and yours. Here Paul has in mind both their ministry to him, in terms of reporting the progress of the Corinthian assembly, and their ministry to the Corinthians in terms of sharing the ministry Paul had with them in Ephesus.

19. Aquila and Priscilla. Having been exiled from Rome (Acts 18:2) Paul first met this couple in Corinth. They have since moved on to Ephesus (cf. also Rom 16:3-5). **The church that is in their house.** Apparently, wherever this couple went they made their home a sanctuary where Christ was honored and believers gathered to share the Word together and worship.

20-24. Greet ye one another with an holy kiss (cf. Rom 16:16; I Thess 5:26; II Cor 13:12; I Pet 5:14). In the custom of the day, this was an expression of mutual affection and friendship. In other words, they were to put away their divisive spirit and unite in the bonds of love. **With mine own hand** has reference to the salutation, not the entire epistle. In Galatians 6:11 Paul remarks that his writing of that epistle with his own hand was something unusual due to his poor sight. Ordinarily, he used a secretary to whom he would dictate his letters and then he would write the salutation with his own hand to authenticate it (Col 4:18; II Thess 3:17). **Anathema,** "devoted to destruction" (cf. Rom 9:3; Gal 1:18,19; I Cor 12:3). **Marantha.** Properly, two words in the Aramaic. It expresses one of two possible ideas. It may be taken in the sense of "our Lord is come," signifying the incarnation. Or it may mean "our Lord cometh," signifying the second coming. The latter seems to be in view here. It is much like John's concluding remarks in Revelation: "even so, come, Lord Jesus" (Rev 22:20). **My love be with you all.** Only their spiritual father could speak to them in this way. His love is extended not only to those who agree with him, but to all in the assembly, even his enemies. The greatest example these Christians have of how to live the Christian life is the great apostle, himself.

BIBLIOGRAPHY

Alford, H. *The Greek Testament,* Vol. II, Revised by E. F. Harrison. Chicago: Moody Press, 1968.

Barclay, W. *Letters to the Corinthians.* Philadelphia: Westminster Press, 1956.

Barrett, C. K. The First Epistle to the Corinthians. In *Harper's New Testament Commentaries.* New York: Harper and Row, 1968.

Boyer, J. B. *For a World Like Ours.* Grand Rapids: Baker, 1971.

Erdman, C. R. *The First Epistle of Paul to the Corinthians.* Philadelphia: Westminster Press, 1928.

Findlay, G. G. Saint Paul's First Epistle to the Corinthians. In *The Expositor's Greek New Testament.* Vol. II. Grand Rapids: Eerdmans, n. d.

*Godet, F. *Commentary on Saint Paul's First Epistle to the Corinthains.* 2 Vols. Edinburgh: T & T Clark, 1957.

*Gromacki, R. G. *Called to Be Saints, An Exposition of I Corinthians.* Grand Rapids: Baker, 1977.

*Grosheide, F. W. Commentary on the First Epistle to the Corinthians. In *The New International Commentary.* Grand Rapids: Eerdmans, 1953.

*Hodge, C. *An Exposition of the First Epistle to the Corinthians.* Grand Rapids: Eerdmans, reprint, 1974.

Ironside, H. A. *Addresses on the First Epistle to the Corinthians.* New York: Loizeaux Brothers, 1938.

*Johnson, S. L. The First Epistle to the Corinthians. In *The Wycliffe Bible Commentary.* Pfeiffer, C. F. and Harrison, E. F., Editors. Chicago: Moody Press, 1963.

Kling, C. W. The First Epistle to Paul to the Corinthians. In *A Commentary on the Holy Scriptures.* Ed. by J. P. Lange. Trans. by P. Schaff. New York: Scribners, 1889.

Lenski, R. C. H. *The Interpretation of Paul's First and Second Epistle to the Corinthians.* Columbus: Wartburg Press. 1957.

Morgan, G. C. *The Corinthian Letters of Paul.* Old Tappan, N. J.: Revell, 1946.

*Morris, L. The First Epistle of Paul to the Corinthians. In *Tyndale New Testament Commentary.* Grand Rapids: Eerdmans, 1976.

Redpath, A. *The Royal Route to Heaven.* Westwood: Revell, 1960.

Rice, J. R. *The Church of God at Corinth.* Murfreesboro: Sword of the Lord, 1973.

Robertson, A. and Plummer, A. A Critical and Exegetical Commentary on the Epistle of Paul to the Corinthians. In *The International Critical Commentary.* New York: Scribner, 1911.

Zodhiates, S. *Conquering the Fear of Death. A Commentary on I Corinthians 15.* Grand Rapids: Eerdmans, 1970.

The Second Epistle To The

CORINTHIANS

INTRODUCTION

II Corinthians is actually the fourth letter that Paul wrote to Corinth (see introduction to I Corinthians). A "previous epistle" was written prior to I Corinthians, and then another "sorrowful letter" was written between I Corinthians and II Corinthians. The second canonical epistle has several features which distinguish it. His first epistle is both practical and instructional but this epistle is intensely personal and autobiographical. In fact, its style appears so spontaneous and emotional that some have questioned its internal unity. For this reason a word needs to be said about the integrity of the epistle.

Authorship. Although the historical evidence is not as early as that of I Corinthians, it is almost equally as strong. External evidence suggests that the second epistle to the Corinthians had not yet reached Rome by the end of the first century (A.D. 96) since it is not quoted by Clement of Rome. However, it was known to Polycarp who quotes 4:14. II Corinthians is further attested in the letter to Diognetus, Athanagoras, Theophilus of Antioch, Tertullian, Clement of Alexandria, Irenaeus, the Muratorian Canon, and Marcion's *Apostolocon.* It is also found in the Old Syriac and the Old Latin, along with the first epistle. By the end of the second century the attestation is replete.

The internal evidence is also very strong. The writer calls himself Paul (1:1; 10:1). Likewise conservative scholarship is unanimous in its agreement that the Pauline authorship of this epistle is unmistakable, not only in content but in style and vocabulary.

Background. II Corinthians is written to the assembly which was founded on Paul's first visit to that city. Since his departure and subsequent ministry in Ephesus the apostle has learned a great deal about the problems fomenting in this little assembly. Problems with worldliness, internal wranglings, and doctrinal defections continue to fester in spite of Paul's efforts in the first epistle.

Opposition to Paul's ministry continues to mount, especially coming from the party which associated itself with "Christ" (cf. 10:7; 11:13). The leader of this group seems to have been especially obnoxious to the apostle (10:7-11). When the news of these conditions reached Paul at Ephesus he made a brief visit to Corinth in order to deal with them (cf. 2:1; 12:14, 21; 13:1-2). At this time the personal vendetta against the Apostle Paul himself was shown. Upon his return to Ephesus the apostle was so distressed he penned a letter to the church of such a severe nature that he later regretted having written it. This he sent to them by Titus (2:3-4, 9; 7:8-12). It is probable that this letter was lost in its entirety. While some have suggested that this letter is preserved in II Corinthians 10-13 (Plummer, *Commentary on Second Corinthians,* p. xviii), this theory is quite unlikely (Bernard, *Expositior's Greek Testament,* v. 3, pp. 21-27). The charges leveled against the apostle by this group are indicated in a number of passages in the epistle. For example, he was accused of being fickle (1:17), authoritarian (1:24), ministering without proper credentials (3:1), cowardice (10:1, 10), failure to maintain proper clerical dignity (11:7), presumption (10:13-17), and fleshliness (10:2). Likewise, the apostle has a few things to say about his accusers. For example, they corrupted the Word (2:17), they were deceptive (3:1), they were Jews masquerading as ministers of Christ (11:23-27), they were domineering (11:20), and bold (11:21), they lacked the spiritual courage to step out on their own and start their own ministry (11: 23-27). Thus it was no small wonder that the apostle was seriously concerned about the spiritual well-being of the church at Corinth.

Titus was to deliver the "sorrowful letter" then return to Paul with a report of the response of the Corinthians and subsequent development. However, Paul had to leave Ephesus earlier than scheduled because of the uprising of the silversmiths (cf. Acts 20:1). He stopped at Troas and apparently was engaging in a very fruitful evangelistic effort in that city. However, Titus tarried much longer than the overstrained and impetuous apostle could stand. He discontinued his minitsry in Troas and crossed over to Macedonia expecting to meet him somewhere along the *Via Egnatia,* the great highway which connected the chief Macedonian towns along the coast. It was therefore "with great relief that the apostle received Titus' report that they had been genuinely grieved by the painful letter (7:9), the offending person had been dealt with (2:6-8), the great majority of the Corinthians were really loyal to the apostle as he had suspected all along (7:14), and Titus himself had developed a new appreciation for this assembly (7:15). Thus it is not surprising in the first seven chapters of II Corinthians to see the apostle pour out his thanksgiving to God in encouragement at the progress this assembly was making. Thus, he sat down immediately and penned II Corinthians from Macedonia (2:3; 7:5-7; 8:1; 9:2-4), probably from the city of Philippi.

Purpose. Thiessen has ably sum-marized Paul's reasons for writing II Corinthians. He did so in order: (1) to explain his sufferings in Asia (1:3-11); (2) to justify himself in his change of plans about returning to Corinth (1:12-2:4); (3) to instruct them as to the treatment of the offender (2:5-11); (4) to express his joy at the good news of their progress (2:12-13); (5) for full reconciliation with himself (6:11-7:16); (6) to urge the Corinthians to participate in the collection for the church at Jerusalem (chs. 8-9); (7) to establish his authority as an apostle (10:1-13:10.).

The unity of II Corinthians has frequently been called into question (cf. Alford, Zahn, Lake, Moffatt, Kummel, and Plummer). However, there is absolutely no external evidence to support the contention that II Corinthians was ever more than one unit. The arguments rest entirely upon internal evidence such as the change of tone in chapters 10-13, certain supposed inconsistencies in 1-9 compared with 10-13, and the reconciling of some statements with Paul's geographical location at the time of writing (10:16). None of these objections bear a great deal of weight. The basic tenor of the epistle is less formal than others of Paul's epistles. It is much more emotional, and therefore, there are more abrupt changes in his thought. Yet the main divisions are clearly visible. Thiessen is probably correct to suggest that the changes in tone between chapters 1-9 and 10-13 are likely due to the particular group Paul is addressing in each of these sections (Thiessen, *Introduction to the New Testament,* p. 210). This peculiarity in style can be demonstrated, not only in other biblical literature, but in secular literature as well.

(Editor's note. The author acknowledges much indebtedness throughout this study to notes originally complied by his late father, Burton C. Mitchell, noted Bible lecturer.)

OUTLINE

I. Introduction. 1:1-11.
   A. Salutation. 1:1-2.
   B. Thanksgiving 1:3-11.

II. Apology for Paul's Ministry. 1:12-7:16.
   A. The Conduct of Paul. 1:12-2:17.
      1. Paul's change of plans. 1:12-2:4.
         a. His concern. 1:12-14.
         b. His plan. 1:15-22.
         c. His explanation. 1:23-2:4.
      2. Paul's charge concerning the offender. 2:5-11.
      3. Paul's confidence in the Corinthians. 2:12-17.
   B. The Calling of Paul. 3:1-6:10.
      1. The superiority of his ministry. 3:1-4:6.
         a. The credentials of his ministry. 3:1-5.
         b. The quality of his ministry. 3:6-4:6.
            (1). The glory of the new covenant. 3:6-11.
            (2). The permanence of the new covenant. 3:12-18.
            (3). The ministry of the new convenant. 4:1-6.
      2. The suffering in his ministry. 4:7-12.
      3. The goal of his ministry. 4:13-5:10.
         a. Hope of the resurrection. 4:13-15.
         b. Confidence in ministry. 4:16-18.
         c. Contemplation of new life. 5:1-10.
      4. The service in his ministry. 5:11-6:10.
         a. Paul's motives. 5:11-15.
         b. Paul's message. 5:16-21.
         c. Paul's methods. 6:1-10.
   C. The Challenge of Paul. 6:11-7:16.
      1. The entreaty for reconciliation. 6:11-7:4.
         a. Sympathy towards Paul. 6:11-13.
         b. Separation from the world. 6:14-7:1.
      2. The encouragement from their response. 7:5-16.
         a. Comfort of Titus. 7:5-7.
         b. Correction of the letter. 7:8-12.
         c. Consolation. 7:13-16.

III. Appeal of Paul's Ministry. 8:1-9:15.
   A. Faithfulness Illustrated. 8:1-5.
   B. Faithfulness Exhorted. 8:6-15.
   C. Faithfulness Delegated. 8:16-9:5.
   D. Faithfulness Directed. 9:6-15.

IV. Authority of Paul's Ministry. 10:1-13:10.
   A. The Defense of the Apostle. 10:1-18.
      1. By his attitudes. 10:1-6.
      2. By his authority. 10:1-11.
      3. By divine commendation. 10:12-18.

COMMENTARY

I. INTRODUCTION. 1:1-11.

A. Salutation. 1:1-2.

1:1. Paul, an apostle. Paul characteristically begins, as in his other epistles, by establishing his authority and his commission (cf. Eph 1:1; Col 1:1; I Tim 1:1; II Tim 1:1; Gal 1:1). This ministry was commissioned him **of Jesus Christ by the will of God.** Paul takes for granted that he fulfills any requisites for the office of apostleship. His is no usurpation of power, but obedience to the call of God. **And Timothy.** This companion of Paul is not mentioned in the introduction to I Corinthians, presumably because Timothy had already been sent to Corinth (I Cor 4:17; 16:10). That he appears here indicates that he has since rejoined the apostle, given his report concerning the affairs at Corinth, and traveled with him to Macedonia. The epistle is primarily addressed to **the church of God which is at Corinth.** That is, the local assembly. But, that it was intended also as a circular letter to be read by other assemblies is implied by the fact that he also addresses **all the saints that are in all Achaia.** This would embrace at least the Christians that were in Athens (cf. Acts 17:34) and in Cenchreae, the eastern port of Corinth (cf. Rom 16:1). **Saints** calls to mind all who have been set apart by God and walk in newness of life

(cf. Rom 1:7; I Cor 1:2; 6:11; II Cor 5:17).

2. Grace be to you and peace. For Paul, grace always precedes peace. Until one has received the grace of God he can know nothing of His peace. "Grace (Gr *charis*) is the infinite love of God that enables Him to pour out infinite favor on the object loved without receiving anything in return. It demands no merit and incurs no obligation. It has been extended to all of humanity by the cross work of Jesus Christ which alone makes God's love available to mankind (I Jn 2:2). Anything that we might place between the provision of God's grace and the power of God's grace has been received by faith. There is nothing that brings this peace so much as the undiluted gospel of God's grace (cf. Eph 2:14; Phil 4:7; Col 1:20; 3:15). **From God our Father and from the Lord Jesus Christ.** The single preposition (Gr *apo*) links the Father and the Son thus, affirming unequivocally the deity of Christ. The reference is to the eternal Father and the incarnate Son (cf. also 13:14).

B. Thanksgiving. 1:3-11.

3-4. Blessed (Gr *eulogētos,* "well spoken of"). This term is used in the New Testament of God and so here. It is a term of adoration and praise. In consideration of God's grace and peace (vs.

2) and in anticipation of His mercies and comforts (vs. 3b) such a pronouncement from the apostle is understood. For he contemplates both who God is and what God does. **Even the Father of our Lord Jesus Christ, the Father of mercies, and the God of all comfort.** The mercies in view here, no doubt, include such great verities as deliverance from the world, sin, and Satan to participation in sonship, light, and life. But the force is even more than this. The stress is that the Father is "characterized" by mercy (cf. Ps 86:5; Dan 9:9; Mic 7:18). **Comfort** (Gr *paraklēsis*) is cognate to "the Comforter" of John 16:7. This term does not connote "sympathy" as much as "empathy" or "encouragement." It has the idea of someone coming alongside to provide support. Since the Comforter abides within (cf. Jn 14:16-17) a twofold process is implied: strength for the inner man and encouragement for the outer man. Paul now turns his thoughts to the everyday problems of life and he does so in the context of the **God of all comfort; Who comforteth us in all our tribulation.** In the general scope of life, God's comfort extends to every area. But the purpose emphasized here is not just for our own good, but **that we may be able to comfort them which are in any trouble.** God's comfort is transferable and intended to be shared.

5. For as the sufferings of Christ abound in us, so our consolation also aboundeth by Christ. As the problems increase so does the consolation. Both, in this case, are measured by the experience of Christ (cf. Lk 24:26, 46; Phil 3:10; Col 1:24; I Pet 1:11). Paul's use of the term "abound" is significant throughout this epistle (cf. II Cor 4:15; 8:2, 7-8, 12).

6-7. Many ancient manuscripts differ in the order of the clauses in these verses. But the sense in every case is basically the same "if we are afflicted, it is for your good, or if we are comforted, it is for your good." Everything else, in these verses, is subordinated to these two main ideas. Paul does not glory in suffering

per se. But, he knows that the fact of suffering identifies us with Christ and with His church (cf. also Rom 8:17). He also knows **that as ye are partakers of the sufferings, so shall ye be also of the consolation.** If we should suffer together, then we know that we shall also rejoice together. Those who share mutual suffering and affliction share also in the joy of consolation. This relationship of intimacy implied by the apostle's terminology stands in stark contrast to the divisive spirit that persisted in Corinth. His readers could not help but compare their own situation against the feelings and experiences expressed by Paul.

8-10. Paul draws upon his recent experience to do two things: to share with his readers his needs and concerns, and also, to explain his change in plans. **We despaired even of life** and the expression, **we had the sentence of death in ourselves** are parallel concepts. Paul's condition, due to external pressures and physical limitations, reached the point where the only way out, visible to him, was death (cf. Acts 14:19). Yet God's purpose, even in this, was being fulfilled so that Paul would come to the end of himself and trust in **God which raiseth the dead.** For Paul has initiated a process of faith that is viewed in a threefold sense, **Who delivered us** (past) . . . **and doth deliver** (present) . . . **he will yet deliver** (future). Faith liberated Paul from bondage to his circumstances and the fear of death (cf. Heb 2:14-15).

11. Helping together probably has reference to their cooperation in interceding on his behalf with the other churches. Paul's thinking in this verse is very much like that in verses 6-7. Since there were many who where sharing together in **prayer for us,** then the fact of Paul's deliverance may also elicit **thanks . . . by many on our behalf.** The preposition "by" (Gr *dia*) is best rendered "by means of." Thus the sense of the verse is: as health was rendered by means of prayer so also thanksgiving to God is rendered by means of many who shared in that prayer.

II. APOLOGY FOR PAUL'S MINISTRY. 1:12-7:16.

A. The Conduct of Paul. 1:12-2:17.

In this opening section the Apostle Paul has three concerns: (1) his change of plans (1:12-2:4); (2) his charge concerning the offender (2:5-11); (3) his confidence in the Corinthians to do what is right (2:12-17). In the opening section he alludes to his desire to come again to Corinth. It was on this score that he had been criticized by his enemies in the assembly. They accused him of promising them a visit with no intention of ever coming. It is this allegation that the apostle answers here.

1. Paul's change of plans. 1:12-2:4.

a. His concern. 1:12-14.

12. The testimony of our conscience may suggest the "ground" of Paul's rejoicing, or the "substance" of his rejoicing. The latter idea seems to fit best with what follows. Paul was able to rejoice in a ministry of **simplicity and godly sincerity.**

13-14. For we write none other things unto you, than what ye read or acknowledge. Paul's epistles are characterized by the same degree of honesty and integrity that characterize his life. **Ye have acknowledged us in part.** Most in Corinth stood with the apostles in affirming his integrity. On the other hand, there was a small contingency of individuals who did not. **We.** This is an editorial use of the pronoun to refer to the apostle himself. **Your rejoicing.** Those who appreciated the apostle's ministry. **Ye are also ours.** Likewise, the apostle rejoiced in those who received his ministry. **In the day of the Lord Jesus.** In the day when all the secrets of men are revealed Paul was confident that these believers would have the assurance that their faith in him was not misplaced.

b. His plan. 1:15-22.

15-16. In this confidence refers to the confidence which elicited their rejoicing in the previous verse. **I was minded to**

come unto you. In Paul's initial itinerary he intended to go immediately from Ephesus to Corinth. **Second benefit** must not be misconstrued as Paul's second visit to them, since he had already visited them twice (cf. 12:14). But, that in his trip he would be seeing them twice: as he explains, **to pass by you into Macedonia, and to come again out of Macedonia unto you.** Thus he would be visiting with them twice before he went on his way to Judea. **And of you to be brought on my way** (Gr *propempō*) "to be brought on my way," "to be aided in my journey"). Following the custom of ancient times, since Paul would be traveling immediately to Judea from Corinth, it would be appropriate for the assembly to assist him financially.

17-18. When I therefore was thus minded, did I use lightness? Here Paul avers the sincerity of his purpose. Nor did he intend any secular advantages to himself **according to the flesh . . . there should be yea, yea, and nay, nay?** The apostle cannot be charged with inconsistency. That which he affirmed he affirms still. That which he denies, he denies still. Hence, **as God is true, our word toward you was not yea and nay.** As the truth of God stands so does the word of the apostle (cf. also Gal 1:8; I Jn 5:10). The trustworthiness of Paul's words are seen in the nature of his gospel.

19. Jesus Christ, who was preached among you by us . . . was not yea and nay. Those who truly knew the Lord as Saviour in the Corinthian assembly could hardly doubt the veracity of this statement. They had received and experienced the reality of saving faith and knew that Paul's words were true.

20-22. For all the promises of God in him are yea (literally, "as many promises of God"). The thrust of this expression is that the promises of God find their affirmation and fulfillment in Christ. **Amen** is equivalent to "yea." Whether one is a Gentile (yea) or a Hebrew (amen) the promises of God are sure. But the force of Paul's analogy is

COMMENTARY

I. PERSONAL: THE APOSTLE OF LIBERTY. 1:1-2:21.

A. Introduction. 1:1-9.

1:1. Paul. Paul was his Latin name; Saul was his Hebrew name. He was born in Tarsus in Cilicia (Acts 9:11; 22:3) of Jewish parents (Phil 3:5). His father was a Pharisee and a Roman citizen (Acts 23:6), so Paul was a Roman citizen by birth (Acts 22:27-28). He studied under the renowned Gamaliel (Acts 5:34, 22: 3). **An apostle.** An apostle is one who is sent with authority to represent and speak for another. He is accredited with special delegated authority and entrusted with a special divine message. Paul claims to be a messenger, an envoy, an ambassador for Christ. He was endowed with all the credentials of his office. He was owned by Christ, commissioned by Christ, and empowered by Christ. **Not of men.** Not from men. The bluntness of Paul's denial is due to the charge of the legalists that he was not one of the Twelve and not a genuine apostle. The preposition (Gr *apo*) signifies origin and separation. Paul already states that the source of his apostleship is not from men, not emanating from men. **Neither by man.** The preposition here (Gr *dia*) implies means, medium, instrument. Paul declares decisively that the means of receiving his apostleship was not a man. "The first preposition denotes the fountain-head whence the apostle's authority springs, the second the channel through which it is conveyed" (J. B. Lightfoot, *The Epistle of St. Paul to the Galatians,* p. 71). Paul was not an ambassador of men, and his gospel was not the word and wisdom of man. Paul's "mission to the Gentiles had apparently been disparaged on the plea that it had been emanated from men, i.e., from the church of Antioch only. Again, the validity of his commission was impugned on the ground that he originally had received the Spirit through a man, i.e.,

through the agency of Ananias, who had been deputed to lay his hands upon him at Damascus" (Frederic Rendall, *The Epistle to the Galatians,* p. 149). Paul knew nothing about apostolic succession, but he experienced an abundant measure of apostolic success. **But by Jesus Christ, and God the Father.** When the preposition (Gr *dia*) is used of a personal agent sometimes it expresses the author of the action as well as its instrument. Here Jesus Christ is both the ultimate source and the mediate agency. Both Christ and God are governed by one preposition and joined by one conjunction, indicating that they are coequal and coeternal. There was no one higher to commission Paul and no lower through whom he was commissioned. He had a divine commission to expose false teaching, to exclaim the gospel, to establish churches, to exhort Christians, and to exalt Christ. **Who raised him from the dead.** Paul had seen the risen Christ (I Cor 9:1; 15:8) and was qualified to be an apostle. The resurrection was God's "amen" to Christ's "It is finished." Paul emphasized the resurrection because some were saying that he had not seen the Lord Jesus Christ and could not be an apostle. It was the risen, glorified Son of God whom Paul had seen on the road to Damascus (Acts 9:3-9). Paul's mission and message were divine, not human.

2. And all the brethren which are with me. Paul implies that there were with him a goodly number of Christian believers, members of the household of faith. Paul associates these unnamed fellow workers with him in sending greetings. **Unto the churches of Galatia.** Not to the church of Galatia. To Paul there was no state or national church. The word church (Gr *ekklēsia*) occurs over one hundred times in the New Testament. Once it refers to the assembly of saints in heaven (Heb 12:23), several times it is used in a wide sense (mostly in whom he considers to be his spiritual children.

2. Paul's charge concerning the offender. 2:5-11.

Since by this time the apostle has heard the report from Titus (cf. vss. 12-14) he now knows that they have, indeed, followed his advice. They have disciplined one offender at least in the assembly and it has produced such radical results the apostle now finds it necessary to give some additional counsel regarding this particular matter (vss. 5-11).

5. If any have caused grief (literally, if there is anyone in the assembly who has caused sorrow). Paul is generalizing in order to state a principle. At the same time he is speaking specifically to the situation recorded in I Cor 5:1-13. **He hath not grieved me, but in part: that I may not overcharge you all.** The sentence structure is awkward here and the sense is difficult to derive from the AV. Here Paul is saying, to paraphrase, "if someone has caused grief in the assembly, his offense is not so much against the apostle as it is against the local assembly, to put it mildly." For this reason the obligation of discipline lies not on the shoulders of the apostle but on the leadership of the local church, and Paul is prepared to go along with their decision (cf. vs. 10). Tasker follows Menzies in suggesting that the offender in view is not the one mentioned in I Corinthians 5:1. On the contrary, he suggests that the person is not guilty of immoral conduct but rude and disagreeable conduct. It is asserted that it is quite contrary to the moral position of Paul to say that he could have ever tolerated the presence of the incestuous person in the church (R. V. G. Tasker, *The Second Epistle of Paul to the Corinthians,* p. 52). To this two things need to be said. First, while this view commends itself, Tasker fails to show how it is concluded without question that the person involved had been guilty of rude and disagreeable conduct. Secondly, Paul has

already cited the fact that his forgiveness, and certainly that of the Lord, has been extended to persons guilty of grossly immoral conduct (cf. I Cor 6:9-11). Therefore, the view favored by the majority of the older commentators is to be preferred here. That is, that the offender involved is the incestuous person mentioned in chapter 5 of I Corinthians.

6-8. Sufficient to such a man is this punishment. Your discipline of this individual is enough. Paul sensed that they had gone far enough in bringing this person to repentance. His advice now is to, **Forgive . . . and comfort . . . lest perhaps such a one should be swallowed up with overmuch sorrow.** The purpose of discipline is not to destroy but to edify and restore. Therefore, when true repentance is evidenced the proper response is to **Confirm your love toward him.** Paul goes on to express why he instructed the church to administer discipline.

9. That I might know the proof of you. Paul needed to know that the Corinthian assembly possessed the maturity and character to deal with sin in their midst. It is now clear to him that they did. In 1:3-4 Paul indicated that God's comfort was designed to be shared. Here is Paul's application of this principle in the context of church discipline. As they had received God's forgiveness they are to forgive.

10. To whom ye forgive any thing, I forgive also. Paul awaits the church's decision. He was prepared to sanction their ruling on the matter. Notice here that there is no hierarchical structure dictating to the local assembly. The ruling authority was the local church.

11. Lest Satan should get an advantage of us. Such an advantage could be gained by Satan either by the despair of an individual Christian, or the disunity of the local assembly through the incident in view. **For we are not ignorant of his devices.** Paul knows that Satan can and will use this incident to distract and diminish the work of God in the Corinthian assembly unless it is properly handled. Satan's first attack is against the gospel (cf. II Cor 4:4). If he can bring disunity to the church, which is the agent of propagating the gospel, then he will also bring dishonor upon the gospel. The church which God can best use is the church which exudes God's forgiveness and consolation (on Satan's devices see also 10:3-4; 11:3, 12-14).

3. Paul's confidence in the Corinthians. 2:12-17.

12-13. When I came to Troas . . . a door was opened unto me of the Lord. The connection of this verse is with verse 4: "that ye might know the love which I have." Further evidence of this love is Paul's behavior while engaged in a very fruitful ministry in Troas: **I had no rest in my spirit.** Paul's concern for the evangelization of the lost was overriden by his concern for the Corinthian assembly, and that was saying something (cf. I Cor 9:16)! It is not love for the lost nor love for the world which distinguishes the believer. It is love for one another (Jn 13:35). **But taking leave of them I went . . . into Macedonia.** This was in hopes of meeting Titus on the way. On Titus' report to Paul about the condition of things in Corinth. See 7:5-6.

14-17. Triumph (cf. Col 2:9-15). The imagery conveyed in the use of this term is of the Roman general who marched in victory with his entourage, consisting of two groups: **Them that are saved, and . . . them that perish.** The former group consisted of those allowed to live as slaves of the empire. They were being led into a new life. The latter group were the condemned. They were being led to their death. Each group carried a burning incense. The one was a **savor of death unto death,** the other was a fragrance of **life unto life.** Calvary was the mighty display of the infinite power of a sovereign God. The human race was divided into two categories: those of life unto life and those of death unto death. The practical lesson here is that the believer is a "savor" of God's infinite power and un-

speakable love wherever he goes. Also, as the believer proclaims this truth, he divides men. This is not a "method" of evangelism, but a proclamation of the triumph of Christ at Calvary. **Who is sufficient for these things?** The implied answer to Paul's question is "I am." Paul's credentials are given in the words **as . . . in the sight of God speak we in Christ** (literally, "but as from sincerity, but as from God, we speak in Christ in the sight of God"). The apostle's adequacy is not within himself, but God (cf. 3:5). This is in contrast to those who merely **corrupt the word of God** (Gr *kapēleuō*, should read, "are peddling the Word of God").

B. The Calling of Paul. 3:1-4:6.

1. The superiority of his ministry. 3:1-4:6

a. The credentials of his ministry. 3:1-5.

3:1. Do we begin again to commend ourselves? The apostle is incredulous that a formal introduction to a church he founded should be necessary. **Epistles of commendation to you.** Such letters of introduction constituted a common practice in New Testament times (cf. Acts 9:1-2; 18:27). Due to the prevailing social, political, and religious climate such letters were both advisable and necessary. Paul here does not disparage their use. He can only be amazed that the Corinthian believers require it of him.

2-3. Ye are our epistle. Paul's converts at Corinth were living testimonials to the genuineness of his ministry. **Our hearts.** Paul employs the plural in agreement with the use of the editorial "we" throughout this passage. **Known and read of all men.** To any who would "take up and read" Paul's ministry was authenticated (cf. I Cor 9:2). **The epistle of Christ ministered by us.** The apostle is always careful to show that the enabling power of his ministry did not reside in himself but in Christ (cf. I Cor 15:9-10). This epistle is distinguished in two ways.

for Christ. Any change in the gospel of Christ is a corruption, interfering with its simplicity, its purity, and its effectiveness. Even the thought of this stirs Paul to the very depths of his being. Note how vehement is his language now, and how he repeated it for greater emphasis.

8. But though we, or an angel from heaven, preach any other gospel. Paul does not say that he or a messenger from heaven was likely to preach any other gospel. He merely uses a future hypothetical possibility to illustrate the case. This passage directly speaks against such claims as that of the Mormons, whose *Book of Mormon* claims angelic authority as delivered by the Angel Moroni and "translated" by their founder Joseph Smith. **Let him be accursed.** An "anathema" on anyone who would proclaim a gospel contrary to that which Paul delivered and had received from God (I Cor 15:3-4). God does not want His Word twisted by unlearned and unstable men unto the destruction of souls (II Pet 3:17). God said what He meant, and He meant what He said. God can do nothing less than put an awful curse on all who reject, pervert and falsify the gospel of His Son. It was the Holy Spirit who moved Paul to pen these serious words. We must never forget that the awful day of doom and destruction is coming when the divine "anathema" pronounced here will be executed (II Thess 1:7-9). May God's people everywhere stand with Paul in opposition to false teaching. May God help us to believe the gospel, to behave the gospel, and to become living epistles of the gospel.

9. As we said before. The language is too emphatic to refer to the verse lightly. Paul no doubt had warned them of the dangers of false teachers as he did the Ephesian elders (Acts 20:29-32). The perfect tense of "said" (Gr *prolegō*) means that it was a certain and clear pronouncement. The Galatians still remember Paul's warning, and therefore their defection is inexcusable. The plural number (we) shows that the previous warning was given by others in addition to Paul. **If any man.** The particle (Gr *ei*) speaks of a fulfilled condition. Paul is not speaking of a future probability (vs. 8), but of an actual, current fact, and he hurls the anathema directly at the legalists. Note the omission in verse 9 of "we or an angel."

B. Paul's Apostleship.
    1:10-2:21.

1. Paul's revelation from Christ.
    1:10-17.

10. For. This introduces a justification of the severe language just used. **Do I now persuade men.** This means to win over, to conciliate, to render friendly to one's self. These rhetorical questions indicate that an attack has been made on Paul for the purpose of discrediting both him and his ministry. He denies the charges. Paul was not softening down unwelcome truths to men, that he might by some means win them over to his way of thinking. Neither was he trying to persuade God to tone down His message. Paul's loyalty to Christ and his sufferings for Christ were evidences that he was not seeking man's approval, but his Lord's "well done." He has no desire to please anyone but Christ, whose he is and whom he serves (Acts 27:23).

11. But I certify you. I make known, inform, tell you plainly, assure you. This word (Gr *gnorizō*) is used to introduce matters of great importance (I Cor 12:3; 15:1; II Cor 8:1). Paul uses a strong word to leave no doubt as to the truth of the statement he is about to make. **Brethren.** Paul addresses them as brethren in Christ, sons of the same heavenly Father. They are deceived, disturbed, and defecting in their devotion and duty to Christ. But they are still regarded as brethren, brethren needing Paul's Spirit-inspired counsel. **That the gospel which was preached of me.** Literally, the gospel gospelled by me. **Is not after man.** Not according to man. Paul sets the record straight. He affirms the divine origin of his message in terms similar to those

13. And not as Moses. What follows is an allegorization of the account given in Exodus 34:29-35. **Put a veil over his face.** The veil was not to hide the glory but to obscure it. The people saw his brightness but not directly. Not only did this veil actually conceal the brightness of the glory but it also concealed the **end of that which was abolished.** The transience of the glory which accompanied the old covenant was not manifestly evident to the children of Israel. And for Paul this has typical significance.

14. Their minds were blinded: for until this day remaineth the same veil. For Israel the same obscurity obtains. Their minds are still blinded to the truth as though the veil upon Moses' face were thrown upon their hearts. **Which veil is done away in Christ.** Only the gospel of God's grace exposes the truth to full view.

15. But even unto this day, when Moses is read, the veil is upon their heart. Unfortunately, as far as the Jews are concerned, Christ is still a stumbling block they cannot see (cf. I Cor 1:23). For the apostle this is no light matter and a concern which caused him great anxiety (cf. Rom 9:1-4). But now the veil is not so much upon the revelation of the glory but upon their own hearts (cf. Lk 24:25; Acts 13:27-29).

16. Nevertheless, when it shall turn to the Lord, the veil shall be taken away. The practice of Moses of removing the veil when he turned to the Lord to speak with Him directly, is in view here (Ex 34:29-35). In the same sense, when Israel turns once again to the Lord, she will see and understand—the veil will be removed.

17. Now connects the reference to "the Lord" in the previous verse with the reference to **the Lord** in the present verse. This Lord is Christ (cf. vs. 14). **Is that Spirit.** While the article does not appear in the original text the AV has properly rendered the sense when it includes "that" before Spirit. Paul is not saying "the Lord is Spirit" (in the same sense that is indicated in Jn 4:24) but "the

Lord is the Holy Spirit, the Third Person of the Godhead." It is also important to note here that Paul is not confusing the two Persons. Jesus said earlier, "I and my Father are one" (Jn 10:30). He bears the same relationship to the Holy Spirit. Here is the ineffable mystery of the Trinity, one in essence yet three distinct personalities. **And where the Spirit of the Lord is, there is liberty.** Indeed, when Israel turns once again to the Lord and the veil is removed, there is glorious liberty that comes with the confrontation with the truth (cf. Jn 8:32; 14:6, 17; 15:26). For further insight into the relationship of the Holy Spirit to the ministry of Christ see Jn 14:16-17, 26; 15:26-27; and 16:7.

18. But we all. Reaching a climax, based upon the experience of Moses and Israel, Paul now applies the truth to all his readers. **With open face beholding as in a glass.** As though looking at a clear reflection in a mirror. **The glory of the Lord.** As Moses' face reflected God's glory at Sinai the face of every believer radiates the glory of Christ. That which was reserved for only the highest under the old covenant is made available to all in the new. Some commentaries have attempted to identify the mirror in this text with Christ, the Word, or the believer's heart. This, however, is difficult to justify from the context. What the apostle has in mind, specifically, is difficult to say. The term "beholding" can have the sense of "reflecting." Thus, in agreement with Lenski (*The Interpretation of I and II Corinthians*, pp. 947-948) the believer himself "reflects" the glory of the Lord just as the face of Moses reflected the glory of the Lord. This view fits most favorably with Paul's imagery.

Yet there is more. For Moses the glory eventually faded away, but under the New Covenant the believer is **changed into the same image.** Paul has already established that, "as we have borne the image of the earthy, we shall bear the image of the heavenly" (I Cor 15:49). The Apostle John says that ultimately we will be just like Christ "because we shall see him as he is" (I Jn 3:2). (See also I Peter 1:4; Galatians 4:19; and John 17:17.) **Even as by the Spirit of the Lord** (literally, "as from the Lord the Spirit"). This transformation takes place by the abiding presence of the Spirit of God.

(3). The ministry of the new covenant. 4:1-6.

4:1. Therefore, seeing we have this ministry, as we have received mercy, we faint not. In light of the superiority and character of the gospel of Jesus Christ under the new covenant, the Apostle Paul vigorously and enthusiastically assumes the task of proclaiming its message everywhere. The expression **we faint not** has the sense that Paul was not derelict in discharging his responsibilities to this ministry.

2. But (the strong adversative). What follows stands in sharp contrast to the last statement of verse 1. What Paul denies of himself he affirms of the false teachers at Corinth (C. Hodge, *Commentary on the Second Epistle to the Corinthians*, p. 82). In that regard, Paul demonstrates that he has **renounced the hidden things of dishonesty.** This may have reference to either disgraceful conduct or secret motives. The latter idea is best since the emphasis is upon "hidden things." The apostle's ministry was one of openness and honesty. He was **not walking in craftiness.** The apostle was not an opportunist nor shrewdly and unscrupulously seeking to achieve his desired aims. **Nor handling the word of God deceitfully** (cf. 2:17). Paul was not "peddling the Word of God" or adulterating it with false doctrine. Paul could say "I have received of the Lord that which also I delivered unto you" (I Cor 11:23). That which Paul preached was exactly as God revealed it to him. It was **the manifestation of the truth.** In contrast to those in the Corinthian assembly who were giving undue stress to human credentials Paul's message commended itself to **every man's conscience in the sight of God.**

3. But if our gospel be hid. Carrying over the analogy of the veil in the preceding chapter, such a veil conceals the truth only from **them that are lost.**

4. In whom the God of this world hath blinded the minds of them which believe not. On Satan's control of the world system see Matthew 4:8-9; John 12:31; 14:30; I Corinthians 10:20; Ephesians 2:2; 6:12; II Timothy 2:26. The "lost" of verse 3 are the "unbelievers" of this verse. Such ones are so controlled by Satan that he effectively shields them from the **light of the glorious gospel of Christ.** There are two vital inferences that must be drawn from this passage. The first is contextual. The apostle effectively categorizes those who find his message difficult to accept. In effect, he is saying that the person who is criticizing his ministry at Corinth is not even saved. He is lost, unbelieving, and has been blinded by Satan. The second inference is theological. For those who inordinately stress human freedom it must be observed here and elsewhere that the unregenerate man is in bondage. He is under Satanic control and is, therefore, incompetent to evaluate the truth of God.

5. For connects with the preceding verse. **We preach not ourselves but Christ Jesus the Lord.** Paul's message was clear and simple and could be summed up in a word, or even better, in a name, i.e. Christ Jesus. The singular object of Paul's preaching was to confront men with the person of Christ. **And ourselves your servants for Jesus' sake.** As a minister of the gospel, Paul is not his own man. He is a slave of his constituents and compelled by his Master.

6. For. The particle connects with the preceding verse and forms the basis for it. **God, who commanded the light to shine out of darkness.** This contemplates the old creation, Genesis 1:3. **Hath shined in our hearts.** This contemplates the new creation. Some suggest that "our" is used editorially to speak of the apostle himself. The reference would thus connect primarily with such passages as Acts 9:3-6; 26:15-16; Galatians 1:15-16. However, the plural "hearts" seems to lend more support to the notion that Paul here has in mind all believers, not just himself. Thus, the miracle of the new birth while not always accompanied by an outward manifestation of lights such as the experience of Paul, nevertheless involves a spiritual illumination concomitant with Paul's experience on the road to Damascus. **To give the light** (literally, "for illumination"). Just as the comfort of God is to be shared (cf. 1:3-4) even so the light which penetrates the darkness and regenerates the soul is to be reflected to others, and for Paul that constituted the essence of the gospel ministry. Specifically, for Paul this light was **the knowledge of the glory of God in the face of Jesus Christ.** This calls to mind Acts 9:3-6. Yet the experience is nonetheless glorious for all who have seen the light (cf. Jn 1:1-14; 9:24-25, 35-41; I Cor 2:10-14).

2. The suffering in his ministry. 4:7-12.

Having discussed his credentials for the ministry (3:1-5), and then in much more detail the specific quality of his ministry (3:6-4:6), Paul now gives attention to his personal suffering in the ministry (4:7-12).

7. We have this treasure in earthen vessels. In the wilderness under the old covenant God dwelt in a tent; today He dwells in the believer's heart. This is unspeakable truth and forms the theological rationale for holy living (cf. I Cor 6:19-20). But the stress here is upon "earthen." An earthenware jar is a brittle one. It depicts humanity in its weakness. The gospel is not a product of human genius or clever intellect (humanity in its strength). Yet it resides in men of clay, **that the excellency of the power may be of God, and not of us.** The quality of the gospel ministry is calibrated by the degree to which it points attention to the God of glory.

8-9. We are troubled on every side, yet not distressed. The believer may be hard pressed but never crushed. He may

be **perplexed** but he need never **despair.** Though he be **persecuted** he will never be abandoned. He may be **cast down** but he'll never be cast out.

10-12. Always bearing about in the body the dying of the Lord Jesus. The persecution and suffering and the trial which confronts the believer are to be understood as the "fellowship of his suffering" (cf. Phil 3:10; I Cor 15:31; 4:9; II Cor 11:23; Rom 8:36; Gal 6:17). **That the life also of Jesus might be made manifest in our body.** This same thought occurs in Romans 8:17. If we share in His suffering we will also share in His glory (cf. II Tim 2:11; I Pet 4:13-14; Rom 6:8-9; Jn 14:19).

We which live (literally, "the living"). **That the life also of Jesus might be made manifest in our mortal flesh.** A diamond is best seen against a black background. The brilliance of the life that is in Christ Jesus is best seen against the background of death. **So then death worketh in us.** Paul relates this to his own personal ministry. **Us** is used editorially to refer to the apostle himself. **But life in you.** Through a ministry of weakness and suffering Paul was able to accomplish a very positive ministry in Corinth (cf. I Cor 2:1-4). The tone is not ironic such as that in I Corinthians 4:8-10.

The Apostle Paul was able to endure suffering in his ministry not only because he knew that his message was vastly superior to anything offered in the old covenant but also because the gospel of Christ assured him of the glorious prospect of going far beyond the present exigencies of life. This subject he deals with in 4:13-5:10.

3. The goal of his ministry. 4:13-5:10.

a. Hope of the resurrection. 4:13-15.

13. We having the same spirit of faith. That is, the same Spirit of 3:17, who is the Holy Spirit, often designated by the effects which He produces (for example, He is called the Spirit of adoption, Romans 8:15; the Spirit of wisdom, Ephesians 1:17; the Spirit of grace,

Hebrews 10:29; the Spirit of glory I Peter 4:14). Here He is so called because He is the Spirit who produces faith. Thus, in much the same way that David expressed himself in Psalm 116:10, Paul extolls the goodness of God. **We also believe, and therefore speak.** The assurance in Paul's heart because of faith caused him to proclaim the gospel with utter confidence in its truth.

14. Knowing. This indicates the basis for the confidence expressed in the preceding verse. **He which raised up the Lord Jesus** refers to the literal, bodily resurrection of Jesus Christ. **Shall raise up us also by Jesus.** Personal affliction and death become of little consequence when measured against the prospect of resurrection. **And shall present us with you.** This prospect was expressed by Jude, who said, Thanks be "unto him that is able to ... present you faultless before the presence of his glory with exceeding joy" (Jude 24; cf. II Cor 11:2 and Col 1:22). The thought is similar to that of I Corinthians 15:19-22 in the idea of "the firstfruits." Throughout Pauline literature the resurrection of Christ is seen as evidence of the resurrection of the believer (Rom 8:11; I Cor 6:14; Eph 2:6; Col 2:12; I Thess 4:14).

15. For all things are for your sakes. Everything the apostle endured to carry the gospel to Corinth was for their benefit. **That** ("in order that"). The ultimate purpose was **the glory of God** and this Paul envisions as being directly proportional to the sum of gratitude offered in thanksgiving to God for His grace.

b. Confidence in ministry. 4:16-18.

16. For which cause. The certainty of the glorious resurrection. **We faint not.** In 4:1 the Apostle Paul uses this expression in response to the superiority of the new covenant. Now he does so in anticipation of the glory of the New Covenant in the resurrection. **Though our outward man perish, yet the inward man is renewed day by day.** The physical body is temporal and passing away. It is subject to decay and through affliction and suf-

fering is utterly worn out. Yet, the believer can rejoice that he has a life within that is increasing in vitality with every passing day. "The inward man" does not have reference to man's soul or immaterial nature but to a new life imparted to the believer (cf. Rom 7:22).

17-18. For our light affliction. Paul is being modest (See 11:16-33). The reader would hardly suspect how intense the affliction was for him. Yet Paul does not patronize his readers here, nor does he use irony. For the afflictions of life are **but for a moment.** And they work **a far more exceeding weight of glory; While we look not at the things that are seen, but at the things that are not seen.** In the sufferings of life the power of God transforms the experience of the faithful Christian into glorious expectation.

Paul's confidence in the ministry expressed in the preceeding verse is justified in 5:1-10. In 4:18 Paul says his eyes are not upon temporal things but heavenly. In the next section he explains what he means by that.

C. Contemplation of new life. 5:1-10.

5:1. For we know. This knowledge is based on 4:13-14. It is the knowledge of faith which has already been ratified in the experience of Jesus Christ. **If our earthly house of this tabernacle were dissolved.** "Earthly" here has the sense of "terrestrial," i.e. that which is upon the earth (cf. I Cor 15:40). "Tabernacle" (Gr *skēnos)* is best rendered as "tent." The figure has reference to the physical body and the transient character of it. **Were dissolved** (Gr *katalyo,* "take down"). Appropriately used to signify "taking down a tent." Here it signifies physical death. **We have a building of God.** The tense shows that Paul reckons himself to be already in possession of this new building. This expresses certainty (Rom 8:30). In contrast to the old body the new body is pictured as a permanent dwelling: **A building of God, a house not made with hands, eternal in the heavens.** There are, generally, three views taken

Further describing the secret infiltration of these enemies who "crept in unawares" (Jude 4). The verb means to come in secretly or by stealth, to creep or steal in. **To spy out.** This infinitive of purpose (Gr *kataskopeō*) means to reconnoiter, to make a treacherous investigation, to examine carefully with hostile intent. **Our liberty which we have in Christ Jesus.** Our emancipation from legalism and ceremonialism. **That they might bring us into bondage.** Expressing the ultimate result they hoped to attain. Their object was to reduce Christians to abject spiritual slavery, completely enslave them by rites, rules, and regulations. These spies operating under false colors were trying to undermine our liberty in Christ.

5. To whom we gave place. Paul refused to yield for a single moment. He held his ground firmly and did not give in an inch. He refused to compromise the truth of God. **By subjection.** The article (Gr *tē*) identifies the submission as that demanded by the legalists. **That the truth of the gospel.** The gospel in its integrity as opposed to the pseudo-gospel of the enemies of the cross. This denotes salvation by faith. This was the reason for Paul's adamant stand in earnestly contending for the faith. He would not let the Gentiles be deprived of the true gospel. The future of Christianity was bound up in this test case, and by God's grace Paul gained the victory. **Might continue with you.** For you and your spiritual welfare. "The idea of firm possession is enforced by the compound verb, by the present tense, and by the preposition" (J. B. Lightfoot, *The Epistle of Paul to the Galatians,* p. 107). Many weak-kneed, jellyfish preachers would have yielded and then justified themselves on the basis of love and expediency, but not the champion Paul.

6. Whatsoever they were. Referring to the Jerusalem apostles, their past privileges and their present position. They had sojourned with Christ and had been appointed by Him. It **maketh no matter to me.** Paul does not say "that the standing and repute of the apostles were matters of indifference to him, but that he was indifferent about receiving his commission from them as recognized dignitaries of the church" (M. R. Vincent, *Word Studies in the New Testament,* Vol. IV, pp. 97-98). Paul received his apostleship directly from Christ and he was independent of the other apostles. **God accepteth no man's person.** Literally, God does not receive the face of man. God looks on the heart and is no respecter of persons. Phillips translates, "God is not impressed with a man's office." **Added nothing to me.** They imparted no new information, no new interpretation, and no new application. There was no correction of, deletion from, or addition to Paul's message. There was not deficiency in Paul's gospel. He preached the truth, the whole truth, and nothing but the truth (Acts 20:27).

7. But contrariwise. Those in repute not only set nothing before Paul, but they heartily approved him and his mission. **Saw.** Perceived the divine source of Paul's apostleship. **The gospel.** There is only one gospel. There is no difference in contents, only in recipients. The same gospel is for all men. **Committed unto me.** Entrusted. The perfect tense speaks of Paul's certain commission. **Uncircumcision . . . circumcision.** Gentiles and Jews respectively. **Peter.** Mentioned not with the idea of excluding the other apostles, but as representing them. The ministry of Paul was primarily, but not exclusively, to the Gentiles. That of Peter was primarily, but not exclusively, to the Jews. Both men were divinely appointed to proclaim a divine message by divine power.

8. Wrought effectually. Energized (Gr *energeō*) by the inward power of the Holy Spirit for the furtherance of the gospel. God gets all the glory for what He accomplished through Peter and Paul. There was material acknowledgment of each other's equal apostleship.

9. James, Cephas, and John. James is named first because of the prominence

10. For we must all appear before the judgment seat of Christ. The judgment seat (Gr *bema*) was an elevated seat in the square at Corinth where Roman magistrates sat to administer justice and where the athletes who distinguished themselves in the arena received their reward. The judgment in view here is is not of the unbeliever but of the believer (cf. I Cor 4:5; Col 3:4). **That every one may receive the things done in his body.** That is, be rewarded for the deeds done in this life **whether it be good or bad.** While it is true that for the Christian there is "no condemnation" (Rom 8:1), it is not correct to assume that God will not hold him responsible for the deeds done in the body. Paul has already explicated this truth in I Corinthians 3:10-15.

4. The service in his ministry. 5:11-6:10.

Now Paul turns his attention to the import of all this in terms of his personal ministry. He discusses his motives (vss. 11-15), his message (vss. 16-21). and his methods (6:1-10).

a. Paul's motives. 5:11-15.

11. Knowing therefore indicates that what follows is inferred from that which precedes it. **The terror of the Lord.** This is best understood in the general sense of "the fear of the Lord" as it is found throughout the Scriptures (cf. Acts 7:1; 9:31; Rom 3:18; Eph 5:21). It denotes a deep reverence for God. Here it is particularly in view of the Judgment Seat, before which we all must stand. **We persuade men.** That is, of his own personal integrity as is also verified by the fact that **we are made manifest unto God; and I trust also are made manifest in your consciences.** "My character is known to God and I trust it is known to you as well."

12. We commend not ourselves again to you. Paul's object was not to glory in his credentials nor to prove his character to the Corinthians, but simply to authenticate his personal integrity. For the most part the Corinthian assembly by this time was convinced of Paul's genuineness but Paul was also aware that he still had enemies in the assembly and the purpose here is to give his followers **somewhat to answer them.**

13. Paul's ministry was never motivated by or directed to self-interest. **Whether we be beside ourselves,** (to paraphrase, "if I appear out of my senses") **it is to God.** Paul may be introducing irony here. Some may well have thought he was insane to waste his time with an assembly that demonstrated so little appreciation for his ministry. Nevertheless, if his actions seemed to betray sound logic, he was only acting in obedience to God. **Or whether we be sober, it is for your cause.** The suggestion is that Paul's enthusiasm and spontaneity is held in check in order not to offend the Corinthian believers.

14. For the love of Christ constraineth us. Whether Paul appeared to be out of control or under control, Christ's love for Paul held him in such a grip, that it constituted the compelling force in everything he did. **Because we thus judge.** We have thus concluded. **That if one died for all, then were all dead:** the first conviction to which Paul comes has to do with the total depravity of man. If the atoning death of Christ was for all, then it must follow that all are dead.

15. They which live should not henceforth live unto themselves. The second conviction to which Paul comes has to do with God's purpose in the redemption of man. He does not thereby release the shackled sinner to live henceforth unto himself but unto the One who **died for them** (cf. Rom 5:12-21; 6:1-8; I Cor 15:21-22; Gal 2:20; Eph 2:5-6). **And rose again.** The resurrection of Christ is as essential to the salvation of the sinner as the death of Christ (Rom 4:24-25). It also provides incentive to holy living.

b. Paul's message. 5:16-21.

16. Now Paul turns his attention to his message (vss. 16-21). **Wherefore** (Gr *hoste,* "so that") is inferential.

Henceforth know we no man after the flesh: For the Apostle Paul the death and resurrection of Jesus Christ has forever destroyed all human distinctions. **Yea, though we have known Christ after the flesh. We** is used editorially for Paul himself. He admits that there was a time when all he knew of Christ was what other men said about Him. **Yet now henceforth know we him no more.** Since the day he was saved, Paul could no longer think of Christ as just another man.

17. Therefore. Paul infers, **if any man be in Christ, he is a new creature.** What Paul particularizes in verse 16 he generalizes in verse 17. The reason Paul could no longer think of Christ in carnal terms is because of the universal truth that has been applied to Him personally. When a man comes into vital union with the risen Lord he is a "new creation" (cf. Jn 3:3; 15:5; 8:1-9; Gal 6:14-15). **Old things are passed away.** The aorist tense indicates a decisive break with the old life at the moment of salvation. **Behold, all things are become new** (literally, "new things have come to be"). Paul changes to the perfect tense to stress the abiding results of the Christian's union with Christ (cf. Isa 43:18-19; 65:17; Rev 21:4-5; Eph 4:24).

18-19. And all things are of God. All the "new things" introduced to the experience of those who are in Christ Jesus. **Who hath reconciled us to himself by Jesus Christ.** "To reconcile" (Gr *katallassō*) is to remove enmity between two enemy parties. In the strictest sense it involves a "change of mind." Since the sinner cannot do this for himself God does it through Jesus Christ in his sacrificial death (cf. Rom 5:9-10). **And hath given to us the ministry of reconciliation.** This is identical to the "word of reconciliation" in the next verse. This is announcing the good news **that God was in Christ, reconciling the world unto himself.** The great message of the apostle was that here was not just another man ("now we know no man after the flesh"). But here at the "end of the age"

Christ, on Calvary's tree, put away sin forever (cf. Heb 10:5-12). **Not imputing their trespasses unto them.** Not to impute is to forgive (cf. Rom 4:5; Col 2:13; II Tim 4:16). The Greek present tense here emphasizes a continuous action (cf. I Jn 1:9).

20. This ministry of reconciliation involves calling upon men to demonstrate a changed life and so Paul considered himself, and all who are truly born again, to be **ambassadors for Christ.** Paul did not usurp authority to himself. His ministry at Corinth was representative. His appeal to them is as though **God did beseech you by us** and his desire is, for the sake of Christ, for them to be **reconciled to God.** The verb is not active but passive. He does not call upon them to change themselves for he has already established that it is God who does the reconciling (vs. 18). Rather he is asking them to submit to the reconciling work of God.

21. For he hath made him to be sin for us, who knew no sin. Three aspects of Paul's concept of imputation are seen in this passage. In verse 19 God imputes not iniquity (cf. Ps 32:2). Here he imputes sin to Christ, the spotless Lamb of God (cf. Jn 1:29; I Pet 1:19). This imputation helps us understand Christ's struggle in the garden of Gethsemane with the cup of sin which would be poured upon Him on the cross. **That we might be made the righteousness of God in him.** Then the righteousness of Christ is imputed to the sinner's account. This truth may be viewed from the side of justification, whereby the sinner is declared righteous upon the merits of Jesus Christ (cf. Rom 3:24-25), or it may be viewed from the side of sanctification, wherein the righteousness of Christ is daily applied. This is the sense enjoined here and is best understood in conjunction with 3:18.

c. Paul's methods. 6:1-10.

6:1. What follows is based upon Paul's teaching in 5:17-21. **As workers together with him** (literally, "working together"). The AV adds "with him."

law could only condemn (Rom 3:19-20). **But by the faith of Jesus Christ.** Not on account of faith but only by means of faith. Faith is not the ground of justification: grace is. It is not faith in our faith, but faith in Jesus Christ. No one is justified except through faith in Christ. Salvation is wholly by divine mercy (Tit 3:5) and not hy human merit. **Even as we have believed in Jesus Christ.** Even the Jews with all their privileges are no better than the Gentiles. Their law was inadequate and insufficient to bring them into a right relationship with God. Therefore it was necessary for Jews to believe in Christ in order to be justified. Since no flesh, Jew or Gentile, could ever be justified by the works of the law, how ridiculous it is to bind the burden of law-works on the Gentiles who were already justified by faith in Christ. Note the progressive order in this verse: knowing, believing, justified.

17. Is therefore Christ the minister of sin? An illogical inference. They were sinners already in spite of being Jews. Christ simply revealed to them the fact of their sin. Since grace does not encourage men to sin (Rom 6:1-2), Christ is not a minister or promoter of sin by causing us to abandon the law as a means of justification. This is a rebuttal to the argument of the legalists that salvation in Christ is insufficient.

18. For if I build again. Return to the law. After Paul had preached that justification is only by faith in Christ plus nothing, it would be folly to seek righteousness by keeping the law. This would be building again that which he destroyed. **Destroyed.** This word means to demolish, dissolve, disunite, pull down. Paul destroyed the teaching that salvation was by works of merit by proclaiming that salvation was by grace through faith in Christ. When Peter lived as a Gentile he tore down the ceremonial law; when he lived as a Jew he tore down the doctrine of salvation by grace. **A transgressor.** If he denied the absolute sufficiency of Christ. Jewish believers were right when they abandoned law-works

as a means of salvation and were justified by faith in Christ; it would be wrong for them to return to law-works now.

19. For I through the law. Through the agency of the law. Paul relates his own expereience. The Old Testament law is powerless to give life; it only condemns the guilty. Under the law, Paul was brought to despair; his only hope was to find salvation elsewhere. The condemnation of the law drove Paul to Christ for salvation. **Am dead to the law.** Better, died to the law. To die to anything is to cease to have any relation to it so that it has no claim or control over one. The law condemned Paul to death, but Christ, his substitute, died for him. Paul died in Christ and is now united with Him in resurrection life. The sentence of death was executed on Paul in the person of the Lord Jesus Christ. Once the law has executed the death penalty it has no more jurisdiction over the one executed, for the law has dominion over a man only as long as he lives (Rom 7:1). Having died with Christ, Paul is dead to the law, and so is every true believer. When Christ died, we died. **That I might live unto God.** Identification with Christ enabled Paul to die unto the law as a means of obtaining righteousness and to live unto God, the source of his righteousness and the object of his new life.

20. I am crucified with Christ. This is Paul's personal testimony, which may be repeated by every believer in Christ (Rom 6:3-11). The Greek perfect tense speaks of completed action in time past and present certainty of results. Having been crucified with Christ when He died on Calvary, Paul is truly dead to everything else except Christ and what He represents. Paul's faith united him to Christ in such a way that Christ's death was his death, and Christ's resurrection was his resurrection. In Christ, Paul found a perfect sacrifice for sin and a perfect righteousness forever. **Christ liveth in me.** This is the union of the vine and the branches. A Christian is one in whom Christ lives. Christ is our life (Col 1:27;

knowledge. The context here implies insight to cope with difficult situations. **By longsuffering, by kindness.** The former is a passive idea the latter is active. In the one there is patient submission to injustice, in the other there is the kind disposition to do good to others, providing enabling gifts, comfort, and assurance (cf. I Cor 12:7-11; Jn 14:16-17; II Cor 1:3-4, 22). **By love unfeigned** (cf. I Cor 13), **By the word of truth** refers to the "preaching" of the truth (cf. 4:2). **By the power of God** has relation to his apostolic ministry (cf. Rom 15:14-21; I Cor 15: 10). **By the armour of righteousness on the right hand and on the left.** This has in mind, primarily, the righteousness of God in justification (cf. Rom 5:1-2). Hence the expression is equivalent to "armor of God" (Eph 6:11) and does not denote one piece of armor, but all of it. By this means Paul was protected on every side.

8-10. Prompted by the expression "on the right hand and on the left" in the previous verse the apostle now analyzes the extremes of life and here shows that regardless of the situation, whether riding the wave of popularity or digging in against the onslaughts of opposition he was always approved a faithful minister of God. As he does in verses 4-5, here too he arranges his thoughts in three groups of triplets. **By honor and dishonor, by evil report and good report: as deceivers, and yet true.** Regardless of the reputation or report that precedes him, Paul never compromised on the integrity of his message. **As unknown, and yet well known; as dying, and, behold, we live; as chastened, and not killed.** In the front lines of the spiritual warfare Paul can be seen weary but undaunted, beaten but not broken, bruised but unbowed. **As sorrowful, yet always rejoicing; as poor, yet making many rich; as having nothing, and yet possessing all things.** Paul had learned to abound and be abased, he had learned to have much, and nothing. For he had learned, on a practical level, the lesson of our Lord in Luke 12:15. "A

man's life consisteth not in the abundance of the things he possesseth."

C. The Challenge of Paul. 6:11-7:16.

1. The entreaty for reconciliation. 6:11-7:4.

This section turns on three imperatives. "Be ye also enlarged" (vs. 13), "be ye not unequally yoked together" (vs. 14), and "receive us" (7:2). Thus Paul deals successively with: (a) sympathy toward himself (6:11-13); (b) separation from the world (6:14-7:1): and (c) surety of reconciliation (7:2-4).

a. Sympathy towards Paul. 6:11-13.

11. O ye Corinthians. Paul addresses his readers by name in only two other places (Gal 3:1; Phil 4:15). In each case it reflects deep emotion. **Our mouth is opened unto you** (literally, "our mouth has spoken freely"). On the use of this expression see also Matthew 5:2; Acts 8:32, 35; and Ephesians 6:19. On its significance in this context compare 3:12. **Our heart is enlarged** (Gr *platynō*, "widen"). This is a common expression from the LXX (cf. Gen 9:27; Ps 4:1; 119:32). To enlarge the heart gives the idea of increasing its capacity for sympathy and understanding.

12. Ye are not straitened in us. This is the antithesis of "enlarged." Paul is saying that there is no want of room in his heart for the Corinthians. **But ye are straitened in your own bowels.** That is, the problem lies with Paul's readers and their ability to receive him.

13. Be ye also enlarged. If the Corinthians would but open themselves to the apostle the problem could be resolved. In the "ministry of reconciliation" there is no room for bickering between the brethren.

On the other hand, Paul's principle of openness does not justify compromise.

b. Separation from the world. 6:14-7:1.

14. Be ye not unequally yoked with unbelievers. In enlarging one's capacity to receive others the apostle is careful to insist that he has only believers in mind. There is no doubt that he makes special reference to the situation in Corinth with all of its vice and pagan associations (cf. I Cor 6:6-20; 8:1-13; 10:14-33).

15. Belial ("worthlessness" or wickedness"). The expression may also be used in the sense of "wicked one" (cf. II Sam 23:6; Job 34:18). Here it is used as a reference to Satan, ("the wicked one" in I Jn 5:19). **Infidel** is the same term used in the previous verse rendered "unbeliever."

16. Temple of God. In Scripture this expression has a variety of meanings: (a) It may have reference to heaven as God's dwelling place (cf. Ps 11:2; Hab 2:20); (b) It may refer to the church as God's temple (Eph 2:20; I Cor 3:16); or (c) It may have reference to the individual believer as a temple of God (I Cor 6:19). The plural pronouns in the Old Testament quotation suggest that Paul had the second idea in mind in this passage. That is, collectively, they constitute the temple of God. Accordingly, the promise of God in Exodus 29:45 and Leviticus 26:11, 12 applies to their situation as well. **I will dwell in them, and walk in them** ("in" is best best rendered "among"). Paul does not quote directly from the Old Testament here, but seems to be employing the language of the Old Testament. **I will be their God, and they shall be my people.** This great promise to Abraham and to his natural seed, is now applicable to all who are sons of Abraham by faith (Gal 3:6-16).

17-18. Wherefore come out from among them, and be ye separate (cf. Isa 52:11-12). **And I will receive you** (Ezk 20:34). **And will be a Father unto you, and ye shall be my sons and daughters** (cf. Isa 43:6; Hos 1:10). Separation from the ungodly and those who compromise their Christian standards is a basic biblical doctrine related to church discipline. This ultimate connection of Paul's thought here is with the "ministry of reconciliation" (5:18). He has shown that it was motivated by "the terror of

the Lord" (5:11), energized by the "love of Christ" (5:14), exemplified by the experience of Paul (6:1-10), and qualified by the promise of God (6:16-18). In what follows, he shows that it provides incentive to holy living. The Apostle Paul always roots practical Christianity in sound Bible doctrine. The exhortation is to holiness before God and ultimately, to reconciliation with the apostle.

7:1. Having therefore these promises, dearly beloved, let us cleanse ourselves from all filthiness of the flesh and spirit, perfecting holiness in the fear of God. The promises of God demand a purity of heart and life on the part of those who receive them.

2. The apostle now turns back upon his previous concern, that is, their relationship to him. Here is the third imperative, **Receive us.** Since they are the temple of God and since their relationship ought to be with God and His people rather than unbelievers and wickedness their hearts should be open to Paul. For he has **wronged no man . . . corrupted no man . . . defrauded no man.** The biblical definition of separation has both a negative and a positive side. The negative, expressed in 6:14-17, is that the believer abstains from fellowship with all who are opposed to God. But the positive side is that the believer is open to all that are truly the children of God and such individuals will be evidenced by the quality of their lives. In this category Paul places himself.

3. I speak not this to condemn you: The apostle does not insinuate that the Corinthian church was reprobate, or that they were not genuine believers. For, Paul practiced what he preached. He says, **ye are in our heart.** This could not be true if they were not believers. Thus, he conveys his unfeigned love to this wayward assembly. **To die and live with you.** Neither death nor any other circumstance of life could destroy Paul's deep affection for the Corinthian believers.

4. Great is my boldness of speech toward you, great is my glorying of you.

This expresses joyful confidence. **I am filled with comfort, I am exceeding joyful in all our tribulation.** And rightly so. He has just received word from Titus that the Corinthians were actively seeking to rectify the evils and abuse in the assembly.

2. The encouragement from their response. 7:5-16.

In this passage Paul discusses: (a) the comfort of his friend Titus (vss. 5-7); (b) the correction of his letter (vss. 8-12), and (c) the consolation of his spirit (vss. 13-16).

a. Comfort of Titus. 7:5-7.

5-6. Upon leaving Troas and coming **into Macedonia** Paul's anxiety over the Corinthian believers was evident (2:12). **Without were fightings.** There were external wranglings all about. **Within were fears.** Not the least bit assuaged by the situation at Corinth. **God, that comforteth** (cf. 1:3-4). **Comforted us by the coming of Titus,** (i.e. his arrival from Corinth) with the news that the church had accepted Paul's letter (the "severe letter," 2:3-4).

7. Your earnest desire, your mourning, your fervent mind toward me. The Corinthians had evidenced toward Titus a repentant spirit and a desire to be reconciled to Paul.

b. Correction of the letter. 7:8-12.

8-10. For though I made you sorry with a letter, I do not repent. Although for a while Paul was sorry that he had written as he did, he is now thankful. **Not that ye were made sorry, but that ye sorrowed to repentance** (on "repentance" cf. Mt. 3:8; Lk 5:32; Acts 5:31; Heb 12:17). The criminal may feel sorry that he is caught, but that is not sorrow **after a godly manner.** What happened at Corinth agitated the believers to realignment with the will and purpose of God. This made all of Paul's efforts worthwhile.

11-12. Revenge. The apostle is not gloating that circumstances have turned out in his favor, but rejoicing that a sense

of justice (Gr *ekdikēsis*) had been aroused in them to the extent that they felt a moral obligation to disipline sin in the assembly. **Not for his cause that had done the wrong, nor for his cause that suffered wrong** refers to the individuals involved in I Corinthians 5. This indicates that the offender's father is still alive, thus making his sin all the more heinous.

c. Consolation. 7:13-16.

13. Therefore we were comforted in your comfort. The "comfort" Paul could not find (vs. 5), is supplied by the report of the spiritual progress at Corinth.

14. I have boasted. In Paul's discussions with Titus, previously, he was convinced that the opposition in Corinth was coming from only a small group of dissenters. But the vast majority of the congregation wanted to do what was right. This conviction is confirmed by Titus' report so that Paul is able to say, **even so our boasting, which I made before Titus, is found a truth.**

15-16. With fear and trembling ye received him. Not that they cower before him but they treat him with respect and honor (Eph 6:5). **I have confidence in you in all things.** Paul concludes this section fully assured that the Corinthian believers will take whatever steps are necessary to restore unity in the church, to enforce discipline, and to be restored to fellowship with himself.

III. APPEAL OF PAUL'S MINISTRY. 8:1-9:15.

Paul is commonly credited with being a great theologian and missionary. But what is often not known of him is that he was also a great financial genius of the early church. Chapters 8 and 9 of this epistle concern the offering for the poor saints at Jerusalem. Concerning this offering several factors may be noted.

It took eight years to accomplish (from the council of Jerusalem in ca. A.D. 49, to Paul's arrest in A.D. 57). It involved thousands of miles of travel, covering four Roman provinces and including most of the Gentile churches. There were at least ten collectors involved. Since it is here that Titus is first introduced to the New Testament narrative, it is likely that this constituted one of his first responsibilities. The full amount collected was apparently significant since it excited the attention of the Roman governor, Porcius Festus, who hoped to get his hands on some of it (Acts 24:17-26). It nearly cost Paul his life and it did cost him much of his freedom.

Pentecost and poverty have long distinguished the Christian church (Acts 2:45). But the problem facing the church at this time was especially acute. On March 23, A.D. 37, in the reign of Caligula, there occurred a great earthquake. It was followed by another in the reign of Claudius, accompanied by widespread crop failures. The Christians, the poorest of all, had their source of help in the church of Antioch. Agabus, the prophet, had announced a famine at hand (Acts 11:28), and the fellowship determined to send relief. Saul and Barnabas were chosen to take the contribution to the elders at Jerusalem (Acts 11:30). They, most likely, were the initiators of its collection. So Paul was quite well trained in famine relief and in the art of taking collections. God is preparing him for something greater. A few years later, at the Council of Jerusalem (A.D. 49), when Paul and Barnabas, again in Jerusalem, were defending themselves and the liberty of the Gentile converts, a special plea was added to the decree. The diaspora and the Christians were to remember the suffering and poverty of the Judaean Christians (Acts 15:23-29). And this, Paul later says, he was very anxious to do (Gal 2:10). From here on a definite plan of missionary giving becomes a primary part of every church Paul establishes (I Cor 16:1 ff.), and he urges it upon all those to whom he writes (Rom 15:26-27).

The peculiar difficulties at Corinth opened up the whole picture of the offering. They demonstrated a special willingness to pledge (II Cor 8:10), and their pledging inspired the Galatians, the Macedonians, and the Romans. Verbal instructions were followed by questions and written instructions regarding how they were to give and how it was to be handled (I Cor 16:1 ff: II Cor 9:1). There was careful, business-like handling of all the finances. Each was to vote their own financial representative (II Cor 8:23). We know who some of these were. From Beroea, there was Sopater, from Thessalonica there were Aristarchus and Secundus, from Asia there were Tychicus and Trophimus, from Galatia there were Gaius of Derbe and possibly Timothy (Acts 20:4). Since no one is specifically mentioned as coming from Achaia, it is likely that Luke or Titus or perhaps even the apostle himself represented them.

The spiritual nature of this offering is evident in the terms Paul uses. He never calls it "money" because he never seems to think of it as such. Instead, he calls it "grace" or "generosity" or "blessing" or "partnership." Thus, Paul speaks of the "grace of giving" as one of the highest Christian virtues. It would seem that such explicit directions for the offering would be adequate and apparently this was the case in Galatia and Macedonia. But Corinth had failed, though she had been first to pledge. Now special action and instructions are necessary. Hence, there is the special attention devoted to the subject in these chapters.

The section turns on the concept of "faithfulness." As this is exemplified in the apostle, in the previous section, it is now exhorted upon the Corinthian believers. His argument is structured as follows: faithfulness illustrated (8:1-5). faithfulness exhorted (8:6-15); faithfulness delegated (8:16-9:5); and faithfulness directed (9:6-15).

A. Faithfulness Illustrated. 8:1-5.

8:1. Moreover indicates a new subject. **We do you to wit of the grace of God bestowed on the churches of Macedonia** (literally, "we want to make known to the law. This blessing is intended for the whole world, but it is only in and through (Gr *en*) Christ. No man is saved apart from Christ and any man may be saved by Christ (Jn 6:37). The promise of the Spirit, the gift which comes to all who accept Christ, is through (Gr *dia*) faith. It is folly indeed to seek for higher or holier blessings by deeds of merit.

2. The purpose of the law. 3:15-29.

15. Brethren. Denoting affection. **Manner of men.** Paul takes an anology from human affairs of everyday life and illustrates his point so clearly that all can understand. **Man's covenant.** Better, human testament. This word (Gr *dia-thēkē*) strictly speaking is not a contract between two parties (Gr *synthēkē*), but a binding will or testament instituted by the first party. **Confirmed.** Ratified. The Greek perfect tense means that the ratification is complete and in force. The matter stands settled. **Disannulleth,** annul, abrogate, make void. **Or addeth thereto.** No new condition may be imposed, no codicil allowed. Since no one can alter, amplify, or annul a man's testament after it has been duly excuted, surely no one can add to God's unconditional promise to Abraham, as the legalists were trying to do. God's promise was not a matter of mutual arrangement and it remains inviolate.

16. To Abraham and his seed. The beneficiaries of the promise were not limited to Abraham. Some may have objected that God's promise to Abraham was only temporary, so Paul adds "and his seed." **The promises.** Plural because frequently repeated (Gen 13:15; 17:8; 18:18; 22:18). **Thy seed, which is Christ.** The promise looked forward to the one descendant of Abraham in whom all the promises were to be fulfilled.

17. Confirmed before God. By repeated ratifications and sealed with God's own oath (Gen 22:16-17; Heb 6:13). The perfect participle indicates the certainty of prior ratification. Unbelief here charges God with perjury. **Four hundred and thirty years after.**

God's ratified promise of long standing certainly could not be rendered inoperative by the law. The law, which was not given for centuries after God's gracious promise, had nothing to do with that promise or with Abraham's justification. If the law had nothing to do with Abraham's justification, how can it have anything to do with anyone's justification? **Cannot disannul.** Does not repeal. The law cannot unconfirm God's confirmed testament. **None effect.** Cancel, render inoperative. The law cannot invalidate the promise which God has validated; it cannot nullify the promise.

18. Inheritance. The messianic blessing. **Of the law.** Derived from the law as its source. **God gave it.** God graciously granted it as a free gift without reserve, with no strings attached. God's promised gift did not contain even one legal stipulation. The perfect tense emphasizes its permanence; it still holds good after the law has come. Note that God gave it, not merely promised it. **By promise.** By promise alone, plus nothing. This excludes all self-effort. A new law may repeal or replace a previous law, but the law cannot affect in any way God's promise. Faith is not superseded by the works of the law. The legalists' stipulation of works meant not merely modification, but cancellation of God's confirmed promise. Grace and faith precede law and works. Grace and faith supersede law and works.

19. Wherefore. Why then the law? What is the meaning and purpose of the law? **It was added.** Not as a codicil. The law was not part of God's original and confirmed testament, and it was not added to it later. The law was not added to grace; it did not become another ingredient of salvation. It was brought in along side of the promise. It was supplemental and subordinate. **Because of transgressions.** Because (Gr *charin*) means for this cause and denotes the aim of the law. Transgression (Gr *parabasis*) means a step beyond a fixed limit into forbidden territory. It is a willful act of gives. That, of course, varies **according to that a man hath.**

13-14. Paul does not intend to merely transfer the burden from one group to another. **But by an equality, that now at this time your abundance may be a supply for their want.** He wants to equalize matters.

15. As the Scripture has it, **He that had gathered much had nothing over; and he that had gathered little had no lack** (cf. Ex 16:18). Hodge (p. 206) observes "property is like manna, it will not bear hoarding."

C. Faithfulness Delegated. 8:16-9:5.

16-17. Titus illustrates the reciprocity implied in verse 14. **But thanks be to God, which put the same earnest care into the heart of Titus for you.** What Paul is asking of the Corinthians in terms of spontaneous loving concern for brethren in need, is reflected in the attitude of Titus toward them. Notice here that Paul understands the character qualities distinctive of a spiritual life are not intrinsic to human nature, but given by God.

18. We have sent with him the brother. All that is known of this individual is what is indicated here. Since his name is not given, it is useless to conjecture who he was. At any rate, he was known **throughout all the churches.**

19. Like Titus, he was **chosen of the churches to travel with us with this grace.** He was selected by the churches to assist the apostles in overseeing the collection for Jerusalem. Most likely, he was one of the men cited in Acts 20:4.

20-21. Such men were selected so that no one would question how the funds were acquired or what was done with them subsequently. **Providing for honest things, not only in the sight of the Lord, but also in the sight of men.** Especially in financial matters, the apostle is scrupulously aware of his vulnerability to criticism.

22. And we have sent with them our brother. Along with the previously unnamed individual (vs. 18), there will be one other who will be accompanying Titus when he arrives.

9:1-2. It is superfluous for me to write. Paul rendered this exhortation, and his earlier one, unnecessary. In fact, it was Paul's understanding that the offering in **Achaia was ready a year ago** and he had cited their **zeal** as an example of sacrificial giving and willingness to give.

3-4. Yet have I sent the brethren, lest our boasting of you should be in vain in this behalf. Of course, Paul knows that the Corinthian church has been derelict in discharging its original commitment in this regard. Thus, while he applies pressure he tactfully suggests that he is only concerned that they be on schedule. **That, as I said, ye may be ready.** In the event they were **unprepared,** it would not only be an embarrassment to the apostle but a disgrace to themselves.

5. Lest those of the assembly at Corinth should interpret the ministry of Paul's three companions in the wrong way, he assures them that they are there only to oversee and to expedite the offering. His desire is only that those who wish to give and who are able to give have the opportunity to do so.

D. Faithfulness Directed. 9:6-15.

6. But this (literally, "as to this, however"). Paul now turns his attention to some positive instruction and encouragement regarding giving. In so doing he provides the church with the clearest and most comprehensive treatment of the subject to be found in the New Testament. His approach is to extract principles from both the Old Testament and experience to demonstrate why and how they are to give. **He which soweth sparingly shall reap also sparingly; and he which soweth bountifully shall reap also bountifully** (cf. Prov 11:24; Lk 6:38; Gal 6:7). One's return is determined by his investment. The Greek expression *ep eulogiais* ordinarily translated "with blessings," here has the sense of "freely." While it does not suggest "undiscriminating'' giving, it does denote ''unrestrained'' giving.

7. Every man according as he purposeth in his heart, so let him give. The apostle does not have a minimum quota, nor yet, a minimum percentage figure in mind. For each individual it is an amount to be determined before the Lord. **Not grudgingly, or of necessity: for God loveth a cheerful giver.** There is to be a willing heart and a sincere desire on the part of the one giving in order to participate. Paul is not so much interested in their money, nor is God, for that matter, as the passage from Proverbs 22:9 indicates. The Greek term *hilaron* from which the English term ''hilarious'' derives, is best rendered as the AV suggests, ''cheerful.'' Giving is not a joke, it is serious business, but it is also a delightful experience.

8. And God is able to make all grace abound toward you. Paul's logic is identical to that of our Lord in Matthew 6:33. When the temporal concerns of life are placed first, God is usually excluded. But when the kingdom of God is placed first, God sees to it that the temporal needs are included. **That ye, always having all sufficiency in all things, may abound to every good work.** Giving is a grace that has reciprocal benefits.

9. As it is written (cf. Ps 112:9), **He hath dispersed abroad; he hath given to the poor: his righteousness remaineth for ever.** Of course, neither Paul nor the psalmist intended to mean that every believer will always be wealthy, nor yet that the believer who gives regularly and faithfully will always be wealthy. Both experience and the context (cf. 8:2) deny this. He only intends to say that the abundance of God's riches are available to those who are rightly related to Him. **His righteousness remaineth for ever.** The righteous acts of the man who readily gives and supplies the needs of others, have eternal value.

10. This should best be rendered ''now he that ministereth seed to the sower and bread for your food will supply you seed sown and increase the fruits of your righteousness.'' The AV renders it as a prayer to God. Actually it is an affirmation of the surety of God's supply.

11. Being enriched in every thing in all bountifulness, which causeth through us thanksgiving to God (literally, ''you shall be enriched . . .''). This unusual use of the participle is not foreign to the New Testament, nor yet to the Apostle Paul (cf. Acts 15:22; Eph 3:17; 4:2; Col 2:2; 3:16).

12-13. Giving consummates in a twofold grace. It **supplieth the want of the saints,** and it is **abundant** (''overflowing'') by means of **many thanksgivings unto God.** The final result is that God is glorified. It will be noted that this process is cyclical. Out of the riches of God's grace He supplies the needs of the believer. The believer, in an expression of gratitude and liberality, shares of his abundance with others. They, in turn, direct their expressions of thanksgiving (''grace'') to God from whom the supply originated. Thus, the cycle is complete. And so Paul says **they glorify God for your professed subjection unto the gospel of Christ, and for your liberal distribution unto them.** The act of giving is evidence of obedience to the gospel.

14. And by their prayer for you. The connection is with ''abundant'' in verse 12. Another positive result of faithful giving is that the recipients are induced to extend the giver before the Throne of Grace. It is in this way that the giver is compensated by the recipient of the gift. This further explains the thought of 8:14.

15. Thanks be unto God for his unspeakable gift. The reference is to the gift of God's Son, but the verse is more than a spontaneous outburst of the writer. It is the supreme illustration of the principles Paul has just enumerated. As the example of Christ is applied to the experience of suffering in I Peter 2:21, so Paul applies the example of Christ to the grace of giving.

28. Ye are all one in Christ. This is a statement of fact, rather than a mere possibility. The point is that "in Christ Jesus" race or national distinction does not exist; class differences vanish, and sex rivalry disappears. These things are not barriers to Christian fellowship. At the foot of the cross all men are equal, and no one enjoys special privileges.

29. If ye be Christ's. Since you Galatians are His, it follows that you are Abraham's seed and heirs according to promise. Christ is heir to all things (Heb 1:2) and you are joint-heirs with Him (Rom 8:17).

C. Paul's Amplification of Liberty. 4:1-31.

1. The coming of God's Son. 4:1-7.

4:1. Child. One of tender years (Gr *nepios*) in contrast to (Gr *teleios*), one full grown. He is illustrating the spiritual immaturity of those living under the law and who are being prepared for faith in Christ. **Differeth nothing from a servant.** He has no more freedom than a slave and is no better off than a slave. **Lord of all.** He is an heir *de jure*, but not *de facto*. He is not enjoying the actual possession of his promised inheritance. He is Lord of all by birthright and by title. Paul's meaning is clear and his purpose is plain. He is warning the Galatians against becoming entangled in the bondage of the law, and he is encouraging them to enjoy the spiritual liberty they have by faith in Christ.

2. Under tutors. Guardians who have the supervision of the person. **Governors.** Stewards who have the supervison of the property. They are the trustees who manage the estate. During his minority, the heir is controlled and restrained by guardians and stewards. **Until the time appointed.** The time appointed beforehand for the termination of his minority status when he attains his inheritance. Under the law men were minors and enjoyed little of the inheritance because they were under tutelage and in servile condition.

3. Even so we. Paul makes the application. **When we were children.** In our minority. **Were in bondage.** The Greek perfect tense implies that we were in a real state of servitude under the legalistic system and not free sons under grace. **Under the elements of the world.** The word elements (Gr *stoicheion*) denotes things placed in a row, thus the letters of the alphabet. Hence, the ABC's or first principles of non-Christian humanity, the elemental lesson in simple symbols of outward things (Col 2:8, 20). The kindergarten department of instruction in religious observances which are external and temporal as contrasted with the permanent spiritual principles of faith in Christ. Under law men were in the process of preparatory training.

4. But when. Marks the beginning of a remarkable change in the state of affairs. **The fullness of the time.** The proper time had arrived for both God and man. The time appointed by the Father and foretold by the prophets. It was a time of outward prosperity and inward corruption. The religions of the world were spiritually bankrupt, devoid of power to change men's lives, and had degenerated into feeble superstitions and meaningless rituals. The pre-messianic period ended right on schedule. **God sent forth his Son.** There was no other way to save man (Acts 4:12). With Christ there is an endless hope; without Christ there is a hopeless end. God sent forth Christ from Himself, from heaven's majesty to earth's misery, to execute His plan and purpose. This reveals Christ's pre-existence, His deity, and His authority. It was the second person of the Trinity who was commissioned. **Made of a woman.** The Son of God became out of (Gr *ex*) a woman, became incarnate and dwelt among us (Jn 1:14). The fact of the miraculous virgin birth agrees perfectly with the language here. Christ did not cease to be God when He became man, the God-man, one person with two natures. **Made under the law.** Not only a human birth but a Jewish birth, subject to all the ordinances of the law.

the metaphor, Paul is still at war. He is casting down strongholds. He is leading captives. Now he is prepared to punish all disobedience. **When your obedience is fulfilled.** Paul does not intend to deal with them quite so severely until he has given them ample time to repent and fall into submission both to the Lord and to himself.

2. *By his authority. 10:7-11.*

7. Paul's attitude is fully justified by his delegated authority, as will be shown in what follows. **Do ye look on things after the outward appearance?** This connects with "those which think of us as if we walked according to the flesh" (vs. 2). If such an individual should **trust to himself that he is Christ's,** let him know that **even so are we.** The opposition indicated here may have derived from the faction within the assembly that identified itself with the name of Christ (I Cor 1:12). At any rate they were giving out that they were from Christ and Paul was not. The apostle was quick to assert that they had no authority or advantage which did not apply equally to him.

8-10. For though ("even if") I should boast somewhat more of our authority implies that Paul is showing restraint. **Which the Lord hath given us for edification, and not for your destruction.** His restraint is due to an overriding desire to help them, not hinder them. **I should not be ashamed** (literally, "I shall not be ashamed"). He contains himself so as to provide no opportunity for criticism. It has been on this account that they have brought charge against him, **For his letters, say they, are weighty and powerful; but his bodily presence is weak, and his speech contemptible.** Paul does not wish to give any cause for them to point the finger again.

11. On the contrary, he intends to demonstrate that his actions will correspond to his words. **Such will we be also in deed when we are present.** He does not give empty threats.

3. *By divine commendation. 10:12-18.*

12-15. Paul does not measure his credentials as his enemies do, **measuring themselves by themselves.** Such an approach Paul says is **not wise.** Rather he will measure his credentials by an objective standard, **a measure to reach even unto you.** What he has in mind is his "track record." Where Paul's enemies cited their authority, he cites his accomplishments. **For we are come as far as to you also in preaching the gospel of Christ.** Paul's critics were not responsible for founding the church at Corinth; he was. Paul is not riding on another's coattails. He is **Not boasting of things without our measure,** i.e. another man's labors. He is an original. Accordingly, he is prepared to take credit even for their spiritual growth; as he puts it: **when your faith is increased, that we shall be enlarged by you.** The principle of 9:10 not only applies to one's material possessions, but also to the investments of one's energies.

16-18. Paul does not intend to allow this situation or any other to inhibit him from going even further. **To preach the gospel in the regions beyond you.** He had no intention of lowering himself to **boast in another man's line of things.** Lest they interpret what he has to say as expressions of self-conceit, Paul shows that in the final analysis, his commendation comes from Christ. Paul was always careful to show that any success he enjoyed in the ministry was not due to his own innate ability but Christ working in him (cf. Rom 15:17-18). Thus, his boast is not in himself, but **in the Lord.**

B. The Boast of the Apostle. 11:1-12:10.

The boasting that Paul is about to engage in stands as an apparent contradiction to what he has said in 10:17-18. Thus, at the outset, he must present the basis for his boast (11:1-15). This he follows with the proof of his boast (vss. 16-33). Then he relates the consequences of his boast (12:1-10).

1. The basis for his boast. 11:1-15.

11:1. Bear with me a little in my folly. Already the apostle is uneasy about what he has to do. For him it is "foolishness." And yet, as repugnant as it is to him, it is necessary.

2. For indicates "reason." What follows answers why they must bear with him. Paul has their own well-being in mind. **I have espoused you to one husband, that I may present you as a chaste virgin to Christ.** They were in danger of being turned from Christ by being turned off to the ministry of the apostle. As an "ambassador for Christ," he realizes he must win them back to himself in order to win them back to Christ.

3. What is implied in the previous verse is expressed here. **I fear, lest by any means, as the serpent beguiled Eve through his subtilty, so your minds should be corrupted from the simplicity that is in Christ.** His deepest concern is that the Corinthians are being seduced from their faithfulness to Christ.

4. Paul could understand **if he that cometh preacheth another Jesus, whom we have not preached.** Or another **spirit** or **another gospel.** If such were the case, **ye might well bear with them.** Paul is being ironic here. The Corinthians would be justified in listening to the false teachers if what they had to say introduced them to a genuine gospel which they had not yet received. The irony of the passage cannot be escaped. That which Paul finds necessary to beg of them in verse 1 they had willingly offered to false teachers.

5-6. Although Paul was **not a whit behind the very chiefest apostles** it was not immediately evident in his personal ministry. He was **rude in speech** and this was apparently offensive to some. Yet he could not have been criticized **in knowledge.** And, as for the message that he preached, the Corinthians had been **thoroughly made manifest . . . in all things.** The AV is misleading here. He has in mind making manifest the things

of the gospel. The tone is clearly ironic and the contrast is with verse 4. They may have criticized his style, but they could add nothing to his sermon.

7. Have I committed an offense in abasing myself? (I Cor 9:1-18). Irony fairly drips from his pen. Their only legitimate criticism was his self-effacing manner. **I have preached to you the gospel of God freely.** In eighteen months of ministry he never once extracted from them a living wage.

8. I robbed other churches is hyperbolic, and intended to shame them. **Taking wages of them, to do you service.** Paul, no doubt, has the Philippian church primarily in mind (Phil 4:15-16). He could have mentioned the fact that he worked with his own hands to sustain a living on his first arrival in Corinth. It is suggestive of his restraint that he does not.

9. And so will I keep myself. Paul's behavior at Corinth was unimpeachable. And he was not going to start now allowing his readers to force him to compromise his principles (cf. Acts 18:3; 20:34-35; I Thess 2:9; II Thess 3:8; I Cor 9:15-18).

10. This is an oath. **No man shall stop me of this boasting in the regions of Achaia.** It is significant that Paul readily receives aid from the Macedonian churches and refuses it from those at Corinth.

11-12. Why? Because he has no interest in them and no desire for their help? No, but **that I may cut off occasion from them which desire occasion.** Those who are looking for things to criticize will find no help from Paul. **That wherein they glory, they may be found even as we.** There is method in Paul's madness. He knows that if they are to bring accusation against his character, theirs had better, at least, match his, i.e. they will be forced to stop merchandizing the gospel.

13. For such are false apostles, deceitful workers, transforming themselves into the apostles of Christ. Until now Paul has been dealing gratuitously with his enemies. He now lays his cards on the table and says what he really thinks of them (cf. Phil 3:2).

14. And no marvel. It is no surprise that they have been able to deceive the Corinthian believers **for Satan himself is transformed into an angel of light.** The passage calls to mind the culmination of our Lord's discussion with the Pharisees in John 8. The specific allusion Paul makes is not altogether clear. Perhaps it is to Job 1:6.

15. Therefore it is no great thing. They were acting only according to their nature. **Whose end shall be according to their works.** Their judgment will not be according to the role they have assumed. One day their true character will be revealed for "that day shall declare it."

2. The proof of his boast. 11:16-33.

16. What Paul is about to do he considers foolishness. It runs crossgrain to every fiber of his being. But the spiritual welfare of a congregation in danger of being led astray is at stake, and it becomes necessary to **boast myself a little.**

17. I speak it not after the Lord. Paul is not here disclaiming inspiration. But, what he is about to do, is out of character with his mission from the Lord.

18. Seeing that many glory after the flesh (literally, "since many glory after fleshly standards"), **I will glory also.** If the Corinthians wish to qualify Paul on strictly human standards he will give them a *curriculum vitae.*

19-20. Paul seems to have a hard time getting into his task, i.e. to boast about himself. However the irony continues to drip from his pen. **Ye suffer fools gladly.** Since you so readily receive fools I shall attempt to qualify myself as one. **Seeing ye yourselves are wise** (cf. I Cor 4:8). This trait seems to be characteristic of their brand of wisdom. Their faulty sense of values also ties in with their warped sense of discrimination. **Ye suffer.** As in verse 19, "ye tolerate." **If a man bring you into bondage, if a man devour you, if a man take of you, if a**

man exalt himself, if a man smite you on the face (cf. Gal 1:7; I Pet 5:3). In this strange turn of events these believers had forsaken their own loving father in the faith and had subjected themselves to spiritual tyrants who were self-seeking and destructive of true spirituality.

21-22. I speak as concerning reproach (literally, "by way of disparagement"), **as though we had been weak.** Such tolerance had hardly been extended to the apostle. **Howbeit whereinsoever any is bold (I speak foolishly,) I am bold also.** While in reality it amounts to nothing, if one wishes to discuss personal qualifications, Paul will advance his own. Here Paul boasts about his nationality. **Hebrews . . . Israelites . . . seed of Abraham** indicate that Paul's enemies were primarily Jewish. On Paul's claim see also Philippians 3:5.

23-27. Then Paul boasts of the cost of his commitment to Christ. **Are they ministers of Christ? (I speak as a fool).** The expression is hypothetical. If they are ministers of Christ as they claim to be, then **I am more.** Discipleship cannot be purchased at bargain prices (Lk 9:23). The cost exacted of the Apostle Paul is measured by the tabulation which follows.

What Paul does here is demonstrate the depth of his commitment by delineating the sufferings and trials he endured because of it. **In deaths oft** (literally, "in many deaths"). This is tantamount to saying "I die daily" (I Cor 15:31). **Forty stripes save one.** Deuteronomy 25:3 forbids the Jews to inflict more than forty stripes upon an offender. Scrupulous in their observance of Moses' law, they were in the habit of giving no more than 39 (so as not to go over the limit of the law). **Once was I stoned** (Acts 14:19). **Thrice I suffered shipwreck, a night and a day I have been in the deep.** Since Paul penned this letter long before the shipwreck recorded in Acts 27 it must be reckoned that the incidents of which he speaks find their mention in Scripture only here. There are numerous occasions recorded in

Acts 13:1-20:5 when Paul traveled by sea. Since Luke, the author of the book of Acts, did not accompany Paul much of that time (apparently only in Acts 16:10-17) it is not surprising that some of the incidentals have been omitted from his account. **Perils of waters** ("perils of rivers"). Along the roads traversed by Paul there were numerous rivers which seasonally swell with flood waters, and which to this day, are legendary for the perils they pose for the traveler. This, especially along the Alpine district and the road extending through Lebanon from Jerusalem to Antioch. **Perils of robbers.** The area from Perga to Antioch in Pisidia was especially known for this (Acts 13:14). **Perils among false brethren.** Halfway through the list of Paul's perils from "outside" he includes his enemies at Corinth. What is implied by this is explicitly stated in 11:13. **In fastings often.** The context does not view this as a ritualistic observance practiced by the Pharisees. Rather it is an "involuntary abstinence." While it is admitted that *nesteia* is ordinarily used of ritualistic fastings (cf. Lk 2:37; Acts 14:23) it is unlikely that such is the sense here. From its connection with **hunger and thirst** it is not unlikely that there is a touch of irony here. No doubt Paul's Jewish adversaries at Corinth made a practice of ritualistic fasting and took pride in it. On the other hand, Paul fasted because the pressures of a faithful ministry required it of him.

28. Besides those things that are without (literally, "not to mention those things which are besides"). To enumerate the things that came upon him **daily** in the **care of all the churches,** Paul could go on. But he chooses not to.

29-30. Instead he chooses to boast, not in his ability to endure hardness, but in his weakness. **Who is weak, and I am not weak?** (cf. I Cor 9:22). **Who is offended, and I burn not?** ("Who is caused to stumble, and I am not indignant?") The apostle is deeply concerned about the weaker brethren and he "burned" with indignation when he thought of

those who would lead them astray. On the relation of his weakness to the evidences of God's strength see also 12:10; 13:9; I Corinthians 4:10.

31-33. Paul's thought here is difficult to connect either with what precedes or what follows. It sounds as though he is about to introduce a discussion of his experiences shortly after his conversion. In this regard he asserts **I lie not.** What he says is in essential agreement with Acts 9:24-25. The only addition is **Aretas the king.** When one correlates this with Acts it must be inferred that Aretas was acting at the behest of the Jews. Why Paul does not continue at this point to pursue this discussion can only be speculated. Perhaps he was interrupted or distracted. At any rate, this is all he says and when he begins chapter twelve, his mind is on a matter of much greater moment.

3. The consequences of his boast.
12:1-10.

This section turns on the concept of "glory" (*Kauchaomai*, "boast"). Paul's adversaries were boasting after the flesh (11:18). Paul's boasting is of another sort.

In coming to this passage, one almost senses an attitude of frustration in the apostle. He has entered into something that is especially obnoxious to him, i.e. boasting of himself. In the previous chapter his focus of attention has been on earthly, physical experiences in the gospel. Yet, there is something even more significant on his mind and one senses that it is a matter he had hoped he could avoid. But, two factors converge to force him to say what he does here. The first is the contempt of Paul's adversaries for his personal appearance and delivery (10:10; I Cor 2:1-4). The second is that the nature of Paul's boasting in chapter 11 requires explanation. Left as it is, one might suspect that Paul derived some sort of warped pleasure from physical suffering. As to the first he will stop their mouths forever. As to the second he will demonstrate that his attitude was fully justified in consequence of his unparalleled spiritual privilege.

25. Mount Sinai. Hagar represents Mount Sinai. **Answereth to.** Belongs to the same or corresponds to. **Jerusalem which now is.** The earthly Jerusalem stands for Judaism and represents the Jewish nation. Jerusalem was the center of apostate Judaism. **Is in bondage with her children.** Jerusalem is a slaving mother of slaving children. A severe condemnation of the legalists from Jerusalem who were trying to seduce the Galatians, and of all who would supplant grace with law.

26. But. Opposes the preceding verse. **Jerusalem which is above.** The heavenly Jerusalem (Heb 12:22-24) is the spiritual city of which all Christians are children. **Free.** Independent of the Mosaic law. The heavenly Jerusalem is a free mother with free children.

27. Written. We have here a quotation from the Septuagint of Isaiah 54:1 which is applied to unfruitful Sarah, who answers to the heavenly Jerusalem. Abraham's spiritual seed shall be more numerous than his natural seed. Isaiah closes the fifty-third chapter with these words, ''He bare the sins of many, and made intercession for the transgressors.'' The next word in ''sing.'' Paul translates it ''Rejoice.'' The grace of God gives men something to sing about. Israel will some day realize the full meaning of Isaiah 53 and experience glorious deliverance and restoration through God's grace.

28. Now. Paul applies the truth to the Galatians. **We brethren.** The best texts have ''ye'' instead of ''we.'' Paul assures the Galatians that they like Isaac are born according to promise, not of mere fleshly descent, as Ishmael. The sons of promise are free.

29. But as then. As then, so now. **Born after the flesh.** Born naturally and are enslaved sinners. **Born after the Spirit.** Born supernaturally and are liberated saints. **Persecuted.** The word (Gr *diōkō*) means drive away, put to flight, harass, molest. The presence of Isaac causes

Ishmael to manifest his true character (Gen 21:9). From Isaac, came the Hebrews; from Ishmael, came the Arabs. From the beginning these two sons of Abraham were unfriendly, and so have been their descendants. The presence of the new nature makes known what the old nature really is. The legalists were persecuting Paul and all who would not abandon grace for law. There are two types of men in the world: those who have been born only of the flesh, and those who in addition have been born of the Spirit. It would be better not to have been born at all than not to be born again. Men of the flesh detest men of the Spirit. No one despises grace like the man who is trying to save himself by his own merit.

30. Cast out. Abraham by divine direction sent Hagar and Ishmael away (Gen 21:10-12). This is an encouragement to all who have been born of the Spirit and a solemn warning to all who are born only of the flesh. Grace, not law, brings the inheritance in the family of God. **Shall not be heir.** The son of the slave girl shall not, no never, by any means share the inheritance with the son of the free woman. Those who seek acceptance with God through obedience to the law, and are destitute of true sonship, have no inheritance. This verdict stands for all who have no higher birth than Ishmael.

31. So then. A deduction from the preceding verse. **Bondwoman.** The absence of the Greek definite article emphasizes Hagar's lower status. God says that His children are the children of promise, saved by grace. It is impossible to be children of both the slave girl and the free woman. It is impossible to be under law and under grace. We belong to Christ and are therefore liberated from the bondage of the law. Christendom is critically infected with the deadly doctrine of the legalists. The crying need of the hour is for uncompromising men to proclaim the liberty in Christ which is the birthright of every believer.

privilege, as though he warranted God's favor in some way. **I shall not be a fool.** Paul will boast, but not in an empty claim. **For I will say the truth: but now I forbear.** What Paul says is absolutely true, yet even now he is reluctant to share it with his readers with the fear that they might **think of me above that which he seeth me to be.** Paul does not even wish to share his glory vicariously. His only interest is to exalt the Lord.

b. The thorn in the flesh. 12:7-10.

7. What follows explains Paul's attitude, **lest I should be exalted above measure through the abundance of the revelations** (literally, "in order that I might not, by the abundant excess of the revelation, be uplifted"). **There was given me a thorn in the flesh** (cf. Gal 4:14) The next expression **the messenger of Satan** is appositional. Just what Paul means by this has excited no small amount of conjecture. Among the views suggested are: (a) temptations from the devil; (b) Paul's opposition from his adversaries; (c) some intense bodily pain; (d) some recurring physical affliction such as eye trouble, epilepsy, or malaria. What is known of it is that it was a tool of Satan, it was painful ("thorn"), and it was accompanied by shame and/or embarrassment to the apostle. A fairly strong argument can be sustained in favor of the view that it was eye trouble (ophthalmia). See also Acts 13:9; 23:1; Gal 4:14-15; 6:11. However, as Alford has observed, "it may also have been something else besides this, and to such an inference, probability would lead us; disorders in the eyes, however sad in their consequences, not being usually of a very painful or distressing nature in themselves" (*Ibid.*, p. 713). W. Ramsey makes a strong case for epilepsy (*St. Paul the Traveller*) as does S. Asch (*The Apostle*).

8-9. So troublesome was this affliction that Paul **besought the Lord thrice, that it might depart** from him. Subsequent to his third request, God gives him an answer: **My grace is sufficient for thee: for my strength is made perfect in weakness.** The trial will remain but accompanied always by the enduring grace of God. And thus for Paul, this and every affliction reminded him **that the power of Christ may rest upon** him.

10. Paul concludes, this is the reason I have such an attitude, i.e. **I take pleasure in infirmities.** Not that I should suffer, but **for Christ's sake.** The thrill of suffering for the sake of Christ is that **when I am weak, then am I strong.** And so Paul concludes his "foolishness" stopping the mouths of his adversaries and establishing once and for all his right to speak as he does.

C. The Credentials of the Apostle. 12:11-18.

Paul has at length concluded a task which has been manifestly repugnant to him. He now goes on to review his credentials as an apostle and to demonstrate why 11:1-12:10 need never to have been written, especially to his own children in the faith. This he discusses in terms of his position (vs. 11), his performance (vss. 12-14) and his integrity (vss. 15-18).

1. His position among the other apostles. 12:11.

11. I am become a fool in glorifying. One can almost visualize the flush of embarrassment. **Ye have compelled me** ("Ye" is emphatic). The sincerity of Paul's affection for these people is measured by the pain he is willing to endure to secure theirs. **For I** (also emphatic) **ought to have been commended of you.** That these people whom Paul loved so much failed to take the initiative in defending him against his critics inflicted a crushing blow to the apostle. **For in nothing am I behind the very chiefest apostles.** His personal and official credentials were as clear as if Peter, James and John visited them. **Though I be nothing.** Not that Paul considered himself, personally, to be on a par with any of the other apostles; only that his credentials were equally as good (cf. also I Cor 4:7; 15:5-8).

2. His performance as a true apostle. 12:12-13.

12. Truly the signs of an apostle were wrought among you. The expression here is elliptical, suppressing a negative reaction, i.e. signs, indeed, were truly demonstrated, but never recognized.

13. For what is it wherein ye were inferior to other churches. In what respect do you find your church handicapped, for not having been founded by one of the other apostles (see I Cor 1:6-7)? **Except it be that I myself was not burdensome to you?** The only fault of his ministry was that he showed them preferential treatment. Against such ingratitude Paul's irony deals a mortal blow. Then, as though the blade did not penetrate enough, he gives it an additional twist with the words **forgive me this wrong.**

3. His behavior as an apostle. 12:14-18.

14. Finally, Paul cites his own behavior as reflective of his integrity. **Behold, the third time I am ready to come to you.** Paul anticipates his third visit (on the chronology see 13:1 and the introductions to both I and II Corinthians). **And I will not be burdensome to you.** Again he still expects nothing in terms of personal remuneration from them. **For I seek not yours, but you.** His intentions were benevolent, not selfish. **Children . . . parents.** Paul was the spiritual father of the Corinthian assembly. Thus, he maintained a parental concern for them. **And I will very gladly spend and be spent.** The apostle considered himself expendable in the interests of the Corinthian assembly. **For you** (literally "in the service of your souls"). **Though the more abundantly I love you, the less I be loved.** This is not a statement of fact, but a condition he was prepared to accept, i.e. to spend himself totally, even if it meant without a return of his affection.

16. But be it so ("but be that as it may") **I did not burden you,** i.e. it must be admitted that I posed no financial burden upon your church. **Nevertheless, being crafty, I caught you with guile.** This is ironic, intended as an additional objection Paul's enemies might propose.

17-18. Not only in terms of Paul's personal ministry there, but also in terms of the ministry of **Titus** and the other **brother,** the **same spirit** was evidenced, and it was clear that they walked in the **same steps.** No devious tactics could be seen in Paul or any of his companions.

D. The Charge of the Apostle. 12:19-13:10.

1. The charge to repent. 12:19-13:10.

19. Again, think ye that we excuse ourselves unto you? (literally, "you have been some time imagining that it is to you that I am defending myself"). If they are under the delusion that Paul has gone through all of this only on their behalf, Paul's answer is: **we speak before God in Christ.** The apostle was not accountable to the Corinthians, only to God. As for them his only concern was their **edifying.** It was not necessary for Paul to defend himself before anyone, much less qualify his apostolic authority. On the other hand it was imperative that the Corinthian believers be brought back into line and into submission to their father in the faith.

20. For I fear, lest, when I come, I shall not find you such as I would. His only fear is that when he arrives in Corinth he will discover, still neglected, all the same problems that he has been dealing with in these two epistles. **And that I shall be found unto you such as ye would not.** Indeed that his dark side should be exposed. And such would be the case if he should arrive to find the abuses and sins reputed of them still persisting.

21. My God will humble me among you, i.e. "that I should be humiliated in your midst." And such would be the case if he arrived and discovered **the unclean-**

terpreters and most modern scholars apply this to the self-mutilation practiced by the heathen priests of Cybele. Paul speaks with satire. **Which trouble you.** Causing so much disturbance and throwing you into confusion.

B. Liberty is Perverted by Lawlessness. 5:13:26.

13. For brethren. A tender title. **Ye.** Emphatic contrast to the false teachers. **Have been called unto liberty.** Ye were called unto liberty, not slavery. Liberty is not an excuse for license. License destroys liberty. **Only use not liberty for an occasion to the flesh.** Some of the Galatians may have already done this, and others were tempted. Liberty must be maintained, not abused. It is abused when it is made the occasion of turning liberty into license. "Occasion" (Gr *aphorme*) is a military term signifying a camping place which becomes a launching pad to capture the opposing army. It is the base of operations for giving way to carnal passions. The flesh is the sinful nature to man, which has been crucified with Christ (2:20), but which seems to possess possibilities of revival. Therefore do not let your liberty become the impulse which will start the old nature to assert itself again. **But.** On the contrary. **By love.** True Christian love is the motive of true Christian conduct. **Serve one another.** Constantly and voluntarily enslave yourselves to one another.

14. For all the law is fulfilled in one word. The whole moral law stands fully accomplished and completed in one precept. **Thou shalt love thy neighbor as thyself.** Such love is produced by the Holy Spirit. Love is the real fulfillment of the law which the legalists were wanting to serve. It was said of the early Christians, "Behold how they love one another," not how they quarrel, criticize, and backbite. Christ did not come to destroy the law . . . but to fulfill (Mt 5:17). Grace does not make one free to sin; it makes him free to serve.

15. But if. Setting in contrast what they were doing with what they should do. **Bite and devour.** Continually biting and devouring like wild animals in deadly combat, i.e. a picture of church strifes. **Take heed.** Watch out. **That ye be not consumed one of another.** Mutual destruction by slander and criticism.

16. Walk in the Spirit. Have the habit of continually walking by the energizing power and under the divine direction of the Holy Spirit. This is the only way of deliverance from selfish lusts. **And ye shall not fulfil the lust of the flesh.** The double negative with the aorist subjunctive means you will never gratify the sinful desires originating in and overflowing from the lower nature. When God saved us, He did not eradicate the old nature, neither did He reform the old life; He gave us an absolutely new life (Jn 3:6). The old nature is "not subject to the law of God, neither indeed can be" (Rom 8:7). The Christian can conquer the self-life and have continual victory by walking by the Holy Spirit.

17. For the flesh lusteth against the Spirit. There is a constant deadly feud being waged. Bunyan shows that both Christ and Satan long for the possession of the city of Man Soul. Romans 7:15-25 is an inspired commentary on this verse. The flesh opposes the Spirit in an effort to prevent the believer from a life of obedience, surrender, and victory. **The Spirit against the flesh.** The Holy Spirit opposes the flesh and gives the believer victory over it. **And these are contrary.** Lined up in hostile, face-to-face conflict. There is mutual antagonism. mutual antagonism. **So that ye cannot do the things that ye would.** So that ye may not keep on doing whatever ye may want to do.

18. But if ye be led of the Spirit. If you are being led continually by the Holy Spirit, then it follows that **ye are not under the law.** Christians have a live-in divine Person to keep them in line, and they do not need an external curb.

19. Now the works of the flesh. Note the plural, works, the complex mixture of evil desires and deeds. The flesh is always active; it never takes a vacation.

with you. Maturity, contentment, unity, and harmony, reflected in these terms, answer to the immaturity, unrest, division, and quarreling so evident in the Corinthian assembly.

12. Greet one another with a holy kiss. This denoted affection and kinship. It was and continues to be common especially in the East. It was practiced even in the West till the thirteenth century.

13. All the saints salute you. This should be properly restricted to Paul's companions at the time. However, the more general truth also finds appropriate emphasis in the apostle. That is, that all the saints, everywhere enjoy a common fellowship and therefore, a mutual interest in the spiritual welfare of one another.

14. The grace of the Lord Jesus Christ, and the love of God, and the communion of the Holy Ghost, be with you all. Amen. In his concluding benediction, Paul not only invokes the fullness of God's provision on behalf of the Corinthian believers, but also in passing, provides one of the clearest expressions in the New Testament on the doctrine of the Trinity. The deity of the Son, of the Father, and of the Holy Spirit are affirmed by virtue of their relation to one another. The distinctive personality of each is implied by the independent activity denoted in the threefold operation of grace, love, and communion.

BIBLIOGRAPHY

Barclay, W. *The Letters to the Corinthians.* Philadelphia: Westminster Press, 1956.

Darby, J. N. *Notes of a Reading on I and II Corinthians.* London: G. Morrish, n.d.

Denny, J. The Second Epistle to the Corinthians. In *The Expositor's Bible.* Nicoll, W. R., Ed. Cincinnati: Jennings and Graham, n.d.

Erdman, C. R. *The Second Epistle of Paul to the Corinthians.* Philadelphia: Westminster Press, 1929.

Gouge, H. L. *The Mind of St. Paul.* London: Edward Arnold, 1911.

Hering, J. *The Second Epistle of St. Paul to the Corinthians.* Allcock, P. J. and Heathcote, A. W., Trans. London: The Epworth Press, 1967.

* Hodge, C. *Commentary on the Second Epistle to the Corinthians.* Grand Rapids: Eerdmans, n.d.

* Hughes, P. E. Paul's Second Epistle to the Corinthians. In *The New International Commentary.* Grand Rapids: Eerdmans, 1975.

Ironside, H. A. *Addresses on the Second Epistle to the Corinthians.* New York: Loizeaux Brothers, 1939.

Kelly, W. *Notes on the Second Epistle to the Corinthians.* Oak Park, Ill.: Bible Truth, 1975.

McPheeters, J. C. The Epistles to the Corinthians. In *Proclaiming the New Testament.* Vol. VI. Grand Rapids: Baker, 1964.

Menzies, A. *The Second Epistle of Paul to the Corinthians.* New York: Macmillan, 1912.

Ockenga, H. J. *The Comfort of God.* New York: Revell, 1944.

Plummer, A. The Second Epistle of St. Paul to the Corinthians. In *International Critical Commentary*. Edinburgh: T. & T. Clark, 1915.

Rendall, G. H. *The Epistles of St. Paul to the Corinthians*. New York: Macmillan, 1909.

Strachan, R. H. The Second Epistle of Paul to the Corinthians. In *Moffatt Commentary*. London: Hodder and Stoughton, 1935.

* Tasker, R. V. G. The Second Epistle of Paul to the Corinthians. In *Tyndale New Testament Commentaries*. Grand Rapids: Eerdmans, 1975.

The Epistle To The

GALATIANS

INTRODUCTION

Authorship. The authorship of Galatians never has been seriously doubted and it has been well said that "whoever is prepared to deny the genuineness of the epistle, would pronounce on himself the sentence of incapacity to distinguish true from false." Findlay says, "No breath of suspicion as to the authorship, integrity, or apostolic authority of the Epistle to the Galatians has reached us from ancient times" (*International Standard Bible Encyclopaedia,* Vol. 2, p. 1156). Lightfoot adds, "Its every sentence so completely reflects the life and character of the apostle to the Gentiles that its genuineness has not been seriously questioned" (*St. Paul's Epistle to the Galatians,* p. 57). Even Baur, father of the radical school of critics in Germany, and the radical Dutch scholars concede that Paul wrote Galatians. Both the internal and the external evidences of Galatians are strong, and it is not necessary to produce extensive proof of its early existence or of its Pauline authorship.

Destination. The letter is addressed to the churches of Galatia. Galatia is the name that was given originally to the territory in North Central Asia Minor, where the invading Gauls settled in the third century before Christ. Gradually the Gallic population was absorbed into other peoples living there, and after a number of political changes, the territory became the property of Rome in 25 B.C. The Romans incorporated this northern section into a larger division of the land which they made a province and called it Galatia. Politically, Galatia was the Roman province which included Isauria, Lycaonia, and parts of Phrygia and Pisidia. Geographically, it was the center of Celtic tribes and included Derbe, Lystra, Iconium, and Antioch of Pisidia. The question is did Paul write to the ethnic Galatia of the north or the geographical Galatia of the south? Paul and Barnabas evangelized the southern section of the Roman Galatia during their first missionary journey (Acts 13:14-14:26). The Epistle to the Galatians agrees with everything that we know about the churches Paul founded on this journey in southern Galatia. Whereas, the existence of churches in northern Galatia is hypothetical. No churches are mentioned in the North Galatia territory, only disciples. "While the evidence for either view is not conclusive, it seems to us that the balance of probability is in favor of the South Galatian theory. While this position is steadily growing in popularity it must be admitted that the North Galatian theory is arguable and has its able defenders. Fortunately, neither the value of the epistle or its interpretation is seriously affected by the question" (D. Edmond Hiebert, *An Introduction to the Pauline Epistles,* p. 83).

Date. The date depends on whether Paul wrote to churches in the North or the South Galatian territory. The North Galatian theory would require A.D. 57, but the South Galatian theory would place it about A.D. 49. Most of the older commentators follow Lightfoot in favor of the North Galatian theory and the later date. Most contemporary commentators follow Ramsay in favor of the South Galatian theory and an early date, A.D. 49 from Antioch just before the council of Jerusalem.

Occasion of the epistle. This epistle was called forth by the activities of the unscrupulous Judaizers. These legalists had vigorously discredited and denounced Paul and his gospel and had persuaded many to turn away from Christianity to Judaism. They claimed that the Jewish law was binding upon Christians and that salvation must be attained by the works of the law. They especially urged the Galatians to submit to circumcision. The purpose of Galatians was to root out the errors of the legalists, to win back the converts to allegiance to Christ, and to expound the doctrine of justification by faith. Paul sets forth grace as opposed to law, faith as opposed to works, and spirit as opposed to flesh.

Permanent value of Galatians. Some look upon this epistle as having little value for our times. But the perverted gospel, which is so severely condemned in this epistle, is the very message which is so prevalent in our days. Christendom is so thoroughly permeated by the leaven of legalism, Judaism, ritualism, Romanism, materialism, and every form of externalism. "A little leaven leaveneth the whole lump" (5:9). The Epistle to the Galatians has a contemporary relevance in its message of justification by faith for modern man, with all his cults and religious systems that seek to gain heaven by human merit, rather than by divine mercy. Erdman says, "Wherever religion has lost its reality, wherever ritual is more regarded than right living, wherever subscription to a creed is substituted for submission to Christ, wherever loud claims of orthodoxy are accompanied by conduct devoid of charity, wherever deeds of self-righteousness are obscuring the glory of the cross, there this epistle should be made to sound out its clarion call to a new dependence upon justifying grace, to a faith that is shown by works, to a walk that is by the Spirit, to a life inspired by love" (Charles R. Erdman, *The Epistle of Paul to the Galatians,* p. 5).

OUTLINE

I. Personal: The Apostle of Liberty. 1:1-2:21.
    A. Introduction. 1:1-9.
    B. Paul's Apostleship. 1:10-2:21.
        1. Paul's revelation from Christ. 1:10-17.
        2. Paul's acceptance by the churches. 1:18-24.
        3. Paul's approval by the apostles. 2:1-10.
        4. Paul's rebuke of Peter. 2:11-21.
II. Polemical: The Doctrine of Liberty. 3:1-4:31.
    A. Paul's Appeal to Liberty. 3:1-7.
        1. Rebuke of the Galatians. 3:1-4.
        2. Reception of the Spirit. 3:5-7.
    B. Paul's Argument for Liberty. 3:8-29.
        1. The promise to Abraham. 3:8-14.
        2. The purpose of the law. 3:15-29.
    C. Paul's Amplification of Liberty. 4:1-31.
        1. The coming of God's Son. 4:1-7.
        2. The conduct of the Galatians. 4:8-21.
        3. The comparison of Hagar and Sarah. 4:22-31.
III. Practical: The Life of Liberty. 5:1-6:18.
    A. Liberty is Imperiled by Legalism. 5:1-12.
    B. Liberty is Perverted by Lawlessness. 5:13-26.
    C. Liberty is Perfected by Love. 6:1-10.
    D. Conclusion. 6:11-18.

COMMENTARY

I. PERSONAL: THE APOSTLE OF LIBERTY. 1:1-2:21.

A. Introduction. 1:1-9.

1:1. Paul. Paul was his Latin name; Saul was his Hebrew name. He was born in Tarsus in Cilicia (Acts 9:11; 22:3) of Jewish parents (Phil 3:5). His father was a Pharisee and a Roman citizen (Acts 23:6), so Paul was a Roman citizen by birth (Acts 22:27-28). He studied under the renowned Gamaliel (Acts 5:34, 22: 3). **An apostle.** An apostle is one who is sent with authority to represent and speak for another. He is accredited with special delegated authority and entrusted with a special divine message. Paul claims to be a messenger, an envoy, an ambassador for Christ. He was endowed with all the credentials of his office. He was owned by Christ, commissioned by Christ, and empowered by Christ. **Not of men.** Not from men. The bluntness of Paul's denial is due to the charge of the legalists that he was not one of the Twelve and not a genuine apostle. The preposition (Gr *apo*) signifies origin and separation. Paul already states that the source of his apostleship is not from men, not emanating from men. **Neither by man.** The preposition here (Gr *dia*) implies means, medium, instrument. Paul declares decisively that the means of receiving his apostleship was not a man. "The first preposition denotes the fountain-head whence the apostle's authority springs, the second the channel through which it is conveyed" (J. B. Lightfoot, *The Epistle of St. Paul to the Galatians,* p. 71). Paul was not an ambassador of men, and his gospel was not the word and wisdom of man. Paul's "mission to the Gentiles had apparently been disparaged on the plea that it had been emanated from men, i.e., from the church of Antioch only. Again, the validity of his commission was impugned on the ground that he originally had received the Spirit through a man, i.e.,

through the agency of Ananias, who had been deputed to lay his hands upon him at Damascus" (Frederic Rendall, *The Epistle to the Galatians,* p. 149). Paul knew nothing about apostolic succession, but he experienced an abundant measure of apostolic success. **But by Jesus Christ, and God the Father.** When the preposition (Gr *dia*) is used of a personal agent sometimes it expresses the author of the action as well as its instrument. Here Jesus Christ is both the ultimate source and the mediate agency. Both Christ and God are governed by one preposition and joined by one conjunction, indicating that they are coequal and coeternal. There was no one higher to commission Paul and no lower through whom he was commissioned. He had a divine commission to expose false teaching, to exclaim the gospel, to establish churches, to exhort Christians, and to exalt Christ. **Who raised him from the dead.** Paul had seen the risen Christ (I Cor 9:1; 15:8) and was qualified to be an apostle. The resurrection was God's "amen" to Christ's "It is finished." Paul emphasized the resurrection because some were saying that he had not seen the Lord Jesus Christ and could not be an apostle. It was the risen, glorified Son of God whom Paul had seen on the road to Damascus (Acts 9:3-9). Paul's mission and message were divine, not human.

2. And all the brethren which are with me. Paul implies that there were with him a goodly number of Christian believers, members of the household of faith. Paul associates these unnamed fellow workers with him in sending greetings. **Unto the churches of Galatia.** Not to the church of Galatia. To Paul there was no state or national church. The word church (Gr *ekklēsia*) occurs over one hundred times in the New Testament. Once it refers to the assembly of saints in heaven (Heb 12:23), several times it is used in a wide sense (mostly in

Ephesians and Colossians), but the vast majority of times it refers to a local assembly of called-out, born-again Christians bonded together for worship and work. Paul addresses this epistle to a group of churches that were relinquishing the essential truths of the gospel of grace and were going back to the works of the law as a means of justification. "The omission of any expression of praise in addressing the Galatians shows the extent of their apostasy" (J. B. Lightfoot, *The Epistle of St. Paul to the Galatians,* p. 73).

3. Grace be to you and peace. Grace was the usual Greek greeting, and peace was the usual Hebrew greeting. By these two words, Paul sums up all the blessing his heart would desire for them. In Christ, God revealed His grace, and through Christ He bestowed His peace. Grace is the sum of all the blessings extended by God; peace is the sum of all the blessings experienced by man. This customary salutation is not a perfunctory thing with Paul. He uses it here even when he has so much fault to find. He does not withhold the wish for divine grace and peace even for those whom he is about to upbraid. **From God the Father, and from our Lord Jesus Christ.** The Father and the Son cooperate fully in the salvation of sinful man.

4. Who gave himself for our sins. Christ voluntarily and vicariously offered Himself on account of our sins. The preposition (Gr *hyper*) speaks of substitution, instead of, in behalf of. Christ who knew no sin, made sin for us that we might be made the righteousness of God in Him (II Cor 5:21). He exchanged places with us; He took all of our sins and gave us all of His righteousness. He was both the purchaser and the price of our redemption. There was no other good enough to pay the price of sin. At Calvary Jesus Christ once for all settled the sin question. Just before He bowed His head and gave up the ghost, He said, "It is finished" (Jn 19:30). Our sins made His sacrifice necessary, and His sacrifice is the only ground of our ac-

ceptance with God. **That he might deliver us from this present evil world.** The purpose of His sacrifice was to deliver us, rescue us, and set us free from this present evil age. It is "out of" (Gr *ek*) rather than "from" this pernicious age; those delivered had been within the grasp of an enemy. Christ not only delivers the believer from the penalty of sin, but also from the power of sin. Salvation is an emancipation out from a state of bondage. This is the keynote of the epistle. The word "rescued" (Gr *exaireō*) is used in Acts 23:27 to speak of Paul's rescue from the mob, and in Acts 7:34 to speak of Israel being taken out of Egypt. Here it has the connotation of rescue from danger and deliverance from bondage. Sin had endangered and enslaved us; Christ delivered us and set us free. All is due to His atoning death. This age is an evil, corrupt and corrupting, deceived and deceiving. The word evil (Gr *ponēros*) means not only evil in its nature but actively and viciously evil in its influence. It is used to describe Satan, the god of this age, who is corrupting man and dragging him to destruction. The substitutional sacrifice of Christ alone can liberate man from Satan. **According to the will of God.** This was all in accordance with God's determinate counsel and foreknowledge (Acts 2:23).

5. To whom be glory for ever and ever. Amen. Paul ascribes praise unto God unto the ages of the ages, in contrast to the present transitory age. This doxology in the salutation takes the place of Paul's usual thanksgiving for his readers.

6. I marvel. This word (Gr *thaumazō*) was used often by Greek orators of surprise at something reprehensible and can be translated "amazed," "astonished," "bewildered." Norley translates it "dumbfounded." Paul is painfully surprised and alarmed at the instability of the Galatians. **That ye are so soon removed.** Not referring to the brevity of time since Paul's visit, but "so quickly" referring to the rapidity of their apostasy. Instead of ushering the legalists out the door (II Jn 10), these churches gullibly listened to their false teaching. The Galatians were very fickle and easily induced to change. False teaching issued in spiritual delinquency. Corrupt teaching always leads to corrupt living. In classical Greek, this word "removed" (Gr *metatithēmi*) was used of a turncoat. The Galatians were deserting Christ and turning renegade. The present tense indicates: (1) that the transfer had begun; (2) that it was in progress; and (3) that it was not yet complete. Paul does not despair because there is some hope of spiritual recovery and restoration. All is not lost, but time is of a premium. The middle voice of the verb implies that the Galatians were transferring themselves from grace to law and from liberty to bondage. They were responsible and accountable for their own defection. **From him that called you.** Their defection was not only from the gospel of God, but from God Himself. This assertion should have startled the Galatians who probably thought they were honoring God by trying to keep His law. Their departure from God was dangerous and dreadful. They were abandoning God and His grace by putting themselves under the law and its curse. **Into the grace of Christ.** God calls in and by Christ's grace. This suggests the permanency of the divine favor in which God calls and through which the blessings of Christ are given. God called the Galatians to salvation which was: (1) purchased at Calvary; (2) offered in and by grace; and (3) to be accepted by faith. All that God requires of man, he Has already provided by grace in Christ. **Unto another gospel.** There are two Greek words which mean "another." One (Gr *allos*) means another of the same kind, a numerical difference; and the other (Gr *heteros*) means another of a different kind, a qualitative difference. Here the meaning is that there is no other gospel, although the legalists had brought them a different kind of teaching, which they claimed to be the gospel. There is an es-

sential difference between the true gospel and a man-made, spurious gospel (cf. II Cor 11:4). There is but one, and only one gospel concerning the eternal Son of God who became incarnate in order to become the propitiation for the sins of the whole world (I Jn 2:2). Christ's finished work at Calvary enables God to be just and the justifier of him who believes in Christ (Rom 3:26). God has no other gospel, and He cannot and will not tolerate the perversion of His gospel.

7. Which is not another. It was different and therefore no gospel at all. A message of salvation by works is not good news to lost sinners. The message of the legalists was diametrically opposed to the gospel of God's grace. When the works of the law are added to grace, you no longer have grace. "If the clause be rendered, whereas there is no other gospel (i.e., than the true), the sense becomes perfectly clear, and it forms an appropriate introduction to the succeeding anathemas by its emphatic testimony to the one true gospel" (Frederic Rendall, *The Epistle to the Galatians,* p. 152). There is no other gospel, only a spurious semblance. **Some that trouble you.** This word (Gr *tarassō*) means to agitate, to trouble, to cause inward commotion, to disturb mentally with fear, excitement, and perplexity. The present tense means that the legalists were in Galatia at the time Paul wrote, and they were confusing the Galatians and shaking their allegiance to Christ. **And would.** The legalists are determined to pervert the gospel, and Paul writes to hinder their success. **Pervert the gospel of Christ.** This word "pervert" (Gr *metastrephō*) is used only three times in the New Testament, and it means to completely change into something of the opposite nature as in Acts 2:20 where the sun is turned into darkness and in James 4:9 where laughter is turned into mourning. The legalists were determined to pervert the gospel by substituting law for grace, circumcision for the cross, works for faith, bondage for liberty, and self for Christ. Any change in the gospel of Christ is a corruption, interfering with its simplicity, its purity, and its effectiveness. Even the thought of this stirs Paul to the very depths of his being. Note how vehement is his language now, and how he repeated it for greater emphasis.

8. But though we, or an angel from heaven, preach any other gospel. Paul does not say that he or a messenger from heaven was likely to preach any other gospel. He merely uses a future hypothetical possibility to illustrate the case. This passage directly speaks against such claims as that of the Mormons, whose *Book of Mormon* claims angelic authority as delivered by the Angel Moroni and "translated" by their founder Joseph Smith. **Let him be accursed.** An "anathema" on anyone who would proclaim a gospel contrary to that which Paul delivered and had received from God (I Cor 15:3-4). God does not want His Word twisted by unlearned and unstable men unto the destruction of souls (II Pet 3:17). God said what He meant, and He meant what He said. God can do nothing less than put an awful curse on all who reject, pervert and falsify the gospel of His Son. It was the Holy Spirit who moved Paul to pen these serious words. We must never forget that the awful day of doom and destruction is coming when the divine "anathema" pronounced here will be executed (II Thess 1:7-9). May God's people everywhere stand with Paul in opposition to false teaching. May God help us to believe the gospel, to behave the gospel, and to become living epistles of the gospel.

9. As we said before. The language is too emphatic to refer to the verse lightly. Paul no doubt had warned them of the dangers of false teachers as he did the Ephesian elders (Acts 20:29-32). The perfect tense of "said" (Gr *prolegō*) means that it was a certain and clear pronouncement. The Galatians still remember Paul's warning, and therefore their defection is inexcusable. The plural number (we) shows that the previous warning was given by others in addition to Paul. **If any man.** The particle (Gr *ei*) speaks of a fulfilled condition. Paul is not speaking of a future probability (vs. 8), but of an actual, current fact, and he hurls the anathema directly at the legalists. Note the omission in verse 9 of "we or an angel."

B. Paul's Apostleship. 1:10-2:21.

1. Paul's revelation from Christ. 1:10-17.

10. For. This introduces a justification of the severe language just used. **Do I now persuade men.** This means to win over, to conciliate, to render friendly to one's self. These rhetorical questions indicate that an attack has been made on Paul for the purpose of discrediting both him and his ministry. He denies the charges. Paul was not softening down unwelcome truths to men, that he might by some means win them over to his way of thinking. Neither was he trying to persuade God to tone down His message. Paul's loyalty to Christ and his sufferings for Christ were evidences that he was not seeking man's approval, but his Lord's "well done." He has no desire to please anyone but Christ, whose he is and whom he serves (Acts 27:23).

11. But I certify you. I make known, inform, tell you plainly, assure you. This word (Gr *gnorizō*) is used to introduce matters of great importance (I Cor 12:3; 15:1; II Cor 8:1). Paul uses a strong word to leave no doubt as to the truth of the statement he is about to make. **Brethren.** Paul addresses them as brethren in Christ, sons of the same heavenly Father. They are deceived, disturbed, and defecting in their devotion and duty to Christ. But they are still regarded as brethren, brethren needing Paul's Spirit-inspired counsel. **That the gospel which was preached of me.** Literally, the gospel gospelled by me. **Is not after man.** Not according to man. Paul sets the record straight. He affirms the divine origin of his message in terms similar to those used to declare the divine origin of his apostleship. Both his mission and his message are independent of man, both received by direct divine revelation.

12. For I neither received it of man. Man had absolutely nothing to do with Paul's gospel. His message was not received from man as a source or through man as a channel. The preposition (Gr *para*) translated "of" emphasizes the idea of transmission and connects the giver with the receiver. Paul did not receive the gospel "from" man. **Neither was I taught it.** Paul was taught the precepts of Judaism at the feet of Gamaliel (Acts 5:34; 22:3), but he received no human instruction or human interpretation of the gospel. But, on the contrary, **by the revelation.** Therefore there was nothing human about it. It was a direct divine communication of previously unknown truth. The word "revelation" is used of the unveiling of divine persons or things, never of one human revealing a secret to another man. Paul refers to his experience on the road to Damascus (Acts 9), which was supplemented during his seclusion in Arabia. **Of Jesus Christ.** This can mean either Christ is revealing or Christ is revealed; both interpretations make good sense. This is a subjective genitive. Christ revealed Himself to Paul. Christ was the subject, sum, and substance of that revelation with the result that Paul became a new man with a new message to proclaim. Paul was not a man-made apostle. He received his commission and his message from Christ.

13. For ye have heard. Paul refers to the time he spent with them. He often related his personal testimony as part of his ministry (Acts 22 and 26). **Of my conversation.** Originally the word (Gr *anastrophē*) meant "up-turning" and then came to mean that thing which would keep on turning up, and means the custom, conduct, or manner of one's life. It refers to Paul's everyday life. **In time past in the Jews' religion.** This was Judaism as a religion of faith and custom, with human traditions superim-

posed upon it; an apostate Judaism as an ethical, unspiritual cult. **How that beyond measure.** Transliterated hyperbole and means according to excess, immeasurable. **I persecuted.** This word (Gr *diōkō*) means put to flight, drive away, harass, trouble, molest, persecute. The imperfect tense denotes continuous action (I kept on persecuting). Paul constantly and relentlessly persecuted the church. **The church of God.** The whole body (Gr *ekklēsia*) of born-again believers. It is God's church; redeemed by God's Son and regenerated by God's Holy Spirit. It is the body of Christ, in whom the Holy Spirit lives and through whom the Holy Spirit ministers. **And wasted it.** This word (Gr *portheō*) means to overthrow, destroy, make havoc, lay waste. The original idea is that of rooting up and leaving devastation behind. The imperfect tense implies that Paul continually, persistently, and violently kept on ravaging the church (Acts 9:13; 26:10-11). Paul had been the supreme Judaistic fanatic of his time.

14. And profited. Literally (Gr *prokoptō*) "to cut forward," hence to blaze a trail or cut a pioneer path. Paul was advancing, pushing forward, and outstripping all others in power and prestige. **In the Jews' religion.** Traditional Judaism was not much like Mosaism in its pristine purity. Paul was a zealous, law-loving Pharisee. **Above many my equals.** He started out with his fellow classmates but soon far surpassed them in his zeal and activities for the traditions of Judaism. **In mine own nation.** My race. **Being more exceedingly zealous.** Paul was an uncompromising partisan, a zealot burning with superabundant zeal. **Of the traditions of my fathers.** Traditions played a large part in the precepts and practices of the Pharisees. By traditions Paul means those hundreds of human commandments built around the Old Testament law and which must be maintained at any cost. Our Lord Jesus distinguished between the written law and man-made traditions and clearly proclaimed that the traditions of man caused the Word of God to be of none effect (Mt 15:1-6; Mk 7:3-13). But for the grace of God, Paul would have lived and died a profound protagonist of Judaism.

15. But. Very strong here, in contrast to the traditions. **When it pleased God.** God's good pleasure in His gracious purpose. **Who separated me.** Refers to God's setting Paul apart for special service. The word (Gr *aphorizō*) means to work off from a boundary, to limit, to separate, to designate, to set apart, to appoint. The Pharisees were the separatists who held themselves off from others. Paul conceives himself a spiritual separatist, separated unto the gospel of God (Rom 1:1). **From my mother's womb.** The preposition (Gr *ek*) makes the temporal starting point. Only God could define the limits of one's life while yet in the womb of his mother. God's plan for Paul's life was determined before he was born (cf. Jer 1:5). **And called me by his grace.** It was by means of grace that God called Paul out of darkness into His marvelous light (I Pet 2:9) and made him a chosen vessel (Acts 9:15), "a vessel unto honor, sanctified, and meet for the master's use, and prepared unto every good work" (II Tim 2:21). **To reveal his Son in me.** Paul was inwardly enlightened. After his vision of Christ, Paul spent three days in solitary communion (Acts 9:9). There "was an inward and spiritual revelation which followed that appeal to eye and ear" (Frederic Rendall, *The Epistle to the Galatians,* p. 154). "The whole subject of discourse in this paragraph is not how Paul made known his gospel, but how he received it" (Ernest DeWitt Burton, *A Critical and Exegetical Commentary on the Epistle to the Galatians,* p. 51). There was altogether a threefold revelation: (1) to Paul; (2) in Paul; and (3) through Paul, and in that order. **That.** In order that, (Gr *hina*). Now the purpose of the revelation is made known. It was not for salvation alone, but for service. We are saved to serve. Salvation is a means to an end, not an end in itself. **I might preach**

him. The final object of God's revelation to Paul was that he should go on proclaiming Christ to others. The present tense (Gr *euagglizomai*) speaks of continued effort, and the accusative case (Gr *auton*) **him,** the person preached. Christ was the sum total of Paul's message, not the law or ceremonies. Paul was not proclaiming a plan of salvation but the person of the Saviour. It is not a matter of one religion against another. Paul has a divine commission to preach Christ. **Among the heathen.** God not only told Paul **whom** to preach, but where to preach, among the Gentiles (Acts 9:15; 22:15; 26:16-19). **Immediately I conferred not.** Paul received his commission from God, and there was no need to consult man. The double compound (Gr *prosanatīlhēmi*) means "to place over and toward," hence to put one's self in communion with another. The real purpose of a conference is to get advice from someone more knowledgeable than yourself. Paul already had been made an apostle and already knew God's plan for his life (Acts 26:14-19); he had no need of man's advice. Paul is establishing his dependence upon God and his independence from man. **With flesh and blood.** Apparently a reminiscence of "flesh and blood hath not revealed it unto thee, but my Father" (Mt 16:17). Flesh and blood suggests human weakness and ignorance and represents human as opposed to divine wisdom. Man could not add anything to God's revelation.

17. Neither. Literally, not even. **Apostles before me.** The Jerusalem apostles were genuine apostles, but so was Paul. Before in order of time, but not in rank; they had more seniority, but not more authority. Paul's call and commission did not come from them nor did he receive confirmation by them. Paul's apostleship was firsthand. There was no human instrumentality in his apostleship. **But.** On the contrary, Paul took the opposite course. **I went into Arabia, and returned again unto Damascus.** Paul avoided Jerusalem and emphasizes his independence of the other apostles. The Holy Spirit has not revealed all we would like to know, but Paul spent considerable time alone with God (cf. Moses and Elijah).

2. Paul's acceptance by the churches. 1:18-24.

18. Then after three years. Paul dates the time from his conversion. During these three years, he had no contact with any of the apostles. **I went up to Jerusalem.** His first visit is recorded in Acts 9:26-30. **To see Peter.** "See" (Gr *historeō*), used only here in the New Testament, is the word from which we get our word "history." It was used to express either: (1) to learn facts from personal inquiry or observation or; (2) to relate facts as a historian would. There was an interchange of facts between Paul and Peter. The purpose of this visit was to become personally acquainted with Peter, not to gain official sanction or recognition. They met on common ground. Peter did not install Paul into the apostleship nor confer anything upon him. Paul uses the old Aramaic name "Cephas." **And abode with him.** The preposition (Gr *pros*) means "toward" him. Paul was facing Cephas in a most personal, intimate, and friendly manner, but not subordinating himself in any way. Paul visited Peter as an equal. **Fifteen days.** Paul's visit was interrupted because the Grecians were seeking his life (Acts 9:29) and the Lord appeared to him while he was praying in the temple and told him to leave quickly (Acts 22:17-18).

19. James. The half-brother of our Lord Jesus Christ. This distinguishes him from James the brother of John. He was a leader in the Jerusalem church (Acts 15).

20. Before God, I lie not. Paul's enemies had accused him of being a slick talker. He asserts his integrity by a solemn affirmation, made as if in the very presence of God. His word was as good as his oath, as Christ taught every man's word should be (Mt 5:33-37).

21. Regions of Syria and Cilicia. "Regions" (Gr *klema*) is the source of our word "climate" and refers to the coastal plains of the countries named. Paul does not describe his ministry here, but it lasted for about six years. During this time Paul was out of contact with Jerusalem. Syria is named first because of its prominence in the Roman Empire and because of the greater significance of Paul's ministry here.

22. And was unknown by face. They did not recognize Paul when they saw him. **Into the churches of Judea.** There were other local churches in Judaea besides the church at Jerusalem. **Which were in Christ.** True churches are in Christ as branches are in the True Vine (Jn 15:5).

23. But they had heard only. The members of the Judaean churches kept on hearing from time to time, as the Greek present tense implies. **Now preacheth the faith.** The saving faith in Christ based on the truth of the gospel which was once for all delivered unto the saints (Jude 3). **Which once he destroyed.** Same word (Gr *portheō*) translated as "wasted" in verse 13. The imperfect tense speaks of continuous action. Before his conversion, Paul's one passion that consumed his time was to root out Christianity.

24. And they glorified God in me. They recognized God's handiwork (Eph 2:10) in Paul and kept on glorifying God for saving, transforming, and using Paul. How different from the reaction of the legalists who were seeking to destroy Paul's ministry. Paul has displayed the divine origin of his apostleship and his independence from the apostolic band.

3. Paul's approval by the apostles. 2:1-10.

2:1. Then fourteen years after. If fourteen years after his conversion, it could be his visit recorded in Acts 11:30; but if fourteen after his first visit, it would be the one recorded in Acts 15:2. Scholars are divided. J. B. Lightfoot and others hold to the traditional view (Acts 15:2) but Sir William Ramsey and many contemporary scholars hold to the other view (11:30). The evidence is not conclusive, so we must be tolerant, and not dogmatic. The exact date is important in establishing the chronology of Paul's mission but not in the exposition of his message. **I went up again to Jerusalem.** The preposition (Gr *ana*) may be used because of the geographical position of Jerusalem, or more probably because of its religious superiority. Paul's contacts with Jerusalem were few and brief. **With Barnabas.** A wealthy Levite of Cyprus. He had keen insight into the character of man and clear understanding of Christianity. He was a philanthropist and had the confidence of the whole church. **And took.** This double compound (Gr *sumparalambanō*) means to take along with as a companion. **Titus.** A Gentile convert. He is not mentioned in the book of Acts, and little is known of him.

2. And I went up by revelation. The Holy Spirit revealed His will to Paul, and Paul was obedient to His divine guidance. Paul did not go merely because of any doubt or difficulty he was experiencing, and neither on his own initiative, nor at the direction of the church of Antioch. **And communicated.** Literally "set up" (Gr *anatithēmi*) for the consideration of others. The real purpose of his visit is to place before the apostles the gospel he is preaching among the peoples in the Gentile lands. **Privately.** To the recognized spiritual leaders, rather than to the whole church body. This does not imply secrecy. **Of reputation.** The apostolic leaders (cf. vss. 6 and 9), were men of eminence, those looked upon as authorities and held in high regard. **Run in vain.** Lest I should be running in vain, thwarted by misunderstanding and opposition. Paul is not expressing any doubt. He desires to maintain unity and fellowship with the apostles in Jerusalem and avoid a split. A schism would have caused division in every church. But he did not go to Jerusalem to determine whether he was preaching the one true gospel but whether they were. But Paul would be running a fruitless race and to no purpose if the message of the legalists was the true gospel. There was so much at stake: is salvation by law or by grace, a matter of human attainment or of divine atonement, by works or by faith.

3. But neither. Not even. **Titus.** This Gentile was accepted as a real Christian just as he was. (Not) **compelled to be circumcised.** Titus was a test case. The legalists failed completely in their demands and position. It is evident that the apostles at Jerusalem did not sanction their teaching that circumcision is necessary for salvation. Paul prevailed against all the pressure brought by the legalists to force the issue. Paul stood firmly and successfully and won the full approval of the apostles. Paul resisted, rejected, and refused the demands of the legalists. Concession was not expedient; it was impossible, and it would have been fatal to Christianity. Paul could not and would not surrender on this vital issue. The gospel of grace would have disintegrated if Paul had circumcised Titus on the demands of the legalists. "Once the Judaizers made their demand regarding Titus, they destroyed all reason for his ever being circumcised" (R. C. H. Lenski, *Interpretation of Paul's Epistles to the Galatians, to the Ephesians, and to the Philippians,* p. 76). Thank God for the undaunted, uncompromising apostle who "kept the faith" (II Tim 4:7, and may He raise multitudes to follow his steps.

4. False brethren. Those who ostentatiously profess to be Christians, but who are destitute of spiritual life. They may have regarded Christ as Messiah, but they knew nothing of salvation through His atoning blood. They were clinging to a salvation-by-works system. **Unawares brought in.** Literally, brought in by the side or on the sly (Gr *pareiserchomai*). These traitors were foisted in unexpectedly, smuggled in surreptitiously and insidiously. **Came in privily.**

Further describing the secret infiltration of these enemies who "crept in unawares" (Jude 4). The verb means to come in secretly or by stealth, to creep or steal in. **To spy out.** This infinitive of purpose (Gr *kataskopeō*) means to reconnoiter, to make a treacherous investigation, to examine carefully with hostile intent. **Our liberty which we have in Christ Jesus.** Our emancipation from legalism and ceremonialism. **That they might bring us into bondage.** Expressing the ultimate result they hoped to attain. Their object was to reduce Christians to abject spiritual slavery, completely enslave them by rites, rules, and regulations. These spies operating under false colors were trying to undermine our liberty in Christ.

5. To whom we gave place. Paul refused to yield for a single moment. He held his ground firmly and did not give in an inch. He refused to compromise the truth of God. **By subjection.** The article (Gr *tē*) identifies the submission as that demanded by the legalists. **That the truth of the gospel.** The gospel in its integrity as opposed to the pseudo-gospel of the enemies of the cross. This denotes salvation by faith. This was the reason for Paul's adamant stand in earnestly contending for the faith. He would not let the Gentiles be deprived of the true gospel. The future of Christianity was bound up in this test case, and by God's grace Paul gained the victory. **Might continue with you.** For you and your spiritual welfare. "The idea of firm possession is enforced by the compound verb, by the present tense, and by the preposition" (J. B. Lightfoot, *The Epistle of Paul to the Galatians,* p. 107). Many weak-kneed, jellyfish preachers would have yielded and then justified themselves on the basis of love and expediency, but not the champion Paul.

6. Whatsoever they were. Referring to the Jerusalem apostles, their past privileges and their present position. They had sojourned with Christ and had been appointed by Him. It **maketh no matter to me.** Paul does not say "that the

standing and repute of the apostles were matters of indifference to him, but that he was indifferent about receiving his commission from them as recognized dignitaries of the church" (M. R. Vincent, *Word Studies in the New Testament,* Vol. IV, pp. 97-98). Paul received his apostleship directly from Christ and he was independent of the other apostles. **God accepteth no man's person.** Literally, God does not receive the face of man. God looks on the heart and is no respecter of persons. Phillips translates, "God is not impressed with a man's office." **Added nothing to me.** They imparted no new information, no new interpretation, and no new application. There was no correction of, deletion from, or addition to Paul's message. There was not deficiency in Paul's gospel. He preached the truth, the whole truth, and nothing but the truth (Acts 20:27).

7. But contrariwise. Those in repute not only set nothing before Paul, but they heartily approved him and his mission. **Saw.** Perceived the divine source of Paul's apostleship. **The gospel.** There is only one gospel. There is no difference in contents, only in recipients. The same gospel is for all men. **Committed unto me.** Entrusted. The perfect tense speaks of Paul's certain commission. **Uncircumcision . . . circumcision.** Gentiles and Jews respectively. **Peter.** Mentioned not with the idea of excluding the other apostles, but as representing them. The ministry of Paul was primarily, but not exclusively, to the Gentiles. That of Peter was primarily, but not exclusively, to the Jews. Both men were divinely appointed to proclaim a divine message by divine power.

8. Wrought effectually. Energized (Gr *energeō*) by the inward power of the Holy Spirit for the furtherance of the gospel. God gets all the glory for what He accomplished through Peter and Paul. There was material acknowledgment of each other's equal apostleship.

9. James, Cephas, and John. James is named first because of the prominence of his leadership in Jerusalem and because of his strict legal tendencies. His support of Gentile freedom was of great importance. **Who seemed to be pillars.** The Jews used this metaphor to refer to their great teachers. The church was looked upon as the temple of God, and these men were regarded as supporters. **Perceived the grace.** As they reflected on the manifestation of God's grace in Paul, they recognized his equality with them, his official status and prerogative, and his independent mission to the Gentiles. **The right hands of fellowship.** Fellowship speaks of cooperation and joint participation. The right hand of fellowship was given to equals and indicated a token of approval and a pledge of fidelity and agreement to work in their respective fields, so that all men would be evangelized by the same gospel. This was the dramatic conclusion of the pact for cooperation in independent spheres of evangelism. The legalists were brushed aside when these five men shook hands as equals in the work of Christ.

10. Only. One stipulation was emphasized. **Remember the poor.** Judaea often experienced famine, and the Christians there suffered most because of social ostracism and religious hatred. **I also was forward to do.** Paul was zealous to keep on remembering the poor and needed no prompting. Such generosity would foster a sense of unity in both Jewish recipients and Gentile givers.

4. Paul's rebuke of Peter. 2:11-21.

11. But when Peter was come to Antioch. The exact time is not stated. Certainly it was after Peter's vision at Joppa (Acts 10:10-16) and his experience in the home of Cornelius (Acts 11:1-8). Peter knew that God is no respecter of persons and that ceremonial uncleanness was a thing of the past. **I withstood him to the face.** This was face to face confrontation between two apostles. Paul set himself against Peter, resisting and reprimanding him. There is no hint of Peter's so-called "primacy." The

false teachers attributed superiority to Peter, whose words and actions were regarded as next to infallible. Peter had no authority over Paul. Paul is not belittling Peter in the eyes of the Galatians; he is proving his own divine commission. How could anyone claim that Paul received his apostleship from any man after he rebuked Peter? **Because he was to be blamed.** Peter incurred reproach by his own inconsistent conduct, and he stood self-condemned without any defense. In this verse Paul introduces an incident which not only proves that he had not received his apostleship from the apostles, but that he actually was so independent of them that he openly rebukes Peter for a course of action wholly inconsistent with the gospel.

12. For before that certain came from James. Certain certified members in good standing in Jerusalem; no doubt they were of the circumcision party who assailed Peter once before (Acts 11:1-3). At that time he successfully defended his actions. It does not say that James sent these men with any special authority or for the purpose of bringing believers under the bondage of the law. However, their presence in Antioch exerted a tremendous influence on Peter. **He did eat with the Gentiles.** The Greek imperfect tense shows that Peter was in the habit of eating with Gentiles; his habit was to publicly fraternize with them. God had revealed to Peter that the Levitical legislation regarding certain foods had been set aside. In obedience to God's revelation, Peter laid aside the obsolete Jewish custom and was eating with Gentiles. **He withdrew and separated himself.** He began to draw back in isolation, holding himself aloof, and having nothing to do with the Gentiles, as if he was afraid of defilement. Peter gradually discontinued his former practice of eating with the Gentiles when the circumcision party arrived. He was trying to change his conduct without letting them know what he had been doing and without breaking off so abruptly that the Gentile brethren would notice it. **Fear-**

ing them. Peter had his eyes on man instead of looking unto Christ, and he was afraid of losing his prestige in Jerusalem and of facing the arrogant attitude of the circumcision party. He concluded that it was more important to keep his Jerusalem friends happy than to avoid the possible risk of estranging Gentile believers. His breach of fellowship with the Gentiles brought about misunderstanding and division in Antioch. Paul recognized that Peter's conduct practically exhibited to the Gentiles that they were not fit company for the circumcised apostle, and was in effect a summons for them to become Jews.

13. And the other Jews dissembled. Other Jews followed the example of Peter, who was trying unsuccessfully to play both ends against the middle without letting either the Gentiles or the Jews know exactly what he was doing. **Barnabas.** Paul's co-laborer in proclaiming grace and liberty was also carried away. The legalists claimed that the law could do something that faith in Christ could not do. They were not only trying to supplement the gospel Paul preached, but to supplant it. **Carried away.** Followed their example. Barnabas was swept off his feet and shaped his conduct by that of others. **Their dissimulation** (Gr *hypocrisis*). The source of our word "hypocrite." It is pretense, playing a part, believing one thing and practicing another. Their inconsistent conduct was hypocrisy because it concealed their true convictions. It was a surrender of Christian liberty, a denial of Christian unity, and an impeachment of the Christian message. Thank God Paul saw the gravity of the situation and did something about it.

14. Walked not uprightly. Literally, straight-footed, forward, unwavering (Gr *orthopodeō*). Peter and company were walking in a crooked path, a path that was likely to lead others astray. They were guilty of appearing to walk one way, but turning aside whenever it was convenient to give another impression. **According to the truth of the gos-**

pel. Their compromising conduct was contrary to the gospel. They had deviated from the standard of God's Word. **I said unto Peter before them all.** Paul severely and publicly rebukes Peter for his inconsistency and his insincerity. The rebuke was as wide as the relapse. Paul, vested with divine authority, took Peter to task. Paul's unsparing, but tactful, rebuke of Peter reveals his apostolic independence of all human authority. Peter did not try to defend himself, but graciously accepted the well-deserved rebuke and later referred to "our beloved brother Paul" (II Pet 3:15-16). **Livest after the manner of Gentiles.** Not under the customs and restrictions of the Jews. Peter's habit had been to live according to Gentile ways, although he was a Jew by birth. With this as a condition, Paul asks Peter a pointed question. **Why compellest.** Indirect compulsion by his example, not by false preaching. He was guilty of compromising conduct by which he was obliging the Gentiles to Judaize, to adopt Jewish customs and observe Jewish statutes.

15. We. Paul includes Peter in holding the doctrine of justification by faith. **Jews by nature.** Born Jews with special privileges and prerogatives, not Jews by proselytism. **Sinners of the Gentiles.** Jews regarded all Gentiles as unclean dogs, sinners without the restraint of the law.

16. Knowing that a man, any man, Jew or Gentile, **is not justified by the works of the law.** Justification is the judicial act of God whereby He declares righteous those who trust in Christ. It is the reversal of His attitude toward the sinner because of the sinner's new relationship to Christ. God did condemn, now He acquits. This means that all the guilt and penalty of the believer is removed forever (Rom 8:1) and that the perfect righteousness of Christ is imputed to him from (Gr *ek*) the works of the law, not resulting from man's deeds of obedience. The standard of the law was so exacting that no one (except Christ) ever kept it, and so the broken law could only condemn (Rom 3:19-20). **But by the faith of Jesus Christ.** Not on account of faith but only by means of faith. Faith is not the ground of justification: grace is. It is not faith in our faith, but faith in Jesus Christ. No one is justified except through faith in Christ. Salvation is wholly by divine mercy (Tit 3:5) and not by human merit. **Even as we have believed in Jesus Christ.** Even the Jews with all their privileges are no better than the Gentiles. Their law was inadequate and insufficient to bring them into a right relationship with God. Therefore it was necessary for Jews to believe in Christ in order to be justified. Since no flesh, Jew or Gentile, could ever be justified by the works of the law, how ridiculous it is to bind the burden of law-works on the Gentiles who were already justified by faith in Christ. Note the progressive order in this verse: knowing, believing, justified.

17. Is therefore Christ the minister of sin? An illogical inference. They were sinners already in spite of being Jews. Christ simply revealed to them the fact of their sin. Since grace does not encourage men to sin (Rom 6:1-2), Christ is not a minister or promoter of sin by causing us to abandon the law as a means of justification. This is a rebuttal to the argument of the legalists that salvation in Christ is insufficient.

18. For if I build again. Return to the law. After Paul had preached that justification is only by faith in Christ plus nothing, it would be folly to seek righteousness by keeping the law. This would be building again that which he destroyed. **Destroyed.** This word means to demolish, dissolve, disunite, pull down. Paul destroyed the teaching that salvation was by works of merit by proclaiming that salvation was by grace through faith in Christ. When Peter lived as a Gentile he tore down the ceremonial law; when he lived as a Jew he tore down the doctrine of salvation by grace. **A transgressor.** If he denied the absolute sufficiency of Christ. Jewish believers were right when they abandoned law-works as a means of salvation and were justified by faith in Christ; it would be wrong for them to return to law-works now.

19. For I through the law. Through the agency of the law. Paul relates his own expereience. The Old Testament law is powerless to give life; it only condemns the guilty. Under the law, Paul was brought to despair; his only hope was to find salvation elsewhere. The condemnation of the law drove Paul to Christ for salvation. **Am dead to the law.** Better, died to the law. To die to anything is to cease to have any relation to it so that it has no claim or control over one. The law condemned Paul to death, but Christ, his substitute, died for him. Paul died in Christ and is now united with Him in resurrection life. The sentence of death was executed on Paul in the person of the Lord Jesus Christ. Once the law has executed the death penalty it has no more jurisdiction over the one executed, for the law has dominion over a man only as long as he lives (Rom 7:1). Having died with Christ, Paul is dead to the law, and so is every true believer. When Christ died, we died. **That I might live unto God.** Identification with Christ enabled Paul to die unto the law as a means of obtaining righteousness and to live unto God, the source of his righteousness and the object of his new life.

20. I am crucified with Christ. This is Paul's personal testimony, which may be repeated by every believer in Christ (Rom 6:3-11). The Greek perfect tense speaks of completed action in time past and present certainty of results. Having been crucified with Christ when He died on Calvary, Paul is truly dead to everything else except Christ and what He represents. Paul's faith united him to Christ in such a way that Christ's death was his death, and Christ's resurrection was his resurrection. In Christ, Paul found a perfect sacrifice for sin and a perfect righteousness forever. **Christ liveth in me.** This is the union of the vine and the branches. A Christian is one in whom Christ lives. Christ is our life (Col 1:27;

3:4). The old self-righteous, self-centered Saul died, and the new Christ-centered Paul lives. Paul's new life is really Christ living His life in and through Paul. It is not a matter of imitation, but of realization. A Christian is not an unregenerate, religious sinner trying to attain salvation by works, but a regenerated saint manifesting the life of Christ through the presence and power of the indwelling Holy Spirit. **In the flesh.** This new life must be lived in the flesh, but not by the flesh. **By the faith.** Not by works. **The Son of God.** Paul specifically states that Christ is the Son of God. **Who loved me and gave himself for me.** Note how personally Paul appropriates to himself the love and sacrifice of Christ, which belong equally to the whole world. Christ is our sovereign, sufficient sacrifice.

21. I do not frustrate the grace of God. Lest someone should misunderstand, Paul says he does not set aside, reject, nullify, or invalidate the grace of God. **For if righteousness come by the law.** Through the agency of the law. False teachers were trying to make of no effect the gospel by adding something (law-works) one must "do" instead of trusting and being united to Christ who has already "done" everything necessary for time and eternity. **Then Christ is dead in vain.** A logical conclusion if righteousness is through the agency of the law. The choice must be made between works and grace, between law and Christ. If salvation is of works, it is not of grace; if it is of grace, it is not of works (Rom 11:6). If salvation is by works, then the atonement of Christ was in vain, a blunder, a useless tragedy, without a cause. But the purpose of the cross has not failed; the message of the cross is not vanity. Salvation must be either by the works of the law or through the atoning death of Christ. It cannot be a combination of both. There are two mutually exclusive teachings prevalent in the world: (1) salvation is by human merit; and (2) salvation is by divine mercy (Tit 3:5). Christ is not a part Saviour, either He

must be all (Col 3:11) or He is nothing at all.

II. POLEMICAL: THE DOCTRINE OF LIBERTY. 3:1-4:31.

A. Paul's Appeal to Liberty. 3:1-7.

1. Rebuke of the Galatians. 3:1-4.

3:1. O foolish Galatians. Paul jolts them with this exclamation of surprise and indignation. The Galatians were not naturally stupid or unintelligent, but were acting as if they were bereft of reason when they questioned the sufficiency of Christ. They did not stop to think how senseless it is to mix law-keeping with faith in Christ, and they were swept along with this false doctrine (cf. Eph 4:14). **Bewitched you** (Gr *baskainō*). The Galatians acted as if subject to some weird occult influence or under the spell of an evil eye. The false teachers had so fascinated them and confused their minds that they seemed to be groping around in a spiritual fog. **That ye should not obey the truth.** These words are not found in the best manuscripts, but they present the fact of the Galatians' defection. **Set forth.** This word was used of public pronouncements and means to present vividly, displaying graphically, post clearly, placard (as on a sign board). **Crucified.** As having been crucified. The Greek perfect tense emphasizes a past completed action resulting in certain and positive present effects. Paul is not speaking of the figure of a dead Christ on a crucifix, but of a risen, ascended Christ who had been crucified and is now alive forever more (Rev 1:18). Paul preached Christ crucified (I Cor 2:2) as man's only and sufficient Saviour. Paul and Barnabas had lifted up Christ before the Galatians, who should have kept their eyes on Him and not heeded the errors of the legalists.

2. Learn of you. Ascertain from your personal testimony, not from hearsay. The mere asking of the question gives the answer and is a decisive argument. **Re-**

ceive ye the Spirit. The Galatians heard the gospel of grace, believed, and received the Holy Spirit. All believers receive the Holy Spirit at the time of salvation. The indwelling of the Holy Spirit is the unmistakable evidence of salvation (Rom 8:9; I Cor 3:16; 6:19-20). By the works of the law. Definitely not. By the hearing of faith. From what source (Gr *ek*). By hearing and believing God's message of grace (Rom 10:17; I Thess 2:13). What the law could not do, grace has done. The works of the law and the hearing of faith are exclusive opposites and cannot tolerate each other. It must be one or the other, not a combination of both.

3. Having begun in the Spirit. Whom ye received at the time of your salvation. The Holy Spirit is the author of the new birth; He is the creator of the new creation in Christ (II Cor 5:17). Are ye now made perfect by the flesh. The word perfect (Gr *epiteleō*) most certainly does not mean sinless, but complete, spiritual maturity. The middle voice implies "making yourselves perfect" by means of self-effort. The present tense indicates that the action is in progress and that there is still time to correct the error. Spirit and flesh indicate the two spheres of moral and spiritual influence, one divine and one human. Turning from the divine to the human is not the way to spiritual maturity. No man can ever do the work of the Holy Spirit. There is a double contrast between having begun and finished, and between Spirit and flesh. There is irony in this thrust. The flesh denotes the unregenerate, depraved self, all that a person is apart from the transforming power of the Holy Spirit. The flesh is incurably evil, it is corrupt, and cannot produce a holy influence. It may be educated, cultivated, reformed, and refined; but it is still flesh (Jn 3:6), still at enmity against God (Rom 8:7-8), and at war against the Spirit (Gal 5:17). It would be the height of folly to descend from the high plane of the Spirit to the low level of the flesh and expect ceremonial circumcision and ritual observance to accomplish what only the Holy Spirit can do. The natural can never produce the supernatural. The old nature can never improve the new nature. Salvation is what God does for man and not what man does for himself. Christ is the Author and the Finisher of our faith (Heb 12:2). What God begins, He finishes (Phil 1:6).

4. Suffered so many things. Because of their identification with Christ, they experienced many hardships. Indications of these persecutions are recorded in Acts 13:45, 50; 14:2, 5; 14:19, 22. Paul refers to them in his second letter to Timothy and then adds, "Yea, and all that will live godly in Christ Jesus shall suffer persecution" (II Tim 3:10-12). If it be yet in vain. Paul is unwilling to believe that they will completely and finally abandon Christ for Judaism; he hopes for better results. It would be vain, useless, and of no purpose for them to forsake grace for law.

2. *Reception of the Spirit. 3:5-7.*

5. Ministereth (Gr *epichorēgeō*). Furnish, lavish, bestow liberally, supply abundantly. God bestows His Spirit abundantly. Worketh miracles among you. We read of miracles at Iconium and Lystra (Acts 14:3, 9-10). Doeth he it. The Greek present tense shows that the work still goes on. Works . . . faith. Once again Paul points to this contrast. Faith in Christ is the means of their new life and the channel of all their spiritual blessings. The gift of the Holy Spirit to them and His mighty works in and among them were dependent absolutely on their faith, not by the works of the law. Divine, supernatural power is not received from a human, natural source. Spiritual power is not produced by fleshly efforts. The Galatians had irrefutable evidence that grace is the way of salvation. The legalists had no evidence that their message was from God. The question raised here has only one answer.

6. Even as. Paul appeals to the witness of the Word of God, and he implies that the experience of the Galatians

and that of Abraham are essentially the same. **Abraham believed God.** Abraham put his trust in God (Gen 15:4-6; Rom 4:3; Jas 2:23) to do for him what he could not do for himself. Abraham's faith was not a meritorious action that deserved a reward. That would have made salvation by works. Works were not involved in obtaining justification. Abraham was justified by faith when he was an uncircumcised Gentile and before he performed any good works. **Accounted to him for righteousness.** Accounted (Gr *logizō*) is common to Greek accounting. It is to reckon, put down on the ledger, credit to one's account. God imputed righteousness to Abraham on the basis of faith, not works. God's accounting changed Abraham's status. The moment Abraham believed, he was justified. Abraham believed God's promise. He had nothing to add, and God required nothing. Abraham committed himself completely and unreservedly to God. Paul shuts the Galatians up to faith alone, not faith plus circumcision and the keeping of the law, as the false teachers would have them do.

7. Know ye. Realize, perceive. **Therefore;** a logical deduction from the previous verse. **of faith.** Believes. Abraham was accepted on the basis of faith. God deals with all men on the same terms. **The same.** These and no others. **Children of Abraham.** Sons with all rights, privileges, and responsibilities. The legalists taught that only the natural descendants of Abraham and those circumcised were his sons. But God says men of faith become his spiritual children. Those who trust in works are aliens, not sons (Rom 2:28-29). Abraham is the father of all believers, Jews and Gentiles.

B. Paul's Argument for Liberty. 3:8-29.

1. The Promise to Abraham. 3:8-14.

8. The scripture. This points to divine inspiration (II Tim 3:16). The word spoken to Abraham was recorded by Moses much later. **Foreseeing** (Gr *pro-oraō*). Anticipating beforehand, seeing a long distance off. God foresaw that Abraham would become a channel of blessing to the Gentiles; God knows the end from the beginning (Acts 15:18). **Justify the brother through faith.** Not the Jews only. Abraham is an example of how Jew and Gentile alike must appropriate salvation, through faith alone, not through faith plus works. How can anyone believe God's Word and entertain the idea that salvation is by human merit? Salvation must be altogether by grace or altogether by works; it cannot be a combination of both (Rom 11:6). The present tense of the word justify signifies that God is justifying now in exactly the same manner He has always done. **Preached before the gospel.** He announced the "good news" beforehand, before the blessing came to the Gentiles. **In thee.** In union with thee as spiritual progenitor. From Abraham would flow blessings to all nations. This speaks of the Messiah and messianic blessings. These blessings are wider than justification by faith, without which no other spiritual blessing could be bestowed.

9. So then. Consequently. Adducing the result in conclusion of the argument just presented. **Blessed.** The Greek present tense shows the blessing to be axiomatic, and the passive voice shows that God is the blesser. **With.** In association and fellowship with (Gr *syn*) Abraham. **Faithful Abraham.** Believing Abraham or Abraham the believer. Abraham was a man of faith. The emphasis is on his faith, not his faithfulness.

10. Of the works of the law. All those who are resting upon their works and counting on justification by their obedience to the law. Two classes of men stand out in opposition: those of faith and those of works. **Are under the curse.** The wrath of God is hanging over them. This curse includes both their present alienation from God and their future, eternal separation from God (Jn 3:18, 36). Those under the law stand condemned, not justified; cursed, not blessed. **Writ-**

ten. The Greek perfect tense indicates that God's Word is a permanent record (Ps 119:89) and shall never be altered, amended, or annulled. Jesus said, "Heaven and earth shall pass away: but my words shall not pass away" (Mk 13: 31). **Every one.** Jew and Gentile. **Continueth not in all things.** All, not just a majority; both small and great in their sum total with no exception. **To do them.** The infinitive expresses purpose. To do them fully, precisely, entirely. Who could be saved on those terms? No one except our Lord Jesus Christ ever perfectly kept the law all the time. To fail in just one point, one time, puts one under the curse (Deut 27:26; Jas 2:10). Men put themselves under the curse by putting themselves under the law.

11. No man is justified by the law. No man ever kept it. A broken law can only curse, not bless. **The just shall live by faith.** God did not design the law to be the means of justification; He designed faith for that purpose. Righteousness and faith are inseparable. Law and righteousness are total strangers. Faith is not a substitute for righteousness; it is that heart trust that brings one into a new relation with God, that of being accepted in Christ (Eph 1:6) and which results in faithfulness, integrity, and steadfastness. The just shall live by faith. This Old Testament verse (Heb 2:4) is quoted three times in the New Testament (Rom 1:17; Gal 3:11; Heb 10:38). The righteous live by faith, not works.

12. The law is not of faith. The two principles of legalism and faith are diametrically opposed to each other and are mutually exclusive of each other as a means of justification. Man can be in only one of two conditions; he is either under the law or he is under grace (Rom 6:14-15). **The man that doeth them shall live in them.** This expresses the principle of the law. Men are not commanded to believe the Old Testament law, but to do it. Failure to render absolute obedience is fatal.

13. Christ hath redeemed us. What the law could not do, God did (Rom 8:3-4). Redeemed (Gr *exagorazō*) means "to buy out from" the slave market so that the liberated slave shall never be put on sale again. Christ paid the ransom price, His precious blood (I Pet 1:18-19), to deliver us from slavery to liberty. The Bible knows nothing of partial redemption. Christ redeemed us completely, freely, and irreversibly. Once acquitted, acquitted forever (Jn 5:24; Rom 8:1). **From the curse of the law.** Out from (Gr *ek*) the curse of a violated law, i.e. from its condemnation. The curse was the effect of sin in separating us from God. We were sentenced to die (Rom 6:23), but Christ died as our substitute (Rom 5:8). The curse of the law was: universal (Rom 3:23), fearful (Ps 9:17), and present (Jn 3:18, 36). The law was of divine origin, holy and heavenly. But it was just as cold, hard, and irresistible as the tablets of stone on which the Mosaic law was written with the finger of God (Ex 31:18). **Being made a curse for us.** The method by which Christ redeemed us. He suffered the just for the unjust that He might bring us to God (I Pet 3:18). He was our only mediator (I Tim 2:5). He became a curse for us (I Pet 2:24) and was made sin for us (II Cor 5:21). He did it for us voluntarily (Jn 10:17-18). This preposition (Gr *hyper*) implies substitution. **For it is written, Cursed.** Deuteronomy 21:23 does not refer to crucifixion, but rather to the ignominious hanging of a body of an executed criminal on a post or stake. God wants Christ to be seen as what He actually became, a curse. Three prepositions give us a vivid picture of redemption. We were under (Gr *hypo*) the curse of the law (vs. 10). Christ came above (Gr *hyper*) us, between us and the curse, and took us out from (Gr *ex*) under the curse having become a curse for us. He took our place; He took all of our sins and gave us all of His righteousness. God was satisfied forever; the law was silenced forever; and the believer is saved forever.

14. That . . . that. Two purpose clauses. The blessing of Abraham is justification by faith. There is no room for the law. This blessing is intended for the whole world, but it is only in and through (Gr *en*) Christ. No man is saved apart from Christ and any man may be saved by Christ (Jn 6:37). The promise of the Spirit, the gift which comes to all who accept Christ, is through (Gr *dia*) faith. It is folly indeed to seek for higher or holier blessings by deeds of merit.

2. The purpose of the law. 3:15-29.

15. Brethren. Denoting affection. **Manner of men.** Paul takes an anology from human affairs of everyday life and illustrates his point so clearly that all can understand. **Man's covenant.** Better, human testament. This word (Gr *diathēkē*) strictly speaking is not a contract between two parties (Gr *synthēkē*), but a binding will or testament instituted by the first party. **Confirmed.** Ratified. The Greek perfect tense means that the ratification is complete and in force. The matter stands settled. **Disannulleth,** annul, abrogate, make void. **Or addeth thereto.** No new condition may be imposed, no codicil allowed. Since no one can alter, amplify, or annul a man's testament after it has been duly excuted, surely no one can add to God's unconditional promise to Abraham, as the legalists were trying to do. God's promise was not a matter of mutual arrangement and it remains inviolate.

16. To Abraham and his seed. The beneficiaries of the promise were not limited to Abraham. Some may have objected that God's promise to Abraham was only temporary, so Paul adds "and his seed." **The promises.** Plural because frequently repeated (Gen 13:15; 17:8; 18:18; 22:18). **Thy seed, which is Christ.** The promise looked forward to the one descendant of Abraham in whom all the promises were to be fulfilled.

17. Confirmed before God. By repeated ratifications and sealed with God's own oath (Gen 22:16-17; Heb 6:13). The perfect participle indicates the certainty of prior ratification. Unbelief here charges God with perjury. **Four hundred and thirty years after.**

God's ratified promise of long standing certainly could not be rendered inoperative by the law. The law, which was not given for centuries after God's gracious promise, had nothing to do with that promise or with Abraham's justification. If the law had nothing to do with Abraham's justification, how can it have anything to do with anyone's justification? **Cannot disannul.** Does not repeal. The law cannot unconfirm God's confirmed testament. **None effect.** Cancel, render inoperative. The law cannot invalidate the promise which God has validated; it cannot nullify the promise.

18. Inheritance. The messianic blessing. **Of the law.** Derived from the law as its source. **God gave it.** God graciously granted it as a free gift without reserve, with no strings attached. God's promised gift did not contain even one legal stipulation. The perfect tense emphasizes its permanence; it still holds good after the law has come. Note that God gave it, not merely promised it. **By promise.** By promise alone, plus nothing. This excludes all self-effort. A new law may repeal or replace a previous law, but the law cannot affect in any way God's promise. Faith is not superseded by the works of the law. The legalists' stipulation of works meant not merely modification, but cancellation of God's confirmed promise. Grace and faith precede law and works. Grace and faith supersede law and works.

19. Wherefore. Why then the law? What is the meaning and purpose of the law? **It was added.** Not as a codicil. The law was not part of God's original and confirmed testament, and it was not added to it later. The law was not added to grace; it did not become another ingredient of salvation. It was brought in along side of the promise. It was supplemental and subordinate. **Because of transgressions.** Because (Gr *charin*) means for this cause and denotes the aim of the law. Transgression (Gr *parabasis*) means a step beyond a fixed limit into forbidden territory. It is a willful act of violating an explicit law, overstepping what is right into the realm of what is wrong. The law was added much later to make men conscious of the existence and the extent of sin (Rom 3:19; 5:20). The law was added to reveal sin, not remove it. To show men the need of righteousness, not to be a means of securing righteousness. The law drives men to despair and to cry out for deliverance (Rom 7:24-25). The law declares man to be a helpless, hopeless sinner. **Till the seed should come.** The law was temporary and preparatory, from Moses to Christ; it was not of permanent duration. It was a temporary institution between the original promise and its fulfillment in Christ. After Christ came, the law was abolished (Rom 10:4) as a means of securing righteousness. **Ordained by angels.** Put in force or promulgated through angels as a channel (Deut 33:2; Acts 7:53; Heb 2:2). God used angels to communicate with Moses. The angels represented God and Moses represented Israel. **Hand of a mediator.** Moses stood between God and Israel (Deut 5:5) and received the tablets of stone (Ex 32:15-16).

20. Mediator. A mediator is a middleman between two parties: He does not act on behalf of one person alone. The presence of Moses implies two other parties, God and Israel. The law was a contract to which both parties agreed to the condition. God said, "If ye will obey," and Israel said, "We will do" (Ex 19:5, 8). Israel was obligated to obey, and God was obligated to bless if they did obey. The law was valid so long as both parties fulfilled the terms of the contract. Israel defaulted and did not live up to her part of the bargain. So then God was no longer obligated to keep His part. The conditions were not kept, and the blessings were not received. Israel therefore had no hope on the basis of keeping the law. **God is one.** The immutable God acted alone when He graciously gave Abraham the promise. He dealt personally and directly with Abraham, not through a mediator. The promise was unconditional, with no stipulation. Its fulfillment depended upon God's faithfulness, not upon Abraham's obedience to a set of rules (Rom 4:13-16).

21. Against the promises. The law has its own specific function; it is different in nature and purpose. It is not opposed to the promise; it is not competitive, but complementary. The law operates in a different area. The law has a ministration of condemnation. Grace has a ministration of righteousness (II Cor 3:9). **If there had been a law.** This premise is assumed to be contrary to fact. There never was such a law. The law was given through Moses (Jn 1:17), but not to be a source or means of justification. **Could have given life.** Capable of imparting life. The very impossibility of such a law is evident, and yet the legalists were urging the Galatians to abandon the righteousness of Christ which was theirs by faith alone and go back to the law. Man by nature is dead in trespasses and sin (Eph 2:1, 5), and he needs a new life. It was not God's plan to make men alive by the law, but by the new birth (Jn 1:12-13). The broken law demands satisfaction and will not accept good works in lieu of the death penalty. The law demands death. It cannot give life. The law demands righteousness, but it cannot provide it. **Verily.** Indeed, in reality as opposed to the mere pretense. **Righteousness should have been by the law.** Better, it would have been by the law.

22. But. In contradiction to the hypothesis of the preceding verse. **The scripture.** The inspired writing (II Tim 3:16; II Pet 1:21). God's recorded will. **Hath concluded all under sin.** Hath confined, shut up, locked up in prison, for care and constraint. This is a universal arraignment (Deut 27:26; Rom 3:9, 19, 22-23), with no exception. All men are prisoners of sin. The law shows that man does not attain justification by human works, but obtains it by divine mercy (Tit 3:5). **That the promise by faith.** This states the reason for the law and the intention of God. The law paves the way for salvation by grace and justification by faith in Jesus Christ. Consciousness of sin is a necessary step to justification. Until a man realizes that he is lost, he will have little or no interest in being saved. The words faith and believe state clearly how God's gift of eternal life is bestowed. Faith always has an object, here the object is our Lord Jesus Christ. A promise is received by faith only. How can legalists, Galatians or anyone else, say that God's promise is received by the works of the law?

23. Before faith came. The personal faith mentioned in the preceding verse. **Kept under the law.** The Greek imperfect tense indicates that we were continually guarded, by a stern and strict jailer to prevent our escape. It was really for protection rather than incarceration for punishment. **Shut up un to the faith.** This expresses the object of being held in custody. It shuts men up to faith in Christ as their only means of freedom. The law imprisoned men so that they might find true liberty in Christ; it cuts off every other way of escape. The purpose of the law was to prepare men for faith in Christ. **Which should afterwards be revealed.** The about-to-be-revealed faith. The law was a preparation for faith in Christ not a substitute for it or a supplement to it. The law sentry was relieved of its duty when Christ came. The legalists claim the law is still on duty and even assign it an unscriptural function. They would place God's liberated sons back in slavery under a terrible task master.

24. Wherefore. So that. **The law was our schoolmaster.** A schoolmaster (Gr *paidagōgos*) is really the trusted boy-leader or child-escort employed to attend a boy from six to sixteen and who watched over his morals and manners. He was not the teacher and he had no authority to punish. His business was to see that the child went to the right place and did the right thing. Such was the purpose of the law, to prescribe right conduct and impose certain checks. The law convicts of sin, restrains from sin, and condemns for sin; but the law cannot save from sin. **Bring us to Christ.** The God-given purpose of the law has led us to Christ; its work is finished. **That we might be justified by faith.** The ultimate purpose of the law.

25. Faith. The faith in Christ. **No longer under a schoolmaster.** The born-again believer is no longer under the boy-leader, who has been discharged from service. We are not under the law, but under grace (Rom 6:15).

26. Ye are. Paul changes from "we" to "ye" to apply the truth to the Galatians. **All.** Jews and Gentiles. **Children of God.** There is a distinction between the term children (Gr *teknon*) and the term sons (Gr *huios*). All Christians are God's children, having been born again and sharing God's nature (II Pet 1:4). The term "son" denotes a legal status, that of a liberated, mature person in possession of the inheritance (fulfilled promise). **By faith in Christ Jesus.** The Word of God knows nothing of the so-called universal Fatherhood of God and the universal brotherhood of man. Only those who exercise faith in Christ are sons of God (Acts 4:12). Faith in our Lord Jesus Christ is the only human condition of salvation (Eph 2:8-10).

27. Baptized into Christ. This is how one becomes united to Christ. This is not baptismal regeneration and does not refer to water baptism, for that never put anyone into Christ. Paul speaks of the baptism of the Holy Spirit which places all true believers into a living union with Christ (I Cor 12:12-13), and with each other (Eph 4:15-16). The Greek passive voice means that this was done for them and not by them. Baptism in water symbolizes, but does not effect, this glorious experience. **Have put on Christ.** Clothed yourself with Christ (Rom 13:14). This implies family likeness to Christ. The Greek aorist middle infers their own deed, with reflexive action, and refers to the custom of investiture. When a boy became of age, he put on a garmet which signified the full privilege of a grown up son enjoying full citizenship.

28. Ye are all one in Christ. This is a statement of fact, rather than a mere possibility. The point is that "in Christ Jesus" race or national distinction does not exist; class differences vanish, and sex rivalry disappears. These things are not barriers to Christian fellowship. At the foot of the cross all men are equal, and no one enjoys special privileges.

29. If ye be Christ's. Since you Galatians are His, it follows that you are Abraham's seed and heirs according to promise. Christ is heir to all things (Heb 1:2) and you are joint-heirs with Him (Rom 8:17).

C. Paul's Amplification of Liberty. 4:1-31.

1. The coming of God's Son. 4:1-7.

4:1. Child. One of tender years (Gr *nepios*) in contrast to (Gr *teleios*), one full grown. He is illustrating the spiritual immaturity of those living under the law and who are being prepared for faith in Christ. **Differeth nothing from a servant.** He has no more freedom than a slave and is no better off than a slave. **Lord of all.** He is an heir *de jure*, but not *de facto*. He is not enjoying the actual possession of his promised inheritance. He is Lord of all by birthright and by title. Paul's meaning is clear and his purpose is plain. He is warning the Galatians against becoming entangled in the bondage of the law, and he is encouraging them to enjoy the spiritual liberty they have by faith in Christ.

2. Under tutors. Guardians who have the supervision of the person. **Governors.** Stewards who have the supervison of the property. They are the trustees who manage the estate. During his minority, the heir is controlled and restrained by guardians and stewards. **Until the time appointed.** The time appointed beforehand for the termination of his minority status when he attains his inheritance. Under the law men were minors and enjoyed little of the inheritance because they were under tutelage and in servile condition.

3. Even so we. Paul makes the application. **When we were children.** In our minority. **Were in bondage.** The Greek perfect tense implies that we were in a real state of servitude under the legalistic system and not free sons under grace. **Under the elements of the world.** The word elements (Gr *stoicheion*) denotes things placed in a row, thus the letters of the alphabet. Hence, the ABC's or first principles of non-Christian humanity, the elemental lesson in simple symbols of outward things (Col 2:8, 20). The kindergarten department of instruction in religious observances which are external and temporal as contrasted with the permanent spiritual principles of faith in Christ. Under law men were in the process of preparatory training.

4. But when. Marks the beginning of a remarkable change in the state of affairs. **The fullness of the time.** The proper time had arrived for both God and man. The time appointed by the Father and foretold by the prophets. It was a time of outward prosperity and inward corruption. The religions of the world were spiritually bankrupt, devoid of power to change men's lives, and had degenerated into feeble superstitions and meaningless rituals. The pre-messianic period ended right on schedule. **God sent forth his Son.** There was no other way to save man (Acts 4:12). With Christ there is an endless hope; without Christ there is a hopeless end. God sent forth Christ from Himself, from heaven's majesty to earth's misery, to execute His plan and purpose. This reveals Christ's pre-existence, His deity, and His authority. It was the second person of the Trinity who was commissioned. **Made of a woman.** The Son of God became out of (Gr *ex*) a woman, became incarnate and dwelt among us (Jn 1:14). The fact of the miraculous virgin birth agrees perfectly with the language here. Christ did not cease to be God when He became man, the God-man, one person with two natures. **Made under the law.** Not only a human birth but a Jewish birth, subject to all the ordinances of the law.

5. To redeem. Buy out of the slave market (3:13). This means both purchase and liberation. The purpose of the incarnation was redemption, to deliver us from the curse of the law and make us sons under grace. Christ came not to explain the law, but to expiate sin, to obliterate a guilty past and initiate a glorious future. **Them that were under the law.** The law is not preceded by the definite article, so law in general. Even Gentiles are not without law to God (Rom 2:14). Christ came to redeem all men (I Tim 2:4-6). **That we might receive.** Receive from the giver for the first time, not recover something we once possessed. It means to get from, not to get back. **The adoption of sons.** Placed and recognized as adult sons. This means full deliverance from the child-servant status. This is based on redemption and implies family likeness with its position, privilege, and prestige. Regeneration gives us the relationship; adoption gives us the position.

6. Because ye are sons. God could not do this while men were still minors under guardians and stewards. As a consequence of sonship and as a proof of sonship (Rom 8:14-16). **God hath sent forth the Spirit of His Son.** Commissioned Him, as He had His Son. Note the parallels: Son and Spirit. The Holy Spirit is called here the Spirit of His Son (Rom 8:9; Phil 1:19; Jn 15:26). **Into your hearts.** Every child of God is indwelt by the Holy Spirit (I Cor 3:16; 6:19-20). He is the earnest of our inheritance (Eph 1:13-14). All guardians and stewards have been discharged; their supervision is no longer needed because believers are full-grown sons indwelt by the Holy Spirit. **Crying Abba, Father.** This cry of deep emotion comes from the indwelling of the Holy Spirit. While an immature child is under supervision, he doesn't fully appreciate his Father; but when he reaches his maturity, he begins to realize who and what his Father is, and so cries out Abba, Father (Rom 8:15). These words were used by Christ in the Garden of Gethsemane (Mk 14:36). Wherever the Aramaic "Abba" occurs in the New Testament, it has the Greek interpetation added. This combination may suggest the impartiality of the Holy Spirit's ministry in all believers, whether they are Jews or Gentiles.

7. Wherefore. On the basis of what has gone before. After God sent His Son for you and His Holy Spirit in you. We are what we are because God sent forth His Son. We have what we have because God sent forth His Spirit, God's work external and internal. The whole Trinity has been involved in making the believer a son and an heir. **Thou art no more a servant.** Paul addresses each one individually and tells him what he is by the grace of God. Though you were once a slave (Gr *doulos*) to the law, you are no longer. **But a son.** How foolish to abandon this high position and privilege for the law state of a slave under the bondage of the law. **And if a son.** This is a Greek first class condition of logic, meaning "since" you are a son. There is no doubt about it. **Then an heir.** Enjoying a new spiritual heritage, not through works of personal merit, but through grace. It is not by placing themselves under the law, but by remaining free from it, that they will obtain the blessing of Abraham.

2. The conduct of the Galatians. 4:8-21.

8. Howbeit then. In your former pagan state. **Ye knew not God.** Ignorant of God, not acquainted with Him. They lived in utter spiritual darkness. Paul is not excusing them, merely stating the fact of their wretched condition. **Ye did service.** Ye slaved and were in bondage. The Galatians had been pagans and had worshipped idols before they were saved. **Which by nature are no gods.** Paul is not denying their existence, but their deity. Paul refers to them as so-called gods (I Cor 8:4-6) and demons (I Cor 10:19-20).

9. But now. Since your salvation. **After that ye have known God.** Having come to God by personal experience, and enjoying fellowship with Him. **Or**

rather are known of God. This explains how the Galatians came to know God. The initiative was not theirs. Paul emphasizes the fact that it is all of grace. God recognizes them as His sons and heirs. The word for "know" (Gr *ginōskō*) often implies a personal relationship between the knower and the known. God knows them in a saving relationship (Mt 7:23; I Cor 8:3). The Greek aorist tense (ingressive) emphasizes the beginning of the action and leaves room for the question about the present. **How turn ye again.** The Greek present tense signifies that they were in the act of turning from grace and liberty to law and bondage. Their defection was just beginning and still in progress, not yet complete. **To the weak and beggarly elements.** These two adjectives express the utter impotence of these elements to do and bestow what was done and given by God sending His Son. These elements are without strength and without resources; they are spiritually powerless and spiritually poverty-stricken. **Ye desire again to be in bondage.** The combination of these words (Gr *palin* and *anōthen*) describes the completeness of their proposed relapse into second childhood. Paul's question shows the absurdity of their desire to be slaves again. They were in the process of leaving the light and liberty of Christianity for the shadow and slavery of legalism. Ritualistic observances are heathenish in principle. They are a system of bondage opposed to God's grace. How can anyone want to exchange the robe of Christ's righteousness for the filthy rags of heathenism, Judaism, or any other "ism"?

10. Ye observe. The Greek present middle implies that they are continually observing for themselves, for their own benefit, some of the requirements of Judaism. They were in the process of launching into legalism and were scrupulously observing with meticulous care certain rules with the belief that such practice would gain merit. This shows the partial success of the legalists.

11. I am afraid of you. He is afraid about or concerning them. **Lest.** Denotes the reason for Paul's fear. **I have bestowed upon you labour.** The perfect tense indicates the finished work of Paul in placarding Christ as the crucified one. Labor (Gr *kopiaō*) means to labor to the point of exhaustion. **In vain.** It is placed before the verb for emphasis and means to no purpose, without effect, without due result. Could it be possible that Paul's labor was merely a mirage and not a miracle? Paul's labor would have been in vain if all that was accomplished was for the Galatians to exchange their pagan religion for the old abrogated legalism of the Jews. Turning to legalism is equivalent to rejecting the gospel and renouncing Christ. Paul's admonition to the Galatians should be a solemn warning to Christians not to sacrifice their spiritual liberty in Christ for the slavery of forms and ceremonies.

12. Brethren. Paul identifies himself with them, and though fearful, he will not give them up. **I beseech you.** I beg you, suggesting the intensity of his appeal. **Be as I am.** The Greek present middle imperative means keep on becoming as I am. Don't give up grace for law, but get all the way out from under the law and come all the way under grace. Paul had been liberated from legalism; he gave it up. Paul laid aside the pedigree, privileges, and prejudices of Judaism for Christ (Phil 3:4-8). He abandoned his own righteousness of the law for the righteousness of God in Christ, and he asks the Galatians to do the same. **For I am as ye are.** Since being saved by grace and being liberated from legalism, Paul is living like a Gentile, in order to be more effective in winning Gentiles to Christ (I Cor 9:21). The bondage of the law does not promote spiritual life, but it endangers Christian liberty. **Ye have not injured me at all.** Ye did me no wrong, no injustice.

13. Ye know. In what unfavorable light his infirmity placed him when he first came among them. **How through infirmity.** Because of illness. An attack of some malady detained Paul and made it necessary to spend more time than he had planned to spend in their region. Some think it may have been an attack of malaria or epilepsy, or perhaps ophthalmia, an oriental eye disease prevalent in the lowlands of Pamphylia. But whatever it was, it occasioned Paul's preaching the gospel to them. **At the first.** Paul's first visit. Some believe this implies a second visit on a subsequent missionary journey. But on Paul's first missionary journey, he retraced his steps after preaching in Derbe (Acts 14:20-25), so he actually visited most of these cities twice on his first tour.

14. My temptation. The best Greek texts have "your" temptation. The trial to which you were subjected by my bodily infirmity and which might have caused you to treat me with indifference. **Ye despised not.** This word (Gr *exoutheneō*) means despise utterly, set at nought, scorn, treat with contempt. **Nor rejected.** Literally, "spit out" (Gr *ekptuō*). Hence to disdain, spurn, loathe. Spitting was a sign of disgust. The ancients expectorated when they saw a person having an epileptic seizure. This may have even been Paul's malady. **But.** On the contrary. **Received me.** In spite of Paul's illness and repulsive appearance, they treated him with great kindness. **As an angel of God.** With veneration (Acts 14:11-18). **As Christ Jesus.** The highest honor.

15. Where is then. What became of the congratulatory spirit? **Blessedness.** The blessedness of being in a state of prosperity resulting from having Paul as their apostle. **I bear you record.** I testify or bear witness. **Plucked out your own eyes.** Literally, dug out, gouged out (Gr *exorussō*). Some infer from these words that Paul had a disease of the eyes and that he needed a new pair of eyes, but there is no conclusive evidence that such was the case. It is a graphic description of their attitude and expresses supreme love and devotion. Paul lamented their changed attitude toward him.

16. Therefore. And so, seeing your love has waned. **Am I . . . become.** The Greek perfect tense signifies permanence of the action. **Your enemy.** Your personal enemy (Gr *echthros*) in a hostile, active sense. Paul has not changed, and the gospel has not changed. Why do they regard him as an enemy? He chides them for their fickle disloyalty. Paul is not their enemy. **Because I tell you the truth.** The legalists accused Paul of not telling the truth and of keeping the Galatians in a retarded spiritual condition by his adamant stand against circumcision as a means of salvation.

17. They zealously affect you. Affect has its root in (Gr *zeō*) a word meaning to boil with heat and is used of intense passions. The legalists were courting, taking a warm interest in, striving after, and earnestly desiring the Galatians. **But not well.** Not honorably. They were zealous for their own cause. Their ulterior motive was to promote Judaism and steal their hearts from Christ. Their great proselyting zeal was condemned by Christ (Mt 23:15). **They would exclude you.** They would separate, isolate, and shut you out from other teachers and from the liberating gospel of Christ. They would exclude you from salvation unless you observed the law. **That ye might affect them.** The purpose of the legalists in excluding the Galatians from salvation was that they, having no hope elsewhere, would court the legalists and seek affiliation with them. With their fawning fallacies they were seeking to monopolize the affections of the Galatians and make them a prey for their false teachings.

18. It is good. It is good to be courted in a good way. It is good for someone to take a warm interest in you in an honorable manner. Paul zealously sought the Galatians for Christ, and he welcomes all such efforts in relation to the gospel of Christ. The motive behind the courting is very important. Paul did not desire a monopoly in serving them, but he did not want them seduced from Christ. **In a good thing.** Paul is speaking primarily of preaching Christ and Him crucified. All true Christians are fervent in their evangelistic zeal and persistent and consistent in seeking the lost for Christ. This differs vastly from the selfish proselyttism of legalists, both ancient and modern.

19. My little children (Gr *teknion*). The usual word for maternal endearment. It expresses the tenderness of Paul and the immaturity of the Galatians. **Of whom I travail in birth again.** For whom I am undergoing the birth pangs (I Cor 4:15; Phm 10). Paul is again experiencing the same painful anguish as when he brought them to Christ. **Until Christ be formed in you.** This word (Gr *morphoō*) means to give outward expression to one's inward nature. Paul wants Christ to be seen in the lives of the Galatians. A living Christ on the inside will manifest Himself on the outside (Gal 2:20; Rom 8:29). As a result of the legalists' propaganda, the Galatians were beginning to trust "self" in their efforts to obey the law, instead of depending on the Holy Spirit to produce a Christlike life in them and through them.

20. I desire. Greek imperfect tense. I was desiring to be present with you. **Change my voice.** Paul was under the handicap of having to write, which is never as effective as the spoken word. If Paul could speak to them, he could straighten matters out in a very short time. **I stand in doubt of you.** Literally, I am perplexed in you. Paul was at his wits' end, not knowing the best way to prevent them from the error into which they were drifting.

21. Tell me. A direct appeal. **Ye that desire to be under the law.** On the verge of adopting law and of becoming subject to all its demands and condemnation. **Do ye not hear the law?** Are you hearing what it really says and heeding what it really means? Paul wants them to learn a very important lesson.

3. The comparison of Hagar and Sarah. 4:22-31.

22. It is written. Not a direct quotation, but a summation of the historical facts. **Abraham had two sons.** Those who claim to be Abraham's sons by their submission to the law forget that Abraham had two sons. Abraham had other sons, but it is clear that Paul is speaking of Ishmael and Isaac (Rom 9:6-9). The status of the mother determined the status of the son. Natural birth is no guarantee of spiritual privilege. The son of the slave girl, Hagar, was rejected; the son of the free woman, Sarah, obtained the inheritance.

23. But. Although sons of the same father. **Was born.** The Greek perfect tense, "has been born," emphasizes the certainty of the distinction between these two births. Ishmael's descendants do not belong to the covenant people; Isaac's descendants have the promise. Slave girls were customarily given by a barren wife, but could not be taken by a husband voluntarily. Sarah, losing hope that the promise would be fulfilled, substituted Hagar for herself and sought to get an heir by proxy. But God had a better idea and later carried out His plan and fulfilled His promise. Ishmael's birth was natural; Isaac's birth was supernatural, through a miraculous intervention of God (Rom 4:18-21).

24. An allegory. Speaking allegorically. Paul uses the historical narrative to illustrate his point for the benefit of the Galatians who were tempted to place themselves under the burden of the law. Paul illustrates the deep distinction and distance between grace and law, between the children of promise and the subject of legalism. An allegory is a veiled presentation of a meaning, metaphorically implied but not expressly stated. The superficial reader sees only the surface, but there is more to see, the facts in their full reality. Paul gives these historical facts a symbolic meaning and uses them to illustrate the already established doctrine of justification by faith. **These are the two covenants.** These two women symbolize the two covenants, law and grace. Hagar represents the Mosaic covenant of law and bondage and is the mother of the child of the flesh. Sarah represents the Abrahamic covenant of grace and liberty and is the mother of the child of promise.

25. Mount Sinai. Hagar represents Mount Sinai. **Answereth to.** Belongs to the same or corresponds to. **Jerusalem which now is.** The earthly Jerusalem stands for Judaism and represents the Jewish nation. Jerusalem was the center of apostate Judaism. **Is in bondage with her children.** Jerusalem is a slaving mother of slaving children. A severe condemnation of the legalists from Jerusalem who were trying to seduce the Galatians, and of all who would supplant grace with law.

26. But. Opposes the preceding verse. **Jerusalem which is above.** The heavenly Jerusalem (Heb 12:22-24) is the spiritual city of which all Christians are children. **Free.** Independent of the Mosaic law. The heavenly Jerusalem is a free mother with free children.

27. Written. We have here a quotation from the Septuagint of Isaiah 54:1 which is applied to unfruitful Sarah, who answers to the heavenly Jerusalem. Abraham's spiritual seed shall be more numerous than his natural seed. Isaiah closes the fifty-third chapter with these words, "He bare the sins of many, and made intercession for the transgressors." The next word in "sing." Paul translates it "Rejoice." The grace of God gives men something to sing about. Israel will some day realize the full meaning of Isaiah 53 and experience glorious deliverance and restoration through God's grace.

28. Now. Paul applies the truth to the Galatians. **We brethren.** The best texts have "ye" instead of "we." Paul assures the Galatians that they like Isaac are born according to promise, not of mere fleshly descent, as Ishmael. The sons of promise are free.

29. But as then. As then, so now. **Born after the flesh.** Born naturally and are enslaved sinners. **Born after the Spirit.** Born supernaturally and are liberated saints. **Persecuted.** The word (Gr *diōkō*) means drive away, put to flight, harass, molest. The presence of Isaac causes Ishmael to manifest his true character (Gen 21:9). From Isaac, came the Hebrews; from Ishmael, came the Arabs. From the beginning these two sons of Abraham were unfriendly, and so have been their descendants. The presence of the new nature makes known what the old nature really is. The legalists were persecuting Paul and all who would not abandon grace for law. There are two types of men in the world: those who have been born only of the flesh, and those who in addition have been born of the Spirit. It would be better not to have been born at all than not to be born again. Men of the flesh detest men of the Spirit. No one despises grace like the man who is trying to save himself by his own merit.

30. Cast out. Abraham by divine direction sent Hagar and Ishmael away (Gen 21:10-12). This is an encouragement to all who have been born of the Spirit and a solemn warning to all who are born only of the flesh. Grace, not law, brings the inheritance in the family of God. **Shall not be heir.** The son of the slave girl shall not, no never, by any means share the inheritance with the son of the free woman. Those who seek acceptance with God through obedience to the law, and are destitute of true sonship, have no inheritance. This verdict stands for all who have no higher birth than Ishmael.

31. So then. A deduction from the preceding verse. **Bondwoman.** The absence of the Greek definite article emphasizes Hagar's lower status. God says that His children are the children of promise, saved by grace. It is impossible to be children of both the slave girl and the free woman. It is impossible to be under law and under grace. We belong to Christ and are therefore liberated from the bondage of the law. Christendom is critically infected with the deadly doctrine of the legalists. The crying need of the hour is for uncompromising men to proclaim the liberty in Christ which is the birthright of every believer.

III. PRACTICAL: THE LIFE OF LIBERTY. 5:1-6:18.

A. Liberty is Imperiled by Legalism. 5:1-12.

5:1. Stand fast therefore. Take a tenacious stand and do not be moved from this position. Keep on standing, and do not bow your neck to the yoke of slavery. **In the liberty.** For the purpose of freedom which belongs to the children of the free woman (4:31). Legalism destroys liberty. **Christ hath made us free.** Christ, the great liberator, definitely, deliberately, and decisively liberated us. The emphasis is on the completeness of our freedom. **And be not entangled again.** Stop being held in the yoke of bondage. Having escaped the slavery of heathenism, they were in danger of the slavery of Judaism. The legalists were trying to yoke the Galations with Judaism. Yoke is a symbol of slavery.

2. Behold, I Paul. The stalwart champion of liberty asserts all his personal and apostolic authority. **If ye be circumcised.** A hypotheticl case, but with awful consequences. The "if" implies that they had not yielded yet to the demands of the legalists. The present tense indicates, not one act, but a practice they were considering as necessary for salvation. If they should receive circumcision under such conviction, they would obligate themselves to keep the whole law, because circumcision is a pledge to live by the law, and it is a badge of Judaism. **Christ shall profit you nothing.** Grace and law are diametrically opposed to each other and mutually exclusive of each other. Christ is of advantage only to the one who trusts Him exclusively. There can be no compromise between grace and law and no combination of faith and works.

3. For I testify again. Paul's emphatic protest and warning addressed to all who were contemplating circumcision. **That he is a debtor to do the whole law.** A debtor is one who assumes an obligation. To accept circumcision as a condition of salvation is to abandon the liberty for which Christ liberated us and to bind one's self to the slavery of legalism. Submission to circumcision commits one to perfect obedience to the whole law; he takes upon himself both the requirements of the law and its curse (Jas 2:10; Gal 3:10).

4. Christ is become of no effect unto you. Literally, ye were brought to nought from Christ. Your relation to Christ is finished, rendered null and void. Without an effective relation to Christ, one deprives himself of spiritual blessing. **Whosoever of you are justified by the law.** Justified as you think, but not really. You who are trying to be justified in the law, trying to seek a right standing with God on the basis of works or merit. One either attains salvation by his own works or he attains it as a free gift of God (Rom 11:6). **Ye are fallen from grace.** The only time this phrase is used in the Bible. Having been saved by grace, the Galatians, who were reverting to the law for Christian living, were actually falling short of the standard of grace by which they were saved. The frustrating result would have been similar to the believer in Romans 7 who was struggling to live under the law (see the discussion on that passage). This does not teach that children of God can lose their salvation by falling out of grace. Paul is contrasting grace and law. Depending on circumcision, or any other work, means renouncing justification by grace through faith and takes one out of the spirit of grace and puts him under the dominion of the law. There cannot be two grounds of salvation, two means of justification, two ways of life. To accept the one means to reject the other. It is either law or grace, either works or faith, either self-righteousness, or the righteousness of God, either circumcision or Christ. The Galatians were in danger of substituting law for Christ as a means of salvation.

5. For we. True born-again believers, who cling to the covenant of grace. **Through the Spirit.** Not through the flesh; not through the law. **Wait.** This compound verb means literally, receive-away-from-out of. It means more than mere waiting passively. It suggests earnest, constant expectancy. This verb occurs eight times in the New Testament each time with eschatological significance. **For the hope of righteousness by faith.** The realization of perfect righteousness.

6. For in Jesus Christ. In vital union with Him, the true sphere of salvation. **Neither circumcision availeth anything.** Circumcision is not strong to effect (Gr *ischuō*) anything; it conveys no spiritual blessing in return for its binding pledge to keep the whole law. **But faith which worketh by love.** Faith is a vital heart trust and personal commitment to Christ (Rom 10:9-10) which identifies the believer with Christ in the sphere of grace. A living faith expresses itself in love. Love does not add anything to faith; it gives it a place to operate. This coincides with the familiar statement, ''Faith alone justifies, but the faith which justifies is not alone.''

7. Ye did run well. You were running nobly, gallantly, and bravely with every prospect of reaching the goal. You were making good progress on the right course. **Who.** Probably refers to some ringleader of the legalists. **Did hinder you.** A military term (Gr *enkoptō*) which pictures an enemy impeding one's progress and preventing him from reaching his goal by cutting off his way and setting up a roadblock. Since Paul is using the figure of a race, this word suggests the ''cutting in'' of one runner on another and thus slowing up his progress and throwing him off course. **That ye should not obey the truth.** The Galatians were turned aside from obedience to the truth by false teaching.

8. This persuasion. The flattering fallacies of the legalist; their sedulous attempts to persuade the Galatians to turn from the course they were already pursuing. **Cometh not of him that calleth you.** This counsel toward ritualism and legalism was not of God, who calls men to liberty. The legalists were not God's

servants, and the Galatians should not have heeded them (Jn 10:45).

9. A little leaven. The false doctrine which appeared so slight and harmless. **Leaveneth the whole lump.** Goes on working slowly, silently, and satanically until the whole lump is corrupted. Leaven is corrupt and produces corruption; its nature is never altered. Doctrinal differences are dangerous. The process of doctoral fermentation was going on but all the assemblies had not been permeated yet. Paul expresses confidence that they will deal with this doctrinal error summarily.

10. I have confidence in you through the Lord. Paul has been persuaded that the Galatians will share his loyalty to Christ, but he doesn't trust them apart from the Lord. **That ye will be none otherwise minded.** Let us say through the influence of false teachers. **He that troubleth you.** The one continually agitating, disquieting, and disturbing your faith. **Shall bear his judgment.** He cannot escape; God will judge him. **Whosoever he be.** It seems unlikely that Paul knew precisely who the leader was.

11. And I, brethren. Paul contrasts himself with the legalists. **If I yet preach circumcision.** As Paul's enemies accused. **Why do I yet suffer persecution?** If Paul preached legalism, he would not be persecuted. The legalists charged Paul with inconsistency and duplicity. They had misconstrued Paul's act of having Timothy circumcised (Acts 16:3). Paul could not be preaching both circumcision and the cross, for they are contradictory. **Then is the offence of the cross ceased.** The offense is the stumblingblock of the cross (I Cor 1:23). The cross uproots the doctrine of salvation by human merit. Salvation is by grace alone, and justification is by faith alone; there can be no compromise. The offensiveness of the cross to the legalists is that salvation is by grace without circumcision and obedience to the law.

12. I would. I could wish. That **they were even cut off.** That they will cut themselves off. All the ancient Greek interpreters and most modern scholars apply this to the self-mutilation practiced by the heathen priests of Cybele. Paul speaks with satire. **Which trouble you.** Causing so much disturbance and throwing you into confusion.

B. Liberty is Perverted by Lawlessness. 5:13:26.

13. For brethren. A tender title. **Ye.** Emphatic contrast to the false teachers. **Have been called unto liberty.** Ye were called unto liberty, not slavery. Liberty is not an excuse for license. License destroys liberty. **Only use not liberty for an occasion to the flesh.** Some of the Galatians may have already done this, and others were tempted. Liberty must be maintained, not abused. It is abused when it is made the occasion of turning liberty into license. "Occasion" (Gr *aphorme*) is a military term signifying a camping place which becomes a launching pad to capture the opposing army. It is the base of operations for giving way to carnal passions. The flesh is the sinful nature to man, which has been crucified with Christ (2:20), but which seems to possess possibilities of revival. Therefore do not let your liberty become the impulse which will start the old nature to assert itself again. **But.** On the contrary. **By love.** True Christian love is the motive of true Christian conduct. **Serve one another.** Constantly and voluntarily enslave yourselves to one another.

14. For all the law is fulfilled in one word. The whole moral law stands fully accomplished and completed in one precept. **Thou shalt love thy neighbor as thyself.** Such love is produced by the Holy Spirit. Love is the real fulfillment of the law which the legalists were wanting to serve. It was said of the early Christians, "Behold how they love one another," not how they quarrel, criticize, and backbite. Christ did not come to destroy the law . . . but to fulfill (Mt 5:17). Grace does not make one free to sin; it makes him free to serve.

15. But if. Setting in contrast what they were doing with what they should do. **Bite and devour.** Continually biting and devouring like wild animals in deadly combat, i.e. a picture of church strifes. **Take heed.** Watch out. **That ye be not consumed one of another.** Mutual destruction by slander and criticism.

16. Walk in the Spirit. Have the habit of continually walking by the energizing power and under the divine direction of the Holy Spirit. This is the only way of deliverance from selfish lusts. **And ye shall not fulfil the lust of the flesh.** The double negative with the aorist subjunctive means you will never gratify the sinful desires originating in and overflowing from the lower nature. When God saved us. He did not eradicate the old nature, neither did He reform the old life; He gave us an absolutely new life (Jn 3:6). The old nature is "not subject to the law of God, neither indeed can be" (Rom 8:7). The Christian can conquer the self-life and have continual victory by walking by the Holy Spirit.

17. For the flesh lusteth against the Spirit. There is a constant deadly feud being waged. Bunyan shows that both Christ and Satan long for the possession of the city of Man Soul. Romans 7:15-25 is an inspired commentary on this verse. The flesh opposes the Spirit in an effort to prevent the believer from a life of obedience, surrender, and victory. **The Spirit against the flesh.** The Holy Spirit opposes the flesh and gives the believer victory over it. **And these are contrary.** Lined up in hostile, face-to-face conflict. There is mutual antagonism. **So that ye cannot do the things that ye would.** So that ye may not keep on doing whatever ye may want to do.

18. But if ye be led of the Spirit. If you are being led continually by the Holy Spirit, then it follows that **ye are not under the law.** Christians have a live-in divine Person to keep them in line, and they do not need an external curb.

19. Now the works of the flesh. Note the plural, works, the complex mixture of evil desires and deeds. The flesh is always active; it never takes a vacation.

Are manifest. Plainly evident to everyone. These works all issue from a heart in rebellion against God and insisting upon doing as it wills (Mt 15:19; Mk 7:21-22). **Adultery.** Illicit sexual intercourse between married partners. **Fornication.** Illicit sexual intercourse between unmarried partners. **Uncleanness.** Moral impurity. **Lasciviousness.** Wantonness, debauchery, lewdness. This word (Gr *aselgeia*) was used to describe an attitude of utter disregard for the opinions and conventions which governed others.

20. Idolatry. Worship of idols, putting anything in the place of God. **Witchcraft.** Sorcery, the profession of magical arts which used various combinations of chemicals (drugs) to deceive and get control of their victims (cf. Rev 21:8). **Hatred.** Enmities, personal animosities (cf. I Jn 3:15). **Variance.** Strife, rivalry, discord, factions, quarrelsomeness. **Emulations.** Jealousies, sedition, constant desire to excel other people and secure their admiration. **Wrath.** Passionate anger, stirring up the emotions of temper resulting in an explosion. **Strife.** Factions, intrigues manifested in party spirit. **Seditions.** Splits, divisions. **Heresies.** Choices based on preferences, sectarian parties.

21. Envyings. Feelings of ill-will. **Drunkenness.** Excessive indulgence in strong drink. **Revellings.** Carousals such as the outrageous feasts to the god Dionysus associated with horrible orgies, not unlike many riotous, wild parties of today. **And such like.** The list is representative, not exhaustive. **They which do such things.** Those whose lives are characterized by the habit of continually doing such things. Such life style is proof positive that one has not become a new creature in Christ (II Cor 5:17), that he is not in the kingdom of God, and that he shall have no share in it. A Christian may fall temporarily into these sins, but he will be miserable until he confesses and forsakes them (Prov 28:13).

22. But the fruit. Singular in number; not nine fruits, but one fruit composed of nine elements. The first three are in relation to God; the next three are in relation to man; and the last three are in relation to one's own inner life. **Of the Spirit.** The Holy Spirit produces this fruit through the believer who is in vital union with Christ (Jn 15:1-8). **Love.** The self-denying, self-sacrificing, Christlike love which is the foundation of all other graces. A divine exposition of this kind of love is found in I Corinthians 13. **Joy.** The joy of the Holy Spirit (I Thess 1:6), that deep, abiding, inner rejoicing in the Lord (Phil 4:4). **Peace.** Tranquillity of soul (Phil 4:7), the peace that Christ gives (Jn 14:27), and which the world cannot take away. **Longsuffering.** Patient endurance and steadfastness under provocation; forbearance under ill-will, with no thought of retaliation. **Gentleness.** Graciousness, kindly disposition. **Goodness.** Beneficence, ready to do good, love in action. **Faith.** Fidelity which makes one true to his promise and faithful to his task.

23. Meekness. Not weakness, but controlled strength. This word conveys the idea of a listening ear to hear what God has to say. It is submission to God and unselfishness to our fellowmen. **Temperance.** Rational restraint of the natural impulses, self-control. **Against such there is no law.** No law forbids the possession and the practice of these virtues. No law is needed to require a man who is bearing much fruit in his life to do right to his fellowman.

24. And they that are Christ's. Belong to Christ by purchase. **Have crucified the flesh.** This is a settled matter (2:20), but the very fact that the flesh and the Spirit are in constant conflict shows that the flesh is very active. When one puts his trust in Christ, he receives the actual benefits of identification with Christ, resulting in breaking the power of cancelled sin and in setting the prisoner free. The Christian is to daily give outward expression of his inward experience and in order to do this, he must constantly reckon himself "to be dead indeed unto sin, but alive unto God through our Lord Jesus Christ" (Rom

6:11). **With the affections and lust.** Emphasizes the completeness of the transaction.

25. If we live in the Spirit. Since we live by the Spirit we derive our life from Him. **Let us also walk in the Spirit.** Let us go on walking, making progress toward spiritual maturity, by the Holy Spirit's indwelling presence and power. The word walk (Gr *stoicheō*) means to walk in a line, keep in rank and file, march in battle order. We need to keep in step with the Holy Spirit.

26. Let us not be desirous of vain glory. Let us cease becoming self-conceited. **Provoking one another.** Challenging one another to combat. **Envying one another.** Pining away with feelings of jealousy over the other's undeserved praise. Such actions toward one another are not consistent with a life of faith, lived by one who has been crucified with Christ and who is keeping step with the Holy Spirit.

C. Liberty is Perfected by Love.
6:1-10.

6:1. Brethren. Members of the same spiritual family. **If a man be overtaken.** Literally, to take before. Sudden temptation seized him unawares before he could escape. This is a probable contingency. **In a fault.** A falling beside, a trespass, a lapse or deviation from truth and uprightness. It is important to distinguish between willful, deliberate sin and sudden, unexpected failure because of overwhelming temptation taking one off guard. **Ye which are spiritual.** Those who are constantly walking by the Spirit and living by the Spirit (5:16, 25), and who are exhibiting the fruit of the Spirit (5:22-23). These are experts in mending souls. **Restore such an one.** This word (Gr *katartizō*) is used as a surgical term, of setting a bone or dislocated joint. It is the same word used in Matthew 4:21 of mending nets. The present imperative signifies to keep on having the habit of restoring the offender to his former condition. Bring him into line. It takes skill to bring one who has slipped off the road

of grace and is struggling in the quicksand of legalism back into his former manner of life and rightful place of unbroken fellowship with Christ. **In the spirit of meekness.** A fruit of the Spirit. This is the opposite of arrogance and harshness; it is tender consideration and forbearance. There must be no self-complacency, no scolding, and no "better-than-thou" attitude. **Considering thyself.** Constantly looking with fixed attention on thyself. **Lest thou also be tempted.** All need this warning; no one is immune from temptation.

2. Bear ye one another's burdens. Have the habit of mutual burden-bearing. Lend a helping hand by lifting heavy loads. Burdens (Gr *baros*) is an overload which we can lighten, a weight too heavy for the individual and capable of being shared with others of the fellowship. **And so.** In this manner. **Fulfil the law of Christ.** Satisfy the requirements of the law and fill it to overflowing.

3. For if a man think himself to be something, when he is nothing. If he has the habit of accounting himself a big number, when he is a zero, he is conceited without a cause. Self-esteem is vanity, and vanity is nothing. The very fact of thinking more highly of himself than he ought to think (Rom 12:3) condemns him; he is weighed in the balances and found wanting (Dan 5:27). **He deceiveth himself.** He is constantly leading his own mind to stray; he deceives no one else. Self-conceit results in self-deception.

4. But let every man prove his own work. Let each one continually and carefully test his own actual accomplishments by objective scrutiny. Such testing is for the purpose of approving. **Then.** After he has done this. **Shall he have rejoicing.** A ground of glorying. **In himself alone.** With regard to himself. **And not in another.** He will not arrive at a wrong conclusion by comparing himself with the other person and decide that he is better than the other person.

5. For every man shall bear his own burden. Each one shall carry his own responsibility, shoulder this own pack, bear his own private load. There is no contradiction between verses 2 and 5; different Greek words are translated "burden." In verse 2 the word is (Gr *baros*) and denotes a heavy, crushing, overtaxing weight; our extra load, which can and must be relieved. Here in verse 5 the word is (Gr *phortion*) and is used to designate a pack carried by a soldier. It is the word used by Christ to describe the burden He lays on His disciples (Mt 11:30), which He says is light. This word is the diminutive form of the Greek *phortos* which is used of the lading or cargo of a ship (Acts 27:10).

6. Let him that is taught in the word. Let him that is being taught in the word. In the early church, there were those whose full time duty it was to give instruction in the Word of God. **Communicate.** Be a partner with, share with, enter into fellowship with financially. **Unto him that teacheth in all good things.** In all material and spiritual things (cf. I Cor 9:10-11). The Christian community was expected to support these gifted teachers.

7. Be not deceived. Stop being led astray into error. **God is not mocked.** God is not ignored, sneered at, ridiculed, treated with contempt by cynical gestures. There can be no double-dealing with God; He is not deceived by hypocrites. **For whatsoever a man soweth.** Keeps on sowing. **That.** Not something different. There is an identity of what is sown and what is harvested. **Shall he also reap.** Eventually there will be a harvest, and the immutable law of sowing and reaping applies (Mt 7:16-19).

8. For he that soweth to his flesh. The one who is constantly (Greek present tense) sowing with a view to the promotion of his own corrupt, sinful nature; that nature which is opposed to God and unrenewed by the Holy Spirit. **Shall of the flesh reap corruption.** Physical, moral, and spiritual rottenness and ruin. **But he that soweth to the Spirit.** Our life here is a sowing of one kind or another. **Shall of the Spirit reap life everlasting.** In opposition to corruption. Eternal life is produced by the Holy Spirit in those who put their trust in Christ. Paul has shown (5:19-25) the intermediate products of the flesh and the Spirit; here he mentions the two final harvests. "For if ye live after the flesh, ye shall die: but if ye through the Spirit do mortify the deeds of the body, ye shall live" (Rom 8:13).

9. And let us not be weary in well doing. Stop (Greek present imperative) getting discouraged and tired of doing good, i.e. sowing to the Spirit. This word "weary" means to retreat in battle, to give up the fight, to flag in one's efforts. The idea is that one may get tired on the job and slacken up his work, or even stop, before the field is plowed and planted. **For in due season.** At its proper season, i.e. harvest time. **We shall reap, if we faint not.** If we do not relax, let down, become exhausted, and faint.

10. As we have therefore opportunity. Occasion, appropriate season. **Let us do good unto all men.** Let us keep on working the good to everyone. **Especially unto them who are of the household of faith.** All born-again believers belong to the same spiritual family. For these we are under special obligation to work good, whenever we have an opportunity.

D. Conclusion. 6:11-18.

11. Ye see how large a letter. Better, with how large letters. **I have written unto you with mine own hand.** I wrote (Greek epistolary aorist). Paul now takes the pen from the amanuensis and writes the rest of the letter.

12. As many as desire to make a fair shew. Make a pretentious display of religion, i.e. put on a good front, present a good looking face to win favor of men and avoid the loss of popularity, position, and prominence. **In the flesh.** In external rites and ritual. **They constrain you to be circumcised.** They are trying to compel you by saying it is absolutely necessary. **Only lest they should suffer persecution.** The legalists were not concerned for the Galatians, or for God, but only about their own comfort and reputation. **For the cross of Christ.** Because of the cross of Christ. The symbol of suffering and shame, which came to those identified with the cross of Christ.

13. For neither. Not even. **They themselves who are circumcised.** Those who are submitting to circumcision, the legalistic circumcision party. **Keep the law.** The legalists were insincere and inconsistent, pretending to be zealous for the law. They felt that merely observing circumcision would compensate for not observing the rest of the law. **But desire to have you circumcised.** They had a twofold selfish purpose in mind: (1) to escape persecution which comes with the cross of Christ; and (2) to brag and boast over the Galatians. **That they may glory in your flesh.** Get credit for proselytizing Gentiles or persuading Gentiles to be circumcised and adopt the legalistic system.

14. But God forbid that I should glory. May it not come to pass to me to be continually glorying. This is a wish for the future. **Save in the cross of our Lord Jesus Christ.** What was a shame to the legalists was the object of glorying to Paul. The cross represents the sacrificial sufferings of Christ; not Paul's sufferings for Christ (II Cor 12:9-10), but Christ's sufferings for Paul (Phil 3:3). **By whom.** Our Lord Jesus Christ. **The world.** The satanic world system which is opposed to God and Christ, both the religious and the irreligious world. **Is crucified unto me, and I unto the world.** The perfect tense emphasizes the present, permanent results of this double crucifixion. Crucifixion means a death of shame. The world has no more power over Paul because it is dead as far as he is concerned and Paul is also dead so far as the world is concerned. This was accomplished by means of the cross of our Lord Jesus Christ. Paul was crucified to the world when he was crucified with Christ (2:20). The old Saul died and was buried with Christ; the new Paul lives.

15. For in Christ Jesus. In living union with Him. **Neither circumcision availeth anything, nor uncircumcision.** Circumcision affects only the body, not the soul. A surgical operation can have absolutely no effect on the old nature. Nothing short of death and the creation of a new nature can be effective, and this comes only when one is identified with the crucified, risen Christ. **But a new creature.** The only thing that is important is to be a new creation in Christ (II Cor 5:17). "He that hath the Son hath life; and he that hath not the Son hath not life (I Jn 5:12).

16. And as many as walk according to this rule. Man needs a standard or a measuring rod to guide his steps. The law was a failure, so God has given us another standard, placing all our hopes of salvation in the crucified, buried, risen, and coming again Christ. **Peace be on them, and mercy, and upon the Israel of God.** Not a different class of believers. Israel of God is in contrast to Israel after the flesh. Those who received the Saviour who came through Israel are true Israelites, spiritual descendants of Abraham.

17. From henceforth let no man trouble me. Paul's apostleship, authority, and gospel had all been questioned. He successfully answered all the criticism, and now he says, "Let's hear no more of such disturbing, distracting attacks." **For I bear in my body the marks of the Lord Jesus.** Let anyone show the like if they want to qualify to speak. There were devotees who stamped upon their bodies the names of the gods whom they worshipped; some slaves had the names or marks of their owners on their bodies; and sometimes soldiers were thus identified. Paul glorified in being a slave of Jesus Christ. The brandmarks, his badge of lifelong, faithful service, were the scars left by scourgings, stones at Lystra, and rods at Philippi (cf. II Cor 11:24-27). Paul had endured hardness as a good soldier of Jesus Christ (II Tim 2:3).

18. Brethren. They remained brethren by the grace of God. This final touch of affection, in spite of the sharp things he said to them. **The grace of our Lord Jesus Christ be with your spirit.** What more fitting benediction could have been given at the close of a letter emphasizing grace instead of law, and spirit rather than flesh. **Amen.**

BIBLIOGRAPHY

Burton, E. de Witt. A Critical and Exegetical Commentary on the Epistle to the Galatians. In *The International Critical Commentary*. Edinburgh: T. & T. Clark, 1921.

Calvin, John. *Commentaries on the Epistles of Paul to the Galatians and Ephesians*. Trans. by William Pringle. Grand Rapids: Eerdmans, 1948.

DeHann, Martin R. *Galatians*. Grand Rapids: Zondervan, 1960.

* Eadie, John. *Commentary on the Epistle of Paul to the Galatians*. Grand Rapids: Zondervan, n.d.

Eerdman, Charles R. *The Epistle of Paul to the Galatians*. Philadelphia: Westminster Press, 1930.

Findlay, George G. *Galatians*. In *The Expositor's Bible*. New York: Hodder and Stoughton, n.d.

Hendricksen, William. Exposition of Galatians. In *New Testament Commentary*. Grand Rapids: Baker, 1968.

Hiebert, D. Edmond. *An Introduction to the Pauline Epistles*. Chicago: Moody Press, 1954.

Ironside, H. A. *Expository Messages on the Epistle to the Galatians*. Neptune, N.J.: Loizeaux Brothers, 1941.

Lenski, R. C. H. *The Interpretation of St. Paul's Epistles to the Galatians, to the Ephesians, and to the Philippians*. Columbus, Ohio: The Wartburg Press, 1937.

* Lightfoot, J. B. *The Epistle of St. Paul to the Galatians*. Grand Rapids: Zondervan, Second Reprint Edition, 1957.

Luther, Martin. *A Commentary on St. Paul's Epistle to the Galatians*. Westwood, N.J.: Revell, reprint ed., n.d.

* Ramsay, Sir William M. *A Historical Commentary on St. Paul's Epistle to the Galatians*. New York: G. P. Putnam's Sons, 1900.

* Rendall, Frederic. The Epistle to the Galatians. In *The Expositor's Greek Testament*. Grand Rapids: Eerdmans, n.d.

* Ridderbos, H. B. The Epistle of Paul to the Churches of Galatia. In *The New International Commentary on the New Testament*. Grand Rapids: Eerdmans, 1954.

Stott, John R. W. *The Message of Galatians*. London: Inter-Varsity Press, 1968.

Strauss, Lehman. *Devotional Studies in Galatians and Ephesians*. Neptune, N.J.: Loizeaux Brothers, 1957.

Tenney, Merrill C. *Galatians: The Charter of Christian Liberty*. Grand Rapids: Eerdmans, 1951.

Wuest, Kenneth S. *Galatians in the Greek New Testament for the English Reader*. Grand Rapids: Eerdmans, 1944.

The Epistle To The

EPHESIANS

INTRODUCTION

The Church of Ephesus. Ephesus was the queen city of Asia Minor, situated about three miles from the Aegean Sea on the Cayster River, and had a population of about 340,000. It was the capital of the proconsular province of Asia and was one of the most important cities visited by the Apostle Paul. Ephesus was noted for the Great Temple of Diana (Artemis), an open-air theatre seating 25,000, a magnificent stadium, and the shrine of Serapis (an Egyptian divinity). Ephesus was famous for its rich culture: oriental religion, Greek philosophy, Roman government, and worldwide commerce.

At the close of his second missionary journey, Paul made a brief visit to Ephesus, left Priscilla and Aquila there to work in his absence, and promised to return (Acts 18:19-21). Apollos spent some time there (Acts 18:24-28). On his third missionary journey, Paul remained in Ephesus for about three years evangelizing the city and the surrounding region. On his last voyage to Jerusalem, Paul met the elders of Ephesus at Miletus (Acts 20:17-38). Others who labored at Ephesus were Timothy (I Tim 1:3), Onesiphorus (II Tim 1:16), Tychicus (II Tim 4:12), and the Apostle John after A.D. 70.

Authorship. The writer identifies himself as Paul (1:1; 3:1). Both the internal and the external evidences are strong for the Pauline authorship.

Date and place of writing. This is one of the Prison Epistles. Paul states that he was a prisoner (3:1; 4:1; 6:20). Paul was in prison three times: (1) at Caesarea for about two years, A.D. 58-60; (2) once in Rome for about two years, A.D. 61-63; and (3) again in Rome about A.D. 67. He probably wrote the Prison Epistles during his first Roman imprisonment, A.D. 61-63. Ephesians was composed about the same time as Colossians. Tychicus was the bearer of both letters (Col 4:7-8; Eph 6:21-22).

Destination. Scholars are divided as to the destination of this epistle: (1) that it was written for and sent directly to Ephesus; (2) that it was a circular letter sent to the churches of Asia Minor, of which Ephesus was the chief; or (3) that it was addressed to Gentile Christians. The oldest and most reliable Greek manuscripts do not have the words "which are at Ephesus" (Gr *en Ephesoi*) in 1:1. Lightfoot maintains that wherever these manuscripts agree, they almost always represent the original text. However, the great majority of Greek manuscripts do include the words "in Ephesus," and there are no Greek manuscripts which include the name of any other city. In Colossians 4:16, Paul mentions "the epistle from Laodicea." Perhaps the autograph copy had a blank space in 1:1, and since most of manuscripts were copies of the letter sent to Ephesus, it came to be known as the Epistle to the Ephesians. No doubt it was a general or circular letter for the churches of Asia Minor. The letter lacks a personal tone; there are no personal greetings and no personal references. After all is said, the value of the epistle is not affected by the problem of its destination.

Purpose. This epistle magnifies the church as a divine institution, sets forth God's purpose of heading up all things in Christ (1:9-10), emphasizes that salvation is only in Christ, and shows that a well-rounded life issues out of salvation by grace through faith.

This epistle is not personal, but general. It is not polemic: Paul is not defending his apostleship as in I Corinthians, not rebuking fickleness as in II Corinthians, not controverting Judaizers as in Galatians, and not battling Gnosticism as in Colossians.

Theme. Ephesians has been called "The Heavenly Epistle" and "The Alps of the New Testament." In it Paul takes us from "the depths of ruin to the heights of redemption." The church is one with Christ: it is the body of which He is the Head (1:22-23); it is the building of which He is the Chief Cornerstone (2:20-22); and she is the bride of whom Christ is the Bridegroom (5:25-32).

Comparison with Colossians. In Ephesians the emphasis is on the dignity of the church, which is the body of Christ. In Colossians the emphasis is on the deity of Christ, who is the Head of that body. Ephesians considers the church's oneness with Christ; Colossians considers the church's completeness in Christ. Ephesians speaks of the Christian being in Christ; Colossians speaks of Christ being in the Christian.

OUTLINE

COMMENTARY

I. INTRODUCTION. 1:1-2.

1:1. Paul. Designated as the human author. **An apostle.** One fully equipped and sent on a mission. Paul claims to be directly commissioned by Christ to represent Him. He was an envoy, an ambassador for Christ. **Of Jesus Christ.** He was owned by Christ and sent from Him; both possessed and commissioned. **By the will of God.** Paul is always conscious of the divine origin and authority of his commission. This assurance sustained him throughout all of his trials. His ministry was not of his own choosing. He could ever say, "By the grace of God I am what I am." **To the saints.**

The separated and holy ones (Ps 4:3). Saints are sinners saved by the grace of God, separated from sin, and set apart for God. They are not sinless, have not attained to certain heights of sanctity, and do not belong to some special religious group. **At Ephesus.** Geographically. **And to the faithful.** Even those who are distinguished for their faithfulness and loyalty to Christ. This is one way to describe Christians. The word means that they are "believers" in Christ. **In Christ.** Spiritually they are in vital union with Christ enjoying blessed fellowship with Him.

2. Grace. That divine, free, and unmerited favor of God. **And peace.** Not only the absence of all strife but the blessing of tranquillity. It is the result of reconciliation between God and man based on faith in and union with the Lord Jesus Christ. Here both words are used as a greeting. **From God . . . and . . . the Lord Jesus Christ.** The source of spiritual blessings, our gracious heavenly Father and our lovely Lord.

II. THE CALLING OF THE CHURCH. 1:3-3:21.

A. The Origin of the Church. 1:3-14.

3. Blessed. This doxology is composed of three stanzas, each of which closes with a similar refrain (vss. 6, 12, 14). This word "blessed" is always used of God in the New Testament, and it means praised or eulogized. **Who hath blessed us.** God is the great giver, and the blessings are already ours. **With all spiritual blessings.** With every kind of spiritual blessing. They are spiritual in nature as opposed to temporal and material, and they are the products of the Holy Spirit. **In heavenly places.** In the realm and sphere of heavenly things as contrasted with earthly things. The adjective expresses quality rather than place. This expression is found several times in this epistle and refers to that exalted sphere of activities to which the believer has

been lifted in Christ. **In Christ.** In vital union with Him. Note how often these words are found in this epistle. "In Christ" is the key to this wonderful passage. Since the saints are in Him, nothing is too good or too great for God to bestow upon them.

4. He hath chosen us. This word (Gr *eklegomai*) means to pick out, to choose. This is a definite statement of God's elective grace concerning believers in Christ. **In him.** In union with Christ. Apart from Christ, there would have been no election and no salvation. God always deals with man in Christ, who is the one and only mediator between God and men (I Tim 2:5). Paul traces man's salvation back to the plan of God's will. **Before the foundation of the world.** Before the projection of the world order. God's choice was eternal; His plan is timeless. The fall of man was no surprise to God, and redemption was no afterthought. God provided for our salvation before one star glittered in infinite expanse. We must be careful not to draw false conclusions from this sublime truth. God is not stating a fatalistic doctrine in which He arbitrarily elects some to heaven and consigns all others to hell. There is no scriptural doctrine of election to damnation. God's election provides for the means as well as the ends. God's infallible Word plainly states, "For whosoever shall call upon the name of the Lord shall be saved" (Rom 10:13). Man either receives or disbelieves God's provisions in Christ. "So far as the human race is concerned, every man may not only accept Christ as Saviour but is urged and invited to do so. The ground of this invitation is the work of the incarnate son . . . Divine foreordination and human freedom are humanly irreconcilable, but like two parallel lines that meet in infinity, they have their solution in God" (Merrill F. Unger, *Unger's Bible Handbook,* pp. 672-674). "To explain an apparent difficulty by denying one or the other of these tenets is to explain away the truth'' (W. Curtis Vaughn, *The Letter to the Ephesians,* p. 13). **That we should be holy and without blame before him in love.** This is the purpose of God's election. The real purpose of God's elective grace is not "pie in the sky by and by," but has to do with a separated life here and now (cf. Rom 8:29). Holiness is the positive side of a Christlike life (Heb 12:14), separated from all evil courses and connections. Blamelessness in character is the negative side of the Christlike life: not sinless, but stainless, without blemish and without defect. God's expectation is for His saints to live on a high spiritual plane.

5. Having predestinated us. Having decided beforehand by marking off the boundaries of His possession in His saints. **Unto the adoption of children.** With a view to our being placed as adult sons (Gal 4:5; Rom 8:15; 9:4). The purpose of His predestination was that we should experience sonship. **By Jesus Christ to himself.** By means of Christ's mediation and for His very own to serve Him and glorify Him. **According to the good pleasure of his will.** It was right for Him to do this.

6. To the praise of the glory of his grace. Literally, the glory, the splendor, of His unmerited favor. The purpose was for God's glory and intended to issue forth in praise. **He hath made us accepted in the beloved.** God accepts us into His family because of our vital relationship with Christ and on no other grounds.

7. In whom we have. A present possession, not a future prospect. **Redemption.** Redemption is deliverance from bondage by means of a price paid. Saints have been liberated from the slavery of self, sin, and Satan, having been bought out of the slave market. "If the Son therefore shall make you free, ye shall be free indeed" (Jn 8:36). **Through his blood.** His blood is the ransom price paid for our salvation. Redemption is effected by the precious blood of Christ (I Pet 1:18-20). Salvation is not a matter of human attainment, but of divine atonement. God makes everything of the blood of Christ: we are redeemed by His blood (Eph 1:7); justified by His blood (Rom 5:9); purged as to conscience by His blood (Heb 9:14); forgiven by His blood (Col 1:14); cleansed by His blood (Rev 7:14); have peace through His blood (Col 1:20); enter the holiest by His blood (Heb 10:19). **The forgiveness of sins.** Remission rests on ransoming. Forgiveness means the bearing away of all our shortcomings. God's remission is unqualified and unchanging. His Word is very specific in telling us what He has done with our sins; He has blotted them out (Isa 43:25; 44:22), He has removed them (Ps 103:11-12), He has cast them behind His back (Isa 38:17), He has cast them into the depths of the sea (Mic 7:19), and He remembers them no more (Heb 8:12). God's forgiveness is free, full, and final. When He forgives, He forgets. **According to the riches of his grace.** Our redemption is measured by the boundless resources of His marvelous, nifinite grace. This is a very rich epistle which reveals our riches in Christ; the riches of His grace (1:7), the riches of the glory of His inheritance in the saints (1:18), the riches in mercy (2:7), the unsearchable riches of Christ (3:8), and the riches of His glory (3:16).

8. Wherein he hath abounded toward us. Which He lavished on us to overflowing. God's grace enriches believers (cf. Rom 5:20). **In all wisdom.** Wise insight and spiritual perception which come from above (Jas 1:5; 3:17). **Prudence.** This is the practical use of wisdom and spiritual discernment.

9. The mystery of his will. God has a plan which was once hidden from human reason for ages (Rom 16:25) but now is divinely revealed (Col 1:26-27). **Which he hath purposed in himself.** Which He set forth in Christ.

10. That in the dispensation. A stewardship or administration to carry out His plan and purpose. **The fulness of times.** The appointed time of the historical ages. **He might gather together in one all things in Christ.** To sum up, to head up all things in Christ in orderly and harmonious completion. Christ is the center of the universe, which some day will be integrated into one harmonious whole.

11. In whom . . . we have obtained an inheritance. Better, we were made the inheritance, we became God's heritage, and became the Lord's portion (Deut 32:9). Zephaniah 3:17 records a remarkable expression, "he will save, he will rejoice over thee with joy; he will rest in his love, he will joy over thee with singing." This is applicable to Gentile saints, as well as to Hebrew saints.

12. That we should be to the praise of his glory. This second refrain praises God the Son.

13. In whom ye also trusted. Faith is the connecting link between man and Christ. **After that ye heard.** They first heard God's good news, called the Word of truth and further described as the gospel of your salvation. Notice the order here. They first heard God's good news and then they put their trust in Christ. ". . . faith cometh by hearing, and hearing by the word of God" (Rom 10:17). **After that ye believed, ye were sealed with that holy Spirit of promise.** They were sealed, not in order to be redeemed, but because they were already redeemed. They had trusted in Christ and now they are sealed in Him. The word seal means to set a seal on one as a mark of ownership. The Holy Spirit ratified God's ownership of believers by fixing His seal on them in a supernatural manner. They were sealed at the same time they believed, not at some later time. The sealing was not something apart from salvation, not something in addition to salvation, and not something subsequent to salvation. All who believe in

Christ are sealed then and there. The seal is: (1) a sign of a finished transaction (Jer 32:9-10; Jn 17:4; 19:30); (2) a sign of ownership (I Cor 16:19-20; II Tim 2:19); and (3) a sign of security (Dan 6:17; Eph 4:30). The Holy Spirit is called the Spirit of promise because Christ promised to send Him (Jn 14:16).

14. Which is the earnest of our inheritance. An earnest (Gr *arrabōn*) is a partial down payment in the first installment and a pledge guaranteeing a complete transaction and payment of the total obligation. Since God has graciously given us the Holy Spirit and we now have a foretaste of heaven, we have His guarantee that He will perform all that He has promised (Phil 1:6). **Unto the praise of his glory.** Paul uses similar, though not identical, terms in ascribing these wonderful blessings to the grace of God. In verse 6, God the Father is praised for selecting us by His mercies; in verse 12, God the Son is praised for securing us by His mediation; and in verse 14, God the Holy Spirit is praised for sealing us by His ministry. We see in each stage of salvation grace, marvelous grace, and nothing but grace. In its past inception, in its present possession, and in its future glory, grace is supreme.

B. The Prayer for the Church. 1:15-23.

There are two prayers in Ephesians. God is both light and love. Paul's first prayer (1:15-23) is for light, and his second prayer (3:14-21) is for love. It is as natural for a regenerate man to pray as it is for an unregenerate man to breathe.

15. Wherefore, on this account, for this cause. This looks back to verses 3-14, and Paul adds prayer to praise. **Faith** and **love** are two great words. Love is the outgrowth of faith, and faith manifests itself by love. Faith works by love (Gal 5:6), and love is the proof of discipleship (Jn 13:35; 15:12; I Jn 3:14).

16. Cease not to give thanks for you. A vital part of Paul's ministry was his intercession for the saints. This was his constant and continual fixed habit. Prayer and thanksgiving go together.

17. That (Gr *hina*). In order that. This introduces the definite purpose and object of Paul's prayer for them. He makes specific requests. **The God of our Lord Jesus Christ.** Paul addresses the throne of grace, the source of all blessings. **The Father of glory.** The one who is all glorious and the source of all that is glorious. **May give unto you the spirit of wisdom and revelation.** Revelation has to do with new truths. The Ephesians were the recipients of God's revelation, and they had knowledge of spiritual truths. The Holy Spirit knows the deep things of God (I Cor 2:11), and He is our teacher (Jn 14:26). Man needs much more than reason and research; he needs a revelation from God. Wisdom is general illumination, the know-how to apply the revealed spiritual truths. **In the knowledge of him.** This is that deep and wide, growing, experimental knowledge (II Pet 3:18). We all need a fuller knowledge of Christ (Phil 3:10).

18. The eyes of your understanding being enlightened. Better, that the eyes of your heart having been enlightened. The heart refers to the whole inner man. The soul has eyes that need to be and can be enlightened, i.e. flooded with divine light. The Holy Spirit opens the eyes and hearts in order that the believer may see the great truths mentioned here. The purpose of spiritual illumination and spiritual perception is that believers may know and experience God's calling, inheritance, and power. **The hope of his calling.** The call from Him and a summons to Him. It is a call to new life in Christ, through Christ, for Christ, and with Christ. It involves perfect deliverance and perfect fellowship. God's calling is a high calling (Phil 3:13-14) to be like Christ and with Christ. **The riches of the glory of his in-**heritance in the saints. God owns the universe, but His most precious possession is the pearl of great price, the church. The saints are the trophies of His grace.

19-20. The exceeding greatness of his power. The transcendent, immeasurable, more-than-sufficient greatness of His dynamic power. Paul heaps up terms that defy description in speaking of God's power. **To us-ward who believe.** We can depend on God's power. It is divine, inexhaustible, irresistible, and available. No one need ever complain of insufficient power to meet temptations, to overcome sinful habits, or to live and witness for Christ. Little power is an indisputable evidence of little fellowship with Christ. Paul prays that we may know: the hope to which He calls us, the riches He possesses in us, and the power He extends toward us. **Which he wrought in Christ.** A demonstration of God's omnipotence; putting forth energetically His infinite power. **When he raised him from the dead.** Resurrection power is available to us. The resurrection of Christ is the attestation of God's acceptance of Christ's sacrifice and the pattern and pledge of the believer's resurrection. **And set him at his own right hand.** This refers to the ascension, exaltation, and enthronement of Christ. God's right hand is the place of honor, privilege, and power. The same omnipotence which seated our Lord amid ineffable glory is pledged to seat the church with Him in the same glory.

21-22. Far above all. The primacy of Christ far above all angelic and celestial beings, His sovereign dominion; He is superior to and authoritatively over all. He is "KING OF KINGS, AND LORD OF LORDS" (Rev 19:16). **Head over all things to the church.** The word church (Gr *ekklēsia*) is used over one hundred times in the New Testament and in most cases refers to a local assembly of believers. In Ephesians it is used in a comprehensive sence referring to all the redeemed, the body of Christ. Christ has sovereign authority over the church, and He will rule and reign supreme.

23. Which is his body. Paul states that the relationship between Christ and His church is similar to that between the head and the body of a human organism. The church is a living organism, not a dead organization. The union of Christ and His church is a real, mystical, perfect, and permanent union. The head directs the body's activities. The church is a living expression of Christ; it is the means by which He effects His plan and purpose; it is the agent through which He accomplishes His work. Believers are not only members of His body, they are members one of another in that body (cf. Rom 12:4-5). **The fullness of him that filleth all in all.** Christ is the full expression of God (Col 1:19; 2:9), and the church is the expression of Christ. The church is filled with His presence, animated with His life, and endowed with His gifts. In Christ the church has everything needed to fulfill its mission.

C. The Character of the Church. 2:1-10.

2:1. And you hath he quickened. The mnain verb in Greek does not occur until verse 5. **Who were dead.** Scripture paints man as he really is. Lost men are spiritually dead, notmerely weakened, incapacitated, disabled, or sick. **In trespasses and sins.** Trespasses (Gr *paraptōma*) refer to stepping out of line of true conduct, a deviation from truth and uprightness. Sins (Gr *hamartia*) are missing the mark of life's divine aim, as an archer misses the "bull's eye." These lead to guilt, and man's need of forgiveness; they lead to death, and man's need of new life. This truth is denied in these days. Men speak of "the better self" and "the good spark." Man needs a new heart, not just a new start; a new life, not just turning over a new leaf; a resurrection, not just reformation.

Signing a pledge card will not suffice. No one can live a life for God until he first receives life from God.

2. Wherein in time past. Paul describes the past manifestation of a man devoid of spiritual life. **Ye walked according to the course of this world.** Before conversion, you walked habitually in a wrong path of conduct conforming to the world's low standard of morality, doing what comes naturally. Life was determined by the spirit and practice of the age in its unregenerate state. **According to the prince of the power of the air.** Dominated by the devil, who administers the corrupt power of unholy spirits. The devil is a real person, whose many aliases reveal his true character. **The spirit that now worketh in the children of disobedience.** Satan exerts himself effectively in the society of unregenerate men (Jn 8:44; I Jn 3:8). The conduct of lost men mark them as children of disobedience.

3. Among whom also we all. We Jews, as well as Gentiles. **Our conversation.** (Gr *anastrephō*), Literally, to turn back and forth, hence to live (II Cor 1:12). **Lusts of our flesh.** Dominated by the desires of the fallen, unregenerate nature. **Fulfilling the desires of the flesh.** Following the evil inclinations of the desires of fleshly appetites. **And were by nature the children of wrath.** Worthy of and subject to wrath (Jn 3:36). The only hope for men in this condition is to experience the grace of God in Christ.

4. But God. God alone can meet man's needs. **Who is rich in mercy.** Wealthy in mercy by His very nature. This is much more than being merciful. Instead of dealing with us as deserving wrath and judgment, He deals with us in compassionate mercy. **His great love.** The source of our salvation (Jn 3:16).

5. When we were dead. Spiritually dead and needing new life in Christ (Jn 1:12-13; I Jn 5:11-12). **Quickened us together with Christ.** He made us alive spiritually by imparting the life of Christ in us. This is what is meant by the new birth. "With Christ" refers to resurrection; literal in His case and spiritual in our case. What God did for Christ, He did for all who put their trust in Him. Note that God did it. We were born from above instantly and once for all. God may have used a powerful preacher, a praying parent, or a tearful teacher; but He did it. He did it when we trusted Christ, not because we prayed so earnestly, repented so bitterly, or resolved so thoroughly. Salvation is by grace plus nothing.

6. And hath raised us up together. Christ was raised in a physical resurrection and we in a past spiritual resurrection. On the basis of that, a future physical resurrection or transformation will occur for all living at the time of Rapture. **Made us sit together.** God set us down alongside of Christ in the heavenly realms and relations. God has already accomplished this. He dealt with us in Christ and sees us in Christ.

7. That in the ages to come. The end in view of God's gracious salvation in Christ. **He might show the exceeding riches of his grace.** God delights to show great grace to great sinners. God will display the trophies of His grace throughout the endless ages of eternity. Saints will be concrete demonstrations of the overflowing wealth of His grace.

8. For by grace are ye saved. The grace mentioned in verse 5. Grace is what God does for man, not what man does for God or for himself. Salvation is God's greatest gift and man's greatest need. The Greek perfect tense denotes the certainty of this God-given salvation; we have been saved in the past, and are just as thoroughly saved in the present. We have a perfect salvation. God gives; man receives. **Through faith.** Grace is God's provision; faith is man's appropriation. Faith is not a meritorious act, but the indispensable channel through which man receives God's free gift (Heb

11:6). **And that.** The word "that" (Gr *houtos*) is neuter and does not refer to faith (which is feminine) or to grace (also feminine), but to the fact of being saved by grace on God's part and conditioned on faith on man's part. **Not of yourselves.** Not through your merits or efforts. **It is the gift of God.** The free gift of God.

9. Not of works. Not based upon or produced by the works of man. **Lest any man should boast.** "He that glorieth, let him glory in the Lord" (I Cor 1:31). Calvin sums up Paul's meaning as follows: "In these three phrases,—not of yourselves,—it is the gift of God,—not of works,—he [Paul] embraces the substance of his long argument in the Epistles to the Romans and to the Galatians, that righteousness comes to us from the mercy of God alone,—is offered to us in Christ by the gospel,—and is received by faith alone, without the merit of works" (John Calvin, *Commentaries on the Epistles of Paul to the Galatians and Ephesians*, Trans. William Pringle, p. 228).

10. For we are his workmanship. We are God's poem (Gr *poiēma*), His masterpiece. In the matter of salvation, we are the product of the will and work of God. **Created in Christ Jesus.** The new birth, in living union with Christ. **Unto good works.** For good works, destined to good works. The purpose of the new creation in Christ. Christ in us still goes "about doing good" (Acts 10:38). We are saved apart from good works, but saved unto good works. Good works are the aim of our salvation and the evidence of our faith (Jas 2:17-18). Works never produce salvation, but salvation always produces good works. A man is not justified by works, but a justified man works. Works are the consequences, not the causes of salvation. They are the fruit, not the root of salvation. One must be a Christian before he can live as a Christian; he must be good before he can do good. One must be **created in**

Christ Jesus unto good works before he can walk in them (Phil 1:6; 2:12-13). God is still working. **By grace** (vs. 8), it was Christ for us; **through faith** (vs. 8), it was Christ in us; and **unto good works,** it is Christ through us.

D. The Progress of the Church. 2:11-22.

11. Wherefore remember. Keep constantly in mind the precious truth just stated. **Gentiles.** All peoples who are not born Jews, as they are classified on the flesh basis and called uncircumcision. **Called the Circumcison in the flesh.** The Jews who proudly claim a religious sanction for racial exclusiveness and exaltation, even though the distinction is quite superficial. **Made by hands.** Handmade and limited to the flesh. Paul tactfully points out that the rite once used as a sign for spiritual promises is used now as a mere superficial thing of little or no value.

12. That at that time. Before your salvation experience. **Ye were without Christ.** Paul speaks of the destitution and desolation of the unregenerate, lost and undone. Being Christless we were: without rest (Mt 11:28); without life (Jn 14:6), without light (Jn 8:12); without salvation (Acts 4:12); and without peace (Col 1:20). **Aliens from the commonwealth of Israel.** We were friendless, estranged and separated from Israel and the theocracy of God's chosen people. **Strangers from the covenants of promise.** We were homeless, not having any share in the Messianic promises. God's Word has thousands of promises, but very few apply to the lost. God's promises are exceeding great and precious, but Christless souls see no value in them. **Having no hope.** We were hopeless. We had aspirations for the present, but cherished no hope for the future. Being Christless, we had no faith, no hope, and no love. **And without God.** We were atheists (Gr *atheos*) in the sense of being without God and in hostility to Him. A terrible picture, but a true one. We had

gods many and lords many, but not the true God. We had no knowledge of God and no saving relationship to Him.

13. But now. A strong, glorious contrast to "at that time" of verse 12. **In Christ.** Our new position in union with Him in contrast to being "without Christ" in verse 12. **Are made nigh by the blood of Christ.** This is what God has done. We are made nigh by the blood of Christ; not by becoming a proselyte of Judaism, not by the sincerity of our repentance, not by the strength of our faith, not by the depth of our devotion, not by the joy of our spiritual experience. A new relationship has been established in a new covenant sealed with the sacrificial blood of Christ, who suffered the just for the unjust, that He might bring us to God (I Pet 3:18).

14. For he is our peace. He Himself, not just what He did. He is our peace with God and with each other without distinction. **Who hath made both one.** Jews and Gentiles united in position and in privilege. A new unity has been established where race and national distinctions disappear in Christ (Gal 3:28). **Hath broken down the middle wall of partition.** The dividing wall of racial and religious enmity has been destroyed once for all. In the temple courts a partition wall divided the court of the Gentiles from the court of Israel with an inscription forbidding a Gentile from going further on pain of death (cf. Acts 21:28). No such division exists in the church.

15. Having abolished. This modifies "hath broken down" and means to make ineffective, null and void. **In his flesh.** In His incarnate state. **The enmity.** The old enmity of personal and national prejudice and exclusiveness between Jews and Gentiles was slain at Calvary. Only Christ crucified can effect so great a task as to reconcile and reunite hostile members of the human family. Christ is the world's only hope. **For to make in himself.** There was no other way to accomplish this except by taking two separate and antagonistic groups and making **one new man.** God's purpose is one new people. Christ's body, the church, is the one new man made up of new men (II Cor 5:17). **So making peace.** He is our peace (vs. 14) and our peacemaker (Col 1:20). He puts an end to the hostility between God and man and between man and man.

16. And that he might reconcile. Previously there had been a state of alienation, estrangement, and enmity, but there has been a change of relations both Godward and manward. Christ has harmonized both the factional and the fractional divisions of mankind. **In one body.** The church, Christ's spiritual body. **By the cross.** "God was in Christ, reconciling the world unto himself" (II Cor 5:19). **Having slain the enmity thereby.** God utterly put an end to the enmity that separated men into antagonistic groups.

17. Preached peace. By His vicarious death He procured peace, and by His servants He proclaims peace. Peace was the first word Christ spoke to His disciples in the upper room on the night of His resurrection (Jn 20:19). **To you which were afar off.** Gentiles were far away from God. **To them that were nigh.** Jews were regarded as near, but just as needy and just as dead in sin.

18. For through him. And only through Him. **We both have access.** A continuous, common, and unhindered approach to God. Through Christ all believers can "come boldly unto the throne of grace" (Heb 4:16). **By one Spirit.** Our access to the Father is through the Son and by the Holy Spirit. All three persons of the Trinity share in the total work of salvation.

19. Now therefore. So then, in the light of all this, because all hostility and enmity are past. **Ye are no more strangers.** Sojourners dwelling near by, but not in the family of God. **Foreigners.** Without full rights and privileges of citizenship. **But fellow-citizens.** Having been born into the family of God, with citizenship in heaven (Phil 3:20). **And of the household of God.** Suggests the fellowship enjoyed by members of God's family.

20. And are built. Paul changes the figure of speech from a family to a spiritual temple in setting forth the unifying character of the church. **The foundation of the apostles and prophets.** The eternal foundation of God's purpose as proclaimed by the apostles and prophets. **Jesus Christ himself being the chief corner stone.** Christ is the stone rejected by the Jewish builders but chosen of God as the Head of the corner (Mt 21:42). He is not only the Chief Cornerstone, He is also the foundation. (I Cor 3:11).

21. In whom. In present, precious, and permanent union with Him. **All the building fitly framed together.** An architectural metaphor. God places each one exactly where He wants him. We would be misfits anywhere else. **Groweth unto an holy temple.** The church is a growing temple in the process of construction. It is holy in the sense of being sanctified in Christ for God's glory. **In the Lord.** He is the center of its unity.

22. Ye also. Gentiles are included. **Built together.** The Greek present tense implies continuous and contemporaneous building together with varied materials (I Pet 2:3-7). **For an habitation of God through the Spirit.** The great objective is to provide a place of habitation for God, who by the Spirit dwells permanently in this holy temple (Jn 14:16-17; I Cor 3:16; 6:19-20). In Old Testament times, God dwelt *with* His people; in New Testament times, God dwells *in* His people. Note the work of the Trinity: in Christ all believers are fitted and formed into one building by the Holy Spirit who regenerates and indwells them so that we are a dwelling place for God.

E. The Function of the Church. 3:1-13.

3:1. For this cause. Refers to the preceding exposition of God's elective grace and for the sake of the holy temple of redeemed men which God is building. **Prisoner of Jesus Christ for you Gen-**

tiles. On behalf of you Gentiles whom the Jews are not willing to accept freely.

2. If ye have heard. Since ye have heard with the understanding. **Dispensation.** Paul refers to his high privilege and sacred trust of the administration of stewardship of God's universal grace to all men. This was given to Paul, and not of his own choosing. **Of the grace of God.** The grace of God is to be shared with others; it is not a personal luxury (Col 1:25; I Pet 4:10). Paul was merely a channel of blessing to the Gentiles.

3. How that by revelation he made known unto me the mystery. The mystery was not unintelligent or mysterious, but merely God's secret until He revealed it. It was unknown and unknowable apart from divine revelation. It did not come to Paul by research or by rationalization, but by revelation (Gal 1:11-12).

4. When ye read. This epistle was to be read in public. **My knowledge.** Having this information you are able to comprehend my God-given insight in the mystery of Christ, God's eternal purpose in Christ.

5. In other ages. Preceding generations. **As it is now revealed.** Up until that time, God's revelation was frequent and partial, now it is full and final. Then there were faint gleams of light in types and symbols, now there is a clear and complete revelation. **By the Spirit.** The Holy Spirit is the agent of inspiration and illumination (Jn 14:26; 16:12-15).

6. That the Gentiles. As truly as the Jews and along with them and on the same terms. The Gentiles are not second-class citizens of heaven. Paul gives a clear statement of the mystery. **Fellowheirs.** Because they are in the same body and the same family by regeneration, they are joint-heirs with Christ (Rom 8:17) and co-heirs with the Jews. **Of the same body.** Fellow-members of the same unitary, corporate body the church (2:15). The church is one body with one head. Anything else would be a spiritual monstrosity. In Christ there is perfect amalgamation of

each and every member. **Partakers of his promise.** Gentiles are fellow-partakers and equal sharers of the same promise. **In Christ by the gospel.** The Old Testament is not silent as to blessings for Gentiles, but it says nothing of a union of all believers of every nationality in the Lord Jesus Christ, so as to form one body of which Christ Himself is the glorified Head. It is all made actual by means of the gospel of the grace of God in its marvelous comprehension and its glorious contents.

7. Whereof I was made a minister. A God-appointed minister. **The gift of grace.** It took divine grace to transform Paul from a blasphemer into a saint, from a Pharisee into an apostle, and from a persecutor of Christians into a preacher of Christ. Then it took divine power and authority to enable Paul to function as a minister of God.

8. Less than the least of all saints. Paul's sense of unworthiness is progressive: (1) the least of the apostles (I Cor 15:9); (2) less than the least of all saints (Eph 3:8); and (3) chief of sinners (I Tim 1:15). Paul's high calling humbled him, and he never got over his own unworthiness. He is ever conscious of his demerit and never thinks of himself more highly than he ought to think (Rom 12:3). **The unsearchable riches of Christ.** The contents of message, the wealth beyond description which God provides for all men in the person and work of Christ. It is a vast and measureless resource, this love and grace of God. If Christ were not too big for our mental comprehension, He would be too little for our spiritual need.

9. And to make all men see. This is Paul's purpose in preaching the unsearchable riches of Christ. He would cause all men to see by turning the light on. Paul was aiming at spiritual enlightenment and spiritual apprehension. **Fellowship of the mystery.** The stewardship of worldwide proclamation of Christ and His gospel. **Hid in God.** The mystery of God's eternal plan and purpose had been concealed from the beginning.

10. To the intent. In order that now. **Might be known.** The mystery had been made known to Paul, and now he wants to make it known. Our great mission in this life is to know Christ and to make Him known. **By the church.** Through the church. The church is God's instrument to make known the grace of God in Christ. **The manifold wisdom of God.** The much-variegated and many-sided wisdom of God. This speaks of the beauty and diversity of God's grace.

11. The eternal purpose. God's purpose runs through the ages, not arbitrarily or capriciously, but according to a definite course and consummation, which he projected in Christ Jesus our Lord.

12. In whom we have boldness. Free speech. It speaks of the absence of fear and restraint and the liberty believers enjoy (Heb 4:16). **And access.** This is our approach to God. **With confidence.** Assurance of acceptance (I Jn 5:14-15). **By the faith of him.** Through faith in Him.

13. That ye faint not. Don't lose heart and give in to evil or behave badly. **At my tribulations for you.** In the thought of my afflictions in behalf of you (II Cor 11:23-28). Paul's imprisonment did not mean that the Word of God was bound, that the purpose of God had failed, or that the servant of God was out of the path of duty (Phil 1:12). Opposition and difficulty are not reasons for abandoning a divinely-appointed task. **Which is for your glory.** Even this experience is your glory.

F. The Fullness of the Church.
3:14-21.

14. For this cause. In view of God's plan in Christ and my relation to it. **I bow my knees.** The usual bodily posture in prayer. The position of the body reflects the condition of the soul. Bow in humiliation, in lowly supplication, in special solemnity, and in unusual urgency. **Unto the Father.** The preposition (Gr *pros*) implies face to face communication.

15. The whole family. God has only one family. Some of the members are already in heaven, and others are here on earth representing and interpreting Christ to the world.

16. That. The purpose of Paul's petition. Grant you. Born-again believers. **According to.** Not out of. **The riches of his glory.** God's endowment, His infinite wealth and resources. You can't possibly ask too much. **To be strengthened.** Paul prays that they will be made mightily strong with spiritual power. The nature of this enduement is divine, dynamic power which comes from God. **In the inner man.** In contrast to the outer man (Rom 7:22), the spiritual man as opposed to the fleshly man. **By his Spirit.** This dynamic power is communicated to us by the Holy Spirit. He is our dynamo, our powerhouse. He resides in us and works through us.

17. That Christ may dwell in your hearts. Christ should be enthroned; He must have first place. It is God's purpose that He dwell in our hearts personally, permanently, and powerfully (2:22). Christ is not a guest or an occasional visitor; He is the rightful owner and lives here (Gal 2:20). **By faith.** Faith is the medium of appropriating Christ. Faith opens the door and receives Him. In some Christ is just present, in others He is prominent, and in still others He is preeminent. **Rooted.** Established and settled securely in the love of Christ. Rooted like a tree growing strong and massive. **And grounded.** Deeply and firmly founded, like a building rising higher and larger.

18. May be able to comprehend. May be strong to comprehend, lay hold of effectually spiritual enlightenment. **With all saints.** This is not an isolated privilege. Each one comprehends a little; all together we fathom the unfathomable. Our comprehension is partial and progressive. **What is the breadth, and length, and depth, and height.** The love of Christ is immeasurable. The breadth extends to all people; its length extends to all time; its depth extends to the lowest condition of human need; and its height extends to the highest heavens. Truly Christ is "able also to save them to the uttermost that come unto God by him" (Heb 7:25).

19. And to know by experience the unknowable, the love of Christ in all its dimensions mentioned above. The love of Christ is knowledge-transcending. **That ye may be filled with all the fullness of God.** Filled with His presence and power, the fullness which God imparts.

20. Now unto him. This ascription of praise to God's ability expresses our assurance of answered prayer. Why should we hesitate to offer our deepest petitions? Note the expressive and exhaustive language. **Is able.** The strength of our confidence is the fact that He is vastly able above and beyond all that we might ask. **To do exceeding abundantly.** Superabundantly, overwhelming, over and above, more than enough. David said, "my cup runneth over" (Ps 23:5), and we can say, "He brought me to the banqueting house, and his banner over me was love" (Song 2:4). **That we ask or think.** Our highest aspirations are not beyond God's power to grant. **According to the power that worketh in us.** This is that omnipotence that raised Christ from the dead and quickened us when we were dead in sins.

21. Unto him be glory in the church by Christ Jesus. Christ and His church constitute one living organism. The church is His body, and He is the Head of that one body. **Throughout all ages.** The duration of our praise and thanksgiving. **Amen.** Paul sealed the doxology with "Amen."

III. THE CONDUCT OF THE CHURCH. 4:1-6:9.

A. The Undivided Conduct of the Church. 4:1-16.

4:1. Therefore. In view of grace revealed, new life imparted, and your high and heavenly calling. **The prisoner of the Lord.** Paul was not seeking sympathy, but declaring his acceptance of his circumstances. He was a prisoner because of his relationship to Christ, his faithfulness to Christ, and his service for Christ. **Walk worthy.** Walk indicates activity and advance step by step. Paul is beseeching the saints to order lives in a worthy manner. **Of the vocation wherewith ye are called.** A vocation (Gr *klēsis*) is a calling or life's work. It behooves Christians to walk worthy of the source, the substance, and the sequence of their high and holy calling of God in Christ. Christians are called to live for Christ (Phil 1:21) and to walk "even as he walked" (I Jn 2:6).

2. With all lowliness. Your high calling should not lead to pride or self-exaltation, but on the contrary to all lowliness of mind and modest opinion of yourself. This means unfailing humility, an utter lack of self-assertiveness, and a deep sense of unworthiness, in every experience and in every relationship. **And meekness.** This is not timidity, cowardice, or servile fear, but self-suppression for the purpose of serving others. It is the spirit that never takes offense and which manifests itself in submission to God's will and gentleness toward men. **With longsuffering.** This is the opposite to short-tempered. The old nature is so quick to take offense that we need longer fuses. The new life in Christ enables one to endure with unruffled temper any wrong suffered without retaliation and to turn the other cheek (I Pet 2:21-23). **Forbearing one another.** Forbearance is restraint under just provocation with a liberal allowance for the faults and failures of others. It is that mutual and enduring putting up with one another, and making allowances for one another (Col 3:13). **In love.** Love beareth all things and endureth all things (I Cor 13:7).

3. Endeavouring. This means to give diligence to do your best in persistent effort, fixed determination, and heroic perseverance. It combines the ideas of haste, eagerness, and zeal. **To keep.** Not produce; it already exists as a reality. **The unity of the Spirit.** Not external, ecclesiastical union, but internal, spiritual unity (Jn 17:21-23). Such unity cannot be legislated or produced by the mechanics of an organization. It is produced and maintained by the Holy Spirit. **In the bond of peace.** Peace with God and with one another is the unifying bond that holds all together.

4. There is one body. The church is a living organism composed only of living members, i.e. blood-bought, born-again, Bible-believing saints. This one body has one head and many members (I Cor 12:12-13). **One Spirit.** The Holy Spirit who is the life and breath of that body, who was instrumental in the regeneration of each member, and who now maintains a vital connection of each member with the other members and with the head. **One hope of your calling.** The same ultimate, glorious reality for both Jews and Gentiles.

5. One Lord. The Lord Jesus Christ, not a series of aeons. "If He is not Lord of all, He is not Lord at all." **One faith.** Not a creed, but a commitment to Christ. One saving experience of trust in Christ, one way of salvation (Rom 10:9-10). **One baptism.** One result of baptizing (Gr *baptisma*), not the act of baptizing (Gr *baptismos*). Scriptural baptism is the outward expression of an inward experience; a public confession of Christ. Men are not made disciples by baptism, but merely profess to be disciples. Water baptism presupposes and pictures the baptism of the Holy Spirit (I Cor 12:12-13). The one baptism is the expression of the one faith in the one Lord which resulted in the baptism of the one Spirit into the one body.

6. One God and Father of all. For all; not a separate God for each nation. **Who is above all.** This speaks of His transcendence and His unshared sovereign power. **And through all.** This speaks of His immanence, His pervading action. **And in you all.** This speaks of His indwelling presence of believers, His personal relationship. The one God rules over all, works through all, and dwells in all.

7. But unto every one of us is given grace. Each member of the body receives from the Sovereign Lord his own integral value, place, responsibility, opportunity, and duty. No one should be idle for each one has a place to fill, which no one else can fill. **According to the . . . gift of Christ.** There is a wide variety of gifts. Each Christian has some gift; no one has all the gifts; and not all have the same gifts. These gifts are not just natural endowments, but specific graces and capacities for service. Since God deems these gifts important, man should not despise them. We should be content with our own gifts and not envy or look down on the gifts of others.

8. Wherefore. Because the living Lord distributes His grace by sovereign love to each member of the body and thus makes them fit to be His gifts for service to men. **When he ascended up on high.** This is a quotation from Psalm 68:18, a Messianic psalm of victory in which God is praised for deliverance. **He led captivity captive.** The inferences drawn from the triumphal return of the King are: (1) the thought of victory; and (2) the bestowal of gifts. The captives are most probably the Old Testament saints in sheol (hades).

9. Ascended . . . descended. Christ's ascension back to heaven after accomplishing the purpose of His incarnation. **The lower parts of the earth.** Probably hades (Mt 12:40; Acts 2:25-35; II Cor 12:2-4).

10. That he might fill all things. The purpose and plan of Christ is to fill all with His presence and His Spirit.

11. He gave. He gave gifts to men, and He gave gifted men to the church, in which and through which they function. **Apostles.** The official title of the Twelve, including Paul. This was a temporary office. Nowhere does God's Word teach apostolic succession. To the contrary, God's Word indicts those who lay claim to the title of apostle as deceivers (Rev 2:2). **Prophets.** These men were both foretellers and forthtellers. They received their message from

God and delivered it for God and to man. They had deep insight into spiritual truths as they interpreted God's message under the power of the Holy Spirit. **Evangelists.** These were the itinerant missionaries who preached the gospel to the unconverted in new areas (Acts 21:8; II Tim 4:5). **Pastors and teachers.** This refers to one office with two functions, i.e. teaching pastors. The word "pastor" is used by Christ referring to Peter (Jn 21:16); by Peter referring to ministers (I Pet 5:2); and by Paul referring to elders (bishops) of Ephesus (Acts 20:28). They were to shepherd the sheep and train the saints.

12. For the perfecting of the saints. With a view to the equipping them for service. The purpose of Christ's gifts is not making saints sinlessly perfect, but of completely outfitting them to be vessels unto honor, sanctified and meet for the Master's use (II Tim 2:21). **For the work of the ministry.** Unto spiritual service. Not doing their work for them, but preparing them for their work. D. L. Moody said, "It is better to put ten men to work than to do the work of ten men." The church is not a spiritual rest home, but a barracks for training soldiers of the cross. **For the edifying of the body of Christ.** With the end in view of building up spiritually the whole body of Christ. Our Lord is interested in quantity, but He is more concerned about quality. All the saints are to be equipped for the work of edification and then be engaged in work of edification.

13. Till we all come in the unity of the faith. This has reference to the whole body of Christ. We should not neglect anyone. The goal is that we attain unity, not uniformity; and our essential work is far from being accomplished. **And of the knowledge of the Son of God.** Paul speaks of true, accurate, and full knowledge which enables saints to cooperate with one another in working out God's plan and purpose. **Unto a perfect man.** As long as our faith in Christ is imperfect and our knowledge of

we cannot be full-grown, mature Christians. **Unto the measure of the stature of the fulness of Christ.** No under-shepherd has finished his work while the sheep fall short of this goal, a full-grown man in Christ. This fullness, this Christlikeness, is that which belongs to Christ and that which is imparted by Christ. God predestined His saints "to be conformed to the image of His Son" (Rom 8:29). It would be wise for all of us to cry out with John, "He must increase, but I must decrease" (Jn 3:30). As long as we have a factious, contentious, immature church, we will not make much headway in evangelizing the world.

14. That we henceforth be no more children. In this verse Paul sets forth the negative results of spiritual unity and maturity. God desires that we be stalwart Christians with doctrinal stability, spiritual perception, responsibility, and direction toward the goal. Too many are content to remain in weakness and immaturity, spiritual infancy. **Tossed to and fro.** Cast about as driftwood on the waves of the sea. This is a picture of instability, helplessness, and restlessness. **Carried about with every wind of doctrine.** Christians should not be whirled around in circles by every shifting wind of false doctrine. If not anchored in Christ, Christians are at the mercy of these ever changing winds which blow unstable souls in every direction. **By the sleight of men.** By the deceit and dishonesty of the religious quacks. The word (Gr. *kubeia*) means "dice-throwing," and the dice are loaded. **And cunning craftiness.** These unscrupulous, scheming frauds stop at nothing to ensnare fickle souls by their clever deceit and treacherous trickery. **Whereby they lie in wait to deceive.** By deliberate planning and scheming deceit, they wrest, twist, and pervert the Word of God (Acts 13:10; Gal 1:7; II Pet 3:16). The Christian's only hope is to "search the scriptures daily, whether those things were so" (Acts 17:11).

15. But speaking the truth in love. Paul now turns to the positive results of spiritual unity and maturity. The truth should always be spoken in love without any tricks or gimmicks. **May grow up into him in all things, which is the head, even Christ.** Ever growing up in all ways, in all respects, and in fellowship with Him and with each other.

16. From whom the whole body. Christ is the source and sustainer of the body. **Fitly joined together.** Harmoniously and closely fitted together, with no one out of place, and with each one contributing his share for the good of the whole body. **And compacted.** Firm and solid adhesion to Christ and to other Christians. **Maketh increase of the body.** When all the members of the body perform faithfully their several functions, it results in the growth and maturity of the whole body. The church is a living organism united to Christ and indwelt by the Holy Spirit so that every member helps and is helped, strengthens and is strengthened, whereby the whole body grows and "increaseth with the increase of God" (Col 2:19). The result is a unified and an edified church.

B. The Unblemished Conduct of the Church. 4:17-5:16.

17. This I say therefore. Paul bears his testimony as to the Christian calling and conduct. **In the Lord.** Speaking in His name as His servant and clothed with divine authority as His apostle. **That ye henceforth walk not as other Gentiles.** Let the daily conduct of your lives conform with your new life in Christ. Make a clean break with your old life and stop living by the standards of behavior of the pagan people. The low standards of the world must be abandoned and repudiated, and the Christian must live ethically and morally in segregation from the world (II Cor 6:14). The church is a colony of heaven living here on earth. **In the vanity of their minds.** Their intellect is empty of truth and filled with false de-lusions and things that lead to nothing. This implies: aimlessness, uselessness, and futility.

18. Having the understanding darkened. Their beclouded intellect and their emotions have been darkened permanently so that they are without the faculty of discernment and are unable to distinguish clearly between right and wrong. **Being alienated from the life of God.** Having alienated themselves completely, they are held in the grips of spiritual death. The cause of their alienation is twofold. **Through the ignorance that is in them.** They were born in moral, ethical, and spiritual stupidity. **Because of the blindness of their heart** (Gr *pōrōsis*). Literally "hardness," covered with a callus (Mk 3:5; Rom 11:25). The heart lost its capacity to feel, and they became insensible, indifferent, and unresponsive to all moral principles and practices.

19. Who being past feeling. Insensible to moral and spiritual impressions and to the appeal of truth. Conscience is not functioning, and there is no hatred of sin and no love for Christ. **Have given themselves over unto lasciviousness.** They abandoned and delivered themselves over once for all to moral degradation, unbridled lusts, excessive immortality, and dissipating debauchery, with no sense of shame or decency and with scorn for all moral restraint. **To work all uncleanness.** Committing themselves to active indulgence in every form of impurity, outrageous sensuality, indecency, and lewd conduct, such that shocks the public. **With greediness.** With insatiable desires to have more, with no regard for the person or property of others. He gets what he wants no matter whom he hurts and no matter what methods he uses.

20. But ye have not so learned Christ. In sharp contrast to the pagan life. Christ teaches men to renounce sin and vice and to cultivate holiness and virtue.

21. If so be that ye have heard him. Since you did hear. **Have been taught by him.** Instructed as to the standards, meaning, and behavior of Christian living. **As the truth is in Jesus.** Embodied in Him and exemplified in His character and conduct, as He lived the truth on the plane of human experience.

22. That ye put off concerning the former conversation the old man. Put off definitely, deliberately, quickly, and permanently once for all the old man as a filthy and repulsive garment. The old man is the unregenerated self, a slave to sin, and headed for judgment. It is the old "I" that has been crucified with Christ (Gal 2:20) and must be so reckoned (Rom 6:9-14). **Which is corrupt according to the deceitful lusts.** The old man is decaying day by day, like a decomposing corpse, and inevitably grows more and more corrupt. The old man is not renewed (Jn 3:6); he must be denounced and replaced.

23. And be renewed. The Greek present tense means continual and progressive renewal. This is the antithesis of the growing corruptness of the old man. **In the spirit of your mind.** That attitude and disposition which determines behavior and conduct. Being renewed with spiritual food, constantly and continually grasping and appropriating new truth.

24. And . . . put on the new man. Clothe yourself once for all. The old man is stripped off and the new man is put on. These two acts are inseparable. The new man is the new life we receive in Christ (II Cor 5:17; Gal 6:17; Col 3:10). **Which after God is created in righteousness and true holiness.** This is not the reformation or renovation of the old man; this is the product of the new birth and results in a new creation. The new man is created after God and in the family likeness of God. The brand new man is known by the Christlikeness exhibited day by day in living out the new life. Righteousness refers to his new conduct toward his fellowmen. Holiness refers to his new conduct towards God. These two are the essential qualities and the evidence of the new man in Christ.

25. Wherefore putting away lying. Paul now describes the old, obsolete, filthy rags of the old man which are to be discarded. Lying is to be put away definitely and deliberately. The Greek middle voice indicates that you will personally receive some benefit from this action. Lying speaks of everything false: deception of every kind, dishonesty in personal relations, unscrupulous practices in public relations, and corruption in the government. **Speak every man truth with his neighbor.** Speaking the truth habitually is the only intelligent and consistent way to deal with our neighbors, or those who are members of the body and of one another, where deceit and dishonesty in any form is unthinkable. We must guard our tongue.

26. Be ye angry, and sin not. This is a permissive imperative, rather than a direct command to be angry. There is a righteous indignation which is not sin (Mk 3:5), but "the wrath of man worketh not the righteousness of God" (Jas 1:20). Do not go on being angry and let it not take root in your heart and degenerate into wrath. **Let not the sun go down upon your wrath.** There is a grave danger in cherished, prolonged anger. We must get cooled off quickly and maintain such control and restraint of our temper that we make a Christlike adjustment to the irritating circumstances.

27. Neither give place to the devil. Satan waits for opportunity to get his foot in the door. The Greek present imperative means: Do not have the habit of giving place to Satan. Uncontrolled anger is an open door and an invitation for Satan to enter in to disrupt and corrupt the body. He can only hurt and harm as he finds a place in some life to do his evil work.

28. Let him that stole steal no more. Let the one who has the habit of stealing stop stealing. There is no place for dishonesty in Christian dealings. **But rather let him labor.** Let him adopt the higher Christian standard and ideals of manly independence and brotherly helpfulness. Let him toil honestly rather than subsist by the labor of others. Instead of robbing others, let him bring forth fruits fit for repentance. **The thing which is good.** As opposed to stealing, honest work is rich and rewarding. **That he may have to give to him that needeth.** That he may accumulate and contribute to the needy.

29. Let no corrupt communication proceed out of your mouth. Corrupt speech comes from a corrupt heart, and pure speech comes from a pure heart. Corrupt speech is like rotten fruit (Mt 7:16-20) or a fish (Mt 13:48) and tainted with moral decay. Corrupt speech will contaminate the thoughts of others. **But that which is good to the use of edifying.** Our speech should be suitable to building up where the need for constructive help exists. We must watch our words (Ps 141:3) and be careful that our speech is "always with grace, seasoned with salt" (Col 4:6). **That it may minister grace unto the hearers.** Our speech should impart a blessing, not a blight. If a rotten word is found in the mind, shut it off at the mouth.

30. And grieve not the holy Spirit of God. The Holy Spirit is a very sensitive person. Paul says stop having the habit of offending the Holy Spirit by rebellious deeds and grievous words (vss. 25-31). **Whereby ye are sealed unto the day of redemption.** Sealed with God's stamp, marking you as God's purchased possession and destined unto the day of complete redemption, when final redemption is realized and we are transformed into His likeness (Phil 3:20-21; I Jn 3:2).

31. Let all bitterness. Let every form of irritability, every inward resentful disposition against others, and hardness of spirit be put away from everyone of you. **And wrath.** This is the rapid boiling up and furious outburst of temper into passionate expression. **And anger.** Anger is the settled disposition of indignation. **And clamor.** Clamor is the loud, railing outburst in a storm of anger. **And evil speaking.** This is the reviling, deliberate insult with abusive words. **With all**

malice. This refers to a vicious disposition of character. Each of these vices is to be put away once and for all. God wants us to make a clean sweep of these unchristian characteristics.

32. Be ye kind. Paul summarized Christian character. Keep on becoming kind towards one another—well disposed, useful, benevolent, gracious and gentle mannered, as opposed to being harsh, hard, bitter, and sharp. The person who is kind is full of benign courtesy, is distinguished by gracious deeds, and is desirous of promoting common interests and conferring reciprocal obligations. This kindness is the outward expression of love in the heart and applies to all contacts and situations. **Tender hearted.** Merciful, compassionate, pitiful. There is a willingness to be understanding of and patient with the faults and failures of others, ready to put kindness into action. **Forgiving one another.** The word "forgive" (Gr *charizomai*) is built on the same root as the word "grace" and means to bestow favor unconditionally. This means that a Christian will always treat the offending party graciously, letting the wrong go without any claim for punishment or reparation. It means pardoning the guilty person instead of displaying resentment or exercising retaliation. Forgiveness is not probation, i.e. merely suspending the sentence under supervision and specific conditions. Forgiveness is not a reprieve, i.e. temporarily postponing the punishment. Forgiveness results in complete reconciliation and restored fellowship. **Even as God for Christ's sake hath forgiven you.** We are to forgive others just as God forgave us. We are to exhibit the life of Christ in and through us, thus giving evidence of having been made partakers of the divine nature (II Pet 1:4). God's forgiveness is the model, the motive, and the measure of our forgiving others. God's forgiveness is free, full, and final. When God forgives, He forgets; so must we.

5:1. Be ye therefore followers of God. Keep on becoming, in your daily conduct, imitators of God, demonstrating the family likeness. Christ is our example in holiness of life, purity of thought, and cleanness of speech. **As dear children.** Beloved children. Paul is describing the walk of heavenly pilgrims. Imitating God is the result of our acceptance in Christ, not its means.

2. And walk in love, as Christ also hath loved us. The distinguishing marks of the Christlike love are forgiveness (4:32) and sacrifice. Our Lord's sacrifice involved death that was voluntary (Jn 10:17-18), vicarious (I Cor 15:3), and victorious (Rom 4:25). Christ's death was a satisfactory sacrifice to God, not to Satan (Anselm), on behalf of us (Rom 5:8). Love is the Christian standard for daily conduct. The Christlike love denies self, takes up the cross daily, and follows Him (Lk 9:23). **For a sweetsmelling savor.** An analogy of the sacrifices by which Israel was made acceptable to God and is a symbol of restored peaceful relations between God and man.

3. But fornication. A perilous, prevalent, perverse sin, which is lightly regarded by many and committed without scruples and without shame. It is illicit sexual intercourse between unmarried partners, similar to, but not identical with, adultery (Mt 5:32; 15:19; Mk 7:21). **And all uncleanness.** Every form of impurity, immorality, and lasciviousness. **Covetousness.** Desiring to possess that which belongs to another; inordinate desire for gain. Here it includes insatiable lusts and sexual greed directed toward the ruin of another's purity. **Let it not be once named among you, as becometh saints.** These sins must be dreaded and detested. Christians are saints and are to live like saints. They are separated unto God, and therefore separated from sin. These sins are not to be mentioned, much less permitted. Such terms taint the imagination, soil the lips, and cultivate sensual lusts. Such conversation is unbecoming saints and incompatible with Christianity.

4. Neither filthiness. Neither implies that the same rule applies as in verse 3.

This means shameful speech, indecent talk, filthy stories, and obscenity as opposed to purity. **Nor foolish talking.** Senseless "fool-talk," silly speech, coarse vulgarity, evil-minded chatter, idle gossip. It is all godless discourse which is wretched in itself and offensive for Christian decency. **Nor jesting.** Quickness in making repartee in a profligate sense, ribaldry, scurrility, buffoonery, levity, making light of sin. **Which are not convenient.** Not compatible with Christianity, beneath a Christian, unbecoming, out of place, not suitable. **But rather giving of thanks.** This is excellent employment for redeemed tongues, and it is a positive virtue which supplants and inhibits these vices.

5. For this ye know. Keep this constantly in mind. **No whoremonger.** Every fornicator without exception, either the one who submits to it, or the one who perpetrates it. **Nor unclean person.** The impure one. **Nor covetous man.** The man of insatiable passion and sensual greed. **Who is an idolater.** Sex idolater, dreadful and debase. **Inheritance in the kingdom of Christ and of God.** All these are excluded from having any share in the kingdom of Christ. An inheritance requires the certitude in character and conduct of the heir as a member of the family of God, and these prove their unfitness by their lifestyle. It is possible for such sinners to be delivered from the power of darkness and to be translated into the kingdom (I Cor 6:9-11; Col 1:12-13).

6. Let no man deceive you. Stop (Greek present imperative) letting a false teacher lead you astray as to the character and consequences of the sins just mentioned. These sins have their apologists: some condone them as innocent pleasure; others excuse them as weakness; still others say this teaching is puritanical and a relic of outmoded standards. **With vain words.** Hollow words, void of truth, empty, speculative, and misleading arguments. For example, Satan said, "Ye shall not surely die" (Gen 3:4). But God, who is righteous, said, "The wages of sin is death" (Rom 6:23). **Because of these things cometh the wrath of God upon the children of disobedience.** The wrath of God is real (Acts 17:30-31) and it is coming. The Greek present tense implies its certainty and its imminence. The children of disobedience are those who in selfish and fleshly abandon are so ready to disobey all moral and religious restraints.

7. Be not ye therefore partakers with them. Stop becoming partakers with them. This is a strong warning against lapsing into these sins. Paul is saying not to get involved in these sins. "If you don't want to do business with the devil, keep out of his shop." Don't become a partaker in the sin, the shame, and the eternal separation from God.

8. For ye were sometimes darkness. In time past, you were so gripped in the ways of moral darkness as to be part of it; not merely in the dark, but part of it. You were so ignorant of God's Word and will and so identified with evil, that you were the very embodiment of darkness. **But now ye are light in the Lord.** At present, you are in union with Him who is the Light of the world (Jn 8:12), and you are light. The Christian is not merely enlightened, he is the light of the world (Mt 5:14-16). Christ has shined in that we might shine out (II Cor 4:6). **Walk as children of light.** It does not say to walk in the light, but as children of light. We are to walk as possessed by the Light and radiating the Light.

9. For the fruit of the Spirit. The spiritual product of walking as light (cf. Gal 5:22). **Goodness.** Moral excellence, benevolence in thought, word, and deed. **Righteousness.** Moral rectitude, integrity and rightness as God sees it and in relation to man. **Truth.** Moral reality, honesty, sincerity, and straightforwardness, as opposed to all that is false.

10. Proving what is acceptable unto the Lord. Constantly learning by discrimination and putting to the test to prove what is well-pleasing to the Lord.

11. Have no fellowship with the unfruitful works of darkness. The Greek present imperative means stop having joint-participation with the barren works of darkness. These works yield no profit and no reward. They do produce bitterness, pain, and disgrace. Darkness suggests action and habits characteristic to a life of sin. **But rather reprove them.** Not just abstain, but expose them by a consistent life. We are to express our disapproval by word and action, by the light of right living and loving example, thus attracting them from the destruction of darkness to the light of salvation in Christ (Jn 3:19-20).

12. For it is a shame. It is degrading and disgraceful, because these practices are vile and corrupt. **Done of them in secret.** Men hide such things because they love the darkness.

13. Made manifest by the light. The character, the course, and the consequences of sin are made clear and tested by the light.

14. Awake thou that sleepest. This is a call from drowsiness to spiritual life. **Arise from the dead.** Stand up from the dead among you. **Christ shall give thee light.** Make day dawn upon you.

15. See then. Take heed by. Looking around thoughtfully and prayerfully, by giving attention to circumstances and consequences, by guarding against everything improper and unbecoming for a Christian. Keep a sharp lookout for those things that would cause you or a brother to stumble. **Walk circumspectly.** This denotes that exact accuracy which is the result of diligent carefulness. **Not as fools.** Men lacking wisdom. **But as wise.** Sensibly and thoughtfully. We need to be careful and prayerful that we do not walk in perilous places, in the pitfalls of perdition, and in the snares of Satan.

16. Redeeming the time. Buy up the opportunity. The Greek present tense denotes keep on buying. There is a price to be paid or we will forgo the bargain. The price is self-denial and strenuous work. There is also opportunity, i.e. to serve the Lord, to witness for Christ, to be a channel of blessing, and to advance the cause of Christ. We must recognize the opportunity, appreciate it, and take hold of it for God's glory. **Because the days are evil.** There are many obstacles in the way, much opposition to God, and much corruption in the world. The days are full of difficulty, danger, darkness, and death. We dare not lose one opportunity by letting things drift aimlessly and carelessly.

C. The Unblamable Conduct of the Church. 5:17-6:9.

17. Be ye not unwise. Stop becoming foolish, senseless, without intelligence, and lacking in wisdom; and start exercising good judgment and reason. **But understanding.** Divinely enlightened by prayer and meditation. **What the will of the Lord is.** Be a Bible Christian; give God's Word the place it deserves, then you will understand what He wants you to be and do. The entrance of God's Word gives light (Ps 119:130). God's will is revealed in God's Word. Our first concern is God's will; it is not what is most profitable, what is most pleasurable, or what is most honorable.

18. And be not drunk with wine. Stop the habit of getting drunk. **Wherein is excess.** Drunkenness leads to riot and ruin. It corrupts character, debauches life, brooks no restraint, defies efforts to reform it, and sinks its victim lower and lower into helplessness and hopelessness. **But.** A strong contrast from the physical to the spiritual, from the debasing to the ennobling. In days of drab routine, disappointment, and depression, men need stimulation and inspiration. The Christian's resource is the Holy Spirit. **Be filled with the Spirit.** Although all Christians have been baptized by the Spirit at salvation, all Christians are not filled with the Spirit, which is their heritage. The fullness of the Holy Spirit was the normal experience of the early Christians. The natural man has not the Spirit (Jude 19; Rom 8:9); the carnal man has the Spirit, but lives by the power and dictates of the flesh; the spiritual man has the Spirit, and the Spirit has

him, and he lives by the power and dictates of the Holy Spirit. The very translated "be filled" (Gr *pleroō*) is full of meaning. The second person plural means "you all," everyone without exception. It is in the imperative mood, which means it is a positive command, a distinct duty. Just as surely as God commanded all men everywhere to repent (Acts 17:30), so He has commanded every born-again believer to be filled with the Spirit. This verb is in the Greek present tense and means keep on being filled moment by moment. God speaks of an abiding reality; yesterday's filling will not do for today. The early Christians were repeatedly filled with the Spirit. This verb is in the passive voice, the voice that presents the subject as receiving the action, rather than doing the action. The filling is what God does. When we are willing to let the Holy Spirit saturate us He will pervade our entire being with His presence and with His power. The filling is not a question of having more of the Holy Spirit, but a question of the Holy Spirit having all of us. Our only choice is to obey or to disobey this divine direction.

19. Making melody. Playing by means of an instrument. This word means to make or let a string twang and signifies to play an instrument as an accompaniment to the voice. **In your heart to the Lord.** Not merely with the lips and the fingers for man, but with the heart for the glory of the Lord.

20. Giving thanks always for all things. See Philippians 4:6. **In the name of our Lord Jesus Christ.** Jesus taught His disciples to use His name in prayer.

21. Submitting yourselves one to another. The way to have happy harmony. This submission is reciprocal, mutual, voluntary, and personal. It is opposed to rudeness, haughtiness, and selfish preference of one's own opinions.

22. Wives, submit yourselves unto your own husbands, as unto the Lord. The duty and manner of submission. The Christian home is a symbol of Christianity, and should be a "little bit of heaven" on earth. The word submit (Gr *hypotassō*) is an old military figure to line up under (Col 3:18) and means to subject yourselves in line in a specialized way. Christian wives will be ordering their lives in proper subjection to their own husbands as required in this relation in the Lord, for subjection to the Lord includes loyal living in the home. Submission is not slavish fear, neither is it forced upon her by a demanding domestic despot, but it is voluntary. There is no hint of inferiority, but a matter of authority and responsibility in the home. Husbands and wives are parts of a unit. The question arises, what if the husband is not a born-again believer? The Word of God gives definite instructions covering such a case (I Pet 3:1-7).

23. For the husband is the head of the wife. The reason of submission. Authority and government are lodged in the husband. The home has its center and unity in the husband. The truest unity is conjugal duality. **Even as Christ is the head of the church.** Headship in a living union where Christ and His church become one. **And he is the saviour of the body.** No husband can ever be savior, but he represents Christ symbolically as good provider and protector.

24. As . . . so. This description of the submissive obedience of wives is clear, concise, complete, and correct.

25. Husbands, love your wives. The plain duty of husbands is now set forth. Husbands are to love their wives, not treat them as inferior subjects. Such love will lift a husband out of a state of arbitrary self-indulgence and capricious self-satisfaction. **Even as Christ also loved the church.** Christ is the husband's ideal example. The measure of Christ's love for the church is to be the measure of the husband's love for his wife. Husbands owe their wives the same kind of love and loyalty as Christ has for His bride; supreme, self-forgetting, self-sacrificing love. In the economy of the family and after the manner of Christ, husbands are to reign in love. The church

is called the body of Christ (1:22-23). **Gave himself for it.** The measure and manifestation of Christ's love for the church. Christ gave Himself both in life and in death on behalf of the church.

26. That he might sanctify. The purpose of His death is set forth in the words sanctify, cleanse, and present. Sanctify means to consecrate, set apart for sacred service. **And cleanse.** The tense of this participle indicates antecedent action to sanctify. First there was the cleansing and then the sanctifying. **With the washing of water by the word.** The washing of water refers to "the washing of regeneration" (I Cor 6:11; Tit 3:5). **By the word.** God the Holy Spirit uses the Word of God to accomplish God's purpose in redemption (Ps 119:9; Jn 15:3; 17:17; I Pet 1:23).

27. That he might present it to himself a glorious church. He Himself as loving, saving, and sanctifying Lord. The Bridegroom presents His bride to Himself. It will then be a glorious church arrayed in glory, with nothing to mar her beauty. **Not having spot, or wrinkle, or any such thing.** In perfect purity. Spots are from without, wrinkles from within. "The world about the church causes the stains, the flesh still in her causes the wrinkles" (R. C. H. Lenski, *The Interpretation of Saint Paul's Epistles to the Galatians, to the Ephesians, and to the Philippians,* p. 635). **But that it should be holy.** Morally pure and wholly consecrated. **Without blemish.** Immaculate, just like the Heavenly Bridegroom.

28. So ought men to love their wives. In the same manner and same measure as Christ loved the church, assumed all responsibility for her, and spared nothing that contributes toward His purpose for her. Husbands are under similar obligations to devote themselves, all they are and have, to their own (individual) wives. **As their own bodies.** Treat them as constituting their own personal bodies. The two have become one in marriage. **He that loveth his wife loveth himself.** For he is completed and perfected in her, with whom he has become one flesh (Mk 10:8).

29. Nourisheth. That it may develop to maturity. **Cherisheth.** To foster with tender care, concern, and comfort. The best and highest interest of the husband is to recognize his complete identity with his wife.

30. For we are members of his body. Consequently we should understand and adopt His principle in our relationships with each other within His church (Rom 12:4-5; I Cor 12:12-27).

31. For this cause shall a man leave his father and mother. In response to this divinely given ideal. **And shall be joined unto his wife.** Once for all glued to his wife. Marriage is a picture of the union of Christ and His church. Paul insists on the sanctity of the family and treats marriage as an inseparable union between a husband and wife. **And they two shall be one flesh.** One unit of flesh by assimilation (Gen 2:24; Mk 10:2-12). God is insisting that both husband and wife joined in perfect union live up to the standard of Christ and His church. They are joined together in body, soul, and spirit and should be set apart to each other in a holy union of sinless human relationship.

32. Great mystery. This holy secret revealed in the Word of God is great. The comparison of the marriage union with the union of Christ and His church is the mystery.

33. Nevertheless let every one of you in particular so love his wife. Husbands measure up to the ideal of Christ in His love for the church. **And the wife see that she reverence her husband.** Wives measure up to the church in its devotion to Christ.

6:1. Children. We come to the duties of children and parents. **Obey your parents.** The word (Gr *hypakouō*) means to hear as under another with listening and attentive ears, to give obedient heed. This duty has been recognized among all people, in all lands, and in all ages. The neglect of this duty is lamented. Disobedience to parents is a sin (Rom 1:30; II

Tim 3:2). **In the Lord.** God commands it. It is a Christian duty for children to obey their parents promptly, habitually, and cheerfully. **For this is right.** It is a moral duty, not merely becoming or an accepted custom (Col 3:20).

2. Honor thy father and mother. Honor is the attitude of love, respect, and disposition of heart that produces obedience. **First commandment with promise.** The second commandment has a general promise, but the fifth has a specific promise (Ex 20:12; Deut 5:16).

3. That it may be well with thee. Both temporal and spiritual prosperity.

4. And, ye fathers. Mothers are included in this exhortation. **Provoke not your children to wrath.** The word provoke means do not irritate, exasperate, rub the wrong way, incite. This is done by a wrong spirit and by wrong methods, i.e. severity, unreasonableness, sternness, harshness, cruel demands, needless restrictions, and selfish insistence upon authority. Such provocation would produce adverse reactions, deaden his affection, check his desire for holiness, and make him feel that he can't possibly please his parents. A wise parent seeks to make obedience desirable and attainable by love and gentleness. Parents must not be godless tyrants. Luther said, "Keep an apple beside the rod to give the child when he does well." **But bring them up in the nurture.** Discipline in general education and culture must be exercised with watchful care and constant training. **And admonition.** Chastening, disciplining, and counsel by the Word of God, giving both reproof and encouragement whenever needed. **Of the Lord.** Proceeding from the Lord, learned in the school of Christian experience, and administered by the parents. Christian discipline is needed to prevent children from growing up without reverence for God, respect for parental authority, knowledge of Christian standards, and habits of self-control.

5. Servants. Bondslave, yet free men in Christ. The Bible does not condone slavery nor does it advocate its violent overthrow. Slavery must ultimately disappear where the gospel is proclaimed, with its implications of human equality, Christian brotherhood, and the lordship of Christ. **Be obedient.** Servants are to be obedient and loyal. **Masters.** Either owners or employers, who have control of the body, but not of the spirit. **With fear and trembling.** Not dread of the master, but respect for authority and anxious to leave no duty undone. **In singleness of your heart.** With genuine readiness of heart and undivided purpose, not with pretense or an ulterior motive, not halfhearted, but sincere. **As unto Christ.** Your Christian duty.

6. Not with eyeservice. Working only while being under the watchful eye of an exacting employer and to make a show and gain human praise. **As menpleasers.** Who have no higher motive than to please their human masters and curry their favor. **But as the servants of Christ.** Rather meet the demands of your station as bondslaves of Christ. **Doing the will of God from the heart.** Even while the servants of men, view your tasks as doing God's will from the heart (literally, "out of the soul").

7. With good will doing service. And not with resentment. This implies enthusiasm and a generous spirit.

8. Knowing that whatsoever . . . any man doeth, the same shall he receive of the Lord. Get back in compensation from the Lord. The Lord remembers and rewards. **Bond or free.** The law of spiritual equity operates without regard to social class or economic status.

9. Ye masters, do the same things unto them. Accept the same Christian principles, with the same attitude, and the same spirit with regard to the will of God and to the authority of Christ. **Forbearing threatening.** Leave off the evil practice of threatening shorter hours, lower wages, and loss of employment by using harsh compulsions and treating them like chattels. **Your Master also is in heaven.** He is ruling and reigning. He keeps accurate records, and we will be judged by the perfect standards of heaven. **Neither is there respect of persons with him.** God does not have a double standard. He weighs the unfaithfulness in servants and the unkindness in masters in the same scales of divine equity and justice.

IV. THE CONFLICT OF THE CHURCH. 6:10-20.

10. Finally. In respect of the rest. Paul has already spoken of the church's heavenly calling and her earthly conduct, now he is revealing her spiritual conflict. **Be strong in the Lord.** Be continuously empowered in union with Him. He is the source of spiritual power. Spiritual battles require spiritual strength.

11. Put on the whole armor of God. God supplied the panoply, the complete armor, but he expects the Christian warrior to put it on. **That ye may be able to stand.** A purpose clause. In order that you may stand your ground and not retreat or fall in the struggle (cf. Jas 4:7). **Against the wiles of the devil.** The devil's wiles are attractive, deceptive, and ensnaring. Satan is a personal enemy, a great adversary, a slanderous accuser, and a malignant foe. He uses clever and crafty methods to deceive. Men dream of a devil that is a hideous, horned, and hoofed monster who haunts the vice dens of the world; but God says he fashions himself into an angel of light and fashions his ministers as ministers of righteousness (II Cor 11:14-15). He is the champion of liberalism, ritualism, rationalism, and every other "ism" that seeks to displace Christ. His aim is to substitute something else and something different for the grace and truth of Christ. Never underestimate the enemy.

12. For we wrestle not against flesh and blood. We are not engaged in a human, physical warfare. Wrestle means to throw or to swing. It is a contest between two opponents that continues until one hurls the other one down and holds him down. The word "against" presents the idea of a personal foe, face-to-face and hand-to-hand conflict to the finish, a life and death struggle. Paul is not describing a Sunday school picnic. **But against principalities.** Principalities refer to the high ranking hierarchy of demonic authority. **Powers.** Invested with authority. **Rulers of the darkness of this world.** The world rulers in revolt against God and limited to "this darkness" here on earth. **Spiritual wickedness.** The army of invisible wicked spirits. **In high places.** The sphere of this conflict is in the heavenlies, where life in Christ is lived (2:5-6).

13. Wherefore take unto you the whole armor of God. Appropriate promptly, for there is no time to lose. No ordinary weapons will do (II Cor 10:4). Confronted by the old subtle serpent out of the pit, we need the panoply of God, which is fully provided and freely given. **Withstand . . . stand.** The purpose of the armor is that we may hold our ground firmly, completely, gloriously, and victoriously.

14. Stand therefore. Take your stand therefore, bent on victory. **Having your loins girt about with truth.** This Greek aorist participle indicates antecedent action to the standing; it means belted around your thighs with the military band of true integrity and sincerity. This band holds the tunic in place and holds the scabbard. It is not an ornament, but an armament. Truth is revealed in the Word of God; it is light from heaven and dispels darkness. **Having on the breastplate of righteousness.** Clothed with the breastplate of righteousness both in character and conduct. The breastplate protects the vital organs in the chest area from the assaults of the enemy. Without it we would be vulnerable, disgraced, and defeated.

15. And your feet shod with the preparation of the gospel of peace. Having bound under (cf. Mk 6:9; Acts 12:8) for firm footing, for sure steps, and for protection. Preparation indicates readiness; prepared to see duty, prepared to do God's will, and prepared to proclaim the gospel of peace.

16. Above all. In addition to all. **Taking the shield of faith.** The shield is the large oblong shield for full protection. Note it is to be taken. Faith is utter dependence on God, upon His presence and His power. Faith puts God between you and the enemy. **Wherewith ye shall be able to quench all the fiery darts of the wicked.** The fire-tipped darts are the arrows dipped in combustible material and set on fire in Satan's malignant efforts to destroy you. The shield will quench every one of them without exception. It will stop the missiles and put out the fire.

17. And take the helmet of salvation. Take means receive or accept it from God. It is the assurance of salvation (II Tim 1:12; I Jn 5:11-13). Salvation is a present possession. The helmet protects the head, the citadel of intelligence, from false teachings and gives confidence and boldness in the conflict. **And the sword of the Spirit, which is the word of God.** This sword is the sharp one used in hand-to-hand conflict. It is the only offensive weapon. It is provided by the Spirit. When the church, or the Christian, used the rotten sticks of culture, science, theories, traditions, or commands of men, defeat is inevitable. God has promised to bless His Word (Isa 55:8-11). Our Lord used this powerful source in the wilderness and met the devil with, "It is written" (Mt 4:4-10). The sword must be unsheathed; the Bible must not lie idle.

18. Praying always. Pray without ceasing (I Thess 5:17) as you engage in battle. Keep the lines of communication open with the Captain of our salvation (Josh 5:13-15; Heb 2:10). Prayer and the Word should never be separated. The searching of the Word must be done with prayer, and prayer will be effectual through knowing the Word. **With all prayer.** Confession, adoration, thanksgiving, petition, intercession, supplication. **In the Spirit.** Not for the Spirit. It is the Holy Spirit who prays in us, through us, and for us (Rom 8:26-27; Jude 20). **Watching.** Be on guard, vigilant, wide awake (Mt 26:41). **Perseverance.** Persistence and importunity (Lk 11:5-8). **Supplication.** Specific requests. **For all saints.** In behalf of all believers. Christians should fight shoulder-to-shoulder and knee-to-knee.

19. And for me. Paul requests prayer for himself. **That utterance.** Freedom of speech. Paul was not trusting in education or experience. **Make known.** With clear fullness and boldness. **The mystery of the gospel.** The divine meaning of the gospel in its universal application to all races on equal terms and conditions. Paul had a message from God, and desired the means to deliver that message.

20. An ambassador in bonds. An ambassador (II Cor 5:20) of the risen Lord, in chains and in prison.

V. CONCLUSION. 6:21-24.

21-22. Tychicus (Acts 20:4; Col 4:7; II Tim 4:12; Tit 3:12), the bearer of this epistle, will inform the recipients of Paul's circumstances and encourage their troubled hearts.

23. Peace. Christ's gift. **Brethren.** In the Lord and in the Lord's work. **Love with faith.** Love of the saints and faith in Christ.

24. Grace will be with all them that love our Lord Jesus Christ. Lord speaks of His deity, Jesus speaks of His humanity, and Christ speaks of His Saviourhood. **In sincerity.** Incapable of being corrupted (I Cor 9:25, 15:52; I Tim 1:17). **Amen.** So let it be. Amen.

BIBLIOGRAPHY

Abbott, T. K. A Critical and Exegetical Commentary on the Epistles to the Ephesians and the Colossians. In the *International Critical Commentary.* Edinburgh: T & T Clark, 1964.

Bruce, F. F. *The Epistle to the Ephesians.* Westwood, N. J.: Revell, 1961.

*Eadie, John. *Commentary on the Epistle to the Ephesians.* Grand Rapids: Zondervan, n.d.

Erdman, Charles R. *The Epistle to the Ephesians.* Philadelphia: Westminster Press, 1931.

Gerstner, John H. *The Epistle to the Ephesians.* Grand Rapids: Baker, 1967.

Hendricksen, William. Exposition of Ephesians. In *New Testament Commentary.* Grand Rapids: Baker, 1967.

*Hodge, Charles. *A Commentary on the Epistle to the Ephesians.* Grand Rapids: Eerdmans, 1950.

Ironside, H. A. *In the Heavenlies.* New York: Loizeaux Brothers, 1937.

Kent, Homer A., Jr. *Ephesians: The Glory of the Church.* Chicago: Moody Press, 1971.

*Lenski, R. C. H. *The Interpretation of St. Paul's Epistles to the Galatians, to the Ephesians, and to the Philippians.* Columbus, Ohio: Lutheran Book Concern, 1937.

Miller, H. S. *The Book of Ephesians.* Houghton, N.Y.: Word-Bearer Press, 1931.

*Moule, H. C. G. *The Epistle of Paul the Apostle to the Ephesians.* Cambridge: Cambridge University Press, 1937.

Paxson, Ruth. *The Wealth, Walk and Warfare of the Christian.* Westwood, N. J.: Revell, 1939.

Robinson, J. A. *St. Paul's Epistle to the Ephesians.* London: Macmillan, 1939.

Simpson, E. K. and Bruce, F. F. Commentary on the Epistles to the Ephesians and the Colossians. In the *New International Commentary.* Grand Rapids: Eerdmans, 1957.

*Summers, Ray. *Ephesians: Pattern for Christian Living.* Nashville: Broadman Press, 1960.

Van Ryn, August. *Ephesians, The Glory of His Grace.* New York: Loizeaux Brothers, 1946.

Vaughn, W. Curtis. *The Letter to the Ephesians.* Nashville: Convention Press, 1963.

Westcott, Brooke Foss. *Saint Paul's Epistle to the Ephesians.* Grand Rapids: Eerdmans, 1958.

Wuest, Kenneth S. *Ephesians and Colossians in the Greek New Testament for the English Reader.* Grand Rapids: Eerdmans, 1953.

The Epistle To The

PHILIPPIANS

INTRODUCTION

The city of Philippi. The city of Philippi anciently bore the name of Krenides meaning "The Little Fountains" because numerous springs surrounded it. When Philip of Macedon, father of Alexander the Great, seized it, he enlarged the site and named it after himself. It was the eastern military outpost of Philip's empire protecting it from the wild Thracians.

We know little of the history of Philippi from then on until it was made a Roman colony by Augustus, as a memmorial of his victory over Brutus and Cassius. A colony was a planned outpost of Rome, a portion of Rome transplanted to the province. The members of the colony were Roman citizens in a place of danger to defend the homeland and its borders. The colony was to Romanize the district in which it was placed. It is interesting and suggestive that Paul refers to the church at Philippi as a colony of heaven (3:20). The city is seldom mentioned in Roman history, but it is spoken of as an important city. It was destroyed or ceased to exist sometime during the Turkish domination. Today it lies in ruins. Archaeologists have uncovered a colonial archway, a marketplace, and an amphitheater. The population of Philippi was dominantly Roman with a large percentage of Greek and oriental.

Philippi was the center of the old licentious Bacchus worship, the newer mystery religions, and the Roman Emperor worship. It also became the center of Christianity.

The church at Philippi. In obedience to the Macedonian call, Paul and his co-laborers, on the second missionary journey, took the gospel into Europe for the first time. There was no synagogue there, so Paul met with the Jews at the riverside. Paul's labors were crowned with success, and a church was established.

Luke remained in Philippi (Acts 19:10-40). After leaving Ephesus on his third missionary journey, Paul went into Macedonia (Acts 20:1-2; II Cor 2:12-13; 7:5-6), and it is reasonable to think he spent some time in Philippi. Three or four months later, on his return from Greece, he evidently spent the Passover at Philippi (Acts 20:6). Luke rejoins Paul here.

The church membership was largely Gentiles, and women occupied a prominent place (Acts 16:12-15; Phil 4:2-3). The church was loyal to Paul and grateful and generous to Paul (Acts 18:5; II Cor 8:1-5; 11:8-9; Phil 4:15-18). The Philippians had not been affected by the false Judaizing teachers, yet Paul warns them of this danger (3:14).

Authorship. The majority of scholars and a preponderance of both internal and external evidence favor the Pauline authorship. There is no reason to question either the authorship or the integrity of Philippians.

Date and place of writing. Philippians was written from Rome during Paul's imprisonment. The references to the "palace" (1:13) and to "Caesar's household" (4:22) confirm this. Paul was a prisoner (1:7, 13-14) and expected a speedy release (1:19, 20, 26; 2:24).

Occasion of the epistle. Epaphroditus had brought a contribution from the church in Philippi (4:18), and became sick nigh unto death (2:27). He was grieved over the sorrow which this sickness caused the Philippians (2:26). When he was well enough, Paul sent him back with this letter of thanks and explanation of Epaphroditus' long absence.

Contents. This "Hymn of Joy" has as its theme the adequacy of Christ for life and for death. The whole atmosphere of this epistle is that of joy. When Paul penned this letter, he was in a Roman prison. Years before in the jail in Philippi, Silas and he "prayed and sang praises to God" (Acts 16:25). Joy, the fruit of the Spirit (Gal 5:22), does not depend on and is not affected by outward circumstances.

The words "sin" and "sins" are not found in this epistle. The words "joy" and "rejoicing" are used eighteen times. We find no murmuring or complaining. Paul counts "it all joy" (Jas 1:2) and is glorying "in tribulation" (Rom 5:3).

Philippians shows us what true Christian experience is, the outward expression of the Christ-life within the believer in the power of the Holy Spirit, apprehending our position in Christ and manifesting Christ in our daily walk.

OUTLINE

I. Rejoicing in Christ as the Principle of Life. 1:1-30.
   A. Introduction 1:1-11.
      1. Salutation. 1:1-2.
      2. Thanksgiving. 1:3-8.
      3. Prayer. 1:9-11.
   B. Rejoicing in the Christian Ministry. 1:12-26.
      1. Proclaiming the gospel. 1:12-20.
      2. Surrendering to Christ. 1:21-26.
   C. Rejoicing in Christian Living. 1:27-30.
II. Rejoicing in Christ as the Pattern of Life. 2:1-30.
   A. The Need of a Pattern. 2:1-4.
   B. Christ the Pattern. 2:5-11.
      1. Preexistence of Christ. 2:5-6.
      2. Incarnation of Christ. 2:7-8.
      3. Exaltation of Christ. 2:9-11.
   C. Example of Paul. 2:12-18.
   D. Example of Timothy. 2:19-24.
   E. Example of Epaphroditus. 2:25-30.
III. Rejoicing in Christ as the Prize of Life. 3:1-21.
   A. True Goal of Life. 3:1.
   B. False Goal of Legalism. 3:2-14.
   C. False Goal of Antinomianism. 3:15-21.
IV. Rejoicing in Christ as the Power of Life. 4:1-23.
   A. Steadfastness in Christ. 4:1-3.
   B. Rejoicing in Christ's Peace. 4:4-9.
   C. Rejoicing in Christ's Provisions. 4:10-19.
   D. Benediction. 4:20-23.

COMMENTARY

I. REJOICING IN CHRIST AS THE PRINCIPLE OF LIFE. 1:1-30.

A. Introduction. 1:1-11.

1. Salutation. 1:1-2.

1:1. Paul. Paul does not mention his apostleship in this epistle. He is not insisting on his apostolic authority; he is not defending some doctrine; he is not enforcing some command. **And Timothy.** Timothy is not the co-author of the epistle, but the co-laborer of the apostle. He was with Paul when the church at Philippi was founded (Acts 16:1) and had been there since (Acts 19:19-22; 20:4). **Servants of Christ Jesus.** A servant is one who gives himself up wholly to another's will, a bondservant, a man of servile condition, one devoted to another to the disregard of his own interest. Paul and Timothy were the property of our Lord Jesus Christ. They were His slaves and of no one else. No man can serve two masters (Mt 6:24). Paul and Timothy had been servants of sin by the first birth, now they are servants of Christ by the second birth. They have been purchased by the blood of Christ and they are owned by Christ. Therefore, they have no will of their own, no business of their own, no time of their own. They are acting for Christ; they are dependent upon Christ; they are obedient to Christ. **To all the saints.** Saints are holy ones both in character and conduct. They are set apart for God to be exclusively His, dedicated to God, holy (holiness of heart and conduct in contrast of the impurity of unbelievers). Saints are set aside for sacred use. **In Christ Jesus.** This is the position of the saints. This is Paul's summation of the Christian life, the most intimate and living union between the believer and his Lord. **Which are at Philippi.** This is the place of their residence, the place of their discipline, the place of their experience, and the place of their service. **With the bishops.** The bishops were the overseers,

guardians, those who had a care for. The word is synonymous with presbyter and elder; they were the spiritual leaders. They were not dictators, but godly examples and undershepherds (I Pet 5:1-4). **And deacons.** Deacons are servants (in their activities for the work and not in their relationship to any other person). "The etymology (Gr *dia, konis*) suggests raising a dust by hastening" (A. T. Robertson, *Word Pictures of the New Testament,* Vol. IV, p. 435). Both bishops and deacons were the recognized officers of the church at this time. There was simple organization in the early church. We must never violate the scriptural principals of (1) the priesthood of all believers and (2) the lordship of Christ.

2. Grace be unto you, and peace. Grace and peace, always in that order. Grace is the foundation and peace is the result. Where there is no grace, there can be no peace. Grace denotes unmerited favor and expresses God's sacrificial love to men. Peace expresses "the tranquil state of a soul assured of its salvation through Christ, a soul fearing nothing from God and content with its earthly lot, of whatsoever sort that is." Peace is that harmony and health of the one who has been reconciled to God through the grace of our Lord Jesus Christ (Rom 5:1-2). **From God our Father, and from the Lord Jesus Christ.** The preposition (Gr *apo*) governs both objects, God and Christ, who form one unit and are placed on a level of equality. A definite affirmation of Christ's deity. God is called our Father because we are His children by the new birth; Christ is called our Lord because we live under Him and serve Him in righteousness.

2. Thanksgiving. 1:3-8.

3. I thank my God. Paul expresses his personal relationship to God. He says in effect, God is mine, and I am His. **Upon every remembrance of you.** This is Paul's basis and the stimulus for his thanksgiving. Paul remembers their acceptance of the gospel, their consistency of faith, their growth in grace, and their burden for lost souls.

4. Always in every prayer of mine for you all. The word prayer (Gr *deēsis*) means supplication, petition, entreaty. Paul was a great prayer warrior. In a day when programs, publicity, and promotion characterize much of the Lord's work, it should be emphasized that without prayer no lasting work will be accomplished for God. **Making request with joy.** Joy is the keynote of this epistle. Paul had been a happy prisoner in Philippi (Acts 16:25).

5. For your fellowship in the gospel. Fellowship is joint participation and cooperation in a common interest and activity. Not fellowship primarily with Paul or with each other, but fellowship in the furtherance of the gospel by their living, loyalty, love, and liberality. They were fellow laborers with Paul to take the whole Word to the whole world.

6. Being confident of this very thing. Paul has been persuaded. The Greek perfect tense signifies past completed action with present existing results. Paul is still firmly confident and will continue to be so. He has no doubts about their salvation or their security. **That he which hath begun a good work in you will perform it until the day of Jesus Christ.** God's beginning the work is a pledge of its completion. What God begins, He will finish (I Sam 3:12). The good work has its initiation in regeneration (past); has its continuation in sanctification (present); and will have its consummation in glorification (future). In the past there was God's unchangeable purpose; in the present there is God's unlimited power; and in the future there is God's unbreakable promise. This is God's guarantee for the final preservation and perseverance of the saints. Salvation is all of God.

7. Even as it is meet for me to think this of you all. Paul gives the reason for his settled persuasion. It was right for him to feel this way concerning them.

Because I have you in my heart. Paul loved them as his own soul. Paul's heart beats in unison with Christ's heart, for Christ lives in and loves through Paul. Paul's love for them was the fruit of the Holy Spirit. **Inasmuch as both in my bonds.** Paul's bonds refer to his present imprisonment. **And in the defense and confirmation of the gospel.** Defense is our word apology, but not with the idea of apologizing (Acts 22:1; 25:16). Defense is the negative side and confirmation (verification) is the positive side of establishing the gospel. Defense means clearing away the objections and removing the obstacles; confirmation means the aggressive advancement in proclaiming the good news. Both words are connected by the same definite article in Greek, and combined to form one complete idea. It is the defense and confirmation of the gospel, not Paul's self-defense. The fate of the apostle was of little concern; the fate of the gospel was then and still is everything. **Ye all are partakers of my grace.** Literally, my co-sharers or fellow-participants in grace.

8. For God is my record. Literally, God is my witness (Gr *martys*). Our word martyr is derived from this word. **How greatly I long after you all.** The word means to long for, desire earnestly, pursue with love. **In the bowels of Jesus Christ.** The word (Gr *splangchnos*) means heart, viscera (literal, vital organs), the seat of the affections. We translate, "with the heart of Jesus Christ with the tender affections and yearnings of Christ."

3. Prayer. 1:9-11.

9. And this I pray. Keep on praying. **That your love may abound yet more and more.** Their love was already in existence and that in no small degree to God, to one another, and to all men. The word abound (Gr *perisseuō*) means to exceed a fixed number or measure, to be over, to abound, to overflow. The Greek present active subjunctive means to keep on overflowing in a perpetual flood of love. **In knowledge and in all judgment.**

The word knowledge means whole, complete, precise, and correct knowledge, knowledge gained by experience. Judgment means perception, delicate discernment, and spiritual understanding. It is keen, intelligent, spiritual insight that selects, classifies, and applies that which knowledge furnishes. knowledge deals with the general principles; judgment deals with the discriminating of those principles.

10. That ye may approve things that are excellent. The word approve (Gr *dokimazō*) means to test, scrutinize, prove, recognize as genuine after examination, to sanction after testing. Some translate "approve things that are excellent" and others, "try the things that differ." The meaning is very similar. For by testing things that differ, we approve the things that are excellent. The Greek present participle means literally to carry different ways to different places. Thus to test things that differ, sift truth from error, discriminate the higher spiritual blessings from the lower material blessings. The criterion is always the Word of God as taught by the Holy Spirit. **That ye may be sincere.** The word sincere means unmixed, unalloyed, pure, free from falsehood, sincere. God wants sterling Christians, not those who are merely "plated" with outward religion. God wants men and women of transparent character, clear as crystal, so that the world will see Christ in their character and in their conduct. **And without offence.** Having nothing for one to strike against, not causing to stumble, without offense. Here the word conveys both ideas of not stumbling and of not causing others to stumble. Stepping-stones not stumbling blocks. **Till the day of Christ.** With a view to His glorious appearance.

11. Being filled. The word (Gr *plēroō*) means to make full, cause to abound, filled to the full. This Greek perfect participle expresses the present results of a past action. They have been filled and are still filled. There is no room for anything else; there is no room for any other fruit. **With the fruits of righteousness.** Righteousness fruit. **Which are by Jesus Christ.** This fruit cannot be produced by human power but only by the Holy Spirit as the believer is in vital union with Christ (Jn 15:4-5). **Unto the glory and praise of God.** This is the spiritual purpose of all Christian endeavor.

B. Rejoicing in the Christian Ministry. 1:12-26.

1. Proclaiming the gospel. 1:12-20.

12. But I would ye should understand. Paul wants the Philippians to be informed that his bonds led to a wider witness. Paul turned his prison cell into a gospel chapel. His chain did not curtail the gospel, but advanced it. **The things which happened unto me.** Paul refers to being mobbed in Jerusalem, unjustly imprisoned, shipwrecked, chained to guards, etc. These things happened not for crimes, but for Christ. **Have fallen out rather unto the furtherance of the gospel.** Paul's affairs turned out just the reverse of what might have been expected. Progress means advancement. This word pictures the pioneer cutting a way before an army and thus furthering its advance. Paul's imprisonment did not hinder his ministry of intercession, his ministry of evangelism, his ministry of writing.

13. So that my bonds in Christ. Paul's bonds were in connection with Christ and His cause. Paul is imprisoned for Christ's sake, and his chains are seen in relation to Christ and thus bear witness for Christ. **Are manifest in all the palace.** The palace of the provincial governor, probably including the barracks of the praetorian guard. The imperial guard was made up of noble soldiers appointed to keep guard over the emperor and the palace. These men had been reached with the gospel. **In all other places.** To all the rest.

14. And many of the brethren in the Lord. The majority of the brethren. **Waxing confident by my bonds.** Paul's courage was contagious. His confinement did not intimidate these brethren. Paul's brave and fearless example brought confidence to them. **Are much more bold.** In a greater degree and with increased zeal. **To speak.** The word denotes the fact of speaking, rather than the substance of speaking. **The word without fear.** The brethren dared fearlessly to proclaim God's Word.

15. Some indeed preach Christ even of envy and strife. Envy and strife are very low motives for preaching the gospel. On account of their jealousy of Paul, they sought to undermine his influence. These men are in contrast to the brethren of verse 14. Strife means rivalry, contention, wrangling. These men were motivated by malice. They had the right message, but they had the wrong motive. **And some also of good will.** These brethren found pleasure and satisfaction in Paul's work. These have the right message and the right motive.

16. The one preach Christ of contention. The word contention (Gr *eritheia*) means self-seeking, the desire to put one's self forward, selfish ambition, a partisan and factious spirit. Their motives were rivalry and ambition. **Not sincerely.** The word (Gr *hagnōs*) means not purely, not chaste, not modest, not immaculate. They are not preaching Christ from pure motives; not from unalloyed love for Christ; but insincerely. **Supposing to add affliction to my bonds.** Their aim was unchristian. Their purpose was to stir up vexation for Paul and to aggravate his sufferings. Their purpose was to triumph over Paul, not to triumph over pagans. They were concerned about promoting a sect, not saving souls.

17. But the other of love. Love both for Christ and for Paul knowing **that I am set for the defence of the gospel.** The same defense that is mentioned in verse 7. The word set (Gr *keimai*) means appointed, placed, destined. We see in these last two verses two types of preachers. They differ in their hearts: in one contention rules, and in the other love

reigns. They differ in spirit: in one there is envy and strife, in the other good will. They differ in the source of their strength: in one there is merely the love of party; in the other there is confidence in the Lord. They differ in their aim: in one the aim is to advance a branch of the church; in the other the aim is to advance the cause of Christ. They differ in conviction: one aims to add affliction to Paul; the other knows that Paul is set for the defense of the gospel.

18. What then? Notwithstanding, every way, whether in pretence. Pretense means an excuse, a pretext, that which is put forward to hide the true state of things. It has the idea of an ulterior motive. **Or in truth.** In sincerity. Paul could not and would not condone false teaching, but he graciously could and would tolerate wrong motives. We find no resentment in Paul's part and no rebuke in his actions. Paul rose above petty jealousy and animosity. Christ was in control, and Paul was out of sight. **Christ is preached.** Paul was bound, but the Word of God was not bound (II Tim 2: 9). **And I therein do rejoice, yea, and will rejoice.** Paul rejoiced because Christ was being openly proclaimed; not because of the wrong motive of some, but in spite of the wrong motive.

19. For I know that this shall turn to my salvation. Paul speaks of his deliverance and his preservation. He was being delivered from discouragement and spurred on to greater endeavors for Christ. He was experiencing victory and blessings in the midst of and in spite of his trials and his tribulations. It was Paul whom the Holy Spirit used to write, "tribulation worketh patience" (Rom 5:3). **Through your prayer.** Through your petition. Paul depended much on the intercession of God's people. **And the supply of the Spirit of Jesus Christ.** The ample supply comes as a result of the supplication. Note the cooperation of the human (petition) and the divine (ample supply). The Holy Spirit is both the gift and the giver.

20. According to my earnest expecta-

tion. The word translated earnest expectation (Gr *apokaradokia*) means to watch with the head erect and outstretched, to direct attention to anything, to wait for in suspense, anxious anticipation, intense desire, persistent expectation. The word is used only here and in Romans 8:19. It comes from (Gr *apo*) away from, (Gr *kara*) head, and (Gr *dokeō*) to watch closely. The idea of eagerness is intensified by (Gr *apo*), which implies abstraction. Paul's attention is drawn away from all other things and concentrated on one thing in order to see its very first appearance. **That in nothing I shall be ashamed.** Put to shame, disgraced. **But that with all boldness.** Boldness means freedom in speaking, fearless, confidence, cheerful courage, assurance, boldness. The absence of fear in speaking boldly was Paul's priviledge as a slave of Jesus Christ. **As always, so now also Christ shall be magnified in my body.** Paul shrinks from using the first person (I will magnify Christ) lest he should seem to magnify himself. The Holy Spirit will use Paul as an instrument to glorify Christ. The idea is that the glory of Christ will be manifest to others through Paul. Paul desires to be a magnifying glass through whom others could more clearly see Christ in all His glory. **Whether it be by life, or by death.** Through life or through death. Paul's utter committal to magnify Christ is seen in his willingness to accomplish it through life or through death. The Holy Spirit will determine which means best suits His purpose.

2. Surrendering to Christ. 1:21-26.

21. For me to live is Christ. Christ lives in Paul (Gal 2:20) and is the source and sustainer of Paul's spiritual life (Col 3:4). Paul is in vital union with Christ and lives in devotion to Christ. **And to die is gain.** The Greek aorist tense implies the state after death; not the act of dying, but the consequences of dying. Death does not interrupt our conscious fellowship with Christ. The moment of

absence here is the moment of presence there (II Cor 5:8). One of the martyrs said to his persecutors as they led him to death, "You take a life from me that I cannot keep, and bestow a life upon me that I cannot lose." The idea of gain is a precious thought on dying. After death Christians will collect the profits of their life's investments for Christ, and God pays rich dividends. It will be gain both in what we lose (sinful body, temptation, sorrow, sufferings, enemies, etc.) and in what we gain (glorified body, personal presence with Christ, joy, reunion with departed saints, etc.). Not all share Paul's view. Some would say to live is wealth, or knowledge, or fame, or fortune, or pleasure, or prestige, or power. But for Paul living in Christ: the commencement of life was being identified with Christ; the continuation of life was daily revelation of Christ; the conduct of life was self-renunciation for Christ; and the consummation of life will be transformation into the likeness of Christ.

22. But if I live in the flesh, this is the fruit of my labor. Paul speaks of life in the flesh because when he moves out of the body, he will still be living. If to go on living in the flesh be Paul's lot, this will issue in more fruit from his work. **Yet what I shall choose I wot not.** This word "wot" or know (Gr *gnōrizō*) has two distinct meanings: transitive, to make known; intransitive, to know, to become acquainted with, to discover. Paul was in a dilemma concerning which to choose between life and death.

23. For I am in a strait betwixt two. The expression means to hold together, compress, constrain. Paul was hard pressed. He was hemmed in on both sides and prevented from inclining either way because of the pressing in upon him from the two considerations. There is a desire to depart; there is a necessity to abide. There is a very strong reason for either choice; he is being pulled in both directions. Paul is in a dilemma and is held back from a decision. **Having a desire to depart.** This word (Gr *analyō*) means to unloose, to undo again, to depart. This word pictures the loosing of the tent pins for breaking up camp (cf. II Cor 5:1) or the loosing of the ship from its moorings, to lift anchor and sail away, sail away from earth to heaven, from time to eternity. **And to be with Christ.** The destination for which Paul yearns. There is no soul sleeping; there is no intermediary probation. **Which is far better.** Very much better. By far the preferable. This is a double comparative and means literally by much more better. Labor for Christ is sweet, but rest with Christ will be sweeter. Whitfield said, "I am often weary *in* the work, but never weary *of* it." Paul was ready to go and willing to wait. Life has its attractions; death has its advantages. Paul desires to live and labor, preferring Christ's purpose.

24. Nevertheless to abide in the flesh is more needful for you. It was necessary and indispensable for Paul to continue abiding in the flesh. Paul's eagerness to be a channel of blessing to the Philippians outweighs his desire for personal gain. He wants to finish the work God gave him to do (II Tim 4:6-8).

25. And having this confidence. Here the Greek perfect tense implies that Paul has been persuaded in time past, and presently thoroughly convinced with this settled conviction. **I know that I shall abide and continue with you all.** The preposition (Gr *para*) stresses the place of Paul's abiding, by the side of you all, denoting continuance in a certain place, or with certain persons, or in certain relations. **For your furtherance and joy of faith.** This states the purpose for which Paul will continue and remain with them. The word furtherance is the same word found in 1:12. Paul will continue abiding with them for the purpose of promoting the progressive advancement of their faith. Paul's purpose is twofold: progress of their faith and joy of their faith. Both words are connected by one definite article in Greek. It is the joy of the faith. Their progress will result in their joy.

26. That your rejoicing may be more abundant in Jesus Christ for me. The word rejoicing (Gr *kauchēma*) is exultation, that of which one glories or can glory, a matter or ground of glorying, reason for boasting. The word does not mean the act of glorying. Their exaltation is the natural result of their joy. Paul desires that their exaltation may constantly overflow, exceed a fixed number or measure, exist in abundance, be over and above, overflow. The sphere in which this blessing is enjoyed is in Christ Jesus, the only legitimate realm for glorying (I Cor 1:31). **By my coming to you again.** Paul refers to his own personal presence with them.

C. Rejoicing in Christian Living. 1:27-30.

27. Only. The emphatic position states Paul's purpose for which he desires to remain alive. Whatever may happen, make this your chief business. **Let your conversation be.** Keep on conducting yourselves. The word (Gr *politeuō*) means to be a citizen, behave as a citizen. Here the present imperative middle describes the subject as acting in reference to himself and for his own benefit, participating in the results of the action. This word is taken from the political life. The church at Philippi was a colony of heaven, and the members are commanded to walk as citizens of heaven, not by outward regulations, but by the power of the indwelling Holy Spirit. Their conduct is to reflect what Christ has done in them. They are to recognize their responsibilities and perform their obligations. God wants all of His children to be holy in character and conduct so that spiritual unity and power may be achieved. Our daily deportment should betray us as pilgrims and strangers down here and as citizens of that "city which hath foundations, whose builder and maker is God" (Heb 11:10). A life worthy of the gospel is a life lived in the power of the Holy Spirit. It is the earthly walk of a heavenly man. Such consistency is: (1) the result of gospel disposition; (2) maintained by gospel principles; (3) conformable to gospel precepts; (4) resembles gospel patterns; and (5) possible through gospel power. **That ye stand fast in one spirit.** The idea is to keep one's ground in battle, and in order to do this, one must be settled on the firm foundation of the Rock of Ages. In one spirit means in the spirit of unity and harmony; for bickering, contention, and self-seeking hinder and mar the gospel witness. One spirit refers to that unity into which the church is fused by the presence and the power of the Holy Spirit (Eph 4:3-4). **With one mind striving together for the faith of the gospel.** To strive at the same time (Gr *synathleō*) with one another, to contend along with, share, or take part in a contest. There is to be a mutual striving together: side by side, shoulder to shoulder, and heart to heart. We get our word "athlete" from this word. The preposition (Gr *syn*) implies cooperation and coordination against common opposition. The Philippians are already contending with united effort, working as a team for the faith once for all delivered unto the saints (Jude 3). Every Christian is an important member of the team, an important link in an important chain extending the gospel of Christ. Christians are friends, not foes; co-workers, not competitors. Since the church has a common objective and a common adversary, Paul pleads for a consistent church, a united church, and a zealous church to resist the adversary, develop Christian graces, establish the true faith, and advance the gospel of Christ.

28. And in nothing terrified by your adversaries. The word terrified (Gr *ptyrō*) means to frighten, scare, alarm. This word was used of horses being scared and startled and turning about or springing aside. God wants fearless fighters with undaunted courage, who will not be startled or intimidated by anything. Such holy boldness is produced by the Holy Spirit. **Your adversaries.** Better, by those opposing you. Christians have adversaries. There is no

middle ground; a person is either for Christ or against Him (Mt 12:30). **Which is to them an evident token of perdition.** This is a legal term denoting proof obtained by an appeal to the facts. The opposition of the adversaries was in fact strong evidence that they were rushing head long into perdition. Perdition never means annihilation. Too bad they didn't realize their final destiny and flee from the wrath to come. **But to you of salvation.** The same evidence was a positive pledge of salvation to the Philippians. **And that of God.** Their salvation was from God. God is the source and origin of salvation.

29. For unto you. To you who are striving and struggling. **It is given.** It is graciously granted. **In the behalf of Christ.** For His sake. **Not only to believe on him, but also to suffer for his sake.** The Christian's privileges are to believe on Him and to suffer for Him, and always in that order. God confers upon us the high honor of suffering with Christ and for Christ (II Tim 2:12; 3:12). Christ suffered to provide salvation; we suffer to proclaim salvation. God crowns the believing in His Son with the suffering for His Son (Mt 5:11-12). A glorious reward awaits all who suffer (II Cor 4:17).

30. Having the same conflict. The conflict (Gr *agōn*) signifies a contest of athletes or the inner conflict of the soul. The inner conflict is often the result of an outward conflict of struggle. Our word agony is derived from this word. **Which ye saw in me.** The Philippians saw Paul beaten and thrown into prison (Acts 16). **And now hear to be in me.** Paul was an example and an encouragement to the Philippians.

II. REJOICING IN CHRIST AS THE PATTERN OF LIFE. 2:1-30.

A. The Need of a Pattern. 2:1-4.

2:1. If. Since. Here we have a first class conditional sentence expressing the condition as a fact in Greek. Since these things are blessed realities, how incongruous for any saint to act as if they were non-existent. **There be therefore.** Paul is expanding the exhortation of 1:28. All the terms used in this verse (2:1) get their coloring from that connection. **Any consolation in Christ.** Any exhortation. The word is always modified by the context. Paul is pleading for unity. Surely an exhortation in Christ must be heeded. **If any comfort of love.** Any consolation. The idea is to make things easier by speaking to a person in trouble. This is the encouragement of tender persuasiveness which love gives, an incentive to action (II Cor 5:14). Love is that unselfish, self-sacrificing love of John 3:16. **If any fellowship of the Spirit.** Any intimate partnership or joint participation. Such common interests and mutual, active participation are the results of the Holy Spirit's work. The fellowship of the Spirit is a blessed reality, not merely a beautiful idea. **If any bowels and mercies.** Bowels is the same word as we find in 1:8 and means tender-heartedness, tender mercies. Mercies means compassionate yearnings and action. These graces present in the lives of the Philippians will result in peace and in power. Unity will prevail, differences will be dissolved, bickerings will cease, and estrangements will be completely healed.

2. Fulfill ye my joy. Fill up to the full. Paul wants his cup of joy full and running over. The Philippians can accomplish this by heeding Paul's admonitions and exhibiting the virtues to which he exhorts them. **That ye be likeminded.** That you all may keep on thinking the same thing. They are to be intent on one thing, one purpose. **Having the same love.** This unity of affection is the fruit of the Holy Spirit. Equally loving and being loved. **Being of one accord.** Literally, souls together. Souls knit together in love by the Holy Spirit, hearts beating in unison, unity in sentiment. **Of one mind.** Thinking one thing. Unity of thought and purpose. Unity is defined as something far deeper than: (1) consent to a common creed; (2) union in a form of worship; and (3) participation in a common task.

It is unity of heart, soul, and mind. This is what Christ can and will do.

3. Let nothing be done through strife. Factious strife, intriguing for office, a desire to put one's self forward, a partisan and factious spirit, self-seeking. **Or vainglory.** Empty, proud, or groundless self-esteem. Ambition and vanity will destroy the unity and harmony of a church. Paul's prohibitions are indicators of what is wrong, which he wishes to correct. Christians should seek the approval of God, not the applause of men. **But in lowliness of mind.** Humility of mind and deportment, a deep sense of one's littleness. This indicates self-forgetfulness in serving others, the spirit which most resembles Christ. The pathway to unity is lowly and lonely. **Let each esteem other better than themselves.** Go on regarding others above themselves. This is that Christlike spirit of humility which fixes its eyes on the excellency of others and judges them from that standpoint.

4. Look not every man on his own things. Keep an eye for the good of others. Have respect for, fix your attention upon with a desire for an interest in others. They were to be attentive to the interests of others as well as their own. Every member of the church should practice unselfishness and due consideration for all the others. **But every man also on the things of others.** Others is the keynote of these verses. This was the dominant feature in the life of our Lord who "came not to be ministered unto, but to minister, and to give his life a ransom for many" (Mk 10:45). A man of the flesh "looks out for number one," but a man of the Spirit lives in submission to Christ and in service to his fellowman.

B. Christ the Pattern. 2:5-11.

1. Preexistence of Christ. 2:5-6.

5. Let this mind be in you, which was also in Christ Jesus. Keep on thinking this in you which was also in Christ Jesus. Paul says in I Corinthians 2:16,

"We have the mind of Christ," and here he exhorts the saints at Philippi to allow that mind to dominate and control their lives. When this is done, saints will not: (1) assert their own virtues; (2) defend their own rights; (3) promote their own selfish interests; or (4) live for themselves. Verse 5 introduces one of the most sublime and wonderful mysteries of the Scriptures, what is called the doctrine of the kenosis. This doctrine of our Lord's self-emptying is used as an example and as an illustration of that lowliness of mind which should be the pattern for all the followers of Christ. Paul is stating accepted facts to enforce the obvious duties of humility and unselfish consideration of others.

6. Who, being in the form of God. The word being (Gr *hyparchō*) is better translated existing or subsisting. This word is much stronger than the verb to be; it does not simply mean being but existing. Christ ever was, is, and ever shall be God. This word denotes prior existence (cf. Jn 1:1; Col 1:17). From all eternity the Son was co-existent, co-equal, and co-eternal with the Father. Christ existed in the form of God. This is the strongest Greek word (Gr *morphē*) to denote the exact image, the image of being and essence. It has no reference to the shape of a physical object, but refers to the expression of being. Christ is brightness of God's glory, "and the express image of his person" (Heb 1:3). Christ is not merely like God; He is God (Jn 1:1; Col 2:9). **Form** signifies the mode in which He expresses His divine essence. Form (Gr *morphē*) "always signifies a form which truly and fully expresses the being which underlines it" (H. A. Kennedy, *The Epistle to the Philippians*, p. 436). No creature could exist in **the form of God**, but Lucifer aspired to this (Isa 14:12-14). To give expression to the essence of deity implies the possession of deity. What Peter, James, and John witnessed on the Mount of Transfiguration was a glimpse of the outward expression of His deity (Mt 17:1-2). Christ's own eternal self-manifesting

characteristics were shining forth from His divine essence. **Thought it not robbery.** This word (Gr *harpagmos*) has two distinct meanings. One, a thing unlawfully seized, and two, a treasure to be clutched and retained. Christ did not cling to His prerogatives of His divine majesty, did not ambitiously display His equality with God. Christ waived His rights to: (1) express His deity; (2) display His divine attributes; and (3) demonstrate His equality with God. He did not regard His position as equal with God as something to be held on to, but as something to be relinquished for the redemption of man. He gave up His throne in glory for a cross of shame and suffering. **To be equal with God.** This confirms the meaning of "form." Christ was on an equality with God. He laid aside His divine glory, but He did not and could not lay aside His divine nature. He laid aside the expression of deity, but He did not and could not lay aside His possession of deity. He laid aside His rights as the Son and took His place as a servant. He put aside the insignia of deity and put on the robes of humanity.

2. Incarnation of Christ. 2:7-8.

7. But made himself of no reputation. He emptied Himself. He divested Himself of His prerogatives. We have an incomplete thought which leaves us with the question "of what?" Certainly not His deity, but only His divine prerogatives and privileges. He did not and could not cease to be God when He was made flesh (Jn 1:14). His deity remained throughout the whole course of His self-imposed humiliation. He gave up something that was His. **Himself** is accusative in Greek. He did not empty something from Himself, but He emptied Himself from something, i.e. the form of God. The figure presented is similar to pouring water from a pitcher into a glass. The form is different, but the substance remains the same. "Jesus Christ the same yesterday, and to day, and for ever" (Heb 13:8). Christ emptied Himself of

His divine glory (Jn 17:3), but not of His divine nature. He emptied Himself of the self-manifestation of His divine essence. "He was not *unable to assert* equality with God. He was able *not to assert it*" (M. R. Vincent, *Word Studies In The New Testament.* p. 433). He stripped Himself of His expression of deity, but not His possession of deity. He restricted the outward manifestation of His deity. In His incarnation, He clothed Himself with humanity. He was like a king temporarily clothing Himself in the garb of a peasant while still remaining king, even though it was not apparent. When Christ became incarnate, He was one person with two natures, divine and human, "each in its completeness and integrity, and that these two natures are organically and indissolubly united, yet so that no third nature is formed thereby. In brief, to use the antiquated dictum, orthodox doctrine forbids us either to divide the person or to confound the natures" (A. H. Strong, *Systematic Theology*, p. 673). Christ emptied Himself in order that He might fill us (II Cor 5:21; 8:9). **And took upon him the form of a servant.** The form of a slave refers to His mode of expression. He veiled Himself with humanity (Heb 2:14-18). The same divine person who existed in the form of God took on Himself the form of a slave. He who was the Sovereign manifested Himself as a slave. When He did this, His person did not change, only the mode of His expression. God refutes all claims of modernism that the Lord Jesus Christ emptied Himself of His deity. **And was made in the likeness of men.** Becoming in the likeness of men. The verb forms emptied, taking, and becoming are punctiliar aorists, expressing simultaneous, but not identical action. Becoming, as opposed to what He was by nature; entering into a new state. Likeness denies identity. It refers to an outward expression that is assumed from the outside and does not come from within. Likeness means similarity, but not sameness. Christ was not identical with man (not

merely a man, and nothing else); He was the sinless Son of God, the God-man. Adam aspired to be like God; Christ condescended to be like man. His humanity was the vehicle through which he manifested Himself as a slave.

8. And being found. Men discovered Him to appear as man. Men recognized Him as a true man. **In fashion as a man.** In appearance. The word form (Gr *morphē*) differs from fashion (Gr *schēma*) as that which is intrinsic from that which is outward. The contrast is between what He is in Himself (God) and what He appears to be in the eyes of men (man). Christ had all the qualities which Adam had before he sinned, but not the sinful nature which came through Adam's fall. **He humbled himself.** This is not the same as "He emptied Himself," but shows how the self-emptying manifested itself. His love for us prompted Him to voluntarily do this. **And became obedient unto death.** The mark of a slave is obedience. When slaves were executed they were crucified. Christ placed Himself on the same plane as the worst of criminals. The cross was a horrible death of shame and suffering. Christ's obedience was **unto death** and not to death. He never was death's slave, but death's master and conqueror. Adam was disobedient unto death; Christ was obedient unto death (Rom 5:19). Christ's death was voluntary, vicarious, and victorious. **Even the death of the cross.** The most despised death of a condemned criminal on an accursed cross.

3. Exaltation of Christ. 2:9-11.

9. Wherefore. Because of His voluntary renunciation, obedience, and death (cf. Mt 23:12). **God also hath highly exalted him.** God exalted him supremely. Christ's exaltation is not only God's attestation of satisfaction in Christ's work, but also God's recognition of Christ's equality with God. Christ emptied Himself; God exalted Him. On earth Christ was God, but appeared as man, back in heaven. He retained His humanity, but He manifests His prerogatives of deity. God graciously granted to Him the name. On earth Christ was crowned with thorns (Mt 27:29), back in heaven He is crowned with glory and honor (Rev 5:12-14). **And given him a name which is above every name.** Probably "KING OF KINGS, AND LORD OF LORDS" (Rev 19:16).

10. That at the name of Jesus every knee should bow. Every created rational and moral being will bow in submission to Christ's lordship. **Of things in heaven, and things in earth, and things under the earth.** Heavenly ones, earthly ones, and subterranean ones. They refer to personal beings, not to impersonal things existing in heaven, existing upon the earth, and existing under the earth.

11. And that every tongue should confess that Jesus Christ is Lord. Every tongue shall profess openly that Christ is Lord. The word Lord is equivalent to the Old Testament word *Jehovah.* God made Him "both Lord and Christ" (Acts 2:36). Men may flaunt Christ's lordship here, but they will be compelled to acknowledge it hereafter. This will not result in their salvation. Subjugation is not reconciliation. When reconciliation is under consideration, only two spheres are mentioned, on earth and in the heavens (Col 1:20), but the things under the earth are omitted. This passage does not teach that ultimately all the lost will be saved, as taught by many cults. No future reconciliation for the lost is anywhere promised in the Word of God. **To the glory of God the Father.** God is glorified when men openly acknowledge Christ as Lord.

C. Example of Paul. 2:12-18.

12. Wherefore. So then. This refers to what precedes. Having the example of Christ's humility to guide us and the exaltation of Christ to encourage us. **My beloved, as ye have always obeyed, not as in my presence only, but now much more in my absence.** There is always a tendency to relax obedience when the spiritual leader is absent, but the Philippians obeyed "much more" in Paul's

absence. **Work out.** Keep on working out thoroughly in your own interests so as to achieve the desired results. Both freedom and responsibility are implied. In verses 12 and 13 we see divine sovereignty and human freedom in blessed cooperation. Our salvation is **worked in** by the Holy Spirit in answer to faith in God's promises and it is *worked out* by the Holy Spirit by our obedience to God's precepts. It is always a matter of trust and obey. The verse does not say "work for" your salvation. The Philippians had already been saved. Salvation is all of grace (Eph 2:8-10), but it is to be manifested in the daily life by glorifying Christ in everything. One must possess salvation first, and then work it out to its ultimate conclusion, namely, Christlikeness. No one can live the Christian life until he has Christ. It is not a matter of the imitation of Christ but the manifestation of Christ the Holy Spirit reproducing the life of Christ in and through the believer. **Your own salvation.** Salvation is a personal relationship; it is a divine work accomplished at Calvary. Salvation should be viewed in three tenses: past, justification; present, sanctification; and future, glorification. **With fear and trembling.** These two words describe the anxiety of the person who distrusts his own ability to meet all the requirements, but nevertheless does his best to discharge his duty. This is not slavish fear, but wholesome, serious caution. It is the constant apprehension of the deceitfulness of the heart, taking heed lest we fall (I Cor 10:12); or stop short of the final goal (II Pet 1:1-11). It is that desirable distrust of our own self-sufficiency and the consciousness that all depends on the grace of God. It is not fear of being lost, but fear of the failure of not walking in lowliness of mind, in true humility, and in unfailing obedience. It is fear of all that would rob us of our spiritual vitality and spiritual victory and of shrinking from all carelessness in matters of faith and life.

13. For it is God which worketh in you. For God is the one continually working effectually in you. This word is used in Galatians 2:8 (wrought effectually) and in I Thessalonians 2:13 (effectually worketh). We are God's workmanship (Eph 2:10). **Both to will and to do.** To keep on willing and to keep on working. God is the source of all we need. The Holy Spirit dwelling within makes the abundant life a reality (not merely a possibility). The energy of God enables a Christian to desire God's will and replace the Christian's weakness with the needed power. "Paul has no sympathy with a cold and dead orthodoxy of formalism that knows nothing of struggling and growth. He exhorts as if he were an Arminian in addressing men. He prays as if he were a Calvinist in addressing God, and feels no inconsistency in the two attitudes. Paul makes no attempt to reconcile divine sovereignty and human free agency, but boldly proclaims both" (A.T. Robertson, *Word Pictures in the New Testament,* Vol. IV, p. 446). **Of his good pleasure.** For the sake of His good pleasure—His sovereign and gracious purpose.

14. Do all things without murmurings. Keep on doing all things apart from murmuring. Murmurings means to mutter, to murmur, an expression of secret and solemn discontent. This word (Gr *gongysmos*) appears many times in the LXX (Septuagint) of the children of Israel in the wilderness and refers to their stubborn spirit. **And disputings.** Disputings refer to the thinking of a man deliberately with himself, rationalizing and calculating. This word is translated "imagination" in Romans 1:21. It has two distinct meanings: (1) inward questionings; and (2) outward disputings or discussions. Used here in the first sense and implies a doubtful spirit. We get our word dialogue from this word. The Christian is called to unquestioned submission to God's will.

15. That ye may be blameless and harmless. That ye may become blameless, faultless, without defect, deserving no censure. This refers to outward conduct, and presents the idea of a person in

whom no grace is defective. It is that moral integrity as expressing itself outwardly. The word harmless means sincere, unmixed, pure, unadulterated. It refers to the inward, intrinsic character. This word is used of unalloyed metal. It describes the saint with not one thing in his heart or motives which ought not to be there. **The sons of God.** Better, the children of God. This stresses the dignity and character of the relationship. Children of God are expected to resemble their Father. **Without rebuke.** Better, without blemish. **In the midst of a crooked and perverse nation.** Crooked means froward, perverse, wicked (in the sense of departing from the truth). This describes the outward perverted conduct of their generation, crooked in mind, heart, and action, bent in all directions. The word perverse (Gr *diastrephō*) is a perfect passive participle and can be translated having been turned out of the way. The Greek perfect tense expresses the existence of a completed action. The word means to warp, twist, corrupt, distort, pervert, turn out of the way. **Among whom ye shine.** Among whom ye are appearing. This refers not to the act of shining, but to the fact of appearing, being recognized as God's children. **As lights in the world.** As luminaries. Christ is the light of the world (Jn 8:12) and His followers are luminaries (Mt 5: 14-16; Eph 5:8), light-bearers, reflecting His light (II Cor 4:6). The picture is that of a procession at night, in a crooked and distorted age, in which torchbearers are going and holding high the blazing torches, so that those following can see how to walk in this sin-darkened world.

16. Holding forth the word of life. The world does not have this Word of Life. Apart from the Word of God, all are spiritually dead (Jn 6:63; I Pet 1:23). There is a connection between life and light. Christ is both the light (Jn 8:16) and the life (Jn 14:6). Christians are to be continually holding forth the Word of Life; they are to offer God's salvation to a lost and dying world. This explains how the saints at Philippi are luminaries.

That I may rejoice in the day of Christ. That I may have cause of glorying or a ground of boasting and exultation. **That I have not run in vain, neither laboured in vain.** The word run means to progress freely and advance rapidly. The idea is to spend one's strength in performing or attaining something. The word laboured means toil with wearisome effort. It refers to labouring to the point of exhaustion. Paul did not want his life to be without fruit or an empty failure.

17. Yea, and if I be offered. But even if I am being poured out as a libation. In the passive, this word (Gr *spendō*) means to be in the act of being sacrificed. "The Philippians are the priests; their faith (or their good works springing from their faith) is a sacrifice: St. Paul's life-blood the accompanying libation" (J. B. Lightfoot, *St. Paul's Epistle to the Philippians,* p. 119). **And service of your faith.** Ministration of your faith. This word (Gr *leitourgia*) is used of a priest's ministration of a sacrifice. **I joy, and rejoice with you all.** I am going on rejoicing together with you all.

18. For the same cause also do ye joy, and rejoice with me. Keep on rejoicing together with me.

D. Example of Timothy. 2:19-24.

19. But I trust in the Lord Jesus. Paul was hoping to send Timothy, and his hope is founded on faith in the Lord Jesus Christ, and all of his plans and purposes center in Christ. **To send Timotheus shortly unto you.** Paul was hoping to send Timothy to be a channel of blessing for the personal benefit of the Philippians, and to learn firsthand just how they were getting along. **That I also may be of good comfort, when I know your state.** Paul is facing possible death and yet he is more concerned over the affairs of the Philippian saints than over his own affairs. He longs for news from his Christian friends which will encourage him.

20. For I have no man likeminded. Not even one was available at this time. There were some of Paul's fellow workers who were not with him in Rome. The word likeminded means equal in soul. Timothy's pastoral concern (shepherd-heart) was a gift from the Holy Spirit, and no one with Paul was so competent or so willing to serve Christ and His church. **Who will naturally care for your state.** Or who genuinely will care for your state. The word care for (Gr *merimnaō*) means to be anxious, solicitous, be troubled with care, extend careful thought, feel an interest in, concern one's self, seek to promote someone's interest. Timothy was spiritually qualified to promote the interest of Christ and His church and is an example for all Christians.

21. For all seek their own. They are constantly seeking after their own affairs. All without exception were striving after, looking for, and searching for their own things. Paul does not say they are not saved, but they are not so self-sacrificing as Timothy. Some will help only when Christ's gain is compatible with their own. So few have a genuine dedication to Christ and an unselfish devotion to His church. **Not the things which are Jesus Christ's.** It is possible to be an admired and eloquent speaker and yet be a self-seeker, using God's gifts for personal aggrandizement, and not sincerely. These were not pursuing Christ's interest and glory, but allowing their own interests to interfere. Therefore the Philippians should appreciate Timothy all the more.

22. But ye know the proof of him. The proven worth, that by which something is tried or proved, a specimen of tried worth. It refers to that which has met the test and has been approved, the sterling life, love, and loyalty of Timothy. **That as a son with the father.** This refers to the personal relationship, the reciprocal affection, and the closest companionship between Paul and Timothy. **He hath served with me in the gospel.** Better, he has discharged the duties of a slave.

23. Him therefore I hope to send presently, so soon as I shall see how it will

go with me. As soon as Paul gets a clear view of his own circumstances relative to his trial, he plans to send Timothy.

24. But I trust in the Lord. I have been persuaded. Paul reached this settled conviction through communion with Christ. Paul's confidence and hope are in Christ. **That I also myself shall come shortly.** Paul was confident that he also would soon come to Philippi.

E. Example of Epaphroditus 2:25-30.

25. Yet I suppose it necessary to send to you Epaphroditus. Suppose (Gr *hēgeomai*) means to consider, regard, think. This is a word that refers to the decision made after weighing all the facts. **My brother** speaks of common origin and parenthood. **And companion in labour.** Fellow worker, cooperator. **And fellow-soldier.** Paul emphasized Christian brotherhood and regards the Christian life as that of a soldier of Jesus Christ (II Tim 2:3-4). **But your messenger, and he that ministered to my wants.** Your apostle and your minister. The word apostle has a dignified tone. Epaphroditus was sent on a misson with a specific commission to minister to Paul's needs on behalf of the church. The word minister means a servant, one who ministers, acts as an official, public servant, or engages in a priestly service. Epaphroditus was duly commissioned and officially appointed by the church.

26. For he longed after you all, and was full of heaviness. Because he was desiring earnestly to see you all and being depressed. The word translated full of heaviness (Gr *adēmoneō*) means to be depressed or rejected, be troubled, distressed, full of anguish or sorrow. This word is used of Jesus in the Garden of Gethsemane (Mt 26:37; Mk 14:33). The word does not refer to homesickness, but to the discomfort and distress of not being at home. Epaphroditus was aggravated and full of heaviness because the Philippians heard that he fell sick. **Because that ye had heard that he had been sick.** Epaphroditus became ill, but he did not quit working.

27. For indeed he was sick nigh unto death. His illness nearly proved fatal. **But God had mercy on him.** God had compassion and intervened and granted recovery no doubt in answer to prayer. **And not on him only, but on me also, lest I should have sorrow upon sorrow.** The word sorrow (Gr *lypē*) means pain, distress, grief, afflictions. The heaping up of one thing upon another, with the idea of accumulation. This would have been true if to Paul's bonds and trials had been added the death of his friend and benefactor.

28. I sent him therefore the more carefully. Or the more earnestly, diligently, hastily. Sooner than might otherwise have been expected. **That, when ye see him again, ye may rejoice.** That ye may recover your cheerfulness, which had been marred by the news of Epaphroditus' illness. **That I may be the less sorrowful.** More free from sorrow. Paul would be more relieved than he would otherwise be. He would have one burden lifted from his heart. If the Philippians have the joy of seeing Epaphroditus again, Paul's own troubles will be lessened, but his prior sorrow (prison, trial) will remain for the present.

29. Receive him therefore in the Lord with all gladness. Receive him to yourselves. **And hold such in reputation.** Keep on holding him in high honor.

30. Because for the work of Christ he was nigh unto death. He drew near, approached death. This means that Epaphroditus was at the point of death. **Not regarding his life.** Having thrown by the side his life. This (Gr *paraboleuomai*) is a gambling term and was used when a person placed all his money on one throw of the dice. Epaphroditus threw down a stake and gambled his life recklessly in the service of Christ and in his devotion to the Apostle Paul. **To supply your lack of service toward me.** That he might fill up to the full the deficiency of your sacred ministration to me. The Philippians were unavoidably absent, so Epaphroditus, as their personal representative, did what they would have done if they had been with Paul. There is no reproach. They lacked the opportunity, not the will. All that was wanting was their ministration in person, which distance prevented them from rendering.

III. REJOICING IN CHRIST AS THE PRIZE OF LIFE. 3:1-21.

A. True Goal of Life. 3:1.

3:1. Finally. Literally, for the rest. **My brethren, rejoice in the Lord.** Keep on constantly rejoicing in the Lord. Paul exhorts them to be joyful Christians. Rejoicing in the Lord is much more than rejoicing in His grace and in His gifts, much more than rejoicing in our salvation and in our service. **To write the same things to you.** To go on writing the same counsel. **To me indeed is not grievous.** Not irksome, not troublesome. It was not wearisome for Paul to repeat his warnings of lurking dangers. **But for you it is safe.** It means your safety.

B. False Goal of Legalism. 3:2-14.

2. Beware. Keep a watchful eye always, constantly look out for. **Dogs** (Gr *kuōn*). The word used here is not that of a household pet (Mt 15:26), but the prowling wild dogs, without a home and without an owner. They were scavengers which ate garbage; they were vicious, attacking every passerby; they were unclean, mangy, flea-ridden dogs. Paul is referring to the false teachers who boasted in their religion, trusted in human attainment rather than divine atonement, trusted in the works of man rather than in the grace of God. They perverted the gospel and substituted something else for the blood of Christ. These false teachers dogged Paul's footsteps, snapping and snarling, biting and barking. **Beware of evil workers.** Deceitful workers (II Cor 11:13). They were mischief-makers who disturbed both the faith and the peace of believers. They were wolves in sheep's clothing, deceiving, deluding, and destroying the flock. **Beware of the concision.** Beware of the

mutilation (Gr *katatomē*) in contrast to circumcision (Gr *peritomē*). Paul refers to those who are not of the true circumcision (Rom 2:28-29; Col 2:11; Eph 2:11) as merely mutilated. Circumcision has no spiritual value in itself. There were those who followed the law, but had no heart for God. They substituted circumcision for the new birth, and rested in the rite without the reality, and trusted in the sign without having the substance. Thus Paul gives a warning against false teachers.

3. For we are the circumcision. Paul presents the true position of the Christian. We who believe in Christ have the true spiritual circumcision of the heart. True circumcision is spiritual, not physical; inward, not outward; reality, not a rite. **Which worship God in the spirit.** Worship by, or render sacred service by, the Holy Spirit. Christians practice priestly service in a spiritual ministry. Their service is inspired by the Holy Spirit, guided by the Holy Spirit, and supported by the Holy Spirit. Sacred service is of the heart, not by ordinances and traditions. **And rejoice in Christ Jesus.** Better, glory or exalt in Christ Jesus, not in external ceremonies or legal observances. Let him that glorieth, glory in the Lord (I Cor 1:31). **And have no confidence in the flesh.** Have no settled persuasion in trusting in the flesh or of relying upon external ceremonies. We have not placed confidence in anything of a fleshy nature. Christians expect nothing from the flesh. The flesh is always flesh; it is always corrupt; it is never improved; it is never changed. One may educate it, or reform it, or give it religion, but it is still flesh. "They that are in the flesh cannot please God" (Rom 8:8).

4. Though I might also have confidence in the flesh. Paul now presents his pedigree. **If any other man thinketh that he hath whereof he might trust in the flesh, I more.** Paul claims to have more ground for boasting than anyone else.

5. Circumcised the eighth day. Ishmaelites were circumcised in the thirteenth year, proselytes from Gentiles in mature age, but Jews on the eighth day (Lev 12:3). **Of the stock of Israel.** Paul was not a proselyte; he was not grafted into the covenant race. Paul's parents were Jews. **Of the tribe of Benjamin.** Not one of the so-called lost tribes, but the tribe that gave Israel their first king, and the tribe that remained true to the Davidic throne when other tribes rebelled. **An Hebrew of the Hebrews.** A full-blooded Jew of Hebrew parents, who retained Hebrew customs and characteristics, as distinct from the Hellenistic Jews (Acts 6:1). Paul was educated at the feet of Gamaliel in Jerusalem and was proficient in the Hebrew language and the Hebrew Scriptures. **As touching the law, a Pharisee.** In distinction from the Sadducees. Paul was of the straightest and strictest sect.

6. Concerning zeal, persecuting the church. Paul was a zealot of Judaism and against Christianity. He was the ringleader from the death of Stephen until his own conversion (Acts 8:1-9:9). Paul was a conscientious, relentless, persistent persecutor of the Christians. **Touching the righteousness which is in the law, blameless.** Paul observed the fine points of the law. He was blameless, faultless, and beyond reproach. He knew and practiced the rules of the rabbi. He scored one hundred percent in Judaism.

7. But what things were gain to me. Gains (plural), assets, profits, anything that would be an advantage. Paul had natural pride in his Jewish attainment. But all these assets did not save him, justify him, give him peace, nor bring him into fellowship with God. **Those I counted loss for Christ.** All those things were on the wrong side of the ledger. They were as worthless stock, and Paul renounced and relinquished them all for Christ. Paul did not exchange one religion for another; he did not exchange one creed for another; he did not exchange one system of rites for another. The word counted (Gr *hēgeomai*) is in the perfect tense and means that Paul had counted, and at the moment of writ-

ing, he still counted all things lost for Christ, not for Christianity, but for Christ crucified, buried, risen, and glorified. Christ alone meets the needs of a soul; Christ alone meets the demands of God's righteous judgment. Paul had no reserve, no retreat, no regrets.

8. Yea doubtless, and I count all things but loss. The word count here is in the present tense. Paul says I am still counting all things but loss. **For the excellency of the knowledge of Christ Jesus my Lord.** Literally, the surpassing superiority of the personal experiential knowledge of Christ, the personal relationship with Him. Excellency is the priceless privilege and the exceeding value of knowing Christ. **For whom I suffered the loss of all things.** Paul was willing to count everything else as a liability and as a disadvantage. **And do count them but dung.** Refuse of any kind, useless, worthless, and harmful. **That I may win Christ.** Better, gain Christ. Christ is the only item on the credit side of Paul's ledger.

9. And be found in him. Discovered to be united to Him and in union with Him. Such union with Christ is real, vital, and fruit-bearing. One is either in Christ or out of Christ. The first question God ever asked man was, "Adam, where art thou?" **Not having mine own righteousness, which is of the law.** A righteousness of mine own, by works, by strict observance of the law, a righteousness that is self-achieved by a series of "do's" and "don't's." Such self-righteousness is worthless. It is the opposite of the righteousness which is of God by faith. This righteousness is derived from God, obtained by faith, and is of infinite value.

10. That I may know him. Not speculate about Him, but know Him. Paul desires a fuller and a richer experience in the knowledge of Christ. Everything else fades into worthlessness before this knowledge which makes Christ Jesus one's Lord. **And the power of his resurrection.** That power exercised when God raised Christ from the dead. Such power is available (Eph 1:19-20) and imparted by the indwelling, risen Christ. **And the fellowship of his sufferings.** Or the joint-partnership in His sufferings. **Being made conformable unto his death.** Christians are to live as those who died with Christ (Rom 6:6-8) and who have been raised to a newness of life (Rom 6:4).

11. If by any means I might attain. Not implying uncertainty; there is no doubt about the realization. The only uncertainty is as to how Paul is going to attain unto the resurrection of the dead: by a martyr's death, by a non-violent death, or by the rapture. Sufferings cannot daunt Paul; death cannot terrorize him. These are just opportunities for a fuller and a richer fellowship with Christ.

12. Not as though I had already attained, either were already perfect. Paul disclaims perfection; he had made great progress in Christlikeness, but the goal is still before him and not behind him. **But I follow after.** I am pressing on. Paul is encouraged, not discouraged, as he keeps up the chase in pursuit of the goal. **If that I may apprehend that for which also I am apprehended of Christ Jesus.** If I may lay hold of that for which I was laid hold of by Christ Jesus. Christ laid hold of Paul on the road to Damascus, and Paul's desire is to lay hold of Christ's purpose for his life. God desires to reveal His Son in Paul (Gal 1:16). Paul desires a fuller apprehension of Christ, a fuller appropriation of Christ, and a fuller appreciation of Christ.

13. Brethren, I count not myself to have apprehended. To have grasped completely. **But this one thing I do.** Paul had a singleness of purpose. Paul's life was summed up in 1:21 where he said, "for me to live is Christ." Nothing could distract Paul and nothing could divert Paul from this one thing. **Forgetting those things which are behind.** Both his old pre-Christian life and his previous progress as a Christian. Paul had no time for the past and scant attention for the present. The future goal claims all of his

attention and all his efforts. It is good to forget all that hinders and to remember all that helps. **And reaching forth unto those things which are before.** Paul was stretching himself out toward the goal, as a runner as he breaks down to the finish line, straining every nerve and muscle.

14. I press toward the mark. Paul was constantly bearing down upon the goal. **For the prize of the high calling of God in Christ Jesus.** Paul found no time to relax; he found someone worth living for. Everything else was a waste of time and energy. Note it is the high calling of God or the upward calling. It was a call from heaven and a call to heaven. It was a call to be like Christ and some day to be with Christ. Paul is in hot pursuit of Christ-likeness.

C. False Goal of Antinomianism. 3:15-21.

15. Let us therefore, as many as be perfect, be thus minded. As many as are spiritually mature, full grown. This does not mean sinless perfection. We have not attained perfection. **If in anything ye be otherwise minded.** If ye think that ye are perfect. **God shall reveal even this unto you.** Such cases are turned over to God. There are three stages of perfection: First, there is positional perfection or justification (Heb 10:14; Col 2:10). Secondly, there is progressive perfection, or sanctification (II Cor 7:1; Eph 4:11-12; Gal 3:3). Thirdly, there is ultimate perfection in heaven or glorificacation (Eph 5:27; I Jn 3:1-2). The Philippians were not all mature; some were satisfied with low attainment and others with a medium attainment. But Paul says God will reveal this to them.

16. Nevertheless, whereto we have already attained, let us walk by the same rule. We need to continue in the same straight path in which we have been walking, guided by the same divine truths and the unchanging principles of faith. We need to hold on to what we have and then strive to go higher.

17. Brethren, be followers together of me. Keep on becoming imitators together of me. Paul is asking them to mimic his good example. Paul lived Christ and Paul preached Christ. It was on this basis that Paul told the Philippians to imitate him (I Cor 11:1). **And mark them which walk so as ye have us for an example.** Observe attentively and follow them as a pattern or model. Paul says keep your eye on your guide.

18. For many walk, of whom I have told you often, and now tell you even weeping. Paul had warned them repeatedly even weeping in deep emotion as he warned them of the enemy. **That they are the enemies of the cross of Christ.** Paul was not talking about erring Christians, but non-Christians. He referred to the anti-legalists, those who were a law unto themselves. They confessed Christ with their lips, but denied Christ with their lives. They taught and practiced loose living; they confused liberty with license. They taught freedom from sin, but really meant freedom to sin. They were religious and made a pretense of piety, but they denied the cross, loved the world, and lived after the flesh.

19. Whose end is destruction. Paul now gives us a description of the enemies of the cross. Paul states the plain, terrible fact that their end is doom and destruction, eternal ruin from the presence of God (II Thess 1:9). They do not realize that they are on the road to hell. **Whose God is their belly.** They admit of no one higher than themselves, and they worship themselves. They live for self-indulgence, for comfort, and for convenience. **And whose glory is in their shame.** Their glory is their shameless conduct. They boast of liberty, yet are slaves to Satan, sin, and self. **Who mind earthly things.** They are living for this world only. They are completely occupied with the material, not the spiritual; with the earthly, not the heavenly.

20. For our conversation is in heaven. Our citizenship is in heaven. Heaven is the Christian's home; he is only temporarily in this world. The church is really a colony of heaven: our names are enrolled in heaven; we are under heaven's government; we share heaven's glory; we enjoy heaven's honor. Heavenly conduct should mark the Christian. Our allegiance is to Jesus Christ. **From whence also we look for the Saviour, the Lord Jesus Christ.** We wait with eager expectation for the Second Coming of Christ. This is the normal attitude of a citizen of heaven. This expectancy of His coming should spur us on to higher and holier giving and living. The greatest event in a colony was the visit of the emperor. Our blessed hope is in the coming of Christ: it is our daily delight; it is our earnest expectation; it is our eager longing. The blessed hope motivates heavenly living (I Jn 3:1-3).

21. Who shall change our vile body. Who shall fashion anew our body of humiliation, the body suited for this world, but not for the next. These earthly bodies are subject to disease, death, and decay. **That it may be fashioned like unto his glorious body.** Conformed to the body of His glory, the body in which He appears in His present glorified state. **According to the working whereby he is able even to subdue all things unto himself.** Better subject, not merely subdue, all things unto Himself.

IV. REJOICING IN CHRIST AS A POWER OF LIFE. 4:1-23.

A. Steadfastness in Christ. 4:1-3.

1. Therefore. For this reason. **My brethren dearly beloved.** This is the same word used when God spoke of Christ at His baptism (Mt 3:17). **And longed for.** These brethren were loved and longed for. Paul had a strong yearning to see them face to face. **My joy and crown.** They were his joy because he had won them to Christ; they will be his crown of reward or wreath of victory at the Second Coming (I Thess 2:19). **So stand fast in the Lord.** Keep on standing firm and hold on to your present possession and your heavenly hopes. They were tempted to defection, and standing firm is difficult when a panic starts.

2. I beseech Euodias, and beseech Syntyche. Euodias means "prosperous journey" and Syntyche means "pleasant acquaintance." These two were women of prominence, leadership, and capability. But they had had a quarrel which is the fruit of the flesh. Paul beseeches or better exhorts or admonishes these two women. He does not use his apostolic authority. Pride, stubbornness, and ambition for prominence usually get in the way of reconciliation. These two women had not been pulling together, and both were equally at fault and were not good examples. **That they be of the same mind in the Lord.** That they agree in the Lord. No doubt they had minds of their own. Paul admonishes them to be of the same mind in the Lord, to think the same thing. Peace and unity must be preserved. It is inconsistent for two Christians to be at variance when they are in Christ; but stubborn pride and selfish ambition get in the way. Christians should be able to resolve their differences, for the scriptural cure is natural, simple, and easy.

3. And I entreat thee also, true yokefellow. It is not known who this peacemaker was. A yokefellow is one who pulls well in double harness. **Help those women which labored with me in the gospel.** Take hold with and lend a helping hand to those women in their efforts to settle their differences and to be reconciled. Paul states that they had labored with him in the gospel. They had earnestly contended in cooperation by the side of Paul. They did not usurp the place of man (I Tim 2:12), but they supplemented Paul's ministry (Tit 2:3-4). Women have access that men do not have, and they have abilities that men do not have, especially in reaching other women and children for Christ. **With Clement also, and with other my fellow-laborers, whose names are in the book of life.** Hence they are real Christians in spite of their bickerings.

B. Rejoicing in Christ's Peace. 4:4-9.

4. Rejoice in the Lord alway: and again I say, Rejoice. The Christian is not gloomy, but glorious. The keynote of this book is joy. Paul exhorts them to keep on rejoicing. Paul kept on rejoicing whether he were in prison or in the palace; in prosperity or in adversity; in health or in sickness. Joy is a fruit of the Spirit and is the result of peace with God (Rom 5:1-2). Joy drives out discord and is contagious. Christians rejoice because they are in living union with Christ.

5. Let your moderation. Your forbearance, considerateness, graciousness, gentleness, sweet reasonableness; overlooking the faults and failures of others. This is the opposite of stubbornness and thoughtlessness. **The Lord is at hand.** Christ may come at any moment (Jas 5:7-9).

6. Be careful for nothing. Stop being anxious and do not have the habit of worrying. In days of tension and trouble, in days of frustration and failure, instead of worrying, take it to the Lord in prayer. **But in everything by prayer and supplication with thanksgiving let your requests be made known unto God.** Prayer is the essence of worship and devotion. Supplication is entreating, earnest pleading for personal needs. Prayer is a general term; supplication is definite and detailed. Thanksgiving should always accompany a prayer or a petition. Thanksgiving for past blessings is good preparation for successful supplications. Care and prayer are mutually opposed. We should be anxious for nothing, prayerful for everything, and thankful for anything. "Casting all your care upon him; for he careth for you" (I Pet 5:7).

7. And the peace of God. This is more than peace with God (Rom 5:1); it is a peace which God has and which Christ gives (Jn 14:27). The peace of God comes to a child of God who trusts and prays. All Christians have peace with God, and all Christians may have the peace of God, i.e. that inward tranquility of soul grounded in God's presence, God's promise, and God's power. One may have peace with God without having the peace of God. Peace with God is dependent upon faith, and peace of God is dependent upon prayer. Peace with God describes the state between God and the Christian, and the peace of God describes the condition within the Christian. **Which passeth all understanding.** Which surpasses all power of human reason or comprehension (Eph 3:20). The peace of God in the Christian will keep peace in the church. "Thou wilt keep him in perfect peace, whose mind is stayed on thee: because he trusteth in Thee" (Isa 26:3). The Christian can put everything into God's hand and let the peace of God rule in his heart (Col 3:15). **Shall keep your hearts and minds through Christ Jesus.** Shall keep safely and continually, garrison, stand guard as an armed sentinel.

8. Finally. In conclusion. **Whatsoever.** Whatsoever introduced six adjectives picturing old-fashioned Christian ideas. **True.** Resting on reality and aiming at reality. **Honest.** Honorable, dignified, worthy of reverence, the combination of gravity and dignity. **Just.** Righteous relations between man and man, and man and God. **Pure.** Stainless, chaste, unsullied. **Lovely.** Lovable, endearing, amiable, gracious, charming, pleasing, winsome. **Of good report.** Attractive, fair speaking. **If there be any virtue.** Mental, moral, and physical excellence. **If there be any praise.** Anything praiseworthy, deemed worthy of praise. **Think on these things.** Meditate on them with careful reflection, not casually and superficially, but constantly and logically. "For as he thinketh in his heart, so is he" (Prov 23:7). Noble thinking produces noble living; high thinking produces high living; and holy thinking produces holy living. All these noble qualities were exemplified in Christ and are produced by the Holy Spirit.

9. Those things . . . do. Paul was the interpreter of the spiritual life, and his life at Philippi was an illustration of this

high and holy thinking. Paul lived what he preached, and he preached by his living. His life spoke more eloquently than his lips. The Philippians can safely follow Paul's example and exhortation. He urges them to keep on doing and practicing those things; converting creed into conduct and profession into performance. **And the God of peace shall be with you.** God will be with you in this turbulent, tempestuous world and bring unity and harmony to you and through you to the church.

C. Rejoicing in Christ's Provisions. 4:10-19.

10. But I rejoice in the Lord greatly. The Philippians had sent a love offering and Paul's cup of joy overflowed. But Paul rejoiced in the Lord, not their gift. **Your care of me hath flourished again.** Literally, you caused your thinking of me to bloom afresh. Their care not only blossomed again, but it bore fruit. **Wherein ye were also careful, but ye lacked opportunity.** Ye were continually taking thought, but, through no fault of your own, you lacked opportunity. Paul traveled far and communication was slow. The Philippians did not lack love, but the opportunity to express it. They had not forgotten Paul; they had not failed Paul.

11. Not that I speak of respect of want. Paul's commendation was not a complaint in disguise; he was not hinting for another gift. Paul does not need gifts to rejoice. Joy is not dependent on outward circumstances, but on the indwelling Christ. Paul's joy bubbles from within, not from without. **For I have learned.** He did not always know this precious truth; he learned it through long, hard experience. **In whatsoever state I am.** In prison and in chains; in want and in hunger. **Therewith to be content.** Self-sufficient, not needing outside help, able to make ends meet. Paul was totally independent of man because he was totally dependent upon God. Paul's satisfaction and sufficiency were in Christ (II Cor 12:9).

12. I know both how to be abased. Humbled, having very little, and running low as a river in a drought, facing poverty. **And I know how to abound.** Overflow in an abundance, having more than enough, facing prosperity. **I am instructed both to be full.** Well-fed with a seven course dinner. **And to be hungry.** Suffer need. Paul had been in God's school of discipline, and earned his advance degree by taking post-graduate courses in difficulty. Paul was a victor over every circumstance, not a victim to any circumstance. He adjusted well to the will of God.

13. I can do all things through Christ which strengtheneth me. In all things I continue to be strong by the One who infuses the power into me. Paul has such strength as long as Christ keeps pouring the power (Gr *dynamis*) into him. A living Christ on the inside is more than sufficient to endure the circumstances on the outside. What Christ wants Paul to do, Christ enables Paul to do. Where the finger of God points, the hand of God provides the way.

14. Notwithstanding ye have well done. Paul commends the Philippians for their loving care in relieving his sufferings. They had avoided such dangers as: (1) the deceitfulness of riches, which choked the Word; (2) contentment in their own circumstances; (3) carelessness about the needs of others; and (4) unfaithfulness in their obligations in stewardship. **That ye did communicate with my affliction.** They became fellow partakers in common with Paul in the furtherance of the gospel. Paul's needs were real and his appreciation was sincere.

15. In the beginning of the gospel. In the early days of Paul's missionary work he left Philippi. **No church communicated with me.** No other church had partnership with Paul or supported him. Paul depended upon God, and God depended upon faithful stewards, Only the church at Philippi was thoughtful in sharing and generous in giving. **Concerning giving and receiving.** Paul uses bookkeeping terms to express their dealings with him. Paul did not have to keep books with any other church at that time. Later Thessalonica and Berea joined in supporting Paul (II Cor 11:8). Not even Antioch contributed anything other than prayers and good wishes.

16. For even in Thessalonica ye sent once and again unto my necessity. Twice while Paul was in Thessalonica the Philippians contributed toward his needs.

17. Not because I desire a gift. This is delicate courtesy; Paul is not seeking another gift. **But I desire fruit that may abound to your account.** The fruit is the returns on their investments. God is a good bookkeeper; He will settle all accounts, and He pays big dividends.

18. But I have all, and abound. More than enough. You have paid me in full. **I am full.** I have been filled and am still full, supplied and satisfied. **Having received of Epaphroditus the things which were sent from you.** The Philippians' stewardship was a barometer of their spiritual condition. One can give without loving, but he cannot love without giving. Love takes the *stew* out of stewardship. The love gift pleased God, relieved Paul, and enriched the Philippians. **An odor of a sweet smell, a sacrifice acceptable, wellpleasing to God.** Their generosity was like a sweet fragrance (cf. Gen 8:20-21; Ex 29:18).

19. But my God shall supply all your need according to his riches in glory by Christ Jesus. The Philippians had met Paul's need out of their poverty by Epaphroditus; God will meet their need out of His riches by Christ Jesus. We see first of all in this verse a great need. God promises to meet all of their need, not all of their wishes, wants, or whims. Men have physical needs, mental needs, social needs, economic needs. Men have not only temporal needs, but spiritual and eternal needs. Men need perpetual pardon, perpetual peace, and perpetual power. Secondly, we see in this verse a great helper. Paul says **But my God.** Paul could not repay the Philippians, but God could and would. Paul does not say my God *can* supply all your needs, but my God *shall* supply all your need. This was Paul's personal testimony and confession of faith. We see next a great supplier. There is a total supply for a total need. God's supply is infinite, abundant, inexhaustible, limitless, boundless. God many times uses the agencies of men to meet our needs. Next we see great resources. God's riches in glory. Paul says according to His riches, not out of His riches, not off the top. God's supply is not according to our deserts, but according to His mercy; not out of debt, but out of grace; not according to our emptiness, but according to His fullness; not according to our poverty, but according to His wealth. God has great riches. Lastly, look at the great and glorious channel by Christ Jesus. "For there is one God, and one mediator between God and men, the man Christ Jesus; Who gave himself a ransom for all, to be testified in due time" (I Tim 2:5-6). There is no other mediator; there is no other channel. With such precious truth before us there can only be concurrence with the past, contentment with the present, and confidence for the future.

D. Benediction. 4:20-23.

20. Now unto God and our Father be glory for ever and ever. Amen. This doxology flows out of the joy of the epistle. For ever and ever means unto the ages of the ages.

21. Salute every saint. No partiality here. **In Christ.** Every saint is in vital union with Christ. **The brethren.** Paul's companions.

22. All the saints salute you. All of God's children join in sending greetings. **Chiefly they that are of Caesar's household.** Not necessarily members of the imperial family, but those connected with the imperial household. Paul had personally won many of them to faith in Christ, and they send greetings.

23. The grace of our Lord Jesus Christ be with you all. Paul closes with this short, simple, sublime benediction. **Amen.**

BIBLIOGRAPHY

Barth, Karl. *The Epistle to the Philippians.* Richmond: John Knox Press, 1962.

Beet, Joseph Agar. *A Commentary on St. Paul's Epistles to the Ephesians, Philippians, Colossians, and to Philemon.* London: Hodder & Stoughton, 1890.

Calvin, John. *Commentaries on the Epistles of Paul the Apostle to the Philippians, Colossians, and Thessalonians.* Trans. by John Pringle. Edinburg: Calvin Trans. Soc., 1951.

Eadie, John. *Commentary on the Greek Text of the Epistle of Paul to the Philippians.* Grand Rapids: Zondervan, n.d.

Erdman, Charles R. *The Epistle of Paul to the Philippians.* Philadelphia: The Westminster Press, 1932.

* Hendriksen, William. A Commentary on the Epistle to the Philippians. In *New Testament Commentary.* Grand Rapids: Baker, 1962.

Herklots, H. G. G. *The Epistle of St. Paul to the Philippians. A Devotional Commentary.* London: Lutterworth Press, 1946.

Ironside, H. A. *Notes on Philippians.* New York: Loizeaux Brothers, 1922.

Kennedy, H. A. A. The Epistle to the Philippians. In *The Expositor's Greek Testament.* Grand Rapids: Eerdmans, n.d.

Lenski, R. C. H. *The Interpretation of St. Paul's Epistles to the Galatians, to the Ephesians, and to the Philippians.* Columbus: The Wartburg Press, 1937.

* Lightfoot, J. B. *Saint Paul's Epistle to the Philippians.* Grand Rapids: Zondervan, 1953.

Martin, Ralph P. The Epistle of Paul to the Philippians. In *Tyndale New Testament Commentaries.* Grand Rapids: Eerdmans, 1959.

Meyer, F. B. *The Epistle to the Philippians.* Grand Rapids: Baker, 1952.

* Moule, H. C. G. *Philippian Studies: Lessons in Faith and Love.* Grand Rapids: Zondervan, n.d.

Plummer, Alfred. *A Commentary on St. Paul's Epistle to the Philippians.* London: Robert Scott, 1919.

* Robertson, A. T. *Paul's Joy in Christ.* New York: Revell, 1917.

Robertspn, A. T. *Word Pictures in the New Testament.* Nashville: Broadman Press, 1931.

Strauss, Leyman. *Devotional Studies in Philippians.* New York: Loizeaux Brothers, 1959.

Tenney, Merrill C. *Philippians: The Gospel at Work.* Grand Rapids: Eerdmans, 1956.

Vincent, M. R. A Critical and Exegetical Commentary on the Epistles to the Philippians and to Philemon. In the *International Critical Commentary.* New York: Scribner's, 1897.

* Wuest, Kenneth S. *Philippians in the Greek New Testament for the English Reader.* Grand Rapids: Eerdmans, 1944.

The Epistle To The
COLOSSIANS

INTRODUCTION

The church of Colossae. Colossae was located in Asia Minor in the Lycus Valley, about one hundred miles east of Ephesus on the main east-west highway. The population was heterogeneous, i.e. native Phrygians, Greek colonists, and Jews. The city was deserted completely about A.D. 700 and today is a place of ruins. The church at Colossae was not mentioned in the book of Acts, and it was not directly founded by the Apostle Paul (2:1). Probably during Paul's stay at Ephesus when "all they which dwelt in Asia heard the word of the Lord Jesus" (Acts 19:23. See also 18:23 and 19:26), Philemon, Apphia, Archippus, Epaphras, and other natives were converted and became effective witnesses in this area (Phm 2, 13, 19, 23; Col 1:6-8; 4:12-13). The membership was composed largely of Gentiles (1:21, 27; 2:13). Its size is not indicated; it attained no prominence in history, and it soon faded from view.

Authorship. The author claims to be Paul (1:1, 23; 4:8), and there is no evidence that anyone else used Paul's name to palm off this powerful polemic.

Date and place of writing. This is one of the Prison Epistles and was written from Rome 61-63 A.D. Tychicus was the bearer of Colossians and Ephesians (Col 4:7-8; Eph 6:21-22).

Occasion of the epistle. Epaphras, who helped evangelize the Lycus Valley, arrived with greetings and with disturbing news from Colossae (1:7-9; 4:12). After Paul's departure from Ephesus, the "grievous wolves" (Acts 20:29 ff.) had entered into the church, playing havoc and leading many away from the truth. The Phrygians had a mystic tendency in their worship of Cybele and were susceptible to incipient Gnosticism, which later developed into strange heresies. This threatening danger was both doctrinal and ethical. There was a false conception of theology characterized by mysticism regarding the person of Christ and the origin and nature of the universe. There was also a false basis of morals characterized by ritualism and formalism. At Colossae there was a strict asceticism, attempting to purify lives by a code of strict prohibitions (2:20-23), and also a wild unrestrained license, antinomianism (3:5-7).

Purpose. Paul writes to express his personal interest in the Colossians and to warn them against reverting to their old vices. He refutes false doctrine and proclaims the truth. He presents a full-length portrait of Christ as supreme, sufficient (2:9-10), Son of Man (humanity), and Son of God (deity).

Relation to the Epistle to the Ephesians. In Ephesians the emphasis is on the dignity of church, which is the body of Christ; in Colossians the emphasis is on the deity of Christ, who is the Head of that body. Ephesians considers the church's oneness with Christ; Colossians considers the church's completeness in Christ. Ephesians speaks of the Christian being in Christ; Colossians speaks of Christ being in the Christian.

OUTLINE

I. Introduction. 1:1-14.
    A. Salutation. 1:1-2.
    B. Thanksgiving. 1:3-8.
    C. Intercession. 1:9-14.
II. Personal: The Christ. 1:15-2:3.
    A. The Person of Christ. 1:15-19.
        1. His relation to God. 1:15a.
        2. His relation to creation. 1:15b-17.
        3. His relation to the church. 1:18-19.
    B. The Work of Christ. 1:20-23.
    C. The Servant of Christ. 1:24-2:3.
        1. Paul's solemn charge. 1:24-27.
        2. Paul's loving care. 1:28-2:3.
III. Polemical: The Church. 2:4-3:4.
    A. The Position of the Church. 2:4-15.
        1. The threatening danger: false philosophy. 2:4-7.
        2. The saving doctrine: person and work of Christ. 2:8-15.
    B. The Responsibility of the Church. 2:16-3:4.
        1. Negatively. 2:16-19.
            a. There must be no submission to former legalism. 2:16-17.
            b. There must be no subservience to false philosophy. 2:18-19.
        2. Positively. 2:20-3:4.
            a. Dead with Christ, we are free from earthly ordinances. 2:20-23.
            b. Risen with Christ, we are bound to heavenly principles. 3:1-4.
IV. Practical: The Christian. 3:5-4:6.
    A. Principles for the Inner Life. 3:5-17.
        1. Vices to put off. 3:5-11.
        2. Virtues to put on. 3:12-17.
    B. Precepts for the Outer Life. 3:18-4:6.
        1. Relation to the domestic life. 3:18-4:1.
            a. Helpmeets and husbands. 3:18-19.
            b. Families and fathers. 3:20-21.
            c. Servants and the served. 3:22-4:1.
        2. Relation to the world. 4:2-6.
            a. Duty of prayer. 4:2-4.
            b. Duty of propriety. 4:5-6.
V. Conclusion. 4:7-18.

COMMENTARY

I. INTRODUCTION. 1:1-14.

A. Salutation. 1:1-2.

1:1. Paul, an apostle. Paul refers to his apostleship because he is unknown to the Colossians. This refers to his authoritative title, signifying equality with the Twelve, because he has seen the risen Christ (I Cor 15:8). It refers to the dignity of his office; he is clothed with authority and endued with power. In his official capacity, he is writing to combat error. **Of Jesus Christ.** Paul is our Lord's ambassador. He bore His commission, did Hid work, and sought His acceptance. Paul's life and work were ordered by Christ. **By the will of God.** This speaks of his divine appointment. His appointment was not by the Twelve, by religious leaders, by his family, nor by himself. This is an assertion of his divine authority, a declaration of his independence of all human authority, and he disclaims any individual merit or personal power. **And Timothy our brother.** Timothy was not an apostle; he was a brother. This trusted companion was with Paul in Rome. As an act of courtesy, Paul includes Timothy in the salutation. Timothy was Paul's spiritual son (I Tim 1:2, 18; II Tim 1:2; I Cor 4:17).

2. To the saints (Gr *hagios*). This speaks of their divine relationship. It means "holy ones," born-again believers, not some special group. It also means "separated ones": separated to God, separated by God, and separated from the world. The main idea is not excellence of character, but separation to God, for His purpose and for His service. **And faithful brethren.** Believing brethren. This refers to their human relationship. They were full of faith, trustful, and trustworthy. They were loyal to Christ. Paul refers to them as brethren. There is no spiritual nobility. God has one spiritual family, and all are on an equality, despite difference of cultural background, social status, or racial origin. **In Christ.** This speaks of the spiritual position of believers in union with Christ. This is a real, mystical union. There is not only filial relation to God, but also brotherly relation to believers. Paul speaks of their faith, fraternity, and fellowship. **Grace.** God's unmerited favor. Grace gives us what we do not deserve; mercy withholds from us what we do deserve. Grace always precedes peace. **And peace.** Peace with God and the peace of God. Peace speaks of the calm tranquility of heart amidst disturbing circumstances. **From God.** The source of grace and peace.

B. Thanksgiving. 1:3-8.

3. We give thanks. Paul begins with thanksgiving because there is much for which to be thankful. Thanksgiving precedes intercession; praise precedes prayer. Paul calls God the Father of our Lord Jesus Christ. **Praying always for you.** Continually. Paul practices what he preached (Eph 6:18).

4. Since we heard of your faith in Christ Jesus. Having heard, because we heard. There were no secret believers. Paul simply refers to your faith; not your great faith, abounding faith, or extraordinary faith. Their faith was in Christ. They trusted Christ; committed themselves to Christ, and had a vital spiritual connection with Christ. Their faith was Christ-centered; they rested in Christ, and they were anchored in Christ. **And of the love.** Love is a fruit of the Spirit (Gal 5:22; Rom 5:5). Love is the evidence of faith (Jn 13:35; 15:12; Gal 5:6; Jas 2:14-20; I Jn 3:14). Love is the characteristic mark of Christianity; it is not superficial friendliness. **To all the saints.** They were not isolationists; there were no sectarian limitations. They loved everyone of whatever position or disposition. This speaks of the depth of brotherly fellowship and the breadth of brotherly concern. They were not indifferent to the needs of others, nor disapproving of the deeds of others, nor critical of the motives of others.

5. For the hope. Because of the hope, not on account of the hope. This states the cause or reason of their love. **Laid up for you in heaven.** Stored up like a treasure, reserved (II Tim 4:8; I Pet 1:3-5). The hope Paul speaks of is still future, and its nature is still unknown, but its possession is absolutely certain. **Whereof ye heard before.** They heard the gospel from Ephaphras before Gnosticism crept in. **The word of the truth of the gospel.** Knowledge of this hope came through the Word. Truth is the very essence of the gospel. Paul speaks of faith; the beginning of the Christian life, which lays hold of Christ. Faith rests in the past. Paul speaks of love; love lives in the present and links together faith and hope. Hope looks toward the future and anticipates the crown (I Jn 3:1-3).

6. Which is come unto you. Present with you. **In all the world.** The gospel was spreading all over the Roman Empire. **Bringeth forth fruit.** Is bearing fruit, keeps on bearing fruit. The gospel is dynamic, and this speaks of its inner energy and transforming power. It is folly to look for fruit before there is life. "By their fruits ye shall know them" (Mt 7:20). **Increasing.** Growing and fruit-bearing are simultaneous. There is inward growth and outward expression. The outward extension of the gospel never stops. We read in John 12:24, "Verily, verily, I say unto you, Except a corn of wheat fall into the ground and die, it abideth alone: but if it die, it bringeth forth much fruit." The church must germinate or terminate; it will either evangelize or fossilize. **Since the day ye heard.** This fruit-bearing and growing began and it continues. **Knew the grace of God in truth.** The grace of God was fully apprehended and should have made them immune from Gnosticism.

7. As ye also learned of Epaphras. Epaphras was their teacher; a native of Colosse; Paul's fellowservant; and a faithful minister of Christ.

8. Who also declared. Made manifest. **Your love.** This is the supernatural of John 3:16 and produced by the Holy Spirit.

C. Intercession. 1:9-14.

9. For this cause. The reason for Paul's intercession. **Do not cease to pray.** Daily and definitely. **Filled with the knowledge of his will.** This is available to all, not for a privileged few. The thoughts, feelings, and emotions are to be saturated with this knowledge of God's Will. The word knowledge here is in contrast with the knowledge of the Gnostics. It is full knowledge, super knowledge, thorough knowledge gained by experience, and deep accurate comprehension. It is not theoretical, but experimental and practical. Notice it is a knowlege of His will, not of His nature. We are not expected to understand and explain the Trinity, but we are expected to understand His plan and His purpose for our lives. This is the foundation of all Christian character and conduct. The cure for Gnosticism is more knowledge of, and obedience to, God's will. **In all wisdom.** This is practical good sense, the ability to use knowledge. **And spiritual understanding.** This is spiritual insight, correct apprehension, inner perception, and clear discernment.

10. That ye might walk worthy. To the end that ye should walk worthy. This is the aim and the result of knowing God's will. Knowledge is not an end in itself, and is not given to satisfy curiosity. Walk refers to the total conduct and course of life. Right knowledge issues in right conduct; right conduct is never the product of wrong knowledge. God wants His children to walk worthy; to be a credit to Christ, to live in conformity with our union with Christ, and in conformity with His purpose for our lives. Our lives should be Christ-centered (Gal 2:20). **Unto all pleasing.** Not pleasing everybody, but pleasing God in everything, in every way, and all the time. **Being fruitful.** This modifies the word walk. Continually bearing fruit. Christians are to be perennial fruit-bearers. **In every good work.** Fruit of right relationship to Christ. This is an evidence of discipleship (Jn 15:8). **Increasing in the knowledge of God.** This speaks of both the sphere where spiritual growth takes place and also the means of that spiritual growth (II Pet 3:18). A fruit-bearing tree grows; one that does not grow ceases to bear fruit.

11. Strengthened with all might. Empowered with all power. We are engaged in a spiritual conflict (Eph 6:10 ff.), and we need spiritual power from God. The word strengthened is in the Greek present tense and indicates that God keeps continuously and progressively filling us with dynamic power. **According to his glorious power.** His limitless omnipotence. This strengthening is not proportioned simply to our need, but according to His abundant supply. **Unto all.** The threefold results of such empowerment: not working miracles, not outburst of eloquence, but producing homely virtues. **Patience.** Literally, "remaining under." This is the opposite of cowardice and despondency. It is forbearance, steadfast endurance, fortitude, and the capacity to see things through. It means remaining under difficulties without succumbing to them. **Longsuffering.** This is the opposite of wrath and revenge. It is self-restraint, even-temperedness, holding out long. Longsuffering does not retaliate in spite of injury or insult (cf. Jas 5:7-11). **With joyfulness.** Not with a long face, not with a sickly smile, but with psalms in the night. "The joy of the Lord is your strength" (Neh 8:10).

12. Giving thanks. Not striving for, not praying for, but giving thanks for three things. **Made us meet.** Made us fit, adequate; not worthy. He qualified us, made us competent and sufficient. This is true of every Christian. There are no degrees of fitness. Fitness depends on privilege and position, not character or experience. The Greek aorist tense points to the instantaneous act of conversion, not a progressive process. It is a present reality. **To be made partakers of the inheritance.** Not purchasers. We have a portion and share of the inheritance as an unearned gift. **In light.** This marks the inheritance as future and as

heavenly. Light speaks of the realm where there is no night and no sin.

13. Delivered us from the power of darkness. God rescued and liberated us from the power, dominion, authority, and tyranny of darkness. Darkness speaks of a miserable, horrible state of being held captive by Satan. Darkness is a symbol of ignorance, falsehood, and sin. **Translated us.** This is an accomplished fact. God transported, transplanted, and transferred us from the devil's dominion to Christ's control. **Into the kingdom of his dear son.** The Son is the object of the Father's love. Paul rules out the system of aeons which the Gnostics placed above Christ. It is Christ's kingdom in which He is sovereign. God removed us from the realm of darkness and he established us as colonists and as citizens in the realm of light (I Pet 2:9).

14. In whom we have redemption. This is a present possession. We have redemption because of our vital union with Christ. Redemption means deliverance, ransom, release, emancipation. Redemption speaks of our release on the payment of a ransom (Mk 10:45; Acts 20:28; Gal 3:13; Tit 2:14). **Through his blood.** The best texts do not contain these words; however this truth is taught elsewhere (Eph 1:7; I Pet 1:18; I Jn 1:7). This deliverance is exhibited by **the forgiveness of sins.** This is the logical result of redemption, the real consequences of salvation. Forgiveness is remission, the sending away and removal of our sins. (Ps 103:12; Mic 7:18; Isa 43:25; 44:22).

I. PERSONAL: THE CHRIST. 1:15-23.

A. The Person of Christ. 1:15-19.

1. His relation to God. 1:15a.

15a. Who is the image of the invisible God. The image expresses Christ's deity in relation to the Father; it is the very stamp of God as He was before the incarnation (Jn 17:5). The word is not *form* (Phil 2:6), but **image.** This is more than a resemblance, more than a representation. It is a manifestation, a revelation. The "Word" of John 1:1 is a divine person, not a philosophical abstraction. In the incarnation, the invisible God became visible in Christ: deity was clothed with humanity (Mt 17:2), deity under some human limitations. Christ in God: visible, audible, approachable, knowable, and available. All that God is, Christ is.

2. His relation to creation. 1:15b-17.

15b. The firstborn of every creature. This expresses Christ's deity and sovereignty in relation to creation. Christ was the firstborn, not the first created. Firstborn signifies priority in time. First, this speaks of His pre-existence, what He was from eternity. He was before all creation; not a part of creation, but apart from creation. He is not a creature, but the Creator. Secondly, this speaks of the supremacy of His position. He is the self-existent, acknowledged Head of creation. Thirdly, this also speaks of being recognized as the Messiah (Ps 89:27). So we have here declared the eternity, the sovereignty, and the lordship of Christ.

16. For by him were all things created. Three prepositions tell the story: (1) *In* Him, sovereign source; (2) *by* Him, divine agent; (3) *unto* Him, for His use and for His glory. The first word "created" (Gr *ktizō*) is in the Greek aorist tense and views creation as a definite, historical act. Creation is a past, perfect work. The second word "created" is in the Greek perfect tense and speaks of the resulting state. Creation stands created, a permanant work. We have a Christo-centric universe, and this is complete denial of the Gnostic philosophy.

17. And he is before all things. Christ existed prior to all creation. He is the great "I am" (Jn 8:58). The Jehovah of the Old Testament is the Jesus of the New Testament. **And by him all things consist.** Through Christ all things hold together, cohere, are sustained, and united. Christ is the personal sustainer and preserver. He maintains harmony and order. All things are created by Him and are controlled by Him. Apart from Christ all things would disintegrate: He holds the stars in their courses, He directs the planets in their orbits, and He controls the laws of the universe. We have a cosmos, not a chaos.

3. His relation to the church. 1:18-19.

18. And he is the head of the body, the church. He is emphatic; He alone, and no one else. He directs, controls, guides, and governs the church. The church is His body; He is its source and its life. He unites the members into one organism. The church is a living organism, composed of living members joined together; an organism through which Christ works, carries out His purposes; and an organism in which Christ lives. **Who is the beginning, the firstborn from the dead.** The Prince of Life (Acts 3:15). The church is also a family, composed of those who share in His resurrection life. The word "beginning" is used in three senses: (1) prior in time; (2) supremacy in rank; (3) creative initiative. Christ is not the first of a series, but the source. Christ is the source of new creation and the sovereign Head of that new creation. **That in all things he might have the preeminence.** He is emphatic; He alone, not angels or men. Christ has unshared supremacy; He has first place; He is in a class by Himself; He is eminent above all others. It is not enough for Christ to be present, nor prominent; He must be preeminent.

19. For it pleased the Father. His good pleasure and purpose. **That in him should all fullness dwell.** Christ is a manifestation of God, the Sovereign Creator, and the Head of the church. The sum total of all the power and attributes are in Christ. The Gnostics distributed the divine powers among various aeons. Paul gathers them all up in Christ. In Christ there is divine perfection: not just a part, nor just almost all, but all divine nature in all its fullness (Eph 1:23; 3:19; 4:13; Col 2:9; 3:11). The word "dwell" indicates permanent residence, not just a temporary visit. Only a divine person could create a world, be the Head of the church, and reconcile a world to God.

B. The Work of Christ. 1:20-23.

20. And, having made peace through the blood of his cross. This for the special benefit of the Docetic Gnostics, who denied the real humanity of Christ. The blood speaks of Christ's redemptive work and the sacrificial aspect of His death. **By him to reconcile . . . unto himself.** Reconcile (Gr *apokatallasō*) means to change completely (Rom 5:6-10). Christ is the chosen and sufficient agent in reconciliation; nothing else is needed. Divine harmony has been restored; all barriers and obstacles have been removed. God took the initiative. Religion is man seeking God; Christianity is God seeking and saving man (II Cor 5:18-20; Eph 1:10; 2:14-16).

21. And you, . . . alienated . . . enemies. Alienated means that we were estranged from God. Enemies means we were hostile and at war with God (Rom 1:30; 8:7; Eph 2:1-2, 12, 19). **In your mind.** The seat of antagonism was the thoughts, attitude, and disposition of their minds. **By wicked works.** The evidence and manifestation of alienation. This indicates willful opposition and personal animosity.

22. In the body of his flesh through death. This emphasizes the reality of His incarnation and humanity. Death speaks of real suffering, not mere appearance. There was an actual atonement; not through His birth, His baptism, His miracles, His teaching; but through His death (Eph 2:15-16; Heb 9:22; 10:19-20). **To present you.** The ultimate purpose of reconciliation (Eph 5:27). **Holy.** The positive side. Christians are consecrated, dedicated, and set apart for God. Christ's righteousness becomes our righteousness. **Unblameable.** This is the negative side. Unblameable is a technical, sacrificial term and means "without flaw, free from defects, without blemish, and stainless in character and conduct." **Unreproveable.** There is no charge and no accusation either here or hereafter. All of this through His precious blood.

23. If ye continue in the faith. Provided that and assuming that there is a continuance in a firm position of faith. The test of reality is steadfastness in faith. There is no doubt insinuated, no threatening danger implied, but a certain necessary condition. Paul is sure that they will continue in the faith. **Grounded.** A firm foundation. The church is built on the rock and there is no shifting (Eph 3:17). **Settled.** Referring to the superstructure or the firm building in a solid fashion. The church is immovably fixed. **And be not moved away.** Not continually shifting away. The church has a stable position and shall never be dislodged. **From the hope of the gospel.** The hope given in the gospel. We read of: the hope of righteousness (Gal 5:5); the hope of His calling (Eph 1:18); the hope of eternal life (Tit 3:7); the living hope (I Pet 1:3-4); and the hope that we have (Heb 6:19). **Whereof I Paul am made a minister.** One who serves.

C. The Servant of Christ. 1:24-2:3.

1. Paul's solemn charge. 1:24-27.

24. Who now rejoice in my sufferings. Paul was in prison and in chains. **For you.** Not in your place, but in your interest, on your behalf, for your benefit, and for your advantage. Afflictions of Christ. These were sufficient for the finished atonement (Jn 1:29; I Jn 2:1-2). The sufferings of Christ provided the gospel and salvation. The afflictions of Paul proclaimed the gospel, and referred to servants. The afflictions of Paul are identified with the afflictions of Christ but are on a different plane. Paul's afflictions could add nothing to the finished work of Christ. The proclamation of the gospel transforms sinners into saints, and saints into martyrs. **For his body's sake.** Not in the sense of atonement, but the announcing of that atonement (Phil 4:11).

25. I am made a minister. Become a servant. Paul's appointment made him a minister of the gospel (Eph 3:7; Col 1:23) a minister of God (II Cor 6:4); a minister of Christ (I Cor 4:1); and a minister of the New Covenant (II Cor 3:6). **Dispensation.** Divine ordering (Gr *oikonomia*). Administration, stewardship, trusteeship. This was Paul's high privilege and sacred trust. Paul was a steward in God's economy; a trustee in God's household; and an administrator of God's business. Paul was on business for the King. **Given.** Not usurped. **For you.** For your benefit and for your blessing. **To fulfill the word of God.** God's purpose was Paul's purpose, and God's Word was Paul's message. Therefore Paul's message was pure and uncorrupted by false teaching (Rom 15:19; II Tim 4:2-5).

26. Even the mystery. Sacred secret. There is no connection here with mystery religions. **Hid.** Unknown in ages past; once concealed, now revealed by the Holy Spirit. **Manifest.** Clear as day. **To his saints.** To all born-again Christians.

27. To whom. God was pleased to make this mystery known (Eph 1:17-18). God willed this change from hidden mystery to manifestation. **Riches.** Glorious wealth. **Christ in you.** The indwelling Christ (Jn 15:5; Gal 2:20; Eph 3:17). Christ is the answer: not the law, not circumcision, not ceremony, not philosophy, not science, not social reform. **Hope of glory.** Pledge of the future.

2. Paul's loving care. 1:28-2:3.

28. Whom we preach. Paul did not proclaim precepts, a creed, a code of ethics, rules or regulations, not a plan, not a program, but a Person (II Tim 1:12). **Warning.** Addressing, admonishing the heart; reproving and convincing of error. This refers to conduct and leads to repentance. **Teaching.** Addressing the intellect; informing, and instructing in faith and morals. This refers to doctrine. **May present.** Paul's aim and purpose. **Every man.** This is repeated three times for emphasis. Paul has no narrow exclusiveness such as the Gnostics. **Perfect in Christ Jesus.** Not sinless, but perfect, complete, full grown, mature.

29. Whereunto. Paul's goal. **I also labour.** Exerting all my strength in weariness and exhaustion. **Striving.** Intense struggling (like an athlete), agonizing in strenuous effort. **His working.** Divine energy and supernatural power in Paul and through Paul. Paul was God's instrument to do God's work, through God's power, and for God's glory.

2:1. Knew. The seriousness of the situation and perils in which Paul stood. Paul desires them to know this so that they will appreciate him, pray for him, and share with him in this great conflict. **Great conflict.** The strain of Paul's soul in his pastoral concern (II Cor 11:28; I Thess 2:2). **For you.** The Colossians, Laodiceans and for others. Paul prayed earnestly for the converts and for the churches.

2. Hearts ... comforted. Confirmed, strengthened, encouraged. Not consoled, but strengthened; not relief, but reinforcements. They were in danger of being shaken. **Being knit together in love.** A closer unity, a vital helpful relationship, being welded together, a unibody. This will safeguard against the corruption and the disruption of false teaching. **All riches.** Complete abundance of inward wealth. **Full assurance.** Confidence, deep convictions, full knowledge of Christ (I Cor 2:12; Eph 3:17-20). **To the acknowledgement.** Personal knowledge of the sacred secret.

3. In whom are hid. Don't look anywhere else. **Treasures.** Our thesaurus or storehouse. These treasures are available and accessible to every believer. Paul confronts the Gnostics with the fact that Christ sums up all wisdom and knowledge.

III. POLEMICAL: THE CHURCH. 2:4-3:4.

A. The Position of the Church. 2:4-15.

1. The threatening danger: false philosophy. 2:4-7.

4. Beguile. Literally, "reason alongside." This means to elude, deceive by false reasoning, and lead astray (Mt 24:4; Acts 20:30; II Cor 11:13; Eph 4:14; I Jn 4:1). **Enticing words.** Attractive arguments, persuasive rhetoric, plausible speech, fast talk, and a smooth line.

5. Your order. This is a military term (Gr *taxis*) indicating an orderly array of disciplined soldiers. The Colossians' ranks had not been broken yet; but the Gnostics were attacking, and Paul was concerned for them. **Stedfastness of your faith in Christ.** Another military word (Gr *stereōma*) signifying solidity. With unbroken ranks, every man was in his place, presenting a solid front. This speaks of the unyielding nature of their faith which was firm and true to Christ.

6. As . . . received Christ Jesus the Lord. This refers to a personal appropriation of Christ, not just believing a truth about Him. By using this unique phrase, Paul discharged both barrels at the same time to lay low the two forms of Gnostic heresy about the person of Christ: (1) the recognition of the historical Jesus in His actual humanity (Docetic Gnostics); and (2) the identity of Christ with this historical Jesus (Cerinthian Gnostics). **So walk.** Live accordingly, keep on walking. Our walk must match our talk.

7. Rooted. Permanently rooted in Christ and firmly anchored in Him. This is what God has done. **Built up.** This is a continual process, being built up constantly like an ever-expanding building. **Stablished in the faith.** This means to make firm or stable. **Abounding.** The natural consequence.

2. The saving doctrine: person and work of Christ. 2:8-15.

8. Beware. Take heed, see to it, be on your guard, keep a watchful eye ever open, be alert to the imminent danger because the enemy is lurking in darkness. **Spoil you.** Carry away captive, carry you off as booty. The picture here is of kidnapping you for the purpose of seducing you from faith in Christ. It is not robbing you of some blessing, but

taking you captive; a picture of a long line of prisoners of war, leading them away into slavery. The false teachers were men-stealers, entrapping and dragging men into spiritual slavery. **Through philosophy.** Love of wisdom. Paul does not condemn knowledge and wisdom, but only this false philosophy, knowledge falsely named (I Tim 6:20). **And vain deceit.** An explanation of this philosophy: empty delusions, vain speculations, hollow sham, devoid of truth, high sounding nonsense. This all amounts to nothing, and cannot meet the needs of the soul. **After the tradition of men.** That which is handed down. Here it refers to foolish theories of the Gnostics. We see here a contrast between human reason and divine revelation (Mk 7:6-9); man's theories versus God's truth; fables versus facts. **After the rudiments of the world.** Anything in a row or series (Gr *stoicheion*) like the letters of the alphabet; elementary, preparatory, and immature. Paul is speaking of the ritualistic and materialistic elements of Gnosticism. This is a contrast between the outward and the material as opposed to the inward and the spiritual. **And not after Christ.** In contradiction to Christ, and to God's Word. Gnosticism stood in the way of Christ, weakened faith in Christ, and took men away from Christ. Such heresy is best met, not by detailed discussion, nor by bitter denunciation, but by the declaration of truth.

9. For in him. This is emphatic, and means nowhere else. **Dwelleth.** Permanent residence. **All the fulness of the Godhead.** The godhood. All attributes and the essence of deity are in Christ; not just divinity, but deity; not God-like, but God; not a nature like God's, but a nature the same as God's. **Bodily.** The incarnation was real. Here our Lord Jesus Christ was one person with two natures: the God-man. Paul disposes of the Docetic theory that Jesus had no human body as well as the Cerinthian separation between the man Jesus and aeon Christ. Paul declares the deity and the humanity of Jesus Christ in corporeal form.

10. And ye are complete in him. God did this in connection with Christ. This is both complete and permanent. Having been completely filled in the past, we are in a state of fullness now. All we need is in Christ (I Cor 1:30). We do not need the emptiness of the Gnostics, since we have the fullness of Christ. We seek no other source of grace and truth; we show no allegiance to anyone else; and we submit to no other authority. Christ is the Head; He is the source of life; and He is sovereign over life.

11. Circumcised. This points to conversion (Rom 4:1; 2:28-29; Phil 3:3). The character of this circumcision is spiritual and not physical. It is without hands; inward and not outward. The extent of this circumcision is the whole body, not just one organ. The author of this circumcision is Christ, not Moses. This circumcision that Paul speaks of is not a rite, but a reality. **Putting off the body . . . the flesh.** Stripping and casting aside as a filthy garment. The flesh is removed from the throne, and the Christian is set free from his sinful nature. The evil nature is not eradicated (I Jn 1:8), but its power is broken. Christ is now on the throne; but the flesh lurks about and tries to usurp the throne. Our physical members are to be instruments not of unrighteousness unto sin, but of righteousness unto God (Rom 6:11-14).

12. Buried with him in baptism. Jointly entombed with Christ; sharing in His experience. Baptism is not a magic rite, but an act of obedience in confessing our faith. Baptism symbolizes our experience of death to the old life and resurrection to the new life (Rom 6:3-5). Baptism is an outward expression of an inward experience. **Through the faith.** Without saving faith, baptism is an empty, meaningless ceremony. Through faith we receive Christ (Jn 1:12-13) and experience the new birth.

13. And you, being dead. Devoid of the life of God, a totally depraved nature (Eph 2:1; 5:6, 11). **Hath he quickened.** Made alive in union with Christ. **Having forgiven you all trespasses.** Graciously pardoning and cancelling the debt (cf. Lk 7:42).

14. Blotting out. Erased, wiped away, obliterated, cancelled the note. This explains the forgiveness. **The handwriting of ordinances.** The hand-written document consisting of ordinances. The bond here is the certification of debt, the instrument of condemnation, the indictment drawn up against a prisoner, and a signed confession of indebtedness. Three expressions describe the law: (1) it is written in ordinances, expressed in decrees and commandments; (2) it was against us, had a valid claim on us; (3) it was contrary to us, because we couldn't meet the claim. Paul states that bond was: (1) blotted out; (2) taken out of the way; (3) and nailed to His cross. This was once for all removal (II Cor 5:21; Eph 2: 15-16; Gal 3:13). In the East, a bond is cancelled by nailing it to the post. Our bond of guilt was nailed to His cross.

15. Having spoiled principalities and powers. Stripped off and away from. The principalities and powers are conquered antagonists stripped of their weapons, disarmed (Mt 12:29; Lk 11: 21-22; Jn 16:11; Rom 8:37-39; I Cor 15: 55-57; Heb 2:4). By His death, Christ conquered His enemies, stripped them of their power, exposed them to public disgrace, held them up in contempt, and led them captives in His triumph.

B. The Responsibility of the Church. 2:16-3:4.

1. Negatively. 2:16-19.

a. There must be no submission to former legalism. 2:16-17.

16. Let no man therefore judge you. Sit in judgment, take you to task, deciding for you, criticizing and condemning. Paul is encouraging the Colossians not to be enslaved by legalism, ritualism, rites, and ceremonies.

17. Which are a shadow. A shadow is not the real thing. There is a difference between the shadow and the substance. Symbols and types may stimulate thought, may awaken emotions, may convey divine truth, and may even strengthen faith; but beyond this they are meaningless and dangerous, and may replace the Living Christ. Mosaic institutions are of value, setting forth man's need for pardon, purity, and holiness; and setting forth God's provision of a great high priest, an atonement, and fellowship with God. Why look at the shadow when we can look to Christ, the Author and the Finisher of our faith. These ceremonies are shadows, superseded, and should be abandoned. Since Christ has come, we no longer need the symbols (Heb 8:13; 10:1).

b. *There must be no subservience to false philosophy. 2:18-19.*

18. Let no man beguile you of your reward. Rob you of your prize. The word means to act as an umpire, denying your claim, defrauding you, and declaring you as unworthy. **Voluntary humility.** This is self-imposed, mock humility which is expressed in **worshipping of angels. Intruding . . . not seen.** This refers to alleged visions, imagined and invented revelations, and the living in a world of hallucinations. **Vainly puffed up.** Inflated with conceit, senseless pride, like a big bag of wind. **Fleshly mind.** Literally, the mind of the flesh. He is dominated by his unregenerated nature and devoid of spiritual enlightenment.

19. And not holding the Head. This one lacks a vital connection with Christ, and has never been a part of the body. **The body.** The figure of the body emphasizes both its unity and its diversity. Christ supplies: (1) nourishment, i.e. life and energy; (2) unity, i.e. knitted together; and (3) growth, i.e. the increase of God.

2. *Positively. 2:20-3:4.*

a. *Dead with Christ, we are free from earthly ordinances. 2:20-23.*

20. Wherefore if ye be dead with Christ. Since ye died at the time of your conversion (Rom 6:2-4, 6, 11; 7:4; II Cor 5:15; Gal 6:14). Death means separa-

tion: the Colossians were separated from the **rudiments of the world.** This refers to the first principle, the childish lessons, and the ABC's of elementary spiritual instructions. **Subject to ordinances.** Pestered by rules and regulations. These are outward forms: outworn, annulled, and superseded.

21. Touch not; taste not; handle not. Specimens of Gnostic rules, of which the Christian stands liberated, but which are still a test of holiness in certain religious groups.

22. Perish with the using. Destined for corruption in their consumption. **After . . . of men.** Human origin, based on the will and the word of men (Mt 15:8-9).

23. A show of wisdom in will worship. An appearance, a masquerading. Will worship is self-imposed worship, prescribed for one's self. **Humility.** Spurious, hypocritical, mock humility. **Neglecting of the body.** Ascetic discipline, severe, harsh, torturing. **Not in any honor.** Not of any value, impotent; not a remedy, it can't deliver. **Satisfying the flesh.** The indulgence of the flesh.

b. *Risen with Christ, we are bound to heavenly principles. 3:1-4.*

3:1. If ye then be risen with Christ. Since you are jointly raised up and new life has begun. **Seek.** Keep on seeking, an outward active. **Things.** Real, heavenly, spiritually things (II Cor 4:18). **Above.** The upward things (Phil 3:14), treasures of heaven (Mt 6:20). Our Head is there; our home is there. **Where Christ sitteth.** The place of exaltation, power, and authority. Paul gives heavenly motives for earthly duties.

2. Set your affection. This is inward active. Keep on thinking about and directing your mind toward heavenly things. We should seek everything in the light of eternity. The Christian must be heavenly-minded, not worrying about earthly things.

3. For ye are dead. Literally, ye died. **Your life . . . hid.** Permanently hidden. We are locked together with Christ in security, and Satan can't break the lock.

4. Christ . . . our life, shall appear (Jn 14:6; Phil 1:21; I Jn 5:11-12). **Shall ye also appear.** Be made manifest (I Jn 3: 1-3).

IV. PRACTICAL: THE CHRISTIAN. 3:5-4:6.

A. Principles for the Inner Life. 3:5-17.

1. Vices to put off. 3:5-11.

5. Mortify. Put to death quickly. The flesh must be kept in the place of death; it must be nailed to a cross. **Members.** Not yourselves. **Fornication.** A perilous, prevalent, perverse sin, which is lightly regarded by many and committed without scruples and without shame. It is illicit sexual intercourse between unmarried partners; similar to, but not identical with, adultery (Mt 5:32; 15:19; Mk 7:21). **Uncleanness.** Impurity in thought and speech, dirty mindedness, indecency. **Inordinate affection.** Depraved passion, uncontrolled lust, an evil desire. **Evil concupiscence.** Wicked craving and sensualness beyond natural expression. **Covetousness.** Greedy desire to have more; entire disregard for the rights of others. **Which is idolatry.** The worship of false gods, putting things in place of God.

6. For which things' sake. God does not regard sin with indifference. **The wrath of God.** God's vengeance and dreadful judgment. **Cometh.** Denotes certainty and imminence (Jn 3:18, 36). **Children of disobedience.** Unbelievers.

7. In which ye also walked. These vices characterized their past, pagan, pre-Christian experience. They were addicted to and practiced these vices (Eph 2:2; I Pet 4:3). **Lived in them.** The Greek imperfect tense implies constant conduct, the habit of existence.

8. But . . . put off all these. Put aside and rid yourselves completely of all these. **Anger.** Uncontrolled temper, a deep-seated emotion of ill will, a settled feeling of habitual hate, revengeful resentment. **Wrath.** Boiling agitation, fiery outburst of temper, violent fit of rage, passionate outbreak of exasperation. **Malice.** Vicious disposition, depraved spite, willful desire to injure, cruel malignity, which rejoices in evil to others. **Blasphemy.** Slanderous talk, reviling, evil speaking, railing insults, reckless and bitter abuse. **Filthy communication out of your mouth.** Obscene speech, shameful speaking, foul-mouth abuse, dirty epithets, unclean stories (Eph 4:29; 5:4).

9. Lie not one to another. The Greek present imperative forbids a continuation of action that is going on. Stop lying (Eph 4:25), there is no such thing as "a little white lie." All lies are big and black. **Seeing that ye have put off the old man.** The old man is the old unregenerated nature derived from Adam and received by the first birth. The old man has not been converted, has not been renewed, and has not been improved; he is corrupt, useless, and must be put off. The word put off means to strip off and discard like a filthy, worn-out garment, and tossed on the rubbish heap.

10. And have put on the new man. Have clothed yourselves with the new man. The new man is the person you are after having been saved. The new man is received from Christ at the time of the second birth, and is the regenerated man, the new nature. **Renewed.** This present passive participle (Gr *anakaineō*) indicates constantly being renewed. This is a continuous process; the new man has not yet matured and is ever in the state of development.

11. Where there is neither Greek nor Jew. In the new man there is an obliteration of distinctions. National privilege has been obliterated; ceremonial standings have been obliterated; cultural standings have been obliterated; and social castes have been obliterated. **Christ is all, and in all.** Christ is absolutely everything.

2. Virtues to put on. 3:12-17.

12. Put on therefore. Clothe yourselves with. This Greek aorist imperative implies a sense of urgency; this command is to be obeyed at once. We now have a characterization of believers: (1) elect of God, i.e. chosen of God; (2) holy, i.e. set apart by God and for God; and (3) beloved, i.e. loved by God. These are the attire of the new man; his spiritual wardrobe of practical righteousness. **Bowels of mercies.** A heart of compassion, mercy in action, and heartfelt sympathy for the less fortunate. **Kindness.** Thoughtfulness of others, unselfishness, sweetness of disposition, gentleness, and graciousness. This is the fruit of the Holy Spirit and refers to the inner attitude. **Humbleness of mind.** This refers to the outward expression of that inner attitude. Humbleness is modesty, it places self last, and regards self as least (Eph 3:8). **Meekness.** Not weakness, but lowliness; delicate consideration for others. It is the opposite of arrogance and self-assertion. Pride has no place in the Christian's life. **Longsuffering.** Patient under provocation. This denotes restraint which enables one to bear injury and insult without resorting to retaliation. It accepts the wrong without complaint. Longsuffering is an attribute of God (Rom 2:4) and a fruit of the Holy Spirit (Gal 5:22).

13. Forbearing one another. Put up with things we dislike and get along with those who disagree. Christians can disagree without being disagreeable. **Forgiving one another.** The word "forgive" (Gr *charizomai*) is built on the same root as the word grace and means to bestow favor unconditionally. This means that the Christian will always treat the offending party graciously. The Christian not only forgives, he forgets. **Quarrel.** A quarrel is a cause of blame, a ground for complaint. He thinks himself aggrieved.

14. And above all these things. On top of all these things, like an outer garment. **Put on charity.** Love is the basis and cloak of all the graces (I Cor 13:13) **bond.** The bond that binds the others together. **Perfectness.** This means completeness, full grown, mature.

15. Let the peace of God. Better, the peace of Christ. This is that heart-peace which Christ demonstrated. It is a tranquility of soul which is not ruffled by adversity nor disturbed by fear. This peace passeth all understanding (Phil 4:7) and is given by Christ (Jn 14:27). **Rule.** Sit as umpire, arbitrate, decide all doubts, settle all questions, and make the final decision. **Hearts.** Thoughts, feelings, desires. **Thankful.** Grateful.

16. Let the word of Christ dwell in you richly in all wisdom. Be at home and dwell permanently (Josh 1:8; Jn 15:7). Let the Word of Christ saturate you and remain in you as a rich treasure.

17. Do all in the name of the Lord Jesus. In all relations of life, act as His representative; obeying His word, trusting in His power, and devoted to His service. We should live Christ-centered lives. All of life must be Christian; belief relates to behavior; creed issues in conduct; and doctrine relates to duty.

B. Precepts for the Outer Life. 3:18-4:6.

1. Relation to domestic life. 3:18-4:1.

a. Helpmeets and husbands. 3:18-19.

18. Wives, submit. This is an old military figure (Gr *hypotassō*) meaning to line up under (Eph 5:22) or to subject yourselves in a specialized way. There is no hint of inferiority, but a matter of authority and responsibility in the home. Wives are to be in habitual subjection with implicit trust. This is voluntary, not forced on her by a demanding despot. The wife is a helpmeet (a help suitable to the husband), not a slave. The family is held together by authority and obedience. The wife's submission is prompted by the husband's love. **As it is fit in the Lord.** As it should be, becoming, and proper. All of life is to be lived in fellowship with Christ. God is emphasizing responsibilities, not rights (Eph 5:22-24).

19. Husbands love your wives. Keep on loving your wives. This is more than human affection; it is produced by the Holy Spirit. The dominate trait of the

Christian husband is self-devotion, not self-satisfaction (Eph 5:25-28). **Be not bitter against them.** Stop being bitter and do not have the habit of being bitter against them. This sin wrecks many marriages.

b. Families and fathers. 3:20-21.

20. Children, obey your parents in all things. This is an old verb and means to listen under, harken, to hear and heed, to obey. Children are to have the habit of hearing and heeding instructions (Eph 6:1-3). **In all things.** Continual, not just occasional obedience. **This is well-pleasing.** Your commendable Christian duty.

21. Fathers, provoke not. Do not have the habit of exasperating your children. This is an old word (Gr *erethizō*) and means to excite, to nag, to vex, to rouse to resentment (Eph 6:2-4). Fathers exasperate their children by: being inconsiderate, being too demanding, being over-corrective, and being unjust and severe. Parents also provoke their children by continual fault-finding, always frowning, never smiling, and holding other children up as examples. The twig is to be bent with caution, not broken. **Lest they be discouraged.** This negative purpose with the Greek present subjunctive (Gr *athymeo*) implies the forbidding of beginning an act. Discouraged means disheartened, depressed, frustrated. Such children are broken in spirit, give up, and feel it is impossible to please. Could this not be the source of the sorrow of so many runaway children?

c. Servants and the served. 3:22-4:1.

22. Servants, obey in all things your masters. Paul does not denounce slavery nor demand its violent overthrow. The slaves are part of a household, and they are without rights. They are to constantly obey and give service, not demand freedom. **Not with eyeservice as menpleasers.** Working only while being under the watchful eye of an exacting master and for the purpose of making a show or gaining human praise. Men-

pleasers are those who have no higher motives than to please their human masters and curry their favor. **In singleness of heart.** Literally, without a fold in the heart, under which to hide a false motive. Christians are to have a genuine readiness of heart and undivided purpose, not with pretense or ulterior motive, not half-hearted, but sincere. **Fearing God.** Rather than the masters according to the flesh. The real motive of service is dreading God's displeasure.

23. Heartily. Literally, out of the soul. Christians are to throw their souls into their work, and labor cheerfully and diligently. As **to the Lord.** This is the real test of Christian service.

24. Knowing . . . inheritance. The heavenly inheritances are full recompense in return for faithful service. **For ye serve the Lord Christ.** Christians are actually employed by Christ. This verb could either be an indicative or an imperative, in which case it would mean, keep on slaving for the Lord.

25. But he that doeth wrong. Slave or master, God will pay either one. **There is no respect of persons.** Literally, receiving of face, judging on the basis of outward appearance. There is respect of persons with man, but not with God. God does not have a double standard; He weighs the unfaithfulness in servants and the unkindness in masters in the same scale of divine equity and justice. There are no partialities, no favorites, and no exceptions with God (I Pet 1:17).

4:1. Masters, give . . . just and equal. Render on your part that which is right and fair; deal equitably. This would solve a lot of problems between management and labor. **Knowing . . . a Master in heaven.** A reminder that God keeps His eye on the character and the conduct of all men, and that "every one of us shall give account of himself to God" (Rom 14:12).

2. Relation to the world. 4:2-6.

a. Duty of prayer. 4:2-4.

2. Continue in prayer. This is an appeal to give constant attention to prayer.

The Christian should persevere steadfastly in intercession (Eph 6:18; Phil 4:6). **Watch in the same.** Literally, keep awake, give strict attention to and be spiritually alert. You must guard against wandering thoughts, and beware of indifferences (Mt 26:41). **With thanksgiving.** The heart is to be thankful.

3. Withal. At the same time (Eph 6:18-19). **That God would open.** Only God can open (I Cor 16:7-9; Rev 3:7). **A door.** A door for the Word, not the door of the prison. Paul is asking them to pray that he will have the opportunity to proclaim the Word of God (I Cor 16:9; II Cor 2:12). **The mystery of Christ.** As opposed to the senseless mysteries of the Gnostics. **For which I am also in bonds.** Paul is conscious that his chains are the result of preaching Christ. Paul is kept in prison, but yet he has opportunities to witness (Phil 1:12).

4. That I may make it manifest. Paul's chief concern is to make the message clear and plain. **As I ought to speak.** As it is my duty; as it is necessary for me to speak (I Cor 2:4; II Cor 2:14, 17).

b. Duty of propriety. 4:5-6.

5. Walk in wisdom . . . are without. It takes wise walking as well as wise talking to win the lost to Christ. The walk refers to one's behavior. Christians are to conduct themselves wisely, to be prudent in their behavior, and to be discreet in their conduct. In order to advance the cause of Christ, we must walk consistently and avoid everything that would turn the unsaved off, and do everything that would turn the unsaved on. **Redeeming the time.** Buying up (Gr *exagorazomai*) the opportunity for one's self; making wise and sacred use of every opportunity; using the time to the best possible advantage. There is the price of self-denial and strenuous work to be paid or we will forgo the bargain.

6. Let your speech be always with grace. Christ was full of grace and truth (Jn 1:14). Christians are to be gracious, pleasant, attractive, winsome, and courteous. **Seasoned with salt.** Not insipid, not flat, not dull, not tasteless. Christians are to have an edge of liveliness, and to be marked by purity, wholesomeness, and hallowed pungency. **That ye may know . . . answer every man.** In order that we can adapt the message to the situation and speak appropriately to each and every man.

V. CONCLUSION. 4:7-18.

7. All my state. My affairs, the things relating to me. **Tychicus.** The bearer of this letter (cf. Eph 6:21).

8. Whom I have sent unto you for the same purpose. Paul has a twofold purpose in sending Tychicus. **That he might know your estate.** Better, that ye may know our estate, the things concerning us. **Comfort your hearts.** Give encouragement, rather than consolation.

9. With Onesimus. The co-bearer of the letter, and Philemon's runaway slave. **Who is one of you.** Now a brother in Christ.

10. Aristarchus my fellow prisoner. From Thessalonica, he accompanied Paul to Jerusalem (Acts 19:29; 24). Now in Rome with Paul. **Marcus.** John Mark who was once rejected by Paul (Acts 15: 36-39) but now commended (II Tim 4: 11). He was a nephew or cousin of Barnabas.

11. And Jesus, which is called Justus. Joshua, a common name. **Who are of the circumcision.** Jewish Christians. **These only.** Not many of Paul's Jewish friends were sympathetic to his mission to the Gentiles. **A comfort.** Our word paregoric comes from this word.

12. Epaphras, who is one of you. Probably one of the founders of the church at Colosse. He brought Paul news of the conditions in the church. **Always laboring fervently for you in prayers.** Strenuous intercession, wrestling with God on their behalf. **That ye may stand.** Stand firm, mature in all the will of God.

13. Great zeal for you. Expending painful toil.

14. Luke, the beloved physician. Luke, the dear and trusted friend, was now with Paul. **Demas.** In II Timothy 4:10-11, he is mentioned as one who deserted Paul for this present world.

15. Nymphas. This Greek word could either be masculine or feminine, depending on the position of the accent. Then some texts read "his" house and others read "her" house. Scholars are divided as to whether this is a man's name or a woman's name. **The church.** Christians did not have church buildings until the third century.

16. And when this epistle is read among you. Read in public to the church. **The epistle from Laodicea.** "The most likely meaning is that the so-called Epistle to the Ephesians was a circular letter to various churches in the province of Asia, one copy going to Laodicea and to be passed on to Colossae as the Colossian letter was to be sent to Laodicea. This was done by copying and keeping the original" (A. T. Robertson, *Word Pictures of the New Testament,* Vol. IV, p. 513).

17. And say to Archippus. He is mentioned in Philemon 2 in such a way as to suggest that he was a member of Philemon's household, probably his son. **Take heed.** Keep an eye on. **Thou hast received in the Lord.** Archippus was called of the Lord, and most probably had some ministerial responsibility in the church at Colosse. **That thou fulfil it.** That you keep on filling to the full, discharge fully. This is a lifetime job. God does not discharge His servants.

18. The salutation by the hand of me Paul. Paul adds this salutation in his own handwriting. **Remember my bonds.** The chain probably clanked as Paul penned the salutation. This is an indirect appeal to pray for his release. **Grace be with you. Amen.**

BIBLIOGRAPHY

Abbott, T. K. A Critical and Exegetical Commentary of the Epistles to the Ephesians and to the Colossians. In the *International Critical Commentary.* Edinburgh: T. & T. Clark, n.d.

Barnes, Albert. *Notes on the New Testament, Explanatory and Practical—Ephesians, Philippians and Colossians.* Ed. by Robert Frew. Grand Rapids: Baker, 1950.

* Bruce, F. F. Commentary on the Epistles to the Ephesians and the Colossians, In *The New International Commentary on the New Testament.* Grand Rapids: Eerdmans, 1957.

Calvin, John. *Commentaries on the Epistles to the Philippians, Colossians and Thessalonians.* Trans. and ed. by John Pringle. Grand Rapids: Eerdmans, 1948.

* Eadie, John. *Commentary on the Epistles of Paul to the Colossians.* Grand Rapids: Zondervan, 1957.

English, E. Schuyler. *Studies in the Epistle to the Colossians.* New York: Our Hope, 1944.

Erdman, Charles R. *The Epistles of Paul to the Colossians and to Philemon.* Philadelphia: The Westminster Press, 1933.

Findlay, G. G. The Epistle of Paul to the Colossians In *The Pulpit Commentary.* Grand Rapids: Eerdmans, 1950.

* Harrison, Everett F. *Colossians: Christ All-Sufficient.* Chicago: Moody Press, 1971.

* Hendriksen, William. Exposition of Colossians and Philemon. *New Testament Commentary.* Grand Rapids: Baker, 1964.

Ironside, Harry A. *Lectures on the Epistle to the Colossians.* Neptune, N. J.: Loizeaux Brothers, 1955.

Lenski, R. C. H. *The Interpretation of St. Paul's Epistles to the Colossians, to the Thessalonians, to Timothy, to Titus and to Philemon.* Columbus, Ohio: The Wartburg Press, 1937.

* Lightfoot, J. B. *Saint Paul's Epistles to the Colossians and to Philemon.* London: MacMillan, 1927.

Maclaren, Alexander. The Epistles of St. Paul to the Colossians and to Philemon. In *The Expositor's Bible.* Grand Rapids: Eerdmans, 1943.

* Moule, H. C. G. The Epistle of Paul the Apostle to the Colossians and to Philemon. In the *Cambridge Bible for Schools and Colleges.* Cambridge: Cambridge University Press, 1932 reprint.

Nicholson, William R. *Popular Studies in Colossians.* Ed. by James M. Gray. Grand Rapids: Kregel, n.d.

Peake, A. S. The Epistle to the Colossians. In The *Expositor's Greek Testament.* Grand Rapids: Eerdmans, n.d.

Robertson, A. T. *Word Pictures in the New Testament.* Nashville: Broadman Press, 1931.

Thomas, W. H. Griffith. *Christ Pre-Eminent, Studies in the Epistle to the Colossians.* Chicago: Moody Press, 1923.

Wuest, Kenneth S. Ephesians and Colossians. In *The Greek New Testament for the English Reader.* Grand Rapids: Eerdmans, 1953.

The First Epistle To The

THESSALONIANS

INTRODUCTION

Historical background. Paul was personally acquainted with the city of Thessalonica and its inhabitants since he founded the church there on his second missionary journey. It had been a Roman free city, in fact the capital of the province of Macedonia, before Paul arrived there. It had a strong city government which was accurately described by Luke (Acts 17:6-7). Thessalonica was also an important city because it was on the Egnatian Way, the main East-West Roman highway.

In the western spread of the gospel, Paul was led by the Spirit all the way. After his first missionary journey with Barnabas, Paul reported his successes as he made his deputation tour of the home churches in Falestine. He began to realize the meaning and power of God's calling him to be the apostle of the Gentiles (Acts 14:27; 15:4). Anxious to return to the work, Paul chose a new companion, Silas, and started out again intending to strengthen the churches and establish new ones (Acts 15:36-41). Very soon, Paul and Silas were joined by Timothy (Acts 16:1-4). It is interesting to note how sensitive to the leading of the Spirit these three missionaries were; in Acts 16:6-9 they followed the Holy Spirit through three changes of course. As they crossed the Galatia-Phrygia border, they intended to go west to Ephesus, the leading city of Asia Minor. They were, however, in some unknown way prevented from doing this, and so followed the Spirit to the north. At the latitude of Mysia, they were again led by the Spirit of the Lord not to go into Bithynia, but instead to turn west once more toward the city of Troas on the Aegean coast.

From Troas the Spirit led Paul and the others across the Aegean to Neapolis, Philippi, and then Thessalonica by means of a vision in which Paul saw a man of Macedonia calling for help. This is how the gospel got started on its way westward.

In Europe, Paul and his companions went first to Neapolis, and then founded the Philippian church, and after their miraculous deliverance from the Philippian jail (Acts 16:11-40), went on through Amphipolis and Apollonia to Thessalonica. The Bible mentions that there was a synagogue there (Acts 17:2); this synagogue was the base of operations for Paul's intensive campaign in founding the Thessalonian church (Acts 17:4). "To the Jew first" was Paul's usual method; it was effective here also, but the Jewish believers were far from a majority of those early believers. We also gather from I Thessalonians 1:9, that most of Paul's success was among Gentiles and that the Thessalonian church became a mainly Gentile church. The majority of the Jews at Thessalonica were opposed to Paul from the very beginning and became vehement enemies of the gospel not only there but throughout the area. They even followed Paul to Beroea to incite riots against him. Paul escaped, in fact, only with his life to go on to Athens where he waited for his companions Timothy and Silas.

It is evident from both Acts and Thessalonians that Silas and Timothy were active fellow workers with Paul throughout the Thessalonian campaign (see the introductory words of each of the Thessalonian epistles). When Paul, throughout these two epistles, reminds the Thessalonians of things which had been taught or spoken among them, he is probably not using the editorial "we" but referring quite literally to the work of his companions as well as to his own personal accomplishments.

It seems unnecessary to make Paul the only one who could preach and teach the message of the Word of God. Furthermore, Timothy could have continued to establish the young church on his return visit as Paul's delegate. Paul's primary ministry in Thessalonica was probably not much more than a month (Acts 17:2). In that time he and his companions worked night and day not only in the gospel but also supporting themselves with their own hands so that no false accusations could be brought against the gospel.

Occasion of the epistle. At any rate, a beginning had been made for the Thessalonian church in the early part of Paul's second missionary journey, and Paul now had occasion in that same journey to write back to this church which he had established. Silas and Timothy had gotten separated from Paul at Beroea. They were to meet Paul in Athens. It was while Paul was waiting at Athens for his companions that he gave his famous Mars Hill sermon and started another church (Acts 17:16-34). Paul used every opportunity to reach the world for Christ. Paul went from Athens to Corinth where he stayed and worked with Priscilla and Aquila (Acts 18:1-4) and where Silas and Timothy also worked (Acts 18:5).

Paul worked for a time in Corinth with the synagogue as his base, but soon made the decision to put all his efforts into working among the Gentiles where he seemed to be more successful. For a year and a half, Paul taught the Word of God at Corinth. It appears that this long stay provided the opportunity to write the Thessalonian epistles. While he was still in Athens, Paul had sent Timothy to help the rapidly growing Thessalonian church (I Thess 3:1-6). It was evidently in response to Timothy's reports that Paul wrote I Thessalonians.

Date and place of writing. In light of the above discussion, it appears that the city of Corinth is the only acceptable site for the place of writing of I Thessalonians. The subscription in the AV which reads, "The first epistle unto the Thessalonians was written from Athens" is an addition to the text which is not to be accepted in light of the facts.

The date of the epistle is quite easily discerned from the fact that it was written during Paul's long stay at Corinth on his second missionary journey (see Acts 18:5; I Thess 3:6). This period itself can be dated by the reference to the proconsulate of Gallio which, according to a mutilated fragment discovered at Delphi, dated from the summer of A.D. 52. Paul arrived in Corinth before the proconsulate of Gallio, perhaps a year earlier, and thus the writing of I Thessalonians must have taken place in the summer or fall of A.D. 51.

Purpose. There seem to be multiple purposes for the writing of this epistle. First, Paul wanted to commend the Thessalonians that they had withstood the temptations of the devil (3:6). They were, too, examples to other believers in the area of steadfastness of faith (1:7). In addition, he writes to admonish them to keep themselves from the immoral practices of the heathen (4:1-8). But the most pressing reason for writing was apparently to reveal information to them about the coming of Christ for His church. Thus, he presents the great doctrine of the Rapture of the church in chapter 4. This would correct any erroneous ideas concerning the relation between the resurrection of the dead and the coming of Christ. It was a source of great comfort to the Thessalonians, as it is for us today.

OUTLINE

COMMENTARY

I. INTRODUCTION. 1:1.

1:1. Paul, and Silvanus, and Timothy. I Thessalonians may well be the earliest written epistle of the New Testament. Paul is writing from Corinth to encourage and strengthen these new Christians (3:1-6). Timothy had just arrived with the news from the Thessalonians of their splendid growth and Paul makes immediate reply (3:6). The salutation here is in form like that of any everyday Greek letter of the Hellenistic world; it includes the names of Paul's fellow ministers, Silvanus (Acts uses Semitic form of his name Silas rather than the Latin form used here) and Timothy, because they were involved like Paul in the preaching at Thessalonica, and because they too have an interest in this letter and its encouragement to the believers.

The letter is addressed to **the church of the Thessalonians which is in God the Father and in the Lord Jesus Christ.** A new entity had come into existence, and the name "church" (Gr *ekklēsia*) is applied to it. The word was common, and originally meant simply an "assembly." Jesus had used the term in His teaching (Mt 16:18) to refer to the Christian community and from that time on the word began to take on a specialized and exclusive meaning. The special group at Thessalonica to which Paul now wrote were those who had believed in Christ in response to the preaching of the gospel there (Acts 17:2-4). These people were probably immediately baptized like those in Philippi (Acts 16:33-34), and became the nucleus of the Christian community there. The word "church" is used over one hundred times in the New Testament, and nearly always has the same technical meaning as here: a local group of baptized believers in Christ. The church is said to be in God the Father and in the Lord Jesus Christ, which limits the word church to its new technical meaning. In the New Testament the word "church" never refers to a building. The people of Thessalonica believe in God and have committed themselves to Christ as the promised Old Testament Messiah (cf. Acts 17:1-4; II Thess 1:1).

Grace be unto you, and peace. This is the normal greeting in an everyday letter except that it has been adapted for Christian use.

II. PERSONAL RELATIONS WITH THE THESSALONIANS. 1:2-3:13.

A. Thanksgiving and Praise. 1:2-10.

2. We give thanks to God always for you. The "we" in these epistles is probably not editoral. Paul and his colleagues in the ministry are honestly thankful for their eager response to the Word of God.

3. The reason for thanksgiving is specifically named: they gave thanks because they remembered the **faith . . . love and . . . hope** of these new Christians. This is Paul's famous trilogy, "Faith, hope, and love live on" (I Cor 13:13)! See also Paul's commendation of the Colossians for the same spiritual qualities (Col 1:4-5), and observe the similar words of the Lord to the pastor of the Ephesian church (Rev 2:2).

It is interesting to note that the word **patience** (Gr *hypmonē*) might be better translated "steadfastness," since it refers to their specific endurance of evil treatment and opposition by the Thessalonian Jews, during which these new Christians had their hopes in the return of Christ and drew their comfort from that alone. The hope of His coming has given strength to endure to Christians of all ages since that time.

4. Knowing, brethren beloved, your election of God. A less vague translation here would be, "We know, brethren beloved by God, that He has chosen you." The fact of election cannot be known until after a person has been saved. Paul explains how he was able to recognize it in the Thessalonians: it was their positive response to the gospel (1:5-9).

5. For our gospel came not unto you in word only. The word **gospel** (Gr *euangelion*) means "good news." This word was adopted as a technical term for the Christian message which is succinctly stated by Paul in I Corinthians 15:1-4 and finds complete expression in the four gospels. **In word only** refers to the effect of the gospel.

It was not mere human words; the words contained a mysterious power, the power of the Holy Spirit to change their lives. Paul describes the power of the message in a similar way when he writes to the Corinthians (I Cor 2:3-4).

6. And ye became followers of us, and of the Lord, having reveived the word. It was because of their "reception" (Gr *dechomai*) of the Word (which means to receive in a respectful, obedient, and favorable way) that they became **followers.** A more literal translation would be, "You became imitators." The **joy of the Holy Ghost** is to be interpreted as a Greek subjective genitive: it is joy inspired by the Holy Spirit. Receiving the Word is receiving Christ, receiving Christ is receiving the Holy Spirit, and He brings joy and gladness. He inspires confidence and liberty in our lives.

7. The effect of the gospel was so powerful that Thessalonians became examples to the whole province of Macedonia of which their town was the capital. The word **examples** (Gr *typos*) is singular in the original and refers not to a number of individual examples of Christian living, but rather to the single pattern of response to the Word. It was this willingness to obey the good news and believe in Christ as the Messiah promised in the Old Testament that Paul praised.

8. For from you sounded out the word of the Lord. It should be observed here that the word "sounded out" (Gr *exēcheō*) means to "bounce off" and is the word from which we get the English "echo." The Thessalonians became a sounding-board from which the gospel would echo across the world. Paul states hyperbolically that he hardly needed to preach where people had heard of the faith of the Thessalonians; he had only to ask, "Have you heard what happened?" The fantastic story of the conversion from idols to God was known everywhere.

9. Ye turned to God from idols to serve the living and true God. The word "turned" (Gr *epistrephō*) corresponds more precisely to our English word "conversion." The Thessalonians were a classic example of Christian conversion. Conversion involves both positive and negative elements; one turns from one thing to something else. Here the positive element is stressed: they turned to God. This was a complete reversal in their religious philosophy. It was not that they "got religion" so much as that they changed religions. They turned from a pagan religion to the Christian God to worship Him through Jesus Christ. Idols were an integral part of life for pagans. I Corinthians 12:2 shows that, whatever the moving force, non-Christians are drawn to idols or false religions. It takes the reality of the true God to draw people away from the power of superstition. In the Christian religion God must be first. The Ten Commandments (Ex 20:1-17) show how that we must worship God alone. It is interesting that the word **serve** (Gr *douleuō*) means literally to be a slave to, and alludes to the Old Testament bondslave who was the personal property of another. So complete is real conversion to Christianity that one is "sold out" completely to God. We belong to Him: it is bondage, but it is a bondage of love. We love Him and want to do only His will. This is, in fact, the very heart of Christianity. God is the living God in contrast to idols which have no life, and the true God in contrast to all the false gods of the pagan world.

10. And to wait for his Son from heaven, whom he raised from the dead, even Jesus, which delivered us from the wrath to come. Wait (Gr *anamenō*) means more than just wait; it emphasizes an expectant and active attempt to live for His glory in the meantime. It is an attitude of faith toward the complete fulfillment of the messianic promises of the Old Testament in the second coming of Christ. These last two verses contain the basic tenets of Christianity: conversion, worship of God, hope in the Second Coming, belief in the resurrection of Jesus, complete faith in salvation from the wrath of God which will surely come upon all those who do not accept Christ.

B. Defense of Paul's Motives. 2:1-12.

2:1-2. For yourselves, brethren, know our entrance in unto you, that it was not in vain: Verses 1-12 imply that there had been slanderous accusations against Paul's work and motives. Part of the purpose of the letter is to show that the allegations were far from the truth. This is important, not just for Paul personally, but for the growth and development of the Thessalonians themselves. If they had begun to believe that Paul's **gospel** was just another philosophical dream, and that Paul was just "in it for the money," they could not have continued to grow in Christ. It was not that Paul's reputation alone was at stake, but that their Christian faith was in danger. Paul's coming to the Thessalonians was not in **vain** (Gr *kenos*). The word denotes what is empty of real meaning and purpose. Paul had come to them because he believed the gospel himself, and truly felt that the people of Thessalonica were eternally lost without that message. The argument is that Paul would have quit at Philippi (vs. 2), and would never have gotten to Thessalonica in the first place, had he been there for the money or for anything less than the call of God. He had no other choice but to go on to Thessalonica, "although" (Greek circumstantial participle of concession) he had already suffered shamefully (Acts 16:20-24), and although he knew that it would happen again (Acts 17:5). Paul and his companions were driven by the purest motives. They were completely committed to their own message and concerned for the welfare of the Thessalonians.

3-4. For our exhortation was not of deceit, nor of uncleanness, nor in guile: Paul appealed to the impartial judgment of his readers. Could they honestly say that Paul and his companions had ever acted like someone trying to deceive? Had there been any hint of impure motives? Had they not rather spoken like men who had been entrusted with the gospel message? Twice in verse 4 Paul uses the word "approved" (Gr *dokimazō*) by God, which means that God has "checked them out" by His own standards and has put His stamp of approval on them. Paul derived a great deal of personal confidence from the fact that God had "entrusted" (Gr *pisteuō*) him with the gospel (see also I Tim 1:11-12). His goal in life was not to "please" men but God (Gal 1:10). Had he not outwardly seemed true to this inner motivation?

5-6. For neither at any time used we flattering words . . . nor a cloak of covetousness. Paul calls upon God as his witness that none of their activities had been **a cloak of covetousness.** The word **cloak** (Gr *prophasis*) means an "excuse," "cover-up," or "front" for an impure motive of greed. We were not after **glory** (Gr *doxa*) says Paul, using the word from which we get our word "doxology." It is interesting that in John 12:43 this same word is used to condemn the Pharisees who "loved the praise of men more than the praise of God." Paul could have claimed that glory, in fact he had been a Pharisee before his own conversion. Now, he could have claimed similar glory as an **apostle** (Gr *apostolos*). He refers to himself and to his companions as **apostles,** since he considers them to be representatives of Christ with a commission, like his own. This word obviously is not limited in its use in the New Testament to the Twelve. That they **might have been burdensome** should rather be translated, "we might have made great demands." It is an idiom requiring this meaning. Elsewhere (e.g. II Cor 11:9) Paul shows that he believes that ministers of the gospel should be supported financially

by the gifts of God's people. The thought of this passage is obvious: they did not even take what they had a right to because they were so motivated to get the gospel out. How could anyone accuse them of impure motives?

7. But we were gentle among you, even as a nurse cherisheth her children. It seems probable, although there is little certainty about the matter, that the text in verse 7 should read, "we came like infants," rather than, "we were gentle among you." If this reading is taken, the meaning would go with the previous verse. Far from coming like authoritative apostles, Paul and the others claimed no more prestige than mere infants. Paul next applies the metaphor of a **nurse** (Gr *trophos*) to himself and his companions. This word comes from a root meaning to "feed," "nourish," "support," and "provide with food." The word can also refer to a "mother," and that translation would probably make better sense here. The word **cherisheth** means to "take warm and tender care of." It is found also in Ephesians 5:29, where a man "takes care of" his own body. The portrait Paul intends to paint in this verse is that of a mother tenderly caring for all the needs of her own children. A few verses later in verse 11 Paul changes the figure to a father, and again it is the father taking care of his own children. It was mother-father love that motivated Paul and his companions, rather than greed as someone must have suggested.

8-9. Also our own souls. According to verse 8, they had made up their minds to share not only the gospel, but also their own lives. In verse 9, Paul asks his readers simply to recall the fact that Paul and his companions worked hard with their own hands to support themselves while they were in Thessalonica in order that they might not be a burden to the people. It was customary in Palestine for rabbis to have a secular trade with which they supported themselves. We learn from Acts 18:3 that Paul's trade was tent making. The two words **labor and travail** are also used in the same context in II Corinthians 11:27 and II Thessalonians 3:8. They denote work which is very tiring and very difficult. Paul did not consider it wrong to receive help from preaching the gospel, in fact he received a gift from the Philippian church while he was at Thessalonica (Phil 4:16). His point here was that he had not made any demands on these people even though he had a right to do so. The word translated **preached** (Gr *kēryssō*) means to "proclaim." Note that in verse 8 the gospel is **imparted**, and in verse 9 it is **preached**. Also note that it is the gospel of God here, meaning that God has given it to Paul to preach.

10. Ye are witnesses, and God also, how holily and justly and unblamably we behaved ourselves among you that believe: Here Paul stresses qualities of conduct which could have been denied by the Thessalonians if they were not true. Their conduct was holy, just, and blameless. It is obvious that these things were true and known by all readers. In this verse the Thessalonians are called "believers" which is synonymous with "Christians" and shows again that the church is made up of believers in Christ.

11-12. Paul again refers to the father figure to sum up and justify their apostolic activities as they founded the church. They **exhorted** (Gr *parakaleō*) the believers, which means literally to "encourage." The noun form of this word is used as a name for the Holy Spirit (Comforter). The second word used here, **comforted** (Gr *paramytheō*) can be used of physical comforting as well as giving mental assurance. We can only guess as to the kind of comfort Paul and his companions may have given, but obviously some kind of consolation was needed in the face of the opposition of these Jews who had almost killed Paul. The third summary

word here, **charged** (Gr *martyreō*), means to "witness" or "testify." It is the word from which we get our English word "martyr." The result toward which all this apostolic activity was directed is again stated by Paul, **That ye would walk worthy of God.** All through the New Testament, the Christian life and conduct are referred to as a **walk**. Here also, Paul is referring to proper Christian conduct which, of course, was quite different from the generally accepted conduct of the day.

C. Reception of the Word of God. 2:13-16.

13. For this cause also thank we God without ceasing, because, when ye received the word of God which ye heard of us, ye received it not as the word of men, but as it is in truth, the word of God, which effectually worketh also in you that believe. Verse 13 is a very important verse because of its implications for inspiration and for the Christian attitude toward the Scriptures. There are several distinctions intended by Paul which do not come across in the translations of this verse. The first is the distinction between the words here translated **received**. The first occurrence (Gr *paralambanō*) is a word which means to "take to oneself." In this context it means to listen to and apply the words that were spoken. It could have been used of the teaching of any philosopher of the day. The second occurrence (Gr *dechomai*) is a word which means primarily "to receive" in the sense of receiving a guest, entertaining someone, or welcoming with open arms a true friend; this word involves much more commitment. This is the word that shows the responsive attitude of all true believers for God's word.

It is also important in this verse to distinguish between the three occurrences of **word** (Gr *logos*). The first occurrence would be literally "word of hearing" and is a technical term for the "preached word" of the prophets and apostles. This same expression translates Isaiah 53:1, "Who hath believed our report?" It is alluded to several times in the New Testament (Jn 12:38; Rom 10:16). Hebrews 4:2 uses this technical term to allude to the promise made to the Israelites that they would enter the promised land. Paul also used the term of his own preaching to the Galatians (Gal 3:2, 5). The meaning in Thessalonians is that the people not only listened to and applied the preaching of the apostles, and gladly recognized this message as something more than a merely human message (**word of men**), but welcomed it for what it really was, the **word of God.** This kind of response to the Word of God is characteristic of every true believer. **Effectually worketh** (Gr *energeō*) means simply to be "effective." It is interesting that this same word is found in the same connection in Galatians 3:2, 5 and that it is the Spirit of God in both passages who causes believers to recognize the Word of God. Although Paul does not refer to the written Word of God in I Thessalonians 2:13, the implications are the same, and the oral message was just as inspired and just as authoritative. It was a word spoken by God (Greek subjective genitive) so that this verse is, in effect, parallel to II Timothy 3:16.

14. For ye, brethren, became followers of the churches of God which in Judea are in Christ Jesus. Paul once more refers to the Thessalonians as **followers** or "imitators" (1:6). This is another reference to the persecution which these people suffered when they became Christians at the hands of their own fellow citizens. Paul himself had been guilty of persecuting Christian churches prior to his conversion. There were already at that early date many churches (plural) in Palestine, and persecution must have been a part of their lives from the very beginning. The persecution in Thessalonica was different only in that it was carried out by Gentiles rather than by Jews.

15. Who both killed the Lord Jesus, and their own prophets, and have persecuted us. Paul's sentence structure in the original emphasizes that the one whom they murdered was Jesus the Lord. Jesus Himself had reminded the Pharisees and the leaders of the Jews that prophets and wise men and Scribes had been subjected to murder and beating by their ancestors (Mt 23:34). Peter denounced the Jews of Jerusalem for the murder of Jesus, even though His death was a part of the determinate council and foreknowledge of God (Acts 2:23). Paul now justly charges the Jews of Thessalonica with their recent persecution of himself.

16. Forbidding us to speak to the Gentiles. Not only did the Jews persecute Paul and his companions at Thessalonica, but time after time in his life they have tried to prevent him from preaching to the Gentiles, thus hindering them from being saved. Jesus had strongly condemned those who would hinder people from believing and being saved (Mark 9:42), and Paul now reinforces that condemnation.

D. Timothy's Service There. 2:17-3:5.

17-20. Being taken from you. The word used here (Gr *aporphanizō*) is colorful and intensely passionate. It is related to our word "orphan," and might be translated "since we have been torn apart." It shows the characteristically strong emotional involvement of Paul with his converts everywhere; they were his children, his relatives, his joy and crown. His heart, he said, was still with them even though they had been separated. Paul had also been unable to get back and visit them personally, but in spite of his strong desire Satan somehow blocked his efforts. Paul assures them of his great love for them, and points forward to the hope of the Second Coming (Gr *parousia*). This is the first use of this term in the New Testament, although it was common in the Hellenistic world for the formal visits of royalty. This word became a technical term for the Second Coming of Christ. It is so used eighteen times in the New Testament and seven of these are in the Thessalonian epistles.

3:1-2. Wherefore when we could no longer forbear, we thought it good to be left at Athens alone. Finally, Paul decided to send Timothy to help the Thessalonians while he himself continued the work in Athens. The **we** seems to be editorial here; he probably really intends "I sent" since he speaks of being left **alone.** It is not possible to know the whereabouts of Silas at this time. **Minister of God** is a variant reading which was probably substituted for the more prestigious "God's fellow-worker" (Gr *synergos*). Paul had used this term when he wrote to the Corinthians to refer to himself and Apollos as "God's fellow-workers" (I Cor 3:9) in distinction to the Corinthian believers themselves who were "God's field," or "God's building" in the metaphor.

The reason Paul sends Timothy to the Thessalonians is, first, **to establish** (Gr *stērizō*). The word means "to stabilize," or to support an already existing structure. In the New Testament this word is used in the figurative sense of stabilizing believers. The other reason is to **comfort** (Gr *parakleō*), which should be translated "encourage" rather than **comfort.** It is the word from which we get the name of the Holy Spirit in John, namely "the Comforter." The same word is used of Christ in I John 2:1, where it means a legal advocate. A better translation might be, "to support and help you in your faith."

3. That no man should be moved by these afflictions. Paul explains Timothy's mission: **moved** (Gr *sainō*) means usually "wave," "wag the tail." Perhaps here it means "wobble," and thus collapse. This would carry on the figure of Timothy's stabilizing or

"buttressing" their faith like a wall. The **afflictions** (Gr *thlipsis*) are those which had just been experienced as reported by Timothy. Paul had warned that they would come.

5. For this cause. Paul again states his reason for sending Timothy: he had to know that the Thessalonians were surviving the temptations of Satan and that Paul's work in Thessalonica had not been in vain.

E. Response to Timothy's Report. 3:6-13.

6. But now when Timothy came from you unto us. The sense of the original here is that Timothy has just now arrived with the news when Paul sat down to write. This clearly shows the occasion and purpose of the letter. When Timothy arrived his news was good, so good in fact, that **brought us good tidings** is the same word (Gr *euangelizomai*) often translated "preach the gospel." Paul was glad to hear of their faith and love, and the fact that they had wanted to see him just as much as he had wanted to see them.

7. Therefore, brethren, we were comforted (Gr *parakaleō*). This is again the word which means "help" or "encourage." Another translation has, "we have been encouraged about you." The encouragement was badly needed. Paul was himself in **affliction and distress.** Both of these words are strong. The first (Gr *anangkē*) is related to the word from which we get "anxiety," while the second (Gr *thlipsis*) means "rubbing" or "pressure," and is the word often translated in the New Testament "tribulation." The thing that gave Paul the needed encouragement was the faith of these converts.

8. For now we live, if ye stand fast in the Lord. The idea is that we can now carry on, since we know that you are holding your ground in the faith. The word **stand fast** is not the usual word for stand; it meant rather "to take a stand." This gives Paul the courage to go on, now that he knows that he has made some real converts.

9-10. For what thanks can we render to God again for you. A better translation would be, "for what thanksgiving" (Gr *eucharistia*); it is the word from which we get the English word "eucharist." **Render** (Gr *antapodidōmi*) has the sense of paying back something owed. The meaning is that we as Christians owe to God joyful thanksgiving and praise for what He has done.

11-12. Now God himself and our Father. Another order is possible: "Now may our God and Father Himself, and our Lord Jesus direct our way to you." The Greek verb is optative (to express a wish), as are the two in verse 12. Paul has a threefold desire, or really a "prayer," since it calls upon God. He asks for himself, that God would direct his path back to the people of Thessalonica. He must, however, leave this desire in the hands of the Heavenly Father. He also asks for them, that the Lord may cause their love to continue to grow beyond all limits both among themselves and toward others outside the church.

13. To the end he may stablish. This is the purpose to which Paul's prayers are directed. **Stablish** (Gr *sterizō*) means to "buttress" or "support" an existing structure; here the personal faith of the Thessalonians is in view. The desire is that they will be strengthened in holiness as they wait for the coming Saviour. **At the coming** (Gr *parousia*), Paul again uses what has become a Christian technical term for the Second Coming. It is qualified here by the words **with all his saints.** The adjective **saints** (Gr *hagios*) is used here in the masculine plural, and may refer to holy persons, namely believers (Eph 1:1), or to holy beings like angels (Mk 8:38). It is possible that both are in view.

III. PRACTICAL EXHORTATIONS. 4:1-5:28.

A. Sanctification. 4:1-8.

4:1. Furthermore then we beseech you, brethren. Vss. 1-12 comprise a key section in the book, perhaps the main point of the letter. The word **furthermore** (Gr *loipos*) may be an indication of this. At any rate, Paul now gets down to business and tells how we should live. This section on practical theology was especially important for the Thessalonians as **Gentiles** (vs. 5) since they had no customary moral traditions like the Jews. The words **beseech** and **exhort** are ordinary words meaning "ask" and "encourage" but here they are tempered with **by the Lord Jesus.** This becomes then an authoritative expression of Christian living. Paul has already passed on this Christian traditional information to the Thessalonians by word of mouth in his preaching. Now, he gives it to them in writing. The topic is very clearly labeled, **how ye ought to walk,** and means precisely, "how you must live and please God." These two verbs are in the present tense in Greek, implying that Christianity is a way of life which characterizes all our activities and not just a few of the things we do. It is also interesting to note from verse 1, that Paul acknowledges the fact that his readers are already living according to Christian standards; he is merely encouraging them to continue to grow as they already have.

2. For ye know what commandments we gave you by the Lord Jesus. Again the word **commandments** shows that these exhortations to purity are Christian moral standards. That these are not to be taken lightly is further indicated in this verse by the reference to Paul's apostolic authority; he is acting through the Lord Jesus, or we might say as His representative.

3. For this is the will of God. Verses 1 and 2 were quite general, while verses 3-8 are specific. In this passage Paul has in mind **sanctification** or "holiness" (Gr *hagiasmos*) as it relates specifically to sexual purity. He says in verse 3 that sanctification means to **abstain from fornication** (Gr *porneia*). This is the general word for any kind of illicit sexual intercourse, prostitution, pre-marital sex, or adultery. Paul is here emphasizing the negative side of sanctification when he tells his readers to abstain (the Greek word means to keep oneself entirely away from).

4. Every one of you should know how to possess. This is the positive side of sanctification in this same matter. A better translation of verse 4, "that each of you know how to take a wife for himself in holiness and honor." The word **vessel** (Gr *skeuos*) is used of the wife as the "weaker vessel" in I Peter 3:7. Sanctity in marriage was something brand new for the Thessalonians who had come from obviously corrupt Gentile culture. They grew up not knowing God, and now that they had turned to God they needed to know and conform to Christian standards.

6. That no man go beyond and defraud his brother in any matter. Several words need explanation here. First, **go beyond** (Gr *hyperbainō*) means quite literally "to overstep" or "break laws." In this context it obviously means to break this moral law. Secondly, if he does break this moral law, a man will, by that very fact, **defraud** (Gr *pleonekteō*) his brother. This word denotes "taking advantage of," "robbing," or "cheating someone" through greed. A comment is also needed on the phrase **in any matter.** The construction in the original language of the New Testament (an article of previous reference) allows only one meaning here. It is not just **any matter** that is in view, but specifically this matter which has just been mentioned, that is unethical sexual activity. The sense of the passage is then that when a man does not live with his own wife as he should, but instead commits adultery with someone else's, he must

know that he has violated, or "robbed" his brother by so doing, and that he deserves the vengeance of God. To show the seriousness of this sin, Paul alludes to Psalm 94:1 where God is called the "God of vengeance." Note that according to verse 7, this kind of conduct is the opposite of **holiness** and is called **uncleanness.** To be sanctified according to God's will must mean to be pure or clean in this matter.

8. He therefore that despiseth. Paul here seems to allude to a saying of Jesus recorded in Luke 10:16, where Jesus gives authority to the apostles, and literally explains, "whoever obeys you obeys me, and whoever rejects you rejects me; the person who rejects me, rejects the one who sent me." Note that "despise" and "reject" translate the same Greek word.

B. Love. 4:9-12.

9. But as touching brotherly love ye need not that I write unto you. This is a way of reminding the Thessalonians about the importance of brotherly love (Gr *philadelphia*) without sounding too harsh. **Taught of God** is one word in in the original and implies that they should automatically know that God expects them to **love** (Gr *agapaō*) **one another.**

11. And that ye study (Gr *philotimeomai*). This word does not refer to **study** in the sense of opening books or reading; it means "to desire," or "to determine." A possibly clearer translation would be, "aspire to live quietly and take care of your own affairs while you work with your hands as we instructed you." We gather from this passage, and from II Thessalonians 3:11, that some of the believers in this church believed that the Second Coming of Christ was very near, and in their zeal, abandoned their jobs. Paul gets into the social implications of the gospel when he tells them to look after their families and continue their secular work. According to verse 12 it would be wrong and harmful to their testimonies to depend upon the church to feed their families. Furthermore this might cause actual poverty and economic recession. These verses are then significant for the Christian work ethic.

C. Comfort for the Bereaved. 4:13-18.

There are several indications in these letters that Paul had given considerable emphasis to the Second Coming when he preached to the Thessalonians. One problem, as we have seen, was that some of the Thessalonians quit work to wait for Jesus to come back. In this section of the letter Paul replies to those who had lost loved ones in death since Paul had left. They wondered about the spiritual welfare of those who had died. What a tragedy, they must have thought, for their friends to have died before the return of the Lord. Would they now miss all the blessings of believers at the Second Coming? Would they still be saved even though they died before the *Parousia?*

13. But I would not have you to be ignorant. Although this sounds insulting to our ears, it was a formula Paul used often to mean simply, "I have something I want to tell you." The same introductory clause is used in Romans 1:13; 11:25; I Corinthians 10:1; II Corinthians 1:8. **Concerning them which are asleep.** This, of course, is not to be taken literally. Paul is not talking about those who are asleep, but about those who are dead. This euphemistic metaphor is common to all languages and religions and is used often in the New Testament (Mt 27:52). The word is also used in the same metaphorical sense in verses 14 and 15. **That ye sorrow not.** This is Paul's purpose for wanting to tell them about the dead. The Greek verb is in the present tense, making possible the translation, "so that you will not continue to grieve as others do." Paul intends to impart knowledge which they

may find comforting. **Others which have no hope.** The word **hope** (Gr *elpis*) is the key to this passage. In the New Testament this word refers to a "certain expectation," rather than something one wishes might happen. The Christian's **hope** is resurrection. It is the doctrine of the resurrection which here provides **hope** concerning the loved ones who have died; we know for certain that they will rise. The certainty of the resurrection for the Christian is based upon the resurrection of Jesus Christ our Lord. An obvious parallel is I Corinthians 15. Christ arose according to the Scriptures and appeared to many as indisputable truth. Paul shows the relationship between the resurrection of Christ and that of Christians in I Corinthians 15:20, the fact is, however, that "now is Christ risen from the dead as the firstfruits of them that slept." So the argument runs that since Christ rose from the dead, so we shall rise at his coming (I Cor 15:23).

14. Them also which sleep in Jesus will God bring with him. Again, it is the resurrection of departed saints which is based on the resurrection of Christ. We believe that Jesus died and rose again (as the firstfruits), so we have the "sure expectation" that God will raise the saints as he raised Jesus. **Bring** (Gr *agō*) could mean that God will bring saints back to the earth with him in the *Parousia,* but that does not seem to follow in the context. Since the first part of verse 14 refers to the death and resurrection of Christ, the last part of the verse should have a corresponding death and resurrection of believers. The death of believers is obvious from **them also which sleep in Jesus,** but the resurrection must be implied in the word **bring.** At the very least, the word must imply a resurrection in order for God to bring them back with Jesus at his coming.

15. For this we say unto you by the word of the Lord. By this Paul intends to make an authoritative announcement (cf. I Cor 7:10). **Shall not prevent them which are asleep.** The word **prevent** (Gr *phthanō*) has the meaning "precede." A better translation would be, "we who are alive, who are left until the coming of the Lord, shall not precede those who have fallen asleep." The construction in the original language (the subjunctive of emphatic future negation) emphasizes the fact that the living have no advantage over the dead at the coming of the Lord. This is clearly demonstrated in the next two verses, where Paul gives the order of events step by step.

16-17. First, **the Lord himself shall descend.** This is qualified by three attendant circumstances each introduced with the same preposition in the original: a command, an archangel's voice, and a trumpet blast. Second, **the dead in Christ shall rise first.** The word **rise** denotes the resurrection of the body, and not "rising" into the air. Likewise **first,** means that this resurrection occurs before the Rapture. Verse 17 indicates the third item in order; "then" means the next thing in order after their resurrection. **We which are alive and remain shall be caught up together with them.** It is important to note that the whole church, including those who have died prior to this event, as well as those who are still alive, is caught up together. There is no advantage either way. It is from the word **caught up** (Gr *harpazō*) in the Latin translation we get our word "rapture." The word in the original means "snatch," or "seize," and denotes a sudden violent taking away. The word pictures being "swept off" into the air as by a tornado. The result of this sweeping away, of course, is that we meet the Lord. Paul points out that these words are to be used by the Thessalonians to comfort one another concerning the welfare of their loved ones who have passed on. They will be reunited at His coming!

D. Apocalyptic Encouragement. 5:1-11.

5:1-2. But of the times and the seasons. Two synonyms for **time** are used; the first (Gr *chronos*) denotes chronological extension or "periods of time." The second (Gr *kairos*) denotes "specific points" in time when designated events occur. Paul states that the Thessalonians have no need for him to write about either "periods of time" which must elapse or "designated points in time" when something, like the Parousia, might occur.

The reason that Paul would not need to write is introduced in 5:2. They know perfectly well **that the day of the Lord so cometh as a thief in the night.** Paul here identifies the Old Testament "Day of the Lord" with the Parousia. The prominent idea associated with that Day in the Old Testament, and in this passage as well, is that of "judgment" and destruction upon the enemies of God. This stands in striking contrast to the previous passage (4:13-18), where the emphasis was **hope** and resurrection. The difference of course is one of focus; it depends upon whether believers or unbelievers are in view. The simile of the **thief in the night** heightens the element of surprise for unbelievers in the day of the Lord. Paul had perhaps taught the Thessalonians the words of the Lord Jesus himself concerning that day; Jesus had also called it "the coming of the Son of man" (Mt 24:37), and had said that the time was unknown to the angels of heaven and to Himself. Jesus had alluded to the flood in the time of Noah and the fact that the people were completely surprised and swept away by the flood.

3. Peace and safety. These were slogans of the Roman Empire. The suddenness of the event is portrayed by yet another simile, that of a pregnant woman's labor pains. Just that quickly **destruction** will be **upon** (Gr *ephistēmi*) **them.** The fact that this verb is in the perfect tense in Greek emphasizes the certainty or reality of the destruction. People in catastrophic situations have wondered "can this really be happening?" Paul is saying that the destruction of the Day of the Lord will not only be sudden, but it will be certain, and those upon whom it comes will definitely **not escape** (emphasized in Greek by the subjunctive of emphatic future negation)!

4-7. But ye. Paul, having focused briefly on the negative aspects of the Parousia, now moves to its positive aspects. This contrast is marked in the Greek text by the use of the emphatic personal pronoun with the adversative conjunction. Paul now makes full use of the symbols, **day** and **night.** His readers, since they have been saved, are **children of light,** which is an Old Testament figure meaning to be characterized by light, as opposed to darkness. Therefore, the negative aspects of his former simile of the thief do not apply to them. He is not trying to scare them with the Second Coming. Instead, he gives several exhortations (the Greek hortatory subjunctive corresponds to the occurrence of "let us" in the English text). The exhortations about not sleeping, and being sober correspond exactly to Paul's exhortation elsewhere to "redeem the time." The idea is that we must take advantage of every opportunity to serve Jesus Christ (Eph 5:16).

8. The metaphors of **faith . . . love and . . . hope** as pieces of armor are given more fully in Ephesians 6:14-17, but originally came from the Old Testament (Isa 59:17).

9. For God hath not appointed us to wrath. This again shows the intended contrast between believers and unbelievers at the time of the Second Coming. God has designed for us as believers that we should **obtain** (Gr peripoiēsis) **salvation by our Lord Jesus Christ** at His coming.

10. Who died for us. These words explain how salvation is **by** Jesus

Christ. His accomplishment of salvation is through his death for us. The purpose for which He died, to put it another way, was in order that we might live together with Him. Again in this verse, it is the resurrection of Jesus Christ which is the basis of our new life in Christ and our hope of the resurrection.

11. Comfort yourselves together, and edify one another. The two verbs are in the present tense in Greek implying a continuing obligation of believers to "encourage" and "build" one another. This is, of course, one of the reasons for fellowship together in the church.

E. Summary Exhortations. 5:12-22.

12. The first exhortation concerns the leaders of the Thessalonian church who **labor among you, and are over you in the Lord, and admonish you.** The words who **are over you** (Gr proistēmi) obviously indicate a governing leadership, and refer to spiritual leaders like pastors, elders, or bishops. Since the church was very young, its leaders must have been appointed by the apostolic missionaries in a manner similar to that mentioned in Acts 14:23. Paul asks his readers **to know** or recognize and appreciate the spiritual leaders. The spiritual nature of their leadership is indicated by **in the Lord.**

13. Esteem them very highly in love. The adverb here (Gr hyperekperissōs) is a double compound with a very intensive meaning which is probably quite adequately translated by **very highly** in the English text. The means of this high regard is suggested by **in love.** The reason for the high regard is that they have earned respect by their work. Paul in fact used the same word to describe their labor as he had used earlier for his own.

14. This verse sums up the responsibilities of Christians one toward another in three areas of ministry. A different imperative verb is used with each distinct group, implying that one's method must change according to the type of ministry. The first imperative (Gr *noutheteō*), **warn,** denotes a rather firm reminder to be used with the **unruly** (Gr *ataktos,* meaning, "incorrigible"). The second imperative (Gr *paramytheō*), **comfort** indicates soothing and comforting words for those who are "depressed" or discouraged (**feeble-minded** has other connotations not found in this verse). The third imperative (Gr *antechomai*), **support** calls for a supportive ministry for those who are weak or sick. The fourth exhortation in the verse is general, **be patient,** and encourages true patience **toward all men.**

15-18. Paying back evil with evil, in a manner similar to the Old Testament "eye for an eye," is not a part of the Christian philosophy; we must pursue what is good in our relationships to all men. Paul encourages other positive attitudes: a continual joy, or looking for the positive possibilities in every situation, persistent prayer, and thanksgiving. These are the things which are in accord with God's will for the Christian.

19-22. Quench (Gr *sbennymi*) means in this context to "suppress." It is, in fact, a synonym of the word **despise** in verse 20. The work of the **Spirit** should never be quenched, stifled, or suppressed. Verse 20 is parallel to verse 19; a gift like prophesying is not to be despised or belittled. Yet, in spite of the fact that the Thessalonians are quite literally called upon to stop these kinds of activities, they are encouraged to continue "testing" all things, that is, applying Christian principles to all situations, and to continue holding fast to that which is good. The idea is that, while they should not hinder someone who is genuinely working for God, neither should they be gullible and accept anyone who claims to be religious. Paul also reminds them that they should continue to **abstain** (Gr *apechō*) from every possible kind of evil. What Paul is calling for here is balance; Christians should neither be overcritical nor gullible.

IV. CONCLUSION. 5:23-28.

23. And the very God of peace sanctify you wholly. Paul's prayer for the Thessalonians here is put in the form of a wish (optative of wish) and might better be translated as, "may the God of peace himself sanctify you completely." The word **sanctify** (Gr *hagiazō*) is related to the word "holiness" and implies that God himself is the ultimate influence in changing a man's life. Holiness is more than a set of rules which can be legally imposed. Holiness or sanctification is the work of God's Holy Spirit who indwells us. Paul, having done all that is within his power to teach the Thessalonians to be holy, now commits them to God who alone can make them holy. **I pray God your whole spirit and soul and body be preserved blameless,** should rather be translated "may your spirit, soul, and body be kept sound and blameless at the coming of our Lord Jesus Christ." Paul is not here giving us a list of the separable parts of man, but is simply asking God to preserve the whole man in safety and holiness so that there will be no reason for shame or punishment at the coming of Christ (cf. Phil 1:10). Again, verse 25 emphasizes that, as it is God who saves, so it is God who keeps; God called them in the first place, and he will preserve them.

25-28. In his close, Paul asks for their continued prayers for him. The affection intended is indicated by the use of the term **Brethren,** the intimate **pray for us,** and the issuing of **a holy kiss** by mail. Prior to the words of benediction, Paul solemnly gives a **charge** (Gr *enorkizō*), by an oath to the Lord, that this letter be **read** aloud (Gr *anaginōskō*) to all the brethren. **The grace of our Lord Jesus Christ be with you. A-men.**

(See page 600 for Bibliography to I and II Thessalonians)

The Second Epistle To The

THESSALONIANS

INTRODUCTION

Authenticity. Although the authenticity of I Thessalonians has never been seriously questioned, being supported by internal evidence and the external support of Marcion, the Muratorian Canon, Irenaeus, Clement of Alexandria, Tertullian, and others, nevertheless the authenticity of II Thessalonians has received serious objection from the more radical schools of theology.

Opponents of the authenticity of II Thessalonians have objected to the difference in tone between this and the first epistle, to the doctrine of the man of sin, in chapter 2, and, oddly enough, to the similarities between the two epistles. However, both internal and external evidence favor Pauline authorship of this epistle as well.

Twice the writer refers to himself as Paul (1:1; 3:17). The general contents, style, vocabulary, theological concepts, etc. are all Pauline in nature. In addition, this epistle is quoted more frequently by the church fathers as Pauline than is the first epistle. Polycarp appears to quote from it; Justin Martyr alludes to it. Irenaeus mentions it directly by name. Both Clement of Alexandria and Tertullian attribute it to the Apostle Paul. It is found in the Muratorian Canon, the Syriac, Old Latin and Vulgate versions, as well as Marcion's Canon. Thus the authenticity of the epistle is only questioned by the extremely biased, and then not forcefully.

Authorship. There can be little question that, like I Thessalonians, this epistle was written by Paul. See the discussion above and that of the introduction to I Thessalonians.

Date and Place of Writing. Like the first epistle, II Thessalonians was written in Corinth. Again the names of Paul, Silas, and Timothy are associated in the salutation (1:1; cf. I Thess 1:1). Acts 18:5 indicates that these three were together in Corinth but shortly thereafter Silas drops out of sight, according to the book of Acts.

The date of this epistle must have been only months after the writing of the first. Circumstances at Thessalonica had not materially changed, yet enough time had elapsed in order to allow the believers there to fall into idleness as a result of Paul's teaching in I Thessalonians. Thus, we may date II Thessalonians during late A.D. 51 or early A.D. 52.

Purpose. As is the Pauline practice, Paul never writes a church but what he commends them. This is his purpose here as well. But the overriding purpose is the correction of errors.

The Thessalonians had misread Paul's intentions in the first letter. They interpreted the coming of the Lord to be upon them in such a way as to require them to sell the houses and lands, give up their jobs, and move to the hilltops in order to wait for the coming of Christ. This attitude had created idleness in the church and was a reproach on the name of the Lord Jesus. Paul had to give them additional instruction concerning the coming of the Lord, the man of sin who will be revealed before the Parousia, and the order of events preceding the second coming of Christ.

This epistle, written to Gentile believers, is especially helpful to new converts to Christianity. New Christians need to understand God's prophetic program and the work ethic of serving until the Lord comes.

OUTLINE

COMMENTARY

I. INTRODUCTION. 1:1-2.

1:1-2. Paul, and Silvanus, and Timothy. The salutation of II Thessalonians is almost the same as that of I Thessalonians (see the comments there). II Thessalonians adds **our** in verse 1, and **from God our Father and the Lord Jesus Christ** in verse 2.

II. PERSONAL RESPONSES. 1:3-12.

A. Thanksgiving and Praise. 1:3-4.

3-4. We are bound to thank God always for you. Although the language is slightly different, Paul begins II Thessalonians in the same way that he begins I Thessalonians, by thanking God for the faith and love of the believers. "Hope" is not mentioned in these introductory remarks; perhaps it is taken for granted. This passage seems to be more direct than the parallel passage in I Thessalonians, in that there is no need to "remember." There is, however, the same warm praise and thanksgiving for the progress and growth of the Christians.

B. Apocalyptic Encouragement. 1:5-12.

5. Which is a manifest token. The word **token** (Gr *endeigma*) refers to the result of a demonstration and thus means "a sign," "proof," or "evidence." Paul says that this is a demonstration of the righteous judgment of God, but the problem comes when we ask, "What is a demonstration?" If we take this to refer back to the "afflictions" of the Thessalonians, then Paul must mean to say that God judges righteously and gives the Thessalonians what they deserve. This hardly seems fair and does not fit the context either, since verse 6 shows that God will in fact bring rest to the Thessalonians when Christ comes. Most commentators take the word **token** to refer back to the whole of verse 4, so that it is the way in which the Thessalonians endured their persecutions which is a sign that God judges righteously. It is not the suffering, but their faith which proves God's righteous judgment. It would seem, however, that the main verbal idea in verse 4 is the "praise," or **glory** which Paul and the apostles give to the Thessalonians; this could certainly be understood as a "sign" of the way God would look upon endurance of the Thessalonians in his righteous judgment at the coming of Christ. **That ye may be counted worthy of the kingdom of God,** is an indication of the purpose of Paul's boasting about the Thessalonians and their faith to other churches. Paul wants them to be **counted worthy** which does not mean "made worthy" but simply recognized as being worthy. Paul does not consider it out of character to praise the Thessalonians for their faithfulness; in fact, that is his main means of encouraging them. Paul praises them for patience, faith, enduring persecutions, and suffering for the sake of the **kingdom of God.**

6. Seeing it is a righteous thing with God to recompense. The word **recompense** (Gr *antapodidōmi)* means to "reward" or "pay back." Paul emphasizes both the negative and the positive aspects of the Second Coming. The enemies of the gospel, those who are now troubling the Thessalonians, will be paid back by God for the suffering they caused; they will suffer themselves. It is interesting that the noun and the verb here are cognate forms, so that the literal translation would be, "God will repay those who trouble you with trouble." In other words, they will get a dose of their own medicine. The theme of God punishing sinners is a primary characteristic of all apocalyptic literature.

7. And to you who are troubled rest. This is the positive side of the second coming of Christ, that God will bring comfort and reward to his saints. The reward for those who are troubled by the troublers is **rest** (Gr *thlibō* is the common New Testament word for **tribulation).** The word "rest" (Gr *anesis)* means primarily "release" or "relaxation." This is the word from which we get our common trademark, "Anacin." Real comfort and relaxation in the future, in spite of temporary

affliction here, are the rewards of all those who serve the living and true God. According to this verse, Christ comes with his **mighty angels,** which may parallel the meaning of the original in I Thessalonians 3:13, where the angels are called His "Holy Ones." Note that the same expression in the original recurs in this chapter (1:10). **The Lord Jesus shall be revealed** could be more literally translated "in the revelation of the Lord Jesus." This is a new word for the second coming of Christ which emphasizes the manifestation of the person of Jesus Christ as a powerful judge.

8. Flaming fire taking vengeance. In flaming fire should probably be taken as a part of verse 7; almost the same apocalyptic imagery is found in Revelation 1:13-14, as well as in Daniel 7:13. The emphasis seems to be upon His manifestation as the Son of Man. He comes with the sword of God's vengeance to destroy those who do not know God. Not "knowing" God may be an extension of the Old Testament idiom of not loving God or serving him rather than a simple lack of knowledge. Another important concept in Old Testament theology was obedience as we see, for example, in Isaiah 66:4, "I also will choose their delusions, and will bring their fears upon them; because when I called, none did answer; when I spake, they did not hear: but they did evil before mine eyes, and chose that in which I delighted not." In Thessalonians, their disobedience is to the gospel of our Lord Jesus (an objective genitive).

9-10. Who shall be punished. The literal translation here would be, "who shall pay the penalty of eternal destruction from the face of the Lord." Again, this is the uniform theme of apocalyptic in general (cf. Isa 2:11, 17; Rev 9:6). **In that day** alludes again to the Old Testament Day of Jehovah which has now been identified with the Revelation of Jesus Christ. Here Paul mentions once more the positive purpose for the Second Coming, namely that the Lord should receive glory from those who believe because of the apostolic witness.

11-12. Wherefore should rather be translated "unto this end." Paul's prayer is the encouragement he desires to impart to them. Only God can accomplish his will in the lives of the believers, so Paul prayed that God would first count them worthy, and then fulfill His good pleasure in their lives. The result of the answer to this prayer will be that God will **be glorified in** the believers (by their good lives), and that the believers will be glorified in God. All this is accomplished by God's wonderful grace.

III. THE DAY OF THE LORD. 2:1-12.

A. Plea for Stability. 2:1-2.

2:1. Now we beseech you, is simply the word (Gr *erōtaō*) "ask," but it is used with considerable authority by Paul in this epistle (see 4:1; 5:12). Another misunderstanding about the Second Coming needs correction, and although oral instruction had been given before, Paul uses this opportunity to underscore it in writing. **By the coming,** is better translated, "concerning the coming of our Lord Jesus Christ and our being gathered to meet Him." Paul is not making some kind of oath, but simply introducing this next aspect of the subject at hand. Several aspects had needed comment in these letters: worshiping God involves waiting for His Son (1:10), ultimate joy and reward comes later at His coming (I Thess 2:17-20), His coming encourages us to holiness now (I Thess 3:13), those who die before His coming will not be cheated out of the Rapture, but will be raised first (I Thess 4:13-18), and now it must be shown that however they had gotten the impression that the Day of the Lord events had already started, it simply was not true.

2. That ye be not soon shaken in mind. This clause indicates the purpose of Paul's authoritative statement. He does not want them to be easily swayed from the position they had already accepted as the Word of God. Nor should they be **troubled** (Gr *throeō*), a word denoting great inward pain and anxiety, which is used elsewhere in the New Testament only twice and both times it is in the same eschatological context of the Second Coming. Their tendency to believe that they were in the midst of the very last days had caused other problems too (see I Thess 4:11; II Thess 3:12). By **spirit** evidently refers to a supposed prophetic utterance which might have come from some non-apostolic source; **nor by word,** which again would be a false message but pretending to be authoritative like the Word that Paul had given (I Thess 2:13). **Letter** (Gr *epistolē*) means a forged letter; in 3:17 he tells them that his letters can afterward be recognized by the sign of a closing greeting in his own handwriting. **That the day of Christ is at hand** (Gr *enistēmi*) should rather be translated, "to the effect that the day of the Lord has come." The word means "to be present"; Paul wants to assure them that the Day of the Lord is not already in progress when he writes. Paul taught that the Lord was "near" (Phil 4:5), and that the era of fulfillment (the last days) was inaugurated with the first coming of Christ, but never implied that the apocalyptic Day of the Lord had already begun.

B. The Man of Sin. 2:3-12.

3. Let no man deceive you by any means: for that day shall not come, except there come a falling away. Part of the sentence is implied in the original, and must be supplied in the translation; the Day of the Lord will not begin without the **falling away** (Gr *apostasia*). Our English word "apostasy" comes, of course, directly from this Greek word, which means literally a "standing away from" or "departure." In the religious sense it is a departure from the faith, and what we have in this passage is called the final apostasy which is to be led by the man of lawlessness. Some have taken the words **falling away** to refer to the Rapture of the Church in order to prove a point; there is no historical support for that translation, however. The religious meaning is illustrated by Paul in I Timothy 1:4, and by the author of Hebrews in 3:12. At any rate, an apostasy must precede the Day of the Lord.

Simultaneously with the great apostasy, or at least another prerequisite to the beginning of the events of the Second Coming, is appearance of the **man of sin.** The better manuscripts read here, "man of lawlessness," but there is no important difference in the name, for the Bible tells us that "sin is lawlessness" (I Jn 3:4). That the man of sin is **revealed** (Gr *apokalyptō*) shows that he exists prior to the time of this revelation or appearance. I John 2:18 states that there were already many antichrists, in the sense of people who are against Christ, existing in that day. It is not certain exactly who this person will be; but the identification of the man of sin with the coming Antichrist of Revelation is the most logical conclusion. He is the "beast out of the sea" (Rev 13:1), the "little horn" of Daniel 7:8. He is the Antichrist, i.e. the false christ who will force himself and his kingdom upon the world one day hence (Rev 13:15-17).

4. Who opposeth and exalteth himself. Because of Paul's familiarity with the language of the Old Testament, there are many similarities to Daniel (especially 11:36). This is, however, a new description of the leader of the forces of evil in the final apocalyptic battle against God. **Opposeth** (Gr *antikeimai*) is present tense in Greek and implies continued, determined, and planned opposition to God. It is a common word for the opposing sides in a battle. **Exalteth himself** shows his extreme pride; he puts himself over everything considered as a god or an object of worship and as it were, seats himself in the Temple of God. **As God** was not a part of the original text, although it is certainly implied that this rebellious person acts as if he were God and sits in the Temple personally, unlike Gaius who in A.D. 40 attempted to have his statue placed in the sanctuary at Jerusalem (see Mk 13:14). **Showing himself** (Gr *apodeiknymi*) has the sense of "attempting to demonstrate" that he is God.

5. Remember ye not. Paul must have put great emphasis upon the second coming of Chrsit and related apocalyptic events when he was with the Thessalonians in order to refer back to that preaching so often. Two grammatical items in the Greek make the meaning clear, "You surely recall, do you not, that during my stay, I told you this repeatedly."

6. And now ye know what withholdeth (Gr *katechō*) is literally, "the thing which holds down." Paul seems to say that for the present **(now)**, there is something (a Greek neuter participle) which is holding back the appearance of the lawless leader of the final rebellion. What that "something" meant to the Thessalonian readers is impossible for us to know with any degree of certainty. It may have been the Roman Empire, or perhaps more generally the social structures of law and order manifested in the Roman Empire. This meaning would explain the shift to the masculine participle **(he who now letteth;** same word) in verse 7. However, there is some good reason to assume that it is the ministry of the Holy Spirit which now hinders the work of the man of sin. The work of the Spirit is exhibited in the church and when the church is **taken out of the way** (vs. 7) the Antichrist will manifest his plan of world domination. This rebel will be revealed in his time, (Gr *kairos*), which elkṓ). This is a very strong and this section, namely, that the Day has not yet begun. The "time" is a divinely predetermined time; no one knows when it will be, but Paul shows that it could not have happened already.

7. The mystery of iniquity. If this is translated, "the mystery of lawlessness," it is easier to see the connection with the man of lawlessness (vs. 3), and the "lawless one" (vs. 8). The idea is that there is already rebellion and lawlessness going on in their day, but that up to that time (**now**) "someone" was restraining it. Obviously, the principle of rebellion to the gospel had been at work in the opposition Paul himself experienced at Thessalonica and other places, but it was not as bad as it might have been. **He who now letteth** (Gr *katechō*) corresponds to "what withholdeth" in verse 6, except that the gender is changed from a restraining thing to a restraining person.

8. That Wicked is the same word translated **man of sin** in verse 3, and **mystery of iniquity** in verse 7; a more consistent translation would be "the lawless one." **Whom the Lord.** Better manuscripts have "the Lord Jesus." **Shall consume.** Again, this is a variant which should read "execute" (Gr *anaireō*). The Lord Jesus will execute this wicked rebel **with the spirit of his mouth.** This last phrase should rather be translated, "with the breath of his mouth" and means, of course, "with a word." This expression occurs only here in the New Testament, but corresponds exactly in meaning with the adjective translated "inspired by God" in II Timothy 3:16, and is related idiom. The Scriptures are the "Word" of God because they are "breathed out" or spoken by Him; in the same sense this "word" to execute the lawless one will be breathed out by the Lord Jesus. It is His word, and only a word from Him will **destroy** (Gr *katargeō*) this archenemy of the gospel. This last word means "to make ineffective"; none of his work through the ages will have any effect on the final accomplishments of the gospel.

God and the Lord Jesus will have the final victory.

9. Even him, whose coming. The word **coming** (Gr *parousia*) is used for the coming or presence of various people in the New Testament; in Thessalonians it is used seven times, and except for this last time refers to the second coming of Christ. This is the Parousia of the Antichrist, corresponding to the Parousia of the Lord Jesus mentioned in verse 8; the events concomitant to each coming are supernatural and roughly concurrent. **After the working of Satan.** The distinction of this coming is that all the activities are satanic; they are the signs of an apostle (see II Cor 12:12), but are perverted and false.

10. In that Day, as in Paul's day, there will be followers on both sides; the Antichrist will have his "believers" too. They are called here **them that perish** (Gr *apollymi*) meaning "the lost" or "those who are perishing." The reason these people are lost is **because they received not** the gospel. Note that the word **received** (Gr *dechomai*) is a vivid attitude indicator; it means "to welcome" as one welcomes a guest he wishes to entertain. This is an opposite attitude to that of the Thessalonians themselves who **received** the gospel message for what it was, the Word of God (see I Thess 2:13). These people will not be able to blame God for being lost; they refused to believe the Word of God and be saved. A better translation of the verse has "because they refused to love the truth and so be saved."

11-12. Since they will not believe the truth, God allows them to believe the great lie. Although God is the sovereign agent behind all that happens, it is clear in this passage that a voluntary, rational choice is made by these people of every age who have **pleasure in unrighteousness.** The word used here (Gr *eudokeō*) means to "make a decision about what is right." The decision was theirs; they decided for unrighteousness rather than for righteousness and

God. The result is that they are condemned, i.e. lost!

IV. GOD'S GRACE. 2:13-17.

A. The Means of Salvation. 2:13-14.

13. Paul now moves into a more positive description of how God saved the Thessalonians by His grace through the preaching of the gospel there earlier (I Thess 1:20). Paul puts his obligation for thanksgiving in the plural, indicating that Silas and Timothy join him in feeling the obligation to give thanks to God concerning the believers. As in I Thessalonians 1:4, Paul addresses the Thessalonians as **brethren beloved of the Lord.** The word **beloved** (Gr *agapaō*) is in the perfect tense in Greek, emphasizing the certainty of the fact that God loves them; the passive voice also stresses once again the point that in salvation God always takes the initiative. The reason for the obligation to give thanks follows, **because God hath from the beginning chosen you to salvation.** Paul gives thanks because God has **chosen** (Gr *haireomai*) the believers to salvation. It is interesting that this word, in the active voice, means "to pick out" as one picks fruit, while in the middle it is a regular word for "making a choice." This is also the word used in the Greek Old Testament for God's choice of Israel rather than the Gentiles; it is now applied here to Gentile believers. God has chosen them from among the Gentiles and has washed them, sanctified them, and justified them, in the name of Jesus (I Cor 6:11). **From the beginning** should probably be instead, "as the first converts to salvation." The word for "first converts" (Gr *aparchē*) is used in six other places in Paul's epistles as a favorite expression to show the continuity between the people of God in the Old Testament and the people of God in the New Testament. Verses 13 and 14 comprise a compendium of the doctrine of salvation where several

significant redemptive concepts are given. Note the concepts of obligation, thanksgiving, brotherly love, the love of God, God's choosing the Thessalonians for salvation, firstfruits, salvation, sanctification by the Holy Spirit, faith, truth, God's calling, the apostolic preaching of the gospel, the attainment of glory, and Jesus Christ as our **Lord. Through sanctification of the Spirit** shows the agency of the Holy Spirit in "setting apart" these believers to salvation, while **belief of the truth** shows the means of salvation is by faith in the gospel.

14. Whereunto he called you by our gospel. Here the **calling** of God corresponds to the "choosing" of God in verse 13. Note that God's call comes through the preaching of the gospel, and that it results in **obtaining of the glory.** The word **obtaining** (Gr *peripoiēsis*) refers generally to "obtaining" or "attaining" to something but more specifically and more technically in the Bible it can refer to God's creation of a people for himself. In the Old Testament God made Israel a "people for his own possession," and that same idea in the New Testament has been applied to both Jews and Gentiles as they are brought into the church which becomes a "people for God's own possession" (see also I Thess 5:9; I Pet 2:9; and cf. Mal 3:17). The interpretation of the special use of this word may be supported by the fact that the next word, **glory,** does not have an article in Greek so that the phrase might be translated, "to the glorious obtaining." This would mean that the Lord Jesus is accomplishing God's intended salvation by his death on the cross.

B. The Manifestations of Salvation. 2:15-17.

15. Therefore, brethren, stand fast, and hold the traditions which ye have been taught, whether by word, or our epistle. Another interesting technical term is the word **traditions,** which comes from a verb meaning "to hand down by tradition." These **traditions** were the gospel itself which had been preached among the Thessalonians. Paul uses the word **taught** here for what was often called "preaching." Actually there is little difference between "teaching" and "preaching" according to the New Testament; the content of the teaching and preaching of the apostles was the gospel, and Paul is saying here that it makes no difference whether these traditions were given orally (**by word**) or in written form (**our epistle**). Either way, this teaching, preaching, or tradition, is the Word of God and is authoritative.

16-17. Now our Lord Jesus Christ himself and God, even our Father. Paul inserted a similar doxological prayer in I Thessalonians 3:11 where he also used the Greek optative mood to make his prayer concerning his readers. In both passages the prayer is directed to God the Father as well as to the Lord Jesus Christ. It is also interesting that this prayer emphasizes encouragement (**consolation** and **Comfort** are cognate) as well as support. One should note also that the word **finally** (3:1) marks the beginning of the conclusion of the letter after the prayer here, just as it does in I Thessalonians 4:1.

V. PRACTICAL EXHORTATIONS. 3:1-18.

A. Mutual Prayer. 3:1-5.

3:1-2. Finally, brethren, pray for us, that the word of the Lord may have free course. Paul again refers to the gospel as **the word of the Lord,** meaning the Lord Jesus. In I Thessalonians 2:13 Paul praised the believers for welcoming their preaching as the Word of God. Paul wants the Word of God to be successful and accomplish its purpose, and so **be glorified** as it was among the Thessalonian believers themselves when they recognized it was the Word of God, believed it, and were

saved. When Paul asked for prayer for Silas, Timothy, and himself, it is the same as asking prayer for the Word of the Lord. They are stewards of the Lord who preach his Word as their primary occupation in life. He also wishes them to pray for their safety in the work, and that they might be protected from evil men who oppose them.

3-5. But the Lord is faithful, who shall stablish you, and keep you from evil. Paul's statement at the end of verse 2 that all men are not of the faith is a classic understatement. Jesus had put it much more strongly, saying that the world hated them (Jn 17:14), and Paul himself had been often badly misused. The unfaithfulness of men, however, provides a transition to the faithfulness of God, which is a favorite subject of Paul's (I Cor 10:13; I Thess 5:24; II Tim 2:13). The faithfulness of God means here that He will support and keep from evil. The word **keep** (Gr *phylassō*) means rather "guard." **From evil,** should rather be translated, "from the evil ONE," since the gender is masculine in the original (cf. Jn 17:15). In verse 4, Paul expresses his emphatic (the perfect tense in Greek stresses the certainty of a fact) confidence in his readers that they will continue to obey the Word of God, just as they have been doing. To that end he again expresses his prayer that the Lord will direct their hearts into the love of God and true courage for Christ. The word translated **patient waiting for** (Gr *hypomonē*) has the idea of steadfastness or endurance rather than patience, and is a different word from the one Paul uses in I Thessalonians 1:10 as an example of **waiting for** Christ to return in the Second Coming. What Paul has in mind here is courage on the part of the Thessalonians to continue to live for God in spite of the problems.

B. The Work Ethic. 3:6-15.

6-9. Now we command (Gr *parangellō*). This is a very strong and authoritative word; it denotes standing beside someone like a drill sergeant and telling him what to do. Paul uses it seldom, and only when he wants to be very serious and very authoritative. Neither the verb nor the noun form is used in I or II Thessalonians except in connection with the so-called "work ethic" (I Thess 4; II Thess 3). To make this commandment even more authoritative it is given **in the name of our Lord Jesus Christ.** This important, indirect command is completed by the infinitive of another unusual word for Paul, **that ye withdraw yourselves** (Gr *stellomai*) which denotes disassociation. The word is used only one other time in the New Testament, and even there it does not have this sense of ecclesiastical separation or censure. Other strong words are also used in this commandment; **walketh disorderly** (Gr *atakios*) indicates a continual pattern of life which is "not subjected" to and cannot be subjected to the authority of Christ. It is also noteworthy that the synonymous descriptive clause uses the cognate noun and verb for the authoritative "traditions" of the gospel. The obvious implications are that the message that was preached by the apostles was the Word of God; it was authoritative, inspired, and canonical. If a person refuses to submit to the authority of the Word of God, he is "walking disorderly." In this Paul reminds them that they must follow the apostolic pattern; **for we behaved not ourselves disorderly** (a cognate form is used). While the apostles were in Thessalonica they supported themselves, working hard day and night so that their demands upon the community would not be too great. Paul states again that as apostles, they had the authority to have both their wages and expenses paid by the community. They had purposely avoided using this privilege for the benefit of the Thessalonians.

10-12. For even when we were with you, this we commanded you, that if any would not work, neither should he eat. Again, the word **commanded** refers back to the problem that arose while the apostles were still present in Thessalonica, namely that some people got so excited about the second coming of Christ they decided to quit work and just wait. It should be noted that Paul does not say that if they could not work they should not "be allowed" to eat, but rather that if anyone did not want to continue working he should decide to stop eating also. Paul has heard that some people have disobeyed his former injunction against that sort of attitude and that they have become **busybodies.** They seem to have been the ancestors of some today who are so heavenly-minded that they are of no earthly good.

According to verse 11, this sort of super-spirituality is really pride and a refusal to submit to the authority of God's Word; the same word **disorderly** is used again (vs. 11), along with the word for a "strict command" which is given in the name of the Lord Jesus Christ (vs. 12). The opposite of that sort of conduct is to eat one's own bread, which he earns by means of working at an occupation while he quietly serves the Lord.

13. But ye. The pronoun is emphatic showing that Paul here speaks to those who are really most spiritual, and whom he has often praised in these epistles. **Be not weary in well doing.** This statement is almost identical with that in Galatians 6:9, except that here Paul uses a Greek construction for the prohibition which implies that these believers are already doing what is noble and right, and that they have not yet begun to despair. The translation might be accurately expanded to "don't ever get depressed; just keep on doing good."

14-15. Note that man. The word **note** (Gr *sēmeioō*) implies that the person who refuses to obey the Word of the Lord while professing to be a "Christian" should be marked out and distinguished in some way from normal believers so that he is disassociated from them. He is not to be treated as an enemy, however, but as a brother. It must be made clear to that person and to the others as well that he is a disobedient Christian, and that if he wishes to associate with believers he must be willing to submit to and obey the Word of God (cf. Mt 18:17).

VI. CONCLUSION. 3:16-17.

16. Now the Lord of peace himself give you peace always by all means. In his closing benediction Paul again reminds the Thessalonians that in the end it is not their own efforts but the Lord Himself who must accomplish His salvation and His peace within them. The **Lord of peace** is probably intended by Paul specifically as a name for Jesus Christ.

17. The salutation of Paul in his own hand is the mark of genuineness for his letter. The Thessalonians need not wonder whether another letter they might get would be authentic. It was implied in II Thessalonians 2:2 that some doubt had been present in their minds when they received a letter purporting to be from Paul. Now they would know his letters by this token.

18. The grace of our Lord Jesus Christ be with you all. A-men. This is the identical conclusion as given in I Thessalonians, the substance of which would come to form a Pauline pattern.

BIBLIOGRAPHY
I & II Thessalonians

Askwith, Edward H. *An Introduction to the Thessalonian Epistles.* London: Macmillan, 1902.

Bruce, F. F. I and II Thessalonians in *New Bible Commentary.* Grand Rapids: Eerdmans, 1953.

Denney, James. The Epistles to the Thessalonians in *Expositor's Bible.* New York: Armstrong & Son, 1903.

*Eadie, John. *A Commentary on the Greek Text of the Epistles of Paul to the Thessalonians.* Ed. by William Young. London: Macmillan, 1877.

*Ellicott, Charles J. *Commentary on the Epistle of St. Paul to the Thessalonians.* Grand Rapids: Zondervan, 1957.

Erdman, Charles R. *The Epistles of Paul to the Thessalonians.* Philadelphia: Westminster Press, 1935.

Findlay, George C. The Epistles of Paul the Apostle to the Thessalonians. In the *Cambridge Greek Testament.* Cambridge: Cambridge University Press, 1911.

Hendriksen, William. Exposition of I and II Thessalonians. In *New Testament Commentary.* Grand Rapids: Baker, 1964.

*Hiebert, D. Edmond. *The Thessalonian Epistles.* Chicago: Moody Press, 1971.

Hogg, Charles and Vine, William. *The Epistles to the Thessalonians*. London: Pickering and Inglis, 1959.

Horne, Charles. The Epistles to the Thessalonians. A Study Manual. In the *Shield Bible Study Studies*. Grand Rapids: Baker, 1961.

Hubbard, David A. I and II Thessalonians in *Wycliffe Bible Commentary*. Chicago: Moody Press, 1962.

Lenski, R. C. H. *The Interpretation of St. Paul's Epistles to the Colossians, to the Thessalonians, to Timothy, to Titus, and to Philemon*. Columbus, Ohio: Lutheran Book Concern, 1937.

MacDonald, William. *Letters to the Thessalonians*. Kansas City, Kansas: Walterick Publishers, 1969.

Milligan, George. *St. Paul's Epistles to the Thessalonians*. London: Macmillan, 1908.

Morris, Leon. The Epistles of Paul to the Thessalonians. In *The Tyndale New Testament Commentaries*. Grand Rapids: Eerdmans, 1957.

_____. The First and Second Epistles to the Thessalonians. In *The New International Commentary on the New Testament*. Grand Rapids: Eerdmans, 1959.

Plummer, Alfred. *A Commentary on St. Paul's First Epistle to the Thessalonians*. London: Robert Scott, 1918.

_____. *A Commentary on St. Paul's Second Epistle to the Thessalonians*. London: Robert Scott, 1918.

*Ryrie, Charles Caldwell. First and Second Thessalonians. In *Everyman's Bible Commentary*. Chicago: Moody Press, 1959.

Stevens, William Arnold. Commentary on the Epistles to the Thessalonians. In *An American Commentary*. Philadelphia: The American Baptist Publication Society, 1890.

*Walvoord, John F. *The Thessalonian Epistles*. Grand Rapids: Zondervan, 1956.

Ward, Ronald A. *A Commentary on First and Second Thessalonians*. Waco, Texas: Word, 1973.

The First Epistle To

TIMOTHY

INTRODUCTION

The three letters addressed to Timothy and Titus (I Timothy, II Timothy, and Titus) constitute what is known as the Pastoral Epistles. It is said that this term was used by Thomas Aquinas. Polycarp, bishop of Smyrna early in the second century, is known to have been aware of this corpus (see C. K. Barrett, *The Pastoral Epistles,* p. 1). But it was not until 1703 that D. N. Berdot, followed later by Paul Anton in 1726, popularized the term "pastoral" to describe these letters.

Authorship. The authorship of the Pastoral Epistles came slowly to be suspected as being non-pauline. In fact, it was not until the last century that these three little epistles became a battleground of biblical criticism. In 1807 Schleiermacher denied the genuineness of I Timothy. His criticisms quickly spread to the other two as well. Today scholars are divided into three camps around the question of authorship: (1) those who hold to Pauline authorship (Godet, Lightfoot, Alford, Lange, Schaff, Ramsay, etc.); (2) those who believe that these epistles should be placed in the second century and consequently are not to be considered Pauline in any sense of the word (Baur, Hatch, Goodspeed, etc.); and (3) those who take a mediating position claiming that while these letters were not written by Paul, they do contain some genuine Pauline fragments (Ewald, Harnack, Moffatt, etc.).

1. *External evidence.* Although these epistles were rejected by Marcion and perhaps Tatian, the early church as a whole received them as wholly authoritative. They were accepted as canonical by Irenaeus (cf. *Adversus Haereses* I,

Preface, I); Tertullian cf. *De Praescriptione Haereticorum 7*); and were included in the Muratorian Canon (ca. A.D. 200). Perhaps the most notable concern over the canonicity of these epistles arises out of their absence from the Chester Beatty Papyrus (P[46]). Yet the church at large supported their inclusion into the canon.

2. *Internal evidence.* Personal references to Paul seem to necessitate pauline authorship. It is highly unlikely that anyone but Paul would have referred to Paul as "injurious" (1:13) or the "chief" of sinners (1:15). Paul identifies himself as author (1:1) and the author exhibits the same sense of divine call that Paul exhibits (1:12; 2:7; II Tim 1:11). The doctrine of the epistles is Paul's doctrine. Like other epistles (e.g. Romans or Philemon), a large number of personal names is introduced into this epistle. This was a Pauline practice. Down through the centuries the church has been identifying elements of each of these epistles as Pauline. Thus, if we are to reject Pauline authorship, the objections of the critics must first be proven (which has not been successfully done) and the direct claim of authorship by Paul must be deleted from each epistle (which will never be done). For an excellent discussion of the problems and positions on Pauline authorship see Donald Guthrie, The Pastoral Epistles, in the *Tyndale New Testament Commentaries.*

Recipient. The recipient of I Timothy was a young resident of Lystra named Timothy (Acts 16:1-3). He was the son of a Greek father (Acts 16:2) and a Jewish mother, Eunice (II Tim 1:5). He had been taught the Scriptures from his youth (II Tim 1:5; 3:15) which is a testimony to the faithfulness of his godly mother and grandmother.

Timothy came to know the Lord as Saviour through the ministry of Paul on his first missionary journey (Acts 14:8-20). When Paul revisited the Lycaonian city of Lystra on his second missionary journey he decided to take young Timothy with him as a fellowlaborer. Timothy was ordained to the ministry by the presbytery, Paul being a party to that ordination (4:14; II Tim 1:6). This "beloved child" in the faith periodically spent his next years laboring with or in behalf of the apostle. In Paul's last epistle, II Timothy, the apostle summons his friend to Rome, hoping to see him once more before he dies (II Tim 4:9, 21).

That Paul loved Timothy dearly is evident from the two epistles addressed to him and the character of those epistles. Once the apostle made reference to the closeness of Timothy to his heart by saying that he had "no man like-minded" (literally, "of equal soul") as Timothy. To Paul, Timothy was brother, a like-minded or soul brother.

Date and place of writing. On the likely assumption that there were two imprisonments of Paul in Rome, the Pastoral Epistles must be dated after Paul's first release from prison in the spring of A.D. 63. The exact date will depend on the order of activity which Paul followed between the two imprisonments. However, we will not severely stray if we place the date of I Timothy in the fall of A.D. 63 or early A.D. 64.

"This epistle was addressed to Timothy, stationed at Ephesus, some time after Paul had left for Macedonia (1:3). He appears to be in Macedonia at the time of writing (perhaps at Philippi), but it is possible that he may have gone on to Greece when he wrote" (D. E. Hiebert, *An Introduction to the Pauline Epistles,* p. 329).

Purpose. Although not the pastor at Ephesus, Timothy was Paul's personal envoy to that city and later became his representative there. Being a "young man," Paul felt Timothy would need encouragement for the task which faced him at Ephesus. This epistle is designed to provide such encouragement. In addition, an epistle from the respected, once-imprisoned apostle would add validity to the credentials of Timothy in the eyes of the Ephesians.

However, it appears that false teachers, perhaps Gnostic Jews, men who sought to be known as "teachers of the law" (1:7), had invaded Ephesus and were spreading their poisonous doctrine. The pernicious effects of this teaching (1:4; 6:4-5) had to be halted. Paul advises Timothy on the exhortation needed to quell this tide of heresy (4:11, 16; 6:2).

Many of the problems that Timothy faced, the young pastor of the twentieth century also faces. Thus the Pastoral Epistles continue to be the young pastor's best manual for church leadership.

OUTLINE

COMMENTARY

I. INTRODUCTION. 1:1-2.

A. Paul the Author. 1:1.

1:1. Paul. The founder of churches who was once the fighter of churches as Saul before meeting Jesus. The preacher who was the persecutor. His name (Gr *Paulos*) means "little." He was "in his own sight" little (I Sam 15:17) and God highly exalted him too (cf. Phil 2:5-11)! Note his evaluation of himself as "the least of all saints" (Eph 3:8) and finally "the chief of sinners" (I Tim 1:15). He exemplified John 3:30, "I must decrease." That's maturing. I Peter 5:6 works today too. No wonder he could say, "Be ye followers of me" (I Cor

11:1). An **apostle.** His official position. An apostle was appointed by the Holy Spirit (I Cor 12:8-11), he had to have seen the risen Christ (Acts 1:22; I Cor 15:8-9), and he must be endued with miraculous powers (II Cor 12:12). There are no apostles in this sense today. **By the commandment of God,** his authority, "No man takes this honor to himself" (Heb 5:4). He makes it plain God "called" him (Gal 1:15-16). There is a divine call. Happy is the church who has a God-called preacher and not a man-made preacher. **God ... our Saviour ... Jesus ... our hope. Our saviour** speaks of His past ministry, **our hope** of His future coming. It is a "blessed hope"

(Tit 2:11-13), "a purifying hope" (I Jn 3:1-3), a "comforting" hope (I Thess 4:13-18).

B. Timothy the Recipient. 1:2.

2. Timothy. This name means "he who honors God." **My own son.** "Son" (Gr *teknon*), is "a child, a born one" and "own" (Gr *gnēsios*) indicates "legitimately born, genuine." He was for real and proved it. Every young preacher needs a spiritual father. Every church should produce preachers! What an honor to both pastor and people to have someone they can call **my own son in the faith.**

The salutation is **Grace** (Gr *charis*),the Greeks' "hello." It means to get what you don't deserve. Salvation is by grace (Eph 2:8-9). **Mercy** (Gr *eleos*) means you don't get what you do deserve. It is only in the Pastoral Epistles that Paul breaks from his usual pattern of saying "grace and peace" and includes "mercy." Preachers need mercy. **Peace** (Gr *eirēnē*) means "to bind together that which has been separated." Christ is our peace (Eph 2:14) and binds us to God.

II. THE CHARGE CONCERNING DOCTRINE. 1:3-11.

Paul begins immediately with his course in pastoral theology on how to "behave in the house of God" (3:15) which is the theme for his whole letter. The basis for correct behavior is correct belief. But correct belief should always issue in correct behavior.

A. Purity of Doctrine (Life). 1:3-4.

3-4. Besought (Gr *parakaleō*) the same word as Romans 12:1. It is a strong word and suggests Timothy had other plans. **Abide** means "stay put" and **charge some** that is "take a strong stand." To build a strong church the pastor has to take a strong stand! There must be purity of doctrine maintained. **No other doctrine,** "other" meaning doctrine of a "different kind" from what he had taught (cf. Gal 1:6-7).

4. Fables or "myths." These and **endless genealogies** were so prevalent among the Jews **Desiring to be teachers of the law** (vs. 7). There were countless legends in the Talmud. These led to questions and doubts. Beware of any teacher or teaching which generates doubts and questions, rather than building godliness.

B. Purpose of Doctrine (Love) 1:5.

5. The **end** or purpose of his charge is "charity" or "love" and not divisions. Some claiming to contend for the faith are contentious about the faith and bring divisions. God is never the author of confusion in churches (I Cor 14:33). This love can only come from a **pure heart** which has been redeemed and cleansed in the blood of Christ. **A good conscience.** There should be "nothing between" not only us and the Saviour but saints as well. Confessing our faults and forgiving others' faults gives a clear conscience. **Faith unfeigned** (Gr *anypokritos*). The Greek word here is the one from which we get "hypocrite." It was a term used of actors, one who pretends to be what he is not!

C. Perversion of Doctrine (Law). 1:6-11.

6. Having swerved (Gr *ektrepō*) is a medical term which means "to twist out of joint" like an arm out of socket. This causes great pain to the whole body.

7. Teachers of the law. The law is good and meant to be used even today, but it must be used for its intended purpose, i.e. "that every mouth may be stopped, and all the world may become guilty before God" (Rom 3:19), so that man turns toward Christ for righteousness (Rom 10:1-4; Gal 2:21; 3:24-25).

9-11. A righteous man, "a saved person" is not under the law but grace. He is not lawless but the controlling force is the Holy Spirit and the grace of God (Gal 3:1-5; Tit 2:11 ff.). The list of sins parallels the Ten Commandments which condemn each sin and bring guilt. **Sound doctrine** can be judged by whether it is a "gospel of the glory of the blessed God," which is the sense here. People are transformed in the church by "beholding . . . the glory of the Lord" (II Cor 3:18) and not a constant bombardment of legalistic preaching or teaching. Paul felt keenly this ministry was a trust.

III. THE CHARGE CONCERNING DUTY. 1:12-20.

A. The Challenge from His Own Ministry. 1:12-17.

Doctrine demands duty. These verses share the extreme gratefulness and humility in Paul. What a contrast to the Pharisaic legalities of his day. Correct behavior by the people begins with the behavior of the pastor. Paul, who greeted Timothy with grace and mercy, realized his salvation and ministry was obtained through grace and mercy.

12. I thank Christ Jesus our Lord. There was no arrogance in Paul. The world is "unthankful." He did not take his privilege for granted. **Enabled me** (literally, "put strength"). Paul knew well his "strength is made perfect in weakness" (II Cor 19:9). **Faithful.** This is required of stewards with a trust (I Cor 4:1-2). **Ministry.** No man takes this honor to himself (Heb 4:5) and Paul did not "handle the Word of God deceitfully" (II Cor 4:2), as did the legalizers.

13. Blasphemer. Formerly, Paul was a blasphemer of Jesus not knowing he was God. A Pharisee couldn't slander God. He "did it ignorantly in unbelief" (Acts 26:9), and thus obtained mercy. **Persecutor,** with the idea of pursuing as one chasing an animal. **Injurious** means one whose contempt breaks forth into outrageous acts of harm. The same gospel that transformed men like this works today as well.

14. Grace . . . was . . . abundant. Regardless of what a man was before he was saved, "where sin abounded, grace did much more abound" (Rom 5:20). Paul appreciated the grace which became the main theme of his ministry. Great churches are built with great em-

phasis on grace. "Amazing Grace" is the theme song and a favorite of those who believe and behave in the house of God as they should.

15. This is a faithful saying or "faithful is the word," as was the familiar formula in Paul's day. He uses it five times. **To save sinners.** The prime purpose of Christ's coming was not to teach nor to heal nor to be an example, but to save sinners. To the self-righteous Pharisees and legalizers, as Paul himself once was, it would be repugnant to say that among sinners, **I am chief.** Someone said, "The beginning of greatness is to be little; it increases as we become less and is perfect when we become nothing."

16. Long-suffering. Paul was the supreme example of II Peter 3:9. We must not wonder why God does not strike down blasphemers today. He is still longsuffering and some are still being saved today. Paul was the pattern and proof of that.

17. Now unto the King eternal, immortal, invisible, the only wise God, be honor and glory for ever and ever. A-men. Sharing his testimony and remembering what manner of man he had been causes Paul to break out with this great doxology. The Lord's Supper should remind us of the longsuffering of God and suffering of the Saviour and cause heartfelt praises today.

B. The Charge to Timothy's Ministry. 1:18-20.

18. Commit (Gr *paratithēmi*) means "to deposit." It is a banking term. With Paul was deposited the responsibility to warn about false teaching. Every preacher would rather preach positive truth, but God's people need warnings as well. **War.** War has been declared by our enemy and we are constantly engaged in **warfare.** It means wounds and bruises, but there are also the medals of honor.

19. Holding (the) **faith.** The definite article is here speaking of "the faith" once delivered (Jude 3). "Stay true to the

Word" is the meaning today. **Good conscience.** Six times in the pastoral epistles Paul speaks concerning the conscience. Some people need an amplifier for that still small voice. It can only be kept clear by judging oneself and confessing sin (I Cor 11:30 ff.; I Jn 1:9). Once the conscience is seared (4:2), even a preacher is capable of committing gross sin. David's conscience wasn't cleared, his sin was ever before him (Ps 51:3), until he confessed it. **Shipwreck.** Many a shipwreck began with unconfessed small sins.

20. Two examples are named. **Hymeneus and Alexander** are mentioned again in II Timothy 2:17, but positive identifications are impossible. The seas are filled with shipwrecked preachers. **Delivered unto Satan.** Probably means excommunication as I Corinthians 5:3-5 indicates. It is scriptural. It certainly was effective and would be today, if done correctly (Mt 18:15 ff.).

IV. THE CHARGE CONCERNING PUBLIC WORSHIP. 2:1-15.

Keep in mind these instructions are concerning how to behave in the house of God.

A. Prayer in the Church. 2:1-7.

In Acts 6:4 the early pastors gave themselves to prayer. Prayer was very prominent and should be to behave properly in the church today.

1. The prescription for prayer. 2:1a.

2:1. Prayer should include more than asking for needs. **Prayers** (Gr *proseuchē*), the common word for talking to God, should include worship and praise. **Intercessions.** Not in behalf of others, as the English word means, but has the idea of coming to God in boldness and confidence (Heb 10:19). **Giving of thanks.** This should be for specific things, not a phrase tacked on at the close of prayer (I Thess 5:18).

2. The people for prayer. 2:1b-2a.

1b. All men. This is certainly intercession and is connected with the "all men" of verse 4.

2a. Kings. Respect for authority runs throughout Scripture. Responsibility to pray for those in authority is also the Christian's obligation.

3. The purpose of prayer. 2:2b-4.

2b. The purpose of prayer for our life here is to live a **quiet** life, means free from outward disturbances, and **peaceable** means inward tranquility. This was especially significant since this was the era of terrible persecution by the Roman emperors such as Nero.

3. This. Refers to praying for all men. It's the right thing to do!

4. Who will have all men to be saved. God certainly doesn't want anyone in hell (II Pet 3:9). But no one will ever go to hell who ought not be there! He doesn't say He "wishes to save all men" for men could then say, "Why doesn't He save all of them." **Knowledge of the truth.** What truth they have known, the unsaved have rejected (Rom 1:19-23) or God would have given them more truth (Jn 7:17).

4. The provisions of prayer. 2:5-7.

5. One God. Emphatically God declares there is no other God beside Him (Isa 43:10 ff.; 44:6-8; 45:5, 21-22; 46:9-10). **One mediator.** God is not one among many but the only one, even as only one God. **The man Christ Jesus.** He spells it out plainly. In Paul's day the Gnostics had a vast system of mediators made up of angels but God declares, not so. The Virgin Mary, Joseph Smith, nor anyone else is such a mediator. He is the Mediator for prayer as well (Heb 4:10;; 10:19-20).

6. Gave himself. Calvary was no accident, no failure! (Jn 10:17-18). **A ransom.** He paid for man's sins in full, not just a down payment (Rom 5:8; I Pet 3: 18). **Testified.** The Lord Jesus did His part and now it is up to man to get this good news to every creature (Mk 16:15).

Christ was obedient in testifying the gospel to man; now men must be obedient in testifying the gospel to other men (Jn 20:21).

7. Whereunto I am ordained a preacher. The primary purpose of any preacher is to preach the gospel to every creature (Mk 16:15). Christ did the work of reconciliation, now man has the word of reconciliation (II Cor 5:18 ff.).

B. People in the Church. 2:8-15.

Paul now deals with issues concerning the place and performance of men and women in the church. He tells how they should behave in the house of God.

1. The men. 2:8.

Therefore. Since "men ought always to pray" (Lk 18:1) and since there is a mediator through whom man can pray, Paul now gives some instructions of how men should pray. **Men.** This is the word for man (Gr *anēr*) in contrast to women;, not the word mankind (Gr *anthrōpos*). Men should pray, not just the ladies' missionary circles or prayer groups. Some take this specifically to mean public prayer in a church and believe it indicates men should do the public praying. The emphasis, however, is that men should pray **everywhere** as opposed to infrequently or not at all. **Holy hands.** Paul stresses the "holy" or "unpolluted" and not the posture of "lifting up" hands, though there is nothing wrong with the raising of hands in prayer. Men who expect to get prayers answered must be men of God, godly men, or God won't hear them (Isa 59:1; Ps 66:18). Toward others there must be no **wrath,** even against the evil rulers of the day. Toward God there must be faith **without . . . doubting** (Mt 13:58; 21:22).

2. The women. 2:9-15.

9-10. In like manner also. He now turns to women and worship. To say Paul was a woman-hater and wrote this as a personal feeling is to misunderstand the teaching of the apostle or to deny the inspiration of Scripture (II Pet 1:21). He is simply admonishing women to perform and function as God designed them to. Women are not in any way inferior to men in Pauline thought. In Christ women are equal to men (Gal 3:28). **Modest.** This is a natural trait of women until they are taught differently. A beautiful and innate quality of womanhood is an emotional need for attention. God designed this quality but says; this need should be fulfilled not by clothes but by conduct. **Good works.** She can win her husband to Christ by her behavior (I Pet 3:1-2).

11-12. The home is the woman's castle. In the church the situation is different (I Cor 14:34 ff.). This is God's order and chain of command "in the house of God." Proverbs 31 gives details of a wise woman's place and function: properly performed, her children "call her blessed" and "her husband . . . praiseth her" (vs. 28).

13-14. The precedent for this order in function is in creation of mankind itself. **Adam was first formed.** He was designed for headship by God. Woman was taken from his side to rule creation by his side (Gen 2:21-22). Of all God's creations, only woman could meet the innermost needs of a man for only woman was designed to meet those needs (Gen 2:20 ff.). As man is the crown of God's creation, so woman is the prized jewel in that crown. The **woman being deceived** or beguiled by Satan indicates a fundamental tendency which shows the woman should not be the leader in the home or the church. Paul speaks later (II Tim 3:6) how women are susceptible to be "led away."

15. Childbearing. Uniquely the woman's body is wondrously designed for childbearing. The "barren womb" is "never satisfied" (Prov 30:16) unless psychologically scarred somewhere along the way, every woman has an inner craving to be a mother. God designed her so. **Saved in childbearing.** Every mother is not going to heaven simply because she is a mother. The most acceptable meaning of this passage is that it refers to the incarnation of Christ as promised to Eve (Gen 3:15) and the woman who believes in this One, the Lord Jesus, shall be saved.

V. THE CHARGE CONCERNING LEADERS. 3:1-16.

In discussing how to behave in the house of God, Paul now turns to the leader. There are two scriptural officers of the church: the bishop (Gr *episkopos*), the pastor or overseer today, and the deacon (Gr *diakonos*). The overseer, the pastor or preacher of the gospel, is to live by the gospel (I Cor 9:14). This is his calling. The deacon serves in the church but does not live by this service. He is nowhere told he is called to this as a living. There are no double standards of Christian living. What *ought* to be true of every believer *must* be true of leaders in the house of God. It is very proper to have standards of conduct for leaders in a local church. Here is a good list to go by.

A. The Pastors. 3:1-7.

3:1. Desireth. What is the call to preach, to pastor God's people? Philippians 2:13 says, "For it is God which worketh in you both to will and to do of his good pleasure." God works from within. He "draws" men to salvation from within and does the same for service, through placing a desire "to do His good pleasure." This is not to be equated with "burden" for some people or particular field. You may have a burden for India and pray for those people every day; but if God has never placed a desire deep in your being to go there and minister to them, you do not have the call of God to India. One has to be sure any desire for a particular field of service is not a selfish desire of the flesh! The word "desire" is a very strong and intense word. Paul said "woe is unto me, if I preach not the gospel" (I Cor 9:16). The call to preach or pastor ("to do His good pleasure") is an intense burning desire for this ministry planted in one's heart by God. **Bishop** means overseer or pas-

tor; I Peter 5:12, "taking the oversight" of God's flock. Hebrews 13:17 says he is to "watch for your souls." This is not to be entered into lightly. Just as there were some disqualifications for soldiers (Deut 20:5-8) and priests (Lev 21:16 ff.) so there are for pastors. Some of the qualifications are absolute and some are relative, but one must not change nor lower the standard, only do all to measure up to God's standard. **Good work.** Pastoring is a good work. It must be approached with that attitude. It is a tragedy to see disillusioned and defeated ex-pastors decrying the ministry.

2. Blameless. It does not mean sinless. There is to be no just cause to blame him. Pastors will never be sinless this side of glory, but they must be blameless. **Husband of one wife.** The traditional and most widely accepted view of Bible-believing, soul-winning preachers has been that a pastor must not be divorced and remarried. History has shown it almost never works for a pastor to be divorced. If he cannot rule his own house how can he rule the church?

Vigilant or "temperate" is the idea; watchful as he oversees the flock. **Sober** or serious-minded about a serious business. It doesn't mean a long-faced person with no humor. A sense of humor is essential or the strain could be too much for any man. **Good behavior** means orderly. It is the outward result of a sober mind. **Hospitality.** He must love people. He must be given to this! A pastor once said, "I don't like people, they bother me." He loved to preach, but he had no business being a pastor. He failed in the pastorate and later became an evangelist. **Apt to teach.** The construction of Ephesians 4:12 indicates definitely a pastor is also a teacher. A God-called pastor most assuredly has the gift of teaching. A pastor must reach the sinner and teach the saint. To not do both is unscriptural and unbalanced.

3. Not given to wine or "not a drinker." **No striker.** This refers to physical acts of violence while **brawler**

means a quarrelsome person, i.e. argumentative. He must keep his cool! **Greedy.** The love of money will certainly ruin a pastor. **Patient** or gentle with the wisdom from above which is peaceable (Jas 3:17). **Covetous** (Gr *aphilargyros*), the literal meaning is no lover of money. He must "be content with such things as he has" (Heb 13:5). The Levites had no inheritance in the land, God was their inheritance (Deut 18:2; Num 18:20). A pastor must set his affections on things above (Col 3:1).

4-5. Ruleth. It must be done by a loving leadership and not a dominating dictatorship. The test of his calling and his success can be measured by the success in his home. His sons in the faith will turn out like the sons of his family!

6. Not a novice (Gr *neophytos*). The Septuagint (LXX) uses this word of newly planted trees. **Let these also first be proved** (vs. 10) and **lay hands suddenly on no man** (5:22) fits here as well.

7. Good report. He must deal with them that are "without" (the secular world) and so must have a good report of them to reach them. **Reproach.** Satan is the accuser. He will see to it that every flaw is seen by the world and do all to ruin God's servant's testimony and effectiveness.

B. The Deacons. 3:8-13.

8. Likewise. Just as a pastor lives in a glass house and represents all a Christian should be, so does the deacon. He must be chosen for what he is and not what he has or who he is in the world's eyes. There are musts for him as well as the pastor or overseer. **Deacon** means servant. They were initially chosen to wait on tables and minister to particular situations in the church (Acts 6:1 ff.). They are not to "run the church." They are to relieve the pastor from tasks that would hinder him from giving himself to prayer and ministering the Word (Acts 6:4). **Grave.** On the positive side, the deacon must be worthy of respect. **Not double-tongued.** It simply means not saying one thing and meaning another.

Not given to much wine. The biblical testimony is consistently against the use of strong drink. The practical application of the principle in modern society is total abstinence for all concerned. **Not greedy of filthy lucre.** The temptation is there even to the most godly deacon. It cannot be tolerated as it is the root of all other evil.

9. The faith. To be a deacon a man must be grounded in the faith. Belief is the basis of behavior. **Pure conscience.** His behavior must conform to his belief so that his conscience is pure.

10. Proved. By his belief and behavior. A new convert cannot be grounded and must not be thrust into prominence.

11. Wives. The construction and context seems to indicate "deaconesses" as Phoebe (Rom 16:1). To be sure these qualities must be in the wives of deacons as well or the deacon's ministry would be blemished and hindered for not ruling his own house well. **Grave.** Same as the deacon (vs. 8). **Not slanderers** (Gr *diabolos*), the word for the devil. A slanderer is a devil indeed. **Sober.** Same as in 3:2. **Faithful in all things.** This covers a multitude of areas in practical matters of the church.

12. See verses 4 and 5 above.

13. Used the office . . . well. The motivation to do so is a positive promise. **Purchase.** Obtain or acquire is the sense. **Good degree.** It means standing or respect in the church. Not a promotion, for that would make the motives wrong. **Great boldness.** Confidence and assurance to speak with authority. This was sought after in the early church (Acts 4:13; 29 ff.).

C. The Purpose of This Charge. 3:14-16.

14. Hoping to come unto thee shortly. Paul planned to come shortly with his apostolic authority to set things in order there, but the problems could not wait and so he writes his instructions.

15. The house of God . . . the church. This most assuredly refers to the local church in Ephesus. The emphasis here is in order and structure in a local church. There has to be order, or organization, a chain of command and a policy of correct behavior for God's work to function properly. No Christian is an island unto himself, nor is anyone to do that which is right in his own sight.

16. Now comes one of the greatest, most profound statements of Scripture. The depths of the truths of verse 15 he calls **the mystery of godliness.** Mystery (Gr *mystērion*) does not mean mysterious but a "secret," now being made known. It was used of Greek rites which were secret. **Godliness.** Godliness is "profitable" (4:8) and "great gain" (6:6). The doctrine which follows will produce this highly treasured godliness. Notice the couplets: "flesh" and "spirit"; "angels" and "nations"; and "world" and "glory." **Was manifest in the flesh.** Christ the eternal Son became flesh (Jn 1:14), to provide salvation which was to be both preached and believed. No wonder it is called "so great salvation" (Heb 2:3). **Justified in the Spirit.** The flesh refers to His humanity and Spirit refers to His deity. He proved to be all He claimed. **Seen of angels.** The holy angels witnessed His every move, such as His birth (Lk 2:9), temptation (Mt 1:13), Gethsemane (Mt 26:53), resurrection (Mt 28:2), and ascension (Acts 1:10). **Preached unto the Gentiles.** This good news is to go to all the world (Mt 28:19). This is the Christian's responsibility after Christ performed the work of reconciliation (II Cor 5:29 ff.). **Believed.** Man's responsibility is to respond to these great truths and believe. **Received up into glory.** What a glorious act the ascension was, as He went back to glory.

VI. THE CHARGE CONCERNING FALSE TEACHING. 4:1-16.

Chapter 1 dealt with the then present false teaching of Judaizers. Now Paul deals with the late false teachers such as the Gnostics. They are identifiable even today, as they were then.

A. The False Teaching. 4:1-5.

4:1. The Spirit speaketh expressly or distinctly. There is no uncertainty but that these **depart from the faith.** This faith is that "which was once delivered unto the saints" (Jude 3) and the "one faith" of Ephesians 4:5. **Giving heed to seducing spirits.** They are active. There are the "deep things of Satan" (Rev. 2:24). **The doctrines of devils.** To some it seems harsh to attribute false teaching as coming from Satan, and one must be careful not to attribute everything with which he disagrees to Satan. The doctrine of devils probably means doctrines taught by demons.

2. Conscience seared. How can they believe such things? As your finger is numb when it has been burned with a hot iron, so too their consciences are numbed by the searing of sin.

3-5. Forbidding to marry . . . meats. The Essenes of the first century felt marriage was only necessary for the preservation of the human race and thus forbade it. The Bible does not teach such a drastic policy. Forced celibacy is not scriptural. **Meats** (Gr *brōma*) means solid food in general and not simply animal meat. All types of ascetic teachings have promoted this error even to the present day. The Bible says "marriage" and "meats" were created by God and are not to be refused. **Thanksgiving.** The blessing at the table is not simply a ritual but is scriptural. Vincent says, "Not declared holy but made holy. Thanksgiving to God has a sanctifying effect. The food itself has no moral quality (Rom 14:14), but acquires a holy quality by its consecration to God; by being acknowledged as God's gift, and partaken of as nourishing the life for God's service" (*Word Studies in the New Testament*, p. 246).

B. The Faithful Teacher. 4:6-16.

6. Remembrance. It is so easy to forget. Thus the need for the Lord's Supper to "remember" His death for sins (I Cor 11:24-25), and to "stir up your pure minds by way of remembrance" (II Pet 3:1). **A good minister** will warn of false teaching **(these things)** as well, though not always a popular thing to do.

7-8. But, in contrast, Paul says, **refuse profane and old wives fables.** Don't get detoured to the profitless trivia. **Exercise** about things that lead unto **godliness. Exercise** (Gr *gumuazo*) is the word from which we get gymnasium. Exercise takes determination and discipline. Godliness comes at a price but it is **profitable... now** here and hereafter. If half the effort that goes into **bodily exercise** were put into spiritual exercise, God's people would be much healthier and stronger spiritually, and much better off.

9. This is ... worthy of all acceptation and that no one can deny. The wise become doers of the Word.

10. We ... labor (Gr *kopiaō*) means to work at it to the point of exhaustion as athletes do. Did you ever watch football players practice and exercise like this? To pay such a price for godliness is done because **we trust in the living God. The Saviour of all men.** When Christ died he made atonement sufficient for the whole world. He is the deliverer, the preserver of all mankind, but the Saviour from sin of those who believe. This does not teach universalism, that all will be saved. When you compare Scripture with Scripture you find Him saying to some, "Depart from me, I never knew you" (Mt 7:23).

11. To timid Timothy, Paul says emphatically, **command** and **teach** these things.

12. Then follows the great verse to encourage youth. Timothy was somewhere between thirty and forty years of age. He was but a youth to the "elders" at Ephesus. The wise elder will not "look down" on those younger than he. The wise youth will be an example of believers so

as to earn the respect of his elders. **Example** (Gr *typos*) is a pattern, type or model. He is to be a model in **word** or speech, in **conversation** or behavior, in **charity** or love, the fruit of the Spirit, in **faith** or faithfulness and in **purity** in motives as well as acts.

13. For a balanced ministry Paul admonishes Timothy concerning three things. **Give attendance to reading** (Gr *anaginōskō*), public reading of Scripture since all did not possess Bibles as we do. **Exhortation** or encouragement, the application of teaching. It is the grounding in the truth for belief that affects behavior. **Doctrine.** This is the basis of Christian belief. "Experience" is quick and easily gotten, but doctrine takes time and a great deal of effort. Yet doctrinally weak believers are immature believers and the pastor who does not give attention to doctrine does not exhibit a love for his people.

14. Neglect not. There is difference of opinion as to whether this meant stop neglecting or don't start neglecting the gift. An entrusted spiritual gift is not to be put under a bushel (Mt 5:15) nor hid in the earth (Mt 25:25) but to be put to use. Every Christian is gifted (I Pet 4:10; I Cor 12:7, 11) and needs to heed this admonition. "The gift to Timothy was through prophecy; that is, it was made known to him by an inspired prophet. The imposition of hands was a symbolic action accompanying the reception of the gift" (H. Kent, *The Pastor's Epistle*, p. 164).

15. Meditate here means "to care for" these things he has just mentioned. Paul then emphasizes the importance of this by saying give thyself wholly to them. To do so will have an effect **(profiting)** that is apparent to all!

16. Take heed ... unto the doctrine of God and you will not be "giving heed... to doctrines of devils" (vs.1). This seems to be the contextual meaning of "save thyself." The hearers also will be saved from "giving heed to seducing spirits."

VII. THE CHARGE CONCERNING THE LAITY. 5:1-6:2.

A. The Older. 5:1-2.

5:1. Rebuke not an elder. Timothy is not to let any man reject his youth, but he is not to rebuke an elder or older person, which is what elder here means and not an official office. There must be respect on the part of each. He should not rebuke with harsh words but entreat or beseech as a member of the family.

2. Treatment of women must be **with all purity.** God's servants must be so discreet. Any impropriety (especially with women) can and has ruined many a pastor's ministry.

B. The Widows. 5:3-16.

3. Widows indeed. There were almost certainly no public "widowages" as there are orphanages in the first century. Those widows, cared for by the church, had to fall into certain guidelines and have certain responsibilities.

4. Nephews (Gr *ekgonos*) is a word which meant descendant, usually a grandson. If widows had descendants it was their obligation to care for these widows. The widows must **show piety** or proper respect toward their family.

5. Now, in contrast widows without relatives to care for them, . . . **a widow indeed, and desolate** has some guidelines to meet before being the responsibility of the church. **Trusteth in God.** She must be a Christian. She should be giving herself to spiritual matters. **Supplication and prayers.** With the hardships and perhaps tragedies she has faced, she can have a heart for others and truly intercede on their behalf. Only eternity will reveal the enormous importance godly widows have played in the ministries of God around the world.

6. Liveth in pleasure. Her way of life is one of pleasure. **Is dead** is a present participle meaning now she is already useless to God and others while she still lives physically.

7-8. Women who are blameless in meeting the spiritual requirements are first to be cared for by **his own,** that is, the children or descendants of verse 4. For a believer not to **provide** for his own house is worse than an infidel, for even they recognize their obligations to widows. Believers must as well.

9-10. The widow with no descendants is not to be **taken into the number,** or "added to the list" to be cared for by the church, unless they meet the following conditions: they must be over sixty years of age and must not be married more than once. **Good works.** To qualify for the good works of others a widow must have had good works herslef.

These good works follow. (1) **Brought up children.** The grand duty and privilege of the homemaker (Tit 2:4-5) is the bearing and rearing of children (I Tim 2:15). Women given to good works are not deceived by the clever but satanic furor of the twentieth century of the role of women in modern life. (2) **Lodged strangers.** The widow should be hospitable if she wants others' hospitality now. **Washed . . . saints' feet.** The whole context is of good works done by women primarily in the home and not religious duties. This does not mean footwashing as an ordinance in the church. **Relieved.** The women should care for those neighbors or fellow Christians who are afflicted.

11. Younger widows refuse. Those under sixty years of age (vs. 9). They are not to be the responsibility of the church for they will usually **wax wanton** (Gr *katastrēniaō*). This word carries the idea of having sexual desires to which she yields and marries again.

12. Having damnation. The idea here seems to be that she marries an unbeliever, setting aside her **first faith.** Paul approves remarriage "in the Lord" (Rom 7:7; I Cor 7:39). The damnation has to be taken as chastening according to I Corinthians 11:30-32 and Hebrews 12:4-11.

13. Under divine inspiration Paul foretells that the tendency of young widows is to be **idle, wandering, . . . tattlers, busybodies.** This fits with I

Timothy 3:6. It should be noted that this is not always the case, but too frequently is the case.

14-15. Because of this, Paul reasons that the **younger women marry, bear children.** This is the design of the Creator for their bodies and personalities. The "barren womb" is never satisfied (Prov 30:16). Under normal conditions this is fulfilling and totally rewarding to a woman. To denigrate this divine desire, as some modern liberationists have done, is to cause women to question God's wisdom. Thus they exhibit that they **are already turned aside after Satan.**

16. Believers are to care for their own relatives so the church can care for those who have no one to care for them.

C. The Elders. 5:17-25.

17. Elders. These are not the same as those in verse 1, but are the pastors of the church who **rule** (cf. Heb 13:7, 17, 24). They **labor in the word,** that is, teach or preach. The word **labor** (Gr *kopos*) is strong word meaning "to work hard to the point of exhaustion." The ministry is hard work and not to be taken lightly. Those who rule **well,** for not all do, are to have **double honor.** This seems best to mean honor for their works' sake as in I Thessalonians 5:12-13, and to receive remuneration as indicated in verse 18.

18. The laborer is worthy of his reward. Men called of God would preach whether they are paid or not, but God ordained they are to live by their ministry (I Cor 9:7-11). Paul compares that even the animals reaped from their toils as was told they should in Deuteronomy 25:4.

19. Accusation (Gr *katēgoria*). This word is used of formal charges before a court. A minister has one solemn possession, i.e. his character. An accusation against him, therefore, is serious and must be witnessed before two or three persons or not at all. This would stop many rumors and save many of God's servants if heeded.

20-21. It must be done decently and in order (I Cor 14:40). When an elder is found guilty God says, **rebuke before all** and it is to be done without **partiality.** If God's people expect Congress and public officials to police themselves, so must God's servants.

22. The charging of God's servants is important. Thus ordination must not be an impulsive act. **Lay hands suddenly on no man** or hastily. Many have been ordained too young or too soon. This could save having to discipline a man later if he is first proved (3:10).

23. Use a little wine, for thy stomach's sake. Obviously he did not advocate drinking but to take the wine for medicinal use as was common. With highly effective, prescribed medicines today there is no justification for believers to hide behind this verse to imbibe!

24-25. Cannot be hid. Time will tell! It is not always evident what is inside a man. Therefore don't rush into ordaining a man until it is quite evident by his works as to his character. Poor character qualities will always surface in a man, given enough time.

D. The Slaves. 6:1-2.

6:1. Slavery is nothing new. Paul faced it. God doesn't advocate revolution here but a resolution through proper attitudes and treatment. **Servants.** Addressed here are believing slaves (Gr *doulos*) under unbelieving masters. The Christian attitude is to **honor** those over you whether they are in public office (Rom 13:1 ff.), or parents in the home (Eph 6:1 ff.), or a boss on the job. God is totally against anarchy. For a Christian not to obey those in authority can cause the name of God to be **blasphemed** or "slandered."

Let them not despise believing masters either. Despise here means "to look down on." The believing master was not under any obligation to free a slave (cf. Philemon). Though equal in Christ, all men are not created equal. Some will never be leaders. Some will always have more than others by virtue of inheritance or harder work. **These things** refers back to the doctrine and duty presented by Paul so that one might behave in the house of God, the church. The believer is to seek godliness and not gain of worldly goods or glory. The rest of this chapter elaborates on this.

VIII. THE CHARGE CONCERNING THE PASTOR. 6:3-19.

A. His Teaching. 6:3-5.

3. If is an "if" of a fulfilled condition and could be translated, "if, as the case is." It was being done. **Teach otherwise** (Gr *heterodidaskaleō*), to teach heresy. **Wholesome** (Gr *hygiainō*), from which we get hygiene or healthy. Any other teaching is unhealthy and doesn't lead to **godliness**.

4. He is proud, "puffed up" or "in a fog." **Knowing nothing** and doesn't even know that he knows nothing. **Doting** (Gr *noseō*) means "to be sick" as opposed to "wholesome" in verse 3. Unhealthy **questions** and **strifes** bring on the diseases of **envy, strife,** etc. and should be avoided in the house of God.

5. Perverse disputing (Gr *diaparathribē*) means "rubbing against" or friction. These false teachers are a continuous friction and destitute of the truth. **Supposing that gain is godliness.**

The Greek construction is really saying that godliness, which is the subject in the original language, is the way or source of gain. There are those today who openly advocate riches and material gain for those who follow their brand of Christianity. They promise you to ride in the biggest car and wear the most expensive clothes.

B. His Living. 6:6-10.

6-8. Conversely the believer is to be "content" which is **great gain.** Too many marriages have gone on the rocks because this principle was violated. Many couples are in a strain financially, putting enormous pressure on their marriage. **Contentment,** when coupled with **godliness,** brings great pleasure and harmony.

9-10. They that will be rich. The word **will** (Gr *boulomai*), is not just an emotional fancy but indicates a calculated and planned procedure to get rich. It causes a **temptation . . . snare, and hurtful . . . lusts.** Money doesn't do this, it is the **love** of money. Riches are neither good nor bad. It is the attitude toward them that is good or bad. Some very wealthy love money far less than poorer people who say they can't afford to tithe!

Coveted (Gr *oregomai*) means "to stretch one's self out to grasp." It causes to err from the faith. Rather one should "set his affections on things above" (Col 3:1).

C. His Goals. 6:11-16.

11-12. But, in striking contrast, the man of God should **flee, follow,** and **fight. Flee** is in the Greek present imperative and denotes a continuous action. The temptation for riches is ever present and Timothy was to constantly run from this desire. Instead he was to **follow** (Gr *diōkō*) or "to run" after **righteousness.** This is not the imputed righteousness which every believer has by faith (Rom 10:1-9), but is a personal and practical righteous living which brings usefulness and rewards. Not defeated by the snares which he flees but clothed with this fruit of the spirit (righteousness, godliness, faith, etc.) he is to **Fight the good fight of faith.** The word **Fight** (Gr *agōnizomai*) is an athletic term meaning "to engage in a contest." This contest is the whole life of the believer striving to win "the prize of the high calling of God in Christ Jesus" (Phil 4:13). It is a **good** fight whereas the fight for money is **evil** (vs. 10).

Lay hold on eternal life. Timothy was already saved and possessed eternal life. The idea here seems to be "get hold" of this eternal life that you have until "the things of earth grow strangely dim." Let it grip you until you get into this race and win the prize. **Called.** This is a "high calling" and every believer has this same calling in life. Timothy had already professed a **good profession** before many witnesses, as every believer should.

13-15. Charge or command. Once again Paul presents the seriousness of what he had said. This charge is not for Paul's sake but to be kept before God and Christ Jesus. God who **quickeneth** or "preserves life" and Christ Jesus who gave a good witness before **Pontius Pilate.** Pilate said, "I find in him no fault at all" (Jn 18:38).

14. Commandment probably refers to the initial command of 1:3-5. The whole book is a charge to be alert to the false teachers and their doctrine. **Until the appearing.** The coming of Christ is the great motivation for godly living (I Jn 3:2-3). What happened to Israel was for our admonition (I Cor 10:6, 11) and what was written to Timothy is for our admonition as well, even until the appearing of our Lord Jesus Christ. God never changes (Heb 13:8). Standards and mores may change in men's minds, but God's standards and qualifications are the same until Jesus comes.

15. In God's own time. He shall show this old world who is boss, who is the **only Potentate, the King of kings, and Lord of lords.** We may often wonder why He doesn't quiet some of the wicked rulers today but "the fulness of time" (Gal 4:4) hasn't come yet for that great moment.

16. Who only (Gr *monos*) the word for "only" expresses uniqueness. Jesus uniquely has immortality. In no uncertain terms Jesus is equated fully with God Himself in this verse.

D. His Duty. 6:17-19.

17-18. With this in mind, Paul says, **Charge them that are rich** to trust only in the living God and not in uncertain riches. There is nothing wrong with being rich, if those who are rich are "rich toward God" (Lk 12:21) and are will-ing to communicate or give of what they have to those in need. Then God will give "richly all things to enjoy." This is the path to true happiness and contentment. It is the summation of Matthew 6:33 and Psalm 37:4. There is nothing wrong with making money if the motive is "that he may have to give to him that needeth" (Eph 4:28).

19. Laying up in store. The proper attitude toward riches and the use of money lays up treasure for the future. The age-old expression, "You can't take it with you," is still true. But the believer can send it on ahead of him in the form of rewards. To do this is what it means to **lay hold on eternal life.**

IX. CONCLUSION. 6:20-21.

A. Plea for Faithfulness. 6:20a.

20a. O Timothy. What a pleading this is. Paul's love for Timothy comes through loud and clear. **Keep** (Gr *phylassō*) means to "guard" in the military sense. Guard that which was committed to thy trust. Paul pleads for Timothy's faithfulness as the requirement of a steward (I Cor 4:2). To each of us are given "gifts and callings" (Rom 11:33). They are sacred; they must not be taken lightly. None of us dares let up his guard for one minute. We must all be found faithful.

B. Plea for Separation. 6:20b-21a.

20b. To not be found faithful is a sin. But, in order to be found faithful, one must avoid the detours of **profane and vain babblings** and **science falsely so called.** This is not to intimate that science is innately evil and to be avoided at all costs. The **science** (Gr *gnōsis*) here means any falsely named wisdom, any wisdom which does not begin with the fear of the Lord.

21a. Failure to avoid this type of so-called wisdom caused some to **erred, concerning the faith.** Err (Gr *astocheō*) means to miss the mark. They miss the mark of God's purpose for them now and they miss the mark of God's prize for them in heaven (Phil 4:13). Believers must separate themselves from those who are drunken with worldly wisdom.

C. Benediction. 6:21b.

21b. Grace be with thee. What a fitting conclusion to a letter to the young pastor, Timothy. It takes the grace of God to shepherd the flock, but thank God His grace is sufficient and available. All of Paul's advice is of no avail unless the grace of God be present in the ministry of Timothy. The same is true today. **A-men.** So let it be, in every place, in every age.

(See page 638 for Bibliography to the Pastoral Epistles)

The Second Epistle To

TIMOTHY

INTRODUCTION

Recorded in II Timothy are the final words of the great apostle. Sometimes referred to as the Apostle Paul's "swan song," this second epistle to his own son in the faith is an exhortation for Timothy to stand strong in the face of insurmountable difficulties. As the final writing of Paul, it is tender, sympathetic, tearful, and yet heroic and stately. It is an exciting and fitting conclusion to the pauline corpus.

Authorship. As with I Timothy, the internal and external evidences for Pauline authorship are strong. Paul again claims to be the author (1:1) and the style and tone are such as you would expect from the soon-to-be-martyred apostle. Everything about the epistle is typically Pauline and there is little reason to question Paul's claimed authorship.

Date and place of writing. The epistle must be dated shortly before Paul's death. If Paul was arrested somewhere in the East, upon his return from Spain, and from there was taken to prison, then the date of the epistle can be fixed in dependence on the date of his arrest. Since it appears that the apostle was released from his first Roman imprisonment about A.D. 63, and since he appears to have traveled immediately to the churches he had established and loved so much in Greece and Asia Minor, we must allow a year or more for traveling from Rome to the eastern Mediterranean world and visits to the beloved churches. But in addition to this, it is inferred that he also accomplished his lifelong desire to preach the gospel where no man had laid a foundation, i.e. in Spain. Another year must be allowed for this task. Thus, with time given for a return to the East and a return voyage to Rome,

the earliest conceivable date for the writing of II Timothy would have been sometime in A.D. 66. Navigation on the Mediterranean comes to a halt during the winter months and thus his arrival in Rome for a second imprisonment can be safely concluded to have taken place in late summer. The writing of this epistle must have then occurred in autumn of A.D. 66.

It is evident that Paul was again a prisoner when he penned II Timothy (1:8, 16). He makes reference to the fact that he is suffering "hardship unto bonds, as a malefactor" (2:9). He is in Rome again. This imprisonment, however, cannot be the one mentioned in Acts 28 for he is no longer permitted to live in a hired dwelling under house arrest (Acts 28:30). Now he is closely guarded in close confinement. During his first imprisonment he was readily accessible to his close friends and had many visitors (Acts 28:17-31; Col 4:10-14; Phil 1:13-14). But now he is virtually all alone (4:11).

Tradition is strong that Paul died in the Neronian persecution which began at the great fire of Rome on July 19, A.D. 64. This persecution continued until Nero's death in A.D. 68. Apparently Paul died in the heat of that persecution, in the city of Rome, about A.D. 66.

Purpose. It appears that Paul's primary purpose in writing II Timothy was to encourage the young minister. This epistle reads like a coach's halftime pep-talk to a discouraged team. Three times in II Timothy the note of suffering hardship is mentioned (1:8; 2:3; 4:5) indicating the need for Timothy's encouragement. Paul instructs Timothy to be a "good soldier of Christ Jesus" (2:3).

The whole tenor of the epistle is a note of encouragement and who better to encourage Timothy than an aged warrior who was about to die.

But a secondary purpose is also seen. Paul wants Timothy to come to Rome as soon as possible (4:9, 21) for the apostle is now convinced that he will never be free again. He longs to see his young son in the faith once more before he dies. Yet with a full and rich life of service to the Lord behind him, Paul can look confidently in the face of death, whether Timothy arrives in time or not. This request, a dying request, and the letter in which it was contained must have had a devastating effect on Timothy. In the midst of Paul's strength and encouragement comes the pathetic appeal for his cloak, left at Troas (perhaps at his arrest), the books, and especially the parchments (4:13). The only worldly possessions the great apostle has left are these, the friendship of the faithful brethren, and the certain knowledge that he has fought a good fight (4:7).

OUTLINE

COMMENTARY

I. INTRODUCTION. 1:1-5.

1:1. Paul, an apostle of Jesus Christ. See comments on I Timothy 1:1. **By the will of God.** It is great to know the will of God for one's life. God has a will (Gr *theléma*) "desire" for each one's life. **Promise of life.** An apostle was sent with a message of the promise of life in Christ Jesus. This is the preacher's message and the people's hope today.

2. My dearly beloved son. Here the aged apostle shows his deep affection for his son in the ministry. The older any preacher gets the more he appreciates his "sons" in the ministry, as should teachers and parents.

3. I thank God. What a comely trait, to be thankful. It is so characteristic of Paul and should be of any pastor (I Thess 5:18). It surely is not characteristic of the world (II Tim 3:2). **Serve.** What a great dividend there was to serve God, as we see in Acts 26:23ff. **Pure conscience.** The five references to conscience in I and II Timothy emphasize its importance. A pastor must have a clear conscience with no unconfessed, hidden sins to be effective like Paul. **Without ceasing.** "Pray without ceasing" (I Thess 5:17). Paul practiced it. No wonder Timothy was used. What an encouragement to Timothy. Paul prayed for young Timothy daily. He prayed for Timothy for years. Much of Timothy's "success" in the ministry must be attributed to Paul's prayers for his son in the faith.

4. Greatly desiring to see thee. This again shows Paul's deep love for Timothy. Every pastor knows this feeling for some pastor who has gone out under his ministry. What an honor for Timothy. What **joy** for Paul.

5. Call to remembrance. Precious memories. **Unfeigned faith** (Gr *anhypokritos*), unhypocritical faith. He was no fake. What a powerful influence godly parents are. How fulfilling to any woman to influence the world so mightily through her children.

II. THE CALL TO COURAGE. 1:6-18.

A. Exhortation to Courage. 1:6-11.

6. Stir up. This is in the present tense and should be "keep stirring up." The gifts of God are without repentance (Rom 11:33) but they must be used and exercised (see note on I Tim 4:14).

7. Fear. It was probably part of Timothy's nature to be fearful. All of God's people need to fear fear itself. God can't use fearful servants (Jud 7:3). To the preacher of old God says, "Be not afraid of their faces" (Jer 1:8). This fear

is not of God! Satan must be resisted and rebuked by faith (Jas 5:7; Mt 16:23). **Power** (Acts 1:8; I Cor 2:3, 4). Paul could identify with Timothy for he knew fear naturally, but also power supernaturally. **Sound mind** (Gr *sōphronismos*). The word here means "disciplined" or "self-control."

8. Therefore. There is no excuse to ever be ashamed of the testimony of our Lord. Paul wasn't (Rom 1:16). **Be not.** This is the Greek subjunctive and means "don't start." Paul had not been guilty of being ashamed of the testimony of the Lord. **Nor of me.** Many were ashamed of Paul and had forsaken him (4:10). **Afflictions.** This is par for the course. One wonders where such afflictions are today!

9. Called. Salvation and service are all by grace, not in human power (Zech 4:6). **Us.** Paul puts Timothy's calling on the same par with his own. This must have added courage to Timothy. **Before the world began** (cf. Gal 1:15). How humbling and awesome the responsibility.

10. The "purpose" of God (vs. 9) is **now made manifest by the appearing.** This refers to His incarnation including His whole life, death, and resurrection. Eternal life, immortality, comes through the gospel (Rom 1:16).

11. Preacher. How shall anyone believe this gospel without a preacher! (Rom 10:14). Men were once glad to be known as "gospel preachers." Paul was. Pastors should be known above all for their "preaching" (Acts 6:4; I Cor 1:18-21). **Teacher.** A pastor must also teach. He must be "apt to teach" (I Tim 3:2).

B. Example of Courage. 1:12-14.

12. Suffer. (Phil 1:29; I Pet 4:12). Paul knew it would cost him to serve as a preacher **nevertheless I am not ashamed** and so Timothy should not be either. The basis is knowing a person, the Lord Jesus, and His power to keep (Phil 3:10). Here the word **know** (Gr *oida*) means "absolute knowledge," beyond a shadow of a doubt. **Keep** (Gr *phylassō*) is a military term meaning "guard." **That which.** What is Paul committing, his salvation or his service? Both could be included in his mind, as it seems in verse 9. **Committed** (Gr *parathēkē*) is a banking term meaning "to deposit." **That day** no doubt refers to the day of Christ and the Judgment Seat of Christ where believers' service and works will be judged (I Cor 3:11 ff.; 4:5).

13. Paul must have had in mind the near end of his ministry and that Timothy was to carry on in his place and so exhorts him **Hold fast.** What was committed unto him, by Paul, **which thou hast heard of me. Form** (Gr *hypotypōsis*) means "pattern" of sound words.

14. Good thing refers to pattern of sound words which was committed or deposited with Timothy. He is to "keep on guard" (same word as in verse 12) even as God keeps what we commit to Him. What an awesome responsibility. What a tragedy that the truth, the faith, or the gospel has not been guarded by churches, denominations, and schools so that eventually Ichabod has been written over many. Paul did what he exhorted Timothy to do in 2:2, i.e. pass on gospel to faithful men. He is to accomplish this by the power of the Holy Spirit. There must be that conscious dependence on His anointing and teaching (Jn 2:27).

C. Experience of Courage. 1:15-18.

15. Here is one of the saddest verses of the New Testament. **Asia** refers to the Roman province of which Ephesus was the capital and would include what was known as Asia Minor or Turkey today. **All . . . turned away.** As you read the letter to the Ephesians it is obvious they were greatly instructed. The indictment of Revelation 2, that they had "left their first love" and were in danger of their church (candlestick) being removed, was solemn. Today there is no local, Bible-believing church in Ephesus. The turning away was not personal but positional from the truth which Paul was

charging Timothy to beware of doing or allowing. No doubt **Phygellus** and **Hermogenes** were well-known for their apostasy.

16. God, in His wisdom, provided the house of Onesiphorus who **oft refreshed** Paul. Who encourages a pastor? Who is his pastor? It is ones like Onesiphorus and his house who Paul says were **not ashamed of my chain** and who, when in Rome, **sought me out.** He looked Paul up when in Rome. No doubt it wasn't easy, but he would not be denied, he **found** him.

18. How many things he ministered unto me. Without complaining Paul seems to cover a multitude of problems and the help Onesiphorus gave. Few people ever realize the enormous pressures and problems a pastor faces as included in the daily "care of all the churches" (II Cor 11:28). What reward there will be **in that day** for those who minister to the ministers!

III. THE CALL TO SERVICE. 2:1-26.

The Lord Jesus used familiar pictures and subjects to bring out great truths and now Paul does the same with seven powerful portraits of the Christian life.

A. As a Son. 2:1-2.

2:1. Thou, in the emphatic position in the Greek sentence. Though others falter and fail, he expects more of Timothy. **My son** (Gr *teknon*), child, used even of adults, is a very affectionate term. How Paul dearly loved him as a son. **Be strong.** This is in the present imperative and indicates the continued growth in strength and stamina one can muster to go on and not turn away (cf. Eph 6:10 ff.). **Grace.** This grace is available for living as well as salvation (Heb 4:16).

2. The same commit thou. Here is the ultimate goal of the ministry. Simply put, it is, pass it on. Paul is saying what I have committed to you, you commit to faithful men who then will pass it on and commit it to others also. The buck may stop with you, but truth must never stop but be given to others also.

B. As a Soldier. 2:3-4.

3-4. As a son he is to be strong; as a soldier he is to endure hardness. A soldier is at war. It may mean wounds and suffering. Remember God didn't start the war, Satan did. See Isaiah 28 and Ezekiel 14. **Endure hardness** (Gr *syngkakopatheo*) has a prefix in Greek. **With.** Paul did not ask Timothy to do something he hadn't done. He says, "I have endured hardness, now you endure it with me." Pastors must lead the way (I Cor 11:1). **Entangleth.** Deuteronomy 20:5-8 warns a man not to go to war if there are unsettled affairs in his life. The battle is serious and a soldier cannot be distracted by entanglements of business or family affairs.

C. As an Athlete. 2:5.

5. Paul now speaks of one of his favorite subjects, that of athletics. **Strive** (Gr *athleo*) means to engage in athletic contests. To win the prize, he must **strive lawfully** (Gr *nominos*) or actually keep the rules of the game. To run the race of life one does not break God's rules and get away with it. As the umpire of the game of life, God calls the fouls real close!

D. As a Farmer. 2:6-13.

6. The husbandman. Now comes the sower or farmer. The athlete gets the crown only at the end of the race. The farmer reaps of his labors before the final harvest. He must be partaker of the firstfruit. Those who labor for the Lord are blessed and rewarded here and hereafter. It does pay to serve Jesus.

7. Consider. "Let this sink in." It would do well to meditate much on these things (Josh 1:8). There are many more lessons and parallels. The seed sown must be understood and bring forth fruit! (Mt 13:23).

8. Lest he become weary or fainthearted, Paul begins to elaborate on the

hardness and suffering that must be endured. **Remember.** The death, burial, and resurrection of Christ are always to be remembered (I Cor 11:23 ff.). **Of the seed of David.** Speaking of His humanity, He was of the lineage of David and rightful heir to the throne of David. **Was raised from the dead.** The Greek perfect tense denotes the certainty of the fact. **My gospel** means the gospel which Paul preached and if anyone preaches any other, he is to be accursed (Gal 1:8, 9).

9-10. Preaching this gospel of the resurrection of Christ brought about Paul's persecution. **Suffer trouble.** God doesn't protect His servants from trouble, but preserves them through trouble. Sufferings or troubles are not always the chastening of God or the result of sins. A good soldier should expect suffering while in an enemy's country (Phil 1:29). This world is not our home. Paul suffered for the gospel's sake, even as an **evil doer.** The Greek word is a technical word meaning malefactor. Persecuting Christians and consenting to their death didn't make him a criminal, but preaching the gospel did, in the eyes of the Jews! How often someone who curses, drinks, and carouses gets saved and stops all that, and then receives persecution from loved ones for trying to live right. "Think it not strange!" (I Pet 4:12 ff.). Paul was bound, but the Word of God wasn't bound, he still witnessed! The facts were that these things were to the "furtherance of the gospel" (Phil 1:12 ff.). The reverse is often true today. People are free but their tongue is bound! **Endure all things.** He said it beautifully in Acts 20:24 when he said, "None of these things move me, neither count I my life dear unto myself...." **For the elect's sake.** It was a joy for Paul to suffer for the gospel because when he did so he was actually suffering on behalf of the elect. The persecution which Paul endured would most certainly be a tremendous source of encouragement for other believers. He did not suffer vicariously for believers, as Christ did, but his strength in suffering incited them to action. He would endure anything to see them saved, and now would endure anything to encourage them.

11. Faithful saying or "trustworthy." You can count on it. **For** connects what he has been saying and the conclusions he now draws from his statements. He is talking about the great doctrine of the substitutionary death of Christ and our identification with Him in His death and resurrection as a fact. **We shall also live with him.** The basis of our eternal life is our personal identification with Christ and acceptance of Him. Because we shall live with Him we should endure hardness gladly.

12. If we suffer, and again you can count on it, we will. **We shall also reign.** The rewards are worth it all. Paul is encouraging Timothy with this great hope of the believer and we should be encouraged as well. **Deny him.** The Greek verb here is future, "if we shall deny him." Two things to remember here. First, Peter denied Christ three times even though he was saved but his reaction was conviction and contrition. Secondly, I John 2:19 tells of those who "went out from us, but they were not of us; for if they had been of us, they would no doubt have continued with us: but they went out, that they might be made manifest that they were not all of us." These were apostate. It must be remembered man only sees the outward, God sees the heart (I Sam 16:7).

13. Believe not (Gr *apisteuō*) refers to unfaithfulness. There is an obvious play on words with **he abideth faithful** (Gk *pistos*). God has to remain true to His character. He cannot be unfaithful or deny Himself.

E. As a Workman. 2:14-19.

14. These things. The momentous facts of verses 11-13 are of such importance that it is foolish to get involved and strive about insignificant words to no profit. A faithful pastor will keep off the side issues. Paul told Timothy to keep reminding those he teaches to do the same.

15. Study (Gr *spoudazō*) is not the normal word you think of as a student but a word used of a workman meaning "give diligence," "endeavor," or "exert oneself." A workman is to give diligence or endeavor to show himself **approved** unto God. Approval means one has been put to the test and measures up, thus winning the approval of the person testing him. The workman here is one who is handling the Word of God and thus the conclusion of studying. It certainly takes diligent study of the Word to **rightly divide** it (Gr *orthotomeō*) meaning "to cut a straight course," or "lay out a road," or "correctly interpret." All of the Word of God is true. There are no contradictions when rightly laid out. You cannot add to nor take away any of it (Rev 22:19).

16. But, in sharp contrast, **shun** or avoid **profane and vain babblings.** As in I Timothy 6:20, this includes false and empty talk. It just leads to more ungodliness. False belief produces foolish behavior.

17. The tragedy is it spreads like a **canker** (Gr *ganggraina*), gangrene! **Hymenaeus and Philetus** were prime examples of how it happens.

18. Erred (Gr *astocheō*) means to deviate or "miss the mark." To get bogged down debating such vain babblings only harms and pollutes and must be avoided. "If any man be ignorant, let him be ignorant" (I Cor 14:28). There are some things and some people you just don't debate. **Resurrection is past.** They probably spiritualized the resurrection of the future as the gnostics of the day taught.

19. Nevertheless. In spite of all the failures of men, **the foundation of God standeth sure.** This foundation is referred to in I Corinthians 3:11. It is Christ. Build on Him and there will be no defection, no apostasy. Remember, "they went out because they weren't of us" (I Jn 2:19). **Knoweth.** He surely does. About His sheep He said, "I know them . . . and they shall never perish" (Jn 10:27-28). To the lost he said, "I never knew you: depart from me . . . " (Mt 7:

23). These were not once sheep who had departed. **Depart from iniquity.** This security never means one can live like the devil. In fact, one who appreciates his salvation never attempts to take advantage of it.

F. As a Vessel. 2:20-22.

20. House. The believer is now part of the great house of God being paralleled here. **Vessels of gold . . . also of wood.** Every family has their special and valued dishes as well as everyday inexpensive ones.

21. In God's house if a man **purge himself** from the vessels of dishonor, **he shall be a vessel unto honor.** A long time before Paul said, "Come out from among them, and be ye separate . . ." (II Cor 6:17). God doesn't play favorites, but He is holy and cannot use unholy vessels. God is constantly on a talent hunt "for them whose heart is perfect toward him" (II Chr 16:2). **Meet** means "usable" or "fit" for His use. **Master** (Gr *despotes*) from which we get despot or lord. He is Lord and must be acknowledged as such to be used. **Prepared** means "equipped."

22. Flee also youthful lusts. The youthful desires for fame, fortune and fun are to be run from, **but** to **follow** (Gr *diōkō*) which means "to pursue" and not just meekly follow. That which the believer is to pursue is a catalogue of Christian graces, i.e. **righteousness, faith, charity, peace.**

G. As a Servant. 2:23-26.

23-25. Once again Paul warns about foolish questions for they lead to strife. **The servant** here refers primarily to a pastor. A true servant obeys his master. **Must not strive** (Gr *machomai*). The word here means "quarrel" or "argue" with emotions heated. Usually there will be more heat than light. It is a sin for anyone to lose patience and especially a minister. **Gentle** in one's manner and **meek** in one's disposition. **Instructing.** Giving the truth from God's Word which shows the need for verse 15 and

being "apt to teach" (I Tim 3:2). **If God peradventure will give them repentance.** Notice God must give repentance. **Repentance** (Gr *metanoia*). Repentance is not sorrow for sin, that is, contrition. Sorrow leads to repentance (II Cor 7:9-10). Repentance is not changing direction or your ways of living; that's a result of salvation. Repentance is changing one's mind from false ideas to the **acknowledging of the truth.** A sinner must be willing to change directions and turn from sin, but that's not a condition of salvation else we have salvation as a result of works or deeds and not of faith (Eph 2:8-9).

26. Here primarily he is talking about those accepting false teaching that they may recover themselves out of the snare of the devil. Satan is behind all false teaching. There is nothing innocent about any of it. Pastors must be good shepherds to lead their flocks and protect them from such wolves.

IV. THE CALL TO FAITHFULLNESS. 3:1-17.

A. Unfaithfulness of the World. 3:1-9.

3:1. The last days. This includes the whole Church Age. Paul stated these conditions would be prevalent in Timothy's day, for he said to him, "from such turn away" (vs. 5). **Perilous times** are evident today as well.

2. Lovers of their own selves. Everyone does that which is right in his own eyes. Selfishness abounds. **Covetous.** People must keep up with the Joneses. Few are content with such things as they have. **Disobedient to parents.** Juvenile deliquency is the term in this generation, but now more common and rampant. **Unthankful.** There is no loyalty or thankfulness for anything but only wanting more. **Unholy, Without natural affection.** Romans 1:26 ff. is accepted as a way of life. The gay crowd, sex out of bounds from God's limits, is accepted by much of society. **Trucebreakers.** One only has to look at Korea and Vietnam to see blantant trucebreaking. **Incontinent**

(Gr *akratēs*) meaning "no power" or "restraint" over oneself. Senseless killings and atrocious sex crimes give evidence to this today. **Fierce,** meaning "not tame" or "savage." **Despisers of those that are good.** The all-American boy is not emulated, but the radicals and immoral celebrities are. The honest, wholesome teenager is so often ridiculed! Those who do good and act good are greatly in the minority.

4. Lovers of pleasure. One would have to be blind not to see that pleasure-seeking is skyrocketing today. The cry of first century Rome was, "Give us bread and the circus." The two "necessities" of life were welfare and entertainment. The situation hasn't changed a bit.

5. Form of godliness. Church attendance is at an all-time high, **but** powerless. No longer are God and His teaching considered in matters of divorce, sex, or abortion. Most Christians and churches are powerless in the community. They only appear to be godly. Inwardly they are impotent because of sin.

6. Lead captive silly women. Eve was the first deceived (I Tim 2:14). A sad fact of life is that Satan consistently attacks the women in the area of discernment. Christian women must be especially dependent upon God to give them doctrinal direction and understanding. Many cults today are directed and dominated by women who have had their discernment taken captive by Satan. A Christian woman must be wise enough to seek the counsel and advice of the pastor and church leaders lest in the areas of doctrine and practice she fall prey to the snares of the devil.

7. Ever learning. This refers to the women led astray. One of the strange phenoma of our day is the great amount of women going to all kinds of Bible studies and religious meetings who seem to gravitate to strange doctrines and unorthodox ideas. They never come for the **truth.** That faith once delivered unto the saints, the old-fashioned fundamentals of the Bible.

8. Withstood (Gr *anthistēmi*) is forceful and means "to set oneself against." The boldness of **Jannes and Jambres** to set themselves against Moses is manifest today in multitudes who adamantly "resist" the truth.

9. Their folly shall be manifest. Apostate individuals and groups have come and gone throughout the ages. They are finally exposed for what they really are. In our day many so-called faith healers and charlatans have faded out or died with their followers disillusioned and dispersed.

B. Faithfulness through His Word. 3:10-17.

10. Full known (Gr *parakoloutheō*) is translated in Luke 1:3 as "perfect understanding." **My doctrine.** Doctrine is foundational and must be the basis of discipleship. Experiences can never be the basis. Paul invites close scrutiny of his whole life and ministry. This should be done with anyone who would be followed.

11. Paul endured much persecution of apostates but God delivered him. **Antioch . . . Iconium . . . Lystra** are but three of the places where Paul suffered persecution.

12. Then he assures that persecutions await all who will live godly. **Shall suffer persecution** is a promise with great prospect (I Pet 3:14).

13. This situation will continue to worsen. **Evil men . . . seducers.** This is an age of evil men and deception. The irony is that evil men are deceiving one another and being deceived. They must learn the truth that whatever a man sows, he also reaps.

14. Continue. Others "swerved" (I Tim 1:6). "Made shipwreck" (1:19). "Erred" (6:20). Stewards must be faithful (I Cor 4:2).

15. Holy scriptures refers to the Old Testament Scriptures taught him by his mother and grandmother (1:5). It is so important to teach the Word of God to children in order to bring them to salvation. Salvation comes through faith

(Eph 2:8-9) and faith comes by the Word of God (Rom 10:17).

16. All scripture refers not to the Old Testament as a whole but to every part of the Old Testament. **Inspiration** (Gr *theopneustos*) means "God breathed out" the Scriptures and not that God breathed into the human authors. The authors themselves were controlled by God so that they were not left to their human limitations (II Pet 1:21). **Doctrine . . . reproof . . . correction . . . instruction.** The Scriptures are not only profitable for salvation but for sanctification and Christian growth as well. They are not only the road map to heaven, but the road map of the Christian life. They are all we need for faith and doctrine.

17. When sanctification takes place in the man of God and he is **perfect** or mature, the Scriptures are for service "furnished unto all good works." Doctrine always should emanate in good works.

V. THE CALL TO THE MINISTRY. 4:1-8.

A. Purpose of the Ministry. 4:1-2.

4:1. Charge thee. Paul's final charge to Timothy. A **charge** is more than a command for a charge carries with it the moral obligation to be carried out. **Judge.** In the light of what has been said in chapter 3 about the last days, Paul reminds Timothy of a day of reckoning. **The quick,** the living, those who are alive and remain (I Thess 4:17) **and the dead,** "for the dead in Christ shall rise first" (I Thess 4:16). Pastors and people alike shall stand at the Judgment Seat of Christ (II Cor 5:10), **at his appearing.** "To whom much is given much is required" (Jas 3:1).

2. Preach the word. This means to herald as the emperor's herald gave a formal message in an authoritative way. Be consistent, he says, always at it. Don't be afraid to **reprove** or **rebuke** but do it with **long-suffering** and **doctrine.** The minister's personal feelings are not

the ground for reproof: doctrine alone is that ground.

B. Perversion of the Ministry. 4:3-4.

3. The time will come and most believe it is here today. **Itching ears** will be "tickled" by preachers who do not preach the Bible. Many pastors bow to the wishes of ungodly congregations who only want to hear what pleases them.

4. Turn away (Gr *apostrephō*) is in the Greek active voice and has the idea of deliberate action by themselves. **Shall be turned** (Gr *ektrepō*) means they are acted upon; it is a medical term meaning "to twist out of place."

C. Priority of the Ministry. 4:5-7.

5. But, in contrast to these, Timothy is to **watch,** which has the idea of being sober and alert. **Endure afflictions.** Satan doesn't play games. He puts up a fight. The preacher must not get discouraged and run. **Do the work of an evangelist.** Every pastor must evangelize, he must be a soul winner. He cannot simply pray and preach. He cannot expect his people to witness if he doesn't. He must preach "Be ye followers of me . . ." (I Cor 11:1). To **make full proof** of his ministry the pastor must be faithful in all the above admonitions.

6. For. Paul's exhortation to Timothy to make full proof of his ministry was given because Paul knew his own ministry was almost over, and he knew the deep satisfaction of having done the same himself. What a horrible feeling it must be to come to the end of one's life and have nothing but regrets at a wasted life. **I.** The "I" here is emphatic. Paul is saying "as for myself." How important to be honest with ourselves. **I am now ready to be offered.** Only one who had finished his course (vs. 7) could say this. **Offered** (Gr *spendomai*). This is a word used of pouring out a drink offering. Paul used it of himself in Philippians 2:17 of pouring out himself for the Philippians. **The time of my departure is at hand.** God's servants are indestructible until their work is done. **Departure** (Gr *analyseos*) was used by the military meaning to take down one's tent. The idea is like the old saying of the Arab who took up his tent and silently stole away. As servants we must silently steal away and soon be forgotten so that only what's done for Christ will last!

7. What a power-packed verse. There are three great statements. **A good fight.** The definite article is in the Greek. Paul is not boasting of what he had done but that he had spent his life in the good fight or contest. **Fight** (Gr *agōn*) was used of the Greek athletic contests. **Fought** (*agōnizomai*) in the perfect tense speaks of completed action and expresses Paul's confidence. We get our word "agonize" from this. It does cost. There aren't many who agonize in their labors for Christ today. **I have finished my course.** Course refers to a race track. He had crossed the finish line. He didn't quit. The Christian's life is not a hundred yard dash; it is a marathon and most often an obstacle course. **I have kept the faith.** The faith is not personal faith in Christ but the whole body of Christian truth, i.e. doctrine. Paul never was detoured by some new wind of doctrine.

VI. CONCLUSION. 4:8-22.

A. Wanting of Timothy. 4:8-13.

8. **Henceforth.** The tragedy of life is what people miss here and hereafter. Only those who have borne their cross will win the crown. **Crown** (Gr *stephonos*) referred to the laurel wreath placed on the winner of the athletic contests. There are five crowns spoken of in scripture, all of which we will cast at Jesus' feet in adoration one day (Rev 4:10-11). This **crown of righteousness** is available to **all them also that love his appearing.** How tragic that multitudes are not taught about the Second Coming of Christ and therefore are cheated out of gaining this crown! No preacher should say the preaching of the Second Coming and all that surrounds it is unimportant!

Like the great crescendo of a symphony, Paul has concluded his message in verse 8 and now adds a few final remarks. Some of these give personal insights to this great man who is in a Roman dungeon awaiting his final appearance before the Roman ruler and then executors.

9. **Do thy diligence.** This is from the same Greek word for "study" in 2:15 and it means here "do your best," to come quickly to me.

10. **Forsaken** here means literally "let me down." Demas was standing with Paul in Colossians 4:14 and Philemon 24. What a disappointment. Even Paul had those moments too! **Having loved this present world.** No matter how much disciplining, one can still turn from faithfulness to this world. Every pastor needs to know this so that he does not falter when someone he has spent many years training turns away. They did it to Jesus too, "And they all forsook him and fled" (Mk 14:50).

11. **Only Luke is with me.** What a man is this beloved physician. Paul is not seeking pity here, but gives insight for pastors to know how that when he came to the end of his ministry he was fortified against discouragement during those lonesome hours. **Take Mark. And bring him.** In the accounts of Acts 13:13 and 15:36-41 Mark seems to have deserted Paul and later Paul and Barnabas had a strong disagreement over Mark. Mark has now proven himself and whatever happened in Acts 13:13 Paul has years before forgiven and forgotten. This is as it should be. Too many pout today over trivial things and never are reconciled.

12. **And** (or but) **Tychicus have I sent to Ephesus.** This implies the others left on their own. Probably Tychicus was the bearer of this letter to Timothy who was in Ephesus (I Tim 1:3).

13. **The cloak.** This was a long heavy cape with a hole in the middle to slip over one's head. It hung down to the knees. It was now needed in this cold damp dungeon. **The books** or scrolls were made from papyrus and the **parchments** were

much better quality made from sheep or goat skins. These parchments may well have been copies of the Old Testament Scriptures. To the very end Paul kept his mind sharp and his heart full by reading. What an example to this young preacher and us today.

B. Warning of Alexander. 4:14-15.

14-15. Alexander the coppersmith did me much evil. Alexander was a common name, so he is identified as "the coppersmith" and no doubt Timothy knew who he was. Paul did not do this to harm Alexander but to prevent Timothy from being hurt by this man. Too often, in our mobile society one of God's servants causes trouble in one place and then travels across the country to cause harm there also. There needs to be honesty about such a person and a warning of others, lest they be hurt too (I Tim 5:24).

C. Witness of Paul. 4:16-18.

16. Answer (Gr *apologia*). From this we get our word apology or defense. He is referring to his trial. **Stood with me** (Gr *paraginomai*). This is a technical word and would refer to a defense lawyer or advocate. **All men forsook me.** The same word used of Demas in verse 10, but he did not let it make him bitter. No matter how it hurts, no root of bitterness can be allowed lest many others be hurt (Heb 12:15).

17. The Lord stood with me and He always will (Heb 13:5). He is all one needs. **Strengthened me** (Gr *endynamoō*) means to pour in strength. It

is always available. There is no need to give in or give up. **That by me the preaching might be fully known.** From this one must conclude that at Paul's trial before Nero he preached the gospel, even as he did before Felix! **I was delivered out of the mouth of the lion.** This referred back to Psalm 22:21. It simply means here he was not immediately executed after his trial and thus he could write this letter. We are much richer for it today.

18. Deliver me . . . preserve me. What security! He was sure of being delivered from evil work here and preserved to the glory up there! Preservation from the wicked one is a certainty for the believer (Eph 1:13; 4:30).

19-21. These last greetings show Paul's deep concern for people. It shows God's concern for people and even the smallest detail. Imagine the wonder that God included these items in the eternal Word of God.

Prisca and Aquila are the close friends of Paul (cf. Acts 18:2, 18, 26; Rom 16:3; I Cor 16:19); **Onesiphorus** is the Ephesian Christian mentioned in 1:18; **Erastus** was the "chamberlain" or treasurer of the city of Corinth, where at the time of this writing he again resides; **Trophimus,** a native Ephesian, had been left sick at **Miletus** (Miletum), on the coast south of Ephesus. For **Eubulus . . . Pudens . . . Linus . . . and Claudia** no positive identification can be made.

22. Grace be with you. You here is plural, not to Timothy alone but even to us also. With Paul we may exclaim, "to whom be glory forever and ever." **A-men.**

(See page 638 for Bibliography to the Pastoral Epistles)

The Epistle To
TITUS

INTRODUCTION

As a companion of Paul, Titus did not enjoy the fame of Barnabas, Silas, or Timothy. He is only mentioned thirteen times in the New Testament. Yet this young Greek (Gal 2:3), converted to Christ directly from heathenism, was one of the most faithful of Paul's own converts.

His home was apparently Syrian Antioch. His name does not come to our attention in a ministerial relation until Paul's third missionary journey. Then the mention of Titus is checkered throughout the latter years of Paul's life.

Authorship. Again, like I and II Timothy, and all the recognized Pauline epistles, Paul claims to be the author of this epistle (1:1). The discussion on authorship in the introduction to I Timothy is pertinent here.

Date and place of writing. It is impossible to date the writing of Titus with pinpoint accuracy. If it was written after Paul's visit to Spain, it would then be dated only shortly before II Timothy. If it was written before this western visit it would have been written during Paul's first year of freedom from house arrest in Rome. On the assumption that it is more likely that Paul would have written the letter as soon after his release as possible, and probably visited the churches of Greece and Asia Minor directly upon being released from prison, we can suggest a date of the fall of A.D. 63 or a bit later.

Establishing the place of writing is equally difficult. At first this may not appear to be the case for the subscription to Titus in the AV reads, "It was written to Titus, ordained the first bishop of the church of the Cretians,

from Nicopolis of Macedonia." This statement, which is not part of the inspired writing of Paul, is in error. It was made on the mistaken assumption that Paul was already in Nicopolis at the time of the penning of Titus. It is evident from 3:12, however, that Paul's intention is to winter at Nicopolis and he has not yet reached that point.

Thus the writing of the Epistle to Titus must have taken place somewhere en route to Nicopolis. The prime suggestion is that it was written at Corinth, following Paul's arrival there from Crete. Although this cannot be maintained dogmatically, there is nothing to suggest that this is not an accurate assumption.

Purpose. Perhaps the chief aim of Paul in writing to Titus was to authenticate the work of Titus on Crete. Titus was Paul's representative there. He would undoubtedly encounter opposition to his leadership there since he was not a native. Paul's epistle to him would add authority to his presence.

In addition, Paul found it necessary to advise Titus of specific instructions which he was to convey to the churches of Crete, the Mediterranean island. The believers of Crete had banded together to worship and pray but had not been organized into proper local assemblies. They were ignorant of church polity or structure. They had no indigenous leadership. Thus Titus was to instruct them in the basic structure of authority in the local church. He would appoint elders in the various churches and dictate the qualifications of those in leadership positions. Paul's instruction to Titus would add validity to the very existence of these churches on Crete. The Epistle to Titus was that instruction.

I Timothy and Titus are quite similar and cover a great deal of the same material. Yet Titus is less personal than I Timothy and much more brief. Also, Titus is characterized by a series of doctrinal summaries, brief capsules of what is most certainly to be believed among the churches.

OUTLINE

COMMENTARY

I. INTRODUCTION. 1:1-4.

1:1. Paul. The common way to begin a letter in Paul's day was with an identification of the author by name and title. Paul did not vary from this form. **Servant** (Gr *doulos*). This is not just a worker but one who is born into slavery and one who gives himself wholly to another's will. This was Paul's view of himself in relation to God and ought to be that of every Christian. On the other hand, he was chosen of God to be an apostle. What a humble and high position he held at the same time. He was an apostle **according** to "or in accord with" **the faith**, the whole body of revealed truth. The church had to try those who "say they are apostles" (Rev 2:2). Paul could stand the test.

2. In hope of eternal life. (Gr *epi*) "upon the basis of" a hope or expectation of eternal life. **Promised before the world began.** God's plan of salvation was not an afterthought (Rev 13:8).

3. In due times. God has a schedule and is always on time. God's plan is revealed in **his word** and His Word is manifested through preaching. On the importance of preaching see Romans 10:13-15 and I Corinthians 1:17-21.

4. Own son (Gr *gnēsios*) means "legitimate born." Titus was another of Paul's converts. What a blessed event. **Common faith** or faith held in common. **Grace, mercy, and peace.** Paul's usual greeting in the Pastoral Epistles.

II. ORDER IN THE CHURCH. 1:5-16.

A. Order in the Church by the Elders. 1:5-9.

5. Crete, one of the largest islands of the Mediterranean where Paul ministered with Titus, probably between his imprisonments. Paul's ministry must have been fantastic. He left a church and converts wherever he went and they needed to **set in order** a church and **ordain elders in every city.**

The qualifications of elders in the church:

6. For the **husband of one wife** and other phrases not dealt with here, see notes on I Timothy 3:2 ff. **Faithful** or "believing" children. Not only believing children but ones **not accused of riot or unruly.** If Proverbs 22:6 is true and it is, "Train up a child in the way he should go; and when he is old, he will not depart from it," then there is no excuse for a Christian's son being accused of "riot" or "dissolute."

7. Bishop or overseer as **the steward of God.** A steward has charge of or governs another's affairs (cf. Heb 13:17). He must not be **self-willed** or "self-pleasing," as the Greek indicates, not arrogant. Then, **not soon angry** or prone to anger. The fruit of the Spirit is temperance, the opposite of this.

8. A lover of good men, really "a lover of all that is good" and not just men. **Temperate.** It means one who is held in check and this is done by the Holy Spirit, for it is a fruit of the Spirit (Gal 5:23).

9. Holding fast or "firmly to" the **Word** which is faithful and trustworthy. **As he hath been taught,** meaning "according to the teaching" of the Lord Himself and the inspired apostles (Is 8:20; Acts 2:42). This is necessary in order to **exhort,** encourage, and help believers and **convince** or convict the **gainsayers,** those who "oppose" or "speak against," as the Greek indicates, because of **sound doctrine.**

B. Disorder in the Church by False Teachers. 1:10-16.

The need for elders arose because of false teachers.

10. These false teachers, **teaching things which they ought not** (vs. 11) are first of all **unruly** or uncontrolled as the children of verse 6. The same word occurs in both places. They balk at and reject any authority over them. And so we see it today. **Vain talkers,** in the sense of "empty" or "useless." **Deceivers** are really "mind" deceivers. **Of the circumcision,** i.e. the Jews.

11. Whose mouths must be stopped (Gr *epistomizō*) originally meant to put something in the mouth as a gag. Why? Because **whole houses** or families were being overthrown by them. There was much at stake. They taught for **filthy lucre** or "shameful gain," which God's true servants must not do (vs. 7).

12. A prophet of their own probably refers to the famed Cretan poet Epimenides, born around 600 B.C. Just as sodomy refers to an infamous sin of which Sodomites were guilty, so "Cretan" became almost synonymous with a liar. They were also **slow bellies.** The Greek here really means "idle gluttons." About such a one God says he should put a knife to his throat (Prov 23:2).

13. This witness is true. Paul confirms these as facts and says **rebuke them sharply.** There was no place for timidity here. **Sharply** (Gr *apotomōs*) meant "to cut off abruptly." **That** meant the purpose of the rebuke was that they may be **sound** or "healthy" in the faith. **Rebuke** was not vindictive but curative, as it should be always.

14. These things, **Jewish fables,** they taught (cf. I Tim 1:4-11) and the **commandments of men** that turn away from the truth of God. This was an ever-present danger of the Jews (cf. Mk 7:7-13).

15. Unto the pure . . . defiled. This is a fascinating verse and much needed today. Paul is referring to the Jewish legalists who were extremists about Old Testament Jewish ceremonial washings. These insisted on the ceremonial washings and were still calling some meats unclean so the need for the teaching of Matthew 15:1-20. People today can go to extremes and see something wrong in everything and every person until they separate themselves into total isolation.

16. They profess . . . but. Profession and performance should not contradict. Faith and works go together. True faith produces true works. **Reprobate** has the idea of being tested but disapproved.

III. OBEDIENCE IN THE CHURCH. 2:1-15.

A. Obedience of Older Men. 2:1-2.

2:1. But. In decided contrast to these false teachers Titus is exhorted. The word **become** has the idea of "conspicuously" becoming to sound doctrine. There would be no question about it.

2. The **aged men** are not the official elders but older men in years. **Sober** means sober minded, sincere. **Grave** means dignified as opposed to frivolous and was used of deacons (I Tim 3:8). **Temperate** means "to curb one's desires and impulses." **Sound,** the familiar word meaning healthy.

B. Obedience of Older Women. 2:3.

3. Healthy doctrine shows up in the **aged women . . . in behaviour** or "demeanor." **As becometh** means as is fitting and not out of place with **holiness.** Every believer's body is the temple of the Holy Spirit and everything done should be fitting the temple of God. **Not false accusers** (Gr *diabolos*) rendered devil in some places and meaning "slanderer." **Not given to much wine.** This is a translation of the Greek perfect participle *douloō*, "to make a slave of." The Greek tense speaks here of a confirmed drunkard. Women are not to be false accusers but **teachers of good things.**

C. Obedience of Young Women. 2:4-5.

4. They should teach the **younger women.** Christian matrons have a responsibility to give their years of experience to the younger women. They are the best teachers of younger women.

To love their husbands . . . their children. This is a friendly companionship in which you do things together. Most homes could use a lot of this teaching.

5. Discreet is the same word as in verse 2 translated "temperate" and can mean sound minded. **Chaste** or pure. **Keepers at home** (Gr *oikourgos*) means "working at home." Again, Paul is no male chauvinist. God ordained women are to work at home, but not as a maid or slave. Being a good homekeeper is not demeaning. There is no higher calling. Every man knows the transforming power in the home of a lovely, godly wife. Her power is felt in a much greater institute than a bank or political office when she influences the home and children for God. **Obedient to their . . . husbands.** What an awesome responsibility this puts on the husband to be a man of God and represent Christ in the home! Why are wives to live like this? **That the word of God be not blasphemed.** What an awful result when wives are out of place and unsubmissive.

D. Obedience of Young Men. 2:6-8.

6. The other side of this coin is for **young men** to be **sober-minded.** This is the same word (Gr *sophroneō*) as in verses 2 and 5, translated "temperate" and "discreet," and has the idea of "curbing one's desires and impulses," or "self-controlled."

7. Showing thyself. He now turns to Titus. **A pattern of good works, pattern** (Gr *typos*) meaning model or type. It is common for young men to have a hero and pastors should be the best human models for them to pattern themselves after. Then, **in doctrine**

showing uncorruptness, that is, no taint of heresy. **Gravity** here means "dignity" and a man of God must have such and then he will win the respect of older men and women as well.

8. Sound speech, that cannot be condemned. Besides being a good pattern as a leader, the pastor must exhibit the wisdom to speak only that which is well thought out and not that which is rash or reprehensible. He should say nothing that will bring blame to his ministry (I Tim 5:14).

E. Obedience of Slaves. 2:9-10.

9. Servants (Gr *doulos*) were slaves in a pagan society. Paul did not get side-tracked into social reform. One cannot reform a lost society. The gospel will transform individuals in society and this is the minister's calling. The trend today is to go around passing out aspirins, in the form of a so-called social gospel, to a sick society when it needs the work of a doctor "delivering" new babes into the kingdom of God. This is a much harder work and is opposed by every demon of hell, but it is the only lasting work and must be done by the man of God. Servants are **to be obedient unto their . . . masters,** not liberated! The context indicates that the obedient lives of Christian slaves should **adorn the doctrine of God.** (vs. 10). **Not answering again** (Gr *antilego*), not "contradicting."

10. Not purloining (Gr *nosphizomai*). The root of this word really means to embezzle or pilfer. Petty thievery was common among slaves and they felt no compunction against it. Too many workers today fall into this same error. Businesses lose millions annually to employees who see nothing wrong with such thievery. Of a Christian this must not be, but he must show **fidelity.**

F. The Basis of Obedience. 2:11-15.

11. Why such restraining of oneself? Why demand obedience and sub-mission of men and women? The **grace of God.** Let no one say grace gives license to sin or to be rude or crude. It would take volumes just to delve into the depths of God's grace but II Corinthians 8:9 sums it up by saying, "For ye know the grace of our Lord Jesus Christ, that, though he was rich, yet for your sakes he became poor, that ye through his poverty might be rich." Oh, how rich He was in glory, and how poor He became as He took our sins upon Himself. Then how rich we became as the "sons of God" and "heirs of God" (Rom 8:16). This is the salvation grace brings. See Ephesians 2:8-10. **Hath appeared** refers to the past act of Christ's first coming to give **himself for us, that he might redeem us** (vs. 14).

12. Our initial response to God's grace must be **denying ungodliness.** Some very blindly accuse those who believe salvation is solely by grace of turning grace into a license to sin. Not so, for grace teaches to deny ungodliness and **worldly lusts.** While in the world the believer is not of the world and his desires are not to be set on this world system and its values. Rather, **we should live soberly.** This same word in different forms is in verses 2, 4, 5, 6 of this chapter. **Righteously,** or in simple terms, just do right no matter what others may do! **Godly** means in a godly manner, not "holier than thou" but with true piety. **In this present world.** The gospel is not a pie in the sky, but it is for the here and now, and it teaches how to really live and not just exist, as the world does.

13. There is a great future as well and grace teaches to look for **that blessed hope.** "If in this life only we have hope in Christ, we are of all men most miserable" (I Cor 15:19). There is much more to come. Jesus is coming again and it will be **the glorious appearing of the great God and our Saviour Jesus Christ.** The Greek construction here is fantastic for the construction makes the **blessed hope** and **glorious**

appearing to be one and the same thing. The one true hope and expectation of the believer is seeing Jesus as He is and being like Him (I Jn 3:2). How the heart of the believer longs for that day (II Tim 4:8). Then the same rule of construction makes **the great God** and **our Saviour Jesus Christ** to be one and the same thing as well. This is a strong statement of the deity of Christ. "Let God be true to every man a liar" but Jesus is **God,** not simply like God or godly, but He is God, for indeed, "the Word was God" (Jn 1:1).

14. Who gave himself. This is why He humbled Himself (Phil 2:5-8) and became a man so He, the God-man, might suffer and die for our sins and **redeem us from all iniquity.** The word redeem (Gr *lutroō*) means "to set free by the payment of a ransom." The believer is now set free from sin to become **zealous of good works.** He is "created in Christ Jesus unto good works" (Eph 2:10), not because of good works which would be contrary to salvation by grace.

15. These things speak . . . with all authority. God's man must be authoritative. Jesus was (Mt 7:29). The scribes weren't!

IV. OBEDIENCE IN THE WORLD. 3:1-11.

A. Obedience in Relationship to Rulers 3:1.

1. Put them in mind or simply remind them **to be subject.** This is in the middle voice and means "put oneself" with the idea of doing it willingly and not being made to do it. **To principalities.** This refers to the principal person or first in authority, such as the king. Then **powers** refer to those of delegated authority under them. **Obey magistrates** reminds us there is a chain of command in the civil realm and believers are to be obedient in civil matters. To do away with this principal would lead to anarchy and chaos. **Every good work.** This seems to indicate the believer's sphere of influence

for good ought to be felt in every realm. Joseph, Daniel, and Moses are good examples of this.

B. Obedience in Relationship to People. 3:2-7.

2. To speak evil of no man, from which we get blaspheme (Gr *blasphēmeō*). Usually this is used with reference to God but here it is to men also. How tragic to hear so much of this done among Christians today, even of one another. While this refers to the world primarily, name-calling is not a Christian's prerogative and especially of a brother in the Lord. **Brawler** means "not a contentious person." It is usually the contentious who speak evil of others. **Gentle** usually refers to our outward conduct while **meekness** to inward attitude. Both are Christlike characteristics.

3. We . . . were . . . foolish. It is so easy to forget what manner of men we once were. **Foolish** means "without understanding" which is true of the natural man (I Cor 2:14). **Disobedient.** Romans 1:18 ff. shows just how far the unbeliever will go to be disobedient to God. He is **deceived** by the deceiver himself and will believe a lie rather than the truth. **Serving** (Gr *douleuō*) or slaving to **divers lusts.** "Whosoever committeth sin is the servant of sin" (Jn 8:34). **Living** (Gr *diagō*) meaning "to pass the time" in **malice** or **envy.** Then, as unbelievers, we were **hateful, and hating one another.** What a history. Who dares write his true autobiography before he knew Christ.

4-5. But, thank God for the "buts" in Scripture. But for the grace of God we would all still be in the same wretched condition as the unbeliever in the world, therefore, beware how you speak against even them! **The kindness . . . of God . . . appeared** showing that **Not by works of righteousness which we have done, but according to his mercy he saved us.** We are not saved because we do not do the above things anymore, but are saved **according to**

his mercy. Salvation comes not by trusting our works of righteousness, but His work of redemption on the cross. Salvation then includes **the washing of regeneration.** (Gr *palinggenesia*) is a compound of "again" and "to become." Jesus spoke of it as being born again. It is the act of the **Holy Ghost** (Jn 3:5-8).

6. It all comes **through Jesus Christ our Saviour.** God thought it, Christ bought it, and the Spirit wrought it.

7. Salvation is not just a narrow escape from hell. What was shed on us abundantly was that **we should be made heirs,** heirs of God and joint-heirs with Christ (Rom 8:16-17). What a "great salvation" (Heb 2:3).

C. Obedience and Our Relationship to Heretics. 3:8-11.

8. **I will that thou affirm constantly.** The word "affirm" is the same word used of the false teachers in I Timothy 1:7. It means to strongly affirm. Affirm that believers are **to maintain good works.** Sometimes this is neglected and believers can take a "who cares" attitude. This must not be so.

9. **But avoid foolish questions.** These admonitions were given over and over to Timothy as well. See I Timothy 1:4; II Timothy 2:23 ff.

10. **Heretick** (Gr *hairetikos*) means "to choose, prefer, or take for oneself." It has the idea of choosing to believe what one wants, in spite of what God says. The Word of God must be the final authority for what we believe. Those who accept so-called "further revelations" which are contrary to the Word of God are heretics and should be rejected.

11. This one is **subverted** (Gr *ektrepō*), meaning twisted. It is a medical term used of such as an ankle that has been sprained. Being condemned of himself (Gr *autokatakritos*) means self-condemned. By his own contentions, the subverted one condemns himself and shows whose camp he is in.

V. CONCLUSION. 3:12-15.

Now comes a number of personal notes which conclude the epistle. This is typical of the apostle.

12. Evidently **Artemas** or **Tychicus** was to replace Titus on the island of Crete. Artemas is unknown to us but Tychicus is well attested in Pauline literature being the bearer from Rome to Asia Minor of the epistles to the Colossians, Ephesians, and to Philemon. Also Tychicus was to be sent by Paul to relieve Timothy in Ephesus (II Tim 4:12). He was the trusted companion of Paul. Both here and in II Timothy 4:21 there is a reference to Paul's plan to winter in **Nicopolis** and in each case he urges his associates to **be diligent to come** to him.

13. **Zenas the lawyer and Apollos.** Zenas the "lawyer" (Gr *nomikos*) is otherwise unknown but Apollos is the eloquent evangelist mentioned frequently in Acts and I Corinthians. Assistance is to be provided to them so **that nothing be wanting unto them.**

14. **Learn to maintain good works.** The Cretan Christians are not only to conduct themselves properly, but are to engage only in honorable occupations and to make themselves practically useful to all the other believers. "The practical side of Christianity is here brought into vivid focus. The words **for necessary uses** can be understood either as necessitous cases or as wants. The more probable interpretation is the former, as RSV 'so as to help cases of urgent need.' All who engage in such works of mercy need never fear that they will be unfruitful" (Donald Guthrie, *The Pastoral Epistles,* p. 210).

15. **Grace be with you all. A-men.** This final benediction is identical with those of I and II Timothy, except for the "all" at the end. In characteristic shortness, yet tenderness, Paul has completed his letter to another son in the faith, Titus.

BIBLIOGRAPHY

Barnes, Albert. *Notes on the New Testament, Explanatory and Practical—Thessalonians, Timothy, Titus, and Philemon.* Ed. by Robert Frew. Grand Rapids: Baker, 1951.

Barrett, C. K. The Pastoral Epistles. In *The New Clarendon Bible.* Oxford: Clarendon Press, 1963.

Bernard, J. H. The Pastoral Epistles. In the *Cambridge Greek Testament.* Cambridge: Cambridge University Press, 1922.

Erdman, Charles R. *The Pastoral Epistles of Paul.* Philadelphia: Westminster Press, 1923.

Fairbairn, Patrick. *Commentary on the Pastoral Epistles.* Grand Rapids: Zondervan, 1956.

* Hendriksen, William. Exposition of the Pastoral Epistles. In *New Testament Commentary.* Grand Rapids: Zondervan, 1956.

* Hiebert, D. Edmond. *First Timothy.* Chicago: Moody Press, 1957.

* _____*Second Timothy.* Chicago: Moody Press, 1958.

* _____*Titus and Philemon.* Chicago: Moody Press, 1957.

Humphreys, A. E. The Epistles to Timothy and Titus. In *Cambridge Bible for Schools and Colleges.* Cambridge: Cambridge University Press, 1925.

Ironside, Harry. *Timothy, Titus and Philemon.* Neptune, New Jersey: Loizeaux Brothers, 1955.

Kelly, William. *An Exposition of the Two Epistles to Timothy.* 3rd Ed. London: C. A. Hammond, 1948.

* Kelly, J. N. D. The Pastoral Epistles. In *Harper's New Testament Commentaries.* New York: Harper and Row, 1963.

Lenski, R. C. H. *The Interpretation of St. Paul's Epistles to the Colossians, to the Thessalonians, to Timothy, to Titus, and to Philemon.* Columbus, Ohio: Lutheran Book Concern, 1937.

Liddon, Henry P. *Explanatory Analysis of St. Paul's First Epistle to Timothy.* London: Longmans, Green and Co., 1897.

* Lilley, J. P. The Pastoral Epistles. A New Translation with Introduction, Commentary, and Appendix. In *Handbooks for Bible Classes.* Edinburgh: T. & T. Clark, 1901.

Moule, H. C. G. *The Second Epistle to Timothy.* London: Religious Tract Society, 1905.

Plummer, Alfred. The Pastoral Epistles. In *The Expositor's Bible.* New York: A. C. Armstrong and Son, 1908.

Simpson, E. K. *The Pastoral Epistles.* London: Tyndale Press, 1954.

Vine, W. E. *The Epistles to Timothy and Titus: Faith and Conduct.* Grand Rapids: Zondervan, 1965.

Wuest, Kenneth S. *The Pastoral Epistles in the Greek New Testament for the English Reader.* Grand Rapids: Eerdmans, 1952.

The Epistle To

PHILEMON

INTRODUCTION

Paul's letter to Philemon is the shortest of his thirteen canonical books (only 430 words in the AV), and is thus placed last in the collection of pauline epistles in our Bible. It was written and sent at the same time as Colossians, about A.D. 62, while Paul was under guard in Rome awaiting trial before Caesar (Acts 25:12; 28:16, 30).

This little letter in Paul's own handwriting (vs. 19) is to Philemon, a well-to-do Christian who resided in Colossae (cf. vss. 2, 23 and Col 4:12, 17) in the Roman province of Asia. Paul had been the principal human agent responsible for the salvation of Philemon (vs. 19), accomplished some five or six years prior through Paul's ministry in Ephesus (Acts 19:10, 26). Paul's purpose in writing is to ask Philemon to reinstate Onesimus, a slave who had run away from Philemon, and who apparently had stolen some valuables (vs. 18).

The backdrop of the whole story is, of course, the first century Roman Empire. There were millions of slaves throughout the empire. Many slaveowners had ten or more, and not a few owned hundreds. These slaves were not of any particular race or nationality, but were composed of the people of Rome's many conquered territories from the East to the West. Roman law governing slavery was quite severe toward the slave. They were considered nothing more than pieces of property to be bought, sold, and used for any purpose whatsoever. Life was not easy for slaves. They could be beaten for minor offenses and even crucified for running away.

In contrast to Roman law was the Old Testament law about slaves. They were treated like household members (Lev 25:53) and became partakers of the covenant (Gen 17:27). They were freed during the sabbatical year (Ex 21:2). Harming a slave resulted in his freedom (Ex 21:26-27), and if someone killed a slave he would be severely punished (Ex 21:20). An escaped slave was to be neither hunted nor returned to his master (Deut 23:15-16). For more on slavery, both Jewish and Roman, see J. B. Lightfoot's introduction to Philemon, and W. Alexander's eight-page section in the introduction to Philemon in *The Bible Commentary*, edited by F. C. Cook.

With this contrast between the Jewish law and the Roman practice of slavery in mind, we see how masterfully Paul sought to bring mercy into the Roman system where Christians were concerned. Paul must also have had the slave Onesimus in mind when he addressed Christian slaveowners in Ephesians 6:5-8 and Colossians 3:22-25, both near the time he wrote this letter to Philemon.

OUTLINE

I. Paul's Prologue. 1-3.
II. Paul's Prayer and Praise for Philemon. 4-7.
III. Paul's Plea for Profitable Onesimus. 8-21.
IV. Paul's Personal Prospects. 22.
V. Paul's Postscript. 23-25.

COMMENTARY

I. PAUL'S PROLOGUE. 1-3.

1. Paul, a prisoner of Jesus Christ. As was customary, Paul first identifies himself to his readers. But here, instead of calling himself an apostle, he reminds Philemon that he is a prisoner for Christ's sake (cf. vs. 9; Eph 3:1; 4:1 and II Tim 1:8). **And Timothy, our brother.** All true believers in Christ are brothers. Timothy was no doubt visiting Paul in Rome, and was not being detained. **Unto Philemon.** All we know about Philemon is contained in this short letter. Residing at Colossae, Philemon was apparently a model Christian. He was an active worker for Christ and also the owner of the slave Onesimus, who had run away.

2. Apphia was no doubt Philemon's wife, and is thus warmly greeted, along with **Archippus,** who may be their son, and who apparently has certain responsibilities in the local congregation of believers at Colossae (Col 4:17). **And to the church in thy house.** The word "church" (Gr *ekklēsia*), as it is used here, refers to a local group of immersed believers who would gather together for worship, prayer, edification, exhortation, fellowship, and the commemoration of Christ's death (the Lord's Supper), and then go forth to serve Christ and to tell others about Him. Since believers did not build meeting houses, they frequently met in homes (Acts 2:4-6; Rom 16:5).

3. Grace to you, and peace. Grace (Gr *charis*) was the common Greek greeting, just as **peace** (Heb *shalōm*) was the ordinary Hebrew salutation. Paul combines both of these terms, heightened with the full Christian meaning of all the blessings of salvation that freely come to us through Christ, and the peace of God that we have because Christ has made peace with God on our behalf. The fact that God the Father and the Lord Jesus Christ together send this grace and peace illustrates their equality in the Godhead.

II. PAUL'S PRAYER AND PRAISE FOR PHILEMON. 4-7.

4. Paul perpetually set a proper example in his prayer life. We should be thankful for other believers and bear them up before the Lord. Paul had a long prayer list which he remembered daily (see Eph 1:15-16; Phil 1:3-4; Col 1:9; I Thess 1:2; and II Tim 1:3). We should follow his example.

5. Hearing. Paul continually heard of Philemon's love and faith from others around him. Philemon was a model believer, both before the Lord, and with regard to other believers. This naturally has a bearing on the request Paul makes of Philemon.

6. This verse expresses the content of Paul's prayer for Philemon. He prays that Philemon might generously share with others, the results of which would glorify God.

7. This was in fact what Paul had been hearing about Philemon. Paul was encouraged because Philemon was such a rest and refreshment to the saints (other believers) in Colossae. **Brother.** Paul refers both to Philemon and to Onesimus (vs. 16) as his brothers. Such ties in the Lord are often more meaningful than even blood relations with those who are unsaved.

III. PAUL'S PLEA FOR PROFITABLE ONESIMUS. 8-21.

8. Wherefore. Because Philemon's heart was so gracious, kind, and loving (vss. 4-7), Paul knows that he does not need to command Philemon with the authority of an apostle to perform his request.

9. Instead, Paul makes a forthright appeal to Philemon to act on a higher plane, that of love. Paul's mention that he is aged, and also a prisoner, is calculated to gain the approval sought from Philemon. Paul must have been nearly sixty years old at that time, and he was a missionary statesman by anyone's standards. Not a young inexperienced preacher, Paul was an elder apostle who knew the mind of Christ. His status as a "helpless" prisoner made his appeal all the more weighty upon Philemon. He was trusting God to speak to Philemon concerning his plea.

10. My son Onesimus. Paul's plea is for Onesimus, Philemon's runaway slave. After Onesimus fled from Colossae he made his way to Rome, and somehow came into contact with Paul, who led him to a saving knowledge of Christ. This is why Paul refers to Onesimus as his son whom he has begotten (in the faith). Paul elsewhere refers to Timothy and Titus in similar fashion (I Tim 1:2; Tit 1:4). It is possible that Onesimus, who willingly returned to Philemon with Paul's letter, stood in the very presence of Philemon as the letter was read.

11. This verse contains a play on words. The name Onesimus (Gr *onēsimos*) means "useful" or "profitable." Paul is saying that Onesimus had previously not lived up to his name, but now (since his salvation) he will not only be useful to Philemon, but already has proven himself such to Paul. True salvation changes one's attitude and his actions (II Cor 5:17).

12. Mine own bowels. Paul's deep affection and admiration for Onesimus must have been evident to Philemon, as he refers to Onesimus as his own heart. Paul multiplies the terms in calling Onesimus his son (vs. 10), his own heart (vs. 12), his brother (vs. 16), and even exhorts Philemon to receive him as he would Paul himself (vs. 17).

13. Paul longed to keep Onesimus with him because he ministered to him in his difficult situation in Rome. Paul lovingly mentions that if Onesimus were in Rome he would only be doing what Philemon himself would do if he could. Certainly, Philemon must have been in tears as he read these affectionate words of his beloved friend and apostle.

14. Paul refused to keep Onesimus because to have done so and then to have sought Philemon's approval may have forced Philemon to grudgingly approve of the situation. But Paul knows that if kindness or helpfulness is in any way forced, it becomes insincere. Philemon's goodness always proceeded willingly from a heart of compassion. We must constantly examine our own lives to insure that proper actions are produced by proper motives.

15. The marvelous providence of God is in view in this verse. Onesimus' departure eventuated in his salvation in Christ. Now he returns to Philemon for the duration of this life, with the happy prospect of spending eternity in heaven with Philemon and all other believers. This does not mean that Onesimus never would have been saved if he had not run away. But God in His providence did turn his evil around for good.

16. Though Onesimus was still Philemon's slave, and as far as we know remained such, in Christ he was the Lord's freeman (I Cor 7:21), and a brother to and a joint heir with Paul and Philemon (Gal 3:28; Rom 8:17). Christian bonds transcend human barriers and exceed mere earthly relationships.

17. Paul had already asked Philemon to receive Onesimus back (vs. 12), but now he put the request in terminology that could scarcely be ignored. He stated that if Philemon regarded him as an associate, a partner in spiritual matters, then he should receive Onesimus as he would Paul himself. There is, of course, no question as to how Philemon would receive Paul! This is also a perfect picture of how God receives sinners who trust Christ as Lord and Saviour. How is that? Just as He receives Christ.

18. Put that on mine account. Paul wants all of Onesimus' wrongs placed on his own account as if they were his. In the same way, Christ takes all the believer's sins on Himself and pays for all completely by His shed blood (I Pet 2:24). Christ is our substitute. He suffered our punishment. No wonder Luther could so aptly say, "We are all the Lord's Onesimi."

19. When Paul wrote his various epistles, he often used a stenographer to do the writing; but here, perhaps because of his great personal concern, he points out that he has written the letter in his own handwriting. Paul's offer to pay all that Onesimus owed must have moved Philemon, as well as the reminder that with regard to eternal values Philemon owed everything to Paul's concern for him (humanly speaking).

20. The apostle makes his final appeal to Philemon, calling him brother, and asking him, as it were, for a personal favor. The language expressing Paul's desire is very heightened. He yearns for that which will bring to his own heart abundant joy in Christ. His final challenge is that Philemon might refresh his heart, even as Philemon has refreshed the hearts of others (cf. vs. 7 where the same expression occurs).

21. Thy obedience refers to the obedience that proceeds from a heart of love, not from the compulsion of Paul's authority as an apostle. **Thou wilt also do more than I say.** The extreme confidence Paul has in Philemon's response is noted here. There is even a hint at possible emancipation, i.e., "more than I say," which was merely to receive Onesimus back.

IV. PAUL'S PERSONAL PROSPECTS. 22.

22. With the plea for Onesimus ended, Paul presents his personal plan of visiting Philemon once his case in Rome is decided. He expects to be released soon (Phil 2:24). He is confident that Philemon will provide some hospitality, and that Philemon's prayers will move God to intervene on his behalf. Prayer does move God. One can also imagine how Paul's intention to visit Philemon must have encouraged him to grant Paul's initial request for Onesimus.

V. PAUL'S POSTSCRIPT. 23-25.

23. Epaphras my fellow prisoner. Epaphras was well known to the Colossians (Col 1:7; 4:12-13). To call him a fellow prisoner (as he did Aristarchus, Col 4:10) must mean that these men were so constantly with Paul that it seemed they were prisoners too.

24. Marcus or John Mark had recovered from his failure on the first missionary journey (Acts 13:13; 15:36-41) and was now with Paul again (cf. II Tim 4:11). **Aristarchus** was one of Paul's converts from Thessalonica who accompanied Paul on much of the third missionary journey (Acts 20:4) and on the trip to Rome (Acts 27:2; Col 4:10). **Demas,** sad to say, later turned back from following Christ (II Tim 4:10). **Luke,** the beloved physician, the author of Luke and Acts, was faithful to the very end (II Tim 4:11). These all sent their greetings to Philemon. Of the eleven persons mentioned in this short letter, Onesimus is precisely in the middle, and is the central character.

25. Paul ends this letter as he began it, with **the grace of our Lord Jesus Christ** directed toward Philemon's entire household. All grace resides in Him who freely gave all He had for us. "Thanks be unto God for his unspeakable gift" (II Cor 9:15).

BIBLIOGRAPHY

Alexander, W. The Epistle to Philemon. In *The Bible Commentary*, Vol IX. Ed. by F. C. Cook. New York: Scribner's, 1881.

Alford, Henry. The Epistle to Philemon. In *The New Testament for English Readers*, Vol. II, Pt. 1. Boston: Lee and Shephard, 1875.

* Ellis, E. Earle. The Epistle to Philemon. In *The Wycliffe Bible Commentary*. Ed. Charles F. Pfeiffer and Everett F. Harrison. Chicago: Moody Press, 1962.

Gaebelein, Frank E. *Philemon: The Gospel of Emancipation*. Wheaton: Van Kampen, 1939.

Hendriksen, William. *Exposition of Colossians and Philemon*. Grand Rapids: Baker, 1964.

* Hiebert, D. Edmond. *Titus and Philemon*. Chicago: Moody Press, 1957.

Lenski, R. C. H. *The Intrepretation of St. Paul's Epistle to the Colossians, to the Thessalonians, to Timothy, to Titus, and to Philemon*. Minneapolis: Augsburg, 1937.

Lightfoot, Joseph B. *Saint Paul's Epistles to the Colossians and to Philemon*. Grand Rapids: Zondervan, 1965.

* Moule, Charles F. D. The Epistles of Paul to the Colossians and to Philemon. In *Cambridge Greek Testament*. Cambridge: University Press, 1958.

Moule, H. C. G. The Epistles to the Colossians and to Philemon. In *The Cambridge Bible for Schools and Colleges*. Cambridge: University Press, 1902.

* Müller, Jac. J. The Epistles of Paul to the Philippians and to Philemon. In *New International Commentary*. Grand Rapids: Eerdmans, 1955.

Oesterley, W. E. The Epistle to Philemon. In *The Expositor's Greek Testament*, Vol. IV. Ed. by W. R. Nicoll. Grand Rapids: Eerdmans, 1961.

Scroggie, William Graham. *A Note to a Friend: Paul to Philemon*. London: Hulbert, n.d.

Vincent, Marvin R. A Critical and Exegetical Commenatry on the Epistles to the Philippians and to Philemon. In *The International Critical Commentary*. New York: Scribner's, 1897.

The Epistle To The

HEBREWS

INTRODUCTION

Purpose. First century Jewish Christians were involved in a traumatic identity struggle. Persecuted by both the Romans and their fellow Jews, they were involved in the always difficult conflict of trying to interpret new thoughts in contrast to long-held traditions. The purpose of Hebrews seems clearly to be one of exhorting Jewish believers to hold fast to their "new and living way" of worshiping God. The author presents the superiority of both Christ and the new convenant which He initiated. Throughout the epistle he tries to stress the continuity and flow of development between the Old Testament faith and the new faith in Christ. In order to accomplish this he makes abundant use of references to the Old Testament. In so doing, he assures the Jewish Christians of the biblical heritage of the new covenant. The author challenges them to "run with patience the race that is set before" them (12:1), even as their Jewish ancestors had done in Old Testament times. In the exhortative style of the epistle we find encouragement, comfort, and warning. The majesty of the Greek itself lends much style to the epistle. The writer uses the grammatical tool of alliteration in a truly remarkable fashion. In Hebrews 1:1 we find the letter "P" alliterated five times in a single verse. He uses the alpha-privative twenty-four times in the epistle. In 7:3 he uses three words, all beginning with the letter "A," in describing Melchizedek as "without father or mother or genealogy." This use of the alpha-privative has been noted since the days of Aristotle as being representative of a superior form of Greek. In summary, it would seem that the purpose is amply illustrated by contrasts between the old and new, always concluding with the superiority of the new. The purpose of the book is complemented by perhaps the most brilliant use of the Greek language that we have in the New Testament.

Authorship. The most intriguing mystery surrounding the book of Hebrews is that of its authorship. For one reason or another, the author of this epistle chose to remain anonymous. Discussion concerning the author's identity dates back to the second century. We are not told whether the writer was Gentile or Hebrew. It seems obvious, however, from the content of the book, that the author was indeed Jewish. The author had a superb knowledge of Jewish tradition and levitical thought. We know that he was familiar with Timothy (13:23). The Greek style and syntax is so outstanding, that many feel that it is the finest in the New Testament. While these facts serve to give us clues regarding the writer's identity, they also, by their very nature, help to confuse the issue. The following is a survey of the arguments, both positive and negative, regarding those who are most popularly thought to have written the book of Hebrews.

Paul. Historically, Paul has been considered the prime candidate as the author of Hebrews. From the second century through the Reformation there was little dissension as to the pauline authorship of the epistle. The strongest arguments for his authorship of the book lie in this early historical tradition held by the church for so many years. In modern times, the *Scofield Bible* even included the heading, "The Epistle of Paul the Apostle to the Hebrews." This heading has, however, been deleted from the *New Scofield Bible* edition. Also in

Paul's favor is the comment in chapter 13 regarding Timothy. The closeness between Paul and Timothy is well known to all readers of Scripture. Paul was also very familiar with the Hebrew tradition and levitical ritual presented so often in the book. He was born a Pharisee, the son of a Pharisee and had an excellent background in the law.

In opposition to his authorship, the basic arguments lie in the excellent quality of the Greek with which the epistle was written. Hebrews presents itself with a generally superior style to any of Paul's letters. It is beautifully written with intricate syntax. Arguments against a Pauline authorship state that it is unusual for Paul not to include his name in the beginning of the epistle. Neither does he refer to his personal experiences as he did in so many other of his epistles. Old Testament quotations in the book of Hebrews are from the Septuagiant (LXX), of which Paul did not make extensive use in his epistles.

Barnabas. The viewpoint that Barnabas was the author of the Epistle to the Hebrews was put forth quite early in the second century by Tertullian. Barnabas was a Levite from Cyprus. As such, he would have been thoroughly familiar with the levitical traditions. He would also be thoroughly acquainted with the Alexandrian school of Jewish thought, which seems to be reflected in the epistle. He was also a mediator between Paul and the Jewish Christians in Acts 9. It is suggested that the author was acting in a similar capacity in Hebrews by explaining to Jewish Christians the principles of the new Christian faith.

The arguments against Barnabas' authorship of the epistle stem more from the fact that there is not more abundant positive evidence for it. While it is true that he was a Levite and would be familiar with many of the concepts presented in Hebrews, this could be said about many other early Christians. Barnabas was well known in the early church. It would seem more evidence would support his authorship, if indeed he had written the book.

Apollos. The view that Apollos was the author of Hebrews first gained credence during the time of the Reformation. Martin Luther, Philip Melanchthon, and some post-Reformation scholars, advocated Apollos as the author of this book. Most of the evidence cited for Apollos stems from information contained in Acts 18:24-28. There we learn that Apollos was an Alexandrian Jew. We further read that he was an eloquent man and "mighty in the scriptures." The writer of Hebrews was indeed an eloquent man as evidenced by the brilliant style of writing. Apollos traveled into Achaia where he became familiar with the church of Corinth and possibly Timothy as well. Verse 28 of Acts 18 tells us that he "mightily convinced the Jews, and that publickly, shewing by the scriptures that Jesus was Christ." Apparently Apollos had quite a ministry in reaching the Jews by means of the Scriptures, showing that Jesus was indeed the Christ. This thought is basic to the book of Hebrews. Many quotes from the Old Testament Scriptures are used, illustrating the newfound excellency of Christ. Apollos also had an excellent reputation in the early church. This was evidenced by Paul's testimony regarding him in I Corinthians.

The greatest weakness in the argument for Apollos' authorship of the epistle is the lack of early historical evidence. It seems logical that if Apollos had indeed written such a remarkable epistle, one of the second century Alexandrian fathers, such as Origen, would have laid claim to one of his own as the author.

Conclusion. One of these three men seems to be the most logical choice as the author of the book of Hebrews. There are both strengths and weaknesses in the arguments for all three. Historically speaking, the strongest arguments lie in the direction of Paul. However, the suggestion of Apollos as the author should not be taken lightly and has much in its favor. Perhaps it is best to conclude as Origen of Alexandria did when he wrote regarding the authorship of Hebrews: "Who the author of the epistle is, only God truly knows." Whoever the author may be, the crucial thing seems to be that he encourages us to be "looking unto Jesus the author and finisher of our faith" (12:2). The author asks that we look to Jesus for everything, drawing from Him the strength and encouragement to live the Christian life that is set before us.

Recipients. The earliest extant manuscripts of Hebrews contain the heading "To Hebrews." From every indication in the epistle, it would appear that these Hebrews were Jewish Christians. From the various warnings throughout Hebrews we are led to believe that the readers were first century Jewish Christians who were worshiping in the synagogue. The warnings further indicate that some of them were in danger of returning to Judaism. Others were backsliding in their Christian faith. This was a real problem in the early church. By returning to Judaism the early Christian could avoid persecution. Judaism was a legal religion, sanctioned and protected under Roman law; Christianity was not, and it is apparent from internal evidence in the epistle itself (10:32) that they had undergone suffering.

It is doubtful that these believers were located in Palestine. The epistle (2:3) seems to imply that the readers themselves had not heard the Lord, but that His words were confirmed to them by those who heard Him. If these believers had been in Palestine, many of them would have the privilege of hearing Christ firsthand and would not need such an affirmation. The other locale that is put forth most often as to the area in which these Jewish Christians lived is Rome. This would seem to be a more logical answer. The author closes the epistle (13:24) by stating that "They of Italy salute you." The word translated "of" would seem to imply that Christian brothers who were from Italy were sending greetings back home by word of the author. This would lend credence to the idea that Rome was the destination to which Hebrews was written. Furthermore, the Roman Christians would be involved in facing the front line of persecution by the emperor Nero. Another possibility would be that the author wrote the epistle from Rome and sent it to Jewish believers in the Diaspora.

Date. We have internal evidence which may assist us in assigning a date to the writing of Hebrews. Timothy is still alive (13:23). This would lead one to believe that we must assign a first century date to the epistle. Throughout the epistle (8:4; 10:8, 11) it is noted that the Jewish sacrificial system was still in effect. This would enable us to affix a date prior to A.D. 70 when the Roman general Titus utterly destroyed Jerusalem and the temple. This ended the temple rituals and the sacrificial system. There is other internal evidence that the Christians to whom Hebrews was written were second-generation Christians (2:3). This would not allow an extremely early date for the epistle. The comments in the epistle regarding persecution under the Roman emperor Nero in the late A.D. 50's or early A.D. 60's. Historical evidence suggests that the Jewish Christians were severely persecuted by A.D. 68 or 69 under Nero. As the epistle implies that the readers had not yet shed blood in their persecution (12:4), it would seem logical to assign a date to the epistle in the mid A.D. 60's, approximately A.D. 64 or 65.

Canonicity. An abundance of evidence from the early church exists regarding the acceptance of Hebrews as part of the biblical canon. The epistle is quoted widely as early as A.D. 95 in the epistle of Clement of Rome. Many of the early church fathers, including Eusebius, Origen, Augustine, and Jerome, considered it to belong to the sacred canon. While there was discussion regarding its authorship, there was little doubt as to its authenticity and validity as a part of Holy Scripture. Hebrews is included in the first official list of the canon published in A.D. 397 by the Third Council of Carthage. There has been little question throughout the centuries as to the genuineness and canonicity of the book of Hebrews.

OUTLINE

COMMENTARY

I. A NEW AND LIVING WAY. 1:1-10:31.

A. The Superiority of Christ. 1:1-5:14.

1. Christ is superior to the prophets. 1:1-3.

Notice that there is no introductory statement. The author of Hebrews runs contrary to New Testament tradition by including no greeting or self-identification. This is similar to what is found in I John. It indicates the urgency with which the author desires to get into the meat of his subject; that is the superiority of Christ to the Old Testament way. **1:1-3. God, who at sundry times and in divers manners spake.** In Old Testament times God spoke to His people in different ways and at different times. His revelation was not given in complete form to any one person. He spoke by such means as dreams, visions, and direct contacts. These were given over a period of hundreds of years to many people. This incomplete, diverse revelation is much different from that given in the last days. **For God . . . Hath in these last days spoken unto us by his Son.** The emphasis here is that the revelation through His Son is superior to that of the prophets. It is a one time, complete revelation from the Father through the person of the Heir, His Son. We are reminded of the parable of Christ in Matthew 21:33-41 regarding the husbandman who sent servants to receive the fruit of his vineyard. They were killed, so he sent his son, who was also murdered. In verses 2 and 3 we find the description of the Son. He is the **heir of all things, . . . he made the worlds;** He is **the brightness of his glory, . . . the express image** (Gr *charaktēr*) **of God.** This is the only place this word is used in the New Testament. It is the impression left by an engraving tool. Such an imprint is the exact representation of the design. Even so Christ is the exact representation of God the Father on earth for all men to see. He upholds **all things by the word of his power.** All by Himself He **purged our sins.** Since this purging was a once-for-all event, He was able to sit **down on the right hand of the Majesty.** This is in direct contrast to the Old Testament saints who had to offer repeated sacrifice for sin and the priests who had to continually stand while making such offerings.

2. Christ is superior to the angels. 1:4-2:18.

It is necessary that the author prove to his readers that Christ was superior to the angels. In the first century world, pagans and Christians alike accorded great significance and power to angels. It is possible that some had taught that Christ was Himself an angel, thus able to do miracles. There is further evidence from Scripture (Col 2:18) that some were even worshiping angels. Thus as the author attempts to prove the over all superiority of Christ, he must prove that He is superior to angels.

4. Being made so much better than the angels. This word **better** (Gr *kreitton*) is used thirteen times in the epistle. It is a key concept in showing the fulfillment of the Old Covenant in the New. The thought here is literally "becoming" (Gr *ginomai*) better than the angels, referring to His majestic position at the throne of God (1:3) culminating the plan of salvation. He has **a more excellent name than they.** Indeed, His is the "name which is above every name" (Phil 2:9). To this name "every knee should bow, of things in heaven" (Phil 2:10). This would include the angels.

5. For unto which of the angels. The author here begins a series of Old Testament quotations. These are designed to show the Hebrew readers, from their own Septuagint, the superiority of Christ above the angels. Verse 5 is a quote from Psalm 2:7. It shows the family relationship between God and Christ. A family relationship is surely superior to any other.

6. And again, when he bringeth in the firstbegotten. This is a quote from Psalm 97:7. This verse indicates the superiority of the Son, because the angels are commanded to worship Him. The word **firstbegotten** (Gr *prototokon*) in all likelihood is a reference to the heir relationship of the Son to the Father. The firstborn was always the chief heir of his father; this is then a term denoting privilege or position.

7. And of the angels he saith. This verse is a quote from Psalm 104:4. It tells us that the angels are made or created (Gr *poieō*). The word **spirits** may be appropriately translated winds (Gr *pneuma*). Even as the wind and fire are servants, so are the angels. As servants, they are inferior to the One who created wind and fire.

8-9. But unto the Son he saith, Thy throne, O God, is for ever. These verses are perhaps the most powerful in the epistle. They are quoted from Psalm 45:6-7. Christ is herein referred to as God (Gr *theos*). Therefore, we have the Father calling the Son, God. This is a majestic reference to the deity of Christ. The words **throne** and **sceptre** further enhance His majesty. His throne is described as **for ever and ever** (literally "unto the age of the age"), further highlighting the eternality of the Son. He has been **anointed . . . with the oil of gladness.** This is a further illustration of his kingship, as kings were anointed with oil during the Old Testament period. He is said to be **anointed . . . above thy fellows.** This can be taken as a reference to His superiority to the angels, His fellow sojourners in heaven.

10-12. And, Thou, Lord, in the beginning hast laid the foundation. These verses quote from Psalm 102:25-27. They indicate the creative power of Christ. **They shall perish; but thou remainest** is again a reference to the eternality of Christ. This is further explained in the statement **thou art the same, and thy years shall not fail.** The angels are created, not eternal. Christ is portrayed as the eternal Creator, therefore, superior. How comforting to the Christian! In 13:8 the author elaborates with the mighty statement that Jesus Christ is **the same yesterday, and today, and for ever.** How good to know that we worship a never-changing, all-powerful God.

13-14. But to which of the angels said he at any time. Again, here is an Old Testament quote, this time from Psalm 110:1. This refers to Christ's position at the right hand of the throne (vs. 3). His position is one of majesty. The verb "sit" (Gr *kathēmai*) is in the present tense in Greek. Therefore, Christ is asked (by implication) to sit continually at the right hand of the Father, where in Romans 8:34 we are told He is making "intercession for us." The concept of making **thine enemies thy footstool** refers to the ancient custom of victorious kings who would place their feet on the necks of defeated kings, indicating their superiority and conquest over them. **Are they not all ministering spirits** again indicates the servant status of angels. One purpose of angels is clearly indicated in that they are **sent forth to minister for them who shall be heirs of salvation.** As such we have a source of strength through the ministry of angels. God graciously provides such beings to minister to us in times of trouble (cf. Ps 91).

2:1. Therefore we ought to give the more earnest heed. In chapter 1 Paul endeavors to impress on the readers the importance of Christ and His message. The message is so crucial that the Father sent His only Son to deliver it. Therefore, we must pay close attention to it. The danger in not giving heed is a slipping away from the truth. The word **slip** (Gr *pararreō*) is a nautical term meaning "to slip anchor." Therefore, if we do not **give the more earnest heed to the things which we have heard,** we are in danger of drifting away from the pier, the safe harbor that is ours in the salvation revealed by Christ.

2-4. For if the word spoken by angels. There is ample evidence that this refers to the Mosaic law. Both Luke (Acts 7:53) and Paul (Gal 3:19) attest to the widely held first century view that the law was given through the mediation of angels. In the law there was explicit detail regarding punishment for **transgression** and **disobedience.** This law, given by angels, was explicit regarding discipline for sin. Thus, how much more important is the penalty for neglecting **so great salvation!** The author reaffirms in three ways the importance of that salvation. First, it was **spoken by the Lord,** Himself. Secondly, it **was confirmed . . . by them that heard him.** This may be an argument against Pauline authorship of the epistle. Paul, in his writings, loudly attests to his personal encounter with Christ (Gal 1:12). It is not like him to cite others' testimony as if he, himself, had not heard Christ. Thirdly, God verified this salvation with **signs and wonders, . . . divers miracles, and gifts of the Holy Ghost.** The latter refers to the distribution of gifts by the Holy Spirit to Christians as recorded in Romans 12 and I Corinthians 2:5-9.

5-9. For unto the angels hath he not put in subjection. The author now reaffirms, for the last time, the superiority of Christ, even in His humanity, over the angels. **The world to come,** probably a reference to the millennial reign, will not be subject to angels, but to Christ and believers. The author quotes Psalm 8: 4-6. This is a discussion of the position of man in the world order. Man was made **a little lower than the angels.** The word **little** (Gr *brachy*) can refer to little in terms of time or quantity. In this passage it refers to the briefness of time in which man is subservient to angels. Man will be ultimately crowned **with glory and honour.** This follows the example of the God-man, Jesus Christ, **who was made a little lower than the angels for the suffering of death,** and then ultimately **crowned with glory and honour,** Himself. Man was originally created to have dominion over all things (Gen 1:26). Some day, in the world to come, that prophecy will indeed come true, as believers and Christ will reign side by side. Angels will then eventually be ministers not rulers.

10. For it became him. The concept of a suffering Messiah was a real stumbling block to the Jewish Christians. The author tackles this problem by declaring that the suffering of the cross was an integral part of the plan of salvation. For God to become truly human, He must suffer and even **taste death** (vs. 9). God, in Christ, desires many sons, but Christ is **the captain** of the sons. This word **captain** (Gr *archēgos*) is used to describe Christ in Acts 5:31 as well as in Hebrews 12:2. It refers in its classical use to the founder of a city or movement, as well as a military leader. Christ is herein portrayed as the author of our faith and the One who goes before us into the battle for that faith. On the significance of the proleptic aorist participle *agogonta* as referring to Christ "bringing many sons unto glory," see P. E. Hughes, *A Commentary on the Epistle to the Hebrews,* pp. 101-102.

11-13. For both he that sanctifieth. These verses establish the intimate blood relationship between Christ and believers. We are all **of one.** We are all sons of the same heavenly Father. Verses 12 and 13 quote from Psalm 22:22 and Isaiah 8:17-18. They further declare the **brethren** relationship among Christ and the believers.

14-15. Forasmuch then as the children. Christ's great victory over death in the resurrection is celebrated here. For years man lived in bondage to the **fear of death.** Christ has set us free from that fear. The only way He could conquer death was to experience it and emerge victorious over it. Through His death He destroyed **him that had the power of death . . . the devil.** The word destroy (Gr *katargeō*) means literally to make ineffective or powerless. In the resurrection Christ broke the back of the devil's ultimate power over man.

16-18. For verily he took not on him the nature of angels. Christ, in the incar-
nation, **took on him the seed of Abraham.** He became a man of Jewish descent from Abraham. His desire was **in all things . . . to be made like unto his brethren.** The author now introduces, for the first time, what is to become the heart of the message of the epistle, i.e., the high priestly nature of Christ. As a man, He is our High Priest. He combines mercy and faithfulness into an inspiring model for believers to follow. His primary role as a High Priest is **to make reconciliation for the sins of the people.** He performs the duty mercifully and faithfully. He knew what it was to suffer, **being tempted.** Therefore, He is in an experienced position to **succor them them that are tempted.** The word **succor** (Gr *boetheō*) means to come to the aid of or help someone. How much easier it is to come to the aid of someone when we ourselves have gone through similar trials. How good it is to know that Christ was fully man, experiencing what we experience, therefore, able to provide just such comfort as we really need (cf. II Cor 1:3-5).

3. Christ is superior to Old Testament leaders. 3:1-5:14.

3:1. Wherefore, holy brethren. The author directly confronts the readers. He greets them as **holy brethren.** Obviously, then, he is speaking to Christians. They are admonished to consider (Gr *katanoeō*) **Christ Jesus.** He wants them to focus on, contemplate on, the person and work of Christ. This is the only New Testament reference to Christ as an **Apostle** (Gr *apostolos*). It indicates one who is sent with authority. Surely Christ is sent from the Father with the utmost authority.

2-6. Who was faithful to him. Here is the beginning of a comparison between the roles of Christ and Moses. Moses was very highly regarded by the first century Jews. The author of Hebrews attempts to make his argument for the superiority of Christ even more valid by showing His superiority over Moses. In accomplishing this, he does not cast aspersions on the ministry of Moses. He is in no way negative. Rather, he elevates Christ. Both were **faithful** in their appointed roles; Christ is, however, **counted worthy of more glory than Moses.** He is the One who has created the household of faith. He, therefore, has more honor than one who is assigned a role in that household. Verse 4, following in apposition to verse 3, is an obvious reference to the deity of Christ. See comments in A. W. Pink, *An Exposition of Hebrews,* pp. 158-60. Christ **builded the house** (vs. 3). **He that built all things is God** (vs. 4). Therefore, Christ is indeed deity in its fullest creative sense. Moses was indeed **faithful in all his house** (vs. 2). He is called a **servant** (Gr *therapōn*). This is the only usage of this word as a noun in the New Testament. It implies one who serves willingly and with position. Moses was not a slave. He was one who served faithfully and willingly and was worthy of an exalted position. Moses was, however, only a servant while Christ was **a son.** Therefore, we see the superiority of a son over a servant: Christ over Moses. The author identifies himself in the household of faith, **whose house are we.** He further identifies those in the **house** as having the characteristic of holding **fast . . . unto the end.**

7-11. Wherefore as the Holy Ghost saith. These verses are taken from Psalm 95:7-11. They are attributed to the **Holy Ghost.** Humanly speaking, they are the words of David. The author prefers to point to the Holy Spirit as the author, testifying to divine inspiration of the Scripture. With these verses the author encourages his readers not to follow in the footsteps of their ancestors. The children of Israel, wandering forty years between Egypt and the promised land, are used for an illustration. Because they did **err in their heart** they were unable to enter into the **rest** of the promised land.

12. Take heed, brethren. The author warns his readers not to allow such a **heart of unbelief** to exist in their lives. Just as in earlier years, **unbelief** kept people from experiencing God's **rest** (vs. 11), so it could in any age.

13-14. But exhort one another daily. This is the suggestion the author offers as a protective measure against becoming **hardened.** The word **exhort** (Gr *parakaleō*) means to encourage or comfort. It is the same word used of the ministry of the Holy Spirit in our lives. It is not a negative warning, but a positive encouragement. It is to be done on a **daily** basis because we are susceptible to the **deceitfulness of sin** on a daily basis. The word **deceitfulness** (Gr *apatē*) refers, not to the deceptiveness of sin, but to its pleasing quality. Many sins are pleasurable to the senses. Therefore, they need to be doubly guarded against. The author then describes those who have been **made partakers of Christ.** The word **are made partakers** (Gr *ginomai*) is in the perfect tense in Greek. Therefore, it implies a relationship begun in the past and definitely existing at that time. He encourages believers to hold on to their **confidence.** Those who truly became part of Christ are those who continue in Him.

15-19. While it is said. The author refers to Psalm 95 in these verses. He asks a series of questions. **For some, when they had heard.** The word **some** (Gr *tines*) should rather be translated by the word **who.** This would help verse 16 fit better into the series of questions following: who, **when they had heard, did provoke: . . . But with whom was he grieved forty years? Was it not with them that had sinned . . . ? And to whom sware he that they should not enter into his rest . . . ?** The answer to all these questions is found in verses 18 and 19: **Them that believed not** and those who were guilty of **unbelief. Unbelief** kept people away from God's rest hundreds of years earlier. It could do the same in the first century. It can do the same today. The only sin that keeps us from God's eternal rest is that of **unbelief** in His Son Jesus Christ, the **Apostle and High Priest of our profession** (vs. 1) (cf. the exposition and comments of H. Kent, *The Epistle to the Hebrews,* pp. 78-80).

4:1-2. Let us therefore fear. Chapter 4 is a continuation of the thought expressed in chapter 3. The author is encouraging his readers to examine themselves, lest they not gain the promised rest because of unbelief. In chapter 3 he showed how this happened to the children of Israel. He brings the point into the present warning against falling **short** of the **promise. The gospel** was **preached** to both the children of Israel and the first century believers. The former were not profited because of a lack of faith. So it could be among the latter, given a similar lack of **faith in them that heard it.**

3-7. For we which have believed. The author testifies that those who **have believed,** himself included, were entering into that rest. It was not a future state, but something to be entered into as a result of belief. Matthew 11:28 speaks of the rest that the believer can obtain in Christ. Both the rest (Gr *anapauō*) of Matthew 11:28 and the rest (Gr *katapausis*) of Hebrews 4:3 come from the same root (Gr *pauō*) meaning to stop or rest. The place of rest for the believer is a place of quiet and relief. This potential for rest has been available **from the foundation of the world.** God rested from His work on the **seventh day.** He offers a share in that rest to all who believe in Him. The fact that the rest is still available is seen in the testimony that **it remaineth that some must enter therein.** The **unbelief** of those earlier, does not negate the promise to those who follow. God states in Psalm 95 that **To day** the promise is still available. If it was still available in David's day the author reasons that it is still available in his day.

8-11. For if Jesus had given them rest. The author summarizes his discussion that the Old Testament rest is still available by faith. The Greek word for Jesus and Joshua is exactly the same. The rest referred to here is the Canaan rest, or the promised land. That would explain the reference in verse 8b to Psalm 95 where hundreds of years later God spoke of the availability of the rest **To-day.** The author succinctly sums it up by stating **There remaineth therefore a rest to the people of God.** Because the rest still exists, the readers must be careful not to miss it because of the same **unbelief** as their ancestors. On the theological significance of "rest" as referring to the present blessing of God, cf. F. F. Bruce, *The Epistle to the Hebrews,* pp. 73-79; *contra,* as the Millennium, see G. H. Lang, *The Epistle to the Hebrews,* pp. 73 ff.

12. For the word of God. The power of the Holy Scripture is beautifully testified in this verse. It is in no way easy to escape this sharp **two-edged sword.** It is not fooled by pretense or external piety. It is able to easily divide **asunder of soul and spirit . . . joints and marrow.** It is a **discerner of the thoughts and intents of the heart.** It cuts deep in order to root out unbelief in the heart.

13. Neither is there any creature. Nothing is hidden from the eyes of God. **All things are naked and opened** to the discerning gaze of God, the One to whom we all must give account.

14-16. Seeing then that we have. Having completed his comparison between Moses and Christ, the author refers again to the concept of Christ as High Priest. Christ is a **great high priest,** one who **passed into the heavens.** The Old Testament priests passed through the veil into the Holy of Holies. Christ is obviously superior as He **passed** through the **heavens** into the very presence of God. There He abides forever (12:1). Christ is able to understand our human **infirmities** and communicate them to the Father. He **was in all points tempted like as we are,** yet was able to remain **without sin.** Because we have a **great high priest** who understands **our infirmities** and who sits next to the very throne of the Father, we can **come boldly** to that **throne.** It is not a **throne** of judgment, but one of **grace.** There we can find **mercy** and **grace** to **help in time of need.** The word **boldly** (Gr *parrēsia*) comes from the term applied to those who were citizens of Greece, able to openly say their true feelings before the throne, a privilege not accorded to slaves. We are citizens of heaven. Because of the finished work of Christ our **great high priest,** we ourselves can enter into God's very presence, openly expressing our needs. We can freely obtain the **grace** and **mercy** we need to guide us on our journey through life.

5:1-4. For every high priest. As the author develops the theme of the high priestly nature of Christ, it is his purpose to show that in that office Christ is also superior. All High Priests had been ordained to their roles. They were to **offer both gifts and sacrifices for sins.** It was important that they had the capacity to have compassion. The word compassion (Gr *metriopatheō*) is the ability to deal gently with people. It involves caring without undue harshness or judgment. It was a necessary character quality in all priests. It characterized Christ's ministry while on earth. This ability stemmed from the patience learned out of one's own **infirmities.** An honest realization of one's own weaknesses aids in the comfort of others. Being human, the priest had to sacrifice for **himself** as well as **for the people.** This ritual is elaborated in Leviticus 16:1-24. The office of a high priest could be practiced only as the result of divine calling. This calling was epitomized in the calling of Aaron. There were those in the Old Testament such as Korah (Num 16:1-35) and Saul (I Sam 13:9-11) who took it upon themselves to offer priestly offerings and they did so with dire consequences.

5-6. So also Christ glorified. Because of the truth of the preceding verse, it must be shown that Christ had a divine calling to the priesthood. Such a calling must excel that of Aaron if Christ's superiority was to be shown. To accomplish this, the author quotes Psalm 2:7, validating the sonship of Christ. Combining that quote with one from Psalm 110:4 reiterates both the heirship and the high priestly authority of Christ. Melchizedec (Gen 14:18-20) was both a king and a priest. Since Christ is said to be a priest **after the order of Melchizedec,** He follows a superior priestly lineage than that of Aaron. His lineage combines both royal and priestly functions. He is both King and Priest!

7-10. Who in the days of his flesh. These verses refer to the struggle of Christ in the Garden of Gethsemane prior to His crucifixion. They paint a most vivid picture of Christ's agony in the garden. He is said to have offered **prayers and supplications.** These were offered with **strong crying and tears.** These are increasingly powerful words to describe Christ's agony and passion. He did not direct these petitions to those around Him who could not help, but, rather to the Father, **that was able to save him from death.** As is the case with all earnest prayer, **he . . . was heard.** His prayers were answered in the resurrection, as He gained victory over death. **He . . . was heard in that** (Gr *apo*) **he feared.** The word in Greek can be correctly translated "because." He received an answer because He prayed with **fear** (Gr *eulabeia*). This denotes a reverential awe for God. This is the correct attitude for all Christians as they pray. Even in His darkest hour, Christ provided a model for us to follow. Christ, in His humanity, had to learn **obedience** through that **which he suffered.** This was a necessary part of His incarnation. He did not need to learn obedience because He was disobedient, but so that He could more fully relate to the human condition.

11-14. Of whom we have many things to say. The author interrupts his discussion of the high priestly role of Christ with a rebuke. He is obviously disappointed with the spiritual growth evidenced by his readers. Regarding their spiritual maturity, he states: **ye are dull of hearing, . . . ye have need that one teach you again, . . . are become such as have need of milk,** and are **unskillful in the word of righteousness.** The author wants to give his readers **strong meat.** He is afraid that they may not, however, be able to digest it. The sign of one who is mature is that he has the ability **to discern both good and evil.** This ability to **discern** is one developed through years of practice. The **senses** are sharpened to the point where false teaching can be easily recognized. The **good and evil** refer to truth and error in teaching, more so than in discerning morality from immorality.

B. The Superiority of a Maturing Faith. 6:1-20.

6:1-3. Therefore leaving the principles. The author is not content to allow his readers to remain in their immature (5:11-14) state. He desires to move on from the basic **principles of the doctrine of Christ.** Surely in the list of six **principles** which follows, he was not attempting to provide an exhaustive creed. This list is not meant to provide all the basic doctrines of Christianity. The doctrines listed, however, can be assumed to be examples of the **first principles of the oracles of God** (5:12). They include two dealing with salvation: **repentance from dead works and faith toward God, . . . the doctrine of baptisms, and of laying on of hands** are two post-salvation expressions of belief. The word **baptisms** is plural signifying either both the Judaistic and the Christian baptisms, or water baptism and Spirit baptism (the latter being the more likely). The **resurrection of the dead, and of eternal judgment** are eschatological doctrines which are learned early in the life of new believers. The author recognizes God's involvement in such a moving on to Christian maturity. He states that it is possible only **if God permit.**

4-6. For it is impossible. In these three verses, the author issues a strong warning to his readers. The exact interpretation of these verses has been widely disputed. See Lenski, *Interpretation of Hebrews,* pp. 185-187, he views the apostate as one who was saved and has fallen from salvation; Bruce, pp. 110-125 and Hughes, pp. 206-222,

view the danger of apostasy as being a real danger to the professing Christian, but do not explain how a true believer could fall from salvation. They imply that the person referred to may only "know" Christ by baptismal profession and not by real experience; Archer, *The Epistle to the Hebrews,* p. 40, and Chafer, *Salvation,* view those referred to here as coming close to salvation, but having their faith aborted by unbelief; Kent, pp. 113-114, and Westcott, p. 165, argue that this is a hypothetical case, maintaining that it is impossible for a true believer to fall from salvation and if he could, it would be impossible for him to be saved again since he would crucify Christ afresh to himself. Perhaps it is best to interpret that the author is referring to those who have actually had a salvation experience. All of the Greek participles used to describe those about whom the author is speaking indicate an actual conversion experience. These are spoken of as having been **once enlightened,** as having **tasted of the heavenly gift,** having been made **partakers of the Holy Ghost,** having **tasted the good word of God, and the powers of the world to come.** The word **taste** (Gr *geuomal*) carries the broader meaning of partaking of something in its entirety. In Acts 10:10 it refers to partaking in a meal, not just tasting the food. In Hebrews 2:9, Christ **tasted** death. He fully partook of it. One who tasted **the heavenly gift,** fully partook of it. The author states that if those who met the above conditions (believers) **fall away,** that they cannot be renewed **again unto repentance.**

Since those referred to in the passage have genuinely experienced salvation, it would be impossible for them to fall away and be renewed (reborn) again to repentance. A true believer is not in danger of losing his salvation. However, there are always those who merely profess Christ (see the Parable of the Sower in Matthew 13) and have never truly been born again. These false professors are in danger of apostasy and all apostates go "out from us, but they were not of us" (I Jn 2:19). Thus, the argument of these verses clearly states that a true believer cannot fall away from God, for he would then be outside the grace of God and the opportunity of salvation. No one can be saved, then become unsaved, and then be saved again.

Ryrie states: "There is no such thing as being saved a second time (though it might be convenient sometimes!); therefore, you cannot retreat but must make progress" (*Biblical Theology of the New Testament,* p. 257). To attempt to reach that moment again in life would indeed be to **crucify . . . the Son of God afresh.** Only once in life do we partake of that substitutionary atonement of the cross. At that point in time, salvation becomes effective throughout the remainder of our lives. All the above participles are in the aorist tense. They indicate a "point in time" experience, one which cannot be relived over and over again. The author does not mean that Christians who sin cannot be renewed, or he would have said so. He states that they cannot be renewed **unto repentance.** The author uses strong language in this warning. He wants his immature readers to be well aware of the dangers of trying to live a halfhearted, lazy Christian life. We cannot undo the hurts that we cause people by living anything less than fruitful, productive lives.

7-8. For the earth which drinketh. The same thought is carried through in these verses. **Earth** that is fruitful bringing **forth herbs . . . receiveth blessing. But that which beareth thorns and briers** is eventually **burned** because of its fruitlessness. The professing Christian living in sin and unfruitfulness is in grave danger with God.

9-13. But, beloved, we are persuaded. Even though the author has thus warned his readers, he is **persuaded better things** of them. He reminds them that he is warning the false professor and not the true professor of Christ. He encourages them by assuring that **God** will not **forget** their **work and labor of love.** He admonishes them to continue in the **same diligence** all the way to **the end** of their lives. They are charged not to be **slothful.** They are to follow after the examples of those who inherited God's **promises** as a result of whole lives lived **through faith and patience.** Such a one was Abraham.

13-17. For when God made promise. The author uses Abraham as an example of one who practiced the diligence of a fruitful life. In so doing, he quotes God's promise to Abraham in Genesis 22:16-17. This is a restatement of His promise in Genesis 12:2-3. God backed up His promise with His own integrity. He signed His name to the promise. "Thus both God's authority and His integrity were at stake," (Ross, *Wycliffe Bible Commentary,* p. 918). Abraham had to wait many years to realize the fulfillment of this promise. He waited with **faith and patience.** He then was rewarded with the fulfilling of the promise through his sons. God had **confirmed** the promise **by an oath.** God realized the importance of oaths to men. He condescended for man's sake and confirmed His promise with such an oath.

18-20. That by two immutable things. These **two things** are God's promise (vs. 17) and His **oath** (vs. 17). God could not break a promise or give a false oath. That would be in total contradiction to His nature. Therefore, these **two things** give us a **strong consolation. We have hope** in God's promises. He is an **anchor** to our **soul.** He is **both sure and stedfast.** He does not withdraw from those who seek **refuge** in Him. We all need to have **hope.** What greater source of **hope** could we have than that which is found in Christ? He has already entered **within the veil** and has been made an eternal **high priest** whose function is to intermediate for us with the Father. Our **hope** of access to the **sure** and **steadfast anchor** of God lies in the person and work of our Saviour and **high** priest, Jesus Christ.

C. The Superiority of the New Priesthood. 7:1-10:21.

1. Christ is a superior priest. 7:1-8:5.

7:1-3. For this Melchizedec. Melchizedec appears in Scripture in only two places: Genesis 14:18-20 and Psalm 110:4. The author of Hebrews draws his preliminary discussion of Melchizedec from the Genesis account. His point is to show that Melchizedec is an Old Testament type of Christ. His basic thrust is to prove the superiority of the Melchizedecian priesthood to the levitical. Then he will show that Christ as a priest after the order of Melchizedec is also superior to the levitical priesthood. These first three verses lay the historical background out of which these arguments are drawn. Melchizedec is said to be **Without father, without mother, without descent, having neither beginning of days, nor end of life; but made like unto the Son of God.** There is no record in Scripture of the genealogy of Melchizedec. This is not to conclude that he was not fully human. It does, however, show a type of Christ, **the Son of God,** who also fits the above description. The name Melchizedec literally means **King of righteousness.** He was **King of Salem** (or Jerusalem). **Salem** means peace. Therefore by his name and location he was the **King** of both **righteousness** and **peace,** two attributes which further link him in type to Christ.

9-10. Now consider how great this man was. Abraham was the grand patriarch of all Judaism. Yet, he gave tithes to Melchizedec. The levitical priests had **a commandment to take tithes of the people.** It was expected that they would demand tithes. Melchizedec made no such demand. Abraham did not have to give him a tithe. Yet he did so, of his own will. The author argues that this shows that Abraham considered Melchizedec superior enough to willingly and humbly tithe of his spoils (Gr *akrothinion*), meaning literally of the top of the heap or the best of the spoils usually reserved for deity. Melchizedec showed his worthiness by accepting the tithe of such a great man of God. He then even proceeded to bless **him that had the promises.** Melchizedec blessed Abraham. How crucial this is. For indeed, **the less is blessed of the better.** Obviously, compared with Melchizedec, even mighty Abraham, founder of Judaism, was **the less.** In verse 8, the author contrasts **here** and **there. Here,** in the levitical priesthood as practiced in the first century, **men that die receive tithes. There,** under the Melchizedecian priesthood, we have no record of the death of the one who received tithes. The Melchizedec priesthood is assumed to live on forever. In a manner of speaking, even **Levi . . . payed tithes** to Melchizedec. Abraham was Levi's great-grandfather. It would not be stretching the idea of Old Testament corporate responsibility too far, to say that Abraham, even Levi himself, the one from whom all priests were to come, paid tithe to Melchizedec.

11-12. If therefore perfection. The word **perfection** (Gr *teleiosis*) means "complete," as when something has fulfilled its role. The question herein is if the **Levitical priesthood** had fulfilled the task of enabling men to relate fully to God, then why would **another** priesthood be necessary? The question demands the answer that **perfection** was not reached by the **Levitical priesthood.** It must be changed to provide that complete relationship between God and man. The levitical priest and the levitical law were intimately connected. If one was to be changed then a change in the other must follow.

13-17. For he of whom these things. Christ was not of the tribe of Levi. He came from Judah, **of which tribe Moses spake nothing concerning priesthood.** In fact, Christ was a priest not after any regulations in **the law of a carnal commandment.** He was ordained by divine commandment. To prove this, Psalm 110:4 is quoted. Christ belonged to a special priesthood ordained by special decree of God, the Father.

18-19. For there is verily a disannulling. The Mosaic law was temporary, that was its original intent. By its nature it included **weakness and unprofitableness.** Therefore, by the **bringing in of a better hope,** the former **commandment** was abrogated or declared void (Gr *athetesis*). Furthermore, through this **better hope,** we have the ability to **draw nigh unto God** (the **perfection** lacking in verse 11).

20-22. And inasmuch as not without. The priesthood of Jesus was the result of **an oath** from God. Psalm 110:4 is quoted as evidence. This **oath** is lacking in the levitical priesthood. Therefore Christ's priesthood is again proved superior. Christ was made **surety of a better testament.** The author introduces here the concept of a superior covenant. He will elaborate on it later. The focus here is on the superiority of Christ who is the **surety** (gr *enguos*) of that **testament.** This is the only usage of this word in the New Testament. It implies a "guarantor" or one who stands good for a debt. Christ Himself stands good for this new **testament.**

23-25. And they truly were many priests. In order to further prove the superiority of Christ, the author shows that in contrast to the old covenant in which **were many priests,** Christ stands alone in **an unchangeable priesthood.** The levitical priests were subject to death, Christ **continueth ever.** Christ **is able ... to save them to the uttermost. By him,** man is able to **come unto God.** The old law could not make such a claim. Christ lives eternally for one purpose, that of making **intercession for** man. The word **intercession** (Gr *entyngchanō*) means to plead for someone. Christ lives eternally for the purpose of pleading for those who would **come unto God.**

26-28. For such an high priest. Christ is herein described as **holy, harmless, undefiled, separate from sinners, and made higher than the heavens.** Because of these attributes he needs not **offer up sacrifice ... for his own sins.** The priests were commanded to offer up sacrifices for their own sin (Lev 16:6) but it is likely that they did so on a **daily** basis, even as others did (Lev 4:2-3). The beautiful thing about this passage is that it shows Christ as both the **high priest** and as the **sacrifice. He offered up himself** on the cross of Calvary as the **sacrifice** for the sins of man. He was the perfect sacrifice. Therefore, He needed be offered only **once.** Christ has all the authority of a superior High Priest, yet all the love necessary to become the very sacrifice for our sin. Again, **the law maketh men high priests which have infirmity.** But Christ who was confirmed not by law, but by **the word of the oath** of the Father (Ps 110:4) is **consecrated** forever. The word **consecrated** (Gr *teleioō*) means to be "made perfect" **for evermore.** How much superior a priesthood is His!

8:1-2. Now of the things which we have spoken. This verse contains the **sum** (Gr *kephalaion*) or the main point of that which the author wishes to say. **We have ... an high priest.** He **is set on the right hand of the throne.** He is **in the heavens.** These are three of the most basic concepts true to the heart of the epistle. Christ is furthermore **A minister of the ... true tabernacle.** This refers to heaven, the **true** abiding place of God, **himself** (7:27). It is not temporary. It is not crude in its construction. It was made by the very hand of **the Lord.** It endures forever.

3-5. For every high priest. It is the main function of **every high priest ... to offer gifts and sacrifices.** Christ is no exception. That which He offered was the ultimate sacrifice, i.e. Himself. The word **offer** (Gr *prospherō*), used of Christ, makes His one sacrifice of Himself correspond to the liturgy of the priests. Again, His superiority to those who must continually **offer** (Gr *prospherein*) **sacrifices** is clearly demonstrated. If Christ **were on earth, he should not be a priest.** The levitical order was already set. Christ would not have qualified to serve under it. Yet that order was only an **example and shadow of**

heavenly things. Christ's priesthood belonged to the order of **heavenly things.** Anything that came before it was a mere **example** or **shadow.** Even **Moses,** as he built the **tabernacle** in the wilderness, was **admonished of God . . . to make the tabernacle . . . according to the** heavenly **pattern.** The word **pattern** (Gr *typos*) originally referred to the mark or imprint left by an engraving tool on a mold. Even as the imprint was a copy of the original, so was the **tabernacle** built by **Moses** to be an **example** of the **heavenly** tabernacle. See S. Wemp, *Preaching from the Tabernacle.*

2. Christ offers a superior covenant. 8:6-10:21.

6. But now hath he obtained. The superiority of Christ is vividly stated in this verse. First, **he** has **a more excellent ministry.** Secondly, **he is the mediator of a better covenant.** Thirdly, this **covenant . . . was established upon better promises.** For the first time, Christ is referred to as **the mediator** (Gr *mesitēs*). This was a legal term given to one who arbitrates between two parties. Christ is indeed the arbitrator between God and men. The concept of the **better covenant** is introduced and elaborated upon in the verses which follow.

7-12. For if that first covenant. The author returns to his argument of 7:11 that **if that first covenant had been faultless,** there would have been no need for a **second.** Obviously, the **first** was not **faultless.** To verify that point the author quotes from Jeremiah 31:31-34 in his next five verses. These are words of God written hundreds of years earlier. They prove that even then a **new covenant** was promised. The author continues his pattern of carefully validating everything he has to say from the Old Testament Scriptures. God Himself found **fault** with the old covenant. That is why He promised that in the future He would **make a new covenant with the house of Israel and with the house of Judah.** This **new covenant** will not be **according to the covenant . . . made with their fathers.** It

will be totally new and different. It is to be based on the **surety** of God's own Son (7:22). This **new covenant** is to be a far more personal one. God's laws will be placed **into their mind** and **hearts.** There will be a close personal relationship between **God** and his **people.** They shall **all . . . know** God, **from the least, to the greatest.** God **will be merciful to** them. **Their sins and iniquities** will He **remember no more.** All believers will be able to daily have access to the Father Himself through the sacrifice of His Son, the High Priest.

13. In that he saith. The writer boldly asserts that the old covenant (or law) is **Now that which decayeth and waxeth old . . . ready to vanish away.** He does so on the testimony of God in Jeremiah which he has just quoted. The old covenant was to the Jews. This new covenant was also given to them, yet it includes all who **come unto God** by the person of Christ. For indeed Christ is able to save them **to the uttermost** (7:25).

9:1. Then verily the first covenant. In chapter 9, the author gives a somewhat detailed account of the old covenant. His purpose, again, is to show the superiority of the new covenant. He does this by showing that the old covenant, even with its **ordinances of divine service** and its **worldly sanctuary,** was totally unable to inwardly cleanse hearts.

2-5. For there was a tabernacle made. The author describes the **tabernacle** in some detail. The Holy Place is called the **sanctuary** (Gr *hagios*). It contained **the candlestick, and the table, and the showbread; . . . after the second veil** is the **Holiest of all** (literally, "holy things among holy things"). It is portrayed as having **had the golden censer** and **the ark.** The **ark** contained the **golden pot, . . . Aaron's rod . . . and the tables of the covenant.** The placing of the **golden censer** with the Holy of Holies has at times been a source of confusion. Actually the **golden censer** (Gr *thymiatērion*) refers to the altar of incense. Exodus 30:6 tells us it is to be placed "before the veil that is by the ark of the testimony" or in the

Holy Place. Do we have an error here in the placement of the altar? Definitely not! The author changes his language from the **wherein was** (Gr *en hē*) of verse 2 to **which had** (a Greek participle) in verse 4. He did not say the altar was in the Holy of Holies. He obviously, however, wanted to make a connection between the altar and the **Holiest of all.** The altar was a type of Christ. "It belonged to the Holiest because it typified Christ's Person and intercessory work in the Holiest of all. . . . It was so near the veil that the moment the curtain was rent in twain from the top to the bottom the fragrant smoke of the incense entered the Holiest, but he does declare it belonged to the Holiest. So then the apparent imperfection is really a most beautiful evidence of the perfection of Holy Writ" (H. A. Ironside, *Studies in the Epistle to the Hebrews,* p. 105). Verse 5 includes the statement, **of which we cannot now speak particularly.** The author wanted to specifically mention the items in the **tabernacle,** but did not see the need to go into detail about them.

6-7. Now when these things. The **priests** themselves could only minister in the **first tabernacle** (Holy Place). The **high priest** went **into the second,** but only **once every year.** The author introduces the concept of the necessity of **blood** in the process of atonement. No one could enter God's presence without the protection of the blood. This **blood** was offered both **for himself, and for the errors of the people.** The word **errors** (Gr *agnoēma*) refers to sins of ignorance as contrasted to purposive acts of disobedience (Num 15:27-28).

8-10. The Holy Ghost this signifying. The **Holy Ghost** is the author of the law and of the first covenantal system. The very nature of the existence and design of the tabernacle (both were God-given) showed **that the way into the holiest of all was** barred. As long as **the first tabernacle** (Holy Place) **was yet standing,** it blocked the way into the **holiest of all.** No Hebrew dared venture through the one into the other (except the High Priest

once a year) until Christ severed the veil at His death. The author acknowledges the temporary nature of the whole tabernacle system when he declares it **a figure for the time then present.** He declares what is perhaps the greatest weakness of the old sacrificial system when he states that it **could not make him that did the service perfect, as pertaining to the conscience.** The cleansing of this time was basically an outward cleansing. It could not reach into the **conscience** of a man, to remove the sting of guilt or hurt. The author further declares the surface nature of the system in implying it **stood only in meats and drinks, and divers washings, and carnal ordinances.** There were many levitical regulations regarding permissible foods and drinks (Deut 14:3-20; Num 6:2-3). There were laws regarding **washings** (Num 8:6-7, 21; Lev 6:27-28). All these were surface. None delved into the heart of a man. They were **imposed . . . until the time of reformation** (Gr *diorthōsis*). This **time** is usually thought as being the time that Christ broke into history, severing the veil; creating **a new and living way** (10:20) to approach the Father. A **way** that would cause men to search the depths of their hearts for anything unclean that would separate them and Christ.

11-12. But Christ being come an high priest. The author describes the better way of Christ. He is **an high priest.** He serves in **a greater and more perfect tabernacle. Christ** serves in heaven. He did not offer the **blood of goats and calves.** Quite the contrary, He shed **his own blood,** obtaining **eternal redemption for us.** Vine, *The Epistle to the Hebrews,* pp. 93-94, notes that the verb "having obtained" is in the middle voice, indicating Christ's personal interest in us and His unutterable love for us. This was not a day to day nor year to year **redemption.** It was one which would stand the test of all time, unto eternity.

13-14. For if the blood of bulls. Again, the contrast between external and internal cleansing is placed before us. **If the blood of bulls and of goats and the ashes of an heifer** were sufficient to cleanse **the flesh,** then **How much more shall the blood of Christ** be able to cleanse deep into the **conscience?** Notice that we are purged in order **to serve.** All of our Christian life must be pledged to glorifying and serving God. He that is able to **save . . . to the uttermost** (7:25) is worthy of our uttermost service.

15-17. And for this cause. We find here the **promise of eternal inheritance.** This **promise** brings out another important meaning of the word **testament** (Gr *diathēkē*). **A testament** can refer to a will. A will only becomes effective **by means of death.** The only way to gain an **inheritance** is through being named in the will of **the testator.** Without **the death of the testator,** the will is of **no strength.**

18-22. Whereupon neither the first testament. The author gives an example of the necessity of **blood** even in the **first testament.** In fact, at Sinai Moses **dedicated** the law with **blood. He sprinkled both the book, and all the people.** This account is taken from Exodus 24:3-8. At a later date he also dedicated **both the tabernacle, and all the vessels of the ministry** by sprinkling them **with blood. Almost all things are by the law purged with blood.** He says **almost all things** because there were rare cases when things were purified with other agents, such as fire or water (Num 31:21-24). The author makes then, a generalized statement that **without shedding of blood is no remission.** The word **remission** (Gr *aphesis*) literally means forgiveness. Simply stated, **without shedding of blood** there is no forgiveness of sin.

23-26. It was therefore necessary. It is acceptable for **the patterns of things in the heavens** to be **purified** with such animal blood. **The heavenly things themselves** must be purged with a much purer **sacrifice.** It is not to be assumed from this, that **the heavenly things** are in any way tainted or in need of such purging. The author is merely drawing a logical conclusion to his discussion. How

much better of sacrifice is required for the real thing than is necessary for the shadows or copies? We discover Christ's responsibility in **heaven.** He is there **to appear in the presence of God for us.** His is not a sacrifice made **often.** Rather, **once** did He appear **to put away sin by the sacrifice of himself.** The word **put away** (Gr *athetesis*) means to annul. Christ has annulled or done away with the grip of **sin** over us. Now through Him we can have victory over **sin.** The phrases **in the end of the world** of verse 26 and **them that look for him** of verse 28 indicate that the author viewed the return of Christ as imminent in his time.

27-28. And as it is appointed. It is appointed for all men **to die.** They only die **once.** After that there is no more opportunity for forgiveness, only **the judgment.** Because men die once and then face **judgment,** the analogy is drawn that Christ died **once.** The writer quotes Isaiah 53:12 in stating, **Christ was once offered to bear the sins of many.** His **second** appearance will be one **without sin.** He comes again to culminate His plan of redemption. He takes believers, **them that look for him,** back into heaven to abide with Him forever. The word **look for** (Gr *apekdechomai*) implies those who eagerly await his coming. Surely, as believers, we all "eagerly await" the splitting of the skies, the sound of the trumpet, signifying the return of Christ for His own.

10:1-3. For the law having a shadow. The **law** was only a **shadow** of the better covenant which was to follow. It was not even the exact likeness or **image** (Gr *eikōn*) of it, but something far less. It can never make its followers **perfect** (Gr *teleioō*), carrying the sense of "complete" or "mature." The author employs logic in concluding that if the above were possible, then the law would have fulfilled itself. It would have done its job and **ceased.** In fact, the exact opposite is true. The law itself creates a **remembrance . . . of sins.**

4-10. For it is not possible. The author makes a strong statement about the inadequacy of the law when he states that **it is not possible that the blood of bulls and of goats should take away sins.** This particular sentence begins with the words **not impossible** (Gr *adynaton*). Placing the words **not impossible** first in Greek adds emphasis to the futility of the task. The author quotes Psalm 40:6-7 in the next five verses. He uses these words of David typologically to refer to Christ. It is developed as a conversation between Christ and the Father. It is not quoted exactly, its purpose being illustrative in nature. Christ came to **do the will** of the Father. It is **by** that **will** that we **are sanctified . . . once for all.**

11-14. And every priest standeth. The point is driven home hard in these verses. **Every priest** offers **daily . . . the same sacrifices.** Over and over again the offerings are made. What an incredible exercise in futility. They **can never take away sins.** In contrast, Christ **offered one sacrifice,** Himself, and **sat down.** Psalm 110:1 is quoted. He sits waiting **till his enemies be made his footstool.** His **one offering** has **perfected** His followers **for ever.**

15-17. Whereof the Holy Ghost. From the Old Testament, as an added validation of the above, the author quotes Jeremiah 31:33-34. He acknowledges the inspiration of the **Holy Ghost** in the Scripture. He sees the work of Christ as the fulfillment of the promise in Jeremiah.

18-21. Now where remission of these is. Once we find **remission** (Gr *aphesis*) or forgiveness for sin, there is no need for additional **offering.** See J. Brown, *An Exposition of the Epistle to the Hebrews,* pp. 458-461, for an excellent discussion on the "assurance of faith." The author makes one of his grandest statements in the entire epistle. Since all the above is true, they can have **boldness** and enter the **holiest,** covered **by the blood of Jesus.** No more need for earthly high priests or offerings. They have access into the **holiest . . . By a new and living way.** When Christ's **flesh** was torn on the cross, so was the **veil** in the temple.

The final barrier into **the holiest** was gone. Christ is the heavenly **high priest** charged with the care of the entire **house of God.** The assurance of our faith does not rest in our ability to believe but in the full satisfaction of the efficacy of Christ's priesthood which provides our acceptance with God (see Owen, p. 199).

II. A NEW AND LIVING FAITH. 10:22-12:29.

A. A Superior Promise. 10:22-37.

22-25. Let us draw near with a true heart. The author encourages his readers to **draw near** to God. He introduces the importance of **faith** in God. This will be elaborated on later in the epistle. Through being **sprinkled** by the blood of Christ, their **hearts** are clean. He speaks of their **bodies** being **washed with pure water.** This refers to Christian baptism. It can also be seen as a fulfillment of the levitical cleansings as portrayed in Leviticus 16:4. The readers are encouraged to **hold fast** to their **faith without wavering** and **one another to provoke unto love and to good works.** They are not to forsake **the assembling of** themselves **together.** Regular church assemblies were the normal practice of the early Christians. Attendace at these assemblies is urged for their own sakes, that they might benefit thereby. They are to exhort **one another.** Apparently, from the context, some were not fulfilling all of the above. Instead of slacking up because of the expected soon return of Christ, they are exhorted to do **so much the more, as ye see the day approaching.**

26-31. For if we sin willfully. There is a difference between this warning and that of 6:4-6. In those verses, there was no doubt that the author was speaking to Christians. There cannot be the same assurance in this passage. The author does not speak of those who had **received . . . the truth** (Christ), but of those who had **received the knowledge of the truth. Knowledge** never saved anyone. II Peter 2:20-21 speaks of false prophets and teachers who had a "knowledge" (the same Greek word *epiginōskō* as Hebrews 10:26 "of the Lord and Saviour Jesus Christ." Even after they gained such **knowledge** they remained as before, **false prophets and teachers.** There is further evidence in verse 29 that they had never accepted the new covenant. There they are said to have **trodden under foot the Son of God.** The phrase **trodden under foot** (Gr *katapateō*) originally referred to a situation where a man was going to buy a piece of land. If he felt the price was right and he was being dealt with fairly, he would step over blood sprinkled on the ground by the owner. If he thought he was being cheated he stepped on the blood in front of witnesses. Thus, those who with their feet tread on Christ, both reject His covenant and cast aspersions on His integrity. For such an act there can be no result but **judgment.** Sinning **wilfully** after receiving **knowledge** of Christ can only be seen as deliberate rejection of that **knowledge.** For such **sin** of unbelief there is no **sacrifice.** If one who **despised Moses' law** was killed **without mercy,** how much greater **punishment** for one who rejected **the Son of God, counted the blood . . . unholy,** and who **hath done despite unto the Spirit of grace?** Deuteronomy 32:35-36 is quoted as testimony to the judgment of God. For those who have **wilfully** rejected Christ it will indeed be a **fearful thing** to one day **fall into the hands of the living God.** Apparently among the readers there were those who had made only an outward commitment to the new covenant. These passages are intended as a warning to them.

32-34. But call to remembrance. In a much softer tone, the writer encourages the readers to remember their earlier years as Christians. They had faithfully **endured a great fight of afflictions.** They had been **made a gazingstock** (Gr *theatrizō*). They were publicly exposed for their faith. They **had compassion** with those (not **me**) who were in **bonds.** They even took **joyfully the spoiling of** their **goods.** They had endured all this with a strong and unwavering faith.

35-37. Cast not away therefore. The readers are encouraged not to throw away the **confidence** that had sustained them in their earlier trials. They are admonished to have **patience** so that they can endure to the end and **receive the promise.** They are to do **the will of God.**

B. A Superior Faith. 10:38-12:29.

1. Old Testament examples of the superior faith. 10:38-11:40.

38-39. Now the just shall live by faith. Habakkuk 2:4 is here quoted. The author closes this chapter with a note of reassurance. He knows that they **are not of them who draw back unto perdition** (Gr *apōleia*). **Perdition** carries the sense of destruction or ruin. He is convinced that his readers are **of them that believe to the saving of the soul.** He is supremely confident in the endurance of a **faith** filled life. This would again reinforce the idea that the readers in chapter 6 are genuine believers.

11:1-3. Now faith is the substance. In this chapter the author gives an elaborate treatise on **faith.** Faith is the **substance** (Gr *hypostasis*) or assurance upon which all **hope** is based. It is the **evidence of things not seen.** Through **faith,** objective reality is not necessary. Through **faith** we can have confidence in the fulfilling of God's promises. The Old Testament fathers **obtained a good** report from God because of their faith. No one saw the act of creation, yet by **faith** we know **that the worlds were framed by the word of God.**

4-7. By faith Abel offered. The writer begins a series of illustrations centered around Old Testament leaders who **by faith** fulfilled God's plan for them. The first section deals with the **faith** of those before the flood. **Abel, Enoch,** and **Noah** are listed. **Enoch** is paid especially high tribute in that it is said that **he pleased God.** There is reassurance in the fact that God **is a rewarder of them that diligently seek him. Noah** had great **faith** in that he **prepared an ark** on the basis of a warning about **things not seen . . .**

through **faith Abel . . . obtained witness that he was righteous, . . . Enoch . . . pleased God** and **Noah . . . became heir of the righteousness.** It should be observed that the author fully accepts the historicity of these events (including the flood). He further reminds that **without faith it is impossible to please him** (vs. 6).

8-12. By faith Abraham. A whole section is reserved to discuss the **faith** of **Abraham** and **Sarah. Abraham** had **faith to go out . . . not knowing whither he went.** Abraham followed God even though he did not know where his journey would lead. Because of their **faith, Abraham** and **Sara** became the parents of a family whose number was **as the stars of the sky . . . and as the sand . . . innumerable.**

13-16. These all died in faith. All of the above had enough **faith** to recognize the **promises** of God even though they were **afar off.** Their goals were not of this **earth.** They looked forward to **a better country.** Because of their **faith, God is not ashamed to be called their God.** In fact, in the Scripture (Mt 22:32) God calls Himself "the God of Abraham . . . Isaac . . . and Jacob."

17-22. By faith Abraham. In this section we find the above three men named, along with **Esau** and **Joseph.** There is some discussion of the phrase **only begotten son** in verse 17. **Isaac** was not **Abraham's** only son. The phrase (Gr *monogenēs*) refers to "uniqueness" or the quality of being one of a kind. **Isaac** was the only child of promise, therefore he was unique. Verse 18 verifies that point. The same word is used of Christ in John 3:16, etc.

23-29. By faith Moses. Another whole section deals with the **faith** of **Moses.** Verse 23 actually deals with the faith of his parents. The rest of the verses speak of his **faith** in rejecting the Egyptian way of life. He refused to **enjoy the pleasures of sin for a season.** The eyes of faith enabled him to see **him** who is **invisible,** i.e. Christ. Through his **faith he kept the passover.** Through the act, he saved the lives of hundreds of Hebrews.

Faith enabled him to lead his people through the **Red sea** to safety.

30-31. By faith the walls of Jericho. Two verses describe acts of **faith** during the conquest of Canaan. The **walls of Jericho** were downed **By faith. Rahab** was saved from destruction because of her **faith.** Yes, even a harlot can be saved **By faith.** Notice again how each of these events is viewed as being historically reliable and literal.

32-38. And what shall I more say? The author wants to go on, but time constrains him. So many more deserve recognition. Verses 33 through 38 list mighty deeds of **faith** done by those throughout biblical history. Daniel, **Who . . . stopped the mouths of lions,** Shadrach, Meshach and Abednego who all **Quenched the violence of fire,** Zechariah who was **stoned** and Elijah who **wandered about in sheepskins** are but a few examples of such **faith.**

39-40. And these all. The important thing is that these all persisted in their **faith** even though they **received not the promise.** Genuine (saving) faith is that which persists until the end, not a mere temporary show of emotion. True faith continues to believe the truth! Again the author shows the superiority of the new covenant. God saved this **better thing** or fulfillment of **the promise** for their age. In fact, **without** those of the new covenant, even the mightiest champion of the **faith** in the Old Testament could **not be made perfect.**

2. The Author and Finisher of the faith. 12:1-29.

12:1-4. Wherefore seeing we also are compassed about. All of the giants mentioned in the previous chapter form an impressive group of **witnesses** to **faith** in God. They provide a source of inspiration and example for the readers. The Christian life is portrayed as a **race.** It must be run with **patience.** It must be run **Looking unto Jesus.** Christ is the beginning and the end. He is the goal of the Christian life. He is both the **author** and the **finisher of our faith.** What a tribute it is to Christ's love for us that it can be said He went to the cross propelled by a sense of **joy** (Gr *chara*). The readers are admonished to **consider** the example of Christ and His willingness to suffer. When they sense they are becoming **wearied and faint,** they have only to look at Christ for encouragement. Apparently they had not yet suffered persecution to the point of shedding **blood.** One look at Christ's shed blood on the cross would silence their complaining.

5-8. And ye have forgotten. In this section the author quotes Proverbs 3: 11-12. The readers have been experiencing suffering. They must be shown that such anguish is really a growth process. Through **chastening** they can come to know God in a personal way **(as with sons).** To not respond to chastening for His sake, is not to belong to His family. These, the author calls **bastards** (or illegitimate children professing to be in God's family, but not His real children). His children receive His discipline. To be able to sin and never be chastened, means one is not truly saved.

9-11. Furthermore we have had fathers. If we have had **reverence** (Gr *entrepomai*) or respect for our earthly **fathers,** how much more should we **be in subjection** to our heavenly **Father?** Earthly fathers are inconsistent in their discipline, but God chastens us so that we might learn to **be partakers of his holiness.** We are **exercised** by discipline. The word **exercised** (Gr *gymnazō*) literally means to train, as for an athletic contest. In other words **chastening** is a training process by which we get in shape spiritually. Its end result is the development **of righteousness.**

12-17. Wherefore lift up the hands. Discouragement and a lack of understanding of God's **chastening** (vs. 11) has caused the readers' **hands** to **hang down** and their **knees** to become **feeble.** The words **hang down** (Gr *pariēmi*) mean to be weakened or listless. The word **feeble** (Gr *paraluō*) means to be disabled, even paralyzed. Together they

are quoted from Isaiah 35:3 and present the picture of those who have become spiritually crippled. Verse 13 is taken from Proverbs 4:25-27. The readers are encouraged to pursue **straight paths** so that the infirmities described above will not **be turned out of the way** (Gr *ektrepō*), a medical term meaning dislocated. Thus the infirmity would be worsened. There would be less chance of it being **healed.** In their dealings with each other they are to pursue **peace . . . and holiness.** The admonition in verse 15 is taken from an illustration in Deuteronomy 29:18. From the context of the entire epistle, we know that there were those among the readers who were not remaining faithful. When a few slip away from the truth, it is easier for **many** to **be defiled.** This entire section consists of warnings to the entire group to help and encourage each other in the faith. **Esau** is an example of what can happen when one takes his eyes off God. He sold his **birthright for one morsel of meat.** Genesis 25:29-34 relates the account. Later, upon realizing the consequences of his act, there was nothing he could do. **He found no place** or opportunity **of repentance** (Gen 27:38). How often the consequences of sin limit our service in later years.

18-21. For ye are not come. Another comparison is drawn between the old and the new. The scene at Mount Sinai in Exodus 19 when God gave the law is vividly described. Under the old covenant when men directly faced God, the scene was one of **blackness, tempest,** and **fear.** Man faced death even by touching where God stood. An animal that strayed onto the holy **mountain** must be **stoned** or killed with a **dart.** In that way it would not be touched, resulting in the death of the one touching it (Ex 19:12-13). This scene, so terrible that Moses is quoted as saying, **I exceedingly fear and quake** (a quote not found in Scripture, but inferred from several passages), is contrasted in verses 22 through 24 with the new **mount** where Christians will confront God.

22-24. But ye are come unto mount Zion. How much better the confrontation between God and man under the new covenant! We **come unto** the very **city of the living God.** The words **are come** (Gr *proserchomai*) are in the perfect tense in Greek, emphasizing the certainty of the fact. Upon acceptance of Christ as personal Saviour, Christians gain access to a figurative **mount Zion.** They must wait, however, until death or the Lord's return to enjoy that access to its fullest. The names of those believers are **written in heaven,** in the Book of Life. In **heaven** we come to **angels, . . . to God, . . . and to the spirits of just men, to Jesus** Himself, and **to the blood.** The **blood** being that which was shed on the cross, ratifying the **new covenant.** This is the only time that a different word for **new** is used. The word **new** (Gr *neos*) refers to newness or recency in time. The **covenant** is literally a **new** one. It was then less than fifty years old. Returning to his prevalent theme, the blood **speaketh better things than that of Abel.** Again, the superiority of the new over the old is clearly demonstrated.

25-27. See that ye refuse not him. The parallel argument that runs throughout Hebrews is present here. In the old covenant, Israel did not hearken to the voice of God as He spoke **on earth** at Mount Sinai. They lived lives that were continually spotted by disobedience and rebellion. They **escaped not** from punishment for their actions. How **much more** then, will those be punished who **turn away** from God as He **speaketh from heaven** through Christ? Exodus 19:18 tells us God's **voice . . . shook the earth.** Haggai 2:6 states that God will again **shake** both **earth** and **heaven** (Gr *ouranos*). **Heaven** refers to the cosmic heavens or the universe. This shaking will be done only **once more,** probably at the occasion of the return of Christ. All that is temporal (that which is made) will be removed. Only the eternal will **remain.**

28-29. Wherefore we receiving a kingdom. The **kingdom** which the readers are in the process of **receiving** (Gr *paralambanō*) is unshakable. The use of the Greek present tense for the word **receiving** indicates that there were those who were accepting Christ at that time, thus **receiving** the **kingdom.** They had not yet, however, experienced its final benefits. The word **grace** (Gr *charis*) impliles gratitude or thankfulness. We must have grateful hearts with which **we may serve God.** The chapter closes with a quote from Deuteronomy 4:24 that **God is a consuming fire.** This was evident in Sinai and should cause Christians to take very seriously the commands of God given in Scripture.

III. A NEW AND LIVING LOVE. 13:1-25.

A. A Loving Continuation. 13:1-19.

13:1-3. Let brotherly love continue. This final chapter is a composite of admonitions which covers a wide range of topics. The author has finished the main thrust of the epistle. In chapter 13 he is focusing on the particular needs and problems of those to whom he is writing. They are encouraged to **continue** (Gr *menō*) or remain in **brotherly love.** His words indicate they had demonstrated such **love** in the past. He encourages them to **continue** in that love. They are encouraged to demonstrate that love by not failing to **entertain strangers.** The author refers to Old Testament incidents such as in Genesis 18-19 where Abraham and Lot, through their hospitality, entertained **angels.** The idea is not to be kind to everyone, hoping to meet an angel, but rather that we never know the blessings we may receive through being kind. They are further encouraged to **remember them that are in bonds.** Some of their fellow Christians were suffering for the faith. Their needs must not be forgotten, especially while the readers are also **in the body** and susceptible to suffering.

4-6. Marriage is honorable in all. Apparently there were potential problems among the readers with illicit sex outside of marriage (**whoremongers**) and in marriage (**adulterers**). The author assures the readers that such activity **God will judge. Marriage is honorable in all. The bed** is **undefiled. The bed** (Gr *koite*) is used in reference to sexual activity in marriage. Unless it is ruined by sin, **the bed** is pure in a religious and moral sense. The author clearly expresses God's approval of marriage and His blessing upon it.

They are also admonished against greediness from a financial point of view. They are to be **content,** not filled with **covetousness.** Deuteronomy 31:6 is quoted to give evidence that God has promised to **never leave . . . nor forsake** us. Because of that assurance **we may boldly** claim God as our **helper.** We need not fear **man.** Psalm 118:6 is the Old Testament verse quoted here to provide comfort and assurance to the readers.

7-14. Remember them which have the rule. The readers are exhorted to **remember** and **follow** those who originally taught them the **word of God.** They probably had already died, considering the use of the word **end** (Gr *ekbasis*) which means the outcome of one's life. This entire passage seems to be one of doctrinal discussion. How powerfully is put the doctrine of Christ in the statement **Jesus Christ the same yesterday, and today, and for ever.** Christ had not changed since the early days of the new covenant. Nor would He ever change.

Apparently there was a doctrinal question among the readers over **meats.** There are specific Old Testament guidelines regarding **meats.** There may have been those who sought to integrate such guidelines into Christianity. The author points out the futility of such discussion. **The heart** is **established with grace; not with meats.** Grace is the key factor. Some may have been critical of Christianity because it did not involve any sacrificial system. The author declares that indeed **We have an altar,** referring to the sacrifice made on the cross of Calvary.

Not only is that sacrifice superior to the old altar system, but those who **serve** under that old system **have no right to eat** of the new sacrifice. This eating refers to the practice found in Leviticus 4:22-35 in which priests actually ate some of the sacrificial meat. Furthermore, the sacrifice that was offered on the Day of Atonement was not to be eaten of, but was to be taken **without the camp** and **burned** (Lev 16:27). This sacrifice on the Day of Atonement is a powerful type of Christ and the two are paralleled in verses 11 through 13. The author encourages his readers to **go . . . without the camp.** He is challenging them to look for the answer beyond the confines of Judaism. This will not be easy. They must be prepared even as was Christ, to suffer **reproach.** They were to look beyond the present, seeking that which was **to come.**

15-17. By him therefore. The author introduces a whole new concept of **sacrifices.** He challanges his readers to **offer the sacrifice of praise to God continually.** They are **to do good and to communicate,** for **with such sacrifices God is well pleased.** The word **communicate** (Gr *koinōnia*) is the word more often translated as "fellowship." It implies sharing with each other, or "generosity," and is to be taken literally. They are to **submit to** and **Obey them that have the rule over you.** Such obedience and submission make it possible for the leaders to fulfill their responsibilities in an attitude of **joy,** not **grief.**

18-19. Pray for us. The author requests prayer for himself. He apparently desires to return to them and believes that their prayers will hasten that return.

B. A Loving Benediction. 13:20-25.

20-21. Now the God of peace. This section contains the only specific reference to Christ's resurrection in the epistle. Christ is portrayed, not as a High Priest, but as a **shepherd.** Christ can care for the readers' needs, keep them safe, and in a general sense, give guidance to their lives. How does He do so? **Through**

the blood of the everlasting covenant. Notice the permanency of the new covenant. It is **everlasting.** God is able to **perfect** (Gr *katartizo*) or to make complete the believer. This is done through **Christ.** The ultimate purpose of the believer is to **do his will.** This is our goal, towards which we must work.

22-25. And I beseech you. The author wants his readers to **suffer** (Gr *anechō*) or "listen to willingly" his **word of exhortation. Timothy** has been **set at liberty,** probably from prison. The author suggests that Timothy and he would like to make a joint trip to visit them. The readers are asked to **Salute all them** that are in charge in the church. He bears a greeting from **They of Italy.** This probably refers to people who were from Italy living where the author was writing from. They were sending greetings back to their homeland and fellow countrymen. The author closes with a bestowal of **Grace** upon all the readers.

BIBLIOGRAPHY

Archer, G. *The Epistle to the Hebrews: A Study Manual.* Grand Rapids: Baker, 1961.

Brown, J. *An Exposition of the Epistle to the Hebrews.* London: Banner of Truth, reprint of 1862 ed.

Bruce, A. B. *The Epistle to the Hebrews.* Edinburgh: T. & T. Clark, 1908.

* Bruce, F. F. The Epistle to the Hebrews. In the *New International Commentary.* Grand Rapids: Eerdmans, 1964.

Davidson, A. B. *The Epistle to the Hebrews.* Edinburgh: T. & T. Clark, 1870.

Delitzsch, F. *Commentary on the Epistle to the Hebrews.* Edinburgh: T. & T. Clark, 1870.

Dods, M. The Epistle to the Hebrews. In the *Expositors Greek Testament,* Vol. 4. Grand Rapids: Eerdmans, n.d.

Farrar, F. W. *The Epistle of Paul the Apostle to the Hebrews.* Cambridge: University Press, 1883.

Hewitt, T. The Epistle to the Hebrews. In the *Tyndale New Testament Commentary.* Grand Rapids: Eerdmans, 1960.

* Hughes, P. E. *A Commentary on the Epistle to the Hebrews.* Grand Rapids: Eerdmans, 1977.

* Kent, H. A. *The Epistle to the Hebrews: A Commentary.* Grand Rapids: Baker, 1972.

Lenski, R. C. H. *Interpretation of the Epistle to the Hebrews.* Columbus: Wartburg Press, 1937.

Manson, W. *The Epistle to the Hebrews.* London: Hodder & Stoughton, 1951.

Moffatt, J. Epistle to the Hebrews. In the *International Critical Commentary.* New York: Scribner's, 1924.

Newell, W. R. *Hebrews Verse by Verse.* Chicago: Moody Press, 1947.

* Owen, J. *Hebrews: The Epistle of Warning* (abridged ed.). Grand Rapids: Kregel, n.d.

Pink, A. W. *An Exposition of Hebrews.* Grand Rapids: Baker, 1963.

Ross, R. W. Hebrews. In the *Wycliffe Bible Commentary.* Chicago: Moody Press, 1962.

Vine, W. E. *The Epistle to the Hebrews.* London: Oliphants, 1952.

* Westcott, B. F. *The Epistle to the Hebrews.* Grand Rapids: Eerdmans, reprint of 1889 ed.

The Epistle of

JAMES

INTRODUCTION

The Epistle of James was one of the last books of the New Testament to be accepted into the canon. One of the earliest lists of authoritative books, the Muratorian Canon (A.D. 170-200), omitted it, but general agreement of its canonicity solidified at the Council of Carthage (A.D. 397). Some early Christian writings did allude to it, and Origen definitely accepted it (A.D. 250). Although Eusebius categorized it among the disputed books, he affirmed that it was received by most churches. The primary cause for reluctance to recognize the epistle lies in a misunderstanding of James' soteriology (2:14-16). However, a close examination of his "justification by works" discussion reveals no disagreement between himself and Paul.

Authorship. The author identifies himself as "James, a servant of God and of the Lord Jesus Christ" (1:1). Four men in the New Testament bore that name: First, the father of Judas (the apostle) not Judas Iscariot (Lk 6:16); second, James, the son of Alphaeus, another apostle (Mt 10:3); third, James, the brother of John and the son of Zebedee (Mt 4:21); and last, the brother of the Lord Jesus (Mt 13:55). Since the first two are rather obscure, neither has been postulated as the author, and the brother of John was martyred too early to receive serious consideration. The Lord's brother not only has overwhelming traditional support, but his prominent position in the Jerusalem assembly makes him the most likely choice (cf. Acts 12:17; 15:13; Gal 1:19; 2:9). Prior to Jesus' death and resurrection, James, along with his brothers did not

believe (Jn 7:5). Perhaps it was Christ's post-resurrection appearance to him that brought about his conversion (I Cor 15:7).

Recipients. The salutation labels the addressees as "the twelve tribes which are scattered abroad," which could have been translated "the twelve tribes of the diaspora (dispersion)." Because the expression was typically applied to Israel, some conclude that James was addressing all Jews. Others interpret the phrase metaphorically, referring to Christians in general. In its content and style the letter concedes partial truth in both views. He wrote to Christian Jews. "Brethren" of James 1:2 and 2:1 addresses fellow Christians, while the style and content anticipate a Jewish reader.

Occasion and date. The date of writing proposed is either early or late and, ironically, for the same reason, i.e. the epistle's apparent contrast to Pauline theology. To those who argue for a late date Paul's "justification by faith" had been abused and exaggerated resulting in the neglect of Christian service. Accordingly, James refutes perversions of this doctrine. Others, contending that he wrote before Paul, explain that his aim centered around the practical, works being emphasized. That being the case, a salient need still existed for a clear exposition of justification, which, of course, was accomplished by Paul. Another indication of an early date is found in James 2:2, where the "assembly" mentioned is actually "synagogue," the place commonly used for worship in the earliest years of Christianity. The epistle probably was written in the middle forties, prior to the Council at Jerusalem, which dates to A.D. 49.

The author's subject matter also implies that he wrote early. New Testament epistles notably involve doctrinal issues, because sufficient time had elapsed for perversions to arise. Nevertheless, James disregards such discussion, which infers that significant heresies had not yet developed. Since the initial church consisted of Jews only, the prevailing Jewish style also suits this period.

Characteristics. Many view the Epistle of James as the foremost Jewish book in the New Testament. Christ's name is found only twice (1:1; 2:1), and the author resorts to the Old Testament freely. Illustrations, such as, Abraham, Rahab, and Elijah, and peculiar expressions, as "your synagogue" and "the Lord of Sabaoth" attest to this.

The author's approach is pragmatic. Wielding warnings and reproofs (there are over fifty imperatives), James resembles the prophets of old.

Contents. Admittedly the book's structure is somewhat loose, but it is an exaggeration to characterize it as a series of independent admonitions. An outline within the epistle offers general advice to those under adverse circumstances (1:19): they should be "swift to hear, slow to speak, and slow to wrath." The first point is modified to "obedience" (1:22), the crowning purpose of hearing. Details may be examined in the separate outline.

OUTLINE

COMMENTARY

I. INTRODUCTION. 1:1.

1:1. The author identifies himself as **James, a servant of God and of the Lord Jesus Christ.** He, as well as Jude, was a brother of the Lord. For further discussion about him see the introduction. The designation **servant** (Gr *doulos*) means "bondslave," and is to be distinguished from an employee. He affirms his life, and therefore what he writes, to be under the direction of the One who owns him.

The twelve tribes which are scattered abroad refers to Christians who were by persecution driven out of and scattered from Jerusalem (Acts 8:1). Since James was the leader of the Jerusalem congregation, it was only natural that he write to them regarding their faith.

II. THE TESTS OF LIFE. 1:2-18.

A. Joy Under Temptations. 1:2-11.

2. The trials which befall Christians should not cause alarm or sorrow. In fact, James urges his readers to **count it all joy.** The child of God may rejoice victoriously in the darkest hour. The following verse explains why. **My brethren:** the recipients are Christians. **When ye fall into divers temptations:** the trials (Gr *peirasmos*) refer to internal and external adversities which would misdirect the servant of God. The verb and adjective join to underline a predominant characteristic of trials; they cannot be anticipated in type or time.

3. Joy amid hardship springs up from an illumined heart. The Christian perceives purpose among persecution and problems. **Knowing** (Gr *ginōskō*) involves experiential knowledge, not merely the accumulation of known facts. **That the trying of your faith worketh patience:** the word for trying (Gr *dokimion*) implies victory over trial, and may be better rendered "the proving of your faith. . . ." **Patience** (Gr *hypomonē*) does not mean waiting without anxiety, but to endure adverse circumstances without letting them sour the attitude.

4. Endurance is a virtue which very few people experience fully. Too often we grasp relief from trouble so eagerly that we fail to receive the entire lesson that God intended for us. **Let patience have her perfect work** cautions us to observe our attitudes more than our circumstances. If one does this, he will realize the road to Christian maturity. Perfection in the absolute sense, however, will be reserved for the life to come (I Jn 1:8).

5. The close connection between verses 4 and 5 is masked in the AV by translating a single Greek word in two ways. **Wanting** (vs. 4) and **lack** (vs. 5) stem from the same word (Gr *leipō*) which implies that the reader might ask after verse 4, "How can I find purpose in this predicament?" **If any of you lack wisdom** (specifically in what God is accomplishing through the trials), **let him ask.** Two characteristics of God's attitude toward giving become apparent; **God, that giveth to all men liberally, and upbraideth not.** Both contrast to man's style of bestowing. He neither displays reluctance to release His gifts, nor humiliates the needy petitioners.

6. The restriction involves the receiver, not the Giver. To **ask in faith** denotes the absence of **wavering** (Gr *diakrinomai*), which suggests an anxious reevaluation, "second thoughts" about one's prayer. This type of person compares to a **wave** which is **driven** and **tossed** by circumstances. Christians, by faith, should persistently avow under any circumstances that God is all He claims to be.

7-8. A "waverer" may expect nothing. He lives in two philosophical worlds, the natural and the supernatural; and while he rejects the natural intellectually, he will not wholly commit himself to God. The

Lord covets servants who will be "one hundred percenters."

9-11. These three verses underscore the urgency of submitting to God's perspective. We are to **rejoice** not because of earthly circumstances but by reason of spiritual realities. A **brother** may be **of low degree** (Gr *tapeinos*), of a "lowly" economic or social status, but there is reason for joy. In God's esteem **he is exalted.** Through the grace of God he has been lifted out of the miry clay (Ps 40:2) and claims a heavenly position in Christ (Eph 1:3). Conversely, the **rich** may rejoice because temporal possessions are not all they have. When they humble themselves repenting of sin, they become children of God and joint-heirs with Christ (Rom 8:17). The illustration of the short-lived flower reminds us how ephemeral this life really is.

B. The Source of Temptations. 1:12-18.

12. Endureth (Gr *hypomenō*) is the verb form of the word "patience" (see 1:3 for its etymology). The **crown of life** is not a tangible wreath as in the Greek games, but the reward is life itself.

13. Since temptation may have beneficial results, some might conclude that God Himself sends it. The author categorically denies that; God is never the source of temptation.

14. The actual source of temptation lies within man, **his own lust** (Gr *epithymia*), his inherent longings.

15-16. The process of evil compares to a life cycle. **Lust** may seem insignificantly small, but it produces sin, which, when it is **finished** (Gr *apoteleō*), literally, has matured enough to bear children, **bringeth forth death.** Lust, so to speak, is the grandmother of death.

17. Not only are God's gifts **good** (useful, practical) and **perfect** (nothing lacking in them), but His liberality is wholly consistent. Fickle man may succumb to "lusts," but He, **the Father of**

lights, does not embrace the faintest shadow of change.

18. If "justification by works" (2:24) causes one to question James' soteriology, he should note here the basis of salvation: **Of his own will begat he. . . .** The verb, **begat** (Gr *apokyeō*), stems from the same root as "bringeth forth" of verse 15. Sin kills, but God regenerates.

III. THE CHRISTIAN LIFE THROUGH TESTING. 1:19-5:20.

A. The Author's Structure. 1:19-20.

19-20. From this point, the practical Epistle of James follows the three categories listed here: (1) **swift to hear** (1:21-2:26), regarding hearing as doing; (2) **slow to speak** (3:1-18), including the vulnerability of excessive talking and the comparison of conduct and speech; and (3) **slow to wrath** (4:1-17), identifying the sources of bitterness. The threefold admonition explains the proper response to the trials of life discussed in 1:2-18.

B. "Quick to Hear." 1:21-2:26.

1. Real Hearing involves doing. 1:21-25.

21. The command to **lay aside all filthiness and superfluity of naughtiness** employs expressions of coarseness rather than immorality. To overcome trials one must shun vulgarity as well as wickedness. **The engrafted word,** the implanted message of the gospel (1:18), should be **received** by Christians (cf. "brethren," 1:19) with unqualified submissiveness. The phrase, **able to save your souls,** points out the inherent efficacy of the gospel which they have already accepted.

22. The Greek present tense in **be ye doers of the word** may be rendered "Continue being doers. . . ." However, the word **be** (Gr *ginomai*), often translated "become," views their obedience as a constant struggle. Hearing profits when it generates a transformed life, but **hearers only**

merely soothe their consciences temporarily, deceiving themselves.

23-24. He who follows this form of irrational thinking sees **his natural face in a glass** (mirror) . . . and goeth his way. He observes, becomes entirely cognizant of the flaws, and promptly **forgetteth.**

25. The **perfect law of liberty** parallels the **glass** of verse 23. James chose two words which contradict each other. **Law** signifies restrictions; **liberty** the absence of them. The apparent misnomer sets forth a momentous teaching. Although God embraces inflexible standards and laws, He freely pardons anyone who trusts in Christ. **Whoso looketh** (Gr *parakyptō*) implies much more than a glance (vs. 24), for the word involves bending over for closer inspection. It pictures a person before a mirror noticing a blemish, then leaning forward to examine and attend to it.

2. Doing involves mercy. 1:26-2:13.

26-27. The word **religion** (Gr *thrēskeia*), has to do with worship in the outward sense, religious service. An uncontrolled **tongue** exposes a spiritual problem. **This man's religion is vain** (Gr *mataios*); it yields no results. **Pure religion and undefiled** involves visiting the forsaken and relinquishing worldly enticements. Without governmental-aid programs **widows** and orphans face hunger and cold alone. Their welfare was the responsibility of Christians. It still is.

2:1. The AV's chapter division here is misleading, for the two previous verses relate closely to this passage. If true religion entails visiting the destitute, it leaves no room for **respect of persons** (Gr *prosōpolēmpsia*), which connotes "receiving because of one's face or appearance."

2-4. A clear illustration dismisses all excuses and exceptions. One might imagine two visitors arriving at a church on a Sunday morning. A chauffeured limousine exhibits a man arrayed in expensive clothing. Another man approaches in an old jalopy, and his cheap suit has almost worn through. When the usher favors the wealthy man, he becomes **partial** and a **judge of evil thoughts. Partial** comes from the same verb (Gr *diakrinomai*) as a word used in 1:6 ("wavering"). By their partiality the offenders have "wavered" in their faith. "judges with evil thoughts" (RSV) explains that their evaluation was based on sinful attitudes.

5. In contrast to these inequitable religionists, God chose **the poor of this world.** Christian paupers possess secret riches both in their present **faith** and in His eternal **kingdom.**

6. Despised (Gr *atimazō*), involves not only attitudes but shameful treatment, as when Jesus was "dishonored" by the Jewish leaders (Jn 8:49). **Oppress** refers to the arrogant flaunting of governmental authority over Christians, as tyrants over helpless peasants. James has Jewish officials in mind when he says they **draw you before the judgment seats** (Gr *kritēria*), Acts 9:2, where Saul traveled to Damascus with official letters to arrest Christians, testifies of the authority which Rome handed over to the Jews. The **judgment seat** speaks of the local court.

7. Not only do they despise the poor and oppress Christians, but the rich direct their assaults against the Lord Himself. **They blaspheme** (Gr *blasphēmeō*) or "speak evil against" **that worthy name by the which ye are called,** i.e. Christians (Acts 11:26).

8. The royal law means "law that is truly royal in its quality" (R.C.H. Lenski, *The Epistle of Hebrews and James,* p. 570), because the definite article is absent in Greek, indicating that quality is emphasized. It is royal or kingly in its relation to other laws. Jesus said that this and the first commandment are so fundamental that on them "hang all the law and the prophets" (Mt 22:40). An individual "loves" himself irrespective of financial or social status. We should love others in the same manner. When we practice the law, we **do well;** it's beautiful!

9. The secular view of success assumes that favoritism must be employed, if one is to "climb the ladder" of accomplishment. Nonetheless, James warns that if one adopts this method, **have respect to persons** (2:1), what he "accomplishes" (AV is **commit,** but the Greek is *ergazomai*) in God's eyes is **sin.** Singular in form, the word **sin** points to quality. **Convinced of the law of transgressors** may be better translated "convicted by . . . ." The word for "convinced" (Gr *elengchō*) means to point out the guilt or fault in someone. **The law** is not the Mosaic code, but the "royal law," the law of love. Partiality represses genuine love.

10. Offend (Gr *ptaiō*) literally means to stumble or trip. Thus, James, for the sake of argument, awards the party pure motives, granting that the sin appears accidental. The result, **guilty of all,** contradicts salvation by works. Since all men are "guilty before God" (Rom 3:19), salvation necessarily is by grace through faith (Eph 3:8-9).

11. A basketball, whether it misses the hoop by an inch or a yard, still fails to score. Likewise, he who shows partiality **becomes a transgressor** just as readily as if he had murdered or committed adultery.

12. So speak ye, and so do. Both of these verbs being in the Greek present tense, which connotes continuous action, this phrase would be better translated, "Continue speaking and continue doing." How may we be motivated to do so? **As they that shall be judged.** The AV phraseology, however, implies a too distant judgment. The verb (Gr *mellō*) means "about to be," denoting imminent retribution. Christians ought to conduct themselves as if judgment may come at any moment. The constraining stimulus should not be a harsh, merciless court, but the **law of liberty,** which assures us we are free from the bondage of sin.

13. Mercy is so basic to Christian living that it is impossible for a true believer not to have it. Of course, the extent may vary, but he that shows none will find **judgment without mercy.**

3. Doing demonstrates faith. 2:14-26.

The last thirteen verses of the second chapter of James have been among the most controversial passages in Scripture, some dividing Paul and James into separate statements in this chapter may appear to oppose Pauline doctrine, a careful analysis demonstrates indissoluble harmony between the two inspired writers. The difference in expression arises from their distinct purposes. Paul wrote to explain the gospel; James had in view its practical implications.

14. If one regards the author's purpose, the discussion will be less difficult to interpret. Many misunderstand this verse because they fail to observe two significant facts. First, James does not state that the hypothetical person "has" faith, but merely a man **say he hath faith.** It distinguishes the one who "possesses" from the one who merely "professes." Secondly, conclusions are based on the question, **can faith save him?** The AV unfortunately gives a wrong impression, for he is not asking about faith in general, but that type of faith which one has who makes claims without producing fruit. This is affirmed by the presence of the definite article in Greek meaning "the faith." "Can that faith save him?" would be a proper translation. Which faith? That which the man claims to have. That being the case, James does not contradict Paul. Both affirm that true saving faith results in a changed life as evidenced by works (Eph 2:8-10).

15-16. When Christians **say** empty platitudes without actually helping those in physical need, **what doth it**

profit? How many words fill a hungry stomach?

17. Even so. As the worthlessness of well-wishers reveal their selfishness, so barrenness in a professing believer's life exposes his insincerity. Significantly, the Greek text states with the article, that "the **faith . . . is dead, being alone.** James refers specifically to the faith which is claimed, not the genuine brand.

18. A man may say. The author communicates his accusation through an assumed third person, allowing his remarks to be received more objectively. The matter of contention is not works *per se,* but the evidence of faith. Pious expressions may **seem to be religious** (1:26), but actions are what people hear."

19. One fixed tenet of these Jewish readers was monotheism, **Thou believest that there is one God;** but doctrine alone does not save. **Thou doest well** inserts a measure of sarcasm, for he quickly points out that **the devils** (Gr *daimonion,* "demons") also affirm that truth. Demonic faith, far from effecting service, exists in terror.

20. Wilt thou know is rhetorical. Having developed his argument to this point, James expects the recognition of truth. The address, **O vain man,** extends beyond empty faith to a person void of reality. As in verse 17, the word **faith** occurs with the Greek definite article meaning "the faith" or "that faith."

21. Abraham is the father of all believers (Rom 4:16), but the reference here, **our father,** links him with his nation, the Jews. That he was **justified by works** appears to contradict Paul's "justification by faith" (Rom 3:28; 4:2; 5:1). Romans 3:20 conclusively declares, "Therefore by the deeds of the law there shall no flesh be justified in his sight." Observe Paul's references to God: "in His sight" plus "before God" in Romans 4:2 (cf. Thomas Manton, *An Exposition of the Epistle of James,* p. 244). Most frequently, the

word for justify (Gr *dikaioō*) in the New Testament speaks of God's positive verdict, the opposite of condemnation. The unjustified man, according to Romans, is a condemned sinner; but in the Epistle of James he is a hypocrite. Consequently, Abraham's justification in this passage consisted of man's verdict. Christians, Jews, and Arabs have "declared righteousness" this man of God, because of the faith demonstrated when he offered his only son.

22. A more accurate translation of **faith wrought with his works** would be "faith operated by means of his works." Salvation is not accomplished through the cooperation of faith and works, but faith finds its channel of expression in works. **By works was faith made perfect** may be rendered "out of works was faith completed." James 1:3-4 embraces the same thought: the development of inner character parallels the extent of testing endured (I Pet 1:7).

23. The author never impugns faith *per se,* but he candidly denounces that brand of self-acclaimed faith which finds no profitable service. Genesis 15:6 was spoken years before Isaac was offered, but it was then that Abraham's faith became evident. His fame resulted from works, the corollary of real faith (Rom 4:19-22); but his relationship with the Lord had been settled years before. He has been **called the Friend of God** for centuries by Jews, Arabs, and Christians.

24. In a court, if a man's motive comes in question, the only means to justify or vindicate his motive is to examine his acts. Genuine faith is conscious of others. "Pure religion" involves a life of ministry, not introspective qualities.

25. Rahab's works were done by faith (Heb 11:31), but actions were necessary to affirm her inner change. Had she remained in sin while acclaiming faith, she would never have been "declared righteous" (justified).

26. The comparison of the human spirit and faith converges around their modes of operation. The spirit (Gr *pneuma*) may also be translated "breath." As a breathless body emits no indication of life, so fruitless faith exhibits nothing more than hypocrisy.

C. "Slow to Speak." 3:1-18.

1. The tongue is destructive. 3:1-12.

3:1. According to the structure provided in James 1:19, the second directive is "slow to speak." The problem is rather obvious: too much talking. Its root cause lies in a proud attitude, which thrives in pretentious self-expression. Being **masters** or teachers (Gr *didaskalos*) could become the means for releasing it. Having too many teachers is like having more foremen than laborers. The Bible clearly commends submissiveness, "a contrite spirit" (Isa 66:2), but humility must not be equated with position. James cautions those who would be leaders to examine their motives. Is the Lord Himself directing you, or are you gratifying desires for self-promotion? **Greater condemnation** or judgment (Gr *krino*) parallels greater responsibility (Lk 12:48).

2. The verb **offend** (Gr *ptaiō*) means to trip or stumble, and thus, the clause may be rendered, "we all are stumbling in many areas." None of us has reached perfection. **Perfect** (Gr *teleios*) describes the man who has reached his goal, the man who is self-controlled. That being the case in speech, he is **able also to bridle the whole body,** because the tongue resists control more than any other area of behavior. **Bridle** pictures restrained guidance.

3-4. Two illustrations emphasize that often what holds the greatest influence may appear insignificant, size having nothing to do with importance. In comparison to the total dimensions of a horse, a **bit** in the mouth appears trivial, yet the animal obeys it. **Ships,** enormous and **driven** by awesome winds, may be steered by a **very small helm** (Gr *pēdalion*), rudder. **Whithersoever the governor listeth** in contemporary language may be translated, "Wherever the pilot wants it to go."

5. Behold, how great a matter a little fire kindleth! The tongue may be compared to a match in size, but its effect is like a raging forest fire.

6. Nowhere else in Scripture is the tongue pictured with such pungent language. It is a **world of iniquity** (Gr *adikia*, literally, unrighteousness), and it spreads throughout the body like a devouring cancer. The **course of nature** (Gr *genesis*) refers to the pattern of history; a sharp tongue may instigate war or prevent an election. The source accounts for its character; **hell,** (Gr *geenna*) originally referred to the Valley of Hinnom, south and west of Jerusalem, where a perpetual fire blazed on its garbage heaps. It became an awesome symbol of the eternal abode of the lost.

7-8. Every is obviously restricted to creatures of sufficient intelligence to be **tamed.** The wildest stallion may be broken, but the tongue continually erupts in outbursts of uncontrolled emotion. This does not necessarily mean that everyone unceasingly makes unintended comments, but it does mean that even the most respected, gracious people have their own seasons of regretful words. **Full of deadly poison** speaks of the death blows words may deliver to good relationships. A single sentence uttered in heated discussion may sever a long friendship.

9-10. Contrasting the actions of the tongue unveils its inconsistency: **bless . . . curse.** Although the offender may excuse his contradictory expressions on the basis of depravity, men **are made after the similitude of God.** Inspite of man's fall and resulting wickedness, he still bears God's image (Gen 1:26; 5:1, 3; 9:6; I Cor 11:7; Eph 4:24; and Col 3:10). Although there is an infinite qualitative difference between them, man resembles God in a way which distinguishes him from the rest of God's creation. The Bible does not clearly specify the nature of the image, and therefore, scholars differ as to the meaning. The main views are: (1) bodily form; (2) dominion over the animal world; (3) moral nature; and (4) personality. Stephen Barabas synthesizes three of these. Man is a "rational, self-conscious, self-determining creature, capable of obedience to moral law, and intended by God for fellowship with Himself." (Merrill C. Tenney, Ed. *Zondervan Pictoral Bible Dictionary,* p. 371). **These things ought not so to be.** A distinction may be seen in Scripture between carnal judging and spiritual discernment. Care must be practiced to aim denunciations against sin and not the sinner. The Lord can forgive the worst offender; thus Christians should hope for God's regenerating power even in unlikely persons.

11-12. Fountain (Gr *pēgē*) would be a "spring" in modern terminology. Just as it would be absurd to think that it produces both **sweet water** and **bitter,** or **salt water** and **fresh,** or that a grape **vine** yields **figs,** so a mouth which condemns men while praising God lacks credibility. That sort of person would have a shallow Christian experiences if one at all.

2. True wisdom is expressed through daily living. 3:13-18.

13. A wise man may desire to manifest his knowledge through teaching, but James says **let him show** a changed life through **works. Conversation** (Gr *anastrophe*) means behavior or conduct.

14. The verse correlates the tongue and wisdom. The former, as an outward sign, may reveal a heart of **bitter envying and strife,** which is founded on pride. To bless and curse **out of the same mouth** (vs. 10) is to elevate oneself above God's truth. A man may judge others for wrongdoing, yet overlook his own failure of the **royal law**

(2:8). **Glory not, and lie not,** both present tense verbs, may be translated "stop glorying and stop lying."

15. If wisdom displays itself apart from good conduct and meekness, it is **not from above.** In fact, it is characterized as **earthly,** wise by the world's standards, **sensual** (Gr *psychikos*), meaning natural as distinguished from spiritual, and **devilish** (Gr *daimoniōdēs*), of demonic influence.

16. The author leaves no doubt about the effects of **envying and strife** of verse 14. **Confusion** (Gr *akatastasis*) opposes that which is established. **Every evil work** specifically means "every foul practice." **Strife** usually begins with gossip and climaxes in direct confrontation.

17. Pure contrasts with **evil** of the previous verse. **Peaceable, gentle, and easy to be entreated** join as opposites of **confusion** (vs. 16). **Full of mercy and good fruits** reminds one that faith apart from works is unprofitable (2:14-26). **Without hypocrisy.** Practicing **partiality** (2:4), **faith without works** (2:17), and **boasting** (2:14) all involve hypocrisy, which originally referred to the "acting" that was performed in theaters.

18. This section, "slow to speak" (1:19), has focused around the uncontrolled tongue. Inner qualities are what season one's speech, and here **peace** is emphasized in two ways: (1) **righteousness is sown,** that is, it has its beginnings in peaceful conditions, not **envying and strife** (vs. 16); and (2) righteousness appears in those who practice peace. The glaring blemish of evangelical churches is inner turmoil and bickering, yet Christian living depends upon **peace.**

D. "Slow to Wrath." 4:1-5:6.

1. Wrath stems from a worldly attitude. 4:1-5.

4:1. James addresses church members who are infected by materialism, given to partiality, and jealous of each other. **War in your members** sounds like Peter (I Pet 2:11) or Paul (Rom 7:23) who agree that carnal desires rage within the believer or thwart his spiritual progress. Since self-control is a fruit of the Spirit (Gal 5:22), His filling is the means of victory.

2. Kill, along with **wars and fightings** of the previous verse, is best taken figuratively. It seems inconceivable that Christians were involved in actual combat and murder without any mention of any governmental intervention. These strong words were chosen to stress the seriousness of their acts.

3. Even when they did **ask,** their prayers went unanswered, because they sought personal gratification, disregarding God's will. "What a picture of the lustful heart tossed about and buffeted on the sea of his own selfish desires, committing murder in his heart attitude, jealous and contentious, forgetting to pray except only to pray amiss, always and ever unrestful and unsatisfied" (Zane Hodges, Lectures on James, unpublished).

4. Ye adulterers and adulteresses. Spiritual adultery was mentioned often in the Old Testament (Isa 57:3-9; Jer 3:20; Ezk 16:32, 35, 38; and Hos 2). It is no more right for a Christian to love both God and the world, than for a man to have two wives. Unfaithfulness would repulse the offended party in either case. **Know ye not.** A common characteristic of backsliding is the voluntary blindness toward the seriousness of sin. **Enmity with God** is something the Christian was delivered from (Rom 5:10), and therefore, his "affair" with the world should cause shame and remorse.

5. Do ye think that the scripture saith in vain expects a negative reply. Could we imagine God's Word going forth without purpose, direction, or power? Since this quote cannot be found in the Old Testament, it appears that James alludes to a principle. In the original, **to envy** (Gr *phthonos*) re-

ceives prominence by its position. This expression, when taken adverbially, "the Spirit that dwells in us lusts jealously," speaks of divine jealousy, a familiar doctrine to these Jews (Ex 20:5; 34:14; Zech 8:2). **Dwelleth** (Gr *katoikeō*) differs from the word which signifies a temporary dwelling. The Holy Spirit's indwelling in the believer is not transient, but He, as it were, makes His residence within us. **Lusteth** (Gr *epipotheō*) speaks of intense desires, which explains why the charge of spiritual adultery was made in the previous verse. Its counterpart, spiritual faithfulness, measures the believer's love for the Lord. Friendship with the world exposes the shallowness of one's spirituality.

2. Wrath stems from a proud attitude. 4:6-17.

6. A sharp contrast exists between worldly and divine jealousy; men want revenge, but **he giveth more grace.** That statement, plus the quote (Prov 3:34), assures the repenting sinner that no offense is too great for God's forgiveness.

7. Verses 7 thorough 10 contain a group of imperatives, the first and the last being almost identical: **Submit . . . Humble yourselves. Submit** (Gr *hypotassō*), a combination of two words, literally means "to place under," hence, subjection or submission. Because of God's never-ending grace, the Christian's logical behavior is total submission to Him, rather than enslavement to the world's allurements (Rom 12:1-2). Two factors should be mentioned regarding **Resist the devil.** First, we should stand against outward opposition, even though we are instructed to flee inner cravings (II Tim 2:22). Secondly, **devil** (Gr *diabolos*), a word meaning "accuser," portrays our enemy scrutinizing the intimate details of one's personal life to expose any fault. Thus the believer must walk in the Spirit with the utmost caution. He must walk worthy (Col 1:9-10).

8. The tense of **Draw nigh** implores the listeners to complete a single, definite act. **Cleanse** and **purify** differ in what they affect. The former, along with **hands** and **sinners**, speaks of actions which may be observed. The latter, addressed to the internal insecurities of the "double-minded" (1:8), is aimed against improper motives and wicked thoughts. Spirituality involves regeneration and revival, not just reformation; a new heart precedes a changed life.

10. Humble yourselves. The man who submits himself to the Lord will be exalted in ways which he himself could never accomplish. This primarily refers to one's spiritual relationship with God.

11. With the **wars and fighting among you** of 4:1, James discussed humility in order to advance a principle. True humility cannot be achieved by one who slanders his brothers. As an appeal to spiritual unity, the word **brother** is mentioned three times. When a man impugns his Christian brother, he proudly sets himself above the law that God has established.

12. The word, **one** is placed first in the original to extol Him above all others. In many older manuscripts He is called **lawgiver** (Gr *nomothetēs*), the one **who is able . . . to destroy,** and also **judge.** These designate God as author, interpreter, and executor of the law. If He alone holds these functions, then **who art thou that judgest another?** Yet, in spite of its haughty character, Christians, through various attempts to rationalize, condone its presence in each other.

13. Go to now, used as an interjection, compares to our expression, "Come now!" James attacks another area where pride frequently erupts: the world of business. God has gifted His chosen people with unusual ability in commercial ventures, and these Christian Jews erred because of wrong attitudes toward it. Careful planning must be included in successful business

methods, but sound principles or management are insufficient. Before making an expensive investment a wise executive considers all factors in painful detail. The folly exposed is disregarding the preeminent fact of life, i.e. God! Carnal men assume extended life without knowing "the Life" (Jn 14:6), taking for granted each day as if they had earned it.

14. Ye know not. In spite of human frailty and ignorance of tomorrow, man arrogantly predicts his life's course. **For what is your life?** The question hopes to shake someone out of apathy and cause him to reassess his priorities. **Vapour** (Gr *atmis*) is used of smoke (Acts 2:19), incense (Ezk 8:11), and of steam. It makes no difference which one is chosen, for all are transient and gone in a moment. Compared to eternity, the span of our lives appears insignificant.

15. The command does not mean to keep adding the phrase, **If the Lord will,** to everything one says. To do such could become another form of pride. At the same time one's behavior and plans should consistently demonstrate dependence upon the Lord. He may determine that at the present time patience through tribulation (Rom 5:3) is a greater need than attaining our goals.

16. Rejoice (Gr *kauchaomai*) could be translated "boast." The noun, **boastings** (Gr *alazoneia*), connotes vain pretensions. A man who brags about future plans while ignoring God's sovereignty is foolish, but more than that his attitude is **evil.** The extent of this marks the depravity of contemporary society.

17. Not only does pride condemn others and boast in its potential, but it overlooks its own failure, and those failures which go unnoticed longest are omissions. It is easier to detect wrong than the absence of right. **To him that knoweth to do good** specifically addresses their lack of submission to

God's will, which is called **sin** (Gr *hamartia*), missing the mark.

3. Extreme wrath often comes from the rich. 5:1-6.

5:1. The author censored pride in the previous chapter, and here, in phraseology similar to the prophetic tones of certain Old Testament literature, he repudiates the **rich. Go to now** appeared in 4:13 where it also was used as an interjection. **Weep and howl for your miseries that shall come upon you** reminds one of ancient apocalyptic outcries (Isa 13:6; 14:31; 15:3; Jer 4:8; Joel 1:5, 13). Audible crying is heightened by outbursts of wailing. **Miseries . . . shall come** contrasts to present Christian suffering under trials. When the Lord comes, the experience will be reversed (5:8) in greater proportions. Who are these **rich men?** This social class receives attention neither as a tangent nor because his recipients were such, but James is indirectly warning his double-minded Christian readers of the life styles they approach.

2. One characteristic of prophetic literature is to view the future as though it were present. The perfect tense of **are corrupted** and **are moth-eaten** pictures the effects of **riches** as already having occurred.

3. The destructive results of **rust** upon **gold and silver** testify to the vanity of riches. It is difficult to affirm conclusively the meaning of **eat your flesh as it were fire,** but perhaps James uses this dramatic phrase to contrast the array of mortal bodies to their final state. Analogous to quotes of Jesus (Mt 6:19-20 and Lk 12:21), **the last days** should be a time for securing heavenly treasure, not earthly wealth ("in" the last days would be a more accurate translation than **for**).

4. Uncontrolled appetites for worldly accumulations have carried them to the worst extremes. Not only did they strive for the greatest profits, but they cheated employees in order to do so. **By fraud** they tricked the laborers out of their wages. The resulting desperate **cries** seemed to be in vain, but eternity reveals them to have **entered into the ears of the Lord of Sabaoth.** That title, often translated "Lord of Hosts," emphasizes His omnipotence; in spite of how things may appear, He is sovereign!

5. In a day of slaughter may be taken in two ways. Some explain the slaughter as the excess killing of animals to prepare for a great feast. Thus, preparations for further indulgence seem to be in order. Others find eschatological significance to the phrase (Jer 12:3), making it refer to their self-fattening process for their own slaughter. Perhaps, the author had both ideas in mind. They anxiously make ready for another "day of slaughter" and feasting, while being ignorant of their own ensuing judgment.

6. The just does not refer to Christ (in favor of this interpretation, see Thomas Manton, *An Exposition of the Epistle of James,* p, 416). It is a common Old Testament expression which emphasizes a believer's faithful life. **Resist** has nothing to do with the good man's opposition to the oppressor's wickedness. It deals with the victim's mute response toward the tyrant abuse.

IV. CONCLUSION. 5:7-20.

7. Be patient (Gr *makrothymeō*) may be translated "endure" or "be long-tempered," as opposed to short-tempered. **The coming of the Lord** will dismiss present inequities, while becoming a special goal for oppressed believers. **The husbandman,** farmer, illustrates the type of patience believers should possess. Plowing, planting, and caring for his crop are all means to an end, i.e. the harvest. He labors because he believes a day of reaping will be enjoyed. Christians likewise should view current trials and hardships as a preparation process that helps conform them to the image of Christ.

8. The command of the previous

verse here becomes personal: **ye also.** **The coming** (Gr *parousia*), often translated "appearance," implies the suddenness of His arrival, and thus urges constant readiness. **Stablish** (Gr *stērizō*) may be translated "fix firmly" or "set fast" and is another indication of the double-mindedness of a certain element among the recipients.

9. The foremost unbefitting response to testing is bitterness; but since Christians are reluctant to assault God for their problems, their bitter attitudes erupt against others. The command, **grudge not,** is appropriate here. As when a judge enters a courtroom, a reverent hush moves over the audience, so the **judge** who is **before the door** should quell slanderous remarks among His people.

10. A man undergoing trying circumstances may be comforted to learn that others have endured worse situations. The word **example** (Gr *hypodeigma*) is positioned first in Greek to receive emphasis. A man's outspoken testimony for the Lord, not only attributes a positive stand for the gospel, it frequently occasions harsh opposition from its enemies. **Of suffering affliction, and of patience** both have definite articles in the original, which signifies "an example of the suffering affliction and the patience" which James has been discussing. **The prophets** stood loyal to their Lord, suffered for it, and now their experience encourages us.

11. We count them happy holds somewhat of a paradox, although it may not have been intended. Objectively as we observe suffering in others, we urge them to endure, because victory will eventually arrive. Yet when we ourselves **fall into divers temptations** (1:2), our immediate human response often is negative. Job, who endured loss of property, family and health, stands out as a specimen (see J. Moulton and G. Milligan, *The Vocabulary of the Greek New Testament*) of enduring faith. His case not only

asserts his patience but demonstrates the purpose and character of his Lord. **The end of the Lord** (Gr *telos*) may be better rendered "the Lord's goal." Our Lord permits suffering, because it leads to His excellent purposes (Rom 8:28; Phil 1:6). Moreover, while critics blaspheme God because of human suffering, Job's record shows the Lord to be "full of pity" (this translation is more accurate than the AV's **very pitiful,** which suggests a negative idea) **and of tender mercy.** Suffering, then, must be attributed either to the means for God's ultimate purposes or (more often) man's own doing through corrupt leaders or personal sin.

12. Swear not etc. is the clearest allusion in this epistle to the Sermon on the Mount (Mt 5:34-37). The importance of this command, **above all things,** has two views: **above** (Gr *pro*) may signify superiority (A. T. Robertson, *A Grammar of the New Testament in the Light of Historical Research,* p. 622), but commonly it means "before." The latter view makes better sense, for the absence of oath-taking could hardly be superior, but speech should be the first notable change when the Spirit receives control.

14. God honors unity in prayer (Mt 18:19), but the healing process here specifically involves **the elders** (Gr *presbyteros*), mature spiritual leaders of the church. No inference can be found of the gift of healing. Moreover, it is the sick who must take the initiative: **let him call.** The oil carries no supernatural powers, but often was used in anointing to symbolize the outpouring of God's Spirit. The phrase, **in the name of the Lord,** points to the real source of healing. Also, the service is to take place in the privacy of the home, since the needy person summoned the elders to him.

15. All too often prayer bears little fruit, but **the prayer of faith,** of unqualified trust, will deliver. Nothing about the passage requires instantaneous healing, nor is there any restriction of medical treatment. The presence of **sins** may be the cause for the sickness, but not necessarily. We must reserve judgment for God alone. **They shall be forgiven** assumes that the one who seeks help from the church also recognizes his personal shortcomings.

16. The two imperatives, **Confess** and **pray**, both in the Greek present tense, call for the habitual practice of openness in two activities. Caution should be observed though; confession should be made only to the extent that the sin is open. Lest anyone regard the prayer of faith to be an impulsive expression of desire, James describes its involvement as **The effectual fervent prayer** with only one adjective in Greek, not two as in the AV. One may observe that our English word "energy" is akin to this modifier (Gr *energeō*), which stresses hard labor. If one becomes desperate about a critical situation, he will not be satisfied uttering a few pious sentences.

17-18. The adverb **much** (vs. 16) leaves the effects of prayer ambiguous. The example of Elijah's answered petition responds to the assumed question by the reader, "How much?" Even the forces of nature may be altered, for three and one-half years! But a doubter may react, "That's fine for a prophet, but what about an average man like me?" Only two qualities are ascribed to this man: (1) **a man subject to like passions as we are:** he fled Jezebel's fury immediately after God sent fire on Mount Carmel (I Kgs 19:1-4); (2) he **prayed earnestly.** His greatness did not lie in special gifts or a superhuman character, but he is distinguished by the way he prayed. One may imagine **earnestly** to hold special significance of a unique manner, but not so. He prayed with all superficial distractions removed. **And he prayed again.** The simplistic wording, in fact, seems to ignore the manner. Prayer is communicating with God, and genuine communication results in visible response. Most public "prayers" are ineffective, because in reality they are intended for man's ears.

19-20. The author speaks to **Brethren** who are in doctrinal error. **Err from the truth** may be rendered "misled from the truth," but the passive voice in no way excuses the sin. **And one convert him** means return or persuade him back to the truth. **Save a soul from death.** Since the word **soul** (Gr *psychē*) may mean "life," the clause may be taken as a warning that backsliding may end in physical death (I Cor 11:30). **Shall hide a multitude of sins** along with the former clause attributes supernatural accomplishments to the one who converts the sinner; God alone can save life or forgive sin. The human connection relates to I Corinthians 3:9, "For we are laborers together with God."

BIBLIOGRAPHY

Adamson, James. The Epistle of James. In *The New International Commentary on the New Testament*. Ed. F. F. Bruce. Grand Rapids: Eerdmans, 1976.

Alford, Henry. *The Greek Testament*. Revised by E. E. Harrison. Vol. IV. Chicago: Moody Press, 1958.

Carr, Arthur. The General Epistle of St. James. In the *Cambridge Greek Testament*. Cambridge: Cambridge University Press, 1930 reprint.

Gaebelein, Frank E. *Practical Epistle of James: Studies in Applied Christianity*. Greatneck, N.Y.: Doniger and Raughley, 1955.

Gibson, E. C. S. The General Epistle of James. In *The Pulpit Commentary*. Grand Rapids: Eerdmans, 1950.

*Johnstone, Robert. *Lectures, Exegetical and Practical, on the Epistle of James.* Grand Rapids: Baker, 1954.

Knowling, Richard J. The Epistle of James. In the *Westminster Commentaries.* London: Methuen and Co., 1904.

Lenski, R. C. H. *The Interpretation of the Epistle to the Hebrews and the Epistle of James.* Minneapolis: Augsburg, 1943.

*Manton, Thomas. *An Exposition of the Epistle of James.* London: Banner of Truth Trust, 1962.

Mayor, Joseph B. *The Epistle of James.* Grand Rapids: Zondervan, 1954.

Mitton, C. Leslie. *The Epistle of James.* Grand Rapids: Eerdmans, 1966.

Oesterley, W. E. *The Expositors Greek New Testament.* Ed. W. R. Nicoll, Vol. IV. Grand Rapids: Eerdmans, 1961.

Plummer, Alfred. The General Epistles of St. James and St. Jude. In *The Expositors Bible.* New York: A. C. Armstrong and Son, 1908.

Plumptre, E. H. The General Epistle of St. James. In the *Cambridge Bible for Schools and Colleges.* Cambridge: Cambridge University Press, 1915 reprint.

*Robertson, A. T. *Studies in the Epistle of James.* Nashville: Broadman Press, 1959.

Ross, Alexander. The Epistles of James and John. In the *New International Commentary on the New Testament.* Grand Rapids: Eerdmans, 1954.

Strauss, Lehman. *James. Your Brother: Studies in the Epistle James.* New York: Loizeaux Brothers, 1956.

*Tasker, R. V. G. The General Epistle of James. In *The Tyndale New Testament Commentaries.* Grand Rapids: Eerdmans, 1960.

*Zodhiates, Spiros. *The Behavior of Belief.* Grand Rapids: Eerdmans, 1970.

The First Epistle Of

PETER

INTRODUCTION

Authorship. Peter identifies himself as the apostle of Jesus Christ in the salutation to his first epistle (1:1). This identity has never been seriously questioned among evangelical scholars. The book was received and used as the authentic and authoritative Word of God by Peter from earliest times in Christian churches. I Peter is quoted by Clement of Rome, Polycarp, and other early fathers of the Christian church.

It is interesting that Peter mentions in the close of his letter that he is writing "through Sylvanus," who was a companion of Paul on his second missionary journey (I Pet 5:12). This probably means that for I Peter, Silas (which is the name used in Acts) was the amanuensis or secretary for Peter. Paul also wrote most of his letters in the same manner.

We should mention that the objections to apostolic authorship have been mainly based on language and style. Could Peter the fisherman have written such a polished book with its many illusions to the Septuagint? We might briefly answer that some "polish" would be assumed with the passing of time between Peter's introduction to Jesus and the writing of the book. Peter's lack of education has often been misunderstood or overemphasized. An important factor to note is that Acts 4:13 does not mean to teach that Peter was stupid or even that he was less educated than his peers. It was confidence and authority that priests detected in Peter and John, but could not discern where they had gotten it since they were not priests but laymen. Their "field was not religion," we

might say today. The clause might be better translated, "they saw that they were laymen rather than formally educated priests." It is ridiculous prejudice which supposes that Peter could not have written such a good book. Furthermore, even if Peter had been incompetent to write the book himself, he might have done quite well with the help of his secretary, Silas. Often, in ancient times, style and precision of expression were attributed more to the amanuensis than to the author of a letter. Sylvanus (or Silas as he is called in Acts) does not appear to be less competent than Paul himself as a preacher of the apostolic message; Paul includes him in all the "we" references in the Thessalonian epistles.

A third authenticating figure is Mark who was with Peter (5:13) in Rome. Since Peter calls him "my son," we assume a very close working relationship. Mark is, of course, John Mark who also wrote the Gospel.

Purpose. Peter wrote to the Christians who lived in the Roman provinces of Pontus, Galatia, Cappadocia, Asia, and Bithynia (1:1). From the tone of the book and its vocabulary we gather that it was a time of persecution and suffering (1:6; 2:12, 15; 4:12, 14-16; 5:8-9). It is not necessary to assume any specific historical period; in fact, we do not have much information about persecution in individual localities throughout the Roman Empire. It is not certain how far and fast official government persecution spread when it did begin. Perhaps persecution started earlier in various communities. No specific information about this is given in the book itself either. It is obvious that Peter writes to encourage faithfulness and praise to God in spite of some assumed persecution. The important thing in this book is the attitude a person takes toward the suffering, persecution, and circumstances of life. Encouragement to praise God in spite of the circumstances seems to recur throughout the book along with the exhortations to holy living and hope.

Characteristics. Peter is a book of praise as much as the Psalms. The salutation itself is an abbreviated Christian psalm of praise for God's grace in Christ. The book mentions suffering and persecution but is not at all pessimistic. 1:3 praises God for the new birth. The Christian life is to be a life of hope, and the greatest hope is the return of Christ and the resurrection. Peter is a real positive thinker; note 3:13-14, "who is he that will harm you . . . and if ye suffer for righteousness' sake, happy are ye." This attitude of praise in spite of persecution is probably not peculiar to Peter but seems to be a part of the apostolic pattern of early Christian preaching. The

readers are also encouraged to live lives of purity as God's people (2:9) and God's servants (2:16). They must submit to and live in accordance with God's will for their lives in this world (2:13-3:12). Peter exhorts his readers to true humility and unity as well (5:1-6), and asks them to follow the example of Christ (2:21).

Date and place of writing. Peter wrote from "Babylon" (5:13), which is an esoteric symbol of Rome. The same symbolism is used in Revelation 17 and 18. Although persecution is mentioned often in the book, no specific persecution is mentioned, and the fact applies only generally to the latter part of the first century for a date. The most probable time seems to be between A.D. 62 and 64. Besides the references to suffering and persecution, the primitive state of the development of the church in the epistle, and the still high regard for the authority of the state (I Pet 2:13-17) support a date before A.D. 64. It was, in fact, during the notorious blood bath begun in A.D. 64 that both Peter and Paul laid down their lives in martyrdom.

OUTLINE

COMMENTARY

I. INTRODUCTION. 1:1-2.

1:1-2. Peter, an apostle of Jesus Christ. This letter opens in the usual manner for New Testament epistles and for all letters of the Hellenistic world, with the name of the writer, the address, and a greeting. Peter names himself as an **apostle** of Jesus Christ, which means that he is sent by the Lord with a commission. With this statement Peter claims a certain authority; his letter must then be received and recognized by the churches as the Word of God. The name **Peter** is the Greek form of the Aramaic "Cephas" and means "a stone." The name was given to Peter by the Lord Jesus; compare John 1:42 and Matthew 16:18. **To the strangers scattered.** The Greek word for **scattered** (Gr *diaspora*) means literally "to sow through," and was a technical term for Jews who lived outside of Palestine. Here it is applied to Gentile Christians who figuratively were sown throughout the world by God to be a witness for Him. Although they live in these various Roman provinces, Peter looked upon these Christians as **strangers,** a word that means something like "landed immigrants," and indicates that they are foreigners to the native residents, and that their permanent homeland and citizenship is in heaven. **Elect** (Gr *eklektos*) is in verse 1 in the original, and means "chosen." The implication is that God has purposely placed these Christians in their respective communities to serve Him; they are selected temporary residents who are representatives of God.

Peter now summarizes his theology within his greeting by referring to the Trinity and their cooperative work in accomplishing our great salvation. **According to the foreknowledge** (Gr *prognosis*) which means more than to merely "know about ahead of time." It is a term emphasizing the biblical idea of foreordination. Compare the use of this word in Acts 2:23 and I Peter 1:20 with reference to Christ, and in Romans 8:29 and Romans 11:2 with reference to God's people. It is especially significant here that Peter uses this word with reference to Gentiles, although he had been a devout Jew himself. Foreordination, with reference to these Christians, was accomplished by God the Father through the agency of the Holy Spirit in **sanctification.** This word (Gr *hagiasmos*) means literally "to set apart" or "make holy." The purpose toward which this activity of the Father and the Holy Spirit is directed is the **obedience and sprinkling of the blood of Jesus Christ.** In other words, the activity of the Father and the **Spirit** is directed toward salvation.

II. THE GLORY OF SALVATION. 1:3-4.

A. Salvation of Hope. 1:3-4.

3. Blessed be the God and Father. The word **blessed** (Gr *eulogēios*) is the word from which we get "eulogy," and means "to be well spoken of" or "to be praised." Peter is expressing a desire that God should be praised by all believers everywhere. Although it would be frowned upon in some churches where gravity is a visible virtue, Peter says in effect "Praise God!" The thing for which Peter wishes to praise God is the very foundation or beginning of our salvation, the new birth. If for no other reason, every Christian should praise God for being born again. It is entirely of God's initiative that we have been included in His family. He **hath begotten us again** by His great mercy and for this reason is worthy of all our praise. The words **begotten again** (Gr *anagennaō*) is used only here and in verse 23 in the New Testament, and means "to give new life to." In other literature outside the New Testament this word is used in a botanical sense, as when the trees, plants, and flowers come to life in the spring. Peter pictures the heart of man as dry, shriveled, and dead in sin until God implants the principles of the new life. When this happens, we sprout into life, leaf out, and grow in the grace and knowledge of our Lord and Saviour Jesus Christ.

Note the ideas of the "sprouting seed" and "new life" which recur in verse 23 where this same word is used. The results of the new birth for which Christians are obligated to praise God are indicated by three words in the original each preceded by the same Greek preposition: observe the words **lively hope** in verse 3, **inheritance** in verse 4, and **salvation** in verse 5. Because of the new birth we have a **lively hope**, which should probably be understood as the hope of the resurrection. We should note that the word **hope** is used in the Bible with the distinctive meaning "confident expectation." Today, of course, **hope** means merely to "want" something to happen, without having any real assurance that it will happen, as in the sentence, "I hope tomorrow will be a sunny day." The resurrection is the central hope of Christianity; it is not merely something that we want to happen, but an assurance we have. We know we shall rise!

Furthermore, Peter tells us that this living hope is built upon the resurrection of Jesus Christ Himself. This is the core of the gospel and all Christian creeds through the ages. To prove a point, Paul, in I Corinthians 15:16, reasoned negatively, "For if the dead rise not, then is not Christ raised." He went on to say, in I Corinthians 15:20, that Christ had in fact risen from the dead, and as Peter points out here, we shall rise also.

4. To an inheritance. The second result of the new birth for which we should praise God is called our **inheritance** (cf. Col 1:5, 12). The idea of an inheritance was much more important to a New Testament Jew than it is to us today. For some of us this spiritual inheritance is the only one we will ever have, but its description as incorruptible, undefiled, and unfading, evokes from us the greatest possible praise to God. This inheritance is more lasting than any earthly inheritance could be. Every stone of earth will crumble, every column will fall, every arch will collapse. Diamonds chip, gold wears away, but this inheritance of ours is a truly "imperishable" commodity. This inheritance is also described as **undefiled,** which means that it has no spot of dirt or pollution on it; it is pure as the driven snow (cf. Jas 1:27). **Fadeth not away.** Furthermore, this inheritance is "unfading," which alludes to the inheritance or "crown" of an athlete which, although considered very valuable, would very quickly fade and lose its beauty. This inheritance is said to be **reserved in heaven for you.** The perfect tense is used in Greek to show the confirmed nature of the reservation; it will not be given to someone else by mistake, it cannot be devalued by taxes, and title insurance is provided.

B. Salvation of Power. 1:5.

5. Who are kept by the power of God through faith. Believers themselves are now declared to be **kept** (Gr *phroureō*) by the power of God. This is a military term for the protection of a city by means of a military garrison. In the picture here, the power of God corresponds to an army base with the sole function of protecting believers. The soldiers of God, His angels, surround us to protect us from the bombardment of various trials and temptations so that we do not become crushed by depression and despair. The soldiers are visible only through the eyes of faith.

Unto salvation. The third result of God's grace in giving us new life in Christ is called **salvation.** This, of course, does not refer to the initial experience of accepting Jesus Christ as Saviour, but to the final, inclusive result of salvation; eternal bliss in the presence and service of God. What does the consummation of salvation include? No one knows, for as Paul said, "Eye hath not seen, nor ear heard" what "God hath prepared for them that love him" (I Cor 2:9). We have not yet seen this full and final manifestation, but Peter tells us that it is **ready to be revealed.** The implication here is that everything is fully prepared and accomplished, but remains to be unveiled. The moment of revelation is called **the last time.** The word **time** (Gr *kairos*) does not denote extension of time but designated time when something is to happen. This corresponds to the day of the Lord in Paul's writings, or the second coming of Jesus Christ. The upshot of all this is that, although a person is truly saved when he gives his life to Jesus Christ, and although he experiences the blessings of salvation every day, these are only the pledges of that glorious salvation to which he looks forward in the Day of Christ.

C. Salvation of Trial. 1:6-9.

6. Wherein ye greatly rejoice. The two words **greatly rejoice** (Gr *agalliaō*) are one word in the original which conveys the idea of a strong, deep, supporting exultation; this verb form in the original may be taken as indicative or imperative, depending on the context. The context of exhortation here seems to favor taking it as imperative. The translation would then be, "Always rejoice in this!" The thought here is parallel to the beginning of verse 3, where Peter implies the imperative "Praise God!" Although you would never realize it to look at the faces of some Christians, God wants us to be happy, and to enjoy all the physical and spiritual blessings which He gives to us. **Though now for a season.** These words indicate a concession in spite of which Christians are commanded to praise God. Another translation puts verse 6 this way, "Continue to praise God for this, even though now for a little while you may have had to suffer various trials." We shall have to learn to live more positive, happy, and praise-filled lives in obedience to this commandment if we want to hear His "Well done" on that day.

7. That the trial of your faith. The purpose toward which this command of praise is directed is that the approved character of our faith might result in praise, glory, and honor for us in that day in which Christ is revealed. Verse 7 is better translated, "So that the genuineness of their faith, more precious than gold which though perishable is tested by fire, may redound to praise and glory and honor at the revelation of Jesus Christ." It is interesting that the three words for the "approval" that God will give to those of true faith on that day are found elsewhere in Scripture with the same sense, for example I Corinthians 4:5, where Paul expresses his disinterest in the praise of men because of his forward look at the future and says, "then shall every man have praise of God."

8-9. Whom having not seen, ye love; in whom, though now ye see him not, yet believing, ye rejoice with joy unspeakable and full of glory:

Receiving the end of your faith, even the salvation of your souls. The mention of the name of Jesus Christ in verse 7 causes Peter to insert here a doxological creed concerning the One who is the center of our faith. In this passage two central concepts of Christianity, love and continual joy, revolve around the central person in Christianity by means of two relative pronouns in the original language, of which the antecedent is "Jesus Christ." It does seem strange that the recurrent theme of praise for our great salvation which pervades this passage is so often absent from our preaching today. Likewise, the two concepts of **love** and **joy,** which according to these verses should characterize all those who possess this great salvation, seem now to be in rather short supply.

D. Salvation of Revelation. 1:10-12.

10-12. Of which salvation the prophets have inquired and searched diligently. To show how great a privilege it is to possess this glorious salvation, Peter refers first to the Old Testament prophets. To describe the excitement and wonder of the prophets concerning salvation and grace, verse 10 uses two emphatic compound words. The objects of this industrious research on the part of the prophets were first, the person specifically in whom all these Messianic prophecies would be fulfilled, and second the precise moment of fulfillment (Gr *kairos*). The prophets knew a great deal about the coming salvation and the coming Saviour. They knew that their prophecies reached far beyond their own times, and even beyond the bounds of their own nation. These things were supernaturally revealed to them. There were certain aspects of the

glorious salvation which they prophesied which continually escaped them, and Peter's point is that the glorious objects of prophetic inquiry have now been openly proclaimed and fulfilled in the preaching of the apostles.

The privilege of living in the age of fulfillment should overwhelm us. This privilege is further emphasized by Peter as he refers in verse 12 to the angels; **which things the angels desired to look into.** The last word in the verse, **look into,** means graphically "stooping down close to get a peek at." The picture is that this is something the angels had always wanted to do (Greek present tense) but have never been able to accomplish. This stresses the point that although prophets and angels have been unable to satisfy themselves as to precisely what salvation is all about, we have the privilege not only of full exposition, but of real possession.

III. THE EXHORTATION TO SANCTIFICATION. 1:13-25.

A. Admonition to Sanctification. 1:13-16.

13. The main verb in verse 13 is an imperative **hope** with a participle in attendant circumstance, **gird up** (Gr *anazōnnymi*) which is a metaphor referring to the ancient oriental custom of tying up one's loose flowing robes in the process of getting ready for hard work. An equivalent contemporary metaphor would be, "let's roll up our sleeves and get right to work on the business of holiness." Observe that the main command is **hope,** which means to assume a confident attitude of expectation toward the **grace** (Gr *charis*). Into this one word **grace** Peter has put all the glorious content of our salvation previously given in verses 3-12; this "package," he says, is now being brought to us (Greek present tense), and we should live with our expectations fixed upon it. The package, **grace,** is on its way now, and will arrive in the revelation of Jesus Christ.

14-15. Not fashioning yourselves.
Again, the main verb is imperative: **be
ye holy.** Holiness is the emphatic demand put upon believers. Here it is to
involve, as a better translation has it,
"all your conduct." The participle of
attendant circumstance **not fashioning
yourselves** (Gr *syschematizo*) means
"to assume the same visible form,"
and likewise assumes the imperative
character of the main word. Holiness
has both a positive side, patterning
oneself after God, and a negative side,
nonconformity to one's former, sinful
life. Pagan standards are to be abandoned; the new model is God Himself
(see Isa 40:25; 41:16, 20).

B. Basis for Sanctification. 1:17-20.

17. And if ye call on the Father.
This clause is the protasis of a logical
premise, and might better be translated
"since you envoke as Father Him who
judges each person impartially according to his deeds, conduct yourselves
with fear." The thought is that since
these Gentiles have named the name of
God, and since He is the one who will
judge all men as a truly just Judge,
conduct here is important. **Pass the
time of your sojourning here in fear.
Pass the time** (Gr *anastrephō*) might
be misunderstood as "twiddle your
thumbs" and tremble. Once again, this
is the main verb in the imperative, and
means "conduct yourself in godly
reverence." Holiness is to pervade
every secret corner of one's life. When
we name the name of God we must
abandon all to Him.

18. Forasmuch as ye know. The participle here implies cause, and gives
reason for conducting oneself with
godly reverence; it is because we know
that we have been redeemed. The word
redeemed (Gr *lytroō*) refers to the payment of a required price to release one
from an obligation. This is one of the
most important words in the Bible
since it succinctly describes the atonement of Jesus Christ and the reason for
His death on the cross. Peter refers to
the fact that his readers, like all Christians, have been released from empty
and meaningless lives by a payment
made on their behalf. The value of the
payment that was made was far greater
than silver or gold in any amount; it
was the blood of Christ, meaning His
death on the cross, which paid the price
of release from traditional, pagan conduct. The command to live holy lives
for our brief sojourn on the earth, in
the interim, as we wait for the consummation of our salvation, is based upon
the great price paid by Jesus Christ.

**19. But with the precious blood of
Christ, as of a lamb without blemish
and without spot.** Note the continuity
that Peter assumes between the Old
and New Testaments in the phrase like
that **of a lamb without blemish or spot.**
This metaphor of Jesus as the sacrificial lamb may have been the first thing
that Peter himself learned about Jesus
(see Jn 1:29-42).

**20-21. Who verily was foreordained
before the foundation of the world.**
The word **foreordained** is the verb
form of the noun in 1:2 translated
"foreknowledge." Here in this verse it
refers to the prior determination on the
part of the Father, to send the Son as
the Saviour of the world. Although He
was predestined before the foundation
of the world, He was not made known
or manifested until **these last times.**
The **last times** (Gr *chronos*) translates
the idea of "extension of time." According to the overall schema of the
Bible, there are two extended periods
of time called "the former times" in
which the prophecies and promises
were made, and the "latter times" in
which the prophecies and promises
were fulfilled. This is, of course,
another reference to the fulfillment of
prophecy in Jesus Christ. The believers
of Peter's day and the New Testament
were the first generation to have these
things preached and made known to
them as fulfilled. In verse 21 Peter
again refers to the privilege and blessing of belief and hope in God.

C. Results of Sanctification. 1:22-25.

22-25. The appeal now goes back to the important ingredient of love mentioned in 1:8. The main verb in these four verses is **love one another;** this is the fourth in a series of imperative main verbs which are all based on the primary description of our glorious salvation in verses three through twelve. The call to holiness in verses 13-25 then involves: hope (vs. 13), holiness (vs. 15), reverence (vs. 17), and now love (vs. 22). Love, not bitterness and separation, is the outcome of holiness. If we have really **purified** (perfect tense in Greek) our lives by obeying the truth, Peter says it will result in unhypocritical brotherly love. This is possible because of our new life in Christ (again the participle in Greek is the perfect tense and implies the reality or certainty of the fact of life in Christ). Here, in verse 23, the living Word of God is the instrument used by the Spirit of God to impart principle of the new life (compare Hebrews 4:12). Peter now quotes from Isaiah 46 and following in praise of the Word of God, which unlike any human or created thing continues its beauty, effectiveness, and life forever. Everything else in the world is like grass; its beauty is only temporary. The grass dies, and its beauty fails. God's Word, however, is living and effective. Note the synonyms for the **Word:** in verse 23 it is the **word of God,** in verse 25 it is first, **the word of the Lord,** and then **the word which by the gospel is preached unto you.** It is interesting that four different expressions are used here in the Greek.

IV. THE COMMITMENT TO THE LORD. 2:1-8.

A. The Exhortations. 2:1-3.

2:1-3. Another vivid word picture is painted by Peter as he refers to Christians as needing milk to grow. The metaphorical allusions are mixed, since Peter goes from "putting on new clothes," to "fussing for milk," to "growing like a plant" unto salvation, to "tasting" the goodness of the Lord, to "stones," and "spiritual houses." One thing is common to all these metaphors, however, and that is the idea of growing to maturity, or becoming what God wants us to be in the world. Again, Peter introduces his thought with a subordinate clause and a participle of attendant circumstance, **laying aside.** This is an everyday word which means "to change clothes"; it is the word used by Paul in Ephesians 4:22 where he speaks of putting off the old man and putting on the new man like a suit of clothes. As Christians, we must take off the ragged and filthy clothes of sin: malice, hypocrisy, deceit, envy, and slander.

In verse 2, the figure changes to a hungry, fussing, sucking baby who wants to be fed. The **milk** with which we long to be fed in the figure is, of course, **the word** (Gr *logikos*). This adjective really means "reasonable" or "rational," and intends to interpret the figure. Peter intends the reader to understand "milk for the mind," rather than for the mouth. We are to **desire** this milk; the word used here denotes a very strong emotion or passion fixed upon something. The figure is again changed to plant growth, where the resulting mature plant or tree is salvation (see 1:3-12). The idea of a tree with perhaps fruit, may have suggested Peter's next figure of "tasting" to see if the Lord is good (quoted from Ps 34:8).

B. The Stone of Stumbling. 2:4-8.

4. As unto a living stone. Since Peter had become very familiar with the Greek Old Testament and the striking continuity between its prophecies of the Messiah and their fulfillment in Jesus Christ on the one hand, and between the people of God in the Old Testament and believers in his own era on the other hand, he is here taken up completely with the beauty of metaphor and allusion. He is thinking now of God's people as a building and of Jesus Christ as the **living stone,** fulfilling the prophecy of Isaiah 28:16, "Behold, I lay in Zion for a foundation a stone, a tried stone, a precious corner stone, a sure foundation." Christ is called a **living stone** because, although He is a part of the figure, He is also a real person. Likewise, those who have come to Christ and have received life through Him are called **living stones.** Since Christ had been rejected by the chief priests and leaders of the Jews, Matthew (21:42) saw this as a fulfillment of the Old Testament. Paul also (I Cor 3:11) looked upon his preaching of Christ as laying a foundation upon which others might build. For Paul too, the church was a "building" (I Cor 3:9).

5. Peter uses the same figure that Paul had used and says, **ye also, as lively stones** or "and like living stones you are yourselves being built into a spiritual house so that you may be a holy priesthood." The preposition used in the original language here implies that the purpose for which these Gentile Christian **stones** are being selected, trimmed, and built into a structure is that they might function as a **holy priesthood.** With this, Peter again changes the figure momentarily from buildings and stones to the priesthood. Since the priesthood in the Old Testament had the function of offering animal sacrifices acceptable to God, in the metaphor the church as the new **priesthood** offers sacrifices through Jesus Christ, but they are **spiritual sacrifices.** The author of Hebrews (13:15) also uses the same figures but more specifically names the sacrifices as those of praise and confessing His name.

6. Another reference to the chosen and valuable cornerstone, Jesus Christ applies this statement also, **he that believeth on him shall not be confounded.** The word **confounded** (Gr *kataischynō*) comes from a textual variation in the Septuagint translation of Isaiah 28:16 which is quoted by the New Testament writers. Paul, in Romans 9:33 and 10:11, seems to define quite well the meaning of being **confounded,** or being "put to shame"; it means to "fail to be saved." Whatever the meaning in the Old Testament, the meaning of the quotation in the New Testament and here is, "the person who believes in Him will certainly not fail to be saved."

7-8. Christianity is a matter of one's attitude toward Jesus Christ. He uses the quotations from Isaiah to show that while believers consider this choice stone to be valuable in that they honor, respect, and worship Him, to the unbelievers and disobedient on the other hand Christ has become a **stone of stumbling and a rock of offense.** According to the Old Testament prophecy and Peter's view of its fulfillment, the "chief cornerstone" and foundation of salvation for some, has become the cause of destruction for others who refuse to believe in Him.

V. THE IMPLICATIONS OF HUMILITY. 2:9-3:12.

A. The Believer's Life in General. 2:9-21a.

9. But ye shows a strong contrast between unbelievers and Peter's readers who are Christians. The figure is changed again, and the focus is on the church (New Testament believers) to which are applied the words **ye are a chosen generation, a royal priesthood, a holy nation, a peculiar people; that ye should show forth the praises of him.** These words are from two Old Testament passages (Ex 19:6; Isa 43:21) and show that Peter considers that the privileges and responsibilities of Israel in the Old Testament are now being transferred to the church as the people of God in his own day. This same continuity is recognized by the other New Testament writers as well (see II Cor 4:6; Col 3:12; Rev 1:6).

Along with the great blessings of being the heirs of God's salvation, however, there are great responsibilities.

Peter sums up these in the words **that ye should show forth the praises of him.** The word **show forth** (Gr *exangellō*) means literally "to tell out," and refers to the "preaching" of the gospel, the good news, or **praises** of God. **His marvelous light** (see II Cor 4:6) is probably a reference to Isaiah 9:1, and Christ as the "Light of the world." See also II Peter 1:3. Another amazing proof of the continuity between the Old Testament and Peter's age of fulfillment, and between Israel and the church, is the application of the Hosea passages (1:6, 9; 2:3, 23) directly to his readers and therefore to the church.

11-12. Dearly beloved, I beseech you. The word **beseech** (Gr *parakaleō*) actually denotes encouragement, and might better be translated, "My dear people, let me encourage you. . . ." Although this is the main verb in these two verses, it is completed by two others which comprise the content of the exhortation to these who are **strangers and pilgrims** (that is, they are in the world of the Gentiles, but no longer of the world.) The first exhortation is to **abstain from fleshly lusts,** and the reason given is that they are in constant battle against the soul or the spirit (cf. Gal 5:24). The second exhortation is to maintain good conduct **among the Gentiles.** It should be noted that **conversation,** as usual in the New Testament, does not refer to talking but to conduct. Note further that the word **honest,** with reference to conduct, does not mean merely the virtue we today call honesty; Peter means rather to say that one's whole life is to be good, in the sense of being "Christian." The purpose toward which all this care in conduct is directed is the glory of God. Even though some people might slander the believers as if they were evildoers, they would in the long run, as they observed their Christian conduct, be forced to glorify God in the **day of visitation.** This phrase comes from Isaiah 10:3 where it is the name for the day of punishment or judgment; since that eschatological **day** is for some a day of judgment and for others a day of vindication and salvation, the term can have either connotation (cf. Lk 1:68 and 19:44).

13. Submit yourselves to every ordinance of man for the Lord's sake. The word **submit** (Gr *hypotassō*) is the key to the whole section 2:11-3:12; it means literally "to arrange under," and is used in various contexts to indicate subjection or subordination. In military contexts it was used for the idea of rank. In various New Testament contexts it is used for the relationship between children and their parents, servants and their masters, or wives and their husbands. Here, Peter seems to command the believers, "fit into your place in the social structure with Christian humility." This idea of subordination to the system controls the whole passage. Notice that the word is used in verse 18 for servants, in 3:1 for wives, and implied in 3:7 for husbands (not subjection to their wives but to the social structure as Christians).

In this passage as well as in Ephesians 5, this word for "submit" is very closely related to the word for "humility" which is found in 3:8 as a summary of this whole passage. The implications of Christian humility for Christian living are first given generally in 2:13-17, and then specifically as they relate to servants, wives, and husbands. **To every ordinance of man** is a difficult phrase to translate; perhaps, "Be subject for the Lord's sake to every human institution." Peter writes that they are to be subject to the king because he is supreme; the king or ruler at this time was the Roman Emperor Nero. Christians respected the office regardless of the personal ethics of the man because they believed he had been appointed by God to rule.

14-17. Or unto governors. Since they are authorized by the king, the reasoning behind this philosophy is that we are all the servants of God (vs. 16) and so are obligated to submit to those whom He allows to be in office. The passage seems to be assuming a good government which recognizes, at least in general, the laws of God according to the Scripture. Government is supposed to punish those who do evil (vs. 14), and reward those who do good. There are times, when government is itself in violation of the power and authority given by God and contrary to Scripture, when the Christian must not submit (Acts 5:29). Peter himself on one occasion boldly refused to submit to authority on the grounds that it was contrary to the will of God (Acts 4:19). The general introduction to the subject of humility is summarized by four brief commandments in verse 17: **Honor all men. Love the brotherhood. Fear God. Honor the king.**

18-21a. Peter now approaches the subject of the implications of humility for specific groups, and deals first with **Servants.** The word used here for **servants** is used of household servants or domestics who received wages for what they did in the household. Out of respect for their **masters** they are to submit or conduct themselves properly under the circumstances of this social institution. This is Christian humility. Their conduct is not to be determined by whether their masters are good and gentle, but by Christian ethics; they must also submit to those who are "crooked" and difficult, since there are some people who are hard to get along with. **For this is thankworthy.** The word **thankworthy** (Gr *charis*) is idiomatic for "what pleases God"; the literal translation would be "grace," which in the New Testament usually has the underlying connotation of something which is acceptable to God. Here, what pleases God is that a man can endure pain while suffering un-

justly for the sake of his godly conscience.

A similar idiom is found in verse 20, **For what glory is it.** Here, the word "glory" is likewise idiomatic. It is not the punishment, or even enduring punishment which is creditable, but doing good, continuing to be humble, and continuing to submit even though your goodness is not recognized. **For even hereunto were ye called.** Peter indicates by this that the humility or submission that is advocated is the will of God for all Christians. At this point Peter introduces the example of Christ.

B. The Atonement of Christ. 2:21b-25.

21b. Christ also suffered for us. That is the suffering of Christ was vicarious is indicated by the preposition **for** (Gr *hyper*), which means "in behalf of" or "instead of." The passion of Christ was the most prominent aspect of the preaching of Christ, and was very familiar to all Christians. No mere human being could ever suffer as He suffered.

Leaving us an example. This, of course, is not the main purpose of the suffering of Christ (a participle of attendant circumstance in Greek) but it does so happen that His conduct even in His passion provides us with a perfect pattern of Christian humility, and this is what Peter offers here. **Example** (Gr *hypogrammos*) was literally something to "write under." Originally a line of writing at the top of a tablet written by the teacher so that the child could write under it and make his letters like the master. Our Lord and Master suffered more than any other, and we are called upon to follow His humility. The figure is emphatic, here, since the word **follow** really means "follow exactly" and there are clear "footprints." The mention of the suffering of Christ leads Peter into a recitation of the essentials of the Messianic nature of the suffering experienced; He suffered, but more important than that, He suffered as the Servant of Jehovah, and as it was predicted of Him in the Old Testament. This was too important to Peter to be left unsaid; he had been rebuked as "Satan" for missing it before (Mk 8:31-33.)

22-23. Who did no sin, neither was guile found in his mouth is a quotation from Isaiah 53:9 and was part of the apostolic preaching identifying Jesus as the Messiah. The silence of Christ in the fact of His extreme suffering is also a prominent idea found in Isaiah 53:7. He as our example in humility left the vindication with God the Father.

24. Who his own self bare our sins in his own body is from Isaiah 53:4-5, and is used to show the vivid and detailed way in which Jesus fulfilled the prophecies and accomplished our redemption. He had no sins of His own (vs. 22); He suffered and died vicariously. He gave His body in death on the cross for the purpose (Greek final clause) that we **being dead to sins, should live unto righteousness. Being dead** (Gr *apoginomai*) means literally to "move away from," and might be better translated, "that we might die to sin and live to righteousness." The thought is that the life of Christian humility which is being exhorted here is a basic part of the reason for Christ's death on the cross. **By whose stripes** (wounds) is another supporting quotation from Isaiah 53:6.

25. For ye were as sheep going astray. Healing is one primary figure for redemption; coming home is another, probably suggested by it. Ezekiel 34:5-6 refers to the people of God as scattered sheep; Peter sees that the church has now been brought back, and since it is Christ who has accomplished this, He is the Shepherd. The word **Bishop** (Gr *episkopos*) meaning "manager" is used in the New Testament as synonymous with "elder" or "pastor," but is here applied to Christ as the ultimate Bishop of souls.

C. The Believer's Life at Home. 3:1-12.

3:1. Likewise, ye wives, be in subjection to your own husbands. This section (3:1-6) is grammatically related to the general statement on humility (2:13-17) by **likewise** (Gr *homoiōs*), and by the general dependent participial clause translated **be in subjection.** The word **subjection** (see on 2:13) says to the women readers, "Your part in applying humility to Christian living is to be a living testimony to your own husbands by the way you fit into the social structure; take your place in marriage seriously and be a good wife." It is obvious that the attitude encouraged here can only be expected from a Christian person; Peter does not imply that women are inferior, and therefore should submit to their husbands. A person who is born again has already submitted to God through Christ. If he wants to live Christian humility, he will also submit to government for God's sake, to his masters or employers, and now in this institution of marriage, the wife will submit to her husband (a good or bad husband) in the same spirit.

Does this mean that the husband is the boss in the institution of marriage? How can it mean anything else? The king is the boss, the employer is the boss, and now in the same context the husband is the boss. Keep in mind that in verse 7 Peter has a word to the husband concerning his part in submitting to the system. This does not mean, of course, that wives must obey their husbands if their husbands command something that will violate the law of God; here, the principle of Acts 4:19 would once more apply. The purpose toward which this unbearable humility is directed is that **they also may without the word be won** (Gr *kerdainō*). This is a business word and means "to make a profit" as opposed to experiencing a loss; it vividly portrays the credit and debit sides of the ledger. In the New Testament, the "business" of the church is "winning" the lost (Mt 28:19); the converts are in the sense of this word, "gains." In this verse Christian wives can win their husbands to the Lord just by applying humility and by being a good wife.

2. Conversation in the Bible means "conduct" or "behavior," and the kind of behavior suggested here is further described by **chaste,** and **coupled with fear,** fear meaning respect or reverence, and implying true humility.

3-4. Whose adorning (Gr *kosmos*) means to refer to the beauty or attractiveness which these husbands will see in their wives. The sense is, "Make sure your primary beauty is found in your heart and not merely in your clothes and jewelry." These verses should not be twisted to condemn the use of cosmetics or jewelry; they merely emphasize that, as far as God is concerned, it is more important to have a **meek and quiet spirit.**

5-6. For after this manner. Peter again turns to the Old Testament for illustrations to support his exhortation to humility. This is the way **holy women . . . who trusted in God adorned themselves. Trusted** (Gr *elpizō*) means literally "hoped" in God, and pictures a life of calm assurance and certainty about the fact that God will reward such humility. These women made themselves beautiful to God by **being in subjection unto their own husbands. Sarah** is the prime example. As Abraham was the father of the faithful, so Sarah is the mother of the faithful. Peter's readers should want to be her **daughters;** this can be accomplished by doing **well.** Doing well in this passage can only mean humbling oneself to submit to one's husband. The meaning of humility for wives becomes terribly clear with the concrete example of Sarah: she obeyed her husband and called him **lord.**

7. Likewise. This is the same word which was used in 3:1 to refer back to 3:18 and 3:13; by it Peter introduces

the third specific group to which he applies the principle of humility. The use of this word implies that the husbands are also to be "subject" in the social institution of marriage which is in view here; the Greek word for subjection is not used but the idea is understood as now applying to husbands, just as it did to servants and wives. In what sense can husbands "be subject" in marriage? Certainly, they cannot be subject to their wives for that would contradict 3:1-6. In a marriage, someone has to be the head of the home; it cannot be a fifty-fifty split of authority, and democracy will not work here since the vote would be tied. The husband is the leader, and yet he must also submit in humility, not to his wife, but to the good of the marriage.

Ye husbands, is now addressing Christian husbands who may or may not have unsaved wives to win to the Lord. **Dwell with them according to knowledge.** The husband has a much greater responsibility than the wife; all the decisions of living together are his. **Giving honor unto the wife** may imply a great deal of humility and self-sacrifice in order to show this honor. In this way the husband can submit without neglecting leadership. **As unto the weaker vessel** does not imply inferiority, but probably does refer to physical strength. **As being heirs together of the grace of life.** The grace of life is the inheritance which has been received together; part of that grace is the wife's, and the husband is to see that she gets it. If the husband does not give honor to the wife, prayers will be hindered. All the responsibility in this verse is with the husband; all the blessing and honor belongs to the wife.

8-9. Finally. This does not signal the end of the letter, but the end of the section (2:11-3:12); this is to introduce another summary or general statement like that at the beginning. Again, the central idea is humility, and the same main verb is implied, namely, "submit" to one another, each one humbly filling his place in the Christian community by being or doing the things listed here. **Be pitiful, be courteous** should rather be translated, "have a tender heart and a humble mind."

10-12. For he that will love life. Although the arrangement of the text does not show it, verses 10-12 are a poem quoted from Psalm 34:13-17 of the Septuagint, the Greek version of the Old Testament. The poem sums up the implications of humility for all the aspects of life in general; it is the epitome of the Christian life. The person who wants a truly happy life, enjoying all God's blessings, must first turn away from evil in both word and deed. On the positive side, he must pursue or "run after" peace. This kind of person can be happy because God's eye is on him for protection, God's ear is open to his prayer.

VI. THE CHRISTIAN ATTITUDE TOWARD SUFFERING. 3:13-4:19.

A. Christians and the World. 3:13-17.

13. And who is he that will harm you. Paul had asked (Rom 8:34) a similar question, "Who can condemn you?" Peter seems to take the view that it is highly unlikely that anyone would deliberately bring harm to someone who is a **follower** (Gr *zēlōtēs*) or "zealot" **of that which is good.**

14. But and if ye suffer for righteousness' sake, happy are ye. This is a future condition with the Greek optative mood indicating the possibility that some of them could suffer in the future, but even if they should suffer, they would in fact be **happy. Happy** does not mean they will be singing about it, but rather that they would in fact be privileged to suffer for the sake of Christ. This is exactly what Jesus had taught in the Beatitudes (Mt 5:10), and what Peter had reminded his readers of in 2:20.

15. But sanctify the Lord God. Following another text, a better translation has, "Have no fear of them, nor be troubled, but in your hearts reverence Christ as Lord." **Be ready always to give an answer** (Gr *apologia*), that is not just a reply, but a defense **of the hope that is in you.** What Peter is suggesting is that suffering may be another opportunity to testify of the saving power of Christ and so win some of the persecutors. The word **hope** refers to the whole system or philosophy of Christianity in general, as well as specifically to the attitude of certainty and assurance about the resurrection and the coming of Christ. **With meekness and fear.** These indicate an attitude of humility toward men, and not fear but reverence and worship toward God.

16-17. Having a good conscience. Again, Peter emphasizes that it is better to suffer for doing good than for doing evil. On these verses, see 2:20.

B. Christ's Ministry on Earth. 3:18-22.

18. For Christ also hath once suffered for sins. Some texts have "died for sins," but most interpreters opt for **suffered** because it fits the context better and is a very common word in this epistle. The word **for** translates three different Greek words in the verse; some translations have four "for's." The reason for the advice in verse 17 is, "Because Christ suffered" (Gr *hoti*). Christ suffered "concerning" (Gr *peri*) sins, and He suffered on our behalf, the Just One "in place of" (Gr *hyper*) unjust sinners. It is made very clear that His suffering was not just an exemplary suffering; it was vicarious, and it was an atonement for our sins. Its purpose was to **bring us to God.**

Peter now moves into the illustrative and hortatory part of his citation of the suffering of Christ. He is writing to those who may very soon have to suffer at the hands of wicked men, and so refers to the fact that Christ had also suffered at the hands of wicked men. This is apparently the meaning of the

cryptic **being put to death in the flesh.**
The word **flesh** is used by Peter to refer
to mankind in 1:24, and this seems here
to be the obvious opposite to the **Spirit**
who raised Christ to life again. At any
rate, it would seem that **flesh** and **Spirit**
have a parallel but opposite meaning;
if Jesus' flesh and spirit are meant
rather than the Holy Spirit, it is difficult to view the resurrection as pertaining to only the spirit and not the body.
Furthermore, the "in-his-flesh, in-his-
spirit" interpretation says nothing as
to the agents of the passive verbs, and
gives no example or encouragement for
Peter's readers.

**19. By which also he went and
preached** connotes the agency of the
Holy Spirit if we retain the AV translation, **by the Spirit** (vs. 18). In this
view, maintaining the continuity between verse 18 and verse 19, the same
Holy Spirit who raised Christ from the
dead had enabled him to preach to the
men of Noah's day through Noah
himself. While this interpretation fits
the context and is legitimate by twentieth century standards, it does require
some juggling of one's natural understanding of the original text. The alternative interpretation is to understand
that before the resurrection someone
"made alive" the human spirit of Jesus
so that in this form He preached to the
spirits in Hades. This interpretation
has problems too; for example, the
content of the preaching is supposed to
be an announcement of victory rather
than the preaching of the gospel
message, but the wrong word is used
(Gr *kēryssō*). Also, according to 4:6,
the gospel is preached to the dead, and
the word there definitely means
"preach the gospel" or "evangelize"
(Gr *euangelizomai*).

**20-21. The ark . . . wherein few,
that is, eight souls were saved by water.**
The mention of Noah and the Ark provides the perfect opportunity to expound on the figurative correspondence between the **ark** and **baptism,** which *doth also now save us.*

Technically, of course, it is not true
that baptism saves; the merely
mechanical performance of the
religious rite would only make a sinner
into a very wet sinner. Peter means to
explain this with **not the putting away
of the filth of the flesh.** What is meant
is just as the Ark had something to do
with the deliverance of those people
from the judgment of the Flood, so
baptism, assuming that a person has
accepted Christ as Saviour and desires
to obey in this ordinance, has
something to do with deliverance from
sin. It's only a picture, a type, and the
correspondence is very close.

**22. Angels and authorities and
powers being made subject unto him.**
The mention of the resurrection and
ascension calls for the declaration of
Christ's victory over the powers; they
have all been subjected to Him (Gr
hypotassō). Just as Christians must
submit to human social structures
(2:13-3:12) to live in true humility, so
the structures themselves together with
all supernatural powers must submit to
Jesus Christ who is over all (cf. Eph
1:21; Col 2:15; Heb 2:5).

**C. Christ's Example in Suffering.
4:1-6.**

4:1-2. Peter now goes back to the
thought of the suffering of Jesus mentioned in verse 18, in order to encourage these believers who might very
shortly have to suffer themselves. **Forasmuch then as Christ hath suffered
for us in the flesh.** No article or preposition occurs before either use of **flesh**
in verse 1 or the use in 3:18; the contexts alone must determine the meaning. **Arm yourselves likewise with the
same mind. Arm** (Gr *hoplizomai*)
means to "equip" or "outfit" as one
would outfit an army unit with the best
possible weapons for a particular battle. The best "weapon" here would be
the same **mind** (Gr *ennoia*) or view
toward the suffering that Christ Himself had. It was not that Christ enjoyed
suffering, but He endured it in order to

accomplish our salvation (3:18). **For** (Gr *hoti*) may indicate the content of the proper view toward suffering at the hands of sinful men, namely that **he that hath suffered . . . hath ceased from sin** (Greek perfect tense, meaning "to have truly stopped"). **That** (Gr *eis*) indicates the reason or purpose for so equipping oneself, that is, so that he need no longer **live the rest of his time in the flesh to the lusts of men, but to the will of God.** "In the flesh" in verse 2 has a preposition which may mean "among."

3. **For the time past of our life may suffice us to have wrought the will of the Gentiles.** This might better be translated, "You have already spent too much time thinking like Gentiles, living in licentiousness, passion, parties, carousing, drinking, and meaningless idolatry."

4. **Wherein they think it strange that ye run not with them.** Peter's readers were, of course, Gentles, and had lived like Gentiles all their lives. Their salvation and conversion to Christianity was much more profound than we can imagine today. It is no wonder that the companions of these people were surprised when they no longer continued to live in sin. **Speaking evil of you** (Gr *blasphēmeo*). Since they were unable to understand the Christians, they abused them.

5-6. **Who shall give account.** There will come a time when they shall have to settle up with God who is **ready to judge the quick** (living) **and the dead. For this cause was the gospel preached also to them that are dead.** The idea here parallels 3:19, although the word **preached** (Gr *euangelizomai*) here is different and means specifically to "evangelize." It is probably impossible to be sure, but to **the dead** could mean that they are dead when Peter writes, but were alive when the gospel was preached to them. At least we know that the Bible does not teach that men have a second chance to be saved after death. **That they might be judged ac-**cording to men in the flesh, but live according to God in the spirit.** If this refers to the opportunity these Gentiles had to be saved while they were still alive, we might rephrase it, "They had a choice between human condemnation by wicked men, or divine life by the Spirit." This interpretation at least allows a consistent meaning throughout the passage for "flesh" and "Spirit."

D. **Christian's Conduct through Suffering. 4:7-19.**

7. **But the end of all things is at hand.** As he continues to develop the theme of the Christian attitude toward suffering, Peter wishes now to reemphasize the positive elements of the Christian life in light of the consummation of all things. **At hand** (Gr *enggizō*) is in the perfect tense in Greek and emphasizes the certainty of the nearness of the end. Although this word is used only once in Peter, it was a frequent topic in the apostolic preaching and in the preaching of Jesus and John the Baptist. An equivalent statement in James 5:8 says that the Parousia of the Lord is very near.

8. **Have fervent charity** means, of course, "warm love" toward each other as Christian brothers; it has nothing to do with either giving money as a contribution or the slippery, formal, outward courtesy of good culture. **Charity shall cover the multitude of sins.** Peter draws support from the Greek Old Testament with the quotation of Proverbs 10:12, which simply means that if a person has true love for others, his shortcomings will not be obvious.

9. **Hospitality . . . without grudging** (Gr *gonggysmos*) is easily understood if difficult to perform; hospitality, again, should not be confused with courtesy which is far less costly. Because of the separation of verses in our Bible, it is easy to overlook the fact that verses 10 and 11 are an exposition of "love" and "hospitality" in verses 8

and 9. **As every man hath received the gift** (Gr *charisma*) does not refer to talents, nor does the word have the article in the original. Not "the gift," but "any gift" (meaning something one gets for nothing) is to be given in the same way that it is received, without grudging. This is the thing that makes us **good stewards** of God's **grace. Minister the same to one another** in this context means being hospitable to one another. In the early church, apostles and preachers were constantly travelling from one town to another spreading the gospel. In this type of ministry, they needed someone to minister to them in return by providing the physical necessities of life. The gospel came as a free gift, so should the support of the gospel preachers. In this passage, both the preaching of the message of the gospel, and ministering to the physical needs of the preachers through genuine Christian hospitality, are to be done to glorify God in the name of Jesus Christ.

12-13. Beloved, think it not strange concerning the fiery trial which is to try you. It is possible that the **Amen** of verse 11 was an attempt to close the letter and Peter may have just now heard of some new development in which some of his readers are involved. If not, then he feels that he needs to say a bit more about the attitude of a Christian toward suffering. Either way **fiery trial** need not refer to literal fire like that of Rome in A.D. 64. The important thing here is to note how they are to look upon whatever trial it is; they are not to consider it **strange** (Why me, Lord?), but to rejoice (consider themselves privileged) that they can share in the sufferings of Christ. Then, in the Revelation of Christ, they will be able to be **glad also with exceeding joy.** Three words for joy are used to emphasize true happiness at His coming, and the translations are necessarily awkward at expressing this.

14. If ye be reproached (Gr *oneidizō*) is present tense and literally, "if you are being reproached"; the word denotes heaping insults upon a person. The reproach here is caused by confessing **the name.** The apodosis of the sentence implies "you are" really fortunate, that is, according to the teachings of Christ (Mt 5:10) and Christianity. **Happy are ye.** The reason they should consider themselves fortunate is because of the presence of the Spirit which is a sign of the approval, blessing, and protection of God. **The spirit of glory and of God. Glory** may be an allusion to the "Shekinah" glory cloud of the Old Testament (Ex 33:9-10; 40:34-35.

15-16. But let none of you suffer as a murderer, or as a thief, or as an evildoer, or as a busybody. Peter again returns to this truth mentioned before in 2:20 and 3:17, to show that it is not suffering in itself which is virtuous, but suffering for the name of the Lord, or **as a Christian** which counts. None of his readers should suppose that just punishment for sin by the government would bring the praise of God. The name "Christian" was applied in New Testament times as a term of derision (Acts 11:26; 26:28). Just being a Christian was at times punishable by death, or lesser penalties. History indicates that many have been killed for admitting to being Christians in these times of persecution by the government. **Let him not be ashamed,** that is, of this name of being a "Christian." Let him rather be proud of it, and use this derogatory name as a means and instrument for bringing glory to God.

17-18. For the time is come. The word **time** (Gr *kairos*) refers to a specific, designated, or predicted time when something is supposed to happen. Peter is again making reference to the end time; these verses are an apocalyptic pronouncement with application from the persecution which is beginning to come upon believers. One of the elements of apocalyptic discourse is **judgment** (Gr *krima*); the meaning here would be rather general, the same as "suffering" or "punishment." The application runs that if in the end time judgment and punishment are to come, and we are now beginning to see suffering and punishment (for being a Christian) of the people of God (this is the meaning of **house of God**), this must mean that the end of time is here, or at least very close. **What shall the end be,** that is, what will happen most certainly before this is all over, to **them that obey not the gospel of God?** There is obviously no doubt at all about what will happen to them; they will be judged, and all the apocalyptic predictions about God's wrath upon His enemies will be fulfilled. Peter is attempting to encourage the believers to gladly face any dangers or suffering for Christ by appealing to the apocalyptic comfort that God will punish the ungodly in that day. He draws support from his deep knowledge of the Old Testament and quotes Proverbs 11:31, **if the righteous scarcely be saved, where shall the ungodly and the sinner appear?**

19. In summary of this section, Peter exhorts, **let them that suffer** (the Greek present tense implies the suffering may already have begun) . . . **commit** (Gr *paradidōmi*). It is interesting that this is the same word Peter used in 2:23 to describe what Jesus did in His suffering for our sins on the Cross; He committed Himself "to him that judgeth righteously." Compare Luke 23:46, where Jesus committed His spirit to God, and Acts 7:59, where Stephen prayed in his martyrdom for the Lord Jesus to receive his spirit. This may be an encouragement to bravery in martyrdom if it becomes inevitable, rather than telling Christians to pray for deliverance.

VI. THE CHRISTIAN AND THE COMING OF THE LORD. 5:1-9.

A. Exhortation to the Elders. 5:1-4.

5:1. The elders which are among you I exhort. The elders (Gr *presby-teros*) are not a group in any one place, since this is a circular letter intended for several different congregations, but probably individuals who have been appointed by the apostles in various cities (see 1:1; Acts 14:23). **Elder** as the title for an office has not to do with age, but respect (which originally came from age). Peter has a special exhortation for these spiritual leaders, and to make it more effective, he briefly lists his superior qualifications. **Who am also an elder.** The original has the compound word (Gr *sympresbyteros*) which means an elder serving along with you who are elders.

Peter is also a **witness of the sufferings of Christ.** The word "witness" (Gr *martys*) is the word from which we get the English word "martyr," but denotes here a person who testifies to the truth of something. A **witness** of the sufferings of Christ, then, does not mean someone who has necessarily seen the sufferings, but someone who testifies to the truth and meaning of what happened. The apostles were all witnesses in the sense that they affirmed Jesus to be the Suffering Servant of Jehovah, who according to the Old Testament, was to accomplish the salvation of God's people. Peter learned this himself (cf. Mk 8:31-33) and was now an authoritative proclaimer of the sufferings of Christ. It should be noted that the prophets (1:11) had the Spirit's **witness** of the sufferings of Christ, long before anyone had "seen" these sufferings.

And also a partaker of the glory that shall be revealed. A **partaker** (Gr *koinonos*) is one who shares in something, or is a partner in it. It is not likely that Peter would call himself a "partner" in something that was not yet revealed; it may be that he means to say that he is a partner in the great glory of salvation which was revealed (partially) to the prophets and now had already been fulfilled in his time. See again 1:3-12, and note especially verse 1:11 concerning the **glory** that was to follow the sufferings of Christ according to the prophets. **Shall be** (Gr *mello*) is a present participle in the original which might be better translated, "the glory that was to be revealed," meaning the prophesied blessing of salvation to the Gentiles. Note in this connection, Acts 2:39 from the preaching of Peter at Jerusalem.

2. The content of Peter's exhortation to the elders is expressed in the first word of verse 2, **Feed the flock of God.** This one word sums up the total pastoral responsibility to the flock, or congregation. The word **feed** (Gr *poimainō*) is a cognate of **flock** (Gr *poimnion*), and is especially important because of the biblical metaphor of the people of God as a flock, and their spiritual leaders as shepherds (Gr *poimēn*). The responsibilities of the shepherds (or elders, the terms are synonymous) are many, but are quite obvious from this metaphor of "tending the flock." Compare Jn 21:16; Acts 20:28; I Tim 3:2-7; Tit 1:11; Phile 14; I Pet 2:25. The shepherd has the total responsibility for the care and welfare of the flock; he does not just **feed.** This basic concept has come down to the present day in the word "pastor" (from the Latin *pascere*, "feed"); it is the key concept in seminary training.

Peter defines his exhortation to the elders with three sets of negative and positive words; two sets of words deal with how to pastor as far as the pastor's attitude is concerned, while the third set deals with how to pastor as far as the method is concerned. **Not by constraint, but willingly** means that the pastor or elder is "called" to this vocation; he does not need to be pressed into it, for he feels called, he wants to do it. This is the proper attitude for the pastor today as well; he should enjoy his work. **Not for filthy lucre, but of a ready mind.** Filthy lucre (Gr *aischrokerdōs*) is an adverb from two words meaning "shameful gain." Since the word is used only one time in all Chris-

tian literature, it is difficult to determine its precise meaning, but we know that it's opposite here is **of a ready mind** (Gr *prothymōs*) which means "eagerly." The passage does not say that there is something wrong with money, or with the pastor getting paid. The Bible clearly teaches that pastors should be paid at least as well as other professional people. The pastor or elder should not choose this vocation just because it is such a lucrative occupation (fortunately, there is no danger of this today!), however, but should be eager to do it.

3. The third set of words, **Neither as being lords over God's heritage, but being examples to the flock,** has to do with method of ministry. Another translation has, "not as domineering over those in your charge." The idea is that there is to be no "browbeating," "whipcracking," or "intimidation."

4. Peter refers to the second coming of Christ as the manifestation of the **chief Shepherd,** when the shepherds will be rewarded with a glorious and unfading crown.

B. Exhortation to the Younger. 5:5-9.

5. Likewise, ye younger, submit yourselves unto the elder. Both words are in the plural; the younger men likewise have an exhortation from Peter. It is to **submit** (Gr *hypotassō*) to the elders. See 2:13-17 for the meaning of this word which here implies that the younger men, the elders or pastors, as well as all Christians in general (in this text, the congregation) must fit themselves into the social structure (here the church) and do their part. The elders are not told to submit because they are the leaders, but it is implied that they submit to the "Chief Shepherd." **Be clothed with humility.** The word **be clothed** (Gr *engkomboomai*) means literally to "tie on" an apron; here the thing to be tied on is **humility,** which is the same word used by Peter in 3:8 in the same close connection with the word "submit." Humility is simply assuming the proper role in relationship to others. Again Peter draws upon the Old Testament to prove his point by quoting Proverbs 3:34.

6. Humble yourselves therefore under the mighty hand of God, that he may exalt you in due time. Due time (Gr *kairos*) sounds like "by and by" or "after sufficient time has passed," but the word really means a specific and designated time; here it refers to God's time, namely the second coming of Christ, and more precisely, at the Revelation. **Humble** (synonymous with humility and submit above) is the opposite of **exalt**; it means literally "think low," but in actual usage in the Bible it does not gender a lack of self-confidence or a low self-image. Humility in the Bible, in fact, is an attitude that will bolster and support self-confidence, for it simply means assuming the role that God has assigned to us in life. True humility does not say, "I'm no good; I can't." It says, "This is what God wants me to do; I shall."

7. Casting all your care. Humility means that we do not have to bear our anxieties; we are told to "toss them over to him" (**casting** is a participle of attendant circumstance which assumes the imperative character of the main verb here). The two words for "care" in verse 7 must be distinguished: the first means anxieties, the second refers to the meticulous, personal concern God has about us. He is interested in us and willing to carry all our anxieties if we are willing to do what He wants us to do.

8-9. Several summary exhortations are now given: **Be sober** is nearly the same in meaning as **be vigilant.** The devil is pictured as a prowling lion who is seeking someone to devour. The mention of suffering twice in the context indicates that the devil is to be blamed for it, but is to be resisted with strong faith.

VIII. CONCLUSION. 5:10-14.

10-11. Verses 10 and 11 are more than a doxology and close; they are a great encouragement to these suffering saints. They promise that God will Himself **make you perfect, stablish, strengthen, and settle** the faithful.

12-14. By Silvanus probably indicates the amanuensis or secretary who assisted Peter. Note that he is a faithful brother (a preacher in his own right, and apostolic companion of Paul for some time). The purpose is restated: to encourage, and testify (solemnly affirm) **that this is the true grace** (note that he means by **grace** the whole system of Christianity). Greetings are included from the **church** (implied by the feminine form of **elected together**) at Rome (which here has the symbolic name of Babylon).

(see page 716 for Bibliography to I and II Peter)

The Second Epistle Of

PETER

INTRODUCTION

Authorship. Peter identifies himself as the "apostle of Jesus Christ" in 1:1 and maintains this claim by implication in 1:14 with reference to the Lord's statement about his death. The claim is assumed in 1:18 when he recalls the Mount of Transfiguration experience, and again in his mention of Paul in 3:15. In 3:1 the author mentions by the way that this is the second epistle to these same general readers.

Although there is little certain external evidence (Origen, A.D. 250 is the first to definitely mention it by name) for the book in the earliest times, it was finally and formally recognized as canonical in A.D. 397 at the Council of Carthage. Origen and Eusebius show that there was dispute about its authenticity at first among some of the churches, but it cannot be denied that quotations and allusions of it occur in Irenaeus, Justin Martyr, the Shepherd of Hermas, the Didache, and Clement of Rome.

In modern times some scholars have questioned the authenticity of the book because of the great dissimilarity in style and content between I and II Peter. Other scholars, however, have demonstrated convincingly that there are definitely similarities in style and content between the two books, as well as between II Peter and the sermons of Peter in Acts. Arguments from style and content seem to cancel each other out; but no one has ever disproved the apparently direct and honest claims of the book itself.

Jude seems to be slightly later in date than II Peter, and attests to the apostolic authorship of the latter by his apparent use of it. There is, in short, no reason to doubt the author's statement in 1:1 that he is the Apostle Peter.

Purpose. Reports on the activity of false teachers among the churches of Asia must have come to Peter shortly after the writing of the first epistle. He seems very concerned about the effect these false teachers might have on his readers, who may have already been depressed by suffering and persecution according to I Peter. The book, then, intends to remind the believers of the importance of supplementing their faith with virtue, knowledge, and steadfastness (1:5-7, 12). Peter also turns to the Old Testament again in this letter to find illustrations for the dangers of listening to the false teachers (ch. 2), and reminds the believers of the approaching day in which the ungodly false teachers will be destroyed (3:1-10). In the light of these facts, Peter encourages his readers to holy lives as they wait for the coming of the Day of God (3:11-13).

Date. This second epistle must have been written quite close to the end of the Apostle Peter's life. He sensed (1:15) that the end was near for him, and wanted to provide written reminders for his readers. The *terminus a quo* would be, according to 3:16, the circulation of several of the epistles of Paul; the *terminus ad quem,* the martyrdom of Peter in about A.D. 67.

OUTLINE

COMMENTARY

I. INTRODUCTION. 1:1-2.

1:1-2. Simon Peter includes both his given Jewish name and the symbolic Christian name given to him by the Lord Jesus (Mt 16:18). **A servant and an apostle.** Apostle claims the authority to be heard in the name of the Lord, but **servant** (Gr *doulos*) is a word of deep humility meaning literally "slave" and implying total and permanent ownership by a master. Paul also used this word to describe his relationship to the Lord (e.g. Rom 1:1) as did Jude the brother of the Lord. It is difficult to see why, if the author here had been an impostor, a false author would have changed the introductory formula in this way and made it different from I Peter. This seems then to be an open and direct claim to acceptance. Here, believers are called those who have **obtained like precious faith with us. Obtained** (Gr *langchanō*) means "to be chosen to a position by divine will or by lot," and suggests exactly the same theology as **elect** in I Peter 1:2. Christians are those who are saved only by the grace of God; they do not **obtain** it

by their own initiative or works. The word **like precious** expresses the same theme as I Peter 1:3-12, namely, the glory of salvation. We have been chosen to the **faith . . . through** (Gr *en*), literally "in" **the righteousness of God and our Saviour Jesus Christ.** In order to show that the titles **God** and **Saviour** both refer to the same person, the translation should be, ". . . in the righteousness or our God and Savior Jesus Christ." Peter clearly calls Jesus **God.**

II. SUPPLEMENTING OUR FAITH. 1:3-21.

A. Christian Virtues. 1:3-14.

3. According as his divine power hath given unto us all things that pertain unto life and godliness. There is no main verb in verse 3, and we must assume that the whole of verses 3 and 4 is preparatory in some way for the major exhortation of the chapter in verse 5, "supplement your faith." Verses 3-4 are perhaps a review for his readers of what was started in I Pet 1:3-9. **Hath given** (Gr *dōreomai*) means "to freely give"; the stress is on "freeness" of the gift. The names Dorothy and Theodore come from this word and mean "God's gift." In the original, the perfect tense also stresses the certainty of the fact and possession of this gift.

The context of the gift is expressed in the words **all things that pertain unto life and godliness.** Everything that has to do with life or serving God has been freely given so that we lack nothing. **Through the knowledge of him** expresses the means through which He gives us these things; it is through knowing Him (objective genitive in Greek). **Him that hath called us to glory and virtue** does not refer to our glory and virtue, but that of Jesus Christ. A better translation would be, ". . . through the knowledge of him who called us by his own glory and excellence." Compare I Peter 2:9, which uses both "called," and "virtue" in the same sense as here.

4. Whereby are given unto us (Gr *dōreomai*). Once more, as in verse 3, the perfect tense is used in Greek to imply the certainty of the unmerited gift of his **great and precious promises.** The word **promises** (Gr *epanggelma*) really is not the promise, but the result of the promise, namely its "fulfillment." Peter proposes in both epistles that we no longer live in the age of prophecy and promise, but in the new age, the age of fulfillment. Taken together, these two words stress that God has in fact freely given to us the very things that He had promised in the Old Testament. The verse corresponds to I Peter 1:12, and emphasizes the privilege of living at a time when through the preaching of the gospel the promises were fulfilled. **That by these ye might be partakers.** The final clause shows the reason that the promises were fulfilled: that they might become partakers of the divine nature. That is, God intended by accomplishing salvation in Christ that believers would share a common quality of life. Peter is

not making new promises for the future, he is proclaiming fulfillment and present reality for his readers; he is a preacher and a witness, not a prophet. That this is true is seen also in his use of the word **partakers** which he had used in the same sense in I Peter 5:1 where he stated that he *was* a partner, not that he would be.

Having escaped (Gr *apopheugō*) is a participle of attendant circumstance and must be translated according to the mood of the main verb; the vague translation **having escaped** implies that we can become partakers of the divine life only in the far-off future after we have safely escaped the corruption of the world. Peter's point is totally different from this: God has made it possible for us to share this new quality of life now by having accomplished the promised salvation in Christ. A more accurate translation would be, ". . . so that through these you might escape from lustful, worldly corruption and share a new divine life." This is the same general idea that was expressed in I Peter 1:3 and 23 where he called it a new birth and used the same word for "corrupt seed" from which we are born.

5. And beside this, giving all diligence, add to your faith. A translation may read, "For this very reason, make every effort to supplement your faith with virtue. . . ." The word **add to** (Gr *epichorēgeō*) originally in the Athenian drama festivals meant "to finance, support, or back a chorus," and financial support is primary to most usage of the word in Christian literature; in 1:11 it means "provide." Here Peter calls upon believers to put everything they have into supporting their faith with virtue, etc. **Faith** is not something the believers could "provide" in this verse (cf. 1:1); faith has been given to them or rather they have been chosen to it. What they are called upon to do here is to "provide" certain items of support for faith. Each item is, in turn, to be supported or supplemented with another. Seven items are needed to support perfect faith; each of them is a philosophical abstraction of an aspect of the Christian life or divine nature that we share.

6-7. To read the list one must understand the main verb "support" with each quality named. The most important item of support to each quality will be the quality which follows in the list. At the end of the list is the quality which support all the others and is most needed in the Christian life, love (cf. I Cor 13). **Temperance** means "self-control," and this is the item that is most needed to support knowledge. An ancient Greek saying put it briefly, "Know yourself." Self-control requires more than anything else **patience,** which should rather be translated "endurance," or "strength of character" (Gr *hypomonē*).

8. For if these things be in you, and abound. Peter now points out how important these items of support to faith really are. If they exist in you and if they abound you will be effective and fruitful. These are the elements of success in the Christian life. **They make you** (Gr *kathistēmi*) has the connotation of "distinguishing as" and could be translated, ". . . they keep you from being ineffective or unfruitful." **In the knowledge of our Lord Jesus Christ.** The word **knowledge** (Gr *epignōsis*) is the same one which recurs in 1:2, 3, 8, and 2:10; it means "knowledge" or "recognition of," and may be equal to the simplex form used in 1:5-6; 3:18. There is an emphasis on knowledge in this chapter: grace and peace are in the knowledge or recognition of God (1:2), all things are in the knowledge or recognition of God (1:2), all things are given through this knowledge (1:3), and knowledge must support virtue (1:5).

9. He that lacketh these things is blind, and cannot see afar off, and hath forgotten that he was purged from his old sins. Verse 9 is a conditional sentence corresponding to the one in verse 8; they are positive and negative reinforcements of the importance of the seven indispensable qualities of the Christian life listed in verses 5-7. The protasis here establishes that the person does not possess these qualities; the apodosis is a metaphor: he is blind. The two circumstantial participles explain first the meaning of the metaphor (**cannot see afar,** Gr *myōpazō*, from which we get "myopia"), and then the application of the metaphor: he has spiritual myopia. He never got close enough to Christianity to focus on the fact that he needed to be cleansed from his sins! It should be obvious that the object of the forgetting here is *not* **that he was purged,** since he had never been cleansed in the first place. What escaped him was "the cleansing"; he never saw that his sins had to be cleansed or washed away before he could live the Christian life.

10. In verse 10, Peter urges his readers to confirm **calling and election,** not memory. It does not seem likely that a person could forget it if his sins had been washed away by the atoning death of Christ, but the whole matter could escape his notice if he were not urged to make sure about it. We cannot be sure of **calling and election** if we have not been **purged** (vs. 9) from our former sin. On the other hand, if these are confirmed by the fact that we have been cleansed from our old sins, it is certain that we **shall never fall** (Greek subjunctive of emphatic future negation)!

11. For so (meaning "in this way") **an entrance** (Gr *eisodos*, with the article, "the way into," and there is only one Way; see Jn 14:6) **shall be ministered** (Gr *epichorēgeō*, see 1:5) unto us. This means that if we make sure our sins are washed away by Christ, God, the richest supporter possible, will back us and provide everything else that is needed on our road to heaven.

12-14. Wherefore refers back to **According as** (1:3) and now introduces a

new paragraph based on the propositions of the previous one. Since we
share a new nature, and have a new
quality of life in Christ, Peter says, **I
will not be negligent to put you always
in remembrance of these things.** A
more accurate translation has, "I intend always to remind you of these
things." What is given here is the purpose for the writing of the letter.
**Though ye know them, and be estab-
lished in the present truth,** is a tactful
concession. **As long as I am in this
tabernacle. Tabernacle** (Gr *skē-
nōma*), meaning "tent," is a Christian
metaphor for the body or this earthly
life as a temporary quarters for the real
person which lives on after death.

**To stir you up by putting you in
remembrance. Stir** (Gr *diegeirō*) is the
word for "wake up" from sleep.
Peter's purpose is to remind them and
wake them up because he feels that
suddenly and unexpectedly he will be
taken from them (alluding to Jn
21:18). He wants them to have a
reminder for reference after his death.

B. Christian Doctrine. 1:15-18.

15-18. The two key verbs in this
paragraph of the letter are **made
known** (16) and **We have** (19). In the
light of the work of false teachers,
these are the things Peter wants them
to remember. **For we have not followed** is not a main verb in the original, but a circumstantial participle of
cause; the reason Peter and the other
apostles preached was not because they
had researched (**followed,** Gr
exakoloutheō) and believed in sophisticated fables (Gr *mythos*) but because
they were eyewitnesses of the greatness
of Jesus Christ. The main verb is **we
made known unto you the power and
coming of our Lord Jesus Christ.** What
is referred to here is the preaching of
the apostles. Peter says that they (the
apostles) preached Christ because they
were eyewitnesses of the gospel events;
the implication is that the false teachers
were not, and therefore should not be

listened to. To further corroborate the
apostolic authority of his message,
Peter vividly recalls actually hearing
the voice of God who proclaimed on
that holy mountain, "This is my beloved Son." Peter and the apostles
knew what they were talking about
when they preached; this is the meaning of the reminder here. Could the
false teachers come up with this kind of
authority?

C. Christian Scriptures. 1:19-21.

19. The other key verb in the passage is **We have also a more sure word
of prophecy.** The meaning here is
clearer in the translation, "We also
have the confirmed, Prophetic Word."
Peter is appealing not only to the
apostolic preaching of Christ, but to
the Old Testament Prophetic Word,
that is, the promises and prophecies
about Christ which have now been
fulfilled. **More sure** (Gr *bebaios*) is a
predicate adjective here. It means
"confirmed," "well-established," and
often used with the promises or prophecies which have been fulfilled in
Christ (cf. I Pet 1:12, "which in the
Gospel have been declared as fulfilled"). They must, at least, believe
the Old Testament. Peter insists in
fact, that they must **take heed** to the
Old Testament; it is like a **light.** This is
of course another simile: they are in the
dark dungeon of sin, they need a lamp
to find their way out; they need it until
dawn. They have, of course, already
seen the light and believed the Old
Testament prophecies about Christ.
Both the verbs are progressive present
in the original; they are "doing well,"
and they are already "paying attention" to the light. This figure suggests
the metaphor of Christ as the light: like
the dawn, He shines into their hearts
(cf. Lk 1:78-79, Jn 8:12).

**20. Knowing this first, that no
prophecy of the scripture.** The word
scripture (Gr *graphē*) is obviously the
Old Testament Scripture and is synonymous here with the Prophetic Word.

Peter uses the same word with the same meaning in 3:16 to refer to the "other Scriptures" which the false teachers pervert. It is also used in I Peter 2:6 to refer to the Old Testament. Paul used it as well in II Timothy 3:16 when he said, "All Scripture is given by inspiration of God." **Is of any private interpretation.** This verse needs to be retranslated. First note that it is not **interpretation** (Gr *epilysis*) really tended here (Gr *ginomai* means "become," "originate"); origin is implied in the word **came** in verse 21 as well as in the process of inspiration described there. The word translated as **interpretation** (Gr *epilysis*) really means "ingenuity." Secondly, note that **private** does not mean the opposite of "public" but means "pertaining to a particular individual" which in this case is the prophet. Thirdly, note that specific reference is made to the Old Testament prophecies, the same Prophetic Word mentioned in verse 19. The implied question is "How can you recognize a real prophetic word?" The reply given is, "No prophecy of Scripture ever arises from human ingenuity, for never did a single Old Testament prophecy come at the impulse of a man; what those men spoke was the Word of God because they were being influenced by the Holy Spirit" (II Pet 1:20-21). In these verses then Peter has made it possible on the basis of his reminder of the apostolic preaching, as well as on the basis of the Old Testament, for his readers to recognize a false prophet when they see one. Now in chapter two he will become more blunt.

21. Prophecy refers to the total revelation of God which did not originate by human invention but as the writers of scripture were **moved by the Holy Ghost,** meaning they were "borne along" by the Holy Spirit. Thus, He moved upon them in such a way that their words were indeed the very word of God!

III. SECURING OUR FAITH. 2:1-22.

A. Warning against False Prophets. 2:1-14.

2:1-3. There were false prophets among the people. The **people** here means the people of Israel, God's chosen people, and Peter believes, like Paul, that ". . . these things happened unto them for examples: and they are written for our admonition" (I Cor 10:11). See also I Peter 2:9 where **people** is applied to the church. Deuteronomy 13:1-5 warned the people that if a false prophet came and tried to draw them away from the worship of God, they should not listen. It was a test to see if they loved God with all their hearts. Peter is telling his readers the same thing; he draws upon all the apocalyptic passages he knows to show that the false teachers are despicable to God and doomed to destruction as His enemies. Peter warns that **there shall be false teachers among you, who privily shall bring in** (that is smuggle into the church false doctrine without the people knowing it) **damnable heresies** (literally heresies of destruction, which means that the faith will be destroyed if people believe these things). The reason the false teachers sneak in heresy is because they deny **the Lord that bought them.** This does not mean that Christ is their Lord (master, despot) or ever was, but He could have been since He had paid the price for their release from sin. They denied Him (renounced) and would not have anything to do with Him when they could have been saved, and so will **bring upon themselves swift destruction.**

The problem for Peter and the church is that **many shall follow** them. Paul mentions the great apostasy of the end times in II Thessalonians 2:3 as well as in II Timothy 4:1. This is harmful to the testimony of the **way of truth** (another name for the church). **Make merchandise of you.** The word (Gr *emporeuomai*) means "exploit." The false teachers are in it only for the money (cf. I Pet 5:2). Their **judgment** and destruction are sure since they have made it obvious that they are the enemies of God, and God's enemies will be judged.

4. Peter again draws from the Old Testament to make it very obvious that the false teachers who are exploiting (or soon will be) his Christians readers will certainly be punished in the day of judgment by our Righteous God. This is the implied apodosis to the "if" clause begun in verse 4 but never completed; verse 9 could be translated, ". . . then the Lord knows how to. . . ." Three terrible examples of God's judgment are given. **For if God spared not the angels that sinned.** In Jude 6 they are called "the angels which kept not their first estate, but left their own habitation." Compare Genesis 6:1-4. These are said to be claimed in darkness until the judgment.

5. The second example is the **old world,** meaning the people who lived in the time of Noah before the Flood. God destroyed the whole world by the **flood** (Gr *kataklysmos*), the great cataclysm, and saved only eight people. The word **saved** here (Gr *phylassō*) means literally "guard" or "protect," and this is exactly what God did for Noah and his family (**eighth** is an idiom which includes the other seven).

6-8. The third classic example (Gr *hypodeigma*) is the destruction of **Sodom and Gomorrah** from which only Lot was **delivered** (Gr *hruomai,* meaning "rescue"). It strikes us very strange that Lot, of all people, should be used as an example of the **righteous.** You will remember, however, that in this instance he is the only person who could be used since he was the only one delivered (except for his daughters who were probably more immoral than he). Perhaps in contrast to the totally wicked population of the cities, he was righteous, or perhaps we do not have as much information as we need to judge. At any rate, we are told that he

vexed his **righteous soul** (Peter uses the word "just" or "righteous" of Lot three times here) **from day to day with their unlawful deeds.** It is interesting that the Flood and Sodom and Gomorrah were used by Jesus as examples of judgment (Lk 17:25-30).

9. These examples were cited by Peter to show that **The Lord knoweth how to deliver the godly . . . and to reserve the unjust unto the day of judgment to be punished. To be punished** is a present participle in the original, and might better be rendered, ". . . and to keep the unrighteous under punishment until the day of judgment." The Lord will deliver the godly, but He will punish the ungodly, and especially these false teachers to whom Peter applies this whole section (vs. 10a).

10-14. Peter now describes them as bold and willful, slandering even the angels of God (cf. Eph 1:21; Col 1:16). But even the angels do not bring a slanderous word against them. **But these, as natural brute beasts** (i.e. "dumb animals," Gr *zōon*). So deserving are these false teachers of judgment, that Peter says they ought to be caught and killed like animals, they will be in fact. As a reward for their wrong doing, they will themselves be wronged in the judgment. **They shall utterly perish in their own corruption,** should rather be translated, ". . . they will be destroyed like them" (i.e. as if they were dumb animals). They revel in the daytime; they are like blots and blemishes, and have an insatiable appetite for sin.

B. Characteristics of False Prophets. 2:15-22.

15-16. They **have forsaken the right way** and the point of the whole description is that they will get what they deserve.

17. These are wells without water. More properly "springs" (Gr *pēgē*); either way they are quite worthless without water. **Clouds** (or mists) are not much help for watering a crop. For these worthless false teachers, the gloom of darkness is reserved.

18. For when they speak. Probably this is a participle of means; it is by their well-modulated, authoritative, bloated vanities that they are able to lure (Gr *deleazō*, a fishing term) **those that were clean escaped** (rather, those who are just now barely escaping). New converts are easy prey for these slick talking pseudo-Christians who are really false teachers. Although they promise freedom (vs. 19), they are themselves slaves of corruption and sin. Here the principle of Romans 6:16 is stated: if anyone is in fact conquered by something, he is actually a slave to it.

20-22. Verse 20 begins with an **if** which must not be overlooked. Peter does not say that these false teachers have escaped from the pollutions of the world. The main verb is **overcome** (Gr *hētaomai*) which is in the Greek present tense, implying that they are now being overcome or conquered by the terrible sins depicted in this chapter; the construction in the original has the effect of a present contrary to fact protasis. The writer, Peter, views the statement as a premise which is contrary to fact. He says, "If it were true that these false prophets were just now being conquered by sin and had already escaped the pollutions of the world (it is not true, but if it were), then they would actually be in worse condition now than when they started." These false teachers, of course, had never really escaped the **pollutions of the world** like true believers (cf. 1:4); if they had, and were now as **entangled** (Gr *emplekō*, meaning "hopelessly trapped" like a fish in a net) as they are in sin, they would be better off if they had never heard of Christianity. According to their pretense, they claim to have been saved; according to fact, they have returned to the most despicable sins. This would be, obviously, like a dog eating its vomit, or a pig which has just

been washed going back to wallow in the mire.

The whole chapter warns the believers to secure the faith which had been preached to them by the apostles against the barbarous attack by obvious frauds who have shown themselves to be worthy of the certain judgment of God which will come upon them.

IV. SERVING IN FAITH. 3:1-13.

A. Purpose of the Epistle. 3:1-2.

3:1-2. This second epistle, beloved, I now write unto you . . . to stir up . . . in remembrance. Another allusion to the purpose of writing the letter (see 1:12, 13, where the same words are used) as being hortatory and didactic, and, of course, an implied claim to apostolic authorship. The reminder is that, although there are false teachers among them who claim to be also representing God, believers must recognize, accept, and obey only the true word of God as found in the Old Testament (**the holy prophets**) and in the preaching of **the apostles** (meaning himself and the others). This is parallel to 1:16-18, and shows the aspects of continuity between the Old Testament and the new age, and the promise and fulfillment theme of the apostolic preaching.

B. Unbelief of Scoffers. 3:3-9.

3. Knowing this first. This is an emphatic reminder of a primary fact (Gr *prōtos*); Peter had used these exact words in 1:20 to stress the primary fact that their preaching did not arise from their own ingenuity but was the Word of God as much as was the Old Testament. The fact here is that **scoffers** will come. Although the great apostasy was a generally known fact from all apocalyptic literature (see I Tim 4:1; II Thess 2:3 which also assume this), Peter now applies it to his own time and specifically to the reports of the false teachers, giving us a hint of the occasion of the letter. For Peter, as well as for Paul (I Tim 4:1), the days in which he lived were the **last days.** In biblical terminology, these were not the former days of promise and prophecy, but the latter days of fulfillment and blessing in Jesus Christ. By calling the false teachers **scoffers** (Gr *empaiktēs*), denoting one who ridicules or scorns, a "satirist"), Peter is in turn ridiculing them and coming to the aid of the truth of the second coming.

4. Before coming to the message of the scoffers Peter stresses their false character and corruption. They heap scorn and ridicule on the message of the gospel (literally "scorners with their scorn") and yet they themselves live (Greek present tense) in lust. Talk about the pot and the kettle—how ludicrous can one get? Once again, it is obvious that these false teachers will be destroyed as the enemies of God in the day of judgment! The ridiculous implication of their question (vs. 4) is: "There is no second coming, we can live any way we want. God will never judge us." This was, of course, in direct opposition to the apostolic preaching which always included the second coming of Christ as the ultimate fulfillment of the prophecies of the Old Testament. **All things continue as they were,** they said, God won't bring judgment upon the living and the dead.

5. But **this they willingly are ignorant of.** A more precise translation would be, "They persistently (Greek progressive present) ignore one obvious fact." The fact is, all things are not the same; God destroyed the world in judgment once, and this confirms rather than disproves the warning that he will do it again (vss. 5-6). **By the word of God** (vs. 5) is emphatic in the original. Creation was by the Word of God; the sky, the dry land, and the water were distinguished by the Word of God (Gen 1:6-7, 9), and the world continues to exist by the Word of God (cf. Col 1:17 where the same word is

used for Jesus Christ as the Living Word of God in exactly the same sense of sustaining the world).

6-7. According to Peter's analogy here, water and the Word were involved in the destruction of the world by the Flood according to verse 6 **(Whereby** is plural and means "by these two things"). With pungent success comes the reply to those satirists who dared to suggest that God would not keep His promise of the second coming: **by the same word** of God, this world is **kept in store.** Both ideas, **kept in store,** and **reserved** are certified as fact by the use of the perfect tense in the original. It is as clear as Peter can make it that God's Word will certainly be fulfilled in this matter as it has been in others, the second coming and the day of judgment will transpire exactly as promised, and these ungodly men will be destroyed!

8. Be not ignorant of this one thing. Be not ignorant (Gr *lanthanō*) is the same word used in verse 5 but here there are no condemning insinuations; we might translate, "Don't allow this fact to escape your notice any longer," or, "You are overlooking something, my friends." **This one thing.** Several things are brought up here, but the one idea supported by them all is that "the day of the Lord will come." This part of the apostolic preaching is the main point that had been challenged by these immoral false teachers, and this is the main reason Peter had written this second letter. His readers needed this encouragement to be true to Christ and the gospel as they waited for the glorious appearing of the Lord. First God does not count time in the same way that we do, to Him **a thousand years** may count **as one day** (cf. Ps 90:4).

9. Secondly, the reason for the delay in the return of Christ is not that the Lord is **slack concerning his promise.** This means that it is not one of God's attributes to be slow about keeping promises, although some (like these false teachers) might consider that to be true. The thought is probably parallel to Habakkuk 2:3 (quoted also by Heb 10:37 in another connection), where the writer says, "The prophecy awaits its time; if it seems to be slow, wait for it. It will surely come." **But** (a strong adversative emphasizing that the reason for the delay is a different matter entirely) **is long-suffering.** Long-suffering (Gr *makrothymeō*) is the regular word for "patience," and has the idea deep concern and feeling for someone over an extended period of time. The reason God has delayed that final day is His patience and concern for men that they might be saved. This same word is used again in verse 15 where God's patience is to be considered as salvation; it is made very plain in the passage that the reason for the delay is not negligence on God's part but concern for salvation. This is also stated in a negative way: **not willing that any should perish.** The word **willing** (Gr *boulomai*) means the same as "want" in English; God does not want men to be lost (He does not elect them to damnation but to salvation). The main verb in this sentence is translated by "God is patient"; the word "want" is a circumstantial participle expressing the reason for God's patience. The reason is both negative and positive as shown in the two complementary infinitives; He is patient because He does not want any to be lost, but wants all to **come to repentance.** Come (Gr *chōreō*) to repentance or "make room" for repentance (as one would make room at home for a welcomed guest) expresses the same thought as I Timothy 2:4, but with different words.

C. Looking for the Day of the Lord. 3:10-13.

10. These facts make it clear that **the day of the Lord will come.** Peter uses the same figure as Paul (I Thess 5:2) to express the imminency of the coming, **as a thief in the night.** The description of the judgment of that day is given in the most vivid apocalyptic terms: weird **noise** (Gr *hroizēdon*, meaning a "rushing" and "sizzling" sound; the Greek, like the English word is onomatopoetic), destruction of all the elements by means of burning, and the leveling of all earthly constructions. The last of these descriptions, **the earth also and the works that are therein shall be burned up,** involves a textual variant; instead of **burned** we should read "discovered," which is difficult to understand, but evidently means that everything which has been constructed upon the earth is razed or pushed away so that the earth itself is exposed and nothing else remains. After the noise and the burning, the bulldozer of God's wrath will level the site in preparation for the new city.

11. Peter now, having reminded his readers of the certainty of the coming Day, encourages them to **holy conversation** (always means conduct in the Bible) **and godliness.** The beginning of verse 11 in this version is a bit misleading because of some textual variations and peculiarities of translation. First, note that Peter is not talking about the dissolution of **things** *per se*, but about the judgment and destruction of ungodly "people," and particularly about "these" ungodly people described in chapter two. He speaks about the coming of Christ as a **day of judgment and perdition of ungodly men** (3:7). Although verse 10 mentions **works** being burned up, it is for the punishment of the ungodly false teachers. Peter begins in verse 11, "In the light of the fact that all these ungodly men are to be destroyed (present tense to make it vivid) in this way, shouldn't you live your lives in holiness and godliness as you eagerly anticipate the coming of the day of God?" Note the contrast between "these" ungodly false teachers, and the emphatic "you" in verse 11. These ungodly false teachers have been trying to lure the Christians into immorality; it should be plain now that, since they will be judged and destroyed, their way is not the way to live.

12-14. Verse 12 continues to mark the contrast in the way the day is viewed by the ungodly and the godly; they tremble because it means punishment and destruction, while the Christian is **Looking for and hasting unto the coming of the day. Looking for** (Gr *prosdokaō*) is used in this context with the sense of "anticipation" with the word **hasting** (Gr *psuedō*) which means "hurry," or "get busy," and is translated **be diligent** in verse 14. The hope or expectation of the Christian, **new heavens and a new earth, wherein dwelleth righteousness,** is the basis for the exhortation to blamelessness and purity of conduct. There will be no false teachers in heaven.

B. Exhortation Against the Unstable. 3:15-16.

15-16. The imperative of verse 15, **account that the long-suffering of our Lord is salvation,** encourages believers to recognize the fact that just because God's day hasn't come yet, they shouldn't follow the false teachers in believing that it's not going to come; they should think of it in God's way: the longer He delays it, the more people can be saved. Peter draws support from Paul, saying that he taught the same thing; this is perhaps a reference to Romans 2:4 where God's patience is twice called "kindness," and "leads" to repentance. It is interesting that Peter should consider Paul **hard to be understood!** He does not say that all of Paul is difficult, only certain things in his epistles (most of which would be written by this time and would already have been read and known according

to this statement). What those things are we can only guess, but Paul also had a great deal to say about the second coming, and since that is the point here, we could assume the connection. Those who had the most problem with Paul's writings (and Peter's too) were the **unlearned** (Gr *amathēs*), which is a rare word meaning literally "not a learner," and, as the opposite of "disciple" (Gr *mathētēs*), means here a non-Christian. Compare I Corinthians 1:18; 2:14. These difficult passages in Paul are also a problem for the **unstable** (Gr *astēriktos*), meaning those who needed support in their faith. Paul often used this word (in its positive form) in praying for God to "strengthen" or "stabilize" his readers, and Peter uses it in I Peter 5:10; II Peter 1:12, and also in the next verse (3:17). The are said to **wrest** (Gr *streblōō*), literally "twist," or "torture," **also the other scriptures.** The mention of **scriptures** shows not only that others existed, but that they were early regarded as the Word of God equal to the prophetic Word of the Old Testament, and the apostolic preaching (see 1:16, 20, 21). The result of contradicting and opposing the Scripture, or the teaching of the apostles as the false teachers had done, was **destruction.**

VI. CONCLUSION. 3:17-18.

17-18. Peter encourages them to be on their guard **beware,** (Gr *phylassō*, meaning "guard," or "protect" yourselves) that they do not get dragged off with these false teachers and fall from their own **steadfastness.** He encourages them rather to **grow in grace, and in the knowledge of our Lord and Savior Jesus Christ.**

BIBLIOGRAPHY

Barnes, Albert. James, Peter, John and Jude. In *Notes on the New Testament, Explanatory and Practical.* Grand Rapids: Baker, 1951.

Brown, John. *Expository Discourses in the First Epistle of the Apostle Peter.* Grand Rapids: Sovereign Grace, reprint of 1848 ed.

English, E. Schuyler. *The Life and Letters of Saint Peter.* New York: Our Hope, 1941.

* Green, E. M. B. Second Epistle General of Peter and the General Epistle of Jude, In *Tyndale New Testament Commentary.* Grand Rapids: Eerdmans, 1968.

Hiebert, D. Edmond. *An Introduction to the Non-Pauline Epistles.* Chicago: Moody Press, 1962.

Jowett, John. *The Epistles of St. Peter.* Grand Rapids: Kregel, 1970.

Kelly, William. *The Epistles of Peter.* London: Hammond, n.d.

* Leighton, Robert. *A Practical Commentary upon the First Epistle General of Peter.* Grand Rapids: Kregel, 1972.

Meyer, F. B. *Tried by Fire,* London: Marshall, Morgan & Scott, 1955 reprint of 1890 ed.

Paine, Stephan. Epistle of Peter. In *Wycliffe Bible Commentary.* Chicago: Moody Press, 1962.

Plummer, Alfred. Second Epistle General of Peter. In *Elicott's Commentary on the Whole Bible.* Grand Rapids: Zondervan, reprint, n.d.

* Selwin, Edward. *First Epistle of St. Peter.* London: Macmillan, 1961.

* Stibbs, Alan. The First Epistle General of Peter. In *Tyndale New Testament Commentary,* Grand Rapids: Eerdmans, 1960.

Thomas, W. H. G. *The Apostle Peter: Outline Studies in His Life, Character and Writings.* Grand Rapids: Eerdmans, 1950.

The First Epistle Of

JOHN

INTRODUCTION

Although this writing does not display the usual features of a letter, nevertheless it has always been classified as an epistle. Like Hebrews, it lacks an opening salutation, but in addition it lacks the epistolary conclusion of a letter. No formal mention of thanksgiving for the readers is given in the opening sentences (a practice never violated by Paul except in Galatians). It does not contain a single proper name (except that of Jesus Christ). In addition it does not locate itself historically, geographically, or personally. Nothing in the epistle is specific or local. The contents of this epistle clearly show that it was intended for a local audience. However, on the basis of contents alone it has properly been judged a letter (not a sermon).

Authorship. Although the author does not identify himself directly in any of the three epistles traditionally ascribed to him, the consensus of scholars is that they are all from the pen of the Apostle John, the son of Zebedee.

Tradition and external evidence make it hard to deny the united assumption that John is the author. There is reference to the gospel and epistles of John in the Muratorian Canon. Various allusions to the epistles are found in Clement of Rome, the Didache, and the Epistle to Diognetus. Polycarp quotes I John and Papias also used it.

There are obvious similarities between the epistles and the gospel. The themes of light and darkness, life and death, Christ and antichrist, love and hate are all prevalent in both. The author claims to be an eyewitness (I Jn 1:1-3) and speaks with authority using "we" as if to include himself with the other apostles.

Date and place of writing. There are no indications in the epistle which assist us in fixing a definite time for its composition. The tone and writer's paternalistic attitude toward his readers suggests an old man is writing to a younger generation. The fact that the destruction of Jerusalem in A.D. 70 is not mentioned would mean that the epistle was either written before the city fell or a sufficient time afterward to make common reference to its destruction unnecessary. Generally, a date around A.D. 90 is accepted as accurate.

There is no hint as to where John was when he wrote this epistle, but since the latter years of the apostle's life were spent in Ephesus, it seems most likely that this is the place of writing. No evidence exists to the contrary.

Purpose. The purpose of the Gospel of John was "that ye might believe that Jesus is the Christ, the Son of God; and that believing ye might have life . . ." (Jn 20:31). The purpose of the first epistle is, "that your joy may be full" (I Jn 1:4), and, "that ye may know that ye have eternal life" (I Jn 5:13). Joy and assurance seem to be the attitudes John wishes to encourage in his readers.

The readers were already believers in Jesus Christ and they worshipped and fellowshipped in rather well-defined churches with membership rolls and local pastors. Evidently false teachers (not unlike those in II Peter and Jude) had caused some basic doctrinal problems (I Jn 1:10). With the emphasis on light and darkness, and the incarnation, and knowing, there must also have been an incipient quasi-Gnostic movement afoot. John, at any rate, with apostolic concern, writes to encourage the believers to joy and assurance in purity of life as they wait for the appearance of Christ.

OUTLINE

COMMENTARY

I. INTRODUCTION. 1:1-4.

1:1-4. That which was from the beginning. We must take verses 1-4 as one long, involved, elliptical sentence, and look for the key main verb, which seems to be "and shew unto you" in 1:2 (Gr *apanggellō*). The word means "declare," "announce," or "make known." What is being "made known" in this letter is the object of the verb here and is multifaceted: it is something which existed from eternity, it is something with which the writer has the most detailed personal acquaintance. It could be called the "Word of Life"; it has made a real appearance in the world of men. Others besides the author have seen it and can prove it. Finally, it existed earlier in close association with the Father and then made its appearance into the world. That object which is now being "made known" more fully in this letter is, of course, Jesus Christ. More succinctly, the author is saying that in this letter, "We are declaring Jesus Christ."

The purpose for this declaration is also given in duplicate form: **that ye also may have fellowship with us** (vs. 3), and **that your joy may be full** (vs. 4). Several of the verbs in this sentence are repeated for emphasis and clarity, and those which support the eyewitness nature of his testimony are given in the Greek perfect tense to stress the certainty of the facts. This should be brought out in the translation; for example, ". . . we have actually heard, in fact have seen him with our own eyes. . . ." **That ye also may have fellowship with us** is the purpose, but not the ultimate purpose, for fellowship with the apostles without fellowship with the **Father, and with his Son Jesus Christ,** would be mundane. Verse 4 should read "that our joy may be truly complete," rather than **your** joy. This makes little difference in the sense, however, since the joy of the apostles is truly complete when the believers have real **fellowship** (Gr *koinōnia*) with the Father and Son.

II. Fellowship with God. 1:5-2:8.

A. Walking in the Light. 1:5-7.

5-7. John has made it clear that the purpose of his writing is that the believers might have true fellowship; he now proceeds to make some subtle philosophical implications about fellowship with God which will apply to the present circumstances of the believers. **God is light, and in him is no darkness at all.** Here are the two great symbols suggesting moral purity and evil; John says literally that there is not even one bit of darkness in God. Therefore, **If we say** introduces the protasis of a general condition used as the premise of a syllogism; the first negative conclusion (vs. 6) is **we lie.** It is obvious that if there are false teachers or any others who claim to have **fellowship** (Gr *koinōnia*) with God (having something in common with God), and at the same time (both verbs are in the progressive present in Greek) continue to live according to the standards of darkness only, there is no way around the conclusion that they are lying! "Walking" (Gr *peripateō*) is the regular metaphor for "living" or "conducting one's life" in these epistles. Now, John may have come right to the point; he is probably dealing with a real situation where there are those who claim that you can have fel-

lowship with God and live any way you please. Exactly this situation had existed earlier, and occasioned the writing of II Peter and Jude. More sophistication had probably been added, but these false teachers or incipient gnostics showed signs of having the same warped logic which would permit practicing known and willful sin. John now states the positive form of the conclusion to the syllogism: **we have fellowship one with another.** The grammar here is ambiguous, but the context makes it obvious that **one with another** means we who walk in the light have fellowship with God. Thus, it is clear that the epistle deals with **fellowship** as fellowship in the life eternal. John's evidences of fellowship are not proofs of whether a believer is right with God, but are proofs of whether one is saved at all! Fellowship here refers to being born again. **And the blood of Jesus Christ his Son cleanseth us from all sin.** If it were not for the atoning death of Christ (the original reading was "Jesus his Son") fellowship with God would be impossible according to the syllogism because of the opposing symbols of light and darkness. What makes the difference is the **blood of . . . Christ,** his atoning death, which **cleanseth us from all sin;** this makes the darkness (here specified as sin) into light.

B. Walking in Sin. 1:8-10.

8-10. Sin must be dealt with; it is a fact. Note the simple style of the Hebrew parallelism, saying the same thing in two different ways, and the repetition of ideas. The correct way of dealing with sin is not to deny it, but to acknowledge it and allow God to cleanse it. **If we confess** (Gr *homologeō*, meaning "acknowledge" or "agree with") **our sins, he is faithful and just** (He can be faithful to us and fulfill His promise, as well as just in accordance with His own righteousness and require the punishment of sin in Christ) so that (non-final clauses with

Gr *hina* are possible in John) He forgives our sins, and cleanses **us from all unrighteousness. If we say that we have not sinned** (vs. 10). This is different from saying that we **have no sin** in verse 8. In verse 8 it is a matter of recognizing what can be classed as sin in our lives; in verse 10 it is a matter of denying that we have ever really (perfect tense in Greek) sinned at all. **We make him a liar, and his word is not in us.**

C. Walking with the Advocate. 2:1-2.

2:1-2. My little children. These words are, of course, not written merely to little children; this is an idiom of endearment, as if to say, "My dear friends." On the other hand, John is assuming apostolic authority and responsibility for these his spiritual children. **These things I write unto you, that ye sin not.** Again, John is assuming some threat that would lure the believers away from Christ (perhaps false doctrine). Obviously, in the light of chapter 1, he is not saying that his writing will enable them to avoid committing their first sin. But, **if any man sin,** that is if any believer who has already acknowledged that he was a sinner, and has already been cleansed from his sin by the atoning sacrifice of Christ, if this person should be led off into sin, would he be eternally lost? He could sin, but he would not be hopelessly lost, because **we have an advocate. Advocate** (Gr *paraklētos*) is the word John used four times in his gospel for the Holy Spirit as the "Comforter." It is not so much "comfort" as "encouragement" or "help" which is usually meant by this word, and the help sought is pictured as an **advocate** (which word comes from the Latin equivalent of our Greek word here) or "attorney." **With the Father** means that he will stand and face the Father for us; the very same words are used of Christ in 1:2 (and in Jn 1:1). If we sin, our trouble with the Father will be darkness or unrighteousness, and

we will be out of **fellowship** (1:6) with Him; but our Advocate who is to get us out of the difficulty is **the righteous One.**

And he is the propitiation for our sins. This very important biblical word **propitiation** (Gr *hilasmos*) denotes the price which must be paid to avoid the divine punishment upon sin. It is, therefore, the "fine" we must pay in court to avoid going to jail. In the Bible, there are other synonyms for this concept of the "fine," such as the "atonement" or "ransom" or "sin offering." One really should study all these words throughout the Old and New Testaments to get the full picture of this important redemptive term. Here, Christ is not only the Righteous Lawyer who is on very familiar terms with the Father (Judge), but he pays our "fine," or, more properly according to the text, He *is* the "fine" or "atonement" for our sins. Exactly in what sense Jesus Christ is the **propitiation** for our sins, John does not say; he assumes this knowledge from 1:7, and from a thorough discussion of the passion of Christ in the Gospel. **For the sins of the whole world** does not mean that the application of the atonement is automatic for all the individuals in the world, but simply that if anyone in the world will believe in Christ and confess his sin, he too will find the atonement sufficient. Christianity is not exclusive like gnosticism; anyone can know Him if they want to.

D. Walking under Commandment. 2:3-8.

3-4. And hereby means "in this way," and is used often in the epistle. **We do know that we know him.** The last occurrence of **know** is in the perfect tense in the original stressing the certainty of the action; we should translate, "In this way we know that we *really* know him," or, "By this we may be sure that we know him." **If we keep his commandments.** 3-6 is another simple syllogism (major premise, minor premise, and conclusion): "Everyone who truly knows Christ keeps his commandments; a certain person does not keep his commandments (regardless of his verbal claim that he truly knows Him); conclusion? Simple: he is a liar!"

5-6. Next, John shows how the syllogism applies with a positive minor premise: keeping His commandments (living according to his moral standards) means not only that we have true knowledge of Him, but also that **love of God** (objective genitive) is **perfected** in him (that is, he is a true Christian). **He that sayeth he abideth in him** (talk is cheap) **ought** to **walk** (live) **even as he** (Christ) **walked.** All of this sounds as if it was meant to deal with the antinomian, gnostic false teachers.

7-8. I write no new commandment unto you, but an old commandment which ye had from the beginning. We must keep in mind that John wrote with his immediate readers and their problems in view. He is reminding them of the preaching of the other apostles. What he writes is not new in that sense; it is the Word which they heard from the apostles. Note the emphasis in chapter 1 on terms like **witness, declare,** and **message.** Note also that in 1:5, the content of the message is "that God is light and in Him is no darkness at all." Now observe that **commandment** (2:7-8) is another didactic term like **message,** and has a content which is quite similar to the content in 1:5, that darkness is vanishing, and true light is already shining. In one sense these readers must accept nothing new (like a new teaching or commandment from false teachers), and in just that sense John's message is not new; it is old. The **old commandment is the word which ye have heard (from the beginning** is not original). The **word** (Gr *logos*) is not, it seems, a verse of Scripture which we know, but the **word** in the sense of the "preaching" of the apostles (cf. "the preaching of the cross," I Cor 1:18).

There is also another sense in which John's readers need a new **commandment,** a new **word,** and they must receive it not from the quasi-Gnostic false teachers, but from the apostle himself. The new **word** is true with respect to them, or (in a different sense) with respect to Christ. The new commandment is, "Darkness is vanishing and the true light is now shining." This new **word** is in fact the major premise for John's third syllogism. How it applies to Christ is left to the reader's ingenuity (obviously He is the Light of the world, etc.); how it applies to the believers is the subject of 9-11.

III. FELLOWSHIP WITH LIGHT AND DARKNESS. 2:9-28.

A. Walking in Love. 2:9-17.

9-11. First, the negative application (vs. 9): if every believer has the True Light shining in his life (major premise), then the person who continually hates (Greek progressive present; his life is characterized by hate) his brother (minor premise: his life is all darkness), is still in darkness (conclusion) to this very moment, and thus is not a believer at all. Next, the positive application (vs. 10) which is just the opposite in its conclusion: the person whose life is characterized by love and light is a true believer. In verse 11, John goes back to the negative application of the light-and-love premise in order to emphasize that hatred (perhaps he has in mind some aspect of the problem with the false teachers) creeps over one's life like the darkness, affecting his walk, and even his knowledge (**knoweth not wither he goeth**), making him in fact spiritually "blind." See II Peter 1:9, where false teachers were also a problem.

12-14. I write unto you little children. John is not, of course, writing to literal children, young men, and fathers in this passage. These are metaphors which refer to the various levels of spiritual maturity among his readers. In one sense, all the believers are like **children** to him (cf. 2:1, 18; 3:7; 5:21). In another sense, John can include himself with them as **children** of God (3:1). In still another sense, as in this passage, some of the believers are less mature (having just recently been converted) than others who may have been saved from the beginning and are in a sense **fathers** in the faith to them. The metaphorical use of age for maturity is not at all unusual in the New Testament. The problem of the changes in tense where **I write** (Gr *graphō*) occurs in these verses is not significant; the six instances all refer to the present letter as he is writing it (the Greek aorist being epistolary). John, however, uses the perfect tense in Greek to stress the certainty of the reality of Christianity for each of the six metaphors (Sins have "really been forgiven," they have "truly known," "have actually conquered," etc.). In this way John assures the readers of his confidence in them, while in the same letter he repeatedly exposes the false teachers for what they really are.

15-17. Love not the world, neither the things that are in the world. This prohibition (present tense in the original, and thus progressive action) would literally be translated, "Don't continue your love for the world . . ." (meaning after you have been saved). This introduces the next (fourth) syllogism on how to tell a real believer from a phony. The major premise is found in verse 17; in the lives of those who really love God, **the world passeth away.** Note that **passeth away** (Gr *paragomai*) is the same word used of the darkness in the last syllogism, and that **world** is the same in meaning as **darkness** (cf. 2:8). It follows then, that one who continues his love for the world while he claims to know and love the Father (vs. 15) is a phony. Loving the world (lust, greed, pride, etc.) is the opposite of doing the will of God. With a positive minor premise (vs. 17), the conclusion is positive: he is a true believer rather

than a false prophet, and he **abideth for ever.**

B. Walking with Apostates. 2:18-28.

18-19. John now moves into his fifth test (another syllogism) by which the believers may determine whether the self-authenticating teachers are true or false. First, it is to be expected that false prophets will arise since **it is the last hour.** The coming of Christ marked the beginning of the "last days" (cf. I Cor 10:11; I Pet 4:7; Heb 9:26); God's promises of blessing were fulfilled, but there were also prophecies of apostasy and the Antichrist yet to come (II Thess 2:3; I Tim 4:1; II Tim 3:1; 4:3; II Pet 2:1; 3:3; Jude 18; I Jn 4:1). In one sense, then, the prophecies are already fulfilled in these false teachers, for they are **antichrists,** that is they are against Christ. **They went out from us, but they were not of us.** The meaning of this play on words is obvious: they associated with the believers but they were not real believers. John uses a contrary to fact condition in Greek to express his proof that the false teachers are impostors.

20-24. But ye have an unction. This is the key concept in the major premise; the word **unction** (Gr *chrisma*) denotes literally the "oil" or "unguent" with which a person has been anointed. In the Old Testament, kings were "anointed" as a part of the inaugural ceremony (I Sam 16:6-13); it involved simply pouring oil on the head of the chosen person. The chosen person then had the "oil" on him and was called the "anointed" (Heb *meshiach,* Gr *christos*). Thus, throughout the New Testament, God's chosen King, the Messiah, is designated the **Christ,** meaning in translation, "the Anointed One" or the one who had the "oil" (Gr *chrisma*). The bpatism of Christ (Mt 3:13-17, et al.), with the Spirit coming upon him, and the voice with its messianic pronouncement, is symbolic of the King's coronation, and announced Him to the world as the anointed King.

The verb form **anoint** (Gr *chriō*) is also used several times in the New Testament to allude to the anointing of Christ, but once it is used of Christians, who are also in a sense (obviously a lesser sense than Christ) **anointed** (II Cor 1:21); in this passage it is clear that the "oil" with which we are **anointed** is the same as that with which Christ was anointed, namely the Holy Spirit (cf. II Cor 1:22). This, in fact, is the meaning behind the name "Christian," for believers are "little christs," "little anointed ones." When John, therefore, uses this word **unction** (Gr *chrisma*), or, as it occurs twice in verse 27, **anointing,** he simply means to say that all believers have the Holy Spirit. Since believers have the Holy Spirit, they have an "edge" on unbelievers and can "know" certain things that unbelievers cannot. So, John says in verse 20, **ye know all things.** Do the gnostic false teachers claim to "know"? Here is truth they cannot know, which even the simplest believer "knows" because he has the Spirit. The truth which makes it possible to tell Christians from **antichrists** is the truth that Jesus is the **Christ.** This is the message which the believers had **heard from the beginning** (compare this clause of verse 24 with verse 7, and note the emphasis on hearing and receiving the Word of God from the apostles, as well as holding to that same **commandment,** or letting it **remain in you**). The major premise of John's syllogism can be rephrased: "Every believer has been anointed with the Holy Spirit, and therefore *knows* that Jesus is the Christ." Add the negative minor premise, "The false teacher **denieth that Jesus is the Christ** (vs. 22)," for the obvious conclusion: "He is a **liar** and an **antichrist.**"

25-27. In case anyone has not been able to follow the logic of it all through the many subtle implications and plays upon words, John states plainly in verse 26, that this is a test to be used on false teachers: **These things have I written unto you concerning them that seduce** (literally, "try to deceive") **you.** It is clear from verse 27 that they do not need to listen to these false teachers; they have been taught the Word of God by the apostles, and they have the indwelling Holy Spirit who will give them assurance and teach them to live by that Word.

28. John's exhortation to them is to the effect that they should continue to live in Christ (Greek present tense), ignore the false teachers, and look forward to the second coming of Christ with joyous confidence.

IV. FELLOWSHIP AND LOVE. 2:29-4:21.

A. Identification of Believers. 2:29-3:10.

29. Every one that doeth righteousness is born of him. This is the summary of the sixth major premise and test to be applied to the false teachers. It is important to note first that **doeth** (Gr *poieō*) is progressive present in the original; this means that John is not talking about a person who performs one or two righteous acts, but about a person whose conduct can be characterized as righteous. Of such a person it may be said that he is "born" (Gr *gennaō*), or rather "has been truly born" (perfect tense) of God.

3:1. That we should be called the sons of God. Note that **sons** (Gr *teknon*) is the word usually translated "children" in the New Testament, and stresses the fact that we are members of God's family by birth; this relates 3:1 to 2:29. John stresses that we are *now* the children of God.

2. It doth not yet appear what we shall be. What we shall be along with all John's stress upon true **birth** and **children** of God, gives us reason to beleive that besides the emphasis on knowledge, the false teachers also believed in some kind of esoteric spiritual rebirth. The argument is that if they do not live righteous lives, they are not born of God; they are, of course, somebody's children, the devil's!

3-5. Every man that hath this hope. The **hope** (Gr *elpis*) is not a "hope-so" chance for the Christian, but a "know-so" expectation which is part of the "knowledge" we have because of the indwelling Holy Spirit. It is because of this "sure expectation" that we "purify" our lives. But the implications here for the false teachers are: they do not purify their lives because they do not have the hope; they do not have the hope because they do not have the Holy Spirit; they do not have the Holy Spirit because they are not children of God, which is obvious because they do not live righteous lives.

6. Whosoever abideth in him sinneth not. Sinneth not (Gr *hamartanō*, progressive present) does not mean that once a person is saved he never sins again! It does mean, however, that once a person is saved he no longer lives in sin; his life is no longer characterized by sin (as the lives of the false teachers here are). This is just the other side of the coin of 2:29. To say, "No one who is alive in Christ lives in sin" is the same as saying, "Everyone who is truly born of God lives righteously."

7-8. Let no man deceive you. It is obvious, again, that the false teachers fail the test; they are not **born of God** (vs. 9) at all, whatever they may have claimed. Their lives, characterized by sin, show that they have not really seen, or truly known God. Living in sin is the opposite to Christianity, for Christ came to take away sin (vs. 5). Sin is a characteristic of the devil, and Christ came to destroy (Gr *luō*) the works of the devil (vs. 8).

9. It is clear that the false teachers are not children of God at all, like John's readers, but are in reality the children of the devil.

10. Whosoever doeth not righteousness is not of God, neither he that loveth not his brother. Being **of God** or of the devil can be determined in another way, to deal more fully with a proposition introduced earlier (2:10); a man cannot make claim to righteous living if he does not love his brother. The word **brother** cannot be restricted always to mean only a true, born-again Christian, as is obvious if the logic is pressed here. It has always been part of the Word that was preached, as well as the Old Testament Word, that love is the fulfillment of the law of God. We are to love God with all our hearts; we are to love our neighbor as ourselves.

B. Living with the Believers. 3:11-24.

11-12. This is the message that ye heard from the beginning, that we should love one another. The same expression, almost verbatim, appears in 1:5, "This then is the message which we have heard of him. . . ." It appears again at 2:7 and 2:25. The formula stresses that what is expressed was an important part of the Word of God. John had also expressed in his Gospel (13:34-35) that love for one another should be an identifying characteristic of Christians. Cain is given as a negative example, and would probably have been suggested by the ruthless attitude of the false teachers.

13-16. If every believer lives righteously and loves his brother, then it is easy to deduce that these people who persist in hatred are not believers. On the other hand, the positive minor premise applied to the principle will give assurance that **we have passed from death unto life** (Gr *metabainō*, perfect tense shows certainty of the fact). John uses the supreme example of sacrificial love here (as he did in Jn 13:34-35) to show what love is ultimately, **he laid down his life for us.** Here, the word **for** (Gr *hyper*) shows the vicarious nature of the atonement; Christ died in our place, and suffered the punishment for us. This is made the basis for the obligation of Christian love.

17-21. Whoso hath this world's good. This translation of the original idiom should not be taken to mean that a person must be rich before he is obligated; the text says only that he has the "sustenance" that his brother needs, understands the need, and refuses to help. Again, the conclusion is obvious: this person does not have the love of God living in him, or to put it another way, he is not a true believer. **Hereby we know that we are of the truth, and shall assure our hearts before him.** The result of the test when applied to the true believer, on the other hand, is comforting assurance, and enables us to look forward to his coming with joyous confidence.

22. Our prayers are likewise answered **because we keep his commandments, and do those things that are pleasing in his sight.** "Keeping" his commandments alludes to "doing righteousness" in 2:29 which is the major premise in this syllogism. **Pleasing** (Gr *arestos*) is also a basic part of the righteousness of believers. This was a common way of expressing this "heart attitude" of Christians; in John 8:29 these words come from the lips of Our Lord Himself. This is not at all like legalism, any more than it is like antinomianism; the believer just naturally wants to do the will of God.

23-24. His commandment is not any one word to which our attention is now directed, but it is simply his will or desire for us (cf. John 6:29 where instead of **commandment** we find **work**). His will for us involves trusting in Him, loving one another, and in general, living the Christian life ("abiding" means living), and enjoying the gift of the Holy Spirit (especially in our confrontation with the false prophets, to which subject he now turns).

C. Warning to the Believers. 4:1-6.

4:1. Believe not every spirit. Spirit does not, of course, refer to merely spiritual or supernatural beings; these could not be tested by John's readers. John has just made mention of the fact that believers are indwelled and led by the Spirit of God; the false prophets also claimed spiritual leading. John warns against believers' accepting from these teachers things that are contrary to what they have already received from the apostles. **But try the spirits.** Try (Gr *dokimazō*) means to check out by a pattern or standard that never changes; the standard intended is the Word of God. John has, in this letter, been reminding them of that Word, and the principles by which these false prophets should be checked. Here he repeats one of them.

2. Hereby know ye the Spirit of God, that is the truly Christian teacher who has the Word of God. **Every spirit that confesseth that Jesus Christ is come in the flesh is of God.** This test is equal to that already given in 2:22; the inference to be made here is that the gnostic or quasi-gnostic teachers denied the incarnation and refused to believe that Jesus was God in the flesh. The deduction to be made concerning the false teachers, then, is that they are not inspired by the Spirit as they claim, but are against Christ, and of the same character as the Antichrist (cf. 2:18).

6. We are of God: he that knoweth God heareth us. Here John includes himself with the other apostles as **spirits** who follow the Spirit of Truth, and thus proclaim the truth. The readers, who truly know God, will recognize and willingly accept the word of the apostles for what it really is, the Word of God (cf. I Thess 2:13).

D. Love and the Believers. 4:7-21.

7-10. Let us love one another. Again John returns to the theme of love, but this time it is as a direct exhortation to the believers in order to show that they are different from the false teachers. Once more the principle is stated that **every one that loveth is born of God, and knoweth God.** The negative minor premise is **He that loveth not knoweth**

not God. The major premise is listed both here and in verse 16 (where it is followed by the positive minor premise) **God is love.** This should be compared to 1:5 where "God is light." The proof of God's love to us is clearly seen in that He sent His only Son into the world to die on the Cross as our **propitiation** (cf. 4:10 with 2:2, and see the comments there). **That we might live through him,** shows the purpose and design of the atonement, as well as the fact that life (that is the new quality of life for the Christian) does not come by knowledge, but rather through the atonement of Christ alone.

11-16. The love of God to us makes us obligated to love one another, for this is the only way we can show that we really have love. Claiming to love God is meaningless without showing love to each other. **Because he hath given us of his Spirit.** This is repeated from 3:24, except that here the word **given** (Gr *didōmi*) is in the perfect tense in the original, showing the certainty of the fact that the apostles rather than the false teachers are moved by the Spirit of God, and are united in their testimony about Christ. **We have seen and do testify** refers again to the testimony of the apostles; this is the same way the epistle started (see 1:1-4). The testimony of Christ is here more general, to include that God has sent the Son as the Saviour of the world.

17-19. Herein is our love made perfect, that we may have boldness in the day of judgment: because as he is, so are we in this world. This verse does not mean to say that we can become perfect in fulfilling the command of love. First, the original does not say, **our love** but "love with us." It is because God is love, and because He lives in us, that love can be truly accomplished with us. God is love, so in a sense, we are love (we are all the world will ever see of love). The whole point is that **We love . . . because he first loved us.**

20-21. The principle of love is repeated here, and once again it is demonstrated that the false teachers do not pass the test. How can they claim to love God if they do not love a brother (person) who is right there before their eyes with a real need. Love in "word" is not real; it remains to be demonstrated.

V. FELLOWSHIP AND ASSURANCE. 5:1-17.

A. Assurance of Victory. 5:1-8.

5:1-3. Whosoever believeth that Jesus is the Christ is born of God. Is born (Gr *gennaō*) should rather be translated, "has been truly born," since it is perfect tense in the original. This is another test for the believers to use on the false teachers. Every person who believes (John does not mean merely intellectual assent, for that would contradict the total message of his writings) that Jesus is the Christ is a real Christian (see again on 2:22; 4:2). He now moves on to reiterate several of the tests in their connections to each other. Since the true believer loves God (the begetter, active voice of Gr *gennaō*, meaning to give birth to), it follows that he will also love other believers (**loveth him also that is begotten of him,** is passive voice of the same verb; in this context John is not referring to Christ, though he does in 5:18). The tests are mixed: **By this we know that we love the children of God, when we love God, and keep his commandments.** Love to God is again defined, it is keeping his commandments which are not **grievous** (Gr *barys*), that is they are not difficult to fulfill because we are truly "born of God" and have therefore easy victory.

4-5. Whatsoever is born of God overcometh the world. Overcometh (Gr *nikaō*) denotes gaining victory over; it is used four times in these two verses (4-5). Its first occurrence is present tense in the original, giving the sense: "The true believer is always victorious over the world." Victory is normal and natural, and that is why His commandments are not difficult. **This is the victory that overcometh** (gnomic aorist) **the world, even our faith.** This could be put, "Our faith is the key to victory over the world." **Faith,** in verse 4, is defined as "believing" that Jesus is the Son of God; the words are cognate and reiterate the same test found in 2:22; 4:2; and 5:1. This faith, saving faith, is what makes us true children of God, which in turn assures us of victory over the world.

6-8. John now gives a description of Jesus Christ as **he that came by water and blood.** No one knows (now) exactly what John had in mind when he used these two symbols. Tertullian's guess seems to fit the facts best: the **water** is a reference to His baptism or inauguration, where the Voice from heaven declared, "This is my beloved Son," and established that Jesus was the Christ. The **blood** is a common symbol for His death, where there were also supernatural miracles to cause even the confirmed and cruel Roman centurion to realize that this man (Jesus) was more than a mere man (Mt 27:54); also, by the Resurrection, the Father confirmed Jesus as the Son of God (Rom 1:4). This interpretation also fits the facts concerning the gnostic-type beliefs of Cerinthus who taught that the Christ came upon Jesus at the baptism but left Him before the Cross; John could have been refuting some such heresy. It is interesting that John called attention to **the water, and the blood** which came from the side of Jesus on the cross (Jn 19:34-35). At any rate, these were important symbols or witnesses to the deity of Christ in John's mind. He also adds a third witness, the indwelling **Spirit.** Thus, according to John's count here, **there are three that bear record.** The rest of verse 7 and the first nine words of verse 8 are not original, and are not to be considered as a part of the Word of God (refer to the marginal notes in any

reference Bible). John's three witnesses then are: **the spirit, and the water, and the blood: and the three agree in one. Agree in one** is an idiom which is properly translated simply, **agree.** Only two or three witnesses were needed to establish the truth of a fact (Deut 19:15; Jn 8:17).

B. Assurance of Eternal Life. 5:9-13.

9. The witness of God is greater. It is greater because he is God; if numbers are important (and John did stress the numbers in Jn 8:17-18, where Christ's own testimony is counted with the Father's for the necessary two), God's testimony is three in one. The point is only that there is plenty of evidence to confirm the fact that Jesus is the Christ. **Which he hath testified** (Gr *martyreō*); the Greek perfect tense is used for this word to stress the certainty of the fact of God's witness.

10. He that believeth on the Son of God hath the witness in himself; by believing, a person mystically lives in Christ, and Christ lives in the believer. The believer also has the Spirit who is once more a third witness. **Because he believeth not the record that God gave of his Son.** There is a play upon the cognate forms **record** (Gr *martyria*), and "gave" (Gr *martyreō*), here, with the latter being in the perfect tense stressing again the absolute certainty of the truth of the witness; the allusion is to the apostolic preaching of which the content is now specified in brief.

11-12. The message of the apostles was essentially, **God hath given to us eternal life, and this life is in his Son.** The one who has the Son, that is in the sense of believing in Him (2:22; 4:2; 5:1), **hath life; and he that hath not the Son of God hath not life.** See again 1:1-4 on giving the testimony or "preaching."

13. In summary and conclusion, John wants to make his purpose clear; **These things have I written unto you that believe on the name of the Son of God.** Note the similarity to John 20:31:

". . . that ye might believe. . . ." which ,was the purpose there, is changed to **. . . that ye may know.** . . . The letter is written so that believers might have "knowledge" or assurance about eternal life. In these last few verses, John refers to "knowledge" nine times by means of four synonyms; it must be clear that there were false teachers who were engrossed in a quasi-Gnosticism.

C. Assurance of Answered Prayer. 5:14-17.

14-17. This is the confidence (Gr *parresia*). This word originally meant "speaking out" boldly, but later came to denote the boldness or confidence without reference to the "speaking." In this book, it means "joyous confidence" toward God; in 2:28 it can be seen as the opposite of shame. **If any man see his brother sin a sin which is not unto death.** It is important to keep the context in mind while focusing on the meaning of the **sin . . . not unto death.** It has been emphasized by John that believers have passed over from death into life (3:14). It is quite possible that John is still on the same track; his concern could be over believers who might have already been influenced by heresy, and are living in sin because they think it has nothing to do with worship of God. He would stress that God would answer prayers like this and restore such backsliders to life in Christ. It may be, too, that some who were in the church and considered to be brothers in Christ (although they were not, they **went out from us, but they were not of us** 2:19) have been so influenced by the false teachers that they have, speaking figuratively, now already passed back over from **life** into death. In this sense the **sin unto death** would be rejection of God's truth to

the point that one died in unbelief. Others suggest that the sin unto death is not a particular act of sin, but any sin that occasions one's untimely death. Therefore, a living person need never fear that he has already committed the sin unto death, since he is still alive. Only total rejection and rebellion against God, and rebellion to God's laws, may cause one to sin **unto death.**

VI. CONCLUSION. 5:18-21.

18. Whatsoever is born of God sinneth not reiterates the principle which has been stated in many different ways throughout the book, that if a person is genuinely born of God (Gr *gennaō* is used in the perfect tense), he will not live in sin (Gr *hamartanō* is used in the present tense to imply a life characterized by sin, rather than an isolated act of sin). John again plays upon the word **born** by using it to refer to Christ; **he that is begotten of God keepeth himself** should rather be translated, "The One who was born of God keeps him." It is because Christ keeps the believer that the evil one cannot touch him.

19-21. The theme of assurance and true knowledge continues its intensity to the very end of the epistle as John repeats in the perfect tense, **we know** (for sure!) **that we are of God . . . we know** (for sure!) **that the Son of God** has come (for sure!), **and hath give us an understanding** (for sure!). The purpose for all this assurance and certainty is, "so that we might enjoy knowledge (Greek present tense denoting not just coming to know, but enjoying continually) of the True One." In place of the benediction is the closing exhortation, **keep yourselves from idols. A-men.**

(see page 735 for Bibliography to I, II, and III John)

The Second And Third Epistles Of

JOHN

INTRODUCTION

These two letters, II and III John, have the distinction of being the shortest books in the Bible. Each of John's Second and Third Epistles contains less than three hundred Greek words and was no doubt written on a single sheet of papyrus.

These two brief letters give insight into the hospitality of Christians to fellow travelers. Since inns in the first century were notoriously flea-infested and rapacious, where would a Christian stay while traveling? The answer was in the home of another Christian. "For example, Paul was entertained by Lydia in Philippi, Jason in Thessalonica, Gaius in Corinth, Philip the evangelist in Caesarea and the Cypriot Mnason in Jerusalem (Acts 16:15; 17:7; Rom 16:23; Acts 21:8, 16)" (John R. W. Stott, *The Epistles of John,* pp. 198-199).

Authorship. Again, the author of II and III John is accepted as being the Apostle John. Such was the belief of the Church Fathers. Eusebius listed these two brief books among the *antilegomena* (*Eccl. Hist.* III. 25). Irenaeus twice quotes from II John in his *Against Heresies.* Clement of Alexandria speaks of John's "longer epistle" which would probably indicate that he was aware of some shorter epistles that John had written.

Date and place of writing. Like the First Epistle of John, these writings offer no hint as to the date of their writing. Their close affinity to I John would probably suggest that they were written shortly after the first epistle.

The common assumption is that they were written from Ephesus, as the first epistle. This is based on the history of John's life after receiving the care of our Lord's mother at the cross (Jn 19:26-27). John was called to be the pastor at the church of Ephesus and there apparently labored until he died, with the exception of the brief interlude on the island of Patmos.

Purpose. It appears that the great purpose of II John was to warn the believers not to give indiscriminate hospitality to strangers or traveling evangelist-teachers. Those who did not meet the sure test of sound doctrine were to be refused hastily.

III John seems to have been penned in order to gain the services of Gaius on behalf of the missionary representative John was sending out. Gaius is encouraged not only to continue in his good work, but to learn from the worthy example of Demetrius and the unworthy example of Diotrephes.

OUTLINE

COMMENTARY

I. INTRODUCTION. 1-3.

1. Only a hint of the identity of the author is given when John calls himself here **the elder** (Gr *presbyteros*). The word is synonymous to "pastor" and "bishop" in New Testament literature. Being used with the article, it implies that John has a superior position of leadership and respect in the Christian community. John the Apostle writes to **the elect lady. Lady** (Gr *kyria*) is the same word as "Lord" in the New Testament, except that it is feminine here (and in vs. 5), and refers not to a literal "lady" but to the "congregation" or "church" in a figurative sense. The church is a **lady** in much the same way as we refer to a ship as "she." As the bride of Christ, it is proper to refer to the church as "she." The adjective **elect** is more important; it defines the church "chosen," and implies the metaphor of the church as the "Bride of Christ." **And her children,** would mean, of course, the members of the church, i.e., the people who make up the church (churches are never merely buildings in the New Testament). **Whom I love in truth.** The references here to truth, love, and knowledge show the similarity to especially I John. **Also all they that have known the truth. Known** is perfect tense in the original, stressing the certainty of the fact of the knowledge; it does not mean all who have ever known the truth in any way, but rather all who "really know the truth," that is, real believers.

2-3. The reason that real believers love each other is because of the indwelling **truth** (which is the Holy Spirit, the Spirit of Truth). **Grace . . . mercy,** and **peace** are part of the standard, Christian greeting formula (cf. I Tim 1:2; II Tim 1:2).

II. EXHORTATION TO LOVE. 4-6.

4. I rejoiced greatly that I found. I found is the same as saying "I learned," and may even mean simply "I heard." This is a way of starting the letter in a positive tone; what follows is the real conciliatory message. Evidently the same problems faced this particular congregation as those to whom I John was written. There were ruthless and immoral teachers who claimed authority and spirituality over the believers and threatened to lead some of them astray. **Walking in truth** is here and elsewhere in the New Testament the same as "living righteously." **As we have received a commandment.** This would be the preaching of the apostles which was recognized by the various churches as the Word of God, and so is here spoken of as coming from the **Father.**

5-6. What John is writing is now a new commandment in the sense that it is different from that apostolic message. This was an important point to make, since the message of the false teachers was new and different rather than being part of the original message. **Love,** and **walking** according to God's commandments are the same message as was given all along.

III. EXHORTATION TO DOCTRINE. 7-11.

7. The reason given for the exhortation to love and righteous living is that **many deceivers are entered into the world, who confess not that Jesus Christ is come in the flesh.** The **deceivers** (Gr *planos*) are the apostolic impostors who are trying to lead astray those who are true believers. They are the same false teachers in view throughout John's first letter. The deceivers have not just **entered into the world,** but according to the original reading of the text, have "gone out into the world," the sense of which is more fully explained in comparison to I John 2:19, where they were professing Christians as became obvious when they left the church. Another of John's descriptions for the impostors is those **who confess not that Jesus Christ is come in the flesh.** Another translation has, ". . . who will not acknowledge the coming of Jesus Christ in the flesh." The words **is come** are in the original a supplemental participle in indirect discourse; however, there may be some of the Old Testament apocalyptic flavor remaining in this word, and John may be alluding to the rejection of the Messiah as the "Coming One." At any rate, the deceivers, because they will not agree to this basic truth, are antichrists (cf. I Jn 2:18, 22; 4:2; 5:1).

8. Look to yourselves simply means "Watch out!" Two alternative possibilities are laid out with the warning in regard to the false teachers. **That we lose not those things which we have wrought.** The text should probably read, "that you do not lose what we have accomplished." It is the apostles who have preached and thus fulfilled the commission and made great gain (salvation) possible for the believers; the apostles will not lose anything themselves, but the believers stand to lose all the blessings of Christianity if they listen to the false teachers. It is the believers also who will receive the reward, which is not a reward for something done, but the gift of salvation by grace.

9. Whosoever transgresseth (Gr *proagō*, rather than *parabainō*) should be translated "Whoever goes too far and refuses to live by the teaching," **hath not God.** Now the standard by which the false teachers are to be tested is called the "teaching," which is another technical term to denote the message or preaching of the apostles. The application of a positive minor premise to this syllogism would change the conclusion to the positive, "has both the Father and the Son," which means that he is a true believer rather than one of the impostors.

10-11. If there come any unto you, and bring not this doctrine. This reveals an interesting characteristic of the primitive church, the itinerant prophets or teachers. These circuit-riding preachers depended upon the people of God in each town along their route for food and sustenance; they could not survive without the help and support of Christians. Any of these who do not bring the distinctively Christian message of the apostles, John says, should not be "received," which means that he must not be supported; the hope is that he will be starved out of his diabolical mission. John says that even a greeting is too good for them! **Bid him God speed** (Gr *chairo*) means only to say "Hello." It was a greeting as common in that day as our "Hi!"

IV. CONCLUSION. 12-13.

12-13. Having many things to write unto you. II John is a mini-version of I John. The author is saying that although he could go on and write much more, he prefers to be with them and speak to them **face to face** (which in the first-century idiom is vividly "mouth to mouth") in order that he might, as it were, restore them to spiritual life in Christ. The greeting from the **elect sister** is, of course, another congregation, perhaps a larger one where John lived.

(see page 735 for Bibliography to I, II, and III John)

OUTLINE

I. Introduction. 1.
II. Prayers for the Beloved. 2-4.
III. Examples of the Believers. 5-8.
IV. Diotrephes and the Brethren. 9-11.
V. Demetrius and His Beliefs. 11.
VI. Conclusion. 13-14.

COMMENTARY

I. INTRODUCTION. 1.

1. The author's identity is given in the same way as it is in II John 1:1 (see comments there). The letter is addressed to **the well-beloved Gaius,** an individual rather than a church congregation as in II John. Since Gaius was a common name, it cannot be said with certainty that this Gaius identifies with Gaius of Derbe (the traditional view, cf. Acts 20:4), Gaius of Macedonia (Acts 19:29), or Gaius of Corinth (I Cor 1:14; Rom 16:23). The traditional view is quite possible; at least we know that this Gaius was a leader in the church, he was very hospitable, and that he was a dear friend, perhaps a convert of John's. The word **well-beloved** (Gr *agapētos*) is simply the adjective "loved," and would quite naturally translate into, "To my dear friend Gaius"; the same word is found referring most probably to the common bond in the one message of the apostolic preaching; the same words were used in the address to the congregation in II John I.

II. PRAYERS FOR THE BELOVED. 2-4.

2-4. Beloved, I wish above all things that thou mayest prosper and be in health, even as thy soul prospereth. This is John's wishful prayer for Gaius. The word **prosper** (Gr *euodoō*), which occurs with **soul** as well as with respect to physical well-being, means literally to "have a pleasant trip," and came to denote "getting along well." John hopes that his letter may find everything going well, and Gaius in good health physically as he is spiritually. **For I rejoiced greatly,** expresses the reason and basis of John's knowledge of Gaius' "prosperous soul." He knows that Gaius is doing well spiritually because of the situation he is about to describe. **Brethren came and testified.** The use of the progressive present tense in the original here indicates that this was not a one-time witness; from "time to time" brethren have come to John and testified of how Gaius had helped them along their way. **The truth that is in thee, even as thou walkest in the truth.** The evidence that the truth is in Gaius is that he **walks** (Gr *peripateō*) in the truth, meaning that he lives according to the message of the apostles, rather than just giving mental assent to it. John has **no greater joy** than hearing that his **children walk in truth.** The use of the word **children** with Gaius may indicate that he was a convert of John's; tradition has it that John later appointed Gaius as the first bishop of Pergamum.

III. EXAMPLES OF THE BELIEVERS. 5-8.

5. Beloved, thou doest faithfully. This indicates the value of the service which has been performed; another translation has, "It is a loyal thing you do. . . ." **Whatsoever thou doest to the brethren, and to strangers.** But these are not to be understood as two separate groups; the brethren are the **strangers** (Gr *xenos*), or those to whom the "hospitality" (Gr *philoxenia*, a cognate) is shown. It is important that aspiring bishops show this quality among others (I Tim 3:2).

6. **Which have borne witness of thy charity** (Gr *agapē*), which is rather "love" as a proof of Gaius' genuine Christianity. The mention of the **church** is perhaps a reference to the larger congregation from which John writes; this also gives some indication of the conduct of meetings where missionaries gave reports and testified before the group. Another indication of the life of the early church is the use of the technical term to denote missionary support, "send forward" (Gr *propempō*), which is translated here as **if thou bring forward on their journey.** The phrase **after a godly sort** is an idiom meaning that Gaius' support is deserved by the missionaries in the Christian system, since they have given themselves to serve as God's representatives.

7. **Because for his name's sake they went forth.** This "going out" is missionary service; it is the corresponding opposite to the "going out" of the false teachers (cf. I Jn 2:19; 4:1; II Jn 10). The itinerant missionaries went out in the name of the Lord (literally, "in behalf of the Name") and unlike representatives of other religious cults, they did not receive anything **of the Gentiles. Gentiles** (Gr *ethnikos*), although it usually signifies Gentiles in contradistinction to Jews, here means non-Christians; God's people have the privilege and responsibility to support God's workers.

8. **We therefore ought to receive such.** Such missionaries are to be **received** by the Christians, meaning that they are to be given food, supplies, and money to help them along their way.

By doing this the Christians at the home base become **fellow helpers** (Gr *synergos*, a technical term for missionaries and workers for the Lord in distinction to laity; used exclusively by Paul except for this one use in John) **to the truth** (**truth** is personified here as God, so that Gaius is working with God).

IV. DIOTREPHES AND THE BRETHREN. 9-11.

9. **I wrote unto the church.** Exactly what was written, we have no way of knowing, since the letter must have been destroyed by Diotrephes or otherwise lost. This indicates something of John's position as an elder who evidently had some kind of supervision of the churches and local bishops. Probably Gaius and Diotrephes were teachers or preachers in the same congregation, although they could have had neighboring churches in the same community. At least they were rivals and Diotrephes was far different in character from Gaius. **Diotrephes, who loveth to have the pre-eminence.** To apply some of the tests given in I and II John, Gaius measures up as a true believer: he walks in the truth (lives righteously), serves God faithfully and obeys the commands, he demonstrates that the love of God is fulfilled in him as he loves and ministers to others. Diotrephes, on the other hand, measures up as a false teacher, an impostor! He loves himself more than anyone else; the word **loveth to have the pre-eminence** (Gr *philoprōteuō*) means literally, "to love first place." He does not receive the word of the apostles as the Word of God, but instead continues to reject it personally (cf. I Thess 2:13, where a cognate word for **receiveth us not** appears). His works are evil, and he shows hate rather than love for the missionaries as well as the members who want to help them.

10. **I will remember his deeds which he doeth, prating, against us with mali-**

cious words. Diotrephes not only refuses to acknowledge the authority of the Apostle John, he is in active opposition to him. **Prating** (Gr *plyareō*) means "to talk nonsense," and is used in the present tense here to denote the way Diotrephes always treats the Word of God through the apostles. He mocks it like the false teachers in II Peter 3:3 who are called "scoffers." **Not content therewith.** There is more to show that he is a false teacher: he not only refuses to receive, welcome, and care for the missionaries himself, but he further shows his malicious nature by attempting to prevent (conative present in Greek) real Christians from doing it, and excommunicating them from the church.

11-12. Beloved is singular and vocative; it again addresses Gaius directly, probably as a younger or aspiring bishop. He must not **follow** (Gr *mimeomai*), meaning to "mimic," an evil pattern, but a good one. Again one of John's syllogisms is applied to Diotrephes in contradistinction to **Demetrius** a real believer, and probably another bishop in the congregation or community: **he that doeth evil hath not seen God. Not seen** is in the perfect tense in the original, and emphasizes the negative certainty of the action here, ". . . has never really seen God at all." Diotrephes is not even a believer! How can he be a leader of believers? He certainly should not be respected, obeyed, or allowed to influence Gaius who aspires to be a minister.

V. DEMETRIUS AND HIS BELIEF. 12.

12. Demetrius, on the other hand, would be a good pattern; he checks out all right. **Hath good report** (Gr *martyreō*), the same word that is used for preaching, or testifying to the truth of the gospel; the perfect tense is used in the Greek to show the certainty of the testimony concerning Demetrius both by all the believers, and by the truth (which is demonstrated in his life). **And we also bear record; and ye know that our record is true. We bear record** is the same word as **report.** John means that in this letter he is now giving his word concerning the genuine Christian character of Demetrius.

VI. CONCLUSION. 13-14.

13-14. I had many things to write, but I will not with ink and pen write unto thee. The same idea is expressed here as in the close of II John, but here the desiderative imperfect tense in Greek occurs with a different verb (had), and a slight variation in vocabulary provides a change in style. The same desire to speak face to face (or as the original idiom has it, "mouth to mouth") is present. **Our friends salute thee. Greet the friends by name.** Friends (Gr *philos*) is used here in place of "children of your elect sister" in II John 13, but this is merely another name for "brethren" or "saints." Jesus called his disciples his friends (Jn 15:13-14). It is easy to see why John would use this term if it is remembered that the literal meaning is "loved ones"; it is a synonym for the word **beloved** in verse 2. **By name** hints that the churches were quite small which must have promoted close, personal, and sincere fellowship and love. "By this shall all men know that ye are my disciples, if ye have love one to another" (Jn 13:35).

BIBLIOGRAPHY

Alexander, Neil. *The Epistles of John: Introduction and Commentary.* New York: Macmillan, 1962.

Bruce, F. F. *The Epistles of John.* London: Pickering & Ingalls, 1970.

*Candlish, Robert. *The First Epistle of John.* Grand Rapids: Zondervan, reprint, n.d.

Conner, Walter. *The Epistles of John.* Nashville: Broadman Press, 1957.

Cotton, John. *An Exposition of First John.* London: 1657.

Dodd, C. H. *The Johannine Epistles.* New York: Harper & Brothers, 1946.

Drummond, R. and Leon Morris. Epistles of John in *New Bible Commentary.* Grand Rapids: Eerdmans, 1954.

*Findlay, George. *Fellowship in the Life External.* Grand Rapids: Eerdmans, 1955 reprint of 1909 ed.

Ironside, H. A. *Addresses on the Epistles of John and Exposition on the Epistle of Jude.* New York: Loizeaux Brothers, 1954.

King, Guy. *The Fellowship.* London: Marshall, Morgan & Scott, 1954.

Law, Robert. *The Tests of Life: A Study of the First Epistle of St. John.* Grand Rapids: Baker, 1968.

*Lenski. *The Interpretation of the Epistles of St. Peter, St. John, and St. Jude.* Columbus: Wartburg Press, 1938.

Plummer, Alfred. The Epistles of St. John. In the *Cambridge Greek Testament.* Cambridge: University Press, 1894.

Ross, Alexander. The Epistles of James and John. In the *New International Commentary on the New Testament.* Grand Rapids: Eerdmans, 1954.

Ryrie, Charles. Epistles of John. In the *Wycliffe Bible Commentary.* Chicago: Moody Press, 1962.

*Stott, John R. W. The Epistles of John. In the *Tyndale New Testament Commentary.* Grand Rapids: Eerdmans, 1964.

Strauss, Lehman. *The Epistles of John.* New York: Loizeaux Brothers, 1962.

Vine, William. *The Epistles of John.* Grand Rapids: Zondervan, reprint ed.

*Westcott, B. F. *The Epistles of St. John.* Grand Rapids: Eerdmans, 1966 revised edition of 1883 ed.

White, R. E. O. *An Open Letter to Evangelicals: A Devotional and Homiletical Commentary on the First Epistle of John.* Grand Rapids: Eerdmans, 1964.

The General Epistle of

JUDE

INTRODUCTION

Authorship. In the normal manner, this author identifies himself in the salutation as Jude, the brother of James. This means that he was also the brother of our Lord (Mt 13:55; Mk 6:3). He preferred not to mention the family relationship to Jesus directly; perhaps the mention of James, who was a leading figure in the church in Jerusalem, was enough to give weight to his identity. His boast, like that of Peter and Paul, was that he was a "slave" of Jesus Christ.

Jude was listed as a disputed book by both Origen and Eusebius; this means only that there were some who did not accept it, but Origen himself quoted it as Scripture, and even states that it was "divine Scripture." However, external evidence for this book is strong. It was quoted by several early church fathers (Polycarp, Clement of Rome, etc.), and is listed in the second-century Muratorian Canon.

The outstanding reason for disputing the authenticity of Jude in ancient and modern times has been the fact that Jude quotes from the apocryphal Enoch, evidently accepting that he is the seventh from Adam. Another problem is the amount of duplication from II Peter, although there could have been a common oral or written source behind both. There is no real reason for not accepting the traditional canonical status of Jude.

Occasion and purpose. Jude, like Peter, writes to encourage believers to continue to hold to the faith against the diabolical attack of false teachers. The Old Testament Scriptures and the common apostolic preaching are the authorities which predict both the presence and the doom of the scoffers. His letter has the stated purpose of en-couraging his readers to contend for the faith (vs. 3). The letter assumes an existing danger of apostasy into immorality and deep sin because of the influence of shrewd and greedy teachers. Jude writes to correct this.

Date and place of writing. Whether before or after II Peter, Jude is at least in the same general period. There is the possibility that both draw heavily from a contemporary oral or written source which is no longer extant. The fact that Jude is more definite in his reference to the false teachers as a present reality to his readers (vs. 4) suggests that he wrote after Peter when the problem had more fully developed.

No hint of who the readers are is given in the book, except that they are perhaps in the Palestine area so that they will know who James (vs. 1) is; they may be Jews or Gentiles. The date must then lie somewhere between about A.D. 65 and 80, perhaps A.D. 67-68. The place of writing is not indicated but quite likely is Jerusalem.

Characteristics. The book is characterized by the strongest apocalyptic condemnation of the ungodly and immoral false teachers. Jude, like Peter, refers to the Old Testament to prove his point about the judgment of God upon sin; unlike Peter, he freely refers also to the apocryphal works that were current. Of all New Testament writers, Jude is more noted for this, but he is not alone in doing it. Matthew, Paul, and the writer of Hebrews all do things with quotations which require strained explanations if we judge their literary practices by twentieth century western standards. The book is definitely in character with the other apostolic writings and there is no reason not to accept it as authoritative today.

OUTLINE

COMMENTARY

I. INTRODUCTION. 1-2.

1-2. Jude. The salutation is normal and unpretentious. The author identifies himself as the brother of James (who was well known as the leader of the church in Jerusalem), but more importantly to him, as the **servant of Jesus Christ.** The word **servant** (Gr *doulos*) is literally "slave" and conveys the picture of a bondslave who belonged to another person. Even though, as the brother of James, Jude was the brother of Christ, he prefers that we know him as the "slave" or property of Christ. Peter (II Pet 1:1) and Paul (Rom 1:1) also spoke of themselves in this way; it is a metaphor of complete dedication. Of the readers, we know only that they were **sanctified . . . preserved,** and **called,** and that they must have lived somewhere in the vicinity of Palestine in order to know who James was. There is a variant in the text which should read "well-loved" rather than **sanctified,** and an acceptable translation would be, "To those who are called, beloved in God the Father and kept for Jesus Christ."

I. OCCASION OF THE EPISTLE. 3-4.

A. Change of the Purpose. 3.

3. Beloved, when I gave all diligence to write unto you. This **diligence** (Gr *spoudē*) is really "eagerness" here and is the object of a circumstantial participle in the original, which seems to be a polite concession in order to introduce the real purpose for writing. It is like saying, "Although I've been wanting to write to you for a long time about our common salvation, I now find that there is a compelling necessity, I must write." **Common salvation** is an abstract term like Christianity. Peter begins the first General Epistle with a discussion of salvation, as he does in his second epistle; so does Paul in all his epistles, and Hebrews and James assume salvation. None of the epistles are primarily evangelistic; they are not like "gospel tracts," but are written to

Christians who have some specific need for correction, reproof, encouragement, or instruction. Here Jude sees that **it was needful for me to write unto.** The word **needful** (Gr *anangkē*) implies a compelling, pressing need; a serious problem has come up among the believers, and it must be dealth with. He had to write to encourage them to **earnestly contend** (Gr *epagōnizoman*) for the faith. This word means either "fight for" someone; here Jude is writing to encourage whatever "agonizing struggle" might be necessary to defend the good name of the **faith.** The **faith** (vs. 3) is synonymous with "common salvation" or Christianity; they are to 'fight for" the honor of the *faith.* Note that the emphasis is not on contention, but on the faith which is now described further as **once delivered unto the saints.** The faith is shown to be synonymous with the apostolic preaching by the use of **deliverer** (Gr *paradidō*) which is a technical term for the preaching or handing down of the gospel message by the apostles (the word is used twice in I Corinthians 15:3 for the message which Paul "delivered" after having "received" it himself). What is being promoted here is the apostolic preaching, that is, the Word of God, not an attitude of constant fighting with other believers. This is reinforced by the use of **once,** which is not the word for "once upon a time" assuming a considerable passage of time, but rather means "once for all," and refers to the siderable passage of time, but rather means "once for all," and refers to the fact that the apostles preached this Word as a final and authoritative message which cannot now be changed by the false teachers.

B. Purpose of the Change. 4.

4. For there are certain men crept in unawares. Jude here (vs. 4) explains why he had to write giving this encouragement; false teachers had sneaked in (Gr *pareisduō*) denotes a "sneak" or furtive attack) and they must continue their fight for the purity of the Word. The same idea had been used by Peter (II Peter 2:1) and by Paul (Gal 2:4) to alert believers of the presence of heresy. Jude says (and so had Peter) that such people as these stand under the condemnation of the Old Testament itself: **who were before . . . ordained to this condemnation** (here and elsewhere in this letter Jude seems to allude to Deuteronomy 13:1-11, where people who lure others away from true worship of God are condemned in the strongest possible terms). The false teachers are further identified with the enemies of God in all apocalyptic literature by the word **ungodly** (Gr *asebēs*); these are by no means Christian brothers with a different opinion. What they have done is called **turning the grace of our God into lasciviousness.** The word **turning** (Gr *metatithēmi*) means "transfer" but what these people have done is called negative transfer; they have "misapplied" the grace of God. While God accepts us and forgives our sin, we cannot and dare not misapply this grace and say that therefore we can sin all we want and still enjoy forgiveness. So that there will be no doubt, these people are further described as those who deny **the only Lord God, and our Lord Jesus Christ.** Note that the titles here both refer to the one person Jesus Christ. These false teachers denounce Him and want no part of being "Christian."

III. THE APOSTATE PAST. 5-7.

A. Israelite Apostasy. 5.

5. I will therefore put you in remembrance. Jude now gives three examples of how Deuteronomy 13:1-11 has applied in history and resulted in death and destruction for the offenders. First, those who **believed not** were destroyed (Num 14:35). That great tragedy, you will remember, was called the "day of bitterness," or "day of testing" in the wilderness before the entrance into the Promised Land. The greatest responsibility was upon those "spies" or scouts who brought the "evil report." They not only disbelieved themselves, but they caused the people of God to despair and disbelieve the Word of God. They were **destroyed.**

B. Angelic Apostasy. 6.

6. Then there were the **angels which kept not their first estate, but left their own habitation** whom he has **reserved** (perfect tense in Greek to show the certainty of the fact) to the day of judgment. On this compare Genesis 6:1-4, the apocryphal interpretation of which both Peter (II Peter 2:4, 9) and Jude accept, at least for the sake of the illustration.

C. Pagan Apostasy. 7.

7. The third example is taken from the fiery destruction of the cities of **Sodom and Gomorrah** and the surrounding cities which committed fornication and went **after strange flesh.** The use of **fornication** (Gr *ekporneuō*), which occurs only here in the New Testament, with "strange flesh" refers to the distinctive and terrible sin of Sodom, homosexuality, for which God destroyed the whole area. The point in this passage is that the people of God were lured away from the true worship of God by the homosexual cities (cf. Gen 18-19) and they were therefore destroyed. In the Bible, the most serious sins are those which draw others away from the true worship of God or hinder others from believing in Christ (cf. Deut 13:1-11; Mk 9:42).

IV. THE APOSTATE PRESENT. 8-16.

A. Activity of the Apostates. 8-10.

8-10. Jude now shows the complete and total corruption of these false teachers to prove their identity with the kind of people mentioned in the above three examples. **Likewise also these filthy dreamers.** The word **filthy** is not in the original text but is mistakenly supplied; **dreamers** (Gr *enypiazomai*) means that they are prophets, or actually false prophets, who claimed to get their teachings by revelation or dreams (cf. Deut 13:1-5). That they are filthy is not to be denied but is brought out by the fact that they **defile** flesh which seems to mean men as opposed to angels, and also connects them with the people of Sodom who went **after strange flesh.** So bold in their false teachings are these men that they **despise** (which means "reject") **dominion** (probably God's rule) **and speak evil of dignities.** These false prophets evidently openly rejected God's Word and all spiritual powers, and were so audacious that Michael the Archangel beside them looks timid! On blaspheming **those things which they know not,** compare Paul's words in I Timothy 1:7. **But what they know naturally, as brute beasts, in those things they corrupt themselves.** Here in a very cryptic sentence would seem to be another reference to their wickedly perverted conduct (homosexuality and gluttony) in which they become completely corrupt, and for which they are to be justly destroyed (both meanings are possible for the Gr *ptheirō*).

B. Warning of the Apostates. 11-16.

11-13. Woe unto them! They are doomed as certainly as **Cain . . . Balaam . . . and Korah.** These false teachers are denounced as being as worthless as **spots** (blemishes) **in your feasts** (vs. 12), rainless **clouds** (vs. 12), fruitless **trees** that have been **plucked up by the roots** (vs. 12), **Raging waves** (vs. 13), and **wandering stars** (stars out of orbit, vs. 13).

14-16. Verses 14 and 15 are quoted from Enoch 1:9 (and 60:8) verbatim. They stress typically the ungodliness of the sinners ("ungodly" recurs four times) and the judgment they deserve and get at the Lord's coming. A clearer translation of verse 16 would be,

"These grumblers and malcontents follow their own lusts; their bloated words are nothing but flatter."

V. EXHORTATION AGAINST APOSTATES. 17-23.

A. Exhortation by the Apostles. 17-19.

17-19. Remember ye the words which were spoken before of the apostles of our Lord Jesus Christ. Spoken before (Gr *proeipon*) has been taken to mean that Jude is a late author writing in another generation than that of the apostles; this is not a valid inference, since the word does not necessarily mean "a long time ago." Paul often used this word to refer to his own previous statements made only weeks or months before; once, in Galatians 1:9, he uses it to refer to his statement in the previous verse! The whole purpose of the letter is to remind them that the Word of God was given once and for all by the apostles. The words were not, of course, spoken **of the apostles** (objective genitive), but "by the apostles," as is obvious from the next verse as well as from the grammatical construction of the original. **There should be mockers in the last time.** There are close verbal correspondences with II Peter 3:3 and I Timothy 4:1 which seems to hint at some kind of oral formula in apostolic times (see II Pet 3:3).

B. Exhortation by Warning. 20-21.

20-21. But ye, beloved, building up yourselves. This is now the positive exhortation of the letter. The main imperative verb is **Keep yourselves in the love of God. Keep** (Gr *tēreō*) means "guard" or "reserve," and its object is **yourselves.** The meaning here seems to be "keep yourselves from being dragged off into a life that is different from what God wants for you." The **love of God** may be objective genitive, meaning the true worship of God;

again compare Deuteronomy 13:3; ". . . for the Lord your God proveth you, to know whether ye love the Lord your God with all your heart and with all your soul." The main exhortation to **keep yourselves** in the love of God is supplemented with three circumstantial participles of means in the original; they answer the question, "How does one keep himself in the love of God?" By **building up yourselves** in the faith, which means learning more about the faith, or growing in the grace and knowledge of the Lord and Saviour. He adds, **by praying in the Holy** Spirit, which may be simply worshipping God as led by the Holy Spirit rather than listening to these false prophets who do not have the Spirit at all (vs. 19). And, thirdly, keep yourselves by **looking for the mercy of our Lord Jesus Christ unto eternal life. Looking for** (Gr *prosdechomai*) means to "anticipate." What is meant here is probably the same exhortation as was given by Paul when he used this very word in a similar connection in Titus 2:13, "Looking for that blessed hope, and the glorious appearing of the great God and Saviour Jesus Christ." It is interesting that Paul also used the word **mercy** in a reference to the Second Coming, "The Lord grant unto him that he may find mercy . . . in that day" (II Tim 1:18). Peter also closed his second epistle with a triple use of a synonym, asking his readers to **look for** the coming of the day of God.

C. Exhortation by Example. 22-23.

22-23. Jude seems to have some mercy himself for the false teachers (more likely, for some of the brethren who may have been influenced by them) and we would translate, "Have mercy on those who waver in doubt; save those you can by snatching them, as it were, from the flames. Show mercy in godly fear, although you hate the clothes they wear, stained as they are by the flesh."

VI. CONCLUSION. 24-25.

24.-25. In closing Jude gives one of the most balanced and beautiful benedictions in the New Testament. It is a prayer fitting for his readers who are threatened both with **falling** and with **fault** because of the false teachers who are trying to lure them into sin with claims of false revelation. Only by recalling the Word of God, i.e. the Old Testament, and especially the preaching of the apostles which showed it to be fulfilled in Jesus Christ, can they be "kept" **from falling**, and "presented" **faultless before the presence of his glory with exceeding joy.**

BIBLIOGRAPHY

Coder, Maxwell. *Jude: The Acts of the Apostates.* Chicago: Moody Press, 1958.

*Green, E. M. B. Second Epistle General of Peter and the General Epistle of Jude. In the *Tyndale New Testament Commentary.* Grand Rapids: Eerdmans, 1968.

Jenkyn, Williams. *An Exposition Upon the Epistle of Jude.* London: Bohn, 1653.

*Manton, Thomas. *An Exposition of the Epistle of Jude.* London: Banner of Truth, 1958 reprint of 1677 ed.

*Mayor, Joseph. *The Epistle of St. Jude and the Second Epistle of St. Peter.* Grand Rapids: Baker, 1965.

Robertson, R. Jude. In the *New Bible Commentary.* Grand Rapids: Eerdmans, 1954.

Wallace, David. Jude. In the *Wycliffe Bible Commentary.* Chicago: Moody Press, 1962.

Wolff, Richard. *A Commentary on the Epistle of Jude.* Grand Rapids: Zondervan, 1960.

THE
REVELATION

INTRODUCTION

In the past decades there has been a great revival of interest in the future. Many people are rushing off to fraudulent fortune tellers or satanic soothsayers in an attempt to learn what will happen in the days hence. An apparent increase in demonic activity, witches' covens, exorcisms, and the occult have accompanied this revival in futuristic thought. Bookstores have been deluged with apocalyptic books. But Christians need not waste their time searching for answers in the fruitless activities of the world. There is only one true source of information about the future and that is the One who holds the future in His hands, the Lord God of the universe. If we are to know what is in store for us and our planet, we must look to God's Word and most particularly to the book of Revelation.

Promised blessing. There are many twentieth-century people who say, "I can't understand Revelation. It's all a big puzzle to me!" In most cases this is true; but we must take heart. God knew many would close their Bibles when they reached its final chapters because the book of Revelation is admittedly difficult to understand. Nowhere in God's Word does it say we will fully understand all that is included in this wonderful, apocalyptic book. God doesn't expect us to understand it perfectly; He doesn't promise we will. What He does promise is found in Revelation 1:3: "Blessed is he that readeth, and they that hear the words of this prophecy, and keep those things which are written therein: for the time is at hand." Even though we are not promised perfect understanding, we are promised a blessing by reading the words of Revelation, or hearing them, and by keeping the things written therein.

This does not mean, however, that Revelation is unintelligible or that we will understand none of it. John was commanded not to seal the words of this prophecy. They were to remain open so that everyone would have opportunity to understand its contents (22:10). If we are promised a special blessing for reading it, apparently the book must be helpful to those who do read it.

Even the very word "revelation" is significant. Literally, it is an apocalypse (Gr *apokalypsis*), a revealing, or an unveiling. The book is not meant to cloud our minds or to mystify, but to clarify, enlighten, and inform. We should expect to gain a fuller understanding of the program of God by reading the Revelation, even if we don't understand everything we read.

Authorship. According to the book itself, the author's name was John (1:4, 9; 22:8). This John is identified almost universally in the early church as the Apostle John. He was a prophet (22:9). He was the central figure among the churches of Asia Minor (chs. 2-3). Substantiating evidence for identifying any other person as author is totally lacking.

Not only does John claim to be author, but a host of Church Fathers present collaborating evidence for Johannine authorship. One needs only to consult the writings of Justin Martyr, Irenaeus, Tertullian, Hippolytus, Clement of Alexandria and Origen to learn the traditional belief that John the Apostle was the author of the Revelation. There is no solid evidence against accepting John as the author, and there is much that confirms it.

Place and date of writing. The evidence for Johannine authorship largely depends on whether or not the Apostle John was ever banished to the Isle of Patmos, as the author of Revelation claims for himself (1:9). There is good reason to believe that the apostle was so banished.

John, the brother of James and son of Zebedee, bore a unique relationship to the Lord as one of the inner circle of the Lord's friends (Mk 5:37; 13:3). Although John is mentioned only three times in the book of Acts (3:1; 4:13; 8:14), nevertheless, tradition establishes that he settled in the Asian city of Ephesus, where he became pastor of the church there. Here he brought Mary, the mother of the Lord, for her care had been committed to John by our Lord from the cross (Jn 19:27). Because he was a faithful pastor and a fearless preacher, the emperor Domitian had John exiled to the forsaken Patmos. Patmos is a tiny, wind-swept, craggy island in the Aegean Sea about thirty-five miles southwest of the coast of Asia Minor. Irenaeus *(Against Heresies,* V, xxx, 3) claims that the aging John was sent there to work in the mines. Origen also confirms that John the Apostle was on the Isle of Patmos.

It was here that John received "the Revelation of Jesus Christ." The emperor sent the preacher to a penal colony to silence him, but God opened the heavens to allow eternal light to shine through this apostle. John claims that he was sent to Patmos, "for the word of God, and for the testimony of Jesus Christ" (1:9).

The emperor Domitian reigned from A.D. 81-96, being assassinated in A.D. 96. Clement of Alexandria mentions that John returned from the Isle of Patmos at the end of his life (*Who Is the Rich Man?* XLII). Eusebius confirms this and dates John's return immediately following the death of Domitian (*Eccl. Hist.,* III, xx). In his *Against Heresies* (III, iii, 4), Irenaeus states that John lived in Ephesus after returning from Patmos until the reign of Trajan (A.D. 98-117). This means, if John was banished to the island during the persecution of Chris-

tians near the end of Domitian's reign (A.D. 81-96), and returned to Ephesus about A.D. 96, the recording of the Revelation must have taken place about A.D. 95-96.

Some scholars (Westcott, Lightfoot, Hort, Salmon, et al.) have followed the statement of Papias that John the Apostle was martyred before the destruction of Jerusalem in A.D. 70 and have thus dated this writing to A.D. 68-69. However, the accuracy of Papias' statement has been questioned and the evidence is just too strong not to accept A.D. 95-96 as the date of Revelation. This means that Revelation is the last recorded writing from the mouth of God to the pen of man.

Interpretation. The sixteenth century French critic, Joseph Scaliger, commented on the wisdom of John Calvin by saying, ". . . he has shown his sense as much by not commenting on the Book of Revelation as he had by the manner in which he had commented on the other Books of the Bible" (Quoted by Henry Blunt, *A Practical Exposition of the Epistles to the Seven Churches of Asia,* p. v). Admittedly, Revelation is a difficult book to interpret. But since Revelation is the only prophetic/apocalyptic book in the New Testament, we must ask ourselves how we will interpret it. In the past those who have asked this question have devised no less than four ways to interpret the events of Revelation.

The preterist interpretation. From the Latin word meaning "past," the preterist approach to Revelation views the book as a record of the conflicts of the early church with Judaism and paganism. Thus, those who espouse this view would hold that chapters 5-11 record the church's victory over Judaism; chapters 12-19 record the church's victory over Rome and paganism; and chapters 20-22 record the ultimate triumph of the church.

Credit is usually given to the Jesuit priest Alcasar (ca. 1613) for originating this view, which was held and popularized by the famous Dutch theologian

Grotius. The persecutions described in the Revelation are held to be those of Nero and Domitian. Thus, the entire book would have been fulfilled by the time of Constantine (A.D. 312).

The idealist interpretation. There are a number of theologians who hold that nothing written in Revelation is real. This basically amillennial interpretation originated with the Alexandrian School of which Origen and Clement of Alexandria are representatives. They say Revelation is not literal but fictional (cf. C. H. Allen, *The Message of the Book of Revelation*). By using allegories, so these theologians say, the book simply points out spiritual lessons, mostly for encouragement. However, there is little encouragement in the Great White Throne Judgment. R. C. H. Lenski (*Interpretation of St. John's Revelation*) is a leading representative of this interpretation in this century.

The historicist interpretation. Third, some say we should interpret Revelation as continuous history. They maintain the events recorded in the book cover a time span from the early church to the coming reign of Christ. Thus, Revelation is symbolic of the continuing struggles of the church against evil. There were earlier proponents, but Joachim, a Roman Catholic scholar, is greatly responsible for the popularization of this view.

According to the historical approach to Revelation, we are today living somewhere in the account of Revelation. This view was especially attractive to the reformers, e.g. Luther, Wycliffe, Newton, etc., for it easily identified opponents of the Reformation with the wicked in Revelation. It is this view which gives rise to a belief in postmillennialism, as well as many cockeyed identifications of present personalities with those of the Apocalypse. Nevertheless, a revival of this view has taken place in the last few years.

The futurist interpretation. Each of the first three approaches outlined above fails to fit the facts. It appears that it is proper to interpret this unveiling of the person of Christ prophetically. This view, coinciding with a premillennial interpretation of the Lord's return for His church, regards Revelation as futuristic. Hence, beginning with chapter 4, all events recorded are yet to be fulfilled. This means that chapters 4 through 19 relate to the period just preceding the Second Coming of Christ in glory; chapter 19 refers to His coming to earth; chapter 20 to His future Millennial Kingdom; and chapters 21 and 22 to the events subsequent to the Millennium. Although this view seems to have been widely held in the early church, it is today rejected by both amillennialists and postmillennialists. Proponents of this view include Walvoord, Ryrie, Kent, and the authors of this commentary.

A word of caution must be added here. There is a great deal of variation in interpretation, even among futurists. Readers should not expect to understand the book of Revelation exactly as does the commentator. There is no surefire way, this side of heaven, to guarantee complete accuracy in the interpretation of every detail of this apocalyptic book. Thus, each of us should engage in ferreting out the truth, but more importantly, we must seek the blessing promised to all who read, hear, and keep the words of this prophecy.

The divine outline. Although there are dozens of ways to divide the book of Revelation in outline form, there is none so simple, yet so profound, as the way God divides it. Chapter 1, verse 19, bears the most natural, perhaps we should say supernatural, division of Revelation. John is commanded to "Write the things which thou hast seen, and the things which are, and the things which shall be hereafter." Past, present and future.

The things which John has seen are recorded in the first chapter, verses 9 through 18. At verse 12, John **turned to see the voice that spoke with me.** What he saw was a vision of seven candlesticks, **And in the midst of them one like unto the son of man.** John saw

Jesus Christ dressed in His priestly garments, with hair that was white like wool, and eyes as the flaming fire. All of this John saw and was commanded to write.

The second division, "the things which are," is recorded in chapters 2 and 3. These present things refer to that which takes place during the age of the church. They include the entire Church Age from its beginning to its consummation, when our great God and Saviour will rapture His church.

The final division is, "the things which shall be hereafter." Literally, this means "the things which happen after these things," the events of chapters 2 and 3.

They are the words of prophecy which constitute the bulk of Revelation, from chapter 4 through the end. These chapters describe the events which will take place after the Church Age has become history.

Bearing these three divisions in mind will greatly assist us in understanding that which is revealed in the Revelation of Jesus Christ (1:19). **The things which thou hast seen** are gone. **The things which are** will soon come to a close and we will see before our eyes **the things which shall be hereafter.** We are living in very exciting days and even a knowledge of Revelation which barely scratches the surface makes them much more exciting. Jesus is coming soon.

OUTLINE

COMMENTARY

I. INTRODUCTION TO THE REVELATION OF JESUS CHRIST. 1:1-20.

A. The Prologue. 1:1-3.

1:1. The Revelation of Jesus Christ. This is a far more accurate designation for this book than the standard, "The Revelation of Saint John the Divine." The book is not a simple guide to the future, as an unveiling of predicted events, but is a grand unveiling of a person, Jesus Christ the Lord.

Things which must shortly come to pass. This expression is similarly found in Daniel 2:28-29, 45 and again in Revelation 4:1; 22:6. The events of "the latter days" are described as **shortly** (Gr *en tachei*) or suddenly taking place. Hence, this book is the culmination of what has been revealed of and by Jesus Christ, and is the closing commentary on the person and work of Christ.

The author of this revelation is God, but the man chosen to record it for posterity was the Apostle John. **He sent and signified by his angel unto his servant John.** The authorship of Revelation by John has been questioned by some ever since the days of Dionysius of Alexandria in the third century A.D., but on insufficient grounds (see introductory notes). This communication is said to be **signified** (sign-i-fied) or revealed through signs or symbols. Thus, one who reads this writing should expect the use, but not abuse, of symbolic representations. The principle of interpretation used must be the literalist approach, unless that which is to be interpreted is obviously symbolic.

3. Blessed is he that readeth. There are three key expressions used here which are the avenues of divine blessing. The promised blessing is to those who read (**readeth,** Gr *anaginōskō*), those who **hear** (Gr *akouō*), and those who **keep** (Gr *tēreō*) that which is written in this book. As stated in the introduction, such a promised blessing must indicate that this book is to be read, heard, and its injunctions kept. Thus, there is no reason to relegate the Revelation to the category of the nonunderstandable or the nonrelevant. It is the capstone of God's revelation; it is the Revelation of Jesus Christ.

B. The Salutation. 1:4-8.

4. John to the seven churches which are in Asia. Having given his prologue, the apostle now addresses the churches of Asia Minor. **Asia** (modern Turkey) was actually the Proconsular Asia which at this time included Phrygia, Mysia, Caria, and Lydia. The seven churches which he will address were, in varying degrees, thriving local assemblies in western Asia Minor at Ephesus, Smyrna, Pergamos, Thyatira, Sardis, Philadelphia, and Laodicea. His greeting to these churches is in the typical Pauline fashion, **Grace be unto you, and peace.**

From him which is, and which was, and which is to come is a graphic description of God the Father. He is without beginning or end: chronologically, He is above time. It is interesting to note that this past, present, and future description of the Father corresponds to the chrono-

logical divisions of the book of Revelation (cf. 1:19). This is a revelation of God the Father about God the Son, which pervades both time and the entirety of this book of Revelation.

And from the seven Spirits which are before his throne. The mention of seven spirits here has evoked a great variance in interpretation. "Some have considered the term an allusion to the Holy Spirit (cf. Isa 11:2-3). Others believe these were seven angels in places of high privilege before the throne of God (cf. 3:1; 4:5; 5:6). The word *spirit* (Gr *pneuma*) is commonly used of evil spirits, that is, demons or fallen angels; of the human spirit (cf. Mk 8:12); and occasionally of holy angels (cf. Heb 1:7, 14). Angels are contrasted to spirits in Acts 23:8-9. Those who favor the seven spirits as referring to the Holy Spirit find justification in Isaiah 11. The message originates in God the Father and the Spirit" (John F. Walvoord, *The Revelation of Jesus Christ,* p. 37).

5-7. And from Jesus Christ. The Third Person of the Holy Trinity is now specifically mentioned as being the co-originator of this revelation. Thus, Christ Jesus is not only the object of the book of Revelation, but the author as well. Of this one who is **the first begotten of the dead, and the prince of the kings of the earth,** several activities are enumerated.

First, He **loved us** (literally, "loves us" for the verb is in the present tense). The love of the Lord for His own will permeate this revelation for it is a grand display of divine love out of, in the midst of, and through divine judgment. Second, He **washed us from our sins in his own blood.** It was this divine love that precipitated the divine plan for the Son of God to give His life a ransom for our sins. Thirdly, having been washed in the blood of the Lamb, He **hath made us kings and priests unto God.** This is better rendered that He has made us a "kingdom (Gr *basileia*), priests unto God." As believers, we are both a priesthood unto God and His kingdom (cf. I Pet 2:9;

Rev 5:10). That kingdom will soon become a reality as the Revelation unfolds.

Fourth, **he cometh with clouds.** We who are loved and bought with His blood, we who are made kings and priests, are not stranded on this planet without a King. The expression "He cometh with clouds" is not an unusual one to be associated with the Lord Jesus. He was received by a cloud into heaven (Acts 1:9). He will come in the clouds of heaven to receive His bride (I Thess 4: 16-18). But this reference to "coming" is an obvious reference to Christ's Second Coming, after the Tribulation, to establish His kingdom here on earth (cf. Mt 24:29-30). This will not be a secret coming but a very public one in which all who **pierced him: and all kindreds of the earth shall wail because of him.** This expression is almost identical to Matthew 24:30. There will be no mistaking the coming King for this book is a revelation of His soon coming.

8. I am Alpha and Omega. Alpha and Omega are the first and final letters of the Greek alphabet. They mean much the same as **the beginning and the ending.** God was before all things (Col 1:17); nothing existed before Him. God is after all things (Ps 102:27); nothing will survive Him. The eternality of God is seen in the phrase, **which is, and which was, and which is to come.** The absolute sovereignty of God is expressed in the phrase, **the Almighty.** Here is a tremendous statement about the person and work of Christ, His eternality, His love for us, His substitutionary atonement, His kingship, His priesthood, His sovereignty. If the Apostle John had stopped writing here, we would have more to appreciate about our Lord than is humanly fathomable. But there is much more.

C. The Patmos Vision. 1:9-18.

9. This tiny verse supplies much of the critical material for a discussion of this apocalyptic book. It gives the author, **John;** it gives a clue to his identity, **who also am your brother, and compan-ion in tribulation;** it gives the place of writing, **the isle that is called Patmos;** and it gives the author's purpose for being on that island, **for the word of God, and for the testimony of Jesus Christ.** John had been banished to Patmos for his stalwart preaching. But he knew that this was the plan of God for his life. He was happy in exile for his exile was imposed for the most noble of causes.

10-11. As verse 9 presents John's physical circumstances, verses 10 and 11 present his spiritual circumstances. **I was in the Spirit on the Lord's day.** Although this expression has frequently been used by preachers to indicate the presence of an unusual blessing of the Spirit's power when they preached on Sunday, as it occurs in context, it has nothing whatever to do with this meaning. John indicates that he fell into a trancelike state of supernatural revelation. This was not an unusual circumstance when God revealed Himself to His servants (cf. Ezekiel—Ezk 2:2; 3:12,14; Peter—Acts 1: 1-11; 11:5; or Paul—Acts 22:17-18).

The Lord's day is commonly used today to refer to Sunday. However, nowhere in Scripture is this the case. The day of Christ's resurrection is consistently called "the first day of the week" and never the Lord's day (Mt 28:1; Mk 16:2, 9; Lk 24:1; Jn 20:1, 19; Acts 20:7; I Cor 16:2). This is probably because every day is the Lord's day; He is Master of all and to be worshipped and served equally on them all (see Romans 14 notes). The adjective **Lord's** (Gr *kyriakos*) is used outside the New Testament to refer to "imperial." It referred to the overseer or lord and, as Adolf Deissmann points out, "the distinctive title 'Lord's Day' may have been connected with the conscious feelings of protest against the cult of the Emperor with its 'Emperor's Day'" (A. Diessmann, *Light from the Ancient East,* pp. 362-364).

This expression, then, must refer to the day of the Lord in the broader sense of the Day of the Lord in the Old Testament. This indicates an elongated period during which God judges the earth and rules over it. Thus, John was projected supernaturally into the future to view the period of judgment which has been promised through divine revelation. Hence, the command is given from **Alpha and Omega** to write what will be revealed unto him and to **send it unto the seven churches which are in Asia.**

12-16. And I turned to see the voice that spake with me. When the apostle first began to receive the divine revelation from God, he heard the voice of the Alpha and Omega and turned to face his Lord. What he saw was astounding. **I saw seven golden candlesticks.** In the Old Testament tabernacle and temple, one of the essential pieces of furniture was the seven-branched candlestick or lampstand. It appears here that there are seven separate lampstands instead of just one seven-branched lampstand for the Lord Jesus is said to stand **in the midst of the seven candlesticks.** This gives the Lord a direct relationship to each of the golden lampstands, which verse 20 identifies as the seven churches of Asia Minor here addressed.

The graphic description of Christ in these verses clearly displays His deity. He is **clothed with a garment down to the foot** (vs. 13) which is indicative of a priest or judge. **Girt about the paps with a golden girdle** (vs. 13) is reminiscent of the golden girdle of the High Priest. **His head and his hairs were white like wool** (vs. 14) corresponds to the description of the Ancient of Days in Daniel 7:9. **His eyes were as a flame of fire** (vs. 14) contributes additional description of the Ancient of Days (cf. Dan 7:13-14). **His feet like unto fine brass** (vs. 15), literally of burnished bronze. This copper alloy may symbolize divine judgment as in the brazen altar of the Old Testament where sacrifice for sin was made (cf. Ex 38:30). Or, in the fact that it is burnished brass, it may mean the trials which Christ's earthly life brought, making Him a sympathetic High Priest (Heb 4:15). **His voice as the sound of many waters** gives

reference to the booming voice of the Almighty God in judgment.

In his right hand the Lord held **seven stars** which, according to verse 20, are **the angels of the seven churches,** i.e. the pastors of the seven churches of Asia Minor. Being in the right hand places them in the place of honor. **Out of his mouth went a sharp two-edged sword.** In his book, *The Military Institutions of the Romans* (pp. 19-21), Flavius Vegetius Renatus stated that the Roman soldiers were to employ the sword, the principle offensive weapon, in a stabbing rather than a slicing action, for this would more surely effect the death of the opponent. Thus, the symbolic sword proceeding out of the Lord's mouth is to indicate the devastating judgment which will fall upon those with whom He is engaged in battle. **And his countenance was as the sun.** This undoubtedly refers to the brilliance of His glory, the same brilliance which prostrated Paul on the Damascus road.

17-18. The response of the Apostle Paul and the response of the Apostle John in meeting the Lord of Glory were identical. **And when I saw him, I fell at his feet as dead.** The glory and majesty of the Lord are overwhelming. John, who had been the closest friend our Lord had while tabernacling among us and the one who had laid his head upon the bosom of the Saviour, now views not his Saviour and friend, but his Sovereign and King. The reaction is not unpredictable.

The Lord quiets the apostle's fears by reminding him that He is indeed alive and will live for evermore, and that He has **the keys of hell and of death.** This was stated simply to assure John that the Lord is sovereign over physical death and over hell (Gr *hades*), the life after death. Hades is to be distinguished from the lake of fire or gehenna, which in 20:13-14 and elsewhere, refers to the abode of the eternal state for those who have not received Jesus Christ as Saviour. Jesus Christ is alive. He is in sovereign control. He is victorious.

D. The Commission to Write. 1:19-20.

19. Write the things. Having now been prepared by God, John is commissioned to write. This recording will follow the divine outline discussed in the introduction.

20. The mystery of the seven stars ... and the seven golden candlesticks. Here is a perfect example of Scripture interpreting itself. It will not always be God's purpose to identify that of which we read, but here the **seven stars** are the angels or messengers of the **seven churches.** This probably has reference to the pastors of each local assembly. **The seven candlesticks** or lampstands are to be understood as the **seven churches** which John has now been commissioned to address.

With these verses comes to an end the record of **the things which thou hast seen.** The past is finished. John is now being "borne along" by the Spirit of God to record the significant events of **the things which are.**

II. LETTERS TO THE SEVEN CHURCHES. 2:1-3:22.

In chapters 2 and 3 are recorded seven letters. To learn of their significance, we must ask the three most important questions one can ask in tackling an interpretation of the Scriptures. They are: "Who is doing the speaking?" "Who is being spoken to?" and "What is being spoken about?"

2:1. Unto the angel of the church of Ephesus write: These things saith he that holdeth the seven stars in his right hand. First, who is doing the speaking? The first verse of the letter gives the graphic description of the speaker, one who holds the seven stars in His right hand and walks in the midst of the seven golden lampstands. Verse 8 identifies the speaker as **the first and the last, which was dead, and is alive.** In addition, 2:12, 18 and 3:1, 7, 14 all give a description of the speaker which corresponds to the description of Christ in chapter 1. Thus, the speaker to the seven churches is the Lord Jesus Christ.

And to whom is Jesus speaking? Each letter is addressed to **the angel** of the church. This word (Gr *angelos*) simply means messenger, the one to whom authority has been given over the local churches, i.e. the pastor.

The question of what is being written about brings us to the heart of these two chapters. John is told to write a letter to each of the seven churches. These were literally seven distinct churches which existed in western Asia Minor during the first century A.D. And yet what is so special about these churches? Why should a condition in each of these local congregations be made a part of the Revelation to the church as a whole? Perhaps the answer is that the message to these local churches reaches beyond that time and place.

We must remember that Christ sent His angel and "sign-i-fied" (Gr *sē-maino*) the message to John (1:1). He used present signs to show the meaning of future events. One approach to answering the question why these particular churches were chosen as the recipients of John's letters is to make the conditions in these seven churches typical of the successive stages through which the church would ultimately pass before the Rapture. This view, popularized by the Scofield Reference edition of the Bible, need not necessarily be adopted. It is, however, an interesting theory. Note will be made at each letter how the church of that location is viewed as symbolic of an age in the history of the church. Just as satisfactory solution may be seen in the possibility that each church had a unique problem but one that was quite typical in all churches of all the centuries since Pentecost.

A. The Letter to the Church of Ephesus, 2:1-7.

This city was the capital of Asia Minor, where John resided both before and after receiving the Revelation on Patmos. The church was established by

Paul on his third missionary journey (Acts 19). The word **Ephesus** (Gr *Ephesos*, "desirable"), is the endearing term a young Greek lad would use to refer to his bride-to-be. How appropriate. When Christ left His church in the world it was as a chaste virgin, the bride of Christ, espoused to the Bridegroom. If an identification with the history of the church is to be made, Ephesus would represent the apostolic era of the first century church.

2-3. I know thy works, and thy labor, and thy patience, and how thou canst not bear them which are evil: and thou hast tried them which say they are apostles, and are not, and hast found them liars. This was an evangelistic church which had labored for the Master (2:2-3). It was a separated church for it would not endure false teachers. It was an orthodox church, trying false apostles and judging them liars.

4-5. But alas, Ephesus was a church that had lost its **first love.** Their emotional fervor and depth of love for God had waned. They no longer exhibited the fervent evangelism they once had. They no longer spontaneously expressed their love and devotion to God as they once did. They must **Remember therefore from whence thou art fallen, and repent.** They must return to fan the flames of evangelism **or else I will come unto thee quickly, and will remove thy candlestick out of his place.** This the twentieth century church should well heed.

6. But this thou hast, that thou hatest the deeds of the Nicolaitanes, which I also hate. The church at Ephesus was a people's church for they hated the deeds of the Nicolaitanes. These, whose name (Gr *Nikolaitēs*) means "conquerors of the people," were a group who argued that there ought to be two classes in the church, clergy and laity. They wanted a hierarchy to rule the church.

B. The Letter to the Church of Smyrna. 2:8-11.

8-11. Smyrna (Gr *Smyrna*) means "myrrh" which is an aromatic sub-stance that comes from a thorny tree but must be crushed to yield its perfume and fragrance. Of the Smyrnean church Christ knew **thy works, and thy tribulation, and poverty.** Tribulation (Gr *thlipsis*) denotes serious trouble. Such trouble was directed toward the church by the Roman emperors. Christians are not to think it strange when they encounter such tribulation but are to be happy when reproached for the name of Christ (I Pet 4:12-19). The church of Smyrna had apparently endured just such a reproach and, as such, may speak of the church throughout the ages, especially during the second and third centuries. The persecution by the Roman government upon local churches was like the crushing of myrrh. At no time in the history of the church was such a fragrance of faithfulness and loyalty to Christ exhibited to the world as during those centuries. Yet each crushing blow gave a "sweet-smelling savor unto God."

C. The Letter to the Church of Pergamos. 2:12-17.

12-13. I know thy works, and where thou dwellest, even where Satan's seat is. Should the seven churches of Asia Minor represent actual periods in the history of the church, **Pergamos** would carry us to about the year A.D. 500. Pergamos is a picture of the church in compromise. This city was an important religious center where the pagan cults of Athena, Zeus, Asclepius, and Dionysos were prominent. Here too were a university and a large library of two hundred thousand volumes, later sent to Egypt as a gift from Antony to Cleopatra.

The word **Pergamos** (Gr *Pergamos*) means "marriage" and signifies the spiritual adultery in which this local church engaged. What the devil could not do by Roman persecution, he tried to do by patronage. Outward assault made the church grow inwardly stronger. Thus, Satan switched his tactics from persecution to protection. There was a time in the history of the church when it became an official institution of the state. State taxes supported it and paid its pastors. This was devastating, for the church no longer was the salt in the world; it was not preaching a gospel that was a stumblingblock.

Satan's seat is literally Satan's throne (Gr *thronos*). This reference is included to indicate the influence Satan had in this city. Some think this is an allusion to the serpent, the symbol of Asclepius which was to be found everywhere in Pergamum (Pergamos). Others suggest that **Satan's seat** refers to the great altar of Zeus which stood high on the Acropolis and dominated the city. Still others hold that the reference is to emperor-worship, Charles citing an inscription from Mytilene which shows that Pergamum was the center of the emperor cult for the whole province. Whatever the case, this church perfectly pictures the spiritual unfaithfulness of the church as a whole.

14. But I have a few things against thee, because thou hast there them that hold the doctrine of Balaam . . . to eat things sacrificed unto idols, and to commit fornication. The doctrine of **Balaam** was being spread (cf. Num 31:16 with Num 25:1-3) which resulted in a union of the church and the world. The Nicolaitan tendencies present in the church of Ephesus had become doctrine in the church of Pergamos. The clergy ruled the laity and a papal system was destined to follow. The hierarchy of Romanism is the result of this doctrine in church history.

D. The Letter to the Church of Thyatira. 2:18-29.

18-29. The church of **Thyatira** may symbolize the period from A.D. 500 to 1500. If a history of the church is assumed in viewing these separate, local churches of Asia Minor, then the worldliness of the church at Thyatira introduced other excesses which became dominant in the church. **Thyatira** (Gr *Thyatira*) means "continual sacrifice." It would be fitting for this to indicate the church from A.D. 500 to 1500, for it was during this period that the papacy insti-

tuted the doctrine of transubstantiation, that each time the priest performed the mass, the wafer became the actual body of Christ and the wine became His literal blood. This continual sacrifice of Christ is a heresy which puts our Lord to shame (Heb 6:6). Symbolic representation of this is made by the introduction of Jezebel in verse 20. **Notwithstanding I have a few things against thee, because thou sufferest that woman Jezebel . . . to teach and to seduce my servants to commit fornication.** As this heathen princess endeavored to unite Judaism with her own pagan religion, so, too, many ungodly practices and excesses in the church have tended to prostitute the teachings which the church inherited from Jesus Christ. The church of Thyatira represents the enlargement of the seeds of corruption which the devil earlier introduced into the churches. The church in every age must be cautious not to allow false teachers to introduce false doctrine into the purity of Christ's teachings. To do so is to become the church of Thyatira.

E. The Letter to the Church of Sardis. 3:1-6.

3:1-2. Sardis (Gr *Sardeis*), which means "remnant," is a local church which pictures reformation. When sin enters the local assembly it must be rooted out. Sardis was apparently such a church. This church received a few warnings, **Be watchful, and strengthen the things which remain** (vs. 2), **remember** (vs. 3), etc., but it never received a direct rebuke from the Lord as the previous churches had. It was not perfect, but it was attempting to live blamelessly before the Lord. In so doing, it symbolizes those local assemblies of all ages which attempt to live righteously before a watching world.

Historically, if each church represents a period in the history of the church, this church would represent the age of the Reformation. Having recognized the abuses so prevalent in the church for over one thousand years, and having become convinced that "the just shall live by faith," Martin Luther lifted his hand against Roman tyranny in Germany. Across the continent others joined him in attempting to reform their beloved church. Protestantism was born and the seeds of corruption were badly bruised.

3-4. Remember therefore how thou hast received and heard, and hold fast, and repent . . . Thou hast a few names even in Sardis which have not defiled their garments. In the history of the church, there has always been a remnant who **have not defiled their garments** with the doctrine of Balaam nor the excesses of the hierarchy, but have sought a return to the "pure religion and undefiled" which the apostles had known. As this desire precipitated the Protestant Reformation, so too it ought to precipitate a reformation in every church in every period of history.

F. The Letter to the Church of Philadelphia. 3:7-13.

7-8. And to the angel of the church in Philadelphia write; These things saith he that is holy, he that is true . . . I know thy works: behold, I have set before thee an open door, and no man can shut it. The sixth message of Jesus Christ is to the church of Philadelphia. Every church has an **open door** to preach the gospel, just as every church has the command to go through that door. However, some local assemblies seem to be more characterized by using that open door than are others. Some churches become more evangelistically active than are others. Still, some periods in the history of the church seem to be more characterized by using that open door than are others.

Thus, this church may symbolically mark the great periods of revival through the history of the church, specifically during the eighteenth and nineteenth centuries. Our Lord commended the Philadelphians for using the opportunities of evangelism afforded by this open door, for keeping His Word, and for their separation and fidelity. Per-

haps the years of Spurgeon, Wesley, Whitefield, Moody, and others best characterize this activity of using the open door, at least until the present. During the last two centuries spiritual awakenings were happening everywhere.

9-13. That the Lord especially loved the church of the Philadelphians is exhibited in the promises given to them. **Behold, I come quickly** (vs. 11); **Him that overcometh will I make a pillar** (vs. 12); **I will write upon him my new name** (vs. 12). God is especially pleased with those who avail themselves of the **open door** (vs. 8) of the gospel. This church is promised deliverance from the hour of trial and from seeing conditions which would discourage them from using the open door. They are promised the crown of reward and, in the symbolism expressed here, a place of prominence in the heavenly temple of eternity. God promised to write on these and all saints His name, the name of His city and His new name. Although it is impossible to say what that new name will be, it is evident that the act of writing His name on us identifies us as His eternal possession. This behooves every Christian to use every available door to witness of the love of Christ at every available time.

G. The Letter to the Church of Laodicea. 3:14-22.

14-15. I know thy works, that thou art neither cold nor hot. Now we come to the final church. The seven churches which John addresses lie within a great semicircle beginning with Ephesus, proceeding northward and eastward through Smyrna and Pergamum, and then southward again to Laodicea. Thus, the church at Laodicea was located about ninety miles due east of the church of Ephesus and about forty-five miles southeast of the church of Philadelphia. The city of Laodicea was founded by the Seleucid king Antiochus II in the middle of the third century B.C. Under the Romans, Laodicea became a wealthy city, making a profitable business from the production of wool cloth. Destroyed by an earthquake about A.D. 60, the town had been rebuilt by the time of the writing of the Revelation.

16. The problem in the church at Laodicea was their lukewarmness toward the Lord. The word translated **luke-warm** (Gr *chliaros*) is used only here in the New Testament. It is a reference to tepid water. Frequently servants of the Lord have passed through periods of lukewarmness. In fact, many churches have become terminally ill with this condition. The word Laodicea (Gr *Laodikeia*) means "the people's rights" or "the judgment of the people." It is the clamoring for the rights of the people within the church which has contributed greatly to the lukewarm condition of many churches. Some have suggested this church represents the early years of this century. That may be true. If ever the rights of the people was a battle cry within the church it is in this century. With respect to the church, people have taken over the churches and the Lord is no longer the Head. Conventions, denominations, boards, councils, and the like, governed by the people, now run many local churches. The end result has been a characteristic lukewarmness toward God and the gospel.

I will spew thee out of my mouth. The church must know that lukewarmness is a sin against God. Perhaps this phrase has reference to the induction of vomiting for churches that are lukewarm make God sick. He cannot tolerate such a condition. The members of the Laodicean church were **neither cold nor hot.** No one accused them of the excesses which characterized other churches. However, no one could accuse them of serving the Lord zealously either. They were simply maintaining the *status quo,* unaggressively pursuing a middle-of-the-road policy. This church was guilty of gross indifference.

17-18. I am rich, and increased with goods, and have need of nothing. Secondly, this church was guilty of gross self-sufficiency. They no longer needed

to rely on the Lord for they were functioning well by committee. The riches of the town of Laodicea had spilled over into the church of Laodicea and they felt they had need of nothing, including the power of the Spirit of God. It is a sad situation when a church boasts of gaining wealth by her own human effort and does not realize in reality that her true state is that she is **wretched, and miserable, and poor, and blind, and naked.**

19. Verse 19 indicates the Lord's reason for delivering these seven messages to seven churches. He says, **As many as I love, I rebuke and chasten: be zealous therefore, and repent.** We have been on the road a long time since the days of the first century church, but I wonder how far we have come? This command to repent and be zealous has been repeated by faithful preachers of the gospel in every century. It needs to be repeated again today.

20. It is almost unbelievable that the Lord Jesus would actually be outside His church bidding entrance. Nevertheless He says, **Behold, I stand at the door and knock.** He is not knocking at the door of the unbeliever's hearts; this verse has nothing whatever to do with salvation. Christ the Lord is pictured as knocking on the door of His church at Laodicea, and, symbolically, at the door of His church in every generation when that church becomes lukewarm and nonproductive.

The conditions of these seven churches seem to indicate various states into which a local church may fall. Perhaps one church may experience all seven conditions during its history. This, however, is not necessary if each pastor and local assembly will take every "open door" as a sign from the Lord to minister. This is the best way to stay fervent and zealous for the Lord.

One can see why an interpretation of these churches representing the successive stages of church history would appeal to the editors of the Scofield Reference edition of the Bible during the early years of this century. It appears as if each church, in order of occurrence, graphically portrays the successive periods of the history of the church, right up to and including the day of dead orthodoxy in the first half of the twentieth century. But how does one explain the dynamic resurgence of the impact of the gospel in the last few years? Where does this fit into the scheme of the seven churches of Revelation?

Perhaps the answer is that today in the waning years of the twentieth century, examples of each type of the seven churches can be found. In the United States alone there are Smyrnean churches, Philadelphian churches and Laodicean churches. Perhaps, too, God is causing more pastors and churches to see the ''open door'' today, more so than even during the eighteenth and nineteenth centuries, so that one great final outbreak of revival may bring glory to His name. Perhaps we are presently experiencing a post-seven-church revival and if that be the case we must become keenly aware that this could be the terminal generation for with the close of chapter 3 the division of **the things which are** (1:19) comes to a close. We must become keenly aware that whoever is to receive the message of salvation prior to the awful Tribulation Period must receive it now. We must ''preach as if never to preach again; as a dying man to dying men.''

III. A VISION OF HEAVEN. 4:1-11.

We now embark on a long journey into the future. In relation to the divinely inspired outline of Revelation 1:19, we are about to chart a course in **the things which shall be hereafter.** From the standpoint of the twentieth century, all that occurs in the Revelation from this time on will be future. Beginning with chapter 4, things to come are unfolded. Chapters 4-5 are the introduction and background to the broad scope of prophetic events in the rest of the book. To some degree, they provide a table of contents for the chapters that follow.

A. The Upward Call. 4:1.

4:1. After this I looked, and, behold, a door was opened in heaven: and the first voice which I heard was as it were of a trumpet talking with me; which said, Come up hither, and I will show thee things which must be hereafter. The striking similarities between the elements of this verse and those of I Thessalonians 4:13-18, which record the Rapture of the church, cannot be coincidence. Here, as a representative of the church at large, John envisions being caught up into heaven to view the future. This event symbolizes the catching up to heaven of all born-again believers before judgment begins. That this is a sign of the Rapture of the church is believed for the following reasons:

(1). Beginning with 4:1, the word ''church'' (Gr *ekklēsia*) does not appear again in Revelation until 22:16, after judgment is completely finished.

(2). There is an obvious transition between chapters 3 and 4. Chapter 3 speaks of the churches; chapter 4 of judgment. Chapter 3 is set on earth; chapter 4 in heaven. Chapter 3 closes the division of **the things which are;** chapter 4 opens the division of **the things which shall be hereafter.**

(3). The first vision of Christ in Revelation pictures Him in the midst of the seven lampstands (which the book itself interprets as the seven churches). But in chapters 4-19 Christ is pictured in heaven (4:1-2; 5:5-6). It is certainly logical to believe the church is there with Him (Jn 14:1-3).

(4). The promise made to the Philadelphian church was that it would be kept from the hour of trial (3:10). In order to escape the terrible judgment of Revelation chapters 4-19, the church must be translated to heaven before that time (I Thess 1:9-10; 5:9).

For these and other reasons, it appears that John's vision of himself being caught up from earth to heaven is a symbolic representation of the Rapture of the church before the events of the Tribulation described in chapters 4-19.

B. The Throne of God. 4:2-3.

2-3. And immediately I was in the spirit: and, behold, a throne was set in heaven, and one sat on the throne. And he that sat was to look upon like a jasper and a sardine stone: and there was a rainbow round about the throne, in sight like unto an emerald. The first thing John envisions in heaven is a throne. This is not symbolism, but a judgment scene set in heaven. This throne is neither the Great White Throne of Revelation 20:11 nor the Judgment Seat of Christ of II Corinthians 5:10. The one sitting on the throne is none other than God Himself. This is clear from the symbolism of verses 3 and 5 and from the direct reference to God in verse 8:

Holy, holy, holy, Lord God Almighty, which was, and is, and is to come.

The jasper stone, mentioned in verse 3 and explained in Revelation 21:11, is a crystal-clear white stone representing the purity and glory of God. On the other hand, the sardius stone is ruby-colored, a blood red. By this is pictured God's redemptive nature.

C. The Twenty-four Elders. 4:4-5.

5. And out of the throne proceeded lightnings and thunderings and voices. The throne itself has an emerald-colored rainbow completely encircling it, and out of the throne proceed lightnings and thunderings. Here again is a contrasting picture of God. This is a throne of judgment, depicted by the lightning and thunder. But mingled with God's righteous judgment is His mercy, represented by the rainbow (Gen 9:13-16).

Those around the throne of God are equally interesting. Verse 4 indicates, **And round about the throne were four and twenty seats: and upon the seats I saw four and twenty elders sitting, clothed in white raiment; and they had on their heads crowns of gold.** The seats upon which these twenty-four elders sit are thrones which indicate they are given positions of authority. Who can these elders be? Opinions vary. Amillenialists like R. H. Charles and Leon Morris see these elders as a superior order of angels (cf. R. H. Charles, *A Critical and Exegetical Commentary on the Revelation of St. John;* Leon Morris, *The Revelation of St. John*). The most logical identification, however, is that they are the raptured church. They are representative of the entire church. As the officials of the church today, no better symbol than the elders could be used in this vision to represent the whole church (Acts 15:6; 20:17; Jas 5:14).

D. The Four Living Creatures. 4:6-8.

There is one more group around the throne that needs identification. They are the four beasts, or as the word is more correctly translated "living ones" or "living creatures" (Gr $z\bar{o}on$). They are described in detail in verses 6-7. These are not grotesque animals but rather living creatures of diverse characteristics. The first is like a lion, the second like a calf, the third has a face like a man, and the fourth is like a flying eagle. Each of them has six wings and is **full of eyes,** which depicts their incessant activity in praising the Lord.

These four living creatures are heavenly cherubim (Ezk 10:15, 20). They complete the symbolism that every living creature in heaven will praise God, both earthly and heavenly beings. Both the raptured church, represented by the twenty-four elders, and the heavenly angels, represented by the four living cherubim, will one day praise the Lord as He ought to be praised today.

E. The Worship of the Lord. 4:9-11.

10-11. The four and twenty elders fall down before him that sat on the throne, and worship him that liveth for ever and ever, and cast their crowns before the throne, saying,

Thou art worthy, O Lord,
to receive glory and honor and power:
for thou hast created all things,
and for thy pleasure they are and were created.

The activity of the twenty-four elders gives us a clue as to our own activity in heaven. They cast their crowns before the throne as they praise the Lord God. These are not the diadems (Gr *diadēma*), or crowns of royalty. They are the crowns that have been won in the arena of faith. They are the crowns (Gr *stephanos*) of faithful service during this life. What better way to praise and honor God than to cast at His feet the tangible evidence of our heavenly reward?

Also the twenty-four elders are said to prostrate themselves before God and worship Him. To worship means to ascribe honor to, and that is exactly what these elders do when they say,

Thou art worthy, O Lord,
to receive glory and honor and power.

IV. THE SEVEN-SEALED SCROLL. 5:1-8:5.

A. The Unopened Scroll. 5:1-4.

5:1. And I saw in the right hand of him that sat on the throne a book written within and on the backside, sealed with seven seals. Chapter 5 finds John viewing another majestic sight. In the right hand of God, sitting on the throne, is a book which has been written upon both inside and out. In the days of the Apostle John, books were usually scrolls (Gr *biblion*) rather than bound books such as we have today. When a scroll was completely filled with writing, it would be rolled a little ways, a seal would be placed on it, and then it would be rolled a little more and sealed again. When it was completely rolled, seven seals would secure its message. To unroll the scroll and reveal the contents, one must break the seals successively.

This sealed scroll recalls the ancient Jewish custom of the kinsman-redeemer (Ruth 4). Under the law, when an owner of property allowed another to take possession of it, a sort of mortgage deed was given to the original property owner. This was a sealed scroll which stated that at some future date a representative kinsman could reclaim that property if the purchase price were met. The landowner's representative must be a legal kinsman, and be worthy of the right to purchase the property. When he had paid the stated purchase price, then, and only then, could he break the seals on the scroll. This worthy seal-breaker was called the "redeemer," for he had regained the property from the hands of another.

2. But here a grave problem arises. John sees a mighty angel proclaiming in a loud voice, **Who is worthy to open the book, and to loose the seals thereof?** Since this is the title deed to the universe and only the purchaser of redemption can receive it from the hand of God, an intensive search is made to discover a man worthy to open the scroll.

3. And no man in heaven, nor in earth, neither under the earth, was able to open the book, neither to look thereon. Though the heavens, the earth, and the netherworld are searched, no man worthy is found. By sin all men have forfeited any worthiness they might conjure up to open the scroll (Ps 14:1-3; Eccl 7:20; Rom 3:10, 23).

4. And I wept much, because no man was found worthy to open and to read the book, neither to look thereon. This caused John to fall into uncontrollable despair and much weeping. No man was found worthy. Was this to be the end of the revelation? Was it possible that the scroll would have to remain sealed and its message unknown forever?

B. The Worthy Lamb. 5:5-7.

5. Suddenly one of the elders said to the greatly sorrowful John, **Weep not: behold, the Lion of the tribe of Judah, the Root of David, hath prevailed to open the book, and to loose the seven seals thereof.** Then John looked up and in the midst of the throne, among the four living creatures, and among the twenty-four elders, **stood a Lamb as it had been slain, having seven horns and seven eyes, which are the seven spirits of God sent forth into all the earth** (vs. 6).

Here was the answer to the angel's question. **Who is worthy to open the book, and to loose the seals thereof?** The

Lamb is worthy. The Lion of the tribe of Judah has met the qualifications to open the scroll. This is none other than the Lion (Gen 49:10) from between the feet of Judah, the Root of David (Isa 11:1), the Prince of Peace (Isa 9:6-7), the Lamb of God (Jn 1:29). This is Jesus Christ the Lord. Interestingly, this motif of the Lamb spans the pages of Holy Writ. On Mt. Moriah, where sacrifice was about to be made, Isaac asked father Abraham, "Where is the lamb?" (Gen 22:7). When John the Baptist viewed Christ for the first time he announced, "Behold the Lamb" (Jn 1:29). Now the Lord Jesus makes another appearance and the heavenly hosts sing, **Worthy is the Lamb** (vs.12).

The title deed is in the hand of God and only Jesus has paid the purchase price. He has purchased all things by His death on Calvary. Since Jesus Christ alone has paid the price for redeeming God's property, He is the only one who is able to take the scroll out of the hands of God. On the cross the title to the redeemed souls of the universe was purchased with Christ's blood and now He steps up and receives the scroll in one of the most dramatic scenes in history.

C. The Praise of the Lamb. 5:8-14.

Jesus Christ, the Redeemer, claims those for whom He died, and immediately the four living creatures and twenty-four elders sing a new song, a song of praise to the Redeemer.

9-12. Thou art worthy to take the book,
and to open the seals thereof:
for thou wast slain,
and hast redeemed us to God by thy blood
out of every kindred, and tongue, and people, and nation;
and hast made us unto our God kings and priests:
and we shall reign on the earth.

Even the angels, ten thousand times ten thousand strong, who could not sing the new song of redemption, join in the celebration of praise to the one worthy to receive the scroll by saying with a loud voice, **Worthy is the Lamb that was slain to receive power, and riches, and wisdom, and strength, and honor, and glory, and blessing.**

Finally, every creature in heaven, on earth, and under the earth sings honor and blessing to the Lamb. Yes, Christ Jesus humbled Himself, came to earth in the form of a man, and died for mankind. "Wherefore God also hath highly exalted him, and given him a name which is above every name: That at the name of Jesus every knee should bow, of things in heaven, and things in earth, and things under the earth; and that every tongue should confess that Jesus Christ is Lord, to the glory of God the Father" (Phil 2:9-11). This is exactly what will happen when the worthy Lamb receives the title deed to the universe from God the Father. Believers will be there to witness this great event. I wouldn't miss it for the world.

Beginning with the sixth chapter, and continuing all the way to chapter 19, the Apostle John is permitted to view the Tribulation Period. Within these important chapters is a series of three judgments: the seals (ch. 6), the trumpets (chs. 8-9), and the bowls (ch. 16). Between the record of each judgment is a parenthetical chapter or chapters which provide additional information about each judgment. For example, the judgment of the seals in chapter 6 is elaborated upon in chapter 7.

You'll recall that the seals are placed on the title deed to the universe which only the worthy Redeemer, Jesus Christ, is legally qualified to open. This is a transaction between Father and Son; the Father is the property owner, and the Son its redeemer. Jesus Christ paid the redemption price with His own life's blood, and now He is fully qualified to open the seals and enter into the possession of His property. With the opening of these seals is ushered in the Tribulation, the seventieth week of Daniel (Dan 9:24-27). The future is revealed as each of the seals is successively broken by the worthy Redeemer.

D. The First Seal. 6:1-2.

At the opening of the first seal by the Lamb of God, the first of the four horsemen of the Apocalypse is revealed to John. The rider held a bow, wore a crown, and went forth as a conqueror.

6:1. And I saw, and behold a white horse: and he that sat on him had a bow; and a crown was given unto him: and he went forth conquering and to conquer. The appearance of the white horse makes one think of the white horse in Revelation 19:11. But the rider revealed by the first seal cannot be Christ, for He is the one who holds the scroll and opens the seal. No, this is not Christ, but one who comes in the name of Christ (Mt 24:5), masquerading as the Christ. He is the Antichrist and therefore comes saying, "Peace, peace," offering a plan of world peace and promising a false Millennium. But remember that Paul said, "When they shall say, Peace and safety; then sudden destruction cometh upon them, as travail upon a woman with child; and they shall not escape (I Thess 5:3). This false christ (II Thess 2:3-12) is the Man of Sin, the covenant-making prince of Daniel 9:26.

E. The Second Seal. 6:3-4.

4. And there went out another horse that was red: and power was given to him that sat thereon to take peace from the earth, and that they should kill one another: and there was given unto him a great sword. With the opening of the second seal a red horse appears. This signifies the second phase of the reign of Antichrist. Having come in peace, he soon plunges the whole world into bloodshed. The peace plan offered by the Antichrist, and so readily accepted by the nations of this world, will now be withdrawn, and he will cause worldwide war and bloodshed.

F. The Third Seal. 6:5-6.

5-6. . . . And I beheld, and lo a black horse; and he that sat on him had a pair of balances in his hand. And I heard a voice in the midst of the four beasts say, A measure of wheat for a penny, and three measures of barley for a penny. When the third seal is opened a black horse appears and its rider has a pair of balances in his hand. Following closely on the heels of war will be famine and starvation. The balances suggest that a system of rationing will be enforced (13:16-17). In the New Testament times a denarius or penny was one day's wages and bought only enough for one person (Mt 20:2, 9). Because of the devastation of war, the production of grain will be greatly curtailed and the whole world will have to ration its food. It is evident that we are rapidly heading for that program even today.

G. The Fourth Seal. 6:7-8.

8. And I looked, and behold a pale horse: and his name that sat on him was Death, and Hell followed with him. And power was given unto them over the fourth part of the earth, to kill with sword, and with hunger, and with death, and with the beasts of the earth. The last horseman of the Apocalypse rides a pale horse, and the rider's name is Death. Actually the word "pale" (Gr *chlōros*) means green-like, as a corpse. This rider, Death, will exterminate those living on the earth by four means: (1) the sword (war); (2) hunger (famine); (3) death (plagues which accompany famine); and (4) wild beasts (which will roam unrestrained in that day of destruction).

H. The Fifth Seal. 6:9-11.

9. The fifth seal depicts the souls of those **slain for the word of God, and for the testimony which they held.** These cannot be the martyrs of the Church Age, for they were raptured before the holocaust of the opening of the seals. They must be those martyred for their faith during the first months of the Tribulation. Their being under the altar is symbolic of the fact that these people have been purchased by the blood of Christ.

10. And they cried with a loud voice, saying, How long, O Lord, holy and true, dost thou not judge and avenge our blood on them that dwell on the earth? When those who have been slain for the Word of God inquire how long it will be until the Lord avenges their blood, they are told to rest with their fellow servants and brethren, for many more will yet join the ranks of the slain.

I. The Sixth Seal. 6:12-17.

12. And I beheld when he had opened the sixth seal, and, lo, there was a great earthquake; and the sun became black as sackcloth of hair, and the moon became as blood. With the breaking of the sixth seal havoc is unleashed on the earth and the Lord's wrath brings cataclysmic judgment. Six literal, catastrophic events will occur: (1) a great earthquake; (2) the sun becomes black; (3) the moon becomes reddened like blood; (4) a universal meteor shower of stars falls to earth; (5) the heavens part as a scroll revealing God on His awesome throne; and (6) every mountain and island are moved when the heavens roll back. The result will be panic and fear when men **hid themselves in the dens and in the rocks of the mountains; and said to the mountains and rocks, Fall on us, and hide us from the face of him that sitteth on the throne, and from the wrath of the Lamb** (6:15-16).

Before the opening of the seventh seal some additional information about this period of tribulation is provided for us in chapter 7. The narrative is not advanced; supplementary material is simply added. Here John sees four angels standing on the four corners of the earth, holding the four winds of the earth. The activity of these angels does not follow the opening of the sixth seal but rather begins before the opening of the first seal. Thus chapter 7 provides information about the whole of the Tribulation Period. This information is provided from the perspective of salvation, not history.

J. An Interlude: Salvation During the Tribulation. 7:1-17.

7:1. And after these things I saw four angels standing on the four corners of the earth, holding the four winds of the earth, that the wind should not blow on the earth, nor on the sea, nor on any tree. The "fours" here represent the universality of these angels' activity. Revelation 7:2-3 depicts a fifth and apparently superior angel arising out of the east and instructing the four angels to **hurt not the earth, neither the sea, nor the trees, till we have sealed the servants of our God in their foreheads** (vs. 3). These angels are restraining judgment long enough to reveal God's grace. They are holding on to the winds of God's judgment so that He may save two great throngs of people during this Tribulation Period.

4. And I heard the number of them which were sealed: and there were sealed a hundred and forty and four thousand of all the tribes of the children of Israel. The first group God chooses to save are "sealed" during the first three and one half years of the Tribulation (vss. 3-8). The purpose of the seal is to indicate ownership, and the reference to their foreheads suggests that they are publicly known as the saved of God.

The number to be sealed is 144,000, and God's revelation to John clearly indicates that this group of 144,000 is composed of 12,000 from each of the twelve tribes of Israel. The 144,000 are Jews. The constant repetition of the phrase **of the tribe of . . . were sealed** (vss. 5-8) is too forceful to allow any other biblical or logical conclusion.

Those today who claim to be among this group would have to know the tribe to which they belonged, and since all such tribal records were destroyed when the Roman General Titus sacked Jerusalem in A.D. 70, there is not a person alive today who can honestly claim to be part of the 144,000. Besides, most who claim to be included in this number are not even Jews but cultists, and God's Word clearly indicates that the 144,000 of

God's sealed servants will be out of physical Israel.

9. After this I beheld, and, lo, a great multitude, which no man could number, of all nations, and kindreds, and people, and tongues, stood before the throne, and before the Lamb, clothed with white robes, and palms in their hands. Because this vast number of Jewish servants faithfully witnesses to the saving power of Christ Jesus, a second group of individuals is saved.

12. Whereas the 144,000 were all Jews, here is a great multitude of saved people who are of all nations, all tribes, all peoples and tongues. They stand before the Lamb in white robes, indicating that they too have been saved by the blood of the Lamb. Along with all the angels and the twenty-four elders, representing the church, this great multitude praises the God of our salvation and the Lamb **saying, Amen: Blessing, and glory, and wisdom, and thanksgiving, and honor, and power, and might, be unto our God for ever and ever. Amen.**

"That they are distinct from the church appears from the following considerations: Those were kept out of the Great Tribulation (3:10); these came out. Those wear white raiment; these wear white robes. Those sit on thrones round about the throne; these stand before the throne. Those wear crowns; these are uncrowned. Those have harps and vials; these have palms in their hands. Those sing a new song; these cry with a loud voice. Those are kings and priests and reign with Him; these serve Him day and night" (J. B. Smith, *A Revelation of Jesus Christ,* p. 135).

14. To John's question concerning the origin of this numberless multitude, one of the elders gives the noteworthy answer, **These are they which came out of great tribulation, and have washed their robes, and made them white in the blood of the Lamb.** As the 144,000 were sealed during the first part of the Tribulation, so too these are saved during the last part. What a wonderful picture of God's mercy. Although the Tribulation

is a time of judgment, yet it will be a time of salvation as well. An election out of Israel will be redeemed with an innumerable multitude of Gentiles. In the midst of justice is found God's merciful salvation, for through the Tribulation come those who have been washed in the blood of the Lamb.

Someone may say, "Well, if multitudes are going to be saved during the Tribulation, then I'll just wait. I don't need to be born again now. After the Rapture I'll get my heart right with the Lord."

I have bad news for those who reason in this manner. No one who hears the gospel today and rejects it will have an opportunity to be saved during the Tribulation. II Thessalonians 2:11-12 says, "And for this cause God shall send them strong delusion, that they should believe a lie: That they all might be damned who believed not the truth, but had pleasure in unrighteousness." Whoever rejects the gospel today will become a victim of the strong delusion spread by the Antichrist during the Tribulation. They will swallow his lie hook, line, and sinker, whether they want to or not. As a result, they cannot believe the truth of the gospel then and will be damned because they reject Christ now. Only those who have not known the gospel story or who have never heard it will have opportunity to believe it during the Tribulation. These will be the multitudes saved in Revelation chapter 7.

K. The Seventh Seal. 8:1-6.

8:1. And when he had opened the seventh seal, there was silence in heaven about the space of half an hour. After the interlude of chapter 7 comes to a close, the first verse of Revelation 8 brings us to another crisis event. Six seals have been opened previously and judgment has poured forth. Now the last of the seals is opened and is followed by an amazing response. There is immediately an ominous hush throughout heaven. Moments before the whole company of angels, living creatures and elders was engaged in tumultous praise of the one sitting on the throne and of the Lamb of God. Now, suddenly, there is silence so intense you can feel it. The final seal has been torn away from the title deed to the universe and the calamities about to be witnessed are so awful that the company of heaven is speechless. This is the calm before the storm and lasts a full thirty minutes. If the coming judgment is so intense that the angels silently gasp in horror, how much more should men be alarmed at this terrible judgment and rush to be cleansed by the blood of the Lamb.

2. And I saw the seven angels which stood before God; and to them were given seven trumpets. As the vision continues, John is shown seven angels who stand before God and receive seven trumpets. These are special angels, for they are called **the** seven angels, a distinct group for a distinct purpose. They are marked by special power, dignity, and service (Heb 1:7, 14). The trumpets are instruments of proclamation. The sounding of the trumpet is always followed by an outstanding announcement or event (cf. Ex 19:16; 20:18; Jer 4:5; I Cor 15:51-52; I Thess 4:16).

The vision of the seven trumpets lends itself to various interpretations. Many scholars, especially amillennial scholars, hold that the seven trumpet judgments are simply a recapitulation of the seven seal judgments. Under this interpretation there is but one series of judgments, with three purposes or perspectives. Hence, the judgment of the seals may be interpreted as referring to one group or for one purpose, the judgment of the trumpets (the same as the seals) given to refer to another group or from another perspective, and the judgment of the vials or bowls (again the same as the seals and trumpets) given to refer to another group or from another perspective. This is the view of A. Plummer in *The Pulpit Commentary;* Leon Morris, *The Revelation of St. John;* and others.

A preferred interpretation is that with the opening of the seventh seal the sec-

ond series of judgments is revealed, i.e. the seven trumpets. As well, with the sounding of the seventh trumpet, the third series of judgments is revealed, i.e. the seven bowls. This does not mean that the judgments of the seven bowls follow the judgments of the seven trumpets, which, in turn, follow the judgments of the seven seals. On the contrary, the seven trumpets are the judgment of the seventh seal and the seven bowls are the judgment of the seventh trumpet. This is the view of Herman Hoyt, *The Glory—the Final Victory of Christ;* W. G. Scroggie, *The Book of Revelation;* John Walvoord, *The Revelation of Jesus Christ;* and others.

Perhaps we may conceive of this as the "firecracker" view. The judgments of the seven seals explode over the seven-year period of the Tribulation as firecrackers which are shot into and light up the night sky. Each seal erupts in succession as does each firecracker, but when the final seal explodes it is like a "Roman candle" out of which spring forth seven additional firecrackers. The seventh seal erupts into the judgments of the seven trumpets. Likewise the final firecracker of the "Roman candle" explodes into seven additional firecrackers, i.e. the seven bowl judgments.

This interpretation admits the increasing severity of the tribulation during the Tribulation Period and indicates that the latter half (the Great Tribulation) is much more devastating than the first. Interestingly, Henry Alford (*The Greek New Testament*) dismisses both interpretations but does not attempt a third solution.

3. And another angel came and stood at the altar, having a golden censer; and there was given unto him much incense, that he should offer it with the prayers of all saints upon the golden altar which was before the throne. Before the trumpets can be sounded, another angel appears, standing before the altar with a gold censer and much incense. Some regard this angel as merely an angel (cf. William R. Newell, *The Book of the*

Revelation), but it probably refers to Christ Jesus in His office as High Priest (cf. Walter Scott, *Exposition of the Revelation of Jesus Christ*). The incense, symbolic of the finished work of Christ, causes smoke to rise to the throne of God along with the prayers of the saints. The reason our prayers have any efficacy at all is because of the sweet savor of Christ's finished work at Calvary and His present intercessory work on our behalf.

5. And the angel took the censer, and filled it with fire of the altar, and cast it into the earth: and there were voices, and thunderings, and lightnings, and an earthquake. Once prayer ascends, judgment descends. The fire represents judgment as do the thunder, lightning, and earthquake. The seven angels are now ready to sound the seven trumpets proclaiming God's judgment.

V. THE SEVEN TRUMPETS. 8:7-11:19.

A. The First Trumpet. 8:7.

7. The first angel sounded, and there followed hail and fire mingled with blood, and they were cast upon the earth: and the third part of trees was burnt up, and all green grass was burnt up. As the first trumpet is blown, John sees hail and fire mixed with blood fiercely falling to the earth. So great is the devastation that one third of the earth's trees and green grass is completely burned up. This is a literal burning up of one third of the earth's vegetation. There is no reason to assume this to be figurative, since we take the plagues of Egypt to be literal (Ex 9:23-24).

B. The Second Trumpet. 8:8-9.

8. And the second angel sounded, and as it were a great mountain burning with fire was cast into the sea: and the third part of the sea became blood. The second angel sounds a trumpet and **as it were a great mountain burning with fire** was cast into the sea. It is not necessary that we identify this instrument of judg-ment with anything in our present realm of experience. It may be a meteoric mass blazing from the sky and falling head-long into the sea. It may be some atomic reaction. Whatever it is, the destruction caused is unbelievable. One third of the sea turns to blood, one third of the marine life is annihilated by this fiery mass, and one third of the ships is destroyed. This will not be any time to be on a pleasure cruise.

C. The Third Trumpet. 8:10-11.

10. And the third angel sounded, and there fell a great star from heaven, burning as it were a lamp, and it fell upon the third part of the rivers, and upon the fountains of waters. As the trumpet of the third angel sounds, there falls a great star from heaven. Perhaps a meteor, a great glowing body will fall to earth and destroy another third of the world's water supply, including underground sources of water. Turning sweet water bitter, this judgment will mean that now two thirds of the world's water will be deadly poison. This bitter star is given the name Wormwood (Gr *Apsinthos*). A species of plant related to our sagebrush, wormwood is always used as a symbol of bitterness. It makes a liquor which leads to mental deterioration and death. From drinking the waters poisoned by the star Wormwood, men will go out of their minds and die in judgment.

D. The Fourth Trumpet. 8:12-13.

12. And the fourth angel sounded, and the third part of the sun was smitten, and the third part of the moon, and the third part of the stars; so as the third part of them was darkened, and the day shone not for a third part of it, and the night likewise. The judgment of the fourth trumpet causes one third of the sun to be blackened, one third of the moon, and one third of all the stars. There will be a great decrease in the amount of light and in the time that reduced light is visible, for the hours of light during the day will be reduced by one third.

Notice the progression of the judgments stemming from the trumpets. First affected will be the trees and grass, then one third of marine life and shipping. Next one third of the pure water and finally one third of the heavenly bodies in respect to both quantity and time. This means that not only is the small amount of food available partially destroyed, but in addition, transportation and means of food distribution are hampered, water for increased food growth is limited, and precious light necessary for food production and harvesting is curtailed. These will be dark days indeed, in more than one sense of the word.

But if you think this is a bleak picture, you haven't seen anything yet. As recorded in verse 13, John spies an angel, more correctly translated an eagle, flying through the heaven and crying in a loud voice, **Woe, woe, woe, to the inhabiters of the earth by reason of the other voices of the trumpet of the three angels, which are yet to sound!** There seems to be little question but that the severity of judgment is becoming noticeably greater.

E. The Fifth Trumpet. 9:1-12.

9:1. With the blowing of the fifth trumpet we see the reason for the eagle's saying, **Woe, woe, woe.**... This trumpet entails the first of these three woes. Revelation 9:1 records that John saw a **star fall from heaven unto the earth: and to him was given the key of the bottomless pit.** The word (Gr *piptō*) translated "fall" should read "fallen" (Greek perfect, active participle, accusative, masculine singular). Thus, John did not see the star as it fell, but saw an already fallen star. The fact that this star is given the key to the bottomless pit must mean it is a being and not an inanimate heavenly body. The Bible frequently uses "star" as a symbol of an angel (1:20). Who is this star? He is the angel over the bottomless pit whose name in Hebrew is Abaddon and in Greek is Apollyon (9:11). Both of these names mean "de-stroyer." This angel is the king over those of the bottomless pit, a fallen star of supreme authority. This is Lucifer, the son of the morning (morning star), who was cast out of heaven to the ground for the pride in his heart (Isa 14:12-15).

2. And he opened the bottomless pit; and there arose a smoke out of the pit, as the smoke of a great furnace; and the sun and the air were darkened by reason of the smoke of the pit. When Satan opens the pit, smoke arises out of it like the smoke of a great furnace and the sun is darkened by the black, smoky air. Out of the smoke come locusts which have been given the power of scorpions. The physical appearance of these locusts is extremely gross. They are like horses prepared for battle, having crowns on their heads, with faces like men and hair like women, but teeth like a lion (vss. 7-8). They will wear breastplates of iron and the sound of their wings will be like the sound of chariots rushing into battle (vs. 9). Their tails will be like scorpions' tails with the power to sting severely and torment those they do sting five months (vs. 10).

4-6. And it was commanded them that they should not hurt the grass of the earth, neither any green thing, neither any tree; but only those men which have not the seal of God in their foreheads. . . . They should not kill them, but that they should be tormented five months . . . And in those days shall men seek death, and shall not find it. Given the title "locusts" because they perform a similar function as these marauding pests, those loosed out of the bottomless pit by their leader, Satan, are actually demons. They gravely torment those who do not have the seal of God in their foreheads. These tormented ones are driven to sorceries, witchcraft, fornication, murders, thefts, and other results of pagan idolatry and demon worship and demon possession. Here is the perfect final fulfillment of I Timothy 4:1-3, which predicts the outbreak of demonic worship in the time of the end.

12. One woe is past; and, behold, there come two woes more hereafter. One woe is past but two are yet to come, even more severe than the first.

F. The Sixth Trumpet. 9:13-21.

13-14. And the sixth angel sounded, and I heard a voice from the four horns of the golden altar which is before God, saying to the sixth angel which had the trumpet, Loose the four angels which are bound in the great river Euphrates. The Euphrates River was considered to be the eastern extremity of the Roman Empire and the dividing line between East and West. Thus, the four loosened angels lead an army arising out of the east. These four wicked angels cannot move but at the command of God. When they are loosed and given permission to move, however, the army of horsemen they lead numbers 200,000,000. This is an almost inconceivable number. At peak strength during World War II the United States had only 12,400,000 soldiers. But when we consider the hordes of the East, we can believe that an army of 200,000,000 horsemen could easily be reached today.

15. And the four angels were loosed, which were prepared for an hour, and a day, and a month, and a year, for to slay the third part of men. This horrible army destroys one third of the populace. Under the fourth seal judgment (6:8), one fourth of the earth had been slain. Now one third is slain. This means that these two judgments alone, not to mention the multitudes who have died because of famine, poisoned water, etc., have reduced the population of the earth by one half since the beginning of the Tribulation.

Whether this mighty army, with its horses having heads like lions, tails like serpents, and fire, smoke, and brimstone issuing out of their mouths, should be considered all human or all demon (equipped with modern weapons of war) is really not important. What is important is the world's reaction to the deadly judgment of the sixth trumpet.

20-21. And the rest of the men which were not killed by these plagues yet repented not of the works of their hands, that they should not worship devils, and idols of gold, and silver, and brass, and stone, and of wood: which neither can see, nor hear, nor walk: neither repented they of their murders, nor of their sorceries, nor of their fornication, nor of their thefts. In spite of the awful judgment inflicted on the world by this invading army, those who survive are still unrepentant. Such is typical of hardened human hearts. They still live in sin and debauchery, they still worship demons and idols, they still murder, practice drug abuse, fornicate, and steal. Without the redeeming power of God in a person's life there is no difference between these unfortunate inhabitants and inhabitants of our planet today. The heart is still deceitful and desperately wicked (Jer 17:9). Whether living in Old Testament times, New Testament times, the twentieth century, or the Tribulation, all men everywhere need to repent and receive the blood of Jesus Christ as an atonement for their sins. Without it, there is no hope.

With the beginning of chapter 10 comes another parenthetical section providing additional information about the events of the Tribulation Period. This parenthesis, like that of chapter 7, does not move the narrative forward but simply adds detail to the events of this time of judgment.

G. An Interlude: Angelic Announcement and Slaying of the Two Witnesses. 10:1-11:14.

10:1. And I saw another mighty angel come down from heaven, clothed with a cloud: and a rainbow was upon his head, and his face was as it were the sun, and his feet as pillars of fire. In the first verse John is permitted to see still another mighty angel. The physical appearance of this angel is significant. The angel originates in heaven, and because he is clothed with a cloud, has a rainbow upon his head and a face like the sun and feet like pillars of fire, many have thought this angel to be Christ. This is an unlikely identification, however.

2. And he had in his hand a little book open: and he set his right foot upon the sea, and his left foot on the earth. Crying with the voice of a roaring lion, the angel stands upon the sea and upon the earth showing his authority in all the earth. His authority, however, is apparently not his own. He swears **by him that liveth for ever and ever, who created heaven, and the things that therein are, and the earth, and the things that therein are, and the sea, and the things which are therein** (vs. 6). In swearing by the Creator, Jesus Christ, this angel shows that he has come in our Lord's authority but is not the Lord Himself.

In the hand of this angel is a little, previously opened scroll. It is not the seven-sealed scroll but a much smaller book. John is commanded to **seal up those things which the seven thunders uttered, and write them not** (vs. 4).

When the seventh angel shall sound his trumpet, then the mystery of God will begin to be known, and this sun-faced angel is anxious that there be no delay **(time** in verse 6 of AV) before it is sounded.

7. But in the days of the voice of the seventh angel, when he shall begin to sound, the mystery of God should be finished, as he hath declared to his servants the prophets. The sounding of the seventh trumpet marks the commencement of the end of the age, and all that was revealed by God through His Old Testament prophets and all the mysteries of the kingdom of Christ will be known.

8-9. And the voice which I heard from heaven spake unto me again, and said, Go and take the little book which is open in the hand of the angel which standeth upon the sea and upon the earth. . . . Take it, and eat it up: and it shall make thy belly bitter, but it shall be in thy mouth sweet as honey. At this point John is commanded to take the little book and eat it. The command to eat the scroll is reminiscent of the similar ex-

periences of Ezekiel (Ezk 2:9-10; 3:1-4) and Jeremiah (Jer 15:16-18). This is a symbolic way of saying that John is to devour its contents, become thoroughly familiar with it, assimilate it, digest its meaning.

The message of the book will be bittersweet (vs. 9). John is delighted with a new revelation but is disturbed with the nature of that revelation. He rejoices in the final glory that will be his Lord's, but grieves that so much more judgment must precede the final glory.

Chapter 11 continues the parenthetical information concerning the time of the seven trumpets.

11:1-2. And there was given me a reed like unto a rod: and the angel stood, saying, Rise, and measure the temple of God, and the altar, and them that worship therein. But the court which is without the temple leave out, and measure it not; for it is given unto the Gentiles: and the holy city shall they tread under foot forty and two months. The rod is a reed of the common type grown in the Jordan Valley. It is lightweight, probably ten or twelve feet long, and ideal for a measuring reed. John is told to measure the temple, the altar and even the worshipers. This temple is the one which will be rebuilt in Jerusalem; the same temple in which the Man of Sin will demand to be worshiped and overthrow Jewish worship (II Thess 2:4). The measuring is an act of claiming or staking out. It is symbolic of God's possession of the temple. The fact that even the worshipers are measured indicates that God is beginning again to deal with the nation Israel. This is Daniel's seventieth week (Dan 9:27).

However, the angel specifically instructs John not to measure the court of the temple, for it is outside the Holy Place and given to the nations who shall tread it under foot forty and two months. Here is that familiar phrase **forty and two months** which is also expressed as **time, and times, and half a time** (12:14), **a thousand two hundred and threescore days** (11:3), or three and one half years. All of these expressions indicate the last half of the seven-year Tribulation Period. Here in 11:2 we are told that the Gentiles will tread the outer court of the city underfoot for three and one half years after the covenant of peace with Israel is broken (cf. Dan 9:27).

3. And I will give power unto my two witnesses, and they shall prophesy a thousand two hundred and threescore days, clothed in sackcloth. At this time chronologically, the Lord's power or authority will be given to two witnesses. During the first half of the Tribulation, God's spokesmen are the 144,000 sealed servants of Israel. However, after these servants finish their ministry and flee to the mountains (12:6), God does not leave this earth without a messenger of the gospel. Two powerful preachers are raised up at the middle of the Tribulation Period and prophesy 1,260 days or three and one-half years. It is the ministry of these two preachers which incites the wrath of Antichrist. These witnesses are clothed in sackcloth and are said to be **the two olive trees, and the two candlesticks standing before the God of the earth** (vs. 4). The figure of olive trees is brought over from Zechariah 4:3, 14 and simply means that they are anointed ones. The figure of the two candlesticks or lampstands refers to the witnesses' character as the bearers of God's light in the dark days of judgment.

It is not possible to say dogmatically who these two witnesses are. They may be just two saints who turn to Christ in the days following the Rapture. Perhaps they are converts of the 144,000. But too, these witnesses strangely fit the descriptions and characteristics of two prior prophets of God. Elijah is a good possibility for the identification of one of them (I Kgs 17:1; Mal 4:4-6; Jas 5:17-18). Perhaps the other is Enoch (Heb 11:5; Jude 14-15) or even Moses (Ex 7:20; 9:14; Mal 4:5; Mt 17:4, 10-11).

5-6. And if any man will hurt them, fire proceedeth out of their mouth, and devoureth their enemies: and if any man will hurt them, he must in this manner be killed. These have power to shut heaven, that it rain not in the days of their prophecy: and have power over waters to turn them to blood, and to smite the earth with all plagues, as often as they will. Whoever these two great preachers are, their ministry for the Lord is outstanding. They will have power: (1) to kill their enemies with fire; (2) to withhold the rain; (3) to turn the waters to blood; and (4) to bring plagues upon the earth. The first two powers make us think of Elijah, the last two of Moses.

7. However, at last the ministry of these two great prophets will come to an abrupt and brutal end. When they have finished their ministry, **the beast that ascendeth out of the bottomless pit shall make war against them, and shall overcome them, and kill them.** Notice that absolutely nothing happens to these two witnesses until they have finished their testimony. They are invincible up to that point. Nothing can thwart the purposes of God. But, as in the case of many other great prophets of God, when their ministry is finished, God permits their enemy to overcome them.

8. And their dead bodies shall lie in the street of the great city, which spiritually is called Sodom and Egypt, where also our Lord was crucified. As if the murder of the two witnesses isn't enough for this godless beast, he also allows their dead bodies to lie in the street of that great city, Jerusalem, here spiritually characterized by Sodom and Egypt. Sodom stands for moral corruption; Egypt for the spiritual darkness of the world. You can imagine the hatred that would allow these two bodies to lie in the street until the stench is unbearable.

10. And they that dwell upon the earth shall rejoice over them, and make merry, and shall send gifts one to another; because these two prophets tormented them that dwelt on the earth. So great is the antagonism toward their preaching of repentance that the whole earth will be jubilant at the news of the death of the two witnesses. Every time a prophet of God preaches to people about their sins there is a certain amount of resentment on the sinners' part. But just imagine, the death of these two witnesses invokes rejoicing throughout the earth to such an extent that a holiday is proclaimed, and they that dwell on the earth will actually send gifts to one another in exultation over the prophets' deaths.

11. The forces of Satan will not have long to glory in their deaths, however, for in three and one-half days **the spirit of life from God entered into them, and they stood upon their feet; and great fear fell upon them which saw them.** Before the very eyes of the multitude, God will raise to life His two prophets and shall call them to come up to Him. They will ascend to heaven in a cloud as their enemies behold them. Here is another great victory for God.

12-13. And they heard a great voice from heaven saying unto them, Come up hither. And they ascended up to heaven in a cloud; and their enemies beheld them. And the same hour was there a great earthquake, and the tenth part of the city fell, and in the earthquake were slain of men seven thousand: and the remnant were affrighted, and gave glory to the God of heaven. So great is the impact of this resurrection to life that in the same hour as the two witnesses ascend into heaven, a great earthquake destroys a tenth of the city of Jerusalem. Seven thousand men are swallowed up as those who remain give glory to the God of heaven out of fear. Thus the second woe dramatically comes to a conclusion.

14. The second woe is past; and, behold, the third woe cometh quickly.

H. The Seventh Trumpet. 11:15-19.

15. And the seventh angel sounded; and there were great voices in heaven, saying, The kingdoms of this world are become the kingdoms of our Lord, and of his Christ; and he shall reign for ever and ever. At verse 15 the narrative of future events resumes with the dynamic announcement that Christ shall reign

forever and ever. This is the beginning of the end, and even though some additional events must take place before the kingdom is established, nevertheless the announcement is made, for victory is in the air. This will be the fulfillment of many Old Testament prophecies (e.g., Ps 2:2; Isa 9:6-7; Dan 2:44).

19. And the temple of God was opened in heaven, and there was seen in his temple the ark of his testament: and there were lightnings, and voices, and thunderings, and an earthquake, and great hail. In the midst of the elders' praise, John sees the temple of God as the heavens open, and in the temple is the ark of His covenant. Lightnings, voices, thunder, an earthquake, and great hail are seen as well.

This event just precedes the final outpouring of judgment and, as has been noted, the judgments are gaining in severity. Since the temple in Jerusalem has been defiled by the beast, it is not surprising to see a heavenly temple from which God rules in holiness. The presence of the ark of the covenant indicates that the judgments about to take place are based on the law, and God always keeps His covenants. As God is faithful to us who will be raptured before this period of tribulation, so too He will be faithful to those who trust in Him during this hour of trial.

VI. THE WORLD AT WAR. 12:1-17.

War is an ugly word. None of us even likes to think of it, for we have experienced too much of it. Yet war seems to be a fact of life because sin is a fact of life. Revelation chapter 12 is one of the most important chapters in the book, for it describes the outbreak of war, past, present, and future. This war first takes place on earth (vss. 1-6), then in heaven (vss. 7-12), and finally back on earth again (vss. 13-17).

A. The Woman. 12:1-2.

12:1. And there appeared a great wonder in heaven; a woman clothed with the sun, and the moon under her feet,

and upon her head a crown of twelve stars. There appears in heaven a great "wonder" (Gr *sēmeion*) or sign. You will recall that Revelation is a book that is "sign-i-fied." Such is the case here. The great wonder that appears in heaven is a woman clothed with the sun.

The imagery of this verse gives us a good clue to the woman's identity. First, the figure of a woman is frequently used as a symbol of religion. Jezebel represents paganism and idolatrous worship (2:20; I Kgs 16:31). The bride of Christ represents the true church (ch. 19). So, too, the woman here represents worship. Second, this woman is clothed with the sun. The moon is under her feet. Her crown is made up of twelve stars. There is only one place in the Bible where similar imagery is used. This is in the dream of Joseph where the sun and moon and eleven stars did obeisance to him. Both Joseph and his father, Jacob, recognized the meaning of this dream (Gen 37:9-11). It referred to the nation Israel, as does the woman here in Revelation chapter 12.

2. And she being with child cried, travailing in birth, and pained to be delivered. This woman, Israel, is pictured as being with child, crying, travailing in birth and being constantly in pain to be delivered. Here is a perfect picture of the nation Israel from the call of Abraham to the birth of Christ. She was constantly expecting the birth of the Messiah, constantly in pain. The identification of the woman with Israel fits all the facts.

B. The Red Dragon. 12:3-4.

3-4. And there appeared another wonder in heaven; and behold a great red dragon, having seven heads and ten horns, and seven crowns upon his heads. And his tail drew the third part of the stars of heaven, and did cast them to the earth: and the dragon stood before the woman which was ready to be delivered, for to devour her child as soon as it was born. Verses 3-4 tell us of another wonder or sign in heaven. This time it is a great red dragon with seven heads, ten horns, and seven crowns upon his heads. This dragon has a tail which drew a third of the stars of heaven with him, casting them to the earth. The dragon is the arch-enemy of the woman and stands ready to devour her child as soon as it is born.

It does not take much effort to identify this dragon. This monster is none other than Satan. The stars which he drew from heaven and cast to the earth are the angels which fell with him when he attempted to usurp the throne of God. This open rebellion against God brought sin forth and caused one third of the angels to be cast out of God's presence (II Pet 2:4; Jude 6).

C. The Male Child. 12:5-6.

5. Verse 5 reveals another personality. The woman is pictured as bringing forth a male child, **who was to rule all nations with a rod of iron: and her child was caught up unto God, and to his throne.** Here the identification is obvious. This male child is Jesus Christ. Israel gave birth to the Messiah after travailing from the days of Abraham. At our Lord's birth the red dragon, Satan, had King Herod all ready to devour the Christ child, but God providentially intervened (Mt 2:13-18). The only person who is said to rule all nations with a rod of iron is Jesus Christ (Ps 2:8-9; Rev 19:15). And, of course, the only person ever caught up to God, to the throne of God, was our Lord (Lk 24:51; Acts 1:9-11). Hence, the male child of the woman Israel is Jesus Christ our Lord, the Messiah of Israel.

During Christ's earthly life Satan did his best to war against Him and devour Him. But time and time again the war went badly for the red dragon. He was defeated at Bethlehem, at Calvary, and finally at the Mount of Olives.

6. And the woman fled into the wilderness, where she hath a place prepared of God, that they should feed her there a thousand two hundred and threescore days. Verse 6 resumes the dealings of God with Israel and reveals what will become of this nation during the last half of Daniel's seventieth week, the Tribulation. Since Satan has been totally unsuccessful in destroying the male child of the woman, he turns his attention to the woman herself. Satan's wrath is vented toward the nation Israel, especially during the final three years of the Tribulation. Thus, Israel is forced to flee into the wilderness where God has prepared a place of shelter and safety for her. When Christ gave His prophecy about the Great Tribulation, He warned, "Then let them which be in Judea flee into the mountains" (Mt 24:16).

Perhaps we can identify this wilderness hideaway. The prophet Isaiah mentions the city of Sela in the wilderness of Moab as a place to hide the outcasts. "Let mine outcasts dwell with thee, Moab; be thou a covert to them from the face of the spoiler; for the extortioner is at an end, the spoiler ceaseth, the oppressors are consumed out of the land"(Isa 16:4). Sela is the Hebrew form of the Greek name Petra, meaning "rock." Located some fifty miles south of the Dead Sea, the city of Petra was the capital of the ancient Edomite Empire. Since it is situated in a fertile basin at an elevation of 3,800 feet above sea level and since it is entered only by a narrow, twisting gorge, the walls of which rise a thousand feet higher, this spot seems to be the perfect hideaway for Israel. Although no identification can be made for certain, perhaps here Israel will be protected for the last three and one-half years of intense persecution.

D. The Archangel. 12:7-12.

7. And there was war in heaven: Michael and his angels fought against the dragon; and the dragon fought and his angels. With verse 7 the scene of war shifts from earth to heaven. Think of the consequences of the statement **and there was war in heaven.** The lines of battle are drawn: Michael and his angels versus the dragon and his angels. In Daniel 12:1 the archangel Michael is depicted as the special guardian of Israel, and now he

performs his task well. "Michael" signifies, "Who is like to God?" We may compare this with the cry of the worldly in 13:4, **Who is like unto the beast?** (A. Plummer, Revelation, in *The Pulpit Commentary,* p. 312).

The war in heaven, literally, "the heavens" of the atmosphere, the air (Gr *ouranos*), appears to rage on for an extended period. Perhaps this great atmospheric battle began during the first three and one-half years of the Tribulation and may have been instigated by the violation of air space under Satan's control when the Lord Jesus raptures His church (Eph 2:2; I Thess 4:17).

9. And the great dragon was cast out, that old serpent, called the Devil, and Satan, which deceiveth the whole world: he was cast out into the earth, and his angels were cast out with him. When the dust settles, not only could the dragon not prevail, but a place is no longer found for him in the atmosphere, and thus he is cast to the earth with his angels. With Satan and his demons cast to the ground, God reigns free and unencumbered in the three heavens. No more does Satan have access to God to accuse the brethren, as he did in the case of Job (Job 1).

In verse 9, five individual titles are given to Satan. In this significant moment he is given a very full description. In addition to being the great dragon, he is that old serpent, which is reminiscent of Genesis 3. He is called both the devil and Satan. The latter is the older name. It transliterates a Hebrew word (Heb *satan*) which means "adversary." When used of angels it did not initially have derogatory associations, and it was used, for example, of the "angel of the Lord" who stood in Balaam's way (Num 22:22). But the term came to be used of that spirit that accuses men before God. He accused Job (Job 1:6), and Joshua the High Priest (Zech 3:1). The title "accuser" became attached to him in an exclusive sense.

"This name for the evil one would have made a specially strong impact on the first century, for there was a well-known and well-hated figure called the delator, the paid informer. He made his living by accusing people before the authorities. Devil (Gr *diabolos*) means 'slanderer.' It is not a large step from 'accuser' to 'slanderer' and thus 'the Satan' is not infrequently referred to as 'the devil.' In addition to accusing and slandering, the evil one deceives. John brings out the scope of this activity by saying that he deceiveth the whole world'' (Leon Morris, p. 161).

Now that Satan has been cast out of heaven, he can place his full-time effort into intensifying his activity on the earth. A solemn woe is pronounced upon the inhabitants of the earth and the sea, for the devil is come down and is possessed with great wrath.

12. Therefore rejoice, ye heavens, and ye that dwell in them. Woe to the inhabiters of the earth and of the sea! for the devil is come down unto you, having great wrath, because he knoweth that he hath but a short time. The devil is aware **that he hath but a short time.** This is a reference to the fact that at the end of three and one-half years, the end of the Great Tribulation, Satan will be bound for one thousand years as Jesus Christ establishes His kingdom and reigns in righteousness on this earth. Being aware of this, we can expect the activity of Satan to dramatically increase after he is cast to the earth.

But the brethren living at that time can still have victory over the red dragon. They have it the same way we have been victorious over him. **And they overcame him by the blood of the Lamb, and by the word of their testimony; and they loved not their lives unto the death** (vs. 11). The blood of Jesus Christ not only cleanses us from sin, it defeats Satan in the process, as it will do for these Tribulation saints.

E. The Remnant. 12:13-17.

13. And when the dragon saw that he was cast unto the earth, he persecuted the woman which brought forth the man child. Beginning with verse 13, the war with Satan returns to earth. Thwarted in his last attempt on earth to destroy Jesus Christ, the male child of the woman, and defeated in the heavens, Satan now turns his attention to the woman as mentioned in verse 6. The anti-Semitism of Satan is the most intense ever, for Israel is symbolic of the worship of God, which Satan hates. As Israel rapidly flees to the wilderness, Satan causes a great flood to go forth in an attempt to destroy her. But, in the providence of God, even the earth aids the woman, and the great flood is swallowed up by the earth. The dragon is now exceedingly wroth with Israel and takes his anger out on those who do not flee to the wilderness. Jews who turn to Christ will be the special target of Satan's wrath as he unleashes an attack on God's chosen people which is unparalleled in history.

As you have realized, chapter 12 is an inset into the narrative of future events. Its lines of truth stretch both back to the days of Christ and forward to the end of the Great Tribulation. It gives us a comprehensive view of the deceptive activity of Satan. Each of us should beware, for even now Satan is bent on destroying whoever stands for God in this world. In this Church Age, we are his target. We must "be sober, be vigilant; because your adversary the devil, as a roaring lion, walketh about, seeking whom he may devour" (I Pet 5:8).

VII. THE RISE OF ANTICHRIST. 13:1-10.

The career of Satan has been a long and infamous one. But from the very moment he lifted his head in pride against God, his goal has always been the same. Lucifer wants to be God. He was not happy with being a beautiful angel. His jealousy of God turned ambition into rebellion. He said, ''I will ascend into heaven, I will exalt my throne above the stars of God: I will sit also upon the mount of the congregation, in the sides of the north: I will ascend above the heights of the clouds; I will be like the most High'' (Isa 14:13-14).

Since Satan's ambition to be God is impossible, he attempts the next best thing. Satan imitates God and by doing so deceives people into believing he is God. This is what he did through the Pharaoh's magicians. This is what he is doing today in leading so many unsuspecting people into satanic cults and the worship of demons.

But it is during the dark days of the Tribulation that Satan will be most successful in imitating God. In fact, during this period of judgment upon the earth Satan will produce a counterfeit trinity. This evil trinity will be composed of Satan, the Antichrist and the False Prophet.

Satan is the opposite of God the Father and occupies His position in the evil trinity. Revelation 12:9 reveals that Satan is a great fiery monster, brilliant, formidable, a great dragon (cf. Ezk 28:12). He is that old serpent who introduced sin into the world (Gen 3:1). He is a deceiver, slanderer, accuser of the brethren. He is the devil (Rev 12:9). He is Satan, the adversary of God and His people (Zech 3:1). And by feigning the Trinity of the Most Holy God, Satan deceives the whole world, being a liar right from the beginning and the father of the lie (Jn 8:44). Through deception, trickery and just plain lying, Satan makes himself out to be God the Father.

A. The Beast Out of the Sea. 13:1-3.

13:1. And I stood upon the sand of the sea, and saw a beast rise up out of the sea, having seven heads and ten horns, and upon his horns ten crowns, and upon his heads the name of blasphemy. In Revelation 13 the other two members of this false trinity are introduced. As Satan is the false Father, verse 1 depicts the rise of the false Son, the false Christ. This beast is a man (who very well could be alive today), for he is expressly called a man in verse 18 of this chapter and is treated as a man in other Scriptures (cf. Dan 7:8; II Thess 2:3-4; Rev 19:19-20).

He is said to arise **out of the sea,** an expression which signifies the Gentile nations.

This false Christ or Antichrist is described as a king (17:10-11). However, the Beast is more than a man, more than a king. He is also a kingdom. The seven heads and ten horns with ten crowns speak of a kingdom. The ten horns are identified as ten kings in 17:12; yet they are united in one beast. In other words, the Antichrist represents a confederation of ten kingdoms or countries. Since a similar description is given in Daniel 7:7-8, this beast's kingdom must be the revived Roman Empire. Ancient Rome was built on seven hills, represented by the seven heads. There is no better way to signify an empire than with the symbol of its king (cf. Dan 7:7, 17, 23).

2. And the beast which I saw was like unto a leopard, and his feet were as the feet of a bear, and his mouth as the mouth of a lion: and the dragon gave him his power, and his seat, and great authority. Further confirmation that the Antichrist's kingdom is the revival of the Roman Empire is seen in verse 2. The description of the false Christ as **like unto a leopard, and his feet were as the feet of a bear, and his mouth as the mouth of a lion** is very meaningful. In Daniel chapter 2, and again in the vision of Daniel chapter 7, the prophet Daniel saw four great successive world empires: the lion, referring to Babylon; the bear, referring to Medo-Persia; the leopard, referring to the Grecian Empire; and the last great empire, which took the dominant elements and characteristics of the first three and combined them in itself. The qualities of strength, brutality, and swiftness were all present in the final empire, the Roman Empire.

3. So closely identified are the ruler and his kingdom that verse 3 speaks of **one of his heads as it were wounded to death; and his deadly wound was healed: and all the world wondered after the beast.** The meaning could be twofold. In order to deceive the world into believing that he is Christ, the Antichrist may receive a deathblow. Since it is questionable whether Satan can actually raise a person from the dead, the Antichrist probably only pretends to be dead and then rises again, deceiving people into believing that he is an authentic savior. But the primary meaning here is that of the kingdom, not the king. This verse signifies that the Roman Empire, although apparently dead, will be revived in order to provide the Antichrist with a base of operations, a kingdom, a throne, and great authority.

B. The Worship of the Beast. 13:4.

4. And they worshiped the dragon which gave power unto the beast: and they worshiped the beast, saying, Who is like unto the beast? who is able to make war with him? At this eventful point in history, Satan will receive something he has always wanted. Through his man, the Antichrist, whom he makes the ruler of the world, Satan will receive worship and praise. Satan takes credit for the miraculous phenomena which take place during the Tribulation. Unable to explain them, the people of the earth believe Satan's lie, given to the world through the Antichrist, and fall down and worship them both. They cry, **Who is like unto the beast? who is able to make war with him?** The unique character of the Beast and his might make the people stare in awe. These same individuals were confronted with the unique character of Jesus Christ and His might before the Rapture and yet they did not believe. Now they believe without reservation in Satan and Antichrist.

Not everyone, however, will worship the impostor Christ. Verse 8 indicates, **And all that dwell upon the earth shall worship him, whose names are not written in the book of life of the Lamb slain from the foundation of the world.** The saved of this period will stand true to God the Father and God the Son even though it means death for many of them.

C. The Blasphemy of the Beast. 13:5-6.

5. And there was given unto him a mouth speaking great things and blasphemies; and power was given unto him to continue forty and two months. In the Trinity of God, Jesus Christ came to earth and spoke the words of God, revealing the thoughts and mind of God. So too the second person of this evil trinity will be the spokesman for Satan. Antichrist's message is not his own but rather that of Satan. Unlike the true Christ, who spoke in praise of God the Father and provided the basis for peace with God by shedding His own blood, the activities of the false Christ will be greatly blasphemous, and he will engage in war.

6. And he opened his mouth in blasphemy against God, to blaspheme his name, and his tabernacle, and them that dwell in heaven. Notice what Antichrist will blaspheme. His main target is God but he also pours out venomous blasphemy against the house of God and the children of God. We won't even be safe from slander when we get to heaven. However, these satanic blasphemies against us can't harm us, safe in the arms of Jesus.

D. The Power of the Beast. 13:7-8.

7. Satan continues to use Antichrist by giving him the power of civil authority **to make war with the saints, and to overcome them.** Those who stand true for the faith during the Great Tribulation will have no civil liberties and will be viciously attacked by the Antichrist and killed in the name of the empire. During this period born-again believers will be persecuted and murdered much as they were in the second century under the original Roman Empire.

That Antichrist is a world ruler is evident from the fact that his power will be **over all kindreds, and tongues, and nations.** Undoubtedly he will be gathering power throughout the first half of the Tribulation but will not receive world rulership until he breaks the covenant of peace with Israel (Dan 9:27). Then, acting as the tool of Satan, the Beast will wage all-out war against Israel and the saints of God throughout the entire globe and will overcome them (Dan 7:25; 9:27; 12:10; Rev 7:9-17). In the will of the Father, many believers will perish as martyrs while others are preserved alive in spite of all the blasphemy and war of the impostor Christ.

E. The Exhortation. 13:9-10.

That will be the heyday of Satan. He will receive praise and worship. He will envision himself as God. The second person of this evil trinity will speak forcefully, for Satan and the majority of the world will fall in line against God and those who represent Him on earth. The dream of world conquest by the Babylonian, Medo-Persian, Grecian, and Roman Empires will now, for the first time, be realized completely under the reign of Satan and Antichrist. A counterfeit millennium will be instituted. All of this is permitted by God in a final display of Satan's evil.

The picture is dark indeed, but if we look a little farther down the road John writes, **And I saw as it were a sea of glass mingled with fire: and them that had gotten the victory over the beast, and over his image, and over his mark, and over the number of his name, stand on the sea of glass, having the harps of God** (15:2). God will permit Satan to force his counterfeit trinity on this earth for a while, but He won't permit it forever. As always in history, God's children are promised and assured of ultimate victory.

VIII. THE RISE OF THE FALSE PROPHET. 13:11-18.

The last half of Rev 13 records John's vision of the third member of the trinity of evil. The dragon (Satan) is the antithesis of God the Father. The first beast, the Beast out of the Sea (Antichrist), is the antithesis of God the Son. Now another beast arises (False Prophet) and is the antithesis of God the Spirit. As the heavenly Trinity is made up of three persons, i.e. Father, Son, and Holy Spirit, this counterfeit, hellish trinity is made up of three persons, i.e. Satan, Antichrist, and False Prophet.

The appearance of the second beast out of the earth is far less pretentious than the first. Instead of seven heads and ten horns with ten crowns, this beast has only two horns. There are a number of ways in which this impostor poses as the counterpart of the Spirit of God.

A. The Beast Out of the Earth. 13: 11-12.

11. And I beheld another beast coming up out of the earth; and he had two horns like a lamb, and he spake as a dragon. First, note that this beast appears on the scene **like a lamb.** He is not a lamb, but appears like a lamb. If he were a lamb, we would think him an impostor of Jesus Christ. But since he appears like a lamb, he imitates the Spirit of Christ. As the Holy Spirit produces Christlikeness in us, this False Prophet will produce Antichristlikeness in the lives of those who worship the Beast.

12. And he exerciseth all the power of the first beast before him, and causeth the earth and them which dwell therein to worship the first beast, whose deadly wound was healed. Second, note that **he exerciseth all the power of the first beast before him.** You will recall our Lord's command, "And, behold, I send the promise of my Father upon you: but tarry ye in the city of Jerusalem, until ye be endued with power from on high" (Lk 24:49). That promised power came in the person of the Holy Spirit. "But ye shall receive power, after that the Holy Ghost is come upon you" (Acts 1:8). Whenever the Spirit of God is mentioned in Scripture, He is always associated with power. During the Great Tribulation the False Prophet imitates the Holy Spirit by exerting the power of Antichrist.

Third, verse 12 continues, **and causeth the earth and them which dwell therein to worship the first beast, whose deadly wound was healed.** The aim of the second beast is to promote the worship of

Antichrist. At no time in his career does he promotes himself. This is true with the Holy Spirit. He causes men and women to worship Jesus Christ. He does not attract attention to Himself, but always points to Christ. Those who place an overemphasis on the baptism and work of the Spirit of God defeat His own purpose. Jesus Christ came to give life; the Holy Spirit is come to teach, comfort, and point men to Christ. Likewise, the False Prophet does not seek attention but seeks to divert attention to the Antichrist.

B. The Wonders of the Beast. 13:13-14.

13. And he doeth great wonders, so that he maketh fire come down from heaven on the earth in the sight of men. Fourth, we learn from verse 13 that the second beast is associated with great wonders and fire. Again and again the Holy Spirit is associated with fire. When the Spirit came upon the church at Pentecost, "there appeared unto them cloven tongues like as of fire, and it sat upon each of them" (Acts 2:2-3).

Here, perhaps, the False Prophet is imitating more than the Holy Spirit at Pentecost. The two witnesses were divinely commissioned and empowered by God and had the ability to perform miracles including the issue of fire out of their mouths devouring their enemies. Not to be outdone by his religious adversaries, the False Prophet also performs wonders or signs including the calling forth of fire. All of this is a part of the strong delusion mentioned in II Thessalonians 2:11.

C. The Worship of the Beast. 13:15-17.

15. And he had power to give life unto the image of the beast, that the image of the beast should both speak, and cause that as many as would not worship the image of the beast should be killed. The final way in which the False Prophet imitates the Holy Spirit is found in verse 15. As Satan's religious leader during the Tribulation, the False Prophet will issue an ecclesiastical edict commanding that

an image of the Beast be made. This will become the focal point of their false system of worship.

The expression **he had power to give life unto the image of the beast** is properly translated "it was given to him to give spirit to the image of the beast." The Greek word here is *pneuma,* which means "spirit" or "breath" and is quite different from the word meaning "life" (Gr *zoē*). The magical power that Antichrist gives the False Prophet is not to give life to an inanimate object but to give the "appearance" of life. The satanic image of the Beast will be given the appearance of breathing and moving, either mechanically like a robot or by being indwelt with one of Satan's demons. Whatever the case, the masses will believe it is alive and will worship it.

16. And he causeth all, both small and great, rich and poor, free and bond, to receive a mark in their right hand, or in their foreheads. The last three verses of this chapter inform us of the universal religious influence of this counterfeit Holy Spirit. The mark is placed in the most conspicuous places of the body, i.e. the forehead or right hand. Again you can see the imitation. As the Holy Spirit is the sealer of the redeemed (Eph 1:13; 4:30), and as 144,000 are sealed out of Israel unto God, now we see the false spirit placing a mark or seal on his followers.

The word "mark" (Gr *charagma*) means an impress made by a stamp, like a brand used on slaves and animals or a stamp placed on an official document. The reason for the mark on the forehead or right hand is clearly indicated in verse 17: **And that no man might buy or sell, save he that had the mark, or the name of the beast, or the number of his name.** Some time ago my daughter was invited to a birthday party held at a kiddieland amusement park. When each child arrived she was stamped on the back of the right hand with a rubber stamp. With that stamp the children could ride any ride all day long; without it they could not ride at all. How similar this must be to those terrible days of the Great Tribulation when without the mark of the Beast no one will be able to buy, sell, or trade. Life will come to a grinding halt without that mark. The False Prophet will ration commodities only to those who have the mark of the Beast.

D. The Number of the Beast. 13:18.

18. Here is wisdom. Let him that hath understanding count the number of the beast: for it is the number of a man; and his number is Six hundred threescore and six. Verse 18 seems to indicate what the mark of the beast is. "Probably the simplest explanation here is the best, that the triple six is the number of a man, each digit falling short of the perfect number seven. Six in the Scripture is man's number. He was to work six days and rest the seventh. The image of Nebuchadnezzar was sixty cubits high and six cubits broad. Whatever may be the deeper meaning of the number, it implies that this title referring to the first beast, Satan's masterpiece, limits him to man's level which is far short of the deity of Jesus Christ" (John F. Walvoord, *The Revelation of Jesus Christ,* p. 210).

Opposed to this is seven, the number of God. His creative activity was completed and He rested on the seventh day. Seven is the number of both completion and perfection. The entire book of Revelation is built around the number seven. We note seven spirits (1:4); seven stars (1:16); seven churches (1:20); seven lamps (4:5); seven seals (5:1); seven horns (5:6); seven eyes (5:6); seven angels (8:2); seven thunders (10:3); seven heads (12:3); seven crowns (12:3); seven plagues (15:1); seven vials (17:1); seven mountains (17:9); and seven kings (17:10). This is God's perfect way of completing His revelation to man.

With this in mind, it is easy to understand that the number assigned to the unholy trinity is 666, less than perfect, but a multiple of man at his best, the highest Satan can attain. Hence, this is an appropriate mark for the trinity of evil: Satan, Antichrist, and the False Prophet. In those dark days of deception, Satan is the unseen ruler, the Antichrist the world political ruler, and the False Prophet the world religious ruler. Together they will lie, murder, ration, and force their way into rulership of the entire world.

IX. THE VICTORY OF THE LAMB. 14:1-20.

A. The Lamb and the 144,000 on Mount Zion. 14:1-5.

14:1-3. And I looked, and, lo, a Lamb stood on the mount Zion, and with him a hundred forty and four thousand. . . . And I heard a voice from heaven, as the voice of many waters, and as the voice of a great thunder. . . . And they sung as it were a new song before the throne, and before the four beasts, and the elders. In the midst of this dismal revelation about the last days of the Tribulation, John is given another parenthetic vision recorded in chapter 14. As if to encourage him as he writes, God allows John to see the Lamb, Christ Jesus, standing on Mount Zion with the 144,000. They are singing a new song before the throne, perhaps one they have been taught by the twenty-four elders. You can almost imagine them singing: "Redeemed how I love to proclaim it! Redeemed by the blood of the Lamb. Redeemed through His infinite mercy, His child, and forever, I am."

B. The Angel with the Everlasting Gospel. 14:6-7.

6. And I saw another angel fly in the midst of heaven, having the everlasting gospel to preach unto them that dwell on the earth, and to every nation, and kindred, and tongue, and people. The gospel to be preached is not the good news of salvation but rather the good news that God is at last going to deal with the world in absolute righteousness and rule the world in His divine sovereignty.

C. The Prophesied Destruction of Babylon. 14:8.

8. And there followed another angel,

saying, **Babylon is fallen, is fallen, that great city, because she made all nations drink of the wine of the wrath of her fornication.** A second angel appears to announce the fall of the great city Babylon (probably a reference to Rome). The consequences of participating in the spiritual degradation of this religious system are clearly outlined by this angel. Any nation that shares in the spiritual corruption induced by Babylon will also share in her condemnation and destruction.

D. The Prophesied Doom of the Beast. 14:9-11.

9-11. And the third angel followed them, saying with a loud voice, If any man worship the beast and his image, and receive his mark in his forehead, or in his hand, the same shall drink of the wine of the wrath of God, which is poured out without mixture into the cup of his indignation. John sees a third angel which predicts the doom of those who bow down and worship the beast. The intensity of this destruction is without mixture of mercy. The agents of destruction are fire and brimstone. Its duration is continuous, for the angels which bring destruction on the worshipers of the beast **have no rest day nor night.**

E. The Blessed Saints. 14:12-13.

13. Suddenly a voice from heaven instructs John to **write, Blessed are the dead which die in the Lord from henceforth: Yea, saith the Spirit, that they may rest from their labors; and their works do follow them.** Those who die as martyrs at the hands of the Beast are called blessed. The **henceforth** indicates that this blessing particularly refers to those who will yet suffer and die under the Beast. Their works will follow them into the presence of the Lord.

Finally, in this parenthetic chapter just before the most severe judgments of the seven bowls, John's heart is encouraged by getting just a glimpse of the battle of Armageddon, where the great winepress of God's wrath will pour forth tremendous judgment. God knows just when we need encouragement. Having received the vision of the seven trumpets and about to embark on the vision of the seven vials, the Apostle John is given encouragement by God by showing him a glimpse of the end and the ultimate victory of God.

This same function the book of Revelation performs for us. Bogged down in the trials and troubles of life, we experience a great uplift and encouragement in reading the Revelation, for it shows us that the victory is ultimately God's. Perhaps this is the blessing promised to everyone who reads or hears the words of this prophecy (1:3).

F. The Vision of the Harvest on Earth. 14:14-20.

14-20. And I looked, and behold a white cloud, and upon the cloud one sat like unto the Son of man, having on his head a golden crown, and in his hand a sharp sickle . . . and gathered the vine of the earth, and cast it into the great winepress of the wrath of God. And the winepress was trodden without the city, and blood came out of the winepress, even unto the horse bridles, by the space of a thousand and six hundred furlongs. Here the Lord is pictured with a golden crown, the victor's crown (Gr *stephanos*), and a sharp sickle or judgment. The great harvest of God is about to begin. Two figures are used here, the harvest (vss. 14-16) and the vine (vss. 17-19). "The ripe harvest is literally a dried or withered harvest (cf. Mt 21:19-20; Mk 3:1, 3; Jn 15:6; Rev 16:12). In other words, the inhabitants of the earth are withered, lifeless and fully ready for judgment. The grapes of the vine are also said to be ripe. This is the vine of the earth and stands in contrast to Christ, the true vine (Ps 80:8; Jn 15:1). The picture here is that all the false religion of man is fully ripe and ready for harvest. Thus the harvest is ready because man in his own efforts, apart from the life of God, has fully developed an apostate religious system'' (Charles Caldwell Ryrie, *Revelation,* p. 92).

The judgment of God on this vile system of worship is not hell but something that happens on earth. It is apparently a reference to the battle of Armageddon (cf. 19:17-19). When the great winepress of God's wrath is trodden outside the city of Jerusalem, the result will be that **blood came out of the winepress, even unto the horse bridles, by the space of a thousand and six hundred furlongs.** So fierce is God's judgment that the blood of those who battle against him will run as deep as the horse's bridle for sixteen hundred furlongs.

''A river of human blood one hundred sixty miles in length, and up to the bridles of the horses in depth, tells an awful story. When the Romans destroyed Jerusalem so great was the bloodshed that Josephus says the whole city ran down with the blood to such a degree that the fires of many of the houses were quenched by it. When Sylla took Athens, Plutarch says the blood that was shed in the market-place alone covered all the ceramicus as far as Dipylus, and some testify that it ran through the gates and overflowed the suburbs. Nor are we to think of any exaggeration or hyperbole in the very definite description of what John here saw as the consequence of the treading of this winepress'' (J. A. Seiss, *The Apocalypse,* Vol. III, pp. 55-56).

Those who trust in God and live righteously must take heart. God will not always stay necessary judgment. John is permitted to see a glimpse of the end of the story so that he may accurately record the terrible judgments of God upon an apostate world. We too must live righteously in the face of unrighteousness, for the ultimate victory of God and vindication of the righteous is the substance of the last chapter of history.

X. THE SEVEN BOWLS OF GOD'S WRATH. 15:1-16:21.

As you read chapters 15-16 of Revelation, you get the definite impression that a climax is coming. There is an air of expectancy, an air of finality. Each of the judgments through the seven seals and seven trumpets is increasingly more severe. But now God's judgment upon this wicked earth is rising to a crescendo. John is permitted yet another vision, this one great and marvelous. He views seven angels bearing the seven last plagues. Judgment is about to be poured out as history has never seen it before.

Notice three important features in Revelation 15-16: God's righteousness; God's wrath, and man's response. That God is righteous and holy in His dealings with mankind is firmly established in Scripture (cf. Gen 18:25; Deut 32:4; Ps 7:9-12; Rom 2:5). Here again we have affirmation of His righteousness.

A. Preliminaries in Heaven. 15:1-8.

15:2. And I saw as it were a sea of glass mingled with fire: and them that had gotten the victory over the beast, and over his image, and over his mark, and over the number of his name, stand on the sea of glass, having the harps of God. These are the martyred dead who did not yield to the beast's demand for blasphemy and thus are pictured as the triumphant.

3-4. And they sing the song of Moses the servant of God, and the song of the Lamb, saying,
Great and marvellous are thy works,
Lord God Almighty;
just and true are thy ways,
thou King of saints.

Someone may ask, ''If God is so righteous, why does He suddenly appear so vengeful? Why does He allow such tremendous wrath to pour out on the earth?'' The answer is simple. Today we view God as He deals in mercy and grace. This is the dispensation of grace. However, God has promised judgment as payment for sin, and He wouldn't be just unless He fulfilled that promise. When the age of grace is passed, the age of judgment is ushered in. In Revelation chapters 4-19 we view God at work in the day of righteous judgment.

5. And after that I looked, and, behold, the temple of the tabernacle of the testimony in heaven was opened. Verses 5-8 of this chapter give clear indication that God is just in delivering judgment on the earth. The picture of the heavenly temple containing the ark of the covenant makes it evident that God is not dealing in grace but according to divine law. Those who have broken God's law are now judged by it.

His agents of judgment are seven angels, clothed in pure and white linen with golden belts. They originate in the heavenly temple, and as they leave to bring judgment, each one receives a golden vial or bowl filled to the brim with the wrath of God (vss. 6-7).

8. And the temple was filled with smoke from the glory of God, and from his power; and no man was able to enter into the temple, till the seven plagues of the seven angels were fulfilled. Throughout the entire span of the seven bowl judgments, the heavenly throne room is filled with smoke from the glory and power of God. All of this suggests the sovereignty of God and His righteousness and justice in bringing judgment to sinful men.

With the beginning of chapter 16, the second important feature of these chapters is noticed. This is God's wrath.

B. The First Bowl. 16:1-2.

16:1. And I heard a great voice out of the temple saying to the seven angels, Go your ways, and pour out the vials of the wrath of God upon the earth. Apparently these seven judgments occur in rapid succession. Immediately the first angel leaves the heavens and proceeds to dump the wrath of God out of his bowl.

2. And the first went, and poured out his vial upon the earth; and there fell a noisome and grievous sore upon the men which had the mark of the beast, and upon them which worshiped his image. When the first bowl is emptied, a foul and painful sore comes to those who

have received the mark of the Beast. This judgment is an evil or malignant sore (Gr *helkos*) rotten and incurable, similar to the boils inflicted on the Egyptians in Exodus 9:9-11. The extent of this affliction is limited to those who have received the mark of the Beast or have bowed to his image. Those few who remain true to God are exempt (cf. Ex 9:8-12).

C. The Second Bowl. 16:3.

3. And the second angel poured out his vial upon the sea; and it became as the blood of a dead man: and every living soul died in the sea. The analogy here is to the first of the ten plagues of Egypt (Ex 7:20-25), in which the Nile River turned to blood, killing all the fish and making the water unfit to drink. The sea's becoming as the blood of a dead man is a vivid picture of a man wallowing in his own blood. One-third of the sea animals died under the second trumpet (8:9). Now the destruction is total and marine bodies as well as men will be wallowing in the blood of the sea.

D. The Third Bowl. 16:4-7.

4. And the third angel poured out his vial upon the rivers and fountains of waters; and they became blood. The third bowl of God's wrath is poured out upon the rivers and fountains of waters, and they too become blood. Rivers of blood pour from the ground, adding to the problem of obtaining fresh drinking water.

Here the angel adds a brief footnote indicating God is righteous in causing the water and sources of water to become blood. This is the unchanging law of divine retribution. Throughout the Tribulation Period the forces of Satan have been spilling the blood of the saints as if it were water. Now, because of these acts of infamy, they are getting their fill of blood. The angel says, **Thou art righteous, O Lord, which art, and wast, and shalt be, because thou hast judged thus. For they have shed the blood of saints and prophets, and thou hast given them** blood to drink; for they are worthy (vss. 5-6).

Again bear in mind that God is not now dealing in grace but in judgment. These bloodthirsty inhabitants of the earth are getting just what they deserve, for they have consistently spilled the blood of the saints. As the Tribulation draws to a close, God deals in harsh justice.

E. The Fourth Bowl. 16:8-9.

8-9. And the fourth angel poured out his vial upon the sun; and power was given unto him to scorch men with fire. And men were scorched with great heat, and blasphemed the name of God, which hath power over these plagues: and they repented not to give him glory. When the temperature climbs into the 90's today, we glibly exclaim, "It's a real scorcher" and turn on the air conditioner. However, we know nothing of the scorching heat that will one day torture the ungodly inhabitants of this earth. With the shortages of energy due to rationing and the great judgments of God, there will be no air conditioners or any other forms of relief from the scorching heat of the sun which has been intensified by God.

F. The Fifth Bowl. 16:10-11.

10. And the fifth angel poured out his vial upon the seat of the beast; and his kingdom was full of darkness; and they gnawed their tongues for pain. The fifth plague of judgment attacks the very throne of the Beast. As in the fifth trumpet judgment, and the ninth plague of Egypt (Ex 10:21-23), there is darkness over the earth. It will be pitch black, so dark you can feel it. But this is only part of this bowl's judgment.

11. And blasphemed the God of heaven because of their pains and their sores, and repented not of their deeds. The sores inflicted upon the worshipers of the Beast are still very painful, and the Beast will not be able to work his magic in curing them. Terrible pain results in this intense darkness. So unbearable is the pain that men will gnaw their tongues

in severe agony. Apparently the darkness aggravates the pain and the results of judgment are compounded.

G. The Sixth Bowl. 16:12-16.

12. And the sixth angel poured out his vial upon the great river Euphrates; and the water thereof was dried up, that the way of the kings of the east might be prepared. The Great Tribulation is fast coming to a climactic end. With the emptying of the sixth bowl the great Euphrates River is dried up. Flowing some eighteen hundred miles from the mountains to the Persain Gulf, this river is too deep to ford and too long to go around. Thus, with the sixth bowl of God's wrath emptied, the Euphrates ceases to be a barrier and opens the way for the kings of the East to march into the battle of Armageddon. Verses 13-16 actually give parenthetic information about this great battle. That is how closely tied the sixth and seventh bowls of wrath are to the triumph of God's judgment at Armageddon.

H. The Seventh Bowl. 16:17-21.

17. And the seventh angel poured out his vial into the air; and there came a great voice out of the temple of heaven, from the throne, saying, It is done. With the emptying of the seventh bowl comes the cry from the heavenly throne, **It is done.** Judgment is soon to be completed. With this cry are the accompanying signs of voices, thunders, lightnings, a great earthquake, the likes of which man has never seen before. Jerusalem is upended and divided into three parts, Babylon is destroyed, islands of the sea disappear, mountains vanish, and hail of the weight of a talent falls out of heaven. Today we talk about hail the size of a golf ball. But when God's righteous judgment is poured out, the hail will weigh nearly one hundred and twenty-five pounds. The destruction will be indescribable.

We have seen God's righteousness in judgment and in His wrath. But what is man's response? Does he fall on his knees and repent for worshiping the

Beast? Not at all. In the final illustration of the hardness of man's heart, no one repents or gives glory to God. Instead they **blasphemed the name of God** (vs. 9), and **blasphemed the God of heaven, and repented not of their deeds** (vs. 11).

21. And men blasphemed God because of the plague of the hail. Even in judgment, when the righteousness of God is fully revealed through His wrath on sin, men and women will continue to harden their hearts, blaspheme His holy name, and choose to worship sin and the Beast.

XI. THE DESTRUCTION OF ECCLESIASTICAL BABYLON. 17:1-18.

By now one is aware that the revelation received by John deals with different events which do not always proceed in chronological order. Occasionally John is drawn aside to receive additional information about something previously introduced but now more fully explained. On these occasions a chapter or two is inset into the narrative. Such is the case with chapters 17-18.

In Revelation 14:8 the destruction of Babylon is foretold. Now John is given greater detail about its fall. Chapters 17-18 deal with the destruction of Babylon, which represents religion and government in the end of the age. Revelation 17 records the destruction of ecclesiastical Babylon, and Revelation 18 records the destruction of political Babylon.

These two events, however, do not take place at the same time. The destruction of Babylon, as representing the false religion of the future world church (ch. 17), best fits into the period of the first three and one-half years of Tribulation. When Christ raptures His church and we go to live forever with Him, it doesn't mean the end of religion. Many churches and religious orders will function with "business as usual," for the Lord Jesus Christ is not even a part of them today. When as born-again believers we are taken to heaven, these religions will continue to thrive and Satan will even permit them to grow. The devil will use false religion for his own evil purposes until he no longer needs it. With the rise of the Antichrist, in the middle of the Tribulation, religious activity of all forms, except that instituted by this beast, will cease, and the great ecclesiastical Babylon will be overthrown. This event is described in Revelation 17.

A. The Description of the Great Harlot and the Beast. 17:1-8.

17:1. And there came one of the seven angels which had the seven vials, and talked with me, saying unto me, Come hither; I will show unto thee the judgment of the great whore that sitteth upon many waters. We are immediately faced with the problem of identifying this great whore or harlot who is about to be judged. Verse 5 indicates that **upon her forehead was a name written, MYSTERY, BABYLON THE GREAT, THE MOTHER OF HARLOTS AND ABOMINATIONS OF THE EARTH.** Hence, Scripture tells us that this harlot is Babylon the Great.

"Names are written on foreheads quite often in this book. Thus God's servants were sealed in this way (7:3; 9:4), and the servants of the Lamb were marked similarly (14:1; 22:4). On the other side, the same is true of the adherents of the Beast (13:16; 14:9; 20:4). So now the character of the harlot is shown by her name, which is displayed on her forehead for all to see. Charles draws attention to passages in Roman authors informing us that Roman harlots wore on their brows labels inscribed with their names. The whore is thus in character" (Leon Morris, p. 206).

The matter of identifying this great city is a subject of much debate. There are many good Bible scholars who believe that this refers to the once great capital of the Babylonian Empire, now lying in ruins. They maintain that the city will one day be rebuilt and become both the religious and commercial center of the world (cf. Jer 50-51). However, this may not be the case. Babylon is frequently used in Scripture to refer to a system of idolatrous religion. It is important to bear in mind that in Revelation, Babylon refers to both a city and a religious system, just as Wall Street refers to both a street and a system of free economy. It is highly likely that this Babylon represents another city and religious system which displays the characteristics of the once evil Babylon.

8. The beast . . . shall ascend out of the bottomless pit, and go into perdition. This beast is the same one referred to in 11:7 as coming out of the abyss. It is said to carry the harlot, and is described as having seven heads and ten horns.

B. The Seven Heads of the Beast. 17:9-11.

9. The seven heads are seven mountains, on which the woman sitteth. The Scripture here interprets itself. The seven heads of this beast are seven mountains. "No reasonable doubt can be entertained as to the meaning of these words. The Seven Hills of Rome were a commonplace with the Latin poets" (H. B. Swete, *The Apocalypse of St. John,* p. 220). These hills were named Palatine, Aventine, Caelian, Esquiline, Viminal, Quirinal, and Capitoline. Later the city spread to the hill Janiculum as well.

10. The identification of the seven heads of the Beast, however, is symbolic of seven kings. These apparently have something to do with Rome. **Five are fallen, and one is, and the other is not yet come.** This must indicate a selective list of kings prior to John's day (more than seven had ruled); one is John's contemporary, and one is yet to come. The Beast himself is identified as the eighth king, whose doom is certain. To identify these kings would mean to hazard an unwise guess.

C. The Ten Horns of the Beast. 17: 12-14.

12. The horns of the Beast are ten kings (Dan 7:23-24). These form the nucleus of the Beast's power. Their power is subject to the Beast's. **One**

hour. This expression is to be understood as meaning unity of purpose not brevity of time. These ten kings are unified under the power of the Beast.

13. Such unity of purpose will cause the ten kings to **give their power and strength unto the beast.** All the resources and armies of these ten nations and their kings are at the disposal of the Beast.

14. These shall make war with the Lamb, but, of course, they are unsuccessful. The Beast attempted to proclaim himself king and exert lordship over the nations of the world, but nothing can alter the fact that Jesus Christ is **Lord of lords, and King of kings.** The faithful and chosen on the Lord's side anticipate a complete victory, and they shall have it.

D. The Destruction of the Harlot. 17: 15-18.

15. And he saith unto me, The waters which thou sawest, where the whore sitteth, are peoples, and multitudes, and nations, and tongues. The religious system of ecclesiastical Babylon is described as a harlot sitting on many waters. She is portrayed as committing spiritual fornication with the inhabitants of the earth. We have already noted that in the book of Revelation the figure of a woman symbolizes religion. Jezebel represents the pagan idolatry of the past (2:20), the sunclothed woman represents Israel (12:1), the bride of Christ represents the true church (21:9), and here we have the great harlot representing the false church. The woman is arrayed in purple and scarlet, bedecked with gold and precious stones and pearls (17:4). That the woman is sitting upon seven mountains, which usually refers to the city of Rome, makes it difficult to escape the conclusion that this woman refers to the Roman Catholic Church.

Even though the Roman Church may be the basis for ecclesiastical Babylon, however, there are certainly Protestant churches, Moslem temples, Jewish synagogues and other forms of religions involved here. This false system of worship described as the great harlot will include many groups as well as the mother church. This is the ecumenical movement at its height. Here we see one world church, based in Rome (religious Babylon) and practicing a system of worship which began back in ancient Babylon. The one-world church movement is part of the program of Antichrist. Ecclesiastical Babylon symbolizes apostate religion, religion without the power or presence of the Holy Spirit.

This composite, apostate church will make political alliances with the nations in order to gain power. The fact that she rules over **peoples, and multitudes, and nations, and tongues** is proof positive that this will indeed be a politically minded ecumenical church. But what will be the future of this ecclesiastical Babylon? What is to become of the one-world church movement and this idolatrous church?

16. And the ten horns which thou sawest upon the beast, these shall hate the whore, and shall make her desolate and naked, and shall eat her flesh, and burn her with fire. By comparing other Scriptures, we may place this annihilation of the one-world church midway through the seven years of the Tribulation. During the first half of this period religious freedom is extended to all. All the religions of the world, apart from those who remain true to Christ, will gather in one great world church. The climax of this gathering is seen in the pomp and ceremony of the harlot riding on the Beast.

With the revival of the Roman Empire, however, the Beast no longer needs the church to sustain his power. Thus he destroys the world church and substitutes the worship of himself. The false system of religion called Babylon, the harlot, will vanish, and the Beast will be unchallenged as world leader and his False Prophet as world religious leader. Using the power he has over the ten horns, the league of ten nations, Antichrist will utterly destroy all forms of religion, even the apostate Christianity

known as eccliastical Babylon centered in the church of Rome.

17. For God hath put in their hearts to fulfill his will, and to agree, and give their kingdom unto the beast, until the words of God shall be fulfilled. All of this is in the will and plan of God. God has never been pleased with systems of worship which do not give Him His rightful place, and counterfeit or divert the honor that is due only to God. Thus the ecumenical movement and those Roman Catholic, Protestant, Jewish, Moslem, and other groups so intimately involved in it are doomed to be destroyed by the Antichrist after he has used them to gain world rulership.

XII. THE DESTRUCTION OF POLITICAL BABYLON. 18:1-24.

The preceding chapter recorded the fall of the great harlot, Babylon the Great. It is likely that this event takes place in the middle of the Tribulation, for the fall of the harlot is the destruction of the false system of religion which Satan has supported through the centuries. It is the destruction of the ecumenical church, the one-world church, after Antichrist no longer needs it.

In chapter 18 we have more information about the fall of political or governmental Babylon. The difference in emphasis between the two chapters is this: In chapter 17 it was the Beast and his ten-nation confederacy who destroyed religious Babylon. In chapter 18 political Babylon is destroyed by God Himself in preparation for the coming of the KING OF KINGS AND LORD OF LORDS.

A. Announcement of the Fall. 18:1-3.

18:1-3. And after these things I saw another angel come down from heaven. . . . And he cried mightily with a strong voice, saying, Babylon the great is fallen. . . . The kings of the earth have committed fornication with her, and the merchants of the earth are waxed rich through the abundance of her delicacies.

The great harlot is fallen. Babylon as a system of religion is demonic. She is unfaithful to God and has spiritually fornicated with the nations of the world, soiling the message of true religion. Babylon is intoxicating and drags down with her the nations which align themselves with this false church. They have an easy form of religion with the harlot; a few dollars can make the church look the other way. It is no wonder they weep over her destruction.

It is evident that with the corruption of this end-time system of religion many people will become wealthy. There is much business transacted in the church of the great harlot. She has accumulated great wealth and is a powerful force in business.

B. A Call to Separation. 18:4-5.

4. And I heard another voice from heaven, saying, Come out of her, my people, that ye be not partakers of her sins, and that ye receive not of her plagues. John is permitted to hear still another voice from heaven. The message given by this voice is reminiscent of God's call to Lot begging him to leave worldly Sodom before total judgment (Gen 19:15-22). Here men and women of the Tribulation Period are urged by God to come out of ecclesiastical Babylon just as the children of Israel were urged to come out of ancient Babylon (Jer 51:45). And why? Because by separating themselves from this apostate form of Christianity they will not partake of her sin and will not have the plagues inflicted on them that are certain to afflict ecclesiastical Babylon (18:6-8).

C. Indictment Against Babylon. 18:6-8.

6-7. Reward her even as she rewarded you. . . . How much she hath glorified herself, and lived deliciously. The indictment against Babylon calls for retributive judgment that is doubled, because the enormity of her sin can require nothing but double severity in judgment. Whereas Babylon had lived "deliciously" (the same root word as is translated "delicacies" in verse 3), now the judgment of God falls on her and delicate living gives way to disastrous plagues. Whereas she anticipated seeing no sorrow, now she sees nothing but sorrow.

8. Therefore shall her plagues come in one day. "There is no reason not to understand her final destruction as coming in one day (vs. 8). It happened before with another Babylon (Dan 5:1, 3-5, 30), and it often occurs with individuals (Lk 12:19-20)" (Ryrie, p. 107). Isn't it ironic that the city which once burned Christians for having allegedly burned it, will itself be burned with literal fire?

D. Consequences of Babylon's Fall. 18:9-19.

9. And the kings of the earth, who have committed fornication and lived deliciously with her, shall bewail her, and lament for her, when they shall see the smoke of her burning. Political and economic Babylon now comes into view. With the destruction of the false church comes the collapse of the financial association between the ecumenical church and the nations. Now the economic and political city, symbolized by Babylon, is destroyed. The kings of the earth lament because of the collapse of the false church. Without her there is no means of supporting their governments, for they are built on an alliance with the false religious system. Hence the confederation of nations and their governments also collapse.

Since Rome is the seat of the apostate church, and is described by the **seven mountains** of Revelation 17:9, it is likely that both the religious and the political city fall. The city which thrived on false religion and financially benefited from it will now economically collapse. The burning of the city is a symbol of the fall of its political and economic might, and the kings of the earth marvel at the destruction of the powerful capital of Antichrist's world empire.

It is almost unbelievable the effect that the collapse of religious and political Babylon will have on the people of the earth. Not only do the kings or heads of state bemoan her fate, but commercial officials do as well. Their source of gain is suddenly gone.

11. And the merchants of the earth shall weep and mourn over her; for no man buyeth their merchandise any more. Babylon will be the center of world trade. The ten-membered alliance of nations which forms the common market will be almost totally dependent upon political and economic Babylon. And suddenly she is gone.

12-13. The merchandise of gold, and silver, and precious stones, . . . flour, and wheat, and beasts, and sheep, and horses, and chariots, and slaves, and souls of men. The goods symbolic Babylon deals in are phenomenal. Everything from gold to the very bodies and souls of men and women is bought, sold, and traded by the commercial activities of this great world center of the Antichrist.

15-16. For many months the world's merchants will have depended on economic Babylon, and now what is left for them? Verses 15-16 give the answer. **The merchants of these things, which were made rich by her, shall stand afar off for the fear of her torment, weeping and wailing, and saying, Alas, alas, that great city, that was clothed in fine linen, and purple, and scarlet, and decked with gold, and precious stones, and pearls!** Commerce comes to an abrupt halt because the world center of trade is destroyed by God Himself.

17-19. For in one hour so great riches is come to nought. And every shipmaster, and all the company in ships, and sailors, and as many as trade by sea, stood afar off, and cried when they saw the smoke of her burning, saying, . . . Alas, alas, that great city, wherein were made rich all that had ships in the sea by reason of her costliness! for in one hour is she made desolate. The great shipping lanes of the oceans will be emptied. All commerce will cease. An economic collapse such as the world could never conceive will grip the throat of the world.

The picture is clear. Antichrist will bring to an end the false system of religion centered in Rome (ecclesiastical Babylon), and then God will bring to an end the world commercial system centered in Rome (political Babylon). Both church and state will collapse. No more will man be able to appease himself with an easy, do-nothing religion. No more will he put his trust in world commerce and finance. The end of the Tribulation is near and man has only the lies of the Antichrist to cling to.

E. The Destruction of Babylon. 18: 20-24.

Suddenly and dramatically the whole tone of Revelation changes. Instead of weeping and wailing, instead of the fierceness of God's judgment on this wicked earth, there is a vibrant tone of rejoicing over the total destruction of Babylon in both her ecclesiastical and political forms.

21-24. And a mighty angel took up a stone like a great millstone, and cast it into the sea, saying, Thus with violence shall that great city Babylon be thrown down, and shall be found no more at all. And the voice of harpers, and musicians, and of pipers, and trumpeters, shall be heard no more at all in thee. . . . And the light of a candle shall shine no more at all in thee. . . . And in her was found the blood of prophets, and of saints, and of all that were slain upon the earth. A mighty angel casts a great millstone into the sea, representing the final fall of Babylon. A dead silence arises from the now-destroyed city. No more merriment, no more wedding celebrations, for the great harlot Babylon is at last destroyed forever. "Joyless, dark, and silent, Babylon stands out as a monument to the utmost vengeance of God. Wickedness had sat enthroned in the midst of that professedly bearing the Name of Christ; but at last, when she had filled to the full her cup of iniquity, God rises in His fierce anger, His indignation burns, and Babylon falls to rise no more. Her destruction is irremediable'' (Scott, p. 373).

XIII. THE SECOND COMING OF CHRIST. 19:1-21.

The first ten verses of Revelation 19 are closely linked to the events of Revelation 18:20-24. Note that Revelation 19:1 begins with the words, **And after these things.** After the destruction of Babylon the whole tenor of the book of Revelation becomes that of rejoicing, for the King is coming.

A. Heavenly Songs of Praises. 19:1-6.

19:1-2. And after these things I heard a great voice of much people in heaven, saying, Alleluia . . . unto the Lord our God: for true and righteous are his judgments; for he hath judged the great whore . . . and hath avenged the blood of his servants at her hand. The song of praise by the angels, the twenty-four elders, the four living creatures, and the multitudes of heaven includes praise for God's righteousness in judging Antichrist's evil system of worship, as well as praise for avenging the blood of so many Tribulation believers martyred by Babylon.

6. The end is near. Excitement and expectancy are in the air. John records, **And I heard as it were the voice of a great multitude, and as the voice of many waters, and as the voice of mighty thunderings, saying, Alleluia: for the Lord God omnipotent reigneth.** The great heavenly hallelujah chorus has begun.

B. The Marriage Supper of the Lamb. 19:7-10.

7. Let us be glad and rejoice, and give honor to him: for the marriage of the Lamb is come, and his wife hath made herself ready. In conjunction with this great song of praise is the marriage supper of the Lamb. Gathered around the Lamb, the Lord Jesus Christ, are those who are His bride. Since the true church of today is the bride of Christ, this scene must take place in heaven. At the Rapture of the church, prior to the Tribula-tion Period, we are joined in marriage to the Bridegroom, Jesus Christ. Now the wedding supper or feast, which always followed the wedding ceremony after a brief interval, takes place.

8. And to her was granted that she should be arrayed in fine linen, clean and white: for the fine linen is the righteousness of saints. In a joyous celebration, we who are the saints of God, raptured up to heaven before the Tribulation, stand before the Lord as bride before Bridegroom arrayed **in fine linen, clean and white: for the fine linen is the righteousness of saints.** Our labors for the Lord, found worthy at the Judgment Seat of Christ, now clothe us. And, from our vantage point in heaven, we join in praising the Lord of Glory, for the great harlot has been overthrown.

With this the stage is set for the most dramatic entrance in history. With the tone of Revelation changed from somber to jubilant, the way is prepared for the Second Coming of Christ. He is about to come as the KING OF KINGS AND LORD OF LORDS. What a joyous day that will be when the seven years of Tribulation are ended, judgment upon the earth is over, and Jesus Christ comes as the Prince of Peace to reign in peace.

C. The Triumphal Re-entry as KING OF KINGS. 19:11-16.

Take a deep breath. We are about to consider the most mind-boggling event of history past, present, or future. The great harlot Babylon has been overthrown. There is fantastic rejoicing and praise in heaven, for the blood of the saints is avenged. Yet this rejoicing only foreshadows the event which immediately follows, the Second Coming of Christ to this earth. No imagination can quite visualize this scene which the saints of all the ages have longingly anticipated. It is marvelous.

Christ first came to earth in the form of a babe in Bethlehem. There was no room for Him in the inn and thus He was born in a stable. His coming was on a quiet, silent night. He came to die for our sins. One day soon He will come again to lead to heaven all who know Him as Saviour. This event we refer to as the Rapture, or the "snatching away" of His church. He will not come to the earth at this time, but only into the clouds, where we are caught up to meet Him. His coming is accompanied with the sounding of trumpets, perhaps heard only by those who are born again, whose ears are tuned to the trump of God.

But the event portrayed in Revelation 19 is neither the coming of the Lord as a babe nor His coming in the clouds to rapture His church. It is His second coming to earth, and He will do so as KING OF KINGS AND LORD OF LORDS. He will come to wage war against the Beast and the False Prophet. He will come to end the years of awful tribulation. He will come as the Mighty Warrior.

11. And I saw heaven opened, and behold a white horse; and he that sat upon him was called Faithful and True, and in righteousness he doth judge and make war. Imagine this dramatic moment. Suddenly the heavens part, not to permit entrance, but to permit the Lord Jesus and His armies to ride out of heaven to do battle with the forces of Antichrist. As if the opening of heaven were not dramatic enough, Christ will ride a white horse through the opening in the skies. There will be no mistaking Him for the Antichrist, who rode a white horse in Revelation 6:2. This is the real conqueror. This is Christ, the Son of the living God.

"The symbolism follows the pattern of a Roman triumphal procession. When a general returned from a successful campaign, he and his legions were granted the right to parade up the Via Sacra, the main street of Rome that led from the Forum to the Temple of Jupiter on the Capitoline Hill. Mounted on a white horse, the general rode at the head of his troops, followed by the wagonloads of booty that he had taken from the conquered nations, and by the chained captives" (Merrill C. Tenney, *The Book of Revelation,* p. 94).

Notice the graphic description of the Divine General who rides the white horse. Revelation 19:12-16 records, **His eyes were as a flame of fire, and on his head were many crowns. . . . And he was clothed with a vesture dipped in blood: and his name is called The Word of God. . . . And out of his mouth goeth a sharp sword, that with it he should smite the nations: and he shall rule them with a rod of iron: and he treadeth the winepress of the fierceness and wrath of Almighty God. And he hath on his vesture and on his thigh a name written, KING OF KINGS, AND LORD OF LORDS.**

The Conqueror's eyes, as a flame of fire, denote the penetrating quality of His judgment. His majesty and sovereignty are indicated by the many crowns on His head. The vesture dipped in blood (cf. Isa 63:3-4) reveals the coming vengeance in battle. Out of His mouth proceeds a sharp sword representing the dissecting and cutting edge of the Word of God, a title He bears (Jn 1:1, 14; I Jn 1:1; 5:7). The description of God's appointment of His son as ruler on the earth is seen in the rod of iron and the unique title of KING OF KINGS, AND LORD OF LORDS. Jesus Christ will be an awesome sight as He rides out of heaven to conquer.

There are many other Scriptures in both the Old and New Testaments which anticipate this glorious coming of Christ. Zechariah 14:3-4 reveals, "Then shall the Lord go forth, and fight against those nations, as when he fought in the day of battle. And his feet shall stand in that day upon the mount of Olives, which is before Jerusalem on the east, and the mount of Olives shall cleave in the midst thereof toward the east and toward the west, and there shall be a very great valley; and half of the mountain shall remove toward the north, and half of it toward the south."

Our Lord Himself tells of other startling phenomena which will accompany His return to this earth. He says, "Immediately after the tribulation of those days shall the sun be darkened, and the moon shall not give her light, and the stars shall fall from heaven, and the powers of the heavens shall be shaken: and then shall appear the sign of the Son of man in heaven: and then shall all the tribes of the earth mourn, and they shall see the Son of man coming in the clouds of heaven with power and great glory" (Mt 24:29-30).

With the heavens opening as a scroll, the plea of Isaiah is fulfilled. The ancient prophet pleaded, "Oh that thou wouldest rend the heavens, that thou wouldest come down, that the mountains might flow down at thy presence, as when the melting fire burneth, the fire causeth the waters to boil, to make thy name known to thine adversaries, that the nations may tremble at thy presence!" (Isa 64:1-2).

Christ Jesus comes to earth this second time to establish a thousand-year reign of righteousness. But before He can do this, the forces of evil, led by Antichrist, must be defeated on the battlefield. Beginning with Revelation 19:17, John previews this great battle.

D. The Vision of Armageddon. 19:17-19.

17-18. And I saw an angel standing in the sun; and he cried . . . , saying to all the fowls . . . , Come and gather yourselves together unto the supper of the great God; that ye may eat the flesh of kings, . . . captains, . . . mighty men, . . . horses, . . . and of them that sit on them. The angel, of course, has reference to the carrion and carnage of the great battle about to take place. So mighty is the Lord in battle that it will take a multitude of fowl to clean up the battlefield upon which His enemies die.

The reason for this battle is simple. Antichrist blasphemes the name of God, lies, cheats, and deceives his way into world leadership. He institutes a false system of religion in which he is the center of worship. When in the middle of the Tribulation the Jews no longer can freely worship God, they flee to the safety of the wilderness. Antichrist is unsuccess-

ful in his attempt to destroy them (12:15-16). His own capital city of Babylon falls as a result of the direct judgment from God (Rev 18). Only one group of people remains against whom Antichrist can vent his wrath, and that is a small band of Jews bottled up in the city of Jerusalem. These **keep the commandments of God, and have the testimony of Jesus Christ** (12:17) and thus become the object of Antichrist's hatred. Zechariah 14:1-2 indicates that all the nations of the earth, who comprise the armies of the world ruler, will be gathered against Jerusalem to battle. It is then the clouds part and King Jesus Christ rides forth with His armies.

This will be the most spectacular battle in history. In his vision of the coming battle (16:13-16) John tells us that Antichrist's troops are mustered by three demons who, like frogs, come out of the mouth of Satan, Antichrist, and the False Prophet. The troops are gathered together in **a place called in the Hebrew tongue Armageddon** (Rev 16:16). This site, which means "the mountain of Megiddo," is adjacent to the plain of Megiddo on the west and the large plain of Esdraelon on the northeast. Here was the scene of many great battles in the Old Testament (cf. Jud 4 and 7).

E. The Doom of Antichrist and the False Prophet. 19:20.

20. Although the armies of the nations will be deployed over an area of some two hundred miles (14:20) and some troops will be fighting directly against Jerusalem (Zech 14:2), the focal point of the battle will be Armageddon. The valley of Esdraelon (Jezreel) is itself fourteen miles wide and twenty miles long, and the blood from the dead and wounded will run to the bridles of the horses (14:20).

When the forces of Antichrist ride against the KING OF KINGS and His armies, there will be no contest. The King is armed only with the sharp sword that goes out of His mouth, and by the power of the Word of God the evil armies are slain. **And the beast was taken, and with him the false prophet.** These two are captured and cast alive into the lake of fire and brimstone. They are still there one thousand years later (20:10) and will remain there forever.

F. The Doom of Satan's Army. 19:21.

21. And the remnant were slain with the sword of him that sat upon the horse, which sword proceeded out of his mouth: and all the fowls were filled with their flesh. The battle of Armageddon is swift and deadly. The remnant of Antichrist's army is quickly slain. When the KING OF KINGS AND LORD OF LORDS rides forth out of heaven, followers of Antichrist become a meal for the fowls of the air. The flesh of kings, captains, military men, horses, the flesh of free men, enslaved men, small and great men will be served up for these fowls. This repulsive sight will result from judgment, the proportions of which the world has never seen before. The victory of Christ Jesus will be total over the world which despised Him.

At the consummation of this great battle, the enemies of Christ are vanquished. Their leaders, the Antichrist and the False Prophet, are **cast alive into a lake of fire burning with brimstone** (vs. 20). Note that only these two are cast into the lake of fire and precede Satan himself into this place of everlasting punishment by a thousand years (20:10). These two men, the civil and religious leaders of the league of nations against God, are cast alive into this horrible torment where a thousand years later they are still said to be suffering the vengeance of eternal fire. This should indicate beyond any doubt that the lake of fire is not annihilation and is not purgatory. It neither annihilates nor purifies these two but torments them everlastingly.

The Bible is very clear. "For God so loved the world, that he gave his only begotten Son, that whosoever believeth in him should not perish, but have everlasting life. For God sent not his Son into the world to condemn the world; but that the world through him might be saved" (Jn 3:16-17). All who avail themselves of this grace of God and receive the atonement of His Son on the cross of Calvary will be given a blessed eternity in heaven with God. On the other hand, those who spurn God's grace must be aware they will face Christ in judgment. They will be His conquered enemy without hope of eternal life in heaven and with the certainty of everlasting punishment in hell. The most serious question a person can ask is, "What must I do to be saved?" God's answer is, "Believe on the Lord Jesus Christ, and thou shalt be saved, and thy house" (Acts 16:31). If we want to go to God's heaven, we have to go in God's way. Jesus Christ said, "I am the way, the truth, and the life: no man cometh unto the Father, but by me" (Jn 14:6).

XIV. THE THOUSAND YEAR REIGN OF CHRIST. 20:1-15.

After seven long and increasingly severe years, the Tribulation is over. Christ Jesus comes to earth again and the forces of Antichrist are defeated in the awesome battle of Armageddon. Now comes the calm after the storm. Chapter 20 of Revelation informs us of the one thousand year reign of Christ on this earth known as the Millennium. Once again this planet will return to an atmosphere similar to the Garden of Eden.

A. Satan Bound. 20:1-3.

20:1-3. And I saw an angel come down from heaven, having the key of the bottomless pit and a great chain in his hand. And he laid hold on the dragon, . . . bound him a thousand years, and cast him into the bottomless pit . . . that he should deceive the nations no more, till the thousand years should be fulfilled: and after that he must be loosed a little season. The reason that the earth will return to an Edenic atmosphere is that an angel, which proceeds out of heaven, seizes Satan and binds him for one thousand years, casting him into the bottomless pit, shutting him up and sealing him there. All of this is done to prevent the devil from deceiving the nations till the thousand years are fulfilled. After that, he is again loosed for **a little season.**

Now you may say, "How do you know that it will actually be one thousand years Christ Jesus reigns in peace and righteousness? This is the only chapter in the Bible that mentions a millennium or thousand year reign." Yes, that is correct; but how many times does God have to say it to make it so? Once should be enough. Note here, however, that He repeats it six times. Verses 2, 3, 4, 5, 6, and 7 all refer to the period of a thousand years. This is a literal, thousand year era when the Lord of Glory will be the King of the earth.

Multitudes of people shall enter the Millennium. New Testament saints (the church) will rule and reign along with Christ (3:21). Old Testament saints shall rule in some sense as well. Other saints will now be resurrected to reign with Christ.

B. Resurrection of Tribulation Saints. 20:4-6.

4-5. And I saw thrones, ... and I saw the souls of them that were beheaded for the witness of Jesus, ... and they lived and reigned with Christ a thousand years. But the rest of the dead lived not again until the thousand years were finished. This is the first resurrection. Great numbers of the nation Israel shall enter the Millennial Kingdom: the 144,000 (14:3-4), those who flee into the wilderness hideaway (12:6), and those who remain in Jerusalem (12:17). Millions of Gentiles who are saved during the Tribulation shall enter the Millennial Kingdom of Christ (Mt 13:41-43, 49-50; 25:41, 46). But no unsaved person will enter the Millennium. They have all been vanquished in battle.

With the Antichrist and False Prophet in the lake of fire, and Satan bound in the bottomless pit, this will be an idyllic place to live. In his vision John does not occupy himself with the details of the

Millennial Kingdom. However, many Old Testament passages describe this blessed reign of Christ. Isaiah 2:2-4 indicates that Jerusalem will be the Lord's capital city and the center of the world. Also, the world will now see for the first time what the United Nations spends millions of dollars each year searching for but never finding, worldwide peace. This peace will come under the administration of the Prince of Peace. Isaiah 2:4 says, "And he shall judge among the nations, and shall rebuke many people: and they shall beat their swords into plowshares, and their spears into pruninghooks: nation shall not lift up sword against nation, neither shall they learn war any more." There will be no world peace until the Millennial Kingdom of Christ, for there can be no peace apart from Him.

Isaiah chapter 11 describes the peace and tranquility of Christ's kingdom. "The wolf also shall dwell with the lamb, and the leopard shall lie down with the kid; and the calf and the young lion and the fatling together; and a little child shall lead them. . . . And the sucking child shall play on the hole of the asp, and the weaned child shall put his hand on the cockatrice' den" (Isa 11:6, 8).

During the blissful one thousand year reign of Christ this earth will have a perfect physical environment. It will also have a perfect spiritual environment because Satan is no longer free to deceive the inhabitants of this planet. It will have a perfect moral environment because the sovereign of this kingdom is Christ Himself (Ps 2:6-9).

C. Satan's Final Fling. 20:7-9.

7-8. And when the thousand years are expired, Satan shall be loosed out of his prison, and shall go out to deceive the nations which are in the four quarters of the earth, Gog and Magog, to gather them together for battle: the number of whom is as the sand of the sea. At the end of the thousand years, Satan will be loosed from the bottomless pit and again deceive the nations, gathering them together for battle. How can there be any who follow Satan if all who enter the Millennium are washed clean in the blood of the Lamb? Although all who enter Christ's kingdom know and love the Lord, soon children will be born to these believing parents. Over the course of a thousand years, hundreds of thousands of children will be born. Because Christ rules in righteousness with a rod of iron, they will worship Him on the outside but not all will worship Him in their hearts. Those who do not come to truly love the Lord during the Millennium and place their trust in Him for salvation will be gathered by Satan at the end of the thousand years in one final, desperate attempt to usurp the throne of God. As in all other attempts, they will be unsuccessful, for God will send fire from heaven and devour them (20:9).

The millennial reign of Christ illustrates two things. First, having a perfect environment doesn't make a sinner into a saint. Those born in the Millennium have the most ideal environment imaginable. There is no war, no famine, no moral corruption. Still, they rally around the devil when he is finally loosed. Second, having a perfect heredity doesn't make a sinner into a saint. Each of these born during the reign of Christ is born to Christian parents. But believing parents do not make a believing child. Children of these millennial saints, numbering as the sands of the sea, turn against God the very first chance they get. Why is this? Is it because of the sinful nature which is part of every human being. Everyone, even those born to believers in the Millennium, must recognize his individual responsibility to receive Jesus Christ as his Saviour from sin and hell.

D. Satan's Doom. 20:10.

10. And the devil that deceived them was cast into the lake of fire and brimstone, where the beast and the false prophet are. With Satan's final armies purged from the earth by fire, Satan is himself now cast into the lake of fire and

brimstone, where the Beast and the False Prophet still are after one thousand years. Satan, the Antichrist and the False Prophet **shall be tormented day and night for ever and ever.** There is no more graphic way of saying that hell (the lake of fire) is a place of torment which lasts forever. The cults are wrong when they say death is annihilation. The scoffers are wrong when they say they will enjoy hell with their friends. Hell is sheer torment forever and ever.

Immediately after John views Satan being cast into the lake of fire, he receives another vision. This time John sees a Great White Throne. There have been other thrones mentioned in this book, but none are like this one. It is pure white, the type of white that makes everything else look dirty. Only the wicked, the unsaved, will appear before this throne of judgment. Unbelievers will have no difficulty in seeing their sin when they stand before the Great White Throne. The one who sits upon this throne is undoubtedly the Lord Jesus Christ, for "the Father judgeth no man, but hath committed all judgment unto the Son" (Jn 5:22).

E. The Great White Throne. 20:11-15.

11. And I saw a great white throne, and him that sat on it, from whose face the earth and the heaven fled away; and there was found no place for them. Verse 11 contains a curious reference to the fact that from the face of Christ the earth and heaven flee away and no place is found for them. The most natural interpretation of this is that at this time the present heaven and earth are destroyed and replaced by the new heaven and new earth. The Bible frequently anticipates the time when this present world will be destroyed (Mt 24:35; II Pet 3:10).

12. And I saw the dead, small and great, stand before God; and the books were opened: and another book was opened, which is the book of life: and the dead were judged out of those things which were written in the books, according to their works. Those who stand before the Great White Throne are the **dead, small and great.** As they appear before God, a single book and many books are opened, and they are judged according to their works. What can these books be? The single book is identified by the verse. It is the Lamb's book of life. Here the names of God's people are recorded from before the foundation of the world. A careful search is made to be absolutely certain that the names of none of these unsaved standing before the Great White Throne are in the book of life. None are, for God keeps careful records and knows who are His own (Jn 10:14). Not one person judged here has received Christ as Saviour. These are the wicked who have died in ages past, now resurrected to be judged.

Next the many books are checked to see the works of these who are to be judged. The book of life is not among these books, which record the deeds of the wicked. They are condemned by the fact that their name is not in the book of life. But the degree of punishment they receive for eternity is decided by the number and atrocity of their evil deeds here on earth. The record of these deeds is the substance of the books.

And death and hell were cast into the lake of fire. This is the second death. And whosoever was not found written in the book of life was cast into the lake of fire. The AV says "death and hell" were cast into the lake of fire, but this should be translated "death and hades" (Gr *hadēs*). No one ever returns from hell. Death claims the body and may be referred to as the ground. Hades claims the soul and is an intermediate state for the wicked until they are raised at the Great White Throne. Hell is the lake of fire, and in these verses John indicates that death gives up the bodies of the wicked and hades gives up the souls of the wicked. Thus both are properly judged and together cast into hell, the lake of fire. This means that the death unsaved men die on earth is only temporary. All will one day be raised and judged. Since their names are not in the book of life,

they cannot inherit eternal life. What they do inherit is the second death. From this final death there is no resurrection. It is eternal separation from God in the darkness and punishment of hell. When the wicked die the first time, their fate is sealed. There is no second chance. When the dead are raised at the end of the Millennium and stand before the Great White Throne Judgment, they receive the fruit of their wicked deeds and rejection of Christ. The wages of sin is death, i.e. eternal death, separation from God and everything desirable forever.

XV. THE NEW HEAVEN AND NEW EARTH. 21:1-22:5.

With the Great White Throne Judgment, the thousand year reign of Christ on this earth comes to an end. The Millennium, with its peace and tranquility, is certainly an improvement over our world today. It's hard to believe that anything could be better than this reign of peace. However, when Christ's thousand year reign comes to a close, the Millennium merges with eternity and there is nothing better than heaven.

A. The Vision of the New Heaven. 21:1-6.

21:1. And I saw a new heaven and a new earth: for the first heaven and the first earth were passed away; and there was no more sea. When God sends a new heaven and a new earth, He doesn't just clean up our polluted streams and rivers. He doesn't simply remake this old planet by knocking off some rough edges. He doesn't renovate the earth. God makes a new earth and as He does a new heaven. In verse 5 He says, **Behold, I make all things new.**

When God saves a sinner, He doesn't just patch him up, wash him off, make him over and reform him. Not at all. He makes him a new creature, a new created being. Old things pass completely away, and all things become new (II Cor 5:17). This is what He will one day do to heaven and earth. "Heaven and earth shall pass away," our Lord tells us (Mt 24:35). The Apostle Peter writes, "But the day of the Lord will come as a thief in the night; in the which the heavens shall pass away with a great noise, and the elements shall melt with fervent heat, the earth also and the works that are therein shall be dissolved, what manner of persons ought ye to be in all holy conversation and godliness, looking for and hasting unto the coming of the day of God, wherein the heavens being on fire shall be dissolved, and the elements shall melt with fervent heat? Nevertheless we, according to his promise, look for new heavens and a new earth, wherein dwelleth righteousness" (II Pet 3:10-13).

The Bible doesn't say much about how this new earth will look, but we know there will be no more seas to separate people. Men and women will be able to roam this new earthly paradise uninhibitedly. It will be far more beautiful than we can conceive.

2. And I John saw the holy city, new Jerusalem, coming down from God out of heaven, prepared as a bride adorned for her husband. Likewise the New Jerusalem, the holy city, is depicted by the simile of the beautiful bride as a place of great adornment. With the descent of the New Jerusalem, we are placed in an even more desirable relationship with God than we have ever had.

3. And I heard a great voice out of heaven saying, Behold, the tabernacle of God is with men, and he will dwell with them, and they shall be his people, and God himself shall be with them, and be their God. God the Son came to dwell among men in order to save them (Jn 1:14). God the Spirit came to dwell among men in order to comfort them (Jn 14:16-18). Now God the Father comes to dwell among men in order to fellowship with them.

B. The Blessings on the Overcomers. 21:7-8.

8. But the fearful, and unbelieving, and the abominable, and murderers, and whoremongers, and sorcerers, and **idolaters, and all liars, shall have their part in the lake which burneth with fire and brimstone: which is the second death.** The environment of the New Jerusalem will be even better than that of the Millennium, for God will exclude each of the above from entrance. It is important to note that those people who are excluded are people whose lives are characterized by these sinful traits. They will be cast into the lake of fire, indicating they are wicked unbelievers. The verse does not say that anyone who has ever committed any of these sins will be excluded. There is a great difference between telling a lie and being a habitual liar. Neither is commendable, but the believer can confess his sin and have it forgiven (I Jn 1:9). The unbeliever is hardened into a life style which is characteristic of his unbelief. Only the unbeliever is excluded from the New Jerusalem.

C. The Description of the New Jerusalem. 21:9-22.

The new heaven, the holy city, is so fantastically beautiful it almost defies words. However, under the guidance of the Holy Spirit, John attempts a description in Revelation chapter 21. Note how he describes it.

First, it is a literal city, **coming down from God out of heaven.** Verse 10 repeats, saying it is a **great city, the holy Jerusalem, descending out of heaven from God.** Its location is not specifically told to us. "The idea is that it comes close to the earth; but it is nowhere said that it ever alights on the earth, or ever becomes part of its material fabric. Though coming into the vicinity of the earth, it is always spoken of as the 'Jerusalem which is above' (Gal 4:26). The nations on the earth 'walk by means of its light,' which implies that it is over them. John could only get a near view of it by being spiritually transported to the top of 'a mountain great and high,' like the greatest altitudes of the Alps or the Himalayas. The prophecies also speak of a future Jerusalem as set at the tops of the mountains, and exalted over the hills (Isa 2:2)" (J. A. Seiss, *The Apocalypse,* Vol. III, pp. 404-5).

12. And had a wall great and high, and had twelve gates, and at the gates twelve angels, and names written thereon, which are the names of the twelve tribes of the children of Israel. The glory of God permeates the city. In his description notice, secondly, that John says it has around it a wall great and high, having twelve gates with an angel posted at each gate. The names written on the gates are of the twelve tribes of Israel, perhaps to remind each of us who dwell therein that we owe our Bible, our Saviour, and much more to Israel for "salvation is of the Jews" (Jn 4:22).

Each of the gates is made of one giant pearl (vs. 21). This should remind us, because of the very process needed to make a pearl, that much suffering was undergone in order to provide an entrance into the holy city. Jesus Christ said, "I am the door: by me if any man enter in, he shall be saved, and shall go in and out, and find pasture" (Jn 10:9). In order to become the door, the Lord had to suffer the anguish of dying on the cross. "But he was wounded for our transgressions, he was bruised for our iniquities: the chastisement of our peace was upon him; and with his stripes we are healed" (Isa 53:5). Jesus Christ paid a great price to be the door of our salvation. He suffered immensely, and it is altogether fitting that the gates into the new Jerusalem be of pearl.

Thirdly, note that the city itself is immense.

16. And the city lieth foursquare, and the length is as large as the breadth: and he measured the city with the reed, twelve thousand furlongs. The length and the breadth and the height of it are equal. A furlong is about six hundred feet, which means that the new Jerusalem is roughly fifteen hundred miles long, fifteen hundred miles wide and fifteen hundred miles high.

Here is a city which covers an area of fifteen hundred miles by fifteen hundred

miles, or 2,250,000 square miles at its base. This means that the base of the New Jerusalem is more than eight times the size of the entire state of Texas or two thirds the size of the United States. And in addition to that, it towers fifteen hundred miles straight up as a gigantic skyscraper. It is of fantastic proportions and certainly capable of housing the bride of Christ.

Fourthly, the shape of this city must either be a pyramid or a cube. Perhaps it is best to think of it as a cube, for this shape is frequently seen in the Scriptures. Both the altar of burnt offering and the altar of incense were of this form (Ex 27:1; 30:2). The Holy of Holies in Solomon's temple was a perfect cube, twenty cubits each way (I Kgs 6:20). Even the Greeks thought this shape to be a symbol of perfection.

18-19. And the building of the wall of it was of jasper: and the city was pure gold, like unto clear glass. And the foundations of the wall of the city were garnished with all manner of precious stones. Fifthly, in John's description, note that the foundations of the city number twelve as well as the gates, and each one bears the name of one of the twelve apostles of the Lamb. Perhaps this is to remind us that the church first flourished with these men (Eph 2:20). Each of the foundations is garnished with all manner of precious stones. The first is clear jasper. The second a brilliant blue sapphire. The third a sky-blue chalcedony. The fourth a bright green emerald. The fifth a red and white sardonyx. The sixth a reddish sardius stone. The seventh a transparent golden chrysolyte. The eighth a sea-green beryl. The ninth a transparent yellow-green topaz. The tenth a green chrysoprasus. The eleventh a violet jacinth. And the twelfth a purple amethyst. Each one concontributing to the unimaginable beauty of this holy city.

18. Finally John describes the whole city as being of **pure gold, like unto clear glass.** Even the street of the city is pure gold, as transparent glass. Gold is the most precious and most expensive commodity. Yet the city foursquare is lavishly made from pure gold, indicating an abode fit to be the dwelling place of God.

After reading the description of the magnificence displayed by this city, you may wonder whether there is anything not included in the New Jerusalem. Yes, there is. You'll recall that verse 4 indicates that **God shall wipe away all tears from their eyes; and there shall be no more death, neither sorrow, nor crying, neither shall there be any more pain: for the former things are passed away.** Do you think you'll be able to get along without these things in heaven? You won't miss them for a minute.

D. The Light of the New Jerusalem. 21:23-27.

23-24. And the city had no need of the sun, neither of the moon, to shine in it: for the glory of God did lighten it, and the Lamb is the light thereof. And the nations of them which are saved shall walk in the light of it: and the kings of the earth do bring their glory and honor into it. Verses 23-24 indicate additional things that won't be in the new city of God. We will have no need of the sunshine, for the Son shall shine through the length, breadth, and height of the New Jerusalem. This thought is repeated in chapter 22, verse 5. Also chapter 22, verse 3 indicates that **there shall be no more curse: but the throne of God and of the Lamb shall be in it; and his servants shall serve him.**

Have you ever wondered what we will do in heaven? Heaven is not a place to sit around under a shade tree, play a harp, and reap the reward of prolonged boredom. With God in our midst, we will have the capacity to know Him more, love Him more, and serve Him more. There will be plenty to do in heaven, and it will cause unimaginable joy. Even those living on the new earth, who seem to be redeemed Israel (Rom 4:13), and the saved multitudes who

come out of the Millennium, will have access to the holy city, and **the nations of them which are saved shall walk in the light of it: and the kings of the earth do bring their glory and honor into it. And the gates of it shall not be shut at all by day: for there shall be no night there. And they shall bring the glory and honor of the nations into it (21:24-26).**

E. The Life of the New Jerusalem. 22:1-5.

22:1-2. And he showed me a pure river of water of life, clear as crystal, proceeding out of the throne of God and of the Lamb. . . . And . . . the tree of life, which bare twelve manner of fruits, . . . and the leaves of the tree were for the healing of the nations. A river of life, clear as crystal, will proceed out of the throne of God and the Lamb, and spanning the river the most remarkable tree, the tree of life which bears twelve kinds of fruit year round, will maintain the constant health of the nations on the new earth.

This is a description of what awaits us in the New Jerusalem. But perhaps the best description of our future eternal home comes from the sentiments of Isaiah and the Apostle Paul: "Eye hath not seen, nor ear heard, neither have entered into the heart of man, the things which God hath prepared for them that love him" (I Cor 2:9, quoting Isa 64:4).

XVI. THE FINAL MESSAGE OF THE BIBLE. 22:6-21.

With chapter 22 the Apostle John completes his commissioned task to **write the things which thou hast seen, and the things which are, and the things which shall be hereafter** (1:19). His visions come to a glorious end. The last few verses of Revelation seem to be given as reinforcement that what John has seen will certainly come to pass.

A. The Assurance of the Lord's Return. 22:6-7.

6. These sayings are faithful and true: and the Lord God of the holy prophets sent his angel to show unto his servants the things which must shortly be done. That the words recorded in Revelation are true is seen in that they are statements of fact, given from the lips of God Himself. That they are faithful is evident in that they will surely come to pass. There is no question in John's mind about this, and there should be none in ours as well.

John has envisioned being caught up into heaven to view the opening of the seven-sealed scroll, the sounding of the seven trumpets, and the pouring out of the seven bowls of God's wrath. He has seen the awful Tribulation Period to come and in the middle of that period the rise of the Antichrist and the False Prophet. He has seen multitudes slain for the testimony of the gospel, and other multitudes receive the mark of the Beast. He has viewed the rise and destruction of Antichrist's capital city, symbolically known as Babylon the harlot. He has seen the ecumenical movement at its height and the collapse of the one-world church. He has seen the common-market nations fall apart economically at the hand of God. And at the end of the Tribulation, John has viewed the Second Coming of Christ to the earth. The KING OF KINGS AND LORD OF LORDS has ridden forth as the heavens opened and has conquered the forces of Antichrist at the fierce battle of Armageddon. John watched as the Antichrist and the False Prophet were cast into the lake of fire.

Then John saw something truly amazing. He viewed Christ as the King of the earth, ruling in righteousness and peace for one thousand years. He saw a society more blissful than any of history. But at the end of this thousand year reign, he saw Satan, loosed from the bottomless pit, spearhead a thwarted coup of God's kingdom and then be cast into the lake of fire to be tormented day and night forever. Likewise those who have rejected

Christ as Saviour were raised from the dead and judged at the Great White Throne Judgment. They too were cast into the lake of fire to be tormented forever and ever.

At this point John received his first glimpse of eternity. The heaven and earth were completely created new, and a new city of Jerusalem descended from God out of heaven. It was more beautiful than John could adequately describe. Time was now swallowed up in eternity, and John's vision was about to come to an end. Before it does, he is assured that the vision is accurate and the Lord will quickly be returning to inaugurate these events.

7. Behold, I come quickly: blessed is he that keepeth the sayings of the prophecy of this book.

B. The Angel and John. 22:8-9.

9. John is overawed by what he has just witnessed and falls down to worship before the feet of the angel who has shown him these things. The angel rebukes him saying, **See thou do it not: for I am thy fellow servant, and of thy brethren the prophets, and of them which keep the sayings of this book: worship God.** Men and angels are never to be the objects of our praise. God alone is worthy.

C. The Command: Seal Not. 22:10-16.

10. And he saith unto me, Seal not the sayings of the prophecy of this book: for the time is at hand. In verse 10 John is commanded not to seal the words of the prophecy of this book. The reason is clear. There is blessing for anyone who keeps the sayings of the prophecies given in Revelation (22:7). Besides, the time is near when the Lord will come quickly, and people will need to understand what God is doing for them (cf. Dan 12:4). The period which will usher in the eternal state is very near, and in John's day, as in ours, the end is always impending, because Christ may return at any moment and the timepiece of Revelation will start ticking away. Therefore, this book is to be opened, read, and heeded as a source of blessing.

11-15. He that is unjust, let him be unjust still: . . . and he that is righteous, let him be righteous still. . . . And, behold, I come quickly; and my reward is with me, to give every man according as his work shall be. I am Alpha and Omega, the beginning and the end, the first and the last. Blessed are they that do his commandments. Verses 11-15 seem to be a unit describing the sealing of one's destiny when the Lord comes. At that time all who are unjust will remain so, all filthy will continue to be filthy, etc. When the Lord Jesus comes to snatch His bride away, before the beginning of the Tribulation, He will then reward the saints according to their works. Salvation is a free gift that cannot be earned. But rewards are given in a response to faithful service. "There is a vast chasm between the meaning of salvation and the meaning of rewards. They are not at all the same. Salvation is appropriated to the sinner; rewards are awarded to the saint. Salvation is identical for all who by faith receive it; rewards are proportionate to one's life of service. Salvation is a gracious gift, given by God to the lost; rewards are a gracious wage paid for faithfully allowing the Lord to work through us" (Woodrow Michael Kroll, *It Will Be Worth It All,* p. 28).

At the Rapture, not only will all opportunity for salvation be gone for unbelievers, but also all opportunity for earthly service to the Lord will be gone for believers. What we are going to do for the Lord must be done now. Our eternal reward depends on our service to Him presently, and He warns each of us that He is coming quickly.

That this is true is confirmed by the One who makes the claim to be coming quickly. He is Jesus Christ the Lord and identifies Himself saying, **I am Alpha and Omega, the beginning and the end, the first and the last** (vs. 13). Alpha and omega are the first and last letters of the Greek alphabet. In other words, Jesus is all. He is the beginning of this revelation,

and the end of it. He is the complete One.

16. Additional titles of the Alpha and Omega are given in verse 16. As if to personally assure us of the authenticity of His revelation to John, He says, **I Jesus have sent mine angel to testify unto you these things in the churches. I am the root and the offspring of David, and the bright and morning star.** It is significant that this is the first time the word "church" occurs in Revelation since the third chapter. All during the Tribulation (chs. 4-19) there is no mention of the church, since as born-again believers we are caught up to be with the Lord before the awful period of judgment begins.

As the offspring of David, the Lord Jesus shows His divine right to sit upon the throne as KING OF KINGS AND LORD OF LORDS for all eternity. As the bright and morning star He shall be our light in the new heaven and new earth, for there is no light there but the Lord Jesus.

D. The Final Invitation. 22:17.

17. And the Spirit and the bride say, Come. And let him that heareth say, Come. And let him that is athirst come. And whosoever will, let him take the water of life freely. At this point, realizing that although what John is recording is in the future it will be read in our present age, God issues a final call for the unsaved to receive Him. That's just like God. A similar call was extended in the Old Testament in Isaiah 55:1, but because the hour of judgment is impending, the call is now ever so much more serious.

Someday each of us will hear God's final call for us. If we receive Christ Jesus as Saviour and accept His sacrifice on the cross as payment for our sins, we have a home in heaven with God throughout eternity. If we reject His call, we may be assured of the eternal torment which is caused by the lake of fire.

E. The Final Testimony. 22:18-19.

18-19. For I testify unto every man. . . . If any man shall add unto these things, God shall add. . . . And if any

man shall take away from the words of the book of this prophecy, God shall take away. . . . Verses 18-19 contain a stern warning about adding to or taking away from the words of the prophecy of the book of Revelation. Anyone who changes these words or their meanings to fit his theology, anyone who claims that they are not the words of God or that they are just myth, anyone who attempts to add to them, is promised the plagues written in this book will afflict him. God shall take away his part from the tree of life and the holy city. This does not mean he will lose his salvation, for anyone who would attempt such a crime is not a believer anyway. Only an unregenerated sinner would attempt to deny the Word, or add to the Word of God. Those who come to our doors and say we need their book or study guide in addition to the Bible are persons contemptible to God and condemned in these verses. The Bible alone is the Word of God. Nothing in addition to it is needed as a guide for our lives. Since there can be no additions or corrections, we must let the Scriptures stand approved as read.

F. The Final Benediction. 22:20-21.

20-21. He which testifieth these things saith, Surely I come quickly. Amen. Even so, come, Lord Jesus. The grace of our Lord Jesus Christ be with you all. Amen. Finally, John concludes the record of the Revelation by repeating the words of Christ, **Surely I come quickly.** This is similar to the expressions found in verses 7 and 12 but with the noticeable addition of the word "surely." This is the final testimony of Christ to us. His return for us is certain. It is imminent. It could be today. John felt that way when he breathed the prayer, **Even so, come, Lord Jesus.**

We have come to the close of the book of Revelation, but it has brought us chronologically to the beginning of eternal life with God. We haven't ended, we've only just begun. History has ended. Life with Jesus Christ our Lord has not. We have nothing to look forward to but endless ages of joy in the presence of our Saviour.

THE BEGINNING

BIBLIOGRAPHY

Barclay, William. *The Revelation of John.* 2 Volumes. Philadelphia: Westminster Press, 1961 (Amillennial).

Beckwith, Isbon B. *The Apocalypse of John.* Grand Rapids: Baker, 1967 (Amillennial).

Charles, R. H. A Critical and Exegetical Commentary on the Revelation of St. John. In the *International Critical Commentary.* 2 Volumes. Edinburgh: T. & T. Clark, 1920 (Amillennial).

Criswell, W. A. *Expository Sermons on Revelation.* Grand Rapids: Zondervan, 1962.

Gaebelein, A. C. *The Revelation: An Analysis and Exposition of the Book of Revelation.* New York: Loizeaux Brothers, 1961.

Hendriksen, William. *More Than Conquerors.* Grand Rapids: Baker, 1939 (Amillennial).

Ironside, Harry. *Lectures on the Book of Revelation.* New York: Loizeaux Brothers, 1955.

* Kelly, William. *Lectures on the Book of Revelation.* London: G. Morrish, n.d.

Kuyper, Abraham. *The Revelation of St. John.* Trans. by John Hendrik De Vries. Grand Rapids: Eerdmans, 1935 (Amillennial).

Lenski, R. C. H. *The Interpretation of St. John's Revelation.* Columbus, Ohio: Lutheran Book Concern, 1935 (Amillennial).

Morris, Leon. The Revelation of St. John. In the *Tyndale New Testament Commentaries.* Grand Rapids: Eerdmans, 1969 (Amillennial).

Newell, William R. *The Book of Revelation.* Chicago: Moody Press, 1935.

Pettingill, William. *The Unveiling of Jesus Christ.* Findlay, Ohio: Fundamental Truth Publishers, 1939.

Ryrie, Charles Caldwell. *Revelation.* Chicago: Moody Press, 1968.

* Scott, Walter. *Exposition of the Revelation of Jesus Christ.* London: Pickering & Inglis, n.d.

Scroggie, W. G. *The Book of the Revelation.* Edinburgh: The Book Stall, 1920.

* Seiss, J. A. *The Apocalypse.* Grand Rapids: Zondervan, 1964.

* Smith, J. B. *A Revelation of Jesus Christ.* Scottdale, Pa.: Herald Press, 1961.

Strauss, Lehman. *The Book of Revelation.* Neptune, N. J.: Loizeaux Brothers, 1965.

Swete, H. B. *The Apocalypse of St. John.* Grand Rapids: Eerdmans, n.d. (Amillennial).

Tatford, Frederick. *Prophecy's Last Word.* Grand Rapids: Kregel, 1969.

* Walvoord, John F. *The Revelation of Jesus Christ.* Chicago: Moody Press, 1966.